Experiencing the Lifespan

SECOND EDITION

Experiencing the Lifespan
SECOND EDITION

JANET BELSKY

MIDDLE TENNESSEE STATE UNIVERSITY

Grateful acknowledgment is made for permission to use the images on the following pages:

Pages xxxii, 72, 134, 232, 292, 388 – Robert Carter; pages 2, 450 – Jupiter Images, Digital Vision/Getty Images, Tatjana Alvegard/Getty Images, Jupiter Images, Christina Kennedy/Getty Images, Altrendo Images/Getty Images, Sean Justice/Getty Images, Seth Joel/Getty Images, ColorBlind Images/Getty Images, Marc Romanelli/Getty Images, Derek Shapton/Masterfile, Photodisc/Getty Images; page 34 – Jupiter Images; page 74 – Larry Williams/zefa/Corbis; page 108 – Digital Vision/Getty Images; page 136 – Tatjana Alvegard/Getty Images; page 170 – Jupiter Images; page 200 – Christina Kennedy/Getty Images; page 234 – Altrendo Images/Getty Images; page 262 – Sean Justice/Getty Images; page 294 – Seth Joel/Getty Images; page 326 – ColorBlind Images/Getty Images; page 358 – Marc Romanelli/Getty Images; page 390 – Derek Shapton/Masterfile; page 420 – Photodisc/Getty Images

Senior Publisher: Catherine Woods

Executive Marketing Manager: Katherine Nurre

Developmental Editor: Elaine Epstein

Media and Supplements Editor: Christine Burak

Photo Editor: Bianca Moscatelli

Photo Researcher: Deborah Anderson

Art Director and Cover Designer: Babs Reingold

Interior Text Designers: Lyndall Culbertson and Chuck Yuen

Chapter-opening Layouts: Lyndall Culbertson

Project Editor: Anthony Calcara

Illustrations: Preparé Inc., Dragonfly Media Group, Christy Krames

Production Manager: Sarah Segal

Composition: Preparé Inc.

Printing and Binding: RR Donnelley

Library of Congress Control Number: 2009935952

ISBN-13: 978-1-4292-1950-1
ISBN-10: 1-4292-1950-5

Printed in the United States of America

Fourth printing

Worth Publishers
41 Madison Avenue
New York, NY 10010
www.worthpublishers.com

ABOUT THE AUTHOR

MTSU Photographic Services

BORN IN NEW YORK CITY, JANET BELSKY always wanted to be a writer but was also very interested in people. After receiving her undergraduate degree from the University of Pennsylvania, she deferred to her more practical and people-loving side and got her Ph.D. in clinical psychology at the University of Chicago. After years in New York teaching at Lehman College and doing clinical work in nursing homes and city hospitals, she moved to Tennessee in 1991 to teach full time. In between teaching three sections of lifespan development every semester, Janet found the time to write a few textbooks in adult development and aging and one trade book, *Here Tomorrow: Making the Most of Life After 50*. Her son Thomas is now an emerging adult working in Orlando, Florida. Janet lives in Murfreesboro, Tennessee, with her husband David, to whom she has been married for more than 31 years. In writing *Experiencing the Lifespan*, she has been able to merge her three enduring life passions—writing, teaching undergraduates about the lifespan, and interviewing people from age 3 to 103. Following her own personal optimally aging (and, hopefully, stimulating neurogenesis!) program, Janet has recently developed a new later life passion—acting in community theater.

BRIEF CONTENTS

CONTENTS

PREFACE

I spent my thirties and forties writing textbooks on adult development and aging. I've spent the past thirty-three years (virtually all of my adult life!) teaching this course covering the lifespan as a whole. *Experiencing the Lifespan* represents the embodiment of my life dream. This book is the culmination of my writing and teaching careers.

It goes without saying that, being a relatively new textbook, *Experiencing the Lifespan*, Second Edition, offers the most up-to-date research. In these pages you will find more than 2000 twenty-first-century citations, spanning everything from the latest neuroscience findings relating to brain development to provocative social policy critiques. But my goal is to do more than rigorously explore the science of development in its myriad, magnificent forms. I've been striving to write a book that is *qualitatively* different, one that advances the art of textbook writing in our field. Here are some features that I hope will make *Experiencing the Lifespan* an experience that delights readers—and, ideally, changes students' lives.

What Makes This Book Special?

Experiencing the Lifespan is written to unfold like a story. The main feature that distinguishes my book relates to the writing style. *Experiencing the Lifespan* reads like a personal conversation rather than a traditional text. Each chapter begins with a vignette constructed to highlight the material I will be discussing. I've designed my narrative to flow from topic to topic; and I've planned every chapter to interconnect. In this text, the main themes that undergird developmental science flow throughout the *entire* book. I want to give people the sense of reading an exciting, ongoing story. Most important, I want them to feel that they are learning about a coherent, *organized* field.

Experiencing the Lifespan is uniquely organized to highlight development. A second mission that has been driving my writing is to highlight lives evolving. How can I convey *exactly* what makes an 8-year-old different from a 4-year-old, or a 60-year-old different from a person of 85? In order to emphasize how children develop, I made the decision to cover all of childhood in a single three-chapter part. This strategy has allowed me to fully explore the magic of Piaget's preoperational and concrete operational stages and to trace the development of aggression, childhood friendships, and gender-stereotyped play. It permits me to show *concretely* how the ability to think through their actions changes as children travel from preschool through elementary school. I decided to put early and middle adulthood in one unit (Part V) for similar reasons: It simply made logical sense to discuss centrally important topics that transcend a single life stage, such as marriage, parenting, and work (Chapter 11), and adult personality and cognitive development (Chapter 12), together in the same place.

For this grandmother, mother, and daughter, getting dressed up to visit this Shinto family shrine and pay their respects to their ancestors is an important ritual. It is one way that the lesson "honor your elders" is taught to children living in collectivist societies such as Japan from an early age.

B. Tanaka/Getty Images

In fact, I've designed this *whole* text to highlight development. I follow the characters in the chapter-opening vignettes throughout each several-chapter unit. I've planned each life stage segment to flow in a developmental way. In the first infancy chapter I begin with a discussion of newborn states. The second chapter in this sequence (Infancy: Socioemotional Development) ends with a discussion of toddlerhood. My three-chapter Early and Middle Adulthood unit starts with an exploration of the challenges of emerging adulthood (Chapter 10), then tackles marriage, parenthood, and career (Chapter 11), and culminates with a chapter tracking adult personality and intelligence through midlife, and exploring "older" family roles such as caring for aging parents and grandparenthood (Chapter 12). In Part VI, Later Life, I begin with a chapter devoted to topics such as retirement that typically take place during the young-old years. Then I focus on physical aging (Chapter 14, The Physical Challenges of Old Age) because sensory-motor impairments, dementing diseases, and interventions for late-life frailty become crucial concerns mainly in the eighties and beyond. Yes, this textbook does—for the most part—move through the lifespan stage by stage. However, it's targeted to highlight the aspects of development—such as constructing an adult life in the 20s or physical disabilities in the 80s—that become salient at particular times of life. I believe that my textbook captures the best features of the chronological and topical approaches.

The birth of a Down syndrome child has a life-changing effect on every family member. Will this big sister become a more caring, sensitive adult through having grown up with this younger sibling?

Experiencing the Lifespan **is both shorter and more in-depth.** Adopting this flexible, development-friendly organization has the advantage of making for a more manageable, teacher-friendly book. With 15 chapters and at roughly 500 pages, my textbook *really* can be mastered in a one-semester course! But not being locked into covering each stage of life in tiny slices gives me the freedom to focus on what is most important in special depth. As you will discover as you read my unusually comprehensive discussions of central topics in our field, such as attachment, parenting, puberty, and adult personality consistency and change, omitting superficial coverage of "everything" allows ample time for students to reflect on the core issues in developmental science in a deeper, more thoughtful way.

Experiencing the Lifespan **actively fosters critical thinking.** Guiding students to reflect more deeply on what they are reading is actually another of my writing goals. One advantage of writing a text that reads like a personal dialogue is that I am able to embed critical thinking within the narrative itself. On a more academic level, this means that as I move from discussing Piaget's ideas on cognition to Vygotsky's theory to the information-processing approach in Chapter 5, I can point out the gaps in each perspective and highlight *why* each approach offers a unique contribution to understanding children's intellectual growth. On a policy-oriented level, after discussing the research relating to day care or teenage storm and stress, I can ask readers to think critically about how to improve the way our society cares for children or to devise strategies for making the wider world more user-friendly for the teenage brain.

Experiencing the Lifespan **has a global orientation and a new focus on U.S. ethnicity.** Intrinsic to getting students to think more critically about our own practices is the need to highlight alternate perspectives on our developing life. Therefore, *Experiencing the Lifespan* is a truly international book. This global orientation is evident in the first chapter, when I introduce the concept of collectivist and individualistic cultures and spell out the differences between the developed and developing worlds. It is front and center in the introductory "Setting the Context" sections that often offer a cross-cultural perspective on the material in each chapter. It is part and parcel of the ongoing discussion. In the childhood section, when discussing topics such as parenting or constructing a self, I have full sections devoted to cultural and ethnic differences. In the adulthood chapters, among other topics, I offer snapshots of marriage in different regions of the world, and explore different societal practices and attitudes

Families come in many forms, and the love you have for your adopted children is no different than if you gave birth. Take it from me as an adoptive mom!

toward death. (In fact, "How do other groups handle this?" is a question that crops up when I talk about practically every topic in the book!) Moreover, this second edition extends my global diversity focus to fully showcase ethnic variations within the United States.

Experiencing the Lifespan **highlights the multiple forces that shape development.** Given my emphasis on cultural variations within our universal human experience, it should come as no surprise that the framework that pervades my writing is the need to adopt a developmental systems approach. Throughout the chapters, I explore the many different influences that interact to predict core life milestones—from puberty to physical aging. Erikson's stages, attachment theory, behavioral genetics, evolutionary theory, self-efficacy, and, especially, the importance of looking at nature *and* nurture and providing the best person–environment fit—all are concepts that I introduce in the first chapter and return to stress as the book unfolds. Another theme that runs through this text is the impact of socioeconomic status, both internationally and in the United States, on shaping everything from breast-feeding practices to the rate at which we age and die.

Experiencing the Lifespan **is applications-oriented, and focused on how to construct a satisfying life.** Because of my background as a clinical psychologist, my other passion is to bring home how the scientific findings translate into strategies to improve the quality of life. So *each* topic in this text ends with an "Interventions" section spelling out practical implications of the research. With its varied Interventions, such as "How Can You Get Babies to Sleep Through the Night?" or "Using Piaget's Theory at Home and at Work," to its adulthood tables such as "How to Flourish During Adulthood" and full sections devoted to "Aging Optimally," *Experiencing the Lifespan* is designed to show how the science of development can be concretely applied to help foster a full life.

Experiencing the Lifespan **is a person-centered, hands-on textbook.** My mission is also to make human life (and our research) come alive for students in a riveting, personal way. So in "Experiencing the Lifespan" boxes in each chapter, I report on interviews I've conducted with people ranging from a 15-year-old socialist-in-the-making to a 70-year-old man with Alzheimer's disease. Because I want to teach students to empathize with the challenges of every life stage, I continually ask readers to "imagine you are a toddler" or "a sleep-deprived mother" or "an older person struggling with the challenges of driving in later life."

Another person-centered feature of my writing is regular questionnaires (based on the research) that students can fill out to think more deeply about their *own* lives: The checklist to identify their parenting priorities in Chapter 7, reproduced here; a scale for "using selective optimization with compensation at home and work" in Chapter 12; surveys for "evaluating your relationships" in Chapters 10 and 11; true/false quizzes at the beginning of my chapters on adolescence (Chapter 9), adult roles (Chapter 11), and later life (Chapter 13) that provide a hands-on preview of the content and entice students into reading the chapter so that they can assess the scientific accuracy of their ideas.

Courtesy of Gilda Morelli

This new member of the Efé people of central Africa will be lovingly cared for by the whole community, males as well as females, from his first minutes of life. Because he sleeps with his mother, however, at the "right" age he will develop his primary attachment to her.

TABLE 7.2: **Checklist for Identifying Your Parenting Priorities**

Rank the following goals in order of their importance to you, from 1 (for highest priority) to 8 (for lowest priority). It's OK to use the same number twice if two goals are equally important to you.

____ Producing an obedient, well-behaved child

____ Producing a caring, prosocial child

____ Producing an independent, self-sufficient child

____ Producing a child who is extremely close to you

____ Producing an intelligent, creative thinker

____ Producing a well-rounded child

____ Producing a happy, emotionally secure child

____ Producing a spiritual (religious) child

What do your rankings reveal about the qualities you most admire in human beings?

In fact, I've devised a *wealth* of hands-on exercises designed to make the content of this course come alive. For instance, in Chapters 3 and 5, I offer step-by-step instructions to test for the A-not-B error in an infant or for the presence of theory of mind in a 4-year-old. In Chapter 6 I ask readers to visit a playground to see in action how the play styles of girls and boys differ. In Chapter 14, I have asked students to think up creative alternatives to nursing homes or come up with ways of changing the driving environment in their community to make it user-friendly for older adults.

Does a girl this age have the memory capacity and self-regulation skills necessary to take proper care of a dog? This is the kind of question that an information-processing perspective on cognition can answer.

Experiencing the Lifespan **is designed to get students to learn the material while they read.** The chapter-opening vignettes, the applications sections with their regular summary tables, the hands-on exercises, and the end-of-section questionnaires (such as "A Research-based Guide for Evaluating Your Relationship" in Chapter 10) are components of an overall pedagogical plan. As I explain in my introductory letter to students on page 2, I want this to be a textbook you don't have to struggle to decode—one that will assist you in *naturally* cementing the concepts in mind. The centerpiece of this effort is the "Tying It All Together" quizzes, which follow each major section. These mini-tests, involving multiple-choice, essay, and critical thinking questions, enable students to test themselves on what they have absorbed. I've also planned the photo program in *Experiencing the Lifespan* to directly illustrate the major terms and concepts. As you page through the text, you may notice how the pictures and their captions feel organically connected to the writing. They function as visual extensions of the narrative itself. When it's important for students to learn a series of terms or related concepts, I provide a summary series of vivid photos. You can see examples in the photographs illustrating the different infant and adult attachment styles on pages 115 and 321, and in Table 3.7 on page 97 highlighting Jean Piaget's circular reactions during infant life.

As you scan this book, you will notice a variety of other special features: "How do we know . . . ?" boxes in some chapters that delve more deeply into particular research programs; "Focus on a Topic" features embedded in every chapter that showcase "hot topics," from ADHD to age discrimination at work; and timelines that pull everything together at the end of some complex sections (such as the chart summarizing the landmarks of pregnancy and prenatal development on pages 56 and 57).

Many Italian men in their late twenties are still living with their parents because they cannot afford to leave the nest. If you were in this situation, how would you react?

What will make this text a pleasure to teach from? How can I make this book a joy to read? These are questions I have been grappling with as I've been glued to my computer—often seven days a week—to produce this decade-long labor of love.

What Makes Each Chapter Special?

Now that I've spelled out my major missions in writing this book, here are a few highlights of each chapter.

PART I: Foundations

CHAPTER 1: The People and the Field

- Outlines the basic contexts of development: social class, culture, ethnicity, and cohort.

- Traces the evolution of the lifespan over the centuries and the twentieth-century evolution of the developmental science theories that have shaped our understanding of life.

- Spells out the concepts, the perspectives, and the research strategies I will be exploring in each chapter of the book.

CHAPTER 2: Prenatal Development, Pregnancy, and Birth

- Discusses pregnancy rituals and superstitions around the world.

- Highlights the latest research on fetal brain development and on maternal emotions during pregnancy.

- Fully explores the experience of pregnancy from both the mother's and father's points of view.

- Looks at the experience of birth historically and discusses policy issues relating to pregnancy and birth in the United States and around the world.

PART II: Infancy
CHAPTER 3: Infancy: Physical and Cognitive Development

- Covers the latest research on early brain development.

- Focuses in depth on basic infant states such as eating, crying, and sleep.

- Offers a global perspective on breast-feeding and undernutrition.

- Provides an in-depth, personal, and practice-oriented look at infant motor development, Piaget's sensorimotor stage, and beginning language.

- Explores the cutting edge findings on infant social cognition.

CHAPTER 4: Infancy: Socioemotional Development

- Provides unusually in-depth coverage of attachment theory.

- Offers an honest comprehensive look at day care in the United States and discusses early childhood poverty.

- Highlights exuberant and shy toddler temperaments and stresses the need to promote the right temperament–environment fit.

PART III: Childhood
CHAPTER 5: Physical and Cognitive Development

- Begins by exploring why we have childhood, illustrating what makes human beings qualitatively different from other species.

- Covers childhood obesity, including its emotional aspects, in depth.

- Showcases Piaget's, Vygotsky's, and the information-processing models of childhood cognition—with examples that stress the practical implications of these landmark perspectives for parents and people who work with children.

- Explores the latest research on ADHD and theory of mind.

CHAPTER 6: Socioemotional Development

- Discusses the development of self-understanding, prosocial behavior, aggression, and fantasy play, and explores popularity throughout childhood.

- Clearly spells out the developmental pathway to becoming an aggressive child.

- Highlights the challenge of emotion regulation and focuses on internalizing and externalizing disorders.

- Covers bullying and cyber-bullying.

CHAPTER 7: Settings for Development: Home and School

- This final childhood chapter shifts from the process of development to the major settings for development—home and school—and tackles important controversies in the field, such as the influence of parents versus peers versus genetics in shaping development and the pros and cons of intelligence testing.

This photograph shows the reality of motherhood today. Young working mothers are spending much *more* time teaching their children than their own, stay-at-home mothers did in the past!

- Offers extensive discussions of ethnic variations in parenting styles and describes the latest research on how to stimulate intrinsic motivation.

- Showcases schools that beat the odds and targets the core qualities involved in effective teaching.

PART IV: Adolescence
CHAPTER 8: Physical Development

- Offers an in-depth look at puberty, including the multiple forces that program the timing of this life transition, and looks at historical and cultural variations in puberty timetables.

- Explores the emotional experience of puberty (an "insider's" view) and the emotional impact of maturing early for girls.

- Provides up-to-date coverage of teenage body image issues, eating disorders, and emerging sexuality.

CHAPTER 9: Cognitive and Socioemotional Development

- Covers the latest developmental science research on teenage brain development and various facets of adolescent "storm and stress."

- Spells out the forces that enable teenagers to thrive and explains what society can do.

- Explores parent–child relationships and discusses teenage peer groups.

PART V: Early and Middle Adulthood
CHAPTER 10: Constructing an Adult Life

- Devotes a whole chapter to the concerns of emerging adulthood.

- Offers extensive coverage of diversity issues that become salient during this life stage, such as forming an ethnic and biracial identity, and interracial dating.

- Gives students tips for succeeding in college as well as spelling out career issues for non-college graduates.

- Introduces career-relevant topics, such as the concept of "flow," and provides extensive coverage of the research relating to selecting a mate and adult attachment styles.

CHAPTER 11: Relationships and Roles

- Focuses directly on the core issues of adult life: work and family.

- Provides an extensive discussion of the research relating to how to have happy, enduring relationships, the challenges of parenting, and women's and men's work and family roles.

- Looks at marriage, parenthood, and work in their cultural and historical contexts.

- Offers research-based tips for having a satisfying marriage and career.

- Discusses job insecurity in our more fragile economy, how being out of work may affect family relationships, and explores the mixed benefits of new technologies on family life.

CHAPTER 12: Midlife

- Describes the complexities of measuring adult personality development, and organizes the discussion according to the "we don't change" and "we do change" points of view.

- Anchors the research on adult intellectual change (the fluid and crystallized distinctions) to lifespan changes in creativity and careers.

- Offers thorough coverage of the latest research on generativity.

- Provides research-based advice for constructing a fulfilling adult life.

- Covers age-related changes in sexuality, menopause, grandparenthood, and parent care.

PART VI: Later Life
CHAPTER 13: Later Life: Cognitive and Socioemotional Development

- Offers an extensive discussion of Carstensen's socioemotional selectivity theory.

- Helps decode the core qualities that make for a happy or unsatisfying old age, and offers a section on "aging optimally."

- Describes the latest research on aging memory, retirement, and widowhood.

- Discusses salient current social issues such as age discrimination in hiring and the later life implications of declining pension income.

- Looks at later life developmentally by tracing changes from the young-old to the old-old years.

Mike Powell/Getty Images

Is the middle-aged fashion designer on the left at his creative peak? According to the research, the answer is yes. How proficient will this young man watching ultimately be at designing suits? For answers, we would want to look at this person's creative talents right now.

CHAPTER 14: The Physical Challenges of Old Age

- Offers a clear developmental look at how normal aging shades into chronic disease and ADL impairments, and looks at the impact of gender, ethnicity, and socioeconomic status on physical aging.

- Focuses on how to change the environment to compensate for sensorimotor declines.

- Provides an in-depth look at dementia, accompanied by compelling firsthand descriptions of their inner experience by people with Alzheimer's disease.

- Explores alternatives to institutionalization and provides a full description of nursing home care.

- Strives to provide a realistic, honest, and yet action-oriented and uplifting portrait of the physical frailties of advanced old age.

CHAPTER 15: Death and Dying

- Explores cross-cultural variations in dying and offers a historical look at death practices from the Middle Ages to today.

- Discusses the pros and cons of the hospice movement, with its focus on dying at home.

- Offers a look at the pros and cons of different types of advance directives and explores controversial topics such as physician-assisted suicide.

Ronnie Kaufman/Getty Images

Although his main goal is to greet this woman in a warm, personal way, in order to remember his new friend's name, this elderly man might want to step back and use the mnemonic strategy of forming a mental image, thinking, "I'll remember it's Mrs. Silver because of her hair."

What's Special to this Edition?

My main mission in preparing this new edition has been to provide you with the latest, most cutting-edge findings in our field. Therefore, *Experiencing the Lifespan* now has roughly 700 new citations, dating just from 2007–2009! In addition to rigorously updating *every* chapter, I've totally rewritten the sections on childhood obesity, on day care, on early childhood poverty, on marriage, and on career development, among others. I've added new sections on hot academic-research-oriented topics from social cognition in infancy to the latest neuroscience findings relating to mild cognitive impairment, and its relation to Alzheimer's disease. I moved Chapter 10: Constructing an Adult Life to the adulthood unit, to provide a more natural flow between its "finding a relationship" and "choosing a career" discussions and the next chapter's exploration of work and marriage during adult life. But, for readers and adopters of the first edition, here are three more overarching changes you'll find in *Experiencing the Lifespan*:

- **More focus on U.S. ethnicity.** Given its compelling importance to so many of our students, I've greatly expanded my treatment of U.S. diversity, by adding new sections on interracial dating and forming a biracial and ethnic identity in Chapter 10, explicitly discussing acculturation issues (in various chapters), and inserting a new section on racial differences in aging and illness rates and access to health care in Chapter 14.

- **More focus (even more than before!) on constructing a satisfying adult life.** Although this book has always been implicitly about how to have a successful life, I've included even more information relating to this centrally important topic, from a table summarizing the research findings on happiness in Chapter 12, to a new section on "optimally aging into the 90s" in Chapter 13. In this edition, you will also find even more extensive discussions of how to construct enduring relationships, and find a fulfilling career.

- **A focus on that newly salient social issue: our more fragile economy.** From a discussion of the emotional impact of job insecurity, to speculations about how male joblessness may change adult family roles (all new to Chapter 11), to a new "focus on a topic feature" devoted to age discrimination in hiring, and emerging research on how declining pension income is affecting retirement plans (in Chapter 13), my enduring social policy orientation in *Experiencing the Lifespan* now includes material relating to this pressing problem now affecting the lives of so many adults.

The Supplements Package

When you decide to use this book, you're adopting far more than just this text. You have access to an incredible learning system—everything from tests to video clips that bring the material to life. The Worth team and several dozen dedicated instructors have worked to provide an array of supplements to my text, to foster student learning and make this course a memorable one: Video clips convey the magic of prenatal development, clarify Piaget's tasks, highlight child undernutrition, and showcase the life stories of active and healthy people in their ninth and tenth decades of life; pre-built PowerPoint slides and clicker questions make class sessions more visual and interactive. My publisher has amassed a rich archive of developmental science materials. For additional information, please contact your Worth Publishers sales consultant or look at the Worth Web site at www.worthpublishers.com/belsky2e. Here are descriptions of the supplements:

DevelopmentPortal for *Experiencing the Lifespan*

Created BY psychologists FOR psychologists, DevelopmentPortal is a breakthrough on-line learning space. Specifically built around the new edition, DevelopmentPortal combines:

- **A Multimedia-enhanced eBook.** The eBook fully integrates the text and its images with a rich assortment of media resources and customization features for students and instructors. The eBook is also available in a stand-alone version outside DevelopmentPortal.

- **Diagnostic Quizzing and Study Plans.** Students take a quiz before starting a new chapter. The results are translated into a personalized study plan, with links to specific sections and resources to help with the questions they missed.

- **Assignment Center.** Instructors can easily construct and administer tests and quizzes based on the Test Bank or their own questions. Quizzes are randomized and timed, and instructors can receive summaries of student results in reports that follow the section order of the chapters.

- **Course Materials.** In this convenient location, students can access all media associated with the book, and instructors will find a variety of videos and pre-made PowerPoint presentations for classroom and on-line presentation.

■ **DevelopmentPortal** contains all the standard functionality you expect from a site that can serve as an independent on-line course, but it is the core teaching and learning components—developed with an advisory board of master teachers and learning experts—that make DevelopmentPortal truly unique.

Now Exclusively On-line for Students! Video Tool Kit for Human Development

The student version of this edition's Video Tool Kit is now available exclusively on-line. It spans the full range of standard topics for the child development course, with over 65 student video activities that contain brief clips of research and news footage from the BBC Motion Library, UNICEF, and other sources. These activities are easily assignable and accessible by an instructor.

For instructors, in addition to the student activities, the Video Tool Kit offers hundreds of additional clips—over 350 in total, all closed captioned and easily downloadable in Quick-Time and MPEG formats for easy integration into a PPT presentation. Clips can be used to introduce central topics, stimulate class discussions, or challenge students' critical thinking skills—either in class or via out-of-class assignments.

The Book Companion Site at www.worthpublishers.com/belsky2e

My Web site provides students with a *virtual study guide, 24 hours a day, seven days a week*. Best of all, these resources are free and do not require any special access codes or passwords. The tools on the site include: *chapter previews* highlighting key points within each chapter; *annotated Web links* related to the study of development, updated regularly to provide students with the chance to explore key topics in more depth; *on-line quizzes* offering multiple-choice practice tests (for every chapter) that allow students to test their knowledge of chapter concepts; *Internet exercises* asking students to expand their knowledge of core concepts with Web-based research; *interactive flashcards* that tutor students on all chapter terminology and allow them to then quiz themselves on the terms; and *frequently asked questions about developmental psychology* that permit students to think critically about lifespan development and that explore such topics as how understanding human development can help students in their careers and lives and how to pursue an advanced degree in developmental psychology.

A password-protected Instructor's Site offers a full array of teaching resources, including PowerPoint slides, an on-line quiz grade book, and links to additional tools (Faculty Guides and the Image and Lecture Gallery).

PowerPoint Presentation Slides

There are two pre-built slide sets for each chapter of *Experiencing the Lifespan* (one featuring a full chapter lecture, the other featuring all chapter art and illustrations). In addition, Video PowerPoint Presentation Slides (on the Instructor's Resource CD-ROM) provide an easy way to integrate the Instructor's Media Tool Kit video clips into these PowerPoint slide sets. For every video clip, PowerPoint slides tie chapter concepts to the selected clip, present explanatory slides introducing each segment, and then follow each clip with discussion questions designed to promote critical thinking and foster the student discussion that is so critical to making this course a success.

Instructor's Resource CD-ROM and the Worth Publishers Video Collection (DVD)

Each features a "best of" collection of 100 of the most popular and compelling clips from the collection. In addition to the videos, the IRCD includes:

■ All figures and tables from the text

■ Chapter art PowerPoint slides for each chapter

■ Enhanced Lecture PowerPoint Slides by Meredyth Fellows, West Chester University of Pennsylvania

■ Video PowerPoint Presentation Slides that make it easy to integrate every video clip from the Instructor's Resource CD

Video/DVD Resources

Journey Through the Lifespan **Developmental Video Series.** *Journey Through the Lifespan* illustrates the story of human growth and development from birth to old age in nine narrated segments. It includes vivid footage of people of all ages from around the world (North America, Europe, Africa, Asia, South America) in their normal environments (homes, hospitals, schools, office buildings) and at major life transitions (birth, marriage, divorce, becoming grandparents). More than one hour of unedited video footage helps students sharpen their observational skills. Interviews with prominent developmentalists, including Charles Nelson, Ann Peterson, Steven Pinker, and Barbara Rogoff, are integrated throughout this video to help show students exactly how researchers approach questions. Interviews with social workers, teachers, and nurses who work with children, adults, and older adults offer students insights into the challenges and rewards of these human service careers.

Assessment

Printed Test Bank. Prepared by Janet Belsky, this Test Bank includes multiple-choice, fill-in, true-false, and essay questions for each chapter of *Experiencing the Lifespan.* Each question is keyed to the textbook by topic, page number, and level of difficulty.

Diploma Computerized Test Bank (Windows and Macintosh on one CD-ROM). This CD-ROM offers an easy-to-use test-generation system that guides you through the process of creating tests. The CD allows you to add an unlimited number of questions, edit questions, format a test, scramble questions, and include pictures, equations, or multimedia links. The accompanying gradebook enables you to record students' grades throughout a course, and it includes the capacity to sort student records and view detailed analyses of test items, curve tests, generate reports, add weights to grades, and much more. The CD-ROM is also the access point for Diploma Online Testing, and Blackboard- and WebCT-formatted versions of the Test Bank.

Diploma Online Testing. With Diploma, you can easily create and administer exams over a network and over the Internet, with questions that incorporate multimedia and interactive exercises. The program allows you to restrict tests to specific computers or time blocks, and it includes an impressive suite of gradebook and result-analysis features. For more information on Diploma, visit http://www.wimba. com/products/diploma/ /.

Online Quizzing at www.worthpublishers.com/belsky. Prepared by Rosemary McCullough at Ave Maria University. Using Worth Publishers' on-line quizzing engine, you can easily and securely quiz students on-line using prewritten multiple-choice questions (not from the Test Bank) for each text chapter. Students receive instant feedback and can take the quizzes multiple times. You can view results by quiz, student, or question and get weekly results via e-mail.

Although our species-specific human maximum lifespan is about 100 to 105 years, a minuscule number of people (one out of many millions!) make it to super-centenarian status, living to 110. Here is a photograph of a Lebanese woman who in 2004 was working and—at an amazing 126 years old—qualified as the oldest person on Earth.

Jamal Saidi/Reuters / Corbis

Course Management

Worth's E-Packs for Blackboard and WebCT provide you with cutting-edge on-line materials that facilitate critical thinking and learning. Best of all, this material is preprogrammed and fully functional in your course management system. Pre-built materials based on my text eliminate hours of work and offer you significant support as you develop on-line courses. This package includes course outlines, preprogrammed quizzes, links, activities, interactive flashcards, and a wide array of other materials.

Print

Instructor's Resources. Prepared by Barbara Nicoll, University of La Verne, and Jean Raniseski, Alvin Community College, the Instructor's Resources include chapter outlines, chapter objectives, springboard topics for discussion and debate, handouts for student projects, ideas for term projects, and a guide to integrating audiovisual material and software into the course. They also include activities and worksheets from our **Teaching Tips Booklet,** a collection of creative activities, worksheets, classroom or small-group discussions, and writing assignments that the Worth team has gathered from instructors across the nation.

Study Guide. Prepared by Lisa Hager, Spring Hill College. Each chapter includes a review of key concepts, guided study questions, and section reviews that encourage students' active participation in their learning. Practice tests help students assess their mastery of the material.

Who Made This Book Possible?

This book was a completely collaborative endeavor engineered by the finest publishing company in the world: Worth (and not many authors can make that statement)! Firstly, heartfelt thanks go to my main editor, Elaine Epstein, for guiding this book to the production stage. Elaine meticulously went over the manuscript line by line several times. She made numerous suggestions that greatly improved my prose. She helped select the photos and made sure every table and figure was correct. She is the person who really kept me going emotionally and kept this book on track.

I owe a lifelong debt to Worth's Publisher, Catherine Woods, who took time from her incredibly busy schedule to help oversee this book. Catherine is that rare person—a low-key, available, author-sensitive editor, who can somehow manage to unflappably help guide an entire company at the same time. A truly lifelong debt goes to Jessica Bayne, my primary editor over almost a decade, for making *both* editions possible and for putting me on this entirely new life track.

Now we move on to the production team. Anthony Calcara coordinated the heroic task of pulling this book together—from manuscript copyediting to galleys to page proof—with aplomb. Associate managing editor Tracey Kuehn has been another unflappable guiding hand. Production manager Sarah Segal pushed everyone to get the book out on time.

Then there are the talented people who have made *Experiencing the Lifespan* look like a breathtaking work of art. As you delight in looking at the fabulous pictures, you can thank Deborah Anderson for her outstanding photo research and Bianca Moscatelli for coordinating the photo program. In fact, in addition to her uncanny ability to pick out just the right pictures to express my concept or idea, Deborah has been so much fun to work with that we became friends. Babs Reingold, Worth's resident artistic genius, was responsible for planning the gorgeous design and layout of the book. Robert Carter is the gifted artist who made the beautiful cover drawings and part openers.

Then there are the Worth people who developed and coordinated the supplements and developed the media package. Thanks go to Christine Burak for ferreting out outstanding ancillary authors and nurturing them along. Kudos go to these authors themselves: Lisa Hager who wrote the Student Study Guide and Barbara Nicoll and Jean Raniseski who prepared the Instructor's Resources Manual. A special debt of gratitude goes to Meredyth Fellows, who I convinced to write these wonderful PowerPoints, and who has been supporting and nurturing my writing all along. Because I realized just how crucial decent supplements can be, I've written the new Test Bank for this edition of *Experiencing the Lifespan*. So now you can pin the blame *directly* on Dr. Belsky when a student complains about that "unfair" test item or grade!

Without good marketing no one would read this book. And, as usual, this arm of the Worth team gets my A+ rating. Many authors complain about "the marketing" of their book. Not me! Kate Nurre, our Executive Marketing Manager, and her staff do an outstanding job. They produced a dazzling advertising brochure. They go to all the conferences. They spend countless hours in the field advocating for my work. Although I may not meet many of you personally, I want take this chance to thank all the sales reps for working so hard to get "Belsky" out in the real world.

Next come the instructor reviewers who make this book—and every textbook— what it is. Special credit goes to David Devonis, Meredyth Fellows, and Jason Spiegelman for having the fortitude to thoughtfully review this edition two times. I want to thank Bernie Ostrowski and Richard Kandus for taking the trouble to personally send me either their own and/or their students' comments and also for being such terrific supports. I am grateful for those special student readers who took the time to personally e-mail and tell me "You did a good job," or

"Dr. Belsky, I like it; but here's where you went wrong." These kinds of comments really make an author's day! Here are the names of *all* the instructors who helped make my writing and thinking so much better during the past ten years:

Dana Van Abbema, *St. Mary's College of Maryland*

Daisuke Akiba, *Queens College*

Cecilia Alvarez, *San Antonio College*

Andrea S. Anastasiou, *Mary Baldwin College*

Emilie Aubert, *Marquette University*

Pamela Auburn, *University of Houston Downtown*

Tracy Babcock, *Montana State University*

Harriet Bachner, *Northeastern State University*

Carol Bailey, *Rochester Community and Technical College*

Thomas Bailey, *University of Baltimore*

Shelly Ball, *Western Kentucky University*

Mary Ballard, *Appalachian State University*

Lacy Barnes-Mileham, *Reedley College*

Kay Bartosz, *Eastern Kentucky University*

Laura Barwegen, *Wheaton College*

Jonathan Bates, *Hunter College, CUNY*

Don Beach, *Tarleton State University*

Lori Beasley, *University of Central Oklahoma*

Martha-Ann Bell, *Virginia Tech*

Daniel Bellack, *Trident Technical College*

Karen Bendersky, *Georgia College and State University*

Keisha Bentley, *University of La Verne*

Robert Billingham, *Indiana University*

Kathi J. Bivens, *Asheville-Buncombe Technical Community College*

Jim Blonsky, *University of Tulsa*

Cheryl Bluestone, *Queensborough Community College, CUNY*

Greg Bonanno, *Teachers College, Columbia University*

Aviva Bower, *College of St. Rose*

Marlys Bratteli, *North Dakota State University*

Bonnie Breitmayer, *University of Illinois, Chicago*

Jennifer Brennom, *Kirkwood Community College*

Tom Brian, *University of Tulsa*

Adam Brown, *St. Bonaventure University*

Kimberly D. Brown, *Ball State University*

Donna Browning, *Mississippi State University*

Janine Buckner, *Seton Hall University*

Ted Bulling, *Nebraska Wesleyan University*

Holly Bunje, *University of Minnesota, Twin Cities*

Barbara Burns, *University of Louisville*

Marilyn Burns, *Modesto Junior College*

Norma Caltagirone, *Hillsborough Community College, Ybor City*

Lanthan Camblin, *University of Cincinnati*

Debb Campbell, *College of Sequoias*

Lee H. Campbell, *Edison Community College*

Robin Campbell, *Brevard Community College*

Kathryn A. Canter, *Penn State Fayette*

Peter Carson, *South Florida Community College*

Michael Casey, *College of Wooster*

Kimberly Chapman, *Blue River Community College*

Tom Chiaromonte, *Fullerton College*

Yiling Chow, *North Island College, Port Alberni*

Toni Christopherson, *California State University, Dominguez Hills*

Wanda Clark, *South Plains College*

Judy Collmer, *Cedar Valley College*

David Conner, *Truman State University*

Deborah Conway, *University of Virginia*

Diana Cooper, *Purdue University*

Ellen Cotter, *Georgia Southwestern State University*

Deborah M. Cox, *Madisonville Community College*

Kim B. Cragin, *Snow College*

Charles P. Cummings, *Asheville-Buncombe Technical Community College*

Karen Curran, *Mt. San Antonio College*

Antonio Cutolo-Ring, *Kansas City (KS) Community College*

Nancy Darling, *Bard College*

Paul Dawson, *Weber State University*

Janet B. Dean, *Asbury College*

Lynda De Dee, *University of Wisconsin, Oshkosh*

David C. Devonis, *Graceland University*

Charles Dickel, *Creighton University*

Darryl Dietrich, *College of St. Scholastica*

Lugenia Dixon, *Bainbridge College*

Benjamin Dobrin, *Virginia Wesleyan College*

Delores Doench, *Southwestern Community College*

Sundi Donovan, *Liberty University*

Lana Dryden, *Sir Sanford Fleming College*

Gwenden Dueker, *Grand Valley State University*

Bryan Duke, *University of Central Oklahoma*

Trisha M. Dunkel, *Loyola University, Chicago*

Robin Eliason, *Piedmont Virginia Community College*

Traci Elliot, *Alvin Community College*

Frank Ellis, *University of Maine, Augusta*

Kelley Eltzroth, *Mid Michigan Community College*

Marya Endriga, *California State University, Stanislaus*

Kathryn Fagan, *California Baptist University*

Daniel Fasko, *Bowling Green State University*

Nancy Feehan, *University of San Francisco*

Meredyth C. Fellows, *West Chester University of Pennsylvania*

Gary Felt, *City University of New York*

Martha Fewell, *Barat College*

Mark A. Fine, *University of Missouri*

Roseanne L. Flores, *Hunter College, CUNY*

John Foley, *Hagerstown Community College*

James Foster, *George Fox University*

Geri Fox, *University of Illinois, Chicago*

Thomas Francigetto, *Northampton Community College*

James Francis, *San Jacinto College*

Doug Friedrich, *University of West Florida*

Lynn Garrioch, *Colby-Sawyer College*

Bill Garris, *Cumberland College*

Caroline Gee, *Palomar College*

C. Ray Gentry, *Lenoir-Rhyne College*

Carol George, *Mills College*

Elizabeth Gersten, *Victor Valley College*

Linde Getahun, *Bethel University*

Afshin Gharib, *California State University, East Bay*

Nada Glick, *Yeshiva University*

Andrea Goldstein, *Kaplan University*

Arthur Gonchar, *University of La Verne*

Helen Gore-Laird, *University of Houston, University Park*

Tyhesha N. Goss, *University of Pennsylvania*

Dan Grangaard, *Austin Community College, Rio Grande*

Julie Graul, *St. Louis Community College, Florissant Valley*

Elizabeth Gray, *North Park University*

Erinn L. Green, *Wilmington College*

Stefanie Gray Greiner, *Mississippi University for Women*

Dale D. Grubb, *Baldwin-Wallace College*

Laura Gruntmeir, *Redlands Community College*

Lisa Hager, *Spring Hill College*

Michael Hall, *Iowa Western Community College*

Andre Halliburton, *Prairie State College*

Laura Hanish, *Arizona State University*

Robert Hansson, *University of Tulsa*

Richard Harland, *West Texas A&M University*

Gregory Harris, *Polk Community College*

Virginia Harvey, *University of Massachusetts, Boston*

Janice L. Hendrix, *Missouri State University*

Gertrude Henry, *Hampton University*

Rod Hetzel, *Baylor University*

Heather Hill, *University of Texas, San Antonio*

Elaine Hogan, *University of North Carolina, Wilmington*

Judith Holland, *Hawaii Pacific University*

Debra Hollister, *Valencia Community College*

Heather Holmes-Lonergan, *Metropolitan State College of Denver*

Rosemary Hornak, *Meredith College*

Rebecca Hoss, *College of Saint Mary*

Frances Raphael-Howell, *Montgomery College*

Cynthia Hudley, *University of California, Santa Barbara*

Alycia Hund, *Illinois State University*

David P. Hurford, *Pittsburgh State University*

Margaret Hellie Huyck, *Illinois Institute of Technology*

Elaine Ironsmith, *East Carolina University*

Jessica Jablonski, *Richard Stockton College*

Sabra Jacobs, *Big Sandy Community and Technical College*

Nina Lyon Jenkins, *University of Maryland, Eastern Shore*

David Johnson, *John Brown University*

Emilie Johnson, *Lindenwood University*

Mary Johnson, *Loras College*

Peggy Jordan, *Oklahoma City Community College*

Lisa Judd, *Western Wisconsin Technical College*

Tracy R. Juliao, *University of Michigan Flint*

Elaine Justice, *Old Dominion University*

Steve Kaatz, *Bethel University*

Jyotsna M. Kalavar, *Penn State New Kensington*

Chi-Ming Kam, *City College of New York, CUNY*

Richard Kandus, *Mt. San Jacinto College*

Skip Keith, *Delaware Technical and Community College*

Michelle L. Kelley, *Old Dominion University*

Richie Kelley, *Baptist Bible College and Seminary*

Robert Kelley, *Mira Costa College*

Jeff Kellogg, *Marian College*

Colleen Kennedy, *Roosevelt University*

Sarah Kern, *The College of New Jersey*

Marcia Killien, *University of Washington*

Kenyon Knapp, *Troy State University*

Cynthia Koenig, *Mt. St. Mary's College of Maryland*

Steve Kohn, *Valdosta State University*

Holly Krogh, *Mississippi University for Women*

Martha Kuehn, *Central Lakes College*

Alvin Kuest, *Great Lakes Christian College*

Rich Lanthier, *George Washington University*

Peggy Lauria, *Central Connecticut State University*

Melisa Layne, *Danville Community College*

John LeChapitaine, *University of Wisconsin, River Falls*

Barbara Lehmann, *Augsburg College*

Rhinehart Lintonen, *Gateway Technical College*

Nancey Lobb, *Alvin Community College*

Carol Ludders, *University of St. Francis*

Vickie Luttrell, *Dury University*

Christine Malecki, *Northern Illinois University*

Marlowe Manger, *Stanly Community College*

Pamela Manners, *Troy State University*

Kathy Manuel, *Bossier Parish Community College*

Jayne D. B. Marsh, *University of Southern Maine, Lewiston Auburn College*

Esther Martin, *California State University, Dominguez Hills*

Jan Mast, *Miami Dade College, North Campus*

Pan Maxson, *Duke University*

Nancy Mazurek, *Long Beach City College*

Christine McCormick, *Eastern Illinois University*

Jim McDonald, *California State University, Fresno*

Clark McKinney, *Southwest Tennessee Community College*

George Meyer, *Suffolk County Community College*

Barbara J. Miller, *Pasadena City College*

Christy Miller, *Coker College*

Mary Beth Miller, *Fresno City College*

Al Montgomery, *Our Lady of Holy Cross College*

Robin Montvilo, *Rhode Island College*

Peggy Moody, *St. Louis Community College*

Michelle Moriarty, *Johnson County Community College*

Ken Mumm, *University of Nebraska, Kearney*

Joyce Munsch, *Texas Tech University*

Jeannette Murphey, *Meridian Community College*

Lori Myers, *Louisiana Tech University*

Lana Nenide, *University of Wisconsin, Madison*

Margaret Nettles, *Alliant University*

Gregory Newton, *Diablo Valley College*

Barbara Nicoll, *University of La Verne*

Nancy Nolan, *Nashville State Community College*

Harriett Nordstrom, *University of Michigan, Flint*

Elizabeth O'Connor, *St. Mary's College*

Susan O'Donnell, *George Fox University*

Jane Ogden, *East Texas Baptist University*

Shirley Ogletree, *Texas State University*

Claudius Oni, *South Piedmont Community College*

Randall E. Osborne, *Texas State University, San Marcos*

John Otey, *Southern Arkansas University*

Carol Ott, *University of Wisconsin, Milwaukee*

Patti Owen-Smith, *Oxford College*

Heidi Pasek, *Montana State University*

Margaret Patton, *University of North Carolina, Charlotte*

Julie Hicks Patrick, *West Virginia University*

Evelyn Payne, *Albany State University*

Ian E. Payton, *Bethune Cookman University*

Carole Penner-Faje, *Molloy College*

Michelle L. Pilati, *Rio Hondo College*

Meril Posy, *Touro College, Brooklyn*

Shannon M. Pruden, *Temple University*

Ellery Pullman, *Briarcrest Bible College*

Samuel Putnam, *Bowdoin College*

Jeanne Quarles, *Oregon Coast Community College*

Mark Rafter, *College of the Canyons*

Cynthia Rand-Johnson, *Albany State University*

Janet Rangel, *Palo Alto College*

Jean Raniseski, *Alvin Community College*

Celinda Reese, *Oklahoma State University*

Ethan Remmel, *Western Washington University*

Paul Rhoads, *Williams Baptist College*

Kerri A. Riggs, *Lourdes College*

Mark Rittman, *Cuyahoga Community College*

Jeanne Rivers, *Finger Lakes Community College*

Wendy Robertson, *Western Michigan University*

Richard Robins, *University of California, Davis*

Melanie Domenech Rodriguez, *Utah State University*

Millie Roqueta, *Miami Dade College*

June Rosenberg, *Lyndon State College*

Christopher Rosnick, *University of South Florida*

Trisha Rossi, *Adelphi University*

Rodger Rossman, *College of the Albemarle*

Lisa Routh, *Pikes Peak Community College*

Stephanie Rowley, *University of Michigan, Ann Arbor*

Randall Russac, *University of North Florida*

Dawn Ella Rust, *Stephen F. Austin State University*

Tara Saathoff-Wells, *Central Michigan University*

Douglas Sauber, *Arcadia University*

Chris Saxild, *Wisconsin Indianhead Technical College*

Barbara Schaudt, *California State University, Bakersfield*

Daniela E. Schreier, *Chicago School of Professional Psychology*

Pamela Schuetze, *SUNY College at Buffalo*

Donna Seagle, *Chattanooga State Technical Community College*

Bonnie Seegmiller, *Hunter College, CUNY*

Chris Seifert, *Montana State University*

Susan Shapiro, *Indiana University, East*

Elliot Sharpe, *Maryville University*

Lawrence Shelton, *University of Vermont*

Shamani Shikwambi, *University of Northern Iowa*

Denise Simonsen, *Fort Lewis College*

Penny Skemp, *Mira Costa College*

Peggy Skinner, *South Plains College*

Barbara Smith, *Westminster College*

Valerie Smith, *Collin County Community College*

Edward Sofranko, *University of Rio Grande*

Joan Spiegel, *West Los Angeles College*

Jason S. Spiegelman, *Community College of Baltimore County*

Carolyn I. Spies, *Bloomfield College*

Scott Stein, *Southern Vermont College*

Stephanie Stein, *Central Washington University*

Sheila Steiner, *Jamestown College*

Jacqueline Stewart, *Seminole State College*

Robert Stewart, Jr., *Oakland University*

Rebecca Witt Stoffel, *West Liberty State College*

Cynthia Suarez, *Wofford College*

Joshua Susskind, *University of Northern Iowa*

Josephine Swalloway, *Curry College*

Emily Sweitzer, *California University of Pennsylvania*

Chuck Talor, *Valdosta State University*

Jamie Tanner, *South Georgia College*

Norma Tedder, *Edison Community College*

George Thatcher, *Texas Tech University*

Shannon Thomas, *Wallace Community College*

Donna Thompson, *Midland College*

Vicki Tinsley, *Brescia University*

Eugene Tootle, *Barry University*

David Tracer, *University of Colorado, Denver*

Stephen Truhon, *Austin Peay Centre, Fort Campbell*

Dunja Lund Trunk, *Bloomfield College*

Mary Vandendorpe, *Lewis University*

Janice Vidic, *University of Rio Grande*

Steven Voss, *Moberly Area Community College*

William Walkup, *Southwest Baptist University*

Anne Weiher, *Metropolitan State College of Denver*

Robert Weis, *University of Wisconsin, Stevens Point*

Lori Werdenschlag, *Lydon State College*

Noel Wescombe, *Whitworth College*

Andrea White, *Ithaca College*

Meade Whorton, *Louisiana Delta Community College*

Wanda A. Willard, *Monroe Community College*

Joylynne Wills, *Howard University*

Nancy A. Wilson, *Haywood Community College*

Steffen Wilson, *Eastern Kentucky University*

Bernadette Wise, *Iowa Lakes Community College*

Steve Wisecarver, *Lord Fairfax Community College*

Alex Wiseman, *University of Tulsa*

Nanci Woods, *Austin Peay State University*

Stephanie Wright, *Georgetown University*

David Yarbrough, *Texas State University*

Nikki Yonts, *Lyon College*

Ling-Yi Zhou, *University of St. Francis*

On the home front, I am indebted to my students at Middle Tennessee State University. As any teacher will tell you, I learn as much—or more—from you each semester as you do from me. I want to thank my interviewees for sharing their lives and thereby making this book really come alive. My department deserves my gratitude for patiently listening to my frustrations with grace and for being such a special group of people that it's a joy to come to Jones Hall at 7 A.M. Thanks go to Jules Seeman for masterfully guiding me through the minefields of life and—at a young 94—for showing me that development is the main theme of living at *every* age. (You will be meeting Jules in an Experiencing the Lifespan box in Chapter 13.) I want to thank my life love, David, for making my life happy and putting this book and my happiness center stage. Thanks also to my baby, Thomas, whom you also will meet throughout this book, for being born and growing up to be such a wonderful person; and for teaching me what living and being human is really all about.

Janet Belsky
July 22, 2009

P.S. As textbook writing and teaching is a continual work in progress, I'd like to regularly update you on what I'll be learning for the next three years. I also want to invite you, the reader, to comment on what I've already written and so help me make this next version of *Experiencing the Lifespan* the best that it can be. With that goal in mind, I've set up a Web site (www.janetbelsky.com) for us all to share insights, critiques, and teaching and reading tips. Let's make this a real ongoing conversation—both students and instructors—as we journey through the lifespan in the semesters to come!

The Foundation

This two-chapter part offers you the foundations for understanding the lifespan journey.

Chapter 1—**The People and the Field** introduces *all* the major concepts and themes in this course. In this first chapter, I'll familiarize you with our discipline's basic terminology, provide a bird's-eye view of the evolving lifespan, offer a framework for how to think about world cultures, and highlight some new twenty-first-century life stages. Most important, in this chapter you will learn about the major theories and research strategies that have shaped our field. Bottom line: Chapter 1 gives you the basic tools you will need for understanding this book.

Chapter 2—**Prenatal Development, Pregnancy, and Birth** lays out the foundation for our developing lives. Here, you will learn about how a baby develops from a tiny clump of cells, and get insights into the experience of pregnancy from the point of view of mothers- and fathers-to-be. This chapter describes pregnancy rituals in different cultures, discusses problems (including infertility) that may lie on the prenatal pathway, and offers an in-depth look at the miracle of birth.

PART I

Chapter 1

CHAPTER OUTLINE

Dear Students,

Welcome to lifespan development! This course is about your past, your future, and who you are now. It's about your parents and grandparents, friends and colleagues, the children you have or expect to have. If you plan to work with children, adults, or older people, this course will give you an important foundation for your career. This semester, starting with the first minutes in the womb, you will get a motion picture of human life.

As we travel through the lifespan, I urge you to look outward to the wider world. While reading the infancy chapters, notice babies at restaurants. In the sections on childhood and adolescence, pay attention to boys and girls at a playground, spend an afternoon with a 4-year-old, watch pre-teens at the mall. Then observe married couples. Interview a middle-aged relative. Talk to a 60-year-old about to retire or an 85-year-old coping with the physical challenges of old age. The purpose of this class is to widen your horizons, to enable you to look at each stage of life in a more empathic way.

How can you fully enjoy the scenery on this semester-long trip and still get a great grade in this course? Following the principle that the more emotionally engaged we are, the more we learn, once again: Make it relevant; make it personal; see the concepts come alive in the world. To help you, I've begun each chapter with a vignette. Enjoy the vignette. It's been constructed to alert you to the major chapter themes. Look at the photos, charts, and the summary tables. Complete each hands-on activity. They also are planned to help you effortlessly solidify the key concepts in mind. My goal is to have you reach the end of each chapter and realize, "I learned a tremendous amount, but this reading never felt like a chore. This is NOTHING like a dry, 'textbook-like' text."

Now that you know my main agendas (stay tuned for more scholarly ones later), let's get started. This chapter introduces all of the basic themes in the course. We begin by introducing the characters that you will be meeting in the introductory vignettes.

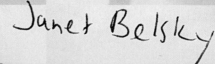

Janet Belsky

The People and the Field

It's Theresa and Sal's fiftieth anniversary and they are having a party. They've been spending a fabulous retirement meeting different people while traveling the country and cruising the world. Now, it's time to get their new friends together for "our celebration of twenty-first-century American life."

One invitation is for Maria and baby Manuel, whom Theresa and Sal met on a cross-country drive to Las Vegas five years ago. What will that precious child be like now that he's in third grade?

David and Doreen, that fascinating couple on last year's Caribbean cruise, get another invitation. As Theresa and Sal are well aware, there is nothing like sitting together night after night at dinner to cement new friendships for life. For Sal, sharing life stories at those nightly dinners was a vivid lesson in how the world has changed. Sal married Theresa, the love of his life, at age 21. During the 1950s, his family would never have tolerated divorcing or waiting until the late twenties to begin adult life. David took until almost age 30 to "find himself," and, after his first marriage broke up, even selected a spouse of a different race. Actually, Sal can't help but be impressed by the commitment of his "young" 40-something friends. Despite their hectic work schedules in this difficult economy, David and Doreen have managed to stay together happily for almost 10 years.

A final invitation goes to those other delightful dinner companions, Kim, her husband Jeff, and baby Elissa. With Elissa, there's got to be incredible catching up to do. Will Theresa and Sal even recognize that adorable 6-month-old now that she's almost one-and-a-half? Theresa's kept up with everyone by e-mail, and everyone's coming to Scranton. Now it's time to reconnect.

Let's start with the children. Kim reports that, since Elissa started walking, her baby does not slow down for a second. Actually, it's kind of depressing. Last year, Elissa went to Theresa with a smile. Now, all she wants is Mom. The changes in Manuel are equally astonishing. At age 8, that child can talk to you like an adult. Still, Theresa sees the same boy she first fell in love with: sunny, kind, and just as gifted mechanically as he was at age 3.

David confides in Theresa that he's concerned about his work schedule because he hardly sees his wife. Does she have any suggestions for staying blissfully married for the next 40 years? Doreen also wants advice from her "second mom." In a few years, when she turns 50, and the kids are in college, Doreen plans to go back to school for a social work degree. But can she make it in the classroom at that age?

Theresa and Sal (bless the Lord) are still feeling okay, but they also have worries. There's the slowness, Theresa's vision problems, and Sal's heart disease. It's lovely to see these young people flowering. The last act has definitely been the best. This celebration is a bit bittersweet. The eighties won't be like the seventies. There isn't much time left.

What does Sal mean that the eighties won't be like the seventies? If you met Theresa and Sal at age 30 or 50, would they be the same vibrant, outgoing people as they are today? Is David's late start in adult life typical? Are Doreen's worries about her middle-aged mental abilities realistic? And what can you do to help ensure that you have a happy married life? Why do 1-year-olds such as Elissa get clingy just as they begin walking, and can we pinpoint the mental leaps that make children at age 8, such as Manuel, seem so adult?

Developmentalists, also called **developmental scientists**—researchers who study the lifespan—are about to answer these questions and hundreds of others about our unfolding life.

developmentalists (developmental scientists) Researchers and practitioners whose professional interest lies in the study of the human lifespan.

lifespan development The scientific field covering all of the human lifespan.

child development The scientific study of development from birth through adolescence.

gerontology The scientific study of the aging process and older adults.

adult development The scientific study of the adult part of life.

normative transitions Predictable life changes that occur during development.

non-normative transitions Unpredictable or atypical life changes that occur during development.

Who We Are and What We Study

Lifespan development, the scientific study of human growth throughout life, is a hybrid latecomer to psychology. Its roots lie in **child development,** the study of childhood and the teenage years. Child development traces its origins back more than a century. In 1877, Charles Darwin published an article based on notes he had made about his baby during the first years of life. In the 1890s, a pioneering psychologist named G. Stanley Hall established the first institute in the United States devoted to research on the child. The field of child development began to take off between World Wars I and II (Lerner, 1998). It remains the passion of thousands of developmental scientists working in every corner of the globe.

Gerontology, the scientific study of aging—the other core discipline in lifespan development—had a slower start. Researchers began to really study the aging process only after World War II (Birren & Birren, 1990). Gerontology and its related field, **adult development,** underwent their phenomenal growth spurt during the final third of the twentieth century.

Lifespan development puts it all together. It synthesizes what researchers know about our unfolding life. Who works in this huge mega-discipline, and what passions drive developmentalists?

- **Lifespan development is multidisciplinary.** It draws on fields as different as neuroscience, nursing, psychology, and social policy to understand every topic relating to human development. A biologically oriented developmentalist interested in day care might examine toddlers' output of salivary cortisol (a stress hormone) when they first arrive at day care in the morning. His anthropologist colleague might look at cultural values relating to the day-care choice. A social policy expert might explore the impact of offering universal government-funded day care in nations such as Finland and France. A researcher interested in the physiology of Alzheimer's disease might examine the plaques and tangles that ravage the brain. A nurse might head an innovative Alzheimer's unit. A research-oriented psychologist might construct a scale to measure the behavioral impairments produced by this devastating disease.

- **Lifespan development explores the predictable milestones on our human journey,** from walking to working, to Elissa's sudden shyness and attachment to her mother. Is Doreen right to worry about her learning abilities in her fifties? What is physical aging, or puberty, or menopause all about? Are there specific emotions we feel as we approach that final universal milestone, death?

- **Lifespan development focuses on the individual differences that give spice to human life,** from Manuel's mechanical talents to Theresa's outgoing personality. Can we really see the person we will be at age 8 (or 83) by age 3? How much does personality or intelligence change as we travel through life? Developmentalists want to understand what *causes* the striking individual differences we see in temperament, talents, and traits. They are interested in exploring individual differences in the timing of developmental milestones, too; examining, for instance, why people reach puberty earlier or later or age more quickly or slowly than their peers.

- **Lifespan development explores the impact of life transitions and practices.** It deals with **normative,** or predictable, **transitions,** such as Theresa and Sal's retirement, becoming parents, or beginning middle school. It focuses on **non-normative,** or atypical, **transitions,** such as divorce, the death of a child, or how the recent declines in the economy affect how we are approaching the world. It explores more enduring life practices, such as smoking, spanking, or sleeping in the same bed with your child.

Chris Hondros/Getty Images

This woman working with youth in Palestine is one of thousands of developmental scientists whose mission it is to help children around the world.

Developmentalists realize that life transitions that we consider normative, such as retiring or starting middle school, are products of living in a particular time in history. They understand that life practices such as smoking or spanking or sleeping in bed with a child vary, depending on our social class and cultural background. They know that our travels through the lifespan are affected by several very basic markers, or overall conditions of life.

Now it's time to introduce several basic **contexts of development,** or broad general influences, which I will be continually discussing throughout this book.

Our cultural background is one force that affects every aspect of development. So, culturally oriented researchers in our field might study how this South Asian wedding ceremony is designed to express this society's messages about how family life should go.

Setting the Context

How does being born in a particular historical time affect our lifespan journey? What about our social class, cultural and ethnic background, or that basic biological difference, being female or male?

The Impact of Cohort

Cohort refers to our birth group, the age group with whom we travel through life. Turn back to the vignette and you can immediately see the heavy role our cohort plays in influencing adult life. Sal reached his late teens in the 1950s, when men married in their early twenties and typically stayed married for life. David, who came of age 30 years later, faced a dazzling array of lifestyle choices in a time when divorce had become common and young people were sensitive to the problems with having long-lasting loving relationships. As an interracial couple, David and Doreen are even taking an unusual life path today! Being in their late forties, this couple is at an interesting cutting point at this moment in history. They are at the tail end of the famous baby boom.

The **baby boom cohort,** defined as people born from 1946 to 1964, is leaving an incredible imprint on the Western world as it moves through society. The reason lies in size. When soldiers returned from serving in World War II to get married, the average family size ballooned to almost four children. When this huge group was growing up during the 1950s, as I just suggested, families were traditional, with the two-parent, stay-at-home-mother family being our national ideal. Then, as rebellious adolescents during the 1960s and 1970s, the baby boomers helped engineer a radical transformation in these attitudes and roles (more about this lifestyle revolution soon). Society is now poised for an explosion of senior citizens as the baby boom cohort floods into its elderly years.

The cohorts living in the early twenty-first century are part of an endless march of cohorts stretching back thousands of years. Let's now take a brief historical tour to get a sense of the dramatic changes in childhood, old age, and adulthood during just the past few centuries, and pinpoint what our lifespan looks like today.

Changing Conceptions of Childhood

At age ten he began his work life helping his father manufacture candles and soap. He hated dipping wicks into wax and wanted to go to sea, but his father refused and apprenticed him to a master printer. At age 17 he ran away from Boston to Philadelphia to search for work.

His father died when he was 11, and he left school. At 17 he was appointed official surveyor for Culpepper County in Virginia. By age 20 he was in charge of managing his family's plantation.

(Mintz, 2004)

contexts of development Fundamental markers, including cohort, socioeconomic status, culture, and gender, that shape how we develop throughout the lifespan.

cohort The age group with whom we travel through life.

baby boom cohort The huge age group born between 1946 and 1964.

In the nineteenth century, if you visited factories such as this cannery, you would see many young children at work—showing how far we have come over the past century in our attitudes about childhood.

While we might imagine that adolescence has always been a life stage, teenagerhood only became a separate "age" during the twentieth century, when mandatory high school attendance helped postpone our entry into adulthood.

emerging adulthood The phase of life that begins after high school, tapers off toward the late twenties, and is devoted to constructing an adult life.

Who were these boys? Their names were Benjamin Franklin and George Washington.

Imagine you were born in Colonial times. In addition to reaching adulthood at a much younger age, your chance of having *any* lifespan would have been far from secure. In seventeenth-century Paris, roughly 1 in every 3 babies died in early infancy (Ariès, 1962; Hrdy, 1999). As late as 1900, almost 3 of every 10 U.S. children did not live beyond age 5 (Mintz, 2004).

The incredible childhood mortality rates, plus the dire poverty, may have explained why child-rearing practices that we would view as abusive today used to be routine. In eighteenth- and nineteenth-century Europe, middle-class babies were farmed out to be nursed by country women. They were separated from their parents during the first two years of life. Child abandonment was common, especially among the poor. In the early 1800s in Paris, about 1 in 5 newborns were "exposed"—placed in the doorways of churches, or simply left outside to die. In cities such as St. Petersburg, Russia, the statistic might have been as high as 1 in 2 (Ariès, 1962; Hrdy, 1999).

In addition, for most of history, people did not have our current sense that childhood is a special life stage (Ariès, 1962; Mintz, 2004). Children, as you saw above, entered their work lives as young as age 9 or 10. During the industrial revolution, in British and U.S. mills, poor boys and girls made up more than a third of the labor force. They worked from dawn till dark (Mintz, 2004).

In the seventeenth and eighteenth centuries, philosophers such as John Locke and Jean Jacques Rousseau had spelled out a different vision of childhood. Locke believed that human beings are born a *tabula rasa*, a blank slate on which anything could be written, and that the way we treat children shapes their adult lives. Rousseau argued that babies enter life totally innocent; he felt we should shower these dependent creatures with love. However, this message could fully penetrate society only when the scientific advances of the early twentieth century dramatically improved living standards, and we entered our modern age.

One force producing this kinder, gentler view of childhood was universal education. During the late nineteenth century in Western Europe and much of the United States, attendance at primary school became mandatory (Ariès, 1962). School kept children from working and insulated these years as a protected, dependent life phase. Still, as late as 1915, only 1 in 10 U.S. children attended high school; most entered their work lives after seventh or eighth grade (Mintz, 2004).

At the beginning of the twentieth century, the developmentalist G. Stanley Hall (1904/1969) identified a stage of "storm and stress," located between childhood and adulthood, which he named *adolescence*. However, it was only during the Great Depression of the 1930s, when President Franklin Roosevelt signed a bill making high school attendance mandatory, that adolescence became a standard U.S. life stage (Mintz, 2004). Our famous teenage culture has existed for only 60 or 70 years!

In recent decades, with so many of us going to college and, sometimes, graduate school, we have delayed the beginning of adulthood to an older age. Developmentalists (for example, Arnett, 2000, 2004, 2007b) have identified a new in-between stage of life in affluent countries. **Emerging adulthood**, lasting from age 18 to roughly the late twenties, is devoted to exploring our place in the world. One reason why twenty-first-century adults, such as David, feel comfortable about postponing marriage or settling down to a career is that today we can expect to live for an amazingly long time.

Changing Conceptions of Later Life

In every culture, a few people always lived to "old age." However, for most of history, largely due to the high rates of infant and childhood mortality, **average life expectancy,** our fifty-fifty chance at birth of living to a given age, was shockingly low. In the New England colonies, average life expectancy was about age 30. In Maryland during Colonial times, it was under age 20, for both masters and their slaves (Fischer, 1977).

Toward the end of the nineteenth century, life expectancy in the United States rapidly improved. By 1900, it was 46. Then, in the next century, it shot up to 76.7. During the twentieth century, life expectancy in North America and Western Europe increased by almost 30 years! (See Kinsella & Velkoff, 2001; Health United States, 2007, CDC.)

This **twentieth-century life expectancy revolution** is perhaps the most important milestone that has occurred in the history of our species. The most dramatic increases in longevity occurred during the early decades of the last century, when medical advances, such as antibiotics, wiped out deaths from many *infectious diseases*. Since these illnesses, such as diphtheria, killed both the young and old, their conquest allowed us to live past mid-life. In the last 50 years, our progress has been slower because we are waging war against another category of disease. The illnesses we now typically die from, called *chronic diseases*—such as heart disease, cancer, and stroke—are tied to the aging process itself.

The outcome is that today life expectancies have zoomed into the upper seventies in North America, Western Europe, New Zealand, Israel, and Japan. As you can see in Figure 1.1, a baby born in affluent parts of the world, especially if that child is female, has a good chance of making it close to our **maximum lifespan,** the absolute biological limit of human life (about age 105).

This extension of the lifespan has changed how we think about *every* life stage. It has moved grandparenthood, once a sign of being "old," down into middle age. If you become a grandparent in your late forties, expect to be called grandma or grandpa for roughly half of your life! Women such as Doreen can start new careers in their fifties, given that today females can expect to live on average for roughly 30 more years (Health United States, 2007, CDC). For well-off older people, such as Theresa and Sal, retirement—at least until recently—has been as long a life stage as childhood and adolescence combined (Clark & Quinn, 2002; see Chapter 13 for some more dismal future projections). Most important, we have moved the real beginning of old age beyond age 65.

Today, most people in their sixties and seventies are active and healthy. But as we approach our eighties, our chance of being disabled by disease increases dramatically. Because of this, developmentalists make a distinction between two groups of older adults. The **young-old,** defined as people in their sixties and seventies, often look and feel middle-aged. They reject the idea that they are old (Lachman, 2004). The **old-old,** people in their eighties and beyond, seem in a different class. Since they are more likely to have physical and mental disabilities, they are more prone to fit the stereotype of the frail, dependent older adult. In sum, Sal is right: Today the eighties are a very different stage of life!

Changing Conceptions of Adult Life

If the medical advances of the early twentieth century made it possible for us to make it to old age, during the last third of the previous century, a revolution in lifestyles transformed the way we live our adult lives. This change in society, which started in Western countries and has spread to many other parts of the globe, occurred when the baby boomers moved into their teenage years.

average life expectancy A person's fifty-fifty chance at birth of living to a given age.

twentieth-century life expectancy revolution The dramatic increase in average life expectancy that occurred during the first half of the twentieth century in the developed world.

maximum lifespan The biological limit of human life (about 105 years).

young-old People in their sixties and seventies.

old-old People age 80 and older.

FIGURE 1.1: **Average life expectancy of men and women in some affluent nations:** Women today can expect to live close to the maximum lifespan in affluent countries. Notice, for instance, the astonishingly high life expectancy for women in Japan. (FYI: As of 2007, the United States ranked 45th globally in average life expectancy.) *Source:* CIA World Factbook (2007 estimates).

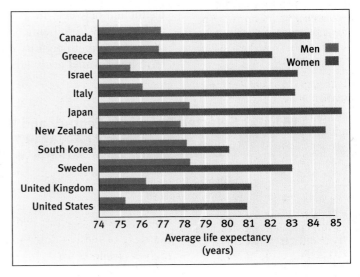

The healthy, active couple in their 60s *(left)* have little in common with the disabled 90-year-old man living in a nursing home *(right)*—showing why developmentalists divide the elderly into the *young-old* and the *old-old*.

A

B

The 1960s "Decade of Protest" included the civil rights and women's movements, the sexual revolution, and the "counterculture" movement that emphasized liberation in every area of life (Bengtson, 1989). People could have sex without being married. Women were free to fulfill themselves in a career. We encouraged men to share the housework and child care equally with their wives. Divorce became an acceptable alternative to living in an unfulfilling marriage. To have a baby, women no longer needed to be married at all.

Today, with women making up roughly half the labor force, only a minority of couples fit the traditional 1950s roles of breadwinner husband and homemaker wife. With roughly one out of two U.S. marriages ending in divorce, we can no longer be confident of following the traditional path of staying together for life. While U.S. divorce rates may be declining, the trend toward having children without being married continues to rise. As of 2005, almost 2 in 5 U.S. babies were born to unmarried women (Centers for Disease Control and Prevention [CDC], 2008). In Northern European nations such as Sweden, the comparable statistic is more than 1 in 2 (Kiernan, 2004).

The timeline on the bottom of this page illustrates these two twentieth-century changes. It charts the progress of the huge baby boom as it moves through society and highlights the emergence of our new life stages. In this book, in addition to dividing the lifespan into its standard categories—infancy, childhood, adolescence, adulthood, and later life—I will be targeting these new phases of life. I'll devote a whole chapter to emerging adulthood. In the late life section, I'll continually emphasize the crucial distinction between the young-old and old-old (being 60 is miles different physically and mentally from being 80 or 95). Throughout the chapters, you will be seeing how the late-twentieth-century changes in adulthood, which amazed Sal in the vignette, have transformed every other stage of life—from infancy to adolescence to old age.

TIMELINE	Selected Twentieth-Century and New Twenty-First-Century Milestones													
	1900	1910	1920	1930	1940	1950	1960	1970	1980	1990	2000	2010	2020	2030
MAJOR SOCIETAL CHANGE	Life Expectancy Takes Off Deaths shift from infectious to chronic diseases								Lifestyle Revolution Women's movement/rise in divorce and single parenthood/more lifestyle freedom					
BABY BOOM COHORT						Born		Teenagers				Young-old →	Old-old	
NEW LIFE STAGES			Adolescence						Old-old		Emerging adulthood			

What do you think of these lifestyle changes? Have they been a benefit or not? On the positive side, we have a much more open society, where anything is possible at any time of life. Doreen can return to school for a new career in her fifties. Theresa and Sal feel free to make good friends of every age and ethnic group. The downside of the lifestyle revolution, at least in the United States, relates to economics. Imagine the challenges of supporting a family alone, and you will understand why the rise in single parenthood and high child poverty rates have gone hand in hand. In fact, in 2007 more than *half* (54%) of all U.S children under age 6 being raised by single moms were living under the poverty line (DeNavas-Walt, Proctor, & Smith, 2008).

Living in poverty has widespread consequences on development. How do you think the educational experiences, health, and life chances of these girls will differ from those of children growing up with affluent parents, given that they are being raised by this poor single mom?

The Impact of Socioeconomic Status

Socioeconomic status (SES) is a term referring to our education and, especially, our income. As you will see throughout this book, living in poverty, in particular, sets people up for a cascade of problems—from being born less healthy to going to lower-quality schools; from living in more dangerous neighborhoods to dying at a younger age. In fact, adults who live under the poverty line in the United States—with an average life expectancy in the mid-sixties—may not even survive to later life! Not only do developmentalists rank people by socioeconomic status, but they rank countries, too.

Developed-world nations are characterized by their affluence, or high median per-person incomes. In these countries—the United States, Canada, Australia, New Zealand, and Japan, as well as every Western European nation, Singapore, Taiwan, and Hong Kong—life expectancy is high (CIA, 2007). Technology is advanced. People have widespread access to higher education and social services. Residents can enjoy the latest advances of twenty-first-century life.

Developing-world countries are at the opposite end of the spectrum. Here, poverty is rampant, and life can be a struggle to survive. In the least-developed nations, much of the population may not have cars, indoor plumbing, clean running water, or access to adequate education and medical care.

Table 1.1 illustrates the dramatic health and wealth gaps among a few of the most- and least-developed countries. Imagine living in a part of the world where

socioeconomic status (SES) A basic marker referring to status on the educational and—especially—income rungs.

developed world The most affluent countries in the world.

developing world The more impoverished countries of the world.

TABLE 1.1: Early Twenty-First Century Health, Wealth, and Lifestyle Gaps Among a Few of the Most- and Least-Developed Nations

	Per Capita Income (average wages per year in U.S. dollars)	Deaths of Children Under Age 5 (per 1,000)	Adult Literacy (percent) (2001)	Cell Phones (per 1,000 people)
Most-Developed Nations				
Ireland	$32,570	7	99+	774
Norway	$35,533	4	99+	815
United States	$36,056	9	99+	451
Least-Developed Nations				
Burundi	$518	196	49	4
Haiti	$1,093	123	50	11
Ethiopia	$366	177	40	0

The lifestyle, health, and educational disparities among the world's least- and most-developed countries are astonishing.

Source: World Health Organization (2005).

Peter Blakely/Corbis

collectivist cultures Societies that prize social harmony, obedience, and close family connectedness over individual achievement.

individualistic cultures Societies that prize independence, competition, and personal success.

infectious diseases such as malaria are common, many of your neighbors are unable to read or write, and you have less than a fifty-fifty chance of living beyond middle age. Babies born in the most impoverished regions of the globe face a twenty-first-century lifespan that has striking similarities to the one developed-world children faced several centuries ago.

The Impact of Culture and Ethnicity

Residents of developing nations, especially those living in rural areas, are less apt to have experienced the late-twentieth-century changes in men's and women's roles. Divorce may be against the law. Arranged marriages still occur, with parents deciding whom their children should wed. Still, if you visited these countries, you might be struck by a shared sense of community and family commitment that we might not find in the West. Is there a way of categorizing cultures according to their basic values? Developmentalists who study culture answer yes.

Collectivist cultures place a premium on social harmony. The family generations expect to live together, even as adults. Children are taught to obey their elders, to suppress their feelings (Matsumoto and others, 2008), to value being respectful, and to subordinate their needs to the good of the wider group.

Individualistic cultures emphasize independence, competition, and personal success. Children are encouraged to openly express their emotions, to believe in their own personal power, to leave their parents, to stand on their own as self-sufficient and independent adults. Traditionally, Western nations score high on indices of individualism. Nations in Asia, Africa, and South America rank higher on collectivism scales (Hofstede, 1981, 2001; Triandis, 1995).

Imagine how your perspective on life might differ if becoming independent from your parents or honestly sharing your feelings were viewed as inappropriate ways to behave. How would you treat your children, choose a career, or select a spouse? What concerns would you have as you were facing death?

As we scan development around the globe, I will regularly distinguish between collectivist and more individualistic societies. At several places in this book, I will pause to highlight research exploring differences among the major U.S. ethnic groups, shown in Figure 1.2. How does being an ethnic minority affect everything from emerging adult attitudes to the chance of developing age-related diseases?

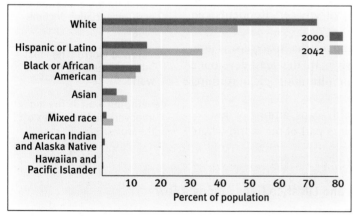

FIGURE 1.2: **The major ethnic groups in the United States, their percentages in the 2000 census, and a few mid-twenty-first-century projections:** By 2042, more than half of the U.S. population is projected to be ethnic minorities. Notice, in particular, the huge increase in the fraction of Hispanic Americans, and the fact that by the mid-twenty-first century the percentage of people who label themselves as "mixed race" is expected to double.
Sources: United States, Factsheet, American Factfinder (U.S. Census Bureau, 2006 community survey; U.S. Census Bureau, AFP, U.S. White Population a Minority by 2042).

As you read this information, keep in mind that what unites us as people far outweighs any minor distinctions based on culture, ethnicity, or race. Moreover, making diversity generalizations is hazardous because of the diversity that exists *within* each nation and ethnic group. In the most traditionally individualistic country (no surprise, that's the United States), people have a mix of collectivist and individualistic worldviews (Christopher & Bickhard, 2007; Keller and others, 2007). As their standard of living rises, residents of classic collectivistic countries, such as China, are developing much more individualistic, Western worldviews.

If the census labels you as "Hispanic American" or "Asian American," you also are probably aware that this broad label masks more than it reveals. As a third-generation Cuban American, do you really have much in common with a recent immigrant from Mexico or Belize? Given that people arrive in the United States from hundreds of culturally different countries, does it really make sense to lump our citizens into a small number of ethnic groups? There is, however, one distinction that we all can agree on. It's called being female or male.

B. Tanaka/Getty Images

For this grandmother, mother, and daughter, getting dressed up to visit this Shinto family shrine and pay their respects to their ancestors is an important ritual. It is one way that the lesson "honor your elders" is taught to children living in collectivist societies such as Japan from an early age.

The Impact of Gender

Obviously, our culture's values shape our life path as males and females. Are you living in a society or at a time in history when men are encouraged to be househusbands and women to be corporate CEOs? But biology is crucial in driving at least one fundamental difference in the pathways of women and men: Throughout the developed world, females outlive males by more than 4 years. Because they must survive child-bearing and carry an extra X chromosome, women are the physiologically hardier sex.

Are boys more aggressive than girls? When we see male/female variations in care-giving, in career interests, and in childhood play styles, are these differences mainly due to the environment (societal pressures or the way we are brought up) or to inborn, biological forces? Throughout this book, I'll examine these questions as we explore the scientific truth of our gender stereotypes and spell out other fascinating facts about sex differences, too. To set you up for this ongoing conversation, you might want to take the "Is It Males or Females?" quiz in Table 1.2. Keep a copy handy. As we travel through the lifespan, you can check the accuracy of your ideas.

TABLE 1.2: Is It Males or Females?

1. Who is more likely to survive the hazards of prenatal development, male or female fetuses? (You will find the answer in Chapter 2.)

2. Who is more vulnerable to experiencing high levels of stress when sent to day care, male or female toddlers? (You will find the answer in Chapter 4.)

3. Who is more aggressive, boys or girls? (You will find the answer in Chapter 6.)

4. Who is more likely to be diagnosed with learning disabilities in school, boys or girls? (You will find the answer in Chapter 7.)

5. Who, when they reach puberty at an earlier-than-typical age, is more at risk of developing problems, boys or girls? (You will find the answer in Chapter 8.)

6. Who is likely to stay in the "nest" (at home) longer during the emerging-adult years, men or women? (You will find the answer in Chapter 10.)

7. Who is more at risk of having enduring emotional problems after being widowed, men or women? (You will find the answer in Chapter 13.)

8. Who lives longer in the face of serious age-related disabilities, men or women? (You will find the answer in Chapter 14.)

9. Who cares more about being closely attached, males or females—or both sexes? (You will find the answer throughout this book.)

Now that I've laid out the framework and highlighted the basic principle that our lifespan is a continuing work in progress varying across cultures and historical times, let's get to the science. After you complete this section's Tying It All Together review quiz, I will introduce the main theories, research methods, concepts, and scientific terms I'll be mentioning in the chapters to come.

TYING IT ALL TOGETHER

1. Tuan, a historian, is arguing that during the twentieth century, conditions for children changed dramatically in very positive ways. He should mention all of the following examples *except* (check the statement that is *false*):

    a. Child mortality used to be high. Today, it is low in the developed world.
    b. Poor infants often used to be abandoned. Today, this practice would be severely condemned.
    c. Children used to start their work lives at a young age. Today, childhood extends through (and even beyond) the adolescent years.
    d. Children used to be the poorest segment of the U.S. population. Today, they are the most affluent group.

2. Maria just became a grandmother; Sara just retired from her job; Rosa just entered a nursing home. If these women live in the United States and are middle class, roughly how old are they likely to be?

3. Jim and Joe are arguing about the impact of the 1960s lifestyle revolution. Jim believes that life is much better today. Joe says that life was better in the 1950s. Argue Jim's position, then Joe's, backing up your points by using the information in this section.

4. Pablo says, "I would never think of leaving my parents or living far from my brothers and sisters. A person must take care of his extended family before satisfying his own needs." Peter says, "My primary commitment is to my wife and children. A person needs, above all, to make an independent life." Pablo has a(n) _____ worldview, while Peter's worldview is more _____.

Answers to the Tying It All Together questions can be found on the last page of this chapter.

Theories: Lenses for Looking at the Lifespan

During his twenties, David was searching for his identity. Manuel's mechanical talents must be hereditary. If Elissa's mother gives her a lot of love during her first years of life, she will grow up to be a loving, secure adult. If any of these thoughts entered your mind while reading about the people in the opening chapter vignette, you were using a major theory that developmentalists use to understand human life.

Theories offer insights into that crucial *why* question. They attempt to explain what causes us to act as we do. They may allow us to predict the future. Ideally, they give us information about how to improve the quality of life. Theories in developmental science may offer broad general explanations of behavior that apply to people at every age. Or they may focus on describing specific changes that occur at particular ages. This section provides a preview of both kinds of theories.

Let's begin by outlining some very broad theories (one is actually a research discipline) that offer general explanations of behavior. I've organized these theories somewhat chronologically, based on their twentieth-century appearance, but mainly arranged according to where each perspective stands on that fundamental issue mentioned earlier: Is it the environment, or the wider world, that determines how we develop? Are our personalities, talents, and traits shaped mainly by biological or genetic forces? This is the famous **nature** (biology) versus **nurture** (environment) question.

theory Any perspective explaining why people act the way they do. Theories allow us to predict behavior and also suggest how to intervene to improve behavior.

nature Biological or genetic causes of development.

nurture Environmental causes of development.

Taking a Different Perspective: Exploring Cognitions

Enter **cognitive behaviorism (social learning theory)**, launched by Albert Bandura (1977; 1986) and his colleagues in the 1970s in a series of studies demonstrating the powerful influence of **modeling,** or learning by watching and imitating what other people do.

Because we are a social species, Bandura argued, modeling is actually the major way we learn. Given that we are continually modeling everything, from the expressions of the person we are talking with to the latest hairstyle, who are we most likely to model as we travel through life?

Bandura's (1986) studies suggest that we tend to model people who are nurturing, or relate to us in a caring way. (The good news here is that being a loving, hands-on parent is the best way to naturally embed your values and ideas.) We model people whom we categorize as being like us. At age 2, you probably modeled anything from the vacuum cleaner to the behavior of the family dog. As we grow older, we tailor our modeling selectively, based on our understanding of who we are.

Modeling similar people partly explains why, after children understand their gender label (girl or boy) at about age 2 1/2, they begin to separate into sex-segregated play groups and prefer to play with their "own group." It accounts for why some at-risk teenagers gravitate to the druggies group at school, and then model the leader who most embodies these group norms (as you will see in Chapter 9). While I will be drawing on the principles of modeling to explain everything from preschool sex-role behavior to predicting whether a given adolescent is having sex, another cognitive behavioral concept developed by Bandura may be even more influential in our field today. It's called self-efficacy.

Self-efficacy refers to our belief in our competence, our sense that we can be successful at a given task. According to Bandura (1989, 1992, 1997), efficacy feelings determine the goals we set. They predict which activities we engage in as we travel through life. When self-efficacy is low, we decide not to tackle that difficult math problem. We choose not to ask a beautiful stranger for a date. When self-efficacy is high, we not only take action but continue to act long after the traditional behavioral approach suggests that extinction should occur.

Let's illustrate by returning to the vignette example of Doreen, who wants to go back to school. If Doreen has extremely poor academic self-efficacy she might be afraid to enroll in the social work program. Furthermore, by exploring her efficacy feelings ("How competent intellectually do I feel?"), we can predict what will happen if Doreen has trouble with tests in her first semester. If her sense of self-efficacy is relatively low, this test-taking trouble might cause extinction—and she will drop out of college. If her efficacy feelings are intense, Doreen will work even harder, spending more hours in the library than before: "I can do it . . . I just need to study more to succeed!"

How do children develop either low or high self-efficacy? How can we improve self-efficacy at any time of life? These are the kinds of questions I will be exploring in later chapters as we examine the vital role that efficacy feelings play from elementary school to old age.

By now, you may be impressed with how behaviorism's simple, action-oriented concepts can help us improve the quality of life. Be consistent. Don't reinforce negative behavior. Reinforce positive things (from traditional behaviorism). Draw on the principles of modeling and stimulate efficacy feelings to help children and adults succeed (from cognitive behaviorism).

Still, many developmentalists, even people who believe that nurture is vitally important, find behaviorism unsatisfying. Aren't we more than just a collection of efficacy feelings or reinforced responses? Isn't there a basic core to our personality, and aren't the lessons we learn in early childhood especially important in adult life?

Notice that behaviorism doesn't address that vital question: What *really* motivates us as human beings? To illustrate the problems that we run into when we don't con-

cognitive behaviorism (social learning theory) A behavioral worldview that emphasizes that people learn by watching others and that our thoughts about the reinforcers determine our behavior. Cognitive behaviorists focus on charting and modifying people's thoughts.

modeling Learning by watching and imitating others.

self-efficacy According to cognitive behaviorism, an internal belief in our competence that predicts whether we initiate activities or persist in the face of failures, and predicts the goals we set.

Although it is likely to have many causes, cognitive behaviorists might explain Oprah Winfrey's triumphant success as due to her intense sense of self-efficacy. Cognitive behaviorists, such as Bandura, believe that by exploring efficacy feelings we can predict a good deal about the lives of people, such as Oprah, who triumph against the odds.

Joseph Marzullo/Retna Ltd.

attachment theory Theory formulated by John Bowlby centering on the crucial importance to our species' survival of being closely connected with a caregiver during early childhood and being attached to a significant other during all of life.

sider basic human motivations, let's listen to John Watson (1924/1998) lashing out at what he calls pathological "love conditioning" destined to produce a whiny, dependent adult: "The child is alone putting blocks together and the mother comes in. . . . The child crawls . . . to the mother . . . climbs into her lap, puts its arms around her neck. The mother fondles her child, kisses it and holds it" (p. 78). Wait a second! Isn't that the way parents and children are supposed to behave?

Attachment Theory: Focus on Nurture, Nature, and Love

According to **attachment theory**, the answer is yes. Attachment theory, put forth by British psychiatrist John Bowlby during the mid-twentieth century, has the same premise as traditional Freudian psychoanalytic theory. (Bowlby was actually trained as a psychoanalyst and worked with Freud's daughter, Anna.) According to Freud and his followers (see the summary Table 1.3), the way our parents treat us during the first years of life either permits us to be loving, successful adults or produces lasting emotional scars. Bowlby agreed that our early life experiences with caregivers shape our lifelong ability to love, but he focused on what he called the *attachment response*.

In observing young children separated from their mothers, Bowlby noticed that, as you saw with Elissa in the introductory chapter vignette, babies need to be physically close to a caregiver during the time when they are beginning to walk (Bowlby, 1969, 1973; Karen, 1998). Disruptions in this biologically programmed attachment response, he argued, if prolonged, can cause serious problems later in life. Moreover,

---

TABLE 1.3: Freudian Facts: *Current* Core Concepts

Bio: Psychiatrist, Jewish, Viennese (1856–1939), author of more than 40 books and monographs

Life Mission

To understand the motives that underlie human behavior (analyze the psyche = psychoanalytic) and promote mental health

Core Principles

1) Our behavior is dominated by our unconscious—motives, thoughts, and feelings derived from early childhood—of which we are not aware. 2) The way our parents treat us in the first five years of life determines our lifelong mental health. 3) The more aware we are of what is motivating our actions, the more in control (and successful) we will be as adults.

Structures of Personality (and relationship to parenting)

Id = there at birth; unconscious instinctual needs. *Ego* = rational, conscious, master controller of personality; grows out of the need to adjust our behavior to the world; works to satisfy our needs in an appropriate way. *Superego* = unconscious moral part of personality; inhibits "id" drives.

Good parenting during early childhood produces a *strong ego*—or a mentally healthy person in control of his actions. Dysfunctional parents make for a life dominated by unconscious impulses, and a symptom-ridden, out-of-control personality.

Goal of Therapy

To explore the *repressed* (made unconscious) pathological childhood experiences that produce psychological problems, make them conscious, and so restore mental health. (Freud beautifully summed up this therapeutic goal as: "Where id there was, ego there will be.")

Current Status

Towering mid-twentieth-century theory of human development, still popular among some mental health workers, but outside the mainstream of current developmental science

---

This table highlights the core principles of the current *psychoanalytic approach—based on my training at a postdoctoral psychoanalytic institute as a young clinical psychologist. I've omitted Freud's famous "oral, anal, and phallic stages" because practicing mental health workers haven't used this part of the theory for decades.*

our impulse to be close to a "significant other" is a basic human need during every stage of life.

How does the attachment response develop during infancy? Is Bowlby right that the quality of our early attachments determines our adult mental health? How can we draw on the principles of attachment theory to understand everything from adult love relationships to widowhood to our concerns as we approach death? Stay tuned for answers as I highlight the principles of this influential theory throughout this book.

Today, unlike Freud's ideas, attachment theory is extremely popular in developmental science. One reason why Bowlby's concepts have such appeal in our field is that they are based on a very modern view of what motivates human beings. Yes, Bowlby did believe that our upbringing (nurture) was important; but he also firmly anchored his theory in biology (nature). Bowlby (1969, 1973, 1980) argued that the attachment response is genetically programmed into our species to promote survival. Bowlby, as it turns out, was an early evolutionary psychologist.

Bowlby believes that the intense, loving bond between this father and his infant son will set the baby up for a fulfilling life. Do you agree with this basic principle of attachment theory?

Evolutionary Psychology: Theorizing About the Nature of Human Similarities

Evolutionary psychologists are the mirror image of behaviorists. They look to nature, or inborn biological forces that have evolved to promote survival, to explain why people act in certain ways. Why do pregnant women develop morning sickness just as the fetal organs are being formed, and why do newborns prefer to look at attractive faces rather than ugly ones? (That's actually true!) According to evolutionary psychologists, these reactions cannot be changed by modifying the reinforcers. They are based in the human genetic code that we all share.

Evolutionary psychology lacks the practical, action-oriented approach of behaviorism, although it does alert us to the fact that we need to pay close attention to basic human needs. Still, this "look to built-in biology" explanation of human motivations is now at the cutting-edge forefront of our field. The reason is that, during the final decades of the twentieth century, most developmentalists rejected the standard behaviorist and Freudian idea that nurture, or our outer world experiences, are all-important. They realized that genetics does matter—often a great deal—in determining the person we will become. Research in an exploding field brought this message home.

Behavioral Genetics: Scientifically Exploring the "Nature" of Human Differences

"I have a genetic tendency to become alcoholic/to develop bipolar disorder/to bite my nails." Have you ever wondered about the scientific basis of these kinds of statements? They come from research in **behavioral genetics**—a field devoted to studying the role genetics plays in understanding why people vary in their personalities or any other human trait. To study the genetic contribution to human differences, behavioral geneticists use twin and adoption studies as their main research tools.

In **twin studies,** researchers typically compare identical (monozygotic) twins and fraternal (dizygotic) twins on a particular trait of interest—be it motor speed, math talents, or mental health. Identical twins develop from the same fertilized egg (it splits soon after the one-cell stage) and are genetic clones. Fraternal twins, like any brother or sister, develop from separate conceptions and so, on average, share 50 percent of their genes. The idea is that if a given trait is highly influenced by genetics, identical twins should be much more alike in that quality than fraternal twins. Specifically, behavioral geneticists use a statistic called *heritability* (which ranges from 1 = totally genetic, to 0 = no genetic contribution) to summarize the extent to which a given behavior is shaped by genetic forces.

evolutionary psychology Theory or worldview highlighting the role that inborn, species-specific behaviors play in human development and life.

behavioral genetics Field devoted to scientifically determining the role that hereditary forces play in determining individual differences in behavior.

twin study Behavioral genetic research strategy, designed to determine the genetic contribution of a given trait, that involves comparing identical twins with fraternal twins (or with other people).

How "genetic" are these children's friendly personalities? To answer this question, researchers compare identical twins, such as these two girls *(left)*, with fraternal twins, like this girl and boy *(right)*. If the identicals (who share exactly the same DNA) are much more similar to each other than the fraternals in their friendliness scores, friendliness is defined as a highly heritable trait.

For instance, suppose you decided to conduct a twin study to determine the heritability of Manuel's mechanical talents. First, you would select a large group of identical and fraternal twins and give both sets of twins various tests of mechanical skills. You would then compare the strength of the test score relationships you found for each twin group. Let's say the identical twins' scores tended to be incredibly similar—almost like the same person taking the tests twice—and the fraternal twins' test scores tended to vary much more from each other. Your heritability statistic would be high, and you then would conclude: "Mechanical talents such as Manuel's are highly genetically determined traits."

In **adoption studies** researchers compare adopted children with their biological and adoptive parents. Here, too, they evaluate the impact of heredity on a trait by looking at how closely these children resemble their birth parents (with whom they share only genes) and their adoptive parents (with whom they share only environments).

Twin studies of children growing up in the same family and simple adoption studies are not difficult to carry out. The most striking evidence for the power of genetics comes from the rare **twin/adoption studies,** in which identical twins are separated in childhood and reunited in adult life. If Joe and James, who have exactly the same DNA, have very similar abilities, traits, and personalities even though they grew up in *different families*, this would be strong evidence that genetics plays a crucial role in making us who we are.

Consider, for instance, the Swedish Twin Adoption Study of Aging. Researchers combed national registries to find identical and fraternal twins adopted into different families in that country—where birth records of every adoptee are kept. Then they reunited these children in late middle age and gave the twins a battery of tests (Finkel & Pedersen, 2004; Kato & Pedersen, 2005).

While genetic forces influenced a wide range of behaviors, specific qualities varied in their heritabilities. The most genetically determined quality, interestingly, was overall IQ (Pedersen, 1996). In fact, if one twin took the standard intelligence test, statistically speaking we could predict that the other twin would have an almost identical IQ despite living apart for an entire life!

Behavioral genetic studies such as these have opened our eyes to the often incredible impact of nature. From the tendency to drink heavily (Agrawal & Lynskey, 2008) to even our chance of getting divorced, qualities we thought *must* be due to how our parents raised us, are influenced by genetic forces (Plomin & others, 2003b).

These studies have given us equally tantalizing insights into the meaning of nurture. It's tempting to assume that children growing up in the same family share the same nurture, or environment. But as you can see in the How Do We Know research box, that assumption is wrong. We inhabit very different life spaces than our brothers and sisters, even when we eat at the same dinner table and share the same room. These environments are shaped in part by our genes (Rowe, 2003).

adoption study Behavioral genetic research strategy, designed to determine the genetic contribution to a given trait, that involves comparing adopted children with their biological and adoptive parents.

twin/adoption studies Behavioral genetic research strategy that involves comparing the similarities of identical twin pairs adopted into different families, to determine the genetic contribution to a given trait.

❋ HOW DO WE KNOW . . .

that our nature affects our upbringing?

For most of the twentieth century, developmentalists assumed that parents treated all of their children the same way. We could classify mothers as either nurturing or rejecting, caring or cold. Then the Swedish Twin/Adoption Study turned these basic parenting assumptions upside down (Plomin, 1994).

Researchers asked middle-aged identical twins who had been adopted into different families as babies to rate their parents along dimensions such as caring, acceptance, and discipline styles. They were astonished to find similarities in the ratings, even though the twins were evaluating different families!

What was happening here? The answer, the researchers concluded, was that the genetic similarities in the twins' personalities *created* similar family environments. If Joe and Jim were both easy, kind, and caring, they evoked more loving parenting. If they were both temperamentally difficult, they caused their adoptive parents to react in more rejecting, less nurturant ways.

This principle—that a child's genetics drives how parents act—does not just apply to personality, but to cognitive stimulation, too, as I vividly saw in my own life. Because my adopted son has dyslexia and is very physically active, in our house we ended up doing active things like sports. As Thomas didn't like to sit still for story time, I probably would have been rated as a "less than optimally stimulating" parent had some psychologist come into my home to rate how much I read to my child.

And now, the plot thickens. When I met Thomas's biological mother, I found out that she also has dyslexia. She's tremendously energetic and peppy. It's one thing to see the impact of nature in my son and his mother revealed. But I can't help wondering. . . . Maureen is a very different kind of person than I am (although we have a terrific time together—traveling and doing active things). Would Thomas have had the *same* kind of upbringing (at least partly) that I gave my son if he had *not* been adopted—and had grown up with his biological mom?

Photodisc Green/Getty Images

The bottom line is that there is no such thing as nature *or* nurture. To really understand human development, we need to explore how nature *and* nurture combine. That is exactly how developmental scientists conceptualize and study the lifespan today.

Imagine how you (and other people) would respond to this grumpy boy versus a sunny, upbeat child and you will understand how *evocative* influences work to make us more like ourselves genetically and why all human relationships are *bidirectional*.

Nature and Nurture Combined

Now let's look at two nature-plus-nurture principles that I will be drawing on again and again in this book.

Our Nature Shapes Our Nurture

Developmentalists now understand that it doesn't make sense to separate nature and nurture into independent entities (see Diamond, 2009). Our genetic tendencies mold and shape our life experiences in two distinctive ways.

Evocative forces refer to the fact that our inborn talents and temperamental tendencies naturally evoke, or produce, certain responses from the human world. A joyous child elicits smiles from everyone. A child who is temperamentally irritable, hard to handle, or has trouble sitting still is unfortunately set up to get the kind of harsh parenting she least needs to succeed. Human relationships are **bidirectional.** Just as you get grumpy when with a grumpy person, fight with your difficult neighbor, or shy away from your colleague who is paralyzingly shy, who we are as people causes other people to react to us in specific ways, driving our development for the good and the bad.

evocative forces The nature-interacts-with-nurture principle that our genetic temperamental tendencies and predispositions evoke, or produce, certain responses from other people.

bidirectionality The crucial principle that people affect one another, or that interpersonal influences flow in both directions.

Nicole Katano/PictureQuest

Because this musically talented girl is choosing to spend hours playing the piano, she is likely to become even more talented as she gets older, illustrating the fact that we actively shape our environment to fit our genetic tendencies and talents.

Active forces refer to the fact that we *actively select* our environments based on our genetic tendencies. A child who is talented at reading will gravitate toward devouring books, and so become an even better reader. His brother, who is exceptionally well coordinated, may play baseball three hours a day and become a star athlete in his teenage years. Because we tailor our activities to fit our biologically based interests and skills, what starts out as minor differences between people in early childhood tend to snowball over time—ultimately producing huge gaps in talents and traits. The unusually high heritabilities for IQ in the Swedish Twin Adoption Study are consistently lower in similar behavioral genetic studies conducted during childhood (Plomin & Spinath, 2004). The reason is that, like heat-seeking missiles, our nature causes us to gravitate toward specific life experiences, so we literally become *more like ourselves* genetically as we travel into adult life (Scarr, 1997).

We Need the Right Nurture to Express Our Nature

Developmentalists understand that even if a specific quality is 100 percent genetic, its expression is 100 percent dependent on the outside world. Let's illustrate by returning to the incredibly high heritabilities for overall intelligence. Suppose you lived in an impoverished developing country, were malnourished, and forced to work as a laborer in a field. In this environment, having a genius-level IQ might be irrelevant, as there would be little chance to demonstrate your hereditary gifts.

Extending this principle to real life, a goal of many developmentalists today is to foster the correct **person–environment fit.** We need to try to select the environment that is right for our talents and skills. How can we use our understanding of our species-specific biology (evolutionary theory) and our unique personal biology (advances in genetics) to provide the right person–environment fit for children, working moms and dads, and older adults? This is a basic challenge we face during the twenty-first century.

Actually, rather than making what we do—as parents, teachers, and health-care professionals—irrelevant, our understanding of the importance of genetics makes the environment we provide for children even *more* crucial. As researchers conduct more sophisticated nature-plus-nurture studies, the message "The environment really matters" comes through loud and clear. From the exciting new studies that show incredibly sensitive care-giving can lessen the impact of a child's being born biologically or genetically "at risk" (see Barry, Kochanska & Philibert, 2008; Diamond, 2009; Rowe and others, 2009) to the fact that sometimes living in a rural setting (with less chance to buy alcohol) makes it less likely for someone with a genetic predisposition to abuse alcohol to drink to excess in his teens (see Agrawal & Lynskey, 2008), the real impact of the nature revolution is to allow us to help change the environment in order to enhance the quality of people's lives.

active forces The nature-interacts-with-nurture principle that our genetic temperamental tendencies and predispositions cause us to actively choose to put ourselves into specific environments.

person–environment fit The extent to which the environment is tailored to our biological tendencies and talents. In developmental science, fostering this fit between our talents and the wider world is an important goal.

Suzanne Krieter/The Boston Globe

This autistic boy is using a specially designed tire swing his family set up in the basement that helps to orient him and calm him down. When a child's problem is biological or genetic, providing nurturing parenting and the best possible environment is more important than ever.

Emphasis on Age-Linked Theories

Now that I've spelled out the basic "nature combines with nurture" perspective that will guide how we view development, let's look at two theories that will also guide us as we travel through the lifespan stage by stage.

Piaget's Cognitive Developmental Theory

A 3-year-old tells you that, "Mr. Sun goes to bed because it's time for me to go to sleep." A toddler is obsessed with flushing different-sized wads of paper down the toilet and can't resist touching everything she sees. Do you ever wish you could get into the minds of young children and understand how they view the world? If so, you share the passion of the number-one genius in child psychology, Jean Piaget.

Piaget, born in 1894 in Switzerland, was a childhood prodigy himself. As the author of several dozen published articles on mollusks, by age 20 he was well on his way to becoming a well-known expert in that field (Wadsworth, 1996; Flavell, 1963). Piaget's interests quickly shifted to studying children when he worked in the laboratory of a psychologist named Binet, who was devising the original intelligence test. Rather than being focused on ranking children according to how much they knew, Piaget became fascinated by the characteristics of children's *incorrect* responses. He spent the next 60 years meticulously devising tasks to map the minds of these mysterious creatures in our midst.

Piaget believed that as they travel from birth through adolescence, children progress through *qualitatively different* stages of cognitive growth (see Table 1.4). The term *qualitative* means that rather than simply knowing less or more (on the kind of scale we can rank from 1 to 10), infants, preschoolers, elementary-school-age children, and teenagers think about the world in *completely* different ways. However, Piaget also believed that there was a basic continuity to cognitive development. Human beings have a built-in hunger to learn and mentally grow. Mental growth occurs through **assimilation**: We fit the world to our capacities or existing cognitive structures (which Piaget calls *schemas*). And then **accommodation** occurs. We naturally change our thinking to fit the world (Piaget, 1971).

Jean Piaget, in his masterful studies spanning much of the twentieth century, transformed the way we think about children's thinking.

Bill Anderson/Photo Researchers, Inc.

TABLE 1.4: Piaget's Stages of Development

Age	Name of Stage	Description
0–2	Sensorimotor	The baby manipulates objects to pin down the basics of physical reality. This stage, ending with the development of language, will be described in Chapter 3.
2–7	Preoperations	Children's perceptions are captured by their immediate appearances. "What they see is what is real." They believe, among other things, that inanimate objects are really alive and that if the appearance of a quantity of liquid changes (for instance, if it is poured from a short, wide glass into a tall, thin one), the amount actually becomes different. You will learn about all of these perceptions in Chapter 5.
8–12	Concrete operations	Children have a realistic understanding of the world. Their thinking is really on the same wavelength as adults'. While they can reason conceptually about concrete objects, however, they cannot think abstractly in a scientific way.
12+	Formal operations	Reasoning is at its pinnacle: hypothetical, scientific, flexible, fully adult. Our full cognitive human potential has been reached. We will explore this stage in Chapter 9.

Piaget's cognitive developmental theory Jean Piaget's principle that from infancy to adolescence, children progress through four qualitatively different stages of intellectual growth.

assimilation In Jean Piaget's theory, the first step promoting mental growth, involving fitting environmental input to our existing mental capacities.

accommodation In Piaget's theory, enlarging our mental capacities to fit input from the wider world.

Ted Streshinsky/Time Life Pictures/Getty Images

With his powerful writings on identity and especially his concept of age-related psychosocial tasks, Erik Erikson (shown here with his wife, Joan) has become a father of our field.

Let's illustrate these two concepts by reflecting on your own thinking while you were reading the previous section. Before beginning this chapter, you probably had certain ideas about heredity and environment. In Piaget's terminology, let's call them your "heredity/environment schemas." Perhaps you felt that if a trait is highly genetic, changing the environment doesn't matter; or you may have believed that genetics and environment were totally separate. While fitting (assimilating) your reading into these existing ideas, you entered a state of disequilibrium—"Hey, this contradicts what I've always believed"—and were forced to accommodate. The result was that your "nature/nurture" schemas became more complex and you developed a more advanced (intelligent) way of perceiving the world! From a newborn who assimilates each object, from a rattle to a pacifier, to his "sucking" schema, to a neuroscientist who incorporates every new discovery into her complex knowledge base, while assimilating everything to what we know, we need to continually accommodate, and so—inch by inch—we cognitively advance.

Piaget was a great advocate of hands-on experiences. He felt that we learn by acting on or physically operating in the world. Rather than using an adult-centered framework, he had the revolutionary idea that we need to understand how children experience life *from their own point of view.* Since the main purpose of this book is to make this material personal and experiential, and to look at life from the perspective of people ranging from age 2 to 92, how can we go beyond cognition and childhood to understand the qualitatively different agendas we have at *every* stage of life? Erik Erikson offered us this basic road map.

Erik Erikson's Psychosocial Tasks

Erik Erikson, born in Germany in 1904—a few years after Piaget—was a psychoanalyst who disagreed with Freud's ideas in several respects. Freud believed that sexuality (what he called *libido*) is the main drive shaping human behavior and that we progress through oral, anal, and phallic stages during the first five years of life. Erikson targeted challenges related to becoming an independent self and social relationships as being at humanity's core. Erikson, however, qualifies as the father of lifespan development because he differed from the Freudians (and Bowlby) in another fundamental way. Rather than believing our personality is formed in early childhood and then doesn't change (recall my Freud Table 1.3), Erikson felt that we continue to develop throughout life. He set out to chart the developmental tasks we face at each stage of life.

Erikson (1963), as Table 1.5 illustrates, spelled out a particular **psychosocial task,** or challenge, that we face during each of eight life stages. These tasks, he argued, build on one another because we cannot master the issue of a later stage unless we have accomplished the developmental milestones of the previous ones.

Erikson's psychosocial tasks In Erik Erikson's theory, each challenge that we face as we travel through the eight stages of the lifespan.

TABLE 1.5: Erikson's Psychosocial Stages

Life Stage	Primary Task
Infancy (birth to 1 year)	Basic trust versus mistrust
Toddlerhood (1 to 2 years)	Autonomy versus shame and doubt
Early childhood (3 to 6 years)	Initiative versus guilt
Middle childhood (6 years to puberty)	Industry versus inferiority
Adolescence (tens into twenties)	Identity versus role confusion
Young adulthood (twenties to early forties)	Intimacy versus isolation
Middle adulthood (forties to sixties)	Generativity versus stagnation
Late adulthood (late sixties and beyond)	Integrity versus despair

TABLE 1.6: Summary of the Major Current Theories in Lifespan Development

	Nature vs. Nurture Emphasis and Ages of Interest	Representative Questions
Behaviorism	Nurture (all ages)	What reinforcers are shaping this behavior? Who is this person modeling? How can I stimulate self-efficacy?
Attachment theory	Nature and nurture (infancy, but also all ages)	How does the attachment response unfold in infancy? What conditions evoke this biologically programmed response at every life stage?
Behavioral genetics	Nature (all ages)	To what degree are the differences I see in people due to genetics?
Evolutionary theory	Nature (all ages)	How might this behavior be built into the human genetic code?
Piaget's theory	Children	How does this child understand the world? What is his thinking like?
Erikson's theory	(all ages)	Is this baby experiencing basic trust? Where is this teenager in terms of identity? Has this middle-aged person reached generativity?

Notice how adults are continually kissing infants and you will understand why Erikson believed that *basic trust* (the belief that the human world is caring) is our fundamental life task in the first year of life. Erikson's second psychosocial task, *autonomy*, makes perfect sense of the infamous "*no* stage" and "terrible twos." It tells us that we need to *celebrate* this not-so-pleasant toddler behavior as the blossoming of a separate self! Think back to elementary school, and you may realize why Erikson used the term *industry*, or learning to work—at friendships, sports, academics—as our basic challenge during our school years, from age 6 to 12.

Erikson's adolescent task, the search for *identity*, has now become a household word. Erikson was particularly interested in issues related to constructing an adult identity. As a young person, he wandered around Europe, thinking he wanted to be an artist before finding his career path as a teacher and psychoanalyst (Coles, 1970).

How have developmentalists expanded on Erikson's task of identity? Is Erikson right that nurturing the next generation, or *generativity*, is the key to a fulfilling adult life? These are just two of the questions I will be exploring as we draw on Erikson's psychosocial tasks to help us think more deeply about the challenges we face at each life stage.

By now, you may be overwhelmed by all these theories and terms. But take heart. You already have the basic concepts you will need for understanding this whole semester well in hand! Now, let's conclude by looking a worldview that says, "Let's embrace *all* of these theories and influences on development and explore how they interact." (For a summary of the various theories, see Table 1.6.)

The Developmental Systems Perspective

A pioneering child psychologist named Urie Bronfenbrenner (1977) was among the earliest lifespan theorists to highlight the principle that real-world behavior has *many* different, complex causes. Bronfenbrenner viewed the child at the center of an expanding circle of environmental influences. At the innermost circle, development is shaped by the relationships between the child and people in his immediate setting, such as parents and teachers. The next wider circles, that indirectly feed back to affect the child, lie in forces such as the parents' work relationships and more general influences such as the neighborhood in which that boy or girl grows up. At the broadest levels, as you saw earlier in the chapter, the child's culture, and his cohort, or the time in history when

developmental systems perspective An all-encompassing outlook on development that stresses the need to embrace a variety of theories, and the idea that all systems and processes interrelate.

he travels through life, crucially shape behavior, too. Bronfenbrenner's plea to examine the total *ecology*, or life situation of the child, forms the heart of a popular contemporary scientific perspective called the **developmental systems approach** (Ford & Lerner, 1992; Lerner, 1998; Lerner, Dowling, & Roth, 2003). Specifically:

- **Developmental systems theorists stress the need to use many different approaches.** There are *many* valid ways of looking at behavior. Our actions *do* have many causes. To fully understand development, we need to draw on the principles of behaviorism, attachment theory, evolutionary psychology, and Piaget. At the widest societal level, to explain our actions, we need to look outward to our culture and cohort. At the tiniest molecular level, we need to look inward to focus on our genes. We have to embrace the input of everyone, from nurses to neuroscientists and from anthropologists to molecular biologists, to make sense of each individual life.

- **Developmental systems theorists emphasize the need to look at the interactions of processes.** As Bronfenbrenner highlighted in his theory, we also need to be aware that every influence on development relates. Our genetic tendencies influence the cultures we construct; the cultures we live in affect the expression of our genes. In the same way that our body systems and processes are in constant communication, continual back-and-forth influences are what human development is all about (see Diamond, 2009).

  For example, let's consider that basic societal marker: poverty. Growing up in poverty might affect your attachment relationships. You are less likely to get attention from your parents because they are under stress. You might not get adequate nutrition. Your neighborhood could be a frightening place to live. Each stress might combine to overload your body, activating negative genetic tendencies and setting you up physiologically for emotional problems.

  But some children, because of their genetics, their cultural background, or their cohort, might be insulated from the negative effects of growing up poor. Others might actually thrive. In a classic study tracing the lives of children growing up during the Great Depression, researchers discovered that if this major historical event occurred at the right time in the life cycle (adolescence), having experienced severe economic hardship made for an enduring sense of self-efficacy. It produced a more competent, resilient adult (Elder & Caspi, 1988). In sum, development occurs in surprising directions for good and for bad. Diversity of change processes and individual differences are the spice of human life.

TYING IT ALL TOGETHER

1. Hernando, a third grader, is having incredible trouble sitting still and paying attention in class. When Hernando's parents consult developmentalists about their son's problem, pick out which comments might be made by: (1) a traditional behaviorist; (2) a cognitive behaviorist; (3) an evolutionary psychologist; (4) a behavioral geneticist; (5) an Eriksonian; (6) an advocate of developmental systems theory.

   a. Hernando has low academic self-efficacy. Let's improve his sense of competence at school.
   b. Hernando, like other boys, is biologically programmed to run around. If the class had regular gym time, Hernando's ability to focus in class would improve.
   c. Hernando is being reinforced for this behavior by getting attention from the teacher and his classmates. Let's reward appropriate classroom behavior.
   d. Did you or your husband have trouble focusing in school? Perhaps your son's difficulties are hereditary.
   e. Hernando's behavior may have many causes, from genetics, to the reinforcers at school, to growing up in our twenty-first century Internet age. Let's use a variety of different approaches to help him.
   f. Hernando is having trouble mastering the developmental task of industry. How can we promote the ability to work that is so important at this age?

2. In the above question, which suggestion involves providing the right person–environment fit?

3. Billy, a 1-year-old, mouths everything—pencils, his favorite toy, DVDs—changing his mouthing to fit the object that he is "sampling." According to Piaget, the act of mouthing everything refers to _____, while changing the mouthing behavior to fit the different objects refers to _____.

4. Samantha, a behaviorist, is arguing for her worldview, while Sally is pointing up behaviorism's fatal flaws. First, take Samantha's position, arguing for the virtues of behaviorism, and then discuss some limitations of the theory.

Answers to the Tying It All Together questions can be found on the last page of this chapter.

Research Methods: The Tools of the Trade

Theories give us the lenses or framework for understanding behavior. *Research* is the way we find out the scientific truth. I already touched on the specialized research technique designed to determine the genetic contributions to behavior. Now let's sketch out the general research strategies that developmental scientists use.

Two Standard Research Strategies: Correlations and Experiments

What impact does poverty have on relationships, personality, or physical health? What forces cause children to model certain people? Does a particular intervention to help memory or improve self-efficacy really work? To answer any question about the impact one condition or entity (called a *variable*) has on another, developmentalists use two basic research designs: correlational studies and true experiments.

In a **correlational study,** researchers chart the relationships between the dimensions they are interested in exploring as they naturally occur. Let's say you want to test the hypothesis that providing a more cognitively stimulating environment at home—for instance, by extensively teaching or reading to your children—leads to better school performance. Your overall game plan is simple: Select a group of children by going to a class. Relate their academic skills to the amount of reading and teaching activities their parents provide.

Immediately, however, you will be faced with decisions related to choosing your participants. Are you going to look at first or second graders, explore the practices of both parents or of mothers alone, solicit your group from a public or private school? You would need to get permission from the school system. You would need to get the parents to volunteer. Are you choosing a **representative sample**—meaning a group that reflects the characteristics of the overall population about whom you want to generalize?

Then you would face your most important challenge—accurately measuring your variables. Just as a broken thermometer can't tell us if we have a fever, if we don't have adequate indices of the concepts we are measuring, we can't conclude anything at all.

With regard to the adult dimension, one possibility might be to directly observe the parents with their children. This technique, called **naturalistic observation**, is appealing because it is very concrete. You are seeing the behavior as it occurs in "nature," or real life. However, a minute's thought suggests this approach presents a huge practical challenge: the need to travel to each home to observe each family on many occasions for an extended time. Plus, when we watch parent–child interactions, or any socially desirable activity, people try to act their best. Wouldn't you be on good behavior if a psychologist arrived at your house to monitor your behavior with your child?

correlational study A research strategy that involves relating two or more variables.

representative sample A group that reflects the characteristics of the overall population.

naturalistic observation A measurement strategy that involves directly watching and coding behaviors.

self-report strategy A measurement strategy that involves having people report on their feelings and activities through questionnaires.

true experiments The only research strategy that can determine that something causes something else; involves randomly assigning people to different treatments and then looking at the outcome.

The most cost-effective strategy would be to give the parents a questionnaire with items such as: "How often do you read to your child?" or "How often do you go to museums?" This **self-report strategy,** in which people evaluate their behavior and ideas anonymously, is the main approach researchers use with adults. Still, this approach has its own biases. Do you think that people can report accurately on their activities? Is there a natural human tendency to magnify our positive behaviors and minimize our negative ones?

Now, turning to measure the child side of your question, a reasonable way to assess academic skills would be to give standard tests measuring abilities in areas such as reading or math (more about these measures, called *achievement tests*, in Chapter 7). Another strategy might be to ask the teacher to evaluate students' skills. Assessments from knowledgeable others, such as teachers or parents, are a very common approach that developmentalists use to assess behavior during the childhood years.

Table 1.7 spells out the uses, and the pluses and minuses, of these four frequently used ways of measuring concepts: naturalistic observation, self-reports, ability measures, and observer reports. Now, returning to our study, suppose you found a relationship, that is, a correlation, between the amount of cognitive stimulation at home and school performance. Could you infer that what parents do *causes* children to perform better in school? The answer is no!

- **With correlations, we may be mixing up the result with the cause.** Given that parent–child relationships are bidirectional, does parental cognitive stimulation really *cause* superior school performance, or do academically talented children provoke parents to act in more cognitively stimulating ways? "Mom, please read to me." "I want go to the science museum." (Remember the How Do We Know story about my son and his reading disability.) This chicken-or-egg argument applies to far more than child–parent relationships, cognition, and personality. Does exercising promote health in later life, or are older adults likely to become physically active because they are *already* in good health?

- **With correlations, there may be another variable that explains the results.** In view of our discussion of the heritability of intelligence, with regard to the cogni-

TABLE 1.7: Common Strategies Developmentalists Use to Measure Specific Variables (Behaviors or Concepts of Interest)

Type	Strategy	Commonly Used Ages	Pluses and Problems
Naturalistic observation	Observes behavior directly; codes actions, often by rating the behavior as either present or absent	Typically during childhood, but also used with impaired adults	**Pluses:** Offers a direct, unfiltered record of behavior **Problems:** Very time intensive; people behave differently when watched
Self-reports	Questionnaires in which people report on their feelings, interests, attitudes, and thoughts	Adults and older children	**Pluses:** Easy to administer; Quickly provides data **Problems:** Subject to bias if the person is reporting on undesirable activities and behaviors
Ability tests	Tests evaluating mental (or physical) skills	Children and adults	**Pluses:** Offers an objective record of performance **Problems:** May not accurately measure that ability in the "real world"
Observer reports	Knowledgeable person such as a parent, teacher, or trained observer completes scales evaluating the person	Typically during childhood; also used during adulthood if the person is mentally or physically impaired	**Pluses:** Offers a structured look at the person's behavior **Problems:** Observers have their own biases

tive stimulation study, the immediate third-force candidate that comes to mind is genetics. Wouldn't parents who are genetically prone to be academic provide a more cognitively enriching home environment and also have children who are more genetically talented in school? In my exercise example above, wouldn't older adults who go to the gym or ski regularly also be likely to watch their diet and generally take better care of their health? Given that these other activities should naturally be associated with keeping physically fit, can we conclude that exercise *alone* accounts for the association we find?

To rule out these other forces, the solution is to conduct a **true experiment** (see Figure 1.3). Researchers take steps to isolate their variable of interest by manipulating that condition (called the *independent variable*), and then randomly assign people to either receive that treatment or another, *control* intervention. The strategy of *random assignment* ensures that any pre-existing differences between participants "wash out." If the group exposed to the treatment does differ as predicted, then it can be concluded that the intervention *caused* the particular result.

The problem is that we could never assign children to cognitively stimulating parents! If a developmentalist decided to give some cognitively stimulating intervention to one group of children and withhold it from another, he could run into serious ethical problems. Would it be fair to deprive the control group of that treatment? In the name of science, is it right to take the risk of doing people genuine harm? Experiments are ideal for addressing important developmental science questions. But to tackle many of the most compelling questions about human development, correlational studies are often required.

Given that researchers need to take such care to "do no harm," you might think the scientific community would be attuned to the hazards of prescribing treatments based on correlational findings. You would be wrong. During the 1990s, U.S. physicians strongly advocated that every older woman take postmenopausal hormone replacement therapy (HRT). HRT was touted as a magic intervention to stave off everything from cancer to heart attacks to Alzheimer's disease. But there was a problem. This advice was based on studies comparing the health of women who chose to take these supplements with that of the overall population. And who do you think these women were likely to be? You guessed it! They were a self-selected, upper-middle-class, health-aware group.

Once researchers at the National Institutes of Health conducted a genuine *clinical trial*—an experiment in which they randomly assigned women to take hormones or not—the study had to be stopped midway. Women taking HRT actually had a

If this committed skier is unusually healthy, is it just because he exercises or because he probably also takes care of his health in other ways? Or maybe he has the stamina for this sport because he is already in exceptionally good health? These questions show how difficult it is to make conclusions about causes from observing correlational relationships.

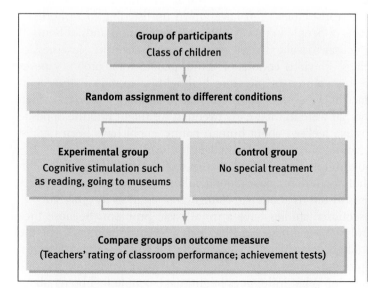

FIGURE 1.3: **How an experiment looks:** By randomly assigning our children to different groups and then giving an intervention, we know that our treatment (cognitive stimulation) *caused* better school skills.

higher risk of developing breast cancer, blood clots, and heart disease. Furthermore, the therapy increased the risk of Alzheimer's disease! (See Alzheimer's Disease Education and Referral [ADEAR] Center, 2004; HealthLink, 2002.)

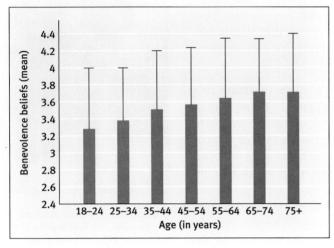

FIGURE 1.4: **"Benevolence beliefs," or faith in humanity across different age groups in a study of U.S. adults:** Notice that, while young people feel worst about human nature, the elderly have the most positive feelings about their fellow human beings.

Source: Poulin & Silver (2008).

Don't you think that these innocent 1950s-era twentysomethings would have a more optimistic view of human nature than young people today? So could we really conclude from a cross-sectional study comparing these now elderly people with the young that "faith in humanity" grows with age?

Designs for Studying Development: Cross-Sectional and Longitudinal Studies

Experiments and correlational studies are standard, all-purpose research strategies. In studying development, however, we have a special interest: "How do people change with age?" To answer this all-important question, scientists also typically use two research techniques—cross-sectional and longitudinal studies.

Cross-Sectional Studies: Getting a One-Shot Snapshot of Groups

Because cross-sectional research is relatively easy to carry out, developmentalists typically use this research strategy to explore changes over long periods of the lifespan (Hertzog, 1996). In a **cross-sectional study,** researchers compare *different age groups at the same time* on the trait or characteristic they are interested in, be it political attitudes, personality, or physical health. Consider a study that (among other questions) explored this interesting issue: "How do our feelings about human nature change with age?"

Researchers gave 2,138 U.S. adults a questionnaire measuring their beliefs in a benevolent world (Poulin & Silver, 2008). Presented with items such as "Human nature is basically good," people ranging in age from 18 to 101 ranked each statement on a scale from "agree strongly" to "disagree." As you scan the findings in Figure 1.4, notice that the youngest age group has the most negative perceptions about humanity. The elderly feel most optimistic about people and the world. If you are in your early twenties, does this mean you can expect to grow less cynical about human nature as you age?

Not necessarily. Perhaps your cohort has special reasons to feel suspicious about human motivations. After all, in our post-9/11 culture you are entering adulthood amidst a drumbeat of fears of a terrorist attack. You have grown up listening to a chorus of pundits cataloguing the sins of people in power, and sat through thousands of hours of *Desperate Housewives*-like TV sitcoms that emphasize the sleaziness of human beings. Previous cohorts of young people were probably never exposed to this volume of messages highlighting human nature at its worst. In fact, if we conducted this same poll during the 1950s, when Theresa and Sal were in their early twenties, we might find the opposite pattern: Positive feelings about human nature might have been highest among the young and declined with age!

The bottom-line message is that cross-sectional studies give us a current snapshot about differences among cohorts (or age groups); but they don't necessarily tell us about real *changes that occur as we grow old.*

Cross-sectional studies have a more basic problem. Because they measure only *group differences,* they can't reveal anything about the individual differences that give spice to life. If you are a real pessimist about people, compared to your friends, will your worldview stay the same as you age? What influences might make people feel better about humanity as they travel through adulthood, and what experiences might make people feel worse? To answer these important questions about how *individuals* develop, as well as to look at what forces make for specific kinds of changes, it's best to be on the scene to measure what is going on. This means doing longitudinal research.

Longitudinal Studies: The Gold-Standard Developmental Science Research Design

In **longitudinal studies,** researchers typically select a group of a particular age and periodically test those people over years (the relevant word here is *long*).

Consider the Dunedin Multidisciplinary and Development Study: An international team of researchers descended on Dunedin, a city in New Zealand, to follow more than 1,000 children born between April 1972 and March 1973, examining them at two-year intervals from age 3 into adult life (Caspi and others, 1995, 1997, 2003; Roberts and others, 2007). At each evaluation, they examined the participants' personalities. They looked at parenting practices and life events. They last gave each person a comprehensive evaluation at age 32 (see Shulruf and others, 2007).

The outcome has been an incredible array of findings, especially related to psychological problems. Can we predict adult emotional difficulties as early as age 3? Do sleep problems in elementary school predict excessive anxiety in adulthood (Gregory and others, 2005)? If you smoke marijuana, would you want to know if you have a genetic vulnerability that puts you at an elevated risk of developing schizophrenic symptoms (Caspi and others, 2005)?

Because the researchers are using cutting-edge technology to examine participants' DNA, they can tackle these vital nature-plus-nurture questions. Plus, like other longitudinal research, this study offers a crystal ball into those questions at the heart of our field: "How will I change as I get older?" "When should we worry about children, and when should we *not* be concerned?"

Longitudinal studies are tremendously exciting, but they have their own problems. For one thing, they involve a tremendous time, effort, and expense. Imagine the resources involved in planning this particular study. Think of the hassles involved in searching out the participants and getting them to return again and again to take the tests. The researchers must fly the overseas Dunedin volunteers back for each evaluation. They need to reimburse people for their time and lost wages. These logistical and financial problems become more serious the longer a study continues. For this reason, we have hundreds of studies covering infancy, childhood, or defined segments of adult life, such as the old-old years. However, ambitious multidisciplinary studies that cover development over many decades are fairly rare (see Shulruf and others, 2007).

The difficulty with getting people to return to be tested presents more than just practical hurdles. It leads to an important bias. Participating in a longitudinal study requires a special commitment. So people who agree to come back to be tested, particularly during adult life, tend to be highly motivated. Think of which classmates are going to come back to your high school reunion. Aren't they apt to be the people who are successful, versus those who have made a mess of their lives? Adults who stay in longitudinal studies, especially for the long haul, are an elite, much better than average group. While longitudinal studies offer us unparalleled information about life, these gold-standard studies have their biases, too.

Critiquing the Research

So to summarize our discussion, how would you go about being a good consumer of the research? When you are evaluating the findings in our field, here are some points to keep in mind:

- Consider the study's participants. How were they selected? Ask yourself, "To what extent can I generalize from this population to the wider world?"
- Examine the study's measures. Are they accurate indices of the behavior the researcher wants to assess? What biases and problems might they have?

cross-sectional study A developmental research strategy that involves testing different age groups at the same time.

longitudinal study A developmental research strategy that involves testing an age group repeatedly over many years.

quantitative research Standard developmental science data-collection strategy that involves testing groups of people and using numerical scales and statistics.

qualitative research Occasional developmental science data-collection strategy that involves interviewing people to obtain information that cannot be quantified on a numerical scale.

- In looking at correlational studies, be alert to competing causal possibilities. What other forces might be responsible for the relationships this researcher finds?
- With cross-sectional findings, beware of making assumptions that this is the way people *really* change with age.
- Look for longitudinal studies and welcome their insights. However, understand—especially during adult life—that these investigations are probably tracing the lives of the best and brightest people rather than the average adult.

Emerging Research Trends

Today, developmental scientists are attuned to these issues. In conducting correlational studies, they use sophisticated statistical techniques to disentangle other influences that might bias their results. They may use several measures, such as teacher ratings and parent input, as well as direct observations, to make sure they are measuring their concepts accurately. They often make efforts to travel to different cultures to check out whether their findings are limited to a particular society or apply to all human beings. Still, along with the emphasis on conducting better-designed, bigger, more global studies, there is an emerging trend. Developmentalists are getting up close and personal, too.

Quantitative research techniques—the strategies I have been describing, using groups of people and statistical tests—are the main approach that researchers use to study human behavior. In order to make general predictions about people, we need to examine the behavior of different individuals. We need to pin down our concepts by using scales or ratings with numerical values that can be tallied and compared. Developmentalists who conduct **qualitative research** are not interested in making numerical comparisons. They want to understand the unique lives of people by conducting in-depth interviews. In this book, I will be focusing mainly on quantitative research because that is how we find out the scientific "truth." But I also will highlight the growing number of qualitative interview studies to put a human face on our developing life.

TYING IT ALL TOGETHER

1. Craig and Jessica are taking a course in research methods at their university and want to test the hypothesis that children who eat excessive sugar at breakfast do poorly at school—but each student decides to tackle this question differently. Craig's plan is to go into children's homes to directly record their sugar consumption at breakfast and relate these data to scores on math and reading tests. Jessica decides to randomly assign one group of children to eat a sugary breakfast (for example, Cap'n Crunch) and another to eat a low-sugar alternative (such as Wheaties), and then have the first-grade teacher rate the math and reading skills of each group. Which student is conducting a correlational study, and which student is conducting a true experiment?

2. In the question above, which student, Craig or Jessica:

   a. will run into real ethical problems conducting the study?
   b. is employing naturalistic observation?
   c. is using expert observer ratings?
   d. will be able to prove that excess sugar consumption *causes* children to do more poorly at school?
   e. may run into the danger of people acting differently because they are being watched?
   f. is conducting a study that—although ethically acceptable—poses enormous practical hurdles in terms of actually carrying out the research?

3. Cecila and Jamel both want to test the hypothesis that people get wiser with age—but each student decides to use a different research strategy. Cecila gives young adults, middle-aged people, and older adults a wisdom questionnaire and compares their scores. Jamel solicits a large group of 20-year-olds, gives them the wisdom questionnaire, and then has them return every five years to take the questionnaire again.

Which student is conducting a cross-sectional study, and which student is conducting a longitudinal study?

4. Plan a longitudinal study to test a developmental science question that interests you. Describe how you would select your participants, how your study would proceed, what measures you would use, and what practical problems and biases your study would have.

Answers to the Tying It All Together questions can be found on the last page of this chapter.

Final Thoughts

This discussion brings me back to my letter that introduced this book and my promise to let you in on my other agendas in writing this text. Because I want to teach you to critically evaluate the research findings, in the following pages I'll be analyzing individual studies and—in the "How Do We Know" features that appear in some chapters—I'll be focusing on research-related issues in more depth. To bring home the personal experience of the lifespan, I've filled each chapter with quotations and vignettes, and—in the "Experiencing the Lifespan" boxes—interviewed people myself. To bring home the basic principle that our human lifespan is a continuing work in progress, I'll be starting many chapters by setting the historical and cultural context before moving on to explore the research. To emphasize the power of our research to improve lives, I'll conclude many sections by spelling out interventions that improve the quality of life.

This book is designed to be read like an unfolding story, with each chapter building on concepts and terms mentioned in the previous ones. It's planned to emphasize how our insights about earlier life stages relate to older ages. I will be discussing three major aspects of development—physical development, cognitive development, and personality and social relationships (*psychosocial development*)—separately. However, I'll be continually stressing how these aspects of development connect. After all, we are not just bodies, minds, and personalities, but whole human beings!

Now, beginning with prenatal development and infancy (Chapters 2, 3, and 4); then moving on to childhood (Chapters 5, 6, and 7); adolescence (Chapters 8 and 9); early and middle adulthood (Chapters 10, 11 and 12); later life (Chapters 13 and 14); and, finally, that last milestone, death (Chapter 15), welcome to the lifespan and to the rest of this book!

SUMMARY

Who We Are and What We Study

Lifespan development is a huge mega-discipline encompassing **child development, gerontology,** and **adult development. Developmental scientists,** or **developmentalists,** chart the universal changes we undergo from birth to old age, explore individual differences in development, study the impact of **normative** and **nonnormative** life transitions, and explore every other topic relevant to our unfolding life.

Several major **contexts of development** shape our lives. The first is our **cohort,** or the time in history in which we live. The huge **baby boom cohort,** born in the years following World War II, has dramatically affected society as it passes through the lifespan. Cohorts of babies born before the twentieth century faced a shorter, harsher childhood, and many did not survive. As life got easier and education got longer, we first extended the growing-up phase of life to include adolescence and, in recent years, with a new life stage called **emerging adulthood,** have extended the start date of full adulthood to our late twenties.

The early-**twentieth-century life expectancy revolution,** with its dramatic advances in curing *infectious disease* and shift to deaths from *chronic illnesses,* allowed us to survive to later life.

Today, **average life expectancy** is within striking distance of the **maximum lifespan** in the most affluent parts of the world, and we distinguish between two groups of elderly, the healthy **young-old** (people in their sixties and seventies) and the frail **old-old** (people in and over their eighties). The second major twentieth-century lifespan change occurred in the 1960s with the sexual revolution, the women's movement, and the counterculture movement. Today, we have enormous freedom to live our own lives the way we want. However, with so many single mothers, U.S. child poverty rates are depressingly high.

Socioeconomic status also greatly affects our lifespan—with people who live in poverty in the United States facing a harsher, more stressful, shorter life. The gaps between **developed world** countries and **developing world** countries are even more dramatic, with the least-developed countries lagging well behind in terms of health, wealth, and technology.

Our cultural and ethnic background also determines how we develop. Scientists distinguish between **collectivist cultures,** which place a premium on social harmony and close extended-family relationships, and **individualistic cultures,** which value independence and personal achievement. We need to make these distinctions cautiously, however. Residents of each nation have a mix of individualistic and collectivist worldviews. Although the census lumps the U.S. population into broad ethnic categories, these divisions mask incredible diversity within each group. Finally, our gender dramatically influences our travels through life. Women outlive men by at least 4 years in the developed world.

Theories: Lenses for Looking at the Lifespan

Theories offer explanations about what causes people to act the way they do. The main theories in developmental science offering general explanations of behavior vary in their position on the fundamental **nature** versus **nurture** question. Behaviorists believe nurture is all-important. According to **traditional behaviorists,** in particular B. F. Skinner, **operant conditioning** and **reinforcement** determine all voluntary behaviors. According to **cognitive behaviorism/social learning theory, modeling** and **self-efficacy**—our internal sense that we can competently perform given tasks—predict how we act.

John Bowlby's **attachment theory** emphasizes both nature and nurture. According to Bowlby, the biological attachment response that develops during early childhood is genetically programmed to promote human survival, and the quality of our attachment relationships in our earliest years is crucial to later mental health. **Evolutionary psychologists** adopt a nature perspective, seeing many actions as genetically programmed into evolution to promote survival. **Behavioral genetics** research—in particular, **twin studies, adoption studies,** and occasionally **twin/adoption studies**—have convinced developmental scientists of the real-world power of nature, revealing substantial genetic contributions to the many ways we differ from each other as human beings.

Developmental scientists today, however, have gone beyond the nature *or* nurture question to explore how nature *and* nurture combine. Due to **evocative** and **active forces,** we shape our environments to go along with our genetic tendencies, and human relationships are **bidirectional**—that is, our temperamental qualities and actions influence the responses of others, just as their actions influence us. A basic developmental science challenge is to foster an appropriate **person–environment fit.** We need to match our biologically based talents and abilities to the right environment. Advances in understanding genetics allow us to better arrange the environment to promote an optimal life.

According to Jean Piaget's **cognitive developmental theory,** children progress through four qualitatively different stages of intellectual development and all learning occurs through **assimilation** and **accommodation.** The other most influential lifespan stage theorist, Erik Erikson, spells out eight **psychosocial tasks,** or challenges, that we must master as we travel from birth to old age.

Most developmental scientists today adopt the **developmental systems perspective.** They welcome input from every theory. They realize that many interacting influences shape who we are. They understand that diversity among people and change processes is the essence of development.

Research Methods: The Tools of the Trade

The two main research strategies scientists use are **correlational studies,** which relate naturally occurring variations among people, and **true experiments,** in which researchers take action to manipulate their variables of interest and randomly assign people to receive a given treatment or not. With correlational studies, there are always competing possibilities for the relationships we find. While experiments do allow us to prove causes, they are often unethical and impractical to carry out. In conducting research, it's best to strive for a **representative sample,** and it's essential to have accurate measures. **Naturalistic observation, self-reports,** tests of abilities, and expert observer evaluations are the main measurement strategies developmental scientists use.

The two major designs for studying development are longitudinal and cross-sectional research. **Cross-sectional studies,** which involve testing people of different age groups at the same time, are very easy to carry out. However, they may confuse differences between age groups with true changes that occur as people age, and they can't tell us about individual differences in development. **Longitudinal studies** are at the heart of our field because they do answer vital questions about how people develop. However, this incredibly informative research—following people over years—is difficult to carry out and based on how atypical, elite volunteers behave and change.

Today our studies are getting more global and statistically sophisticated. **Quantitative research**—studies involving groups of participants, and using statistical tests—is still the standard way we learn the scientific truth. But developmentalists are now occasionally conducting **qualitative research**—interviewing people in depth.

KEY TERMS

developmentalists
  (developmental scientists),
  p. 3
lifespan development, p. 4

child development, p. 4
gerontology, p. 4
adult development,
  p. 4

normative transitions,
  p. 4
non-normative transitions,
  p. 4

contexts of development,
  p. 5
cohort, p. 5
baby boom cohort, p. 5

ANSWERS TO TYING IT ALL TOGETHER

Setting the Context

1. d. Rates of child poverty have increased in tandem with the rise in single parenthood.

2. Maria is probably in her late forties or early fifties; Sara is probably in her sixties; and Rosa is most likely in her eighties.

3. Jim might argue that life is better today because we have a more open society, with considerable individual freedom — especially for women and minority groups. Joe might counter that these same late-twentieth-century lifestyle changes have produced higher divorce rates and increased female and child poverty.

4. Pablo has a collectivist worldview, while Peter's worldview is individualistic.

Theories: Lenses for Looking at the Lifespan

1. (1) c, (2) a, (3) b, (4) d, (5) f, and (6) e.

2. b. As Hernando and other children need to run around, regular gym time would help to foster the best person-environment fit.

3. assimilation; accommodation.

4. Samantha might argue that behaviorism is an ideal approach to human development because it is simple, effective, and easy to carry out. Behaviorism's easily mastered, action-oriented concepts — be consistent, reinforce positive behavior, draw on principles of modeling, and stimulate efficacy feelings — can make dramatic improvements in the quality of life. Also, because behaviorism doesn't blame the person, but locates problems in the learning environment, it has special appeal.

Sally might argue that behaviorism's premise that nurture is all-important neglects the powerful impact genetic forces have in determining who we are. So the theory is far too limited — offering a wrongheaded view about development. We need the insights of attachment theory, evolutionary psychology, behavioral genetics, plus Piaget's and Erikson's theories to fully understand what motivates human beings.

Research Methods: The Tools of the Trade

1. Craig is conducting a correlational study; Jessica's is a true experiment.

2. (a) Jessica, (b) Craig, (c) Jessica, (d) Jessica, (e) Craig, and (f) Craig.

3. Cecila is conducting a cross-sectional study; Jamel's is a longitudinal study.

4. After coming up with your hypothesis, you would need to adequately measure your concepts — choosing the appropriate tests. Your next step would be to solicit a large representative sample of a particular age group, give them these measures, and retest these people at regular intervals over an extended period of time. In addition to the huge investment of time and money, it would be hard to keep track of your sample and entice participants to undergo subsequent evaluations. Therefore, a huge bias would relate to who stays in the study versus who drops out. Because the most motivated fraction of your original group will continue, your results will probably reflect how the "best people" behave and change over time (not the typical person).

Chapter 2

Prenatal Development, Pregnancy, and Birth

It's hard to explain, different from anything that's happened before, Kim told me. Your whole self shifts. You are all about two people now. When you wake up, shop for groceries, or plan meals, this other person is always with you. You are always thinking, "What will be good for the baby? What will be best for the two of us?"

Feeling the first kick—like little feathers brushing inside me—was amazing. It was as if she woke up to tell me, "I'm here, Mommy." Another incredible thing was seeing the ultrasound. It's frightening when you go for that test. You wonder, "Will there be something wrong?" But when I saw her shape and heart, the feeling was unbelievable. At first, I felt like I could never explain this to my husband. But Jeff is wonderful. I think he really gets it. So I feel very lucky. I can't imagine what this experience would be like if I was going through these nine months completely alone.

Now that it's the thirtieth week and I'm confident that my little girl can survive, there is another shift. I'm feeling calmer, more in control, totally focused on the moment she will arrive: What will it be like to hold my baby in my arms? Will she be born healthy?

Actually, the downside has always been the fear that she will be born with some problem. I keep going back to the beginning. Did I do something that could have caused harm before the nausea and tiredness hit, which made me realize that I was pregnant? Could my baby have a birth defect?

Another downside is that, until recently, I still felt really nauseous and tired. Some days, I could barely make it to work. (Everything they told you about morning sickness only lasting through the first trimester is wrong—at least for me!)

But most amazing is what happens with strangers, when I'm at the store or walking around the mall. People light up and grin, wish me good luck, or give me advice. It's like the world is watching out for me, rooting for me, cherishing me.

Setting the Context

The concern and awe Kim is getting from the wider world may be built into our humanity. Many societies see pregnancy as a special time of life. Pregnant women are often pampered, kept calm and happy. Their desires and cravings are satisfied. But we also see pregnancy as a uniquely vulnerable time. In some cultures, pregnant women are shielded from funerals. Rituals—such as the nine-day Navajo Blessing Way ceremony—may be performed to ensure that all goes well. In previous eras, societies used special good luck charms to keep evil spirits away—a pregnancy girdle in medieval England, a bell placed between the breasts in Brazil, a small sack of garlic worn in Guatemala (Aldred, 1997; Von Raffler-Engel, 1994), a cotton pregnancy sash in Japan (Ito & Sharts-Hopko, 2002).

We have the same uneasy feelings in the twenty-first-century developed West. If they are religious, people may turn to prayer: "Have to trust God that his baby be okay," said one African American mother-to-be. And then, she added, hopefully, "He gave me a sign. . . . God doesn't lie" (quoted in Jesse, Schoneboom, & Blanchard, 2007, p. 159). Perhaps you have friends who refuse to tell anyone they are pregnant

AP Photo / Matt York

In this traditional southern Indian ceremony performed at the sixth or eighth month of pregnancy, family members and friends gather around to protect the woman and fetus from "the evil eyes." Rituals such as this one are common around the world and embody our fears about this special time of life.

until after the first three months: "It might be bad luck." In traditional societies, the message—better hold off on celebrating—has been built into formal rituals. In Bulgaria, the first kick was the signal for a woman to bake bread and take it to the church. In Bali, at the seventh month, a prayer ceremony takes place to recognize that there is now, finally, a real person inside whom the spirits need to protect from harm (Kitzinger, 2000; Von Raffler-Engel, 1994).

As these thoughts and fears reveal, pregnancy is a uniquely exciting and frightening time of life. There can be wonderfully uplifting emotions, when women are totally absorbed with the baby and with their physical state. At the same time, there is a sense of danger and fear about the hazards that lie on the journey ahead. Let's keep these different feelings in mind as we turn to explore the science of what happens during the baby's nine months in the womb.

In the first part of this chapter, I'll trace prenatal development, describing what happens, stage by stage, as the baby grows. Then our focus shifts to the mother-to-be, as I examine the inner experience of being pregnant and the emotions of expectant dads. Next, we'll tackle the anxieties related to the baby, describing the external and internal threats to fetal development that, thankfully, only occur infrequently. Finally, we'll look at the event that Kim is anxiously awaiting: birth. What is this amazing experience really like? What was labor and delivery like in previous centuries, and what birth options do women in the developed world have today? I'll conclude this chapter by describing the newborn and exploring the major threats after birth—arriving in the world too soon and/or too small and infant mortality.

The First Step: Fertilization

Before embarking on this chapter-long journey, however, it is vital to understand the starting point. What are the structures involved in reproduction? What is the physiological process involved in conceiving a child? What is taking place at the genetic level when a sperm and an egg unite to form a new human being?

The Reproductive Systems

The female and male reproductive systems are shown in Figure 2.1. As you can see, the female system has several basic parts:

- Center stage is the **uterus,** the pear-shaped muscular organ that will carry the baby to term. The uterus is lined with a velvety tissue, the *endometrium*, which thickens in preparation for becoming pregnant and, if that event does not occur, is shed at the end of the monthly cycle, during menstruation.
- The lower section of the uterus, protruding into the vagina, is the **cervix.** During pregnancy, this thick uterine neck must perform an amazing feat: be strong enough to stay intact for nine months under the pressure of the expanding uterus; be flexible enough to open fully at birth.
- Branching from the upper ends of the uterus are the **fallopian tubes.** These slim, pipe-like structures serve as conduits to the uterus.
- The feathery ends of the fallopian tubes surround the **ovaries,** the almond-shaped organs where the **ova,** the mother's egg cells, reside.

The Process of Fertilization

The pathway that results in **fertilization**—the union of sperm and egg—begins at **ovulation.** This is the moment, typically around day 14 of a woman's cycle, when a mature ovum erupts from the ovary wall. **Hormones**—chemical substances released

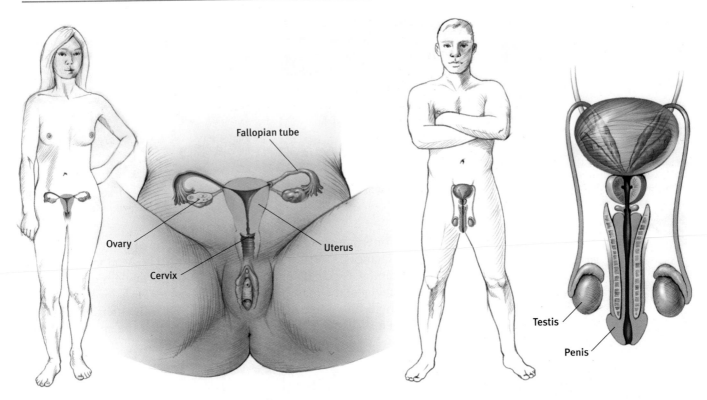

FIGURE 2.1: **The female and male reproductive systems**

into the bloodstream that target certain tissues and body processes and cause them to change—orchestrate the process of ovulation as well as the other events that program pregnancy.

At the moment of ovulation, the feathery ends of the fallopian tube, reacting to signals showing the site of the rupture, move to that location. As they suction the ovum in, the fallopian tube begins vigorous contractions that launch the ovum on its three-day journey toward the uterus.

Now the male's contribution to forming a new life arrives. In contrast to females, whose ova are all mainly formed at birth or early in life, the **testes**—the male structures comparable to the ovaries—are continually manufacturing sperm. An adult male typically produces several hundred million sperm a day. During sexual intercourse, these millions of cells, released at ejaculation, are expelled into the vagina, where a small proportion enter the body of the uterus and wend their way up the fallopian tubes.

To promote pregnancy, the best time to have intercourse is right around ovulation. (Readers not interested in becoming pregnant, be forewarned: The hormones triggering ovulation are sensitive to erotic cues. So this event may occur in response to intense sexual arousal—at erratic times of the month.) The ovum is receptive for about 24 hours while in the tube's wide outer part. Sperm take a few hours to journey from the cervix to the tube. However, sperm can live almost a week in the recesses of the uterus and cervix, which means that intercourse several days prior to ovulation may also result in fertilization (Marieb, 2004).

Although the ovum emits chemical signals as to its location, the tiny tadpole-shaped travelers cannot easily locate the single cell or make the perilous journey upward into the tubes. So, of the estimated several hundred million sperm expelled at ejaculation, only 200 to 300 reach their destination, find their target, and begin to burrow in.

What happens now is a team assault. The sperm drill into the ovum, piercing its outer layers and penetrating through toward the center. Suddenly, one reaches

uterus The pear-shaped muscular organ in a woman's abdomen that houses the developing baby.

cervix The neck, or narrow lower portion, of the uterus.

fallopian tube One of a pair of slim, pipe-like structures that connect the ovaries with the uterus.

ovary One of a pair of almond-shaped organs that contain a woman's ova, or eggs.

ovum An egg cell containing the genetic material contributed by the mother to the baby.

fertilization The union of sperm and egg.

ovulation The moment during a woman's monthly cycle when an ovum is expelled from the ovary.

hormones Chemical substances released in the bloodstream that target and change organs and tissues.

testes Male organs that manufacture sperm.

The sperm surround the ovum.

One sperm burrows in (notice the large head).

The nuclei of the two cells fuse. The watershed event called fertilization has occurred.

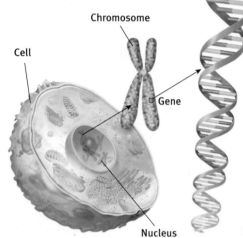

FIGURE 2.2: **The human building blocks:** The nucleus of every human cell contains chromosomes, each of which is made up of two strands of DNA connected in a double helix.

the innermost part. Then, the chemical composition of the ovum wall changes, shutting out the other sperm. The head of this sperm, containing its genetic blueprint, lies inside the nucleus of the ovum. The nuclei of the male and female cells move slowly together. When they meld into one cell, the landmark event called fertilization has occurred. What is taking place genetically when the sperm and egg combine?

The Genetics of Fertilization

The answer lies in looking at **chromosomes,** ropy structures composed of long ladder-like strands of the genetic material **DNA.** Arrayed along each chromosome are segments of DNA called **genes,** which function as the templates for creating the proteins responsible for carrying out all the physical processes of life (see Figure 2.2). Every cell in our body contains 46 chromosomes, with the exception of the sperm and ova, each of which has half this number, or 23. When the nuclei of these two cells, called *gametes*, combine at fertilization, their chromosomes align in pairs to again comprise 46. So nature has a marvelous mechanism to ensure that each new human life has an identical number of chromosomes and every new human being gets half of its genetic heritage from the parent of each sex.

You can see the 46 paired chromosomes of a male in Figure 2.3. Notice that each chromosome pair (one member of which we get from our mother and one from our father) is a perfect match, with one exception—the sex chromosomes (X and Y). The X is far longer and heavier than the Y. Because each ovum carries an X chromosome, our father's contribution to fertilization determines our sex. If a lighter, faster-

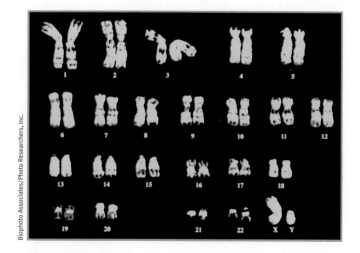

FIGURE 2.3: **A map of human chromosomes:** This magnified grid, called a karyotype, shows the 46 chromosomes in their matched pairs. The final pair, with its X and Y, shows that this person is a male. Also, notice the huge size of the X chromosome compared to the Y.

swimming, Y-carrying sperm fertilizes the ovum, we get a boy (XY). If the victor is a more resilient, slower-moving X, we get a girl (XX).

In the race to fertilization, the Y's are statistically more successful; scientists estimate that 20 percent more male than female babies are conceived. But the prenatal period is particularly hard on developing males. If a family member learns that she is pregnant, the odds still favor her having a boy; but because more males die in the uterus, only 5 percent more boys than girls make it to birth (Werth, 2002). And throughout life, males continue to be the less hardy sex, dying off at higher rates at every age. Recall from our discussion in Chapter 1 that, throughout the developed world, women outlive men by at least four years.

TYING IT ALL TOGETHER

1. Sketch the female reproductive system and label the uterus, fallopian tubes, cervix, and ovaries.

2. What is the parallel structure to the ovary in the male reproductive system?

3. Tiffany feels certain that if she has intercourse at the right time, she will get pregnant—but asks you, "What is the right time?" Give Tiffany your answer carefully, referring to the text discussion, and then tell her the chain of events that leads from ovulation to fertilization.

4. If your aunt is pregnant, statistically speaking, she is more likely to have a _____, and _____ is responsible for the child's sex.

   a. boy; your aunt
   b. girl; your uncle
   c. boy; your uncle
   d. girl; your aunt

Answers to the Tying It All Together questions can be found on the last page of this chapter.

Prenatal Development

Now that we have an overview of the starting point, let's chart prenatal development, tracing how the microscopic fertilized ovum divides millions of times and differentiates into a living, breathing child. This miraculous transformation takes place in three distinct stages.

First Two Weeks: The Germinal Stage

The first approximately two weeks after fertilization—the time when the cell mass has not yet fully attached to the wall of the uterus—is called the **germinal stage** (see Figure 2.4 on page 40). Within 36 hours, the fertilized ovum, now a single cell called the **zygote**, makes its first cell division. Then, the tiny cluster of cells continues to divide every 12 to 15 hours as it wends its way on a roughly three-day trip down the fallopian tube. When the mass of cells passes into the uterine cavity, it sheds its outer wall and differentiates into layers. Now called a **blastocyst**, the rapidly dividing cells form a hollow ball of roughly 100 cells. The next major challenge is **implantation**—the several-day process of embedding into the uterine wall.

The blastocyst seeks an ideal landing site on an upper section of the uterus. Meanwhile, hormones have prepared the uterus to receive the cell mass. The outer layer of the blastocyst develops projections. At about day 9, these tentacles burrow in. From this landing zone, blood vessels proliferate that will make up the **placenta**, the lifeline that passes nutrients from the mother's system to the developing baby. After implantation, the next stage of prenatal development begins. This is the all-important embryonic phase.

chromosome A threadlike strand of DNA located in the nucleus of every cell that carries the genes, which transmit hereditary information.

DNA (deoxyribonucleic acid) The material that makes up genes, which bear our hereditary characteristics.

gene A segment of DNA that contains a chemical blueprint for manufacturing a particular protein.

germinal stage The first 14 days of prenatal development, from fertilization to full implantation.

zygote A fertilized ovum.

blastocyst The hollow sphere of cells formed during the germinal stage in preparation for implantation.

implantation The process in which a blastocyst becomes embedded in the uterine wall.

placenta The structure projecting from the wall of the uterus during pregnancy through which the developing baby absorbs nutrients.

FIGURE 2.4: **The events of the germinal stage:** The fertilized ovum divides on its trip to the uterus, then becomes a hollow ball called a blastocyst, and finally fully implants in the wall of the uterus at about 14 days after fertilization.

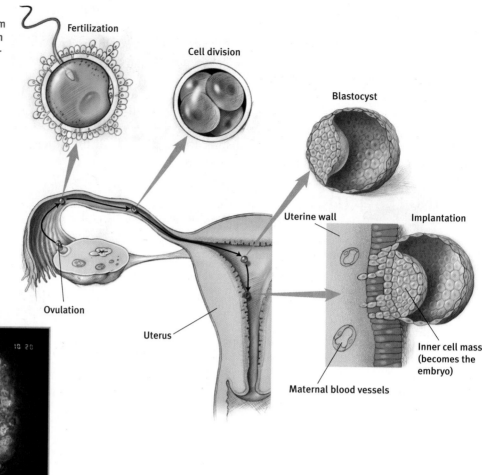

Fertilization

Cell division

Blastocyst

Uterine wall

Implantation

Ovulation

Uterus

Maternal blood vessels

Inner cell mass (becomes the embryo)

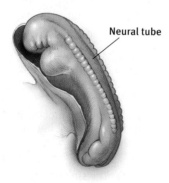

Andy Walker/Midland Fertility Services/Photo Researchers, Inc.

This is a photo of the blastocyst, the roughly 100-cell ball, soon to attach itself to the uterine wall. When implantation occurs, this event will signal the end of the germinal phase.

Neural tube

FIGURE 2.5: **The neural tube:** This structure is one of the first to form after implantation. The brain and spinal cord will develop from it.

Week 3 to Week 8: The Embryonic Stage

Although the **embryonic stage** lasts roughly only six weeks, it is the most fast-paced period of development. During this brief time, all the major organs are constructed. By the end of the embryonic stage, what began as an ill-defined clump of cells now looks like a recognizable human being!

One early task after implantation is to form the mechanism that makes all future development possible. After the baby is hooked up to the maternal bloodstream—which will nourish the fetus as it grows—nutrients must be pumped to the rapidly differentiating cells. So by the third week after fertilization, the circulatory system (our body's transport system) forms, and its pump, the heart, starts to beat.

At around the same time, the rudiments of the nervous system appear. Between 21 and 24 days after fertilization, an indentation forms along the back of the embryo and closes up to form the **neural tube** (see Figure 2.5). The uppermost part of this cylindrical structure will become the brain. Its lower part will form the spinal cord. Although scientists now know we can indeed "grow" new brain cells throughout life, almost all of those remarkable branching structures, called **neurons,** which cause us to think, to respond, and to process information, originated in cells formed in the neural tube during our first months in the womb.

Meanwhile, the body is developing at an astounding rate. At day 26, arm buds form; by day 28, swellings erupt where the legs will form. At day 37, rudimentary feet start to develop. By day 41, elbows, wrist curves, and the precursors of fingers can be seen. Several days later, ray-like structures that will turn into toes emerge. By about week 8, the embryo is only about the length of a thumb, but its internal organs are all in place. What started out looking like a curved stalk or twisted dinner napkin, then a strange outer-space alien, now appears like a distinctly *human* being.

Principles of Prenatal Development

Imagine that you wanted to spell out some guiding principles related to the sequence of development just described. In looking at the photographs of the developing embryo on this page, can you identify three basic patterns that underlie this rapid transformation to a fully formed human being?

- You might notice that from a core cylindrical shape, the arms and legs grow outward and then (not unexpectedly) the fingers and toes protrude. So the first principle is that growth follows the **proximodistal sequence,** from the most interior (proximal) part of the body to the outer (distal) sides.

- You might also notice that from the initial swelling that makes the embryo look mainly like a mammoth head, the arms emerge and the legs sprout. So development takes place according to the **cephalocaudal sequence,** meaning from top (*cephalo* = head) to bottom (*caudal* = tail).

- Finally, just as in constructing a sculpture, development begins with the basic building blocks and then fills in details. A head is formed before eyes and ears are carved; legs are constructed before feet and toes are chiseled. So the **mass-to-specific sequence,** or gross (large) structures before smaller refinements, is the third basic principle of body growth.

Keep these principles in mind. As you will see when I discuss physical development in infancy and childhood, the same patterns apply to growth and to our unfolding motor abilities *after* the baby leaves the womb.

Week 9 to Birth: The Fetal Stage

During the embryonic stage, basic body structures sprout almost day by day. In the final period of prenatal growth—the **fetal stage**—development occurs at a more leisurely pace. From the eyebrows, fingernails, and hair follicles that develop from weeks 9 to 12 to the cushion of fat that accumulates during the final weeks before birth, it takes a full seven months to transform the fully formed embryo into a resilient baby ready to embrace life.

Why does our species need this prolonged period of refining and elaborating that lasts for so many months? One reason is to allow time for the neurons composing that masterpiece organ—the human brain—to move into place. Let's now look at this crucial process of making a brain.

embryonic stage The second stage of prenatal development, lasting from week 3 through week 8.

neural tube A cylindrical structure that forms along the back of the embryo and develops into the brain and spinal cord.

neuron A nerve cell.

proximodistal sequence The developmental principle that growth occurs from the most interior parts of the body outward.

cephalocaudal sequence The developmental principle that growth occurs in a sequence from head to toe.

mass-to-specific sequence The developmental principle that large structures (and movements) precede increasingly detailed refinements.

fetal stage The final period of prenatal development, lasting seven months, characterized by physical refinements, massive growth, and the development of the brain.

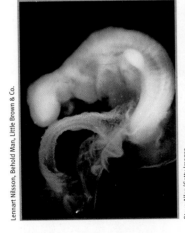
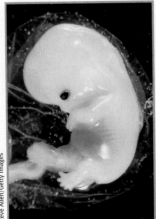
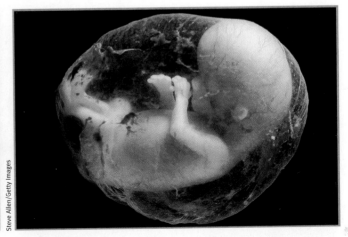

At about week 3, the embryo (the upside-down U across the top) looks like a curved stalk.

At week 4, you can see the indentations for eyes and the arms and legs beginning to sprout.

At week 9, the baby-to-be has fingers, toes, and ears. All the major organs have developed and the fetal stage has begun!

Lennart Nilsson, Behold Man, Little Brown & Co.

Steve Allen/Getty Images

Steve Allen/Getty Images

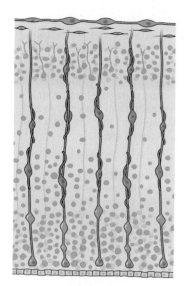

FIGURE 2.6: **Forming a brain: climbing neurons:** During the earlier part of the fetal period, the neurons destined to make up the brain ascend these ladder-like filaments to reach the uppermost part of what had been the neural tube.

Source: Huttenlocher (2002).

During the late embryonic stage, a mass of cells forms within the neural tube that will eventually produce the billions of neurons that compose our brain. From this zone, the new neurons begin to migrate to a region just under the top of the differentiating tube. This period of cell formation and migration, diagrammed in Figure 2.6, concludes when all of the neurons assemble in their "staging area" by the middle of the fetal period. Then, they assume their mature form. The cells lengthen and develop characteristic branches. They start to interlink. This vital process of interconnecting—which is responsible for every human thought and action—will continue until almost our final day of life.

Figure 2.7 shows the mushrooming brain. Notice that the brain almost doubles in size from month 4 to month 7. By now, the brain has already assumed the wrinkled structure of an adult.

This massive growth has a profound effect. At around month 6, the fetus shows signs of consciousness. It reacts to sound (Crade & Lovett, 1988). Its heart beats faster in response to loud noises. If a doctor shines a light inside the uterus, it tries to shield its face (Kisilevsky, Low, & Muir, 1992). And around this time—provided the lungs are mature enough to take in oxygen and expel carbon dioxide—a few babies can even be born and survive. Today, the **age of viability**, or earliest date at which babies *possibly* can live, has dropped to a remarkable 22 weeks—almost halving the 38 weeks the fetus would normally spend in the womb. By week 25, with the best medical care, the chance of survival increases to one in two (Werth & Tsiaras, 2002). Then, week-by-week, these odds rapidly increase.

Still, it is vitally important that the fetus stay in the uterus as long as possible. As you will see later in this chapter, being born too early (and too small) can make a tremendous difference in terms of health. During the last two months alone, in addition to maturing neurologically and in many other ways, the fetus gains almost five pounds.

Figure 2.8 shows the fetus during the final month of pregnancy, when its prenatal nest becomes cramped and birth is looming on the horizon. Notice the major support structures the developing baby requires: the placenta, projecting from the uterine wall, which supplies nutrients from the mother to the fetus; the **umbilical cord,** protruding from what will be the baby's bellybutton, the conduit through which nutrients flow; the **amniotic sac,** the fluid-filled chamber within which the baby floats. This tough, encasing membrane provides vital insulation from infection and harm.

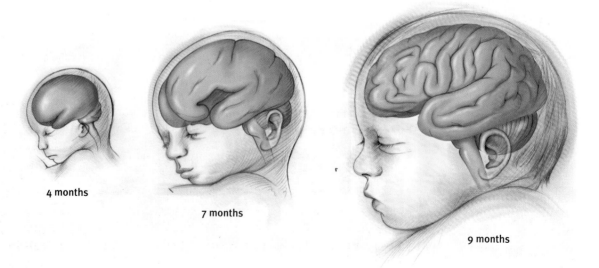

4 months

7 months

9 months

FIGURE 2.7: **The expanding brain:** The brain grows dramatically month by month during the fetal period. During the final months, it develops its characteristic folds.

At this stage of prenatal development, first-time mothers and fathers may be running around, buying the crib or shopping for baby clothes. Especially in affluent countries, middle-class women, such as Kim, may be marveling at the many items their precious son or daughter "must have": a pacifier, a receiving blanket, a bassinet . . . and what else?! As you saw in the vignette, parents-to-be are anxiously focused on that upcoming event: birth. What is happening physically and emotionally during *all* nine months from the mother's—and father's—point of view?

TYING IT ALL TOGETHER

1. Rapid organ formation; neural migration to the top of the brain; the blastocyst: Match each term or process to the appropriate prenatal stage.

   a. embryonic, fetal, germinal
   b. germinal, fetal, embryonic
   c. fetal, germinal, embryonic
   d. germinal, fetal, embryonic

2. A pregnant friend asks you, "How does my baby's brain develop?" Describe the process of neural migration—when it occurs, and when it is complete.

3. Give a concrete example of (a) the cephalocaudal sequence, (b) the proximodistal sequence, and (c) the mass-to-specific sequence.

Answers to the Tying It All Together questions can be found on the last page of this chapter.

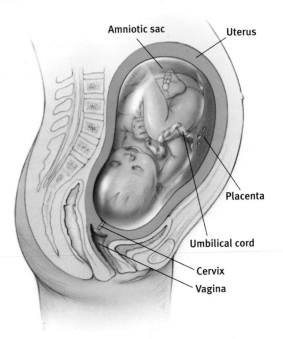

FIGURE 2.8: **Poised to be born:** This diagram shows the fetus inside the woman's uterus late in pregnancy. Notice the placenta, amniotic sac, and umbilical cord.

Pregnancy

The 266- to 277-day **gestation** period (or pregnancy) is divided into three segments. These phases, called **trimesters,** comprise roughly three months each. (Because it is difficult to know exactly when fertilization occurs, health-care professionals date the duration of pregnancy from the woman's last menstrual period.)

Pregnancy differs, however, from the carefully patterned process of prenatal development. Although there are some classic symptoms, there really is no universal pregnancy experience at all.

To bring this point home, ask a few mothers to describe their pregnancies. One person might complain about being violently ill for the entire nine months; another might feel physically better than ever. Some women adore looking pregnant and joyously look forward to the baby; others despise their bodies and feel demoralized and depressed.

Scanning the Trimesters

With the strong caution that variability—from person to person (and child to child)—is the norm, let's now offer a trimester-by-trimester overview of what pregnancy *can* be like.

First Trimester: Often Feeling Tired and Ill

After the blastocyst implants in the uterus—a few days before the woman first misses her period—pregnancy often signals its presence through some unpleasant symptoms. Many women feel faint. (Yes, fainting can be an early sign of pregnancy!) They may get headaches or have to urinate frequently. Like Kim in the vignette, they may feel incredibly tired. Their breasts become tender, painful to the touch. So, many women do not need that definite tip-off—a missed menstrual period—to realize they are carrying a child.

age of viability The earliest point at which a baby can survive outside the womb.

umbilical cord The structure that attaches the placenta to the fetus, through which nutrients are passed and fetal wastes are removed.

amniotic sac A bag-shaped, fluid-filled membrane that contains and insulates the fetus.

gestation The period of pregnancy.

trimester One of the 3-month-long segments into which pregnancy is divided.

The trigger for these varied symptoms is a flood of hormones. After implantation, the production of *progesterone* (literally *pro*, or "for," *gestation*)—the hormone responsible for maintaining the pregnancy—surges. The placenta produces its own unique hormone, *human chorionic gonadotropin* (HCG), thought to prevent the woman's body from rejecting the "foreign" embryo.

Given this hormonal onslaught, the massive body changes, and the fact that the blood supply is being diverted to the uterus, the tiredness, dizziness, and headaches make perfect sense. What about that classic symptom mentioned in the chapter-opening vignette—morning sickness?

Morning sickness—waves of nausea and sometimes vomiting—affects at least two out of every three women during the first trimester (Beckmann and others, 2002). This well-known pregnancy symptom is not just confined to the morning. Many women feel queasy on and off all day. A few get so violently ill that they cannot keep any food down. And men can sometimes develop morning sickness along with their wives! This phenomenon, which occurs around the world, has its own name: *couvade* (Brennan and others, 2007).

But morning sickness seems senseless: Doesn't the embryo need all the nourishment it can get? Why is there a mechanism during the first months of pregnancy that causes women to feel revolted by particular foods?

Consider these clues: The queasiness is at its height during the period of intense organ formation, and, like magic, one day toward the end of the first trimester, usually (but not always) disappears. Munching on crackers or bread products is helpful. Strong odors also make many women gag. Evolutionary psychologists theorize that, in the days before refrigeration, morning sickness may have evolved as a way of preventing the mother from eating spoiled meat or toxic plants, which could be particularly dangerous to the baby while its basic body structures were being formed (Bjorklund & Pellegrini, 2002).

In support of this theory, crackers—the traditional treatment for morning sickness—do not spoil. To alleviate mothers' distress, health-care professionals advise eating more frequently and consuming smaller (less potentially toxic) quantities of food. If you have a friend who is struggling with morning sickness, you can give her this heartening information: Some research suggests that women who experience morning sickness are more likely to carry their babies to term.

This brings up the topic of pregnancy anxieties. Why are some women reluctant to announce the news until after three months have elapsed? The reason is that during the first trimester, roughly 1 in 10 pregnancies are destined to end in **miscarriage** (fetal death). For women in their late thirties, the chance of miscarrying during the first 12 weeks escalates to roughly 1 in 5. Many of these miscarriages are inevitable. They are caused by genetic problems in the developing embryo that are incompatible with life.

Second Trimester: Feeling Much Better and Connecting Emotionally

Another reason that the first months of pregnancy have a tentative quality is that mothers-to-be still don't feel the baby inside. But during the second trimester, the fetus makes its presence physically known.

By week 14, the uterus dramatically expands, often creating a need to shop for maternity clothes. The wider world may begin to notice the woman's expanding body: "Are you really pregnant?" "How wonderful!" "Take my seat."

Around week 18, an event called **quickening**—a sensation like bubbles that signals the baby kicking in the womb—appears. As Kim described in the vignette, and as you can see below, the woman feels viscerally connected to a growing human being:

When I felt him move, I found myself fantasizing about this new person, visualizing what he would look like—seeing him growing up, getting married, becoming a wonderful person. That's when the magic really kicked in.

miscarriage The naturally occurring loss of a pregnancy and death of the fetus.

quickening A pregnant woman's first feeling of the fetus moving inside her body.

This mystical sense of connection varies from woman to woman. Some mothers-to-be are intensely bonded to their babies from the minute they learn they are pregnant. For many, however, the sense of being totally attached intensifies during the second trimester when they experience some watershed event such as feeling the baby move (Righetti and others, 2005). Whenever it happens, this feeling is vital. Although attachment can blossom at any point, feeling intensely connected to one's baby during pregnancy predicts being a sensitive, attuned mother after the child enters the world (Salisbury and others, 2003).

Another landmark event that alters the emotional experience of pregnancy occurs during the beginning of the third trimester, when, as you saw in the vignette with Kim, the woman realizes she is finally able to give birth to a living child. This important late-pregnancy marker explains why some societies build in celebrations at month 6 or 7 to welcome the baby to the human community.

Third Trimester: Getting Very Large, and Waiting for Birth

Look at a pregnant woman struggling up the stairs and you'll get a sense of her feelings during this final trimester: backaches (think of carrying a bowling ball); leg cramps; numbness and tingling as the uterus presses against the nerves of the lower limbs; heartburn, insomnia, and anxious anticipation as focus shifts to the birth ("When will this baby arrive!"); uterine contractions occurring irregularly as the baby sinks into the birth canal and delivery draws very near. What is going on physiologically in the brain—not just the body—during late pregnancy and throughout this landmark time?

Exploring the Pregnant (and New Motherhood) Brain

New research offers fascinating clues. In one study, scientists measured women's anxiety at the midpoint of the second trimester and again at week 32 (during trimester three). No matter what the initial stress level, during late pregnancy the typical pattern was for a person to become less anxious than before. Just as the body's normal fever response is attenuated during late pregnancy to protect the soon-to-be-born baby (Mouihate and others, 2008), the woman's physiology may prepare her for the rigors of birth by becoming biologically less reactive to stress. But here is the kicker: When moms in this study deviated from this pattern by getting *more anxious* during late pregnancy, they were more likely to give birth to a baby that was premature (Glynn and others, 2008). Could doctors eventually be able to predict the risk of a woman giving birth early by tracking pregnancy stress levels over time? And suppose there is another evolutionary function of this pre-birth change. Might feeling less anxious operate to make new mothers more competent, sophisticated caregivers when confronting the challenges of early infant life?

The idea that giving birth may have intellectual benefits brings me to the research relating to a tantalizing phenomenon called "baby brain." Many expectant mothers complain that they are in a mental fog, unable to think as clearly as before. Researchers have clearly documented learning deficits in pregnant rats. With women, studies also show thinking processes become more hazy during this time of life—but only when scientists measure performance on complex, real-world tasks (see DeAngelis, 2008, for review). The animal researchers find that after giving birth, these pre-birth cognitive deficits more than reverse. Mother rats and monkeys perform better on learning and memory tasks than those who have never been pregnant. Furthermore, these changes may be long lasting, as they seem to permanently pump up the neurons in the memory centers of animals' brains (Kinsley & Lambert, 2008). Might the same neural

Focusing on your work can be impossible when you are suffering from "baby brain" and can't stop fantasizing about that wonderful new person inside of you.

©Imagemore Co., Ltd./Corbis

changes at birth also occur in our species and operate to make women more resilient cognitively as they age? Stay tuned for more data relating to this surprising potential motherhood benefit in the third edition of this book.

Pregnancy Is Not a Solo Act

I don't know what it's like for you and your partner to hear the baby's heartbeat, or see the ultrasound together, or feel the first kick. I lived through nine months of pregnancy by myself. No one understood how lonely I felt. I thought this was supposed to be the happiest time of your life. I found myself losing weight instead of gaining and being depressed most of the time.

When I told my husband I was pregnant, he got furious and told me we can't afford this baby. I'm frightened. All I know is that God is the provider of life and abortion is a sin.

So far, I've been discussing findings related to stress, as if the brain magically operated in isolation from the real world. But as these quotations reveal, the emotional experience of pregnancy differs dramatically from woman to woman. What forces can turn this joyous time of life into nine months of distress?

One influence, as suggested above, lies in economic concerns. Studies around the globe show that low socioeconomic status puts pregnant women at risk of feeling demoralized and depressed (Rahman, Harrington, & Iqbal, 2003; Stewart, Dean, & Gregorich, 2007). Imagine coping with the stresses associated with being poor—worrying about making ends meet, perhaps not getting adequate prenatal care—and you will understand why pregnancy is more likely to be one of life's great joys when an expectant mom is comfortably upper middle class.

The main force, however, that predicts having a joyous pregnancy applies to both affluent and economically deprived women alike: feeling loved. Women with high self-efficacy have a built-in buffer for coping with this life change. One interesting study suggested that feeling "in control" during pregnancy even mutes the physiological stress response (Nierop and others, 2008). However, as you saw with Kim in the introductory chapter vignette, the bottom-line research theme is that having caring *relationships* matters most (Glazier and others, 2004; Rahman, Harrington, & Iqbal, 2003; Rubertsson, Waldenström, & Wickberg, 2003; Savage and others, 2007). In fact, in tracking Hispanic women through late pregnancy and the first months after giving birth, researchers found that having a loving partner was especially helpful at staving off postpartum depression for women who had suffered from depressive symptoms before entering the pregnant state (Diaz and others, 2007).

Does this mean going through pregnancy without a partner is *always* a terrible thing? The answer is no. For women without a mate, nurturing family members or close friends are an incredibly important support. Consider this comment of an impoverished single woman in an interview study who was ranked as "thriving" during this time of life: "We've always been a close-knit family, and they were there to get me through. . . . They called me every night to make sure I was eating right" (Savage and others, 2007, p. 219).

Suppose, like the woman quoted at beginning of this section, you were married but your spouse was actively hostile to your pregnancy. If you had the choice, wouldn't you much rather be going through this life journey with a loving family or a good friend?

What About Dads?

This brings up the emotions of the standard partner in the pregnancy journey: dads. Given the attention we lavish on pregnant women, it should come as no surprise that fathers have been relatively ignored in the research exploring this major transition of life. But fathers are also bonded to their babies-to-be. They can feel just as devastated when a pregnancy doesn't work out. Listen to these heartrending stories about miscarriage, taken from a rare study exploring this event from the perspective of men (McCreight, 2004).

I had to be strong for Kate. I had to let her cry on me and then I would . . . drive up into the hills and cry to myself. I was trying to support her even though I felt my whole life had just caved in, you know, my whole life just ended then and there.

(quoted in McCreight, 2004, p. 337)

One father in this study had scanned the ultrasound image of the baby onto his screen saver and took enormous pleasure in looking at it. Three weeks later, when the fetus died in the womb, he could not bear to let the image go, even though every sight of the photo evoked waves of intense grief. Although the men in this study complained that their emotions were often marginalized (one angrily reported having friends call to ask only: "How is your wife doing?"), losing a child—particularly late in pregnancy—can be an unforgettable life trauma for men.

Is pregnancy *normally* a stressful time for men? The answer can be yes (Condon, Boyce, & Corkindale, 2004). Put yourself in the place of a father-to-be. Perhaps you wonder: "Will the child take away from my relationship with my wife?" "Can I be an involved father and support the family?" "Will I *really* be able to handle these two demanding roles?"

Men usually don't have the safety valve of discussing their worries with friends and family. As you saw in the quotation above, our culture expects them to be strong on their own.

So, by returning to the beginning of the chapter, we now know that the widespread cultural practice of pampering pregnant women makes excellent psychological sense—for both the mother *and* her child. But we also need to understand that expectant fathers need cherishing, too!

Table 2.1 summarizes these female findings in a brief "stress during pregnancy" questionnaire. Now, let's return to the baby and tackle that fear that Kim talked about in the opening chapter vignette: "Will my child be healthy?"

Because she is being cherished and pampered by a huge loving family, this single mom is likely to find the pregnancy journey very fulfilling.

TABLE 2.1: Measuring Stress in Mothers-to-Be: A Short Section Summary Questionnaire

1. Has the woman gotten less anxious during the third trimester, or is she more upset? (Rising anxiety levels in late pregnancy may predict giving birth prematurely.)

2. Does this woman have serious financial troubles, or is she living in poverty?

3. Is this woman having marital problems, and does her husband want this baby?

4. Is the woman a single mother? If so, does she have a supportive network of friends and family?

TYING IT ALL TOGETHER

1. Your friend Samantha just learned she is pregnant. Describe how she is likely to feel during each trimester.

2. Another pregnant friend complains to you, "I keep forgetting appointments, and I just can't seem to think as clearly as before." Give her a good news tip about how this symptom *might* change after the baby is born.

3. As a nurse-practitioner you want to be on the alert for signs of depression in your patients. List two *wider world* forces—mentioned in the text—that will tip you off that a woman may need special help coping with pregnancy.

4. As a clinic director, you are concerned about the fact that men are often left out of the pregnancy experience. Design a few innovative interventions to make your clinic responsive to the needs of fathers-to-be.

Answers to the Tying It All Together questions can be found on the last page of this chapter.

Threats to the Developing Baby

In this section, we explore the prenatal reasons for **birth defects,** or health problems at birth. In reading this "what can possibly go wrong" catalogue, keep these encouraging thoughts in mind: The vast majority of babies are born healthy. Only 4 percent have a birth defect of any kind. While some birth defects are indeed very disabling, many are treatable or very mild. Many birth defects result from a complex nature-plus-nurture interaction. Fetal genetic vulnerabilities combine with often unknown environmental hazards in the womb. However, in this section, we separate the causes of these problems into two categories: toxins that flow through the placenta to impair the baby's development; genetic diseases.

Threats from Outside: Teratogens

The universal fears about the growing baby are expressed in mountains of cultural prohibitions: "Don't use scissors or your baby will have cut lips" (a cleft palate) (Afghanistan); "Avoid looking at monkeys [Indonesia] or gossiping [China] or your baby will be deformed." The rules are particularly rigid surrounding what to eat. In Sicily, iced drinks are supposed to make the fetus shiver. Or the off-limit items might be spicy meats or all "hot foods" (Von Raffler-Engel, 1994).

If you think these practices are strange, consider the standard mid-twentieth-century medical advice: Physicians put women in the United States on a strict diet if they gained over 15 pounds. (The recommended weight gain is now 25 to 35 pounds.) They encouraged mothers-to-be to drink two beers each night to relax and routinely prescribed medications to combat nausea, especially during the first trimester (Von Raffler-Engel, 1994; Wertz & Wertz, 1989). Today, these once "up-to-date" medical pronouncements might qualify as fetal abuse! What *can* hurt the developing baby? At what times during prenatal development is damage most apt to occur?

A **teratogen** (from the Greek word *teras,* "monster," and *gen,* "creating") is the name for any substance that crosses the placenta to harm the fetus. A teratogen may be an infectious disease; a medication; a recreational drug; environmental hazards, such as radiation or pollution; or even the hormones produced by a pregnant woman who is under extreme stress. Table 2.2 describes potential teratogens in these categories.

Basic Teratogenic Principles

Teratogens typically exert their damage during the **sensitive period**—the timeframe when a particular organ or system is coming "on line." For example, the infectious disease called rubella (German measles) often damaged a baby's heart or ears, depending on the week during the first trimester when a mother contracted the disease. The sedative thalidomide, prescribed in Europe during the late 1950s to prevent morning sickness, impaired limb formation, depending on which day after fertilization the drug was imbibed. In general, with regard to teratogens, the following principles apply:

1. **Teratogens are most likely to cause major structural damage during the embryonic stage.** Before implantation, teratogens have an all-or-nothing impact. They either inhibit implantation and cause death, or they leave the not-yet-attached blastocyst unscathed. It is during the time of organ formation (after implantation through week 8) that major body structures are most likely to be affected. This is why—unless expectant mothers have a chronic disease that demands they continue this practice—physicians advise women not to take any medications during the first trimester (American Academy of Pediatrics [AAP], Committee on Drugs, 2000).

2. **Teratogens can affect the developing brain throughout pregnancy.** As you saw earlier, because the brain is forming well into the second and third

birth defect A physical or neurological problem that occurs prenatally or at birth.

teratogen A substance that crosses the placenta and harms the fetus.

sensitive period The time when a body structure is most vulnerable to damage by a teratogen, typically when that organ or process is rapidly developing or coming "on line."

TABLE 2.2: Examples of Known Teratogens and the Damage They Can Do

Teratogen	Consequences of Exposure
Infectious Diseases	
Rubella (German measles)	If a pregnant woman contracted rubella during the embryonic stage, the consequence was, not infrequently, mental retardation, blindness, or eye, ear, and heart abnormalities in the baby—depending on the week the virus entered the bloodstream. Luckily, women of childbearing age are now routinely immunized for this typically minor adult disease.
Cytomegalovirus	About 25% of babies infected with this virus develop vision or hearing loss; 10% develop neurological problems.
AIDS	HIV-infected women can transmit the virus to their babies prenatally through the placenta, during delivery (when blood is exchanged between the mother and child), or after birth (through breast milk). Rates of transmission are much lower if infected mothers take the anti-AIDS drug AZT or if newborns are given a new drug that blocks the transmission of HIV at birth. If a mother takes these precautions, does not breast-feed, and delivers her baby by c-section, the infection rate falls to less than 1%. While mother-to-child transmission of HIV has declined dramatically in the developed world, it remains a devastating problem in sub-Saharan Africa and other impoverished regions of the globe (AVERT, 2005).
Herpes	This familiar sexually transmitted disease can cause miscarriage, growth retardation, and eye abnormalities in affected fetuses. Doctors recommend that pregnant women with active genital herpes undergo c-sections to avoid infecting their babies during delivery.
Toxoplasmosis	This disease, caused by a parasite found in raw meat and cat feces, can lead to blindness, deafness, and mental retardation in infants. Pregnant women should avoid handling raw meat and cat litter.
Medications	
Antibiotics	Streptomycin has been linked to hearing loss; tetracycline to stained infant tooth enamel.
Thalidomide	This drug, prescribed in 1960s Europe to prevent nausea during the first trimester, prevented the baby's arms and legs from developing if taken during the embryonic period.
Anti-seizure drugs	These medications have been linked to developmental delays during infancy.
Anti-psychotic drugs	These drugs may slightly raise the risk of giving birth to a baby with heart problems.
Antidepressants	Although typically safe, third-trimester exposure to selective serotonin reuptake inhibitors and tricyclic antidepressants has been linked to temporary jitteriness and excessive crying and to eating and sleeping difficulties in newborns. Rarely, these drugs can produce a serious syndrome involving seizures and dehydration.
Recreational Drugs	
Cocaine	This drug is linked to miscarriage, growth retardation, and learning and behavior problems.
Methamphetamines	This drug may cause miscarriage and growth retardation.
Environmental toxins	
Radiation	Japanese children who had been exposed to radiation from the atomic bomb during the second trimester had extremely high rates of severe mental retardation. Miscarriages were virtually universal among pregnant women living within 5 miles of the blast. Pregnant women are also advised to avoid clinical doses of radiation such as those used in X-rays (and especially cancer treatment radiation).
Lead	Babies with high levels of lead in the umbilical cord may show impairments in cognitive functioning (Bellinger and others, 1987). Maternal exposure to lead is associated with miscarriage.
Mercury and PCBs	These pollutants are linked to learning and behavior problems.
Stress	High stress levels during pregnancy have been linked to lower infant mental and motor milestone scores and to miscarriage and premature delivery. But as women experiencing severe stress are less likely to take care of their health, the direct physiological impact of stress hormones on the fetus is unclear.
Vitamin Deficiencies	In addition to eating a balanced diet, every woman of childbearing age should take folic acid supplements. This vitamin, part of the B complex, protects against the incomplete closure of the neural tube during the first month of development—an event that may produce *spina bifida* (paralysis in the body below the region of the spine that has not completely closed) or *anencephaly* (failure of the brain to develop—and certain death) if the gap occurs toward the top of the developing tube.

General sources: Buitelaar, Huizink, & Mulder, 2004; Huttenlocher, 2002 and the references in this chapter.

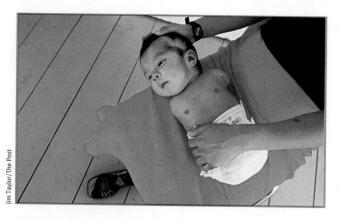

This Honduran baby is a testament to the horrible damage teratogens can potentially cause during the embryonic period, as his condition was believed to be due to his mother's exposure to pesticides during early pregnancy.

trimesters, the potential for neurological damage extends for all nine months. Japanese fetuses exposed to that incredibly severe teratogen, radiation from the atomic bomb, during the second trimester were born with microcephaly (a small brain) and severe mental retardation (Huttenlocher, 2002). Typically, however, during the second and third trimesters, exposure to teratogens increases the risk of **developmental disorders**. This umbrella term refers to a host of conditions that compromise normal development—from delays in reaching basic milestones, such as walking or talking, to serious learning problems and hyperactivity.

3. **Teratogens operate in a dose-response fashion.** With toxic substances, there is often a threshold level above which damage occurs. For instance, women who drink more than four cups of coffee a day throughout pregnancy have a slightly higher risk of miscarriage; but having an occasional Diet Coke is perfectly fine (Gilbert-Barness, 2000).

4. **Teratogens exert their damage unpredictably, depending on fetal and maternal vulnerabilities.** Still, mothers-to-be metabolize potential toxins differently, and babies differ genetically in susceptibility. So the damaging effects of a particular toxin can vary. On the plus side, you may know a child in your local school's gifted program whose mother drank heavily during pregnancy. On the negative side, we do not know where the teratogenic threshold lies in any particular case. Therefore, during pregnancy, erring on the side of caution is best.

Finally, while the damaging impact of a teratogen can show up during infancy, not infrequently it manifests itself years later in learning difficulties during school (Dombrowki and Martin, 2007) or during the adult years. An unfortunate example of this teratogenic time bomb took place in my own life. My mother was given a drug called diethylstilbestrol (DES) while she was pregnant with me. (DES was routinely prescribed in the 1950s and 1960s to prevent miscarriage.) During my early twenties, I developed cancerous cells in my cervix—and, after surgery, had three miscarriages before ultimately being blessed by adopting my son.

The Teratogenic Impact of Medicines and Recreational Drugs

The fact that some medications are potentially teratogenic presents dilemmas for women. Do you cut down on your anti-epilepsy drugs and risk having a seizure that could hurt the baby because your normal dose is linked to infant developmental delays? (Thomas and others, 2008.) Should you abandon your anti-psychotics and risk the mental health consequences, given that these drugs carry a slight risk of producing heart problems in your unborn child? (Reis and Kallen, 2008.) And suppose you are among the millions of women taking antidepressant drugs. You know that continuing your medications into the third trimester may make your newborn groggy or, more rarely, suffer from seizures at birth (Boucher, Bairam, & Beaulac-Baillargeon, 2008). But you also worry, based on reading this chapter, that stopping your meds will cause excessive anxiety and, possibly, raise the risk of a premature birth.

As these comments illustrate, with medications and pregnancy, it can be a difficult balancing act. Sometimes there are no perfect choices.

With all recreational drugs, the choice is clear. Each substance is potentially teratogenic. So just say *no!*

Because tobacco and alcohol are woven into the fabric of daily life, let's now focus on these widely used teratogens. What *can* happen to the baby when pregnant women smoke and drink?

developmental disorders Learning impairments and behavioral problems during infancy and childhood.

SMOKING Each time she reads the information on a cigarette pack, a pregnant woman gets a reminder that she may be doing her baby harm. Still, in surveys, roughly one out of every nine pregnant women in the United States continues to smoke (Martin and others, 2003). As more developing-world women than ever now have this addiction, the dangers smoking poses to the fetus are also a global public health concern (Islam & Gerdtham, 2006).

The main danger with smoking is giving birth to a smaller-than-normal baby, an event that, as you will see later, has the potential to raise the risk of learning and behavior problems (Behrman & Butler, 2006; Dean and Davis, 2007; Pajer, 2008). Nicotine constricts the mother's blood vessels, reducing blood flow to the developing fetus and so not allowing a full complement of nutrients to reach the child. Heavy smoking during the first two trimesters, in particular, compromises fetal length. Ironically, this slowed up prenatal development may help promote childhood obesity, as an accelerated "catch-up" growth process takes place after the baby is born (Vielwerth and others, 2007).

The good news is that one in four pregnant U.S. smokers take the difficult step of quitting for the health of their baby, and almost all cut down. The bad news is that some studies show even six cigarettes a day can raise the risk of giving birth to a small child (LeClere & Wilson, 1997).

ALCOHOL As you saw earlier, it used to be standard practice to encourage pregnant women to have a nightcap to relieve stress. In Italy, drinking red wine during pregnancy was supposed to produce a healthy, rosy-cheeked child! (See Von Raffler-Engel, 1994.) During the 1970s, as evidence mounted for a disorder called **fetal alcohol syndrome (FAS)**, these prescriptions were quickly revised. Whenever you hear the word *syndrome*, it is a signal that the condition has a constellation of features that are present to varying degrees. The defining qualities of fetal alcohol syndrome include a far-smaller-than-normal birth weight; an abnormally small cranium, or brain; facial abnormalities (such as a flattened face); and developmental disorders ranging from serious mental retardation to seizures and hyperactivity (Dean and Davis, 2007; Wedding and others, 2007).

Women who binge-drink (have more than four drinks at a time) (Jacobson & Jacobson, 1994) or who regularly consume several drinks throughout their pregnancies are at highest risk of giving birth to a baby with fetal alcohol syndrome. Their children, at a minimum, may be born with a less severe condition called *fetal alcohol spectrum disorder*, characterized by deficits in learning and impaired mental health (Wedding and others, 2007). As alcohol crosses the placenta, it affects the developing systems that program the stress response; so it's no wonder that drinking during pregnancy might set the fetus up for excessive jumpiness or anxiety during life (Weinberg and others, 2008). But granted that heavy drinking is definitely off limits, what about having one glass of wine a day?

Every U.S. public health organization recommends no alcohol during pregnancy (Wedding and others, 2007). Interestingly, our European counterparts, such as the British Royal College of Obstetricians and Gynaecologists, take a more permissive stance: "One drink per day is perfectly acceptable" (RCOG, 1999). Still, having as little as five drinks a week does slightly raise the risk of stillbirth (Aliyu and others, 2008). Plus, fetal alcohol syndrome ranks as the number-one preventable birth defect in the United States (Wedding and others, 2007). Therefore, when someone offers a pregnant woman a glass of wine, it's wise for her to just say no.

Measurement Issues

Why is there *any* controversy about the minimum safe level to smoke or drink? For answers, imagine the challenges you would face as a researcher exploring the impact of these teratogens on the developing child. You would have to ask thousands of pregnant women to estimate how often they indulged in these "unacceptable" behaviors.

This boy has some of the facial features characteristic of fetal alcohol syndrome. He also has serious learning problems.

fetal alcohol syndrome (FAS) A cluster of birth defects caused by the mother's alcohol consumption during pregnancy.

Could you trust these *self-reports* of, say, one drink or five cigarettes a day? With regard to alcohol, there is the additional problem of documenting content. How much liquor was really in that "one" margarita you mixed last night? (Greenfield & Kerr, 2008.) You would then have to track the children for decades, looking for learning and behavior problems that might appear as late as the teenage years. Then, because your study is correlational, any problems you found might be due to a variety of influences. Wouldn't women who drink during pregnancy be likely to be poorly nourished? (Guerrini, Thomson, & Gurling, 2007.) Might they not be more prone to smoke and/or be less committed mothers once their babies arrived? Could you really isolate the difficulties you found years later to a single teratogen given these multiple "at-risk" forces?

When we see a pregnant woman smoking or drinking, we have all sorts of vengeful emotions: "She is doing terrible damage to her child!" With the diseases we turn to now, there is no person to blame, no question of how much of which substance was too much. The child's fate was sealed at conception. However, the emotional issues can be even more wrenching: "Should I terminate this pregnancy?" "What will happen to my child?"

Threats from Within: Chromosomal and Genetic Disorders

When a birth defect is classified as "genetic," there are two main causes. The child might have an unusual number of chromosomes, or the problem might be caused by a specific faulty gene (or set of genes).

Chromosomal Problems

As we know, the normal human chromosomal complement is 46. However, sometimes a baby with a missing or extra chromosome is conceived. The vast majority of these fertilizations end in first-trimester miscarriages, as the mass of cells cannot differentiate much past the blastocyst stage.

Still, babies can be born with an abnormal number of sex chromosomes (such as an extra X or two, an extra Y, or a single X) and survive. In this case, although the symptoms vary, the result is often learning impairments and sometimes infertility.

Survival is also potentially possible when a child is born with an extra chromosome on a specific other pair. The most common example—happening in roughly 1 in every 2,000 births (EUROCAT, 2004)—produces a baby with Down syndrome.

Down syndrome typically occurs because a cell-division error, called *nondisjunction*, in the egg or sperm causes an extra chromosome or piece of that copy to adhere to chromosome pair 21. (Notice, if you turn back to Figure 2.3 on page 38, that this is the smallest matching set.) The child is born with 47 chromosomes instead of the normal human complement of 46.

This extra chromosome produces familiar physical features: a flat facial profile, an upward slant to the eyes, a stocky appearance, and an enlarged tongue. Babies born with Down syndrome are at high risk for heart defects and childhood leukemia. Here, too, there is a lifespan time-bomb impact. During midlife, many adults with Down syndrome develop Alzheimer's disease (Schupf and others, 2003). The most well-known problem with this familiar disorder, however, is mild to moderate mental retardation.

A century ago, Down syndrome children rarely lived to adulthood. They were shunted to institutions to live out their severely shortened lives. Today, due to modern medical advances, infants with this condition in the United States now have an average life expectancy of 58 (Bellenir, 2004). Ironically, this dramatic longevity gain can be a double-edged sword. Elderly parent caregivers may worry what will happen to their middle-aged child when they die or become physically impaired (Gath, 1993).

Down syndrome The most common chromosomal abnormality, causing mental retardation, susceptibility to heart disease, and other health problems; and distinctive physical characteristics, such as slanted eyes and stocky build.

This is not to say that every baby with Down syndrome is destined to be dependent on a caregiver's help. These children can sometimes learn to read and write (Turner & Alborz, 2003). They can live independently, hold down jobs, marry and have children, construct richly fulfilling lives (Bellenir, 2004). Do you know a child with Down syndrome like the toddler in the photo below who is the light of her loving extended family's life?

Although women of any age can give birth to Down syndrome babies, the risk rises exponentially among older mothers. Over age 40, the chance of having a Down syndrome birth is 1 in 100; over age 45, it is 1 in 25 (Bellenir, 2004). The reason is that, with more time "in storage," older ova are more apt to develop chromosomal faults.

Down syndrome is typically caused by a random event. A spontaneous genetic mistake has occurred in one ovum or, more rarely (in an estimated 5 percent of cases), in one sperm. Now let's look at a different category of genetic disorders—those passed down in the parents' DNA to potentially affect *every* child.

Genetic Disorders

Most illnesses—from cancer to heart disease to schizophrenia—are caused by complex nature-plus-nurture interactions. They result from several, often unknown genes acting in conjunction with murky environmental forces. The conditions we turn to now are different: These illnesses are caused by a *single*, known gene.

Single-gene disorders are passed down according to three modes of inheritance: They may be *dominant, recessive,* or *sex-linked.* To understand these patterns, you might want to look back at the paired arrangement of the chromosomes in Figure 2.3 (page 38) and remember that we get one copy of each gene from our mother and one from our father. Also, in understanding these illnesses, it is important to know that one member of each gene pair can be dominant. This means that the quality will always show up in real life. If both members of the gene pair are not dominant (that is, if they are recessive), the illness will manifest itself only if the child inherits two of the faulty genes.

Dominant disorders are in the first category. A person who inherits one copy of the faulty gene always gets the disease. In this case, if one parent harbors the problem gene (and so has the illness), each child the couple gives birth to has a fifty-fifty chance of also getting ill.

Recessive disorders are in the second category. Unless a person gets two copies of the gene, one from the father and one from the mother, that child is disease free. In this case, the odds of a baby born to two carriers—that is, parents who each have one copy of that gene—having the illness are 1 in 4.

The mode of transmission for **sex-linked single-gene disorders** is more complicated. Most often, the woman is carrying a recessive (non-expressed in real life) gene for the illness on *one* of her two X chromosomes. Since her daughters have another X from their father (who doesn't carry the illness), the female side of the family is typically disease free. Her sons, however—with just one X chromosome that might code for the disorder—have a fifty-fifty chance of getting ill, depending on whether they get the normal or abnormal version of their mother's X.

Because their single X leaves them vulnerable, sex-linked disorders typically affect males. But as an intellectual exercise, you might want to figure out under what conditions females can get this type of disease. If you guessed that it's when the mother is a carrier (having one faulty X) and the dad has the disorder (having the gene on his single X), you are right!

Table 2.3 visually decodes these different modes of inheritance and describes a few of the best-known single-gene diseases. In scanning the first illness on the chart, Huntington's disease, imagine your emotional burden as a

single-gene disorder An illness caused by a single gene.

dominant disorder An illness that a child gets by inheriting one copy of the abnormal gene that causes the disorder.

recessive disorder An illness that a child gets by inheriting two copies of the abnormal gene that causes the disorder.

sex-linked single-gene disorder An illness, carried on the mother's X chromosome, that typically leaves the female offspring unaffected but has a fifty-fifty chance of striking each male child.

The birth of a Down syndrome child has a life-changing effect on every family member. Will this big sister become a more caring, sensitive adult through having grown up with this much loved younger sibling?

Lauren Shear/Photo Researchers, Inc.

TABLE 2.3: Some Examples of Dominant, Recessive, and Sex-Linked Single-Gene Disorders

Dominant Disorders

- **Huntington's disease (HD)** This fatal nervous system disorder is characterized by uncontrollable jerky movements and irreversible intellectual impairment (dementia). Symptoms usually appear around age 35, although the illness can occasionally erupt in childhood and in old age. There is no treatment for this disease.

Recessive Disorders

- **Cystic fibrosis (CF)** This most common single-gene disorder in the United States is typically identified at birth by the salty character of the sweat. The child's body produces mucus that clogs the lungs and pancreas, interfering with breathing and digestion and causing repeated medical crises. As the hairlike cells in the lungs are destroyed, these vital organs degenerate and eventually cause premature death. Advances in treatment have extended the average life expectancy for people with CF to the early thirties. One in 28 U.S. Caucasians is a carrier for this disease.*

- **Sickle cell anemia** This blood disorder takes its name from the characteristic sickle shape of the red blood cells. The blood cells collapse and clump together, causing oxygen deprivation and organ damage. The symptoms of sickle cell anemia are fatigue, pain, growth retardation, ulcers, stroke, and, ultimately, a shortened life. Treatments include transfusions and medications for infection and pain. One in 10 African Americans is a carrier of this disease.*

- **Tay-Sachs disease** In this universally fatal infant nervous system disorder, the child appears healthy at birth, but then fatty material accumulates in the neurons and, at 6 months, symptoms such as blindness, mental retardation, and paralysis occur and the baby dies. Tay-Sachs is found primarily among Jewish people of Eastern European ancestry. An estimated 1 in 25 U.S. Jews is a carrier.†

Sex-Linked Disorders

- **Hemophilia** These blood-clotting disorders typically affect males. The most serious forms of hemophilia (A and B) produce severe episodes of uncontrolled joint bleeding and pain. In the past, these episodes often resulted in death during childhood. Today, with transfusions of the missing clotting factors, affected children can have a fairly normal life expectancy.

*Sickle cell anemia may have remained in the population because having the trait (one copy of the gene) conferred an evolutionary advantage: It protected against malaria in Africa. Scientists also speculate that the cystic fibrosis trait may have conferred immunity to typhoid fever.

†Due to a vigorous public awareness program in the Jewish community, potential carriers are routinely screened and the rate of Tay-Sachs disease has declined dramatically.

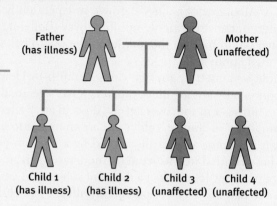

Father (has illness) — Mother (unaffected)

Child 1 (has illness) Child 2 (has illness) Child 3 (unaffected) Child 4 (unaffected)

Here, the gene is dominant, and there is a 1-in-2 chance that each child of an affected parent will have the disease.

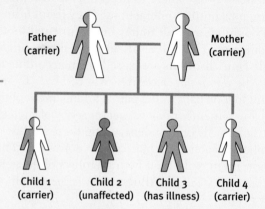

Father (carrier) — Mother (carrier)

Child 1 (carrier) Child 2 (unaffected) Child 3 (has illness) Child 4 (carrier)

Here, both parents are carriers, and each child has a 1-in-4 chance of having the disease.

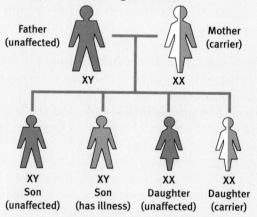

Father (unaffected) XY — Mother (carrier) XX

XY Son (unaffected) XY Son (has illness) XX Daughter (unaffected) XX Daughter (carrier)

Here, the mother has the faulty gene on her X chromosome, so the daughters are typically disease-free, but each son has a 1-in-2 chance of getting ill.

genetically at-risk child. People with Huntington's develop an incurable dementia in the prime of life. As a child you would probably have watched a beloved parent slowly lose his memory and bodily functions, and then slowly die. You would know that your odds of suffering the same fate are 1 in 2. (Although babies born with lethal dominant genetic disorders typically die before they can have children, Huntington's disease has remained in the population because it, too, operates as an internal time bomb, showing up during the prime reproductive years.)

With the other illnesses in the table—programmed by recessive genes—the fears relate to bearing a child. If both you and your partner have the Tay-Sachs carrier gene, you may have suffered the trauma of seeing a child die in infancy. With cystic fibrosis, your affected child would be subject to recurrent medical crises as his lungs filled up with fluid, and he would face a dramatically shortened life. Would you want to take the 1-in-4 chance of having this experience again?

The good news, as the table shows, is that the prognoses for some routinely fatal childhood single-gene disorders are no longer as dire as in the past. With hemophilia, the life-threatening episodes of uncontrolled bleeding can be avoided by supplying the missing blood factor through transfusions. While surviving to the teens with cystic fibrosis used to be a rare event, babies born with this disorder can now expect on average to live to their 20s and sometimes beyond (CysticFibrosis.com, n.d.). Still, with Tay-Sachs or Huntington's disease, there is *nothing* medically that can be done.

In sum, the answer to the question "Can single-gene disorders be treated and cured?" is "It depends." Although people still have the faulty gene—and so are not "cured" in the traditional sense—through advances in nurture (or changing the environment), we have made remarkable progress in treating what used to be uniformly fatal diseases.

Our most dramatic progress, however, lies in advances in **genetic testing.** Through a simple blood test, people can now find out whether they carry the gene for these (and other) illnesses.

These diagnostic breakthroughs, however, bring up difficult issues. Would you want to know whether you have the gene for Huntington's? Suppose an employer got hold of your test results and, in view of your poor genetic profile, denied you a job? Because of the potential for workplace discrimination and because people have a right *not* to know their future physical fate, some people argue that Congress should ban genetic testing in the workplace (Krumm, 2002).

The inspiring story of Nancy Wexler, the psychologist who helped discover the Huntington's gene and whose mother died of the disease, is instructive here (see the How Do We Know box on page 56). While Nancy will not say whether she has been tested, her sister Alice refused to be screened because she felt not knowing was better emotionally than the anguish of living with a positive result.

Interventions

The pluses of genetic testing are clearer when the issue relates to having a child. Let's imagine you and your spouse have been tested and know you are carriers of the gene for cystic fibrosis or another serious genetic disorder. If you are contemplating having children, what should you do?

Sorting Out the Options: Genetic Counseling

Your first step would be to consult a **genetic counselor,** a professional skilled in both genetics and counseling, to help you think through your choices. Genetic counselors are experts in risk assessment. In addition to laying out the odds, they describe advances in treatment. For example, they would inform couples who are carriers for cystic fibrosis about life-prolonging biological strategies on the horizon, such as gene therapy. They would also highlight the interpersonal and economic costs of having a child with this disease. But they are trained never to offer specific advice. Their goal is to permit couples to make a *mutual decision* on their own (Bodenhorn & Lawson, 2003).

Now, suppose that, armed with this information, you and your partner go ahead and conceive. Let's briefly scan the major tests that are available to every woman carrying a child.

genetic testing A blood test to determine whether a person carries the gene for a given genetic disorder.

genetic counselor A professional who counsels parents-to-be about their own or their children's risk of developing genetic disorders, as well as about available treatments.

about the gene for Huntington's disease?

Nancy Wexler and her sister got the devastating news from their physician father, Milton, more than 30 years ago: "Your mother has a fatal illness. She will die of dementia in a horrible way. Your chance of getting it is fifty-fifty. There is nothing we can do. But that doesn't mean we are going to give up." In 1969, Milton Wexler established the Hereditary Disease Foundation, surrounded himself with scientists from around the world, and put his young daughter, Nancy, a clinical psychologist, in charge. The hunt was on for the Huntington's gene.

A breakthrough came in 1979, when Nancy learned that the world's largest group of people with Huntington's lived in a small, inbred community in Venezuela—descendants of a woman who harbored the gene mutation that caused the disease. After building a pedigree of 18,000 family members, collecting blood samples from thousands more, and carefully analyzing the DNA for differences, the researchers hit pay dirt. They isolated the Huntington's gene.

Having this diagnostic marker is the first step to eventually finding a cure. So far the cure is elusive, but the hunt continues. Nancy still serves as the head of the foundation, vigorously agitating for research on the illness that killed her mother. She works full time as a professor in Columbia University's Neurology and Psychiatry Department. But every year, she comes back to the village in Venezuela to counsel and just visit with her families—her relatives in blood.

Courtesy of Nancy Wexler, http://www.hdfoundation.org/

Tools of Discovery: Prenatal Tests

Blood tests performed during the first trimester are now able to show (with reasonable accuracy) various chromosomal conditions, such as Down syndrome. Perhaps the best-known test for assessing the fetus was highlighted in our introductory vignette: the **ultrasound**.

TIMELINE Prenatal Development, Pregnancy, Prenatal Threats, Tools of Discovery

	Germinal stage (weeks 1 and 2)	Embryonic stage (weeks 3–8)	Fetal stage (weeks 9–38)
PRENATAL DEVELOPMENT	Zygote → blastocyst, which implants in uterus.	All major organs and structures form.	Massive growth and refinements; brain develops; live birth is possible at 22–24 weeks.
THREATS	At fertilization: chromosomal and single-gene diseases.	Teratogens can cause basic structural abnormalities.	Teratogens can impair growth, affect the brain, and so cause developmental disorders. They can also produce miscarriage or premature labor.

Ultrasounds, which provide an image of the baby in the womb, are used to date the pregnancy and assess the fetus's growth, in addition to revealing various structural abnormalities and confirming the results of blood tests suggesting that the child might have a particular disorder such as Down syndrome (Wapner and others, 2003).

As you saw in the vignette, this famous test has an interesting side benefit. By making the baby visually real, the ultrasound visits have become emotional landmarks on the pregnancy journey itself. Have you ever had a friend proudly display a precious photograph of his baby's ultrasound? If you are a parent, perhaps you have shown your own child this priceless image of what he looked like before entering the world.

In this ultrasound photo, you can clearly see the baby's head, arms, hands, and fingers. Now, imagine the emotional impact on parents when they see this image.

Because these tests are noninvasive, advances in ultrasound technology and maternal blood testing may be the wave of the future in testing for fetal problems. The two procedures we turn to now, while usually safe, are a bit more risky, as they require actually entering the womb. So when they consider taking these tests, women rely on their personal values—specifically, whether they would consider terminating a pregnancy even if their baby had a serious genetic disease (van den Berg and others, 2008).

During the first trimester, **chorionic villus sampling (CVS)** can diagnose a variety of chromosomal and genetic conditions. A physician inserts a catheter into the woman's abdomen or vagina and withdraws a piece of the developing placenta for analysis. As this test carries a risk of miscarriage, and limb impairments, CVS is recommended only for couples at high risk of carrying a child with a particular disease.

During the second trimester, a safer test, called **amniocentesis,** can be used to determine the fetus's genetic fate. Aided by an ultrasound, the doctor inserts a syringe into the woman's uterus and extracts a sample of amniotic fluid. The cells can reveal a host of genetic and chromosomal conditions, as well as the sex of the fetus.

Amniocentesis is carefully timed for a gestational age (typically week 14) when there is enough fluid to safely siphon out and time to decide whether or not to carry the baby to term. However, it, too, carries a small chance of infection and miscarriage, depending on the skill of the doctor performing the test. Moreover, as culturing the cells for analysis takes several weeks, by the time the results of the "amnio" arrive, quickening may have occurred. The woman must endure the trauma of a full labor should she decide to terminate the pregnancy at this late stage.

The summary timeline spanning these pages illustrates these tools of discovery, the threat zones for problems, and the landmarks of pregnancy from both the maternal and fetal points of view. Now that we have a good understanding of what normally occurs and what can go wrong, let's pause to look at what happens when the pregnancy journey is unfulfilled.

ultrasound In pregnancy, an image of the fetus in the womb that helps to date the pregnancy, assess the fetus's growth, and identify abnormalities.

chorionic villus sampling (CVS) A relatively risky first-trimester pregnancy test for fetal genetic disorders.

amniocentesis A second-trimester procedure that involves inserting a syringe into a woman's uterus to extract a sample of amniotic fluid, which is tested for a variety of genetic and chromosomal conditions.

	First trimester (month 1–month 3)	Second trimester (month 4–month 6)	Third trimester (month 7–month 9)
PREGNANCY	Morning sickness, tiredness, and other unpleasant symptoms may occur; miscarriage is a worry.	Woman looks pregnant. Quickening occurs (around week 18). Mother can feel intensely bonded to baby.	Woman gets very large and anxiously waits for birth.
TOOLS OF DISCOVERY	Ultrasound Blood tests Chorionic villus sampling (CVS) around week 10	Ultrasound Amniocentesis (around week 15)	Ultrasound

Dung Vo Trung/Corbis

Infertility

Been riding an emotional and financial roller coaster for the past five years. Had uterine surgery—Dr. took a cyst out. Had artificial insemination with my husband's sperm. Dr. gave me Clomid [a fertility drug], but I'm still not pregnant. All of my friends have babies. I know I was meant to be a mother. Why is this happening to me?

Some societies view a woman's ability to bear children as vital to the well-being of the whole community. When women are pregnant, the spirits will provide a bountiful harvest. Many cultures view bearing children as critical to the success of a marriage. In fact, the practice of throwing rice at a just-married couple is actually a fertility rite (Kitzinger, 2000). And as you can see in the fertility chatline quotation above, many people view having a child as critical to their own well-being.

Infertility, defined as the inability to conceive a child after a year of unprotected intercourse, affects an estimated 1 in 6 U.S. couples (Turkington & Alper, 2001). This event (no surprise) produces anxiety, depression, and often stress on other relationships. Imagine the pain of jealously witnessing friends and family members drift effortlessly into pregnancy, when your own dream of having a child is dashed month after agonizing month (Peterson, Gold, & Feingold, 2007; Strauss, 2002).

Infertility can affect women (and men) of every age. However, just as with miscarriage and Down syndrome, female infertility rates tilt upward at older ages. Within the first six months of trying, roughly 3 out of 4 women in their twenties are able to conceive. At age 40, only 1 out of 5 achieves that goal (Turkington & Alper, 2001). Because of their more complicated anatomy, we tend to assume infertility is usually a "female" problem. Not so! Male issues are *equally* likely to be involved when a couple cannot conceive (Turkington & Alper, 2001). And yes, just as with women, male infertility is more common at older ages.

To attack the multiple reasons for infertility, we have a twenty-first-century medical arsenal. To demonstrate the need for multiple weapons, Figure 2.9 offers another look at the female reproductive system, showing some places on the complex chain from ovulation to implantation where problems may arise.

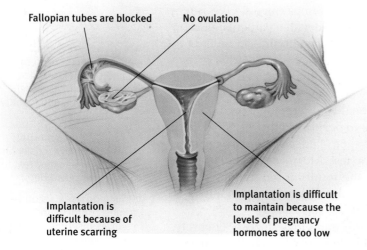

FIGURE 2.9: Some possible missteps on the path to reproduction: In this diagram, you can see some problems that may cause infertility in women. You can also use it to review the ovulation-to-implantation sequence.

Fallopian tubes are blocked

No ovulation

Implantation is difficult because of uterine scarring

Implantation is difficult to maintain because the levels of pregnancy hormones are too low

INTERVENTIONS: Assisted Reproductive Technology

Each problem on the reproductive chain has its treatment—from fertility drugs to stimulate ovulation to hormonal supplements to foster implantation; from surgery to help clean out the uterus and the fallopian tubes to artificial insemination (inserting the sperm into the woman's uterus through a syringe). Then, some couples turn to that ultimate medical weapon: **assisted reproductive technology (ART).**

Assisted reproductive technology refers to any strategy in which the egg is fertilized outside the womb. The most widely used ART procedure is **in vitro fertilization (IVF).** After the woman has been given fertility drugs (which stimulate multiple ovulations), her eggs are harvested and put in a laboratory dish, along with the partner's sperm, to be fertilized. A few days later, the fertilized eggs are inserted into the uterus. Then, the couple anxiously waits to find out if the cells have implanted in the uterine wall.

In vitro fertilization, which was initially developed to bypass blocked fallopian tubes, has spawned amazing variations. The sperm may be placed directly in the woman's fallopian tube or injected into the ova. The fertilized eggs may be inserted into a "carrier womb"—a surrogate mother, who carries the couple's genetic offspring to term (Turkington & Alper, 2001). In view of these modifications, you may be wondering: Can babies conceived this way be normal? One study suggests that the risk of birth defects with in vitro conceptions is roughly double the normal rate—about 9 percent (Hansen and others, 2002). But most couples willingly accept these odds in their desperate quest to have a child.

The real problem lies in the daunting commitment of time and money. There is the day-by-day monitoring and the invasive procedures to harvest and insert the eggs; the roller-coaster emotions involved in waiting to see whether pregnancy occurs (Salmela-Aro & Suikkari, 2008). ART is expensive—with average current costs in the United States well over 10,000 dollars per reproductive round. Medical insurance often doesn't cover the expense (Johnson & Chavkin, 2007). Moreover, success is far from assured. In 2005, according to the Centers for Disease Control, the odds of a woman under age 35 getting pregnant after a round of in vitro treatments was less than fifty-fifty. Over age 40, the success rate slid down to 1 in 6 (CDC, 2005 Assisted Reproductive Technology [ART] report, National Summary, retrieved Oct. 10, 2008).

The final insult is that some of these conceptions are doomed to end in miscarriage. Inserting several fertilized eggs into a woman's uterus increases the odds that one of these conceptions will implant. However, if all "take," there is the possibility that none of the tiny babies will survive. So a couple may have to decide whether to undergo a distressing in-utero procedure called "fetal reduction" to increase their odds of having a living child (Britt & Evans, 2007).

What happens when *any* woman gives birth? The answer brings us to the final stop on the pregnancy pathway—labor and birth.

infertility The inability to conceive after a year of unprotected sex. (Includes the inability to carry a child to term.)

assisted reproductive technology (ART) Any infertility treatment in which the egg is fertilized outside the womb.

in vitro fertilization An infertility treatment in which conception occurs outside the womb; the developing cell mass is then inserted into the woman's uterus so that pregnancy can occur.

🌸 TYING IT ALL TOGETHER

1. Teratogen A caused limb malformations. Teratogen B caused developmental disorders. Teratogen A wreaked its damage during the_____ stage of prenatal development and was taken during the_____ trimester of pregnancy, while teratogen B probably did its damage during the _____stage and was taken during the _____ trimester.

2. Seto and Brandon's mothers contracted rubella (German measles) during different weeks in their first trimester of pregnancy. Seto has heart problems; Brandon has hearing problems. Which teratogenic principle is illustrated here?

3. Your friend Monique is planning to become pregnant and asks you if it will be OK for her to have a glass of wine with dinner each night. What should your answer be?

   a. Go for it! Teratogens operate in a dose-response fashion, and this is definitely too low a dose to do harm.
   b. Go for it! The stress-reducing benefits of a glass of wine would outweigh any harm.
   c. Absolutely not. Even one glass of wine per night is certain to harm the fetus.
   d. Don't press your luck. Even if a drink per night probably is not teratogenic, it raises the risk of stillbirth; so it's best to avoid alcohol completely.

4. Latasha gives birth to a child with Down syndrome, while Jennifer gives birth to a child with cystic fibrosis. Which woman should be more worried about having another child with that condition, and why?

5. To a friend who is thinking of choosing between chorionic villus sampling (CVS) and amniocentesis, mention the advantages and disadvantages of each procedure.

6. Devise a checklist to help infertile couples determine whether in vitro fertilization might be an appropriate strategy.

Answers to the Tying It All Together questions can be found on the last page of this chapter.

Birth

During the last weeks of pregnancy, the fetus' head drops lower into the uterus. On their weekly visits to the health-care provider, women, such as Kim in the vignette, may be told, "It should be any minute now." The uterus begins to contract as it prepares for birth. The cervix thins out and softens under the weight of the child. Anticipation builds . . . and then—she waits!

> *I am 39 weeks and desperate for some sign that labor is near, but so far NOTHING—no softening of the cervix, no contractions, and the baby has not dropped—the idea of two more weeks makes me want to SCREAM!!!*

What sets off labor? One hypothesis is that the trigger is a hormonal signal that the fetus sends to the mother's brain. Once it's officially under way, labor proceeds through three stages.

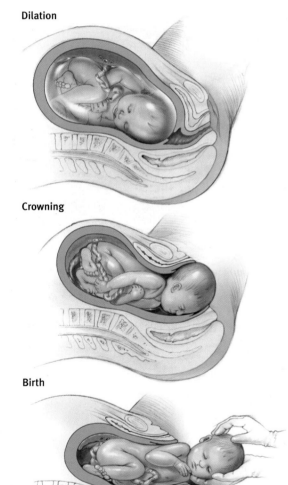

Dilation

Crowning

Birth

FIGURE 2.10: Labor and childbirth: In the first stage of labor, the cervix dilates; then in the second stage, the baby's head emerges and the baby is born.

Stage 1: Dilation and Effacement

This first stage of labor is the most arduous. The thick, protective cervix, which has held in the expanding fetus for so long, has finished its job. Now it must *efface*, or thin out, and *dilate*, or widen from a tiny gap about the size of a dime to the width of a coffee mug or a medium-sized bowl of soup. This dramatic transformation is accomplished by *contractions*—muscular, wavelike batterings against the uterine floor. The uterus is far stronger than a boxer's biceps. Even at the beginning of labor, the contractions put about 30 pounds of pressure on the cervix to expand to its cuplike shape.

The contractions start out slowly, perhaps 20 to 30 minutes apart. They become more frequent and painful as the cervix more rapidly opens up. Sweating, nausea, and intense pain can accompany the final phase—as the closely spaced contractions reach a crescendo, and the baby is poised for the miracle of birth (see Figure 2.10).

Stage 2: Birth

The fetus descends through the uterus and enters the vagina, or birth canal. Then, as the baby's scalp appears (an event called *crowning*), parents get their first exciting glimpse of this new life. The shoulders rotate; the baby slowly slithers out, to be captured and joyously cradled as it enters the world. The prenatal journey has ended; the journey of life is about to begin.

Stage 3: The Expulsion of the Placenta

In the ecstasy of the birth, the final event is almost unnoticed. The placenta and other supporting structures must be pushed out. Fully expelling these materials is essential to avoid infection and to help the uterus return to its pre-pregnant state.

Threats at Birth

Just as with pregnancy, a variety of missteps may happen during this landmark passage into life: problems with the contraction mechanism; the inability of the cervix to fully dilate; deviations from the normal head-down position as the fetus descends and positions itself for birth (this atypical positioning, with feet, buttocks, or knees first, is called a *breech birth*); difficulties stemming from the position of the placenta or the umbilical cord as the baby makes its way into the world. Today, these in-transit troubles are easily surmounted through various obstetrical techniques. This was not true in the past.

Birth Options, Past and Present

For most of human history, pregnancy was a grim nine-month march to an uncertain end (Kitzinger, 2000; Leavitt, 1986; Wertz & Wertz, 1989). The eighteenth-century New England preacher Cotton Mather captured the emotions of his era perfectly when, on learning that a woman in his parish was pregnant, he darkly thundered, "Your death has entered into you!" Not only were there the hazards involved in getting the baby to emerge from the womb, but a raging infection called childbed fever could quickly set in and kill a new mother (and her child) within days.

Women had only one another or lay midwives to rely on during this frightening time. So birth was a social event. Friends and relatives flocked around, perhaps traveling miles to offer comfort when the woman's due date drew near. Doctors were called to the scene in emergencies, but they were of little help. Because this age of modesty made it impossible to view the female anatomy directly, the training in "male midwifery" schools was all academic. In fact, due to their clumsiness (using primitive forceps to yank the baby out) and their tendency to unknowingly spread childbed fever by failing to wash their hands, eighteenth- and nineteenth-century doctors often made the situation worse (Wertz & Wertz, 1989).

Techniques gradually improved toward the end of the nineteenth century, but few wealthy women dared enter hospitals to deliver, as these institutions were hotbeds of contagious disease. Then, with the early-twentieth-century conquest of many infectious diseases, it became fashionable for affluent middle-class women to have a "modern" hospital birth. By the late 1930s, the science of obstetrics gained the upper hand, fetal mortality plummeted, and birth became genuinely safe for the first time (Leavitt, 1986). Today, in the developed world, this conquest is virtually complete. In 1997, there were only 329 pregnancy-related maternal deaths in the United States (Miniño and others, 2002).

This watershed medical victory was accompanied by discontent. The natural process of birth had become an impersonal event. Women began to protest the assembly-line hospital procedures; for example, the fact that they were strapped down and sedated in order to give birth. They eagerly devoured books describing the new Lamaze technique, which taught controlled breathing, allowed partner involvement, and promised undrugged birth without pain. During the women's movement of the 1960s and early 1970s, the natural-childbirth movement fully arrived (Wertz & Wertz, 1989).

Natural Childbirth

Natural childbirth, a vague label for returning the birth experience to its "true" natural state, is now firmly embedded in the array of labor and birth choices available to women today. To avoid the medical atmosphere of a traditional maternity ward, some women choose to deliver in homelike birthing centers. They may use certified midwives rather than doctors in their quest for a less medical birth. They may avoid the routine epidural in order to ease their pain, and draw on the help of a *doula,* a nonmedical pregnancy and labor coach. At the most daring end of the spectrum, mirroring the traditional practice in non-Western cultures, women may choose to give birth in their own homes. (Table 2.4 describes some natural birth options, as well as some commonly used medical procedures.)

Public domain. In "Richard W. Wertz and Dorothy C. Wertz, Lying-In: A History of Childbirth in America, 1977, p. 78"

This classic nineteenth-century illustration shows just why early doctors were clueless about how to help pregnant women. They could not view the relevant body parts!

natural childbirth A general term for labor and birth without medical interventions.

TABLE 2.4: **The Major Players and Interventions in Labor and Birth**

Natural-Birth Providers and Options

Certified midwife: Certified by the American College of Nurse Midwives, this health-care professional is trained to handle *low-risk* deliveries, with obstetrical backup should complications arise.

- *Plus:* Offers a birth experience with fewer medical interventions and more humanistic care.

- *Minus:* If the delivery suddenly becomes high risk, an obstetrician may be needed on the scene.

Doula: Mirroring the "old style" female experience, this person provides loving emotional and physical support during labor, offering massage and help in breathing and relaxation, but not performing actual health-care tasks, such as vaginal exams. (Doulas have no medical training.)

- *Plus:* Provides caring support from an advocate.

- *Minus:* Drives up the birth expense.

Lamaze method: Developed by the French physician Ferdinand Lamaze, this popular method prepares women for childbirth by teaching pain management through relaxation and breathing exercises.

- *Plus:* Offers a shared experience with a partner (who acts as the coach) and the sense of approaching the birth experience with greater control.

- *Minus:* Doesn't necessarily work for pain control "as advertised"!

Bradley method: Developed by Robert Bradley in the 1940s, this technique is designed for women interested in having a completely natural, nonmedicated birth. It stresses good diet and exercise, partner coaching, and deep relaxation.

- *Plus:* Tailored for women firmly committed to forgoing any medical interventions.

- *Minus:* May set women up for disappointment if things don't go as planned and they need those interventions.

Medical Interventions

Episiotomy: The cutting of the perineum or vagina to widen that opening and allow the fetus to emerge (not recommended unless there is a problem delivery).*

- *Plus:* May prevent a fistula, a vaginal tear into the rectal opening, which produces chronic incontinence and pain.

- *Minus:* May increase the risk of infection after delivery and hinder healing.

Epidural: This most popular type of anesthesia used during labor involves injecting a painkilling medication into a small space outside the spinal cord to numb the woman's body below the waist. Epidurals are now used during the active stage of labor—effectively dulling much of the pain—and during c-sections, so that the woman is awake to see her child during the first moments after birth.

- *Plus:* Combines optimum pain control with awareness; because the dose can be varied, the woman can see everything, and she has enough feeling to push during vaginal deliveries.

- *Minus:* Can slow the progress of labor in vaginal deliveries, can result in headaches, and is subject to errors if the needle is improperly inserted. Concerns also center on the fact that the newborn may emerge "groggy."

Electronic fetal monitor: This device is used to monitor the fetus's heart rate and alert the doctor to distress. With an external monitor, the woman wears two belts around her abdomen. With an internal monitor, an electrode is inserted through the cervix to record the heart rate through the fetal scalp.

- *Plus:* Shown to be useful in high-risk pregnancies.

- *Minus:* Can give false readings, leading to a premature c-section. Also, its superiority over the lower-tech method of listening to the baby's heartbeat with a stethoscope has not been demonstrated.

C-section: The doctor makes an incision in the abdominal wall and the uterus and removes the fetus manually.

- *Plus:* Is life-saving to the mother and baby when a vaginal delivery cannot occur (as when the baby is too big to emerge or the placenta is obstructing the cervix). Also is needed when the mother has certain health problems or when the fetus is in serious distress.

- *Minus:* As a surgical procedure, it is more expensive than vaginal delivery and can lead to more discomfort after birth.

*Late-twentieth-century research has suggested that the once-common U.S. practice of routinely performing episiotomies had no advantages and actually hindered recovery from birth. Therefore, the episiotomy rate in the United States declined from 2 out of 3 women in the mid-1980s to 1 in 3 by the turn of the century (Goldberg and others, 2002).

At the medical end of the spectrum, as Table 2.4 shows, lies the arsenal of physician interventions designed to promote a less painful and safer birth. Let's now pause for a minute to look at the last procedure listed in the table: the cesarean section.

The Cesarean Section

A **cesarean section** (or **c-section**), in which a surgeon makes incisions in the woman's abdominal wall and enters the uterus to remove the baby, is the final solution for problems that occur during labor and delivery. This operation exploded in popularity during the 1970s, rising from 5 to 16 percent of all U.S. births (Wertz & Wertz, 1989). Since then, the c-section rate has continued to escalate. C-sections account for roughly one in three U.S. deliveries today (Martin and others, 2005).

Today, women have a variety of birth choices in the developed world. The woman in this photo is having a water birth.

This explosion in c-sections—throughout much of the developed world—is setting off alarm bells. Why might this operation be overused? To bolster their argument that higher fees to the doctor may be partly to blame, critics cite the fact that in different nations rates of this operation vary in interesting ways related to social class. In Italy, which has paid-for medical care, poor women are far more likely to have this procedure (Cesaroni, Forastieri, & Perucci, 2008). Among Brazilian women, affluent private-pay patients are twice as likely to receive this operation than the poor. In fact, an astonishing three out of four private-pay babies in Brazil arrive in the world via the c-section route (Potter and others, 2008).

Some c-sections (roughly one in three in the United States) are planned to occur before the woman goes into labor because the physician knows in advance that there will be dangers during a vaginal birth. However, one survey suggested, what mainly is driving up the "section rate" in the United States are unexpected c-sections—ones that occur after labor has begun (Joesch, Gossman, & Tanfer, 2008). Is this propensity to perform c-sections during labor due to doctors' fears of legal liability ("I might get sued unless I immediately get this baby out") or prudent medical practice ("I want to take every precaution that this child is born healthy")? We don't know. What we do know is that while c-sections are typically very safe, women who have this operation tend to experience more discomfort in the first months after birth than those with uncomplicated vaginal deliveries (Declercq and others, 2008). These new mothers are also at risk of having negative feelings about their birth experience, and *possibly* more vulnerable to experiencing post-partum depression, especially when they had been avidly counting on having a vaginal birth (Lobel & DeLuca, 2007).

Here is a quotation explaining why a doctor might choose to perform a c-section and why, at least initially, having this operation can be a let-down for a woman committed to having a child the "natural" way.

> It all started on Sunday, April twenty-first. I arrived with my doula and was feeling contractions. Twelve hours later, my cervix had only dilated 1/2 centimeter, and I was given a Pitocin drip [a labor-stimulating drug]. Terrible, terrible contractions. But I only dilated to 4 centimeters by the next morning—and the doctor said that if things didn't change by 3 P.M. I needed a c-section. I freaked, as for months I had been planning a vaginal birth. Then the moment of my section, I saw the most beautiful sight in the world emerge—and forgot everything else.

As a final comment, while I've been bemoaning the overuse of c-sections, I've been neglecting the real global problem: It's the horrifying *lack of access* to this standard lifesaving operation in the least developed regions of the world. In Haiti, only 2 percent of pregnant women have c-sections. In Senegal, the statistic is 1.6 percent (Stanton, Ronsmans, & the Baltimore group on Cesareans, 2008). This translates into higher maternal mortality—many women dying when a c-section or other

cesarean section (c-section) A method of delivering a baby surgically by extracting the baby through incisions in the woman's abdominal wall and in the uterus.

Phanie/International Waterbirth

simple medical intervention might save their life. So let's remember that poor mothers-to-be in the developing world approach birth with a more basic concern than their affluent twenty-first-century counterparts. Their worry is not "Will I need a c-section?" It's not "What type of birth method should I use?" Unfortunately, all too often, it's still "Will I survive my baby's birth?"

TYING IT ALL TOGETHER

1. Melissa says that her contractions are coming every 10 minutes now. Sonia has just seen her baby's scalp emerge. In which stages of labor are Melissa and Sonia?

2. To a friend interested in having the most natural birth possible, spell out some of these options.

3. Lo Sue is a great advocate of c-sections; Sara is vehement about the overuse of this operation. First, make Lo Sue's pro-cesarean case, and then, make Sara's anti-cesarean case.

Answers to the Tying It All Together questions can be found on the last page of this chapter.

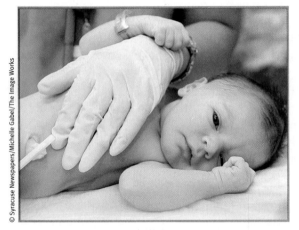

This baby has an excellent Apgar score. Notice his healthy, robust appearance.

Apgar scale A quick test used to assess a just-delivered baby's condition by measuring heart rate, muscle tone, respiration, reflex response, and color.

low birth weight (LBW) A body weight at birth of less than 5 1/2 pounds.

very low birth weight (VLBW) A body weight at birth of less than 3 1/4 pounds.

neonatal intensive care unit (NICU) A special hospital unit that treats at-risk newborns, such as low-birth-weight and very-low-birth-weight babies.

infant mortality Death during the first year of life.

The Newborn

Now that we have examined the process by which the baby arrives, let's turn our attention to that tiny arrival. What happens after the baby is born? What are the main dangers that babies face after birth?

Tools of Discovery: Testing Newborns

The first step after the newborn enters the world is to evaluate its health in the delivery room with a checklist called the **Apgar scale.** The child's heart rate, muscle tone, respiration, reflex response, and color are rated on a scale of 0 to 2 at one minute and then again at five minutes after birth. Newborns with five-minute Apgar scores over 7 are usually in excellent shape. However, if the score stays below 7, the child must be monitored or resuscitated and kept in the hospital for awhile.

Threats to Development Just After Birth

After their babies have been checked out medically, most mothers and fathers are eagerly poised to leave the hospital and take their robust, full-term baby home. But other parents must hover at the hospital and anxiously wait. The reason, most often, is that their child has arrived in the world too small and/or too soon.

Born Too Small and Too Soon

In 2004, one out of every eight U.S. babies were *preterm*, or premature—they arrived in the world more than three weeks early. About one in every eleven U.S. babies were categorized as having **low birth weight.** They entered the world weighing less than 5 1/2 pounds. Babies can be designated low birth weight because they either arrived before their due date or did not grow sufficiently in the womb. Earlier in this chapter, I highlighted poor health practices, such as maternal smoking, as risk factors for low birth weight. But often, uncontrollable influences—such as an infection that prematurely ruptures the amniotic sac, or a cervix that cannot withstand the pressure of the growing baby's weight—cause this too-early or excessively small arrival into life.

Most low-birth-weight babies are fine. The truly vulnerable newborns are the 1.4 percent classified as **very low birth weight,** babies weighing less than 3 1/4 pounds.

When these frail babies are delivered, often *very* prematurely, they are immediately rushed to a major medical center to enter a special hospital unit for frail newborns—the **neonatal intensive care unit.**

> *At 24 weeks my water broke, and I was put in the hospital and given drugs to stop the labor. I hung on, and then, at week 26, gave birth. Peter was sent by ambulance to Children's Hospital. When I first saw my son, he had needles in every point of his body and was wrapped in plastic to keep his skin from drying out. Peter's intestines had a hole in them, and the doctor had to perform an emergency operation. But Peter made it! A week later another surgery was needed to close a valve in Peter's heart. Now it's four months later, and my husband and I are about to bring our miracle baby home.*

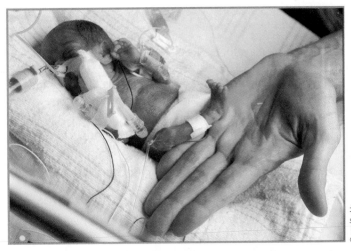

This baby weighing less than one pound was incredibly lucky to make it out of the womb alive—but she is at high risk for having enduring problems as she travels through life.

Is this survival story purchased at the price of a life of pain? Enduring health problems are a serious risk with newborns such as Peter, born far too soon and excessively small (Donohue and others, 2008). The intellectual abilities of these babies often lag behind those of their peers well into the older childhood years (Bayless, Cate, & Stevenson, 2008; Bayless & Stevenson, 2007). And what about the costs? Astronomical sums are required to keep critically ill babies such as Peter alive—expenses that can bankrupt families and are often borne by society as a whole (Caplan, Blank, & Merrick, 1992).

However, there is no question that with babies such as Peter, we must vigorously intervene. It is difficult to make predictions about how these tiniest babies will fare (Caplan, Blank, & Merrick, 1992). Developmental lags during infancy are virtually guaranteed. But many very-low-birth-weight babies outgrow their early problems with special care (Dezoete, MacArthur, & Tuck, 2003). Even with enduring disabilities, some of these miracle babies can have a full life. Sitting before me in her wheelchair every day this semester as I teach this course is Marcia, whose 15-ounce body at birth would have easily fit in the palm of your hand—and whom no doctor believed was capable of surviving. My student, as the Experiencing the Lifespan box on page 66 describes, is partially deaf, blind in one eye, and suffers from the disorder cerebral palsy. But rarely have I met someone so upbeat, joyous, and fully engaged in life.

The Unthinkable: Infant Mortality

Some babies are not as lucky as Peter or Marcia. Premature deliveries and low birth weight rank as the most common causes of **infant mortality,** the term for deaths occurring within the first year of life. In the least developed regions of the globe, where infant mortality rates are highest, infants may die soon after birth due to labor and delivery traumas. Or they may succumb to infectious diseases such as pneumonia and diarrhea (Islam & Gerdtham, 2006; see the next chapter). In the developed world—where infant morality is generally very low (see Figure 2.11)—babies who do not make it beyond their first year tend to be born around the age of viability, or have serious genetic disorders like Tay-Sachs disease.

The good news is that, in recent years, U.S. infant mortality is at low ebb. By the early twenty-first century, of every 1,000 births, only roughly seven babies died before age 1 (Heron and others, 2009). The bad news is our dismal standing compared to many other industrialized countries. Why does the United States rank a

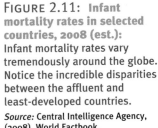

FIGURE 2.11: **Infant mortality rates in selected countries, 2008 (est.):** Infant mortality rates vary tremendously around the globe. Notice the incredible disparities between the affluent and least-developed countries.
Source: Central Intelligence Agency, (2008), World Factbook.

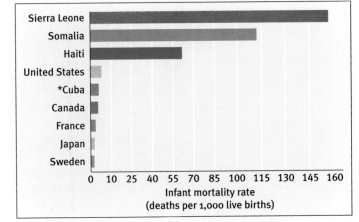

Infant mortality rate
(deaths per 1,000 live births)

*Although clearly classified as a developing country, Cuba prides itself on its exceptional universal free health care.

The service elevator at Peck Hall takes forever to get there, then moves in extra-slow motion up to the third floor. If, as sometimes happens, it's out of service, you are out of luck. It's about a 30-minute drive from my dorm in the motorized wheelchair, including the ramps. When it rains, there's the muck—slowing you up—keeping you wet. So I try to leave at least an hour to get to class.

My goal is to be at least five minutes early so I don't disrupt everything as I move the chair, back and forth, back and forth, to be positioned right in front. Because my bad eye wanders to the side, you may not think I can read the board. That's no problem, although it takes me weeks to get through a chapter in your book! The CP [cerebral palsy], as you know, affects my vocal cords, making it hard to get a sentence out. But I won't be ashamed. I am determined to participate in class. I have my note-taker. I have my hearing amplifier turned up to catch every sound. My mind is on full alert. I'm set to go.

I usually can take about two courses each semester—sometimes one. I'm careful to screen my teachers to make sure they will work with me. I'm almost 30 and still only a junior, but I'm determined to get my degree. I'd like to be a counselor and work with CP kids. I know all about it—the troubles, the physical pain, what people are like. I've got tons of experience starting from day one.

I'm not sure exactly what week I was born, but it wasn't really all that early; maybe two months at the most. My problem was being incredibly small. They think

my mom might have gotten an infection that made me born less than one pound. The doctors were sure I'd never make it. They told Mom and Dad to prepare for the fact that I would die. But I proved everyone wrong. Once I got out of the ICU and, at about eight months, went into convulsions, and then had a stroke, everyone thought that would be the end again. They were wrong. I want to keep proving them wrong as long as I live.

I've had tons of physical therapy, and a few surgeries; so I can get up from a chair and walk around a room. But it took me until about age five to begin to speak or take my first step. The worst time of my life was elementary school—the kids who make fun of you; call you a freak. The parents were the meanest. When someone did invite me to their house, the answer was often, "You can't let that cripple come." In high school, and especially here at MTSU, things are much better. I've made close friends, both in the disability community and outside. Actually, I'm a well-known figure, especially since I've been here so long! Everyone on campus greets me with a smile as I scoot around.

In my future? I'd love to get married and adopt a kid. OK, I know that's going to be hard. Because of my speech problem, I know you're thinking it's going to be hard to be a counselor, too. But I'm determined to keep trying, and take every day as a blessing. Life is very special. I've always been living on borrowed time.

humiliating forty-first in this basic marker of a society's health? (Central Intelligence Agency, World Factbook Rank Order Infant Mortality Rate, retrieved Oct. 10, 2008.) The main cause lies in socioeconomic inequalities, stress leading to poor health practices, and unequal access to high-quality prenatal care.

The ethnic disparities in infant mortality are particularly troubling. In 2004, African American infant mortality rates stood at 13.6 deaths per 1,000 live births—more than double the national average (CDC National Vital Statistics Reports, 2007). Black women are more susceptible to high blood pressure or pregnancy-induced diabetes. Both conditions are risk factors for premature births. Because they may not have the economic resources to see a doctor, African American mothers-to-be are less likely to get prenatal care at the earliest possible time. Emotional distress also can take a toll. In one interesting poll, even perceived experiences with racism were associated with a Black pregnant mother's propensity to give birth to a smaller child (Dominguez and others, 2008). The main issue, however, for people of any race, as I just suggested, relates to socioeconomic status. Low-income women in general are at far higher risk of delivering prematurely or having their baby die before age 1.

The bottom line is that economics shapes every aspect of the pregnancy journey—from the emotions of the mother to the anxieties of the father to the health of the child. This same message, "Socioeconomic status matters," will be a continual theme as we explore the baby's journey through life.

✿ TYING IT ALL TOGETHER

1. Baby David gets a two-minute Apgar score of 8; at five minutes, his score is 9. What does this mean?

2. Bill says, "Pregnancy and birth are very safe today." George says, "Hey, you are very wrong!" Who is right?

   a. Bill, because worldwide maternal mortality is now very low.
   b. George, because birth is still unsafe around the world.
   c. Both are partly correct: Birth is typically very safe in the developed world, but maternal and infant mortality remains unacceptably high in the poorest regions of the globe.

3. If Latisha goes into labor at 26 weeks and has a very-low-birth-weight baby, what can you predict about this child's development?

   a. Due to medical advances, the baby will have no developmental problems.
   b. The baby will probably have developmental lags and *possibly* more enduring problems.
   c. The baby will certainly have severe impairments throughout life.

4. Sally brags about the U.S. infant mortality rate, while Samantha is horrified by it. First, make Sally's case and, then, Samantha's, referring to the chapter points.

5. You want to set up a program to reduce infant mortality in the African American community. List some steps that you might take.

Answers to the Tying It All Together questions can be found on the last page of this chapter.

Final Thoughts: Biological Parenthood and Early Bonding

Before we move on to our lifespan journey, a final comment is required. In this chapter, you learned a good deal about the intense feelings of attachment (or mother-child bond) that begin before the baby emerges from the womb. During the early 1970s, as the natural-childbirth movement was gaining steam, advocates suggested that to fully attach to your baby it was important to hold that child right after birth. This premise left out not only every adoptive parent but also the millions of women whose babies needed to stay in the hospital for their first months of life.

AP Photo/Watertown Daily Times, John Hart

Families come in many forms, and the love you have for your adopted children is no different than if you gave birth. Take it from me as an adoptive mom!

This "up-to-date" pronouncement, as it turned out, was another example of misplaced scientific advice. Parent–child love, or attachment, does not lock in according to a rigid timetable. To bond with a baby, you don't need to personally carry that child inside (or share the same set of genes). So just a small reminder is needed for later chapters when we scan the beautiful mosaic of families on our landscape today: The bottom-line blessing is being a parent, not being pregnant. Parenting is far different from personally giving birth!

In Chapter 3, we begin by catching up with Kim and her baby girl, Elissa, who is now about four months old.

SUMMARY

The First Step: Fertilization

Every culture cherishes pregnant women. Some build in rituals to announce the baby after a certain point during pregnancy, and many use charms to ward off fetal harm. Pregnancy is a time of intense mixed emotions—joyous expectations coupled with uneasy fears.

The female reproductive system includes the **uterus** and its neck, the **cervix;** the **fallopian tubes;** and the **ovaries,** housing the **ova.** To promote **fertilization** the optimum time for intercourse is when the egg is released. **Ovulation** and all of the events of pregnancy are programmed by **hormones.** At intercourse, hundreds of millions of sperm, produced in the **testes,** are ejaculated, but only a small fraction make their way to the fallopian tubes to reach the ovum. When the single victorious sperm penetrates the ovum, the two 23 **chromosome** cells (composed of **DNA,** segmented into **genes**) unite to regain the normal complement of 46 that form every body cell.

Prenatal Development

During the first stage of pregnancy, the two-week-long **germinal phase,** the rapidly dividing **zygote** travels to the uterus, becomes a **blastocyst,** and faces the next challenge—**implantation.** The second stage of pregnancy, the **embryonic stage,** begins after implantation and ends around week 8. During this intense six-week period, the **neural tube** forms and all the major body structures are constructed—according to the **proximodistal, cephalocaudal,** and **mass-to-specific** principles of development.

During the third stage of pregnancy, the **fetal stage,** development is slower paced. The hallmarks of this stage are enormous body growth and construction of the brain as the **neurons** migrate to the top of the tube and differentiate. Another defining landmark of this seven-month phase occurs around week 22, when the fetus can possibly be **viable,** that is, survive outside the womb if born.

Pregnancy

The nine months of **gestation,** or pregnancy, are divided into **trimesters.** The first trimester is often characterized by unpleasant symptoms, such as morning sickness, and a relatively high risk of **miscarriage.** The landmarks of the second trimester are looking clearly pregnant, experiencing **quickening,** and often feeling more intensely emotionally connected to the child. During the third trimester, the woman's uterus gets very large, and she anxiously awaits the birth.

New research suggests that pregnancy and birth might change the brain. Stress levels tend to decrease in preparation for birth. Mental processes can become foggy during pregnancy, but might improve beyond pre-pregnancy levels after a woman gives birth. However, the emotional experience of being pregnant varies dramatically, depending on socioeconomic status and, most importantly, social support. To really enjoy her pregnancy, a woman needs to feel cared about and loved. Fathers, the neglected pregnancy partners, also feel intensely bonded to their babies, and may find that pregnancy is a stressful time.

Threats to the Developing Baby

About 4 percent of babies are born with a **birth defect.** One cause is **teratogens,** toxins from the outside that exert their damage during the **sensitive period** for the development of a particular body part. In general, the embryonic stage is the time of greatest vulnerability, although toxins can affect the developing brain during the second and third trimesters also, producing **developmental disorders.** While there is typically a threshold level beyond which damage can occur, teratogens have unpredictable effects, depending on the vulnerabilities of the baby and mother and other forces. Damage may not show up until decades later.

Any recreational drug is potentially teratogenic. Smoking during pregnancy is a risk factor for having a smaller-than-optimal-size baby. Drinking excessively during pregnancy can produce **fetal alcohol syndrome,** or *fetal alcohol spectrum disorder.* Conducting studies that explore the causal impact of small amounts of alcohol (or any recreational drug) on the baby is difficult, as so many forces are correlated with engaging in these problematic health practices. However, the best advice to women is to avoid all recreational drugs when carrying a child.

The second major cause of birth defects is internal—chromosomal problems and single-gene diseases. **Down syndrome** is one of the few disorders in which babies born with an abnormal number of chromosomes survive. Although Down syndrome, caused by having an extra chromosome on pair 21, produces mental retardation and other health problems, people with this condition do live fulfilling lives.

With **single-gene disorders,** a specific gene passed down from one's parents causes the disease. In **dominant disorders,** a person who harbors a single copy of the gene gets ill, and each child born to this couple (one of whom has the disease) has a fifty-fifty chance of developing the condition. If the disorder is **recessive,** both parents carry a single copy of the "problem gene" that is not expressed in real life, but they have a 1-in-4 chance of giving birth to a child with that disease (that is, a son or daughter with two copies of the gene). With **sex-linked disorders,** the problem gene is recessive and lies on the X chromosome. If a mother carries a single copy of the gene, her daughters are spared (because they have two X's), but each male baby has a fifty-fifty risk of getting the disease. Through advances in **genetic testing,** couples (and individuals) can find out if they harbor the genes for many diseases. Genetic testing poses difficult issues with regard to workplace discrimination, and whether people want to find out if they have incurable adult-onset diseases.

Couples at high risk for having a baby with a single-gene disorder (or any couple) may undergo **genetic counseling** to decide whether they should try to have a child. During pregnancy, blood tests, an **ultrasound,** and more invasive tests such as **chorionic villus sampling** (during the first trimester) and **amniocentesis** (during the second trimester) allow us to determine the baby's genetic fate.

Infertility is tackled by a variety of treatments, including **assisted reproductive technologies (ART),** such as **in vitro fertilization (IVF).** IVF, in which the egg is fertilized outside of the womb, is arduous and expensive and offers no guarantee that a baby will result.

Birth

Labor and birth consist of three stages. During the first stage of labor, contractions cause the cervix to efface and fully dilate. During the second stage, birth, the baby emerges. During the third stage, the placenta and supporting structures are expelled.

For most of human history, childbirth was life-threatening to both the mother and the child. During the first third of the twentieth century, birth became much safer. This victory set the stage for the later-twentieth-century **natural childbirth** movement. Today women in the developed world can choose from a variety of birth options, although the rate of **cesarean sections** seems to be excessive in this day and age. Impoverished, developing-world women do not have this luxury or choice. Their main concern is surviving the baby's birth.

The Newborn

After birth, the **Apgar scale** and other tests are used to assess the baby's health. While most babies are healthy, **low birth weight** can compromise development. Most vulnerable are **very-low-birth-weight** infants. While some of these most fragile babies have serious, enduring problems, others outgrow their difficulties, although they typically need monitoring in the **neonatal intensive care unit** during their early weeks or months of life.

Infant mortality is a serious concern in the developing world. While rates of infant mortality are generally very low in developed-world countries, the United States has a comparatively dismal standing compared to other affluent countries on this basic health parameter. African American women—and low-income mothers in the United States—are at higher risk than affluent women of having a baby die before age 1. Economics looms large in the prenatal and pregnancy experience and every other experience of our developing life.

KEY TERMS

uterus, p. 36

cervix, p. 36

fallopian tube, p. 36

ovary, p. 36

ovum, p. 36

fertilization, p. 36

ovulation, p. 36

hormones, p. 36

testes, p. 37

chromosome, p. 38

DNA (deoxyribonucleic acid), p. 38

gene, p. 38

germinal stage, p. 39

zygote, p. 39

blastocyst, p. 39

implantation, p. 39

placenta, p. 39

embryonic stage, p. 40

neural tube, p. 40

neuron, p. 40

proximodistal sequence, p. 41

cephalocaudal sequence, p. 41

mass-to-specific sequence, p. 41

fetal stage, p. 41

age of viability, p. 42

umbilical cord, p. 42

amniotic sac, p. 42

gestation, p. 43

trimester, p. 43

miscarriage, p. 44

quickening, p. 44

birth defect, p. 48

teratogen, p. 48

sensitive period, p. 48

developmental disorders, p. 50

fetal alcohol syndrome (FAS), p. 51

Down syndrome, p. 52

single-gene disorder, p. 53

dominant disorder, p. 53

recessive disorder, p. 53

sex-linked single-gene disorder, p. 53

genetic testing, p. 55

genetic counselor, p. 55

ultrasound, p. 56

chorionic villus sampling (CVS), p. 57

amniocentesis, p. 57

infertility, p. 58

assisted reproductive technology (ART), p. 58

in vitro fertilization (IVF), p. 58

natural childbirth, p. 61

cesarean section (c-section), p. 63

Apgar scale, p. 64

low birth weight (LBW), p. 64

very low birth weight (VLBW), p. 64

neonatal intensive care unit (NICU), p. 65

infant mortality, p. 65

ANSWERS TO TYING IT ALL TOGETHER QUIZZES

The First Step: Fertilization

1. Make your drawing from memory and compare it to the diagram on page 37.

2. The testes

3. Tell Tiff that the best time to have intercourse is around the time of ovulation, as fertilization typically occurs when the ovum is in the upper part of the fallopian tube. The chain of events that lead to fertilization begins with sexual intercourse, during which millions of sperm are ejaculated. A few find their way to the fallopian tubes and drill into the ovum. When one sperm burrows to the nucleus the two nuclei merge to form a single 46-chromosome cell.

4. c. Roughly 5 percent more boys than girls are born. Your uncle (the dad) determines the baby's sex: If a Y-carrying sperm penetrates the ovum, the baby is a boy (XY); if the sperm carries the X chromosome, the child is a girl (XX).

Prenatal Development

1. a. During the embryonic stage, organs rapidly form; the neurons migrate to the top of the brain during the fetal stage; in the germinal stage, the blastocyst forms.

2. From the neural tube, a mass of cells differentiates during the late embryonic phase. During the next few months, the cells ascend to the top of the neural tube, completing their migration by week 25. In the final months of pregnancy, the neurons elongate and begin to assume their mature structure.

3. (a) The head develops before the arms. (b) The arms develop before the hands. (c) The fingers develop before fingernails. (Now, see if you can come up with different examples than mine!)

Pregnancy

1. During the first trimester, Samantha will probably feel tired and have morning sickness. In the second trimester, she will feel better physically and experience an intense sense of emotional connectedness when she feels the baby move. During the third trimester, she is likely to feel uncomfortable and be excitedly waiting for labor and birth.

2. Tell your friend, "After the baby is born, these thinking problems should evaporate. Moreover, emerging research suggests that pregnancy may pump up the neurons in our memory centers, and so possibly heighten cognitive alertness during new motherhood and throughout life."

3. Two forces that put a pregnant woman at emotional risk are being under economic stress and, especially, feeling isolated—not having a supportive partner or loving social network.

4. You may come up with a host of interesting possibilities. Here are a few: Include dads in all pregnancy and birth educational materials the clinic provides; strongly encourage men to be present during prenatal exams; alert female patients about the need to be sensitive to their partners; set up a clinic-sponsored support group for fathers-to-be.

Threats to the Developing Baby

1. Teratogen A most likely caused damage during *the embryonic stage* of development and was taken during *the first trimester* of pregnancy. Teratogen B probably did its damage during *the fetal stage* and was taken during the *second or third trimesters*.

2. Teratogens exert damage during the sensitive period for the development of a particular organ.

3. d. Although there should be no problem with one glass of wine, it can raise the risk of stillbirth, slightly—so it's best to totally abstain.

4. Jennifer. Down syndrome is typically caused by an unlikely, random event. With cystic fibrosis, that single-gene recessive disorder, the mom (in this case, Jennifer) has a 1-in-4 chance of giving birth to another child with that disease.

5. Tell your friend that the plus of chorionic villus sampling is finding out a child's genetic fate in the first trimester. However, this procedure is more dangerous, carrying a slight risk of limb malformations and, possibly, miscarriage. Amniocentesis is much safer and can show a fuller complement of genetic disorders, but must be performed in the second trimester—meaning you will have to undergo the trauma of a full labor should you decide to end the pregnancy.

6. You can devise your own checklist. Mine would include the following questions:

    Are your fallopian tubes blocked? Is there a problem with the sperm reaching or penetrating the egg? Are you and your mate relatively wealthy (or do you have exceptional health insurance)? Could you (women especially) spend several days each month undergoing a difficult procedure? Do you live near a major medical center or could you regularly travel to visit one? How important is it to you to have your own "biological child"? Could you live with a higher risk of miscarrying (or the difficult ethics of choosing fetal reduction) and a slightly higher chance of having a child with a birth defect?

Birth

1. Melissa is in stage 1, effacement and dilation of the cervix. Sonia is in stage 2, birth.

2. "You might want to forgo any labor medications; and/or give birth in a birthing center under a midwife's (and doula's) care. Look into new options such as water births, and, if you are especially daring, consider giving birth at home."

3. Lo Sue: This operation has saved countless lives—and we vitally need it to protect the baby and sometimes the mother's health. Sara: Birth is a natural process that should occur in a natural way. The remarkably high contemporary c-section rates—and the fact that this procedure is far more common when this operation is paid for—suggests that many of these operations may be unnecessary. While very safe, women do have more discomfort and may be more at risk of depression after having a c-section if they were counting on a vaginal birth.

The Newborn

1. Baby David is in excellent health.

2. c. While birth is very safe in the developed world, maternal and infant mortality remain serious problems in the least developed countries.

3. b. Developmental lags are predictable, and while many babies do outgrow their problems, some children do have enduring disabilities.

4. Sally: The United States—like other developed countries—has made tremendous strides in conquering infant mortality. Today, only 7 out of every 1,000 babies die in the first year of life. Samantha: The fact that the United States has higher infant mortality rates than many other developed countries is incredibly distressing. Low-income women in our nation are at serious risk of getting less than optimal (or inadequate) prenatal care.

5. You can come up with your own suggestions. Here are a few of mine: Increase the number of nurse practitioners and obstetrician-gynecologists in under-served African American neighborhoods; provide special monetary incentives to health-care providers to treat these women; provide better preventative health care by offering free screening for pregnancy-compromising conditions more common in the African American community, such as diabetes and high blood pressure; launch a vigorous public awareness campaign encouraging Black woman to see a health-care provider in the first trimester; make it easier for women to actually see a health-care provider by providing incentives to employers to encourage pregnant employees to take time off work to get prenatal care; and rid society of racism, which adds to pregnancy-related stress!

Infancy

This two-chapter part is devoted to infancy and toddlerhood (the period from birth through age 2). How does a helpless newborn become a walking, talking, loving child?

Chapter 3—**Infancy: Physical and Cognitive Development** starts by offering an overview of brain development, then explores those basic newborn states: feeding, crying, and sleeping. Next, I chart sensory and motor development. What exactly do babies see? How do newborns develop from lying helplessly to being able to walk? What can caregivers do to keep babies safe as they travel into the world? Finally, I'll offer an overview of infants' evolving cognition and their first steps toward language, the capacity that allows us to really enter the human community.

Chapter 4—**Infancy: Socioemotional Development** looks directly at what makes us human: our relationships. First, I'll explore the attachment relationship between caregiver and child, then examine poverty and day care during the first years of life. The final part of this chapter focuses on toddlerhood—the age from roughly 1 to 2 1/2. Toddlers are intensely attached to their caregivers and passionate to be independent. During this watershed time of life, when we are walking and beginning to talk, we first learn the rules of the human world.

PART II

Chapter 3

Infancy: Physical and Cognitive Development

In Chapter 2, I talked to Kim at the beginning of the third trimester, anxiously waiting for her child's birth. Now, let's pay her a visit in the first months of new motherhood and meet Elissa, her baby girl.

She's been here for less than four months—fifteen weeks and two days, to be exact—and I feel like she's been here forever. For me, it was total love at first sight and, of course, the same for Jeff. But the real thrill is watching a wonderful new person emerge day by day. Take what's happening now. At first, she couldn't care less, but since a few days ago, it's like, "Wow, there's a world out there!" See that baby seat? Elissa can make the colored buttons flash by moving her legs. Now, when I put her in it, she bats her legs like crazy. She can't get enough of those lights and sounds. Notice the way she looks at your face—like she wants to get into your soul. She really loves this blue smiley-face cushion I bought for 25 cents at a yard sale. Every time she sees it she starts to gurgle, reach, and laugh.

Elissa doesn't cry much—nothing like other babies during the first three months. Actually, I was worried. In the hospital, I asked the doctor whether there was something wrong. Crying is vital to communicating what you need! The same is true of sleeping. I'm almost embarrassed to tell you that I have the only baby in history who has been regularly giving her mom a good night's sleep since she was 2 months old.

Breast-feeding is indescribable. It's like I am literally making her grow. Plus, she's getting my total, undivided attention. I feel so blessed that Jeff makes enough money for me to take off work for the first five months—especially when I think of my friend, Nora, who was forced to abandon this incredible experience when she had to go back to her job at Walmart right after her son's birth.

Pick her up. Feel what it's like to hold her—how she melts into you. But lately she's starting to squirm more. See those push-ups, like a rocking machine? It's almost as if she's saying, "Mom, I can't wait to turn over—can't wait to get moving into the world." I plan to be there with my video camera to document every step now that she's really traveling into life.

Elissa is poised at a milestone. Past the first three months of life, she is fully waking up to the world. This chapter charts babies' transformation from lying helplessly to moving into the world and the other amazing physical and cognitive changes that occur during the first two years of life. To set the overall context, I begin by offering some highlights of the remarkable—and surprising—brain changes that occur as we travel through life. Then, my focus returns to life's first two years. Here, I'll be discussing those basic newborn states: eating, crying, and sleeping, as well as exploring emerging vision and the motor skills that Kim and her husband are so eager to observe. The final sections of this chapter offer a tour of developing cognition and chart babies' pathway to mastering language, the capacity that makes our species unique.

What does this young baby see and understand about the tremendous loving object he is facing? That is the mystery we will be exploring in this chapter.

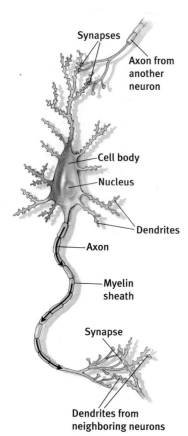

FIGURE 3.1: The neuron and synapses: Here is an illustration of the remarkable structure that programs every developing skill, perception, and thought. Notice the dendrites receiving information at the synapses and how impulses flow down the long axon to connect up with the dendrites of the adjoining cells.

Setting the Context

What causes the remarkable changes—from seeing to walking to speaking—that unfold week by week during infancy? To get an answer, let's step back and scan the changes that are taking place in that masterpiece structure—the human brain—from birth to our adult years.

The Expanding Brain

The **cerebral cortex,** the outer, furrowed mantle of the brain, is the site of every conscious perception, action, and thought. With a surface area 10 times larger than the monkey's and 100 times larger than the rat's, our cortex is what makes human beings stand apart from any other species on earth.

Because of our immense cortex, humans are also unique in the amount of brain growth that occurs outside of the womb. After birth, our brain volume quadruples. It takes two decades for this expansion to be complete. The fastest growth occurs during infancy. In fact, the cortex only comes "on-line," or starts fully taking over our behavior, a few months *after* birth.

During the first two years of life, as the cortex expands, the brain grows from 25 percent to 75 percent of its final weight (Johnson, 2001). This expansion builds on the framework that was put in place before birth.

Recall from Chapter 2 that by the middle months of the fetal period the cells destined to compose the brain have migrated to the top of the neural tube. During the final months of pregnancy, and especially the first year of life, they assume their mature form. The cells form long **axons**—fibers that conduct impulses away from the cell body. They sprout **dendrites**—treelike, branching ends. As the dendrites proliferate at junctions, or **synapses,** the axons and dendrites interconnect (see Figure 3.1).

Synaptogenesis, the process of making these myriad connections, programs every human skill—from Elissa's vigorous push-ups to composing symphonies or solving problems in math. Another transformation that is critical for our abilities to emerge is called **myelination:** The axons form a fatty encasing layer around their core. Just as a stream of water prevents us from painfully bumping down the slide at a water park, the myelin sheath serves as the lubricant that permits the neural impulses to speedily flow.

Synaptogenesis and myelination occur at different rates in specific regions of the brain. In the visual cortex, the part of the brain responsible for interpreting visual stimuli, the axons are fully myelinated by about age 1. In the frontal lobes, the region of the brain involved in higher reasoning, the myelin sheath is still forming into our early twenties or beyond (Huttenlocher, 2002).

This makes sense. Seeing is a skill we need soon after birth. Visual abilities, as you will learn in this chapter, develop rapidly during our first year of life. But we won't really need the skills to compose symphonies, do higher math, or competently make our way in the complex world until we become full adults. So there are clear parallels between our unfolding real-world abilities and the way our brain matures.

Neural Pruning and Brain Plasticity

So far, you might imagine that the basic neural principle underlying development is that more extensive connections equal superior skills. Not so! Neural loss is critical to development, too. Following an initial phase of lavishly producing synapses, each region of the cortex undergoes a period of synaptic pruning and neural death. This shedding timetable also reflects our expanding abilities. It begins around age 1 in the visual cortex. It starts during late childhood in the frontal lobes (Giedd, 2008; Huttenlocher, 2002; Nelson, Thomas, & De Hann, 2006). In the same way that careful weeding is critical to sculpting a beautiful garden, we need to get rid of the unnecessary neurons and connections to permit the cells that are really essential to flourish and flower.

Why does the brain undergo this frantic phase of overproduction, followed by cutting back? Neuroscientists believe that having this early oversupply is useful, as it allows us to "recruit" surplus neurons and redirect them to perform other functions, should we have a major sensory deficit or experience a serious brain insult early in life (Amedi and others, 2003; Huttenlocher, 2002; Nelson & Thomas, 2008). Actually, our cortex is surprisingly malleable, or **plastic** (able to be changed), particularly during infancy and the childhood years.

Using technologies such as fMRI, which measures the brain's energy consumption, researchers find that among people blind from birth—but not those who lose their sight at older ages—metabolism in the visual cortex is intense while reading Braille (Amedi and others, 2003; Lambert and others, 2004). Moreover, when neuroscientists stimulate the visual cortex of congenitally blind adults, their Braille reading is disrupted. This suggests that without early environmental stimulation from the eye, the neurons programmed for vision are literally captured, or taken over, to strengthen our abilities in touch (Westerman and others, 2007).

A similar process occurs with language, which is normally represented in the left hemisphere of the brain. If an infant has a left-hemisphere stroke, with intense verbal stimulation, the right hemisphere takes over, and language develops normally (Rowe and others, 2009). Compare this to the outcome for someone who has a left-hemisphere stroke once pruning has occurred and language is located firmly in its appropriate places. For these unfortunate adults, the result can be devastating—a permanent loss in comprehending language or being able to form words (Huttenlocher, 2002).

The bottom-line message is that our understanding of brain plasticity epitomizes the basic nature-combines-with-nurture principle that governs all of human life. Yes, the blueprint for our uniquely human cortex is laid out at conception. But environmental stimulation is vital in strengthening specific neural networks and determining which connections will be pruned (Westerman and others, 2007). Before the pruning phase, our brain is particularly malleable—permitting us to grow a somewhat different garden should disaster strike (Thomas & Johnson, 2008). Still, as synaptogenesis is a lifelong process, we continue to grow, to learn, to develop intellectually, from age 1 to age 101.

Keeping in mind the basic brain principles—(1) development unfolds "in its own specific neurological time" (you can't teach a baby to do something before the relevant part of the brain comes on-line); (2) stimulation sculpts neurons (our wider-world

cerebral cortex The outer folded mantle of the brain, responsible for thinking, reasoning, perceiving, and all conscious responses.

axon A long nerve fiber that usually conducts impulses away from the cell body of a neuron.

dendrite A branching fiber that receives information and conducts impulses toward the cell body of a neuron.

synapse The gap between the dendrites of one neuron and the axon of another, over which impulses flow.

synaptogenesis Forming of connections between neurons at the synapses. This process, responsible for all perceptions, actions, and thoughts, is most intense during infancy and childhood but continues throughout life.

myelination Formation of a fatty layer encasing the axons of neurons. This process, which speeds the transmission of neural impulses, continues from birth to early adulthood.

plastic Malleable, or capable of being changed (used to refer to neural or cognitive development).

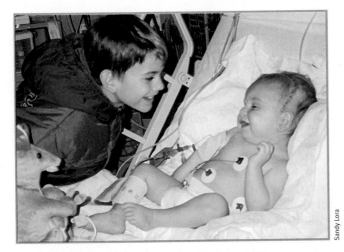

This resilient baby has survived three major surgeries in which large sections of his brain had to be removed. Remarkably—because the cortex is so *plastic* at this age—he is expected to be left with few, if any, impairments.

experiences actually physically change our brain); and (3) the brain is still "under construction" (and shaped by those same wider-world experiences) for as long as we live—now it's time to explore how the expanding cortex works magic during the first two years of life.

TYING IT ALL TOGETHER

1. Cortez and Ashley are arguing about what makes the human brain unique. Cortez says it's the immense size of our cortex. Ashley says it's the fact that we "grow" most of our brain after birth and that the human cortex continues to mature for at least two decades. Who is right—Cortez, Ashley, or both students?

2. Latisha said she wouldn't bother reading this section on the developing brain because she learned that stuff in high school. She knows that the myelin sheath speeds neural impulses. She realizes that the more synaptic connections the neurons form, the higher the level of development. Is Latisha prepared for the test, and if not, where is she wrong?

3. When children with epilepsy have recurring life-threatening seizures, surgeons may remove the portion of the brain in which the seizures are taking place. Remarkably, these children go on to live relatively normal lives. The process that is responsible for this phenomenon is _____.
   a. neural pruning
   b. brain plasticity
   c. myelination

4. Draw a neuron, labeling the axon, dendrites, myelin sheath, and synapses.

Answers to the Tying It All Together questions can be found on the last page of this chapter.

Basic Newborn States

Visit a newborn and you will see a set of simple activities: She eats, she cries, she sleeps. In this section, we spotlight each basic state.

Eating: The Basis of Living

Eating, the foundation for living, undergoes amazing changes during infancy. Let's briefly scan these transformations and then discuss two environmental, or wider-world, nutritional topics that loom large in the first years of life.

Developmental Changes: From Newborn Reflexes to Two-Year-Olds' Food Cautions

Newborns seem to be eating even when they are sleeping—a fact vividly brought home to me by the loud smacking noises that rhythmically erupted from my son's bassinet. The reason is that babies are born with a powerful **sucking reflex**—they suck virtually all the time. Newborns also are born with a **rooting reflex.** If *anything* touches their cheek, they turn their head in that direction and begin to suck.

Reflexes are automatic activities. Because they are not programmed by the cortex, they are not under conscious control. It is easy to see why the sucking and rooting reflexes are vital to promoting survival the minute we leave the womb. If newborns had to learn to suck, they might die of starvation before they mastered that skill. Without having the rooting reflex built in at birth, babies might have considerable trouble finding the breast.

Sucking and rooting have clear functions. What about the other infant reflexes shown in Figure 3.2? Do you think the grasping reflex may have helped newborns survive during hunter-gatherer times? Can you think of why newborns, when stood on a

sucking reflex The automatic, spontaneous sucking movements newborns produce, especially when anything touches their lips.

rooting reflex Newborns' automatic response to a touch on the cheek, involving turning toward that location and beginning to suck.

reflex A response or action that is automatic and programmed by noncortical brain centers.

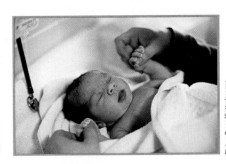

Rooting: Whenever something touches their cheek, newborns turn their head in that direction and make sucking movements.

Sucking: Newborns are programmed to suck, especially when something enters their mouth.

Grasping: Newborns automatically vigorously grasp anything that touches the palm of their hand.

FIGURE 3.2: **Some newborn reflexes:** If the baby's brain is developing normally, each of these reflexes is present at birth and gradually disappears after the first few months of life. In addition to the reflexes illustrated here, other newborn reflexes include the Babinski reflex (stroke a baby's foot and her toes turn outward), the stepping reflex (place a baby's feet on a hard surface and she takes small steps), and the swimming reflex (if placed under water, newborns can hold their breath and make swimming motions).

table, take little steps (the stepping reflex)? Whatever their value, these reflexes, and other characteristic ones, must be present at birth. They also must disappear as the cortex grows.

As the cortex matures, voluntary processes replace these special newborn reflexes. Now that she is almost 4 months old, Elissa no longer sucks continually. Her sucking is governed mainly by *operant conditioning*. When her mother's breast draws near, Elissa sucks in anticipation of that important reinforcer: "Mealtime has arrived!" Still, Sigmund Freud named infancy the oral stage for good reason: During the first year or two of life, the basic theme is, "Everything goes immediately into the mouth."

This impulse to taste everything leads to some scary moments as children begin to crawl and walk. There is nothing like the sickening sensation of seeing a baby put a forgotten pin in his mouth, sample the cleanser, or taste a possibly poisonous plant. My personal heart-stopping experience occurred when my son was almost 2. I'll never forget the frantic race to the emergency room after Thomas toddled in to joyously share a new treasure, an open box of pills!

Luckily, there is a mechanism that may help to protect toddlers from sampling every potentially lethal substance they encounter during their first travels into the world. Between ages 1 1/2 and 2, children may revert to eating only a few familiar foods, such as peanut butter sandwiches and apple juice. Evolutionary psychologists believe that, like morning sickness, this behavior is adaptive. By sticking to foods they know, children reduce the risk of poisoning themselves when they begin to walk (Bjorklund & Pelligrini, 2002). Although it is temporary, this 2-year-old food caution gives caregivers headaches. In one Dutch survey, roughly 2 out of 3 mothers complained that their toddler was either often not hungry at mealtime or rejected specific foods (de Moor, Didden, & Korzilius, 2007). So while not eating anything is a cause for serious concern, moms need to be aware: Picky eating is *normal* during the second year of life.

What is the best diet during the first months of life? When is poor childhood nutrition a truly widespread problem? These questions bring up two important nutrition-oriented topics: breast-feeding and malnutrition around the world.

Breast Milk: The Best First Food (with some qualifications!)

During the late nineteenth century, U.S. babies who were lucky enough to survive the hazards of birth faced enormous perils during their early months of life. Paramount among these threats was a disease called summer diarrhea, which caused a spike in infant mortality in sweltering city tenements. The children of immigrant Eastern European Jews, however, were virtually immune to summer diarrhea. They also were less likely to die of other infectious diseases. The reason, argued historians, was that Jewish custom dictated exclusive breast-feeding for a prolonged time (Preston, 1991).

A century ago, because it protected babies against the hazards of impure milk, the decision to breast-feed was a life-saving act. That choice has an impact today. Breast milk provides immunities to middle ear infections and gastrointestinal problems (Bhandari and others, 2003). It makes toddlers more resistant to coming down with colds and the flu (Dubois & Girard, 2005). Breast-fed babies even tend to get higher scores on intelligence tests (Karns, 2001; Mortensen and others, 2002).

Still, we need to be cautious. These studies typically involve correlations. And, as we know, just because there is a relationship between two variables does not mean one causes the other. The research exploring breast milk's benefits rarely controls for that important "third variable"—social class. Western women—like Kim—who breast-feed for months tend to be better educated and wealthier, and so probably provide their children with optimum care in many other ways (Yeoh and others, 2007). In fact, when researchers control for parents' IQ scores, the widely cited link between breast-feeding and IQ evaporates (Der, Batty, & Deary, 2006; Gibson-Davis & Brooks-Gunn, 2007). Is it *really* breast milk that makes for superior health, or everything else that goes along with infants getting this natural first food?

Despite these cautions, health care experts take a strong stand. Every major public health organization advocates that infants be exclusively breast-fed for the first six months of life (American Academy of Pediatrics [AAP], 2005; World Health Organization [WHO], 2003a).

How many women follow the six-month recommendation? The answer, from Scotland to Korea to Peru, is relatively few (Dungy and others, 2008; Earle, 2002; Hla and others, 2003; Stewart-Knox, Gardiner, & Wright, 2003). As I described earlier, in the developed world, extended breast-feeding is more typical among upper-middle-class women. Given that formula is expensive and breast milk is free, why don't more moderate- and low-income mothers make this choice?

A major reason, as you saw in the introductory vignette, has to do with the need to return to work (Flower and others, 2008; Guendelman and others, 2009). Although U.S. worksites are mandated by law to permit new mothers to pump their milk, imagine the problems you would face following the six-month recommendation as a restaurant server or supermarket clerk, or someone like Kim's friend Nora who had to return soon after delivery to a physically demanding job. Women in Western countries complain that breast-feeding is not practical. They may be ashamed to breast-feed in public. They may not get the support from their families and society that allows them to persevere (Flower and others, 2008; Gill, Reifsnider, & Lucke, 2007; Hauck, Hall, & Jones, 2007).

Would you get uncomfortable—like this male rider on the subway—if a new mother sitting next to you suddenly popped out her breast to nurse?

How do you feel when you see a woman breast-feeding at the mall or hear about someone who continued to offer the breast to her child until age 2 or even 3? If we encouraged women to openly breast-feed and to continue this practice for as long as they wanted, would we be living in a kinder, gentler, more family-friendly culture today?

Malnutrition: A Serious Developing-World Concern

Breast milk is an equal-opportunity food. It potentially gives *every* child a chance to thrive during the first months of life. However, there comes a time—at around 6 months of age—when a baby must be given some solid food. This is when the stark inequalities in global nutrition hit (Caulfield and others, 2006).

How many children in the developing world suffer from **undernutrition,** having a serious lack of adequate food? For answers, epidemiologists often look at the prevalence of a state called **stunting,** the percentage of children under age 5 in a given region who rank below the fifth percentile in height, according to the norms for their

undernutrition A chronic lack of adequate food.

stunting Excessively short stature in a child, caused by chronic lack of adequate nutrition.

micronutrient deficiency Chronically inadequate level of a specific nutrient important to development and disease prevention, such as Vitamin A, zinc, and/or iron.

age (Caulfeld and others, 2008; UNICEF, 2002a). This very short stature is a symptom of *chronic* inadequate nutrition, which takes a long-term toll on cognition, on health, and on every activity of life (Caulfield, 2008).

The good news is that during the last decades of the twentieth century, poor nations made tremendous progress in reducing stunting. In 1980, roughly half of all children under age 5 in developing countries were stunted. By 2000, the figure had dropped to less than a third (UNICEF, 2002a). The tragedy is that life-threatening early childhood nutritional disorders, such as Kwashiorkor (described in the Experiencing the Lifespan box), are still serious problems in some nations, even when there is ample food to go around. **Micronutrient deficiencies**—inadequate levels of nutrients such as Iron or Zinc or Vitamin A—are rampant in Africa and South Asia. As you

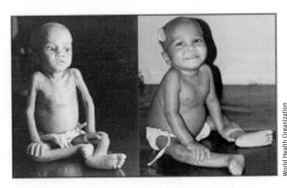

World Health Organization

The stunted baby on the left placed next to a normally developing child his age brings home the dramatic physical toll that chronic, severe undernutrition produces even during the first year of life.

EXPERIENCING THE LIFESPAN: A PASSION TO ERADICATE MALNUTRITION: A CAREER IN PUBLIC HEALTH

What is it like to battle malnutrition in the developing world? Listen to Richard Douglass describe his life and career:

I grew up on the South Side of Chicago—my radius was very small, maybe 4 or 5 blocks in either direction. Then, I spent my junior year in college in Ethiopia, and it changed my life. I lived across the street from the hospital, and every morning I saw a flood of people standing in line. The same people would wait all day and night, and in the mornings a cart would come and take away the dead. I had been Premed, but when I saw the lack of doctors I realized I needed a larger mission. I got my Master's and then my Ph.D. in public health.

In public health we focus on primary prevention— monitoring food and water—how to prevent diseases and save thousands of people from getting ill. You learn a methodology that you apply to any phase of life. So I've worked in Chicago to eradicate syphilis, helped pioneer the field of elder abuse. But my heart is still in Africa, where I spend much of my time. So now let me tell you about my work in Ghana.

My focus for the past 10 years has been on Kwashiorkor, a disease that is responsible for 4 percent of deaths of African children under 5 years old. It's a nemesis throughout the developing world. What it literally means is "the disease that happens when the second child is born." The first child is taken off the breast too soon and given a porridge that doesn't have amino acids, and so the musculature and the diaphragm break down. You get a bloated look (swollen stomach), and then you die. If a child does survive, he ends up stunted, and so looks maybe 5 years younger.

Once someone gets the disease, you can save their life. But it's a 36-month rehabilitation that requires the family to take that child to the clinic for treatment every week. It would be a terrible challenge in our

country. In Ghana it can mean traveling a dozen miles by foot. Most importantly, the day that you go to the clinic you can't go to the marketplace—and then you don't have money for food. So a single mom with two or three kids is going to drop out of the program as soon as the child starts to look healthy. Because of male urban migration in Africa, the family is in peril. If a family has a grandmother or great-auntie, the child will make it because this woman can take care of the children; then they all eat. So the presence of a grandma is saving kids' lives.

Most malnutrition shows up after wars and cataclysmic events. The tragedy is that in Ghana there is tons of food. So it's a problem of ignorance, not poverty. The issue is partly cultural. First, among some groups, the men eat, then women, then older children, then the babies get what is left. So all the meat is gone, the fish is gone, and then you just have that porridge. We have been trying to impose a cultural norm that the mother is responsible for monitoring the family's education—and the way to do that is for everyone to sit around the dining table, thereby ensuring that the children get to eat. And we think it will work. The other issue is just pure public health education—teaching families "just because your child looks fat doesn't mean that he is healthy."

I feel better on African soil than anywhere else. There is a sincerity about the people. With poor people in the developing world who are used to being exploited, they are willing to write you off in a heartbeat if you give them a reason; but if you make a promise and follow through, then you are part of their lives forever. I keep going back to my college experience forty years ago in Ethiopia . . . watching those people standing at the hospital, just waiting to die. Making a difference for them is the reason why I was born. At age 62, I'm at the pinnacle of my life.

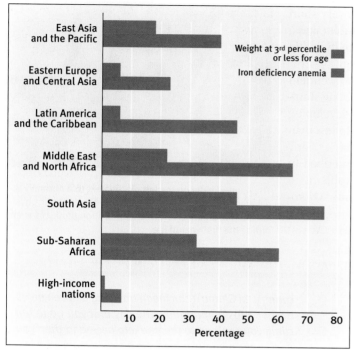

FIGURE 3.3: **Estimated prevalence of severe underweight (a major sign of stunting) and iron deficiency anemia in different regions, 2006:** An unacceptable number of children are malnourished in the developing world. While the most alarming rates of undernutrition are clearly in South Asia, the place where the prevalence of this problem is increasing is sub-Saharan Africa.

Source: Caulfield and others (2006).

can see in Figure 3.3, iron deficiency anemia even affects 1 in 12 children in affluent areas of the world (Caulfield and others, 2006).

This brings up an important issue. How many young children are stunted or chronically hungry in the United States? According to yearly polls sponsored by the U.S. Department of Agriculture, in 2006 roughly one in six U.S. children were classified as "food insecure." Their parents—typically single mothers—reported they could sometimes not afford to provide a balanced diet, or worried that their money for food might run out at the end of the month. Four percent of U.S households suffered from what the bureau calls "severe food insecurity." One or more family members need to skimp on their actual food intake due to lack of funds (USDA, Economic Research Service, 2009). However, the United States does provide young children with a social safety net in the form of the nutrition-related entitlement programs described in Table 3.1. So, in our nation as well as in other developed countries, poor children don't experience the intense, *ongoing* hunger that limits the life chances of such a high fraction of children around the globe.

TABLE 3.1: Major U.S. Federal Nutrition Programs Serving Young Children

Food Stamp Program (SNAP, Supplemental Nutrition Assistance Program): This mainstay federal nutrition program, which served 10 million U.S. households in 2004, provides electronic cards that participants can spend like money to buy food. To qualify for food stamps, a family must have an income less than 130 percent of the federal poverty line and have no more than $2,000 in resources. Although families with young children make up the majority of food stamp recipients, others—single working adults, the homeless, and legal working immigrants who entered the United States before 1996—also qualify for this aid.*

Special Supplemental Nutrition Program for Women, Infants, and Children (WIC): This federally funded grant program is specifically for low-income pregnant women and mothers with children under age 5. To be eligible, a family must be judged nutritionally at risk by a health-care professional and earn below 185 percent of the poverty line. WIC offers a monthly package of supplements tailored to the family's unique nutritional needs (such as infant formula and baby cereals) plus nutrition education and breast-feeding support. In 2008, this program served over 8 million women, infants, and children.*

Child and Adult Care Food Program (CACFP): This program reimburses child-care facilities, day-care providers, after-school programs, and providers of various adult services for the cost of serving high-quality meals. Surveys show that children (roughly 3 million in 2003) in participating programs have higher intakes of key nutrients and eat fewer servings of fats and sweets than do children who attend child-care facilities that do not participate.

Source: U.S. Department of Agriculture (USDA), www.fns.usda.gov/fsp/faqs.htm, accessed November 7, 2005; Food Research and Action Center, www.frac.org/html/federal_food_programs, accessed November 19,2008.

*The WIC and Food Stamp programs not only improve children's health, but parent participation in these services is related to a lower risk of child abuse and neglect (Lee & Mackey-Bilaver, 2006).

Crying: The First Communication Signal

At 2 months, when Jason started crying, I was clueless. I picked him up, rocked him, and kept a pacifier glued to his mouth; I called my mother, the doctor, even my local pharmacist, for advice. Since it immediately put Jason to sleep, my husband and I took car rides at three in the morning—the only people on the road were teenagers and other new parents like us. Now that my little love is 10 months old, I know exactly why he is crying, and those lonely countryside tours are long gone.

Crying, that vital way we communicate our feelings at any age, reaches its lifetime peak at around five weeks after birth (St James-Roberts, 2007). Moreover, from Alaska to the Amazon rain forest, babies get fussier during the late afternoon hours (Barr, 2000; St James-Roberts, 2007). Interestingly, a distinctive change in crying occurs at about month 4. As the cortex comes on-line, crying rates dramatically decline, and babies begin to selectively use this basic mode of communication as a tool to express their needs.

It's tempting to think of crying as simply a negative state. However, because this basic communication is as vital to survival as sucking, when babies cry too little, as Kim worried, this can be a sign of a neurological problem (Zeskind & Lester, 2001). When babies cry, we pick them up, rock them, and give them loving care. So, up to a certain point, crying helps cement the infant–parent bond.

Still, there is a limit. When a baby cries continually and cannot be soothed, she may have that bane of early infancy—**colic.** Watch a baby with colic, screaming with pain, and you can understand why this condition is often linked to digestive system problems (Miller-Loncar and others, 2004). But one expert argues that the true cause of colic may lie in the immature nervous system. After they exit the cozy womb, some babies react with intense distress when bombarded by challenging stimuli, such as being handled or fed (St James-Roberts, 2007).

Still, despite what some grandmas (unhelpfully) tell new mothers, inept or anxious parenting does not produce colicky babies. In one study, half of all women with "high crying" newborns were rated 100 percent on providing sensitivity of care (St James-Roberts, 2007). So we need to beware of blaming severely stressed-out parents for this basically biological problem of early infant life.

The good news is that colic is short-lived. Most parents find, to their relief, that around month 4, their baby suddenly becomes a new, pleasant person overnight. For this reason, developmentalists become concerned only when excessive crying does not decline after month 5 (Barr, 2000).

Imagine having a baby with colic. You feel completely helpless. You cannot do anything to quiet the baby down. There are few things more damaging to parental self-efficacy than an infant's out-of-control crying (Keefe and others, 2006).

INTERVENTIONS: What Quiets a Young Baby?

What normally soothes a crying baby? One strategy is to provide a pacifier, a breast, a bottle, or anything that satisfies the need to suck. Another is clasping the baby to your body and rocking, or **swaddling** (wrapping) him.

An especially powerful soother is skin-to-skin human contact. And the practices of the !Kung San hunter-gatherers of Botswana offer Westerners a lesson here. In this collectivist culture, where mothers strap infants to their bodies and feed them on demand, babies still do get colic, but the frequency of this early infant ailment is dramatically reduced. When researchers compared the babies of European women who adopted this strategy—continuously carrying their babies around, offering the breast on demand—with a comparison group that practiced standard Western care, on average the infants given continuous care cried 50 percent less (St James-Roberts, 2007).

Kangaroo care, or using a baby sling, can even help premature infants grow (WHO, 2003b). In one experiment demonstrating this point, developmentalists had a group of mothers with babies in an intensive care unit carry their infants in baby slings for one hour each day. They then compared these children's development with that of a preemie group given standard care. At 6 months of age, the kangaroo-care babies scored higher on developmental tests. Their parents were rated as providing a more nurturing home environment, too (Feldman & Eidelman, 2003b).

colic A baby's frantic, continual crying during the first three months of life; caused by an immature nervous system.

swaddling Wrapping a baby tightly in a blanket or garment. This technique is calming during early infancy.

kangaroo care Carrying a young baby in a sling close to the caregiver's body. This technique is useful for soothing an infant.

Not only are these Mongolian babies getting protection from the intense winter cold, but by being lavishly swaddled, they may feel like they have re-entered their mother's cozy womb.

Dean Conger/Corbis

PART II ▮ Infancy

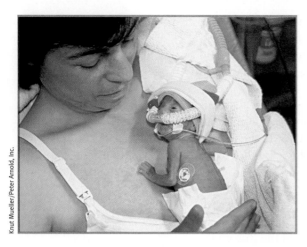

For very premature babies, kangaroo care can make a critical difference in survival. Now, imagine how this mother feels being able to touch her ICU baby and take action to help him live.

Imagine having your baby whisked away at birth to spend weeks in the care of strangers. Now, think of being able to caress his tiny body, the sense of self-efficacy that would flow from feeling personally responsible for helping him thrive. So it makes sense that any cuddling intervention can have a long-term impact on both the baby and the parent–child bond.

Another calming influence on babies is infant massage. From helping premature infants gain weight, to treating toddler (and adult) sleep problems; from increasing immune function, to reducing pain, massage actually enhances well-being from the beginning to the end of life (Field, Diego, & Hernandez-Reif, 2007).

We all know the power of a cuddle or a relaxing massage to immediately soothe our troubles. Can a good deal of holding and stroking in early infancy have the long-term effect of *generally* insulating us against stress? Consider this interesting study with rats.

Because rodent mothers (like humans) differ in the "hands-on" contact they give their babies, researchers classified female rats who had just given birth into high licking and grooming; average licking and grooming; and low licking and grooming groups. During adulthood, the rats that had been lavishly licked and groomed reacted to stress in a far calmer way than the other two groups (Menard & Hakvoort, 2007). We need to be *very cautious* about generalizing this finding to humans. Fully advocating for the !Kung San approach to caregiving might be asking too much of modern moms. Still, the implication is clear: During the first months of life (or, for as long as you can), keep touching and loving 'em up!

Cuddles can calm us from day 1 to age 101. However, the events that cause crying also undergo fascinating developmental changes. The same swaddling or long car ride that magically quieted a 2-month-old evokes agony in a toddler who cannot stand to be confined. First, it's swaddling, then watching a mobile, then seeing Mom enter the room that has the power to soothe. In preschool, it's monsters that cause wailing; during elementary school, it's failing or being rejected by our social group. As teenagers and emerging adults, we weep for lost love. Finally, among mature adults and old folks (as we reach Erikson's stage of generativity), we stop crying for ourselves and cry when our loved ones are in pain. Our crying shows just where we are developmentally throughout our lives!

Sleeping: The Main Newborn State

If crying is a crucial baby (and adult) communication signal, sleep is the quintessential newborn state. Visit a relative or friend who has recently given birth. Will her baby be crying or eating? No, she is almost certain to be asleep. Full-term newborns typically sleep for 18 hours out of a 24-hour day. As Figure 3.4 shows, although they cycle through different stages of arousal, newborns are in the sleeping/drowsy phase about 90 percent of the time (Thoman & Whitney, 1990). And there is a reason for the saying, "She sleeps like a baby." Perhaps because it mirrors the whooshing sound in the womb, noise helps newborns zone out (Anders, Goodlin-Jones, & Zelenko, 1998). The problem for parents, of course, is that babies wake up and start wailing, like clockwork, every three to four hours.

Developmental Changes: From Signaling, to Self-Soothing, to Shifts in REM Sleep

During the first year of life, infant sleep patterns gradually adapt to the human world. Nighttime awakenings become less frequent. Then, by about 6 months of age, there is a milestone. The typical baby sleeps

FIGURE 3.4: Newborns sleep most of the time: During each 24-hour period, newborns cycle through various states of arousal. Notice, however, that babies spend the vast majority of their time either sleeping or in the getting-to-sleep phase.

Source: Adapted from Thoman & Whitney (1990).

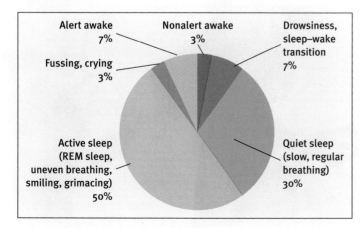

for 6 hours a night. At age 1, the typical pattern is roughly 12 hours of sleep a night, with an additional morning and afternoon nap. During year two, the caretaker's morning respite to do housework or rest is regretfully lost, as children give up the morning nap. Finally, by late preschool, sleep often (although not always) occurs only at night (Anders, Goodlin-Jones, & Zelenko, 1998).

In addition to its incredible length and on-again-off-again pattern, infant sleep differs physiologically from our adult pattern. When we fall asleep, we descend through four stages, involving progressively slower brain-wave frequencies, and then we cycle back to reach **REM sleep**—a phase of rapid eye movement, when dreaming is intense and our brain-wave frequencies look virtually identical to when we are in the lightest sleep stage (see Figure 3.5). When infants fall asleep, they immediately go into the REM phase and spend most of their time in this state. It is not until adolescence that we have the genuinely adult sleep cycle shown in chart A, with four distinct stages (Anders, Goodlin-Jones, & Zelenko, 1998).

Parents are thrilled to say, "My child is sleeping through the night." Is this perception really true? The answer, as researchers discovered, will come as a surprise. When developmentalists used time-lapse photography to monitor nightly sleep, they discovered that babies *never* sleep through the night. Most still wake up several times a night, even at age 2. However, by about 6 months of age, many develop the skills to become **self-soothing**—able to put themselves back to sleep when they do wake up (Goodlin-Jones, Burnham, & Anders, 2000). There is an interesting gender difference here: When it comes to self-soothing, baby girls are superior to baby boys (Goodlin-Jones and others, 2001).

Imagine that you are a new parent. Your first challenge is to get your baby to develop the skill of nighttime self-soothing. Around age 1, because your child is now put into the crib while still awake, there may be issues with getting your baby to *go* to sleep. During preschool and elementary school, the sleep problem shifts again. Now, it's concerns are about getting the child *into* bed: "Mommy, can't I stay up later? Do I *have* to turn off the lights?"

As you might expect, during the first months of life, issues related to getting the baby to sleep through the night are the top-ranking parental concern (Smart & Hiscock,

REM sleep The phase of sleep involving rapid eye movements, when the EEG looks almost like it does during waking. REM sleep decreases as infants mature.

self-soothing Children's ability, usually beginning at about 6 months of age, to put themselves back to sleep when they wake up during the night.

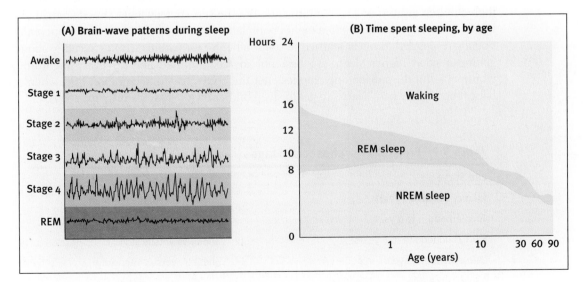

FIGURE 3.5: **Sleep brain waves and lifespan changes in sleep and wakefulness:** In chart A, you can see the EEG patterns associated with the four stages of sleep that first appear during adolescence. After we fall asleep, our brain waves get progressively slower (these are the four stages of non-REM sleep) and then we enter the REM phase during which dreaming is intense. Now, notice in chart B the time young babies spend in REM. As REM sleep helps consolidate memory, is the incredible time babies spend in this phase crucial to absorbing the overwhelming amount of information that must be mastered during the first years of life?

Source: Adapted from Roffwarg, Muzio, & Dement (1966).

2007). Although it may make them cranky, parents expect to be sleep-deprived with a very young baby; but once a child has passed the 5- or 6-month milestone, they get agitated if the infant has never permitted them a full night's sleep. Parents expect periodic sleep problems when their child is ill or under stress, but not the zombie-like irritability that comes from being chronically sleep-deprived for years. There is a poisonous bidirectional effect here: Children with chronic sleep problems produce irritable, depressed parents (Karraker & Young, 2007; Meltzer & Mindell, 2007). Irritable, overstressed parents can provoke childhood problems with sleep (Seifer and others, 1996).

INTERVENTIONS: What Helps a Baby Self-Soothe?

What should parents do when their baby signals (cries out) from her crib? At one end of the continuum stand the traditional behaviorists: "Don't reinforce crying by responding—and be consistent. Never go in and comfort the baby lest you let a variable reinforcement schedule unfold, and the child will cry longer." At the other, we have John Bowlby with his emphasis on the attachment bond, or Erik Erikson with his concept of *basic trust* (see Table 3.2). During the first year of life, both Bowlby and Erikson imply that caregivers should sensitively respond whenever an infant cries. These academic perspectives—still hotly debated by developmentalists—evoke strong passions among parents, too:

> I feel the basic lesson parents need to teach children is how to be independent, not to let your child rule your life, give him time to figure things out on his own, and not be attended to with every whimper.

> I am going with my instincts and trying to be a good, caring mommy. Putting a baby in his crib to "cry it out" seems cruel. There is no such thing as spoiling an infant!

Where do you stand on this "Teach 'em" versus "Give unconditional love" controversy? Based on our discussion of what quiets early crying, at the beginning of life, our bias should clearly be to respond. But after month 3 or 4, there may be advantages to gently heeding the behavioral advice.

To demonstrate this point, let's return to the study of the European mothers who adopted the totally baby-centered !Kung San approach. Remember that, during their first months of life, the infants who were continuously carried and fed on demand cried less than children given standard Western care. But the very strategy that calmed crying during early infancy produced *more* night crying later on, as the babies who were unconditionally responded to never learned to self-soothe. So for parents who care vitally about getting a good night's sleep, it's best not to react immediately to every nighttime whimper—but this advice only applies after the cortex has fully come on-line, when a baby theoretically can "learn" to get to sleep on her own (St James-Roberts, 2007).

TABLE 3.2: Erikson's Psychosocial Stages

Life Stage	Primary Task
Infancy (birth to 1 year)	**Basic trust versus mistrust**
Toddlerhood (1 to 2 years)	Autonomy versus shame and doubt
Early childhood (3 to 6 years)	Initiative versus guilt
Late childhood (6 years to puberty)	Industry versus inferiority
Adolescence (teens into twenties)	Identity versus role confusion
Young adulthood (twenties to early forties)	Intimacy versus isolation
Middle adulthood (forties to sixties)	Generativity versus stagnation
Late adulthood (late sixties and beyond)	Integrity versus despair

According to Erikson, in the first year of life, our mission is to feel confident that the human world will lovingly satisfy our needs. Basic trust is the foundation for the challenges we face at every other life stage.

But the real bottom line is to go with your "mommy (or daddy) instincts" (Connell-Carrick, 2007). For parents, who hate the idea of letting a baby "cry it out," sacrificing some sleep may not be an overwhelming price to pay. The same principle "do what works for you" applies to that other controversial sleep issue—having a baby share the parents' bed.

To Co-sleep or Not to Co-sleep: A Cultural and Personal Choice

It was a standard nighttime routine in our house—one by one we'd wander in and say, "Mommy I'm afraid of witches and ghosts," and soon all four of us would be happily nestled in our parents' huge king-sized bed. I never realized that—in the 1950s, in our uptight, middle-class New York suburb—this family bed sharing qualified as a radical act.

How do you feel about **co-sleeping** or sharing a bed with a child? If you live in the United States and feel queasy about my parents' decision, you are not alone. Until recently, experts in our individualistic society vigorously cautioned parents against co-sleeping (see Ferber, 1985). Behaviorists warned that sharing a bed with a child could produce "excessive dependency." Freudian theorists implied that bed sharing might even place a child at risk for sexual abuse.

In collectivist cultures, where co-sleeping is routine, people would laugh at these ideas (Latz, Wolf, & Lozoff, 1999; Yang & Hahn, 2002). Japanese parents, for instance, often separate to give each child a sleeping partner. The Japanese believe that co-sleeping is crucial to raising a loving, bonded-to-family adult (Kitahara, 1989). Today, in the West, co-sleeping has come out of the closet. Surveys show that, yes, like my parents, many people do it (Ball, 2007; Germo and others, 2007; McKenna and Volpe, 2007). Some mothers and fathers, though, are still reluctant to admit that fact (Goldberg & Keller, 2007). Therefore, Table 3.3 provides three typical anti-bed-sharing stereotypes and some relevant research so you can decide which choice works best for you.

© Yellowdog Productions

This blissfully co-sleeping couple seems at peace with their decision—but they may be reluctant to advertise this behavior to potentially disapproving family members and friends.

TABLE 3.3: Classic Co-sleeping Stereotypes and Some Relevant Research

1. Stereotype: Co-sleeping makes a child less independent and mature.

Relevant research: Among California parents of preschoolers, researchers looked at three groups: people who actively chose to co-sleep with their child; "reactive co-sleepers," who reluctantly brought a child into their bed because of sleep troubles; and solitary sleepers—those who slept apart from their babies (Keller & Goldberg, 2004). The preschoolers whose parents had actively chosen to co-sleep were rated as more self-reliant (for example, able to dress themselves) and socially independent (for example, more able to make friends by themselves) compared to the other two groups. Although a variety of forces could explain this correlation, according to this finding, co-sleeping promotes greater maturity and independence, not less!

2. Stereotype: Co-sleeping disrupts parents' and children's sleep.

Relevant research: Co-sleeping infants do awaken more often at night than solitary sleepers. However, co-sleeping babies get back to sleep in a shorter time (Latz, Wolf, & Lozoff, 1999; Mao and others, 2004). With regard to adults, one EEG sleep study found that parents who shared a bed with their infant spent a bit less time in the deepest sleep stages. However, because they did not have to go into the child's room, these parents did not spend fewer hours sleeping than the non-bed-sharing moms and dads (Mosko, Richard, & McKenna, 1997). Bottom line: Co-sleeping is not detrimental to sleep.

3. Stereotype: Co-sleeping is dangerous because it can cause a baby to be smothered.

Relevant research: Here, there *may* be a few concerns. While some authors argue that co-sleeping helps regulate babies' breathing and so may help prevent suffocating at night (see St. James, 2007), bed-sharing infants spend a good fraction of their sleep time face down (Mao and others, 2004). This sleep position, as you can see in the Focus on a Topic feature on page 88, does not offer the best protection against the ultimate smothering tragedy, SIDS.

co-sleeping The standard custom, in collectivist cultures, of having a child and parent share a bed.

In this next section, we turn to thoroughly explore the issues raised by the third stereotype in the table. What is the risk of a baby's smothering while sleeping, or succumbing to that terrifying event called sudden infant death syndrome?

WHEN SLEEP IS LETHAL

Sudden infant death syndrome (SIDS) refers to the unexplained death of an apparently healthy infant, often while sleeping. Although it strikes only about 1 in 1,000 U.S. babies, SIDS is a top-ranking cause of infant mortality in the United States and the rest of the developed world (Karns, 2001).

SIDS is more common among premature and low-birth-weight babies than full-term infants; this condition seems to have a biological basis (Lipsitt, 2003). Two clearly environmental, or nurture, forces also raise a baby's risk of SIDS: living in a house where adults smoke and, especially, being put to bed face down (Blackwell and others, 2004; Carpenter and others, 2004).

What causes SIDS? Research suggests that a genetic variation affecting the development of the autonomic nervous system—which regulates the breathing cycle—might predispose vulnerable infants to this tragic event (Hunt, 2005; Weese-Mayer and others, 2004). As most SIDS deaths take place between months 2 and 5, one developmentalist suggests that SIDS might be caused by a problem with the transfer from subcortical to cortical functions, when the reflex of shaking one's head in response to breathing problems is waning and the cortex has not yet fully come on-line. When children with initially weak reflexes (or those who are biologically vulnerable) are placed in stressful situations, such as sleeping face down, their breathing mechanism can be overwhelmed (Lipsitt, 2003).

In the early 1990s, when having the baby's face immersed in bedding was recognized as a risk factor for SIDS, the American Academy of Pediatrics launched a campaign alerting parents to put infants to sleep on their backs. The Back to Sleep campaign was highly effective. From 1992 to 1997 there was a 43 percent reduction in SIDS deaths in the United States (Gore & DuBois, 1998).

Table 3.4 offers a summary in the form of practical tips our research tour offers for caregivers and other people dealing with infants' eating, crying, and sleeping. Now, it's time to move on to sensory development and moving into the world.

sudden infant death syndrome (SIDS) The unexplained death of an apparently healthy infant, often while sleeping, during the first year of life.

TABLE 3.4: Infants' Basic States: Summary Tips For Caregivers (and Others)

Eating

- Don't worry about continual newborn sucking and rooting. These are normal reflexes, and they disappear after the first months of life.
- As the baby becomes mobile, be alert to the child's tendency to put everything into the mouth and baby-proof the home (see the next section's discussion).
- Try to breast-feed exclusively for the first six months. But if you cannot breast-feed, don't buy into the stereotype that your child will be *immeasurably* worse off.
- Family members and friends should encourage and support breast-feeding. Employers should make efforts to encourage and support breast-feeding in the workplace.
- After the child is weaned, provide a balanced diet. But don't get frantic if a toddler limits her intake to a few "favorite foods" at around age 1½; this pickiness is normal and temporary.

Crying

- Appreciate that crying is crucial—it's the way babies communicate their needs—and realize that this behavior is at its peak during the first months of life. The frequency of crying sharply declines and the reasons why the child is crying become far clearer after early infancy.

continued

TABLE 3.4 *continued*

- If a baby has colic, hang in there. This condition typically ends at month 4. Moreover, understand that colic has nothing to do with insensitive mothering.

- During the day, carry a young infant around in a "baby sling" as much as possible, and if possible, feed the baby immediately. In addition, employ infant massage to soothe the baby.

Sleeping

- Expect to be sleep-deprived for the first few months, until the typical infant learns to self-soothe; meanwhile, try to take regular naps. After that, expect periodic sleep problems and understand that children will give up their daytime nap at around age 2.

- To promote self-soothing, after 4 months of age, don't go to the infant at the first whimper. However, when crying may signal genuine problems, do check on the baby.

- Co-sleeping—having a child sleep in your bed—is a personal decision. Although most of the stereotypes about co-sleeping are wrong, this practice may not be completely safe with young infants, as bed-sharing may slightly increase the risk of SIDS.

TYING IT ALL TOGETHER

1. You're a nurse in the obstetrics ward, and new parents often ask you why their babies continually make sucking noises and turn their heads toward anything that touches their cheek and then suck. What should you say?
   a. The sucking noises are called the sucking reflex; the head-turning response is the rooting reflex.
   b. These behaviors are programmed by the lower brain centers to automatically occur at birth, because if infants had to learn to eat, they would die.
   c. These behaviors will start to disappear after about three months as the cortex matures.
   d. You should make all of these comments.

2. As a neonatal nurse, you want to design a questionnaire to predict which of your patients are most likely to abandon breast-feeding or persist. What questions might your informal survey include?

3. Your sister and her husband are under an enormous amount of stress because of their colicky 1-month-old's continual crying. Based on this section, give your sister and her husband two bits of advice for soothing their child. What encouraging information can you give your relatives about colic?

4. Jorge tells you that he's thrilled because last night his 6-month-old finally slept through the night. Is Jorge's child ahead of schedule, behind schedule, or right on time for this milestone? Is Jorge right in saying, "My child is sleeping *through* the night"?

5. Take a poll of your classmates, asking them if they believe in co-sleeping and whether they would immediately go in to quiet a crying infant. Do you find any differences in their answers by ethnicity, by gender, or by age?

Answers to the Tying It All Together questions can be found on the last page of this chapter.

Sensory and Motor Development

Sleeping, eating, and crying are easy to observe; but what is it like to really be a newborn? Suppose you could enter into Elissa's consciousness or, better yet, time-travel back to your first days of life. What would you experience through your senses?

One sense is definitely operational before we leave the womb. Using ultrasound, researchers can see startled reactions in response to noise in fetuses 6 or 7 months old, showing that rudimentary hearing capacities exist before birth (Fernald and others, 1998).

Table 3.5 lists some other interesting facts about newborn senses. Now, let's focus specifically on vision because the research in this area is so extensive, the findings are so astonishing, and the studies devised to get into babies' heads are so brilliantly planned.

preferential-looking para-digm A research technique to explore early infant sensory capacities and cognition, drawing on the principle that we are attracted to novelty and prefer to look at new things.

habituation The predictable loss of interest that develops once a stimulus becomes familiar; used to explore infant sensory capacities and thinking.

TABLE 3.5: Some Interesting Facts About Other Newborn Senses

Hearing: Fetuses can discriminate different tones in the womb (Lecanuet and others, 2000). Newborns prefer women's voices, as they are selectively sensitive to higher-pitched tones. At less than 1 week of age, babies recognize their mother's voice (DeCasper & Fifer, 1980). By 1 month of age, they tune in to infant-directed speech (described on page 104), communications tailored to them.

Smell: Newborns develop preferences for certain smells within the first week of life. They prefer the odor of breast milk to that of amniotic fluid (Marlier, Schaal, & Soussignan, 1998). They also know the distinctive smell of their mother's breast milk and will preferentially turn toward a pad soaked with that fluid (MacFarlane, 1975). Smelling mom's milk helps soothe babies. In one study, 3-day-olds cried more vigorously when facing a scentless breast (one covered with a transparent film) (Doucet and others, 2007).

Taste: Newborns are sensitive to basic tastes. When they taste a bitter, sour, or salty substance, they stop sucking and wrinkle their faces. They will suck more avidly on a sweet solution, although they will stop if the substance grows too sweet. Having babies suck a sweet solution before a painful experience, such as a heel stick, reduces agitation and so can be used as a pain-management technique (Fernandez and others, 2003; Gibbins & Stevens, 2001).

What Do Newborns See?

Imagine you are a researcher who wants to figure out what a newborn can see. What do you do? As the accompanying photo series reveals, you would put the baby into an apparatus, present images, and watch the movement of her eyes. Specifically, researchers use the **preferential-looking paradigm**—the principle that human beings are attracted to novelty and look selectively at new things. As the photos show, they also draw on a process called **habituation**—the fact that we naturally lose interest in a new object after some time.

You can easily notice preferential looking and habituation in operation right now in your life. If you happen to see or hear something new, you look up with interest. After a minute, you habituate and go back to focus on reading this book.

By showing newborns small- and large-striped patterns and measuring preferential looking, researchers have found that at birth our ability to see clearly at distances

In this preferential-looking study, as an image pops up on the screen, this little girl is at first enthralled. She then *habituates* and gets interested in a new activity (picking at her dress). Finally (hooray!), another enticing new image appears on the screen.

Charles E. Maurer

is very poor. With a visual acuity score of roughly 20/400 (versus our ideal adult 20/20), a newborn would qualify as legally blind in many states (Kellman & Banks, 1998). Because the visual cortex matures quickly, vision improves rapidly, and by about age 1, infants see just like adults.

What visual capacities *do* we have at birth? A century ago, the first American psychologist, William James, described the inner life of the newborn as, "one buzzing, blooming confusion." In reading the following studies exploring **face perception** (making sense of human faces), you can judge whether or not James was correct.

Focusing on Faces

Face-perception research offers startling evidence that, from their first days out of the womb, babies selectively attend to the social world. When newborns are presented with the paired stimuli in Figure 3.6, they spend more time looking at the face pattern than at the scrambled pattern. They will track or follow that face-like stimulus longer when it is moved from side to side (Farroni, Massaccesi, & Simion, 2002).

The story gets more interesting. Newborns can make amazing distinctions. During their first week of life, they prefer to look at a photo of their mother compared to one of a stranger. They can pick out their mother's face from another face with similar features, although not if their mother's hair is covered by a scarf (Bushnell, 1998; Pascalis and others, 1995).

Most interesting, newborns prefer attractive-looking people! Researchers selected photos of attractive and unattractive women, then took infants from the maternity ward and measured preferential looking. The attractive faces got looked at significantly longer—61 percent of the time (Slater and others, 1998). By 3 to 6 months of age, this preference for good-looking people gets more sophisticated. Babies preferentially look at good-looking infants and children. They even prefer handsome men and pretty women of different racial groups (Slater, 2001). Unhappily, our tendency to gravitate toward people for their looks seems somewhat biologically built in. (In case you are interested, more symmetrical faces tend to be rated as better-looking.)

We also seem pre-wired to gravitate to *relationships*. Newborns look longer at faces when the "eyes" are gazing directly at them (Farroni, Menon, and Johnson, 2006; Frischen, Bayliss, & Tipper, 2007). They can even mimic facial expressions that an adult makes, such as sticking out the tongue (Meltzoff & Moore, 1977). So if you have wondered why you get uncomfortable when someone stares at you, or have agonized at your humiliating tendency to mimic everyone else's gestures and facial tics, this research offers answers. It's not a personal problem. It's built into our human biology, beginning from day one.

With experience, our sensitivity to faces—and the emotions they reveal— markedly improves. But a fascinating study using preferential looking suggests that early experience also shapes what we learn *not* to see (Kelly and others, 2007).

Researchers tested European American babies at 3, 6, and 9 months of age for their ability to discriminate between different faces within their own racial group and those belonging to other ethnicities (African American, Middle Eastern, and Chinese faces). They first habituated the babies to one photo, and then presented a different image of another person of that same ethnic group.

While the 3-month-olds always looked preferentially at the new photo, showing that they could "see" facial differences between every ethnicity, by 9 months of age, these European American babies could only discriminate between faces in their own ethnic group. So if you have wondered why you think that "all Chinese look alike," (if you aren't Chinese), or have puzzled about why "foreigners" (that is, members of other racial groups) look so similar, it's a genuine misperception. Moreover, you developed this erroneous idea during your very first year of life!

In conclusion, William James was wrong. Newborns don't experience the world as a "blooming and buzzing confusion." We arrive in life with a remarkably well-developed sensory apparatus. We have a built-in antenna to tune into the human

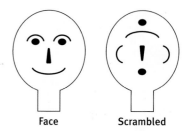

Face   Scrambled

FIGURE 3.6: Babies prefer faces: When shown these illustrations, newborns looked most at the face-like drawing. Might the fact that infants are biologically programmed to selectively look at faces be built into evolution to help ensure that adults give babies loving care?

face-perception studies Research using preferential looking and habituation to explore what very young babies know about faces.

world. However, visual skills also change dramatically as we mature, in sometimes surprising ways.

Now we turn to trace how another type of visual capacity gradually comes on-line—the ability to see and become frightened of heights.

Seeing Depth and Fearing Heights

Imagine you are a researcher facing a conundrum: How can I determine when babies develop **depth perception**—the ability to "see" variations in heights—without causing them harm? Elinor Gibson's ingenious solution: Develop a procedure called the **visual cliff**. As you can see in Figure 3.7, Gibson and her colleague placed infants on one end of a table with a checkerboard pattern while their mothers stood at the opposite end (Gibson & Walk, 1960). At the table's midpoint, the checkerboard design moved from table to floor level, so it appeared to the babies that, if they crawled beyond that point, they would fall. Even when parents smiled and encouraged their children to crawl to them, 8-month-old infants refused to venture beyond what looked like the drop-off—showing that by this age depth perception exists. Do younger babies have this perception and fear?

To answer this question, other developmentalists dangled 2-month-old infants above the drop-off side of the table. The babies' heart rates declined (a sign of interest), showing that by this age they "saw" the difference in depth but were not afraid (Campos, Langer, & Krowitz, 1970). Babies start to *fear* heights about month 6 or 7, around the time they are getting ready to crawl. At this age, their heart rates *accelerate* (showing anxiety) when they are held near the drop-off side (Schwartz, Campos, & Baisel, 1973). Still, once again, there is a nurture (or wider-world experience) component to the age when this biologically programmed fear appears. Early crawlers' fear of heights develops at a younger age (Bertenthal, Campos, & Kermoian, 1994).

In sum, while our ability to *see* differences in depth does appear soon after birth, the sick feeling we have when leaning over a balcony—"Wow, I'd better avoid falling into that space below"—only emerges later, when babies are getting mobile and really need that fear to protect them from getting hurt. Now, we move onto the mobility side of life.

FIGURE 3.7: The visual cliff: Even though his mother is on the other side, this 8-month-old child gets anxious about venturing beyond what looks like the drop-off point in the table—demonstrating that by this age babies have depth perception. By using the strategies discussed in the text, researchers then use the same creative visual cliff apparatus to see if babies too young to crawl also see and fear heights.

Mark Richards/Photo Edit, Inc.

Expanding Body Size

Our brain may expand dramatically after birth. Still, it's far out-paced by the blossoming of the envelope in which we live. Our bodies grow to 21 times their newborn size by the time we reach adulthood (Slater, 2001). This growth is most pronounced during infancy, then drastically slows down during childhood, to dramatically increase in velocity again during the preadolescent years. Still, looking at overall height and weight statistics is not that revealing. This body sculpting occurs in a definite way.

Imagine taking time-lapse photographs of a baby's head from birth to adulthood and comparing your photos to snapshots of the body. You would not see much change in the overall size and shape of the head. In contrast, the body would dramatically elongate and thin out. Newborns start out with tiny "frog" legs timed to slowly straighten out by about month 6. Then comes the stocky, bowlegged toddler, followed by the slimmer child of kindergarten and elementary school. So during childhood, growth follows the same principle as it did inside the womb: Development proceeds according to the *cephalocaudal sequence*—from the head to the feet.

Now, think of Mickey Mouse, Big Bird, and Oscar the Grouch. They, too, have relatively large heads and small bodies. Might our favorite cartoon characters be entic-

depth perception The ability to see (and fear) heights.

visual cliff A table that appears to "end" in a drop-off at its midpoint; used to test for infant depth perception.

ing because they mimic the proportions of a baby? Did the deliciously rounded infant shape evolve to seduce adults into giving babies special care and love?

Mastering Motor Milestones

Actually, all three growth principles spelled out in the previous chapter—*cephalocaudal*, *proximodistal*, and *mass-to-specific*—apply to the achievement of infant *motor milestones*, the exciting progression of physical abilities during the first year of life. First, babies lift their head, then pivot their upper body, then sit up without support, and finally, stand (the cephalocaudal sequence). Infants have control of their shoulders before they can make their arms and fingers obey their commands (proximodistal sequence, from interior to outer parts).

But the most important principle programming motor abilities throughout childhood is the *mass-to-specific* sequence (large before small and detailed). From the wobbly first step at age 1 to the home run out of the ballpark during the teenage years—as the neurons gradually undergo mylenation—big, uncoordinated movements are honed and perfected as we move from infancy to adult life.

Variations (and Joys) Related to Infant Mobility

Charting these milestones does not speak to the joy of witnessing them unfold—that Kodak moment when Kim's baby, Elissa, finally masters turning over, after those vigorous practice "push-ups," or when she first connects with the bottle, grasps it, and awkwardly moves it to her mouth. I'll never forget when my own son, after what seemed like years of cruising around holding onto the furniture, finally ventured (so gingerly) out into the air, flung up his hands, and, *yes, yes*, took his ecstatic first step!

Nor do the standard motor milestone charts mention the hilarious glitches that happen when a skill is first being developed—the first days of creeping, when a baby can only move backward and you find him huddled in the corner in pursuit of objects that get steadily farther way. Or when a child first pulls herself to a standing position in the crib, and her triumphant expression changes to bewilderment: "Whoops, now tell me, Mom, *how do I get down?*"

Actually, rather than viewing motor development in static stages such as sitting, then crawling, then walking, contemporary researchers stress the variability and ingenuity of babies' passion to get moving into life (Adolph, 2008). Consider the "creeping" or belly-crawling stage. Some babies scoot; others hunch over or launch themselves forward from their knees, roll from side to side, or scrape along with a cheek on the floor (Adolph & Berger, 2006). When they first go down stairs, some infants bump down sitting or slide down face first (Berger, Theuring, & Adolph, 2007). Did you know that children reach with their feet before their hands, or that, when they begin to walk, babies' sitting abilities temporarily get worse? And can I really say that there was a day when my son definitely mastered walking? When walking, or any other

The tiny frog legs of very early infancy straighten out by month 6 and then become longer and fully functional for carrying us around (as toddlers)—demonstrating the cephalocaudal principle of development.

Babies first joyously lift their heads and upper torsos, then sit up (at about month 5 or 6), and finally, at around age 1, take their first unforgettable steps—demonstrating that the cephalocaudal principle also applies to motor milestones.

major motor skill first occurs, children do not make steady progress (Adolph & Berger, 2006). They may take their first solo step on Monday and then revert to crawling for a week or so before trying, oh so gingerly, to tackle toddling again.

But suppose a child is definitely behind schedule. Let's say your son is almost 15 months old and has yet to take his first solo step, or your daughter is sliding toward 4 years of age and is in danger of being expelled from nursery school because she still is incapable of regularly making it to the toilet in time? And what about the fantasies that set in when an infant is clearly ahead? "Only 10 months old, and he's already walking. Perhaps my baby is special, a genius."

What typically happens is that, within weeks, the worries become a memory and the fantasies about the future are shown to be completely wrong. Except in the case of children who have developmental disorders, the rate at which babies master motor milestones has no relation to their later intelligence. Different regions of the cortex, as we now know, develop at different times. Why should our timetable for walking or grasping an object predict development in a complex function such as grasping the point of this book?

An interesting exception to the rule that early infant individual differences don't predict later cognition involves an ability that doesn't appear on the milestones chart. It concerns *habituation*, discussed in the earlier section exploring vision. In looking at a variety of infant abilities longitudinally, one researcher was astonished to discover that babies who quickly habituated to stimuli, and then later preferentially looked at a new stimulus when it was paired with an "old" one (showing they remembered what they had seen before), had superior scores on elementary school intelligence tests (Fagan, 1988, 2000). The reason is that processing a stimulus quickly and remembering it is a general capacity that underlies a variety of intellectual skills, from recalling facts better, to mastering language (Heimann and others, 2006), to more effortlessly absorbing the messages of this text.

But even if a baby's early locomotion (physically getting around) does not mean he will end up an Einstein, moving into the world does usher in many cognitive advances.

© Moodboard/Corbis

At 8 or 10 months of age, getting around is a challenge that babies approach in a variety of creative, unique ways.

The Mind-Expanding Effects of Travel

Developmentalists have explored the mind-expanding changes linked to crawling, the one motor milestone that many normal babies actually skip. Crawling provokes more interest in objects at distances (Anderson, Campos, & Barbu-Roth, 2004). Early crawlers—compared to other babies—are "mature" in the relationship area, too. They are more attuned to a caregiver's facial expressions. They get more upset when their parent leaves the room (Campos and others, 2000).

In interviewing mothers of newly crawling babies, developmentalists discovered that crawling is linked to changes in the parent–child bond (Campos and others, 2000). When their infants started crawling, women reported that they saw their children as more independent—individuals with a mind of their own. Many said this was the first time they began to get angry with and discipline their child. So as babies get mobile, the basic parenting agenda emerges: A child's mission is to explore the world. Parents' job, for the next two decades, lies in setting limits to that exploration, as well as giving love.

INTERVENTIONS: Baby-Proofing, the First Person–Environment Fit

Mobility presents perils. Now safety issues become a major concern. How can caretakers encourage these emerging motor skills and still protect children from getting hurt? The answer is to strive for the right person–environment fit—that is, to **baby-proof** the house.

baby-proofing Making the home safe for a newly mobile infant.

Get on the floor and look at life from the perspective of the child. Cover electrical outlets and put dangerous cleaning substances on the top shelf. Unplug countertop appliances. Take small objects off tables. Perhaps pad the furniture corners, too. The challenge is to anticipate possible dangers and to stay one step ahead. There will come a day when that child can pry out those outlet covers or ascend to the top of the cleanser-laden cabinet. As Kim from the chapter-opening vignette is about to learn, those exciting motor milestones have a definite downside, too!

TYING IT ALL TOGETHER

1. You're watching through a one-way mirror as a researcher explores how well newborns can hear. The infant is wearing headphones, and the psychologist presents a tone and watches the baby's face to see if the child looks up with interest. The strategy the researcher is using is called the_____ paradigm.

2. Alicia's daughter has been regularly participating in a visual cliff study. When the baby is placed on the cliff side at 2 months of age, she should _____. At 7 months, she should _____. (Choose from a, b, and c to fill in the blanks.)
   a. show no fear, but give signs that she "sees" the difference by looking interested
   b. be terribly frightened
   c. not notice the drop-off at all

3. Cotonia says that babies can see the world remarkably accurately soon after they emerge from the womb. Jason says that visual capacities grow gradually over the first year of life. First, make Cotonia's case, and then make Jason's, citing the research discussed in this section.

4. Charlie crawled and walked at a very young age, and grew bored before other babies in a habituation test at the local university. His excited parents are sure that Charlie is gifted and are saving up to send him to Harvard. Which, if any, of Charlie's behaviors might support his parents' dreams?

5. List some steps that you would take to baby-proof the room you are sitting in right now.

Answers to the Tying It All Together questions can be found on the last page of this chapter.

Cognition

Why exactly *do* infants have an incredible hunger to explore, to touch, to get into every cleanser-laden cabinet and remove all those outlet plugs? For the same reason that, if you landed on a different planet, you would need to get the basics of reality down.

Imagine stepping out onto Mars. You would roam the new environment, exploring the rocks and the sand. While exercising your walking schema, or habitual way of physically navigating, you would need to make drastic changes. On Mars, with its minimal gravity, when you took your normal earthling stride, you would probably bounce up 20 feet. Just like a newly crawling infant, you would have to accommodate, and in the process reach a higher mental equilibrium, or a better understanding of life. Moreover, as a good scientist, you would not be satisfied to perform each movement only once. The only way to pin down the physics of this planet would be to repeat each action over and over again. Now, you have the basic principles of Jean Piaget's **sensorimotor stage** (see Table 3.6 on page 96).

Piaget's Sensorimotor Stage

Specifically, Piaget believed that during our first two years on this planet, our mission is to make sense of physical reality by exploring the world through our senses. Just as in the above Mars example, as they *assimilate*, or fit the outer world to what they are already capable of doing, infants *accommodate* and so gradually mentally advance. (Remember my example in Chapter 1 of how, in the process of assimilating this information to your current knowledge schemas or mental slots, you are accommodating and so expanding what you know.)

sensorimotor stage Piaget's first stage of cognitive development, lasting from birth to age 2, when babies' agenda is to pin down the basics of physical reality.

TABLE 3.6: Piaget's Stages: Focus on Infancy

Age	Name of Stage	Description
0–2	**Sensorimotor**	The baby manipulates objects to pin down the basics of physical reality. This stage ends with the development of language.
2–7	**Preoperations**	Children's perceptions are captured by their immediate appearances. "What they see is what is real." They believe, among other things, that inanimate objects are really alive and that if the appearance of a quantity of liquid changes (for example, if it is poured from a short, wide glass into a tall, thin one), the amount actually becomes different.
8–12	**Concrete operations**	Children have a realistic understanding of the world. Their thinking is really on the same wavelength as adults. While they can reason conceptually about concrete objects, however, they cannot think abstractly in a scientific way.
12+	**Formal operations**	Reasoning is at its pinnacle: hypothetical, scientific, flexible, fully adult. Our full cognitive human potential has been reached.

Let's take the "everything goes into the mouth" schema that figures so prominently during the first year of life. As babies mouth each new object—or, in Piaget's terminology, assimilate everything to their mouthing schema—they realize that objects have different characteristics. Some are soft or prickly. Others taste terrible or great. Through continual assimilation and accommodation, by age 2, babies make a dramatic mental leap—from relying on their small set of reflexes to reasoning and using symbolic thought.

Circular Reactions: Habits That Pin Down Reality

By meticulously observing his own three children, Piaget discovered that the basic set of actions driving all these advances during infancy were what he called **circular reactions**—habits, or action-oriented schemas, which the child repeats again and again.

From the newborn reflexes, during months 1 to 4, **primary circular reactions** develop. These are repetitive actions that begin by accident, centered on the child's body. A thumb randomly makes contact with his mouth, and a 2-month-old removes that interesting object, observes it, and moves it back in and then out. Waving her legs is an activity that captivates a 3-month-old for hours on end.

At around 4 months of age, **secondary circular reactions** appear. These are action-oriented schemas centered on sights and sounds in the *outside* environment. As Kim noticed with Elissa, at about this age, the child seems to literally wake up to the wider world. Let's see how Piaget described his daughter Lucienne's first secondary circular reactions:

Lucienne at 0:4 [4 months] is lying in her bassinet. I hang a doll over her feet which . . . sets in motion the schema of shakes. Her feet reach the doll . . . and give it a violent movement which Lucienne surveys with delight. . . . After the first shakes, Lucienne makes slow foot movements as though to grasp and explore. . . . When she tries to kick the doll, and misses . . . she begins again very slowly until she succeeds [without looking at her feet]. (Flavell, 1963, p. 103; original source, Piaget, 1950, p. 159)

During the next few months, secondary circular reactions become better coordinated. By about 8 months of age, for instance, babies can simultaneously employ two circular reactions, using both grasping and kicking together to explore the world.

Then, around a baby's first birthday, **tertiary circular reactions** appear. Now, the child is no longer constrained by stereotyped schemas. He can operate just like a real scientist, flexibly changing his behavior to make sense of the world. A toddler gets captivated by toilet paper, unrolling sheets and throwing different-sized wads into the bowl. At dinner, he gleefully spits his food out at varying velocities and hurls his bottle off the high chair in different directions just to see where it lands.

circular reactions In Piaget's framework, repetitive action-oriented schemas (or habits) characteristic of babies during the sensorimotor stage.

primary circular reactions In Piaget's framework, the first infant habits during the sensorimotor stage, centered on the body.

secondary circular reactions In Piaget's framework, habits of the sensorimotor stage lasting from about 4 months of age to the baby's first birthday, centered on exploring the external world.

tertiary circular reactions In Piaget's framework, "little-scientist" activities of the sensorimotor stage, beginning around age 1, involving flexibly exploring the properties of objects.

How important are circular reactions in infancy? Spend time with a young baby, as she bats at her mobile or joyously pinwheels her legs. Try to prevent a 1-year-old from ejecting plates off a high chair, flushing objects down the toilet, or methodically inserting bits of cookie into your open computer drive. Then, you will understand: Infancy is all about the insatiable drive to repeat interesting acts. (See Table 3.7 for a recap of the circular reactions, as well as a look at the sensory-motor substages.)

Piaget's concept of circular reactions offers a new perspective on those obsessions that drive adults crazy during what researchers call the **little-scientist phase** (and parents call the "getting into everything" phase). This is the time, around age 1, when the child begins experimenting with objects in a way that uncannily mimics how a scientist behaves: "Let me try this, then that, and see what happens." The reason it is impossible to derail a 1-year-old from putting oatmeal into the computer, or clogging the toilet with toys (making a plumber a parent's new best friend), is that circular reactions allow infants to pin down the basic properties of the world.

TABLE 3.7: The Circular Reactions: A Summary Table (With a Look at Piaget's Substages)

Primary Circular Reactions: 1–4 months

Description: Repetitive habits center around the child's own body.

Examples: Sucking toes; sucking thumb.

Rommel/Masterfile

Secondary Circular Reactions: 4 months–1 year

Description: Child "wakes up to wider world." Habits center on environmental objects.

Examples: Grabbing for toys; batting mobiles; pushing one's body to activate the lights and sounds on a swing.

Substages: From 4 to 8 months, children use single secondary circular reactions such as those above; from 8 to 12 months, they employ two circular reactions in concert to attain a goal (i.e., they may grab a toy in each hand, bat a mobile back and forth, coordinate the motions of toys).

Christina Kennedy/Photo Edit, Inc.

Tertiary Circular Reactions: 1–2 years

Description: Child flexibly explores the properties of objects, like a "little scientist."

Examples: Exploring the various dimensions of a toy; throwing a bottle off the high chair in different directions; flushing different objects down the toilet; putting different kinds of food in the computer.

Substages: From 12 to 18 months, the child experiments with concrete objects; from 18 to 24 months, his little-scientist behavior transcends what is observable and involves using symbols to stand for something else. (I'll be describing the many advances ushered in by this ability to reason symbolically later in this chapter and in Chapter 5.)

David Young-Wolff/Photo Edit, Inc.

little-scientist phase The time around age 1 when babies use tertiary circular reactions to actively explore the properties of objects, experimenting with them like "scientists."

Why do *specific* circular reactions, such as flushing objects down the toilet or filling the computer with food, become irresistible during the little-scientist phase? This question brings us to Piaget's ideas about how babies progress from reflexes to the ability to reason and think.

Tracking Early Thinking

How do we know when infants begin to actually think? According to Piaget, one hallmark of thinking is deferred imitation—repeating an action that was witnessed at an earlier time. When Piaget saw Lucienne, at 16 months of age, mimic a tantrum she had seen another child have days earlier, he realized she had the mental skills to keep that image in her mind, mull it over, and translate it into action on her own. Another sign of reasoning abilities is the beginning of make-believe play. To pretend you are cleaning the house or talking on the phone like Mommy, you must realize that something *signifies*, or stands for, something else.

But perhaps the most important sign of emerging reasoning is **means–end behavior**—when the child is able to perform a totally separate, or different action, to get to a goal. Turning a doorknob to open a door and get outside, manipulating a switch to turn on the light, screwing open a bottle to extract the juice—all of these are examples of "doing something different" to reach a particular end.

If you have access to a 1-year-old, you might try to construct your own means–end task. First, show the child something she really wants, such as a cookie or a toy. Then, put the object in a place where the baby must perform a different type of action to get the treat. For instance, you might put the cookie in a clear container and cover the top with Saran Wrap or a piece of fabric. Will the baby simply, ineffectively bang the side of the container, or will she figure out the *different* step (removing the cover) essential to retrieving what she wants? If you conduct your test by putting the cookie in an opaque container, the baby must have another basic understanding: She must realize that—although she may not immediately see it—the cookie is still there.

Object Permanence: Believing in a Stable World

Object permanence refers to the understanding that objects still exist even when we no longer see them—a perception that is, obviously, fundamental to our sense of living in a stable world. Suppose you felt that this book disappeared when you averted your eyes or that your house rematerialized out of nothing when you entered your driveway. Piaget believed that this perception is not inborn. Object permanence develops gradually throughout the sensorimotor stage.

Piaget's observations suggested that during babies' first few months, life is a series of disappearing pictures. If an enticing image, such as her mother, passed her line of sight, Lucienne would stare at the place from which the image had vanished as if it would reappear out of thin air. (The relevant phrase here is "out of sight, out of mind.") Then, at around month 5, when the *secondary circular reactions* are first flowering, there was a milestone. An object dropped out of sight and Lucienne leaned over to look for it, suggesting that she knew it existed independently of her gaze. Still, this sense of a stable object was fragile. The baby quickly abandoned her search after Piaget covered that object with his hand.

Hunting for hidden objects becomes a well-established activity as children approach their first birthday. Actually, for 9- or 10-month-olds, uncovering objects that adults hide underneath covers becomes a totally absorbing game. Still, around this age, children make a surprising mistake called the **A-not-B error** (see Figure 3.8). If you put an object in full view of a baby into one out-of-sight location, have the baby get it, and then move it to another place while the child is watching, she will look for it in the initial place!

See if you can perform this classic test if you have access to a 10-month-old: Place an object, such as a toy, under a piece of paper (A). Then, have the baby find it in that place a few times. Next, remove the toy as the infant watches and put it under a

---

means–end behavior In Piaget's framework, performing a different action to get to a goal—an ability that emerges in the sensorimotor stage as babies approach age 1.

object permanence In Piaget's framework, the understanding that objects continue to exist even when we can no longer see them, which gradually emerges during the sensorimotor stage.

A-not-B error In Piaget's framework, a classic mistake made by infants in the sensorimotor stage, whereby babies approaching age 1 go back to the original hiding place to look for an object even though they have seen it get hidden in a second place.

different piece of paper (B). What happens? Even though the child saw you put the toy in the new location, he will probably look under the A paper again, as if it had migrated unseen to its original place!

By about their first birthday, children seem to master the basic principle. Move an object to a new hiding place and they will look for it in the correct location. However, as Piaget found when he used this strategy but *covered* the object with his hand, object permanence does not fully emerge until children are almost 2 years old.

Emerging object permanence explains many puzzles about development. Why does peek-a-boo become an all-time favorite activity at around 8 months? The reason is that a child now thinks there is *probably* still someone behind those hands, but doesn't absolutely know for sure.

Emerging object permanence offers a wonderful perspective on why younger babies are so laid back when you remove an interesting object, and then become increasingly possessive as they travel into their second year of life. Those toddler tantrums about objects do not signal a new, awful personality trait called "the terrible twos." They simply show that children have become much smarter. They now have the cognitive skills to know that objects still exist when you take them away. Finally, the emerging concept of object permanence, or fascination with disappearing objects, plus means–end behavior, makes perfect sense of that irresistible attraction to flush toys down the toilet or the compulsion to stick bits of cookie in a computer drive. What could be more tantalizing during the little-scientist phase than taking a new action to get to a goal plus causing things to disappear and possibly reappear? It also explains why you can't go wrong if you buy your toddler nephew a pop-up toy.

But during the first year of life, there is no need to arrive with any toy. Buy a toy for an infant and he will push it aside to play with the box. Your nephew probably much prefers fiddling with the light switch or buttons on the TV to any fancy mechanical gadget from Toys'R'Us. Toys only become interesting once we realize that they are different from real life. So a desire for dolls or action figures—or for anything else

This child is thrilled with his Jack-in-the-box toy because he is just getting the concept of object permanence.

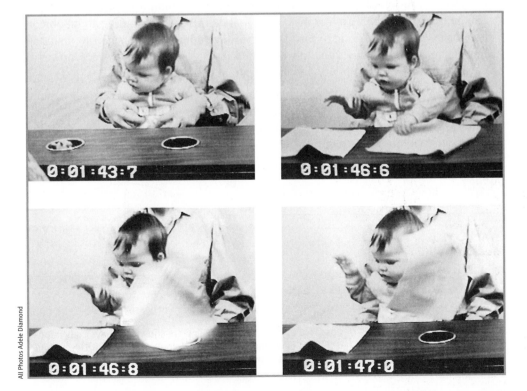

FIGURE 3.8: **The A-not-B error:** Before filming these images, researchers had this baby find a covered object in the hole on the right several times. Then, as you can see in the top images, they placed an object in the hole on the left, made sure the infant was watching, and covered each hole with a cloth. Interestingly, notice that, even while focusing her attention on the correct hiding place, this baby automatically repeated her previous action and picked up the cloth on the right.

that requires make-believe play—shows that a child is emerging from the sensorimotor period and making the transition to symbolic thought. With the concepts of circular reactions, emerging object permanence, and means–end behavior, Piaget masterfully made sense of the puzzling passions of infant life!

Critiquing Piaget

Despite its brilliance, however, Piaget's theory has serious holes. Piaget's problem was that he had to rely on babies' actions (for instance, taking covers off hidden objects) to figure out what they actually knew. He did not have those creative strategies like preferential looking and habituation to decode what babies might understand or cognitively grasp before they can physically respond. Using these techniques, developmentalists realized that infants understand far more than Piaget gave them credit for.

Now, let's look at several criticisms researchers have made about Piaget's conceptions about infant life:

- **Infants grasp the basics of physical reality at a younger age than Piaget believed.** To illustrate this point, developmentalist Renée Baillargeon (1993) presented babies under age 1 with the physically impossible events shown in Figure 3.9. She rotated a screen so that it appeared to pass through a solid object (see B below). She showed a tall rabbit—clearly moving behind a screen—that mysteriously materialized on the other side of the gap it had to pass through to reach the place where it arrived (see A below). Even young infants looked astonished when they saw these physically impossible events. You could almost hear them thinking, "I know that's not the way objects should behave."

- **Infants' understanding of physical reality emerges gradually.** Moreover, Baillargeon and other researchers have found that babies' understanding of the properties of objects does not arrive in huge, qualitatively different chunks. While babies as young as 3½ months old were surprised when the screen passed through the solid object, the impossible traveling rabbit provoked astonishment only around month 4 or 5. It takes infants until about 12 months of age to have other basic insights about the way objects operate, such as the fact that if you are searching for a hidden toy that is tall, you need to look in a tall container rather than a short one (Wang & Kohne, 2007). The bottom-line message is that infants' understanding about objects grows *slowly* during the first year of life. So developmentalists began to abandon Piaget's model of unitary, qualitatively different stages. Today they trace how specific abilities, such as memory or categorization, *gradually emerge.*

Table 3.8 summarizes some insights scientists have derived about babies' emerging cognitive skills by using this more gradual, specific approach. Now, let's conclude by touching on a new, hot topic related to infant cognition. What do young babies *really* understand about human beings?

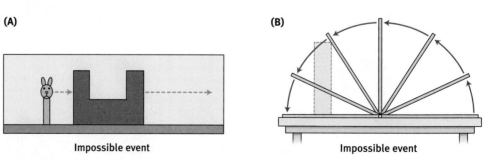

(A)   **(B)**

Impossible event   Impossible event

FIGURE 3.9: **Baillargeon's impossible events:** When babies were shown the physically impossible sequences illustrated in A and B, even by 4 months of age, they looked surprised. The bottom line: Infants understand basic principles about the physical world far earlier than Piaget believed.
Sources: Baillargeon & Graber (1987); Baillargeon & DeVos (1991); Baillargeon (1987).

> ### TABLE 3.8: Infant Memory and Conceptual Abilities: Some Interesting Findings
>
> **Memory:** By using deferred imitation (see the text discussion), researchers find that babies as young as 9 months of age can "remember" events from the previous day. Infants will push a button if they saw an adult performing that act 24 hours earlier. In another study, most 10-month-olds imitated an action they saw one month earlier. There even have been cases where babies this age saw an action and then remembered it a year later.*
>
> **Forming categories:** By 7 to 9 months of age, babies are able to distinguish between animals and vehicles. They will feed an animal or put it to bed, but even if they watch an adult put a car to bed, they will not model her action. So the first classification babies make is between something that moves by itself or cannot move on its own. (Is it alive, like an animal, or inanimate?) Then, categorization abilities get more refined depending on familiarity. Eleven-month-old infants, for example, can often distinguish between dogs and cats but not among dogs, rabbits, and fish.
>
> **Understanding numbers:** By about 5 months of age, infants can make differentiations between different numbers—for instance, after seeing three dots on a screen, they will look preferentially at a subsequent screen showing four dots. Babies also have an implicit understanding of addition and subtraction. If they see someone add one doll to another, or take away a doll from a set, they look surprised when they see an image on a screen showing the incorrect number of dolls.
>
> *Source:* Mandler, 2007.
>
> * Because deferred imitation, like habituation, reflects the child's memory capacities, a preverbal baby's skill in this area predicts the rapidity of language development and later IQ scores.

social cognition Any skill related to understanding feelings and negotiating interpersonal interactions.

joint attention The first sign of "getting human intentions," when a baby looks at an object an adult is pointing to or follows a person's gaze.

Moving on from Piaget: A Note on Emerging Social Cognition

Social cognition refers to any skill related to managing and decoding people's emotions, and getting along with other human beings. One hallmark of being human is that we are always making inferences about people's inner feelings and goals, based on their actions. ("He's running, so he must be late." "She slammed the door in my face, so she must be angry.") How early in development do these judgments first occur? Piaget would say certainly not before age 2 (or even much later) because infants in the sensorimotor period can't think conceptually. Here is just one example of many studies that have proved Piaget wrong.

Babies of about 10 months of age watched a computer animation of a circle struggling to climb up a hill while a triangle and square looked on. Then, the infants saw the triangle push the square to the top. In the next frame, they watched as the square pushed the struggling circle down. After those images appeared, the hill was removed, and the babies observed the circle either approach the "helpful" triangle or the "mean" square. The babies looked much longer when they saw the circle gravitate to the nasty square. They seemed to be thinking: "If Mr. Square treated you like that, why would you *ever, ever* choose him?" (Hamlin, Wynn, & Bloom, 2007.)

So at an incredibly young age, babies start to clue into human motivations. (More about how this crucial human ability to "mind read" gradually develops in Chapter 5.) Another sign of first decoding human intentions is an infant landmark called **joint attention.** If a person the baby is watching points to something—or gazes in a

When his mom points to an interesting object outside of the window, this 2-year-old shows he has mastered a vital human skill—*joint attention.*

specific direction—a 1-year-old will begin to look at the object being pointed to, rather than the individual's hand or face (Harris, 2006; Mundy and others 2007). Joint attention, understanding what people are trying to communicate with gestures ("I want you to look at that"), sets the stage for that milestone—understanding what people are trying to communicate with words.

TYING IT ALL TOGETHER

1. You are working at a child-care center and you notice Darien repeatedly opening and closing a cabinet door. Then Jai comes over and pulls open the door. You decide to latch it. Jai—undeterred—pulls on the door and, when it doesn't open, begins jiggling the latch. And then he looks up, very pleased, as he manages to figure out how to open the latch. Finally, you give up and decide to play a game with Sam. You hide a stuffed bear in a toy box while Sam watches. Then Sam throws open the lid of the box and scoops out the bear. Link the appropriate Piagetian term to each child's behavior: circular reaction; object permanence; means–end behavior.

2. Jose wants to argue, based on this section, that Piaget's theory falls short. Identify which statement is *not* a critique of Piaget's theory.

   a. Cognitive development takes place in qualitatively different stages, but not the ones Piaget described.
   b. Infants grasp the facts about physical reality at an earlier age than Piaget assumed.
   c. Children's understanding of the physical world emerges gradually.
   d. Infants understand much more about human intentions than Piaget believed.

Answers to the Tying It All Together questions can be found on the last page of this chapter.

Language: The Endpoint of Infancy

Piaget believed the onset of language signals the end of the sensorimotor period because its emergence showed that children could see that a symbol stands for something else. True, in order to master language, you must grasp the idea that the abstract word-symbol *textbook* refers to what you are reading now. But the real miracle of human language is that we can string together words in novel, immediately understandable ways. What causes us to master this amazing feat, and how does beginning language evolve?

Nature, Nurture, and the Passion to Learn Language

The essential property of human language is its elasticity. How can I come up with this totally new sentence, and why can you understand its meaning, although you have never seen it before? Why does every language have a **grammar**, with nouns, verbs, and rules for organizing words into sentences? According to linguist Noam Chomsky, the reason is that our species is biologically programmed to make "language." We alone possess a language-generating capacity in our genetic code, which Chomsky named the **language acquisition device (LAD)**.

Chomsky developed his nature-oriented concept of a uniquely human LAD in reaction to the behaviorist B. F. Skinner's nurture-oriented proposition that we learn to speak through being reinforced for producing specific words (for instance, Skinner argued that we learn to say "I want cookie" by being rewarded for producing those sounds by getting that treat). This pronouncement was another example of the traditional behaviorist principle that "all actions are driven by reinforcement" run amok (see Chapter 1). It defies common sense to suggest that we learn to generate billions of new sentences by having other people reinforce us for every word!

grammar The rules and word-arranging systems that every human language employs to communicate meaning.

language acquisition device (LAD) Chomsky's term for a hypothetical brain structure that enables our species to learn and produce language.

Still, Skinner's nurture-oriented perspective on language is correct in one respect. I speak English instead of Mandarin Chinese because I grew up in New York City, not Beijing. So the way our genetic program for making language gets expressed depends totally on our environmental milieu. Once again, nature plus nurture work together to explain every activity of life!

Currently, developmentalists typically adopt a **social-interactionist view** on this core human skill. They focus on the social motivations that propel language (Camaioni, 2001; Hoff-Ginsberg, 1997). Babies are passionate to communicate. Adults are passionate to help babies learn to talk. How does the infant passion to communicate evolve?

Tracking Emerging Speech

The pathway to actually producing language occurs in defined stages. Out of the reflexive crying of the newborn period comes *cooing* (*oooh* sounds) at about month 4. At around month 6, delightful vocal circular reactions called **babbling** emerge. Babbles are alternating consonant and vowel sounds, such as "da-da-da," that infants playfully repeat with variations of intonation and pitch. Even at this stage the environment is shaping language. In one study conducted in France, adults who listened to tapes of 8-month-olds were able to pick out from babble sounds whether the baby babbler was French or Chinese (de Boysson-Bardies, Sagart, & Durand, 1984).

The first word emerges out of the babble at around 11 months, although that exact landmark is difficult to define. There is little more reinforcing to paternal pride than when your 8-month-old genius continually repeats your name. But when does "da-da-da" really refer to Dad? In the first, **holophrase** stage of true speech, one word, liberally accompanied by gestures, literally says it all. When your son says "ja" and points to the kitchen, you know he wants juice . . . or was it a jelly sandwich, or was he referring to his big sister Jane?

Children accumulate their first 50 or so words, centering on the important items in their world (people, toys, and food) slowly (Nelson, 1974). Then, typically between ages 1 1/2 and 2, there is a vocabulary explosion as the child begins to combine words. Because children pare communication down to its essentials, just like an old-style telegram ("Me juice"; "Mommy, no"), this first word-combining stage is called **telegraphic speech.** In Table 3.9, you can see a summary of these basic language landmarks, along with examples and the approximate time during infancy when each milestone occurs.

In the same way as you saw earlier with the critique of Piaget's ideas about cognition, there is a difference between knowing something and being able to actively demonstrate that knowledge. Children's ability to understand what other people say (their *receptive language abilities*) far outpaces their ability to verbalize or speak (their *expressive language skills*). In one study, babies demonstrated that they knew the difference between the complex sentences, "Where is Big Bird washing Cookie

social-interactionist view An approach to language development that emphasizes its social function, specifically that babies and adults have a mutual passion to communicate.

babbling The alternating vowel and consonant sounds that babies repeat with variations of intonation and pitch and that precede the first words.

holophrase First clear evidence of language, when babies use a single word to communicate a sentence or complete thought.

telegraphic speech First stage of combining words in infancy, in which a baby pares down a sentence to its essential words.

TABLE 3.9: Language Milestones from Birth to Age 2*

Age	Language Characteristic
2–4 months	**Cooing:** First sounds growing out of reflexes. *Example:* "oooo"
5–11 months	**Babbling:** Alternate vowel–consonant sounds. *Examples:* "ba-ba-ba," "da-da-da"
12 months	**Holophrases:** First one-word sentences. *Example:* "ja" ("I want juice.")
18 months–2 years	**Telegraphic speech:** Two-word combinations, often accompanied by an explosion in vocabulary. *Example:* "Me juice"

Babies vary a good deal in the ages at which they begin to combine words.

There is nothing more thrilling than being able to have a real father-to-daughter discussion for the first time when your toddler begins to combine words. But what might infant-directed speech sound like delivered in Japanese?

Monster?" and "Where is Cookie Monster washing Big Bird?" when they were only in the holophrase stage (Hirsh-Pasek & Golinkoff, 1991).

Moreover, just as they selectively tune in to faces, babies are selectively attuned to speech sounds that are directed toward them. Caregivers, just as interested in connecting to babies, speak to infants in characteristic ways (Hoff-Ginsberg, 1997).

Infant-directed speech (IDS) (what you and I call *baby talk*) has distinctive attributes. It uses simple words, exaggerated tones, elongated vowels, and it occurs at a higher pitch than we would use in speaking to adults (Hoff-Ginsberg, 1997). Although IDS can sound ridiculous to adult ears ("Mooommy taaaaking baaaaby ooooout!" "Moommy looooves baaaaby!"), when babies are spoken to this way, they perk up and their heart rate decelerates (a sign of interest)(Santesso, Schmidt, & Trainer, 2007). So people naturally use infant-directed speech with babies, just as we are compelled to pick up and rock a child when she cries.

IDS is adopted by adults around the world (Matychuk, 2004; Englund & Behne, 2005). Parents who are well educated, however, adopt more complex constructions when talking to their babies. More clauses and more words per sentence dot their IDS speech (Huttenlocher and others, 2007). So these children are exposed to a richer set of learning experiences when being taught language via this kind of talk. But does IDS actually operate as a learning tool? Does it really help babies begin to master language? The answer seems to be yes.

Developmentalists presented infants with made-up words either in adult intonations or in infant-directed speech (Thiessen, Hill, & Saffran, 2005). When reinforced for showing that they heard the breaks between the nonsense words, the babies who heard the utterances spoken in IDS performed better. Listen carefully to someone speaking to an infant in "baby talk." Doesn't this mode of communication seem tailor-made to emphasize exactly where one word ends and another begins?

✿ TYING IT ALL TOGETHER

1. "We learn to speak by getting reinforced for saying what we want." "We are biologically programmed to learn language." "Babies are passionate to communicate." Identify the theoretical perspective reflected in each of these statements: Skinner's operant conditioning perspective; Chomsky's language acquisition device; a social-interactionist perspective on language.

2. Baby Ginny is 4 months old; Baby Jamal is about 7 months old; Baby Sam is 1 year old; Baby David is 2 years old. Identify each child's probable language stage by choosing from the following items: babbling; cooing; telegraphic speech; holophrases.

3. A friend makes fun of adults who use baby talk when speaking to infants. Given the information in this section, is she right?

Answers to the Tying It All Together questions can be found on the last page of this chapter.

infant-directed speech (IDS) The simplified, exaggerated, high-pitched tones that adults and children use to speak to infants that function to help teach language.

Final Thoughts: Babies "Connect" with the Human World

Have the studies in this chapter stimulated your interest in designing your own "out of the box" research to get into infants' heads? As developmentalists continue to use their brainpower to design creative studies and our knowledge of neural function expands, what more will we know about babies' brains in the next 10 or 20 years?

Just as we come equipped with a passion to master life, one basic message of this chapter is that—from face perception, to joint attention, to early language—we arrive on this planet with a strong impulse to connect with the human world. The next chapter focuses on this number-one infant (and adult) agenda by intensively exploring attachment relationships during our first two years of life.

SUMMARY

Setting the Context: Brain Blossoming and Sculpting

Because our uniquely large **cerebral cortex** develops mainly after birth, during the first two years of life, the brain mushrooms. **Axons** elongate and develop a fatty cover called myelin. **Dendrites** sprout branches and at **synapses** link up with other cells. **Synaptogenesis** and **myelination** program every infant ability and human skill. Although cortical development continues for two decades, the brain does not simply "develop more synapses." Each brain center undergoes a period of rapid synaptogenesis, followed by gradual pruning (or cutting back). Before pruning occurs, the brain is particularly **plastic,** allowing us to compensate for early brain insults—but synaptogenesis and learning occur throughout life.

Basic Newborn States

Eating undergoes dramatic changes during infancy. We emerge from the womb with **sucking** and **rooting reflexes,** which jump-start eating, as well as a set of other special birth **reflexes,** which disappear after the early months of life. Although the "everything into the mouth" phase of infancy can make life scary for caregivers, a 2-year-old's food caution can partially protect toddlers from poisoning themselves.

Because of its many health benefits, every public health organization advocates exclusive breast-feeding for the first six months of life—unless the mother has a serious disease. However, only a minority of women worldwide follow the recommendation. Upper-middle-class women in North America are more likely to breast-feed for longer. Low-income mothers (or any mothers) who must immediately return to work find it difficult to breast-feed.

After weaning, **undernutrition** is a serious concern in the developing world. Although global rates of **stunting** (height retardation due to chronic lack of adequate food) are declining, they are still alarmingly high. Because our country provides food-related entitlement programs—although very poor children may occasionally go hungry and have **micronutrient deficiencies**—in the United States, undernutrition and stunting are virtually unknown.

Crying is at its height during early infancy and declines around month 4 as the cortex comes on-line. **Colic,** excessive crying that disappears after early infancy, is basically a nervous system biological problem. Strategies for quieting crying babies include rocking, holding, **swaddling,** and providing an outlet for the urge to suck. Providing intense skin-to-skin contact through infant massage and **kangaroo care** not only helps quiet babies; these

practices also help infants—especially at-risk premature babies—physically grow. These practices may also generally insulate us against stress.

Sleep is the basic newborn state, and from the 18-hour, waking-every-few hours newborn pattern, babies gradually adjust to falling asleep at night. **REM sleep** lessens and shifts to the end of the cycle. Babies, however, really do not ever sleep through the night. At about 6 months, many learn **self-soothing,** putting themselves back to sleep when they wake up. Although the decision about whether to "let a baby cry it out" or respond immediately is personal, after the first months of life, self-soothing can be fostered by holding off immediately going into an infant's room. **Co-sleeping** (or bed sharing)—the norm in collectivist cultures—although still controversial in the West, is also a personal choice.

Sudden infant death syndrome (SIDS)—when a young baby stops breathing, often at night, and dies—is a main cause of developed-world infant mortality. SIDS has environmental correlates, being more common in homes where adults smoke and when babies lie face down. It also may have biological causes. Rates of SIDS deaths have been reduced due to a public health effort urging parents to put babies to sleep on their backs (not stomachs).

Sensory and Motor Development

The **preferential-looking paradigm** (exploring what objects babies look at) and **habituation** (the fact that we get less interested in looking at objects that are no longer "new") are used to determine what very young babies can see. Although at birth visual acuity is poor, it improves very rapidly. **Face-perception studies** show that newborns look at facelike stimuli, recognize their mothers, and even prefer good-looking people from the first weeks of life. **Depth perception** studies using the **visual cliff** show that although they notice differences in depth at a very young age, babies only get frightened of heights around the time they begin to crawl.

Infants' bodies lengthen and thin out as they grow. The cephalocaudal, proximodistal, and mass-to-specific principles apply to how the body changes and emerging infant motor milestones. Although they do progress through stages when getting to walking, babies show incredible creativity and variability and take one step forward and one step back when they first attain skills. There is no relationship between early motor development and later cognitive abilities, but habituation speed (signaling better memory for a stimulus) does correlate with later intelligence. Crawling is linked to widespread maturational changes, plus the need to **baby-proof** the home.

Cognition

During Piaget's **sensorimotor stage,** babies master the basics of physical reality through their senses and begin to symbolize and think. **Circular reactions** (habits the baby repeats) help babies pin down the basics of the physical world. **Primary circular reactions**—body-centered habits, such as sucking one's toes—emerge first. **Secondary circular reactions,** habits centered on making interesting external stimuli last (for example, batting mobiles), begin around month 4. **Tertiary circular reactions, "little-scientist"** activities—like spitting food at different velocities just to see where the oatmeal lands—are the hallmark of the toddler years. A major advance in reasoning that occurs around age 1 is **means–end behavior**—being able to do something new and different to get to a goal.

Piaget's most compelling concept is **object permanence**—knowing that objects still exist when you no longer see them. According to Piaget, this understanding develops gradually during the first years of life. When this knowledge is in the process of developing, infants make the **A-not-B error,** looking for an object in the place where they first found it, even if it has been hidden in another location before their eyes.

Using preferential looking, and watching babies' expressions of surprise at physically impossible events, researchers have discovered that babies know more about physical reality (and everything else) at a younger age than Piaget believed. Piaget's model of distinct qualitative stages also does not fit the continuous way knowledge unfolds. Developmentalists exploring **social cognition** find that **joint attention** and other signs of our crucial human ability to understand intentions appears as early as 9 to 12 months of age.

Language: The Endpoint of Infancy

Language, specifically our use of **grammar** and our ability to form infinitely different sentences, sets us apart from any other animal on earth. Although B. F. Skinner believed that we learn to speak through being reinforced, the more logical explanation is Chomsky's idea that we have a biologically built-in **language acquisition device (LAD). Social-interactionists** focus on the mutual passion of babies and adults to communicate.

First, babies coo, then **babble,** then use one-word **holophrases,** and finally, at 1½ or 2, progress to two-word combinations called **telegraphic speech.** Caregivers naturally use **infant-directed speech** (exaggerated intonations and simpler phrases) when they talk to babies. IDS helps teach infants to master this core human skill.

ANSWERS TO TYING IT ALL TOGETHER QUIZZES

Setting the Context: Brain Blossoming and Sculpting

1. Both Cortez and Ashley are right. We are unique in our massive cerebral cortex, in growing most of our brain outside of the womb, and in the fact that the human cortex does not reach its adult form for more than two decades.

2. Latisha is partly right (with regard to the myelin sheath) and partly wrong. Synaptic loss and neural pruning are essential to fostering our emerging abilities.

3. b. Their remarkable brain plasticity may allow young children to recruit neurons to compensate for the part of the brain that the surgeons remove.

4. Make your drawing from memory and then see how closely it mirrors the illustration in Figure 3.1 on page 76.

Basic Newborn States

1. d. All these statements are right. The sucking reflex (automatic sucking) and rooting reflex (head turning and sucking) are there at birth to help ensure the infant's survival. As the cortex matures, these reflexes disappear.

2. Your survey might include these kinds of questions: Do you plan to go back to work full-time right after the baby's birth? What is your household income and the highest school grade you've completed? (Low SES is related to prematurely abandoning this practice.) Do your employer and culture support breast-feeding? How do your family feel? Most important: What are your own priorities? Would you breast-feed your baby, even if engaging in this act was difficult or embarrassing? How vital do you think breast-feeding is to infant health?

3. Tell your sister and her husband to get a baby sling and carry the child around (kangaroo care) and be sure to feed the baby on demand, as these are proven techniques to reduce excessive crying. (Also, they might make heavy use of a pacifier and learn baby massage!) Give your relatives the encouraging information that colic is short-lived—typically going away by month 4.

4. Jorge's child is right on schedule, but he's wrong to say his child is sleeping through the night. The baby has simply learned to self-soothe.

5. The answers here will depend on the class.

Sensory and Motor Development

1. The *preferential-looking paradigm.*

2. a and b. At 2 months, Alicia's baby should show interest in the visual cliff, but no fear (a). At 7 months, the child should be afraid of the cliff (b).

3. Cotonia should cite the evidence from face-perception studies that babies understand remarkable things about faces from the first weeks of life. Jason might discuss the visual cliff studies. While babies can see differences in depth early on, infants only start to fear heights at about the time they become mobile.

4. Charlie's early motor skills will have no relationship to his later cognitive abilities, although his parents are right that babies, like their son, who habituate quickly do tend to do well on childhood intelligence tests.

5. Your answers might include installing electrical outlet covers; putting sharp, poisonous, and breakable objects out of a baby's reach; carpeting hard floor surfaces; padding furniture corners; installing latches on cabinet doors; and so on.

Cognition

1. Circular reaction = Darien; means–end behavior = Jai; object permanence = Sam.

2. a. Developmentalists criticize the *idea* that development occurs in qualitatively distinct stages; they haven't suggested different qualitative benchmarks.

Language: The Endpoint of Infancy

1. The idea that we learn language by getting reinforced reflects Skinner's operant conditioning perspective; Chomsky hypothesized that we are biologically programmed to acquire language; the social-interactionist perspective emphasizes the fact that babies and adults have a passion to communicate.

2. Baby Ginny is cooing; Baby Jamal is babbling; Baby Sam is speaking in holophrases (one-word stage); and Baby David is using telegraphic speech.

3. NO, your friend is wrong!!! Baby talk—or in developmental science terms, infant-directed speech (IDS)—gets an infant's attention and helps promote early language.

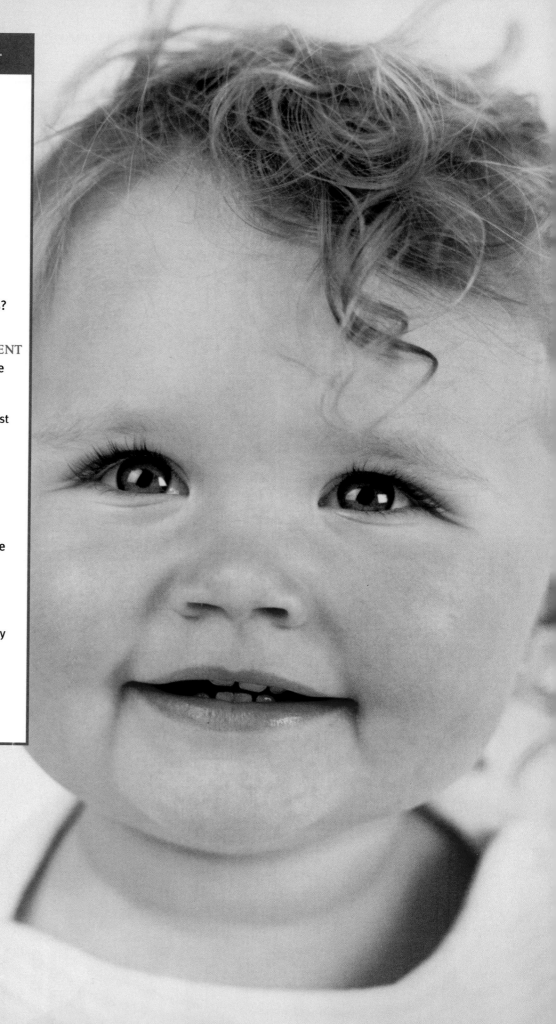

Chapter 4

CHAPTER OUTLINE

Infancy: Socioemotional Development

Now that we've talked to Kim during pregnancy and visited when Elissa was a young baby, let's catch up with mother and daughter now that Elissa is 15 months old.

Elissa had her first birthday in December. She's such a happy baby, but now if you take something away, it's like, "Why did you do that?" Pick her up. For a second everything is fine, and then her face changes and she squirms and her arms go out toward me. She's really busy walking, busy exploring, but she's always got an eye on me. The minute I make a motion to leave, she stops what she is doing and races near. I think Elissa has a stronger connection to her dad, because now that I'm working, Jeff has arranged his schedule to watch the baby late in the afternoon . . . but when she's tired or sick, it's still Mom.

It was very difficult to go back to work. You hear terrible things about day care, stories of babies being neglected. I looked at the center in town, but there were just so many kids. Finally, I settled on a neighbor who watches a few toddlers in her home. I saw how much this woman loves children and felt secure knowing who would be caring for my child. But you still get worried, feel guilty. The worst was Elissa's reaction—the way she screamed the first week when I left her off. But it's obvious that she's happy now. Every morning she runs smiling to Ms. Marie's arms.

It's bittersweet to see my baby separating, running into the world, becoming her own little person—with some very strong likes and dislikes. The clashes are becoming more frequent now that I'm turning up the discipline, expecting more in terms of behavior from my "big girl." But the main thing is that it's hard to be apart. I think about Elissa 50 million times during the day. I speed home to see her. I can't wait to see her glowing face in the window, how she jumps up and down, and we run to kiss and cuddle again.

Imagine being Kim, with your child the center of your life. Imagine being Elissa, wanting to be independent but vitally needing your mother close. In this chapter, we focus on **attachment,** the powerful bond of love between caregiver and child.

My discussion of attachment—which takes up much of this chapter—starts a conversation that we will continue throughout this book. Attachment is not only the emotional basis of infancy, but of all of human life. After exploring this core one-to-one relationship, we turn outward to explore the wider world, first examining how that basic marker, socioeconomic status, affects young children's development, then spotlighting day care, the setting where so many developed-world babies spend their days.

The last section of this chapter focuses directly on **toddlerhood,** the famous time lasting roughly from age 1 to 2 1/2 years. (Your tip-off that a child is a toddler is that classic endearing "toddling" gait that characterizes the second year of life.)

Attachment: The Basic Life Bond

Perhaps you remember being intensely in love. You may be in that wonderful state right now. You cannot stop fantasizing about your significant other. Your moves blend with your partner's. You connect in a unique way. Knowing that this person is there gives you confidence. You can conquer the world. You feel uncomfortable when you are separated. Your world depends on having your lover close. Now, you have some sense of how Elissa feels about her mother and the powerful emotions that flow from Kim to her to child.

Setting the Context: How Developmentalists (Slowly) Got Attached to Attachment

During much of the twentieth century, U.S. psychologists seemed oddly indifferent to these intense feelings. In an age when psychology was dominated by behaviorist ideology, studying love, the province of the poets, seemed too unscientific. Behaviorists minimized our human need for attachment, suggesting that the reason babies wanted to be close to their mothers was because this "maternal reinforcing stimulus" provided food. Worse yet, you may remember from Chapter 1 that the early behaviorist John Watson seemed *hostile* to attachment when he crusaded against the dangers of "too much" mother love:

> When I hear a mother say "bless its little heart" when it falls down, I . . . have to walk a block or two to let off steam. . . . Can't she train herself to substitute a kindly word . . . for . . . the pick up . . . the coddling? . . . Can't she learn to keep away from the child a large part of the day? [And then he made this memorable statement:] . . . I sometimes wish that we could live in a community of homes [where] . . . we could have the babies fed and bathed each week by a different nurse. (!)
>
> (Watson, 1928/1972, pp. 82–83)

European psychoanalysts, such as John Bowlby, felt differently. They were discovering that attachment was far from dangerous. It was crucial to infant life.

Consider a heart-rending mid-twentieth-century film that showed the fate of babies living in orphanages (Blum, 2002; Karen, 1998). In these clean, impeccably maintained institutions, Watson and the behaviorists would have predicted that infants should thrive. So why did babies lie listless on cots—unable to eat, literally withering away?

Now, consider the fact that ethologists—the forerunners of today's evolutionary psychologists—were observing that *every* species had a biologically preprogrammed attachment response (or drive to be physically close to their mothers) that appeared at a specific point soon after birth. When the famous ethologist Konrad Lorenz (1935) arranged to become this attachment-eliciting stimulus for a set of goslings, the outcome was the classic photograph you can see here. Lorenz became the adored Pied Piper the baby geese were willing to follow to the ends of the earth.

However, it took a rebellious psychologist named Harry Harlow, who studied monkeys, to convince U.S. psychologists that the behaviorist meal-dispenser model of mother love was wrong. In a classic study, Harlow (1958) separated baby monkeys from their

The adoring expressions on the faces of parents and babies as they gaze at each other make it obvious why the attachment relationship in infancy is our basic model for romantic love in adulthood.

Ethologist Konrad Lorenz arranged to become the first living thing that newly hatched geese saw at their species-specific critical time for attachment. He then became the goslings' "mother," the object whom they felt compelled never to let out of their sight.

Rick Gomez/Masterfile

Nina Leen/Time Life Pictures

mothers at birth and raised them in a cage with a wire-mesh "mother" (which offered food from a milk bottle attached to its chest) and a cloth "mother" (which was soft and provided contact comfort). The babies stayed glued to the cloth mother, making occasional trips to eat from the wire mom. In stressful situations, they scurried to the cloth mother for comfort. Love had won hands down over getting fed!

Moreover, there were serious psychological consequences for the monkeys who were raised without their moms. The animals couldn't have sex. They were frightened of their peers. After being artificially inseminated and giving birth, the "motherless mothers" were uncaring, abusive parents. One mauled her baby so badly that it later died (Harlow and others, 1966; Harlow, C. M., 1986).

Then, in the late 1960s, John Bowlby put the evidence together—the orphanage findings, Lorenz's ethological studies, Harlow's research, his own clinical work with children who had been hospitalized or separated from their mothers (Hinde, 2005). In a landmark series of books, Bowlby (1969, 1973, 1980) argued that there is no such thing as "excessive mother love." Having a loving **primary attachment figure** is crucial to our development. It is essential to living fully at any age. By the final decades of the twentieth century, attachment moved to the front burner in developmental science. It remains front and center today.

In Harlow's landmark study, baby monkeys clung to the cloth-covered "mother" (which provided contact comfort) as they leaned over to feed from the wire-mesh "mother"—vividly refuting the behaviorist idea that infants become "attached" to the reinforcing stimulus that feeds them.

Exploring the Attachment Response

Bowlby (1969, 1973) made his case for the crucial importance of attachment based on evolutionary theory. He believed that, as is true of other species, human beings have a critical period when the attachment response "comes out." As was true of Lorenz's ducks, he argued, attachment is biologically built into our genetic code to allow us to survive. Although the attachment response is programmed to emerge during our first years of life, **proximity-seeking behavior**—our need to make contact with an attachment figure—is activated whenever our survival is threatened at *any age.*

Bowlby believed that threats to survival come in two categories. They may be activated by our internal state. When Elissa clings only to her mother, Kim knows her baby must be ill or tired. When you go to the hospital, you make sure that your family is by your side. You want to know that you can easily reach your "significant other" by cell phone when you have a fever or the flu.

They also may be evoked by dangers in the external world. When we are children, it's a huge dog at the park or a nightmare that causes us to run anxiously into our parent's arms. As adults, it's a professor's nasty comment or a humiliating experience at work that may provoke a frantic call to our primary attachment figure, be it our spouse, our parents, or our best friend.

Although we all need to touch base with our significant others when we feel threatened, adults and older children can be separated from their attachment figures for some length of time. During infancy and early childhood, simply being physically apart from a caregiver causes intense distress. Now, let's trace step-by-step how human attachment unfolds.

Attachment Milestones

According to Bowlby, during their first three months of life, babies are in the **preattachment phase.** Remember that during this reflex-dominated time infants have yet to really wake up to the world. However, at around 2 months there is a milestone called the **social smile.** Bowlby believed that this first real smile does not show attachment to *a* person. Because it pops up in response to any human face, it is just one example of an automatic reflex, such as sucking or grasping, that evokes care and love from adults.

attachment The powerful bond of love between a caregiver and child (or between any two individuals).

toddlerhood The important transitional stage after babyhood, from roughly 1 year to 2 1/2 years of age; defined by an intense attachment to caregivers and by an urgent need to become independent.

primary attachment figure The closest person in a child's or adult's life.

proximity-seeking behavior Acting to maintain physical contact or to be close to an attachment figure.

preattachment phase The first phase of John Bowlby's developmental attachment sequence, during the first three months of life, when infants show no visible signs of attachment.

social smile The first real smile, occurring at about 2 months of age.

Kevin Fitzgerald/Getty Images

A baby's first social smile, which appears at the sight of any face at about 2 to 3 months of age, is biologically programmed to delight adults and charm them into providing love and care.

Still, a baby's eagerly awaited first smile can be an incredible experience if you are a parent. Suddenly, your relationship with your child shifts to a different plane. Now, I have a confession to make: During my first two months as a new mother, I was worried, as I did not feel anything for this beautiful child I had waited so long to adopt. I date Thomas's first endearing smile as the defining event in my lifelong attachment romance.

At roughly 4 months of age, infants enter a transitional period, called **attachment in the making.** At this time, recall from my discussion of Piaget's sensorimotor substages, the environment-focused secondary circular reactions are unfolding. The cortex is coming on-line. Babies may show a slight preference for their primary caregiver. But still, an outgoing 4- or 5-month-old can be the ultimate party person, happy to be cuddled by anyone—Grandma, a next-door neighbor, or a stranger at the mall.

By around 7 or 8 months of age, this changes. At this age, as you saw in Chapter 3, babies are hunting for hidden objects—showing that they have the cognitive skills to miss their caregivers. Now that they can crawl, or walk holding on to furniture, children can really get hurt. The stage is set for **clear-cut** (or *focused*) **attachment**—the beginning of the full-blown attachment response. This phase of intense attachment will last throughout the toddler years.

Separation anxiety signals this normal milestone. When Elissa was about 7 or 8 months old, Kim probably noticed one day that her baby got upset when she left the room. Then, **stranger anxiety** appears. As you saw in the chapter-opening vignette, infants get agitated when any unfamiliar person picks them up. So, as children travel toward their first birthday, the universal friendliness of early infancy is a thing of the past. While they may still joyously gurgle at the world from their caregiver's arms, it's normal for babies to forbid any "stranger"—the next-door neighbor or even a loving Grandma who lives far away and flies in for a visit—to invade their space.

Between ages 1 and 2, the distress reaches a peak. A child may cling and cry when mom or dad makes a motion to leave. It's as if an invisible string connects the caregiver and the child. In one classic study at a park, 1-year-olds tended to play within a certain distance from their mothers. Interestingly, this zone of optimum comfort (about 200 feet) was identical for both the parent and the child (Anderson, 1972).

To see these changes in action, pick up a young baby (such as a 4-month-old) and an older infant (perhaps a baby about 10 months of age) and compare their reactions. Then, observe 1-year-olds at a local park. Can you measure this attachment zone of comfort? Do you notice the busy, exploring toddlers periodically checking back to make sure a caregiver is still there?

attachment in the making The second phase of John Bowlby's developmental attachment sequence, lasting from about 4 to 7 months of age, when infants show a slight preference for their primary caregiver.

clear-cut attachment The critical period for human attachment, lasting from roughly 7 months of age through toddlerhood, characterized by separation anxiety, the need to have a caregiver physically close, and stranger anxiety.

separation anxiety The main signal of clear-cut attachment at about 7 months of age, when a baby gets visibly upset by a primary caregiver's departure.

stranger anxiety A signal of the onset of clear-cut attachment at about 7 months of age, when a baby becomes wary of unfamiliar people and refuses to be held by anyone other than a primary caregiver.

Spencer Grant/Photo Edit, Inc.

A few months ago, this child would probably not have objected to being held by his family's next-door neighbor; but everything changes at 7 or 8 months of age, during the phase of clear-cut attachment, when stranger anxiety emerges.

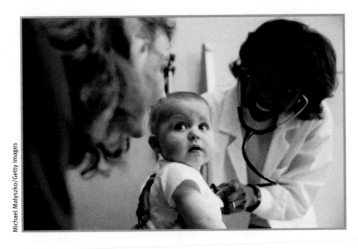

As she *social references* her mom, this baby is getting important data: Is that giant putting the strange object on my chest really safe?

Social referencing is the term developmentalists use to describe this checking-back behavior. Social referencing helps alert the baby to which situations are dangerous and which ones are safe. ("Should I climb up this slide, Mommy?" "Does Daddy think this object is okay to explore?")

Imagine you are a baby who is beginning to social reference. Wouldn't it be logical to be especially attuned to your caregiver's negative facial cues ("That's bad! Don't go near that!") as you explored the world? To test this idea, researchers trained mothers to show happy, calm, or disgusted facial expressions while their 12-month-olds approached a new toy. Simultaneously, they took EEG recordings from the babies' brains. As they predicted, neural activity was most intense when a parent made the upset face (Carver & Vaccaro, 2007). Perhaps because it helps alert us to danger, our species seems pre-wired to be highly attuned to distressing social signals, such as anger or anxiety (LoBue, 2009). But there is a fascinating age when this sensitivity shifts. As I will describe in Chapter 13, the elderly screen out negative emotions and preferentially focus on happy events!

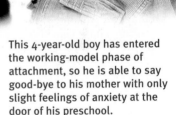

Returning to attachment—and the first two years of life—when does the clear-cut attachment response, or need to be physically close to a caregiver, go away? Although the marker is hazy, children typically leave this stage at about age 3. They still care just as much about their primary attachment figure. But now, according to Bowlby, they have the cognitive skills to carry a **working model,** or internal representation, of this number-one person in their minds (Bretherton, 2005).

This 4-year-old boy has entered the working-model phase of attachment, so he is able to say good-bye to his mother with only slight feelings of anxiety at the door of his preschool.

The bottom-line message is that our human critical period for attachment is timed to unfold during our most vulnerable time of life—when children are first moving into the world and are most in danger of getting hurt. Moreover, what compensates parents for the frustrations of having a Piagetian "little scientist" is enormous gratifications. Just when a toddler is continually messing up the house and saying "No!" parents know that their child's world revolves totally around them.

A toddler's messiness is easy for a grandfather to tolerate when she looks up at him with love—showing why the attachment response overshadows everything else during Piaget's "little-scientist" stage.

social referencing A baby's practice of checking back and monitoring a caregiver's expressions for cues as to how to behave in potentially dangerous exploration situations; linked to the onset of crawling and clear-cut attachment.

working model According to Bowlby's theory, the mental representation of a caregiver that allows children beyond age 3 to be physically apart from a primary caregiver and predicts their behavior in relationships.

Do children differ in the way they express this priceless sense of connection? And if so, what might these differences mean about the quality of the infant–parent bond?

Attachment Styles

These were the questions Mary Ainsworth set out to answer when she developed a classic test of attachment—the **Strange Situation** (Ainsworth, 1967; Ainsworth and others, 1978).

The Strange Situation procedure begins when a caregiver—typically the mother—and a 1-year-old enter a room full of toys. After the child is given time to explore, an unfamiliar adult enters the room. Then, the mother leaves the baby alone with the stranger and, a few minutes later, returns to comfort the child. Next, the mom leaves the baby totally alone for a minute; the stranger enters; and finally, the mother returns (see Figure 4.1). By observing the child's reactions to these stressful separations and reunions through a one-way mirror, developmentalists categorize infants as either *securely* or *insecurely attached*.

Securely attached children use their mother as a secure base, or anchor, to confidently venture out to explore the toys. When she leaves, they may or may not become highly distressed. Most important, when she returns, their eyes light up with joy. As I described with Elissa when Kim comes home, their close relationship is apparent in the way they run and melt into their mothers' arms. **Insecurely attached** children react in the following three ways (see Figure 4.2):

- Infants classified as **avoidant** seem excessively detached. They rarely show signs of separation anxiety. Most important, they show little feeling—positive or negative—when their primary attachment figure returns. They seem wooden, unreactive, without much sense of attachment at all.

- Babies with an **anxious-ambivalent attachment** are at the opposite end of the spectrum—clingy, overly nervous, too frightened to freely explore the toys. Terribly distressed by their mother's departure, these infants may show contradictory emotions when she returns—clinging and then striking out in anger. Often, they are inconsolable, unable to be effectively comforted when their attachment figure comes back.

- Children showing a **disorganized attachment** behave in a bizarre manner. In this worst-case scenario (which tends to be found, most frequently, in cases of abuse), the child freezes, runs around erratically, or may look frightened and try to flee when the caregiver returns.

Developmentalists point out that the insecure attachments you can see in Figure 4.2 do not show a weakness in the *underlying* sense of connection. Avoidant infants

Strange Situation A procedure developed by Mary Ainsworth to measure variations in attachment security at age 1, involving a series of planned separations and reunions with a primary caregiver.

secure attachment The ideal attachment response, when a 1-year-old child responds with joy at being reunited with the primary caregiver in the Strange Situation.

insecure attachment A deviation from the normally joyful response to being reunited with the primary caregiver in the Strange Situation, signaling a problem in the caregiver–child relationship.

avoidant attachment An insecure attachment style characterized by a child's indifference to the primary caregiver when they are reunited in the Strange Situation.

anxious-ambivalent attachment An insecure attachment style characterized by a child's intense distress at separation and by anger and great difficulty being soothed when reunited with the primary caregiver in the Strange Situation.

disorganized attachment An insecure attachment style characterized by responses such as freezing or fear when a child is reunited with the primary caregiver in the Strange Situation.

synchrony The reciprocal aspect of the attachment relationship, with a caregiver and infant responding emotionally to each other in a sensitive, exquisitely attuned way.

Both photos: Mary D. Ainsworth

Separation

Reunion

FIGURE 4.1: The Strange Situation: These scenes are from the original Strange Situation study. At left, the baby cries frantically after the mother and the stranger have left the room. At right, the baby is reunited with the mother as the stranger looks on.

Secure Attachment The child is thrilled to see the mother.

Avoidant Attachment The child is unresponsive to the mother.

Anxious-Ambivalent Attachment The child cannot be calmed by the mother.

Disorganized Attachment The child looks frightened by the mother or behaves bizarrely.

FIGURE 4.2: **Secure and insecure attachments: A summary photo series**

are just as bonded to their caregivers as babies ranked secure. Anxious-ambivalent infants are not more closely attached even though they show such intense separation distress. To take an analogy from adult life, when a person who cares deeply about you pretends to be indifferent, is this individual less in love? Is a lover who can't let his partner out of sight more attached than a person who allows his significant other to have an independent life? Although its outward expression differs, *every* infant is closely attached.

The Attachment Dance

Look at a baby and a caregiver together and it is almost as if you are seeing a dance. The partners are alert to each other's signals. They know when to come on stronger and when to back off. They are absorbed and captivated, oblivious to the world. This blissful **synchrony,** or sense of being totally emotionally in tune, is what makes the infant–mother relationship our ultimate model for romantic love (Bornstein & Tamis-LeMonda, 2001). Ainsworth and Bowlby believed that the parent's "dancing potential," or sensitivity to a baby's signals, produces secure attachments (Ainsworth and others, 1978). Were they correct?

The blissful rapture, the sense of being totally engrossed and in tune with each other, is the reason why developmentalists use the word *synchrony* to describe parent–infant attachment.

THE CAREGIVER Decades of studies suggest that the answer is yes. Sensitive caregivers tend to have babies who are securely attached. Parents who are overly intrusive, misread their baby's signals, and especially those who are depressed, are more likely to have infants ranked insecure (Raikes & Thompson, 2006).

Depressed parents react to their babies' visual cues at a slower tempo—so they are less in sync with their infant's natural "dance" (Beebe and others, 2008). Moreover, to effectively dance, it seems crucial to be able to reach out to your baby with joy. In one longitudinal study, researchers found new mothers who were unusually responsive to infant photos showing happy expressions later played with their toddlers in the most sensitive way (Donovan and others, 2007). Watch the dance of attachment. What you

probably notice is a caregiver's incredible pleasure in seeing her baby's delight. Isn't this thrill in seeing our loved one happy what being in love is *really* all about?

Still, there clearly are other forces involved in attachment, as the most joyful, sensitive caregivers sometimes have children who are insecurely attached. Some depressed, poorly dancing parents have securely attached daughters and sons (Barry, Kochanska, & Philibert, 2008). The main reason, as you may have guessed, is that there are *two* partners in the dance.

THE CHILD Listen to any mother comparing her babies ("Sara was fussy; Matthew is much easier to soothe") and you will realize that not all infants are born with the same dancing talent. Specifically, babies differ in their **temperament**—meaning their characteristic, inborn behavioral styles of approaching the world.

In a pioneering study, developmentalists classified a group of middle-class babies into three temperamental styles: *Easy* babies—the majority of the children—had rhythmic eating and sleeping patterns; they were happy and easily soothed. More wary babies were labeled *slow to warm up*. One in 10 babies were ranked as *difficult*—hypersensitive, unusually agitated, extremely reactive to every sight and sound (Thomas & Chess, 1977; Thomas, Chess, & Birch, 1968). Here is an example:

> My 5-month-old wakes up screaming from every nap. Everything seems to bother her—bright sunlight, a rough blanket, any sudden noise. I thought colic was supposed to go away by month 3. I'm getting discouraged and depressed.

Now, look back at the stressful experiences a baby must go through during the Strange Situation. Do you see why some developmentalists have argued that biologically based differences in temperamental "reactivity"—not the quality of a mother's caregiving—determine attachment status at age 1? (See, for example, Kagan, 1984.)

Does a baby's biology (nature) or poor caregiving (nurture) produce insecure attachments? As you might imagine—given the nature-plus-nurture message of this book—the answer is, a little of both. In one fascinating study, researchers found that biologically hardy babies—those who had a gene associated with resilience to stress—were securely attached, even with less sensitive parents. However, a genetically vulnerable baby needed extremely responsive care-giving to be classified as secure (Barry, Kochanska, & Philibert, 2008). So an incredibly nurturing mother or father can shift a temperamentally "at risk" infant from insecure to securely attached.

But with the most biologically vulnerable infants, there is a limit to how much the most sensitive parent can achieve (Kochanska & Coy, 2002). Suppose a child was extremely premature or autistic, or had some serious disease. Would it be fair to label the baby's attachment issues as the caregiver's fault?

Moreover, because "it takes two to tango" (that is, the dance is bidirectional), a child's temperament affects the parent's sensitivity, too. To use an analogy from real-life dancing, imagine waltzing with a partner who couldn't keep time with the music; or think of a time when you tried to soothe a person who was too agitated to connect. Even a prize-winning dancer or someone with world-class relationship skills would feel incompetent and inept.

THE CAREGIVER'S OTHER ATTACHMENTS And, to continue the analogy, it takes more than two to tango. Just as a woman's attitudes about being pregnant depend on feeling supported by the wider world (recall Chapter 2), it is difficult to be a sensitive caregiver if your other attachment relationships are not working out. When mothers are unhappily married, for instance, their babies are more likely to be rated as insecurely attached (Moss and others, 2005.)

Figure 4.3, illustrating how the caregiver, the baby, and the parent's other relationships interact to shape attachment, brings home the importance of adopting a

temperament A person's characteristic, inborn style of dealing with the world.

FIGURE 4.3: **Three pathways to insecure attachment** Above left: The mother is too depressed to connect. Above center: The child has temperamental vulnerabilities. Above right: The caregiver's other attachment relationships make it difficult to "dance" with her baby.

developmental systems approach. The quality of the attachment dance is shaped by different forces. By assuming that problems were due simply to the parent's personality, Bowlby and Ainsworth were taking an excessively limited view. What about the general theory? Is attachment to a primary caregiver universal? Do infants in different countries fall into the same categories of secure and insecure?

Is Infant Attachment Universal?

From Chicago to Capetown, from Naples to New York, Bowlby's and Ainsworth's ideas about attachment get high marks (van IJzendoorn & Sagi, 1999). Babies around the world do get attached to a primary caregiver at roughly the same age. Interestingly, as you can see in Figure 4.4, the percentages of infants ranked secure in different countries are remarkably similar—clustering at roughly 60 to 70 percent (Sroufe, 2000; Tomlinson, Cooper, & Murray, 2005).

The most amazing validation of the universal quality of attachment comes from the Efé, a close-knit, communal hunter-gatherer people living in Africa. Efé newborns freely nurse from any available lactating woman, even when their own parent is around. They are dressed, bathed, and cared for by the whole community. But, because they sleep with their mothers, Efé babies still develop a primary attachment to a mom at the typical age! (See van IJzendoorn & Sagi, 1999.)

So far, you might be thinking that during the phase of clear-cut attachment, babies are connected to only one person. You would be wrong. Elissa was attached to her father and day-care provider, as well as to Kim. However, typically there is a single caregiver whom the child most prefers. This number-one attachment figure does *not* have to be the mother. It might be Grandma, or the father, or the day-care provider—the person the baby spends the most time with, or the caregiver who seems most attentive to the infant's needs. And, just as you and I may connect differently with each of our "significant others," a baby

FIGURE 4.4: **Snapshots of attachment security (and insecurity) around the world:** Around the world, roughly 60 to 70 percent of 1-year-olds are classified as securely attached—although there are interesting differences in the percentages of babies falling into the different insecure categories.

Source: van IJzendoorn & Sagi (1999), p. 729.

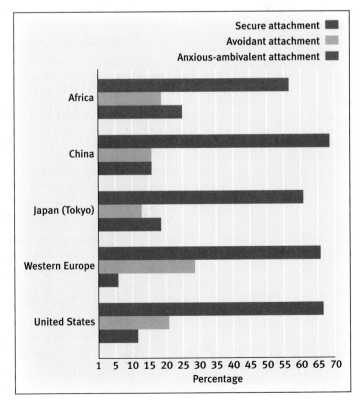

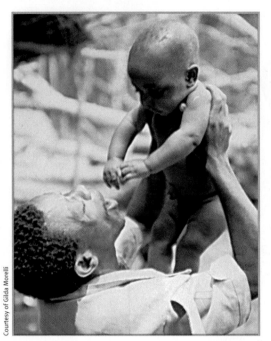

This new member of the Efé people of central Africa will be lovingly cared for by the whole community, males as well as females, from his first minutes of life. Because he sleeps with his mother, however, at the "right" age he will develop his primary attachment to her.

can be securely attached to his father and insecurely attached to his mom (Grossmann, Grossmann, & Zimmermann, 1999). The child's attachment to the primary caregiver predicts development best. Now, let's look at that important question: How *does* attachment relate to the way children develop and behave?

Does Infant Attachment Predict Success in the Wider World?

Bowlby's core argument, when he developed his concept of the working model, is that our attachment relationships in infancy serve as an inner model that determines how we relate to other people and feel about ourselves (Bretherton, 2005). A baby who acts avoidant with his parents will be aloof and uncaring with friends; he may be unresponsive to a teacher's demands. An anxious-ambivalent infant will behave in a needy way in her other love relationships. A secure baby is set up to succeed socially.

In general, research supports Bowlby's idea. Babies who are securely attached are more confident and mature (NICHD Early Child Care Research Network, 2006). Insecure attachment predicts having problems controlling one's emotions and social difficulties down the road (Donovan and others, 2007; Kochanska, Philibert, & Barry, 2009; O'Connor & McCartney, 2006; Stacks, 2007; Vando and others, 2008).

However, there is a strong caution. The link between infant attachment security and how a child behaves in other areas of life is strongest when we study behavior over a short timeframe. As we get further away from the testing date, predictions are less reliable (Sroufe and others, 2003). So, yes, you can get insights into how your 1-year-old nephew will act in preschool or day care from seeing how he relates to his mom and dad. However, you are on shakier ground if you want to extend that crystal ball much further into his future life.

One obvious reason is that we may revise our working model over time as our dance with our parents changes. How much does attachment change as children travel from infancy to adult life?

Does Infant Attachment Predict Adult Relationships?

Imagine your challenge as a researcher who wanted to study attachment security from infancy to adulthood—the time and expense involved in testing babies in the Strange Situation, and then tracking families for decades; the need to develop new age-appropriate measures of attachment as the children grow up. Luckily, we do have these incredible infant-to-adult studies (Grossmann, Grossmann, & Kindler, 2005; Sagi-Schwartz, & Aviezer, 2005; Simpson and others, 2007). Let's look at one investigation and explore the lessons it offers us about love and life.

In the early 1970s, a University of Minnesota research team recruited low-income women during their pregnancies (Sroufe and others, 2002, 2003). Then, they tracked the lives of these impoverished mothers and their babies for almost 30 years. By age 19, 90 percent of the children had experienced at least one disruptive attachment-related event—from parental drug or alcohol problems to neglect, abuse, or serious maternal depression—at some point during their childhood years.

Although the majority of the 1-year-olds were initially securely attached, these stresses took their toll. By age 19, the fraction of children labeled secure slid down to 1 in 3. Moreover, as you might imagine, children who had experienced the most intense

Courtesy of Gilda Morelli

stress were most likely to have become insecure (Weinfield, Sroufe, & Egeland, 2000).

As an example, let's look at the life of a child named Tony, whom the researchers ranked as securely attached during infancy. In preschool and early elementary school, Tony, like many other securely attached children in the study, was succeeding at school and with friends. Then, as Tony was approaching adolescence, his parents went through a difficult divorce, and his mother began to rely on her son as the man of the house.

When Tony was 14, tragedy struck again: Tony's mother was killed in a car accident. To compound his loss, Tony's father moved to another state, taking his other two children and leaving Tony with an aunt. It should come as no surprise that as a teenager Tony, robbed of every attachment figure, got into serious trouble in school and at home. Angry and depressed throughout this time, Tony was rated as insecurely attached. But when Tony was retested at age 26, he was recovering. He met a loving woman and got married. He was a devoted father. Although Tony's attachment status is still classified as avoidant/insecure, he's on the path to becoming more secure (Sroufe and others, 2005).

So the most blissful infancy cannot inoculate us against unhappy experiences—and attachment insecurity—later on. The good news is that children can also move in the opposite direction, becoming secure after facing terrible traumas during their first years of life (Sroufe and others, 2005). Perhaps you have a friend whose family fled the fighting in a war-torn country, like Rwanda or Iraq, and now is excelling socially as a young adult.

For an ultimate good-news story, let's return to Harlow's motherless monkeys, who grew up without any attachment figure at all. In an effort to bring these animals back into the social world, Harlow's research team put young monkeys into a cage with the traumatized animals. (Older animals routinely rejected their socially clueless agemates.) After spending months being nuzzled and played with by their "therapists," the monkeys stopped huddling in corners. They were playing just like their peers. The motherless monkeys could even be taught mother love. When a baby hung in there and clung to an uncaring mother, the infant often brought the parent emotionally back to life! (See C. M. Harlow, 1986.)

In Harlow's experiments, female monkeys that had been raised in isolation did not know what to do with their babies, ignoring or even attacking them. However, if an infant kept clinging to its mother and nuzzling her, there was a reasonable chance that it could teach its mother how to respond with love.

Wrapping up Attachment

The bottom-line message is that early life is more of a sensitive period (or zone of special sensitivity) for attachments than a make-or-break time when inadequate mothering leaves permanent scars. And, while it does provide us with a beautiful beginning, being securely attached in infancy is no guarantee of staying secure throughout life. Finally, when we see insecure attachments, we should beware of automatically blaming the mother. The quality of the attachment dance depends on a variety of forces, from the baby's temperament to the mother's other life dances. Now, we turn to explore two other crucial influences that can affect a baby's attachment relationships and everything else: poverty and day care.

TYING IT ALL TOGETHER

1. List an example or two of "proximity seeking in distress" in your own life within the past few months.

2. Baby Muriel is 1 month old, Baby Janine is 5 months old, and Baby Ted is 1 year old. List each infant's phase of attachment.

low income According to child advocates, the real minimum income it takes for a family to decently make ends meet in the United States; defined as twice the poverty line.

3. Match each of these terms to the correct definition: (1) social referencing; (2) working model; (3) synchrony; (4) Strange Situation.

   a. A researcher measures a child's attachment at age 1 in a series of separations and reunions with the mother.
   b. A toddler keeps looking back at the parent while exploring at a playground.
   c. An elementary school child keeps an image of her parent in mind to calm herself when she gets on the school bus in the morning.
   d. A mother and baby relate to each other as if they are totally in tune.

4. Your cousin is the primary caregiver of her 1-year-old son. On a recent visit to her house, you notice that the baby shows no emotion when his mother leaves the room, and—more important—seems totally indifferent when she returns. How might you classify this child's attachment?

5. Manuel is arguing for the validity of attachment theory as spelled out by Bowlby and Ainsworth. Which argument should Manuel make (that is, which alternative is true)?

   a. Infants around the world get attached to a primary caregiver at roughly the same age
   b. A child's attachment status as of age 1 never changes.

You can find Answers to the Tying It All Together questions on the last page of this chapter.

FIGURE 4.5: **Poverty rates by age, 2007:** Very young children are more likely to be poor than almost any other age group in the United States. (The poverty rates for women over age 75, although not shown on the chart, are higher.)

Source: Bureau of the Census, Current Population Survey, Annual Social and Economic Supplement, http:pubdb3.census.gov, retrieved Nov. 22, 2008.

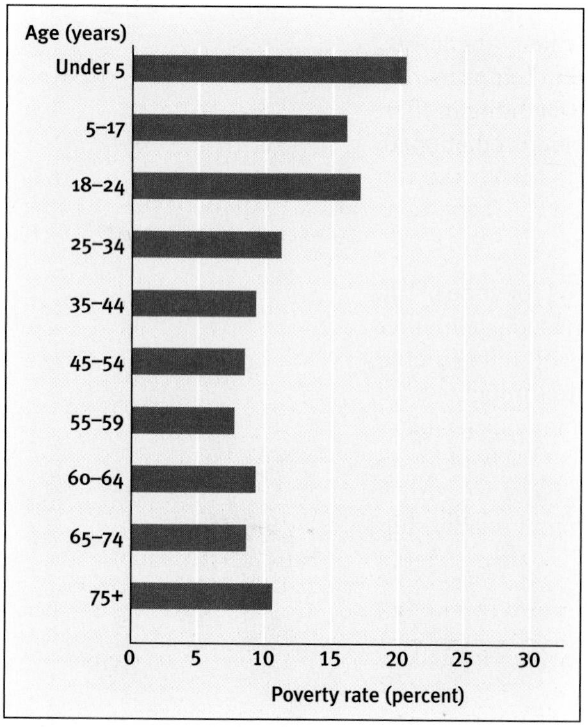

Note: These statistics refer to data collected before the 2008 economic meltdown. As an exercise, you might want to check out the comparable U.S. Census Bureau poverty rates for today.

Settings for Development

What happens to children in the United States, such as those from the Minnesota Study, who spend their first years of life in poverty? And what about that crucial wider-world setting of early childhood—day care?

The Impact of Poverty in the United States

In Chapter 3, I examined the physical effects of extreme poverty—the alarming rates of stunting in the least developed regions of the world. In the United States, you may remember, we don't have the kind of poverty that causes undernutrition. Still, being poor during early childhood can seriously compromise a developing life. What fraction of American infants and toddlers live in poverty? How does poverty affect children's well-being?

The Prevalence of Poverty

The federal government defines the poverty line as an income level that theoretically allows people to pay for shelter, clothing, and food, with a small bit of money left for extras. In 2007, for instance, a U.S. family of four with an annual income of $21,650 or less qualified as living in poverty. Unfortunately, however, if you estimate how much it *really costs* to live in your community, you will understand why child advocates argue that the official figure is set too low. It takes roughly *twice* that income, or about $42,400 a year, for a family that size to really make ends meet (Fass & Cauthen, NCCP, 2008). So let's consider both the official marker and this cut-off for **low income**—the funds it *actually* requires to live—as we explore how common early childhood poverty is in the United States.

What percentage of U.S infants and toddlers are financially deprived? In 2007, using the stringent government statistic, the answer was roughly 1 out of every 5. Adopting the low-income criterion, the figure rose to an amazing 43 percent (Douglas-Hall & Chau, 2008)! Worse yet, as you can see in Figure 4.5, poverty is especially common in the first five years of life. Notice that young children are more likely to live in poverty than all other age groups in the United States (except women over age 75) (Bureau of the Census, 2008).

One cause is single motherhood. It is very difficult for a woman who is raising a baby alone to work, pay for child care, and still have money to make ends meet. Inadequate wages are also to blame (Fass & Cauthen, 2008). The kinds of entry-level jobs (those paying 8 or 10 dollars an hour) available to many people in their early twenties can't adequately support a family—even when a parent works full time. In fact, in 2007, more than half of all children living in low-income families had a mother or father with a full-time job (Douglas-Hall & Chau, 2007).

Poverty and Development

Living in poverty negatively affects children's mental health (Ashford and others, 2008; Wadsworth & Santiago, 2008). It can seriously impair the dance of attachment, as you will see below. However, early childhood poverty has its most devastating impact on academic performance (McCartney and others, 2007; Mistry and others, 2004). You might be surprised to know that simply being poor during the first four years of life makes it statistically much less likely for a child to graduate from high school (Duncan & Brooks-Gunn, 2000).

Relating in a sensitive, caring way to your baby (and other children) can be very difficult if you are an impoverished, stressed-out single mom.

Why can early-childhood poverty have such enduring effects? One possibility is that it is difficult to make up for what you have lost if you enter school "left behind," not knowing your letters or numbers, without those basic building blocks required to succeed (McCartney and others, 2007; Votruba-Drzal, 2006). Low-income children are less likely to go to museums, have enriching toys, or attend quality preschools (Gerber, Whitebook, & Weinstein, 2007; McCartney and others, 2007). As one social critic powerfully put it: Who is more likely to do well on reading and math tests, children who "spent the years from 2 to 4 in lovely Montessori schools . . . in which . . . attentive grown-ups read to them from story books . . . or the ones who spent those years at home sitting in front of a TV . . .?" (Kozol, 2005, p. 53.)

Early-childhood poverty is also associated with being born with health-compromising conditions—such as low birth weight—that affect learning (Li-Grining, 2007, recall Chapter 2). Being born into a poor family amplifies the impact of having an at-risk temperament, too. Imagine that you are a single mother arriving home, exhausted from a low-wage job, or a laid-off worker, fruitlessly searching for work. How would you deal with the kind of temperamentally irritable infant I described in the previous section, a baby who was impossible to soothe? In summarizing more than 60 relevant studies, developmentalists found that affluent mothers tended to react to the challenge of having a "difficult" baby by making special efforts to calm their child's distress. Stressed-out, low-income women were more prone to yell, hit, and scream (Paulussen-Hoogeboom and others, 2007). So, although money cannot buy us loving mothers, it can buy any mother breathing space to try to do her best.

Moreover, poor children may not even have the *concrete* breathing space to learn (Evans, 2006). If a young child lives in crowded, substandard housing and is subject to continual comings and goings, it's a bit like a brain impeded by excessive neural connections before pruning has occurred: Too much stimulation prevents information from getting in. And if the child lives in a dangerous urban area, she cannot escape the household chaos by venturing outside. Her neighborhood is likely to be a frightening place.

As parents understand when they struggle to buy a house in a section of town they can't quite afford, where you live makes a difference in your child's life chances. In one survey of low-income urban families, even when researchers controlled for other forces, the quality of the neighborhood affected a preschooler's ability to concentrate. If a mother responded "yes" to items such as "the streets here are dangerous," her 4-year-old was more likely to do poorly on "school readiness" skills, such as being able to color between the lines (Li-Grining, 2007). Notice the basic developmental systems message here. To understand development, *even in early childhood,* we need to

consider more than a child's genetic capabilities and what's happening at home. We need to look at the wider world.

Still, poor families are not left to flounder in the United States. There are government programs designed to improve disadvantaged children's academic and social chances.

INTERVENTIONS: Giving Disadvantaged Children a Boost

The most famous program to help low-income preschoolers is **Head Start**. The purpose of his well-known program is to offer the kind of high-quality preschool experience that will make poverty-level children as ready for kindergarten as their middle-class peers. In 2006, almost one million children aged 3 to 5 were enrolled in Head Start (Stebbins & Knitzer, NCCP, 2007).

Early Head Start extends these benefits to children under age 3. The primary emphasis of this program is to help low-income parents become more effective caregivers. One special focus of Early Head Start is getting fathers involved with their babies. The program also reaches out to support low-income pregnant women with home visits and other services.

Do these interventions work? The answer is "yes" (USDHHS, 2008). The problem is that these programs only reach a fraction of the children in need. In 2007, for instance, fewer than one in five eligible preschoolers participated in Head Start (Stebbins & Knitzer, NCCP, 2007). Then there is the issue of what happens when these children begin their academic careers. Can we really expect a one-year program to work miracles at making up for the impact of attending inadequate schools? As you will vividly learn in Chapter 7, low-income children attend the poorest-quality kindergartens. Their educational experiences—without adequate books, with mold-encrusted classrooms, and teachers who often quit just a few months into the school year—qualify as a national shame (Kozol, 1988, 2005).

Still, high-quality preschool experiences of any kind can offer disadvantaged children (and any child) a crucial cognitive boost (Weigel, Lowman, & Martin, 2007; Zigler & Finn-Stevenson, 2007). Moreover, the gains children show after attending these programs are partly due to what they directly absorb in the classroom and also the result of how school changes the learning atmosphere at home (McCartney and others, 2007). Imagine picking up your 4-year-old at the end of the day and having the teacher drum in the message: "Be sure to read to your child, and practice writing letters to reinforce what we are doing here." Yes, we might legitimately feel ambivalent about this early academic pressure. Shouldn't the first years of life *really* be all about learning through play? But, particularly for parents who need special encouragement (not those micromanaging moms who make producing a 3-year-old Einstein their main mission in life), outside pressure works.

This brings up the primary educators: parents. Mothers and fathers at *every* income level differ in their dancing skills and the teaching experiences they provide. Every study agrees: What happens at home matters most (Lugo-Gil & Tamis-LeMonda, 2008; McCartney, 2004). Some affluent parents leave the dancing to others. Some poverty-level parents work overtime to nurture and stimulate their daughters and sons.

Can we identify some core qualities of these special low-income moms and dads? In one interesting study, researchers found that, if people felt good about their own childhoods and were basically happy and optimistic, they could put aside their life problems and offer their children the ultimate in tender loving care (Kochanska and others, 2007). As a student of mine commented, "I don't see my family in your description of poverty. My mom is actually my hero. We grew up very poor, but in terms of parenting, we had the very best."

Head Start A federal program offering high-quality day care at a center and other services to help preschoolers aged 3 to 5 from low-income families prepare for school.

Early Head Start A federal program that provides counseling and other services to low-income parents and children under age 3.

The Impact of Child Care

It's easy to insulate ourselves from stories of poverty if we are comfortably well off. Child care affects everyone, from millionaires in mansions to middle-class urban parents to the rural poor. More than half of all women in developed countries return to work during their baby's first year of life (McCartney, 2004). In the opening vignette, Kim's anxiety about leaving her daughter in another person's care is echoed by women around the world. When researchers questioned first-time Israeli mothers about their parenting worries, having to "separate from my baby and return to work" ranked first (Kaitz, 2007).

Perhaps this explains why, when they have infants and toddlers, many parents in the United States struggle to keep child care in the family. They may depend on grandma or juggle full-time work schedules so that one spouse is always home (Kreader, Ferguson, & Lawrence, 2005). People who use paid caregivers have several options. Well-off families often hire a nanny or babysitter. Less-affluent parents, or those who want a more inexpensive option, like Kim, may turn to **family day care,** where a neighbor or local parent cares for a small group of children in her home.

The big change on the child-care landscape is the dramatic increase in licensed **day-care centers**—larger settings that cater to children of different ages. By the late 1990s, more than 1 in 2 U.S. preschoolers attended these facilities (Shonkoff & Phillips, 2000b). The comparable figure for infants and toddlers was more than 1 in 5 (see Figure 4.6).

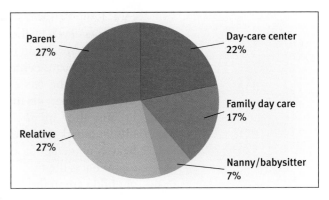

FIGURE 4.6: **Day-care arrangements for infants and toddlers with employed mothers, late 1990s:** Notice that, while most infants and toddlers with working mothers are cared for by other family members, 1 in 5 attend licensed day-care centers.

Source: Shonkoff & Phillips (2000b), p. 304.

Child Care and Development

Imagine that, like Kim, you are the mother of an infant and must return to work. You probably wonder, "Will my child be securely attached if I see her only a few hours a day?" You would also worry about finding a child-care provider and the quality of care your child would receive: "Will my baby have the attention she needs at the local day-care center?" "What is the *real* impact of putting my child in someone else's care?"

To answer these questions, in 1989, developmentalists began the National Institute of Child Health and Human Development (NICHD) Study of Early Child Care. They selected more than 1000 newborns in 10 regions of the United States and intensively tracked the progress of these children, measuring everything from attachment to academic abilities, from mental health, to mothers' caregiving skills. They looked at the hours each child spent in day care and assessed the quality of the settings in which the children were placed. The original NICHD newborns are now being followed as they travel into their teens (NICHD Study of Early Child Care and Youth Development, 2009).

The good news is that putting a baby in day care does not weaken the attachment bond. Most infants attending day care are securely attached to their mothers. The most important force that promotes attachment is the *quality* of the dance—whether a woman is a sensitive caregiver—not whether or not she works. Moreover, as I emphasized earlier, what happens at home is the crucial influence affecting how children develop, far outweighing long hours spent in day care during the first years of life (Belsky and others, 2007).

However, when we look *just* at the impact of spending those long hours, the findings are less upbeat. As I described in the previous section, attending **preschool**—that more teaching-oriented setting serving children ages 3 to 5—has clear cognitive benefits. At their most recent evaluation, the NICHD researchers found that children who attended good preschools had a vocabulary advantage over their peers that persisted into sixth grade (Belsky and others, 2007). But, when we look generally at day care—that setting encompassing the infant and toddler age group—there is troubling news.

Earlier NICHD research first raised alarm bells by reporting that children who spent long hours in day care were slightly more likely to be rated as "difficult to control" by caregivers and kindergarten teachers (NICHD, Early Child Care Research Network, 2003, 2004, 2006). Now, we have the findings for children through sixth grade. By this time, the negative kindergarten finding dissipates, but only for children in family day

family day care A day-care arrangement in which a neighbor or relative cares for a small number of children in her home for a fee.

day-care center A day-care arrangement in which a large number of children are cared for at a licensed facility by paid providers.

preschool Teaching-oriented childcare setting, serving children aged 3 to 5.

care. Long hours in *center care* continue to predict an elevated risk of having "acting-out issues" even by the end of elementary school (Belsky and others, 2007).

These results do not offer much comfort to the millions of working families who rely on day-care centers. But luckily, the correlations are weak (McCartney, 2004). They could be caused by what researchers call *selection effects*. This means that stressed-out parents may send a difficult infant or toddler to the local day-care center because they are *already* having problems with that particular child at home. Still, this landmark study suggests that mothers and fathers might be hesitant about relying heavily on center-based care during their child's early years of life.

What is the trouble with day-care centers? For answers, let's scan the overall state of child care in the United States.

Exploring the Quality of Child Care in the United States

Visit several facilities and you will immediately see that U.S. day care varies dramatically in quality. In some places, babies are warehoused and ignored. In other settings, every child is nurtured and loved.

The essence of high-quality day care again boils down to the dance—that is, the attachment relationship between caretakers and the children in their care. As I implied earlier, children develop attachments to their day-care providers. If a particular day-care teacher is sensitive and responsive, a child in her care tends to be ranked as securely attached (Ahnert, Pinquart, & Lamb, 2006; de Schipper and others, 2008).

Child-care providers and moms agree: To be effective in this job, you need to be patient, caring, and empathic (Berthelsen & Brownlee, 2007). Yes, it's important to be knowledgeable about development (Harrist, Thompson, & Norris, 2007); but what really matters, especially during the first two years of life, is adoring young children and being committed to this field (Torquati, Raikes, & Huddleston-Casas, 2007).

You also need to work in a setting where you have the luxury of being able to relate to children in a close one-to-one way (McCartney, 2004). A telling finding illustrating this point comes from a study conducted in the Netherlands. Researchers videotaped teachers at 64 Dutch preschools in two situations. In one, the teacher was playing with three children; in the other, she was playing with five. Teachers acted more empathic and listened more when they were in the smaller, three-child group. They were far more likely to criticize and get angry when dealing with the group of five (de Schipper, Riksen-Walraven, & Geurts, 2006). These differences in teachers' tone and style were especially pronounced when dealing with younger children (the 3-year-olds). So group size really matters; and the lower the child-teacher ratio, the better, especially earlier in life.

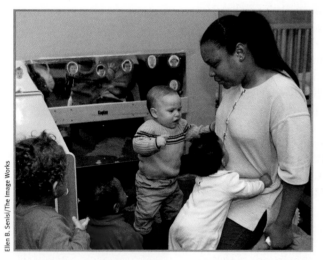

Can this day-care worker give enough attention to the babies and toddlers in her care? Unfortunately, with a caregiver-child ratio at over 3 to 1 at this center, the answer may be no.

Another important dimension is consistency of care (Harrist, Thompson, & Norris, 2007). Forming an attachment takes time. Therefore, it is no surprise that children are more likely to be securely attached to their child-care provider when they are at a given setting for a longer time (Ahnert, Pinquart, & Lamb, 2006). Unfortunately, children tend to get moved around a lot. The NICHD researchers found a typical child in the study experienced more than five different care arrangements from 3 months to 4 years of age (Belsky and others, 2007).

Then, there is the problem that, because of the abysmal pay (typically about 7 dollars an hour), day-care workers may be tempted to quit. One parent in a focus-group study bitterly commented: "We pay firefighters good money to sit around and hope there is not a fire . . . and what do we pay our child-care providers? . . . They are not *hoping* our kids are going to grow up . . . they are *helping* the kids grow up . . . and they get diddly squat!" (Harrist, Thompson, & Norris, 2007, p. 319.)

Combine these terrible salaries with burnout from feeling overwhelmed. While the recommended caregiver-to-child ratio for toddlers is 4 to 1 (McCartney, 2004) as of this writing, only eight states have followed this guideline (Stebbins & Knitzer, NCCP, 2007). Some allow as many as one caregiver per 12 children, even during the first year of life.

In sum, now we have clues as to why day-care centers are at risk of providing inadequate care. The primary culprit is size. In family day care, there is a smaller number of children and probably more caregiver stability (since the person is watching the children in her home) than in a large facility, where "teachers" keep leaving and babies are warehoused in larger groups (Gerber, Whitebook, & Weinstein, 2007). In fact, in one research summary, developmentalists discovered that secure attachments to care providers were more common among children attending family versus center-based care (Ahnert, Pinquart, & Lamb, 2006).

INTERVENTIONS: Choosing Child Care

Given all of these issues, what should working parents do? The take-home message is not "avoid a day-care center," but rather "choose the best possible place." Look for low staff turnover; check to see if the caregivers are empathic and warm; if you have an infant or toddler, make sure your baby will spend the day in a small group. As with Kim, you might find these conditions at your next-door neighbor's house. Perhaps you'll find these attributes at the largest child-care facility in town.

While loving, one-to-one care is most crucial, parents also might look at a facility's physical attributes. One researcher developed a scale rating the environment of preschool classrooms: Are the furniture and toileting facilities child-sized, and is the space user-friendly—for instance, when children paint, is there a sink close by for them to wash their hands? Three-year-olds in preschools rated "excellent" on these dimensions scored higher on tests of cognitive competence than children who attended facilities ranked only "adequate" or "poor" (Maxwell, 2007).

Finally, look to your child. Just as they have more problems in the Strange Situation, highly anxious infants (and extremely active toddlers) are especially vulnerable to less-than-optimal day care (Crockenberg, 2003; Crockenberg & Leerkes, 2005). Parents might consider their baby's gender, too. Although no more temperamentally difficult than girls, boys have more trouble managing their emotions during infancy (Calkins and others, 2002). Therefore, boys are somewhat less likely to develop secure attachments to their day-care providers and are more vulnerable to the negative effects of being sent to center care (Sagi and others, 2002; Ahnert, Pinquart, & Lamb, 2006).

Table 4.1 pulls together these messages. And, if you are a working parent who relies heavily on day care, keep these heartening thoughts in mind: There are *many*

TABLE 4.1: Choosing Day Care: A Section Summary

Overall Considerations

- Consider the caregiver(s). Are they nurturing? Do they love babies? Are they interested in providing a good deal of verbal stimulation to children?
- Ask about stability, or staff turnover. Have caregivers left in the last few months? Can my infant have the same caregivers when she moves to the toddler room?
- Look for a low caregiver-to-baby ratio (and a small group). The ideal is one caregiver to every two or three babies.
- Look at the physical setting. Is it safe and clean, set up with children's needs in mind? (With toddlers, look for a variety of age-appropriate play materials, clearly defined social spaces and more private nooks, child-sized furniture, clear pathways for children to circulate, and sensitive placement of play areas, such as areas for painting situated near sinks.)

Additional Suggestions

- For infants and toddlers in full-time care, limit exposure by having a child take occasional vacations or building in special time with the child every day.
- Consider a child's temperament. Highly anxious babies—or very active toddlers—have special trouble coping with less-than-optimal care.
- Consider a child's gender. Boys are more vulnerable to the negative effects of low-quality day care.

Background sources: the authors cited in this section.

exceptional day-care programs. A silver lining of the current economic downturn may be less staff turnover and (hopefully) more incentive for people to make this crucial job their life career. Every study shows that *your* responsiveness is what matters most. You are your child's major teacher and the major force in making your child secure.

Now that I have thoroughly examined attachment, poverty, and day care, it's time to turn directly to the topic I have been implicitly talking about all along—being a toddler.

 TYING IT ALL TOGETHER

1. Hugo is discussing poverty during early childhood in the United States with Heloise. Which of the following statements should he *not* be making?

   a. Being poor during early childhood can greatly impair cognitive development and the attachment relationship.
   b. Young children are the poorest segment of the U.S. population (with the exception of women over age 75).
   c. Poverty rates during early childhood are lower in the United States than in other Western nations.

2. Discuss (or list) a few forces not mentioned in the text that might negatively affect intellectual development and mental health in poor children.

3. Nancy has just put her 6-month-old in day care, and she is terribly anxious about the impact that decision may have on her child. Give a "good news" statement to ease Nancy's mind, and then be honest and give a "not such good news" statement based on the research.

4. You are making a presentation to a senate special committee investigating early child care. What should you tell the senators about day care in the United States? What improvements can you recommend?

Answers to the Tying It All Together questions can be found on the last page of this chapter.

Toddlerhood: Age of Autonomy *and* Shame and Doubt

Imagine time-traveling back to when you were a toddler. Everything is entrancing—a bubble bath, the dishwasher soap box, the dirt and bugs in your backyard. You are just cracking the language barrier and finally (yes!) traveling on your own two feet. Passionate to set sail into life, you are also intensely connected to that number-one adult in your life. So, during our second year on this planet, the two agendas that make us human first emerge: We need to be closely connected, and we want to be free, autonomous selves. This is why Erik Erikson (1950) used the descriptive word

autonomy Erikson's second psychosocial task, when toddlers confront the challenge of understanding that they are separate individuals.

self-conscious emotions Feelings of pride, shame, or guilt, which first emerge around age 2 and show the capacity to reflect on the self.

socialization The process by which children are taught to obey the norms of society and to behave in socially appropriate ways.

TABLE 4.2: Erikson's Psychosocial Stages

Life Stage	Primary Task
Infancy (birth to 1 year)	Basic trust versus mistrust
Toddlerhood (1 to 2 years)	**Autonomy versus shame and doubt**
Early childhood (3 to 6 years)	Initiative versus guilt
Late childhood (6 years to puberty)	Industry versus inferiority
Adolescence (teens into twenties)	Identity versus role confusion
Young adulthood (twenties to early forties)	Intimacy versus isolation
Middle adulthood (forties to sixties)	Generativity versus stagnation
Late adulthood (late sixties and beyond)	Integrity versus despair

autonomy to describe children's challenge as they emerge from the cocoon of baby-hood (see Table 4.2).

Autonomy involves everything from the thrill a 2-year-old feels when forming his first sentences to the joy children take in dressing or feeding themselves. But it also involves those not-so-pleasant behaviors we associate with the "terrible twos." How common is difficult behavior at this special age? As you can see in Figure 4.7, very (Morawska & Sanders, 2007; Beernick, Swinkels, & Buitelaar, 2007). Angry outbursts and having problems sitting still and "listening" are *normal* during this magic age, when children's life passion is to explore the world (recall Piaget's little-scientist behaviors).

Erikson used the words *shame* and *doubt* to refer to the situation when a toddler's drive for autonomy is not fulfilled. But feeling shameful and doubtful is also vital to shedding babyhood and entering the human world. During their first year of life, infants show joy, fear, and anger. At age 2, more complicated, uniquely human emotions emerge—pride, shame, and guilt. The appearance of these **self-conscious emotions** is a milestone—showing that a child is becoming aware of having an actual self. The gift (and sometimes curse) of being human is that we are capable of self-reflection, able to get outside of our heads and observe our actions from an outsider's point of view. Children show signs of this uniquely human quality between age 2 and 3, when they feel ashamed and clearly are proud of their actions for the first time (Kagan, 1984).

Socialization: The Challenge for 2-Year-Olds

Shame and guilt are vital in another respect. They are essential to **socialization**—the process of being taught to live in the human community.

When do parents begin to seriously socialize their children—or turn up the heat on rules and discipline? For answers, developmentalists surveyed U.S. middle-class parents about their rules for their 14-month-olds and returned with the same questionnaire when the children just turned 2 (Smetana, Kochanska, & Chuang, 2000). While rules for 14-month-olds centered on safety issues ("Stay away from the stove!"), by age 2, parents were expecting their children to "share," "sit at the table," "brush your teeth," and "don't disobey, bite, or hit." Therefore, the pressure to begin to act "like adults" comes on strong as children reach their second birthdays. No wonder 2-year-olds are infamous for those tantrums called "the terrible twos"!

Figure 4.7 shows just how difficult it is for 1-year-olds to follow socialization rules when their parents are around. At what age do children have the self-regulating abilities to follow unwanted directions when a parent *isn't* in the room? To answer this question related to early *conscience*—the ability to adopt internal standards for our behavior, or have that little voice inside us that says, "even though I want to do this, I know it's wrong"—researchers devised an interesting procedure. Accompanied by their mothers, young children enter a laboratory full of toys. Next, the parents give an unwelcome instruction—telling the children either to clean up the toy area or not to touch another easily reachable set of enticing toys. Then, the moms leave the room, and researchers watch what the children do through a one-way mirror.

Not unexpectedly, children's ability to "listen to a parent in their head" and stop doing what they want improves dramatically

This toddler has reached a human milestone: She can feel shame, which means that she is beginning to be aware that she has a separate self.

FIGURE 4.7: Typical and unusual difficult toddler behaviors, based on a survey of Dutch parents of 6491 infants aged 14 to 19 months: Notice that it's normal for toddlers not to listen, have temper tantrums, and refuse to sit still or share—but the other difficult behaviors in red should be warning signs of a real problem.

Source: Beernick, Swinkels, & Buitelaar, 2007

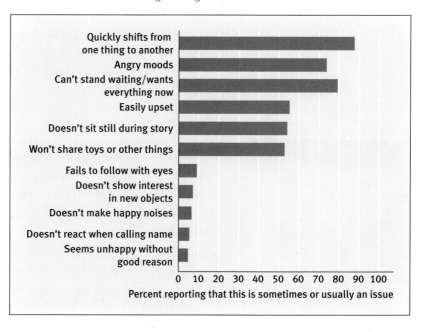

❀ HOW DO WE KNOW . . .

that shy and exuberant children differ dramatically in self-control?

How do researchers measure differences in toddler temperament? How do they measure later self-control? Their first step is to design real-world situations tailored to elicit the three primary emotions—fear, anger, and joy—and then observe how toddlers act.

In the situation specially designed to measure differences in fear, a child enters a room filled with frightening toy objects, such as the dinosaur with huge teeth shown below or a black box covered with spider webs. The experimenter asks that boy or girl to perform a mildly risky act, such as putting a hand into the box. To measure variations in anger, the researchers restrain a child in a car seat for a minute or two and then rate how frustrated the toddler gets. To tap into differences in exuberance, the researchers entertain a child with a set of funny puppets. Will the toddler respond with hysterical gales of laughter or be more reserved?

Several years later, the researchers set up a situation tailor-made to provoke noncompliance by asking the child, now age 4, to perform an impossible task (throw Velcro balls at a target from a long distance without looking) to get a prize. Then, they leave the room and watch through a one-way mirror to see if the boy or girl will cheat.

As it turns out, toddlers at the high end of the fearless, joyous, and angry continuum show less "morality" at age 4. Without the strong inhibition of fear, their exuberant "get closer" impulses are difficult to dampen down. So they succumb to temptation, sneak closer, and look directly at the target as they hurl the balls (Kochanska & Knaack, 2003).

from age 2 to 4 (Kochanska, Coy, & Murray, 2001). Still, the really interesting question is: Which girls and boys are best at this feat of self-control?

As some of you might guess, temperament is crucial. Fearful toddlers are more compliant at age 2. They are far less likely to cheat on a game at age 4 than more emotionally intense, uninhibited girls and boys (Aksan & Kochanska, 2004; see the How Do We Know box). The bottom line is that the exuberant, joyful, fearless, intrepid toddler explorers—no surprise—are more difficult to socialize! (See Kochanska & Knaack, 2003.)

FOCUS ON A TOPIC: ## BEING EXUBERANT AND BEING SHY

Adam [was a vigorous, happy baby who] began walking at 9 months. From then on, it seemed as though he could never stop.

(10 months) Adam . . . refuses to be carried anywhere. . . . He trips over objects, falls down, bumps himself.

(12 months) The word osside appears. . . . Adam stands by the door, banging at it and repeating this magic word again and again.

(16 months) Adam and his mother take a five-hour plane ride to visit his grandparents. . . . He is miserable unless he is going up and down the aisles.

(19 months) Adam begins attending a toddler group. . . . The first day, Adam climbs to the highest rung of the climbing structure and falls down. . . . The second day, Adam upturns a heavy wooden bench. . . . The fourth day, the teacher [devastates Adam's mother] when she says, "I think Adam is not ready for this."

. . .

(13 months) Erin begins to talk in sentences the same week as she takes her first steps. . . . Rather suddenly, Erin becomes quite shy. . . . She cries when her mother leaves the room, and insists on following her everywhere.

(15 months) Erin and her parents go to the birthday party of a little friend. . . . For the first half-hour, Erin stays very close to her mother, intermittently hiding her face on her mother's skirt.

(16 months) Father and Erin go to a small grocery store where the friendly owner . . . praises her beautiful eyes and hair. . . . Erin bursts into tears.

(18 months) Erin's mother takes her to a toddlers' gym. Erin watches the children . . . with a "tight little face". . . . Her mother berates herself for raising such a timid child.

(Lieberman, 1993, pp. 83–87, 104–105)

My exuberant son—shown enjoying a sink bath at 9 months of age—began to have problems at 18 months, when his strong, joyous temperament collided with the need to "please sit still and listen, Thomas!"

Observe any group of 1-year-olds and you will immediately pick out the Erins and the Adams. Some children are wary, careful, and shy. Others are whirlwinds of activity, constantly in motion, literally bouncing off the walls. I remember my own first toddler group at the local Y, when—just like Adam's mother—I first realized how different my exuberant son was from the other children his age. After enduring the horrified expressions of the other mothers as Thomas whirled gleefully around the room while everyone else sat obediently for a snack, I came home and cried. How was I to know that the very qualities that made my outgoing, joyous, vital baby so charismatic during his first year of life might go along with his being so difficult to tame?

The definitive longitudinal studies tracing children with shy temperaments have been carried out by Jerome Kagan. Kagan (1994) classifies about one in five middle-class European American toddlers as inhibited. Although they may be perfectly comfortable in familiar situations, these 1-year-olds, like Erin, get nervous when confronted with anything new. Inhibited 13-month-olds shy away from approaching a toy robot, a clown, or an unfamiliar person. They take time to venture out in the Strange Situation, get agitated when the stranger enters, and cry bitterly when their parent leaves the room.

Babies who are destined to be inhibited toddlers show precursors of their later shyness. At 4 months of age, they fret and cry when confronted with a new object such as a mobile (Moehler and others, 2008). Inhibited toddlers are also more prone to be rated fearful throughout the childhood years. Their basic biological tendency toward shyness even shows in adulthood. Using MRI brain-scan technology, Kagan's research team found that, as young adults, his inhibited toddlers showed more activity in the limbic system (especially the part of the brain coding negative emotions) when shown a stranger's face on a screen (Schwartz and others, 2003). So for all of you formerly very shy people (your author included) who think you have shed that intense childhood wariness, you still carry your physiology inside.

Still, if you think you have come a long way in conquering your *incredible* childhood shyness, you are probably correct. Many highly anxious toddlers (and exuberant explorers) get less inhibited as they move into elementary school and the teenage years (Degnan & Fox, 2007; Feng, Shaw, & Silk, 2008).

INTERVENTIONS: **Providing the Right Temperament–Socialization Fit**

Faced with a temperamentally timid toddler such as Erin or an exuberant explorer like Adam or Thomas, what specifically can parents do to help?

Socializing a Shy Baby

To see what works best for excessively shy babies, one researcher considered two different parenting strategies (Arcus, 2001). Did the mother quickly pick up her 4-month-old the minute he got agitated, or let him cry a bit? At months 9 and 13, did she set limits for her baby, or avoid ever saying no to her inhibited child?

Interestingly, parents who emotionally insulated their infants ended up with the most inhibited toddlers. Parents of fearful children should take special care to foster a secure attachment (Gilissen and others, 2008). However, they should temper their natural tendency to overprotect their anxious babies, and later avoid micromanaging or overly controlling their timid daughters and sons (Feng, Shaw, & Silk, 2008; McLeod, Wood, & Weisz, 2007). Gently exposing a fearful baby to new situations teaches that child to cope.

Raising a Rambunctious Toddler

With fearless explorers, it's tempting for adults to adopt a socialization strategy called **power assertion**—yelling, screaming, and hitting a child who is bouncing off the walls. Parents should resist this tendency. Power assertion is linked to lower levels of conscience development and strongly predicts behavior problems down the road (Brotman and others, 2009; Kochanska & Knaack, 2003). To reduce the risk of later "acting-out problems," it's important to redirect the behavior and provide positive reinforcement—praising and loving the child up—whenever you can (Bakermans-Kranenburg and others, 2008; Gardner and others, 2007). Sensitive, loving parenting is the real route to socializing conscience—getting an exuberant toddler to *want* to be good for mom and dad (Kochanska and others, 2008). As my husband insightfully commented, "Punishment doesn't matter much to Thomas. What he does, he does for your love."

Table 4.3 offers a capsule summary of our discussion, showing these different toddler temperaments, their infant precursors, their pluses and potential later dangers, and lessons for socializing each kind of child. Now, let's look at some general temperament-sensitive lessons for raising every child.

An Overall Strategy for Temperamentally Friendly Childrearing

Clearly, the main key to socializing children is to foster a secure, loving attachment. However, another key is to understand each child's *specific* temperament and work with that baby's unique behavioral style. This principle was demonstrated decades ago, in the classic study mentioned earlier in this chapter, in which developmentalists classified babies as "easy," "slow-to-warm-up," and "difficult."

In following the difficult babies as they traveled into elementary school, the researchers found that these highly intense infants were much more likely to have problems with their teachers and peers (Thomas & Chess, 1977; Thomas, Chess, & Birch, 1968). However, some children did learn to compensate for their biology and to shine. The key, the researchers discovered, lay in a parenting strategy labeled **goodness of fit.** Parents who took special steps to arrange their children's lives to minimize their vulnerabilities and accentuate their strengths had infants who later did well.

Understanding that their child was easily overwhelmed by stimuli, these parents kept the environment as predictable as possible. They did not compound the problem and get hysterical when faced with their child's distress. They may have offered a quiet environment for studying and encouraged their child to do activities that took advantage of his or her gifts. They specifically worked to fit the environment to their son's or daughter's temperamental style.

power assertion An ineffective socialization strategy that involves yelling, screaming, or hitting out in frustration at a child.

goodness of fit An ideal parenting strategy that involves arranging children's environments to suit their temperaments, minimizing their vulnerabilities and accentuating their strengths.

TABLE 4.3: Exuberant and Inhibited Toddler Temperaments: A Summary

Inhibited, Shy Toddler

- **Developmental precursor:** Responds with intense motor arousal to external stimulation in infancy.

- **Plus:** Easily socialized; shows early signs of conscience; not a discipline problem.

- **Minus:** Shy, fearful temperament can persist into adulthood, making social encounters painful.

- **Child-rearing advice:** Don't overprotect the child. Expose the baby to unfamiliar people. Spend plenty of time interacting sensitively with the child to teach social skills (see Chapter 6).

Exuberant Toddler

- **Developmental precursor:** Emotionally intense but unafraid of new stimuli.

- **Plus:** Joyous; fearless; outgoing; adventurous.

- **Minus:** Less easily socialized; potential problems with conscience development; at higher risk for later "acting-out" behavior problems.

- **Child-rearing advice:** Avoid power assertion and harsh punishment. Redirect the behavior and provide lots of positive reinforcement and love.

This strategy applies to more than raising children. A basic message of this book is the need to select the environments that fit us temperamentally so that we can really flower.

TYING IT ALL TOGETHER

1. If Amanda has recently turned 2, what prediction are you *not* justified in making about her?
   a. Amanda wants to be independent, yet closely attached.
   b. Amanda is beginning to show signs of self-awareness and can possibly feel shame.
   c. Amanda's parents haven't begun to discipline her yet.

2. To a colleague at work who confides that he's worried about his timid toddler, what words of comfort can you offer?

3. Think back to your own childhood: Did you fit into either the shy or exuberant temperament type? How did your parents cope with your personality style?

Answers to the Tying It All Together questions can be found on the last page of this chapter.

Final Thoughts

How can we best foster goodness of fit, or person–environment fit, throughout life? How much do our inborn temperament (nature) and the external world (nurture) shape the people we become? What happens to babies who are shy or exuberant, difficult or easy, as they journey into elementary school, adolescence, and adult life? How do Ainsworth's categories of attachment play out in adult romantic relationships, and what conditions evoke the clear-cut attachment response at other life stages? Stay tuned as we revisit and explore these tantalizing questions in the rest of this book.

SUMMARY

Attachment: The Basic Life Bond

For much of the twentieth century, many psychologists in the United States—because they were behaviorists—minimized the mother–child bond. European psychoanalysts such as John Bowlby were finding, however, that **attachment** was a basic human need. Harlow's studies with monkeys convinced U.S. developmentalists of the importance of attachment, and Bowlby transformed developmental science by arguing that having a loving **primary attachment figure** is biologically built in and crucial to development. Although threats to survival at any age evoke **proximity-seeking behavior**—especially during **toddlerhood**—being physically apart from an attachment figure elicits distress.

According to Bowlby, life begins with a three-month-long **preattachment phase,** which is characterized by the first **social smile.** After an intermediate phase called **attachment in the making,** at about 7 months of age, the landmark phase of **clear-cut attachment** begins, signaled by **separation anxiety** and **stranger anxiety.** During this period spanning toddlerhood, children need their caregiver to be physically close, and they rely on **social referencing** to monitor their behavior and ensure that their attachment figure is there. After age 3, children can tolerate separations, as they develop an internal **working model** of their caregiver—which they carry into life.

To explore individual differences in attachment, Mary Ainsworth devised the **Strange Situation.** Using this test, involving a planned series of separations, and especially reunions, developmentalists label 1-year-olds as **securely** or **insecurely attached.** Securely attached 1-year-olds use their primary attachment figure as a secure base for exploration and are delighted when she returns. **Avoidant** infants seem indifferent. **Anxious-ambivalent** children are inconsolable and sometimes angry when their caregiver arrives. Children with a **disorganized attachment** react in an erratic way and often show fear when their parent reenters the room.

Caregiver–child interactions are characterized by a beautiful **synchrony,** or attachment dance. Although the caregiver's responsiveness to the baby is a major determinant of attachment security at age 1, infant attachment is also affected by the **temperament** of the child and depends on the quality of a caregiver's other relationships, too.

Cross-cultural studies support the idea that attachment to a primary caregiver is universal, with similar percentages of babies in various countries classified as securely attached. Even in an African tribe where infants are cared for by many different adults, children still get attached to their mothers. Although babies have one preferred attachment figure, infants can become attached to other caregivers, too.

As Bowlby predicted in his working-model concept, securely attached babies have superior social and emotional skills. Long-term predictions are hazardous, however, because secure attachments during infancy do not insulate us from life traumas (or from becoming insecure). Conversely, some babies with terrible early attachment experiences can construct loving, secure lives.

Settings for Development

Poverty during the first years of life can have a serious impact on later cognitive and emotional development. Two federal programs targeted to low-income children and families, **Head Start** and **Early Head Start,** as well as high-quality preschool experiences, improve school readiness among disadvantaged children. However, their impact may be erased by years of inadequate education. Poverty-level parents differ greatly in their sensitivity and "teaching." Rather than socioeconomic status, children's unique home life matters most.

Going back to work in a baby's first year of life is common, but parents in the United States and other countries tend to be anxious about putting their infants and toddlers in "non-family" care. The U.S. options for "paid care" include using nannies (for affluent parents), **family day care** (where a person takes a smaller number of children in her home), and putting a child in a larger, **day-care center.**

The NICHD Study of Early Child Care showed that the best predictor of being securely attached at age 1 is being a sensitive parent, not the number of hours a child spends in day care. Another piece of good news from this definitive U.S. child-care study is that attending **preschool** has enduring cognitive benefits. Unfortunately, however, children who spend many hours in day-care centers are at a slightly higher risk of being labeled "difficult," even by sixth grade. One reason is that, while settings vary, day care for infants and toddlers in the United States leaves a good deal to be desired.

Having loving, consistent care providers and being in a setting where caregivers can relate in a close to one-to-one way are the core components of quality "non-family" care. Because day-care workers are so poorly paid in the United States, staff turnover is a serious problem. Issues related to their larger size may explain why day-care centers in particular can be problematic. Rather than avoiding day-care centers, parents should search for loving, consistent, one-to-one care, as well as the "child friendliness" of a given physical setting. Be aware that babies who are more temperamentally difficult and male infants seem most vulnerable to poor-quality care. Also be aware that your sensitivity as a parent is what matters most.

Toddlerhood: Age of Autonomy *and* Shame and Doubt

Erikson's term **autonomy** captures the essence of toddlerhood, the landmark time of life when we shed babyhood, become able to observe the self, and so really enter the human world. **Self-conscious emotions** such as pride, shame, and guilt emerge and are crucial to **socialization,** which begins in earnest at around age 2. Having trouble focusing and obeying is normal during toddlerhood. Temperamentally fearful children show earlier signs of "conscience," following adult prohibitions, when not being watched. Exuberant, active toddlers are especially hard to socialize.

As young babies, shy toddlers react with intense motor activity to stimuli. They are also more inhibited in elementary school and adolescence and show neurological signs of wariness to strangers as adults. Still, over time (and with temperamentally sensitive parenting), many extremely shy toddlers and fearless explorers lose these qualities as they move into their elementary school years.

To help an inhibited baby, be empathic and sensitive, but don't overprotect or over-control the child. Socialize a fearless explorer by avoiding **power assertion**—yelling and screaming—and providing lots of positive reinforcement or love. While fostering loving, secure attachments are the real key to effectively raising children, another key to strive for is **goodness of fit**—tailoring one's parenting to a child's unique temperamental needs.

KEY TERMS

attachment, p. 109
toddlerhood, p. 109
primary attachment figure, p. 111
proximity-seeking behavior, p. 111
preattachment phase, p. 111
social smile, p. 111
attachment in the making, p. 112

clear-cut attachment, p. 112
separation anxiety, p. 112
stranger anxiety, p. 112
social referencing, p. 113
working model, p. 113
Strange Situation, p. 114
secure attachment, p. 114
insecure attachment, p. 114
avoidant attachment, p. 114

anxious-ambivalent attachment, p. 114
disorganized attachment, p. 114
synchrony, p. 115
temperament, p. 116
Low income, p. 120
Head Start, p. 122
Early Head Start, p. 122

family day care, p. 123
day-care center, p. 123
preschool, p. 123
autonomy, p. 127
self-conscious emotions, p. 127
socialization, p. 127
power assertion, p. 130
goodness of fit, p. 130

ANSWERS TO TYING IT ALL TOGETHER QUIZZES

Attachment: The Basic Life Bond

1. Your responses will differ, but any example you give, such as "I called mom when that terrible thing happened at work," should show that in a stressful situation your immediate impulse was to contact your attachment figure.
2. Muriel = preattachment; Janine = attachment in the making; Ted = clear-cut attachment.
3. (1) b, (2) c, (3) d, (4) a.
4. The baby has an avoidant attachment.
5. b. A child's attachment status *can* change over time.

Settings for Development

1. c. The United States actually has the highest child poverty rate in the West.
2. Possible answers might include not being able to buy nutritious foods, greater chance of being exposed to environmental toxins, such as peeling paint from living in deteriorated housing, less access to health care, and so on.
3. The good news is that the quality of Nancy's parenting is the main force in determining her child's attachment (and emotional health). The bad news is that many day-care centers leave a good deal to be desired and long hours spent in these centers is associated with a slightly higher risk of having "acting-out issues" in school.
4. Tell the senate committee that, with so many less-than-adequate settings, we have an imperative need to raise the overall quality of day care in the United States. Pass laws mandating (not simply recommending) small child-to-caregiver ratios; pay day-care workers decently; give this job the status it deserves! Also (when the economy recovers), consider passing laws that require employers to offer paid-for leave to parents who want to stay home after a child's birth.

Toddlerhood: Age of Autonomy *and* Shame and Doubt

1. c. Parents typically start serious discipline around age 2.
2. You might tell him that most children grow out of their shyness, even if they do not completely shed this temperamental tendency. But be sure to stress the advantages of being shy: His baby will be easier to socialize, not likely to be a behavior problem, and may have a stronger conscience, too.
3. These answers will be totally your own.

Childhood

In this three-chapter segment covering childhood, the first two chapters trace children's unfolding abilities. In the final chapter, I'll explore the two basic settings within which children develop: home and school.

The first part of Chapter 5—**Physical and Cognitive Development** examines children's expanding motor skills and focuses on health issues such as obesity. Then comes the heart of this chapter: an exploration of children's minds. If you have ever wondered about the strange ways preschoolers think, want a basic framework for teaching, or would like to understand how memory and reasoning develop, this section is for you. This chapter also charts developing language and two crucial types of social knowledge that children master during the preschool years.

In Chapter 6—**Socioemotional Development** my focus shifts to personality and relationships. Here, I'll be tracing growing self-awareness, aggression, caring acts, play, friendships, and popularity from preschool through elementary school. A special focus of this chapter is on boys and girls who are having trouble relating to their peers and adults.

The first half of Chapter 7—**Settings for Development: Home and School** tackles children's family lives. Is there an ideal way of parenting? Why do some children thrive in spite of devastatingly dysfunctional early lives? What is the impact of spanking, child abuse, and divorce on the child? In the second section on school, you will learn all about intelligence tests, what makes schools successful, and how teachers can make every child eager to learn.

PART III

Chapter 5

Physical and Cognitive Development

As the 3-year-olds drift in to Learning Preschool, Ms. Angela fills me in:

"We do free play, then structured games. Then we go outside. At 11 we have snack. We focus on the skills the kids need for school and life: Sit still; follow directions; listen; share. During free play, they need to remember three rules: Four kids to an activity center; clean up before you leave; don't take the toys from one center when you go to another place."

In the kitchen corner, Kanesha is busy pretending to scrub pots. "What is your name?" "You know!" says Kanesha, looking at me as if I'm totally dumb. "This is a picnic," Kanesha continues, giving me a plate: "Let's have psghetti and Nadia makeacake." We are having a wonderful time talking as she loads me up with plastic food. The problem is I'm feeling that we aren't communicating. Who is Nadia, that great cook? Then some girls run in with Barbies from the dress-up corner: "Our babies need some food!" We're happily feeding our toys when Ms. Angela pipes up: "No moving stuff from the play centers! Don't you remember our four kids to a center rule?" . . .

I move to the crafts table, where Moriah, a dreamy frail girl, and Manuel are surrounded by paper: "Hey!" Moriah yells, after Manuel cuts his paper into pieces, "Manuel has more than me!" Manuel tenderly gives Moriah his bunny, and gives me a heart-melting, welcoming smile: "I'm [holds up three fingers]." (Moriah and Manuel are obviously interested in what I'm doing.) "I'm taking notes for a book." "Taking nose," both children giggle and hold their noses. Moriah is making beautiful circles with paste. Manuel tries to copy her but can only make random lines. These children are so different in their physical abilities, even though they are the same age. But, oh, no, here come the kids from the kitchen corner with plastic vegetables, forgetting the "don't move the toys" and "four children to a center" rules! Luckily, it's time for structured games.

Ms. Angela shows the class cards picturing a sun, an umbrella with raindrops, and clouds, and asks: "What is the weather today?" Manuel proudly picks the umbrella. "How many people think Manuel is right?" Everyone raises a hand. "Who feels it's sunny?" Everyone yells: "Me!" "Who thinks it's cloudy?" Everyone agrees. Then Ms. Angela puts on a tape: "Dance fast, fast . . . slower slower . . . Now speed up!" The kids frantically dance around, and it's time to go outside. Soon the wind starts gusting (it really is about to rain), and everyone gets excited: "Let's catch the wind. . . . Oh, he ran away again!" And now (whew!) it's 11:00 and time for snack.

These 3-year-olds have amazing skills. They can cut, climb, follow directions, tell me about their lives, and (occasionally) remember the teacher's rules. But they clearly have miles to go before they reason like adults. What were the children thinking during the pretend feedings, and why was Kanesha sure I *had* to know her name? Why did Moriah assume Manuel had more paper when he cut his sheet into pieces, and why did *everyone* have so much trouble remembering the center's rules? This chapter offers answers to these questions and many others as we explore physical and cognitive development during **early childhood** (age 3 through kindergarten) and **middle childhood** (elementary school).

My discussion begins by focusing on children's developing bodies. Then, you will get a wealth of insights into children's minds—as I chart different perspectives on developing cognition, trace unfolding language, and discuss how two uniquely human *social cognitive skills* emerge. But before tackling these topics let's set the context by looking at a larger question. *Why* does our species take so long to grow up?

Setting the Context

Human beings must wait more than a decade before we become physically "adult." Actually, our species spends more of its lifespan in a childhood state than any other mammal does. Macaque monkeys are able to reproduce at age 4; our closest cousins, the chimpanzees, at age 8 (Poirier & Smith, 1974).

Postponing adulthood is dangerous because, the longer we live in an immature condition, the greater our risk of dying without passing on our genes. Why did childhood evolve? The reason, according to evolutionary theorists, is that we face two special social learning tasks that make us different from any other animal on earth (Bjorklund & Pellegrini, 2002).

Special Social Learning Tasks

One challenge that sets us apart from other animals is our need to learn the rules of living in *different* cultures (Bjorklund & Harnishfeger, 1995; Geary & Flinn, 2001). Three-year-olds growing up in any society on earth have to be *socialized* to relate to their fellow human beings. But if you have spent time in a different country, you were probably struck with the differences in the relationship rules. Do you smile or avoid making eye contact when you are walking down the street? Should you speak openly about your feelings or act more reserved? Learning the rules of living in specific societies requires a long period of time.

The main skill, however, that separates us as a species lies in our remarkable ability to build on the knowledge that has been passed down before. Three-year-olds born in biblical times had the same biology as the preschoolers in the introductory vignette; but these twenty-first-century children will grow up to use cell phones and surf the Internet. They might even take vacations on the moon or Mars.

What mental quality allowed humanity to take off? According to evolutionary psychologists, the core talent that explains all our scientific and cultural achievements is our finely honed ability to put ourselves in other people's heads and make sense of their inner motivations. You saw the beginnings of this special mind-reading skill toward the end of Chapter 3, when I described that 1-year-old landmark in social cognition called *joint attention*. Scientists now know monkeys show rudimentary joint attention. Apes can even decode the meaning of different human emotions, just as older infants do (Buttelmann, Call, & Tomasello, 2009; remember Chapter 4). But, because they cannot use language, our closest mammal cousins are never able to progress to the point where they can collectively draw on each other's insights to really transform the wider world. ("Oh, yes, now I understand what you were trying to do. Let's see if we can work together to improve on that.")

Because our exceptional "mind-reading ability" and its associated skill, language, are at the heart of what makes us human, in the concluding sections of this chapter, I'll be continuing Chapter 3's discussion by focusing on how these two talents fully come on-line during the early childhood years.

Imagine that these chimps could *really* share what insights were going on in each others' minds. Wouldn't they be the species that was constructing cities and traveling into outer space?

Markus Botzek/Zefa/Corbis

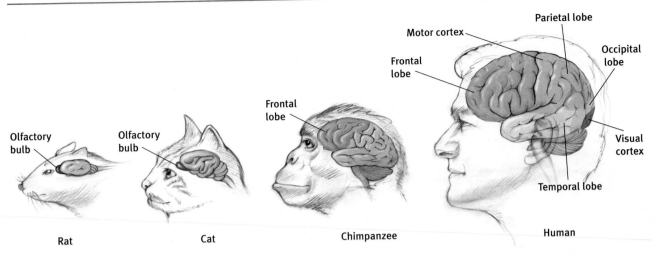

Rat

Cat

Chimpanzee

Human

FIGURE 5.1: **The human cortex and that of some other species:** Notice the size of our cortex in comparison to other species. Also notice the dramatic increase in the size of our frontal lobes. It is our mammoth cortex and especially our huge frontal lobes that are responsible for everything that makes our species unique.

Slow-Growing Frontal Lobes

All this special human learning explains why our huge *cerebral cortex* takes two decades to mature. The *myelin sheath*—the fatty neural cover—continues to grow, even into our twenties. *Synaptogenesis* (the process of making billions of connections between neurons) is on an extended blossoming and pruning timetable, too. This is especially true in the region of the brain responsible for reasoning and thinking through our actions—the **frontal lobes.**

Figure 5.1, which compares the size of our cortex to that of several other species, shows the huge frontal lobes positioned front and center at the top of the brain. During early childhood, the neurons in the visual and motor cortices are well into their pruning phase, which explains why vision develops so rapidly during early infancy (recall Chapter 3) and why we master basic physical milestones, such as walking, at a relatively young age. However, the frontal lobes are only in their early phase of intense synaptogenesis at the time we start toddling around. Pruning in this part of the brain will not start until about age 9.

Their slow frontal-lobe timetable accounts for why the 3-year-olds in the vignette had so much trouble controlling their behavior. It explains why our ability to plan, think through, and inhibit our actions steadily improves throughout childhood and adolescence. It even accounts for the high expectations we have of children when the frontal lobes begin their pruning phase in late elementary school. We expect fourth and fifth graders to be able to understand long division and to be responsible for completing their homework. After all, they can sometimes beat us at baseball and outscore us at the bowling alley, too.

In addition to allowing us to have the inner control to decide to do our homework (rather than watching TV) and the cognitive abilities to grasp long division, the frontal lobes are crucial to mastering every physical ability, from playing tennis, to tight-rope walking, to being able to inhibit our immediate urges and think "I have to get to the toilet" at about age 2 or 3. Keeping in mind that the slow-growing frontal lobes are the master programmer of *every* skill in this chapter, let's begin by looking at physical development in the flesh.

TYING IT ALL TOGETHER

1. In discussing the qualities that distinguish us from other species, Brandy can list all of the following uniquely human characteristics *except:*
   a. We easily grasp other people's inner motivations.
   b. We are able to communicate our insights through language.
   c. We have extremely varied cultures.
   d. We have the ability to keep learning new things.

2. When Steven played hide-and-seek with his 4-year-old nephew, he realized that while Ethan could run very well, the child was having a lot of trouble not betraying his

frontal lobes The area at the uppermost front of the brain, responsible for reasoning and planning our actions.

hiding place and understanding the rules of the game. The reason is that Ethan's _____ cortex is on an earlier developmental timetable than his _____ lobes.

3. If you learn that a colleague was in an accident and has "frontal lobe" damage, what kinds of impairments might you expect?

Answers to the Tying It All Together questions can be found on the last page of this chapter.

What tips us off immediately about the ages of the children in these two photographs relates to the *cephalocaudal principle* of development. We know that the children in the top photo are preschoolers because they have squat shapes and relatively large heads, while the longer bodies in the bottom photo are typical of the middle childhood years.

Physical Development

Go to the mall and look at children of different ages and you will immediately see the *cephalocaudal principle* of physical growth discussed in Chapters 2 and 3. Three-year-olds have relatively large heads and squat, rounded bodies. As children get older, their limbs get longer and their bodies thin out. Although from age 2 to 12 children double their height and weight, after infancy the rate of growth slows down considerably (National Health and Nutrition Examination Survey, 2004). Because they grow at similar rates, boys and girls are roughly the same size until they reach the preadolescent years.

Now, visit a playground or take out samples of your childhood artwork to see the *mass-to-specific* principle—the steady progression from clumsy to sure, swift movements year by year. Three-year-olds have trouble making circles; third graders can draw detailed bodies and faces. At age 4, children catch a ball with both hands; by fourth grade they may be able to hit home runs. You can see the dramatic changes from mass to specific in a few skills in Table 5.1.

Two Types of Motor Talents

Developmentalists divide physical skills into two categories. **Gross motor skills** refer to large muscle movements, such as running, jumping, climbing, and hopping. **Fine motor skills** involve small, coordinated movements, such as drawing circles and writing one's name.

The stereotype that boys are better at gross motor abilities and girls at fine motor tasks is true—although in most areas the differences are small. The largest sex difference in sports-related abilities occurs in throwing speed. During preschool and

TABLE 5.1: Selected Motor Skill Milestones: Progression from Age 2 to Age 6	
At age 2	**At age 4**
Picks up small objects with thumb and forefinger; feeds self with spoon	Cuts paper, approximates circle
Walks unassisted, usually by 12 months	Walks down stairs, alternating feet
Rolls a ball or flings it awkwardly	Catches and controls a large bounced ball across the body
At age 5	**At age 6**
Prints name	Copies two short words
Walks without holding on to railing	Hops on each foot for 1 meter but still holds railing
Tosses ball overhand with bent elbows	Catches and controls a 10-inch ball in both hands with arms in front of body

throughout middle childhood, boys can typically hurl a ball much faster and farther than girls (Geary, 1998; Thomas & French, 1985). Does this mean that girls can't compete with boys on a Little League team? Not necessarily. The boys will have a gross motor advantage: They may be better at running the bases, and they probably will be faster pitchers and more powerful hitters. But the female talent at connecting with the ball, which involves fine motor coordination, may even things out.

Apart from their gender, what accounts for the dramatic differences we can observe between individual preschoolers in their motor skills? To a large degree, nature forces are responsible. Just as children are genetically programmed to be early or late walkers, developmental timetables vary for reaching motor milestones, from catching a ball to being able to draw a human form.

Suppose your 5-year-old nephew is ahead of the other children his age in the motor skills listed in Table 5.1. Does that predict anything about how he will perform intellectually in first grade? Based on the fact, as you learned in Chapter 3, that there is no relationship between when we start walking and our later IQ, you would probably say no. You might reconsider that idea.

Among more than 3,000 kindergartners, developmentalists measured a variety of fine motor skills (such as the ability to draw a person and copy figures) and gross motor skills (such as hopping or skipping). Since the frontal lobes are involved in *generally* controlling our behavior, the researchers predicted that children who performed well at these feats of physical coordination might be better able to control their behavior in first grade.

They were correct (Beaver, Wright, & Delisi, 2007). Moreover, perhaps because preschool talents like drawing or copying forms demand special concentration, children with advanced fine motor abilities were superior at mastering first grade math (Luo and others, 2007).

This finding suggests that to improve "school readiness" we might train children to improve their fine motor skills—for instance, by giving preschoolers special practice drawing or writing. The problem, however, is that we must beware of going too far. Expecting 4-year-olds to write "just like adults," or even to master sports like baseball, is destined to produce frustration for parents and children alike. As young children don't have the frontal-lobe capacities to write well or play organized games, the focus during preschool should be on providing activities—such as cutting or pasting paper, or scaling the monkey bars—appropriate to young children's unfolding motor skills (Zaichkowsky & Larson, 1995). In early childhood, we need to walk a fine line: Provide plenty of chances for preschoolers to exercise their physical talents, but take care not to push; and be sure to provide the right person–environment fit.

Now that we know what kinds of environments encourage ideal physical development, it's time to look at what can go wrong.

Environmental Threats to Growth and Motor Skills

The main environmental force impairing growth and motor skills is the problem discussed in Chapter 3: lack of adequate food. In addition to causing stunting, undernutrition impairs gross and fine motor skills because it compromises the development of the bones, muscles, and brain. Even more important, when children are chronically hungry, they are too tired to move much and so don't get the experience crucial to developing their physical skills.

During the 1980s, researchers observed how undernourished children in rural Nepal helped maximize their growth rate by cutting down on play (Anderson & Mitchell, 1984). Play, as you will see in the next chapter, does more than exercise our

While the boys in the top photograph may have an advantage in the gross motor skills needed to win a potato sack race, the girl in the lower photo might surpass many of the boys in the fine motor talents involved in forming handwritten words.

gross motor skills Physical abilities that involve large muscle movements, such as running and jumping.

fine motor skills Physical abilities that involve small, coordinated movements, such as drawing and writing one's name.

body mass index (BMI) The ratio of weight to height; the main indicator of overweight or underweight.

childhood obesity A body mass index at or above the 95th percentile compared to the U.S. norms established for children in the 1970s.

bodies. It is crucial at teaching social cognition, or helping children learn how to get along with their peers (Pellegrini, Dupuis, & Smith, 2007). So the lethargy that malnutrition produces is as detrimental to children's relationships as it is to their developing bodies and brains. Notice how, after skipping just one meal, you become listless, unwilling to talk, and less interested in reaching out to people in a loving way.

Keeping in mind that undernutrition *remains* the top-ranking twenty-first-century global public health threat to physical development, let's now turn to the problem that is currently ringing alarm bells, especially in the developed world: childhood obesity.

Childhood Obesity

Have you ever wondered about the source of the numbers in the charts showing the ideal weights for people of different heights? These statistics come from a regular U.S. national poll called the National Health and Nutrition Examination Study (NHANES). Since the 1960s, the federal government has literally been measuring the size of Americans by charting average caloric intakes, heights, and weights. The statistic researchers use to monitor overweight is called **body mass index (BMI)**—the ratio of a person's weight to height. If a child's BMI is at or above the 95th percentile, compared to the norms in the first poll, that boy or girl qualifies as obese.

Childhood obesity started to balloon about 30 years ago. During the late 1980s, the NHANES researchers were astonished to find that the fraction of elementary school children qualifying as "seriously overweight" had roughly doubled over a decade (see Figure 5.2). As of 2006, roughly 1 in 6 U.S. elementary school children were defined as obese—more than four times the number in the original poll (National Center for Health Statistics, 2007; Ogden, Carroll, & Flegal, 2008). To bring this difference home, if you entered a second- or third-grade classroom in the early 1970s, one or two children might stand out as seriously overweight. Five or six boys and girls would fit that category today.

This rise in the fraction of children at the top of the weight charts is also a serious European concern. From Germany (Apfelbacher and others, 2008) to Great Britain (Ebbeling, Pawlak, & Ludwig, 2002), obesity rates more than doubled in the last decade of the twentieth century alone. Obesity is also an issue in rapidly developing countries such as China.

However, there is an interesting difference between the developed and developing worlds. In affluent nations, low-income children are more prone to be overweight (Lamerz and others, 2005; Sturm, 2004). In poor regions of the world, childhood obesity is a disease of the well-off (Berkowitz & Stunkard, 2002; Ebbeling, Pawlak, & Ludwig, 2002).

In the United States, there is an ethnic as well as a socioeconomic dimension to the epidemic. Obesity rates are highest among Latino and African American boys and girls (Ogden, Carroll, & Flegal, 2008).

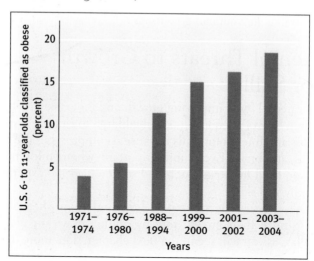

FIGURE 5.2: Percentage of U.S. children aged 6–11 who are classified as obese, selected years: This chart shows that the prevalence of child obesity almost doubled during the 1980s and at least until 2003–2004 has continued to rise.

Source: Adapted from National Center for Health Statistics, CDC, Prevalence of Overweight among Children and Adolescents, 2003–2004, April 2006 (retrieved, 1/7/09).

Obviously, our genetics have not changed. The real problem lies in an assault by a host of "obesogenic" environmental forces (Maziak, Ward, & Stockton, 2008). Families are eating out more often because working parents don't have the time to prepare nutritious, sit-down meals. Meals consumed outside of the home tend to be more calorie-dense (think of those "loaded" baked potatoes and huge hamburger platters) (Sturm, 2004). Restaurant portion sizes have expanded (notice also the popularity of those "all you can eat" buffets). High-calorie foods such as French fries and packaged snacks are relatively inexpensive. Plus, with the Internet and TV, playing outside—that typical childhood vehicle for burning up calories—has sharply declined. In fact, many parents prefer their sons and daughters to stay in the house because roaming the neighborhood can be unsafe. Moreover, with funding cutbacks and the pressure to focus on academics, most U.S. public schools no longer offer daily gym (Berg, 2004; Berkowitz & Stunkard, 2002; Sturm, 2004).

David Young-Wolff/Photo Edit

This photo shows just why heavy TV viewing promotes putting on pounds—total inactivity plus a tendency to gorge on high-calorie snacks, like buttered popcorn.

Everyone agrees that lack of physical activity is a primary culprit (DuBose and others, 2008; Fussenegger, Pietrobelli, & Widhalm, 2008). In one ambitious study, researchers followed a large group of Massachusetts children, from preschool to early adolescence, using electronic sensors to monitor their activity levels. The most active children had far lower BMIs as they traveled into adolescence (Moore and others, 2003). Time spent sitting and watching television, the researchers found, was also an independent predictor of subsequent body fat (Proctor and others, 2003).

There probably is a poisonous "nature evokes nurture" influence in operation here. Children who are genetically prone to be heavy may watch more TV because when they do participate in sports they may be teased: "He is too slow and clumsy. Let's not choose Fatty for the team." Less activity and more TV watching, in turn, makes children put on more pounds.

Gym teachers may do little to prevent this teasing. Physical education instructors, studies show, have especially negative attitudes toward obese children—judging them low on intelligence and clumsy. This message gets through. In one focus group study, overweight middle schoolers said that they avoided sports partly because they got comments from the coaches like: "You can't be good at this game" (Puhl & Latner, 2007).

This brings up the impact of prejudice. How deep-rooted are negative attitudes against heavy children? The answer, according to one review, should come as no surprise: very (Puhl & Latner, 2007). In a classic study, elementary schoolers were shown pictures of an overweight child, a child in a wheelchair, another with facial disfigurements, and several others with disabilities. When asked, "Whom would you choose as a friend?" the children ranked the obese boy or girl last. As early as age 3, children describe chubby boys and girls as "mean" and "sloppy." Worse yet, these reviewers concluded that in recent years anti-fat prejudices have grown more intense (Puhl & Latner, 2007). The unfortunate by-product of targeting obesity as a "huge" contemporary problem is that children who fall into that category are even more likely to be teased and scorned.

Since he is likely to be teased by the other kids (and perhaps even be put down by his teacher) for being "fat and clumsy," it makes sense that this boy would decide to sit on the sidelines during gym.

Attitudes seem less harsh in other cultures. In Hong Kong, obesity is more acceptable, less likely to negatively affect children's self-esteem (Marsh and others, 2007). There are differences by ethnicity—with African Americans generally more weight tolerant than their Caucasian counterparts (more about this in Chapter 8). So it makes sense, in one study, that overweight Black girls still felt very good about their physical appearance, even in the face of being teased at school (Tyler and others, 2009). And finally, there are dramatic variations from family to family. Parents who care vitally about physical beauty or have dysfunctional attitudes about their own bodies, hold especially negative stereotypes about overweight people—and are prone to continually nag their children about weight (Puhl & Latner, 2007).

Image Sources/Getty Images

Nagging backfires. Parents who make mealtime a battle ("You can only eat this much!") are as likely to produce overeating, or eating disorders, as to goad their child into shedding pounds (Puhl & Latner, 2007). And being nagged about being fat does very little for anyone's self-esteem.

There is also a danger in erring in the opposite direction. At a mall, researchers approached over 1,000 adults walking with their child and asked each parent to estimate this son or daughter's BMI. While adults with normal-weight children gave accurate estimates, moms or dads with an obese child saw their child as thinner than that boy or girl really was (Akerman, Williams, & Meuniser, 2007). Could this tendency to minimize problems—maybe we should just call it the need of loving parents to see their children as "just right"— actually be helping to perpetuate the childhood obesity epidemic?

Pediatricians seem to suffer from the same inattention. In scanning the medical records of 60,000 Cleveland children, researchers found that doctors rarely gave weight-related diagnoses when a patient's BMI clearly revealed that child was overweight (but not excessively so). They only listed "weight" as a health issue when a young patient was seriously obese (Benson, Baer, and Kaelber, 2009). Are medical personnel missing the chance to intervene at the very weight-gain stage when children might be best helped? For readers who plan to be nurses or doctors, how would you feel about bringing up this sensitive topic if a "somewhat" overweight older child arrived at your clinic for care?

Table 5.2 summarizes these delicate issues in a set of interventions for parents, teachers, and health-care providers. Still, because the *general* obesogenic environ-

---

TABLE 5.2: Physical Development: A Summary and Practical Messages

General Principle

Provide activities appropriate to children's unfolding capacities; for example, preschoolers don't have the physical capacities to play organized sports like T-ball. They need to run around on the playground, climb, jump, and exercise their bodies in a way that fits their developing skills.

Overweight

Advice for parents:

1. Find ways to make your child more physically active. Cut down on TV watching and access to the Internet. Drawing on the child's interests, focus on building some regular activity into the daily routine.

2. If your family lives within a mile or so of school, have the child walk or bike, rather than being driven, to class.

3. Try to eat family meals at home, and cut down on fast-food meals.

4. Avoid monitoring your son or daughter's food consumption and nagging about weight. This practice is likely to backfire, as the child may sneak food later. Also, nagging is likely to affect the child's self esteem—and so ironically lead to more eating, as a child may rely on food to cope with his distress.

5. Don't make weight a huge issue. Appreciate what is really important—your child's inner qualities; but don't ignore reality. If your son or daughter is genuinely overweight, take action by following the advice suggested above.

Advice for teachers:

1. Be alert to students' tendency to put down or tease their overweight classmates and actively teach the message that this kind of targeting is hurtful and mean (see the next chapter for advice on how to socialize "caring behavior").

2. Don't succumb to negative stereotypes about heavy children yourself!

Advice for health-care professionals:

1. During health-care visits, be careful to note a child's BMI; and when that girl or boy is in the "overweight" category, don't shy away from gently mentioning that fact. Then, advise parents and older children of the weight-control strategies suggested above.

Sources: The references in this chapter.

ment is mainly to blame, we need help from the wider world. Pass laws similar to ones in Western Europe that forbid soft-drink manufacturers from advertising on television shows targeted to children (Fussenegger, Pietrobelli, & Widhalm, 2008). Develop programs, such as pilot efforts in the United States, to incorporate physical exercise into classroom time (DuBose and others, 2008). Build walkable, bike-friendly communities (Maziak, Ward, & Stockton, 2008)—ones that discourage the use of cars. Can you think of some ways to provide a better person–environment fit, by redesigning your community to make physical activity a *natural* part of daily life?

✿ TYING IT ALL TOGETHER

1. You are astonished at the physical changes in your 7-year-old niece, Brittany, since you last saw her several years ago. Which example refers to the cephalocaudal principle and which to the mass-to-specific principle? (a) Brittany could barely draw a circle; now she can draw a detailed face; (b) Brittany's body has become much longer and skinnier.

2. Jessica has terrific gross motor skills but trouble with fine motor skills. Select the two sports from this list that Jessica would be most likely to excel at: long-distance running, tennis, water ballet, the high jump, bowling.

3. You are giving advice to an international panel on obesity. Based on the research, which suggestion should you make?

   a. Encourage families to eat out more.
   b. Use peer pressure to help goad children into losing weight.
   c. Pass laws that forbid advertising candy on children's television shows.

4. Your friend is concerned because her daughter, Tara, has been gaining weight. What is the best advice to give?

   a. Keep reminding Tara that she is too fat.
   b. Encourage Tara to be more physically active.
   c. Carefully monitor exactly what Tara eats.

Answers to the Tying It All Together questions can be found on the last page of this chapter.

Cognitive Development

In this section, we turn to the heart of this chapter: cognition. How do children develop intellectually as they travel from age 3 into elementary school? In our search for answers, we explore three very different perspectives on mental growth. Let's begin with the ideas of the master theorist Jean Piaget.

Piaget's Preoperational and Concrete Operational Stages

Recall from Chapter 1 that Piaget believed that through assimilation (fitting new information into their existing cognitive structures) and accommodation (changing those cognitive slots to fit input from the world), children undergo qualitatively different stages of cognitive growth. In Chapter 3, I discussed Piaget's sensorimotor stage. Now, it's time to tackle the next two stages, illuminated in Table 5.3 on page 146: the preoperational and concrete operational stages.

As their similar names imply, we need to discuss these two stages together. **Preoperational thinking** is defined by what children are missing—namely, the ability to step back from their immediate perceptions. **Concrete operational thinking** is defined by what children possess: the ability to reason about the world in a more logical, adult-like way.

When children leave infancy and enter the stage of preoperational thought, they have made tremendous mental strides. Still, they often seem on a different planet

preoperational thinking In Piaget's theory, the type of cognition characteristic of children aged 2 to 7, marked by an inability to step back from one's immediate perceptions and think conceptually.

concrete operational thinking In Piaget's framework, the type of cognition characteristic of children aged 8 to 11, marked by the ability to reason about the world in a more logical, adult way.

TABLE 5.3: Piaget's Stages: Focus on Childhood

Age	Name of Stage	Description
0–2	Sensorimotor	The baby manipulates objects to pin down the basics of physical reality. This stage ends with the development of language.
2–7	Preoperations	Children's perceptions are captured by their immediate appearances. "What they see is what is real." They believe, among other things, that inanimate objects are really alive and that if the appearance of a quantity of liquid changes (for example, if it is poured from a short, wide glass into a tall, thin one), the amount becomes different.
8–12	Concrete operations	Children have a realistic understanding of the world. Their thinking is really on the same wavelength as adults'. While they can reason conceptually about concrete objects, however, they cannot think abstractly in a scientific way.
12+	Formal operations	Reasoning is at its pinnacle: hypothetical, scientific, flexible, fully adult. Our full cognitive human potential has been reached.

from adults in terms of the way they reason about the world. The problem is that pre-operational children take things at face value. They are unable to look beyond the way objects immediately appear. By about age 7 or 8, children can mentally transcend what first hits their eye. They have entered the concrete operational stage.

The Preoperational Stage: Taking the World at Face Value

We saw some vivid examples of these "from another planet" ways of thinking in the preschoolers' conversations and actions in our chapter-opening vignette. Now, let's enter the minds of young children and explore the ways they reason about physical substances and the social world.

STRANGE IDEAS ABOUT SUBSTANCES The fact that preoperational children are locked into immediate appearances is illustrated by Piaget's (1965) famous **conservation tasks**. In Piaget's terminology, *conservation* refers to our knowledge that the amount of a given substance remains identical despite changes in its shape or form.

In the conservation of mass task, for instance, an adult gives a child a round ball of clay and asks that boy or girl to make another ball "just as big and heavy." Then she reshapes the ball so it looks like a pancake and asks, "Is there still the same amount now?" In the conservation of liquid task, the procedure is similar: Present a child with two identical glasses with equal amounts of liquid. Make sure he tells you, "Yes, they have the same amount of water or juice." Then, pour the liquid into a tall, thin glass while the child watches and ask, "Is there more or less juice now, or is there the same amount?"

Typically, when children under age 7 are asked this final question, they give a peculiar answer: "Now there is more clay" or "The tall glass has more juice." "Why?" "Because now the pancake is bigger" or "The juice is taller." Then, when the clay is remolded into a ball or the liquid poured into the original glass, they report: "Now it's the same again." The logical conflict in their statements doesn't bother them at all. In Figure 5.3, you can see these two procedures illustrated step by step as well as some examples of additional Piagetian conservation tasks you might want to perform with children you know.

Why can't young children conserve? For two reasons, Piaget believes. First, children don't grasp a concept called **reversibility**. This is the idea that an operation (or procedure) can be repeated in the opposite direction. Adults automatically accept as

conservation tasks Piagetian tasks that involve changing the shape of a substance to see whether children can go beyond the way that substance visually appears to understand that the amount is still the same.

reversibility In Piaget's conservation tasks, the concrete operational child's knowledge that a specific change in the way a given substance looks can be reversed.

Type of conservation	Initial step and question	Transformation and next question	Preoperational child's answer
Number	Two equal rows of pennies.  "Are these two rows the same?" (Yes.)	Increase spacing of pennies in one line.  "Now is the amount of money the same?"	 "No, the longer row has more."
Mass	Two equal balls of clay. 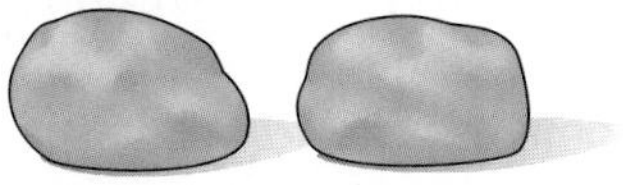 "Do these two balls have the same amount of clay?" (Yes.)	Squeeze one ball into a long pancake shape. 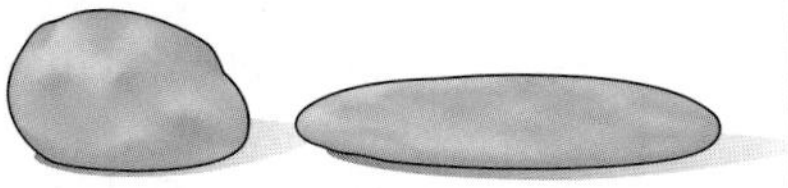 "Now is the amount of clay the same?"	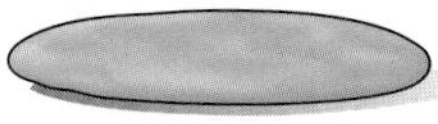 "No, the long, thin one has more clay."
Volume or liquid	Two glasses of the same size with liquid.  "Do these glasses have the same amount of juice?" (Yes.)	Pour one into a taller, narrower glass.  "Now do these glasses have the same amount of juice?"	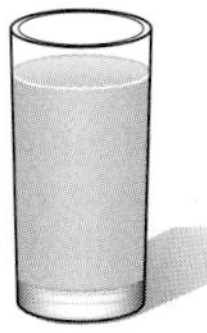 "No, the taller glass has more juice."
Matter*	Two identical cubes of sugar. 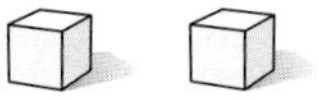 "Do these cubes have the same amount of sugar?" (Yes.)	Dissolve one cube in a glass of water. 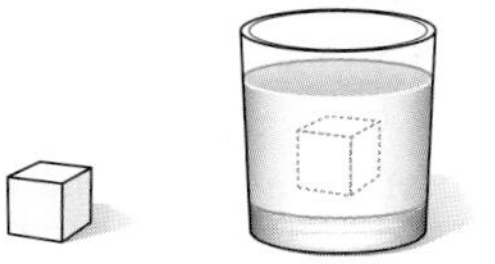 "Now is there the same amount of sugar?"	 "No, because you made one piece of sugar disappear."

*That is, the idea that a substance such as sugar is "still there" even though it seems to have disappeared (by dissolving).

FIGURE 5.3: **Four Piagetian conservation tasks:** Can you perform these tasks with a child you know?

given the fact that we can change various substances, such as our nail polish, hairstyle, or the color of our room, and simply reverse them to their original state. Young children lack this fundamental *schema*, or cognitive structure, for interpreting the world.

A second issue lies in an overall perceptual style that Piaget calls **centering**. Young children, Piaget believed, get fixated on the most striking feature of what they immediately see. They interpret things according to what first hits their eye, rather than taking in the entire visual array. In the conservation of liquid task, they get captivated by the height of the liquid. They don't notice that the width of the original container makes up for the height of the current one. When children reach concrete operations, they are able to **decenter**. They can step back from the immediate appearance of a substance and scan the whole picture—understanding that an increase in one dimension makes up for a loss in the other one.

Centering—the tendency to fix on what is visually most striking—causes children to make mistakes on a variety of real-world tasks. It affects **class inclusion**. This is the knowledge that a general category can encompass subordinate elements. Spread 20 Skittles and a few Gummi Bears on a plate and ask a 3-year-old, "Would you rather have the Skittles or the candy?" and she is almost certain to say, "The Skittles," even when you have determined beforehand that both types of candy have equal appeal. She gets mesmerized by the number of Skittles and does not notice that "candy" is the label for both.

centering In Piaget's conservation tasks, the preoperational child's tendency to fix on the most visually striking feature of a substance and not take other dimensions into account.

decentering In Piaget's conservation tasks, the concrete operational child's ability to look at several dimensions of an object or substance.

class inclusion The understanding that a general category can encompass several subordinate elements.

FIGURE 5.4: **A problem with seriation:** When asked to "put these sticks in order, from biggest to smallest," this kindergartner may center on the uppermost part of the table and identify the sticks numbered 2 and 5 as the biggest.

Centering interferes with **seriation**—the child's capacity to put objects in order according to some principle, such as size. Place sticks of different lengths in various positions on a table and tell a 5-year-old to arrange them from the smallest to the biggest, and she is likely to pick the sticks that protrude farthest first. Because, as you can see in Figure 5.4, she looks at (centers on) what first hits her eye, she doesn't consider the actual length of each stick.

These failures are a symptom of a more basic cognitive difficulty. According to Piaget, young children don't have the abstraction skills to understand the concept of a category within which we can classify objects. They don't grasp the idea that it is possible to rank objects in a series at all.

This tendency to focus on immediate appearances explains why, in the opening vignette, Moriah believed that Manuel had more paper when he cut his sheet into sections. Her attention was captured by the spread-out pieces, and she believed that now there must be more paper than before.

The idea that "bigger" automatically equals "more" extends to every aspect of preoperational thought. Ask a 3-year-old if he wants a nickel or a dime, and he will choose the first option. (This is a great source of pleasure to older siblings asked to equally share their funds.) Perhaps because greater height means "older" in their own lives, children even believe that a taller person has been on earth for a longer time:

> *I was substitute teaching with a group of kindergarten children—at the time I was about 22—and, when I met a student's mother at the end of the week, she was shocked. "When I asked Ben about you," she said, "he told me you were much older than his regular teacher." This teacher was in her mid- to late fifties and looked it. However, then we figured out the difference. This woman was barely 5 feet tall, whereas I am 6 feet two!*

PECULIAR PERCEPTIONS ABOUT PEOPLE Young children's tendency to believe that "what hits my eye right now is real" extends to people. It explains why a 3-year-old thinks her mommy is transformed into a princess when she dresses up for Halloween, or cries bitterly after her first visit to the beauty salon, believing that her short haircut has transformed her into a boy. It makes sense of why a favorite strategy of older sisters and brothers (to torture younger siblings) is to put on a mask and see the child run in horror from the room. As these examples show, young children lack a concept called **identity constancy**. They don't realize that people are still their essential selves despite changes in the way they visually appear.

I got insights into this identity constancy deficit at my son's fifth birthday party, when I hired a "gorilla" to entertain the guests (some developmental psychologist!). As the hairy six-foot figure rang the doorbell, mass hysteria ensued—requiring the

seriation The ability to put objects in order according to some principle, such as size.

identity constancy In Piaget's theory, the preoperational child's inability to grasp that a person's core "self" stays the same despite changes in external appearance.

When her dad puts on a mask, he suddenly becomes a scary monster to this 4-year-old girl because she has not yet grasped the principle of identity constancy.

There was one shadow that would constantly cast itself on my bedroom wall. It looked just like a giant creeping towards me with a big knife in his hand.

Our basement was a big hangout. But take away the kids and it was horrifying. I used to believe that Satan lived in my basement. The light switch was at the bottom of the steps, and whenever I switched off the light it was a mad dash to the top. I was so scared that Satan was going to stab my feet with knives.

Boy, do I remember my mom's doll that sat on the top of my dresser. I called it "Chatty Kathy." This doll came to life every night. She would stare at me, no matter where I went.

My mother used to take me when she went to clean house for Mrs. Handler, a rich lady. Mrs. Handler had this huge, shiny black grand piano, and I thought it came alive when I was not looking at it. It was so enormous, dark, and quiet. I remember pressing one of the bass keys, which sounded really deep and loud and it terrified me.

I remember being scared that there was something alive under my bed. I must tell you I sometimes still get scared that someone is under my bed and that they are going to grab me by my ankles. I don't think I will ever grow out of this, as I am 26.

Can you relate to any of these childhood memories collected from my students? Perhaps your enemy was that evil creature lurking in your basement, under your bed, or in the shadows in your room; the frightening stuffed animal on your wall; a huge object (with teeth) such as that piano; or your local garbage truck.

Now, you know where that master storyteller Stephen King gets his ideas. King's genius is that he taps into the preoperational kinds of thoughts that we have papered over, though not very well, as adults. When we read King's story about a toy animal that clapped cymbals to signal someone's imminent death, or about Christine, the car with a mind of its own, or about the laundry-pressing machine that loved human blood—these stories fall on familiar childhood ground. Don't you still get a bit anxious when you enter a dark basement? Even today, on a very dark night, do you have an uneasy feeling that some strange monster might be lurking beneath your bed?

gorilla to take off his head. After the children calmed down, and the gorilla put on his head again to enact his skit, guess what? Pure hysteria again! Why did that huge animal cause such pandemonium? The reason is that the children believed that the gorilla, even though a costumed figure, was really alive.

Animism refers to the difficulty young children have in sorting out what is really alive. Specifically, preschoolers see inanimate objects—such as dolls or costumed figures—as having consciousness, too. Look back at the vignette and you will notice several examples of animistic thinking—for example, the Barbies that were hungry or the wind that ran away. Now, think back to when you were age 5 or 6. Do you remember being afraid the escalator might decide to suck you in? Or perhaps you recall believing, as in the Experiencing the Lifespan box, that your dolls came alive at night.

Listen to young children talking about nature, and you will hear delightful examples of animism: "The sun gets sleepy when I sleep." "The moon likes to follow me in the car." The practice of assigning human motivations to natural phenomena is not something we automatically grow out of as adults. Think of the Greek thunder god Zeus, or the ancient Druids who worshiped the spirits that lived within trees. Throughout history, humans have regularly used animism to make sense of a frightening world.

A related concept is called **artificialism.** Young children believe that everything in nature was made by human beings. Here is an example of this "daddy power" in action from Piaget's 3-year-old daughter, Laurent:

L was in bed in the evening and it was still light: "Put the light out please" . . . (I switched the electric light off.) "It isn't dark"—"But I can't put the light out outside" . . . "Yes you can, you can make it dark." . . . "How?" . . . "You must turn it out very hard. It'll be dark and there will be little lights everywhere (stars)."

(Piaget, 1951/1962, p. 248)

His animistic thinking causes this 4-year-old to believe that the bear is really going to enjoy the ride he is going to provide.

animism In Piaget's theory, the preoperational child's belief that inanimate objects are alive.

artificialism In Piaget's theory, the preoperational child's belief that human beings make everything in nature.

Animism and artificialism are perfect illustrations of Piaget's concept of assimilation. The child knows that she is alive and so applies her "alive" schema to every object. Having seen adults perform heroic physical feats, such as turning off lights and building houses, a 3-year-old generalizes the same "big people control things" schema to the universe at large. Imagine that you are a young child taking a family tour around the American West. After you visited that gleaming construction called Las Vegas, wouldn't it make perfect sense to you that people had carved out the Grand Canyon and the Rocky Mountains, too?

The sun and moon examples illustrate another basic aspect of preoperational thought. According to Piaget, young children believe that they are the literal center of the universe, the pivot around which everything else revolves. Their worldview is characterized by **egocentrism**—the inability to understand that other people have different points of view from their own.

By *egocentrism*, Piaget does not mean that young children are vain or uncaring, although they will tell you they are the smartest people on earth and the activities of the heavenly bodies are at their beck and call. Many of their most loving acts show egocentrism. There is nothing more touching than a 3-year-old's offer of a favorite "blankee" if he sees you upset. The child is egocentric, however, because he naturally assumes that what comforts *him* will automatically comfort you.

You can easily pick out examples of egocentrism when having a conversation with a young child. In the opening vignette, for instance, remember that Kanesha got disgusted that I didn't automatically know her name. She didn't feel she had to give me background information about Nadia, this person who cooked so beautifully, because she felt I must know everything that was in her head.

Piaget views egocentrism as a perfect example of centering in the human world. Young children are unable to decenter from their own mental processes. They don't realize that what is in their mind is not in everyone else's awareness, too.

The Concrete Operational Stage: Getting on the Adult Wavelength

Piaget discovered that the transition from preoperations to concrete operations happens gradually. First, children are preoperational in every area. Then, between ages 5 and 7, their thinking gets less static, or "thaws out" (Flavell, 1963). A 6-year-old, when given the conservation of liquid task, might first say the taller glass had more liquid, but then, after it is poured back into a very wide glass, become unsure: "Is it really bigger or not?" She has reached the tipping point when she cannot assimilate her experiences to her existing preoperational schemas and is poised to reason on a higher cognitive plane.

By age 8, the child has reached this higher-level, concrete operational state: "Even though the second glass is taller, the first is wider" (showing decentering); "You can pour the liquid right back into the short glass and it would look the same (illustrating reversibility). Now, she doesn't realize that she ever had a different idea: "Are you silly? Of course it's the same!"

Piaget also found that specific conservations come in at different times. First, at about age 5, children learn numbers and then later master conservation of mass and liquid. They may not figure out the most difficult conservations until age 11 or 12. Imagine the challenge of understanding the last task in Figure 5.3 (see page 147)—realizing that when a packet of sugar is dissolved in water, it still exists, but in its basic molecular form.

Still, according to Piaget, age 8 is a landmark for looking beyond immediate appearances, for understanding seriation and categories, for decentering in the physical and social worlds, for abandoning the tooth fairy and the idea that our stuffed animals are alive, and for entering the planet of adults.

Table 5.4 shows examples of different kinds of preoperational ideas. Now test yourself by seeing if you can classify each statement in Piagetian terms.

egocentrism In Piaget's theory, the preoperational child's inability to understand that other people have different points of view from their own.

TABLE 5.4: Can You Identify the Type of Preoperational Thought from These Real-World Examples?

Here are your possible choices: (*a*) no identity constancy, (*b*) animism, (*c*) artificialism, (*d*) egocentrism, (*e*) no conservation, and (*f*) inability to use classification.

_____ 1. Heidi was watching her father fix lunch. After he cut her sandwich into quarters, Heidi said, "Oh, Daddy, I only wanted you to cut it in *two* pieces. I'm not hungry enough to eat four!" (Bjorklund & Bjorklund, 1992, p. 168).

_____ 2. My 2-year-old son and I were taking our yearly trip to visit Grandma in Florida. As the plane took off and gained altitude, Thomas looked out the window and said with a delighted grin, "Mommy, TOYS!"

_____ 3. Melanie watched as her father, a professional clown, put on his clown outfit and then began applying his makeup. Before he could finish, Melanie suddenly ran screaming from the room, terrified of the strange clown.

_____ 4. Your child can't understand that he could live in his town and in his state at the same time. He tells you angrily, "I live in Newark, not New Jersey."

_____ 5. As you cross the George Washington Bridge over the Hudson River to New Jersey, your child asks, "Did the same people who built the bridge also make the river?"

Answers: 1 (e), 2 (d), 3 (a), 4 (f), 5 (c)

INTERVENTIONS: Using Piaget's Ideas at Home and at Work

Piaget's concepts provide wonderful insights into the mysterious workings of young children's minds. For teachers, the theory explains that you need the same-sized cups at a kindergarten lunch table so that an argument won't erupt, even if the children poured each drink from identical cans. Nurses now understand that rationally explaining the purpose of a painful medical procedure to a 4-year-old may not be as effective as providing a magic doll to help the child cope.

The theory makes sense of why forming a Little League team with a group of 4- or 5-year-olds is an impossible idea. Grasping the rules of a game requires abstract conceptualization—a skill that preoperational children do not yet possess. It tells us why young children are terrified of their dreams, the dark, and scary clowns at the amusement park. So for parents who feel uneasy about playing into their child's fantasies when they provide "anti-monster spray" to calm those bedtime fears, one justification is that, according to Piaget, when your child is ready, she will naturally grow out of her ideas.

Piaget's concepts also give us wonderful insights into children's specific passions at different ages. They explain the power of pretending in early childhood (more about this in Chapter 6) and the irresistible lure of that favorite childhood holiday, Halloween. When a 4-year-old child dresses up as Batman, he may be grappling with the challenge of understanding that you can look different yet still remain your essential self. The theory accounts for why third or fourth graders become captivated with games, such as checkers and soccer, and can be avid collectors of items such as baseball cards. Now that they can understand the concept of rules and categories, concrete operational children are determined to exercise their new conceptual and classification skills.

On a larger scale, the theory explains why "real school" (around the world), the academic part, begins at about age 7. Children younger than this age—those still in the preoperational stage—don't have the intellectual tools to understand reversibility, a concept critical to understanding mathematics (if 2 plus 4 is 6, then 6 minus 4 must equal 2). Even having the capacity to fully empathize with the teacher's agenda or grasp the purpose of school is a concrete operational skill.

The fact that age 8 is an important coming-of-age marker is symbolized by the classic movie *Home Alone*. The plot of this film would have

In late elementary school, children take great pride in collecting, classifying, and trading items like Yu-Gi-Oh cards because they are practicing their new concrete operational skills.

Suzanne Kreiter/The Boston Globe/The New York Times

been unthinkable if its hero were 5 or even 6. If the star was 11, the movie would not be interesting because by this age a child could competently take care of himself. Eight is that fragile point when we begin to make the transition to really being able to make it "home alone." It is the age when we shift from worrying about monsters—things that are not real—to grappling with the kinds of dangers that we really face as adults.

Evaluating Piaget

Piaget has clearly transformed the way we think about young children. Still, as you saw with infancy, in important areas, Piaget was incorrect.

I described a major problem with Piaget's ideas in Chapter 3: In the same way as he minimized what babies know, Piaget underestimated preoperational children's cognitive capacities. In particular, Piaget overstated young children's egocentrism. If even 1-year-olds can decode other people's feelings, the first awareness that we live in "different heads" must dawn on children at a far younger age than 8. (As I mentioned earlier, I'll be charting this mind-reading ability later in the chapter.)

We might also take issue with Piaget's idea that we automatically grow out of animism by age 8 or 9. Maybe he was giving us too *much* credit here. Do you have a good luck charm that keeps the plane from crashing, or a favorite place you go for comfort where you can literally hear the trees whispering to you?

Most children around the world eventually do learn to conserve (Dasen, 1977, 1984). But, because nature interacts with nurture, the ages at which they master specific conservation tasks vary from place to place. An interesting example comes from a village in Mexico where weaving is the main adult occupation. Young children in this collectivist culture grasp conservation tasks involving spatial concepts when they are younger than age 7 or 8, because they have so much hands-on training in activities relating to this kind of skill (Maynard & Greenfield, 2003). This brings up a crucial dimension that Piaget's theory leaves out: the impact of teaching in promoting cognitive growth.

Lauren Greenfield/VII Photo

Because this girl growing up in Mexico gets so much practice at weaving, we might expect her to grasp concrete operational conservation tasks related to spatial concepts at a relatively early age.

Vygotsky's Zone of Proximal Development

Piaget gives the impression of a child working alone to construct a more adult view of the world. We can't convince young children that their dolls are not alive or that the width of the glass makes up for the height. They have to grow out of those ideas on their own. The Russian psychologist Lev Vygotsky (1962, 1978, 1986) had a different perspective. Vygotsky believed that people propel mental growth.

Vygotsky was born in the same year as Piaget. He showed as much brilliance at an exceptionally young age, but—unlike Piaget, who lived to a ripe old age—he died of tuberculosis in his late thirties. Still, Vygotsky's writings have given him towering status in developmental science today. One reason is that Vygotsky was, at heart, an educator. He offered a framework for understanding how what *we* do helps children to advance cognitively.

According to Vygotsky, learning takes place within the **zone of proximal development,** which he defined as the difference between what the child can do by himself and his level of "potential development as determined through problem solving under adult guidance or in collaboration with more capable peers" (Vygotsky, 1978, p. 86). Teachers must tailor their instruction to a child's proximal zone. Then, as that child becomes more competent, the instructor should slowly back off and allow the student more responsibility for directing a particular learning activity. This sensitive pacing has a special name. It is called **scaffolding** (Wood, Bruner, & Ross, 1976).

You saw scaffolding in operation in Chapter 3 in my discussion of infant-directed speech, the simplified language that adults use when talking to babies. Recall that

zone of proximal development In Vygotsky's theory, the gap between a child's ability to solve a problem totally on his own and his potential knowledge if taught by a more accomplished person.

scaffolding The process of teaching new skills by entering a child's zone of proximal development and tailoring one's efforts to that person's competence level.

baby talk has a very adult function. It permits caregivers to penetrate a young child's proximal zone for language and so helps scaffold emerging speech. Now, let's explore scaffolding firsthand, as we listen in on a mother teaching her 5-year-old daughter how to play her first board game, Chutes and Ladders:

> *Tiffany threw the dice, then looked up at her mother. Her mother said, "How many is that?" Tiffany shrugged her shoulders. Her mother said, "Count them," but Tiffany just sat and stared. Her mother counted the dots aloud, and then said to her daughter, "Now you count them," which Tiffany did. This was repeated for the next five turns. Tiffany waited for her mother to count the dots, then modeled her mother's actions and moved her piece. On her sixth move, however, Tiffany counted the dots on the dice on her own after her mother's request. . . . During the next few moves, her mother still had to ask Tiffany to count how many dots she had. But eventually, Tiffany threw the dice and counted the dots herself and continued to do so, practicing counting and moving the pieces on both her own and her mother's turns.*

(Bjorklund & Rosenblum, 2001)

Notice that this mother was a superb scaffolder. By pacing her interventions to Tiffany's emerging capacities, she paved the way for her child to master the game. But this process did not just flow from parent to child. Tiffany was also teaching her mother how to best respond. Just as your professor is getting new insights into lifespan development from the process of teaching every single class—or at this very minute, as I struggle to write this page, I'm learning how to better connect with Vygotsky's ideas—education is a *bidirectional*, mind-expanding duet (Scrimsher & Tudge, 2003).

In our culture, we have definite ideas about what makes a good scaffolder. Enter a child's proximal zone. Actively instruct, but also be sensitive to a child's input and responses. However, in collectivist societies, such as among the Mayans living in Mexico's Yucatán Peninsula, children learn mainly by observation. They listen in on adult conversations. They watch. They are not explicitly taught the skills they will need for adult life (Rogoff and others, 2003). So the very qualities our culture sees as vital to socializing children are not necessarily part of the ideology of good parenting in other regions of the globe.

This girl in Thailand is learning to weave just by observing her mother—a strategy that we might find strange in our teaching-oriented culture.

INTERVENTIONS: Becoming an Effective Scaffolder

In our teaching-oriented society, what exactly do superior scaffolders do? Let's list a few techniques:

- They take care to foster a secure attachment, as they realize that nurturing, responsive interactions are a basic foundation for learning (Laible, 2004).

- They break a larger cognitive challenge, such as learning Chutes and Ladders, into smaller, more manageable steps (Berk & Winsler, 1999).

- They give nonthreatening (but clear) feedback about failure—for instance, hesitating and looking at the correct alternative when the child makes a mistake (Gallimore & Tharp, 1992; Rogoff, 1990).

- They continue helping until they know the child has fully mastered the concept before moving on, as Tiffany's mother did earlier.

- They set an overall framework for the learning task and build in motivation. So, in teaching reading, a first-grade teacher might say: "This is a book about lions. It's about how the author makes friends with a cub. Ooh, this looks like a really interesting book. I can't wait to see what the author says!" (Clay & Cazden, 1992).

TABLE 5.5: Piagetian and Vygotskian Perspectives on Life and Learning

	Lev Vygotsky (1896–1934)	Jean Piaget (1896–1980)

Biography	Russian, Jewish, communist (reached teenage years during the Russian Revolution) believed in Marx	Swiss, middle-class family
Basic Interests	Education, literature, literary criticism. Wanted to know how to stimulate thinking.	Biology, mollusks. Wanted to trace the evolution of thought in stages.
Overall Orientation	Look at interpersonal processes and the role of society in cognition	Look for universal developmental processes
Basic Ideas	1. We develop intellectually through social interactions.	1. We develop intellectually through physically acting on the world.
	2. Development is a collaborative endeavor.	2. Development takes place on our own inner timetable.
	3. People cause cognitive growth.	3. When we are internally ready, we reach a higher level of cognitive development.
Implications for Education	Instruction is critical to development. Teachers should sensitively intervene within each child's zone of proximal development.	Provide ample materials to let children explore and learn on their own.

In Chapter 7, we'll be looking at these qualities as they relate to elementary school teaching. For now, think of a master scaffolder, or teacher, who stood out in your life. List that person's qualities. Keep your list handy to see if your items fit the teaching talents you'll read about two chapters from now.

Table 5.5 compares Vygotsky's and Piaget's perspectives and offers capsule summaries of the different backgrounds that shaped these world-class geniuses' ideas (Vianna & Stetsenko, 2006). Although typically described in opposing terms, these two theories form an ideal complementary pair. Piaget gave us unparalleled insights into the developing structure of childhood cognition. Vygotsky offered us an engine to transform children's lives.

The Information-Processing Perspective

Vygotsky filled in the missing social pieces of Piaget's theory and provided us with a framework for stimulating mental growth. But he did not address the gaps in the theory itself. Exactly *why* are children able to decenter? What specific skills allow children to understand that the width of the glass makes up for the height?

Piaget never mentions how crucial abilities such as memory, concentration, and planning develop. Ms. Angela, the preschool teacher in the opening vignette, might wonder (with good reason) if she was asking too much of her 3-year-olds to remember those free-play rules. Elementary school teachers might want tips for teaching spelling to a third-grade class. Parents might be looking for guidelines as to what to expect from a child at a particular age: "Can my six-year-old daughter take responsibility for caring for a puppy?" "When will my son have the organizational skills to get ready for school on his own?" Clinical psychologists and caregivers would want to understand why a particular child has so much trouble focusing and obeying at school and at home. To get this information, everyone would gravitate toward the *information-processing approach*.

Information-processing theorists view mental growth as continuous rather than progressing in qualitatively distinct stages. They break cognitive processes into components and divide thinking into specific steps. Let's illustrate this approach by examining the information-processing perspective on memory, the basis of all thought.

Does a girl this age have the memory capacity and self-regulation skills necessary to take proper care of a dog? This is the kind of question that an information-processing perspective on cognition can answer.

Making Sense of Memory

Information-processing theorists believe that on the way to becoming "a memory," information passes through different stores, or stages. First, we hold stimuli arriving from the outside world very briefly in a sensory store. Then, features that we notice enter the most important store, called working memory.

Working memory is where the "cognitive action" takes place. Here, we keep information in awareness and act to either process it or discard it. Working memory is made up of limited-capacity holding bins. It also consists of an "executive processor," which allows us to focus on what we need to remember as well as to manipulate the material in working memory to prepare it for permanent storage (Baddeley, 1992). Once we have processed what we need to learn through working memory, it enters a more long-lasting store, and we can recall that information at a later time.

You can get a real-life example of the fleeting quality of working memory when you get a phone number from information and immediately make the call from a landline phone. You know that you can dial the seven-digit number without having to write it down, and your memory will not fail *if you get to finish*. If you are interrupted and lose your focus, the number mysteriously evaporates. In fact, for adults, the typical bin size of working memory is about the size of a local phone number: seven chunks (in this case, digits) of information.

Interestingly, by examining age changes in working memory, information-processing researchers have offered an explanation for why young children can't conserve. Memory-bin capacity expands dramatically between ages 2 and 7—from about two to five bits of information (Dempster, 1981). During preschool, there are also dramatic advances in children's ability to focus on relevant information (Garon, Bryson, & Smith, 2008). These changes, developmentalists speculate, may explain why children reach concrete operations at roughly age 7 or 8 (Case, 1999; Pascual-Leone, 1970). By this age, we finally have the memory capacities to step back from our immediate impressions and remember that what we saw previously (such as a wider glass) compensates for what we are seeing right now.

Exploring Executive Functions

Executive functions refer to any skill related to managing our memory, controlling our cognitions, planning our behavior, and inhibiting our responses. Executive functions are programmed by the brain's master planner—the frontal lobes. Now, let's look at three examples of executive functions that make children in concrete operations radically different thinkers than they were at age 4 or even 5.

OLDER CHILDREN REHEARSE INFORMATION A major way we learn new information is through **rehearsal**. We repeat material again and again to embed it in memory. In a classic study, developmentalists had kindergartners, second graders, and fifth graders memorize objects (such as a cat or a desk) pictured on cards (Flavell, Beach, & Chinsky, 1966). Prior to the testing, the research team watched the children's lips to see if

information-processing theory A perspective on cognition in which the process of thinking is divided into steps, components, or stages much like those a computer operates.

working memory In information-processing theory, the limited-capacity gateway system, containing all the material that we can keep in awareness at a single time. The material in this system is either processed for more permanent storage or lost.

executive functions Any frontal-lobe ability that allows us to inhibit our responses and to plan and direct our thinking.

rehearsal A learning strategy in which people repeat information to embed it in memory.

selective attention A learning strategy in which people manage their awareness so as to attend only to what is relevant and to filter out unneeded information.

they were using the strategy of repeating the names of the objects to themselves. Eighty-five percent of the fifth graders used rehearsal; only 10 percent of the kindergartners did. So one reason why older children are superior learners is that they understand that they need to rehearse.

And, furthermore, as children get older, their rehearsal strategy becomes better thought out. Researchers asked third, fifth, and eighth graders to memorize a series of words (Ornstein, Naus, & Liberty, 1975). They presented each word individually and gave the children time in between each presentation to rehearse aloud. Third graders just repeated the previous word, for example, saying, *yard, yard, yard, yard.* Older children allotted their rehearsal time more strategically, saying *yard, yard, man, desk,* to make sure they kept in mind all the words they needed to recall.

To bring home the message of this research: If your final exam in this class is cumulative, you know you need to spend most of your time memorizing the last section of this book but still need to go back and review what you learned for the other tests. In third grade, you *never* would have grasped this fundamental studying strategy.

OLDER CHILDREN UNDERSTAND HOW TO SELECTIVELY ATTEND The ability to manage our awareness so we focus on what we need to know and filter out extraneous information is called **selective attention.** In a classic study illustrating young children's problems in this area, researchers presented boys and girls of different ages with cards. On one half of each card was an animal photo; on the other half was a picture of some household item (see Figure 5.5). The children were instructed to remember only the animals.

As you might expect, older children were far better at recalling the animal names. But now comes the interesting part: When the children were asked how many household items they could recall, the performance differences between the age groups evaporated—suggesting that the young children wasted effort looking at the objects they did not need to know (Bjorklund, 2005). This suggests that, in addition to having smaller memory bins, young children tend to clog their existing bin space with irrelevant information. They can't focus their attention as well on what is relevant and filter out extraneous stimuli.

OLDER CHILDREN ARE SUPERIOR AT INHIBITION In the opening vignette, you saw the enormous problems young children have inhibiting their impulses when the 3-year-olds ran into the different activity centers without stepping back and thinking, "That's not what I'm supposed to do." The most fascinating example of inhibition problems occurred during the weather report. Because the temptation to say yes was so strong, the children could not restrain themselves from putting up their hands and agreeing when the teacher asked *any* question about the weather that day.

To measure differences in inhibition directly, researchers have developed ingenious strategies (Garon, Bryson, & Smith, 2008). Sometimes, they ask children to per-

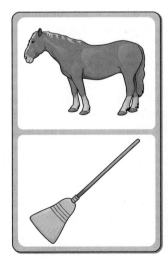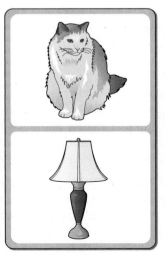

FIGURE 5.5: A selective attention study: In this study measuring *selective attention,* children were asked *only* to memorize the animals on the top half of the cards. Then researchers looked for age differences in their memory for the irrelevant household items.

form some action that contradicts their immediate tendencies, such as instructing them to say the word *black* when they see the word *white* (Diamond, Kirkham, & Amso, 2002). Or, in what are called *delay of gratification* studies, they may tell children, "you can get a small treat now or a larger one if you wait."

Children's ability to master the last task in particular improves markedly during preschool. The typical 3-year-old can delay gratification for one minute; most 4-year-olds can wait for five (Garon, Bryson, & Smith, 2008). In fact, notice that many activities in the chapter-opening vignette—such as the center rules or even the move faster and slower dance—were designed to train children in the vital skill of delaying gratification, or controlling their immediate responses.

The bottom line is that if you think self-control is difficult for you, imagine being a young child. And never, ever tell a 4- or 5-year-old to keep a "big secret." Her automatic response will be to immediately blurt it out!

Given that the exciting news is on this child's mind and the frontal lobes are still under construction, there is no such thing as a secret!

INTERVENTIONS: Using Information-Processing Theory at Home and at Work

So, to bring us back to the questions at the beginning of this section, teachers *cannot* assume that their third graders will automatically understand how to memorize spelling words. Scaffolding study skills, such as the need to rehearse, or teaching strategies to promote selective attention, such as putting large stars next to the relevant words for a test, should be an integral part of education, beginning in elementary school.

Parents will probably need to regularly remind a child, even at age 6 or 7, to feed the dog. Expect activities requiring many different information-processing tasks, such as getting dressed and remembering to take homework and pencils to class, to be a challenge *throughout* elementary school (and beyond). Actively scaffold organizational strategies, such as helping a second grader get everything ready for school before bedtime and teaching that child to put important items such as a book bag in specific places. For everyone else, the information-processing research suggests that executive functions, such as using learning strategies, selectively attending, and inhibiting our behavior, are processes that improve gradually over *many years* (Garon, Bryson, & Smith, 2008).

Table 5.6 summarizes these practical messages and provides some additional information-processing tips. Now let's look at the insights the information-processing

---

TABLE 5.6: **Information-Processing Tips for Adults to Use with Young and Older Children**

Early Childhood

1. Don't expect a child to remember, without considerable prompting, regular chores such as feeding a pet, the details of a movie or show, or the name of the person who telephoned.

2. Expect the child to have a good deal of trouble with any situation that involves inhibiting a strong "prepotent impulse"—such as not touching toys, following unpleasant rules, or keeping a secret.

Middle Childhood

1. Don't assume that the child knows how to best master school-related memorization tasks. Actively teach the need to rehearse information, selective attention strategies (such as underlining important points), and other studying skills.

2. Scaffold organizational strategies for school and life. For example, get the child to use a notebook for each class assignment and to keep important objects, such as eyeglasses, in a specific place.

3. Expect situations that involve many different tasks, such as getting ready for school, to present problems. Also expect activities that involve *ongoing* inhibition to give children trouble, such as refraining from watching TV or using the Internet before finishing their homework. Try to build in a regular structure for mastering these difficult executive-functioning tasks: "The rule is that at 8 or 9 P.M., it's time to get everything ready for school"; "Homework must be completed by dinnertime, or the first thing after you get home from school."

4. To promote selective attention (and inhibition), have a child do homework, or any task that involves concentration, in a room away from tempting distractions such as the TV or Internet.

perspective offers caregivers, teachers, and health-care providers who are interested in understanding children with problems focusing and obeying—boys and girls with attention deficit/hyperactivity disorder, or ADHD.

ATTENTION DEFICIT/HYPERACTIVITY DISORDER

Attention deficit/hyperactivity disorder (ADHD), defined by excessive restlessness and distractibility, is the top-ranking health disorder among U.S. children—affecting roughly 4 million children. Although preschoolers also have this label, ADHD is typically diagnosed in elementary school. During middle childhood, problems sitting still and focusing become clearly apparent and cause widespread, serious trouble in school and at home (Thorell & Rydell, 2008).

ADHD is mainly a male problem—striking two to three times as many boys as girls (Bauermeister and others, 2007). Today, roughly one out of ten 10-year-old boys in the United States is taking medications for this problem! (Castle and others, 2007.)

As ADHD runs in families (Waldman, 2007), researchers are feverishly trying to pin down the neurological problem that might be involved. One popular theory is that people with ADHD have a lower-than-normal output of the neurotransmitter dopamine (Williams, 2008). Scientists also find abnormal patterns of neural activation when these children perform learning tasks (Durston & Konrad, 2007; Hale and others, 2007; Smith and others, 2008). Still, there is no definitive biological test or marker that is diagnostic of ADHD.

According to one expert, a core difficulty with this condition lies in problems with inhibition (Barkley, 1998, 2003). When told, for instance, "Don't touch the toys," boys and girls diagnosed with ADHD have unusual trouble not touching.

These children have special problems with selective attention, too. Researchers asked elementary school children to watch a story on TV (Siklos & Kerns, 2004). In one condition, toys were in the room. In another, there were none. When asked to explain the point of the story, the children diagnosed with ADHD performed just as well as the control group when the toys were not present, but they did more poorly when these distracting objects were around. So, even when they are just as intellectually capable, competing stimuli derail children with ADHD.

As you might imagine, performing several different activities under time pressure, such as getting dressed and ready for school by 7:00 A.M., present immense problems for boys and girls with this condition (Pugzles Lorch and others, 2004). Furthermore, as one study showed, getting verbal feedback about their performance may not be enough to help these children stay on task. In this research, elementary schoolers with ADHD were only helped to focus when given money or another immediate external reward (Durston and others, 2007).

These problems explain why even the most intellectually gifted child with ADHD can have considerable trouble in school. Classrooms are highly distracting environments. Taking tests demands having the inner resources to delay gratification and focus on your own.

The same issues with inhibition, time management, and selective attention lead to failures at home. In dealing with their child's difficulties, parents may resort to *power-assertion* disciplinary techniques. They may lash out at a 9-year-old who seems incapable of getting his things in order. They may scream at a child who seems unwilling to "just sit still." So boys and girls with ADHD are sometimes *least* likely to get the

attention deficit/hyperactivity disorder (ADHD) The most common childhood learning disorder in the United States, disproportionately affecting boys, characterized by excessive restlessness and distractibility at home and at school.

sensitive, loving parenting that they most need. Their problems controlling their behavior also set these children up to fail socially with their peers (Andrade and others, 2009; Mrug and others, 2009; more about these issues in the next chapter). Given these dangers, what should a caring adult do?

INTERVENTIONS: Helping Children with ADHD

The standard treatment for ADHD is to provide psycho-stimulant medications, such as Ritalin. Drugs are useful particularly at reducing the impulsivity, or inhibition problems, basic to ADHD (Barkley & Murphy, 2006; Sutcliffe, Bishop, & Houghton, 2006). Medications are most effective when combined with therapeutic interventions, such as using reinforcement for appropriate behavior (Olfson and others, 2003; Monastra, 2008).

Another strategy is to foster the best possible person–environment fit (Murphy, 2005). Don't put unreasonable demands on a child to do difficult processing tasks. Provide a non-distracting environment during activities that demand selective attention, such as completing homework and taking tests.

Interestingly, perhaps because it helps stimulate dopamine production, boys and girls with ADHD learn better in noisy environments. So, to enhance a school-aged child's ability to focus on his homework, it may help to provide high levels of "white" background noise (Soderlund, Sikstrom, & Smart, 2007). Offering regular exercise can be beneficial, too. Researchers gave an elementary school class periodic recess and then compared their classroom behavior on recess and non-recess days. On recess days, the children with ADHD showed lower rates of "inappropriate behavior." In fact, regular recess helped *every* child stay on task and focus better on work (Ridgway and others, 2003).

Formal schooling is a fairly recent development on the human landscape. Our ancestors never needed to sit in a classroom for hours. To what degree might this contemporary problem be partly a product of poor childhood–society fit? (See, for instance, Panksepp, 1998; Timimi, 2004.)

This brings up the controversy surrounding the diagnosis of ADHD. Are we overmedicating children for a condition that may sometimes not be "real"? Although diagnosed in terms of a category—"this person has this condition or not"—ADHD symptoms appear on a continuum (Frazier, Youngstrom, & Naugle, 2007). Where should we *really* put the cutting point between normal childhood inattentiveness and "a problem" in need of drugs? Especially troubling is the male tilt to ADHD. As you will see in the next chapter, boys are biologically programmed to run around. Without denying that ADHD can cause considerable heartache to children and adults in today's world, what role might cultural forces play in the frequency of this diagnosis—and its knee-jerk treatment via medicine—at this particular moment in history?

Royalty-Free/Corbis

Making the environment as free of distractions as possible and providing "white" background noise is the best strategy for helping this boy diagnosed with ADHD stop daydreaming and focus on his schoolwork.

Wrapping up Cognition

Now that I have reached the end of our survey of cognition, it is clear why our species needs a decade (or two) beyond infancy to master the intellectual challenges of the adult world. Now, imagine the insights we would be missing if we left out any theory. What if you want to make sense of the strange ideas preschoolers have, or need a general framework for stimulating intellectual growth? What if you were looking for some guidance as to what to expect from children in terms of listening, following directions, and sitting still? You would have to turn to Piaget,

Vygotsky, and the information-processing perspective. Has a particular theory been especially valuable in helping you understand the children you know?

TYING IT ALL TOGETHER

1. While spending the day with your 3-year-old nephew Mark, you observe many examples of preoperational thought. Give the Piagetian label—egocentrism, animism, no conservation, artificialism, identity constancy—for each of the following:

    a. Mark tells you that the big tree in the garden is watching him.
    b. When you stub your toe, Mark gives you his favorite stuffed animal.
    c. Mark tells you that his daddy made the sun.
    d. Mark says, "There's more now," when you pour juice from a wide carton into a skinny glass.
    e. Mark tells you that his sister turned into a princess yesterday when she put on a costume.

2. In a sentence explain the basic mental difference between an 8-year-old in the concrete operational stage and a preoperational 4-year-old.

3. Four-year-old Christopher can recognize every letter of the alphabet, and he is beginning to sound out words in books. Drawing on Vygotsky's theory, what should Chris's parents do?

    a. Buy only alphabet books because their son will succeed at recognizing all the letters.
    b. Buy some "easy-to-read" books just above their son's skill level.
    c. Challenge Chris by getting him books with more complicated stories.

4. Which of the following is *not* an example of an executive function?

    a. A fourth grader rehearses the items he has to learn for a spelling test.
    b. An eighth grader decides "I have to do my homework" right after he gets home from school, rather than watch TV.
    c. You blurt out that you are giving your husband a trip for his birthday.

5. Laura's son has been diagnosed with ADHD. On the basis of what you have read in this chapter, suggest some environmental strategies she might use to help her child.

Answers to the Tying It All Together questions can be found on the last page of this chapter.

Language

So far, I have been looking at the cognitive and physical milestones in this chapter as if they occurred in a vacuum. But that uniquely human ability, language, is vital to every childhood advance. Vygotsky (1978) actually put *using* language—or speaking—front and center in everything we learn.

Inner Speech

According to Vygotsky, learning takes place when the words a child hears from parents and other scaffolders migrate inward to become talk directed at the self. For instance, using the example of Chutes and Ladders described earlier, after listening to her mother say "Count them" a number of times, Tiffany learned the game by repeating "Count them" to herself. Thinking, according to Vygotsky, is really **inner speech.**

Support for this interesting idea comes from listening to young children monitoring their actions. A 3-year-old might say, "Don't touch!" as she moves near the stove; or she might remind herself to be "a good girl" at preschool that day. After videotaping children during a selective attention task, researchers found that preschoolers typically recognized when they were talking out loud to themselves. Furthermore, when

asked, the children reported that "telling myself things helps me do well on this game" (Manfra & Winsler, 2006). We may feel the same way as adults. If something is *really important*—and if no one is listening—have you ever given yourself instructions "Be sure to do X, Y, and Z!" out loud?

Developing Speech

How does language *itself* unfold? Actually, during early childhood language does more than simply unfold. It explodes.

By our second birthday, we are just beginning to put together words (see Chapter 3). By the time we reach kindergarten, we basically have adult language nailed down. When we look at the challenges involved in mastering language, this achievement becomes more remarkable. To speak like adults, children must be able to articulate word sounds. They must be able to string units of meaning together in sentences. They must produce sentences that are grammatically correct. They must be able to understand the meanings of words.

The individual word sounds of language are called **phonemes.** When children begin to speak in late infancy, they can only form single phonemes—for instance, they call their bottle *ba.* They repeat sounds that seem vaguely similar, such as calling their bottle *baba,* when they cannot form the next syllable of the word. By age 3, while children have made tremendous strides in producing phonemes, they still—as you saw in the vignette—have trouble pronouncing multisyllabic words (like *psghetti*). Then, early in elementary school, these articulation problems tend to disappear—but not completely. Have you ever had a problem pronouncing a difficult word (like nuclear) that you were perfectly able to read on a page?

The basic meaning units of language are called **morphemes** (for example, the word *boys* has two units of meaning: *boy* and the plural suffix *s*). As children get older, their average number of morphemes per sentence—called their **mean length of utterance (MLU)**—expands. A 2-year-old's sentence, "Me juice" (2 MLUs), quickly becomes, "Me want juice" (3 MLUs), and then, at age 4, "Please give me the juice" (5 MLUs). Also around age 3 or 4, children begin to be fascinated by producing extremely long, jumbled-together sentences strung together by *and* ("Give me juice and crackers and milk and cookies and . . .").

This brings up the steps to mastering grammar, or what is called **syntax.** What's interesting here are the classic mistakes that young children make. As parents are well aware, one of the first words that children utter seems to be *no.* First, children typically add this word to the beginning of a sentence ("No eat cheese" or "No go inside"). Next, they move the negative term inside the sentence, next to the main verb ("I no sing" or "He no do it"). A question starts out as a declarative sentence with a rising intonation: "I have a drink, Daddy?" Then it, too, is replaced by the correct word order: "Can I have a drink, Daddy?" Children typically produce grammatically correct sentences by the time they enter school.

Without doubt, however, the most amazing changes occur in **semantics**—understanding word meanings. Here, the progression is unbelievable. Children go from three- or four-word vocabularies at age 1 to knowing about 10,000 words by age 6 (see Slobin, 1972; Smith, 1926)! While we have the other core abilities basically under our belts by the end of early childhood, our vocabularies continue to grow from age 2 to 102.

One classic mistake young children make while learning language is called **overregularization.** At around age 3 or 4, they often misapply general rules for plurals or past tense forms even when exceptions occur. A preschooler, for instance, will say *runned, goed, teached, sawed, mouses, feets,* and *cup of sugars* rather than using the correct irregular form (Berko, 1958).

According to Vygotsky, by talking to her image in the mirror "out loud," this girl is learning to monitor her behavior. Have you ever done the same thing when no one was watching?

inner speech In Vygotsky's theory, the way by which human beings learn to regulate their behavior and master cognitive challenges, through silently repeating information or talking to themselves.

phoneme The sound units that convey meaning in a given language—for example, in English, the *c* sound of *cat* and the *b* sound of *bat.*

morpheme The smallest unit of meaning in a particular language—for example, *boys* contains two morphemes: *boy* and the plural suffix *s.*

mean length of utterance (MLU) The average number of morphemes per sentence.

syntax The system of grammatical rules in a particular language.

semantics The meaning system of a language—that is, what the words stand for.

TABLE 5.7: Challenges on the Language Pathway: A Summary Table

Type of Challenge	Description	Example
Phonemes	Has trouble forming sounds	*Baba, psghetti*
Morphemes	Uses few meaning units per sentence	*Me go home*
Syntax (grammar)	Makes mistakes in applying rules for forming sentences	*Me go home*
Semantics	Has problems understanding word meanings	*Calls the family dog a horsey*
Overregularization	Puts irregular pasts and plurals into regular forms	*Foots; runned*
Over/underextension	Applies verbal labels too broadly/narrowly	*Calls every old man grandpa; tells another child he can't have a grandpa because grandpa is the name for his grandfather alone.*

Another interesting error lies in the semantic mistakes children produce. Also at around age 3, children often use what are called **overextensions** —meaning they extend a verbal label too broadly. In Piaget's terminology, they may assimilate the word *horsey* not just to horses but to all four-legged creatures, such as dogs, cats, and lions in the zoo. Or they may use **underextensions** —making name categories too narrow. A 3-year-old may tell you that only her own pet is a dog and insist that all the other neighborhood dogs must be called something else. As children get older, through continual assimilation and accommodation, they sort these glitches out.

Table 5.7 summarizes these language challenges. As an exercise, you might want to have a conversation with a 3- or 4-year-old child. Can you pick out examples of overregularization, overextensions or underextensions, problems with syntax (grammar), or difficulties pronouncing phonemes (word sounds)? Can you figure out the child's MLU?

TYING IT ALL TOGETHER

1. A 5-year-old is talking out loud and making comments such as "Put the big piece here," while constructing a puzzle. What would Vygotsky say about this behavior?

2. You are listening to a 3-year-old named Joshua. Pick out the example of overregularization and the overextension from the following comments.

   a. When offered a piece of cheese, Joshua said, "I no eat cheese."
   b. Seeing a dog run away, Joshua said, "The doggie runned away."
   c. Taken to a petting zoo, Joshua pointed excitedly at a goat and said, "Horsey!"

Answers to the Tying It All Together questions can be found in the answers section of the book.

Specific Social Cognitive Skills

Language makes us capable of some uniquely human *social cognitive* understandings. We are the only species that can see ourselves traveling through time and reflect on our past and future. We are the only species, as I mentioned early in this chapter, who regularly transports ourselves into other people's heads, decoding what people are thinking and feeling from their own point of view. How do children learn they have

overregularization An error in early language development, in which young children apply the rules for plurals and past tenses even to exceptions, so irregular forms sound like regular forms.

overextension An error in early language development in which young children apply verbal labels too broadly.

underextension An error in early language development in which young children apply verbal labels too narrowly.

an ongoing life history? When do we *fully* grasp that "other minds" are different from our own?

Constructing Our Personal Past

Autobiographical memories refer to remembering the contents of our personal life histories: from our earliest memories at age 3 or 4, to our high school graduation, to that incredible experience we had at work last week (Nelson, 2000; Nelson & Fivush, 2004). Children's understanding that they have a unique autobiography is scaffolded through a specific kind of talk. Caregivers reminisce with young children: "Remember going on a train to visit Grandma?" "What did we do at the beach last week?" These *past-talk conversations* are teaching a basic lesson: "You have a life story, an ongoing, enduring self" (Nelson, 1999, 2000; Nelson & Fivush, 2004).

Past-talk conversations typically begin with parents doing all the "remembering" at about age one or two, when children are just beginning to speak (Harley & Reese, 1999). Then, during preschool as children's language skills improve, adults directly question children about events that have been shared: "What did we do on the train when we went to Grandma's?" "Whom did we see at the beach?" Gradually, children become full partners in these mutual stories, and finally, at age 4 or 5, initiate past-talk conversations on their own (Nelson & Fivush, 2004). Let's look at the dramatic changes that take place in children's past-talk discussions from age 4 to 6:

INTERVIEWER TO 4-YEAR-OLD: Tell me about the Easter egg hunt.

CHILD: I find the golden basket.

INTERVIEWER: You won the golden egg? So tell me more about finding the golden egg.

CHILD: In the tree.

INTERVIEWER TO 6-YEAR-OLD: Can you tell me about the ballet recital?

CHILD: It was driving me crazy.

INTERVIEWER: Really?

CHILD: Yes, I was so scared because I didn't know any of the people and I couldn't see mom and dad. They were way on top of the audience. . . . Ummm, we were on a slippery surface and we all did "Where the Wild Things Are" and we . . . Mine had horns sticking out of it . . . And I had baggy pants.

(adapted from Nelson & Fivush, 2004)

What can adults do to stimulate the kinds of rich descriptions this 6-year-old produced? The key is to actively question young children about experiences you shared (Boland, Haden, & Ornstein, 2003; Nelson & Fivush, 2004). Parents differ in this tendency. Some rarely talk to a child about what they have done together or ask simple questions such as "What happened at the beach?" Others actively scaffold memories of the past by providing extensive hints. For instance, if a father asks, "What happened when we went to the beach?" and his son doesn't respond, he helps the child by adding details: "Do you remember that we took a walk . . . and what did we pick up?" Needless to say, highly stimulating parent scaffolders—or even parents who are trained to ask these probing questions—have children with richer, more differentiated autobiographical selves (Reese, Haden, & Fivush, 1993; Reese & Newcombe, 2007).

When children start regularly engaging in past-talk conversations, at around age 4 or 5, they use their experiences to connect with other people. Whether we are reminiscing about high school or discussing an amazing event at work, sharing our personal autobiographies is the glue that bonds us to other people at any age. But to really share their personal experiences, children must understand that other people have different experiences from their own. Now, let's turn to when that special awareness fully locks in.

autobiographical memories Recollections of events and experiences that make up one's life history.

When they get home, this mother can help her daughter construct her "personal autobiography" by starting a dialogue about their wonderful day at the beach and—most important—encouraging the child to talk about her memories.

Paul Avis/Getty Images

Making Sense of Other Minds

Listen to 2- and 3-year-olds having a conversation, and you will get the feeling they are talking "at" each other. It's almost as if you are hearing two disconnected monologues, or mental ships passing in the night. At around age 4 or 5, children really start relating in *give-and-take* ways. They have reached a human landmark called **theory of mind**, the understanding that we all live in different heads (Lillard, 1998; Wellman, 1990). Developmentalists have devised a special procedure to demonstrate this milestone—*the false-belief task.*

With a friend and a young child, see if you can perform the test for the presence of theory of mind shown in Figure 5.6 (Wimmer & Perner, 1983). Hide a toy in a particular place (location A) while the child and your friend watch. Then, have your friend leave the room. Once she has left, move the toy to another hiding place (location B). Next, ask the child where *your friend* will look for the toy when she returns. If the child is under age 4, he will typically answer "the second hiding place" (location B), even though your friend could not possibly know the toy has been moved. It's as if the child doesn't grasp the fact that what *he* observed can't be in your friend's head, too.

Having a theory of mind is not only vital to having a real give-and-take conversation, it is crucial to grasping a painful fact: Other people may not have your best interests at heart. One developmentalist had children play a game with "Mean Monkey," a puppet the experimenter controlled (Peskin, 1992). Beforehand, the researcher had asked children which sticker they really wanted. Then, she had Mean Monkey pick each child's favorite choice. Most 4-year-olds quickly figured out how to play the game and told Mean Monkey the opposite of what they wanted. Three-year-olds never seemed to catch on. They consistently pointed to their favorite sticker and always got the "yucky" one instead.

A remark from one of my students brings home the real-world message of this research. She commented that her 4-year-old nephew had reached the stage where he was beginning to tell lies. Under age 4, children don't fully have the mental abilities to understand that their parents don't know the thoughts in their head. So lying is an important cognitive advance!

The false-belief studies convinced developmentalists that Piaget's ideas about preoperational egocentrism had serious flaws. While perspective-taking abilities continue to develop throughout life—and change in major ways around age 8—children grasp the principle that there are other minds out there years sooner than Piaget would have predicted. Even the age-4 marker is not accurate. Children show signs of theory of mind well before they can articulate their understanding in words.

Consider this ingenious study: Researchers had toddlers watch two kinds of false-belief sequences (Onishi & Baillargeon, 2005). In one, the person who left and then returned looked for the hidden object in the place where she logically should have, in hiding place A. In the other, the person returned to look for the object in the second hiding place (location B). By 18 months of age, infants appeared surprised when the adult looked in the second hiding place. It was as if they were thinking: "Hey, she wasn't in the room, so how could she possibly know the object was moved?"

Actually, this finding should come as no surprise. As I reminded you at the beginning of this chapter, *joint attention*—the tendency to follow a person's gaze or the direction of a pointing finger—first occurs at around age 1. This landmark in beginning social cognition ("Mommy must want me to look at that!") suggests the earliest glimmers of the idea that "there are other minds out there" starts at a very young age. So that late preschool social cognitive landmark, mastering false-belief tasks, is the endpoint of *gradual improvements* in the ability to "get into other people's heads," that begins as early as babyhood (Blakemore, 2008; Moll & Tomasello, 2007; Perner, Rendl, & Garnham, 2007; Sirois & Jackson, 2007; Sodian & Thoermer, 2008).

theory of mind Children's first cognitive understanding, which appears at about age 4, that other people have different beliefs and perspectives from their own.

(1) Another adult and a young child watch while you hide a toy in a place like a desk drawer.

FIGURE 5.6: **The false-belief task:** In this classic test for *theory of mind*, when children under age 4 are asked, "Where will Ms. X look for the toy?" they are likely to say, "Under the bed," even though Ms. X could not possibly know the toy was moved to this new location.

Source: Based on Wimmer & Perner (1983).

(2) The other adult [Ms. X] leaves the room.

(3) You hide the toy under the bed and then ask the child, "Where will Ms. X look for the toy?"

Neuroimaging studies suggest that when we make judgments about other people's mental states, regions of the frontal lobes light up. So theory-of-mind abilities are yet another class of uniquely human talent programmed by this quintessentially human part of the brain (Blakemore, 2008). Although most children have mastered false-belief tasks by the time they turn 5, boys and girls with superior language skills and executive functions achieve this landmark sooner (Hughes & Ensor, 2007). But more than simply advanced intellectual abilities predict when children fully attain theory of mind. Babies who are securely attached—those with responsive caregivers—

Although this big sister probably doesn't intend it, her teasing may be stimulating her 3-year-old sibling's emerging theory of mind.

A. Inden/Zefa/Corbis

tend to develop this mind-reading capacity at a younger age (McElwain & Volling, 2004). So sensitively responding to a baby's feelings helps to scaffold the basic life understanding that other people have different points of view.

You might be interested to know that bilingual preschoolers—because they must sensitively switch languages depending on their conversational partner—also tend to develop theory of mind capacities at a younger-than-typical age (Kovács, 2009). Hands-on experience competing with siblings also helps. Perhaps because they are always jockeying for objects—for instance, by saying, "Hey, I want that toy." "Do you?" (Jenkins and others, 2003; Ruffman and others, 1998; Smith, 1998)—having older brothers and sisters also helps to stimulate early theory of mind (Ruffman and others, 1998). Plus, when you are the youngest child in the family, you may be more motivated to develop your "mind-reading" abilities to help you survive (Cummins & Allen, 1998). To illustrate, using an example from the Piaget section, after repeatedly being fooled, a 3-year-old might finally comprehend: "My big brother has a different agenda. When he tells me to take that big piece of money [the nickel], I'd better do the opposite of what he says!"

Interestingly, children and adults with autism, that severe developmental disorder involving difficulties with language and the inability to form relationships, have particular trouble with theory-of-mind tasks (Baron-Cohen, 1999; Steele, Joseph, & Tager-Flusberg, 2003). So autism is a particularly devastating condition because it hinders the ability to genuinely relate to other minds.

TYING IT ALL TOGETHER

1. Andrew said to Madison, his 3-year-old son: "Remember when we went to Grandma and Grandpa's last year? . . . It was your birthday, and what did Grandma make for you?" This _____ conversation will help scaffold Madison's _____.

2. Pick out the statement that would *not* signify that a child has developed a full-fledged theory of mind:

   a. He's having a real give-and-take conversation with you.
   b. He realizes that if you weren't there, you can't know what's gone on—and tries to explain to you what happened while you were absent.
   c. When he has done something he shouldn't do, he is likely to lie.
   d. He's learning to read.

3. Discuss some strategies for stimulating theory of mind.

Answers to the Tying It All Together questions can be found on the last page of this chapter.

Final Thoughts

In summary, during early childhood we lay down the foundations for mature self-awareness and the tools for relating to others. In the next chapter, I will draw on this discussion of emerging social cognition as well as the other theories in this chapter by focusing directly on personality and relationships throughout the childhood years. How can we use Piaget's distinctions between the preoperational and concrete operational stages to understand elementary school children's ideas about themselves and others? Can the principles of information-processing theory allow us to pinpoint why some children have trouble relating to their peers? What insights does Vygotsky's concept of the zone of proximal development offer for children who are having self-esteem problems, and what insights did this master theorist have about childhood play? Now, we look at these questions and many others as we turn to the socioemotional side of life.

SUMMARY

Two Major Learning Challenges

Childhood comprises two phases—**early** and **middle childhood**—and this decade-long period before we are physically able to reproduce lasts longer in our species than in any other animal. We need this time to master the rules of living in particular societies, to absorb the lessons passed down by previous generations, and to take advantage of our finely tuned ability to decode intentions—the talent that has allowed us to advance. The **frontal lobes**, in particular, take two decades to become "adult." As this region of the brain—involved in higher reasoning and planning—develops, every childhood ability improves.

Physical Development

Physical growth slows down after infancy. Girls and boys are roughly the same height during preschool and much of elementary school. Boys are a bit more competent at **gross motor skills**. Girls are slightly superior in **fine motor skills**. Although advanced motor skills can predict early school learning, we need to be careful not to push young children too hard. Undernutrition impairs physical development by making children too tired to engage in the exercise crucial to promoting physical skills.

The prevalence of **childhood obesity**—defined as a **body mass index (BMI)**, or height-to-weight ratio, at the 95th percentile—has dramatically increased in recent decades. While a variety of forces are implicated in this increasingly global problem, the decline in physical activity is particularly important. Although prejudices against overweight children are intense—and begin at very young ages—parents and health-care professionals may sometimes err on the side of not paying attention to this problem. The best way to combat overweight is to change the "obesogenic" environment as a whole.

Cognitive Development

Piaget's preoperational stage lasts from about age 3 to 7. The concrete operational stage lasts from about age 8 to 11. **Preoperational thinkers** focus on the way objects and substances (and people) immediately appear. **Concrete operational thinkers** can step back from their visual perceptions and reason on a more conceptual plane. In Piaget's **conservation tasks**, children in preoperations believe that when the shape of a substance has changed, the amount of it has changed. One reason is that young children lack the concept of **reversibility**, the understanding that an operation can be repeated in the opposite way. Another is that children **center** on what first captures their eye and cannot **decenter**, or focus on several dimensions at one time. Centering also affects **class inclusion** (understanding overarching categories) and **seriation** (putting objects in a series from small to big). Preoperational children believe that if something *looks* bigger visually, it always equals "more."

Preoperational children lack **identity constancy**; they don't understand that people are "the same" in spite of changes in external appearance. Their thinking is characterized by **animism** (the idea that inanimate objects are alive) and by **artificialism** (the belief that everything in nature was made by humans). They are **egocentric**, unable to understand that other people have different perspectives from their own. Although Piaget's ideas offer a wealth of insights into children's thinking, he may have underestimated what young children know. Children in every culture do progress from preoperational to concrete operational thinking—but the learning demands of the particular society make a difference in the age at which specific conservations are attained.

Lev Vygotsky, with his concept of the **zone of proximal development**, suggests that learning occurs when adults tailor instruction to a child's capacities and then use **scaffolding** to gradually promote independent performance. Education, according to Vygotsky, is a collaborative, bidirectional learning experience.

Information-processing theory provides another perspective on cognitive growth. In this framework on memory, material must be processed through a limited-capacity system, called **working memory**, in order to be recalled at a subsequent time. As children get older, their memory-bin capacity expands, and the executive processor fully comes on-line. These advances may explain why children reach concrete operations at age 7 or 8.

Executive functions—the ability to think through our actions and manage our cognitions—dramatically improve over time. Children adopt learning strategies such as **rehearsal**. They get better at **selective attention**. They are better able to inhibit their immediate responses. The research on rehearsal, selective attention, and inhibition provides a wealth of insights that can be applied in real life.

Attention deficit/hyperactivity disorder (ADHD), the most frequently diagnosed childhood disorder in the United States, is far more prevalent among boys than girls. ADHD is largely genetic, but there is no specific brain test for it. Children with ADHD have trouble with executive functions such as inhibition, selective attention, and time management. They tend to have trouble at home and school. Medication can be effective in controlling the impulsivity. Another key to helping children with ADHD is to change the wider world and strive for a better person–environment fit. ADHD is a controversial diagnosis today.

Language

Language makes every other childhood skill possible. Vygotsky believed that we learn everything through using **inner speech.** During early childhood, language abilities expand dramatically. **Phonemic** (sound articulation) abilities improve. As the number of **morphemes** in children's sentences increases, their **mean length of utterance (MLU)** expands. **Syntax**, or knowledge of grammatical rules, improves. **Semantic** understanding (vocabu-lary) shoots up. Common language mistakes young children make include **overregularization** (using regular forms for irregular verbs and nouns), **overextension** (applying word categories too broadly), and **underextension** (applying word categories too narrowly).

Specific Social Cognitive Skills

Autobiographical memories, the child's understanding of having a personal past, are socialized by caregivers through past-talk conversations during the first years of life. Questioning children about shared life events is key to putting them in touch with their personal autobiography.

Theory of mind, a child's knowledge that other people have a different perspective from their own, is measured by the false-belief task. Children typically pass this milestone at about age 4 or 5, although glimmers of this uniquely human quality—programmed by the frontal lobes—may appear at age 1½. Intellectual skills, responsive caregiving, being bilingual, and having older siblings to compete with are related to the early development of theory-of-mind capacities. Children with autism have special trouble mastering theory-of-mind tasks.

KEY TERMS

early childhood, p. 137
middle childhood, p. 137
frontal lobes, p. 139
gross motor skills, p. 140
fine motor skills, p. 140
body mass index (BMI), p. 140
childhood obesity, p. 142
preoperational thinking, p. 145
concrete operational thinking, p. 145

conservation tasks, p. 146
reversibility, p. 146
centering, p. 147
decentering, p. 147
class inclusion, p. 147
seriation, p. 148
identity constancy, p. 148
animism, p. 149
artificialism, p. 149
egocentrism, p. 150

zone of proximal development, p. 152
scaffolding, p. 152
information-processing theory, p. 155
working memory, p. 155
executive functions, p. 155
rehearsal, p. 155
selective attention, p. 156
attention deficit/hyperactivity disorder (ADHD), p. 158
inner speech, p. 160

phoneme, p. 161
morpheme, p. 161
mean length of utterance (MLU), p. 161
syntax, p. 161
semantics, p. 161
overregularization, p. 161
overextension, p. 162
underextension, p. 162
autobiographical memories, p. 163
theory of mind, p. 164

ANSWERS TO TYING IT ALL TOGETHER QUIZZES

Setting the Context

1. d.
2. Ethan's *motor* cortex is on an earlier developmental timetable than his *frontal lobes*.

3. This is a disaster! Your colleague might have trouble with everything from regulating his physical responses, to analyzing problems, to inhibiting his actions.

Physical Development

1. (a) = mass-to-specific; (b) = cephalocaudal.
2. Long-distance running and the high jump would be ideal for Jessica, as these sports heavily tap into gross motor skills.
3. c.
4. b.

Cognitive Development

1. (a) = animism; (b) = egocentrism; (c) = artificialism; (d) = can't conserve; (e) = (no) identity constancy.
2. Children in concrete operations can step back from their current perceptions and think conceptually, while preoperational children can't go beyond how things immediately appear.
3. b.
4. c.
5. Don't put your son in demanding situations involving time management. When he studies, provide a distraction-free environment with "white" background noise. Liberally use external rewards, such as prizes, to help your child focus. Make sure your son gets plenty of physical exercise, and encourage his teacher to offer everyone regular recess. Avoid power assertion (yelling and screaming), and go out of your way to provide lots of love.

Language

1. Vygotsky would say it's normal—the way children learn to think through their actions and control their behavior.
2. b. = overregularization; c = overextension.

Specific Cognitive Skills

1. This *past-talk* conversation will help stimulate Madison's *autobiographical memory*.
2. d.
3. Promote a secure attachment. Work to stimulate language. Encourage a preschooler to interact and play, especially with older children.

Chapter 6

Socioemotional Development

It is recess at Black Fox Elementary School. Eight-year-old Manuel and his best friend Josh, the class leaders, burst into the yard and start a game of tag, with a ball. Soon six or seven other boys join in, having a great time, wrestling, jostling, chasing one another around. But then, things get serious, changing fast and furiously. In comes Moriah, who had been hanging out with a small group of girls.

"Can I play?"

"No girls allowed!" say the boys.

Then, Matt barges in, disrupting the game, shoving and hitting, taking over the ball. A few minutes later, Jimmy, an anxious child who generally plays alone, timidly tries to enter the group.

"Get out!" erupts Matt, "You wuss! You girl!"

Matt pushes Jimmy down roughly and (as usual) a few boys start to laugh. Jimmy starts to cry and slinks away. But suddenly, Manuel slows down.

"Hey, cool it, guys," he says. "Hey, man, are you all right? Come join us."

Manuel comforts Jimmy, manages to tell the other boys to lay off, and does his best, as usual, to keep Matt from messing up the game without getting him too angry—as he knows from experience how that will turn out.

Have you ever wondered why some children, such as Manuel, are incredibly caring, while others, like Matt, are insensitive, aggressive, and rude? Perhaps you are curious about what makes people popular, or want to help children like Jimmy and Matt, who are having problems with their peers. Have you puzzled over why boys love to wrestle or wondered why elementary school children love to hate the other sex? Maybe you simply want to understand your own and other people's behavior in a deeper way. If so, this chapter, covering children's emotional and social development, is for you.

In the first half of this chapter, I'll tackle topics in personality; then, explore relationships in depth. My goal is to give you insights into the myriad challenges in *social cognition* that children face as they travel from preschool through elementary school. But this chapter has another purpose: to allow us to help boys and girls, such as Matt and Jimmy, who are having problems relating in the world. With this goal in mind, let's begin, again, by highlighting that basic life challenge—managing our emotions.

Setting the Challenge

In Chapter 5, you saw how the ability to inhibit our immediate impulses, programmed by the expanding frontal lobes, explains every developing cognitive and physical skill. We need the same self-regulation abilities to succeed socially and emotionally, too. When we get angry, we must cool down our feelings, rather than lash out. We have to overcome our anxieties and talk to that scary professor, or conquer our shyness and go to a party because we might meet that special person who will be the love of our life. **Emotion regulation** is the term developmentalists use for the skills involved in managing our feelings so that they don't get in the way of a productive life (Bridges, Denham, & Ganiban, 2004; Calkins, 2004).

Children with **externalizing tendencies** have special trouble with this challenge. Like Matt, they act on their immediate emotions and often behave disruptively and aggressively. Perhaps you know a child who bursts into every social scene, fighting, bossing people around, wreaking havoc with his classmates and adults.

Children with **internalizing tendencies** have the opposite problem—coping with intense anxiety. Like Jimmy, they hang back in social situations. They seem timid and self-conscious; they often look frightened and depressed.

The beauty of being human is that we vary in our temperamental tendencies—to be shy or active, boisterous or reserved. Because cultural values differ, you might think that if Jimmy grew up in a collectivist society that put a premium on being self-effacing, his shyness might not be a liability. If Matt was raised in a war-like culture, his tendency to aggressively barge in would help him socially succeed. You would be wrong. Socially anxious boys and girls—those, like Jimmy, who tremble at every interaction—*are* unpopular in India (Prakash & Coplan, 2007) and Asia (Chen & French, 2008) as well as the West. Highly aggressive children—if they are impulsive and unable to regulate their feelings—are rejected around the globe. Serious externalizing and internalizing tendencies *universally* present problems during the childhood years.

In Chapter 4, you learned about the temperaments that put toddlers at risk for having internalizing and externalizing problems—being highly exuberant or inhibited. Now, let's look at what happens when these tendencies evolve to the point where they cause genuine suffering during preschool and, especially, elementary school.

✿ TYING IT ALL TOGETHER

1. Krista, a school psychologist, is concerned about two students: Paul, who bursts out in rage and constantly gets into trouble for fighting and misbehaving; and Jeremy, who is timid, anxious, and seems sad most of the time. Krista describes Paul as having _____ tendencies and Jeremy as having _____ tendencies, and she says that issues with emotion regulation are a problem for _____.

   a. externalizing; internalizing; Paul
   b. externalizing; internalizing; both boys
   c. internalizing; externalizing; both boys
   d. internalizing; externalizing; Jeremy

Answers to the Tying It All Together questions can be found on the last page of this chapter.

Personality

How do children's perceptions about themselves change as they get older, and how do these changes affect self-esteem? What makes children (and adults) act in caring or hurtful ways?

Observing the Self

Developmentalist Susan Harter (1999) has explored the first questions in a series of studies examining how children view themselves. To make sense of her findings, Harter draws on Piaget's distinction between preoperational and concrete operational

---

emotion regulation The capacity to manage one's emotional state.

externalizing tendencies A personality style that involves acting on one's immediate impulses and behaving disruptively and aggressively.

internalizing tendencies A personality style that involves intense fear, social inhibition, and often depression.

self-awareness The ability to observe our abilities and actions from an outside frame of reference and to reflect on our inner state.

self-esteem Evaluating oneself as either "good" or "bad" as a result of comparing the self to other people.

thinking—a difference I will be highlighting throughout this chapter. So let's take another look at the mental leap that Piaget believes takes place when children reach age 7 or 8.

Children in the concrete operational stage:

- Look beyond immediate appearances and think abstractly about inner states.

- Give up their egocentrism and realize they are but one person among many others in this vast world.

To examine how these changes affect **self-awareness**—the way children reflect on who they are as people—Harter asks boys and girls of different ages to describe themselves. Here are two examples illustrating the responses she finds:

> *I am 3 years old and I live in a big house. . . . I have blue eyes and a kitty that is orange. . . . I love my dog Skipper. . . . I'm always happy. I have brown hair. . . . I'm really strong.*

> *I'm in fourth grade this year, and I'm pretty popular. . . . That's because I'm nice to people and can keep secrets, although if I get into a bad mood I sometimes say something that can be a little mean. At school I'm feeling pretty smart in . . . Language Arts and Social Studies. . . . But I'm feeling pretty dumb in Math and Science. . . . Even though I'm not doing well in those subjects I still like myself as a person.*

(adapted from Harter, 1999, pp. 37, 48)

Notice that the 3-year-old talks about herself mainly in terms of external facts. The fourth grader's self-descriptions are internal and psychological; anchored in her feelings, abilities, and inner traits. The 3-year-old describes herself in totally unrealistic positive ways as "always happy." The fourth grader lists her deficiencies and strengths in many areas of life. Moreover, while the younger child talks about herself as if she were living in a bubble, the older child focuses on how she measures up compared to her classmates. So Harter believes that during concrete operations, children start to realistically evaluate their abilities and decide whether they like or dislike the person they see. **Self-esteem**—the tendency to feel good or bad about ourselves—first becomes a *major issue* during elementary school.

Actually, studies around the world show that self-esteem tends to decline during early elementary school (Frey & Ruble, 1985, 1990; Harter & Pike, 1984; Lee, J., Super, & Harkness, 2003; Super & Harkness, 2003). A mother may sadly notice this change when her 8-year-old daughter starts to make comments such as, "I am not very pretty" or "I can't do math." (What happened to that self-confident child, who just a few years earlier felt she was the most beautiful, intelligent kid in the world?) Caring teachers struggle to cope with the same comparisons, the fact that their fourth graders are exquisitely sensitive to who is popular, which classmates are getting A's, and who needs special academic help.

This makes perfect sense when we look at Erik Erikson's psychosocial stages. Erikson, as you can see in Table 6.1, labeled the developmental task during middle

When they reach concrete operations, children delight in ranking one another on everything from who is the smartest to who is the most popular. As a result, these elementary school children are now in danger of developing self-esteem "issues" for the first time.

TABLE 6.1: Erikson's Psychosocial Stages

Life Stage	Primary Task
Infancy (birth to 1 year)	Basic trust versus mistrust
Toddlerhood (1 to 2 years)	Autonomy versus shame and doubt
Early childhood (3 to 6 years)	Initiative versus guilt
Middle childhood (6 years to puberty)	**Industry versus inferiority**
Adolescence (teens into twenties)	Identity versus role confusion
Young adulthood (twenties to early forties)	Intimacy versus isolation
Middle adulthood (forties to sixties)	Generativity versus stagnation
Late adulthood (late sixties and beyond)	Integrity versus despair

In Erikson's framework, during elementary school, our challenge is to learn to work for what we want, and the danger is feeling inferior, that we don't measure up to other people.

childhood (from age 6 to 12) as **industry versus inferiority**. During elementary school, we first wake up to the realities of life. We understand that we are not just completely wonderful. We need to work for what we want to achieve. We are vulnerable to feeling inferior, to having the painful sense that we don't measure up.

Having this sense of inferiority is essential. It produces industry or the passion to work to improve ourselves. However, it is a double-edged sword. Not everyone is beautiful or brilliant. We all *do* vary in the qualities the world prizes. So, while children differ in self-esteem, some feelings of inferiority are inevitable during elementary school and throughout life.

Still, all is not lost because entering concrete operations produces another change. Notice that the fourth grader I quoted above compares her abilities in different areas such as personality and school. So as they get older, children's self-esteem doesn't hinge on one quality. Even if they are not doing well in one area, they can take comfort in the places where they really shine.

According to Harter, children draw on five areas to determine their overall self-esteem: *scholastic competence* (their academic talents); *behavioral conduct* (whether they are obedient or "good"); *athletic skills* (their performance at sports); *peer likeability* (their popularity with other children); and *physical appearance* (their looks). To diagnose how a given child feels in each domain, Harter devised the kinds of questions you can see in Figure 6.1.

An examiner points to a girl to a preschooler's right and says, "This girl isn't good at doing puzzles." She then points to a girl to the child's left and says, "This girl is good at doing puzzles." Then she asks the child to point to the appropriate circle under each girl. If "this really fits me," the child points to the large circle. If "this fits me a little bit," the child points to the small circle.

Really True for Me	Sort of True for Me					Sort of True for Me	Really True for Me
☐	☐	Some kids are often *unhappy* with themselves.	BUT	Other kids are pretty *pleased* with themselves.		☐	☐
☐	☐	Some kids feel like they are *just as smart* as other kids their age.	BUT	Other kids aren't so sure and *wonder* if they are as smart.		☐	☐

FIGURE 6.1: How do children view themselves? Harter has devised this questionnaire format to measure children's feelings of competence in her five different areas of life. The item in the top panel is derived from Harter's scale designed for young children; the questions in the bottom panel are from a similar scale for elementary school children.

Source: Harter (1999), pp. 121–122.

Here the elementary school child reads the items and checks the box that applies to her.

As you might expect, children who view themselves as "not so good" in several of these domains often report low self-esteem. However, to really understand a given child's self-esteem, it is important to know that person's unique priorities—the value that boy or girl attaches to doing well in a particular area of life.

To understand this point, you might take a minute to rate yourself along Harter's five dimensions: your people skills, your politeness or good manners, your intellectual abilities, your looks, and your physical abilities. If you label yourself "not so good" in an area you don't really care about (for me, it would be my physical skills), it won't make a dent in your self-esteem. If you care deeply about some particular area where you don't feel you are succeeding, you would probably get pretty depressed.

This discounting process ("It doesn't matter if I'm not a scholar; I have great relationship skills") is vitally important. It lets us get self-esteem from the areas in which we shine. The problem is that some children take this discounting to an extreme. They minimize their problems in *essential* areas of life.

Two Kinds of Self-Esteem Distortions

Normally, we base our self-esteem on the signals we receive from the outside world: "Am I succeeding or not doing so well?" However, when children have externalizing problems, a disconnect may occur. Faced with clear evidence that they *are* failing—for instance, being rejected by their peers—they deny reality and blame other people to preserve their unrealistically high self-worth (Diamantopoulou, Rydell, & Henricsson, 2008; Miller & Daniel, 2007; Thomaes, Stegge, & Olthof, 2007). Perhaps you know an adult whose difficulty managing his anger gets him into continual trouble at home and at work, but who copes by taking the position, "I'm wonderful. It's all their fault. I didn't do anything wrong." Because this person seems impervious to his flaws and has so much difficulty regulating his emotions, he cannot take the needed steps to change his behavior and so ensures that he continues to fail.

Children with internalizing tendencies have the opposite problem. They tend to be highly self-critical. They read failure into neutral situations. They are at risk of developing **learned helplessness** (Abramson, Seligman, & Teasdale, 1978), the feeling that they are powerless to affect their fate, and so should not even attempt to succeed. They give up at the starting gate, assuming, "I know I'm going to fail, so why should I even try?"

So children and adults with externalizing and internalizing tendencies face a similar danger—but for different reasons. When people minimize their real-world difficulties or assume they are totally incompetent, they cut off the chance of working to improve their behavior and so ensure that they *will* fail.

Table 6.2 summarizes these self-esteem problems and their real-world consequences. Then, Table 6.3 offers a checklist, based on Harter's five dimensions, for evaluating yourself. Are there areas where you gloss over your deficiencies and say,

According to Susan Harter, even when they are failing in other areas of life, children can sometimes derive their self-esteem from the skills in which they shine. Do you think this girl can use this science prize to feel good about herself, even if she understands that she is not very popular with the other kids?

industry versus inferiority Erik Erikson's term for the psychosocial task of middle childhood, involving the capacity to work for one's goals.

learned helplessness A state that develops when a person feels incapable of affecting the outcome of events, and so gives up without trying.

TABLE 6.2: **Externalizing and Internalizing Problems, Self-Esteem Distortions, and Consequences—A Summary Table**

Description	Self-Esteem Distortion	Consequence
Children with externalizing problems		
Act out "emotions," are impulsive and often aggressive.	May ignore real problems and have unrealistically high self-esteem.	Continue to fail because they don't see the need to improve.
Children with internalizing problems		
Are intensely fearful.	Can read failure into everything and have overly low self-esteem.	Continue to fail because they decide that they cannot succeed and stop working.

TABLE 6.3: Identifying Your Self-Esteem Distortions: A Checklist Using Harter's Five Domains

You have *externalizing issues* if you regularly have thoughts like these:

1. **Academics:** "When I get poor grades, it's because my teachers don't give good tests or teach well." "I have very little to learn from other people." "I'm much smarter than practically everyone else I know."

2. **Physical skills:** "When I play baseball, soccer, etc., and my team doesn't win, it's my teammates' fault, not mine." "I believe it's OK to take physical risks, such as not wearing a seatbelt or running miles in the hot sun, because I know I won't get hurt." "It's all statistics, so I shouldn't be concerned about smoking four packs a day or about drinking a six-pack of beer every night."

3. **Relationships:** "When I have trouble at work or with my family, it's typically my co-workers' or family's fault." "My son (or mate, friend, mother) is the one causing all the conflict between us."

4. **Physical appearance:** "I don't think I have to work to improve my appearance because I'm basically gorgeous."

5. **Conduct:** "I should be able to come to work late (or turn in papers after the end of the semester, talk in class, etc.)." "Other people are too uptight. I have a right to behave any way I want to."

Diagnosis: You are purchasing high self-esteem at the price of denying reality. Try to look at the impact of your actions more realistically and take steps to change.

You have *internalizing issues* if you regularly have thoughts like these:

1. **Academics:** "I'm basically stupid." "I can't do well on tests." "My memory is poor." "I'm bound to fail at science." "I'm too dumb to get through college." "I'll never be smart enough to get ahead in my career."

2. **Physical skills:** "I can't play basketball (or some other sport) because I'm uncoordinated or too slow." "I'll never have the willpower to exercise regularly (or stick to a diet, stop smoking, stop drinking, or stop taking drugs)."

3. **Relationships:** "I don't have any people skills." "I'm doomed to fail in my love life." "I can't be a good mother (or spouse or friend)."

4. **Physical appearance:** "I'm basically unattractive." "People are born either good-looking or not, and I fall into the not category." "There is nothing I can do to improve my looks."

5. **Conduct:** "I'm incapable of being on time (or getting jobs done or stopping talking in class)." "I can't change my tendency to rub people the wrong way."

Diagnosis: Your excessively low self-esteem is inhibiting your ability to succeed. Work on reducing your helpless and hopeless attitudes and *try for change.*

"I don't have a problem"? Do you have pockets of learned helplessness that are preventing you from living a full life?

INTERVENTIONS: Promoting Realistic Self-Esteem

This discussion shows why school programs focused *just* on raising self-esteem—those devoted to simply instilling the message, "You are a terrific kid"—are missing the boat (Miller & Daniel, 2007; Swann, Chang-Schneider, & McClarty, 2007). Self-esteem must be anchored in reality. It must come from children's genuine achievements in the world. Actually, telling boys and girls who are not being wonderful that they are wonderful can be dangerous if it encourages a child with externalizing tendencies—who really is having serious troubles—to adopt the worldview "I'm great no matter what I do." For any child who is having difficulty in important areas, it's important to: (1) enhance *self-efficacy*, or the feeling "I can be competent" (Miller & Daniel, 2007) and (2) promote *realistic* perceptions about the self. As a caring adult, how might you carry out this two-pronged approach?

Giving this child "good boy" stars just to boost his self-esteem is likely to backfire—making him think "I'm the greatest" no matter how he behaves!

Michael Newman/Photo Edit, Inc.

ENHANCING SELF-EFFICACY. Using Lev Vygotsky's terminology, one key to fostering self-efficacy is to enter the child's proximal zone and put success within striking distance of the developing self. So if a child, like Jimmy, is very shy, you might move him to a smaller class, where it would be easier to comfortably relate. If a second-grader has problems reading, you would first determine the child's actual skill level, then tailor your teaching upward from that point, regularly reinforcing that boy or girl for each small success. As developmentalist Carol Dweck has demonstrated, one key to enhancing academic self-efficacy is to praise children for effort ("You are trying so hard!"), rather than to make comments about basic ability ("You are incredibly smart!"). In her studies, elementary schoolers, who were praised for being "very intelligent" after successfully completing problems, later had *lower* self-efficacy. They were afraid to tackle other challenging tasks ("I'd better not try this or everyone might learn I'm really dumb!") (Molden & Dweck, 2006; Mueller & Dweck, 1998).

Bill Aron/ Photo Edit

How can this teacher get her fourth grader to tackle challenging new school tasks? Praise him for effort ("You are such a brave, hard worker") rather than making comments like, "You are a basically brilliant kid."

ENCOURAGING ACCURATE PERCEPTIONS. But, if a child has internalizing problems, bringing home the message "Yes, you can change" may not be enough. We need to attack the helpless and hopeless perceptions that become more stable, rigid, and ingrained as children travel into the early teenage years (Cole and others, 2008). So, with a boy such as Jimmy, you might provide realistic feedback to change his overly critical self-image: "I don't think the kids hate you. Manuel really wanted you to join the game." And, for children like Matt, who discount their failures at the price of preserving an unrealistic sense of self-esteem, you should reinforce the child when she does well but gently give accurate feedback, too (Thomaes, Stegge, & Olthof, 2007).

There is a way of softening this painful "You are not doing so well" message that is the price of entering the real world. Harter (1999, 2006) finds that feeling loved by their attachment figures provides a cushion when children understand they are having trouble in an important area of life. So, to return to the beginning of this section, school programs (and adults) that convey the message "I love you" plus foster self-efficacy ("You can succeed if you work hard") are the key to *true* self-esteem (Miller & Daniel, 2007).

Self-Esteem, Asian Style

So far, I have been emphasizing the value of enhancing self-esteem. It seems like a "no-brainer" that adults must lavishly praise children when they succeed and encourage them when they fail. It seems self evident that it's important to have (realistically) high self-esteem. If you were raised in a more collectivist society, you might not share this "obvious" mindset at all.

Researchers arranged for Chinese and U.S. fifth graders to succeed or fail at an academic task. Then, they watched parents in these two countries react. When informed that their child had done well, Chinese parents made very few positive statements ("Good job!" "That's wonderful!"). They were far more critical than their American counterparts when informed that a son or daughter's performance was poor. You might assume this negative approach—downplaying success and emphasizing failure—would make the Chinese children discouraged. You would be wrong. These fifth graders improved more than the U.S. boys and girls on a subsequent test (Ng, Pomerantz, & Lam, 2007)!

Why might Chinese parents take pains to minimize their children's successes? This child-rearing method

This Chinese dad would probably react more negatively to his daughter's performance on this paper than other mothers and fathers because, in his culture, raising self-esteem is not a crucial child-rearing goal.

Cindy Charles/ Photo Edit

makes sense if we return to that cultural difference spelled out in Chapter 1. In individualistic societies, it's fine to brag about our achievements. In collectivist countries, people discuss themselves in more self-critical ways (Heine & Hamamura, 2007; see Brown and others, 2009). So comments from a Western perspective that signal low-self esteem ("I'm not very smart") are normal in China and Japan because the collectivist worldview emphasizes being submissive and *not* standing out from the group.

Once again, culture matters. Child-rearing goals are not universal. Even your feelings about yourself might be different if you grew up in another part of the world.

Now that we've explored children's self-perceptions, it's time to focus on two qualities that make us human: our tendencies to act in caring and then hurtful ways.

What qualities made hundreds of New York City firefighters run into the burning Twin Towers on September 11, knowing that they might be facing death? This is the kind of question that developmentalists who study prosocial behavior want to answer.

Doing Good: Prosocial Behavior

Throughout the morning of September 11, 2001, the nation was riveted by the heroism of the firefighters who ran into the flaming World Trade Center buildings, risking almost certain death. We marveled at the "ordinary people" working high in the Twin Towers whose response to this emergency was to help others get out first.

Prosocial behavior is the term developmentalists use to describe such amazing acts of self-sacrifice as well as the minor acts of helping and caring that people perform during daily life. Prosocial behaviors are fully in swing by preschool (Eisenberg, 2003). Children help the teacher clean up the blocks. They share their toys and give their cookie to a friend.

Prosocial activities become more frequent during elementary school (Fabes and others, 1996). Older children are more likely to act prosocially because they have better skills. They can get a bandage when their playmate cuts his finger or call that injured child's parent on the cell phone. Moreover, children in concrete operations have the perspective-taking skills to effectively tailor their help to another person's needs. So, while a 3-year-old might give a hurt friend her *own* teddy bear, a 9-year-old would search for the other child's favorite stuffed animal. The older child would understand that her hurt friend's father was the best person to offer comfort—not her own dad.

Will this caring 3-year-old become an especially prosocial adult? According to the research described in the text, her chances are good.

Individual and Cultural Variations

Amidst these developmental changes lie tantalizing individual differences. In one longitudinal study, developmentalists measured how often young children engaged in sharing and helping activities in preschool classrooms. Then, they followed these boys and girls until they were adults. Amazingly, the amount of spontaneous sharing that children showed at ages 3 and 4 was related to reports of prosocial behavior in elementary school, during adolescence, and also in young adulthood (Eisenberg and others, 1999). So, if your 4-year-old niece seems unusually caring, you can predict that she may grow up to be an especially kind and caring adult.

If people differ in their prosocial tendencies, do cultures? Are children in less individualistic societies more prosocial than in the West? Making culture-by-culture comparisons is risky because, in some societies, people may be socialized to be highly prosocial within their own group and callous to "outsiders" (Eisenberg & Fabes, 1998). What we can say is that in collectivist cultures specific prosocial behaviors, such as sacrificing one's own desires to help one's parents, are more of a norm (Chen & French, 2008). There may be cultural differences in specific prosocial judgments, too.

Consider this dilemma: "I'm the captain of the spelling team. My best friend Joe is dying to compete, but he can't spell well. Should I put Joe on the team, even though that may cause the group to lose? Where do my allegiances lie—to my friend or to the team?" When researchers presented these types of vignettes to fifth graders in China and Canada, the top priority for the Chinese children was to protect the team. Perhaps because our culture prizes individual relationships, the Canadian children felt the true prosocial action was to help a friend (Fu and others 2007). To bring this message home, would you agree with the author E. M. Forster's controversial individualistic-oriented comment, "If I had the choice to betray my friend or my country, I hope I would have the strength to stick up for my friend"?

Decoding Altruism

The fact that cultures differ in their prosocial attitudes brings up an interesting point. We all act prosocially for non-prosocial reasons: to get praise ("I'll lend Sara money because everyone will think I am a generous person"); out of fear of punishment ("I'd better help Sara because otherwise she'll be furious with me"); or for the well-known adult motive for "charitable" donations, to show how successful we are ("If I give a Belsky Building to the college, everyone will know I'm very rich"). Genuinely prosocial behaviors involve **altruism**. They are motivated by the desire to help *apart* from getting external rewards. Acting altruistically, in turn, depends on experiencing a specific emotional state (Eisenberg, 1992, 2003).

Empathy is the term developmentalists use for directly feeling another person's emotion. You get incredibly anxious when you hear your boss berating a co-worker. You were overcome by horror as you watched the Twin Towers burn.

Sympathy is the more muted feeling that we experience *for* another human being. You feel terrible for your co-worker, but don't feel her intense distress. Your heart went out to the people who perished in the Twin Towers that day. Studies suggest that, rather than empathy, sympathy is actually related to behaving in an altruistic way (Eisenberg, 1992, 2003; Trommsdorff, Friedlmeier, & Mayer, 2007).

The reason is that simply experiencing another person's distress can provoke a variety of reactions, from becoming immobilized with fear to behaving in a far from caring way. We can vividly see this when, out of empathic embarrassment, we burst out laughing after a waiter spills a restaurant tray, or when we become paralyzed by terror as we see a highway crash. So, to act altruistically, children need to use their emotion-regulating capacities to mute their empathic feelings into a less intense sympathetic response (Eisenberg, 1992; Saarni, 1999).

Behaving altruistically also involves having the information-processing skills to consider different alternatives and select a prosocial act. It requires feeling confident of having the talents to help. Just as I would not be likely to run into a flaming building unless I was a firefighter, the reason children in elementary school typically give for not acting prosocially is that they do not have the skills (Denham, 1998; Eisenberg & Fabes, 1998). So interestingly, children who lack self-confidence (those prone to internalizing disorders) as well as those who are relatively non-empathic (children with externalizing problems) are often less prosocial than their peers (Saarni, 1999).

Finally, people tend to act prosocially when they are happy, which explains why, when we are immersed in our own problems, we are unlikely to reach out to a friend. It gives us another reason why children with serious internalizing or externalizing problems are less likely to behave in prosocial ways (Eisenberg & Fabes, 1998).

prosocial behavior Sharing, helping, and caring actions.

altruism Prosocial behaviors that we carry out for selfless, non-egocentric reasons.

empathy Feeling the exact emotion that another person is experiencing.

sympathy A state necessary for acting prosocially, involving feeling upset *for* a person who needs help.

To respond altruistically to his injured playmate, this boy had to transform his empathy into sympathy, and also had to feel confident that he could take action to help.

Now, returning to the chapter-opening vignette, we can decode the qualities that made up Manuel's caring stand. He muted his empathic anxiety into sympathy. He used his information-processing capacities to select a prosocial act. He had the self-confidence and happiness to want to act prosocially. But we still haven't answered that critical question: Exactly what *causes* children like Manuel to act in altruistic ways?

As with other human qualities, both nature and nurture are involved. Twin studies suggest that there is a genetic component to the tendency to act prosocially (Knafo & Plomin, 2006; Gregory and others, 2009). Parent readers can relate to this idea of inborn differences when they wonder: "Why is this child naturally so much kinder than my other daughter or son?" The way we socialize children matters, too. Let's now look at techniques any adult can use to help promote children's prosocial acts.

INTERVENTIONS: Socializing Prosocial Children

Giving concrete reinforcements, such as stars or a big prize, for being kind and helpful, as it turns out, is relatively ineffective at fostering prosocial behavior. (In order to teach a child to be altruistic, it doesn't make sense to provide a self-centered motive to be kind!) What works best is to pay attention to prosocial acts and attribute those actions to the child's basic personality—for instance, saying, "You really are a caring person for doing that," instead of "That was a nice thing you did" (Eisenberg, 1992, 2003). So if you regularly notice the kind things your niece does *and* praise her lavishly for being a kind person, you may be helping to socialize her into becoming a caring adult.

Most studies exploring prosocial behavior center on a discipline style called **induction** (Hoffman, 1994, 2001). Caregivers who use induction actively scaffold altruism. When a child has done something hurtful, they carefully point out the ethical issue and try to promote the development of an other-centered, sympathetic response. Now, imagine that classic situation when your 8-year-old daughter has invited everyone in class but Sara to her birthday party. Instead of punishing your child—or giving that other classic response "Kids will be kids"—here's what you should say: "It's hurtful to leave someone out when everyone else is getting an invitation. Think of how terrible Sara must feel!"

Induction is effective for several reasons: It offers children feedback about exactly what they did wrong. It moves them off of focusing on their own punishment ("Oh, now I'm really going to get it!") to the *other* child's distress ("Oh gosh, she must feel hurt"). Most important, induction allows for reparations, the chance to make amends. The bottom line is that induction works because it stimulates the emotion called guilt.

Shame Versus Guilt and Prosocial Acts

Think back to an event during childhood when you felt terrible about yourself. Perhaps, for instance, it was the day you were caught cheating and sent to the principal. What you may remember was feeling so ashamed. Developmentalists, however, make a distinction between feeling ashamed and experiencing guilt. **Shame** is the feeling we have when we are *personally* humiliated. **Guilt** is the emotion we experience when we have violated a personal moral standard or hurt another human being.

Although they appear superficially similar, shame and guilt have different effects. Shame causes us to withdraw from people. When we feel ashamed, we want to retreat, slink away, and crawl into a hole (Thomaes, Stegge, & Olthof, 2007). We also feel furious at being humiliated and want to strike back. Guilt connects us to people. We feel terrible about what we have done. We try to apologize and make amends. So shame diminishes us as people. Guilt can cause us to emotionally enlarge (Tangney, 2003).

This suggests that socialization techniques involving shame are especially poisonous. If, when you arrived at the principal's office, he shamed you ("In the next school assembly, I'll tell everyone what a terrible person you are!"), you might quickly change your behavior, but at a high emotional price. You would feel humiliated and depressed. You might decide you hated school. But if the principal induced guilt ("I felt so disappointed because you're such a good kid"), you could take action to

When parents, like the father in the photograph at the right, use *shame* to discipline, a child's impulse is to get furious. But by pointing out how disappointed she is in her "good girl," the mother in the photograph at the left can produce *guilt*—and so ultimately have a more prosocial child.

enhance self-efficacy ("Oh, Dr. Jones, what can I do to make it up?"). You might end up feeling better about yourself and more connected to school. Has feeling guilty and then apologizing ever made you feel closer to someone you love?

Table 6.4 summarizes these section messages for promoting prosocial behavior and offers an additional tip. And, for readers who are thinking, "I'm prosocial, even though I didn't grow up in that kind of home," there is the reality that people can draw on their shaming childhood experiences to construct enormously prosocial adult lives. Perhaps you know someone who grew up in an abusive family whose mission is to work with abused children; or you have seen a young person learn altruism from stepping in to take care of her siblings when her parents were emotionally impaired. While providing a loving environment is the best way to teach love, people become altruistic out of adversity, too. You will learn more in Chapter 12 about how some adults transform their childhood tragedies into blessings and construct exemplary prosocial lives.

Now that we have thoroughly analyzed what makes us do good (or the angel side of personality), let's tackle the darker side of what makes us human: aggression.

TABLE 6.4: How to Produce Prosocial Children: A Summary Table

- Pay attention to kind behaviors. Then when a child has done something kind and considerate, tell him that he is "really a caring person."

- Avoid giving children treats or special privileges to reward prosocial acts. Instead, praise the child effusively and point out the positive impact of her behavior.

- When the child has hurt another person, use induction: Clearly point out the moral issue, and alert him to how the other person must feel.

- Avoid teasing and shaming. When the child has done something wrong, tell her you are disappointed and give her a chance to make amends.

- Don't think that you have fulfilled your responsibility to teach altruism by having a child participate in school or church drives to help the unfortunate. Morality isn't magically learned on Sunday. It must be taught in an ongoing way during *day-to-day* life.

Doing Harm: Aggression

Aggression refers to any act designed to cause harm, from shaming to shoving, from gossiping to starting unprovoked wars. It should come as no surprise to parents that physical aggression is at its life peak at around age 2 ½ (Dodge, Coie, & Lynam 2006; Van Aken and others, 2008). During this critical age for socialization, children are being vigorously disciplined but don't often have the capacity to inhibit their responses. Imagine being a toddler who is continually being ordered by giants to do impossible things, such as sharing and sitting still. Because being frustrated provokes aggression, it makes perfect sense that biting, hitting, and throwing tantrums are normal during "the terrible twos."

induction The ideal discipline style for socializing prosocial behavior, involving getting a child who has behaved hurtfully to empathize with the pain he has caused the other person.

shame A feeling of being personally humiliated.

guilt Feeling upset about having caused harm to a person or about having violated one's internal standard of behavior.

aggression Any hostile or destructive act.

As preschoolers become more skilled at regulating their emotions and can make better sense of adults' rules, rates of open aggression (yelling or hitting) dramatically decline (Côté and others, 2008). As children get older, the reasons for aggression change. Preschool fights center on objects, such as toys. During elementary school, when children have developed a full-fledged sense of self-esteem, aggression becomes more personal. We strike out when we have been wounded as human beings (Coie & Dodge, 1998). How do researchers categorize aggressive acts?

Types of Aggression

One way developmentalists classify aggression is by its motive. **Instrumental aggression** is the name for hurtful behavior that is actively initiated to achieve a goal. Johnny kicks Manuel to gain possession of the block pile. Sally spreads a rumor about Moriah to replace her as Sara's best friend. **Reactive aggression** occurs in response to being hurt, threatened, or deprived. Manuel, infuriated at Johnny, kicks him back.

When you decide to go after your classmate's purse (*instrumental aggression*), you may feel really powerful and good; however, she is going to get furious (*reactive aggression*) and want to bop you over the head!

Its self-determined nature gives instrumental aggression a more calculated, "cooler" emotional tone. When we behave aggressively to get something, we plan our behavior more carefully. We may feel a sense of self-efficacy as we carry out the act. Reactive aggression, in contrast, involves white-hot, disorganized rage. When you hear that your best friend has betrayed you, or even when you have a minor frustrating experience such as being caught in a traffic jam, you get furious and want to blindly lash out.

This feeling is normal. According to a classic theory called the *frustration–aggression hypothesis*, any time human beings are thwarted, we are biologically programmed to retaliate or strike back.

In addition to its motive—instrumental or reactive—developmentalists distinguish among different forms of aggression. Hitting and yelling are direct forms of aggression. A more devious type of aggression is called **relational aggression**, any act designed to hurt the person's social relationships (Merrell, Buchanan, & Tran, 2006). Not inviting Sara to a birthday party, spreading rumors, or tattling on a disliked classmate qualify as relationally aggressive acts.

Because it targets self-esteem and often involves more sophisticated social skills, relational aggression follows a different developmental path than openly aggressive acts. Just as rates of open aggression are declining, during middle childhood, relational aggression rises. In fact, the overabundance of relational aggression during late elementary school and early adolescence (another intensely frustrating time) may explain why we tend to remember those ages as the "meanest" times of life.

Traditionally, developmentalists assumed that relational aggression was more common in females (Crick & Rose, 2000; Putallaz and others, 2007). But we now know that boys also engage in this behavior at high rates—especially at older ages (Card and others, 2008; Vaillancourt and others, 2007). In one longitudinal study, yes, girls were more relationally aggressive at the beginning of high school, but these sex differences evaporated by senior year (Mayeux & Cillessen, 2008)!

Excluding someone from your group is a classic sign of *relational aggression*—which really gets going in middle childhood. Can you remember being the target of the behavior shown here when you were in fourth or fifth grade?

Table 6.5 summarizes the different types of aggression and gives examples from childhood and adult life. While scanning the table, notice that we all behave in *every* aggressive way. Also, I must emphasize that being aggressive is not "bad." It's vital to making our way as competent adults. Children who are popular, as you will see later in this chapter, don't abandon being aggressive. They use aggression *effectively* to get what they want (Hawley, Little, & Card, 2008: Mayeux & Cillessen, 2008; Pellegrini and others, 2007b; Pellegrini, 2008; Roseth and others, 2007). Still, aggression does produce serious social problems when children make this behavior their typical life mode.

Mary Kate Denny/Photo Edit, Inc.

Masterfile Royalty Free

TABLE 6.5: Aggression: A Summary of the Types

What Motivated the Behavior?

Instrumental aggression: Acts that are actively instigated to achieve a goal.

Examples: "I'll hit Tommy so I can get his toys." "I'll cut off that car so I can get ahead of him." "I want my boss's job, so I'll spread a rumor that he is having an affair."

Characteristics: Emotionally cool and more carefully planned.

Reactive aggression: Acts that occur in response to being frustrated or hurt.

Examples: "Jimmy took my toy, so I'm going to hit him." "That guy shoved me to take my place in line, so I'm going punch him out." "Joe took my girlfriend, so I'm gonna get a gun and shoot him."

Characteristics: Furious, disorganized, impulsive response.

What Was Its Form?

Direct aggression: Everyone can see it.

Examples: Telling your boyfriend you hate his guts. Beating up someone. Screaming at your mother. Having a tantrum. Bopping a playmate over the head with a toy.

Characteristics: At its peak at about age 2 or 3; declines as children get older. More common in boys than in girls, especially physical aggression.

Relational aggression: Carried out indirectly, through damaging or destroying the victim's relationships.

Examples: "Sara got a better grade than me, so I'm going to tell the teacher that she cheated." "Let's tell everyone not to let Sara play in our group." "I want Sara's job, so I'll spread a rumor that she is stealing money from the company." "I'm going to tell my best friend that her husband is cheating on her because I want to break up their marriage."

Characteristics: Occurs mainly during elementary school and may be at its peak during adolescence, although—as we all know—it's common *throughout* adult life.

Understanding Highly Aggressive Children

You just saw that, as they get older, boys and girls typically get much less openly aggressive. However, a percentage of children remain unusually aggressive into elementary school (Hay, 2007; Vaillancourt and others, 2007). These children are labeled with externalizing disorders defined by high rates of aggression. They are classified as defiant, antisocial kids.

THE PATHWAY TO PRODUCING PROBLEMATIC AGGRESSION. Longitudinal studies suggest that there may be a poisonous two-step, nature-plus-nurture pathway to being labeled as a highly aggressive child:

STEP 1: *The toddler's exuberant (or difficult) temperament evokes harsh discipline.* When toddlers are highly active and temperamentally fearless, as you saw in Chapter 4, caregivers are tempted to adopt *power-assertion* disciplinary techniques. They shame, threaten, scream, and hit: "Sit down. Shut up. You are an impossible kid." Deciding that "this child is basically impossible" (Johnston, Hommersen, & Seipp, 2009) or physically punishing a toddler who has special trouble controlling his behavior is especially likely to backfire. Notice from the findings in Figure 6.2 on page 184 that, when parents reported regularly spanking a "temperamentally difficult" 15-month-old, the chances of that child's having externalizing problems were magnified at age four (Mulvaney & Mebert, 2007). So, unfortunately, the very toddlers who need sensitive, empathic parenting the most are sometimes set up to get the harshest, most punitive care.

STEP 2: *The child is rejected by teachers and peers in school.* Typically, the transition to being defined as an "antisocial child" occurs during early elementary school. As impulsive, by now clearly aggressive, children travel outside the family, they get

instrumental aggression A hostile or destructive act initiated to achieve a goal.

reactive aggression A hostile or destructive act carried out in response to being frustrated or hurt.

relational aggression A hostile or destructive act designed to cause harm to a person's relationships.

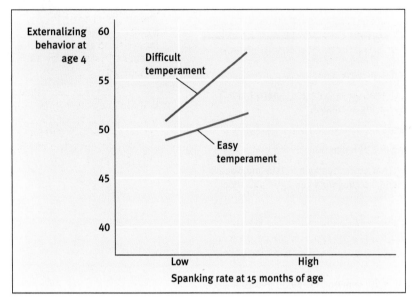

Externalizing behavior at age 4

Difficult temperament

Easy temperament

Low   High

Spanking rate at 15 months of age

FIGURE 6.2: **The relationship between mothers' reports of spanking at 15 months and externalizing behavior at age 4, for temperamentally difficult and easy children, from a longitudinal study:** In this research, notice that if a child was temperamentally easy, being regularly spanked during toddlerhood slightly increased the risk of having later externalizing problems. However, this discipline style had a huge negative impact on development for toddlers with difficult temperaments. Bottom line: power assertion is poisonous for a temperamentally at-risk child.

Source: Mulvaney & Mebert, 2007.

rejected by their classmates and teachers. Being socially excluded is a powerful stress that provokes feelings of paranoia and amplifies aggression at any age (DeWall and others, 2009). Moreover, because aggressive children often *generally* have trouble controlling their behavior, during elementary school, they may also start failing in their academic work. This amplifies the frustration ("I'm not making it in any area of life!") and compounds the tendency to lash out ("It's their fault, not mine!").

A HOSTILE WORLDVIEW. As I just implied, aggressive children also think differently in social situations. They are less able to thoughtfully process feelings (Garner, Dunsmore, & Southam-Gerrow, 2008). They may have a **hostile attributional bias** (Crick & Dodge, 1996). They see threat in benign social cues. When a child gets accidentally bumped at the lunch table, he sees a deliberate provocation. Another aggressive child decides that you are her enemy when you look at her the wrong way. So the child's behavior actually provokes a more hostile world.

To summarize, let's enter the mind of a highly aggressive child like Matt in the chapter-opening vignette. As a toddler, your fearless temperament continually got you into trouble with your parents. You have been harshly disciplined for years. In school, you start failing academically and are shunned by your classmates. So you never have a chance to really interact with other children and improve your social skills. In fact, your hostile attributional bias makes perfect sense. You are living in a "sea of negativity" (Jenson and others, 2004). And yes, the world *is* out to do you in!

Finally, just as you saw with ADHD in Chapter 5, there is a gender difference in the risk of being defined as "an acting-out, antisocial child." Because they are more "exuberant" and far more physical when they play, boys are several times more likely than girls to show the kind of aggressive behavior that gets them labeled with an externalizing problem in elementary school (Card and others, 2008; Hay, 2007; Joussemet, 2008).

How *do* boys and girls relate when they play? Now, let's turn to this question and others as we move to the second part of this chapter: relationships.

Regularly using power assertion to discipline an exuberant toddler (which makes him angry and defiant) and then having him be shunned by the other children for his disruptive behavior in elementary school—that's the two-step recipe for producing a highly aggressive child.

TYING IT ALL TOGETHER

1. You interviewed a 4-year-old and a fourth grader for your class project in lifespan development, but mixed up your interview notes. Which interview statement was made by the 4-year-old?

   a. "My friend Megan is better at math than me."
   b. "Sometimes I get mad at my friends, but maybe it's because I'm too stubborn."
   c. "I have a cat named Kit, and I'm the smartest girl in the world."

2. Identify which of the following boys has internalizing or externalizing tendencies and then, for one of these children, design an intervention program using principles spelled out in this section: Ramon sees himself as totally wonderful, but he is having serious trouble getting along with his teachers and the other kids; Jared is a great student, but when he gets a B instead of an A, he decides that he's "dumb" and gets too depressed to work.

3. When the teacher yells at Zack, Austin and Gabriel both cringe and feel like crying. In addition, Gabriel feels really sorry for Zack. Although both children feel _____ for Zack, Gabriel feels _____. Who is more likely to reach out to comfort Zack?

4. A teacher wants to intervene with a student who has been teasing a classmate. Identify which statement is guilt-producing, which is shame-producing, and which involves the use of induction. Then, name which response(s) would help promote prosocial behavior.

   a. "Think of how bad Johnny must feel."
   b. "If that's how you act, you can sit by yourself. You're not nice enough to be with the other kids."
   c. "I'm disappointed in you. You are usually such a good kid."

5. Alyssa wants to replace Brianna as Chloe's best friend, so she spreads horrible rumors about Brianna. Brianna overhears Alyssa dissing her and starts yelling and slapping Alyssa. Of the four types of aggression discussed in this section—*direct, instrumental, reactive, relational*—which two describe Alyssa's behavior, and which two fit Brianna's actions?

6. Mario, a fourth grader, feels that everyone is out to get him, and he has been labeled as a highly aggressive child. Outline the two-step developmental pathway that may have produced this problem and give the name for Mario's negative worldview.

Answers to the Tying It All Together questions can be found on the last page of this chapter.

hostile attributional bias The tendency of highly aggressive children to see motives and actions as threatening when they are actually benign.

rough-and-tumble play Play that involves shoving, wrestling, and hitting, but in which no actual harm is intended; especially characteristic of boys.

Relationships

Think back to the times you spent pretending to be a superhero or supermodel, getting together with the girls or boys to play, the hours you spent with your best friends, and whether you were popular at school. Now, beginning with play, moving on to the play worlds of girls and boys, then friendships and popularity, and finally tackling bullying—that issue in the chapter-opening vignette—we look at each topic related to childhood relationships one by one.

Play

Developmentalists classify children's "free play" (the non-sports-oriented kind) into different categories. *Exercise play* describes the exciting running and chasing behavior in the chapter-opening vignette. **Rough-and-tumble play** is the name for the shoving, wrestling, and fighting that was so apparent with boys on the playground. Actually, rough-and-tumble play is classically boy behavior. As you will see later, it seems biologically built into being male (Bjorklund & Pellegrini, 2002; Pellegrini, 2006).

Rough-and-tumble play is not only tremendously exciting, but it seems to be genetically built into being "male."

Photodisc/Getty Images

Exploring Fantasy Play

Fantasy play, or *pretending*, is different. Here, the child takes a stance apart from reality and makes up a scene, often with a toy or other prop. While fantasy play can also be very physical, this "as if" quality makes it unique. Children must pretend to be pirates or superheroes as they wrestle and run. Because fantasy play is at the heart of early childhood, let's delve into pretending in depth.

THE DEVELOPMENT AND DECLINE OF PRETENDING. Fantasy play begins to emerge in late infancy, as children realize that a symbol can stand for something else. Mothers actually help scaffold emerging fantasy play. In a classic study, developmentalists watched 1-year-olds with their mothers at home. Although toddlers often initiated a fantasy episode, they needed a parent to expand on the scene (Dunn, Wooding, & Hermann, 1977). So a child would pretend to make a phone call, and his mother would amplify the scenario by picking up the real phone and saying, "Hello, this is Mommy speaking. Should I come home now?"

At about age 3, children transfer the skill of pretending with moms to peers. **Collaborative pretend play**, or fantasizing *together* with another child, really gets going at about age 4 (Smolucha & Smolucha, 1998). Because they need to work together to develop the scene, the ability to collaboratively pretend shows that preschoolers have a *theory of mind*—the knowledge that the other person has a different perspective. (You need to understand that your fellow playwright has a different script in his head.) Collaboratively pretending, in turn, teaches young children the vital skill of getting along with different minds (Jenkins & Astington, 2000).

Anyone with regular access to a young child can see these changes firsthand. When a 2-year-old has his "best friend" over, they play in parallel orbits—if things go well. More likely, a titanic battle erupts, full of instrumental and reactive aggression, as each child attempts to gain sole possession of the toys. By age 4, children can really play *together*. At age 5 or 6, they can pretend together for hours—with only a few major fights that are usually quickly resolved.

For these 4-year-old girls (a.k.a. princesses who have dressed up to feed their baby dolls), their *collaborative pretend play* is teaching them vital lessons about how to compromise and get along.

Although fantasy play can continue into early adolescence, when children reach concrete operations, their interest shifts to structured games (Bjorklund & Pellegrini, 2002). At age 3, a child pretends to bake in the kitchen corner; at 9 he wants to actually bake a cake. At age 5, you ran around playing pirates; at 9, you were interested in hitting the ball like the Pittsburgh Pirates do.

THE PURPOSES OF PRETENDING. Interestingly, around the world, when children pretend, their fantasy play has some universal plots. Let's listen in at a U.S. preschool:

BOY 2: I don't want to be a kitty anymore.

GIRL: You are a husband?

BOY 2: Yeah.

BOYS 1 AND 2: Husbands, husbands! (Yell and run around the playhouse)

GIRL: Hold it, Bill, I can't have two husbands.

BOYS 1 AND 2: Two husbands! Two husbands!

GIRL TO THE TWO BOYS: We gonna marry ourselves, right?

(adapted from Corsaro, 1985, pp. 102–104)

fantasy play Play that involves making up and acting out a scenario; also called *pretend play*.

collaborative pretend play Fantasy play in which children work together to develop and act out the scenes.

Why do young children always play "family," and why do they have to assume the "correct" roles when they play mommy and daddy? For answers, let's turn to Lev Vygotsky's insights about this central activity of early childhood.

Play allows children to practice adult roles. Vygotsky (1978) believed that pretending allows children to rehearse being adults. The reason girls love pretending to be mommy and baby is that women are the main child-care providers in every society

Laura Dwight/Photo Edit, Inc.

around the world. Boys play soldiers because this activity offers built-in training for the wars they may face as adults (Pellegrini & Smith, 2005).

Play allows children a sense of control. As the following preschool conversation suggests, pretending may have a deeper psychological function, too:

GIRL 1: Yeah, and let's pretend when Mommy's out until later.

GIRL 2: Ooooh. Well. I'm not the boss around here, though. 'Cause Mommies play the bosses around here.

GIRL 1: And us children aren't. (Shakes head sadly)

GIRL 2: So . . . when you grow up and I grow up we'll be the bosses. . . .

GIRL 1: (Doubtfully) But maybe we won't know how to punish.

GIRL 2: I will. I'll put my hand up and spank 'em. That's what my mom does.

GIRL 1: My mom does too sometimes.

(adapted from Corsaro, 1985, p. 96)

While reading the previous two chapters, you may have been thinking that the so-called carefree years of early childhood are far from stress-free. We expect children to regulate their emotions when their frontal lobes aren't fully functional. We discipline toddlers and preschoolers when they are not really capable of understanding the rules of the mysterious adult world. Vygotsky (1978) believed that, in response to their feelings of powerlessness, young children enter "an illusory role" in which their desires are realized. In play, *you* can be the spanking mommy or the queen of the castle, even when you are small, and sometimes feel like a slave.

Courtesy of Dr. William Corsaro

Imagine that, like the supersized preschooler shown here (Professor William Corsaro), you could spend years going down slides, playing family, and bonding with 3- and 4-year-olds—and then get professional recognition for your academic work. What an incredible career!

To penetrate the inner world of preschool fantasy play, sociologist William Corsaro (1985, 1997) went undercover. He spent months in a nursery school as a member of the class. (No problem. The children welcomed their new playmate, whom they called Big Bill, as a clumsy, greatly enlarged version of themselves.) As Vygotsky would predict, Corsaro found that preschool play plots often centered on mastering upsetting events. There were separation/reunion scenarios ("Help! I'm lost in the forest." "I'll find you.") and danger/rescue plots ("Get in the house. It's gonna be a rainstorm!"). Sometimes, play scenarios centered on that ultimate frightening event, death:

CHILD 1: We are dead, we are dead! Help, we are dead! (Puts animals on their sides)

CHILD 2: You can't talk if you are dead. . . .

CHILD 1: Oh, well, Leah's talked when she was dead, so mine have to talk when they are dead . . . Help, help, we are dead!

(adapted from Corsaro, p. 204)

Notice that these themes are basic to Disney movies and fairy tales. From *Finding Nemo, Bambi,* and *The Lion King* to—my personal favorite—*Dumbo,* there is nothing more heart-wrenching than being separated from your parent. From the greedy old witch in *Hansel and Gretel* to the jealous queen in *Sleeping Beauty,* no scenario is as sweet as triumphing over evil and possible death.

Play furthers our understanding of social norms. Corsaro (1985) found that death was a touchy play topic. When children proposed these plots, their partners might try to change the script. This relates to Vygotsky's third insight about play: Although children's play looks unstructured, it has clear boundaries and rules. Plots involving two husbands or dead animals waking up make children uncomfortable because they violate the rules of adult life. Children get especially uneasy when a play partner proposes scenarios with gory themes, such as cutting off people's heads (Dunn & Hughes,

2001). Therefore, play teaches children how to act and how not to behave. Wouldn't you want to retreat if someone showed an intense interest in decapitation while having a conversation with you?

Now that we know play has many benefits, let's look at how health-care professionals and teachers might use these insights in their work.

INTERVENTIONS: **Helping Children Through Play**

Based on the idea that play allows us to cope with our fears, nurses on a pediatric ward might be alert to a child's pretend play to get clues into a patient's concerns about an operation. Then, they might enact their own pretend sequence to speak directly to the child's anxieties (for example, "Little Joe Bear went to sleep for awhile, but when he woke up he began to feel better, and now he's all well, and you will be, too").

Preschool teachers could see problems looming on the horizon if one of the 4-year-olds in class was obsessed with playing "I'll kill you and cut off your head." They might try to help that child tone down his violent fantasies and encourage him to play in more appropriate ways (Bartolini & Lunn, 2002).

Still, we have to be cautious about intervening in play. By managing (or micromanaging) make-believe, we may be keeping children from learning important lessons on their own. If we decide how children *must* play, we might be going against nature, too. Many teachers get anxious about rough-and-tumble play. Misinterpreting this basic play mode as real aggressive acts, they tend to vigorously punish the very play activity that boys most love (Ardley & Ericson, 2002; Smith and others, 2002b). Why do female teachers recoil from rough-and-tumble play? The reason will be clear as we explore that other fundamental characteristic of play: Boys and girls live in separate play worlds.

Girls' and Boys' Play Worlds

[Some] girls, all about five and a half years old, are looking through department store catalogues, . . . concentrating on what they call "girls' stuff" and referring to some of the other items as "yucky boys' stuff." . . . Shirley points to a picture of a couch . . . "All we want is the pretty stuff," says Ruth. Peggy now announces, "If you come to my birthday, every girl in the school is invited. I'm going to put a sign up that says, 'No boys allowed!'" "Oh good, good, good," says Vickie. "I hate boys."

(adapted from Corsaro, 1997, p. 155)

Does this conversation bring back any childhood memories of being 5 or 6? How does **gender-segregated play** develop? What are the characteristics of boy versus girl play, and what causes the sexes to separate into these different, often warring camps?

Exploring the Separate Societies

Visit a neighborhood playground and observe children of different ages. You might notice that toddlers show no sign of gender-segregated play. By preschool, children begin to play mainly in sex-segregated groups (Pellegrini and others, 2007a). In early elementary school, gender-segregated play is firmly entrenched. On the playground, boys and girls can sometimes play in mixed groups (Fabes, Martin, & Hanish, 2003). Still, children rarely join a play group unless another member of their own sex is present (Martin & Fabes, 2001). With friendships there is a real split: Boys are almost always best friends with boys and girls with girls (Maccoby, 1998).

Actually, children are intensely interested in the other society. They thrill at teasing, at chasing, at making raids on the "enemy" gender camp (Thorne, 1993). Some girls try to cross the divide and play with the boys. Still, during elementary school, attempts to unite the sexes can be met

A visit to any elementary school lunchroom vividly brings home the fact that middle childhood is all about *gender-segregated play.*

Ellen B. Senisi/The Image Works

with resistance. One 11-year-old girl described the teachers in her school who tried to get the boys and girls to play together as "geeky ughs" (Maccoby, 1998).

Now, go back to the playground and look at the *way* boys and girls relate. Do you notice that boy versus girl play differs in these following ways?

Boys excitedly run around; girls calmly talk. Boys' play is more rambunctious. Even during physical games such as tag, girls play together in calmer and more subdued ways (Maccoby, 1998; Pellegrini, 2006). The difference in activity levels is striking if you have the pleasure of witnessing one gender playing with the opposite sex's toys. In one memorable episode, after my son and a friend invaded a girl's stash of dolls, they gleefully ran around the house bashing Barbie into Barbie and using their booty as swords.

Boys compete in groups; girls play collaboratively, one-to-one. Their exuberant, rough-and-tumble play explains why boys tend to burst on the scene, running and yelling, dominating every room. Another difference lies in play group *size*. Boys get together in packs. Girls prefer playing in smaller, more intimate groups (Maccoby, 1990, 1998; Ruble, Martin, & Berenbaum, 2006).

Boys and girls also differ in the *way* they relate. Boys try to establish dominance and compete to be the best. This competitive versus cooperative style spills over into children's talk. Girl-to-girl collaborative play really sounds collaborative ("I'll be the doctor, okay?"). Boys give each other bossy commands ("I'm doing the operation. You lie down now!") (Maccoby, 1998). Girl-to-girl fantasy play involves nurturing themes. Boys prefer the warrior, superhero mode.

The intensely stereotypic quality of girls' fantasy play came as a shock to me when I spent three days playing with my visiting 7-year-old niece. We devoted day one to setting up a beauty shop, complete with nail polishes and shampoos. We used my sink for hair washing. We had a table for massages and a makeover section featuring all the cosmetics I owned. Then, we opened for business for the visiting relatives and, of course—by charging for our services—made money for toys. We spent the last day playing with a "pool party" Barbie combo my niece had carefully selected at Wal-Mart that afternoon.

Boys' and girls' different play interests show why the kindergartners in the vignette at the beginning of this section came to hate those "yucky" boys. Another reason why girls turn off to the opposite sex is the unpleasant reception they often get from the opposing camp. In observing at a preschool, researchers found that while active girls played with the boys' groups early in the year, they eventually were rejected and so forced to play with their own sex (Pellegrini and others, 2007a). Therefore, boys are the first to erect the barriers: "No girls allowed!" Moreover, the gender barriers are *generally* more rigid for males.

Boys live in a more exclusionary, separate world. My niece did choose to buy the Barbies, but she also plays with trucks. She loves soccer and baseball, not just doing her nails. So, even though they may say they hate the opposite sex, girls do sometimes cross the divide. Boys are more likely to avoid that chasm—refusing to venture down the Barbie aisle or consider buying a toy labeled "girl." So boys live in a more roped-off gender world (Boyle, Marshall, & Robeson, 2003).

Now, you might be interested in what happened during my final day of pretending with the pool party toys. After my niece said, "Aunt Janet, let's pretend we are the popular girls," our Barbies tried on fancy dresses ("Oh, what shall I wear, Jane?") in preparation for a "popular girls" pool party, where the dolls met up ("Hello, Sara! I'm *so* glad to see you") to discuss—*guess what*—where they shopped and who did their hair!

What Causes Gender-Stereotyped Play?

Why do children, such as my niece, play in these incredibly gender-stereotyped ways? Answers come from exploring three interacting forces: biology (nature), socialization (nurture), and cognitions (or thoughts).

A BIOLOGICAL UNDERPINNING. Ample evidence suggests that gender-segregated play is biologically built in. Children around the world live in separate play societies

gender-segregated play Play in which boys and girls associate only with members of their own sex—typical of childhood.

gender schema theory An explanation for gender-stereotyped behavior that emphasizes the role of cognitions; specifically, the idea that once children know their own gender label (girl or boy), they selectively watch and model their own sex.

This boy is learning to be more "boy-like" as he aggressively pounds a peg into this traditionally male toy, given to him by his parents.

This image of 5-year-old girls getting together to enjoy their dolls and reinforce one another for activities such as braiding Barbie's hair shows us exactly why gender-segregated play powerfully reinforces traditional gender-role behavior.

(Maccoby, 1998). Troops of juvenile rhesus monkeys behave *exactly* like human children. The males segregate into their own groups and engage in rough-and-tumble play (Pellegrini, 2006). Grooming activities similar to my niece's beauty-shop behaviors are a prominent activity among young female monkeys, too (Bjorklund & Pellegrini, 2002; Suomi, 2004).

Actually, when pregnant rhesus monkeys are injected with the male sex hormone testosterone, their female offspring also engage in rough-and-tumble play (Udry, 2000). Could a similar effect apply to females in our species, too?

To answer this fascinating question, one developmentalist measured the naturally occurring testosterone levels of women pregnant with female fetuses (Udry, 2000). He took maternal blood samples during the second trimester—the time, you may recall from Chapter 2, when the neurons are being formed. Then, years later, when the daughters were about age 17, he asked them to fill out sex-role questionnaires.

Girls who had been exposed to comparatively high levels of prenatal testosterone were more interested in traditionally male occupations, such as engineering, than the lower-hormone-level prenatal group. They were less likely to wear makeup. Even in their twenties, they showed more stereotypically male interests (such as race-car driving). So, depending on the dose, prenatal exposure to testosterone may program us to have more "feminized" or "masculinized" brains.

THE AMPLIFYING EFFECT OF SOCIALIZATION. The wider world helps biology along. Parents buy dolls for their daughters and trucks for their sons. They tend to play with their male and female children in gender-stereotyped ways.

Peers play a powerful role in this programming. When they play in mixed-gender groups, children act in less stereotypically masculine or feminine ways (Fabes, Martin, & Hanish, 2003). So, in the chapter-opening vignette, if Manuel and his friends had let Moriah and her friends join their game of tag, they would have felt forced to tone down their rough-and-tumble play. Therefore, the actual act of splitting into separate play societies trains children to behave in ways typical of their own sex (Martin & Fabes, 2001).

Same-sex playmates reinforce one another for selecting the most gender-stereotyped activities ("Let's play with dolls." "Great!"). They mutually model one another as they play together in "gentle" or "rough" ways. The pressure to toe the gender line is also promoted by powerful social sanctions. Popular children tend to closely fit the gender stereotypes. Girls labeled as tomboys are less well liked than "typical" girls. Sensitive, anxious boys rank especially low on the male popularity totem pole (Chen & French, 2008; Coplan, Closson, & Arbeau, 2007).

THE IMPACT OF COGNITIONS. A cognitive process reinforces these external messages. According to **gender schema theory** (Bem, 1981; Martin & Dinella, 2002), once children understand which basic category (girl or boy) they belong in, they selectively attend to the activities of their own sex.

When do children first grasp their gender label and start this lifelong practice of observing and modeling their group? By the time they begin really talking, at about age 2½, children typically have their gender identity nailed down (Maccoby, 1998). Although they may not learn the real difference until much later (here, it helps to have an opposite-sex sibling to see naked), 3-year-olds can tell you that girls have long hair and cry a lot and boys fight and play with trucks. At about age 5 or 6, when they are mastering the similar concept of identity constancy (the knowledge that your essential self doesn't change when you dress up in a gorilla costume), children grasp the idea that once you start out as a boy or girl, you stay that way for life (Kohlberg, 1966). However, mistakes are still common. I once heard my

5-year-old nephew ask my husband, "Was that jewelry from when you were a girl?"

In sum, my niece's beauty-shop activities had a clear biological basis, although a steady stream of nurture influences from adults and playmates helped this process along. Her behavior was also promoted by identifying herself as "a girl" and then spending hours selectively attending to and modeling the women in her life.

But is the sex-segregated childhood play world changing? My students describe having more close friends of the opposite gender during elementary school than I recall from when I was growing up. Do you think our less gender-defined adult culture could be making for less gender-stereotyped play? Were your best friends during elementary school the same sex as you?

Children spend hours modeling their own sex, demonstrating why *gender schema theory* (the idea "I am a boy" or "I am a girl") also encourages behaving in gender-stereotyped ways.

Friendships

This last question brings us to that important topic: friends. *Why* do children choose specific friends, and what benefits do childhood friendships provide?

The Core Qualities: Similarity, Trust, and Emotional Support

The essence of friendship is feeling a sense of similarity. As you just saw, we gravitate toward people who are "like us" both in gender and general worldview (Rubin, Fredstrom, & Bowker, 2008). So in preschool, an active child will tend to make friends with a classmate who also likes to run around. A 4-year-old who loves the slide will most likely become best buddies with a child who shares this passion, too (Rubin, Bukowski, & Parker, 2006).

Mirroring the way they describe themselves, however, young children describe their friendships in terms of external qualities: "She's my best friend because we go down the slide together." As children get older, they shift to talking about inner qualities in describing their friends: "Josh and I are best buddies because he is funny and such a great guy." Around this age, children also develop the concept of loyalty ("I can trust Josh to stand up for me") and the sense that friends share their inner lives (Hartup & Stevens, 1997; Newcomb & Bagwell, 1995). Listen to these fourth and fifth graders describing their best friend:

> He is my very best friend because he tells me things and I tell him things.
> Me and Tiff share our deepest, darkest secrets and we talk about boys, when we grow up, and shopping.
> Jessica has problems at home and with her religion and when something happens she always comes to me and talks about it. We've been through a lot together.

(quoted in Rose & Asher, 2000, p. 49)

Left: Preschool best friends connect through their shared passion for physical activities such as going down slides.
Right: In late elementary school best friends bond by sharing secrets and plans.

These quotations would resonate with the ideas of personality theorist Harry Stack Sullivan. Sullivan (1953) believed that a chum (or best friend) fulfills the developmental need for self-validation and intimacy that emerges at around age 9. Sullivan also believed that this special relationship serves as a stepping-stone to a truly adult romance.

The Protecting and Teaching Functions of Friends

In addition to offering emotional support and validating us as people, friends stimulate children's personal development in two important ways:

Friends protect and enhance the developing self. Perhaps you noticed this protective function in the quotation earlier in which the fourth grader spoke about how she helped her best friend when she had problems at home. Friends help insulate children from being bullied at school (Rubin, Fredstrom, & Bowker, 2008; Scholte and others, 2009). They become especially important safe zones of comfort as we become teenagers and begin separating from our parents and moving into the wider world (Rubin, Bukowski, & Parker, 2006). You also may have noticed that the reasons for shedding a friendship often center on not being protected: The person we *thought* was a friend let us down in our hour of need.

Friends teach us to manage our emotions and handle conflicts. Your parents will love you no matter what you do, but the love of a friend is contingent. So to relate to a friend, children must be able to modulate their emotions and attune themselves to the other person's needs (Bukowski, 2001; Denham and others, 2003).

This is not to say that friends don't have arguments. In Western cultures, disagreements among friends are often intense. Friendships differ, however, during the conflict resolution phase. Friends are more likely to deal with conflicts by negotiating and compromising (Rubin, Fredstrom, & Bowker, 2008). They are committed to preserving their attachment bond.

This is not to say that friends are always positive influences. They can bring out a child's worst self, too, by encouraging relational aggression ("We are best friends, so you can't play with us") and daring one another to engage in dangerous behavior ("Let's sneak out of the house at 2 A.M."). I will be exploring this dark side of friendship when we look at the pathways to committing delinquent acts during the adolescent years. However, in general, Sullivan seems to be right: Friends do help teach us how to relate as adults.

Popularity

Friendship is a symmetrical, one-to-one relationship. It involves relating on an equal level to a single human being. Being popular is a group concern. It requires having the talent to rise to the top of the social totem pole.

Although children differ in social status in preschool, you may remember from your own childhood that "Who is popular?" becomes an absorbing question during later elementary school. Entering concrete operations makes children highly sensitive to making social comparisons. The urge to rank classmates according to social status is heightened by the confining conditions of childhood itself. In adulthood, popularity fades more into the background because we are free to select our own social circles. Children are required to make it on a daily basis in a classroom full of random peers.

Who Is Popular and Who Is Unpopular?

How do children vary in popularity during the socially stressful elementary school years? Here are the categories researchers find when they ask third, fourth, or fifth graders to list the two or three classmates they like most and really dislike:

- *Popular children* are frequently named in the most-liked category and never appear in the disliked group. They stand out as being really liked by everyone.

- *Average children* receive a few most-liked and perhaps one or two disliked nominations. They rank around the middle range of status in the class.

• *Rejected children* land in the disliked category often and never appear in the preferred list. They stand out among their classmates in a negative way.

In addition to these distinctions, some children may be classified as neglected. They receive no nominations, positive or negative, and so don't appear on the classroom radar screen. Others may be labeled controversial. Their names turn up frequently in both the most-liked and most-disliked lists. The class clown or a very aggressive child who is also socially skilled fit this interesting "love 'em or hate 'em" type (Putallaz and others, 2007). However, these categories are small and unstable. What is highly relevant is the popularity–unpopularity distinction. What qualities make children popular? Most importantly, what traits make children disliked by their peers?

Popular children tend to be friendly and outgoing, prosocial and kind (Mayberry & Espelage, 2007). But researchers have also identified a subset of popular children who are both prosocial and instrumentally aggressive (Hawley, Little, & Card, 2008; Roseth and others, 2007). They rise to the top of the social hierarchy by having the talent to aggressively beat out their adversaries and then reach out to enlist the group as allies in a caring way (Pellegrini, 2008). Rejected children lack this sophisticated balance of skills. They are *simply* highly aggressive. Or, like Jimmy, they shrink back from competing at all. Specifically:

Rejected children have externalizing (and sometimes internalizing) disorders. Children with externalizing tendencies—especially if they are physically aggressive—quickly fall into the rejected category. These are the boys and girls, like Matt in the opening vignette, who make aggression their major life mode (Putallaz and others, 2007; Hawley and others, 2007). Anxious children—those prone to internalizing disorders—may or may not be rejected (Gazelle, 2008). However, a *socially inept*, anxious child, like Jimmy, is likely to be avoided as early as first grade (Gazelle & Ladd, 2003).

Moreover, a poisonous nature-evokes-nurture interaction can set in when a child enters school extremely shy. As children pick up on the fact that people are avoiding them, their shyness becomes more intense. So they may become less socially competent—and increasingly likely to be rejected—as they advance from grade to grade (Booth-LaForce & Oxford, 2008).

An unfortunate bidirectional process is also occurring. The child's anxiety makes other children nervous. They get uncomfortable and want to retreat when they see this person approach. In response to your own awkward encounters, have you ever been tempted to walk in the opposite direction when you saw a very shy person approaching in the hall?

Rejected children don't fit in with the group. Children who stand out as different are also at risk of being rejected: Girls who don't like to play with Barbies; boys who are very quiet (Chen & French, 2008); low-income children in middle-class schools (Zettergren, 2007)—all may be set up for rejection during elementary school.

Middle School Meanness

In elementary school, popular children are well liked by both the teachers and their classmates. In middle school, the group norms take a different tilt. Now, being rebellious is more of an "in thing," and some aggressive children who are disliked by adults may be in the popular group (Chen & French, 2008). Now, the talents that help children rise to the top of the social ladder are not necessarily prosocial skills.

When researchers followed several hundred children from fifth to ninth grade (Cillessen & Mayeux, 2004), they found that, for girls in particular, high levels of relational aggression became more linked to being in the popular group year by year. Furthermore, as you can see in Figure 6.3, by ninth grade, being defined as popular became less closely linked to measures of being liked. This explains that familiar paradox: In middle school and high school, children in the "in-group" or popular crowd may be *personally* disliked by much of the class (Kosir & Pecjak, 2005; Prinstein & Cillessen, 2003).

His shyness may set this boy up for social rejection in first grade because his anxiety will make the other children uneasy and he may not have the courage to reach out to his classmates.

FIGURE 6.3: How being popular relates to being personally liked for girls in middle school: In this study, children in different grades were asked which classmates were popular and which classmates they liked the most. Notice that, by ninth grade, there was little relationship between being viewed as in the "popular" group and being seen as well liked. Did you *really* like the kids in the "in-crowd" at your school?

Source: Cillessen & Mayeux (2004), p. 153.

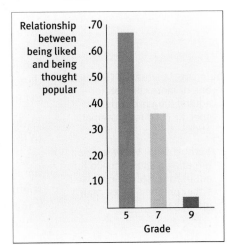

Alistair Berg/Getty Images

Will this socially isolated elementary school boy get it together and shine in high school and college? Provided that he is not very aggressive, the answer may be yes.

You might be interested to know that there is a potential downside to being in the teenage popular group. In a fascinating longitudinal study conducted in a high school, boys and girls in the "in-group" who were *highly aware* of their status ("We are the class stars!") tended to get more aggressive over time (Mayeux & Cillessen, 2008). Just as we might imagine, letting popularity "go to your head" can have negative consequences for personality down the road!

The Fate of the Rejected

What about being in the out-group? Is being rejected during childhood a risk factor for having future problems? The answer is "sometimes." Highly aggressive "antisocial" children are at risk for having serious difficulties during adolescence and their early adult years (stay tuned for more about this in Chapter 9). But some traits that get children ranked low-status during childhood do not translate into an unhappy adult life. Consider an awkward little girl named Eleanor Roosevelt, who was socially rejected at age 8, or a boy named Thomas Edison, whose preference for playing alone got him defined as a "problem" child. Because they were so different, these famous adults were dismal failures during elementary school. To get insights into the fleeting quality of childhood peer status, you might organize a reunion of your fifth- or sixth-grade class. You might be surprised at how many "average," "neglected," or "rejected" classmates flowered during their high school or college years.

FOCUS ON A TOPIC:

BULLYING

bullying A situation in which one or more children (or adults) harass or target a specific child for systematic abuse.

cyberbullying Victimizing or targeting a specific child (or adult) for systematic abuse either on-line or via e-mail messages.

Children who are shy can excel in the proving ground of life. This is not the case on the proving ground of the playground. While aggressive boys and girls who are also disorganized and impulsive may be a target of harassment, children who are unassertive and anxious are especially vulnerable to **bullying**—being regularly teased, made fun of, and verbally or physically abused by their peers.

Who tends to be bullied? Studies around the world agree: Boys and girls who are anxious, rejected, or low in the social hierarchy are typical targets (Deveci, Acik, & Ayar, 2008; Putallaz and others, 2007; Scholte and others, 2009). They turn into victims, as you can see in my true confession in the Experiencing the Lifespan box, when they can't (or won't) strike back. Being targeted breeds more anxiety and further victimization. School becomes such an aversive experience that some bullied children turn off to what happens in class, even when they are highly competent in school (Beran & Lupart, 2009; Ladd, Herald-Brown, & Reiser, 2008).

Where does most bullying take place? When researchers looked at three middle school settings—school dances, the cafeteria, and the hallway—they found that most incidents of bullying occurred in the lunchroom. Virtually none occurred at school dances, one reason being that middle schoolers who were victimized avoided these events (Parault, Davis, & Pellegrini, 2007).

Unfortunately, however, in this day and age, children cannot decide that "I won't go to the dances" or feel comforted that "this will stop once I am at home." In one huge on-line poll, roughly 1 in 3 boys and girls reported experiencing **cyberbullying**—being harassed either via e-mail or in on-line chat rooms. Reports from its victims show how frightening cyberbullying can be. One 11-year-old wrote, "… a friend from school e-mailed me: 'Tomorrow—watch your back—we are coming for you.' It made me feel so bad I started to cry" (quoted in Hinduja & Patchin, 2008, p. 142). A boy reported: "I was talking to someone in a chat room. . . . They told me they were going to harm me and I was scared because . . . they (somehow) knew where I lived" (quoted in Hinduja & Patchin, 2008, pp. 142–143).

Cyberbullying is like a drive-by shooting. Cruel statements people might be ashamed to make face-to-face are not off limits. No one can spot you as you anonymously attack. Real-life bullying is an up-front, in-your-face, often social event. As you saw in the chapter-opening vignette, typically one child (or a few children) start the harassment while another group provides the perpetrator positive reinforcement by looking on and laughing. Children sometimes engage in bullying for social reasons—like getting acceptance from their peers (Olthof & Goossens, 2008). A negative, rejecting school climate is one crucial wider-world "context" that provokes this behavior, too (Barboza and others, 2009). So interventions to prevent bullying emphasize not changing the person, but reversing the classroom norms (Breakstone, Dreiblatt, & Dreiblatt, 2009).

Imagine that this chilling message anonymously arrived on your cell phone one morning and you will get a flavor of why *cyberbullying* is a particularly terrifying event.

EXPERIENCING THE LIFESPAN: MIDDLE-AGED REFLECTIONS ON MY MIDDLE-CHILDHOOD VICTIMIZATION

It was a hot August afternoon when the birthday present arrived. As usual, I was playing alone that day, maybe reading or engaging in a favorite pastime, fantasizing that I was a princess while sitting in a backyard tree. The gift, addressed to Janet Kaplan, was beautifully wrapped—huge but surprisingly light. This is amazing! I must be special! Someone had gone to such trouble for me! When I opened the first box, I saw another carefully wrapped box, and then another, smaller box, and yet another, smaller one inside. Finally, surrounded by ribbons and wrapping paper, I eagerly got to the last box, and saw a tiny matchbox—which contained a small burnt match.

Around that time, the doorbell rang, and Cathy, then Ruth, then Carol, bounded up. "Your mother called to tell us she was giving you a surprise birthday party. We had to come over right away and be sure to wear our best dresses!" But their excitement turned to disgust when they learned that no party had been arranged. My ninth birthday was really in mid-September—more than a month away. It turned out that Nancy and Marion—the two most popular girls in class—had masterminded this relational aggression plot directed at me.

Why was I selected as the victim among the other third-grade girls? I had never hurt Nancy or Marion. In fact, in confessing their role, they admitted to some puzzlement: "We really don't dislike Janet at all." Researching this chapter has offered me insights into the reasons for this 50-year-old wound.

Although I did have friends, I was fairly low in the classroom hierarchy. Not only was I shy, but I was that unusual girl—a child who genuinely preferred to play alone. But most important, I was the perfect victim. I dislike competitive, status situations. When taunted or teased, I don't fight back.

As an older woman, I still dislike status hierarchies and social snobberies. I'm not a group (or party) person. I far prefer talking one-to-one. I am happy to spend hours alone. Today, I consider these attributes a plus (after all, having no problem sitting by myself for many thousands of hours was a prime skill that allowed me to write this text!), but they caused me anguish in middle childhood. In fact, today, when I find myself in status-oriented peer situations, I can still catch glimmers of my long-ago, nervous, third-grade self!

INTERVENTIONS: Attacking Bullying and Helping Rejected Children

For instance, in the *Olweus Bully Prevention Program*, administrators plan a school assembly to discuss bullying early in the year. Then, they form a bullying-prevention committee composed of children from each grade. Teachers and students are kept on high alert for bullying in their classes. The goal is to develop a schoolwide norm to not tolerate peer abuse (Olweus, Limber, & Mihalic, 1999).

Anti-cyberbullying Web sites and in-school "stop-bullying" programs are currently very popular. More neglected are the classic victims of this abuse—boys and girls, such as Jimmy in the opening vignette, who are rejected and/or socially shy. What can we do to help these children succeed?

In following a group of shy 5-year-olds, researchers found that if a child developed friends in kindergarten or first grade, that boy or girl became less socially anxious over time (Gazelle & Ladd, 2003). So, to help a temperamentally anxious child, parents need to immediately connect their son or daughter—preferably in preschool—with a playmate who might become a close friend. Another strategy is to model what a caring relationship is all about. In one longitudinal study, mothers who researchers ranked as highly sensitive when relating to their shy 2-year-olds had 4-year-olds who were more prone to reach out to a friend (Gazelle & Spangler, 2007).

Actually, in helping children at risk for *both* internalizing and externalizing disorders, it's best to intervene early on. As I've been implying in this chapter and Chapter 4, providing loving, sensitive parenting during infancy and toddlerhood is especially important with any temperamentally "at-risk" child. We also need to understand that with active explorers, the same traits that *can* spell trouble are potential life assets. In an amazing decades-long study, when researchers measured temperament during infancy and then looked at personality during adulthood, the *one* quality that predicted being highly competent at age 40 was having been rated "disinhibited" and fearless during the first year of life (Blatney, Jelinek, & Osecka, 2007). So, with the right person-environment fit, a "difficult to tame" toddler may turn into the caring soldier in this photo or a true prosocial hero, like the firefighters on 9/11!

U.S. Defense Department

What was this incredibly brave prosocial Iraq War soldier really like at age one or two? Probably a fearless handful!

🌸 TYING IT ALL TOGETHER

1. When Melanie and Miranda play, they love to make up pretend scenes together. Are these two girls likely to be about age 2, age 5, or age 9?

2. In watching boys and girls at recess in an elementary school, which *two* observations are you likely to make?

   a. The boys are playing in larger groups.
   b. Both girls and boys love rough-and-tumble play.
   c. The girls are quieter, and they are doing more negotiating.

3. Erik and Maria are arguing about the cause of gender-stereotyped behavior. Erik says the reason why boys like to run around and play with trucks is biological. Sophia argues that gender-stereotyped play is socialized by adults and other children. First, argue Erik's position and, then, make Sophia's case by referring to specific data in this section.

4. You are fondly remembering your best friend in later elementary school. Which of the following statements is *not* likely to fit this relationship?

   a. You and your best buddy rarely fought or argued.
   b. You and your best buddy were very similar in interests.
   c. You and your best buddy supported and protected each other.

5. If Madison is in the popular kids' crowd, she may be (highly aggressive and prosocial/simply highly prosocial/simply highly aggressive) and being in this crowd (will have totally positive effects/can have negative effects) on her later personality.

6. Which of the following children is at risk of being rejected in elementary school?

   a. Miguel, a very shy, socially anxious child
   b. Lauren, a tomboy who hates "girls' stuff"
   c. Nicholas, a highly aggressive child
   d. All of these children

7. (a) If a child is being bullied, name the quality that may be making her an easy target.
   (b) Then, to a parent of a shy preschooler, offer advice to help reduce the chance of

that boy or girl being rejected in elementary school. (c) Finally, give a piece of parenting advice to a mother or father of a highly exuberant toddler. (Give a brief answer to each question.)

Answers to the Tying It All Together questions can be found on the last page of this chapter.

Final Thoughts

The underlying message of this chapter has been that parents play a vital role in shaping children's emotional and social skills. But another strong message is that peers are vital in socialization, too. How critical a role do parents versus peers play in determining our behavior and the kind of adult we become? Can we identify some overall strategies for good parenting? What specifically can schools do to help children thrive both socially and academically? Stay tuned for answers in the next chapter, as we shift from looking at the process of development to examining the wider-world settings in which children develop: home and school.

SUMMARY

Setting the Context: Emotion Regulation

Emotion regulation, the ability to manage and control our feelings, is crucial to having a successful life. Children with **externalizing tendencies** often "act out their emotions" and behave aggressively. Children with **internalizing tendencies** have problems managing intense fear. Both of these temperamental tendencies, at their extreme, cause problems during childhood.

Personality

Self-awareness changes dramatically as children move into middle childhood. Concrete operational children think about themselves in psychological terms, realistically scan their abilities, and evaluate themselves in comparison with peers. These more realistic self-perceptions explain why **self-esteem** normally declines during elementary school. Erikson's terms **industry** and **inferiority** also capture the self-esteem challenges children face during middle childhood. Relationships, academics, behavior, sports, and looks are the five areas from which elementary school children derive their self-esteem.

Children with externalizing tendencies minimize their difficulties with other people and may have unrealistically high self-esteem. Children with internalizing tendencies tend to be excessively self-critical, prone to low self-esteem, and may develop **learned helplessness**, the feeling that they are incapable of doing well. Because both attitudes keep children from working to improve their behavior, the key to helping *every* child is to focus on enhancing self-efficacy, promote realistic views of the self, and offer love. Stimulating self-esteem, however, is not an issue in Asia, where the cultural ideal is to be self-effacing and modest.

Prosocial behaviors—caring, helpful acts—become more varied and mature as children develop. There also is consistency, with prosocial preschoolers tending to be prosocial later on. Acts defined as most prosocial vary by culture.

Altruism—prosocial behavior that is genuinely non-egocentric—involves transforming one's **empathy** (directly experiencing

another's feelings) into **sympathy** (feeling for another person); being self-confident (not overly anxious); and being happy. The best way to socialize altruism is to use **induction** (getting a child who has behaved hurtfully to understand the other person's feelings) and to induce **guilt**. Child-rearing techniques involving **shame** (personal humiliation) backfire, making children angry and less likely to act in prosocial ways.

Aggression, or hurtful behavior, is also basic to being human. Rates of open aggression (hitting, yelling) dramatically decline as children get older. **Instrumental aggression** is hurtful behavior we initiate. **Reactive aggression** occurs in response to being frustrated or hurt. **Relational aggression** refers to acts of aggression designed to damage social relationships. Relational aggression increases during late elementary school and middle school, and is present in girls and boys.

A two-step pathway may produce a highly aggressive child. When toddlers are very active (exuberant) or difficult, caregivers may respond harshly and punitively—causing anger and aggression. Then, during school, the child's "bad" behavior causes social rejection that leads to more aggression. Highly aggressive children may have a **hostile attributional bias**. This "the world is out to get me" outlook is understandable, since aggressive children may have been living in a rejecting environment since their earliest years. Because boys tend to act out their feelings they are more likely to be diagnosed as having "problematic aggression" than girls.

Relationships

Play is at the heart of childhood. **Rough-and-tumble play**, play fighting and wrestling, is typical of boys. **Fantasy play** or pretending—typical of all children—begins in later infancy and becomes genuinely mutual at about age 4, with the beginning of **collaborative pretend play**. Fantasy play declines during concrete operations, as children become interested in organized activities.

Fantasy play may help children practice adult roles; offer a sense of mastery and teach the need to adhere to social norms.

Through examining fantasy play, adults can get insights into children's inner concerns.

Gender-segregated play unfolds during preschool, and in elementary school girls and boys typically play mainly with other members of their own sex. Boy-to-boy play is rambunctious, while girls play together in quiet, collaborative ways. Boys tend to compete in groups; girls play one-to-one. Boys' play is more excluding of girls. Gender-stereotyped play seems to have a strong biological basis, but this behavior is also socialized by parents and, especially, by peers as children play together in same-sex groups. According to **gender schema theory**, once children understand that they are a boy or a girl, they attend to and model behaviors of their own sex.

In childhood (and adulthood) we select friends who are similar to ourselves, and when children get older, inner qualities such as personality, loyalty, and sharing feelings become important. Friends provide children with vital emotional support and teach them to get along with others.

Friendship is a symmetrical relationship. Popular children may rise to top of the social totem pole, by combining prosocial behavior and instrumentally aggressive acts. Rejected children either have serious externalizing tendencies or are socially anxious; or they don't conform to the group norms. In elementary school popular children are well liked by their classmates, but during middle school and high school, children who are at the top of the social hierarchy may be relatively disliked by their peers. Although unpopular children with externalizing problems are at risk for having later problems, shy children and those who don't fit the childhood social mode may flower as they get older.

Children who are unpopular, who are anxious, and, especially, who don't fight back are vulnerable to **bullying**. Today, in addition to in-school harassment, **cyberbullying** has become a major concern. Bully-prevention programs help to change the atmosphere at school. A good way to help the main victims of bullying—socially anxious children—is to get them connected with a friend. The main way to help temperamentally at-risk children—those prone to externalizing and internalizing problems—is to offer sensitive parenting during the first years of life. Exuberant toddlers—those most "at risk" of having later problems—may be incredibly successful as adults.

KEY TERMS

emotion regulation, p. 172	learned helplessness, p. 175	aggression, p. 181	fantasy play, p. 186
externalizing tendencies, p. 172	prosocial behavior, p. 178	instrumental aggression, p. 182	collaborative pretend play, p. 186
internalizing tendencies, p. 172	altruism, p. 179	reactive aggression, p. 182	gender-segregated play, p. 188
self-awareness, p. 173	empathy, p. 179	relational aggression, p. 182	
self-esteem, p. 173	sympathy, p. 179	hostile attributional bias, p. 184	gender schema theory, p. 190
industry versus inferiority, p. 174	induction, p. 180	rough-and-tumble play, p. 185	bullying, p. 194
	shame, p. 180		cyberbullying, p. 194
	guilt, p. 180		

ANSWERS TO TYING IT ALL TOGETHER QUIZZES

Setting the Context: Emotion Regulation

1. b.

Personality

1. c.
2. Ramon = externalizing tendencies. Jared = internalizing tendencies. *Suggested intervention for Ramon:* Point out this child's misperceptions ("You are not just the best. In fact, you are having trouble in X, Y, Z areas."), but cushion criticisms with plenty of love. Stimulate self-efficacy by entering Ramon's proximal zone, and reinforce him for appropriate behavior. *Suggested intervention for Jared:* Continually point out reality. ("No one can always get A's. In fact, you are a fabulous student.") Get Jared to identify his "hopeless and helpless" ways of thinking, and teach him to substitute more accurate perceptions.

3. Empathy; sympathy. Gabriel is more likely to reach out and comfort Zack.

4. a. = induction; good for promoting prosocial behavior; b. = shame; bad strategy; and c. = guilt; good for promoting prosocial behavior.

5. Alyssa = instrumental, relational. Brianna = direct, reactive.

6. Step 1: Mario's exuberant temperament as a toddler evoked harsh discipline from his parents, which made him angry and hostile. Step 2: Then, Mario was rejected by his peers and teachers in school, which made him even more defiant. Mario has a hostile attributional bias.

Relationships

1. About age 5

2. a and c.

3. Erik can argue that gender-stereotyped play must be biologically built in as this behavior occurs in primates and appears in societies around the world. He can also mention the study showing masculine-type interests during adulthood may be programmed by prenatal testosterone. Sophia can say that parents teach traditional gender-role behavior by buying children gender-stereotyped toys and playing with their sons and daughters in "feminine" or "masculine" ways. Most important, peers powerfully socialize "girl" or "boy" behavior as they segregate into same-sex play groups. Children are highly motivated to conform to these "correct" ways of acting or risk being socially excluded.

4. a.

5. If Madison is in the popular kids' crowd she may be *highly aggressive and prosocial,* and being in this crowd *can have negative effects* on her later personality.

6. d.

7. (a) She is anxious and has trouble standing up for herself. (b) Get your child involved with a friend; foster a secure attachment. (c) Provide lots of love!

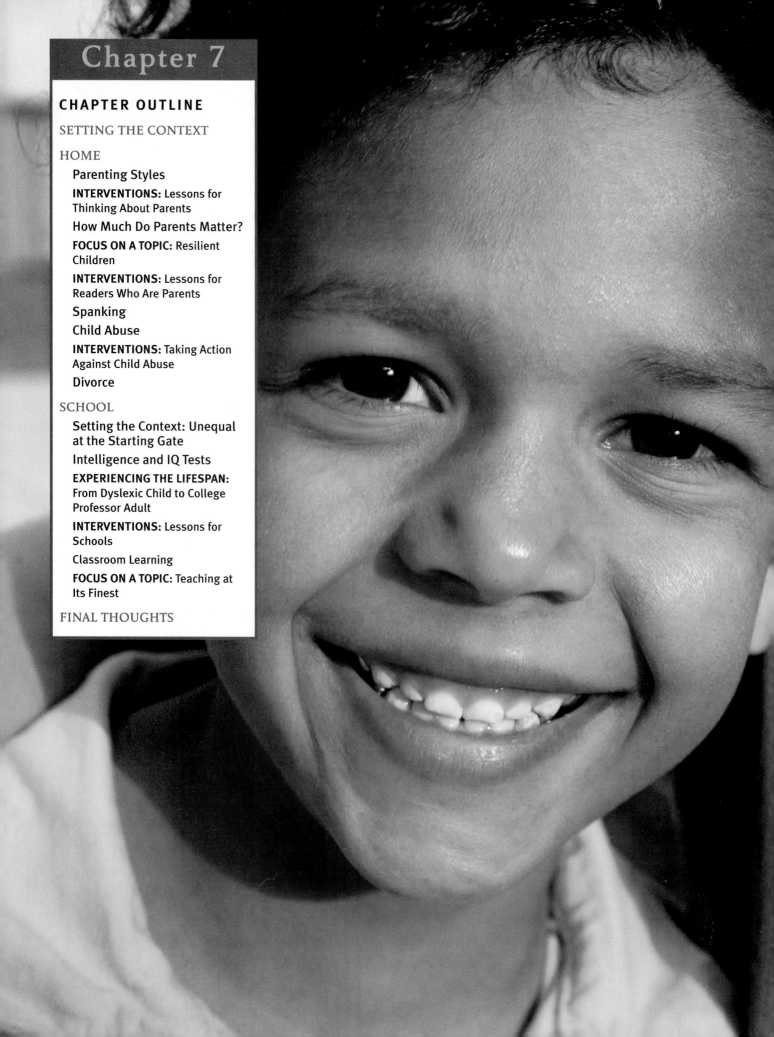

Settings for Development: Home and School

Manuel's parents migrated from Mexico to Las Vegas when he was a baby. Leaving their close extended family was painful, but they knew their son would not have much of a future in their small rural town.

At first, life was going very well. The Las Vegas economy was booming. José joined the Culinary Workers' Union. Maria got a housekeeping job at Caesar's Palace. They sent money to relatives regularly and made a down payment on a condo—carefully chosen to be in the best school district in town. Most important, their baby was turning into an exceptional boy. At age 5, Manuel could repair household appliances. He put together puzzles that would stump a 10-year-old child. He was picking up English beautifully, even though his parents, who only spoke Spanish, could not help him much with reading English and preparing for school.

Then, when Manuel was age 7, everything changed. José was laid off. He started to drink heavily. He came home late to regularly yell at his wife. Maria fell into a depression. This totally involved mother, who had been so strict but very loving—managing her son's activities, teaching him values—was barely able to pay any attention to her child. Although Manuel's first-grade teacher recommended he be tested for the gifted program, when the district psychologist got around to performing the evaluation a year later, Manuel didn't make the cutoff. His performance IQ was off the charts. But growing up in a Spanish-speaking family was a real handicap. His verbal IQ was only 95. And this was the worst time for Manuel to be tested: Maria had recently taken her belongings, moved out, sent for her mother, and filed for divorce.

It's two years later and life is getting back to normal. Maria's becoming the caring mother she used to be. After a rocky third-grade year, Manuel is returning to his old terrific self. The fourth-grade teacher is wonderful. She's creative, gives the children responsibility, understands Manuel's talents, and appreciates diverse kids. The thorn in Maria's side is Grandma—or, to be exact, Manuel's attitude toward Grandma. Having her mother in the house has been a godsend. Manuel doesn't have to stay home alone at night when Maria works double shifts to keep the family above the poverty line. But Manuel is beginning to be ashamed to bring friends home to see that "old world" lady. He wants to be a regular American boy. The downside of seeing your baby blossom beautifully in this country is watching your heritage get lost.

Is it typical for children, like Manuel, to have a difficult year or two after their parents get divorced? Given that we vitally need to succeed in the wider world, how important are the lessons we learn from our parents as opposed to our peers? What was that test Manuel took, and what strategies can teachers use to make every child eager to learn? Now, we tackle these questions, and others, as I focus on the main settings within which children develop: home and school.

While my discussion applies to all children in every home and school, in this chapter, I'll pay special attention to children such as Manuel, whose families differ from the traditional two-parent, middle-class, European American norm. So let's begin our exploration of home- and school-related topics by setting the context: scanning the tapestry of families in the twenty-first-century United States.

Parenting grandmothers, such as this woman helping her grandson with his homework, show that strong, loving families in the United States come in many forms. What *exactly* is this grandma doing right? This is the question we will explore in this section.

Setting the Context

At the turn of the century, roughly 7 out of 10 U.S. families with children were categorized as "two-parent." That umbrella category covers a range of family types. There is the *traditional two-parent family*—never-divorced couples with biological children. There are *blended families*—spouses have divorced and remarried, so children grow up with stepparents and, often, stepsiblings. There are *adoptive parents*, *gay parents*, *foster parents*, and *grandparent-headed families*.

Then there are the legions of *one-parent families*. With regard to this category, as you can see in Figure 7.1, we can make two generalizations. The majority of single-parent families are headed by women (typically mothers). Because two out of three mother-headed families are classified as low income, most children who grow up in a one-parent family experience economic hardship as a fact of life.

Finally, there is the beautiful mosaic of U.S. ethnic families—people, like Manuel and his mother, who vary in immigration status and everything else. What is your country of origin? What generation American are you? (Check out the stereotypes in Table 7.1 for some interesting facts about this immigrant flood.)

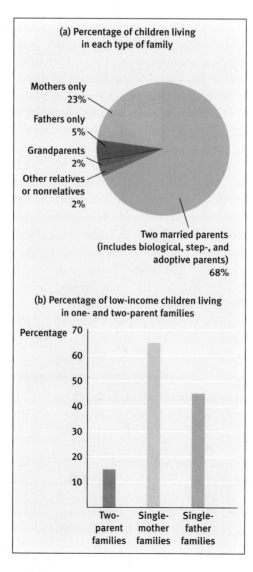

FIGURE 7.1: **Living arrangements of children in U.S. families:** The first chart (a) shows that the two-parent family is still the most common one—although this family form includes a wide variety of "traditional" and more nontraditional families. The second chart (b) shows the dramatic income differences between two-parent and single-parent families.
Source: Fields (2003); Fields & Casper (2001).

Home

Can children thrive in every family? The answer is yes. The key lies in what parents do. We already know generally what parents need to do: promote a secure attachment and be sensitive to a child's unique temperamental needs. Can we outline an overall discipline style that works best? Decades ago, developmentalist Diana Baumrind decided that we could.

Parenting Styles

Think of a parent you really admire. What is that mother or father doing right? Now, think of parents who you feel are not fulfilling this job. Where are they falling short? Most likely, your list will center on two functions. Are these people loving and nurturing? Do they provide consistent discipline or rules? By classifying parents on these two dimensions—being responsive or child-centered, and providing "structure" or rules—Baumrind (1971) and other researchers spelled out the following four **parenting styles:**

- **Authoritative parents** rank high on both nurturing and setting limits. They give their children reasonable

TABLE 7.1: Stereotypes About "Immigrant America" and Some Statistical Facts

Stereotype #1: Immigrants are taking over the country.

Fact: While the phrase "taking over the country" may too strong, as I suggested in Chapter 1, the United States is experiencing a remarkable influx of immigrants from every corner of the globe. In 2008, 70 million people were first- or second-generation immigrants, roughly 1 in 4 Americans. When we look at Hispanic Americans—currently 14 percent of the population and the largest minority group in the United States—the phrase "becoming more numerous" rings especially true. With a median age of 27, compared to 41 for European Americans, the face of the United States is poised to become far more Latino. By the mid-twenty-first century, this major minority group may outnumber whites.

Stereotype #2: Immigrants are poorly educated.

Fact: True and false, depending on their region of origin. Only half of all first-generation Hispanic Americans are high school graduates. However, with a whopping 1 in 4 Asian immigrants arriving with graduate degrees (versus 8.4 percent for Whites), new immigrants from the Far East are educationally miles ahead of native-born Americans.

Stereotype #3: Immigrants—particularly Hispanics—commit a disproportionate share of crimes.

Fact: Definitely false! Less than 1 percent of first-generation Hispanics are in prison (compared to more than 1 in 10 native-born African Americans and roughly 2 percent of Whites)—making newly arrived Latinos an incredibly law-abiding group. Unfortunately, however, over time, comparisons become less upbeat. Although incarceration rates never reach the alarming levels for African Americans, the percentage of second- and third-generation Hispanic Americans who have been in prison equals that of native-born Whites.

Stereotype #4: Immigrants don't want to learn the language or customs of the United States.

Fact: Once again, this (racist) stereotype is totally false. Even when they are raised in non–English-speaking families, more than half of all immigrant children say they prefer to speak English. By the third generation, English has become *everyone's* native tongue. Unfortunately, however, as I suggested above, the second and third generation also pick up some less-positive American customs. While the overwhelming majority of first-generation Mexican American children grow up in two-parent families, by the third generation, only slightly more than half make that claim. Among second-generation Asian Americans, rates of single motherhood are double that of their parents.

Source: Rumbaut, Biennial Meeting, Society for Research in Adolescence, March, 2008.

freedom and lots of love but also have clear expectations and consistent rules. These families set high standards for their children's behavior. There are defined bedtimes, rules for completing homework, and specific household chores. However, if a daughter wants to watch a favorite TV program, these parents might relax the rule that homework must be finished before dinner. They could let a son extend his regular 9:00 P.M. bedtime for a special event. Although authoritative parents believe firmly in structure, they understand that rules don't take precedence over human needs.

- **Authoritarian parents** are more inflexible. Their child-rearing motto is, "Obey the rules and do what I say." In these families, bedtimes and homework rules are not negotiable. While authoritarian parents typically love their children deeply, their upbringing style can appear to be inflexible, rigid, and cold.

- **Permissive parents** are at the opposite end of the spectrum from authoritarian parents. Their parenting mantra is, "Provide total freedom and unconditional love." In these households, there may be no set bedtimes and no childhood chores. The child-rearing principle here is that children's wishes rule.

- **Rejecting-neglecting parents** are the worst of both worlds—low on structure and low on love. Their child-rearing motto is, "Minimize involvement with my child." In this house, children are neglected, ignored, and emotionally abandoned. They

parenting style In Diana Baumrind's framework, how parents align on two dimensions of childrearing: nurturance (or child-centeredness) and discipline (or structure and rules).

authoritative parents In the parenting-styles framework, the best possible child-rearing style, in which parents rank high on both nurturance and discipline, providing both love and clear family rules.

authoritarian parents In the parenting-styles framework, a type of childrearing in which parents provide plenty of rules but rank low on child-centeredness, stressing unquestioning obedience.

permissive parents In the parenting-styles framework, a type of childrearing in which parents provide few rules but rank high on child-centeredness, being extremely loving but providing little discipline.

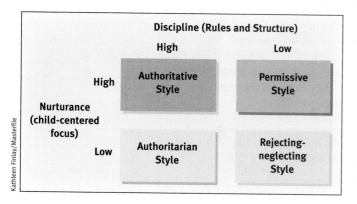

Kathleen Finlay/Masterfile

FIGURE 7.2: **Parenting styles:** A summary diagram.

Source: Adapted from Baumrind (1971).

are left to literally raise themselves (see Figure 7.2 for a visual recap).

When Baumrind observed 1960s middle-class California parents and classified them into the first three categories (the fourth style, rejecting-neglecting, was added later), she found that the children of "authoritative" parents were more successful and socially skilled. Many late-twentieth-century studies confirmed this finding (Maccoby & Martin, 1983): Authoritative parenting works best.

Questioning and Criticizing the Styles Framework

At first glance, Baumrind's authoritative category offers a wonderful blueprint for the right way to raise children: Provide firm structure and lots of love. However, if you take a minute to classify your own family along these dimensions, you may find a problem. Your mother might have been permissive and your father authoritarian, or vice versa.

Parents, not infrequently, differ in their discipline styles. Does this confuse children or is there an advantage to being exposed to contrasting approaches? The following study offers tantalizing clues (McElwain, Halberstadt, & Volling, 2007).

Developmentalists compared how married couples said they would react to their preschooler's negative outbursts: "Would you be supportive and soothing if your child had a temper tantrum (Poor honey!) or respond in a harsher, more authoritarian way (Go to your room!)?" When both moms and dads reported being very soothing, boys in particular were rated as less socially skilled than when one parent was highly supportive and the other was strict. Could being exposed to different parenting styles be beneficial because it teaches children to relate better to the diversity of "other minds"?

Even if this finding sometimes *can* be true, I must highlight a crucial qualification. *Fighting* about discipline is tailor-made to poison family life. So, if one parent is strict and the other is more permissive, the key is to value what the other person brings to the family or, at a minimum, to agree to disagree.

My real message, however, is that it's too simplistic to say that children are raised according to a single discipline style. Actually, Baumrind's categories do not reflect the complexity of real-life parenting in *several* important ways:

CHILDREARING INVOLVES A WIDE VARIETY OF BEHAVIORS. For one thing, being a good parent involves far more than providing love and discipline. Parents arrange the environment. They may move to a different part of town or, as in the opening chapter vignette, a different country for the sake of their children. They teach values, help with homework, arrange after-school activities (see McDowell & Parke, 2009), and advocate for their daughters and sons. Spend a day with a couple and their children. How many of their activities have nothing to do with *any* defined parenting style?

During that day, you may also notice that this family's parenting is difficult to categorize. In some areas of life, they might seem authoritarian. In others, they might appear too permissive from your point of view. One reason is that parents have different child-rearing priorities and goals.

rejecting-neglecting parents In the parenting-styles framework, the worst child-rearing approach, in which parents provide little discipline and little nurturing or love.

CHILD-REARING APPROACHES VARY BY CULTURE AND ETHNICITY. Baumrind's authoritative style reflects a middle-class, individualistic, North-American cultural perspective on childrearing: It's okay for children to negotiate with their parents and disagree with adult rules (Tamis-LeMonda and others, 2008). People living in more collectivist nations, such as Japan or China, have a different point of view: Respect your elders; be obedient; don't criticize (Mistry, Chaudhuri, & Diez, 2003). Are there ethnic differences in the premium parents put on having obedient, respectful children in the United States?

To get insights into this interesting question, developmentalists videotaped Latino, African American, and European American mothers and their third-grade daughters discussing a difficult issue (Dixon, Graber, & Brooks-Gunn, 2008). As the researchers predicted, during their conversations, the European American girls acted less respectful. They were more likely to talk back or ignore their moms. Moreover, when their daughters did talk back, African American and Latino mothers said they found this experience incredibly upsetting. Not so true for the European American moms! These middle-class White women seemed less sensitive to the need to have their daughters treat them with respect.

This study was carried out in the urban Northeast. I doubt that researchers would find the same tolerance for back talk if they polled Caucasian mothers living in my Tennessee town. Still, the bottom-line message is that our cultural background matters. Standards about what constitutes acceptable child behavior—even in Western countries—vary a good deal.

The same lack of agreement applies to disciplinary techniques. As you will see later in this chapter, many African American parents (as well as Evangelical Protestants) believe strongly in the value of spanking—a child-rearing style that most developmentalists rank as authoritarian. However, while upper-middle-class European American families who rely heavily on physical punishment are more likely to have children with emotional difficulties, this is not the case for African American parents—especially those who feel that this approach really works (McLoyd and others, 2007).

How do you feel about spanking? What importance would you put on your children being respectful to you? In what ways do your personal parenting values reflect your family's ethnic background or cultural worldview?

CHILD-REARING APPROACHES CHANGE, DEPENDING ON THE ENVIRONMENT. The fact that attitudes about parenting differ from culture to culture is evident when we look throughout history. You may remember from Chapter 1 that, during the eighteenth and nineteenth centuries, affluent parents in cities such as Paris sent their newborns away to be nursed by women in the countryside. Today, we would consider these practices abusive. In that era, they were vital to ensuring that babies would survive.

Difficult life conditions affect parenting decisions today. For children such as inner-city African Americans growing up in very dangerous neighborhoods, authoritarian parenting is related to high achievement (Dearing, 2004). If your mission is to shield your child from the drug dealer on the corner, you don't have the luxury of allowing much negotiation over rules (Burton, 2001). Think of how your parenting style would change if you moved to a war-torn country or a crime-ridden area of your town. Safety would be your *first* priority, before anything else.

In sum, let's accept the idea that parents should provide clear standards and plenty of love. However, let's understand that parenting styles are affected by people's priorities. Plus, good parents vary their child-rearing strategies to provide the best discipline–environment fit.

If you asked this loving dad from Africa (who has just become a new American) about the right way to discipline his baby girl, you would almost certainly hear a more positive idea about using physical punishment than if you questioned a developmental scientist—showing that other cultures and ethnic groups *legitimately* differ about how to bring up children in a caring, nurturing way.

INTERVENTIONS: Lessons for Thinking About Parents

How can you use this section's insights to relate to parents in a more empathic way in your career and daily life?

- Be culture-friendly. Don't impose your own parenting priorities on other people. Understand that there are a variety of valid child-rearing goals.

- Be aware that dangerous environments demand a more vigilant, rule-oriented kind of parenting—one that may look rigid and less child-centered from a middle-class European American view.

- Before you blame a mother or father for being too strict (or too lax), try to understand the pressures this family is facing. Rather than being judgmental, it is best to be caring and work to provide parents with support.

How Much Do Parents Matter?

My discussion, however, assumes that parents are in the driver's seat—that what happens at home is the crucial force in determining how children turn out. Why then do so many wonderful parents have children with terrible problems? Why do some children with terrible early lives succeed brilliantly as adults?

FOCUS ON A TOPIC: RESILIENT CHILDREN

His aristocratic parents spent their time gallivanting around Europe; they never appeared at the nursery doors. At age 7, he was wrenched from the only person who loved him—his nanny—and shipped off to boarding school. Insolent, angry, refusing to obey orders or sit still, he was regularly beaten by the headmaster and teased by the other boys. Although gifted at writing, he was incapable of rote memorization; he couldn't pass a test. When he graduated at the bottom of his boarding school class, his father informed him that he would never amount to anything. His name was Winston Churchill. He was the man who stood up to Hitler and carried England to victory in the Second World War.

Churchill's upbringing was a recipe for disaster. He had neglectful parents, behavior problems, and was a total failure at school. But this dismal childhood produced the leader who saved the modern world.

Resilient children, like Churchill, confront terrible conditions such as parental abuse, poverty, and the horrors of war and go on to construct successful, loving lives. What qualities allow these children to thrive? Developmentalists who study these unusual boys and girls find that resilient children often have special talent, such as Churchill's gift for writing, or superior cognitive skills. They are adaptable and able to regulate their emotions. They have a high sense of self-efficacy and an optimistic worldview (Brodhagan & Wise, 2008). They possess a strong faith or sense of meaning in life (Wright & Masten, 2005).

Clearly, being resilient depends on "good genetics"—having an "easy" temperament and superior intellectual and social skills (Deater-Deckard, Ivy, & Smith, 2005). But the quantity of environmental setbacks also matters. If you are exposed to a series of tragedies—for instance, war, losing your parents, or having an overload of problems at critical points in your development—it's more difficult to preserve your efficacy feelings or rebound to construct a happy life (Wright and Masten, 2005).

Not only is the amount and timing of life stress important, so is the presence of "social supports." Children who succeed against incredible odds typically have at least one close, caring relationship with a parent or another adult (such as Churchill's nanny). In impoverished U.S. neighborhoods, a teacher may step in to turn a promising student's life around by agitating for a college scholarship or admission to an elite private school (Abelev, 2009). Like a plant that thrives in the desert, resilient children have the internal resources to extract love from their parched environment. But they cannot survive without any water at all.

resilient children Children who rebound from serious early life traumas to construct successful adult lives.

Might these children have specific resilience-promoting genes? Emerging neuroscience research suggests that they may (Diamond, 2009). Consider this finding from the Dunedin Study, the mammoth investigation that tracked children born in this New Zealand city I discussed in Chapter 1. At their age-26 evaluation, the Dunedin researchers questioned study participants about stressful events they had experienced over the previous five years. Then, the scientists genotyped each person and looked for the presence of the long form of a gene that regulates the production of the neurotransmitter serotonin.

If a person's life was relatively free of stress, having this gene did not make a difference to mental health. The findings were different if these young people experienced four or more upsetting life changes. Forty-three percent of the severely stressed study participants with short forms of the gene developed a major depression. The rate for their long form counterparts was less than half as high. Actually having the same long forms of this gene also makes teens growing up in harsh, poverty-level environments less vulnerable to becoming addicted to cigarettes or abusing alcohol (see Brody and others, 2009). So some lucky people seem blessed by their biology to calmly rebound from life stress.

The Library of Congress

Abandoned by his father at about age 9 to be cared for by a teenaged sister for several years after his mother's premature death, raised in a dirt-floor Kentucky shack without any chance to attend school—Abraham Lincoln grew up to become our most beloved president and perhaps the greatest man of the nineteenth century. What qualities made this incredibly resilient child thrive? The answer: Towering intellectual gifts, a remarkable drive to learn, optimism, self-efficacy, and—most of all—a world-class talent at understanding human motivations and connecting with people in a caring, prosocial way. By the way, while he guided a battered nation, "father Abraham"—shown here with his son—also made time to be a totally *permissive*, hands-on dad.

Making the Case That Parents Don't Matter

How important is our biology (nature) versus our upbringing (nurture) in the adult we become? Twin and adoption studies, you may remember from Chapter 1, come down firmly on the "a good deal is genetic" side. In fact, because they involve correlations, some behavioral geneticists have severely criticized Baumrind's findings: Couldn't the link between authoritative parenting and successful children be explained by shared genetic tendencies? Parents who handle childrearing competently pass down the same biological predispositions for competence that cause their children to succeed (Rowe, 1981, 1983, 2003; Scarr, 1997). Or, because our genetic temperament evokes certain reactions, wouldn't easy, mellow babies produce authoritative parents? (Think of how hard it would be for you to act authoritative with a child who was bouncing off the walls. Your main impulse would probably be to hit and yell or give up!) Therefore, don't children's inborn personalities drive parenting styles, not the reverse (Deater-Deckard, 1996; Plomin & Bergeman, 1991)?

About 15 years ago, a rebel psychologist named Judith Harris proposed the most interesting twist on the "parents don't matter" argument. Harris (1995, 1998, 2002, 2006) actually believes that the environment has a dramatic impact on our development. But she makes the surprising case that—rather than our parents—our peers (or social group) socialize us to become adults.

Harris begins by taking aim at the main principle underlying attachment theory—that the lessons we learn from our parents transfer to our other relationships.

Look at these exuberant boys, passionate to fit in with their friends. Then, ask yourself whether these children are acting the same way they were taught to behave at home. Suddenly, doesn't Judith Harris's theory that "peer groups shape our development" make a good deal of sense?

Learning, Harris believes, is context-specific. We cannot use the same *working model* with our mother and with the classroom bully, or we would never survive. Furthermore, because we live our lives in the wider world, she argues, the messages we absorb from the culture of our contemporaries must take precedence over the lessons we are taught at home.

Any parent can relate to Harris's ideas about peer group power when she is horrified to witness her preschooler automatically picking up every bad habit from the other children the first week after entering nursery school. The most compelling evidence for Harris's theory, however, comes from looking at what happens to boys and girls such as Manuel. Turn back to Table 7.1 on page 203 and you will notice that children who immigrate to this country quickly come to prefer English—the language of the wider society—to the tongue they speak at home. From divorce, to non-marital parenthood, to the tendency to break the law, by the second generation, every immigrant group blends in more with the American norm. So the rapidity with which **acculturation**, assimilation to *any* new culture, occurs is a vivid testament to the fact that Harris has an important point.

These arguments that genetics and the values of the wider culture shape our development alert us to the fact that, when we see children "acting out" at a restaurant or at school, we cannot leap to the conclusion that "it's all the parents' fault." As developmental systems theory would predict, a variety of influences—from temperament, to peer groups, to everything else—affect how children behave. But you may be thinking that the idea that parents are *not* important goes way too far.

Many developmentalists agree. For children to fully realize their genetic potential, parents should try to provide the *best* possible environment (Ceci and others, 1997; Kagan, 1998; Maccoby, 2002). In fact, when children are temperamentally vulnerable, as you know from previous chapters, superior parenting is required.

Making the Case for Superior Parenting

Imagine, for instance, that your toddler is very active and has trouble regulating his emotions. You know from reading this book that your child's temperament puts him at risk of having externalizing problems as he travels into school. You are determined not to let that pattern unfold. So you inhibit your use of *power assertion*. You take care to provide lots of love. You carefully work to arrange the environment to minimize your child's vulnerabilities and highlight his strengths.

Actually, when a child is biologically vulnerable, developmentalists find again and again that sensitive caregiving can make a critical difference (see Diamond, 2009). From research suggesting that intense parental "linguistic input" is vital at stimulating cortical plasticity—and so promoting normal language development—when infants have damage to the language centers of the brain (Rowe and others, 2009) to the studies I have been highlighting in previous chapters that track inhibited or exuberant toddlers as they move into elementary school, the message is the same: With "at-risk" children, superior parenting matters most.

So yes, resilient children can flower in the face of difficult life conditions and less-than-ideal parenting styles. But when a baby needs special nurturing, the importance of high-quality nurturing shines through.

INTERVENTIONS: Lessons for Readers Who Are Parents

Now, let's summarize our whole discussion by shifting gears and talking directly to the parent readers of this book:

There are no firm guidelines about how to be an effective parent—except to be loving, set high standards, and provide consistent rules. But it also is critical to be flexible. Adapt your discipline to your life situation and especially to your unique child. You will face special challenges if you live in a dangerous neighborhood (where you

acculturation Among immigrants, the tendency to become more similar in terms of attitudes and practices to the mainstream culture after time spent living in a new society.

corporal punishment The use of physical force to discipline a child.

TABLE 7.2: Checklist for Identifying Your Parenting Priorities

Rank the following goals in order of their importance to you, from 1 (for highest priority) to 8 (for lowest priority). It's OK to use the same number twice if two goals are equally important to you.

_____ Producing an obedient, well-behaved child

_____ Producing a caring, prosocial child

_____ Producing an independent, self-sufficient child

_____ Producing a child who is extremely close to you

_____ Producing an intelligent, creative thinker

_____ Producing a well-rounded child

_____ Producing a happy, emotionally secure child

_____ Producing a spiritual (religious) child

What do your rankings reveal about the qualities you most admire in human beings?

may have to exert more control) or have children who are "harder to raise" (where you may have to work harder to stay loving and attached). Your ultimate power is limited at best.

However, try to see this message as liberating. Children cannot be massaged into having an idealized adult life. Your child's future does not totally depend on you. Focus on the quality of your relationship, and simply enjoy these wonderful years. And if your son or daughter is having problems, draw heart from Winston Churchill's history. Predictions from childhood to adult life can be hazy. Your unsuccessful child may grow up to save the world!

Table 7.2 offers a checklist for you to evaluate your personal child-rearing priorities and think more deeply about the qualities you believe are most important to instill in a child.

Now that I've covered the general territory, we turn to specifics. First, let's look at that controversial practice mentioned earlier, spanking; then, focus on the worst type of parenting, child abuse; and finally, explore the life transition described in the chapter-opening vignette, divorce.

Today, when children misbehave in school, we put them in "time-out" rather than paddling them, as we would have done in the past, because we now believe that corporal punishment may teach children that it's fine to hit.

Spanking

Poll your friends and family members about their opinions relating to **corporal punishment**—any discipline technique using physical measures such as spanking—and you are likely to get strong reactions. Some people firmly believe in the biblical principle, "Spare the rod and spoil the child." They may blame the decline in spanking for every social problem. Others blame corporal punishment for *creating* those same social problems. They believe that parents who rely on "hitting" are implicitly teaching children the message that it is okay to respond in a violent way.

Because many Europeans agree with the idea that corporal punishment offers a model of violence, in most E.U. countries, using physical discipline in school and at home is now against the law (Benjet & Kazdin, 2003). Where do North American parents stand on the issue of corporal punishment, and what do developmentalists say?

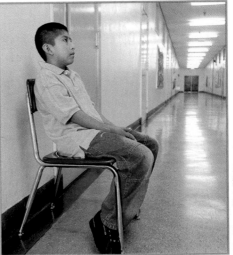

Michael Newman/Photo Edit, Inc.

To answer the first question, in the mid-1990s, researchers polled more than 900 U.S. parents, asking them about milder forms of corporal punishment ("Do you spank your child on the bottom with your hand?"), as well as more severe practices ("Do you hit your child with a belt?") (Straus & Stewart, 1999).

Most people said they refrained from physically punishing an infant, but almost everyone (94 percent) reported using this discipline with preschoolers. Moreover, although most parents said they used only mild forms of corporal punishment, such

as spanking, more than one in four reported that they hit their child with a hard object such as a brush or a belt.

The fact that preschool is when parents often use corporal punishment was confirmed by a more recent twenty-first-century poll (Barkin and others, 2007). However, with only 1 in 10 people saying they "often spanked" their child, this survey revealed that, for contemporary U.S. parents, physical punishment is not a preferred discipline mode. The most "popular" current discipline strategies are time-out and removal of privileges (each used by about 40 percent of the sample) and, to a lesser extent, getting sent to one's room.

Who tends to rely more on spanking? As I mentioned earlier, in the United States, African Americans and Evangelical Protestants are most likely to use this discipline technique (Barkin and others, 2007; Grogan-Kaylor & Otis, 2007). One Canadian poll suggested that upbringing matters, with people who were spanked as children believing more in the value of this approach. But there is an important caution. In this survey, adults who felt they had been abused said they bent over backwards not to use corporal punishment with their own daughters and sons (Gagne and others, 2007). So, if you believe that during your childhood physical punishment got out of hand, you probably are passionate about *never* hitting your child.

What do developmentalists advise? Here, there is considerable debate. Some people argue that using physical punishment is *never* appropriate (Gershoff, 2002; Straus & Donnelly, 1994). As I suggested earlier, these psychologists feel that hitting a child models violence. It conveys the message that it is acceptable for big people to give small people pain. Spanking, they point out, is also a shame-inducing technique. While it may produce immediate compliance, it is tailor-made to impair prosocial behavior and conscience development down the road (Andero & Stewart, 2002; Benjet & Kazdin, 2003).

Others disagree, believing that mild spanking is not necessarily detrimental (Baumrind, Larzelere, & Cowan, 2002; Larzelere & Kuhn, 2005). They suggest that if we totally rule out corporal punishment, we run the risk that caregivers will resort to more emotionally damaging kinds of verbal abuse, such as saying, "I hate you. You will never amount to anything." Still, these psychologists have the following guidelines about when physical punishment can—and should not—be used:

Adults should never hit an infant. Babies don't know what they are doing wrong. Moreover, infants who are hit regularly have higher baseline rates of the stress hormone cortisol, so spanking a baby may set that child up to be chronically anxious and depressed (Bugental, Martorell, & Barraza, 2003). For a preschooler, a few swats on the bottom can be an effective disciplinary technique, especially when a child is engaging in dangerous activities—such as running into the street—that need to be immediately stopped (Larzelere & Kuhn, 2005). Still, when parents use physical punishment, they should accompany this action with a verbal explanation ("What you did was wrong because . . ."). Ideally, they should reserve a spanking as a backup technique when other strategies, such as time-outs, fail.

The problem is that, as you just saw, sometimes spanking is *not* a backup strategy. Moreover, as I suggested in the previous chapter, toddlers and preschoolers for whom physical punishment is genuinely detrimental—those at risk for externalizing problems—are at risk of getting spanked the most (Grogan-Kaylor & Otis, 2007). Therefore, parent training is important. We need to emphasize the behavioral principle that positive reinforcement (giving rewards for good behavior) is more effective than *any* punishment, be it spanking or being sent to one's room. Actually, although there are many reasons for this finding, E.U. countries that outlaw corporal punishment, such as Sweden, have far lower rates of violent crime than the United States. Plus, what starts out as "normal" spanking can escalate and turn into that worst-case type of parenting, child abuse.

Child Abuse

Child maltreatment—the term for any act that endangers children's physical or emotional well-being—comprises four distinct categories. *Physical abuse* refers to bodily injury that leaves bruises. It encompasses everything from overzealous spanking to battering that may lead to a child's death. *Neglect* refers to caregivers' failure to provide adequate supervision and care. It might mean abandoning the child, not providing sufficient food, or even failing to enroll a son or daughter in school. *Emotional abuse* describes acts that cause serious emotional damage, such as terrorizing or exploiting a child. *Sexual abuse* covers the spectrum from rape and incest to fondling and exhibitionistic acts.

Everyone can identify serious forms of maltreatment, but there is a gray zone as to exactly what activities cross the line (Whitaker, Lutzker, & Shelley, 2005). Does *every* spanking that leaves bruises qualify as physical abuse? If a single mother is forced to leave her toddler in an 8-year-old sibling's care when she goes to work, should we classify her as neglectful? Are parents who walk around naked in the house guilty of sexual abuse? Emotional abuse is very difficult to prove and prosecute, although this type of maltreatment can also leave devastating inner scars (Egeland, 2009).

Even if we had the clearest definitions, it would be impossible to pin down the actual incidence of child abuse. Rates of maltreatment in the United States have declined since the early l99os, but at almost one million documented cases in 2006, they are still unacceptably high (U.S. Department of Health and Human Services [USDHHS], n.d.; United States Children's Bureau, 2006). Worse yet, most cases are probably not reported to the authorities (Dubowitz & Bennett, 2007). They may be found "accidentally" when a child is discovered with welts, or possibly severely stunted and near death. What might provoke this kind of violence, and how might caring adults intervene?

Exploring the Risk Factors

As developmental systems theory would predict, several categories of influence may combine to provoke caregivers to act in a physically or emotionally abusive way:

Parents' personality problems are important. People who abuse their children often have psychological disorders such as depression and, especially, substance abuse (Dubowitz & Bennett, 2007). They tend to be temperamentally angry and hypersensitive to infant distress (Shay & Knutson, 2008)—responding with rage when their children cry. They may have unrealistic developmental expectations; for example, believing that children should be able to sit still or be totally toilet trained at a very young age (Bissada & Briere, 2001; Goodman, Emery, & Haugaard, 1998).

Serious life stress is part of the picture. Parents who maltreat their children are often coping with an overload of problems, from domestic violence (Casanueva & Martin, 2007) to severe poverty (Child Welfare Information Gateway, 2008). They tend to be isolated from caring family or friends (Bissada & Briere, 2001).

Children's vulnerabilities are often influential. Then, there is the contribution of the child. Children with difficult temperaments and babies who cry excessively (Reijneveld and others, 2004) are more at risk of being abused. The fact that abusive parents may target just one child was brought home to me when I was working as a clinical psychologist at a city hospital in New York. A mother was referred for treatment by the court for abusing what she called her "spiteful" 10-year-old although she never harmed his "sweet" 3-year-old brother. So disturbances in the attachment relationship are often a core ingredient in the poisonous recipe for producing a battered child.

child maltreatment Any act that seriously endangers a child's physical or emotional well-being.

FIGURE 7.3: **Chance of a maltreated boy's showing resilience to "antisocial behavior," as a function of his internal strengths and exposure to multiple stresses, in a study conducted in the U.K.:** Notice that having a high IQ and positive temperament protects an abused child from developing externalizing problems. But as the number of life stresses increases, more boys succumb, and being temperamentally resilient may not matter at all.

Source: Jaffee and others, 2007, *Child Abuse and Neglect,31,* p. 245.

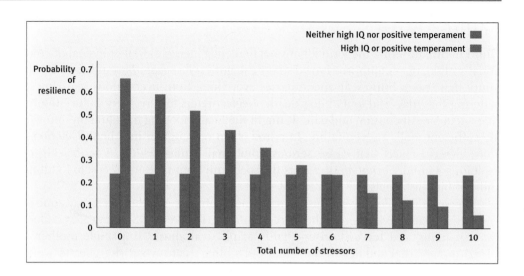

As you learned in Chapter 4, maltreated children tend to have insecure attachments. They often have academic and social difficulties (Egeland, 2009), problems regulating their emotions (Ford, 2005), and difficulty accurately identifying other people's feelings (Masten and others, 2008). Particularly when they are physically abused, they are often unusually aggressive with their peers (Teisl & Cicchetti, 2007). These same deficits, in turn, place these children at higher risk of engaging in domestic violence and maltreating their own children as adults. But it is crucial to point out that children who have been abused are not fated to repeat those behaviors (Trickett, Kurtz, & Pizzigati, 2004). As I suggested in the previous section, some victims of abuse go overboard to *never* physically punish their daughters and sons.

Given our discussion of resilience, it should also come as no surprise that individual children vary in how they cope with this terrible life stress. Figure 7.3 offers interesting insights into what makes a particular maltreated boy either hardy or prone to break down. Notice that (once again) high intelligence and an adaptable temperament promote resilience. But the number of environmental blows matters, too. If you live in a high-crime neighborhood, your parents have substance-abuse problems, and you experience other family and neighborhood stresses, it's hard not to develop externalizing problems, no matter how biologically resilient you are. To use my earlier analogy, even genetically hardy plants cannot survive in the face of a total tsunami—that is, a whirlwind of devastating environmental events.

INTERVENTIONS: Taking Action Against Child Abuse

What should you do if you suspect child abuse? Teachers, social workers, and health-care professionals are required by law to report the case to child protective services. In 18 states as well as most Canadian provinces, the law impels *any* concerned citizen to speak up (Mathews & Kenny, 2008). Children in imminent danger are removed from the home, and the cases are referred to juvenile court. Judges do not have the power to punish abusive parents, but they can place their children in foster care and possibly limit or terminate their parental rights.

Imagine you are a judge who must make the heart-wrenching decision to take a child away from his parents. If you leave the child in an abusive home, that boy or girl may be re-injured or neglected (see Fluke and others, 2008). But you also know that being separated from a primary attachment figure can leave emotional scars. This is why it's preferable, if possible, to keep the child in the family and provide intensive support to help parents be more effective caregivers (National Clearinghouse on Child Abuse and Neglect Information, 2005). The same principle—promoting effective parenting—applies to the family situation we turn to now: divorce.

Divorce

Child abuse affects a small fraction of children. Millions of children each year see their parents' marriage break up. How does divorce affect children, and what forces affect how children adjust?

Let's start with the bad news. Studies around the globe comparing children of divorce with their counterparts in intact married families show that children of divorce are at a statistical disadvantage—academically, socially, and in terms of physical and mental health (Amato, 2000, 2001; Lowenstein, 2005). However, these general comparisons are misleading because they paint an overly grim picture. Three out of four children whose parents divorce don't have major mental health problems (Kelly, 2003). When children growing up in divorced families perform more poorly academically or have emotional problems, their difficulties might mainly reflect the economic stresses of living in a single-parent family—or experiencing the turbulent transitions that often go along with this change—not the trauma of seeing their parents' marriage break up (Kelly, 2003; Teachman, 2008).

Moreover, the psychological difficulties children tend to show after divorce often begin before the couple splits up (Kelly, 2003). Imagine your parents are continually fighting. The family atmosphere is tense. Like Manuel's mother in the chapter-opening vignette, your mother (or father) is depressed and angry. She cannot give you the attention you need. Around the time of the separation, researchers find, child-rearing tends to become more disorganized as couples struggle with their feelings and try to rearrange their lives (Hetherington, 1999). Because of their own inner turmoil, many parents have trouble talking openly about their situation—leaving their children confused, angry, and sad. Fortunately, however, most parents do regroup and regain their equilibrium after a year or two (Kelly, 2003).

What forces help children rebound from this trauma? One key is to keep daily life as consistent as possible. Unfortunately, right after they divorce, about one out of every two families moves. But relocation places another loss and stress on a child (Austin, 2008). Another is to empower children by giving them some voice in what happens with regard to visitation and custody. In one poll of divorced parents and their children, everyone agreed that having child input was important, but that it might be too threatening for sons and daughters to have total say. As a teenager named Sophie commented, "I don't think they should have the final decision. . . . But they should be able to say, 'I would prefer this and this'" (quoted in Cashmore & Parkinson, 2008 p. 94).

The main key to long-term adjustment, however, lies in the quality of care the parent who gets custody provides. Can the custodial mother or father be an effective parent? (See Wolchik and others, 2005.) It is also important to look at the relationship between the parents. When husbands and wives battle over visitation rights, continually bad-mouth each other, or try to turn the children against a former partner, children suffer most (Baker, 2005; Siegler, 2005).

Would it be better for couples, such as Maria and José in the vignette, to stay together for the sake of the children? The answer is probably no. Children in two-parent families with spouses embroiled in chronic conflict are also vulnerable to mental health problems (Rhoades, 2008). Witnessing domestic violence (no surprise) is incredibly destructive to children's emotional well-being (El-Sheikh and others, 2008; Ireland & Smith, 2009; Reading, 2008). Therefore, staying together "for the sake of the children" only makes sense if parents can really "get it together"—at least fairly well—and get along.

Figure 7.4 on page 214 illustrates the problems associated with divorce on a timeline and suggests some interventions that counselors might make. In Chapter 11, I'll explore divorce from the adult point of view. Now, let's turn to that other major setting within which children develop: school.

Should this unhappy couple stay together "for the sake of their daughter"? The answer, as you can see in the text, depends on whether they can stop continually getting into these terrible arguments.

Royalty-Free/Masterfile

FIGURE 7.4: Timeline of divorce, with interventions to minimize problems for children.

Sources: Pedro-Carroll (2005); Pruett, Insabella, & Gustafson (2005); Wolchik and others (2005).

Timeline (1–2 years)			
Family arguments →	Separation, chaotic parenting →	Divorce →	Reorganizing life
Interventions			
Couple counseling	Offer emotional support to children. Minimize other life changes.		Foster authoritative custodial parenting.
	Encourage open discussion with children about what is happening; give them some voice in visitation.		Discourage parents from using their children as pawns to express their anger.
	Support parents as they adjust to their new lives.		Discourage parents from fighting over custody.

🌀 TYING IT ALL TOGETHER

1. Montana's parents make firm rules but value their children's input about family decisions. Pablo's parents have rules for everything and tolerate no ifs, ands, or buts. Sara's parents don't really have rules. At their house, it's always playtime and time to indulge the children. Which parenting style is being used by Montana's parents? Pablo's parents? Sara's parents?

2. Chloe grew up in a happy middle-class family, but Amber and Sierra both had difficult childhoods. Sierra is struggling in college and often feels very unhappy, but both Amber and Chloe are doing well at school. To which student does the term resilient best apply?

3. Melissa's son Jared, now in elementary school, was premature and has a difficult temperament. What might Judith Harris advise about best fostering this child's development, and what might this chapter recommend?

4. Your sister is concerned about a friend who uses corporal punishment with her baby and her 4-year-old. She asks you what the experts say. Pick out the following *two* positions developmentalists might take?
   a. Never spank children of any age.
   b. Mild spanking is okay for the infant.
   c. Mild spanking is okay for the 4-year-old, as a backup.
   d. If the child has a difficult temperament, regular corporal punishment might help.

5. As an elementary school teacher, you are worried about a student who has been coming to school without a coat or jacket this winter. You've also seen what you're pretty sure are burn marks on the child's arms. What kinds of abuse seem to be involved? What should you do? What should the ideal goal be?

6. Your friend Crystal recently had the courage to leave her abusive husband after years of constant fighting. Crystal is feeling good about the separation, but she is worried that maybe she should have stayed with her spouse for the sake of their daughter. Did Crystal make the right decision? What advice can you give Crystal about helping her child?

Answers to the Tying It All Together questions can be found on the last page of this chapter.

School

What was that test Manuel took, and what does intelligence really mean? What makes for good teaching and superior schools? Before looking carefully at these school-related topics, let's begin by setting the framework—stepping back and, once again, exploring the impact of that basic marker, poverty, on young children's cognitive skills.

Setting the Context: Unequal at the Starting Gate

In Chapter 4, you learned that living in poverty for the first years of life has damaging effects on cognition. Figure 7.5 reveals that devastation directly by offering sobering statistics with regard to an entering U.S. kindergarten class (Lee & Burkam, 2002). Notice that children from low-income families, on average, do markedly worse than their upper-middle-class counterparts on tests of reading readiness and math. When we compare poverty-level Latino and African American children to the wealthiest European Americans, the test score gap widens to a chasm. The most disadvantaged children enter school academically several years behind their most affluent counterparts.

The reasons for these inequalities become apparent when developmentalists visit young children's homes to rate aspects of family life. As one national survey showed, children growing up in poverty-level U.S. families had few books. Their parents infrequently read to them. They rarely had home computers. They practically never went to museums (Bradley and others, 2001a).

I must emphasize that low-income parents care as much about their sons' and daughters' education as do corporate CEOs. But when you are working long hours to provide the bare necessities, children's basic needs—and safety—take priority over anything else. Here is how one parent at an inner-city school described the situation:

> *I mean some of us are scraping to put food on the table, clothes on their backs . . ., keeping the kids off of the street corner. That's our job, you know, taking care of business and making sure that they have the opportunity to go to school each day. 'Cause with no clothes, or if they wind up in trouble with the system, then school ain't a possibility for them.*

(quoted in Lawson, 2003, pp. 91–92)

For immigrant families, language barriers add to the difficulties. The downside of being a nation of immigrants is that, as you saw in the chapter-opening vignette, many young children need to grapple with the challenge of learning a new language at school (Lee & Burkam, 2002). Among first-generation children of Mexican origin, such as Manuel, fewer than 1 in 10 have parents who speak English "very well" (Rumbaut, 2008).

You would think that, when children start a race miles behind, they should be given every chance to catch up. The reality is the reverse. From class size, to the quality of teacher training, to the attractiveness of the physical building—kindergartens serving poor children rank at the bottom of the educational heap. Here is the dismal—but not unexpected—conclusion that one group of researchers reached:

FIGURE 7.5: Socioeconomic status and kindergartners' scores on tests of readiness for reading and math: As children's socioeconomic status rises, so do average scores on tests of math and reading readiness. Notice the dramatic differences between low-income and affluent children.

Source: Lee & Burkham (2002), p. 18.

This dispiriting photo of an inner-city school powerfully brings home the vast educational inequalities that impoverished U.S. children encounter, starting as early as kindergarten.

Peter Byron / Photo Edit

achievement tests Measures that evaluate a child's knowledge in specific school-related areas.

WISC (Wechsler Intelligence Scale for Children) The standard intelligence test used in childhood, consisting of a Verbal Scale (questions for the child to answer), a Performance Scale (materials for the child to manipulate), and a variety of subtests.

mentally retarded The label for significantly impaired intellectual functioning, defined as when a child (or adult) has an IQ of 70 or below accompanied by evidence of deficits in learning abilities.

specific learning disability The label for any impairment in language or any deficit related to listening, thinking, speaking, reading, writing, spelling, or understanding mathematics; diagnosed when a score on an intelligence test is much higher than a child's performance on achievement tests.

The consistency of these findings across aspects of school quality that are themselves very different from one another is both striking and troubling. The least advantaged of America's children, who also begin their formal schooling at a substantial cognitive disadvantage, are systematically mapped into our nation's worst schools.

(Lee & Burkam, 2002, p. 77)

Now, let's keep these inequalities in mind as we explore the controversial topic of intelligence tests.

Intelligence and IQ Tests

What does it mean to be intelligent? Ask your classmates the question, and they will probably mention both academic and "real-life" skills (Sternberg, Grigorenko, & Kidd, 2005). Conceptions of what it means to "be intelligent" also differ from society to society and among different ethnic groups. Latino parents, for instance, focus more heavily on social competence (getting along with people), while our mainstream culture views intelligence in terms of purely cognitive traits (Sternberg, 2007).

Traditional intelligence tests reflect the mainstream view. They measure only cognitive abilities. Intelligence tests, however, differ from **achievement tests**, the yearly evaluations children take to measure their knowledge in various subjects. The intelligence test is designed to predict a person's general academic potential, or ability to master *any* school-related task. Do the tests measure mainly genetic capacities? Do they have any relevance beyond school? To approach these surprisingly cloudy hot-button issues, let's examine the intelligence test that children typically take today: the WISC.

Examining the WISC

The **WISC (Wechsler Intelligence Scale for Children)**, now in its fourth revision, was devised by David Wechsler and is the current standard intelligence test. As you can see in Table 7.3, the WISC samples a child's performance in a variety of areas. However, it is divided into two sections—one involving answering questions (the Verbal Scale), and the other involving manipulating materials (the Performance Scale). This allows testers to give a child a separate IQ score for each part.

Achievement tests are administered to groups of children. The WISC is given individually to a child by a trained psychologist, a process that includes several hours of testing and concludes with a written report. If the child scores at the 50th percentile for his age group, his IQ is defined as 100. If that child's IQ is 130, he ranks at roughly the 98th percentile, or in the top 2 percent of children his age. If a child's score is 70, he is at the opposite end of the distribution, performing in the lowest 2 percent of children that age. Put on a graph, this score distribution, as you can see in Figure 7.6, looks like a bell-shaped curve.

When do children take this time-intensive test? The answer, most often, is during elementary school, when there is a major issue about classroom work. School personnel then use the IQ score as one component of a multifaceted assessment, which also includes achievement test scores, teachers' ratings, and parents' input, to determine whether a boy or girl needs special help (Sattler, 2001). If a child's low score (under 70) and other behaviors warrant this designation, she may be classified as **mentally retarded**. If a child's IQ is far higher than would be expected, compared to her performance on achievement tests, she is classified as having a **specific learning disability**—an umbrella term for any impairment in language or difficulties related to listen-

FIGURE 7.6: **The bell-shaped curve:** The WISC scores are arranged to align in a normal distribution. Notice from the chart that about 68 percent of the population has scores between 85 and 115 and about 95 percent of the scores are between 70 and 130.

TABLE 7.3: The WISC-III Subtests and Sample Kinds of Items

Verbal Scale

Subtest	Sample (simulated) Item
Information (tests factual knowledge)	Who is George Bush?
Similarities (analogies)	Cat is to kitten as dog is to _____.
Vocabulary (defining words)	What is a table?
Comprehension (social judgment)	What do you do if you are lost in Manhattan?
Arithmetic	Mary has five apples and gives two away.
	How many does she have left?
Digit span (memory)	Repeat these seven digits forward . . . backward. . . .

Performance Scale

(involves manipulating, arranging, or identifying materials within a time limit)

Picture completion	What is missing in this picture?
Block design	Arrange these blocks to look like the photograph on the card.
Picture arrangement	Arrange these pictures in the correct sequence to tell a story.
Object assembly	Put these puzzle pieces together.
Coding	Using the key above, put each symbol in the correct space below.

Source: WISC-III, Psychological Corporation (Wechsler, 1991).

dyslexia A learning disability that is characterized by reading difficulties, lack of fluency, and poor word recognition that is often genetic in origin.

gifted The label for superior intellectual functioning characterized by an IQ score of 130 or above, showing that a child ranks in the top 2 percent of his age group.

ing (such as ADHD), thinking, speaking, reading, spelling, or math (see Shaywitz, Morris, & Shaywitz, 2008).

Although children with learning disabilities often score in the average range on IQ tests, they have considerable trouble with schoolwork. Many times, they have a debilitating neurological impairment called **dyslexia** that undercuts every academic skill. Dyslexia involves a host of reading-related difficulties. At the core of this familiar diagnosis is an "unexpected" difficulty. The child is motivated, has had good instruction, and does well on general tests of intelligence, but still is struggling to read (Shaywitz, Morris, & Shaywitz, 2008).

My son, for instance, has dyslexia, and our experience shows just how important having a measure of general intelligence can be. Because Thomas was falling behind in the third grade, my husband and I arranged to have our son tested. Thomas was defined as having a learning disability because his IQ score was above average but his achievement scores were well below the norm for his grade. Although we were aware of our son's reading problems, the testing was vital in easing our anxieties. Thomas—just as we thought—was capable intellectually. Now, we just had to get our son through school with his sense of self-efficacy and self-esteem intact!

Often, teachers and parents urge testing for a happier reason: They want to confirm their impression that a child is intellectually advanced. If the child's IQ exceeds a certain number, typically 130, or in the top 2 percent (see Figure 7.6), she is labeled **gifted** and eligible for special programs. In U.S. public schools, intelligence testing is mandated by law before children can be assigned to a gifted program or remedial class (Canter, 1997; Sattler, 2001).

Table 7.4 on page 218 offers a fact sheet about dyslexia. The Experiencing the Lifespan box on page 219 provides a firsthand view of what it is like to deal with—and

Bob Daemmrich/The Image Works

This second grader, taking a subtest of the WISC Performance Scale, will be tested for at least an hour and a half. Then, the examiner will write a report and compare his scores with those of other children his age. If this boy's IQ is at least 130—ranking him at roughly the top 2 percent of his age group—he will be eligible for his school's gifted program.

TABLE 7.4: Some Interesting Facts About Dyslexia

- Reading difficulties are shockingly prevalent among U.S. children. According to one 2005 survey, more than 1 in 4 high school seniors were reading below the most basic levels. The figures were higher for fourth graders—over 1 in 3 had trouble grasping the basic points of a passage designed for their grade.

- Specific learning disabilities (including dyslexia) are a mainly male diagnosis—affecting roughly three times as many boys as girls around the world. However, because a referral bias favors boys, there may be more undiagnosed females with dyslexia than had previously been thought.

- Researchers have implicated genes on chromosomes 2, 6, 15, and 18 in dyslexia. While there is strong evidence that dyslexia is inherited and "genetic" in origin (23 to 65 percent of children with dyslexia have a parent who has the condition), problems learning to read may have a variety of causes.

- Late-appearing language (entering the word-combining phase of speech at an older-than-typical age, such as close to age 2½ [see Chapter 3]) and phonemic deficits (the inability to differentiate sounds [see Chapter 5]) are early predictors of dyslexia.

- Children prone to dyslexia may even be identified during their first weeks after birth—by looking at the pattern of their brain waves evoked by different sounds. These newborns have a slightly slower shift from positivity to negativity on "event-related potentials" when exposed to noises of different frequencies (Guttorm and others, 2005).

- Although many children with dyslexia eventually learn to read, this condition persists to some extent into adulthood. Early interventions—involving massive instruction in teaching "at-risk" kindergartners and first graders to identify phonemes—are quite effective. After second or third grade, however, it is more challenging to bring children up to grade level.

- Boys and girls with dyslexia are at higher risk for developing other mental health problems—such as depressive and anxiety disorders. About 15 to 50 percent also have ADHD.

Source: Shaywitz, Morris, & Shaywitz, 2008.

---

triumph over—this debilitating condition. Now that we have explored the measure and when it is used, let's turn to that vital issue—what the scores really mean.

Decoding the Meaning of the IQ Test

The first question we need to grapple with in looking at the meaning of the test relates to a basic measurement criterion called **reliability.** When people take a test thought to measure a basic trait, such as IQ, more than one time, their results should not really vary. Imagine that your IQ score randomly shifted from gifted to average, year by year. Clearly, this test score would be worthless. It would not tell us anything about a stable attribute called intelligence.

The good news is that, in general, IQ test performance does typically remain fairly stable. In one amazing study, people's IQ scores remained fairly similar when they first took the test in childhood and then were retested more than a half-century later, in old age (see Deary and others, 2000). Still, when we look at individual children, the IQ can change dramatically. Scores are most likely to shift when children have undergone major life stresses.

This research tells us exactly why Manuel in the chapter-opening vignette was being tested at the wrong time: We should never evaluate a child during a family crisis such as a divorce. But being reliable is only the first requirement. The test must be **valid.** This means it must predict what it is supposed to be measuring. Is the WISC a valid test?

If our predictor is academic performance, the answer is yes. A child who gets an IQ score of 130 will most likely perform well in the gifted class. A child whose IQ is 80 will probably need remedial help. But now, we turn to the really controversial question: whether the test measures genetic learning potential or biological smarts.

reliability In measurement terminology, a basic criterion of a test's accuracy that scores must be fairly similar when a person takes the test more than once.

validity In measurement terminology, a basic criterion for a test's accuracy involving whether that measure reflects the real-world quality it is supposed to measure.

Aimee Holt, a colleague of mine who teaches our school psychology students, is beautiful and intelligent, the kind of golden girl you might imagine would have been a great childhood success. When I sat down to chat with Amy about her struggles with dyslexia and other learning disabilities, I found first impressions can be very misleading:

When I was in first grade, the teachers at school told my parents I was mentally retarded. I didn't notice the sounds that went along with the letters of words. I walked into walls and fell down a lot. My parents refused to consider putting me in a special school and finally got me accepted at a private school, contingent on getting a good deal of help. I spent my elementary school years being tutored for an hour before school, an hour afterwards, and all summer.

Socially, elementary school was a nightmare . . . I have memories of kids laughing at me, calling me stupid. There was a small group of people that I was friendly with, but we were all misfits. One of my closest friends had an inoperable brain tumor. Because of my problems coordinating my vision with my motor skills, I couldn't really participate in normal activities, such as sports or dance. By seventh grade, after years of working every day with my wonderful reading teacher, I was reading at almost grade level.

Then when we moved to Tennessee in my freshman year of high school, I felt like a completely new person had emerged. Nobody knew that I had learning difficulties. We moved to a rural community, so I got to be a top student, because I'd had the same classes in my Dallas private school the year before. In the tenth and eleventh grades, I was making A's and B's. I got a scholarship to college, where I was a straight-A student (with a GPA of 3.9).

My mom is the reason I've done so well. She always believed in me, always felt I could make it; she never gave up. Plus, as I mentioned, I had an exceptional reading teacher who ended up working as a leader in the field. My goal was always to be an elementary school teacher, but, after teaching for years and realizing that a lot of the kids in my classes were not being accurately diagnosed, I decided to go back to graduate school to get my Ph.D.

Today, in addition to teaching, I do private tutoring with children like me. First, I get kids to identify word sounds (phonemes) because children with dyslexia have a problem decoding the specific sounds of words. I'll have the children identify how many sounds they hear in a word . . . "Which sounds rhyme, which don't?" . . . "If I change the word from cat to hat, what sound changes?" Most children naturally pick up on these reading cues. Kids with dyslexia need to have these skills directly taught.

Many children I tutor are in fourth or even sixth grade and have had years of feeling like a total failure. They develop an attitude of "Why try? I'm going to be a failure anyway." I can tell them that I've been there and that they can succeed. So I work on academic self-efficacy—teaching them to put forth effort. Most of these kids are really intelligent, but as they progress through school, their verbal IQ drops because they are not being exposed to written material at their grade level. I try to get them to stay in the regular classroom, with modifications such as books on tape and oral testing, to prevent that false drop in their knowledge base. I was so fortunate—with a wonderful mother, an exceptional reading teacher, getting the help I needed at exactly the right time—that I feel my mission is to give something back.

ARE THE TESTS A GOOD MEASURE OF GENETIC GIFTS? When we are evaluating children living in poverty (or boys and girls growing up in immigrant families who may not be familiar with our cultural norms), logic tells us that the answer should be no. The test score cannot offer a good portrait of a child's innate abilities. Look back at the items on the WISC Verbal Scale (Table 7.3 on page 217), in particular, and you will immediately see that if parents stimulate a child's vocabulary, she will be at a clear advantage. If a family cannot afford to take their children to museums or buy books and learning toys, their children will be handicapped on the test.

Our logical impression that the test can't reflect the genetic capacities of disadvantaged children is scientifically correct. For low-income children, the IQ score mainly reflects environmental forces. For upper-middle-class children, the test score is more reflective of genetically based abilities and gifts (Turkheimer and others, 2003).

Now, imagine that you are an upper-middle-class child. You were raised by attentive parents, regularly read to, and taken to museums. Your IQ score is only 95 or 100. Is your potential limited for life?

DO IQ SCORES PREDICT REAL-WORLD PERFORMANCE? When, as often happens, a student comes up after this class lecture and proudly admits that his IQ is 130 or 140, he is not thinking of school learning. He is assuming that his score measures a basic "smartness" that carries over to every life activity. In measurement terminology, this student would agree with the ideas of theorist Charles Spearman. Spearman believed that a score on an IQ test reflects a general underlying, all-encompassing intelligence factor called "**g**."

Psychologists hotly debate the existence of "g." Many do believe that the IQ test *generally* predicts intellectual capacities. They argue that we can use the IQ score as a summary measure of a person's cognitive potential for any life task (Herrnstein & Murray, 1994; Rushton & Jensen, 2005). Others believe that people have unique intellectual weaknesses and strengths. There is no one-dimensional quality called "g" (Eisner, 2004; Schlinger, 2003; Sternberg, 2007). These critics argue that it is inappropriate to rank people on a single continuum from highly intelligent to not very smart (Gould, 1981; Sternberg, Grigorenko, & Kidd, 2005).

Tantalizing evidence for "g" lies in the fact that people differ in the speed with which they process information (Brody, 2006; Rushton & Jensen, 2005). You may remember from Chapter 3 that infants who easily grasp the essence of a stimulus and habituate more quickly later perform at high levels on intelligence tests. Intelligence test scores also correlate with various indicators of life success, such as occupational status. However, the problem is that the gateway to high-status professions, such as law and medicine, is school performance, which is what the tests predict (Sternberg, 1997; Sternberg, Grigorenko, & Bundy, 2001).

One problem with believing that IQ tests offer an X-ray into basic intellectual capacities is that people may carry around their test-score ranking as an inner wound. A psychologist supervisor once confessed to me that he was really not that intelligent because his IQ was only 105. He devalued the criterion the scores were supposed to predict—his many years of real-life success—by accepting what, in his case, was an invalid score!

A high test score can produce its own real-world problems. Suppose the student who told me his IQ was 140 decided he was so intelligent he didn't have to open a book in my class. He might be in for a nasty surprise both in college and in life when he found out that what *really* matters is your ability to work. Or that person might worry: "I'd better not try in Dr. Belsky's class because, if I do put forth effort and *don't* get an A, I will discover that my astronomical IQ test score was wrong." (Recall the research I mentioned in Chapter 6 that showed how telling elementary schoolers "you are smart" made them afraid to tackle challenging academic tasks.)

Even the firmest advocate of "g" would admit that people have different talents. Some of us are marvelous mechanically and miserable at math, wonderful at writing but hopeless at reading maps. If a child such as Manuel in our chapter-opening vignette is so gifted mechanically, shouldn't we nurture that talent, even though he does not qualify as exceptional in every area of life?

Toward a Broader View of Intelligence

But if intelligence involves different abilities, such as mechanical talents, perhaps we should go beyond the IQ test to measure those skills in a broader way. Psychologists Robert Sternberg and Howard Gardner have devoted distinguished careers to providing this broader view of what it means to be smart.

STERNBERG'S SUCCESSFUL INTELLIGENCE. Robert Sternberg (1984, 1996, 1997) is a man on a mission. In hundreds of publications, this contemporary psychologist has transformed the way we think about intelligence. Sternberg's passion comes from the heart. He began his school career with a problem:

As an elementary school student, I failed miserably on the IQ tests. . . . Just the sight of the school psychologist coming into the classroom to give a group IQ test sent me into a wild

"**g**" Charles Spearman's term for a general intelligence factor that he claimed underlies all cognitive activities.

Camille Tokerud Photography, Inc./Getty Images

Iconica/Getty Images

Being an inspired writer (*creative intelligence*) or knowing how to put up a tent and camp alone in the woods (*practical intelligence*) doesn't necessarily go along with being a "genius" at school. That's why Robert Sternberg believes that the standard IQ test (which measures *analytic intelligence*) does not tap into many of the skills we need to be successful in life.

panic attack. . . . You don't need to be a genius to figure out what happens next. My teachers in the elementary school grades certainly didn't expect much from me. . . . So I gave them what they expected. . . . Were the teachers disappointed? Not on your life. They were happy that I was giving them what they expected.

(1997, pp. 17–18)

Sternberg actually believes that traditional intelligence tests can do damage in the school environment. As you might imagine, the relationship between IQ scores and schooling is somewhat bidirectional. Children who attend inferior schools, or who miss months of classroom work due to illness, perform more poorly on intelligence tests (Sternberg, 1997). Worse yet, Sternberg argues, when schools decide to assign children to lower-track, less demanding classes on the basis of their low test scores, their IQs gradually decline year by year.

Most importantly, Sternberg (1984) believes that conventional intelligence tests are too limited. Although they do measure one type of intelligence, they do not cover the total terrain.

IQ tests, according to Sternberg, measure only **analytic intelligence**. They test how well people can solve academic-type problems that have a single, defined solution. They do not measure **creative intelligence**, the ability to "think outside the box," to come up with innovations, or to formulate problems in new ways. Nor do they measure a third type of intelligence called **practical intelligence**, common sense, or "street smarts."

Brazilian street children who make their living selling flowers and who don't have any formal education show impressive levels of practical intelligence. They understand how to handle money in the real world. However, they do poorly on measures of traditional IQ (Sternberg, 1984, 1997). Others, such as Winston Churchill, can be terrible scholars who flower after they leave their academic careers. Then, there are the people who excel at IQ test-taking and traditional schooling but fail abysmally once they enter the real world. Sternberg argues that to be **successfully intelligent** in life requires a balance of all three "intelligences."

GARDNER'S MULTIPLE INTELLIGENCES. Howard Gardner (1998) did not have Sternberg's problem with intelligence tests:

As a child I was a good student and a good test taker . . . but . . . music in particular and the arts were important parts of my life. Therefore when I asked myself what optimal human development is, I became more convinced that [we] had to . . . broaden the definition of intelligence to include these activities, too.

(1998, p. 3)

Gardner is not passionately opposed to standard intelligence tests. Still, he believes that using the single IQ score is far less informative than trying to measure children's unique talents and gifts. (Gardner's motto is: "Ask not *how*

analytic intelligence In Robert Sternberg's framework on successful intelligence, the facet of intelligence involving performing well on academic-type problems.

creative intelligence In Robert Sternberg's framework on successful intelligence, the facet of intelligence involved in producing novel ideas or innovative work.

practical intelligence In Robert Sternberg's framework on successful intelligence, the facet of intelligence involved in knowing how to act competently in real-world situations.

successful intelligence In Robert Sternberg's framework, the optimal form of cognition, involving having a good balance of analytic, creative, and practical intelligence.

Being a terrific guitarist (*musical intelligence*) or a world-class gymnast (*kinesthetic intelligence*) doesn't necessarily mean that you will also shine in reading or math. That's why Howard Gardner believes that schools need to broaden their focus to teach to the *different* kinds of intelligences that we all possess.

intelligent you are, but *how are* you intelligent.") According to Gardner's (2004; Gardner & Moran, 2006) **multiple intelligences theory**, human abilities come in eight, and possibly nine, distinctive forms.

In addition to the verbal and mathematical skills measured by traditional IQ tests, people may be gifted in *interpersonal intelligence*, or skillful at understanding other people. Their talents may lie in *intrapersonal intelligence*, the skill of understanding oneself, or in *spatial intelligence*, the ability to grasp where objects are arranged in space. (You might rely on a friend who is gifted in spatial intelligence to understand just how to arrange the furniture in your house or remember where an item is located by simply scanning a room.) Some people have high levels of *musical intelligence*, *kinesthetic intelligence* (the ability to use the body well), or *naturalist intelligence* (the gift for dealing with animals or plants and trees). There may even be an *existential (spiritual) intelligence*, too.

EVALUATING THE THEORIES. These different perspectives on intelligence are very exciting. Some of you may be thinking, "I believe that I'm gifted in practical or musical intelligence. I always knew there was more to intelligence than being successful at school!" But let's use our practical intelligence to critique these approaches. Why did Gardner select these particular eight abilities and not others (Barnett, Ceci, & Williams, 2006; White, 2006)? Yes, parents may marvel at a 6-year-old's creative or kinesthetic intelligence. But unfortunately, it is analytic intelligence that will get this child into the gifted program at school, not his artistic productions or how well his body moves (Eisner, 2004).

We can also criticize Sternberg's ideas. Is there really such a thing as creative or practical intelligence apart from a particular field? For instance, adopting the idea that there is a single "creative" intelligence might lead to the conclusion that Michelangelo would also be a talented musician or that Mozart could beautifully paint the Sistine Chapel.

The bottom line is that neither Gardner nor Sternberg has developed good replacements for our current IQ test. But this does not matter. Their mission is larger than changing the way we test children. They want to transform the way school systems teach (Gardner & Grigorenko, 2007; Sternberg & Moran, 2006).

INTERVENTIONS: **Lessons for Schools**

Gardner's theory has been enthusiastically embraced by teachers who understand that intelligence involves more than having traditional academic skills (see, for instance, Kunkel, 2007). However, to fully implement his ideas requires revolutionizing the way we structure education. Therefore, the most widespread use of multiple intelligences theory has been in helping "nontraditional learners" succeed in

multiple intelligences theory In Howard Gardner's perspective on intelligence, the principle that there are eight separate kinds of intelligence—verbal, mathematical, interpersonal, intrapersonal, spatial, musical, kinesthetic, naturalist—plus a possible ninth form, called spiritual intelligence.

traditional schools (Schirduan & Case, 2004). Here is how Mark, a dyslexic teenager, describes how he uses his spatial intelligence to cope with the maze of facts in history:

> I'll picture things; for example, if we are studying the French revolution . . . Louis the 16th . . ., I'll have a picture of him in my mind [and I'll visualize] the castle and peasants to help me learn.

(quoted in Schirduan & Case, 2004, p. 93)

Sternberg's research team has conducted an experiment demonstrating that teaching with every type of intelligence in mind produces better classroom performance. The researchers divided third-grade classes at a public school into two groups. One was taught social studies by standard methods. The other was given instruction balanced among the three types of intelligence. The children taught according to Sternberg's theory performed at a higher level even on standard multiple-choice tests (Sternberg, Torff, & Grigorenko, 1998)!

So the real potential of these innovative ideas is to enrich the way standard classrooms operate. How exactly do classrooms operate?

Classroom Learning

The diversity of intelligences, cultures, and educational experiences at home is matched by the incredible diversity of American schools. There are small rural schools and large urban schools, public schools and private schools, and highly traditional schools where students wear uniforms and schools that teach to Gardner's intelligences. There are single-sex schools, charter schools, religious schools, magnet schools that cater to gifted students, and alternative schools for children with behavior problems or learning disabilities.

Can students thrive in every kind of school? The answer is yes, *provided* schools have an intense commitment to student learning and teachers can excite students to learn. The rest of this chapter focuses on these challenges.

Examining Successful Schools

What qualities make a school successful? We can get insights from surveying elementary schools that are beating the odds. These schools, while located in low-income areas and serving large numbers of children whose parents do not speak English, have students who are thriving.

In the Vista School, located on a Native American reservation in Washington State, virtually all the children are eligible for a free lunch. However, Vista consistently boasts dramatic improvements on statewide reading and math tests (Borko and others, 2003). According to Ms. Thompson, the principal, "Our job is not to make excuses for students, but just to give them every possible opportunity. At Vista, teachers refuse to dumb down the curriculum. We offer tons of high-level conceptual work" (quoted in Borko and others, 2003, p. 177).

At Beacon Elementary School, also in Washington State, two out of every three students exceed state-mandated writing standards despite coming from impoverished backgrounds. Here, Susie Murphy, the principal, comments: "You can . . . say, these kids are poor. You just need to love them. Or you can come to a school like this where the philosophy is that the best way to love them is to give them an education so they can make choices in their life" (quoted in Borko and others, 2003, p. 186). Beacon teachers, she continues, "are here in this building by choice. They are committed to proving that kids who live in poverty can learn every bit as well as other kids" (p. 192).

A school's physical appearance can also make a real difference in whether children "beat the odds." This boy attends a model public school, designed and built by a well-known architect and located in an impoverished section of New York City.

Tony Cenicola/The New York Times/Redux

intrinsic motivation The drive to act based on the pleasure of taking that action in itself, not for an external reinforcer or reward.

extrinsic motivation The drive to take an action because that activity offers external reinforcers such as praise, money, or a good grade.

At Beacon, teachers are also committed to providing high-level challenging work. The school regularly builds in opportunities for the teachers to share ideas: "We have mini-workshops in geometry, or problem solving. Our whole staff talks about the general focus and where math is going" (p. 194).

Lest you think that a shared passion for excellence and mutual collaboration is mainly important in schools serving disadvantaged children, let's take a trip to Bennett Woods elementary school in Michigan, where, within a few years, students went from scoring at the middle of the heap to the top on that state's annual reading tests. What turned this school—serving mainly middle-class children—around? Teachers credited the new principal. She instituted extensive in-service training for teachers. She insisted that every boy and girl be immersed in children's literature, beginning in first grade. (In the primary grades, each student had a book bin of 10 or more books *currently* being read at school.) She allowed the teachers to experiment and use their creativity to creatively teach (Pressley and others, 2007).

The bottom line is that successful schools set high standards and believe that every child can succeed. Teachers offer an excess of nurture—both to their students and to one another. In terms of Baumrind's parenting-styles framework, these schools are authoritative in their approach.

Now that we have the general outlines for what is effective, it's time to tackle the challenge *every* teacher faces: getting students to be eager to learn.

Producing Eager Learners

> But to go to school on a summer morn,
> O! it drives all joy away;
> Under a cruel eye outworn,
> The little ones spend the day
> In sighing and dismay.
>
> —William Blake, "The Schoolboy" (1794)

Jean Piaget believed that the hunger to learn is more important than food or drink. Why, then, do children over the centuries lament, "I hate school"? The reason is that learning loses its joy when it becomes a requirement instead of an activity we choose to engage in for ourselves.

THE PROBLEM: AN EROSION OF INTRINSIC MOTIVATION. Developmentalists divide motivation into two distinct categories. **Intrinsic motivation** refers to self-generated activities—actions we take purely from our inner desires. When Piaget described our hunger to learn, he was referring to intrinsic motivations. **Extrinsic motivation** refers to activities that we undertake in order to get external reinforcers, such as praise or pay, or a good grade.

Unfortunately, the learning activity you are currently engaged in falls into the extrinsic category. You know you will be tested on what you are reading. Worse yet, if you decided to pick up this book for an intrinsic reason—because you wanted to learn

Compare the activities of the kindergarten class of "little scientists" at left with those of the second graders in the photograph at right and you will immediately understand why by about age 8 many children begin to say, "I hate school."

about human development—the very fact that you might be graded would make your basic interest fall off.

Numerous studies show that when adults give external reinforcers for activities that are intrinsically motivating, children are less likely to want to perform those activities for themselves (Patall, Cooper, & Robinson, 2008; Stipek, 1996). In one classic example, researchers selected preschoolers who were intrinsically interested in art. When they gave a "good player" award (an outside reinforcer) for the art projects, the children later showed a dramatic decline in their interest in doing art for fun (Lepper, Greene, & Nisbett, 1973). This research makes sense of the question you may have wondered about: "Why, after taking that literature class, am I so much less interested in reading on my own?"

Young children enter kindergarten brimming with intrinsic motivation. When does this love affair with school turn sour? Think back to your childhood, and you will realize that the enchantment typically ends during the early years of elementary school, when teachers begin to provide those external reinforcers—grades (Stipek, 1997). To make matters worse, during first or second grade classroom learning becomes more abstract and removed from life. Boring, rote activities, like filling in worksheets and memorizing multiplication tables, have replaced the creative hands-on projects of kindergarten. Ironically, then, school has been transformed into the very setting where Piaget's little-scientist activities are *least* likely to occur.

Then, as children fully enter Piaget's stage of concrete operations—at around age 8 or 9—they begin really comparing their performance to that of their peers. This competitive orientation erodes intrinsic motivation (Dweck, 1986; Self-Brown & Mathews, 2003). The focus shifts from "I want to improve for myself" to "I want to do *better* than my friends."

In sum, several forces explain why children naturally come to dislike school: School involves extrinsic reinforcers (grades). School learning, because it often involves rote memorization, is not intrinsically interesting. In school, children are not free to set their own internal learning goals. Their performance is judged by a fixed outside standard: how they measure up to the rest of the class.

It is no wonder, therefore, that studies in Western nations document an alarming decline in intrinsic motivation as children travel through school (Lepper, Corpus, & Iyengar, 2005; Spinath & Steinmayr, 2008). Susan Harter (1981) asked children to choose between the following two statements: "Some kids work really hard to get good grades" (referring to extrinsic motivation) or "Some kids work really hard because they like to learn new things" (measuring intrinsic motives). When she gave her measure to hundreds of California public school children, intrinsic motivation scores fell off from third to ninth grade.

Still, external reinforcers can be vitally important. They are sometimes the hook that gets us intrinsically involved. Have you ever reluctantly read a book for a class assignment and found yourself captivated by the subject matter? Perhaps you enrolled in this course because it was a requirement for graduation but are becoming so interested in the material that you want to make some aspect of developmental science your future career. Given that extrinsically motivating activities are basic to school and life, how can we make them work best?

THE SOLUTION: MAKING EXTRINSIC LEARNING PART OF US. To answer this question, Edward Deci and Richard Ryan (1985, 2000) make the point that extrinsic learning tasks vary on a continuum. We engage in some types of extrinsic learning totally unwillingly: "I have to take that terrible anatomy course because it is a requirement for graduation." We enthusiastically embrace other extrinsic tasks, which may not be inherently interesting, because we identify with their larger goal: "I want to memorize every bone of the body because that information is vital to my plan to become a nurse." In the first situation, the learning activity seems completely irrelevant. In the second, the task has become intrinsic because it is connected to our inner self. Therefore, the key to transforming school learning from

Masterfile

Using computers in the class-room can draw on children's basic interest in video games to make academics intrinsically more interesting. But in order to make this learning *truly* intrinsic, this teacher cannot microman-age or hover over her students, or be overly critical. These boys need to feel that they can control their learning and master the concepts at their own pace.

a chore into a pleasure is to make extrinsic learning relate to children's internal goals and desires.

The most boring tasks take on an intrinsic aura when they speak directly to children's passions. Imagine, for instance, how a first grader's motivation to sound out words might change if a teacher, knowing that a particular student was captivated by dinosaurs, gave that child the job of sounding out dinosaur names. Deci and Ryan believe that learning becomes intrinsic when it satisfies our basic need for relatedness (attachment). Think back, for instance, to the discussion of schools that beat the odds. Now imagine how motivated those children were to learn to read and write when they understood that their success would make their beloved school proud. Finally, extrinsic tasks take on an intrinsic feeling when they foster our need for autonomy, or offer us choices of *how* to do our work (Patall, Cooper, & Robinson, 2008; Ryan and others, 2006).

Studies around the globe suggest that when teachers and parents take away children's autonomy—by controlling, criticizing, or micromanaging learning tasks—they erode self-efficacy and intrinsic motivation (Chirkov & Ryan, 2001; Moorman & Pomerantz, 2008). We can see this principle in our own lives. By continually denigrating our work, or hovering over every move, a controlling supervisor has the uncanny ability to turn us off to the most intrinsically interesting job.

Our basic need for autonomy offers clues as to why high-level conceptual learning tasks might be effective with *every child*. One researcher asked third-grade teachers to abandon their typical strategy of teaching writing skills by having children fill in sentences or copy words. He urged them to do activities such as writing creative essays and not to worry about what learning objectives they did or did not cover in class. This change produced a dramatic shift from extrinsic motivations (children saying "I'm doing this for a good grade") to intrinsic motivations (students reporting "I really love this stuff"). Moreover, to the teachers' surprise, their classes performed just as well on the standard end-of-year achievement exam as if they had specifically drilled in material that would appear on the test.

Most exciting, the low-ability students did not find the higher-level tasks overwhelming. Their scores on the end-of-year tests increased the *most*. So giving high-level conceptual work may be the most intelligent strategy for students across the board (Miller, 2003)!

Table 7.5 summarizes these three messages for teachers: Focus on relevance, enhance relatedness, and provide choices or autonomy. The table also pulls together other teaching tips based on our discussion of Gardner's and Sternberg's perspectives on intelligence and our look at what makes schools successful. Now, let's conclude our discussion by paying a visit to a class that embodies all of these teaching lessons.

TABLE 7.5: Lessons for Teachers: A Recap of This Chapter's Insights

1. **Foster relevance.** For instance, in teaching reading, tailor the books you are assigning so that they fit children's passions. And entice students to learn to read in other ways, such as getting first and second graders energized by telling them that they will now be able to break a code that the world uses just like a detective!

2. **Foster relatedness.** Develop a secure, loving attachment with every student. Continually tell each child how proud you are when that person tries hard or succeeds.

3. **Foster autonomy.** As much as possible, allow your students to select among several equivalent assignments (such as choosing which specific books to read). Don't give time limits, such as "It's 9:30 and this has to be done by 10:00," or hover, take over tasks, or make negative comments. Stand by to provide informational comments and careful scaffolding (see Chapter 5) when students ask. Build in assignments that allow high-level thinking, such as using essays in preference to rote work such as copying sentences or filling out worksheets.

TABLE 7.5 (continued)

Teaching Tips Based on Gardner's and Sternberg's Theories

1. Offer balanced assignments that capitalize on students' different kinds of intelligence—creative work such as essays; practical-intelligence activities such as calculating numbers to make change at a store; single-answer analytic tasks (using Sternberg's framework); and classroom time devoted to music, dance, the arts, and caring for plants (capitalizing on Gardner's ideas).

2. Explicitly teach students to use their different intelligences in mastering classroom work.

Additional Teaching Tips

1. Don't rely on IQ test scores, especially in assessing the abilities of low-income and ethnic-minority students.

2. Avoid praising children for being "brilliant." Compliment them for hard work.

3. Go beyond academics to teach children interpersonal skills.

4. Strive for excellence. Expect all students to succeed.

5. Foster collaborative working relationships with your colleagues.

6. Minimize grade-oriented comparisons (such as who got As, Bs, Cs, etc.). Emphasize the importance of *personal improvement* to students. Experiment with giving grades for individual progress.

FOCUS ON A TOPIC: ## TEACHING AT ITS FINEST

When you enter Cindy Jones's fourth-grade classroom in Murfreesboro, Tennessee, you immediately realize that this teacher is special. You see a corner cluttered with evidence of enduring attachments—letters and gifts from former students now living around the world and provocative sayings that dot the walls: "Teachers are united mind workers." "Fair means everyone gets what they need. Not everyone gets the same." There are creative projects on display, and canned goods stacked to be delivered to families in need. Clearly offering caring, making learning intrinsically motivating, and teaching to different intelligences is what this class is about.

To help foster Gardner's interpersonal and intrapersonal intelligences, Cindy has divided the class into teams: the Red Hot Patriots, the Shooting Stars, and the Lightning Bolts. In making up the teams, Cindy strives for a balance. She puts students with learning problems together with children who are reading at the twelfth-grade level; pairs popular children with those who are rejected or very shy. Children get points for taking responsibility and for doing something positive for another child. Cindy tells me:

> Don't let them know, but I arrange the points so that every team wins each third week. I also tone down the competition by giving points for rooting for and helping the other teams. When children say they want to switch to be with a friend, I never say yes. Life involves relating to all kinds of people. That's an important lesson I want to instill. When conflicts come up, they take the responsibility to have a group pow-wow to work things out.

The teams are the subtext that keeps the year humming along. But each day unfolds according to a specific plan:

8:30–9:30 (CURRENT EVENTS) The morning begins with a high-intensity curtain raiser that combines relevance and autonomy: Cindy has the children bring in some interesting fact they learned from reading the newspaper or watching the news. Her goal here is "to seize the teachable moment," or to relate this material to the academic content in class. So, when a girl reports that she heard that a woman just died at age 107, Cindy says, "Let's calculate her birth date. What events were happening when she was a little girl? Imagine the way the world will have changed when you get that old."

9:30–10:30 (CENTERS) During this hour, the students circulate in small groups among areas designated for reading, computer activities, and using worksheets to practice for the upcoming statewide exams. Now, I wonder, how will Cindy handle this completely extrinsic task? The answer, I discover, is to connect this activity to children's feelings of autonomy and relatedness: "Slow and steady." "Fill everything in." "You can do it." "Get mad at the test-makers. You need an attitude for these terrible tests." "Josh, I'm going to put a tattoo on your hand so when you invite me to your wedding, it will say 'Josh, slow up.'" For a girl with serious reading problems: "Brittany, would you be the class role model for a child in kindergarten this year?"

10:30–11:30 (GRAMMAR) Now comes a hilarious exercise in understanding the purpose of punctuation, showing how the most rote learning can be fun: "I bought

PAPER . . . BAGS . . . FISH . . . GLUE . . . paper bags . . . fish . . . glue . . . Suppose I bought two things? . . . three things? . . . Or, suppose I decided to buy fish glue?" "Who got that one right, and who had trouble?" "David, I'm so glad you are explaining that to Jason, just like he gave you help on spelling last week."

Then there is some downtime before lunch listening to classical music, followed by an afternoon seminar discussing how the children feel about the piece: "Was the composer successful in conveying his ideas?" The day ends with a test, during which Cindy and I *leave the room.* Cindy explains, "I make it clear to the children that I trust them . . . but they also work to earn my trust."

Because this class—like any other—has its share of students who are hard to manage, at the end of the day Cindy has a few children fill out a sheet listing goals for improvement, which they take home. The difference is that here the children assume responsibility for monitoring their *own* behavior: Cindy asks questions like, "Think carefully: Do you give yourself a smiley-face sticker for focusing today or not talking back?" Then, in the evening, she calls parents to brainstorm about problems and discuss the child's progress: "I try to call or e-mail when there is good news to report, not just when something goes wrong." In fact, the intimate dance of attachment between parents and this teacher makes this class stand out. There is a seamless web of socialization between what happens at school and what goes on at home.

Perhaps the most defining moment of my day spent observing this class occurred when Cindy reminded these fourth graders that there would be a holiday the next Monday and the students all groaned and said, "Oh no!" Outstanding teachers can make school such an exciting experience that children hate vacation time!

TYING IT ALL TOGETHER

1. If Devin, from an upper-middle-class family, and Adam, from a low-income family, are starting kindergarten this fall, you can predict that (pick one):
   a. Both children will perform equally well on school readiness tests, but Adam will fall behind because he is likely to go to a poor-quality kindergarten.
   b. Devin will outperform Adam on school readiness tests, and the gap will probably widen because Adam will go to a poor-quality kindergarten.

2. Malik hasn't been doing well in school, and his achievement test scores have consistently been well below average for his grade. On the WISC, Malik gets an IQ score of 115. What is your conclusion?

3. You are telling a friend about the deficiencies of relying on a child's IQ score. Pick out the *two* arguments you might make.
   a. The tests are not reliable; children's scores *typically* change a lot during the elementary school years.

    b. The tests are not valid predictors of school performance.

    c. As people have different abilities, a single IQ score may not tell us very much about a child's unique gifts.

    d. As poor children are at a disadvantage in taking the test, you should not use the test as an index of "genetic school-related talents" for low-income children.

4. Josh doesn't do well in reading or math, but he excels in music and dance, and he gets along with all kinds of children. In terms of Sternberg's theory of successful intelligence, Josh is not good in _____, but he is skilled in _____ and _____. In terms of Gardner's theory of _____, Josh is strong in which intelligences?

5. A friend of yours, who is the principal of a school, asks for some tips to help her children succeed. Based on this section, you can give all of the following suggestions *except*:

    a. Have your teachers regularly meet to work together and share ideas.

    b. Be sure your teachers make the material very simple so that all students experience success.

    c. Make sure that your teachers share a commitment to having every child learn.

    d. Encourage your teachers to give the children high-level creative work.

6. (a) Define intrinsic and extrinsic motivation. (b) Give an example of a task in your life right now that is driven by each kind of motivation. (c) From reading the chapter, can you come up with some ways to make the unpleasant extrinsic tasks you do feel more intrinsic?

Answers to the Tying It All Together questions can be found on the last page of this chapter.

Final Thoughts

Throughout this chapter, you may have noticed a few fundamental themes. Outstanding teachers like Cindy, as well as outstanding parents, have clear priorities. They provide structure or high standards for their children. They understand each child's gifts and weaknesses. They flexibly tailor their behavior to the needs of a given child.

    I also hope that this discussion has encouraged you to think more deeply about the many forces involved in development, what it means to be intelligent, and what schools can do to make learning a positive experience for every child. And I hope you have been sensitized to the crucial role that the cultural and social context plays in development, too. Other societies and ethnic groups have a good deal to teach us about the child-rearing values we personally hold dear. Children who grow up in poverty have trouble performing well on intelligence tests or in school. We need to provide the kind of environment that allows parents to effectively parent and school systems to teach in a way that permits *every* child to succeed.

SUMMARY

Home

The composition of two-parent families varies dramatically, from the never-divorced two-parent family to different types of blended families. Most single-parent families are headed by women, and boys and girls growing up in these families are at risk of being poor. There are dramatic variations by ethnicity and immigrant status, too. Children, however, can thrive in any kind of family, depending on the care parents provide.

According to Diana Baumrind's **parenting styles** approach, based on the dimensions of providing rules and nurturing, discipline styles can be classified as **authoritative, authoritarian, permissive,** and **rejecting-neglecting.** Although studies show that authoritative parents who provide clear rules and are also highly child-centered tend to raise the most well-adjusted, competent children, we can question this framework. Sometimes, it is helpful to have parents with different child-rearing styles. Good parents do far more than just provide discipline. Parenting attitudes differ by ethnicity and culture. Difficult environments demand a stricter, more authoritarian child-rearing approach.

Resilient children, boys and girls who do well in the face of traumatic early experiences, tend to have an adaptable temperament, other talents, one close, secure attachment, and not be faced with an overload of stresses. There may be specific genes that promote resilience, too.

Some behavioral-genetic researchers argue that children's biologically based temperament shapes parenting. Judith Harris believes that peer groups (and the wider society)—not parents—are the main socializing force in children's lives. Although statistics related to **acculturation** support Harris' theory, we now have overwhelming evidence that high-quality parenting matters greatly, especially when children are "at risk." Parents need to be flexible, tailoring their childrearing to their environment and to their children's needs. They should also relax and enjoy these fleeting years.

Corporal punishment, particularly mild spanking, is most common in the United States during the preschool years. While not currently the preferred punishment, spanking is more widely accepted among certain groups. Experts differ as to whether an occasional spanking is detrimental, but no developmentalist believes that it is ever appropriate to hit a baby. Positive reinforcement for good behavior is preferable to punishment. Severe corporal punishment qualifies as child abuse.

The behaviors that constitute the four forms of **child maltreatment**—physical abuse, neglect, emotional abuse, and sexual abuse—can *sometimes* be hard to classify. The true prevalence of abuse in the United States is unclear. However, in general, parents' personality problems, intense environmental stress, and lack of attachment to a given child are the main risk factors that provoke abuse. Abused boys and girls often have serious emotional and academic problems and are at risk for committing antisocial acts later in life. However, children vary in how they cope with this trauma, and victims of abuse do construct successful, loving adult lives. When children are maltreated, it is preferable not to break up the family, but to give parents the help they need to parent more effectively.

Children of divorce are at risk for a host of negative life outcomes. However, most boys and girls survive this common childhood transition without serious emotional scars. The key to making divorce less traumatic lies in minimizing other changes in the child's life, giving children some say in custody arrangements, not having parents fight over the children and, especially, promoting high-quality custodial parenting. Living in a conflict-ridden or violent two-parent home may be as bad—or worse—for children as divorce.

School

Many children from low-income families enter kindergarten well behind their affluent counterparts in basic academic skills. These inequalities at the starting gate are magnified by the fact that poor children are likely to attend the poorest-quality kindergartens.

Achievement tests measure a child's body of knowledge. IQ tests measure a child's basic potential for classroom work. The **Wechsler Intelligence Scale for Children (WISC)**, with its Verbal and Performance Scales, is the main childhood IQ test. This time-intensive test, involving a variety of subtests, is given individually to a child. If the child's IQ score is below 70—and if other indicators warrant this designation—that boy or girl may be labeled **mentally retarded**. If the child's score is much higher than his performance on achievement tests, he is classified as having a **specific learning disability**, such as **dyslexia**. If a child's IQ score is at or above 130, she is considered **gifted** and is eligible to be placed in an accelerated class.

IQ scores satisfy the measurement criterion called **reliability**, meaning that people tend to get roughly the same score if the test is taken more than once. However, stressful life experiences can artificially lower a child's score. The test must also be **valid**, meaning that it predicts what it was devised to measure: performance in school. While some psychologists claim that performance on the test reflects a single, overall quality called **"g"** that relates to cognitive performance in every area of life, others feel that intelligence involves multiple independent abilities. These critics argue that it is inappropriate to rank people as intelligent or not based on their IQ scores. For disadvantaged children in particular, the IQ score cannot be viewed as an index of genetic gifts.

Robert Sternberg and Howard Gardner argue that we need to expand our measures of intelligence beyond traditional tests. Sternberg believes that there are three types of intelligence: **analytic intelligence** (academic abilities), **creative intelligence**, and **practical intelligence** (real-world abilities, or "street smarts"). **Successful intelligence** requires having a balance among all three of these skills. Gardner, in his **multiple intelligences theory,** describes eight (or possibly nine) distinct types of intelligences. Although neither of these psychologists has developed alternatives to conventional IQ tests, their ideas have generated excitement and have been used to transform how some schools teach.

Schools that serve poor but high-achieving children share a mission to have every child succeed. They assume that poor children can do well at high-level conceptual work. Teachers support and mentor one another. These same attributes apply to unusually successful schools in middle-class neighborhoods, too.

Why do many children come to dislike school? The reason is that classroom learning is based on **extrinsic motivation** (external reinforcers such as grades), which impairs **intrinsic motivation** (the desire to learn for the sake of learning). School learning is inherently less interesting because it often involves rote memorization. Being evaluated in comparison to the class also erodes a child's interest in learning for its own sake. Studies show a disturbing decline in intrinsic motivation as children progress through elementary school.

Teachers (and parents) can make extrinsic learning tasks more intrinsic by offering material relevant to children's interests, fostering relatedness (or a close attachment), and giving students choices about how to do their work. Because it offers more autonomy, conceptual work is preferable to rote learning tasks for students of every kind of ability. With exceptional teaching, students can love school!

KEY TERMS

parenting style, p. 202

authoritative parents, p. 202

authoritarian parents, p. 203

permissive parents, p. 203

rejecting-neglecting parents, p. 203

resilient children, p. 206

acculturation, p. 208

corporal punishment, p. 209

child maltreatment, p. 211

achievement tests, p. 216

WISC (Wechsler Intelligence Scale for Children), p. 216

mentally retarded, p. 216

specific learning disability, p. 216

dyslexia, p. 217

gifted, p. 217

reliability, p. 218

validity, p. 218

"g," p. 220

analytic intelligence, p. 221

creative intelligence, p. 221

practical intelligence, p. 221

Sternberg's successful intelligence, p. 221

Gardner's multiple intelligences theory, p. 222

intrinsic motivation, p. 224

extrinsic motivation, p. 224

ANSWERS TO TYING IT ALL TOGETHER QUIZZES

Home

1. Montana's parents = authoritative. Pablo's parents = authoritarian. Sara's parents = permissive

2. Amber

3. Judith Harris' advice = Get your son in the best possible peer group. This chapter's recommendation = Provide exceptionally sensitive parenting.

4. a. and c.

5. These are possible symptoms of neglect and physical abuse. You should report the problem to child protective services. The goal is to teach the parents to parent more effectively so that this student can remain with his family or eventually be reunited with the family if he must be removed from home.

6. Tell Crystal she made the right decision as living in an atmosphere poisoned by chronic fighting might have devastating consequences for her child's mental health. *Your advice:* Encourage your child to express her feelings, and try to give her *some* input into custody decisions. Minimize other life disruptions (e.g., see if you can keep your daughter in the same neighborhood or school). Don't bad-mouth your former spouse or continually battle over custody arrangements.

School

1. b.

2. Malik has a learning disability.

3. c. and d.

4. Analytic intelligence . . . creative intelligence and practical intelligence . . . multiple intelligences . . . Josh's strengths are in musical, kinesthetic, and interpersonal intelligence.

5. b.

6. (a) Intrinsic motivation is self-generated—we work at something simply because it gives us joy. Extrinsic motivation refers to activities propelled by external reinforcers like grades. (b) Ask yourself: Am I doing this because I love it or only because this activity results in an external reward? (c) 1. Make disliked, extrinsic tasks relevant to a larger personal goal. ("Cleaning the house will help me become a more organized person. Plus, it's great exercise, so I'll become healthier.") 2. Increase your sense of autonomy or feeling of having choices around this activity. ("I'll do my housecleaning at the time of day that feels least burdensome while I listen to my favorite CD.") 3. Enhance attachments ("If my significant other comes home to a clean house, she'll feel wonderful!")

Adolescence

This two-chapter part dealing with the teenage years actually progresses a bit chronologically. That's because my first topic, puberty, can begin to take place as early as age 9 or 10.

In Chapter 8—**Physical Development**, I'll actually spend a good deal of time tracking puberty, that early adolescent total body change. However, I'll also be focusing on two other major teenage body-oriented topics: body image concerns (and eating disorders) and adolescent sexuality.

Chapter 9—**Cognitive and Socioemotional Development** begins by examining the dramatic advances in reasoning and morality that take place during adolescence. Next, I'll be looking carefully at teenagers' emotional states and offering insights into which children are at risk for having problems and flourishing during this special decade of life. The last part of this chapter is all about relationships—how teenagers behave with their parents; how they act with their peers.

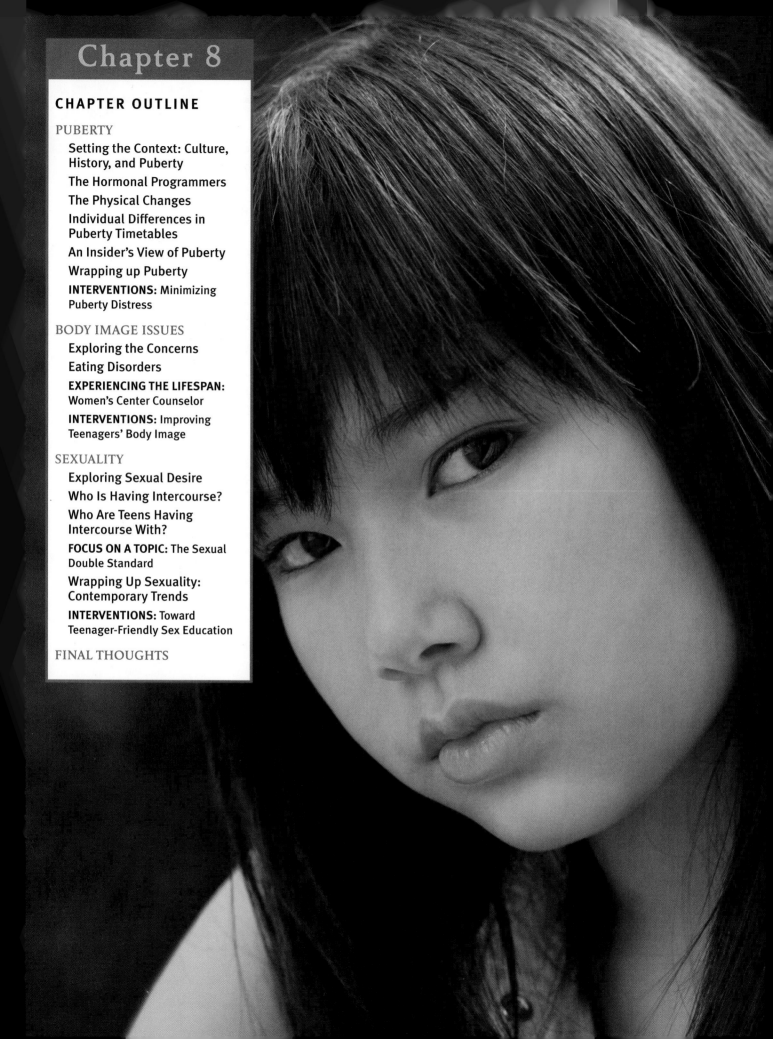

Chapter 8

CHAPTER OUTLINE

Physical Development

Samantha and her twin brother, Sam, were so much alike—in their physical features, their personalities, their academic talents. Except for the sex difference, they almost seemed like identical twins. Then, when Samantha was 10, she started to tower over Sam and the rest of the fifth-grade class.

Yes, there was a downside to being first to develop—needing to hide behind a locker when you dressed for gym; not having anyone to talk to when you got your period at age 10. But, oh, what fun! From being a neglected, pudgy elementary school child, by sixth grade, Samantha leaped into the ranks of most popular, especially with the older boys. At age 12, Samantha was smoking and drinking. By 14, she regularly defied her helpless parents and often left the house at 2 A.M.

Samantha's parents were frantic, but their daughter couldn't care less. Everything else was irrelevant compared to exploring being an adult. It took a life-changing tenth-grade trip to Costa Rica with Caroline, and a pregnancy scare, to get Samantha on track. Samantha had abandoned Caroline, her best friend during elementary school, for her new "mature" friends. But when the girls got close again that memorable summer, Caroline's calming influence woke Samantha up. Samantha credits comments like "Why are you putting yourself in danger by having unprotected sex?" with saving her life. Plus, her lifelong competition with her brother didn't hurt. Although Sam was also an early developer, when he shot up to 6 feet in the spring of seventh grade, he was great at sports and also an academic star.

Now that Samantha is 30, married, and expecting her first child, it's interesting for the three of them to get together and really talk (for the first time) about the teenage years. Sam remembers the thrill of getting so much stronger and his first incredible feelings of being in love. Samantha recalls being excited about her changing body, but she also remembers constantly dieting and obsessively worrying about being too fat. Then, there is Caroline, who says she sailed through middle school because she didn't begin to menstruate until age 14. Everyone goes through puberty, but why does everyone react in such different ways?

|ow do children feel during **puberty,** the name for all of the internal and external changes related to physically becoming adult? This chapter focuses on this question and many others as we explore physical development during the teenage years. I'll begin by thoroughly tracking puberty—examining what sets off this total body transformation, exploring how the changes unfold, focusing on how teens react to their changing bodies. Why did Samantha—but not Sam—have trouble coping with being an "early-maturing" child? What can we do to make puberty a less stressful experience for every boy and girl?

Next, I'll discuss body image issues such as Samantha's dieting frenzy, and finally offer an in-depth look at sexuality during this watershed time of life. As you read though the following pages, you might think back to when you were 10 or 12 or 14. How did you feel about your body during puberty? When did you begin dating and fantasizing about having sex?

puberty The hormonal and physical changes by which children become sexually mature human beings.

puberty rite A "coming of age" ritual, usually beginning at some event such as first menstruation, held in traditional cultures to celebrate children's transition to adulthood.

secular trend in puberty A century-long decline in the average age at which children reach puberty in the developed world.

menarche A girl's first menstruation.

spermarche A boy's first ejaculation of live sperm.

These photographs of fourth graders and high school juniors at the prom offer a vivid visual reminder of the total body transformation that takes place as children travel through puberty during early adolescence.

Puberty

Compare photos of yourself from late elementary school and high school to get a vivid sense of the incredible changes that occur during puberty. From the size of our thighs to the shape of our nose, we become a totally different-looking person during the early teenage years. Although children's timetables vary, today puberty—which lasts about five years from start to finish—typically is a pre-teen and early adolescent change (Archibald, Graber, & Brooks-Gunn, 2003). Moreover, today, as you saw with Samantha, who started menstruating at age 10 and has just gotten pregnant at age 30, the gap between being physically able to have children and actually *having* children can be twice as long as infancy and childhood combined.

This lack of person–environment fit, when our body is telling us to have sex and society is telling us to "just say no" to intercourse, explains why teenage sexuality is such a widespread worry today. Our concerns are fairly recent. They are a product of living in the twentieth-century developed world.

Setting the Context: Culture, History, and Puberty

As my sisters and I went about doing our daily chores, we choked on the dust stirred up by the herd of cattle and goats that had just arrived in our compound. . . . These animals were my bride wealth, negotiated by my parents and the family of the man who had been chosen as my husband. . . . I am considered to be a woman, so I am ready to marry, have children, and assume adult privileges and responsibilities. My name is Telelia ole Mariani. I am 14 years old.

(quoted in Wilson, Ngige, & Trollinger, 2003, p. 95)

For this rural Vietnamese boy, reaching puberty means it's time to assume his adult responsibilities as a fisherman. This is the reason why having *puberty rites* to mark the end of childhood makes excellent sense in less industrialized cultures, but not in our own.

As you can see in this quotation from a girl in rural Nigeria, throughout most of history and even today in a few agrarian cultures, having sex as a teenager was considered "normal." The reason is that reaching puberty was often society's signal to find a spouse (Schlegel, 1995; Schlegel & Barry, 1991). The fact that a young person's changing body has traditionally meant entering a new adult stage of life led to a different cultural attitude toward the physical changes. In industrialized societies, we need to minimize puberty because we don't want teenagers to act on their sexual feelings for years. In many agrarian cultures, the community would get together to celebrate the changes in a coming-of-age ceremony called the **puberty rite**.

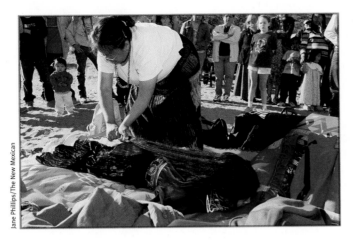

As the female mentor symbolically welcomes her into adulthood, this newly menstruating Navajo girl is undergoing a traditional cultural ritual that will be an unforgettable highlight of her life. Plus, the female tourists watching this ceremony are getting insights into a very different, positive way of looking at menarche!

Celebrating Puberty

Puberty rites were more than just parties. They were thrilling events, carefully scripted to highlight a young person's entrance into adult life. Typically, children were removed from their families and, under the supervision of same-sex role models, asked to perform challenging tasks. There was intense anxiety ("Can I really do this thing?") and feelings of awe and self-efficacy as the young person returned, to be joyfully reunited with the community in a different, adult way (Weisfeld, 1997).

So at his fourteenth or fifteenth birthday, a boy might be spirited away by the males in the village to a secret campsite, to hunt, raid an enemy camp, and perhaps be initiated into the mysteries of sex (Weisfeld, 1997). A girl's first menstruation was the signal for a community-wide festival to celebrate her arrival into womanhood.

Consider, for instance, the traditional Navajo four-day Kinaalda ceremony (Markstrom & Iborra, 2003). At the beginning of her first or second menstrual cycle, guided by a female mentor, a girl performed the long-distance running ritual, sprinting for miles. (Imagine your motivation to train for this event, when you understood that the length of your run symbolized how long you would live.) The female role model massaged the girl's body and painted her face and supervised her in the grinding of corn (a symbol of fertility) for a cake. On the final day, the girl served the cake during a joyous, all-night community sing. The Navajo believe that, when females begin menstruating, they possess special spiritual powers, so everyone would gather around for the girl's blessings as they gave her a new adult name.

Today, however, girls may reach puberty at age 10 or even 9. At that age—in *any* society—could people be ready for adult life? The answer is no. In the past, we reached puberty at a much older age.

The Declining Age of Puberty

You can see this dramatic age decline, called the **secular trend in puberty**, illustrated in Figure 8.1. In the 1860s, the average age of **menarche**, or first menstruation, in Northern Europe was over 17 (Tanner, 1978). By the 1960s, in the developed world, it dropped to well under 13 (Parent and others, 2003). A century ago, girls could not get pregnant until their late teens. Today, many girls can have babies *before* they enter their teenage years.

Researchers use menarche as their marker for charting the secular trend in puberty because it is an obvious sign of possibly being able to have a child. The male signal of fertility, **spermarche**, or

FIGURE 8.1: **The secular trend in puberty:** Notice that the average age of menarche dramatically declined in developed countries during the first half of the twentieth century. What impact do you think this change alone has made on teenage pregnancy rates?

Source: Tanner (1978), p. 103.

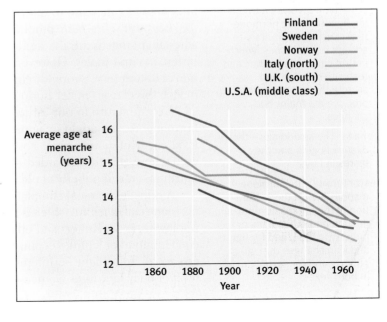

If they had grown up a century ago, these seventh graders at a summer computer camp would really have looked like girls. Due to the *secular trend in puberty*, they look like women today.

first ejaculation of live sperm, is a hidden event. But at least through the mid-twentieth century, the age of puberty has also been declining for boys.

In addition, because it reflects better nutrition, in the same way as with stunting rates in early childhood (remember Chapter 3), we can use the secular trend in puberty as an index of a nation's economic development. In the United States, African American girls begin to menstruate at close to age 12. In impoverished African nations, such as Senegal, the average age of menarche is over 16 (Parent and others, 2003)!

Given that nutrition is intimately involved, what *exactly* sets puberty off? For answers, let's focus on the hormonal systems that program the physical changes.

The Hormonal Programmers

Puberty is programmed by two independent command centers. One system, located in the adrenal glands at the top of the kidneys, begins to release its hormones at about age 6 to 8, several years before children show any observable signs of puberty. The **adrenal androgens**, whose output increases to reach a peak in the early twenties, eventually produce (among other events) pubic hair development, skin changes, body odor, and, as you will see later in this chapter, our first feelings of sexual desire (McClintock & Herdt, 1996).

About two years later, the most important command center kicks in. Called the **HPG axis**—because it involves the hypothalamus (in the brain), the pituitary (a gland at the base of the brain), and the **gonads** (the *ovaries* and the *testes*)—this system produces the major body changes.

As you can see in Figure 8.2, puberty is set off by a three-phase chain reaction. At about age 9 or 10, pulsating bursts of the hypothalamic hormone stimulate the pituitary gland to step up production of its hormones. This causes the ovaries and testes to secrete several closely related compounds called *estrogens* and the hormone called **testosterone** (Ebling, 2005; Sisk & Foster, 2004).

As the blood concentrations of estrogens and testosterone float upward, these hormones unleash a physical transformation. Estrogens produce females' changing shape by causing the hips to widen and the uterus and breasts to enlarge. They set in motion the cycle of reproduction, stimulating the ovaries to produce eggs. Testosterone causes the penis to lengthen, promotes the growth of facial and body hair, and is responsible for a dramatic increase in muscle mass and other internal masculine changes.

Boys and girls *both* produce estrogens and testosterone. Testosterone and the adrenal androgens are the desire hormones. They are responsible for sexual arousal in females and males. However, women produce mainly estrogens. The concentration of testosterone is roughly eight times higher in boys after puberty than it is in girls; in fact, this classic "male" hormone is responsible for *all* the physical changes in boys.

Now, to return to our earlier question: What primes the triggering hypothalamic hormone? As you might imagine, the signal is set off when the body reaches a certain level of maturation (Sisk & Foster, 2004). This explains why developing world children whose growth is retarded—boys and girls whose bodies are stunted due to poor nutrition—reach puberty at older ages.

A critical chemical stimulating puberty in animals—and possibly humans—is a hormone called *leptin*, which is tied to the level of body fat (Elshafie and others, 2008; Kaplowitz, 2008; Rutters and others, 2008). Underfeeding laboratory rats inhibits the concentration of leptin, keeping them in a prolonged infantile state (Parent and others, 2003). You might be interested to know that severe dieting and reaching a low level of body fat causes women to stop menstruating and ovulating, too.

adrenal androgens Hormones produced by the adrenal glands that program various aspects of puberty, such as growth of body hair, skin changes, and sexual desire.

HPG axis The main hormonal system programming puberty; it involves a triggering hypothalamic hormone that causes the pituitary to secrete its hormones, which in turn cause the ovaries and testes to develop and secrete the hormones that produce the major body changes.

gonads The sex organs—the ovaries in girls and the testes in boys.

testosterone The hormone responsible for the maturation of the organs of reproduction and other signs of puberty in men, and for hair and skin changes during puberty and for sexual desire in both sexes.

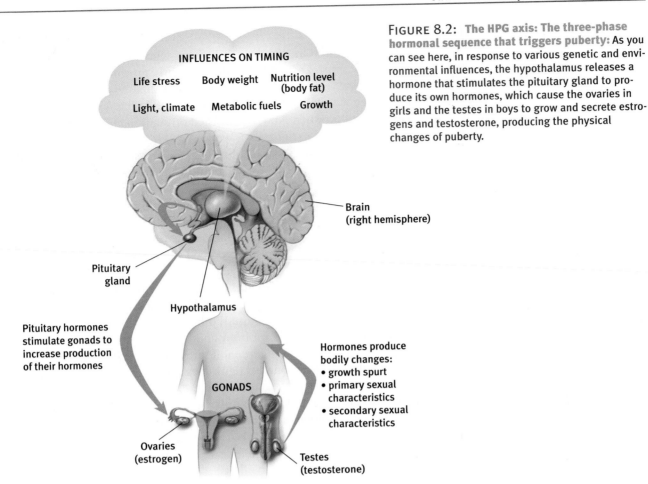

FIGURE 8.2: The HPG axis: The three-phase hormonal sequence that triggers puberty: As you can see here, in response to various genetic and environmental influences, the hypothalamus releases a hormone that stimulates the pituitary gland to produce its own hormones, which cause the ovaries in girls and the testes in boys to grow and secrete estrogens and testosterone, producing the physical changes of puberty.

Brain (right hemisphere)

Pituitary gland

Hypothalamus

Pituitary hormones stimulate gonads to increase production of their hormones

GONADS

Hormones produce bodily changes:
• growth spurt
• primary sexual characteristics
• secondary sexual characteristics

Ovaries (estrogen)

Testes (testosterone)

But in making sense of the puzzle of puberty, we need to take into account more than simply the amount of body fat. As Figure 8.2 illustrates, the hypothalamic trigger is sensitive to a variety of signals—from leptin levels, to exposure to heat and light (given comparable nutrition, children who live in warmer climates tend to reach puberty comparatively early), to environmental stress (more about this fascinating force later) (Ebling, 2005). This complexity is mirrored by the diversity of the physical changes.

The Physical Changes

Puberty causes a total *psychological* as well as physical transformation. As the hormones flood the brain, they affect the neurotransmitters, making teenagers more emotional and more interested in taking risks (as you will see in Chapter 9). Scientists divide the physical changes into three categories:

- **Primary sexual characteristics** refer to all of the body changes directly involved in reproduction. The growth of the penis and menstruation are examples of primary sexual characteristics.

- **Secondary sexual characteristics** is the label for the hundreds of other changes that accompany puberty, such as breast development, the growth of pubic hair, voice changes, and alterations in the texture of the skin.

- The **growth spurt** merits its own special category. At puberty—as should come as no surprise—there is a dramatic increase in height and weight.

Now let's offer a motion picture of these changes, first in girls and then in boys.

primary sexual characteristics Physical changes of puberty that directly involve the organs of reproduction, such as the growth of the penis and the onset of menstruation.

secondary sexual characteristics Physical changes of puberty that are not directly involved in reproduction.

growth spurt A dramatic increase in height and weight that occurs during puberty.

For Girls

As you saw with Samantha in the chapter-opening vignette, the first sign of puberty in girls is the growth spurt. During late childhood, girls' growth picks up speed, accelerates, and then a few years later begins to decrease (Abbassi, 1998). On a visit to my 11-year-old niece, I got a vivid sense of this "peak velocity" phase of growth. Six months earlier, I had towered over her. Now, she insisted on standing back-to-back to demonstrate: "Look, Aunt Janet, I'm taller than you!"

About six months after the growth spurt begins, girls start to develop breasts and pubic hair. On average, girls' breasts take about five years to grow to their adult form (Tanner, 1955, 1978).

Interestingly, menarche tends to occur relatively late in this process, in the middle to final stages of breast and pubic hair development, when girls' growth is winding down. So you can tell your 12-year-old niece, who has just begun to menstruate, that, while her breasts are still "works in progress," she is probably about as tall today as she will be as an adult.

When they reach menarche, can girls get pregnant? Yes, but there is often a window of infertility until the system fully gears up. Does puberty unfold in the same way for every girl? The answer is no. Because the hormonal signals are so complex, the timing of specific changes varies a bit from child to child. In some girls, pubic hair development (programmed by the adrenal androgens) is well underway before the breasts begin to enlarge. Occasionally, a girl does grow much taller after she begins to menstruate.

There are also fascinating differences in the *rate of change*. In following prepubescent girls in Greece, researchers found that if a child began puberty earlier, the process often took longer to unfold. Girls who developed breasts first didn't necessarily reach menarche earlier than their peers. Late beginners often went through puberty at a faster rate (Pantsiotou and others, 2008). Scientists also observe this catch-up growth—or accelerated maturation—in boys and girls whose growth has been retarded due to famine. Once children get adequate nutrition, the hormones that program development go into overdrive. It's almost as if the body is saying, "It's time to get going very fast" (Parent and others, 2003).

In tracking puberty in females, researchers focus on charting pubic hair and breast development because they can measure these external secondary sexual changes in stages. The internal changes are equally dramatic. During puberty the uterus grows, the vagina lengthens, and the hips develop a cushion of fat. The vocal cords get longer, the heart gets bigger, and the red blood cells carry more oxygen. So, in addition to looking very different after puberty, girls become much stronger (Archibald, Graber, & Brooks-Gunn, 2003). The increases in strength and stamina and height and weight are really incredible in boys.

For Boys

In boys, researchers also chart how the penis, the testicles, and pubic hair develop in distinctive stages. However, because these organs of reproduction begin developing first, boys still look like children to the outside world for at least a year or two after their bodies start changing. Voice changes, the growth of body hair, and that other clearly visible sign of being a man—needing to shave—all take place after the growth of the testes and penis are well underway (Tanner, 1978). Now, let's pause to look at perhaps the most obvious signals that a boy is becoming a man—the transformations in size, shape, and physical strength.

You may recall from Chapter 5 that, during elementary school, boys and girls are roughly the same size. Then, during the puberty growth spurt, everything changes. Males shoot up an incredible average of 8 inches, compared to 4 inches for girls (Tanner, 1978).

Because that landmark change, shaving, occurs fairly late in the sequence of puberty, we can be sure that this 14-year-old boy has been looking like a man for some time in the ways that you and I can't see.

Michael Newman/Photo Edit, Inc.

During puberty, boys also become much stronger than the opposite sex.

One reason lies in the tremendous increase in muscle mass. Another lies in the dramatic cardiovascular changes. At puberty, boys' hearts increase in weight by more than one-third. In particular, notice in Figure 8.3 that, compared to females, after puberty, males have many more red blood cells and a much greater capacity for carrying oxygen in their blood (Tanner, 1978). The visible signs of these changes are a big chest, wide shoulders, and a muscular frame. The real-world consequence is that after puberty males get a boost in gross motor skills that gives them a biological edge in everything from soccer to sprinting; from cycling to carrying heavy loads.

Do you have access to a group of seventh- or eighth-grade boys? If so, you might notice that growth during puberty takes place in the opposite pattern to the one that occurs earlier in life. Rather than following the *cephalocaudal* and *proximodistal* sequences (from the head downward and from the middle of the body outward), at puberty, the hands, feet, and legs grow first. While this happens for both sexes, because their growth is so dramatic, these changes are especially obvious in boys.

Their unusually long legs and large feet explain why, in their early teens, boys look so gawky (and unattractive!). Adding to the problem is the crackly voice produced by the growing larynx, the wispy look of beginning facial hair, and the fact that during puberty a boy's nose and ears grow before the rest of his face catches up. Plus, the increased activity of the sweat glands and enlarged pores leads to the condition that results in so much emotional agony: acne. Although girls also suffer from acne, boys are more vulnerable to this condition because testosterone, which males produce in abundance, produces changes in the hair and skin.

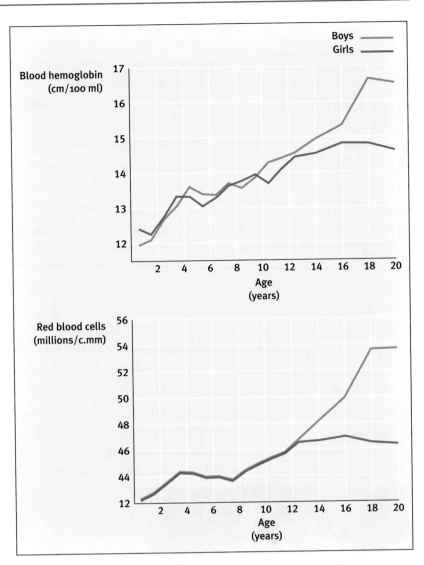

FIGURE 8.3: **Changes in blood hemoglobin and red blood cells during puberty in males and females:** At puberty, increases in the amount of hemoglobin in the blood and in the number of red blood cells cause children of both sexes to get far stronger. But notice that these changes are more pronounced in boys than in girls.

Source: Tanner (1955), p. 103.

Are Boys on a Later Timetable? A Bit

Now, visit a sixth-grade class and you will be struck by the gender difference mentioned in the chapter-opening vignette. Boys, on average, appear to reach puberty two years later than girls. But appearances can be deceiving. In girls, as I mentioned earlier, the externally visible signs of puberty, such as the growth spurt and breast development, take place toward the beginning of the sequence. For boys, the more hidden developments, such as the growth of the testes, are the first changes to occur (Huddleston & Ge, 2003).

If we look at the *real* sign of fertility, interestingly, the timetables of girls and boys are not very far apart. In one study, boys reported that spermarche occurred at an average age of roughly 13, only about six months later than the average age of menarche (Stein & Reiser, 1994).

Figure 8.4 on page 242 graphically summarizes a few of the changes I have been discussing. Now, let's explore the numbers inside the chart. Why do children undergo puberty at such different ages?

FIGURE 8.4: **The sequence of some major events of puberty:** This chart shows the ages at which some important changes of puberty occur in the average boy and girl. The numbers below each change show the range of ages at which that event begins. Notice that girls are on a slightly earlier timetable than boys, that boys' height spurt occurs at a later point in their development, and that there are dramatic differences from child to child in the timing of puberty.

Source: Adapted from Tanner (1978), pp. 23, 29.

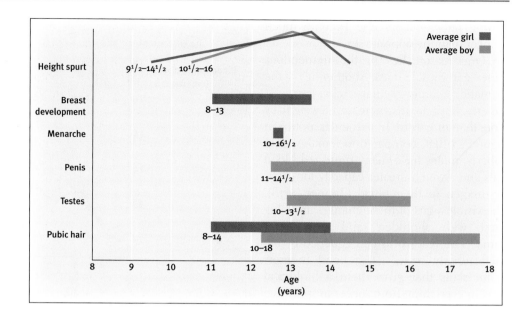

Look at female middle school friends—such as these girls getting ready for a dance—and you will be struck with the differences in puberty timetables. In this section, you will find out why children mature earlier or later than their peers.

Individual Differences in Puberty Timetables

I'm seventeen already. But I still look like a kid. I get teased a lot, especially by the other guys. . . . Girls aren't interested in me, either, because most of them are taller than I am. When will I grow up?

(adapted from an on-line chat room)

The gender difference in puberty timetables can cause anxiety. As an early-maturing girl, I vividly remember slumping to avoid the humiliation of having my partner's head encounter my chest in sixth-grade dancing class! But nature's cruelest blow may relate to the individual differences in timing. What accounts for the five-year difference in puberty timetables between children who live in the same environment (Parent and others, 2003)?

Not unexpectedly, genetics is critically important. In one twin study, researchers found that the onset of the male growth spurt (and boys' eventual adult height) was completely determined by "genetic forces" (Silventoinen and others, 2008).

There are also interesting genetic ethnic differences. Asian Americans tend to be slightly behind other U.S. children in puberty timetables (Sun and others, 2002). African American boys and girls are ahead of other North American groups (Freedman and others, 2002; Rosenfield, Lipton, & Drum, 2009). In one turn-of-the-century survey, the average African American girl reached menarche at about her twelfth birthday, a full six months earlier than the typical European American girl (Wu, Mendola, & Buck, 2002).

But remember that in impoverished African countries—where children are poorly nourished—girls begin to menstruate, on average, as late as age 16. You might also recall from Chapter 5 that, in the United States, obesity rates are skyrocketing among African American elementary school girls and boys. This brings us to an interesting question: Given that body fat is linked to the onset of puberty, does childhood "obesity" generally affect when children physically mature?

Overweight and Early Puberty

If a third grader is seriously overweight, will that child reach puberty at a younger-than-normal age? And, given that more elementary school children *are* seriously overweight today, is the secular trend in puberty continuing?

The answer to both of these questions is yes—but interestingly, the evidence is clearest for girls. Having a high BMI (body mass index) definitely predicts a female child's early entry into puberty (Adair, 2008; Kaplowitz, 2008; Rosenfield, Lipton, & Drum, 2009). Based on the conclusions of an international panel, while the data are "insufficient" for boys, the twentieth-century trend to earlier menarche that you saw in Figure 8.1 (on page 237) shows few signs of leveling off (Euling and others, 2008). Although scientists suggest that estrogen-like chemicals in food might be partly to blame, a main culprit, many experts feel, is the alarming rise in childhood body size (Buck Louis and others, 2008; Kaplowitz, 2008).

So far, it seems as if we have targeted the main lifestyle influence involved in the current secular trend in puberty: It's the obesity epidemic. But remember that the hypothalamic timer is influenced by many environmental forces. Now, let's look at the most interesting nurture force that may program puberty—our nurturing during early life.

Anxiety, Angry Parents, Absent Fathers, and Early Puberty

Drawing on an *evolutionary psychology* perspective, about two decades ago, developmentalists devised a compelling hypothesis. When family stress is intense, they argued, it would make sense to build in a mechanism to accelerate sexual maturity and free a child from the inhospitable nest (Belsky, Steinberg, & Draper, 1991; Ellis, 2004). According to this theory, an unhappy early life increases the level of stress hormones, which prompts the body to put the hypothalamic signal forward, causing a child to reach puberty at a younger age.

You may be amazed to know that this prediction has considerable support, but once again, mainly for girls. Early-maturing girls more often report unhappy childhoods (Ellis, 2004; Moffitt and others, 1992). They are more likely to recall experiencing violence from their fathers during their early years (Tither & Ellis, 2008). In one longitudinal study, while genetics was by far the most important predictor of early menarche (when a mom reached that milestone), mothers' use of power assertive techniques—yelling, shaming, rejecting—was also associated with daughters menstruating at a younger age (Belsky and others, 2007).

Another fascinating family risk factor—for both girls and boys—relates to growing up in the absence of a biological father. The presence of a stepfather doesn't alter the age of puberty much. What seems to be influential is being raised by a single mother, particularly during a child's first years of life (Bogaert, 2005; Ellis, 2004; Quinlan, 2003).

So with puberty, we can vividly see the developmental-systems principle that a variety of forces combine to influence every aspect of who we are and that all systems interrelate. This basic biological process seems sensitive to our emotional state. What happens to us, hormonally, years later may be affected by our relationships during our earliest years. And since we know that many forces set off the hypothalamic timer, the fact that mental distress might affect puberty makes excellent biological sense.

Table 8.1 summarizes these points by spelling out questions that would predict a female (and possibly male) child's chance of reaching puberty at a younger-than-average age. If you were an early maturer, how many—if any—of these forces applied to you?

TABLE 8.1: Questions to Ask to Predict an Elementary School Child's (Particularly a Female Child's) Chances of Reaching Puberty Early

1. When did this child's parents reach puberty? Ask about first menstruation for mother; voice change for father; 12 or under = early for mother; under 14 = early for father.
2. Is this child African American?
3. Is this child overweight?
4. Has this child's family life been stressful and unhappy?
5. Did this child grow up in a single-parent, mother-headed family?

Now that I've described the physical process, it's time to shift to an insider's perspective. In this next section, we explore how children feel about three classic signs of puberty—breast development, menstruation, and first ejaculation—and then look at whether it *really* matters if a boy or girl reaches puberty relatively early or late.

An Insider's View of Puberty

FIGURE 8.5: **Getting your first bra:** To measure how girls undergoing puberty feel around their parents—without asking them directly—researchers used this specially constructed card and asked children of different ages to describe what is happening and "How do the mother, the father, and the girl feel?"

Source: Brooks-Gunn and others (1994), p. 549.

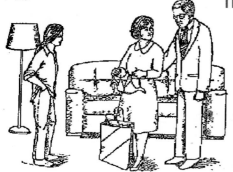

If you think back to how you felt about your changing body during puberty, you probably remember a mixture of emotions: fear, pride, embarrassment, excitement. Now, imagine how you would react if a researcher asked you to describe your inner state. Would you want to talk about how you *really* felt? The reluctance of pre-teens to discuss what is happening ("Yuck! Just don't go there!") explains why, when researchers study reactions to puberty, they often ask adults to remember this time of life. When developmentalists do explore young teenagers' feelings, they tend to use indirect measures, such as having children tell stories about pictures, to reveal their inner concerns.

The Breasts

In a classic study, researchers used this indirect strategy to explore how girls feel in relation to their parents while undergoing that most visible sign of becoming a woman—breast development (Brooks-Gunn and others, 1994). They asked a group of girls to tell a story about the characters in a drawing that showed an adult female (the mother) taking a bra out of a shopping bag while an adolescent girl and an adult male (the father) watched (see Figure 8.5). While girls often talked about the mother in the picture as being excited and happy, they typically described the teenager as humiliated by her father's presence in the room. Moreover, girls in the middle of puberty told the most negative stories about the fathers, suggesting that body embarrassment is at its height when children are actually undergoing the physical changes.

Because society strongly values this symbol of being a woman (and our contemporary culture definitely sees bigger as better!), other research suggests that U.S. girls feel proud of their developing breasts (Brooks-Gunn & Warren, 1988). However, among girls in ballet schools, where there are strong social pressures to look prepubescent, breast development evokes distress (Brooks-Gunn & Warren, 1985). The same principle—that children's reactions to puberty depend on the messages they get from the wider world—holds true for menstruation, too.

Imagine how these girls auditioning at a premier ballet academy in New York City will feel when they develop breasts and perhaps find that their womanly body shape interrupts their career dreams, and you will understand why children's reactions to puberty depend totally on their unique environment.

Chris Hondros/Getty Images

Menstruation

Think of being a Navajo girl and realizing that, when you begin to menstruate, you enter a special spiritual state. Compare this with the less-than-glowing portrait Western societies traditionally have painted about "that time of the month" (Brooks-Gunn & Ruble, 1982; Costos, Ackerman, & Paradis, 2002). From the advertisements for pills strong enough to handle *even* menstrual pain to its classic description as "the curse," it's no wonder that previous cohorts of girls approached this milestone with feelings of dread (Brooks-Gunn & Ruble, 1982).

Luckily, contemporary upper-middle-class, baby boom mothers may be trying to change these ingrained cultural scripts. When 18- to 20-year-old students at Oregon State University were asked in 2006 to write about their "first period experiences," 3 out of 4 women recalled their moms as being supportive or thrilled ("She was incredibly excited"; "She treated me like a princess"). One person wrote that, the day after she told her mother, "I saw an expensive box of chocolates and a card addressed to me. It said 'Congrats on becoming a woman'" (quoted in Lee, 2008, p. 1332).

Positive responses such as these make a difference. In contrast to the findings of earlier studies, about half of these young women described menarche as overwhelmingly positive or "no big deal." But I have to admit that negative emotions linger on. Even when they described their mothers as incredibly supportive, 1 in 3 students remembered feeling "horrified" or "disgusted" or, more likely, ambivalent—both ashamed and happy—when menarche arrived.

First Ejaculation

Daughters must confide in their mothers about menarche because this change demands specific coping techniques. Spermarche, as I mentioned earlier, is a hidden experience—one that doesn't require instructions from the outside world. Who talks to male adolescents about first ejaculation, and how do teenagers feel about their signal of becoming a man? Listen to these memories from some 18-year-olds (Stein & Reiser, 1994):

> *I woke up the next morning and my sheets were pasty. . . . After you wake up your mind is kind of happy and then you realize: "Oh my God, this is my wet dream!"*
>
> (quoted in Stein & Reiser, 1994, p. 380)

> *My mom, she knew I had them. It was all over my sheets and bedspread and stuff, but she didn't say anything, didn't tease me and stuff. She never asked if I wanted to talk about it—I'm glad. I never could have said anything to my mom.*
>
> (quoted in Stein & Reiser, 1994, p. 377)

Most of these boys reported that they needed to be secretive. They didn't want to let *anyone* know. And notice from the second quotation—as you saw earlier with fathers and pre-teen girls—that boys also view their changing bodies as especially embarrassing around the parent of the opposite sex.

Is this tendency for children to hide the symptoms of puberty around the parent of the other gender programmed into evolution to help teenagers emotionally separate from their families? We can only speculate about this interesting idea. Where we do have scientific information is on the emotional impact of being early or late.

Being Early: It Can Be a Problem for Girls

Imagine being an early-maturing girl. How would you feel if you looked like an adult while everyone else in your class still looked like a child? Now imagine being a late maturer and thinking, "What's wrong with my body? Will I *ever* grow up?"

Actually, the timing of development definitely matters, but again for girls, not boys. Study after study conducted over the last 30 years in the developed world agrees: *Early-maturing girls are vulnerable to having a host of difficulties during their adolescent years.*

As you saw with Samantha in the chapter-opening vignette, early-maturing girls often are more popular (Michael & Eccles, 2003). The bad news is that the problems attached to this popularity can outweigh the pluses.

EARLY-MATURING GIRLS ARE AT SPECIAL RISK OF DEVELOPING ACTING-OUT, EXTERNALIZING PROBLEMS. Because we select friends who are "like us," early-maturing girls tend to gravitate toward becoming friends with older girls and boys. So they may get involved in "adult activities" such as smoking and drinking at a younger age (see, for instance, Negriff, Fung, & Trickett, 2008).

Because they are so busy exploring adulthood, the result can be a disconnect from school (Archibald, Graber, & Brooks-Gunn, 2003). In one classic study, early-maturing

This 13-year-old cheerleader is getting a lot of attention from the 18-year-old football star. Unfortunately, she may be too young to assert herself and say no if they start to date and he pressures her to have sex.

girls tended to get worse grades than their classmates in the sixth and seventh grades (Simmons & Blyth, 1987). Once set in motion, this poor performance can be difficult to reverse. In another classic longitudinal study, by their twenties, early-maturing girls were several times less likely to have graduated from high school than their later-developing peers (Stattin & Magnusson, 1990).

Then, there is the main concern with having a mature body early on: having unprotected sex. Because they may not have the cognitive abilities to resist this social pressure and often have older boyfriends, early-maturing girls are more likely to have intercourse at a younger age (Golub and others, 2008). They are less likely to use contraception, making them more vulnerable to becoming pregnant as teens (Ellis, 2004). How would you feel if you were a sixth- or seventh-grade girl being pursued by high school boys? Would you have the presence of mind to "just say no"?

EARLY-MATURING GIRLS ARE AT SPECIAL RISK OF GETTING ANXIOUS AND DEPRESSED. As if this were not enough, early-maturing girls are also more prone to feel bad about themselves (Kaltiala-Heino, Kosunen, & Rimpela, 2003). In particular, they are vulnerable to being dissatisfied about their weight (Ge and others, 2001). The reason is that early-maturing girls tend not only to be heavier when they approach puberty, but also may end up being shorter because their height spurt occurs at an earlier point in their development than that of other girls (Adair, 2008; Must and others, 2005). Late-maturing girls feel better about their bodies because they are more likely to fit the ultra-slim model shape. Maturing early sets girls up for a poor body image and low self-esteem.

So far, I've been painting a dismal portrait of early-maturing girls. But, as with any aspect of development, it's important to look at the whole context of a person's life. Early maturation is less likely to produce problems for African American girls (Mrug and others, 2008). As I mentioned in Chapter 5, African American girls may be more comfortable about their blossoming shape because they have a healthier, more inclusive idea about body size (more about this later).

Moreover, these negative effects happen only when girls enter the high-risk setting of dating and having older friends (Stattin & Magnusson, 1990). If a girl attends a single-sex school, has strong family or religious values, or, unlike Samantha in the vignette, stays close to her elementary school friends, her puberty timetable will not matter.

Another fascinating influence that affects children's chances of getting into trouble relates to the educational structure of their town. In another classic study exploring puberty, developmentalists traced the lives of two groups of pre-teens in Milwaukee: boys and girls in school districts with separate junior high schools (what we now call middle school) and those who attended a K–8 (kindergarten through eighth grade) school (Simmons & Blyth, 1987).

You might think that the early-maturing girls in K–8 schools would have more problems because they look so different from everyone else. You would be wrong. Girls who transferred to a junior high school had more troubles. In fact, for *every child* who moved to the larger, more anonymous junior high, academic performance tended to decline and self-confidence typically became shakier. Therefore, many of the problems that seem to be basic to reaching puberty, such as getting more anxious or becoming less interested in academics, may be in part a function of changing schools.

Wrapping Up Puberty

Now, let's summarize the messages of our discussion:

- **Children's reactions to puberty depend on the environment in which they physically mature.** Negative feelings are more likely to occur when society looks down on a given sign of development (as with menstruation) or when the physical changes are not valued in a person's particular group (as with breast development in ballerinas). Changing schools during puberty magnifies the stress of the body changes (Eccles & Midgley, 1989; Eccles & Roeser, 2003).

- **With early-maturing girls, we need to take special care to arrange the right body–environment fit.** While having an adult body at a young age can be dangerous for girls, wider-world influences, such as staying in the same school from kindergarten through eighth grade, can reduce the tendency for early-maturing girls to get into trouble as teens.

- **Communication about puberty can be improved—especially for boys.** While many contemporary moms may be doing a fine job discussing menstruation with their daughters, boys, in particular, seem to enter puberty without any guidance about what to expect (Omar, McElderry, & Zakharia, 2003).

`INTERVENTIONS:` Minimizing Puberty Distress

Given these findings, what are the lessons for parents? What changes should society make?

LESSONS FOR PARENTS. It's tempting for parents to avoid thoroughly discussing puberty because children are so sensitive about their changing bodies. This reluctance is a mistake. Developmentalists urge parents to make an effort to discuss what is happening with a same-sex child. They advise beginning these discussions when the child is at an age when talking is emotionally easier, before the actual changes take place. Fathers, in particular, need to make special efforts to talk about puberty with their sons (Graber, Petersen, & Brooks-Gunn, 1996; Paikoff & Brooks-Gunn, 1991).

Finally, parents with an early-maturing daughter need to be alert to potential "acting-out problems" and poor self-esteem. They should make special efforts to get their child involved in positive activities, especially with friends her own age and, possibly, to switch their pre-teen to a more nurturing K–8 school.

LESSONS FOR SOCIETY. This brings up the influence of the wider environment. Should we move *any* child to a large middle school during a time of intense bodily change? (See Eccles & Roeser, 2003.) If we cannot switch to K–8 school systems, at a minimum, we should try to make middle schools more intimate, perhaps by having schools within a school, in which groups of students attend all their classes together in separate, cozy units.

We also need to provide adequate education about puberty. However, if you think back to what you personally wanted to know about your changing body ("My breasts don't look right"; "My penis has a strange shape"), you will realize that simply laying out biological facts is not enough. In one turn-of-the-century U.S. survey, adolescents reported that they got their first formal education about puberty at around age 13, or even 15 (Omar, McElderry, & Zakharia, 2003)—*after* the changes had taken place. (That's like locking the barn door after the horses have been stolen!) Sex education

It is extremely difficult for children who are in the midst of puberty to adjust to a huge middle school like this one—having to make new friends, being a small fish in a sea of unfamiliar faces. This is why most developmentalists believe that during the prime puberty years, children should ideally attend smaller K—8 schools.

David Frazier/Photo Edit

classes in the United States focus heavily on what not to do, telling teenagers, "Don't have intercourse," and emphasizing the hazards of teen pregnancy (Guttmacher Institute, 2007). Suppose our society really *celebrated* puberty, as the Navajo do? Perhaps this might start us on a revolution where we celebrated every body size.

 TYING IT ALL TOGETHER

1. Reading about traditional puberty rites, Luis thinks that they sound like an awesome idea but that they wouldn't make much sense in the twenty-first century. What is the *main* reason why our culture would find it difficult to celebrate puberty today?

2. You notice that your 11-year-old cousin is going from looking like a child to looking like a young woman. (a) Outline the three-phase hormonal sequence that is setting off the physical changes; (b) name the three classes of hormones involved in puberty; (c) identify which change is happening first.

3. Both Kendra and Anthony are 12 years old. Kendra recently shot up in height and is just beginning to develop breasts. Anthony still looks physically like a child. Statistically speaking, you can predict that Kendra [is already menstruating/is not yet menstruating] and that Anthony [has not yet reached puberty/may or may not have reached puberty].

4. All of the following facts about Brianna suggest that she may be on an earlier puberty timetable *except*:

   a. She is African American.
   b. She experienced "harsh," rejecting parenting.
   c. Her mother was an early maturer.
   d. She is a dancer and she is very thin.

5. Which girl is at highest risk for getting into trouble (e.g., with drugs, academics, or having unprotected sex) as a teen?

   a. Kimberly, who matured early and goes to the local middle school
   b. Jennifer, who matured early and goes to an all-girls school
   c. Melanie, who matured late and goes to a K–8 school

6. You are on a national advisory committee charged with developing programs to help children deal better with the changes of puberty. On the basis of what you've read in this chapter, what recommendations might you make?

Answers to the Tying It All Together questions can be found on the last page of the chapter.

Body Image Issues

What do you daydream about?
Being skinny.

—Amanda (quoted in Martin, 1996, p. 36)

Puberty is a time of intense physical preoccupations, and there is hardly a teenager who isn't concerned about some body part. How important is it for young people to be *generally* satisfied with how they look?

Consider this finding: Susan Harter (1999) explored how feeling competent in each of five dimensions—scholastic abilities, conduct, athletic skills, peer likeability, and appearance (see Chapter 6)—related to teenagers' overall self-esteem. She found that being happy about one's looks far outweighed *anything else* in determining whether adolescents generally felt good about themselves. This finding is not just true of teenagers in the United States. It appears in surveys that Harter and her colleagues have conducted in a variety of Western countries among people at various stages of life. If we are happy with the way we look, we are almost certain to be happy with who we are as human beings.

Feeling physically appealing is centrally important to everyone. But given the premium society puts on female beauty, girls (no surprise) are more likely than boys to

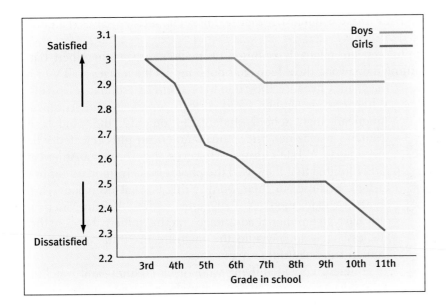

FIGURE 8.6: **Satisfaction with physical appearance among boys and girls in the third through the eleventh grade:** Girls feel increasingly dissatisfied with their physical appearance as they get older. Boys feel just about as self-assured in high school as they were in third grade.

Source: Harter (1999), p. 163.

Exactly when did our culture develop the idea that women should be unrealistically thin? Historians trace this change to the 1960s and 1970s, when extremely slim actresses like Audrey Hepburn became our cultural ideal.

feel unhappy with their looks. As Figure 8.6 shows, this gender gap in satisfaction widens grade by grade as children travel through adolescence. Also, notice that the gender split begins well before puberty, during elementary school, when children reach concrete operations and begin to compare themselves to their peers.

Still, while this tendency for women to be more critical of their appearance may be ageless, one reason that females today are at high risk for low self-esteem is that, especially in Western cultures, we expect women to be abnormally thin. For this reason, let's now turn specifically to look at worries about weight (and body shape) in girls and boys.

Exploring the Concerns

Puberty sets off a dieting epidemic among females in the Western world. Surveys show that roughly 1 out of every 2 U.S. teenage girls is actively trying to lose weight (Ricciardelli & McCabe, 2004). Although boys also worry about being too heavy, males may have another concern: They want to build their muscles up—spending hours at the gym, sometimes using protein powders and anabolic steroids to increase their body mass (Field and others, 2005; McCabe & Ricciardelli, 2005).

These preoccupations may be promoted in part by biological forces. As you will see in the next chapter, the hormones of puberty make children intensely self-conscious. A variety of environmental influences, however, are also involved. Teenagers become more interested in dieting when they start dating. Another force that sets off the obsession to diet is peer pressure: feeling "my friends will like me more if I lose weight" (Meyer and Gast, 2008); getting teased about one's body size ("Ha ha. You are really getting fat!") (Compian, Gowen, & Hayward, 2004; Jackson & Chen, 2008).

Especially influential culprits are the media. In several experiments, researchers showed teenagers advertisements featuring fashion models. Compared to control groups who watched other kinds of ads, girls and boys who saw the models were more dissatisfied with their body shape (Baird & Grieve, 2006; Hargreaves & Tiggemann, 2003). So *both* genders are vulnerable to feeling bad about themselves when they are exposed to unrealistic media images of how people should look.

The fat mania still hits females far harder. However, unfortunately, body-oriented pressures on men seem to be on the rise. In examining past issues of *Sports Illustrated*, researchers found a recent trend to more male photos highlighting appearance (those Abercrombie and Fitch ads are a good example). This increased emphasis on the body-as-external-object takes a toll. When boys see body-oriented advertisements targeting performance-oriented qualities such as "how to increase your energy"—versus ads

During puberty, children of both sexes get attuned to every facial flaw. But unlike girls who are focused on being super thin, teenage boys often spend time building up their muscles.

discussing strategies to "make better abs"—they feel better about themselves (Farquhar & Wasylkiw, 2007).

Still, some children are relatively immune to media messages. In Albert Bandura's social learning framework, these teenagers don't model the images on TV or in magazines because they don't see them as "similar to myself." When one researcher asked African American and European American high school students to describe the models in women's magazines, the African American girls rejected what they saw as "White culture." However, the European American girls admitted that they used the photos as their standard for how to look because, in their words, "this is what everybody cares about" (Milkie, 1999). As I suggested earlier, African American girls have an emotional advantage entering puberty because they are less likely to buy into the mainstream "thin" ideal. Black women feel beautiful at many sizes!

Because most African Americans don't buy into the idea that the key to beauty lies in being slim, they can be joyous and comfortable with bodies that come in many sizes.

Interestingly, identifying with Black culture—and watching its media—may inoculate a female teenager against being unhappy with her shape. In a longitudinal study conducted with Latina girls, teens who reported watching mainly mainstream TV felt worse about their bodies as time went on. Girls who said they frequently watched Black-oriented programs did not show *any* drop in physical self-worth (Schooler, 2008).

In cultures that appreciate ample-sized females, rates of eating disorders are far lower than in the West. So the negative impact of globalization—transporting the Western "thin" ideal around the world—may be a universal increase in these serious diseases (Striegel-Moore & Bulik, 2007). What exactly *are* eating disorders like?

Eating Disorders

Ten lbs a week! You can do it! I know you can. Just make a plan…like at the beginning of the week, of what you'll allow yourself to eat that day.

Scales are evil! But I'm obsessed with them! I'm on the damn thing like 3 times a day!

(Gavin, Rodham, & Poyer, 2008, pp. 327–328)

As these quotations from a "pro-anorexia" chat room suggest, **eating disorders** differ qualitatively from "normal" dieting. Here, being thin is the *sole* focus of life. Imagine waking up and planning each day around eating (or not eating). You monitor every morsel. You are hyper-alert to images relating to food or body shape (Smeets and others, 2008). Let's now look at two classic forms this total obsession can take: anorexia and bulimia.

eating disorder A pathological obsession with getting and staying thin. The two best-known eating disorders are *anorexia nervosa* and *bulimia nervosa.*

anorexia nervosa A potentially life-threatening eating disorder characterized by pathological dieting (resulting in severe weight loss and extreme thinness) and by a distorted body image.

Anorexia nervosa, the most serious eating disorder, affects roughly 1 in 1000 teenagers, the vast majority of whom are girls. To qualify for this diagnosis, a person must have starved to the point of being 85 percent of ideal body weight or less. (This means that if your ideal weight for your height is 110 pounds, you now weigh *less than* 95 pounds [American Academy of Pediatrics, Committee on Adolescence, 2003].) Another basic feature of this disorder—among both girls and boys—is a distorted body image (Striegel-Moore & Bulik, 2007). Even when people look skeletal, they feel fat and are driven to cut their food intake down to virtually nothing. A child with anorexia may consume a single pea for lunch, misuse laxatives, and continuously exercise.

Anorexia is a dangerous, life-threatening disease—with a mortality rate of roughly 5 percent (Chavez & Insel, 2007). When a person reaches two-thirds of her ideal weight or less, that's a signal the child needs to be hospitalized and fed—intravenously, if necessary—to stave off death (Diamanti and others, 2008). A student of mine who runs a self-help group for people with eating disorders at our university provided a vivid reminder of the enduring physical toll anorexia can cause. Alicia informed the class that she had permanently damaged her heart muscle during her teenage bout with this devastating disease.

Bulimia nervosa is typically not as life-threatening because the person's weight often stays within a normal range. However, because this disorder involves bingeing (periodic eating sprees in which thousands of calories may be consumed in a matter of hours) and either purging (getting rid of the food by inducing vomiting) and/or fasting, bulimia can seriously compromise health. In addition to producing deficiencies of basic nutrients, the purging episodes can cause mouth sores, ulcers in the esophagus, and the loss of enamel in the teeth due to the throat and mouth being exposed to stomach acid (American Academy of Pediatrics, Committee on Adolescence, 2003).

Because of their higher prevalence among upper-middle-class females, psychoanalytic theorists typically viewed the search for perfection and anger at authority figures as the root of anorexia and bulimia. Bombarded by pressures to be perfect, they reasoned, the girl unconsciously gets back at her parents by choosing to be "perfect" at controlling her weight (Muuss, 1986). Now, we know that there is a strong hereditary component to developing eating disorders, especially in girls (Striegel-Moore & Bulik, 2007).

This does not rule out a nature-plus-nurture combination, however. Girls who develop eating disorders often report having mothers who are critical, disapproving, and micromanage their lives (Blodgett Salafia and others, 2007). When a susceptible girl has a rejecting, nagging mother ("What are you doing? You messed up again!"), this produces intense distress, feelings of incompetence, and ultimately the sense that, "The only way I can control my life is to control my weight" (Cooley and others, 2008; Meno and others, 2008; Perry and others, 2008; see Figure 8.7).

At bottom, therefore, eating disorders reflect more than problems with eating. They are a symptom of a general temperamental tendency to feel anxious and depressed (Johnson & Wardle, 2005). Studies show that elementary-school girls who go on to develop eating disorders as teenagers are prone to making negative comparisons: "I'm less popular, less good-looking than so-and-so" (Ricciardelli & McCabe, 2004; Stice & Whitenton, 2002). At the core of any eating disorder lies low *self-efficacy*—a sense of being helpless and generally out of control of one's life. (See my interview with the women's center counselor in the Experiencing the Lifespan box on page 252.)

But for readers who know a young person who is struggling with this affliction, there is upbeat news: One 20-year-long study suggested that most adolescents grow out of eating problems as they age (Keel and others, 2007). Marriage, parenting, and grappling with the challenges of adult life tend to lessen the fixation on thinness that is a toxic by-product of living in today's body-obsessed culture.

bulimia nervosa An eating disorder characterized by cycles of bingeing and purging (by inducing vomiting or taking laxatives) in an obsessive attempt to lose weight.

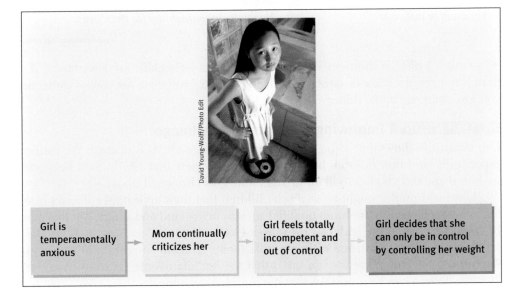

David Young-Wolff/Photo Edit

| Girl is temperamentally anxious | → | Mom continually criticizes her | → | Girl feels totally incompetent and out of control | → | Girl decides that she can only be in control by controlling her weight |

FIGURE 8.7: **A possible pathway to developing an eating disorder.**

Now that we know the diagnostic categories and risk factors for eating disorders, it's time to get an insider's perspective. Here is what Mary, a counselor at my university's women's center, told me when we sat down to chat about her clients with eating disorders:

With eating disorders, denial is big. A lot of times, people won't bring their problem in as the issue that troubles them but, after talking for a while, they finally feel comfortable enough to say that they abuse laxatives or exercise incessantly. Sometimes a person talks seemingly innocently and I'm thinking: "Hmm, sounds like you have an eating disorder."

You won't find it in the standard diagnostic criteria, but to me the key is, "Is this person's self-worth defined by how much she weighs?" Also, with eating disorders the whole day focuses around what the person is going to eat. Because secrecy is involved, a fair amount of planning goes into a binge. A person might go to the drive-through at six fast food restaurants to hide the fact that she is buying six meals that she will eat right now.

So there's the obsession about obtaining the food, the obsession about what the food is going to be, and the obsession about weight. Gaining half a pound becomes a crisis. Losing half a pound makes the person's day. People often have a magic number where everything in life is going to fall into place. Sometimes I get a call from a client who says, "I always thought if I weighed such-and-such everything would be OK." Then they do a reality check and say, "I think I need help."

It's a progressive disease. You start out bingeing and purging once every few weeks. Somebody who is pretty well into the illness will be doing it several days a week. A good day is when you fight the urge. A bad day is when you skip class or put your

At this clinic in Florida, teenagers and women with eating disorders participate in group therapy to learn how to cope with their anxiety and reduce the feelings of low self-efficacy that are at the root of their debilitating symptoms.

kid at the babysitter so you can binge and purge all day. Every case is individual, but I feel at the core of all eating disorders is the sense that "I'm not good enough." I frequently find people have controlling parents who don't let them make decisions, telling them exactly what to wear, exactly what to eat: "You have to make 'our family' look good, get the highest grades, be in such-and-such activity." You are not allowed to have problems. "Everything's OK in this family." These are people who are used to being controlled by everyone—parents, boyfriends. They don't have the concept of directing their life. They come in saying, "I hate to take up your time but my boyfriend wants me to be here."

My goal is to have them take control of their life. We work on self-esteem issues, a sense of having value. Most people are more than willing to talk about how worthless a person they are. So that's my opening. It's a slow process. The most gratifying experience is seeing people grow, become assertive, take responsibility for their lives.

Table 8.2 offers a summary of these influences in a checklist for determining if a person has serious body dissatisfaction. If these forces ring true for you or someone you love, here are a few strategies that might help.

INTERVENTIONS: Improving Teenagers' Body Image

Our discussion shows that some dissatisfaction with one's body is normal. We cannot expect girls (and now boys) to be immune from a society that asks human beings to try to reshape their bodies to fit an unattainable goal (Brownell, 1991).

Our first impulse might be to teach children that their appearance doesn't matter. What really counts are inner qualities such as being kind and smart. But this may be impossible when the wider world is saying otherwise, and, as you saw from Harter's research, feeling satisfied with our looks looms critically important in determining our self-esteem. What we can say is that the "standards" are far from objective. How we behave can be crucial in shaping our physical appeal.

TABLE 8.2: Is a Teenager at Risk for Serious Body Dissatisfaction? A Checklist

(Background influences: Has this child reached puberty? Is this child female, European American, upper-middle class, and dating?)

1. Is this child becoming obsessed with dieting (or, if male, becoming obsessed with building up his muscles)?

2. Has this child been teased about weight by friends?

3. Does this child obsessively read fashion magazines (or if male, "body-centered" male magazines)?

4. Is this child temperamentally prone to anxiety and depression, low self-efficacy, and self-esteem?

5. If female, does this teen have a micromanaging mother who expects her to "act perfect"?

Consider this study exploring physical attractiveness in a preschool class (Hawley and others, 2007). Raters, who had never met the class, first ranked each child's looks from photographs. Then, the children's teachers made the same ratings. Amazingly, there was no relationship between the two assessments. Children who teachers judged as the best looking turned out to be the class leaders—the boys and girls who had superior social skills. So the actual shape of our nose or the size of our body may matter less to beauty than we think. Our personality, as it shines forth in action, weighs heavily in how other people see our looks!

How can we convince teenagers (or anyone else) that who we are as people can determine how attractive we appear? The good news is that many boys and girls intuitively grasp this idea. When Harter (1999) surveyed a group of teenagers about how they viewed the connection between looks and self-esteem, about 60 percent said they believed that the external image shaped their feelings: "When I look in the mirror and don't like what I see, I feel bad about myself." The other 40 percent said: "When I am feeling upset and look in the mirror, I don't like the way I look." Teenagers who adopted the idea that there is an "objective image" out there were much more likely to feel vulnerable and unhappy with their appearance. Those who understood that their feelings about themselves determined what they (and others) saw were more upbeat about both their looks and their lives.

This finding may explain why programs designed to prevent adolescent eating disorders that use hands-on exercises to teach children the message that "I am in control of my own beauty" tend to be particularly effective. It's especially important to inoculate girls against the media images that equate beauty with being pencil thin and to give teens a sense of self-efficacy about their own ability to determine how they look (Stice and others, 2008). This need to empower children of *both* sexes to resist outside pressures also looms large as we turn now to the final topic in this chapter, sexuality.

TYING IT ALL TOGETHER

1. Kimberly, an eleventh grader, tells you, "I am ugly," but knows she is terrific in sports and academics. According to Harter's studies, is Kimberly likely to have high or low self-esteem?

2. Daniel works out at the gym, trying to build up his muscle mass. Amy is regularly on a diet, trying for that Barbie doll figure. Jasmine, who is far below her ideal body weight, is always exercising and has cut her food intake down to virtually nothing. Sophia, whose weight is normal, goes on periodic eating sprees followed by purges. Identify which *two* of these teenagers have a genuine eating disorder, and name each person's specific problem.

3. Your teenage daughter says, "Mom, I look in the mirror and think I'm fat and ugly." According to this chapter, what should your response be?

   a. "Looks don't matter—you've got brains and you're a good person, and those are the things that really count."

    b. "It's all in your power. If you feel good about yourself as a person, you'll feel like you look good, and other people will probably see you as attractive."

    c. "It's all in your power. Just lose all that extra weight and you'll look great!"

4. You are an adolescent specialist interested in setting up a prevention program for teens at risk of developing eating disorders. Devise a checklist to identify people who would be most likely to benefit from your program.

Answers to the Tying It All Together questions can be found on the last page of this chapter.

Sexuality

548: Immculate ros: Sex sex sex that all you think about?

559: Snowbunny: people who have sex at 16 r sick:

560: Twonky: I agree

564: ooooCaFfEinNe; no sex until ur happily married—Thtz muh rule

566: Twonky: I agree with that too.

567: Snowbunny: me too caffine!

(quoted in Subrahmanyam, Greenfield, & Tynes, 2004, p. 658)

Sex is the elephant in the room of teenage life. Everyone knows it's a top-ranking issue, but the adult world shies away from even mentioning it. Celebrated in the media, ignored (or condemned) by society, the minefield issue of when and whether to have sex is left for teenagers to decide on their own as they filter through the intense conflicting messages and—as you can see above—vigorously stake out their positions in on-line chats.

    It is a minefield issue that contemporary young people negotiate in different ways. Take a poll of your classmates. Some people, as with the teenagers quoted above, may advocate abstinence, believing that everyone should remain a virgin until marriage. Others are likely to believe that having sex within a loving relationship is fine. Some students, if they are being honest, will admit, "I want to try out the sexual possibilities, but I promise to use contraception!"

    This increasing acceptability (within limits) of carving out our own sexual path was highlighted in a survey polling sexual attitudes of the seniors at a U.S. high school in 1950, 1972, and 2000 (Caron & Moskey, 2002). Over the years, as you might imagine, the number of seniors who decided "It's okay for teenagers to have sex" shot up from a minority to more than 70 percent. But at the turn-of-the-century poll, more teens than ever agreed with the idea that a person could decide to *not* have sex and still be popular. The majority of students felt confident they would always use birth control when they were sexually active, and could resist the pressure from romantic partners and wait to have intercourse until they got married—if they desired. How are these encouraging attitudes being translated into action? Let's begin our exploration of teenage sexual practices in the United States at the starting gate—with desire.

Exploring Sexual Desire

> *David, age 14: Since a year or so ago, I just think about sex and masturbation ALL THE TIME! I mean I just think about having sex no matter where I am and I'm aroused all the time. Is that normal?*
>
> *Expert's reply: Welcome to the raging hormones of adolescence!*

(adapted from a teenage sexuality on-line advice forum)

At what age does sexual desire begin? Although scientists had long assumed that the answer was probably in the middle of puberty, when testosterone is pumping through the body, research with homosexual adults caused them to rethink this idea. When gay women and men were asked to recall a watershed event in their lives—the age when they first realized that they were physically attracted to a person of the same sex—their responses centered around age 10. At that age the output of the adrenal androgens is rising but testosterone production has not yet fully geared up (McClintock & Herdt, 1996). So our first sexual feelings seem to be programmed by the adrenal androgens and appear well before we undergo the visible changes of puberty, by about fourth grade!

How do sex hormone levels relate to the intensity of teenagers' sexual interests? According to researchers, we need a threshold androgen level to prime our initial feelings of sexual desire (Udry, 1990; Udry & Campbell, 1994). Then, signals from the environment feed back to heighten the interest in sex. As children see their bodies changing, they begin to think of themselves in a new, sexual way. Reaching puberty evokes a different set of signals from the outside world. A ninth-grade boy finds love notes in his locker. A seventh-grade girl notices men looking at her differently as she walks down the street. It is the physical changes of puberty and how outsiders react to those changes that usher us fully into our lives as sexual human beings. Now, let's look directly at which young people begin to act on those desires by having intercourse as teens.

Being ogled and eyed by men as you walk down the street—these experiences help stimulate androgen production and cause intense feelings of sexual desire.

Who Is Having Intercourse?

Today, the average age of first intercourse in the United States is the late teens (Zimmer-Gembeck & Helfand, 2008). But about 1 out of 7 teenagers has made their "sexual debut" by age 15 (Guttmacher Institute, Facts on American Teens' Sexual and Reproductive Health, 2007).

As developmental systems theory suggests, a variety of forces predict what researchers call the *transition to intercourse*. One influence, for both boys and girls, is biological—being on an earlier puberty timetable. There's also a U.S. social class and ethnic difference, with low-SES children and African American boys, on average, becoming sexually active at younger ages (Zimmer-Gembeck & Helfand, 2008). There also may be an interesting intergenerational family effect. In one study, young teens who were sexually active had mothers and even grandmothers who were more likely to get pregnant during their teens (Johnson & Tyler, 2007). So, sexually speaking, girls sometimes model what their mothers and grandmothers do.

This brings up the crucial role of peer-modeling. As I suggested earlier in our discussion of early-maturing girls, we can predict a teenager's—particularly a female teenager's—chance of having intercourse by looking at the company she chooses. Having an older boyfriend, or girlfriend (no surprise), dramatically raises the chance of becoming sexually active (Marin and others, 2006). In one classic study, developmentalists discovered that if a virgin girl's two best friends were nonvirgins, they could predict that the girl would have made the transition to intercourse within the next

To learn whether their daughters are sexually active, parents might try to find out about the sexual activities of these best friends. Knowing that your daughter has an older boyfriend can also alert a parent to the fact that her child may be in the danger zone.

Spencer Grant/Photo Edit

The image of this girl gleefully reading the sex-laden articles in *Cosmo* may be a tip-off that she is poised to make the transition to intercourse.

year (Billy & Udry, 1985). So to understand whether your daughter has become sexually active, look to the behaviors of her social group.

You also might want to look at what your child watches on TV. In one fascinating study, researchers were able to predict which virgin boys and girls were likely to become sexually active from looking at their prior TV watching practices. Teens who reported watching a heavy diet of programs rated high in sexually oriented talk were twice as likely to have intercourse in the intervening year as the children who did not (Collins and others, 2004).

Since a remarkable eighty percent of TV programs feature sexual innuendos (Grule and others, 2008), we might predict that simply watching a good deal of TV would promote the transition to intercourse. We would be wrong. In another study following more than a thousand U.S. teens, researchers discovered that (contrary to their predictions) extremely frequent TV viewing was related to a lower risk of having sex (Grule and others, 2008)! With any media, it's the content that matters—whether a child watches sexually explicit cable channels (Bersamin and others, 2008), gravitates to Internet porn, or avidly consumes adult magazines like *Cosmo* rather than sticking to *Seventeen* (Walsh, 2008).

Should we blame *Cosmo* reports such as "101 Ways to Drive Him Wild in Bed" for *causing* teenagers to start having sex? A bidirectional influence is probably in operation here. If a teenager is *already* very interested in sex, that boy or girl will gravitate toward media that fit this passion. For me, the tip-off was raiding my parents' library to read the steamy scenes in that forbidden book, D.H. Lawrence's *Lady Chatterley's Lover*. Today, parents know that their daughter has entered a different mental space when she abandons the Discovery Channel in favor of *Sex and the City* DVDs. (For boys, it's when your passion shifts from playing Internet games to watching Internet porn.) Swimming in this sea of media sex would then naturally further inflame a teenager's desires.

Who Are Teens Having Intercourse With?

Internet pornography celebrates anonymous sex. Many intercourse episodes on TV involve one-night stands (Grule and others, 2008). Are children imitating these kinds of models when they actually start having intercourse? With roughly 3 in 4 U.S teens reporting they first had sex with a steady dating partner, the encouraging answer is no (Child Trends fact sheet, 2008). But as about 1 in 2 sexually active teens also report having intercourse outside of a committed relationship, let's pause to look briefly at what these non-romantic encounters are like.

Do teens who have intercourse with a person they are not dating hook up with strangers, or have sex with a good friend? For answers, we have a rare interview study in which researchers asked high schoolers in Ohio about their experiences with "non-committed" sex (Manning, Giordano, & Longmore, 2006).

As it turns out, of the teens who admitted to a non-romantic sexual encounter, 3 out of 4 reported that their partner was a person they knew very well. One boy described the day he and his best friend decided it was "time" to lose their virginity in these words: "It's like I wouldn't really consider dating her … but I've known her so long … anytime I feel down or she feels down, we just talk to each other" (quoted in Manning, Giordano, & Longmore, 2006, p. 469). Sometimes, the goal of having sex was to change a friendship to a romance: "After we started sleeping together … having a relationship came up." Or, a teenager might fall into having sex with an ex-boyfriend or girlfriend: "Well, it (sex) kind of happened like towards the end when we were both friends" (quoted in Manning, Giordano, & Longmore, 2006, p. 470).

So far, I have painted a relatively benign portrait of these more casual "friends with benefits" experiences. Wrong! For teenage girls, engaging in non-committed sex—especially with a number of partners—is a serious risk factor for getting depressed. But in one study, boys who said they had a good deal of casual sex reported high self-esteem (Grello, Welsh, & Harper, 2006)! This brings me to that interesting topic: the supposedly clashing sexual agendas of women and men.

FOCUS ON A TOPIC: THE SEXUAL DOUBLE STANDARD

It's different for boys, it's like . . . if they have sex with somebody and then they are rewarded . . . and all the guys are just like "That's great!" You have sex, and you're a girl and it's like "Slut." That's how it is . . .

(quoted in Martin, 1996, p. 86)

These complaints from a 16-year-old girl named Erin refer to the well-known **sexual double standard**. Boys are expected to want sex; girls are supposed to resist. Teenage boys get considerable reinforcement for "getting to home base." Intercourse is fraught with ambivalence and danger for girls: "Should I do it? Will he love me if I do it? Will he love me if I don't? Will I get pregnant? What will my friends and my parents think?"

Is it really the case, then, that teenage boys are more likely to be having sex than teenage girls? If we look at the statistics for U.S. European Americans, the reverse is true. Actually, more girls (45 percent) report having had sex by their senior year than boys (41 percent) (Child Trends fact sheet, 2008)! The fact that a majority of European American males in the United States are still virgins by age 17 suggests that there is something wrong with seeing teenage boys as simply passionate to have sex.

Basic to the stereotype of the double standard is the idea that girls are looking for committed relationships and that boys mainly want sex. A rare study in which researchers actually interviewed an ethnically mixed group of boys undergoing puberty about their attitudes came to a different conclusion (Tolman and others, 2004). Many of these eighth graders said that they wanted a girlfriend for the emotional connection. They were yearning for the kind of intimate relationship they could not get with their male friends. Read what one 13-year-old named Skater had to say:

Eric Glenn/Getty Images

> [I want] Someone with the same interests as me. . . . Not just like [a] makeout body, you know . . . , like you don't just hang around them to make out, you just hang around them like regular friends. . . . [And then he added that this relationship would be different] 'cause it would feel more open . . . we'd feel closer.

(quoted in Tolman and others, 2004, p. 240)

Here is how another 13-year-old boy named Boo talked about his girlfriend of about a year:

> She's, like, one of the few people that actually like cares about me . . . I'm more able to tell her things. . . . Like, other people, like my other friends, they would just be, like, whatever, go away or I'll see you next week. [And then he added] I'd be lost [if we broke up].

(quoted in Tolman and others, 2004, p. 240)

The boys in this study stressed the importance of needing to act macho when they were around their male friends. (Several mentioned that it was important to show that they wanted to "get some" in order to prove that they were not gay.) But they also expressed considerable ambivalence about just having sex.

And it's not just girls who feel bad when external pressures lead them to compromise their inner selves. One 13-year-old described his first French kiss (in a game of kiss or dare at a party) as "terrible, disgusting and nasty, 'cause like I didn't really want to. . . . It was like a big rip-off. . . [He pauses.] In a way, that's just, like, rude to myself" (quoted in Tolman and others, 2004, p. 246).

Yes, in surveys, teenage boys report having sex as a higher priority in their relationships than do girls. But both teenage boys and girls put their highest priority on intimacy (Ott and others, 2006). It's really all about attachment and love—not just about raging hormones—for *both* sexes during the adolescent years.

Are male teenagers intensely interested in caring and closeness? The adoring expressions on the faces of this couple tell us that adolescent boys' love relationships involve far more than just physical desire.

sexual double standard A cultural code that gives men greater sexual freedom than women. Specifically, society expects males to want to have intercourse and expects females to remain virgins until they marry and to be more interested in relationships than in having sex.

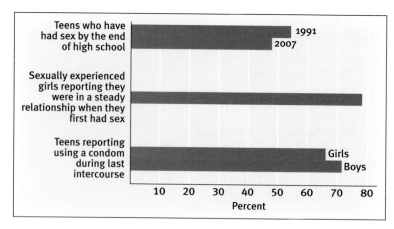

Wrapping Up Sexuality: Contemporary Trends

In summary, teenagers today feel more comfortable about charting their own sexual path. Most sexual encounters occur in committed relationships. Boys are primarily interested in love, not "just having sex." These changes are mirrored in the encouraging statistics in Figure 8.8: fewer U.S. teenagers having intercourse; most adolescents using condoms when they do have sex; the fact that the "transition to intercourse" typically happens in a serious dating relationship for girls.

FIGURE 8.8: Encouraging snapshots of twenty-first century teenage sexuality in the United States: This news about teenage sex is good! Fewer young people are having intercourse, most first intercourse occurs in a committed relationship, and most sexually active adolescents report using condoms.

Source: Child Trends fact sheet, 2008.

Still, with 4 out of every 10 girls getting pregnant before age 20, the United States remains the teenage pregnancy capital of the Western world (Klein and the Committee on Adolescence, 2005). And, unfortunately, reversing a 15-year-long slide, 2006 statistics show a slight up-tick in the number of U.S. teenage births (Moore, 2008). Compared to the rates for teens in Western Europe, the prevalence of gonorrhea and chlamydia among U.S. adolescents is very high (Guttmacher Institute, 2006). Another ominous trend is the recent popularity of oral sex. In 2002, a higher fraction of teenagers reported they had engaged in oral sex (55 percent) than had actually made the transition to intercourse (46 percent) (Child Trends fact sheet, 2008).

Young people report many advantages to choosing oral sex. Because teenagers often don't define this activity as "real" sex, you can engage in oral sex and still say that you are a virgin (Chambers, 2007). Obviously, oral sex eliminates at least one major risk: You can't get pregnant. Young people also see oral sex as less emotionally dangerous: There's less potential for getting hurt, less chance of getting a bad reputation and feeling guilty or bad about oneself (Halpern-Felsler and others, 2005). Interestingly, the teenagers most likely to report only oral sex are the very young people who might feel that having intercourse would be a special threat. Oral sex is most popular among affluent, upper-middle-class teens (Child Trends Data Bank, 2005a).

How do you feel about this trend toward oral sex? Do you see it as an example of a dangerous practice and a new route to low female self-esteem, as it's mainly boys who get the benefits of this activity? Or do you see it as an intelligent way of dealing with a body that wants to "just say yes" when society is saying no?

INTERVENTIONS: Toward Teenager-Friendly Sex Education

All of this leads back to the issue alluded to in my discussion of puberty: the best way to educate teenagers about sex. Given that many adolescents today see oral sex as a guilt-free alternative to intercourse, we need to stress that this activity does carry the risk of getting a sexually transmitted infection (STI). At a minimum, any sex education program adults develop should be sensitive to the complex attitudes, feelings, and perceptions that contemporary teenagers bring to their exciting, emerging new sexual selves.

Unfortunately, however, many sex education courses in the United States focus heavily on avoiding STIs and urging teens to "just say no." In 21 states, public school sex education programs are required by law to stress abstinence (Guttmacher Institute, 2006). Longitudinal studies show teenage abstinence programs and their associated virginity pledges don't work! Worse yet, when they do have sex, teens who make these pledges are less likely to use contraception and so are more vulnerable to getting pregnant than their peers (Rosenbaum, 2009). Teenagers want more from sex education than mere moralizing or memorizing a frightening list of sexually transmitted diseases (Nayak & Kehily, 2008). Consider,

How likely is this couple to progress from making out to having intercourse? If they are affluent and live in the United States, they may put their limit at oral sex, so they can say that they are still virgins.

TABLE 8.3: Designing a Teenager-Friendly Sex Education Program: A Summary Table

1. Know your group. Understand that sexual practices vary by SES, ethnicity, and family of origin. Then, tailor your interventions to your cultural group.
2. Be aware of peer influences—and try to foster a group norm of responsible sexuality. For girls, bring home the message that even if your friends are having sex you can still remain a virgin. For everyone, stress that having an older boyfriend or girlfriend doesn't mean you "need to" have sex.
3. Assess your group's "media watching" practices and work to counter TV, Internet, or magazine images that celebrate random sex.
4. As every girl could benefit from interventions focused on increasing self-efficacy, build in the message that "you have control of your body." It's especially important to tell girls that often having sex outside of committed relationships is destined to produce low self-esteem.
5. Don't neglect boys. Pay special attention to teaching boys to resist the peer pressure to be "players."
6. Design your program to provide information about contraception (rather than just stressing abstinence). Also, focus on oral sex in addition to simply "targeting" intercourse.
7. Go beyond providing information just about sex. Teach teens about handling *relationships*.

for instance, this comment from a girl named Kristin, when she was asked what a course of this type should teach:

> *Umm what are the right circumstances and wrong circumstances to have sexual intercourse. . . . But umm, I think they should learn about what emotional steps they should go through to see if they are prepared to have sexual intercourse.*

(quoted in Martin, 1996, p. 124)

Another 16-year-old, named Tracy, added that in her sex education course,

> *They just taught, like, VD and stuff like. . . . Maybe they could have stressed more, talked about relationships or something. 'Cause when I [started] high school, . . . I had no clue of what boys were like, you know.*

(quoted in Martin, 1996, p. 125)

So, with sex education, what teenagers are really hungering for is information about *relationships*, not just information about sex.

Table 8.3 pulls together this section's insights by spelling out some considerations in devising a teenage sexuality program. Although contemporary young people in the United States are doing far better at negotiating the minefield of sexual choices than teenagers were a few decades ago, clearly, the adult world can do more to help.

TYING IT ALL TOGETHER

1. As a parent you are determined to talk to your children about sex when they are experiencing their *first* sexual feelings. What should your target age be?

   a. Around age 10, when the output of the adrenal androgens is rising
   b. Around age 12, when testosterone levels are rising
   c. Around age 10, when the output of testosterone is rising

2. Your friend thinks her teenage daughter may be having sex. So she asks for your opinion. All the following questions are relevant for you to ask *except*:

   a. Is your daughter's best friend having sex?
   b. Is your daughter's school teaching about contraception?
   c. Is your daughter watching sexually explicit cable channels and reading *Cosmo*?
   d. Does your daughter have an older boyfriend?

3. Tom is discussing recent trends in teenage sex. Which statement should he make?

   a. Today, more teenage boys than girls have sex during high school.
   c. Today, rates of teenage births are at their lowest ebb ever.
   d. Today, oral sex may be a substitute for intercourse, especially among affluent kids.

4. Based on what you have learned in this chapter, spell out in a sentence how you would change the current focus of U.S. sex education classes to make these programs genuinely responsive to teenagers' needs.

Answers to the Tying It All Together questions can be found on the last page of this chapter.

Final Thoughts

Any program to help teenagers cope with their changing bodies and emerging sexual feelings has to take into account what teenagers are really like "as people." Are adolescents really emotionally vulnerable, more prone to take risks, and to get into trouble as the stereotypes of teenagerhood suggest? What new reasoning capacities emerge as children leave childhood behind? In the next chapter, I'll turn to these topics as we explore cognition and personality during the teenage years.

SUMMARY

Puberty

Today, the physical changes of **puberty** occur during early adolescence, and there can be decades between the time children physically mature and the time they fully enter adult life. Because in agrarian societies a person's changing body used to be the signal to get married, many cultures devised **puberty rites** to welcome the physical changes. The **secular trend in puberty** has magnified the separation between puberty and full adulthood, the fact that **menarche** (and **spermarche**) have been occurring at much younger ages.

Two hormonal command centers program puberty. The adrenal glands produce **adrenal androgens** starting in middle childhood. The **HPG axis**, the main system that sets the bodily changes in motion, involves the hypothalamus, the pituitary, and the **gonads** (ovaries and testes), which produce estrogens and **testosterone** (found in both males and females). Leptin levels and a variety of environmental influences trigger the initial hypothalamic hormone.

The physical changes of puberty are divided into **primary sexual characteristics, secondary sexual characteristics**, and **the growth spurt**. Although in females puberty begins with the growth spurt and menarche occurs late in the process, the rate and sequence of this total-body transformation varies from child to child. Because for males the externally visible changes of puberty occur later and the organs of reproduction are the first to start developing, the puberty timetables of the sexes are not as far apart as they appear to be.

The striking individual differences in the timing of puberty are mainly genetically programmed. African American children tend to reach puberty at a younger age. For girls, being overweight is tied to reaching puberty earlier, and this change may be accelerated by childhood stress. Growing up in a single-mother family has been linked to developing at an earlier-than-average age for girls and boys.

How children feel about their changing bodies varies, depending on the social environment. Breast development often evokes positive emotions. Feelings about menstruation seem more positive than in the past because today's mothers are more apt to celebrate this change. First ejaculation is rarely talked about. Children tend to be embarrassed about their changing bodies when they are around the parent of the opposite sex.

Girls who mature early are at greater risk of getting into trouble as teens (for example, taking drugs, getting pregnant, or doing poorly in school) because they get involved with older friends. Because they often end up heavier and shorter, these girls tend to have a poor body image and are more prone to be anxious and depressed. Research shows that it is better for *all* children to attend a school that offers K–8 education during this time of dramatic body change.

Parents need to talk about puberty with their children, especially their sons. We need to be alert to the potential for problems with early-maturing girls, and schools should be structured to provide the best person–environment fit for adolescents undergoing puberty. We need more sensitive education about puberty in schools.

Body Image Issues

How children feel about their looks is closely tied to their overall self-esteem. Girls tend to feel worse about their looks than boys do, partly because society expects women to be unrealistically thin. However, the body pressure on males is getting more intense. At puberty, many girls start to diet. Boys sometimes diet and also tend to focus on building up their muscle mass. Media images and cultural norms play an important role in causing teenage body distress.

The **eating disorders** called **anorexia nervosa** (severe underweight resulting from obsessive dieting) and **bulimia nervosa** (chronic bingeing and, often, purging) are most likely to strike upper-middle-class teenage girls. Genetic vulnerabilities and maternal rejection that produces feelings of low self-efficacy may put girls at special risk. We need to convince children that beauty is less "objective" than it appears and that how we feel about

ourselves is important in determining our physical appeal. We also need to inoculate teenagers against the destructive media images that promote unrealistic ideals of slimness.

Sexuality

Teenagers today feel freer to make their own sexual decisions, including whether or not to begin to have intercourse. While sexual desire is triggered by the adrenal androgens, and first switches on around age 10, sexual signals from the outside world feed back to cause children to really become interested in sex.

Risk factors that predict making the transition to intercourse include, among others, race, SES, family and peer influences, and gravitating to sex-laden media. Most teens have their first inter-course experience in a romantic relationship. Non-committed sex most often takes place with someone a teen knows well. Although the **sexual double standard** suggests that boys just want sex and girls are interested in relationships, teenage boys are as interested in close relationships and love as girls are.

The good news about teenage sexuality in the United States is that rates of sexual activity are declining and fewer children are having intercourse during their high school years. However, there is a recent slight increase in U.S. teenage pregnancies, and more upper-middle-class U.S. teens than ever are engaging in oral sex. Sex education programs in high schools need to focus more on helping teenagers deal with relationships, rather than simply stressing abstinence or the risk of getting sexually transmitted diseases.

KEY TERMS

puberty, p. 235

puberty rite, p. 236

secular trend in puberty, p. 237

menarche, p. 237

spermarche, p. 237

adrenal androgens, p. 238

HPG axis, p. 238

gonads, p. 238

testosterone, p. 238

primary sexual characteristics, p. 239

secondary sexual characteristics, p. 239

growth spurt, p. 239

eating disorder, p. 250

anorexia nervosa, p. 250

bulimia nervosa, p. 251

sexual double standard, p. 257

ANSWERS TO TYING IT ALL TOGETHER QUIZZES

Puberty

1. Today, puberty occurs a decade or more before we can fully reach adult life.

2. (a) The initial hypothalamic hormone triggers the pituitary to produce its hormones, which cause the ovaries and testes to mature and produce their hormones, which, in turn, produce the body changes. (b) Estrogens, testosterone, and the adrenal androgens. (c) Your cousin will start growing taller.

3. Kendra is probably *not yet menstruating*. Anthony *may or may not* have reached puberty.

4. d.

5. a.

6. *Possible recommendations*: Encourage communities to adopt K–8 schools. Push for more adequate, "honest" puberty education at a younger age, possibly in a format—such as on-line—where children can talk anonymously about their concerns. Institute a public awareness program encouraging parents to talk about puberty with a same-sex child. Encourage mothers to speak positively about menstruation and have dads discuss events such as spermarche with sons. Make everyone alert to the dangers associated with being an early-maturing girl and develop formal interventions targeted to this "at-risk" group.

Body Image Issues

1. Unfortunately, low self-esteem.

2. Jasmine and Sophia have eating disorders. Jasmine has the symptoms of anorexia nervosa; Sophia has the symptoms of bulimia nervosa.

3. b.

4. Your checklist might include the following items: Is this child female, European American, and temperamentally anxious with a very low sense of self-efficacy? Does this teen have a critical, micromanaging mom—especially one with "eating issues" of her own? Is this girl obsessed with reading fashion magazines and currently trying to diet down to "model-sized" proportions?

Sexuality

1. a.

2. b.

3. c.

4. Sex education programs should focus on helping teens deal with relationships—and provide concrete information about contraception—rather than simply stressing abstinence or frightening children about sexually transmitted diseases.

Chapter 9

CHAPTER OUTLINE

Cognitive and Socioemotional Development

Samantha's father began to worry when his daughter was in sixth grade. Suddenly, his sweet little princess was becoming so selfish, so moody, and so rude. She began to question everything, from her 10 o'clock curfew to why poverty exists. At the same time, she had to buy clothes with the right designer label and immediately have the latest CD. She wanted to be a total individual, but her friends shaped every decision. She got hysterical if anyone looked at her the wrong way. Worse yet, Samantha was beginning to hang out with a bad crowd—staying out all night; not doing her homework; cutting class.

Her twin brother, Sam, couldn't have been more different. Sam was obedient, an honor student, captain of the basketball team. He seemed to mellowly sail into his teenage years. Actually, Sam defied the categories. He was smart and a jock; he really had heart. Sam volunteered with disabled children. He effortlessly moved among the brains to the popular kids to the artsy "Goths" groups at school. Still, this model child could also give his parents palpitations. The most heart-stopping example happened when the police picked up Sam and a carload of buddies for drag racing on the freeway. Sam's puzzled explanation: "Something just took over and I stopped thinking, Dad."

If you looked beneath the surface, however, both of his children were really great. They were thoughtful, caring, and capable of having the deepest discussions about life. They simply seemed to get caught up in the moment and lose their minds—especially when they were with their friends. What really is going on in the teenage mind?

Think of our contradictory stereotypes about the teenage mind. Teenagers are supposed to be idealistic, thoughtful, and introspective; concerned with larger issues; pondering life in deeper ways; but also impulsive, moody, and out of control. We expect them to be the ultimate radicals, rejecting everything adults say, and the consummate conformists, dominated by the crowd, driven by the latest craze, totally influenced by their peers. After I trace how adolescence became a defined life stage, the chapter you are about to read will make sense of these contradictory ideas.

Setting the Context

Youth are heated by nature as drunken men by wine.

Aristotle (n.d.)

I would that there were no age between ten and twenty-three . . . , for there's nothing in between but getting wenches with child, wronging the ancientry, stealing, fighting. . . .

William Shakespeare, *The Winter's Tale*, Act III

As the quotations above illustrate, throughout history, wise observers of human nature have described young people as being emotional, hotheaded, and out of control. When, in 1904, G. Stanley Hall first identified a new life stage characterized by **"storm and stress,"** which he called "adolescence," he was only echoing these time-less ideas. Moreover, as the mission of the young is to look at society in fresh, new ways, it makes sense that most cultures would view each new generation in ambiva-lent terms. They would praise young people for their energy and passion; they also would fear them as a menace and threat.

However, until fairly recently, young people never had years to explore life or rebel against society because they had to take on adult responsibilities at an early age. As you may remember from Chapter 1, adolescence only became a distinct stage of life in the United States during the twentieth century, when—for most children—going to high school became routine (Mintz, 2004; Modell, 1989; Palladino, 1996).

As this famous 1930s photo-graph of a migrant family travel-ing across the arid Southwest to search for California jobs illus-trates, during the Great Depres-sion, there was no chance to go to high school and no real ado-lescence because children had to work to support their families at a very young age.

Look into your family history and you may find a great-grandparent who finished high school or college. But a century ago, these events were fairly rare, as the typical U.S. child left school after sixth or seventh grade to find work (Mintz, 2004). Unfortunately, how-ever, during the Great Depression of the 1930s, there was little work to actually find. Idle and at loose ends, many young people took to roaming the countryside, angry, demoralized, and depressed. Alarmed by the sit-uation, the federal government took action. At the same time as it instituted the Social Security system to provide for the elderly (to be discussed in Chapter 13), the Roosevelt administration implemented an ambi-tious national youth program to lure young people to school. The program worked. By 1939, 75 percent of all U.S. teenagers were attending high school.

High school boosted the intellectual skills of a whole cohort of Americans. But it produced a genera-tion gap between these young people and their less-educated, often immigrant par-ents and encouraged teens to spend their days together as an isolated, age-segregated group. Then, during the 1950s, when entrepreneurs began to target products to this new, lucrative "teen" market, we developed our familiar adolescent culture with its distinctive music and dress (Mintz, 2004; Modell, 1989). The sense of an adolescent society bonded together (against their elders) reached its height during the late 1960s and early 1970s. With "Never trust anyone over 30" as its slogan, the huge teenage baby boom cohort rejected the conventional rules related to marriage and gender roles and transformed the way we live our adult lives today.

In this chapter, I will be exploring the experience of being adolescent in the con-temporary developed world—a time in history when we expect teenagers to go to high school (and now often college) and society insulates young people from adult respon-sibilities for a decade or more. First, I'll enter the mysterious teenage mind, making sense of why adolescents, like Samantha and Sam, seem both remarkably mature and immature. Then, I'll turn to relationships, charting how teenagers separate from their

TABLE 9.1: Stereotypes About Adolescence: True or False?

T/F	1. Adolescents think about life in deeper, more thoughtful ways than children do.
T/F	2. Adolescence is when we begin to develop our personal moral code for living.
T/F	3. Adolescents are highly sensitive to what other people think.
T/F	4. Adolescents are unusually susceptible to peer influences.
T/F	5. Adolescents are highly emotional compared to other age groups.
T/F	6. Adolescents are prone to taking risks.
T/F	7. Many adolescents are emotionally disturbed.
T/F	8. Rates of substance abuse and suicide are comparatively high during adolescence.
T/F	9. Adolescents reject their parents' basic ideas and worldviews.
T/F	10. Getting in with a bad crowd makes it more likely for teenagers to "go down the wrong path."

(Answers: 1. T, 2. T, 3. T, 4. T, 5. T, 6. T, 7. F, 8. F, 9. F, 10. T)

parents and relate to one another in groups. This chapter ends by touching on some issues that affect the millions of young people living in impoverished regions of the world who still can't count on having a life stage called adolescence at all.

Before beginning your reading, you might want to take the "Stereotypes About Adolescence: True or False?" quiz in Table 9.1. In the following pages, I'll be describing why each stereotype is either right or wrong.

The Mysterious Teenage Mind

Thoughtful and introspective, but impulsive, moody, and out of control; peer-centered conformists and rebellious risk takers: Can teenagers *really* be all these things? In our search to explain these contradictions, let's first look at three classic theories of teenage thinking; then turn to the exciting research related to teenage storm and stress.

Three Classic Theories of Teenage Thinking

Have a thoughtful conversation with a 16-year-old and a 10-year-old and you are likely to be struck by the remarkable mental growth that occurs during adolescence. It's not so much that teenagers know much more than they did in fourth or fifth grade, but that adolescents *think* in a different way. With an elementary school child in the concrete operational stage, you can have a rational talk about daily life. With a teenager, you can have a rational talk about *ideas*. This ability to reason abstractly about concepts is the defining quality of Jean Piaget's formal operational stage (see Table 9.2 on page 266).

Formal Operational Thinking: Abstract Reasoning at Its Peak

Children in concrete operations are able to look beyond the way objects immediately appear. They realize that when Mommy puts on a mask, she's still Mommy "inside." They understand that when you pour a glass of juice or milk into a different-shaped glass, the amount of liquid remains the same. Piaget believed that, when children reach the **formal operational stage** at around age 12, this ability to think abstractly takes a qualitative leap. Teenagers are able to reason logically in the realm of pure thought. Specifically, according to Piaget:

Adolescents can think logically about concepts and hypothetical possibilities. Ask fourth- or fifth-graders to put objects such as sticks in order from small to large and they will have no problem performing this *seriation* task. But present a similar task

"storm and stress" G. Stanley Hall's phrase for the intense moodiness, emotional sensitivity, and risk-taking tendencies that characterize the life stage he labeled *adolescence*.

formal operational stage Jean Piaget's fourth and final stage of cognitive development, reached at around age 12 and characterized by teenagers' ability to reason at an abstract, scientific level.

TABLE 9.2: Piaget's Stages: Focus on Adolescence

Age	Name of Stage	Description
0–2	Sensorimotor	The baby manipulates objects to pin down the basics of physical reality.
2–7	Preoperations	Children's perceptions are captured by their immediate appearances. "What they see is what is real." They believe, among other things, that inanimate objects are really alive and that if the appearance of a quantity of liquid changes (for example, if it is poured from a short, wide glass into a tall, thin one), the amount actually becomes different.
8–12	Concrete operations	Children have a realistic understanding of the world. Their thinking is really on the same wavelength as adults'. While they can reason conceptually about concrete objects, however, they cannot think abstractly in a scientific way.
12+	Formal operations	Reasoning is at its pinnacle: hypothetical, scientific, flexible, fully adult. Our full cognitive human potential has been reached.

verbally: "Bob is taller than Sam, and Sam is taller than Bill. Who is the tallest?" and the same children will be lost. The reason is that, during adolescence, we first become capable of logically manipulating concepts in our minds (Elkind, 1968; Flavell, 1963).

Moreover, if you give a child in concrete operations a reasoning task that begins, "Suppose snow is blue," she will refuse to go further, saying, "That's not true!" Adolescents in formal operations have no problem tackling that challenge because, once our thinking is liberated from concrete objects, we are comfortable reasoning about concepts that may *not* be real.

Adolescents can think like real scientists. When our thinking processes occur on an abstract plane, we have the capacity to approach problems in a genuinely scientific way. We can devise a strategy to rule out alternative interpretations and scientifically prove that something is true.

Piaget designed an interesting exercise to reveal the emergence of this new scientific thought: He presented children with the pendulum apparatus shown in Figure 9.1 and the set of four strings and different weights. Notice that two of the strings are shorter than the other two and that the bigger weights also differ in their heaviness. Children's challenge, as described in the figure, was to find out which influence determined how quickly the pendulum swung from side to side. Was it the length of the string, the heaviness of the weight, or the height from which the string was released?

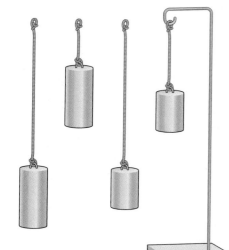

FIGURE 9.1: Piaget's pendulum apparatus: A task to assess whether children can reason scientifically: Piaget presents the child with the different weights and string lengths illustrated here and shows the boy or girl how to attach them to the pendulum (and to one another). Then he says, "Your task is to discover what makes the pendulum swing more or less rapidly from side to side—is it the length of the string, the heaviness of the weight, or the height (and force) from which you release the pendulum?" and watches to see what happens.

Think about how to approach this problem and you may realize that it's crucial to be systematic—keeping everything constant but the factor whose influence you want to assess (remember my explanation of an experiment in Chapter 1). To test whether it's the heaviness of the weight, you must keep the string length and the height from which you drop it constant, varying only the weight. Then, you need to isolate another variable, keeping everything else the same. And when you vary the length of the string, keeping everything else the same, you will realize that the string length alone affects how quickly the pendulum swings.

Elementary school children, Piaget discovered, approach these types of problems haphazardly. Only adolescents can use this careful systematic strategy to solve reasoning type tasks (Flavell, 1963; Ginsburg & Opper, 1969).

HOW DOES THIS CHANGE IN THINKING APPLY TO REAL LIFE? This new ability to think hypothetically and scientifically explains why it's not until we're in high school that we can thrill to a poetic metaphor or comprehend chemistry experiments (Kroger,

2000). It's only during high school that we can join the debate team and argue the case for and against capital punishment, no matter what we *personally* believe. In fact, reaching the formal operational stage explains why teenagers are famous for debating *everything* in their lives. A 10-year-old who wants to stay up till 2 A.M. to watch a new video will just keep saying, "I don't want to go to bed." A teenager will lay out his case logically, point by point: "Mom, I got enough sleep last night. Besides, I only need six hours. I'll just be lying in bed with my eyes open. I can sleep after school tomorrow."

But, do *all* adolescents really reach formal operations? The answer is definitely no. For one thing—rather than being universal—formal operational reasoning only occurs in scientifically oriented Western cultures. Worse yet, even in our society, most people don't make it to Piaget's final stage. In a classic study, one researcher discovered only a fraction of U.S. adults approached the pendulum problem scientifically. More disheartening, when asked to debate a controversial issue, such as capital punishment, most people did not even realize that they needed to use logic to construct their case (Kuhn, 1989).

Still, even if many of us never reason like real scientists or master debaters, we can vividly see the qualities involved in formal operational thinking if we look at how adolescents—especially older teenagers—reason about their *own lives.*

If you are a traditional emerging-adult student, you might think back to the complex organizational skills it took to get into college. You may have learned about your options from an adviser, researched each possibility on the Internet, visited campuses, and constructed different applications to showcase your talents. Then, when you got accepted, you needed to reflect on your future self again: "This school works in terms of finances, but is it too large? How will I feel about moving far from home?" Would you have been able to mentally weigh these different possibilities, and project yourself into the future in this way, at age 10, 12, or even 14?

The bottom line is that reaching concrete operations allows us to be on the same wavelength as the adult world. Reaching formal operations allows us to *act* in the world like adults.

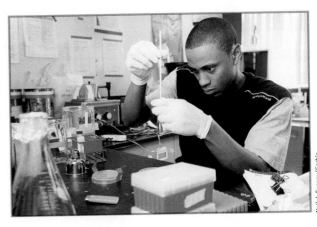

The advances in scientific thinking that allow teenagers to solve the pendulum problem are the core qualities that make it possible for this University of Maryland undergraduate to be a real research collaborator in his professor's chemistry lab.

Discussing your plans with an adviser, filling out college applications, and realistically assessing your interests and talents involve the kind of future-oriented adult thinking that only becomes possible in late adolescence. So, even if they don't reason at the formal operational level on Piaget's laboratory tasks, these Portland, Maine, high school seniors are probably firmly formal operational in terms of thinking about their own lives.

Kohlberg's Stages of Moral Judgment: Developing Internalized Moral Values

This new ability to reflect on ourselves as people allows us to reflect on our personal values. Therefore, drawing on Piaget's theory, developmentalist Lawrence Kohlberg (1981, 1984) argued that it is only during adolescence that we become capable of developing a moral code that guides our lives. To measure this moral code, Kohlberg constructed ethical dilemmas. He then had people reason about these scenarios and asked raters to chart the responses according to the three levels of moral thought outlined in Table 9.3 on page 268. Before looking at the table, take a minute to respond to the "Heinz dilemma," the most famous problem on Kohlberg's test of moral judgment:

A woman was near death from cancer. One drug might save her. The druggist was charging . . . ten times what the drug cost him to make. The . . . husband, Heinz, went to everyone he knew to borrow the money but he could only get together about half of what it cost. [He] asked the . . . druggist to sell it cheaper or let him pay later. But the druggist said NO! Heinz broke into the man's store to steal the drug. . . . Should he have done that? Why?

TABLE 9.3: Kohlberg's Three Levels of Moral Reasoning, with Sample Responses to the Heinz Dilemma*

Preconventional level:

Description: Person operates according to a punishment-and-reward mentality.

Reasons given for acting in a certain way: (1) to avoid being punished by the authorities; (2) to serve one's own interests, although the person also shows signs of recognizing that other people may have different interests

Examples: (1) Heinz shouldn't steal the drug because he will go to jail. (2) Heinz should steal the drug because his wife will love him more.

Conventional level:

Description: Person's morality centers on the need to obey society's rules.

Reasons given for acting in a certain way: (1) to be a "good person" in one's own and other people's eyes; (2) the need to keep the social system going and avoid a breakdown in society

Examples: (1) Heinz should steal the drug because that's what "a good husband" does; or Heinz should not steal the drug because good citizens don't steal. (2) Heinz can't steal the drug—even though it might be best—because, if one person decides to steal, so will another and then another, and then, the laws would all break down.

Postconventional level:

Description: Person has a personal moral code that transcends society's rules.

Reasons given for acting in a certain way: (1) talks about abstract concepts, such as taking care of the welfare of all people; (2) belief in universally valid moral principles that transcend anything society says

Examples: (1) Although it's wrong for Heinz to steal the drug, there are times when rules must be disobeyed to provide for people's welfare. (2) Heinz *must* steal the drug because the obligation to save a human life transcends every other consideration.

*Within each general moral level, the reasons and examples numbered (1) reflect a slightly lower sub-stage of moral reasoning than those numbered (2).

Source: Adapted from Reimer, Paolitto, & Hersh, 1983.

---

preconventional level of morality In Lawrence Kohlberg's theory, the lowest level of moral reasoning, in which people approach ethical issues by considering the personal punishments or rewards of taking a particular action.

conventional level of morality In Lawrence Kohlberg's theory, the intermediate level of moral reasoning, in which people respond to ethical issues by considering the need to uphold social norms.

postconventional level of morality In Lawrence Kohlberg's theory, the highest level of moral reasoning, in which people respond to ethical issues by applying their own moral guidelines apart from society's rules.

If you thought in terms of whether Heinz would be personally punished or rewarded for his actions, you would be classified as operating at the lowest level of morality, the **preconventional level**. Responses such as "Heinz should not take the drug because he will go to jail," or "Heinz should take the drug because, if he does this good thing, then his wife will treat him well," suggest that—because your focus is solely on the external consequences for Heinz—you are not demonstrating *any* internalized moral sense.

If you made comments such as "Heinz should [or shouldn't] steal the drug because it's a person's duty to obey the law [or to stick up for his wife]," or "Yes, human life is sacred, but the rules must be obeyed," your response would be classified at the **conventional level**—right where adults typically are. This shows that your morality revolves around the need to uphold society's rules.

People who reason about this dilemma using their own moral guidelines *apart* from the rules of society are operating at Kohlberg's highest **postconventional level**. As the table shows, a response showing postconventional reasoning might be, "No matter what society says is wrong or right, Heinz had to steal the drug because nothing outweighs the universal principle of saving a life."

When he conducted studies with different age groups, Kohlberg discovered that at age 13, preconventional answers were universal in every culture. By age 15 or 16, most children around the world were reasoning at the conventional level. Still, many of us stop right there. Although some of Kohlberg's adults did think post-conventionally, using his *incredibly* demanding criteria, almost no person consistently made it to the highest moral stage (Reimer, Paolitto, & Hersh, 1983; Snarey, 1985).

HOW DOES KOHLBERG'S THEORY APPLY TO REAL LIFE? Kohlberg's categories get us to think more deeply about our own values. Do you have a moral code that guides your actions? Would you intervene, no matter what the costs, to save a person's life? These categories give us insights into other people's moral priorities, too. While reading about Kohlberg's preconventional level, you might have thought: "I know someone just like this. This person has no sense of ethics. He only cares about whether or not he gets caught!"

However, Kohlberg's research has been severely criticized. For one thing, Kohlberg was wrong when he said that children can't go beyond a punishment-and-reward mentality. Even four-year-olds understand: "If you get an unfair prize, you should give it to the person who really deserves it." They also realize that "stealing is wrong" (Nunner-Winkler, 2007).

We can question the link between talk and actions. Does how people reason about artificial scenarios relate to qualities, such as sympathy and self-efficacy, which predict acting prosocially in real life? (Recall my discussion of *prosocial behavior* in Chapter 6.) In fact, when a group of outstandingly prosocial teenagers—in this case, community leaders who set up programs for the homeless—took Kohlberg's test, researchers rated their answers at the very same conventional level as non-prosocial teens! (See Reimer, 2003.)

Concerns about the *validity* of Kohlberg's scale (does it predict real-world morality?) are heightened when we look around. We all know people who can spout the highest ethical principles but behave pretty despicably: the minister who lectures his congregation about the sanctity of marriage while cheating on his wife; the chairman of the ethics committee in the state legislature who has been taking bribes for years.

Still, when he describes the changes in moral reasoning that take place during adolescence, Kohlberg has an important point. Teenagers are famous for questioning society's rules, for seeing the injustice of the world, and for getting involved in idealistic causes (as you can see in the Experiencing the Lifespan box on page 270). Unfortunately, this ability to step back and see the world as it should be, but rarely is, may produce the emotional storm and stress of teenage life.

Taking to the streets of Austin to march for immigrant rights may be a life-changing experience for this Latina teen. It's also a developmental landmark, as advances in moral reasoning make adolescents highly sensitive to the world's injustices.

Bob Daemmrich/Photo Edit

Elkind's Adolescent Egocentrism: Explaining Teenage Storms

This was David Elkind's (1978) creative conclusion when he drew on Piaget's concept of formal operations to make sense of teenagers' emotional states. Elkind argues that, when children make the transition to formal operational thought at about age 12, they suddenly see beneath the surface of adult rules. A sixth-grader realizes that his 10 o'clock bedtime, rather than being carved in stone, is an arbitrary number capable of being contested and changed. As you will see in the Experiencing the Lifespan box on the next page with Olivia, the social activist, a 14-year-old becomes acutely aware of the difference between what adults *say* they do and how they really act. The same people who tell you to appreciate diversity or to treat everyone equally, as Olivia realized, let the rich kids cheat. The same parents and teachers who punish you for missing your curfew or being late to class can't get to the dinner table or a meeting on time.

The realization that the emperor has no clothes ("Those godlike adults are no better than I am"), according to Elkind, leads to anger, anxiety, and the impulse to rebel. From arguing with a ninth-grade English teacher over a grade to testing the limits by drinking or driving very fast, teenagers are well known for protesting anything just because it's "a rule."

More tantalizing, Elkind draws on formal operational thinking to make sense of the classic symptom Samantha showed in the chapter-opening vignette—the fact that young teenagers are unusually sensitive to what other people think. According to

EXPERIENCING THE LIFESPAN: OLIVIA, A TENTH-GRADE SOCIAL ACTIVIST

In my niece Olivia's room there are no photos of teen idols, no cosmetics, no closet overflowing with clothes. The peace symbols and posters with titles such as "U.S. out of my uterus" show that this 16-year-old has a clear moral vision. Here's how Olivia explains the passions that dominate her life:

I volunteer at a soup kitchen on weekends. I am active in the Young People's Socialist League—that's a grassroots organization centering on social justice. I went to a couple of their protests against local greengrocers. They pay illegal immigrants, like, $2 an hour and take advantage of the fact that they can't complain to the police.

I began to get into social activism in eighth grade. I had a really cool teacher, and he lent me a book called *Marx for Beginners*. After reading that, I became really enraged at the fact that for so many thousands of years the common man has been screwed over, and still is being screwed over, and continues to be screwed over all over the world. The capital is there, the money is there, and so the fact that poverty exists is really remarkable. We have such vast inequalities in wealth. So basically my anger at that prompted me to get involved in the Young People's Socialist League.

My friends are wonderful, but a lot of the other kids at school are really superficial. In our town, you have a lot of racial and class divisions. Everyone talks about what a diverse community it is, but the white kids live on the north end and the poor minority kids live on the south end. At school, there's a lot of separatism in the races. You might be friendly on the surface, but there's no real mixing. There's also this mad scramble to get into college. Parents are putting a lot of pressure on the kids. If they don't get a 95, there is going to be hell to pay. Some kids in the AP chemistry class were cheating . . . white kids from the north end. And they had already been inducted into the National Honor Society. So when these kids were caught, the department pretended like the whole thing never happened. If you are white and it looks like your parents have money, or if you are the kind of kid who looks like they are going to an Ivy League school, they are not interested in whether you cheat or not. It's a very Machiavellian system.

I try to do the best job I can, but I'm not interested in the "get the grade, get the grade" mentality. I told my parents if they pressured me about grades, I wasn't going to college. My plan is to apply to the United World College for my senior year. That's this real cool, rigorous academic program. They take high school students to places where you can make a difference, like in India and Africa. In Westchester we are the third richest county in the nation, so you don't get a chance to see real poverty. I'm trying to learn more about the income inequality gap between nations. It's really of mammoth proportions. I want to spend these years taking time to read as much as I can.

Elkind, when children first become attuned to the flaws in other people's behavior, this feeling turns inward to become an obsession with what others think about their *own* personal flaws. This leads to a state named **adolescent egocentrism**—the distorted feeling that one's *own* actions are at the center of everyone else's consciousness.

So 13-year-old Melody drives her parents crazy. She objects to everything from the way they dress to how they chew their food. When her mother arrives to pick her up from school, she will not let this humiliating person emerge from the car: "Oh, Mom, I don't know you!" She does not spare herself: A minuscule pimple is a monumental misery; stumbling and spilling her food on the cafeteria lunch line is a source of shame for months ("Everyone is laughing at me! My life is over!"). According to Elkind, this intense self-consciousness is caused by one facet of adolescent egocentrism called the **imaginary audience**. By that term, he meant that young teens, such as Melody, literally feel that they are on stage, with everyone watching everything they do.

A second component of adolescent egocentrism is the **personal fable**. Teenagers feel that their own lives are totally special and unique. So Melody believes that no one has *ever* had so disgusting a blemish. She has the *most* embarrassing mother in the world.

These mental distortions explain the exaggerated emotional storms we laugh about, especially during the early adolescent years. Unfortunately, the personal fable can also lead to tragic acts. Boys, as you saw in the chapter-opening vignette, may put their lives at risk by drag racing on the freeway because they imagine that they can

Lauren Greenfield/VII

Look at the worried expressions on the faces of these freshmen cheerleaders and you can almost hear them thinking, "If I make a mistake during the game, everyone will laugh at me for my whole life!" According to David Elkind, the *imaginary audience* can make daily life intensely humiliating for young teens.

never die. A girl does not bother to use contraception when she has sex because, she reasons, "Yes, *other* girls can get pregnant, but that will never happen to me. Plus, if I do get pregnant, I will be the center of attention, a real heroine."

Studying Three Aspects of Storm and Stress

Are teenagers really unusually sensitive to other people's reactions? Is Elkind (like other wise observers from Aristotle to Shakespeare to G. Stanley Hall) on target in saying that risk-taking is intrinsic to being a "hotheaded youth"? Are teenagers really intensely emotional and/or more likely to be emotionally disturbed? Now, let's turn to the research related to these three core aspects of teenage storm and stress.

Are Adolescents More Socially Sensitive?

In the previous chapter, you learned that, when they reach puberty, children become highly attuned to their body size and often start to diet. You saw that we can predict whether a particular teenager has become sexually active by looking at that person's social group.

When researchers tried to pinpoint what concerned teenagers they discovered, as Elkind believed, that everything comes down to: "What will other people think?" From being overweight to deciding whether to have intercourse (or oral sex), from having a fight with their parents to getting pregnant as an unmarried teen, the issue is: "Will I be laughed at or rejected? How will my friends respond?" (Bell & Bromnick, 2003.)

The fact that they are so socially sensitive suggests that our stereotype of adolescents as incredibly motivated to conform to their peers must be true. The reality, as developmentalist Laurence Steinberg discovered, is more complicated.

Steinberg's research team adapted Susan Harter's scenario approach with 13- to 18-year-olds by asking questions such as: "Some people go along with their friends. But other people refuse. Which is most like you?" To their surprise, they discovered that the tendency to say, "I'd definitely resist peer pressure," grew steadily over the teenage years (Steinberg & Monahan, 2007). Unfortunately, however, as you can see in the research in the How Do We Know box on page 272, this determination to "just say no" can be overwhelmed in the heat of the moment. In emotionally charged situations, teenagers *are* more vulnerable to negative peer influences than to adults. All of which may explain why the most level-headed adolescents, like Sam in the chapter-opening vignette, sometimes do crazy things with their friends (Steinberg, 2005; 2008).

What compounds this tendency to take risks in groups is a tendency to favor immediate gratifications over future rewards. Steinberg and his colleagues used a computer game in which people from age 10 through their twenties could choose to get a smaller amount of money right now or wait some time for a larger reward. While by late adolescence, there were no meaningful age differences, teens under age 16 accepted a smaller payoff to get a reward sooner than older players did (Steinberg and others, 2009). Or, as my student puzzled when he confessed to the class about a high-speed chase with the police that landed him in Juvenile Detention at age 15: "It's like I couldn't see that I might be getting into serious trouble. All I thought of was the thrill of possibly getting away."

Are Adolescents Risk Takers?

Doing something and getting away with it. . . . You are driving at 80 miles an hour and stop at a stop sign and a cop will turn around the corner and you start giggling. Or you are out drinking or maybe you smoked a joint, and you say "hi" to a police officer and he walks by. . . .

(quoted in Lightfoot, 1997, p. 100)

adolescent egocentrism David Elkind's term for the tendency of young teenagers to feel that their actions are at the center of everyone else's consciousness.

imaginary audience David Elkind's term for the tendency of young teenagers to feel that everyone is watching their every action; a component of adolescent egocentrism.

personal fable David Elkind's term for the tendency of young teenagers to believe that their lives are special and heroic; a component of adolescent egocentrism.

George Shelley/Masterfile

Imagine being the boy driving this car—listening to deafening music, captivated by your friends, perhaps thinking, "To prove myself to that gorgeous girl in the back seat, I need to go very fast." Now, we understand from the developmental science research that our fears about carloads of teenagers have a realistic basis!

❋ HOW DO WE KNOW . . .

that adolescents make riskier decisions when they are with their peers?

Their heightened sensitivity to social stimuli gives us strong indirect evidence that teenagers might tend to do more dangerous things in arousing situations with their friends. An ingenious laboratory study vividly demonstrated the truth of this statement (Gardner & Steinberg, 2005). Researchers asked younger teenagers (aged 13 to 16), emerging adults (aged 18 to 22), and adults (aged 24-plus) to play a computer game in which they had the chance to earn more points by taking risks, such as continuing to drive a car after a traffic light had turned yellow. They assigned the members of each age group to two conditions: They either played the game alone or they played it while two friends were watching and giving advice.

The chart below shows the intriguingly different findings for young teenagers and for people over age 24. Notice that while being with other people had no significant impact on risky decision making in the adults, it had an enormous effect on young teens, who were much more likely to risk crashing the car by driving farther after the yellow light appeared when they were playing the game in the presence of their friends. The bottom line: Watch for risky behavior when groups of teenagers are together—a fact to consider the next time you see a car full of adolescents in the next lane, barreling down the road with music playing full blast!

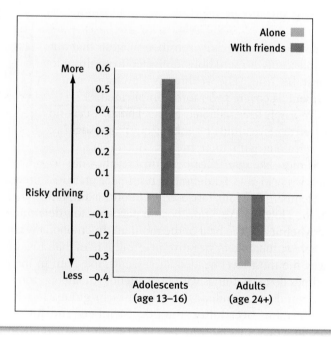

Last Friday we dropped acid. . . . At school you have to be straight and set your mind on something, but when you are free to be with your closest friends you can get wild and uninhibited. It's a different way to relate—a different way of being close.

(quoted in Lightfoot, 1997, p. 99)

These quotations from teens in an interview study, plus Steinberg's laboratory findings, show that (no surprise) the second storm-and-stress stereotype is *definitely* true. From the thrill of taking that first drink to the lure of driving very fast, pushing the envelope—sometimes in dangerous ways—is a basic feature of teenage life (Dahl, 2004; Steinberg, 2004, 2008).

Consider data from yearly University of Michigan sponsored polls exploring teens' use of social drugs (see, for instance, Johnson and others, 2009). The vast majority of all U.S. high school seniors report having sampled alcohol. Roughly 2 in 10 older

TABLE 9.4: Three Stereotypes and Surprising Facts About Alcohol and Teens

Stereotype #1: Teenagers who drink heavily are prone to abuse alcohol later in life.

Research answer: "It depends." Beginning to drink at an atypically early age (under 16) is a risk factor for persistent problems (Pitkanen, Lyyra, & Pulkkinen, 2005). However, during the late teens and twenties, drinking—at least in Western societies—is normative. So we can't predict well from a person's consumption at these peak-use ages to the rest of adulthood.

Stereotype #2: Involvement in athletics protects a teen from abusing alcohol.

Research answer: "False." Actually, participation in high school sports is *positively* correlated with drinking (Barnes and others 2007; Peck, Vida, & Ellis, 2008)—especially for boys. In one study, identifying oneself as a jock predicted generally getting involved in delinquent acts (Miller and others, 2007)! The best conclusion, however, is that sports neither promote nor discourage heavy drinking. We need to look at other core factors such as "aggressiveness" that may cause some teens to gravitate to athletics and also to abusing alcohol (Peck, Vida, & Eccles, 2008).

Stereotype #3: Middle childhood problems are risk factors for later excessive drinking.

Research answer: "Both true and surprisingly false." As you might expect, childhood externalizing problems are one predictor of adult problem drinking (Englund and others, 2008; Pitkanen and others, 2008). However, two longitudinal investigations—conducted in the United States and Great Britain—revealed that, for girls, *high* academic achievement was a risk factor for heavy drinking in the early twenties (Englund and others, 2008; Maggs, Patrick, & Feinstein, 2008)! To explain away this uncomfortable finding, researchers suggest that girls who do well academically may be more likely to go to college, where, as many of you are well aware, the whole environment strongly encourages drinking to excess.

adolescents—depending on the poll—admit to binge drinking (defined as having five or more drinks at a time for males and four or more drinks in a row for females) in the previous month. (Table 9.4 showcases some interesting research facts related to alcohol and teens.)

The good news, as you can see in Figure 9.2, is that, in contrast to our images of rampant teenage substance abuse, most high school seniors do not report using *any* drugs. The percent of teens who use any given illicit substance—other than marijuana and alcohol—has hovered in the single digits for years (as reported in University of Michigan News Service, Dec. 11, 2008). The bad news is that, for a significant minority of young people, regular overuse of that consummate social lubricator—alcohol—remains a potent lure.

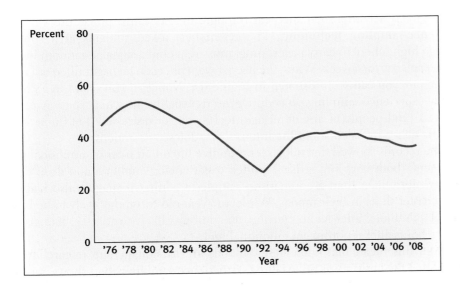

FIGURE 9.2: Trends in prevalence of illicit drug use, reported by U.S. high school seniors from the mid-1970s to 2008: Contrary to our stereotypes, only 2 in 5 U.S. high school seniors reports using any illicit drugs (including alcohol) over the past year. Notice also that drug use was actually somewhat more common during the late 1970s and early 1980s—among the parents of today's teens, during their own adolescence.
Source: Monitoring the Future Studies, University of Michigan

Petr David Josek/Associated Press

This image of underage drinkers—taken in the Czech Republic—enjoying "shots" at a New Year's party would be familiar around the world. In addition to being an exciting, forbidden—but easily available—"adult" substance, liquor is a potent anxiety-reducer. Plus, notice how chugging down drinks together is helping these teens to bond as a group.

Now, let's look at the temptation to engage in activities that are physically dangerous or against the law. You might notice from the quotations earlier that there is truth to Elkind's concept of the personal fable. For many teenagers, doing things that can get you into trouble and not getting caught is part of the thrill of being alive (Lightfoot, 1997). This tendency to tempt fate and engage in risky activities is the glue that binds teenagers to their friends. It makes for lifelong memorable experiences, too. When the adolescents quoted at the beginning of this section meet up again at age 30 or 40, they can reminisce about the time they did acid together, or drove too fast and barely missed getting pulled over by that cop.

Do you remember doing something that was against the law with your friends at age 14 or 15 and then advertising your act to everyone at school? In analyzing teenage social networking sites—that terrific modern medium for eavesdropping into what young people are *really* into today—one researcher confirmed that showcasing these kinds of exploits is still a core part of the adolescent experience. More than 8 out of every 10 teenagers mentioned participating in some type of risky behavior on their blog. One in six teens bragged about having engaged in an actual criminal act (Williams and Merten, 2008).

Younger children also rebel, disobey, and test the limits. But, if you have ever seen a group of teenage boys hanging from the top of a speeding car, you know that certain kinds of risks adolescents take can be threatening to life. At the very age when they are most physically robust, teenagers—particularly male teenagers—are most likely to die of preventable causes such as accidents (Dahl, 2004; Spear, 2008). So, yes, parents can legitimately worry about their children—particularly their sons—when they haven't made it home from a party yet and it's already 2 A.M.!

Are Adolescents More Emotional, More Emotionally Disturbed, or Both?

By reading the previous sections, it should also come as no surprise that the third major stereotype about teenage storm and stress is also correct. Adolescents *are* more emotionally intense than adults. Developmentalists could not arrive at this conclusion by using surveys in which they asked young people to reflect on how they *generally* felt. They needed a method to chart the minute-to-minute ups and downs of teenagers' emotional lives.

Imagine that you could get inside the head of a 16- or 17-year-old as that person went about daily life. Several decades ago, Mihaly Csikszentmihalyi and Reed Larson (1984) accomplished this feat through an innovative procedure called the **experience-sampling technique**. The researchers asked students at a suburban Chicago high school to carry pagers programmed to emit a signal at random intervals during each day for a week. When the beeper went off, each teenager filled out a chart like the one you can see illustrated in Figure 9.3. Notice, if you scan Greg's record, that the experience-sampling procedure gives us insights into what experiences make teenagers (and people of any other age) feel joyous or distressed. Let's now look at what the charts revealed about the intensity of adolescents' moods.

The records showed that adolescents *do* live life on an intense emotional plane. Teenagers—both boys and girls—reported experiencing euphoria and deep depression far more often than a comparison sample of adults. Teenagers also had more roller-coaster shifts in their moods. While a 16-year-old was more likely to be back to normal 45 minutes after feeling terrific, an adult was likely to still feel happier than average hours after reporting an emotional high.

Does this mean that adolescents' moods are irrational? The researchers concluded that the answer was no. As Greg's experience-sampling chart shows, teenagers

experience-sampling technique A research procedure designed to capture moment-to-moment experiences by having people carry pagers and take notes describing their activities and emotions whenever the signal sounds.

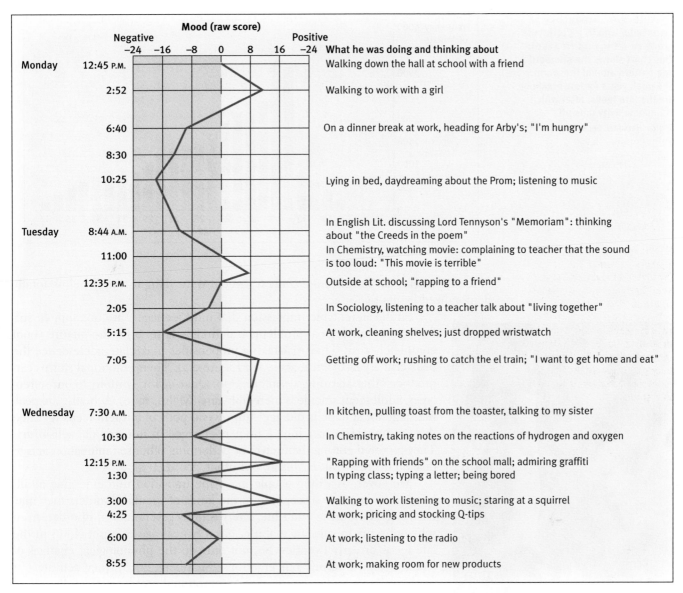

FIGURE 9.3: **Three days in the life of Gregory Stone: An experience-sampling record:** This chart is based on three days of self-reports by a teenager named Greg Stone, as he was randomly beeped and asked to rate his moods and what he was doing at that moment. By looking at the ups and downs of Greg's mood, can you identify the kinds of activities that he really enjoys or dislikes? Now, as an exercise, you might want to monitor your own moods for a few days and see how they change in response to your own life experiences. What insights does your internal mental checklist reveal about which activities are most enjoyable for you?

Source: Adapted from Csikszentmihalyi & Larson (1984), p. 111.

don't get excited or down in the dumps for no reason. It's hanging out with their friends that makes them elated. It's a boring class or boring job that makes them very, very bored.

Does this mean that most adolescents are emotionally disturbed? Now, the answer is *definitely* no. Although the distinction can escape parents when their child wails, "I got a D on my chemistry test; I'll kill myself!," there is a difference between being highly *emotional* and being emotionally disturbed.

Actually, when developmentalists ask teenagers to step back and evaluate their lives, they get a very upbeat picture of how young people generally feel. Surveys around the world routinely show that most adolescents are confident, zestful, and hopeful about the future (Gilmand and others, 2008; Offer and others, 1988). Based on asking questions such as "Do you feel competent . . . close to family and friends . . . good about the world?" in one U.S. poll, researchers classified an amazing 4 out

FIGURE 9.4: Frequency of arrests by age in a California study of offenders (n 2350): This chart shows the standard age pattern around the world: The peak years for law breaking are the late teens, after which criminal activity falls off.

Source: Natsuaki, Ge, & Wenk (2008).

Most teens are upbeat and happy, and suicide is very, very rare during the adolescent years. But specific signs of distress, such as this boy's *nonsuicidal self-injury* (cutting behavior), seem surprisingly prevalent among affluent adolescents, especially girls.

of 10 adolescents as "flourishing." Only 6 percent were "languishing," feeling totally demoralized by life (Keys, 2007).

So the stereotypic impression that most teenagers are unhappy or suffer from psychological problems is definitely false. Still, the picture is not completely rosy. Their risk-taking propensities make late adolescence the peak crime years (Warr, 2007; see Figure 9.4). Their emotional storms can produce other alarming symptoms, too. Once again, contrary to our stereotypes, adolescent suicide is incredibly rare (Males, 2009). Actually, the peak life stage for suicide is old age! But several polls of affluent teens revealed that an amazing 1 in 3 high schoolers engaged in **nonsuicidal self-injury**. They reported cutting themselves or performing other self-mutilation acts to deal with stress (Yates, Allison, & Luthar, 2008).

Moreover, as young people make the transition into emerging adulthood, they become susceptible to the kinds of mental disorders they may have to battle during adult life. *Every* serious psychological disorder, from schizophrenia to substance abuse, has a typical age of onset either in the late teens or early twenties. So, not only do the physiological changes of teenagerhood intensify our emotions (Steinberg, 2008), they activate our predispositions to developing specific emotional problems as adults.

I saw this distressing process happen with a close colleague and his wife, both of whom have suffered from serious mood disorders. Their children were all successful, well adjusted, and happy throughout elementary school. But, when they became older teenagers, their family history of depression kicked in. *Each* child began to develop symptoms of this devastating disease.

Different Teenage Pathways

The bottom-line message is that, yes, some teenage risk-taking is normal, but the dire scenarios about teenagers as an age group in terrible emotional trouble are totally wrong. Yes, crime rates do escalate and specific symptoms of distress such as "cutting" erupt during the teens. But a remarkable percentage of adolescents are flourishing during this time of life. As diversity at this life stage—and at every age—is the norm, the really relevant question is: "Who gets emotionally derailed and who thrives during these special years?"

Which Teens Get into Serious Trouble?

As I just mentioned, for children who are genetically vulnerable, getting seriously emotionally derailed—that is, developing a mental disorder—is a tragedy that we may not be able to predict. However, when we look at "acting out" or delinquent behaviors, we can see early warning signs of what is to come.

At-risk teens tend to have emotional problems earlier on. It should come as no surprise that, if an elementary school child is having externalizing problems, that boy or girl is especially vulnerable to getting into trouble as a teen (see Chapter 6). One reason is that, as I will describe later in this chapter, children whose aggressive behavior is causing them to fail socially gravitate toward antisocial groups of friends, who then give one another reinforcement for doing dangerous things.

Actually, any situation that disconnects children from conventional reinforcements is a warning sign—be it failing at school or simply failing to connect with any healthy passion in life (Hunter & Csikszentmihalyi, 2003). Even young people who say that their only goal in life is "just having fun" are more likely to engage in delinquent acts (Dubois and others, 1999).

At-risk teens tend to have poor family relationships. Feeling disconnected from one's parents is also a potent indicator of later troubles (Allen and others, 2007; Choi, He, & Harachi, 2008). For instance, in the study I just mentioned, which explored "cutting" among privileged teens, boys and girls who engaged in these self-injury behaviors often blamed their parents: "My family is too critical"; "I'm under excessive pressure to perform"; "My parents don't love me for who I am" (Yates, Allison, & Luthar, 2008).

Teenagers who say they don't get along with their parents actually complain about too little and too much involvement. They may report: "My mother and father are clueless about my life," or "My parents want to micromanage every act" (Goldstein, Davis-Kean, & Eccles, 2005). In essence, these young people are describing an insecure attachment. Teenagers want to know they can disagree with their parents and be listened to and respected. They need to be able to openly discuss their feelings and still understand they are unconditionally loved (Allen and others, 2003). Furthermore, while it's tempting to blame mothers for this disconnect, let's not neglect the role of dads. In one study, middle schoolers who reported that their fathers criticized them, rather than listening to their point of view, were also at risk for later acting out (Allen and others, 2007).

So, to use the attachment metaphor spelled out in Chapter 4, with adolescents, *both* parents must be exceptionally skillful dancers. They must provide limits and respect their child's need for independence. They should understand when to back off and when to stay close.

Still, when we see correlations between teenagers' reporting distant family relationships and their getting into trouble, is it *simply* parents who are at fault? Imagine that you are a teen who is having casual, unprotected sex or taking drugs. Wouldn't you lie to your parents about your activities? And when you lied, wouldn't you feel even more alienated: "My family knows nothing about my life?" (Warr, 2007.)

Yes, it's easy for experts to *say* that being authoritative and keeping lines of communication open are vital in parenting adolescents. But take it from me (I've been there), when your teenager is on the road to trouble, confronting him about his activities—or snooping into his email, and then saying "you've been lying to me"—is apt to backfire (Warr, 2007). So it can be very difficult for frantic parents to understand how to *really* act authoritatively in a much-loved son's or daughter's life.

At-risk teens begin getting into trouble at younger ages. Another classic warning sign occurs when a child starts to engage in problem behaviors, such as drinking, taking drugs, or cutting classes during middle school. As you saw with early-maturing girls in Chapter 8, when teenagers get involved in deviant activities at a young age, their problems tend to escalate during subsequent years (Campa and others, 2008; Natsuaki, Ge, & Wenk, 2008).

However, it is important to make a distinction between what adolescent specialists call **adolescence-limited turmoil** (antisocial behavior

nonsuicidal self-injury Cutting, burning, or purposely injuring one's body to cope with stress.

adolescence-limited turmoil Antisocial behavior that, for most teens, is specific to adolescence and does not persist into adult life.

If you interviewed this 17-year-old who has been picked up for stealing and dealing drugs, you might find a history of externalizing behaviors during elementary school, poor family relationships, and deviant behaviors that began to escalate in the young teenage years. (Or, because every person is different, you might not find any of these classic risk factors!) The good news—as you will see on the next page—is that even severe *adolescence-limited turmoil* infrequently leads to *life-course difficulties.*

Doug Menuez/Getty Images

during the teenage years) and **life-course difficulties** (antisocial behaviors that continue into adult life) (Moffitt, 1993). From the teenage rebel Benjamin Franklin, who ran away to Philadelphia at age 17 (see Chapter 1) to that angry school failure Winston Churchill (discussed in Chapter 7), some of the most difficult teenagers can become exceptional adults. Perhaps you have a friend who used to stay out all night partying, drinking, or taking drugs but became an extremely responsible parent. Or you may know someone who was continually in trouble in high school who is now succeeding incredibly well after finding the right person–environment fit at work. If so, you understand a main message of the next chapter: We change the *most* during our emerging-adult years.

Which Teens Flourish?

In high school I really got it together. I connected with my lifelong love of music. I'll never forget that feeling when I got that special history prize my senior year.

All I remember was my church group—getting involved with mission work. It actually was my best time of life.

Now that we have spelled out the risk factors for trouble, what makes children flourish as teens? As you might imagine, these attributes offer a good mirror image of the very qualities I just described: Teenagers thrive when they have close family relationships and prosocial friends; when, as you can see above, they are succeeding academically; or have a special passion, such as music or mission work (Masten, 2004). Having a strong religious faith is especially helpful (Miller, 2008). Religion offers teenagers insulation from getting into trouble. It provides solace in the face of life stress: As one 17-year-old boy (whose brother had been killed) explained: "Sometimes . . . I feel like I'm going to explode. So I go in my room, close the door and pray. And *wow* it's like peace" (quoted in Miller, 2008, p. 297). The church embeds teens in a caring, prosocial community, too.

Actually, the impact of the wider community may be especially crucial during adolescence because, during this pivotal life stage, children are separating from their parents and moving into the world. To paraphrase the old saying: "It may take a village to raise a child, but it *really* takes a nurturing village to help a teenager thrive." (Table 9.5 offers a checklist based on these considerations to help you evaluate whether a child you love is at risk of getting into trouble or is set up to flourish as a teenager.)

The determined expression on 15-year-old Michelle Wie's face as she tees off during the men's U.S. Open in Hawaii says it all: Having a life passion and special skill the world prizes allows teenagers to really thrive.

AP Photo/Ronen Zilberman

If the answer to most or all of these questions is "false," a boy or girl is at high risk of getting into trouble in adolescence. The more "true" responses, the greater the probability that the child will flourish as a teen.

TABLE 9.5: **Predicting Whether a Child Is Likely to Have Problems or to Flourish as a Teenager: A Section Summary Checklist**

T/F	1. Does this child have close family relationships?
T/F	2. Does this child have nurturing relationships with other competent and caring adults?
T/F	3. Does this child live in a community with good schools and is he "connected to school"?
T/F	4. Does this child have close friends who are prosocial?
T/F	5. Is this child religious?
T/F	6. Does this child have a life passion or a special talent?

Source: Adapted from Masten (2004), p. 315, and the sources in this section.

Wrapping Things Up: The Blossoming Teenage Brain

Now, let's put it all together: the delightful mental growth; the heightened morality; the intense emotionality; and sensitivity to what others think. Give teenagers an intellectual problem and they can reason in mature, adult ways. But younger teens in particular tend to be overly sensitive to the lure of immediate rewards and get overwhelmed in arousing situations when with their friends.

According to adolescence specialists, these qualities make perfect sense when we look at the developing brain. During teenagerhood, a dramatic pruning occurs in the frontal lobes (Giedd, 2008; Spear, 2008), meaning executive functions are gradually reaching their peak. At the same time, puberty heightens the output of certain neurotransmitters, which provokes the passion to take risks. As Laurence Steinberg (2008) has beautifully described it, it's like starting the engine of adulthood with an unskilled driver. This heightened activation of the "socioemotional brain," with a cognitive control center still "under construction," makes adolescence—particularly the earlier teenage years—a potentially dangerous time (Steinberg and others, 2008).

But from an evolutionary standpoint, it is developmentally logical to start with an emotional engine in high gear. Teenagers' risk-taking tendencies propel them to venture forth and experience what life has to offer. Their awareness of social cues helps them confront the challenge of forming loving relationships as adults. Although it can make for a more dangerous few years, the unique qualities of the adolescent mind are beautifully tailored to help young people separate from their families and begin to construct a successful adult life (Dahl, 2004; Steinberg, 2008).

INTERVENTIONS: Making the World Fit the Teenage Mind

Table 9.6 below summarizes these messages in a chart for parents. Now, let's explore the ramifications of our discussion for society as a whole.

Don't punish adolescents as if they were mentally just like adults. Given the evidence that the adolescent brain is a work in progress, it doesn't make sense to have the same legal sanctions for teenagers who commit crimes that we have for adults. Rather than simply locking adolescents up, it seems logical that at this young age we focus on rehabilitation. In fact, because teenagers' frontal lobes are undergoing so much growth, adolescence may offer a special neurological window of opportunity to turn people's lives around. As Laurence Steinberg (2008) and virtually every other adolescence expert has suggested with regard to the legal system, "less guilty by reason of adolescence" is the way to go.

Limit adolescents' access to potentially dangerous adult activities. Moreover, given adolescents' susceptibility to immediate, heat-of-the-moment influences, Steinberg (2008) makes the point that trying to teach teenagers to carefully think through their decisions may not be effective. We need to provide external barriers to risky behavior, too. Raising the age of getting a driver's license to 17 or 18; increasing the cost of cigarettes to help deter children from smoking; vigilantly enforcing laws against

life-course difficulties Antisocial behavior that, for a fraction of adolescents, persists into adult life.

TABLE 9.6: Tips for Parents of Teens

1. Understand that strong emotions may not have the same meaning for your child that they do for you. So try not to take random comments like "I hate myself" or "I'm the dumbest person in the world" very seriously. Also, let negative comments such as "I hate you" roll off your back. Just because your child gets furious at you, don't think she doesn't love you!

2. Do worry if you see a general pattern developing, with your child becoming more withdrawn, angry, or depressed over weeks or months. Getting involved with peers who are clearly in trouble or starting down a problem path at a young age is a warning sign that your child may need special help.

3. Keep the lines of communication open and know when to get involved and when to back off.

4. Both you and your spouse should avoid harshly criticizing your child, and be careful not to put your son or daughter under unrealistic pressure to "just succeed."

5. Try to get your child connected with her religious faith, or some passion or activity she really loves.

youth development program Any after-school program, or structured activity outside of the school day, that is devoted to promoting flourishing in teenagers.

underage drinking—all these measures offer teenagers some insulation from getting into trouble until their brains finish growing up.

Capitalize on adolescents' strengths. At the same time, we need to harness the brain capacities that *can* lead to dangerous risk taking in a positive way. Have teens channel their risk-taking energies into painting, producing poetry, or public service. Capitalize on adolescent's burgeoning sense of morality. Get teenagers involved in arousing challenges related to making a difference in the world.

Youth development programs fulfill this mission. They provide positive efficacy-promoting, responsibility-enhancing activities for teens (Dworkin, Larson, & Hansen, 2003; Kurtines and others, 2008; Woodland, 2008; Wood, Larson, & Brown, 2009). From 4H clubs, to teenage church groups, to starring in high school plays, these programs ideally foster qualities that developmentalist Richard Lerner has named the five Cs: competence, confidence, character, caring, and connections. They provide the kind of environment that allows young people to flourish and thrive (Lerner, Dowling, & Anderson, 2003; Lerner and others, 2005).

Can after-school programs turn vulnerable young people around? And, if so, which activities work best? Researchers got insights into these questions when they traced the lives of eighth-graders who were failing at academics and in their family lives, as they traveled into their emerging-adult years (Peck and others, 2008).

Involvement *specifically* in school-sponsored activities, such as high school clubs, upped the chances of college attendance from less than 50-50 to over 75 percent. (In contrast, you might be interested to know that working during high school was *negatively* related to going to college). In fact, participating in school-related extracurricular activities also has long-term benefits. Provided a child really gets immersed in a given activity for at least two years, one longitudinal study suggested involvement in high school activities predicts academic competence, confidence, and occupational success years down the road (Gardner, Roth, & Brooks-Gunn, 2008; Linver, Roth, & Brooks-Gunn, 2009). Given these findings, we can't help but think: Even if a teen is not basically a scholar, get that boy or girl connected to school!

Change high schools to provide a better adolescent–environment fit. Feeling strongly identified with one's high school, as you might imagine, is related to thriving emotionally as a teen (Bizumic and others, 2009). The problem, however, is that many Western high schools are far from enticing places. In one international poll, although teens were generally upbeat about other aspects of their lives, they rated their high school experience as only "so-so" (Gilman and others, 2008). How can we turn this situation around? Again, the experience-sampling method offers clues.

In charting the emotions of students during various high school periods, Csikszentmihalyi and his colleagues found that passive activities, such as listening to lectures and watching videos, almost always produced boredom. Teenagers were happiest when they were directing their own learning, either while working on group projects or by themselves (Shernoff and others, 2003). Given that the main mode of instruction in traditional high schools (and unfortunately college) involves lectures, it makes perfect sense for many young people to zone out in their classes and find school an unpleasant place.

In surveys, teenagers say that they are yearning for the same kinds of academic experiences that characterize high-quality elementary schools (described in Chapter 7). They want more autonomy-supporting activities—that is, work that encourages them to think independently (Greene and others, 2004). They are yearning for teachers who respect their point of view (LaRusso, Romer, & Selman, 2008). They would love more courses that are relevant to their own lives (Wagner, 2000).

These high school girls are taking enormous pleasure in, and deriving a tremendous feeling of self-efficacy from, spending their Thanksgiving serving dinners to the homeless and impoverished elderly in their south Texas town. Was some teenage service learning experience life-changing for you?

Bob Daemmrich/The Image Works

Service-learning classes, involving hands-on volunteer activities, in particular, can make a lasting difference in later development (McIntosh, Metz, & Youniss, 2005; Reinders & Youniss, 2006). Here is what one African American young man had to say about his junior-year course in which he volunteered at a soup kitchen: "I was on the brink of becoming one of those hoodlums the world so fears. This class was one of the major factors in my choosing the right path" (quoted in Yates & Youniss, 1998, p. 509).

Finally, we might rethink the school day to take into account teenagers' unique sleep requirements. As you may recall from your own adolescence, the hormones of puberty push the sleep cycle to begin at a late hour (Carskadon, Acebo, & Jenni, 2004; Dahl, 2004). The typical teenager goes to bed well after 11 P.M. and often must get up by 6 or 7 A.M. to get to school on time. Because adolescents actually need at least nine hours of sleep to function at their best, during the school week, the average teen accumulates a net sleep deficit of roughly two hours per night (Hansen and others, 2005; Loessi and others, 2008). Spending one's school days in a zombie-like state is destined to make even the most intrinsically motivating class torture. It is tailor-made to make any person irritable and depressed. Therefore, simply starting the school day a couple of hours later might go a long way toward reducing adolescent storm and stress!

Take a minute to think back to your days in high school—what you found problematic; what helped you cope; what may have allowed you to thrive. Do you have other ideas about how we might change schools, or any other aspect of the environment, to help teenagers make the most of these special years?

Until now, I've been emphasizing the current mainstream developmental science message: "Because of their brain immaturity, teens are in need of special help." But I cannot responsibly end my discussion without pointing out that there are critics of this popular contemporary model (Males, 2009): Do we really know enough about how the brain functions to make these kinds of neural attributions? (Many researchers might say no.) Worse yet, doesn't the "brain deficit" label marginalize teenagers and ignore the many ways in which adolescents show remarkable restraint? Given the easy availability of social drugs, for instance, today's typical teen is an incredibly law-abiding child. The high prevalence of happiness—and strikingly *low* suicide rates—also speak to the basic resilience of this life stage. In their push to invoke biology, might academics and the public be overstating the dangers of the teenage mind?

Many of the very adults who see the teenage mind up-close-and-personal might answer yes. In contrast to our stereotypes about this being an "impossible" life stage, in U.S. polls, the vast majority (75 percent) of parents of teens say they can talk very well about things that matter with their child. A whopping 9 out of every 10 moms and dads report feeling very close to their teenage daughter or son (Bandy & Moore, 2008). If parents typically find adolescence a joy, why does society love to hate this time of life?

Could this have been you in high school, particularly toward the end of the week? Did you decide not to take early-morning classes this semester because you realized the same thing would happen to you today? Do you think that we are making a mistake by resisting teenagers' biological clocks and insisting that their school day start at 8 A.M.?

Are fathers and their adolescent sons emotionally distant? In contrast to our stereotypes, if you asked this dad—like most U.S. parents—he would probably say he actually feels incredibly close to his almost-grown-up baby boy.

TYING IT ALL TOGETHER

1. Robin, a teacher, is about to transfer from fourth grade to the local high school, and she is excited by all the things that her older students will be able to do. Based on what you have learned about Piaget's formal operational stage and Kohlberg's theory of moral reasoning, pick out which two *new* capacities Robin is likely to find among her high school students.

    a. The high schoolers will be able to memorize poems.
    b. The high schoolers will be able to summarize the plots of stories.
    c. The high schoolers will be able to debate different ideas even if they don't personally agree with them.
    d. The high schoolers will be able to develop their own set of moral principles.

2. Eric is the coach of a basketball team. The year-end tournament is tomorrow, and the star forward has the flu and won't be able to play. Terry, last year's number-one player, offers to fill in—even though this is a clear violation of the conference rules. Eric agonizes about the ethical issue. Should he take the risk of depriving his guys of their one shot at the championship, or go against the regulations and put Terry in? For each of the following possible decisions, fill in the moral reasoning level (preconventional, conventional, or postconventional) that Eric is using:

a. Yes. We need to put Terry in because that's our best shot at winning.
b. No. Going against the basic rules of the tournament is wrong.
c. No. If someone finds out, the team will be in huge trouble.
d. Yes. If I put Terry in, the team will feel that I went all out for them and maybe vote me coach of the year.
e. No. If it were a question of saving someone's life, I would feel justified in going against the rules and putting Terry in. But my guys have to understand that any victory would be meaningless if it violated the basic principle that honesty comes first.

3. A 14-year-old worries that everyone is watching every mistake she makes; at the same time, she is fearless when her friends dare her to take life-threatening risks like bungee jumping off a cliff. According to Elkind, this feeling that everyone is watching her illustrates _____; the risk taking is a sign of _____; and both are evidence of the overall process called _____.

4. Your 15-year-old nephew, Sanjay, is spending the summer with you. He's a typical teenager, so you can expect all of the following *except:*

a. intense mood swings.
b. depression, as most adolescents have psychological problems.
c. a tendency to engage in risky behavior when this normally level-headed kid is with his friends.

5. There has been a rise in teenage crimes in your town, and you are at a community meeting to explore possible solutions. Given what you know about the teenage mind, which of the following interventions should you *definitely* support?

a. Push the state legislature to punish teenage offenders as adults. Let them pay for their crimes!
b. Consider instituting a teenage curfew and heavily taxing the sale of liquor.
c. Encourage the local high school to expand their menu of exciting after-school clubs.
d. Think about postponing the beginning of the school day to 10 A.M.
e. Devote more high school lecture time to warning teens not to get into trouble.

Answers to the Tying It All Together questions can be found on the last page of this chapter.

Teenage Relationships

What exactly are teenager/parent interactions like? Now, it's time to tackle this question, as we look directly at those basic adolescent relationship agendas—separating from parents; connecting with one's peers.

Separating from Parents

When I'm with my dad fishing, or when my family is eating dinner, and we get going on some story, or just when Mom and I share a laugh—it's times like these when I feel completely content, loved, the best about life, the world and myself.

In their original experience-sampling study, Csikszentmihalyi and Larson (1984) discovered that teenagers' most uplifting experiences occurred when they were with their families—sharing a joke around the dinner table or having a close moment with Mom or Dad. Unfortunately, however, taken as a whole, those moments were few. In fact, teenagers generally felt much more upbeat with their friends than with their parents. When adolescents were with their families, unhappy emotions outweighed positive ones 10 to 1.

The Issue: Pushing for Autonomy

Why does family life produce a few peak moments and so many dramatic lows? As developmentalists point out, if our home life is basically good, our family provides our cocoon. Home is the place where we can relax, be totally ourselves, and feel completely loved. However, in addition to providing our safe haven, our parents must be a source of pain. The reason is that parents' job is both to love us and to limit us. When this parental limiting function gets into high gear, teenage distress becomes acute. Consider this quotation from a child in the original experience-sampling study:

> *Finally, I get a Sunday off; I don't have to work, so I can sleep a little later. But now I have to go to church. . . . They always wake you up, and they act like they are always cheerful . . . but they are really hostile if you don't want to go . . . [then on the way things get worse]. . . I asked them to change the channel—they were listening to some opera stuff. They just ignored me. . . . Jesus Christ, at least they could answer me!*
>
> (quoted in Csikszentmihalyi and Larson, 1984, p. 141)

What specifically do teenagers and their parents argue about? Studies dating from the Depression era, to the 1960s, to today agree: Conflicts do not typically occur over large concerns such as politics, the state of the world, or even the merits of being religious, but rather the minutiae of daily life—going to church, doing your homework, or cleaning your room (Laursen & Collins, 1994; Montemayor, 1983; Smetana, Daddis, & Chuang, 2003). Conflicts relating to independence loom large ("Why can't I stay out late?"; "Everyone at school is going to that party"; "You have too many rules!"). Interestingly, the most intense differences of opinion are apt to occur just when Steinberg finds that teenage risk-taking tendencies reach their height—around the early to middle teens (Goede, Branje, & Meeus, 2009).

The Process: Separating to Become Close in a New Way

Actually, parent–adolescent conflict tends to flare up while children are in the midst of puberty (Steinberg, 2005). When Steinberg and a colleague videotaped sons and mothers having a conversation, they found that, if a boy was undergoing puberty, he was most likely to challenge, to contradict, and to argue with his parent's point of view (Steinberg & Hill, 1978). From an evolutionary perspective, the hormonal surges of puberty may propel this struggle for power ("You can't tell me what do!") that sets in motion the dance of separation intrinsic to becoming an independent adult.

Even the physical changes of puberty may promote the impulse to separate. Parents are probably less interested in cuddling their suddenly shaving, six-foot-tall son or having their 120-pound daughter sit on their lap. Being that pre-teens find the "symptoms" of puberty so embarrassing (recall Chapter 8), children may also put a halt to much of the kissing and hugging as they struggle to hide their developing bodies from their families' sight.

Passing a driving test and *finally* getting the keys to the car is a joyous late-teenage transition into adult liberation. It's almost the developed-world equivalent of a puberty rite!

As teenagers push for freedom, they are given more decision-making opportunities and gradually establish a new, more equal, adult-like relationship with their moms and dads (Gutman & Eccles, 2007). Although conflict may be intense during mid-adolescence, it tends to subside during the later teenage years (Goede, Branje, & Meeus, 2009).

By late adolescence, the urge to rebel becomes less alluring. Now, it's important to either get going on preparing for college or a career. Your main agenda shifts to constructing an adult life. Even the major social markers of independence at around age 16 or 17 eliminate sources of family strain. Think about how getting your first real job, or getting your license and perhaps your first car, removed an important area of family conflict. You no longer had to ask your parents for every dime or rely on mom or dad to get around.

These eagerly awaited adult milestones put distance between parents and teenagers in the most basic physical way. The experience-sampling charts showed that ninth-graders spent 25 percent of their

Being able to have a real woman-to-woman talk with your grown-up daughter can make the older teenage years a delight.

time with family members. Among high school seniors, the figure dropped to 14 percent (Csikszentmihalyi & Larson, 1984).

So the actual process of separating from our families makes it possible to have a more harmonious family life. The delicate task for parents, as suggested earlier, is to keep an eye on their sons and daughters but increasingly to allow them space to shape their own lives (Steinberg, 2001). One mother of a teenager explained what ideally should happen when she said: "I don't treat her like a young child anymore, but we're still very, very close. Sort of like a friendship, but not really, because I'm still in charge. She's my buddy" (quoted in Shearer, Crouter, & McHale, 2005, p. 674).

Cultural Variations on a Theme

In individualistic societies the typical pattern is for parents encourage their children to construct an independent life. As you saw in the quotation earlier, the ideal is an adult-to-adult relationship that is less hierarchical, more like a friendship. What about teenagers who grow up in immigrant families with more collectivist norms? Do they have the same clashes with their parents? Do they need to feel independent from their families, too?

To explore this question, researchers asked three sets of immigrant teenagers—Korean Americans, Armenian Americans, and Mexican Americans—to respond to different scenarios related to parent–child differences of opinion: "A popular band is giving a concert. You and your friends want to go, but your parents say no. What would you do and why?" They then compared the answers of these first-generation ethnic-minority children with those of European Americans of the same age. To see if their findings differed by stage of adolescence, the researchers gave the questionnaires to people in their mid-teens, late teens, and early twenties (Phinney and others, 2005).

As it turned out, the immigrant children were more likely to say that they would automatically listen to their parents. (Recall the Chapter 7 discussion of ethnic differences in arguing with mothers.) But the Mexican Americans and Armenian Americans in their early twenties did speak about the need to follow their own desires. Therefore, with some, but not all, immigrant children, the push to be autonomous still does happen, but not until the twenties rather than at age 15!

Ask the teenage sons posing for this photograph with their Latino father and Native American mom if they agree with the individualistic idea that it's important for them to separate from their parents and they might say no. For ethnic-minority teens, adolescence can be a time to connect with your heritage and, in the case of the emerging-adult son on the right, embed your European American girlfriend into your warm, caring family.

Immigrant and ethnic-minority teenagers may have an interesting push/pull issue. On the one hand, they may feel closer to their parents as they connect with their ethnic roots and encounter discrimination in the wider world (Grotevant & Cooper, 1998). But coming from a first-generation immigrant family can make for more distance. You want to become a "real" American. You think: "My parents have such old-fashioned attitudes. They have nothing to do with my life." As Judith Harris' peer group socialization theory might predict (recall Chapter 7), anytime children must create a radically different adult lifestyle, parent–child disagreements may go beyond bickering about family rules. They may involve a basic separation in attitudes and worldviews (Arnett, 1999).

This line of reasoning suggests that a risk factor for distress specific to immigrant teens involves issues related to *acculturation*. Teens may be more likely to get into trouble when they believe their un-acculturated parents inhabit a totally different life-space (Choi, He, & Harachi, 2008); or they may feel overstressed by having to take on the parental role with a non-English-speaking mom and dad. One teacher who works with first-generation Chinese American teens commented in an interview study: "The kids may be doing the interpreting and translating . . ., they may be the de-facto parents" (quoted in Lim and others, 2009, p. 40). Now, combine these pressures with a sense of being disconnected from the mainstream culture yourself. As a teen in this same study anguished, "It's other people's country. . . I feel helpless" (quoted in Lim and others 2009, p. 41). Luckily, however, these feelings of adolescent alienation have an antidote: connecting with a compatible group of peers.

clique A small peer group composed of roughly six teenagers who have similar attitudes and who share activities.

crowd A relatively large teenage peer group.

Connecting in Groups

Go to your local mall on a weekend or after school and you will see teenagers in groups, "hanging out" with friends. Why exactly do *groups* of friends become important during adolescence? What function does this typical teenage arrangement serve?

Defining Groups by Size: Cliques and Crowds

Developmentalists classify teenage peer groups into categories. **Cliques** are intimate groups having a membership size of about six. Your group of closest friends would constitute a clique. **Crowds** are larger groupings. Your crowd comprises both your best buddies and a more loose-knit set of people you get together with less regularly.

In a pioneering 1960s observational study in Sydney, Australia, one researcher found that these different-sized groups serve a fascinating purpose: They are the vehicles that convey teenagers to relationships with the opposite sex (Dunphy, 1963).

As you can see in the photos in Figure 9.5, children enter their pre-teen years belonging to unisex cliques, the close associations of same-gender best friends that I talked about in Chapter 6. Relationships start to change when cliques of boys and girls enter a public space and "accidentally" meet. You may observe this fascinating stage of development at your local mall. Notice the bands of sixth- or seventh-grade girls who have supposedly arrived to check out the stores, but who really have another agenda: They know that Sam or José and his buddies will be there. A major mode of interaction when these groups meet is loud teasing. When several cliques get together to walk around the store or go to a movie, they have melded into that larger, first genuinely mixed-sex group called a crowd (Cotterell, 1996).

The crowd is an ideal medium to bridge the gap between the sexes because there is safety in numbers. Children can still be with their own gender while they are crossing into that "foreign" land. Gradually, out of these large-group experiences, small heterosexual cliques form. You may recall this stage during high school, when your dating activities occurred in a small group of girls *and* boys. Finally, at the end of adolescence, the structure collapses. It seems babyish to get together as a group. You want to be with your romantic partner alone.

How accurate is this 50-year-old study? You might be surprised to know that the progression outlined in this research still rings remarkably true (Smetana, Campione-Barr, & Metzger, 2006; see also Child Trends Data Bank, 2008): First, teenagers get together in large mixed-sex crowds; then, they align into smaller groups; then, they go out in pairs, or form one-to-one relationships, or date.

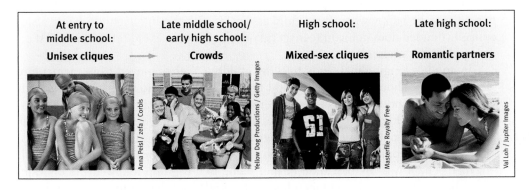

At entry to middle school:	Late middle school/ early high school:	High school:	Late high school:
Unisex cliques	→ Crowds	Mixed-sex cliques	→ Romantic partners

FIGURE 9.5: **The steps from unisex elementary cliques to adult romantic relationships: A visual summary:** Unisex cliques meld into large heterosexual crowds, then re-form as heterosexual cliques, and then break up into one-to-one dating relationships. Does this sequence match your own teen experience?

What Is the Purpose of Crowds?

Crowds have other functions. As I implied earlier, they allow teenagers to connect with people who share their values and ideas. Just as we select friends who fit our personalities, we gravitate to the crowd that fits our interests. We disengage from a crowd when its values diverge from ours. As one academically focused teenager lamented: "I see some of my friends changing. . . . They are getting into parties and alcohol. . . . We used to be good friends . . . and now, I can't really relate to them anymore. . . . That's kind of sad" (quoted in Phelan, Davidson, & Yu, 1998, p. 60). Adventuresome teenagers, such as Sam in the chapter-opening vignette, may move from crowd to crowd to explore different lifestyles (Cotterell, 1996; Stone & Brown, 1998).

Crowds also offer a roadmap for finding "our kind of people" in an overwhelming social world (Smetana, Campione-Barr, & Metzger, 2006). Interestingly, distinctive crowds are most prominent in large high schools. If you went to a small school, you can probably recall having a circle of friends, but your class was less likely to be split into clear crowds, such as "the Goths" or "the brains," who shared activities, attitudes, and a special type of dress. Therefore, one developmentalist has suggested that the impersonal, large public high school plays a vital role in the development of the teenage crowd (Cotterell, 1996). When each class is filled with unfamiliar faces, it is helpful to develop an easy mechanism for finding a smaller set of people just like you. Teenagers adopt a specific look—like having blue hair and wearing grungy jeans—to signal: "I'm your type of person. It's okay to be friends with me."

As you pass this group of "punks" on the street, you may think, "Why do they dress in this crazy way?" But for this group, their outlandish hair and clothes are a message that "I'm very different, and I don't agree with what society says," and most important, they are a signal to attract other fellow minds: "I'm like you. I'm safe. I have the same ideas about the world."

What Are the Kinds of Crowds?

Interestingly, in affluent societies, there is consistency in the major crowd categories. The academics (also called brains, the nerds, the grinds, eggheads), the popular kids (also known as hotshots, preppies, elites, princesses), the deviants (burnouts, dirts, freaks, druggies, potheads), and a residual type (Goths, alternatives, grubs, loners, caters, independents) appear in high schools throughout the West (Sussman and others, 2007).

How much mixing occurs among different crowds? To answer this question, researchers went into a large public high school and asked the students to map the crowds at school according to their status and their relative social closeness (that is, how similar they were in values and ideas) (Stone & Brown, 1998). As it turns out, many teens, such as Sam in the introductory vignette, do straddle different crowds (Lonardo and others, 2009). However, unlike Sam, they typically tend to be friends with children in adjacent groups. So a boy in the jock crowd would, most likely, associate with the popular kids. He would have little to do with the groups that were ranked socially very different, such as the deviants (or the bad kids).

Moreover, the jocks and the popular kids tend to be the highest-status crowds. The brains are only marginally well liked (Sussman and others, 2007). So, although *parents* may be happy when their child associates with the intellectuals, being academically minded does not gain teenagers kudos in the peer world (at least in the standard public high school).

In another longitudinal study tracking children as they moved from elementary school to high school, researchers found that the children who were in specific high school crowds tended to travel certain emotional pathways (Prinstein & La Greca, 2002). Notice in Figure 9.6 that the boys and girls who ended up in the high-status popular kids and jocks crowds became more self-confident during their teenage years. (These are the people who would tell you, "I wasn't very happy in elementary school, but high school was my best time of life.") The brains group followed the opposite path—happiest during elementary school but less self-confident as teens. (Once again,

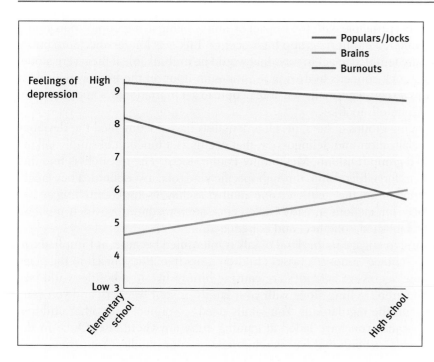

FIGURE 9.6: **Feelings of depression in late elementary school and high school for children who ended up in three different high school crowds:** In this "follow-back" study, researchers tested children in grades four and six and then looked at their depression levels in high school and explored their particular high school crowds. Notice that the boys and girls in the high-status "populars" and "jocks" crowds became happier during high school. The children destined to be in the "brains" crowd felt happiest during elementary school. The teens who became "burnouts" were more depressed than any other group both in late elementary school and in high school. If you remember being in one of these high school crowds, how do these findings relate to your feelings in elementary school versus high school?

Source: Prinstein & La Greca (2002), p. 340.

being academically oriented is associated with feeling great in elementary school, but it doesn't give teenagers much mileage in terms of self-esteem.)

Finally, as the figure shows, the teenagers in the deviant burnout group were most apt to be depressed before adolescence and *stayed* at the low end of the happiness continuum in high school (see also Heaven, Ciarrochi, & Vialle, 2008). We already know that failing socially in middle childhood predicts gravitating toward groups of "bad" peers. Now, let's explore in detail why joining that bad crowd makes a teenager even more likely to fail.

"Bad Crowds"

The classic defense that parents give for a teenager's delinquent behavior is, "My child got involved with a bad crowd." Without ignoring the principle of selection (birds of a feather flock together), there are powerful reasons why bad crowds *do* cause kids to do bad things.

For one thing, as we know, teenagers are incredibly swayed by groups of friends. Moreover, each group has a leader, the person who most embodies the group's goals. So, if your child joins the brains group, his school performance is likely to improve because everyone will be jockeying for status by competing for grades. (In fact, one middle school study confirmed that parents are right to feel overjoyed when their child associates with the brainy kids. Best friend's GPA in seventh grade was the *most* influential force predicting a child's own grades the following year) (Cook, Deng, & Morgano, 2007). However, in delinquent groups, the pressure is to model the most antisocial member. Therefore, the activities of this most acting-out leader set the standard for how the others want to behave.

So, in the same way you felt compelled to jump into the icy water at camp when the bravest of your bunkmates took the plunge, if one group member begins robbing stores or selling drugs, the rest must follow the leader or risk being called "chicken." Moreover, when children compete for status by getting into trouble, this creates ever-wilder antisocial modeling and propels the group toward taking increasingly risky actions.

As a group euphoria sets in and people start surging for the stage, these teenagers at a rock festival in England might trample one another—and then later be horrified that they could ever have acted this way.

Combine this principle with the impact of simply being in a group. When young people get together, a euphoric group high occurs. Talk gets louder and more outrageous. People are tempted to act in ways that would be unthinkable if they were alone. From rioting at rock concerts to driving 100 miles an hour on the freeway with their buddies, groups *do* cause normally sensible people to act in irrational, sometimes dangerous ways (Cotterell, 1996).

By videotaping groups of boys, developmentalists have documented the **deviancy training**, or socialization into delinquency, that occurs as a function of simply talking with friends in a group (Dishion, McCord, & Poulin, 1999). The researchers find that "at-risk" pre-teens forge friendships through specific kinds of conversations: They laugh; they egg one another on; they reinforce one another as they discuss committing antisocial acts. So peer interactions in early adolescence are a medium by which problem behavior gets established, solidified, and entrenched.

The pressure to engage in this kind of talk is intensified because, as I implied earlier, friendship "choice" among "at-risk" children is not free. Put yourself in the place of a child whose aggressive activities are causing him to live in a hostile world (see Chapter 6). You aren't getting along with your family or your teachers, and you can't fit in socially with the regular kids. You vitally need to connect with other children like yourself because you have failed at gaining entry anywhere else. Once in the group, your *hostile attributional bias* is reinforced by your buddies. Your friends tell you that it's fine to go against the system. For the first time, you may find acceptance in an unfriendly world.

In middle-class settings, the popular kids—and, of course, the jocks—are not immune from getting into trouble, for instance, by abusing alcohol or having unprotected sex (Cook, Deng, & Morgano, 2007). (At this point, any reader who has lived through high school or gone to a college frat party is probably saying, "Duh!") But in affluent communities, it's mainly children with emotional problems who gravitate toward the hardcore druggy or delinquent groups. In economically deprived neighborhoods, however, there may be few achievers to hang out with. Flourishing is difficult because the whole community is a toxic place. The only major crowd may be the antisocial group called a gang.

The **gang**, a close-knit, delinquent peer group, embodies society's worst nightmares. Gang members share a collective identity, which they often express by adopting specific symbols and claiming control over a certain territory, or turf (Shelden, Tracy, & Brown, 1997). This predominantly male group is found in many different cultures and historical eras. However, with gangs, the socioeconomic context looms large: Adverse economic conditions promote gangs.

Gangs provide teenagers with status. They offer a child physical protection in dangerous neighborhoods (Shelden, Tracy, & Brown, 1997). There may be economic motives to join. When young people have few options for making it in the conventional way, gangs offer an alternative pathway to making a living (for example, by selling drugs or stealing). So, in dangerous neighborhoods, what starts as time-limited adolescent turmoil is more likely to turn into a life-course criminal career.

This suggests that simply moving inner city children to safe middle-class communities might be able to turn them around. Not so fast! In one large-scale intervention, when impoverished ghetto families were randomly assigned by lottery to move to subsidized housing in an affluent suburban town, the "mover" teenagers actually did worse than the children who were left behind (Fauth, Leventhal, & Brooks-Gunn, 2007; see Figure 9.7)! Actually, when we think more deeply, it makes sense that simply relocating disadvantaged children to a potentially unfriendly place might backfire. If a specific group of teens is defined as "not like us"—in this case, perhaps labeled as "those scary kids who live in subsidized housing"—these young people will end up feeling even more isolated from a caring, nurturing community than before. Once again, it takes a whole *nurturing* village for adolescents to thrive.

deviancy training Socialization of a young teenager into delinquency through conversations centered on performing antisocial acts.

gang A close-knit, delinquent peer group. Gangs form mainly under conditions of economic deprivation; they offer their members protection from harm and engage in a variety of criminal activities.

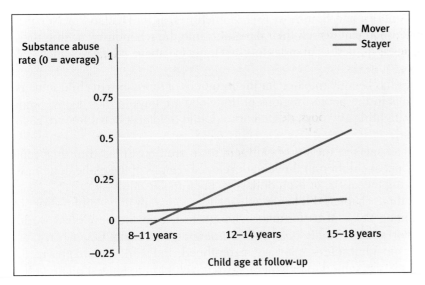

FIGURE 9.7: **Rates of substance abuse for inner-city children who moved to a middle-class community and those who stayed:** In the "moving to opportunity study," children who were relocated from an inner-city neighborhood to an affluent community ended up worse off as teens than those who remained. This graph shows the upsetting findings with regard to substance abuse.

Source: Fauth, R. C., Leventhal, T., & Brooks-Gunn, J. (2007).

🌸 TYING IT ALL TOGETHER

1. Chris and her parents are arguing again. If they're like most families, you can be pretty sure that their arguments concern which of the following topics?

   a. How their community treats the homeless
   b. How late Chris's curfew should be
   c. Issues such as Chris's cleaning her room and doing chores

2. Based on this chapter, at what age might arguments between Chris and her parents be most intense: age 14, 18, or 21?

3. Your pre-teen niece, Heather, hangs around with a small group of girlfriends. You see them at the mall giggling at a group of boys. According to the standard pattern, what is the next step?

   a. Heather and her friends will begin going on dates with the boys.
   b. Heather and her clique will meld into a large heterosexual crowd.
   c. Heather and her clique will form another small clique composed of both girls and boys.

4. Mom #1 says, "Getting involved with the 'bad kids' makes teens get into trouble." Mom #2 disagrees: "It's the kid's personality that causes him to get into trouble." Mom #3 says, "You are both correct—but also partly wrong. The kid's personality causes him to gravitate toward the 'bad kids,' and then, that peer group encourages antisocial acts." Which mother is right?

5. You want to set up a program to help prevent "at-risk" pre-teens from becoming delinquents. First, make up a short checklist to assess who might be appropriate for your program. Then, applying the principles in this chapter, set up a program to turn your potentially "troublemaking teens" around.

6. Moving inner-city children to affluent communities has definite academic and emotional benefits (true or false).

Answers to the Tying It All Together questions can be found on the last page of this chapter.

Final Thoughts: A Note on Adolescence Worldwide

It also takes a nurturing society for adolescence to exist. So many contemporary children growing up in the most impoverished areas of the world still can't count on having this extra decade insulated from adult life. Unfortunately, adolescence has been eliminated for the approximately 1 million children who enter the sex trade every year (UNICEF, 2002b). Some of these boys and girls are street children, living in gangs in

This 14-year-old soldier in Sierra Leone and this teenage prostitute on a Rio de Janeiro street offer a stark testament that, in many areas of the world, young people still do not really have an adolescence.

AP Photo/Adam Butler

Miguel Rio Branco/Magnum Photos

cities in Latin America and Southeast Asia. Sometimes, as in Thailand or Nepal or Nigeria, impoverished parents sell their daughters into the sex industry or ship them to other countries as domestics in order for the family to survive (Gajic-Veljanowki & Stewart, 2007).

Adolescence has been eliminated for the hundreds of thousands of child soldiers. Many combatants in the poorest regions of the globe are boys in their teens. Some are coerced into fighting as young as age 8 or 10 (Child Soldiers Global Report, 2008; UNICEF, 2002b).

Yes, many teenagers in the world's affluent areas are flourishing. But unacceptably large numbers of children in the least-developed regions of the globe don't have the luxury of being teenagers, or even of having a reasonable adult life.

In the next three chapters, I'll be directly focusing on adult life, mainly—but not exclusively—among those of us fortunate enough to live in the developed world. Chapter 10 explores that new life stage called emerging adulthood. Chapter 11 tackles the three classic adult roles—marriage, parenthood, and work. In Chapter 12, I'll look at how we change (and don't change) as we travel into the longest phase of the lifespan, middle age.

SUMMARY

The Mysterious Teenage Mind

Wise observers have described the special "hotheaded" qualities of youth for thousands of years. However, adolescence, first identified by G. Stanley Hall in the early 1900s and characterized by **"storm and stress,"** became a fully distinctive life stage in the United States during the twentieth century, when high school became universal and "isolated" teens together as a group.

According to Jean Piaget, when teenagers reach the **formal operational stage,** they can think abstractly about hypothetical possibilities and reason scientifically. Although even most adults don't typically reason like scientists, older teenagers use the kinds of skills involved in formal operations to plan their lives in an adult way.

According to Lawrence Kohlberg, reaching formal operations makes it possible for people to develop a set of values that guide their lives. By examining how they reason about ethical dilemmas, Kohlberg has classified people at the **preconventional level** (a level of moral judgment in which only punishment and reward are important); the **conventional level** (moral judgment that is based on obeying social norms); and the highest, **postconventional level** (moral reasoning that is based on one's own moral ideals, apart from society's rules). Kohlberg's criteria may not adequately measure real-world morality. Despite this issue and other criticisms of Kohlberg, adolescence is when we first become attuned to society's contradictions and flaws.

According to David Elkind, this new ability to evaluate the flaws of the adult world produces **adolescent egocentrism**. The **imaginary audience** (the feeling that everyone is watching everything one does) and the **personal fable** (the feeling that one's life is utterly unique) are two components of this intense early-teenage sensitivity to what others think.

Studies suggest that some, but not all, storm-and-stress stereotypes about teenagerhood are true. Adolescents are sensitive to social cues and immediate reinforcements. In arousing situations, they are more influenced by their peers. This tendency to take risks, especially with friends, makes early adolescence a potentially more dangerous time. Research, using the **experience-sampling technique,** shows teens are more emotionally intense than adults. Contrary to our stereotypes, however, most adolescents are upbeat and happy. Many flourish during this life stage. Still, an alarming percentage of affluent teens tend to engage in **nonsuicidal self-injury**; others begin to develop the emotional problems that they will battle as adults.

The minority of teenagers who get into *serious* trouble tend to have prior emotional problems (especially with aggression) and to feel distant from their families. Antisocial activities that start early are a risk factor for delinquency down the road. However, **adolescence-limited turmoil** only infrequently becomes **life-course difficulties.** Many problem teens go on to construct fulfilling adult lives. Children who thrive as teens have personal

strengths, interpersonal resources, and tend to live in nurturing communities.

The unique characteristics of the developing teenage brain may make early adolescence a relatively dangerous life stage. The frontal lobes are still maturing. Puberty may heighten teenagers' social sensitivities and emotional states. The lessons for society are: Don't punish teenagers who break the law in the same ways that adult offenders are punished; provide external barriers that limit teenagers' chances of getting into trouble; channel teenage passions in a positive way through **youth development programs**; connect children to high school; adjust the school day to fit adolescent sleep needs. While the "immature brain" conception of adolescence is currently very popular, critics suggest that it may minimize teenagers' considerable strengths.

Teenage Relationships

Teenagers' conflicts with their parents tend to center on mundane issues (cleaning up their room, curfew, and so on), and struggles are most intense during puberty. In late adolescence, children ideally develop a more adult, friend-like relationship with their parents. Cultural differences affect the separation process, the extent of conflict, and the degree to which parents and their children become "friends."

Teenage peer groups comprise **cliques** and **crowds**. These different-sized groups function to convey adolescents, in stages, toward romantic involvement. Crowds, such as the jocks or the brains, give teenagers an easy way of finding people like themselves in large high schools. The popular kids and the jocks (in contrast to the lower-status brains) feel better about themselves in high school than during elementary school. Children who enter delinquent groups tend to be unhappy before high school and remain the unhappiest during their teenage years.

Entering a "bad crowd" smooths the way to more antisocial behavior. The reason is that the group members model the most antisocial leader and compete for leadership by trying to perform the most delinquent acts. **Deviancy training**, in which pre-teens egg one another on by talking about doing dangerous things, leads directly to antisocial behavior as "at-risk" children travel into high school. **Gangs**, mainly male teenage peer groups that engage in criminal acts, are most common in impoverished crime-ridden communities. In impoverished regions of the world, young people may not have an adolescence at all.

KEY TERMS

storm and stress, p. 265
formal operational stage, p. 265
preconventional level of morality, p. 268
conventional level of morality, p. 268

postconventional level of morality, p. 268
adolescent egocentrism, p. 270
imaginary audience, p. 270
personal fable, p. 270

experience-sampling technique, p. 274
nonsuicidal self-injury, p. 276
adolescence-limited turmoil, p. 277
life-course difficulties, p. 278

youth development program, p. 280
clique, p. 285
crowd, p. 285
deviancy training, p. 288
gang, p. 288

ANSWERS TO TYING IT ALL TOGETHER QUIZZES

The Mysterious Teenage Mind

1. c and d.
2. a. preconventional; b. conventional; c. preconventional; d. preconventional; e. postconventional
3. the imaginary audience; the personal fable; adolescent egocentrism
4. b.
5. b, c, and d.

Teenage Relationships

1. b and c.
2. At age 14.
3. b.
4. Mom #3 is correct.

5. Checklist: (1) Is this child unusually aggressive and being rejected by the mainstream kids? (2) Does this child have poor relationships with his parents? (3) Is this child failing at school? (4) Does this child have few interests in life, other than having fun?

Your possible program: Have your group get involved with high school clubs, and be sure to get these teens involved in service-learning opportunities. (You also might work to generally improve the overall quality of the local high school—by encouraging more hands-on, nurturing classes.) Possibly institute group sessions with the teens and their parents to problem-solve about issues. Definitely try to get your group connected with a different set of (prosocial) peers.

6. False.

Early and Middle Adulthood

This three-chapter book part spans the time from high school graduation (at roughly age 18) until society labels us as senior citizens (in our mid sixties)—a lifespan chunk that covers almost 50 years!

Chapter 10—**Constructing an Adult Life** tackles the challenges of making it to full adulthood—a process that may take a decade or more after we reach age 18. In this chapter, among other topics, you will learn what it is like to enter the work world without a college degree and get tips for succeeding in college, choosing a fulfilling career, and finding a mate. If you are a traditional college student or a twenty-something young adult, this chapter is all about your life.

Chapter 11—**Relationships and Roles** continues this focus on work and love by exploring marriage, parenthood, and careers. In the marriage section, you will get insights into how different societies view this core relationship, how marriages naturally change over time, and, especially, get the benefit of the latest research findings related to how to have a satisfying relationship that lasts. In the parenthood section, you'll find out how becoming parents changes a marriage and learn what twenty-first-century motherhood and fatherhood is really like. The last section of the chapter addresses work: How have our career lives been changing? What makes for happiness in this vital role?

Chapter 12—**Midlife**. In much of this chapter, my focus is, "How do people change over the adult years?" Once again, as I survey the research on personality and intellectual change, you'll be getting a wealth of insights into what makes for a fulfilling adult life. The last sections of this chapter cover topics specific to middle age: grandparenthood, caring for elderly parents, and age-related changes in sexuality.

Chapter 10

CHAPTER OUTLINE

Constructing an Adult Life

After graduating from high school in the middle of his class, David looked forward to pursuing his dream of becoming a lawyer. But his freshman year at State U was a nightmare. His courses felt irrelevant. He zoned out during lectures. The work seemed impossibly hard. Especially after a night of clubbing, he couldn't make it to class. David knew he was too immature to get through sophomore year, much less graduate. The only solution seemed to be to drop out for a while and extend his part-time sales associate job to 40 hours a week.

David was getting by financially—and having much more fun—although he still needed to rely on his parents for help with the car payments and rent. Then, headquarters eliminated his branch store, and David was suddenly fired. What followed was a series of temporary jobs that never paid more than $500 a week. Finally, David's parents intervened and encouraged their wayward son to enroll in bartending school.

After getting his certificate, David spent some time with a buddy in Florida, then moved to California and got a job tending bar at a Hilton. Next came a year at the Amsterdam Marriott, followed by some exciting months traveling through the Far East. Then, at age 25, completely broke, David moved back home with his parents for six months.

David thought about returning to college, but rejected that idea. Academics just aren't his thing. He's passionate to go into business—perhaps get a loan to start his own restaurant. The reason is that he met a wonderful woman named Clara. If things continue to progress, they plan to get engaged. After all, David's life plan was to be established in a career and have a family by age 35. Life should be an eternal adventure, but at age 28, it's time for a person to consider growing up!

Can you relate to David's experience—his need to take time off from school, to travel, his worries about constructing an adult life? If so, you might agree with the young people in Figure 10.1 on page 296. You are no longer children, but you have not yet entered the real-world activities that mark full adulthood: financial independence, marriage, parenthood, starting a career. Because it does not fit neatly into the category "adult" or "adolescent," until recently, developmentalists overlooked this in-between period when we are constructing an adult life. The problem, says Jeffrey Arnett (2004, 2007a), is that we need a new category. We need to label *emerging adulthood* as a distinct life stage.

This chapter is devoted to this new life phase. First, I'll explore the features of emerging adulthood; then, examine *identity*, our major psychological challenge during these years. The last half of this chapter centers on those crucial emerging adult concerns: career, college, finding love.

FIGURE 10.1: **Have you reached adulthood?** When asked, "Do you feel that you have reached adulthood?" people of different ages responded differently. Notice that people aged 18 to 25 are unsure about the answer to this question. They are often on the fence, saying "yes and no." If you are in this age group, how would you answer this question?

Source: Arnett (2004).

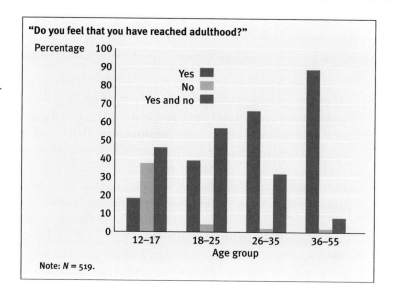

"Do you feel that you have reached adulthood?"

Percentage

- Yes
- No
- Yes and no

Age group: 12–17, 18–25, 26–35, 36–55

Note: *N* = 519.

For this nineteen-year-old married couple who are parents, there may be no emerging adulthood, as they have been thrust into taking on this important adult responsibility at an unusually young age.

Karen Kasmauski/Science Faction/Corbis

Emerging into Adulthood

As you learned in Chapter 1, **emerging adulthood** starts after high school and tapers off by our late twenties. Its function is exploration, trying out options before committing to adult **roles**. Emerging adults are not quite ready to settle down. They feel too young to get married or to have children. They are not financially or emotionally secure. Like David in the vignette, they may be exploring many trial pathways—moving from job to job, entering and then exiting college, traveling the world, testing out relationships before they commit (Arnett, 2007a).

Emerging adulthood is characterized by testing out different possibilities, focusing on self-development, and feeling "in between." But more than simple personal freedom or exploration are involved. Emerging adulthood is *generally* the most challenging, change-inducing stage of life:

We need to totally re-center our lives. During adolescence, we are protected by our parents. Now, our task is to take control of ourselves and act like "real adults" (Tanner, 2006). We used to be able to count on the standard roles of marriage or supporting a family to make us feel adult. No more! Today, people in Western nations view the top three characteristics of adulthood in internal terms. Being an adult means accepting responsibility, supporting yourself, and making your own independent decisions about life (Arnett, 2007a; Fadjukoff, Kokko, & Pulkkinen, 2007).

We move from a highly structured environment into a fluid, unstructured path. During adolescence, high school organizes our days. We wake up, go to class; we are all basically on an identical track. Then, at age 18, our lives diverge. Many of us go to college; others enter the world of work. Some people get married; others decide to never enter that state. Emerging adults live alone or with friends, stay with their parents or move far away. For some emerging adults, constructing "an adult life" takes decades. For others—people who have children, get married, and enter the work world at age 18 or 19—there may be no life stage called emerging adulthood at all. So emerging adulthood is defined by variability—as we each set sail on our own. Why did this structure-free life stage emerge?

Setting the Context: Culture and History

Emerging adulthood is a product of living in the developed world at this moment in history. This longer trip to adulthood—taking time to decide on a career, putting off marriage—was made possible by our dramatic twentieth-century longevity gains. Imagine reaching adulthood a half-century ago. With a life expectancy in the mid-sixties, you could not have afforded the luxury of spending almost a decade constructing an adult life. Now, with life expectancy floating up to the late seventies in industrialized nations, putting off adult commitments until an older age makes excellent sense.

Emerging adulthood has been promoted by social changes. A half-century ago, high school graduates could easily climb to the top rungs of a career. Today, most emerging adults enter college. In the United States and Canada, it typically takes at least six years to get an undergraduate degree, especially because so many of us need to work to help pay for our college years (Cote & Brynner, 2006).

Finally, our attitude toward adulthood has shifted. Emerging adulthood took hold in an individualistic, late-twentieth-century Western culture that stressed self-expression and "doing your own thing," in which people often make dramatic life changes *throughout* adult life.

Longevity, higher education, and personal freedom made emerging adulthood possible. Still, the forces that drive this new life stage vary from place to place. For snapshots of this variability, let's travel to Southern Europe, Scandinavia, and then the United States.

emerging adulthood The phase of life that begins after high school, tapers off toward the late twenties, and is devoted to constructing an adult life.

role The characteristic behavior that is expected of a person in a particular social position, such as student, parent, married person, worker, or retiree.

cohabitation Sharing a household in an unmarried romantic relationship.

nest-leaving Moving out of a childhood home and living independently.

The Mediterranean Model: Living with Parents until Entering Adult life

In Spain and Italy a seriously sagging economy and a preference for hiring men with families makes it difficult for young people to find jobs. In fact, even before the 2008 economic downturn, Italy had one of the highest youth unemployment rates in the European Union (E.U.) (reported in Buhl & Lanz, 2007). The Italian and Spanish cultures have strong norms against **cohabitation**, or living together and having babies before marriage. Students often attend universities close to home. So young people in these southern E.U. countries typically spend their emerging adult years in their parents' house (Arias & Hernandez, 2007; Arnett, 2007b; Buhl & Lanz, 2007). In Spain and Italy, financial issues make the markers of being adult—marriage, family, and career—difficult to reach until people are in their thirties and can find decently paying work.

Many Italian men in their late twenties are still living with their parents because they cannot afford to leave the nest. If you were in this situation, how would you react?

The Scandinavian Plan: Living Independently with Government Help

At the opposite extreme are nations such as Sweden, Norway, Denmark, and Finland, where promoting young people's independent adulthood is a strong societal goal. Here the government subsidizes university attendance. Employers make a special effort to hire young workers. A strong social safety net provides free health care and other benefits to citizens of every age. So in Scandinavia, because young people can survive economically, **nest-leaving**—moving out of one's parents' home to live independently—routinely occurs at about age 18.

Moreover, because being married is not seen as important for having children, in these Northern European nations, the traditional timing of these adult roles is reversed. Swedish women have their first baby at an average age of 28. The typical age of settling down to marriage is 30 for women and 32 for men. For Scandinavian emerging adults, the twenties really can qualify as a stress-free interlude—a time for exploring, for traveling the world, and for enjoying life (Buhl & Lanz, 2007; Cook & Furstenberg, 2002).

The United States: Alternating Between Independence and Dependence

Emerging adulthood in the United States has features of both the Scandinavian and Southern European scenes. Unmarried couples often live together during their emerging-adult years. And—although not as common as in Sweden—many American women have babies before they get married (recall Chapter 1). As in Scandinavia, our U.S. individualistic culture encourages moving out of our parents' home at 18. But, like in Italy, the United States does not actively help young people emerge into work. This makes for a bumpier, less predictable pathway to constructing an adult life (Cook & Furstenberg, 2002).

This erratic up-and-down path became evident when researchers tracked several hundred New York State young people from ages 17 to 27, looking at their progress toward reaching classic adulthood markers such as financial independence, marriage, and living on their own (Cohen and others, 2003). Yes, there was an overall shift to more mature adult status as people moved deeper into their twenties. But notice from Figure 10.2 that, when we look at individuals, we see variability and movement backward and forward toward the benchmarks of being adult. So, at age 22, a man might be cohabiting with the idea of getting married. At 25, he might break up with his fiancée and begin dating again. A woman could be financially independent at 21, then slide backward, depending on her parents' help after losing her job or deciding to return to school.

Although backsliding is normal, it can have emotional costs. In following a huge sample of young Australian women, researchers found that "normative," forward-looking transitions, such as getting married or leaving school, resulted in higher life satisfaction. Backward movement, such as having a relationship break up or leaving the work world to return to the classroom, were linked to lower feelings of happiness (Lee & Gramotnev, 2007).

If you are in your mid- or upper-twenties, take a minute to think about your own progress to adulthood in terms of relationships, career, and becoming financially independent. Does your pathway also show these ups and downs? Did lagging behind in your timetable ever make you feel demoralized or anxious when a step toward adulthood didn't work out? This last question brings up that interesting topic: When *should* emerging adulthood begin and end?

FIGURE 10.2: **The ups and downs of the emerging-adult years:** In a 10-year study tracing how young people develop from age 17 to 27, researchers discovered that many emerging adults move backward and forward on their way to constructing an adult life. These graphs illustrate the adult pathways of five different people in the areas of financial independence and romantic relationships.

Source: Cohen and others (2003).

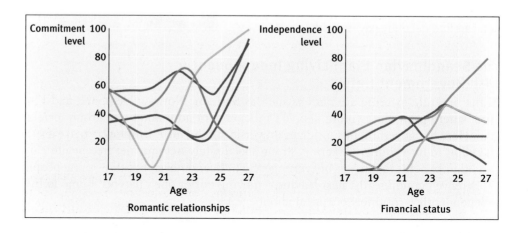

Beginning and End Points

In the United States, we often view the beginning of emerging adulthood as the time when young people first move out of their parents' house. Its exit point is that hazy age when we expect people to settle down in terms of relationships and career.

Leaving Home: Past and Present

Historically, this entry point has undergone fascinating changes. Traditionally—as is still true in many regions of the world—young people in the United States moved out of their parents' house only when they fully entered adult roles. Women left home when they got married. Men moved out when they were financially established, or if work was not available in their area, to search out a job (Modell, 1989).

During the last half of the twentieth century, the draft at World War II, plus the mushrooming number of people attending college, made it socially acceptable for young people to leave their families simply to be independent. This change also anchored the milestone for moving out at around age 18 (Goldscheider & Goldscheider, 1999).

Today, age 18, or after we finish high school, remains the frequent U.S. target date for leaving the nest. But in the United States, as in Southern Europe, this push to declare our independence by moving out—especially in today's economic climate— can be unrealistic because it's so difficult for young people to find a decent job. So the current U.S. nest-leaving pattern is fuzzy, as emerging adults leave home and— as with David in the vignette—periodically move back into their parents' house on their way to constructing an adult life (Aquilino, 2006; Goldscheider & Goldscheider, 1999).

What are these moves back like? Most often, rather than being propelled by mutual love or the desire to be close, they are promoted by the younger generation's need for help. They tend to happen at specific cutting points, such as after graduating from college, or, as I suggested above, leaving the work world and going back to school. The good news is that, even if their prior relationships were rocky, parents typically accept these re-entries (Aquilino, 2006; Ward & Spitz, 2007). Moms and dads are well aware that, in this difficult economy, today's emerging-adults often need to move back for refueling and rest.

This 22-year-old is working as a server in a restaurant and living at home while looking for a journalism job. Do you think this return to the nest feels to her like a return to childhood?

The bad news is that—as I suggested earlier—moving back may make emerging adults feel as if they are sliding into a life state they thought they had left behind (Arnett, 2007a; Lee & Gramotnev, 2007; White, 2002). For insights into how living with one's parents can interfere with a person's normal, developmental need to become adult, let's listen to comments of two emerging adults from different parts of the world.

One 19-year-old Australian female complained:

I think I'd feel a lot more mature if I was out of home. . . . My parents often say, "I wouldn't do that because this could happen." . . . That doesn't give me time to learn or grow as an individual.

(quoted in White, 2002, p. 225)

But Martin, a 24-year-old emerging adult in the Czech Republic, had a more ambivalent view:

"Well the bad thing is that you are under a regime at somebody else's place; they still think you are a child . . . But the advantages are incredible. . . . That's really a good living that I have here."

(quoted in Macek, Bejcek, & Vanickova, 2007, p. 462)

Martin's comment brings up an interesting male/female difference in moving out. Men are more likely to live with their parents than women during their emerging-adult years (Ward & Spitze, 2007). Do you think that mothers and fathers give live-in sons more space to be adult—greater freedom to come and go—than they give their daughters? Is

social clock The concept that we regulate our passage through adulthood by an inner timetable that tells us which life activities are appropriate at certain ages.

age norms Cultural ideas about the appropriate ages for engaging in particular activities or life tasks.

on time Being on target in a culture's timetable for achieving adult life tasks.

off time Being too late or too early in a culture's timetable for achieving adult life tasks.

the nest more male-friendly because—as Martin implies—sons tend to get the perks of living at home, such as meals and laundry, without having to do the household chores? What role might the fact that men tend to marry at an older age than women play in these interesting gender differences in moving out?

Finally, I must emphasize that nest-leaving is not a universal U.S. norm. Because living together is more expected in collectivist cultures, immigrants from Asia and Latin America—as well as ethnic-minority young people in general—don't feel as compelled to move out in order to be independent, as European-heritage young people do. Minority emerging adults, particularly if their parents are struggling economically, may choose to live at home for very adult-centered reasons—to help their families with the finances and the chores (Phinney, 2006). Particularly when they are strongly identified with their culture, family obligations (taking care of mom and dad) are important values for ethnic-minority youth (Kiang & Fuligni, 2009). In sharp contrast to European Americans, Asian-heritage young people actually see taking care of their parents as a landmark *signaling* that they have become adult (Arnett, 2007b).

So the bottom-line issue is not where a child is living, but how that person is acting. Is my son behaving responsibly (Nelson and others, 2007)? Do I see signs that my daughter is working toward her adult goals (Aquilino, 2006)? Even the most laid-back parent is likely to get uneasy when a child is still living at home by a certain age, especially if that person is making little progress in constructing an adult life (Ward & Spitze, 2007). When *do* we expect people to finalize their passage to adulthood? The answer brings up a classic concept in adult development.

The Ticking of the Social Clock

Our feelings about when we should get our adult lives in order reflect our culture's **social clock**, the idea that we chart our adult progress by referring to shared **age norms** (Neugarten, 1972, 1979). These age norms act as guideposts that tell us which behaviors are appropriate at particular ages. If our passage matches up with the normal timetable in our culture, we are defined as **on time**; if not, we are **off time**—either too early or too late in terms of where we should be at a given age.

So in the twenty-first-century developed world, exploring different options is considered "on time" during our twenties, but these activities quickly become off time if they extend well into the next decade of life. A parent whose 35-year-old son is "just dating" and shows no signs of deciding on a career or moves back home for the third

When this not-so-young man in his 40s *finally* proposed to his long-time 38-year-old girlfriend, she and her family were probably thrilled. Feeling "off time" in the late direction in your social clock timetable can cause considerable distress.

David Young-Wolff/Photo Edit, Inc.

or fourth time may become impatient: "Will my child ever grow up?" A woman traveling through her thirties may get uneasy: "I'd better hurry up if I want a family," or "Do I still have time to go to medical school?"

Society sets the general social clock guidelines. Today, it's fine to get married in our thirties (or fifties). But in my mother's World War II cohort, any middle-class woman who didn't land a husband by her mid-twenties was labeled an "old maid." But personal preferences make a difference, too. In one interesting undergraduate survey, developmentalists found that they could predict a given student's social clock timetable by asking a simple question: "Is having a family your main passion in life?" People who said that "marriage is my top-ranking agenda," or "I can't wait to be a mom or dad," were less interested in exploring different options. They often had an earlier timetable for entering adult life (Carroll and others, 2007). Furthermore, as a longitudinal study revealed, students with strong family priorities did tend to get married and have children at a younger age (Salmela-Aro, Aunola, & Nurmi, 2007). So the limits of emerging adulthood are set both by the wider culture and shaped by our own individual priorities and goals.

The problem, however, as we all are well aware, is that our personal social clock agendas are not totally under our control. You cannot simply "decide" to marry the love of your life at a given age. This sense of being "out of control," combined with the pressures to get our adult life in order, may partly explain why emerging adulthood is both an exhilarating *and* emotionally challenging time. On the plus side, people exult: "I want to be young like this forever." "I am incredibly free." On the minus side, during the early twenties, rates of mental disorders such as depression reach their life peak (Schulenberg & Zarrett, 2006).

For some young people, the problem lies in failing at the task of taking adult responsibility. As one emerging adult anguished: "My life looks like a . . . gutter and effort to fight that gutter . . . then back in the gutter . . . I just don't have any control over myself" (quoted in Macek, Bejcek, & Vanickova, 2007, p. 466). For others, there may be serious economic troubles or, as you saw with David, the painful realization that you don't have the skills to get a college degree. Or some emerging adults may simply have the frightened feeling of not knowing where they are going in life: "We do have more possibilities . . . but that's why it's harder" . . . "You study and you wonder what it is good for" (quoted in Macek, Bejcek, & Vanickova, 2007, p. 468). The reason for this inner turmoil is that, during emerging adulthood, we undergo a fundamental mental makeover. We decide *who* to be as adults.

For a surprising number of people, coping with the demands of college can seem like an insurmountable challenge. You need to struggle with the anxious feeling of "can I make it academically?" plus take responsibility for handling all those fast-paced deadlines, all on your own. This shock of first bumping up against adult realities helps explain why, during the early twenties, emotional problems are at their peak.

❀ TYING IT ALL TOGETHER

1. You are giving a toast at your friend Sarah's twenty-first birthday party, and you want to offer some predictions on what the next years might hold for her. Given your new understanding of emerging adulthood, which of the following would *not* be a safe prediction?

   a. Sarah may not reach all the standard markers of adulthood until her late twenties.
   b. Sarah's pathway to adulthood will flow smoothly, with steady, predictable steps forward toward adult life.
   c. Sarah might need to move back in with her parents at some point during the next few years.

2. If Maria moves back home after graduation so that she can pay off her college loans more quickly, what is the main risk she may face?

3. Which of the following two people is most likely to be worrying about a social clock issue: Martha, age 50, who lost her job as a project manager and wants to apply to nursing school, or Lee, age 28, who has just become a father?

4. Statistically speaking, which college freshman might make the transition to adult life earlier—John, who can't wait to start a family, or Sam, whose main focus is establishing his career?

Answers to the Tying It All Together questions can be found on the last page of this chapter.

Constructing an Identity

Erik Erikson was the theorist who highlighted the challenge of transforming our childhood self into the person we will be as adults. As you may remember, he called this process the search for **identity** (see Table 10.1 on page 302).

Time spent wandering through Europe to find himself sensitized Erikson to the difficulties young people face in constructing an adult self. Erikson's lifelong

identity In Erikson's theory, the life task of deciding who to be as a person in making the transition to adulthood.

Myrleen Ferguson Cate/Photo Edit

TABLE 10.1: Erikson's Psychosocial Stages

Life Stage	Primary Task
Infancy (birth to 1 year)	Basic trust versus mistrust
Toddlerhood (1 to 2 years)	Autonomy versus shame and doubt
Early childhood (3 to 6 years)	Initiative versus guilt
Late childhood (6 years to puberty)	Industry versus inferiority
Adolescence (teens into twenties)	**Identity versus role confusion**
Young adulthood (twenties to early forties)	Intimacy versus isolation
Middle adulthood (forties to sixties)	Generativity versus stagnation
Late adulthood (late sixties and beyond)	Integrity versus despair

fascination with identity as a major developmental task, however, crystallized when he worked as a psychotherapist in a Massachusetts psychiatric hospital for troubled teens. Erikson discovered that many of his young patients suffered from a problem he labeled **identity confusion**. They had no sense of *any* adult path. They found it impossible to move ahead:

> [The person feels as] if he were moving in molasses. It is hard for him to go to bed and face the transition into . . . sleep; and it is equally hard for him to get up . . . Such complaints as . . . "I don't know" . . . "I give up" . . . "I quit" . . . are often expressions of . . . despair.
>
> (Erikson, 1968, p. 169)

Some young people felt a frightening sense of falseness about themselves: "If I smoke a cigarette, if I tell a girl I like her, if I make a gesture . . . this third voice is at me all the time—'You're doing this for effect; you're a phony'" (quoted in Erikson, 1968, p. 173). Others could not cope with having any future at all and planned to end their lives on their eighteenth birthday or some other symbolic date.

This total derailment, which Erikson called confusion—an aimless drifting, or shutting down—differs from the active search process he labeled *moratorium* (1980). Taking time out to explore various paths, Erikson argued, is crucial to forming a solid adult identity. Having witnessed Hitler's Holocaust, Erikson believed vehemently that young people must discover their *own* identities. He had seen a destructive process of identity formation firsthand. To cope with that nation's economic problems after World War I, many German teenagers leaped into pathological identities by entering totalitarian organizations such as the Hitler Youth.

Can we spell out the different ways people tackle the challenge of constructing an adult identity? Decades ago, James Marcia answered yes.

Marcia's Identity Statuses

Marcia (1966, 1987) actually devised four different **identity statuses** to expand on Erikson's powerful ideas:

- **Identity diffusion** best fits Erikson's description of the most troubled teens—young people drifting aimlessly toward adulthood without any goals: "I don't know where I am going." "Nothing in life has any appeal."

- **Identity foreclosure** describes a person who adopts an identity without any self-exploration or thought. At its violent extreme, foreclosure might apply to a Hitler Youth member or a young person who becomes a terrorist in his teens. In general, however, researchers define young people as being in foreclosure when they uncritically adopt a life path handed down by some authority: "My parents want me to take over the family business, so that's what I will do."

identity confusion Erikson's term for a failure in identity formation, marked by the lack of any sense of a future adult path.

identity statuses Marcia's four categories of identity formation: identity diffusion, identity foreclosure, moratorium, and identity achievement.

identity diffusion An identity status in which the person is aimless or feels totally blocked, without any adult life path.

identity foreclosure An identity status in which the person decides on an adult life path (often one spelled out by an authority figure) without any thought or active search.

This young person may fit Marcia's category of *identity diffusion*. She seems listless and depressed.

The young man in the background plans to take over this barber shop when his father retires. People who follow their parents' career choices without exploring other possibilities are in *identity foreclosure*.

This college student, volunteering as a tutor in a local public school to see if she wants a career as a teacher, is in *identity moratorium*.

South African singer Buddy Masondo *(left)*, following his life's passion, is in *identity achievement*.

- The person in **moratorium** is engaged in the exciting, healthy search for an adult self. While this internal process may provoke anxiety, because it involves wrestling with different philosophies and ideas, it is critical to arriving at the final stage.

- **Identity achievement** is the end point: "I've thought through my life. I want to be a musician and songwriter, no matter what my family says."

Marcia's categories offer a marvelous framework for pinpointing what may be going wrong (or right) in a young person's life. Perhaps while reading through these descriptions you were thinking, "I have a friend or co-worker in diffusion. Now, I understand exactly what this person's problem is!" How do these statuses *really* play out in life?

The Identity Statuses in Action

Marcia originally believed that, as we move through adolescence, we naturally pass from diffusion to moratorium to achievement. Who thinks much about adulthood in ninth or tenth grade? At that age, your agenda is to cope with puberty. You test the limits. You sometimes act in ways that seem tailor-made to undermine your adult life (see Chapter 9). Then, as older adolescents and emerging adults, we all undertake a moratorium search as adulthood looms in full view. At some point during our twenties, we have reached achievement, finalizing our search for an adult identity.

However, in real life, identity pathways are more erratic. People move backward and forward in statuses *throughout* their adult years (Cote & Brynner, 2006; Waterman, 1999). A woman might enter college exploring different faiths, then become a committed Catholic, start questioning her choice again at 30, and finally settle on her

moratorium An identity status in which the person actively searches out various possibilities to find a truly solid adult life path. A mature style of constructing an identity.

identity achievement An identity status in which the person decides on a definite adult life path after searching out various options.

spiritual identity in Bahai at age 45. As many older students are aware, you may have gone through moratorium and firmly believed you were in identity achievement in your career, and now have shifted back to moratorium when you realized, "I need a more secure, fulfilling job."

Actually, this lifelong moratorium shifting is good. It's unrealistic to think we need to reach a final identity as emerging adults. The push to rethink our lives, to change directions, to have plans and goals, is what makes us human. It is essential at any age. Moreover, revising our identity is vital to living fully since our lives are always prone to being disrupted—as we change careers, become parents, are widowed, or adapt to our children leaving the nest (McAdams, 2001b).

The bad news is that many people seem stuck in unproductive places in their identity search. In some studies, an alarming 1 in 4 undergraduates is locked in diffusion (Cote & Brynner, 2006). They don't seem to have *any* career goals. Or, as I see in my classes, some students may be sampling different paths, but without much Eriksonian moratorium joy. Is your friend who keeps changing his major and putting off graduation really excitedly exploring his options, or is he afraid of entering the real world? Are non-college emerging adults like David, who spend their twenties moving from job to job, really in moratorium, or are they randomly drifting into adult life? Rather than being universal, does Erikson's concept of a zestful moratorium search mainly apply to emerging adults who have intellectual and emotional advantages and are blessed by entering the work world during a good economy? In what ways has the economic downturn changed your social clock timetable, or limited your moratorium search, or shaped your *own* career identity?

FOCUS ON A TOPIC: ETHNIC IDENTITY, A MINORITY THEME

The fact that identity challenges are shaped by our given life situation (rather than being universal) and continue well beyond the twenties is highlighted by examining **ethnic identity**—our sense of belonging to a specific ethnic category such as "Asian American." If, like me, you are part of the mainstream culture, you rarely think of your ethnic identity. For minorities, issues related to coping with one's minority status ("I'm a Chinese American") are more salient, although they wax and wane at different times of life. For instance, being one of the only Chinese Americans in a mainly European American college or workplace heightens someone's ethnic consciousness at *any* life stage (Phinney, 2006).

People cope with this consciousness in various ways. They may develop dual minority and mainstream identities (acting Black in one setting and not another); or reject one identity in favor of another ("I never think of myself as Black, just as American," or "I never think of myself as American, just Black") (Phinney, 2006). The best strategy is to feel connected to your unique heritage and also reach out, seeing yourself as firmly embedded in the *universal* human community (Anglin & Wade, 2007; Chen, Benet-Martinez, & Bond, 2008; Tadmor, Tetlock, & Peng, 2009). Arriving at this milestone may mean coming to terms with prejudice in the wider world. As one "achieved" 21-year-old Mexican American put it: "Even though a person may be racist . . . I'm not going to tell myself I shouldn't like myself because I'm Mexican" (Phinney, 2006, p. 125).

The challenges for **biracial** or **multiracial** emerging adults, people from mixed racial or ethnic backgrounds (like President Obama), can be particularly poignant. These young people face the danger of feeling adrift without *any* single ethnic home. But, here, too, coping with this hurdle and reaching identity achievement can have benefits that apply to every other aspect of life. Fascinating research suggests having a biracial or bicultural background pushes people to think in more creative, complex ways about life (Tadmor, Tetlock, & Peng, 2009). It can work to promote a special kind of

ethnic identity How people come to terms with who they are as people relating to their unique ethnic or racial heritage.

biracial or multiracial identity How people of mixed racial backgrounds come to terms with who they are as people in relation to their heritage.

inner security, too. As one biracial woman in her early thirties put it: "When I was younger I felt I didn't belong anywhere. But now I've just come to the conclusion that my home is inside myself" (Phinney, 2006 p. 128).

Making sense of one's "place in the world" as an ethnic minority is literally a minority identity theme. But every young person has to grapple with those two universal identity issues: choosing a career and finding love. The rest of this chapter tackles those agendas.

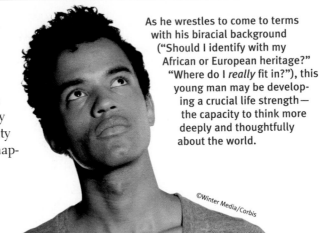

As he wrestles to come to terms with his biracial background ("Should I identify with my African or European heritage?" "Where do I *really* fit in?"), this young man may be developing a crucial life strength— the capacity to think more deeply and thoughtfully about the world.

©Winter Media/Corbis

TYING IT ALL TOGETHER

1. You overheard your psychology professor saying that his daughter Emma shows symptoms of Erikson's identity confusion. Emma must be _____ (drifting, actively searching for an identity), which in Marcia's identity status framework is a sign of _____ (diffusion, foreclosure, moratorium).

2. Joe said, "Because we Malloys have worked for generations on the family farm, I know that this must be my career." Kayla replied, "I don't know what my career will be. I'm searching out different possibilities." Joe's identity status is _____, while Kayla's status is _____ (moratorium, foreclosure, diffusion, or achievement).

3. The following is *not* a criticism of Marcia's identity status framework.

   a. Rather than reaching identity achievement in their twenties, people can cycle back and forth in identity statuses throughout life.
   b. Rather than being a universal experience, going through moratorium may be a luxury of "coming of age" in a good economy.
   c. Very few people reach identity achievement today.

4. Confronting the challenge of having a biracial or multiracial identity tends to make people think in more rigid ways about the world. (True or False)

Answers to the Tying It All Together questions can be found on the last page of this chapter.

Finding a Career

In a famous statement, Sigmund Freud, when asked to sum up the definition of ideal mental health, answered with the simple words, "the ability to love and work." Let's now look at finding ourselves in the world of work.

Teens' Career Dreams

When did you begin seriously thinking about your career? What influences are drawing you to psychology, nursing, or business—a compelling class, a caring mentor, or just the conviction that this field would fit your talents best? How do young people feel about their careers, their futures, and the act of working?

To answer these kinds of questions, Mihaly Csikszentmihalyi and Barbara Schneider (2000) began a pioneering study of teenagers' career dreams. They selected 33 U.S. schools and interviewed students from sixth to twelfth grade. To chart how young people felt—when at home, with friends, when working at school—they used the *experience-sampling method* (discussed in Chapter 9). Now, let's turn to their insights, plus those of other researchers.

TABLE 10.2: Expected Occupations of Teens in Csikszentmihalyi and Schneider's Study

Rank	Career Goal	Percentage of Teens (n = 3,891)
1.	Doctor	10
2.	Businessperson	7
3.	Lawyer	7
4.	Teacher	7
5.	Athlete	6
6.	Engineer	5
7.	Nurse	4
8.	Accountant	3
9.	Psychologist	3
10.	Architect	3

Source: Adapted from Csikszentmihalyi & Schneider (2000).

The Up Side: High Goals

Every teenager, Csikszentmihalyi and Schneider discovered, expects to go to college. As you can see in Table 10.2, almost everyone plans to have a professional career. The tendency to aim high appears regardless of gender or social class. Whether male or female, rich or poor, adolescents in Western countries have lofty career goals (see also Arnett, 2007c; Hechhausen and others, 2008).

Having high ambitions—at least with regard to schooling—is actually positive. In one California study, high school seniors who had unusually optimistic educational expectations ("I can make it through college") were less likely to engage in delinquent behaviors, happier, and prone to still be enrolled in school four years down the road (Hechhausen and others, 2008).

The Down Side: Unrealistic Ideas

Teenagers, however, are understandably vague in appreciating the barriers to implementing their actual dream *careers*. Can 10 percent of the teenage population (see Table 10.2) really make it through medical school? Is a psychology Ph.D. a good bet if a person hates reading? What happens when you find out that you need to have an incredibly high GPA to enter your university's nursing program, or that you can't go to law school because you'll never, ever get those astronomical scores on the LSAT? Career disappointment seems to lurk right around the corner for many young people as they emerge from the cocoon of high school.

Can we predict who is set up to cope with these kinds of setbacks and move more easily into a satisfying career? Without minimizing the often vital role of external barriers, such as dealing with poverty or a poor economy, clues come from looking at internal qualities: whether young people are "planful" and adaptable (Pizzolato, 2007)—specifically, whether teenagers like to work.

A Core Ability: Enjoying Work

Using the experience-sampling records and interviews, Csikszentmihalyi and Schneider (2000) classified the teenagers in their study into two categories: workers and players. *Workers* enjoy being productive. They relish striving toward goals. *Players* hate the idea of working. They speak in terms of what they want to avoid, rather than what they want to do. So being at the upper end of the player spectrum puts a teenager at risk of being in career diffusion during the emerging-adult years. One player high school senior in the study vividly described this feeling of drifting into life when she told the researchers: "None of my friends really know what they want to do. I mean, you know, they want to go to college . . . but no one is really sure exactly where they are going to be. . . . They just talk about how they want to, you know, be friends and have barbecues" (quoted in Csikszentmihalyi & Schneider, 2000, p. 86).

Can we identify which boys and girls are most likely to be players—or are apt to emerge into adulthood identity diffused? Because personality is somewhat consistent, as you might expect, children with internalizing and externalizing problems are at special risk of having problems making the transition into adult life (Dennissen, Asendorpf, & van Aken, 2008). Imagine being very anxious, or well aware of your troubles with focusing or controlling your hostile emotions, and you can understand why, for young people with these more difficult temperaments, even the act of searching for a job (or relationship) can be a stressful, frightening task. But all is not lost. Emerging adulthood can be a watershed life stage in terms of personal growth.

A Core Development: Personality Growth

Actually, several longitudinal studies suggest the twenties are the time of life when our personalities change the most (Clausen, 1991; Costa & McCrae, 2002; Eichorn and others, 1981; Haan, Millsap, & Hartka, 1986). Moreover, the good news is that, during emerging adulthood, there *is* a general tendency to grow more mature. Emerging adults are more prone to weigh their options in making decisions. They think about life in more complex ways (Labouvie-Vief, 2006). During their twenties, people begin to see their failures as life lessons rather than simply unredeemable, devastating defeats (Gottlieb, Still, & Newby-Clark, 2007). (More about these signs of mature adulthood in Chapter 12.)

When researchers gave personality tests to a group of 17-year-olds and then retested them at age 27, aggression, in particular, declined, and people tended to improve most dramatically in self-control. Interestingly, in this study, the emerging adults who changed very little were those who were most mature as teens (Donnellan, Conger, & Burzette, 2007). So, if an adolescent is already a mature, resilient worker, you aren't likely to see much difference in his basic personality as he travels into adulthood. Expect much more "growing up" for many—but not all—young people who are not doing so well during their teenage years (see also Cramer, 2008; Johnson and others, 2007).

What causes these upward shifts in a basic temperamental trait that developmentalists call *conscientiousness* (to be described in Chapter 12)? One possibility is that, as the frontal lobes fully mature, we naturally develop adult self-control. But interesting evidence suggests that rather than being biologically driven, real-world events unique to this crucial life stage propel emotional growth. In the longitudinal study I mentioned earlier, suggesting that childhood externalizing problems predicted a rocky passage into adulthood, teenagers with this least-conscientious temperament were likely to become far less hostile and angry if they got satisfying, responsible jobs (Dennissen, Asendorpf, & van Aken, 2008). Therefore, even the most at-risk emerging adults can get it together if they find the right person-environment fit at work. An absorbing inner state may have the power to transform players into workers and help lock *all of us* into the right career.

A Core Goal: Finding Flow

Think back over the past week to the times you felt really energized and alive. You might be surprised to discover that events you looked forward to—such as relaxing at home or watching a favorite TV program—do not come to mind. Many of life's most uplifting experiences occur when we connect deeply with people. Others take place

For this graduate student who is puzzling over the meaning of a difficult paper in his field, the hours may simply fly by. Intensely challenging activities that fully draw on our talents and skills produce that marvelous inner state called " flow."

when we are immersed in some compelling task. Csikszentmihalyi names this intense task absorption **flow**.

Flow is very different from simply "feeling happy or good." We enter this state when we are immersed in an activity that stretches our capacities, such as the challenge of climbing a mountain or decoding a difficult academic problem, or (hopefully) getting absorbed in mastering the material in this book. People also differ in the kinds of activities that cause flow. For some of us, it's hiking in the Himalayas that produces this feeling. For me, it has been writing this book. When we are in flow, we enter an altered state of consciousness in which we forget the outside world. Problems disappear. We lose a sense of time. The activity feels infinitely worth doing for its own sake. Flow makes us feel completely alive.

Csikszentmihalyi (1990), who has spent his career studying flow, finds that some people rarely experience this feeling. Others feel flow several times a day. If you feel flow only during a rare mountain-climbing experience or, worse, when robbing a bank, Csikszentmihalyi argues that it will be difficult to construct a satisfying life. The challenge is to find flow in ways related to your career.

Flow depends on being *intrinsically motivated*. This means we must be mesmerized by what we are doing right now for its own sake, not for an extrinsic reward. But there also is a future-oriented dimension to feeling flow. Flow, according to Csikszentmihalyi, happens when we are working toward a goal.

For example, the idea that this book will be published two years from now is the ultimate goal that is pushing me to write this very page. But what really riveted me to my chair for hours this morning is the actual process of writing itself. Getting into a flow state is often elusive. On the days when I can't construct a paragraph, I get anxious. But if I could not regularly find flow in my writing, I would never be writing this book.

Figure 10.3 shows exactly why finding flow can be difficult. Reaching that state depends on a delicate person–environment fit. When a task seems beyond our capacities, we become anxious. When an activity is too simple, we grow bored. Ideally, the activities in which we feel flow can alert us to the careers in which we want to spend our lives. Think about some situation in which you recently felt flow. If you are in moratorium or worry you may be in career diffusion, can you use this feeling to clue you in to a particular field?

Drawing on the compelling concept of flow, plus my discussion of identity, let's now explore two different paths that emerging adults follow.

FIGURE 10.3: **The zone of flow:** Notice that the flow zone (white area) depends on a delicate matching of our abilities and the challenge involved in a particular real-world task. If the task is too difficult or beyond our capacities, we land in the upper, red area of the chart and become anxious. If the task is too easy, we land in the lower, gray area of the chart and become bored. Moreover, as our skills increase, the difficulty of the task must also increase to provide us with the sense of being in flow.

Which theorist's ideas about teaching and what stimulates mental growth does this model remind you of? (Turn page upside down for answer.)

Source: Adapted from Csikszentmihalyi (1990).

Answer: Vygotsky.

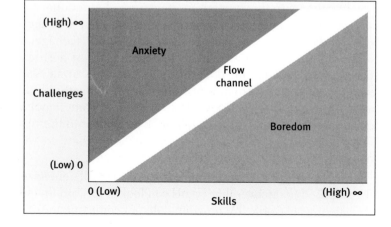

Emerging into the Workforce Without a College Degree

Roughly 2 of every 3 U.S. high school graduates enroll in college (Fouad & Bynner, 2008). Then, the ranks start to thin. Like David in the chapter-opening vignette, half of all entering freshmen don't make it to graduation within the next five years (U.S. Department of Education, 2008). By their mid-twenties, slightly more than 1 in 4 U.S. emerging adults has completed a four-year degree (Fouad & Bynner, 2008). What is the fate of the legions of emerging adults who do not finish college?

People who do not go to college or who never get their degree can have very fulfilling careers. Some may excel at Robert Sternberg's practical or creative intelligence (described in Chapter 7) but do not do well at academics. When they find their person–environment fit in the work world, they blossom. Consider the career of that college failure, the famous filmmaker named Woody Allen, or even that of Bill Gates, who found his undergraduate courses too confining and left Harvard to pioneer a new field.

Unfortunately, however, as I suggested earlier, young people like David in the opening vignette, who emerge directly into the workforce, tend to have a difficult time. They are less likely to reach identity achievement in their careers by their thirties or forties than their counterparts who do complete a college or graduate school degree (Fadjukoff, Kokko, & Pulkkinen, 2007). They tend to shift from job to job or remain chronically unemployed and spend their first working years in the **secondary labor market**, a group of jobs offering low pay and little security. Because the stereotype of "unreliable teenager" can linger, it is not until a worker reaches the mid-twenties that some employers view that young person as good promotion material at a job.

Moreover, non-college emerging adults are at a double disadvantage when they search for work. Many **primary labor market** jobs—those that offer good salaries and benefits such as health care—require an associate's degree, technical certification, or a B.A. (Rosenbaum, 2001).

Still, in interviewing a group of these non-college young people, researchers found that a satisfying experience was possible if a job offered a chance for advancement, friendly co-workers, and an opportunity to enhance work skills. One key to happiness was a quality that psychologists call *planful competence*—the ability to have a proactive "worker like" strategy to finding work. People did best when they reached out for help to friends and to other adults and had an open-minded, flexible approach to potential careers. Another key to satisfaction, as you may already have guessed, was being in flow:

> *During my first weeks as a server, I was terrified that I wouldn't be able to keep up. Now, I am in the flow of things. I served 20 customers on Saturday. Time passed so quickly. When closing rolled around, I thought it was like 7 o'clock.*

> *When I paint houses I enter a kind of altered state—I will be working for 14 hours and I get amazed when I notice it's dark.*

In theory, the United States has many avenues for finding flow-inducing careers: job fairs, Internet sites, and word of mouth. However, despite a U.S. movement toward establishing high schools in which teens choose a career track in tenth or eleventh grade (any developmentalist could inform these well-meaning administrators that age 15 or 16 is *far, far* too young to commit to a work identity!), we leave young people to sink or swim when it comes to actually *finding* work.

This disconnect between school and jobs does not exist in some other countries. In Japan, employers develop close relationships with specific educational institutions (Rosenbaum, 2001). When looking for workers, companies turn to these feeder

Photodisc

This twenty-something, high school graduate can only find work in the low-wage, *secondary labor market*. For young people who do not go to college, it can take years to find a satisfying career identity or land a better paying *primary labor market job.*

flow Csikszentmihalyi's term for feeling total absorption in a challenging, goal-oriented activity.

secondary labor market A category of low-wage jobs providing few benefits and little security.

primary labor market A category of jobs offering good salaries and benefits such as health care and retirement plans.

schools and hire students the faculty recommends. This practice not only makes for a less stressful **school-to-work transition**, it also helps with a classic teenage complaint: "My courses are totally irrelevant; I am just marking time to get my degree." Suppose you knew your performance in high school or college was critical to your future employment. Wouldn't you be more highly invested in your classes?

Germany offers another model for the school-to-work transition. In their late-elementary-school or early-teenage years, non–college-bound students enter a vocational track that leads to a job in a particular industry. The centerpiece of the German program is an apprenticeship system. Employers partner with schools to offer on-the-job training. Graduates emerge with a job in a particular firm (Cook & Furstenberg, 2002).

Many of us would instinctively reject the German approach because it labels people as "non-college material" at an early age. The great benefit of the U.S. system, in contrast to many other industrialized countries, is that we give people continual second chances. Theoretically, we can reinvent ourselves in the work world no matter how poorly we performed in school. Moreover, many guidance counselors now encourage every high school senior to enroll in college, no matter how dismal their grades (Kerckhoff, 2002; Rosenbaum, 2001).

One observer, however, suggests that this uncritical positive stance has costs: It contributes to a kind of preoperational thinking, a magical fantasy that "college will turn me around." In truth, the best predictor of succeeding in college is succeeding in high school. Only 1 of 5 public high school graduates with an average of C or below receives a four-year college degree (Engle, n.d.). By comparison, more than 3 of 4 A-average high school students go on to get their degree.

INTERVENTIONS: Helping Young People Find Careers Outside the College Path

Because finishing college is a long shot for a young person in the lower half of a public school class, experience in the work world may be a more productive route to advancing in a career (Rosenbaum, 2001). Employers look for qualities such as reliability, initiative, and the ability to get along with co-workers—skills that can best be demonstrated by a track record at work.

Joining the work world directly from high school does not mean never returning to college, as many readers are well aware. In many European countries, the social clock for college is actually *programmed* to start ticking a few years after high school (Arnett 2007c). The reasoning is that time spent traveling or at a job helps young people hone in on what they want to study during their college years.

As conscientiousness shifts upward during the twenties, putting off college for a few years may improve academic performance. I cannot tell you how many times students have told me, "I was too young to be in college at 18. Now, I have the motivation to succeed." Their grades show it, too!

Still, we should not let society off the hook. The more structured school-to-work transitions in Germany and Japan suggest that the United States can do more to strengthen the link between school and work, for both non–college-bound young people and people bound for Ph.D.'s (Kerckhoff, 2002).

Why do I regularly see my emerging-adult relatives—even those with the best credentials—flounder? Why don't college career centers *really* function as conduits to work? Suppose there was a vigorous national effort to develop links among high schools, colleges, and relevant employers in each community. If you knew that your high school teachers or college professors had the power to get you your first post-graduation job, wouldn't you be more committed to class and feel more secure about emerging into the world of work?

Table 10.3 pulls together some career-search tips based on this discussion of emerging adulthood, identity, and finding a career. Let's turn next to the setting you are in right now.

school-to-work transition
The change from the schooling phase of life to the work world.

TABLE 10.3: Some Career-Search Tips

1. Don't be overly concerned that you have not decided on a particular career during college. Many people take considerable time to explore various possibilities before settling on a satisfying career.

2. Conduct an active moratorium career search by reaching out to other people for advice and exploring a number of potential fields.

3. Use the activities that give you flow as guidelines for choosing a satisfying career. If you feel in diffusion right now, remember that your work orientation can change dramatically if you find a job that gives you a sense of flow.

4. Don't feel you must go directly to college—especially if academics are not your "thing." Build up a track record at work. If you do decide to take the college path later, you may be a better student.

Emerging Directly into College

College offers a marvelous opportunity for exploring your identity. You can venture far from your hometown or stick close by, be a big fish in a little pond (attending a small private school) or be a little fish in a big pond (enrolling in a large university). Whether you want to explore deaf culture or agriculture, some school will fit your needs. What do the studies exploring college satisfaction suggest about being successful during these special years?

As you can see by looking at the flow chart in Figure 10.4, a variety of forces combine to predict college happiness and success (Tinto, 1987). The bottom-line message is that the key to college fulfillment lies in becoming emotionally connected to school.

This sense of being embedded in a caring community explains why students at small residential colleges are often highly satisfied with their undergraduate experience (Astin, 1999; Engle, n.d.). It tells us why living off campus and working more than 20 hours per week increases the risk of dropping out (Bozick, 2007). It explains why students who get heavily involved in college activities develop closer friendships (Bohnert, Aikins, & Edidin, 2007). It accounts for the fact that developing close campus friendships not only promotes college satisfaction, but also fosters academic success (Boute and others, 2007).

Table 10.4 on page 312 offers a few tips for helping conquer this new academic world. Now, let's look at some suggestions for generally making the most of your undergraduate years.

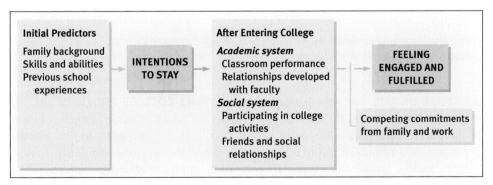

FIGURE 10.4: Predicting college success—a flow chart: What we bring to college, in terms of family background, skills, and school experiences, affects our motivation to succeed as undergraduates. Once in college, our academic talents and relationships with the faculty, as well as our school activities and relationships with friends, help foster the sense of engagement that is vital to succeeding happily. Competing commitments (yellow box), however, tend to interfere with forming an emotional connection to college life.

Source: Adapted from Tinto (1987).

TABLE 10.4: Tips for "Making the Grade" in College

When planning your semester: Find out about each teacher before you enroll in classes; balance your schedule to include a few more difficult and easier courses; and, if you aren't an early morning person, avoid 8 or 9 A.M. classes. Then:

1. Ask for *concrete* information about the tests and papers. ("Will the exams come mainly from lectures and/or the reading?" "What *exactly* are you looking for in a term paper?")

2. Do the assigned reading before you come to class and be SURE to attend every day. (I know it's difficult when no one is watching, but it's essential for performing well and becoming an adult!)

3. Form study groups with your classmates before exams. Start studying early, and, perhaps, take a minute to mentally go over the high points of each lecture after you leave class.

And, if you follow the above steps and fail the first test, e-mail or visit your teacher to ask for advice.

INTERVENTIONS: Making College a Flow Zone

IMMERSE YOURSELF IN THE COLLEGE MILIEU. Following this advice is easy at a small residential college: You live on campus. The college experience is at your doorstep, ready to be embraced. At a large university, especially a part-time commuter school, you'll need to make active efforts to get involved in campus life. Choose, if possible, to live in a college dormitory or move close to school. If you are taking a full load of classes, try to avoid working full time. Join a college organization, or two, or three. Working for the college newspaper or becoming active in the drama club not only will provide you with a rich source of friends, but can help promote your career identity, too.

CONNECT YOUR CLASSES TO POTENTIAL CAREERS. Because the link between college courses and specific careers is often ill defined, take steps to institute your personal school-to-work transition. Set up independent studies involving volunteer work. If you are interested in science, work in a professor's lab. If your passion is politics, do an internship with a local legislator. In one study, college seniors mentioned that the highlight of their undergraduate experience occurred during a mentored project in the real world (Light, 2001).

MAKE CONNECTIONS WITH YOUR PROFESSORS. College takes on a different flavor when students feel close ties with professors. Take several courses with a favorite nurturing professor. Visit your adviser every semester, and—if this person doesn't seem all that responsive—ask your favorite instructor to be your adviser. (She will be flattered.) As this senior describes, feeling cared about by a professor can be a peak experience in your personal life:

> He began by asking me which single book had the biggest impact on me. He was the first professor who was interested in what matters to me. . . . You can't imagine how excited I was.

(quoted in Light, 2001, pp. 82–83)

CAPITALIZE ON THE DIVERSE HUMAN CONNECTIONS COLLEGE PROVIDES. As you saw during adolescence, the crowds and cliques we select as undergraduates propel the direction of our future self (Astin, 1993). At college, it is tempting to find a single clique and then not reach out to other crowds. Resist this impulse. Students—particularly European Americans—report that one of the major growth experiences college offers is the chance to get to know people of different backgrounds, religions, and races (Hu & Kuh, 2003). Let's see what another undergraduate had to say:

> I have re-evaluated my beliefs. . . . At college, there are people of all different religions around me. . . . Living . . . with these people marks an important difference. . . . [It] has made me reconsider and ultimately reaffirm my faith.

(quoted in Light, 2001, p. 163)

How can you break out of your social circle and promote your own Eriksonian moratorium search? One strategy, again, is to spend your first years living in a diverse college residence hall. Another is to participate in the *inclusive* activities on campus that provide you with flow. Writing for the newspaper or becoming active in student government will not only help you establish your identity, but will also smooth your way to that other central goal of constructing an adult life—finding love.

TYING IT ALL TOGETHER

1. Your 15-year-old nephew continually gets into trouble at school and home, and his parents are concerned about what will happen when he enters the world of work. Based on the information in this section, what can you legitimately say to your relatives about how troubled teens fare, work-wise, as emerging adults?

2. Hannah confesses that she loves her server job—but only during busy times. When the restaurant is hectic she gets energized. Time flies by. She feels exhilarated, at the top of her form, like a multitasking whiz! Hannah is describing a _____ experience.

3. As a member of the President's Commission on youth development, you've been asked to offer advice for improving the school-to-work transition in the United States. Give two suggestions based on what the Germans and Japanese do.

4. Your cousin Juan, who is about to enter his freshman year, asks you for tips about how to succeed in college. Based on the information in this section, pick out the advice you should *not* give:

   a. Get involved in campus activities.
   b. Be sure not to live in a dorm or you will just party.
   c. Get to know at least one professor personally.

Answers to the Tying It All Together questions can be found on the last page of this chapter.

College is an ideal time to connect with people from different backgrounds. So go for it!

Finding Love

How do twenty-first-century emerging adults negotiate Erikson's first task of adult life (see Table 10.5)—**intimacy**, the search for a soul mate or enduring love? How do romantic relationships develop, and why do they sometimes fall apart? What insights

TABLE 10.5: Erikson's Life Stages and Their Psychological Tasks

Life Stage	Primary Task
Infancy (birth to 1 year)	Basic trust versus mistrust
Toddlerhood (1 to 2 years)	Autonomy versus shame and doubt
Early childhood (3 to 6 years)	Initiative versus guilt
Late childhood (6 years to puberty)	Industry versus inferiority
Adolescence (teens into twenties)	Identity versus role confusion
Young adulthood (twenties to early forties)	**Intimacy versus isolation***
Middle adulthood (forties to sixties)	Generativity versus stagnation
Late adulthood (late sixties and beyond)	Integrity versus despair

*Although we began to tackle the early adult search for intimacy in this section, I'll be continuing this discussion in Chapter 11, when we discuss marriage.

intimacy Erikson's first adult task, involving connecting with a partner in a mutual loving relationship.

does the social science research offer for finding an ideal mate? We now explore these questions one by one.

Setting the Context: Different Partner Choices

Daolin Yang, 77, a grandfather, is retired and lives in Hebie Province, China. . . . At age 15, he married his wife Yufen, then 13, in a village. . . . A matchmaker proposed the marriage on behalf of the Yang family. They have been married for 62 years and reared three children. . . . He says that they married first and dated later. It is "cold at the start and hot in the end." The relationship gets better and better over the years.

(Xia & Zhou, 2003, p. 231)

This long-lasting love story reminds us that searching for a mate on our own is a uniquely Western phenomenon. Throughout history, families have routinely taken over that responsibility. Even today in our multicultural nation (see the Experiencing the Lifespan box below), among certain groups, mate-selection choices are carefully controlled. Still, the basic recent thrust in our individualistic society is for young people to have *much more* latitude than ever in the partners they can select. Let's explore two ways that mate-selection processes in the United States and the developed world have widened over the past thirty or so years.

The Growth of Interracial (and Inter-ethnic) Dating

During much of U.S. history, deciding to date outside of your "own kind" (even religiously) was a daring act. By the beginning of the twenty-first century, 1 in 3 European Americans reported getting romantically involved with someone of a different ethnicity or race. More than half of all African Americans, Hispanic Americans, and Asian Americans had also made that claim (Yancey & Yancey, 2002).

Openness—especially to interracial dating—varies from person to person. In sampling online personal advertisements, one researcher found (no surprise) that

---

EXPERIENCING THE LIFESPAN: ANOTHER PERSPECTIVE ON U.S. DATING AND MATING

To keep in mind that selecting love relationships on our own is far from universal, even in our choice-oriented society, listen to Alara, an immigrant from India:

Dating is not allowed in my religion. That is a very strict rule. If I was to date someone and he was not Hindu, I couldn't marry him. If I met a Hindu I might be allowed to see him, but it wouldn't be dating in the traditional sense. You can't date for the experience. It's always for the purpose of marriage.

We have loosened up a bit. My parents had an arranged marriage. My mother's and father's parents were best friends—and my two grandpas decided that my parents would marry each other when they were little children. Mom says if she had had a choice she would not have married Dad. They used to argue all the time. Now that we are grown up, Mom moved back to Pittsburgh and teaches school there, and my dad still lives in Springfield. They still say they are married, but they really don't talk much.

When I was in kindergarten, we moved from India to Pittsburgh, where there is a large Indian community. Eight years ago, my dad got a better job offer, and we moved to western Massachusetts. In Pittsburgh, all my friends were Indian, either Hindu or Muslim; after we went to Springfield I didn't have one Indian friend. They were all Americans. They were real cool, but I always felt their values were different.

My brother is 29 and about to get married. He met Shukla, his fiancée, at a friend's wedding. She lives in California. Every time he visits, her mom chaperones them. They are not allowed to be alone together. My sister is also engaged, but, once again, when they see each other, my mom always has to be there.

I did have a problem with our practices, but I've accepted them. When I lived at home, I didn't date. Then, when I went to college I went crazy for about a year. I fell in love with a Baptist guy, but after a while I realized I had to end the relationship. My mom, it would have broken her heart. I care too much about my family. People would look down on my parents if I married outside our religion. And, suppose I married my Baptist boyfriend, I mean, what religion would my children be? I want to give my children a firm sense of identity. So I'm comfortable waiting until I meet the right Hindu man.

adults who identified themselves as "cultural conservatives" and/or said they were "highly religious" were likely to specify only wanting a partner of their own race (Yancey, 2007). Who dates outside their ethnic group specifically during the college years? What happens to undergraduates who make this choice?

To answer these questions, researchers polled students the summer before they entered a large multicultural California state university. Then, they tracked those undergraduates' dating practices over the next four years (Levin, Taylor, & Caudle, 2007). As you might imagine, having close friends of different ethnicities during high school predicted dating outside one's ethnic group. Being highly identified with one's own ethnicity made people more likely to date only people in their "group." Students who did get involved with someone of a different ethnicity (about half the sample) ended up more accepting and less racially biased at the end of college. But they also reported getting some negative feedback from members of their own group. So, although times are changing, if you do get involved with a person of another race or ethnicity, be prepared for a comment or two from your fellow Asian Americans, African Americans, or European Americans to "stick to your own kind."

homophobia Intense fear and dislike of gays and lesbians.

It's a pleasure to see this college couple deeply in love; but, even today, they may get hassled by a few Asian American and African American undergraduates around campus for not sticking to their "own" racial group.

More Acceptance of Same-Sex Romance

About 10 years ago at my Southern university, I remember being disturbed by the snickering that would sometimes erupt when I mentioned issues related to being gay. No more! Although the gay rights movement exploded on the scene in the late 1960s in New York's Greenwich Village, it's most revolutionary strides took place within the twenty-first century's first years. As one expert put it, in an astonishingly few years, the announcement of "I'm gay" went from evoking shock waves to producing yawns— "So what else is new?" (Savin-Williams, 2001, 2008).

This is not to say that **homophobia**, or intense fear and dislike of gays and lesbians, is absent today. Discrimination continues to be rampant in many areas of the world, where coming out can mean death. (In 2007, the Iranian President, for instance, responded to an interviewer who asked about his country's treatment of homosexuals with this amazing comment: "Oh, we don't have *those* people in our nation.") Stereotypes such as the ones described in Table 10.6 on page 316 are widespread. Being shunned for one's sexual orientation is a common experience among ethnic minorities, especially for older cohorts of men (David & Knight, 2008; Wilson & Yoshikawa, 2004). During their early teenage years, gay young people—even in liberal nations such as Holland—report more distant family relationships and comparatively low self-esteem (Bos and others, 2008). In the United States, without supportive teachers, gay and bisexual adolescents remain highly vulnerable to being victimized at school (Darwich and others, 2008). But for a young person who is upper-middle-class, European American, and in a liberal high school, coming out can be a teenage coming-of-age event. In an era in which hip college students define themselves as "mostly straight," "sometimes gay," or "occasionally bisexual," even limiting one's sexual orientation to a certain category can be passé (Diamond & Savin-Williams, 2003; Thompson & Morgan, 2008).

This cake decoration, created in Seattle for the first annual Gay Wedding Show, is a perfect sign of how the landscape of love has seriously widened in the United States. However, it might not fly so well at a wedding show that was taking place in Egypt or Iran!

TABLE 10.6: Homosexual Stereotypes and Scientific Facts

Stereotype: *Overinvolved mothers and distant fathers "cause" boys to be homosexual.*

Scientific Fact: There is no evidence that this or any other parenting problem causes homosexuality. The causes of homosexuality (which occurs in many mammals and so may play an adaptive function in evolution) are unknown—however, recent research suggest levels of prenatal testosterone may help program a fetus' later gender orientation (see Chapter 6).

Stereotype: *Through counseling, homosexuals can change their sexual orientation from gay to straight.*

Scientific Fact: Outcome studies exploring "reparation therapy"—strongly discouraged by every major U.S. mental health organization but practiced by a few Christian ministries—are nonexistent. One researcher did conduct a telephone poll of people who said they had successfully undergone this therapy (Spitzer, 2003). Although complete change was rare, these people did report that they had changed their orientation from predominantly homosexual to heterosexual. The strong caution here is that this study comes from a very self-selected sample—men and women anxious to report success.

Stereotype: *Homosexual couples have lower-quality relationships—their interactions are "psychologically immature."*

Scientific Fact: Researchers compared the relationships of committed gay couples with their heterosexual counterparts via a variety of strategies. They explored each partner's attachment security (see the discussion of this important attribute later in the chapter). They gave questionnaires in which partners rated their concerns in the relationship. They directly observed how people related by videotaping the couple discussing a problem area. The finding: NO differences in the quality of heterosexual and homosexual relationships were discovered. There was one exception, however: Lesbian couples were rated as relating more harmoniously when being observed (Roisman and others, 2008).

Stereotype: *Homosexual parents have pathological family interactions and disturbed children.*

Scientific Fact: British researchers compared groups of lesbian-mother, two-parent-heterosexual, and single-mother families (Golombok and others, 2003). They rated the parents and their elementary-school-aged children on various measures of child rearing and mental health. Boys and girls raised in lesbian families had no problems with their gender identity and had no signs of impaired mental health. In fact, the lesbian mothers showed some signs of superior parenting—hitting their children less frequently and engaging in more fantasy play.

Coming out to your friends or announcing your sexual orientation in school is very different than telling mom and dad. What happens when young people make this announcement to their parents, and how is it received?

FOCUS ON A TOPIC: COMING OUT TO MOM AND DAD

Imagine you are a parent and your child has just informed you that he is gay. You may have suspected the truth for years, but the revelation can hit like a bombshell. Believing that this lifestyle is just fine in the abstract is different from feeling that this lifestyle is just fine for *your child*. If this is your only child, you may feel a sense of mourning as you realize that your fantasies of grandparenthood will be less easily fulfilled. You may worry about telling other family members or feel anxious about what "the neighbors" will think. Most importantly, you have fears for the future: Will your baby have trouble finding fulfilling love? In a series of interviews with U.S. teenagers and emerging adults, Rich Savin-Williams explored what happened when young people deliver this news (Savin-Williams, 2001; Savin-Williams & Ream, 2003).

You may have heard stories of parents banishing gay offspring from the house. These events, according to Savin-Williams, are very rare. Only 4 percent of the young people in his study described parental rejection or verbal abuse. Many parents did wrestle with intense feelings. However, after a short period of adjustment, the majority rallied around their child. Few sons or daughters felt that their relationship with their parents deteriorated after coming out. The majority reported that they felt either closer or just as close as before.

Coming out is a gradual process. People first must be clear about their feelings. Then, they typically confide in a good friend. Finally, they decide if and when to tell their family the news. Most of the people in Savin-Williams's study made the announcement to their parents at about age 19. There was considerable variability, however—from the young people who came out as young as age 13 to those who said they would never tell.

Imagine you are a gay emerging adult who has yet to come out to your parents. How can you predict how they will respond? Studies show the key lies in knowing your family. If your parents are highly traditional (for instance, religious) and believe being gay is an individual choice that you can control, it's a good bet they may have trouble with the news (Heatherington & Lavner, 2008). According to Savin-Williams, if your family is highly homophobic and you feel that coming out may put you in genuine jeopardy, you should trust your gut instincts and not tell. However, if you and your parents have a close, caring relationship, revealing your sexual orientation will not make a dent in that enduring bond.

The caution is that Savin-Williams's upbeat findings came only from young people who felt comfortable enough to tell their families, not from those who were reluctant to disclose. Still, this research makes an important point: Gay young people are like all young people. We cannot assume that they are alienated or distant from their parents. We cannot assume that they relate in any stereotyped way. Diversity is a hallmark of family relationships among young people with same-sex orientations, just as it is with other teenagers and emerging adults (Savin-Williams, 2008).

This brief look at the changing social context of finding a mate tells us nothing about how people really connect. Do opposites attract, or do we choose our mirror selves? How do relationships develop and progress?

Traditional Looks at Love: Similarity and Structured Relationship Stages

Bernard Murstein's now-classic **stimulus-value-role theory** (1970) views mate selection as a three-phase process. During the **stimulus phase**, we see a potential partner and make our first decision: "Could this be a good choice for me?" "Would this person want me?" Since we know nothing about the person, our judgment is based on superficial signs, such as looks or the way the individual dresses. In this assessment, we compare our own reinforcement value to the other person's along a number of dimensions (Murstein, 1999): "True, I am not as good-looking, but she may find me desirable because I am better educated." If the person seems of equal value, we decide to go on a date.

When we start dating, we enter the **value-comparison phase**. Here, our goal is to select the right person by matching up in terms of inner qualities and traits: "Does this person share my interests? Do we have the same values?" If this person seems "right," we enter the **role phase**, in which we decide how to work out our shared lives.

So, at a party, Michael scans the room and decides that Samantha with the tattoos and frumpy-looking Abigail are out of the question. He can do much better than that! Erika, surrounded by all those men, may be *too* beautiful. He gravitates to Ashley, who seems very appealing. Her dress and her way of speaking suggest that she might be athletic or intellectual, and maybe—like him—a bit shy. As Michael and Ashley begin dating, he discovers, to his delight, that they really are on the same wavelength. They enjoy the same movies; they both love the mountains; they have the same worldview. The romance could still end. On their third or tenth date, there may be a revelation that "this person is way too different." But if things go smoothly, Michael and Ashley will begin planning their future. Should they move to California when they graduate? Will their wedding be small and intimate or big and expensive?

The "equal-reinforcement-value partner" part of Murstein's theory explains why we expect couples to be similar in their social status. We're not surprised if the best-looking girl in high school dates the captain of the football team. When we find what appear to be serious partner status mismatches, we search for reasons to explain these discrepancies (Murstein, Reif, & Syracuse-Siewert, 2002): "That handsome young lawyer must have low self-esteem to have settled for that unattractive older woman." "Perhaps he chose that woman because she has millions in the bank."

stimulus-value-role theory Murstein's mate-selection theory that suggests similar people pair up and that our path to commitment progresses through three phases (called the stimulus, value-comparison, and role phases).

stimulus phase In Murstein's theory, the initial mate-selection stage, in which we make judgments about a potential partner based on external characteristics such as appearance.

value-comparison phase In Murstein's theory, the second mate-selection stage, in which we make judgments about a partner on the basis of similar values and interests.

role phase In Murstein's theory, the final mate-selection stage, in which committed partners work out their future life together.

Most important, Murstein's theory suggests that opposites definitely do *not* attract. In love relationships, as in childhood and adolescent friendships, the driving force is **homogamy** (similarity). Our goal is to find a soul mate, a person who matches us not just in external status, but also in basic interests, needs, and attitudes about life.

Our personal choices promote homogamy. We actively put ourselves in situations that give us a sense of flow. If your passion is politics, you might join the college Democrats and meet your soul mate. If you are devoted to your religion, you could find the love of your life at a local Bible study group. The fact that "birds of a feather" naturally flock together actually has a fascinating, not-so-obvious benefit. As you will see in the next chapter, sharing common passions helps keep marital passion alive.

Homogamy is also promoted by our need to have our partner mesh with our family and friends. It is an illusion that people choose a mate entirely on their own. Because we enter the landscape of adult love embedded in a network of other close relationships, the input of family and friends weighs heavily in our romantic choices. So you actively select someone who will get along with your Mom and Dad (if you are close to your parents). It's certainly going to make things much easier if friends really like your significant other, too. Conversely, if family and friends start criticizing your choice ("He's not right for you"), won't that put a chill in your own feelings of love?

So far, I have stressed the importance of finding a similar mate. But the issue is a bit deeper than that. Actually it's best to choose a partner who is similar to "our ideal self"—the person we would like to be. In a fascinating series of studies, researchers found that, when people believe their significant other embodies key elements of their best self ("I fell in love with him because he's incredibly smart, and that's always been my goal"), they tend to grow emotionally as people, becoming more like their ideal. Moreover, really prizing a mate's best qualities ("He's my intellectual role model") has another benefit. When couples really idolize and value each other's strengths, relationships tend to grow more loving over time (Rusbult and others, 2009).

If you are currently in a relationship, you now might list the specific qualities that attracted you to your significant other. What do these attributes say about your own personal goals? Do you feel that simply being together is helping you grow as a human being in these important areas of life?

The bottom-line message is that, in most areas of life, the principle is "the more similar, the better." Along one interesting dimension, however, it may be preferable to choose a partner who is the opposite of you. When psychologists asked unattached undergraduates to describe their ideal mate, in accordance with the homogamy principle, the young people selected someone with a similar personality. But when the researchers actually examined happiness among long-married couples, they found that people tended to get along best when one partner was more dominant and the other more submissive (Markey & Markey, 2007).

Logically, it makes sense that matching up two strong personalities might not be good for romantic bliss (you'd probably fight). Two passive partners might be destined to frustrate each other ("Why doesn't my lover take the lead?"). Yes, it's best to be similar in most ways, but not all!

David Young-Wolff/Photo Edit

Admiring each other's talents in their shared life passion ("I love how brilliant my significant other is at science. I want to be just like that") predicts future happiness for this young couple. It also may make these people feel like they are becoming superior scientists, just from being together.

homogamy The principle that we select a mate who is similar to us.

New Looks at Love: Irrationality, Unpredictability, and Attachment Styles

So far, I have looked at love as a realistic process of matching up. We choose people based on homogamy. We get involved in structured stages. We select a person that embodies our ideal self. But romance is far more irrational and unpredictable in the real world.

Irrationality and Unpredictability

Actually, researchers find that rather than seeing a realistic image, people in highly satisfying relationships tend to view their mates through rose-colored glasses (Murray & Holmes, 1997). They inflate their partner's virtues. They describe their partner in more glowing terms than either friends or the person would describe their own personality (Murray and others, 2000). They become insensitive to attractive alternative potential partners (Maner, Rouby, & Gonzaga, 2008). They overestimate the extent to which they and their mate are alike in terms of values and goals (Murray and others, 2002). So science confirms George Bernard Shaw's classic observation: "Love is a gross exaggeration of the difference between one person and everyone else."

Moreover, the inner experience of commitment does not translate neatly into stages such as stimulus, value-comparison, and role phases. People have doubts and ups and downs; their feelings about the relationship and their partner fluctuate.

To get firsthand insights into this emotional ebb and flow, researchers asked couples who were seriously dating to graph their chances (from 0 to 100 percent) of marrying their partner (Surra & Hughes, 1997; Surra, Hughes, & Jacquet, 1999). They then had the young people return each month to chart changes in their commitment level and asked them to describe the reasons for any dramatic relationship turning points, for better or worse.

You can see interesting examples of these turning points in Table 10.7. Notice that relationships do often hinge on homogamy issues ("This person is really right for me") and the input of family and friends. Other causes may be turning points, too — from social comparisons ("Our relationship seems better than theirs") to the simple insight, "I'm really too young to get involved."

Sometimes, people know when their relationship has reached a critical turning point. As one woman reported, "He told me to sit down and . . . and then he just looked at me and he said, 'I love you'" (quoted in Surra, Hughes, & Jacquet, 1999, p. 139). At other times, everything seems to be going according to schedule, when an event that has nothing to do with you or your partner intrudes: "I talked to my dad . . . who felt he got married too young so he was a little bit more encouraging against getting married" (quoted in Surra, Hughes, & Jacquet, 1999, p. 138).

One of the most interesting findings in this study and others is that we can often predict the outcome of a relationship by looking at its overall features. Some relationships accelerate gradually to a higher level of commitment, with couples getting closer and closer over time. Others are **event-driven**, punctuated by intense highs and lows. People start out passionately involved, then repeatedly fight and break up, to become passionately involved again. Event-driven relationships are more fragile. Dramatic ups and downs are a sign that a romance is less likely to endure (Arriaga, 2001; Surra, Hughes, & Jacquet, 1999).

So the reality is that real-world love doesn't operate according to a structured plan. It helps to exaggerate your partner's good qualities and soul-mate-like similarity to you. (That's what love is all about!) Relationships have unpredictable twists and turns. If a romance involves *many* dramatic twists and turns, however, that relationship is at risk of being derailed. In fact, when researchers asked women who were in

TABLE 10.7: Some Major Positive (+) and Negative (−) Turning Points in a Relationship

Personal Compatibility/Homogamy

We spent a lot of time together. +

We had a big fight. −

We had similar interests. +

He was acting like a jerk. −

She said she was still upset about me going out without her. −

Compatibility with Family and Friends

My friends kept saying that Sue was bad for me. −

She met my whole family. +

I fit right in with his family. +

Her dad just hated me. −

We had a better relationship than my friends did. +

Other Random Forces

I just turned 21, so I don't want to be tied down to anyone. −

The guy I used to date started calling me. −

We always got along better in hot weather. +

Source: Adapted from Surra, Hughes, & Jacquet (1999).
If you are in a relationship, have you experienced any of these turning points?

event-driven relationship An erratic love relationship characterized by dramatic shifts in feelings and sense of commitment, with couples repeatedly breaking up, then getting back together again.

blissful long-term relationships to reflect on how their romance developed, they never mentioned rationality or spoke in terms of structured relationship phases. At some point, they just "fell" mysteriously in love (Levitt, 2006).

Now, let's take a different perspective, as we shift from exploring relationships to examining the personalities of the partners in a romance.

Adult Attachment Styles

Think back to Chapter 4's discussion of the different infant attachment styles. Remember that Mary Ainsworth (1973) found that *securely attached* babies run to Mom with hugs and kisses when she appears in the room. *Avoidant* infants act cold, aloof, and indifferent in the Strange Situation when the caregiver returns. *Anxious-ambivalent* babies are overly clingy, afraid to explore the toys, and angry and inconsolable when their caregiver arrives. Now, think of your own romantic relationships, or the love relationships of family members or friends. Wouldn't these same attachment categories apply to adult romantic love? Cindy Hazan and Phillip Shaver (1987) had the same insight: Let's draw on Ainsworth's dimensions to classify people into specific **adult attachment styles**.

People with a **preoccupied/ambivalent** type of insecure attachment fall quickly and deeply in love (see the How Do We Know box on the facing page). But, because they are engulfing and needy in their relationships, they often end up being rejected or feeling chronically unfulfilled. Adults with an **avoidant/dismissive** form of insecure attachment are at the opposite end of the spectrum—withholding, aloof, reluctant to engage. You may have dated this kind of person, someone whose main mottos seem to be "stay independent," "don't share," "avoid getting emotionally close" (Feeney, 1999).

Securely attached people are emotionally fully open to love. They give their partner space to differentiate, yet are firmly committed. Like Ainsworth's secure infants, their faces light up when they talk about their partner. Their joy in their love shines through.

Decades of studies exploring these different attachment styles show that insecurely attached adults have trouble with relationships. Securely attached people are more successful in the world of love.

Securely attached adults have happier marriages. They report more satisfying romances (Feeney, 1999; Mikulincer and others, 2002; Morgan & Shaver, 1999). They are more likely to be romantically involved (Bookwala, 2003). Securely attached adults are more sensitive to their partner's signals. They freely reach out and give support to their partners during times of need (Davila & Kashy, 2009). Not being terrified about being "left" or insensitive to a partner's feelings, if their loved one disappoints them, securely attached people are more forgiving (Burnette and others, 2009). They even are more biologically laid back—less prone to show heart rate increases or other signs of physiological distress—when discussing problems with their mates (Roisman, 2007).

Securely attached people are also open to being cared for with love. When avoidant/dismissive adults are upset, as one study showed, they respond best to a hands-off caregiving approach, preferring to receive rational advice. Securely attached adults are soothed by touching, kissing, having their loved one listen and offer emotional support (Simpson and others, 2007). Using the metaphor of mother–infant attachment, described in Chapter 4, people with secure attachments are wonderful dancers. They excel at being emotionally responsive and in tune.

Recall that Bowlby and Ainsworth believe that the dance of attachment between the caregiver and baby is the basis for feeling securely attached in infancy and for dancing well in every other relationship in life. If you listen to friends anguishing about their relationship problems, you will hear similar ideas: "The reason I act so clingy and jealous is that, during my childhood, I felt unloved." "It's hard for me to warm up and respond to kisses because my mom was so rejecting and cold." How enduring are adult attachment styles, and how much can they change?

To answer this question, researchers measured the attachment styles of several hundred women at intervals over two years (Cozzarelli and others, 2003). They found that almost one-half of the women had changed categories over that time. So the good

adult attachment styles The different ways in which adults relate to romantic partners, based on Mary Ainsworth's infant attachment styles. (Adult attachment styles are classified as secure, or preoccupied/ ambivalent insecure, or avoidant/dismissive insecure.)

preoccupied/ambivalent insecure attachment An excessively clingy, needy style of relating to loved ones.

avoidant/dismissive insecure attachment A standoffish, excessively disengaged style of relating to loved ones.

secure attachment The genuine intimacy that is ideal in love relationships.

that a person is securely or insecurely attached?

How do developmentalists classify adults as either securely or insecurely attached? In the *current relationship interview*, they ask people questions about their goals and feelings about their romantic relationships; for example, "What happens when either of you is in trouble? Can you rely on each other to be there emotionally?" Trained evaluators then code the responses.

People are labeled securely attached if they coherently describe the pluses and minuses of their own behavior and of the relationship, if they talk freely about their desire for intimacy, and if they adopt an other-centered perspective, seeing nurturing the other person's development as a primary goal. Those who describe their relationship in formal,

stilted ways, emphasize "autonomy issues," or talk about the advantages of being together in nonintimate terms ("We are buying a house"; "We go places"), are classified as avoidant/dismissive. Those who express total dependence ("I can't function unless she is nearby"), anger about not being treated correctly, or fears of being left are classified as preoccupied/ambivalent.

This in-depth interview technique is extremely time intensive. But many attachment researchers argue that it reveals a person's attachment style better than questionnaires in which people simply check "yes" or "no" to indicate whether items on a scale apply to them.

Avoidant/dismissive insecure attachment
- **Definition:** Unable to get close in relationships.
- **Signs:** Uncaring, aloof, emotionally distant. Unresponsive to loving feelings. Abruptly disengages at signs of involvement. Unlikely to be in a long-term relationship.

Secure attachment
- **Definition:** Capable of genuine intimacy in relationships.
- **Signs:** Empathic, sensitive, able to reach out emotionally. Balances own needs with those of partner. Has affectionate, caring interactions. Probably in a loving, long-term relationship.

Preoccupied/ambivalent insecure attachment
- **Definition:** Needy and engulfing in relationships.
- **Signs:** Excessively jealous, suffocating. Needs continual reassurance of being totally loved. Unlikely to be in a loving, long-term relationship.

Source: Crowell, Fraley, & Shaver (1999).

news is that we can change our status from insecure to secure. And—as will come as no surprise to many readers—we can also move in the opposite direction, temporarily feeling insecurely attached after a terrible experience with love. The best way to understand attachment styles, then, is as somewhat enduring, consistent, and related to our early life experiences (Simpson and others, 2007), arising in part from our current experiences in love.

One reason attachment styles have a tendency to stay stable is that they operate as a self-fulfilling prophecy. A preoccupied, clingy person does tend to be rejected repeatedly. An avoidant individual remains isolated because piercing that armored shell takes such a heroic effort. A secure, loving person gets more secure over time because his caring behavior evokes warm, loving responses (Davila & Kashy, 2009). Are there normal developmental changes toward attachment security as we get older? Stay tuned for Chapter 12, where we examine research relevant to this question as we chart how personality changes from emerging adulthood through middle age.

By now, you are probably impressed with the power of the attachment-styles framework in offering guidelines for how to sensibly select a mate. Bowlby's (1969) analyses of the universal forces that drive security-seeking are equally powerful at offering insights into love relationships that make little rational sense. Remember that our biologically programmed attachment response is activated when we are upset (see Chapter 4). Therefore, it makes perfect sense that we would cling to exciting, unreliable partners (who are bad for us). The principle that feeling vulnerable—or being in physical pain—evokes the attachment response even explains why victims of abuse have trouble shedding their addiction to a battering mate. We may not need years of therapy to understand these so-called pathological love choices. We can treat them as examples of distortions of the normal human impulse to seek security when we are in distress (Morgan & Shaver, 1999). Attachment theory allows us to look at *every* love relationship through a fascinating, new lens.

INTERVENTIONS: Evaluating Your Own Relationship

How can you use *all* of the information in this section to help predict more intimate, smoother-sailing love? Select someone who is similar in values and interests and be sensitive to how this person meshes with the people you really care about. Choose someone who embodies the person you want to be in important ways—but it's best if you each differ a bit on the need to take charge. Focus on the outstanding "special qualities" of your significant other. Be wary of stormy, event-driven relationships. Look for a partner who is securely attached and secure as a human being. Take care, however, to note the message of the research on relationship turning points: If things don't work out, it easily may have *nothing* to do with you, your partner, or any problem basic to how well you get along! If you want to evaluate your own relationship, you might take the questionnaire based on these chapter points in Table 10.8.

TABLE 10.8: Evaluating Your Own Relationship: A Section Summary Checklist

	Yes	No
1. Are you and your partner similar in interests and values?	☐	☐
You don't have to be clones of each other, but the research shows that the more similar you are in attitudes and basic worldviews, the greater your chances of a happy relationship.*		
2. Do your other "attachment figures," such as close friends and family, like your partner?	☐	☐
Not everyone needs to adore your partner, but if your most central attachment figures really dislike your partner, problems may arise.		
3. Do you each believe that in key ways your partner embodies your ideal self?	☐	☐
Seeing your partner as someone you want to be like predicts staying together happily as well as growing emotionally toward your ideal.		
4. Do you see your partner as utterly wonderful and unique?	☐	☐
Deciding that this person has no human flaws is not necessary—but seeing your partner as "unique and special" also predicts being happy together.		
5. Is your relationship progressing toward greater commitment at a fairly steady rate?	☐	☐
If you and you partner have minor arguments, that's fine; but if you both repeatedly have huge fights, break up, and get back together, that's not a good sign.		
6. Is your partner able to fully reach out in love, neither intensely jealous nor aloof?	☐	☐
Some jealousy or hesitation about commitment can be normal, but in general, your partner should be securely attached and able to love.		

If you checked "yes" for all six of these questions, your relationship is in excellent shape. If you checked "no" for every question, your "relationship" does not exist! One or two no's mixed in with yes's suggest areas that need additional work.

*Recall that it may be best if one of you has a stronger, or more dominant, personality.

TYING IT ALL TOGETHER

1. If Latoya is discussing how relationships have changed in recent decades with James, which statement should she *not* be making?
    a. Today there is more interracial and inter-ethnic dating.
    b. Today, same-sex relationships are much more acceptable.
    c. Today, there is practically no pressure to date within one's own ethnic group.

2. Natasha and Akbar met at a friend's New Year's Eve party and just started dating. They are about to find out whether they share similar interests, backgrounds, and world-views. This couple is in Murstein's (choose one) *stimulus/value-comparison/role* phase of romantic relationships.

3. Catherine tells Kelly, "To have a happy relationship, find someone as much like you as possible." In what ways might Catherine be somewhat wrong?

4. Kita is clingy and always feels rejected. Rena runs away from intimate relationships. Sam is affectionate and loving. Match the attachment status of each person to one of the following alternatives: *secure, avoidant-dismissive,* or *preoccupied*

Answers to the Tying It All Together questions can be found on the last page of this chapter.

Final Thoughts

So far, I have talked about finding love as if this agenda operated in a vacuum—disconnected from the rest of life. But, just as getting a satisfying job can help players become responsible workers, entering into a loving relationship may boost young people to grow more mature. In tracking emerging adults through their twenties, German researchers found that emerging adults who formed committed relationships in their middle twenties became less neurotic and more outgoing. In Italy, where emerging adults tend to live with their parents, entering a romantic relationship severely shortened a young person's social clock timetable for leaving the nest (Lanz & Tagliabue, 2007). Like David in the introductory vignette, when emerging adults find a partner, they may think, "It's time to stop exploring, to get my career together, to *really* grow up." So personality shapes our social clock passage, our social clock passage shapes personality, and reaching one adult social clock marker also ripples out to affect every other adult benchmark.

In the next chapter, I'll continue to explore these connections as I focus directly on those major adult roles: marriage, parenthood, and work. What happens when people get married, and how do marriages change over time? How does having a child change a couple's relationship, and what is motherhood and fatherhood really like? Do careers go through specific phases, and what strategies—other than finding flow—can you use to have a satisfying work life? Then, in Chapter 12, we'll return to personality and once again tackle that important question: Over the years, do we *really* get more mature?

SUMMARY

Emerging Adulthood

Psychologists have identified a new life phase called **emerging adulthood**. This in-between, not-quite-fully-adult time of life, beginning after high school and tapering off by the late twenties, involves testing out adult **roles**. The main challenge of this least-structured life stage is taking adult responsibility for our lives. This new developed-world life stage differs from person to person and country to country. In Southern Europe, young people typically live at home until they marry and have trouble becoming financially independent. In Scandinavia, **cohabitation** and having babies before marriage are widespread. Here, government help, plus a norm stressing independence, make **nest-leaving** at age 18 routine. In the United States, there is tremendous variability, with people moving backward and forward on the way to constructing an adult life.

Today, U.S. adults are supposed to leave the nest at age 18, but they tend to periodically move back in with their parents. A danger of moving back is the potential to slide into a less adult state. Sons tend to stay in the nest longer. Ethnic-minority young people don't feel the same pressure to move out and may actually live at home to help their families as "full adults."

Social clock pressures, or **age norms**, set the boundaries of emerging adulthood. Exploring is **on time**, or appropriate, in the twenties, but **off time** if it extends well into the thirties. Although society sets the overall social clock guidelines, people also have their own personal timetables for when to get married and reach other adult markers. Social clock pressures, plus other forces, make emerging adulthood both an exhilarating life stage and a time of special stress.

Constructing an Identity

Deciding on one's **identity**, Erikson's first task in becoming an adult, is the major challenge facing emerging adults. Erikson believed that exploring various possibilities and taking time to ponder this question is critical to developing a solid adult self. At the opposite pole lies **identity confusion**—drifting and seeing no adult future.

James Marcia identified four **identity statuses: identity diffusion** (drifting aimlessly), **identity foreclosure** (leaping into an identity without any thought), **moratorium** (exploring different pathways), and **identity achievement** (settling on an identity). In contrast to Marcia's idea that we progress through these stages and reach achievement in the twenties, people shift from status to status throughout life, and moratorium may be a luxury reserved for privileged young people living in good economic times. Finding a secure **ethnic, biracial, or multiracial identity** is a special challenge for minority youth.

Finding a Career

Researchers find that teenagers have high career goals. The downside is that many people may not be able to fulfill these lofty dreams. Teenagers who are workers seem better able to lock into a career identity. Players (or highly work-averse teenagers)—and children with internalizing and externalizing disorders—may be more likely to end up in diffusion. However, during emerging adulthood, we generally get more mature, and even acting-out player teenagers can become conscientious when they lock into a satisfying job.

Flow is a feeling of total absorption in a challenging task. The hours seem to pass like minutes, intrinsic motivation is high, and our skills are in balance with the demands of a given task. Flow states can alert us to our ideal careers.

Although most high school graduates do enter college, only about one in four complete their degree. Young people who emerge directly into the workforce tend to have trouble establishing a satisfying work life, and end up in the **secondary labor market**, rather than in more desirable **primary labor market** jobs.

Being planful and finding a sense of flow are the keys to feeling satisfied when emerging directly into the work world.

Japan and Germany offer models for a well-organized **school-to-work transition**, and they suggest that the United States could do more to strengthen the connection between high school and careers. Although the U.S. unstructured pathway has the benefit of giving everyone second chances, it leaves people on their own to search for jobs. Another problem is the contemporary emphasis on college for all. Because the odds of making it through college are far lower for students in the bottom half of their high school class, experts suggest first developing a track record at work.

For young people who emerge into college, the key to undergraduate satisfaction lies in feeling engaged at school. Tips for achieving this goal include living on or near campus, avoiding full-time work, using these years to explore career-relevant work, making connections with professors, and getting to know other students of different ethnic backgrounds.

Finding Love

Erikson's second emerging-adult task, **intimacy**—finding committed love—has changed dramatically in recent decades. Inter-ethnic dating and gay relationships have become far more acceptable. Still, **homophobia**, an intense fear and dislike of gays, exists, and there is a bit of pressure to date within one's own kind. When gay young people come out to their families—if they generally have close, loving relationships with their parents—they are not in danger of losing that enduring love.

Stimulus-value-role theory spells out a three-stage process leading to marriage. First, we select a potential partner who looks appropriate (the **stimulus phase**); then, during the **value-comparison** phase, we find out whether that person shares our interests and worldview. Finally, during the **role phase**, we plan our lives together. **Homogamy**, people's tendency to choose similar partners and partners of equivalent status to themselves, is the main principle underlying this theory.

The chances of finding a homogamous partner are enhanced by the fact that people select activities where they find similar others and strive to have their social group (family and friends) approve of their mate. Actually, however, it's best to choose a partner who is similar to our "ideal self," and there is one exception to the principle that selecting by similarity is best: Relationships in which one person is dominant and the other partner is submissive make for the most harmonious romantic life.

A good deal of irrationality is involved in romance. We tend to idealize a partner and exaggerate our similarities. Relationships have turning points rather than progressing in a smooth, patterned way. Stormy, **event-driven relationships** are less likely to endure.

Researchers have spelled out three **adult attachment styles**. Adults ranked as insecurely attached—either **preoccupied/ambivalent** (overly clingy and engulfing) or **avoidant/dismis-**

sive (overly aloof and detached)—have poorer-quality relationships. **Securely attached** adults tend to be successful in love and marriage. Adult attachment styles (which are somewhat enduring and also can change), and Bowlby's ideas about security-seeking in distress, offer fascinating insights into real-world romance.

KEY TERMS

emerging adulthood, p. 296
role, p. 296
cohabitation, p. 297
nest-leaving, p. 297
social clock, p. 300
age norms, p. 300
on time, p. 300
off time, p. 300
identity, p. 301
identity confusion, p. 302
identity statuses, p. 302

identity diffusion, p. 302
identity foreclosure, p. 302
moratorium, p. 303
identity achievement, p. 303
ethnic identity, p. 304
biracial or multiracial identity,
   p. 304
flow, p. 308
secondary labor market,
   p. 309
primary labor market, p. 309

school-to-work transition,
   p. 310
intimacy, p. 313
homophobia, p. 315
stimulus-value-role theory,
   p. 317
stimulus phase, p. 317
value-comparison phase,
   p. 317
role phase, p. 317
homogamy, p. 318

event-driven relationship,
   p. 319
adult attachment styles,
   p. 320
preoccupied/ambivalent
   insecure attachment,
   p. 320
avoidant/dismissive insecure
   attachment, p. 320
secure attachment, p. 320

ANSWERS TO TYING IT ALL TOGETHER QUIZZES

Emerging Into Adulthood

1. b.
2. Maria's parents are likely to have no problem with her moving back, but she runs the risk of feeling like a child while living under their roof.
3. Martha, who is starting a new career at age 50; she will be most worried about the ticking of the social clock.
4. John, who can't wait to start a family.

Constructing An Identity

1. drifting; diffusion
2. foreclosure; moratorium
3. c.
4. False

Finding a Career

1. You should tell these parents that, realistically, their son may have more trouble constructing a work life. But, if he finds a satisfying job, chances are he will settle down and become more mature.

2. flow
3. *Possible suggestions, based on the German and Japanese models:* Have a high school track specifically devoted to preparing teens for careers that don't require college. Set up apprentice programs connected to specific workplaces—and make sure that these industries commit to hiring people after their training. Develop connections between local employers and schools and colleges—and have these people specifically hire students the school recommends
4. b.

Finding Love

1. c.
2. *value-comparison* phase
3. Actually, it's best to find a partner who is similar to one's "ideal self." Also, partners who have dominant personalities might be better off with more submissive mates (and vice versa).
4. Kita's status is preoccupied. Rena is avoidant/dismissing. Sam is securely attached.

Chapter 11

Relationships and Roles

Home at 3 A.M. from closing the restaurant and hopefully to bed by 4. Then, Doreen wakes up and gets the kids ready for school to make it to her accountant job by 9.

David's first marriage to Clara ended in a disastrous divorce. He feels blessed to have this second chance for happiness at age 35. David and Doreen met at a community-wide faith celebration. They share the same values. They understand what marriage is all about—it's about commitment, sacrifice, and forgiveness. The racial difference hasn't mattered. They are together in their passion for the Lord.

This time around, David is trying to be the best possible husband. One divorce in a lifetime is one more than enough! He helps the twins with their homework. He cooks the family dinners so Doreen can sit down with the kids when she comes home stressed out from work.

David's manager job at O'Charley's is exhausting. He would love a less hectic, more laid-back career. With the frantic cell phone calls that arrive from his staff at all hours, this so-called 40-hour job is more like an 80-hour week. Worse yet, with his weekend and evening work schedule, David seems to never see his wife. But in this terrible economy—and with many restaurants in Murfreesboro closing—David needs to count his blessings that he still has a (hope, hope) secure, decently paying job. Working nights also has real fatherhood benefits. David can pick up the kids from school, take them to soccer practice, and get in good family time before leaving for work at 5. It's a 24/7 struggle, but this marriage must work for life!

Do you know someone like David who is struggling to be a caring husband, an involved father, and to support a family? Perhaps you know a person who is working at a high-stress job and dreaming of a more fulfilling career. If so, you know a twenty-first-century adult.

This chapter is devoted to the main role challenges involved in being fully adult. Here, I'll be building on our emerging adult love and career discussion by focusing directly on marriage, parenthood, and work as we travel from our twenties to the senior citizen years. Before you begin your reading, you might want to take the quiz about family and work in Table 11.1 on page 328. In the following pages, you will learn *why* each stereotype is right or wrong.

Although I will discuss them separately, I must emphasize again that we cannot look at marriage, parenthood, and career as separate parts of life. Our work situation determines if we decide to get married. Having children changes a marriage and—as you saw with David—affects our feelings about our careers. As *developmental systems theory* suggests, marriage, parenthood, and career are tri-directional, interlocking roles. Moreover, how we approach these core adult roles depends on the time in history and the society in which we live.

327

TABLE 11.1: Stereotypes About Family and Work: A Quiz

Write "True" or "False" next to each of the following statements. To see how accurate your beliefs about family and work are, look at the correct answers, printed upside down below the table. As you read through the chapter, you'll find out exactly *why* each statement is true or false.

_____ 1. Americans today are not as interested in getting married as they were in the past.

_____ 2. Poor people often don't get married, because they are basically less interested in having a permanent commitment.

_____ 3. People are happiest in the honeymoon phase of a marriage.

_____ 4. Having children brings married couples closer.

_____ 5. People who don't have children are self-absorbed and narcissistic.

_____ 6. Becoming a mother makes people more mature.

_____ 7. Mothers used to spend more time with their children than they do today.

_____ 8. Men work longer hours today than they did in the 1950s.

_____ 9. The average workweek in the United States is 40 hours.

_____ 10. People who are well educated and have wealthy parents "have it made" career-wise—even when they feel depressed and/or bad about themselves.

_____ 11. Mothers worry more about their work interfering with their time with the children than fathers.

Answers: 1. F, 2. F, 3. T, 4. F, 5. F, 6. F, 7. F, 8. F, 9. F, 10. F, 11. F

Marriage

Ask friends to describe their ideal marriage (or relationship) and you may hear phrases such as "soul mates," "equal sharing," and "someone who fulfills my innermost self" (Amato and others, 2007). This concept of lovers for life, who split careers and child care equally, is a product of living in the contemporary, developed world.

Setting the Context: The Changing Landscape of Marriage

Throughout much of human history, as I implied in Chapter 10, people often got married based on practical concerns. With many marriages being arranged by the brides' and grooms' parents, and with daily life being so difficult, couples did not have the luxury of marrying simply for love. In addition, in the not-so-distant past, life expectancy was so low that the typical marriage only lasted a decade or two before one partner died.

Then, in the early twentieth century, as social conditions improved and medical advances allowed people to routinely live into later life, in the United States and other Western nations, we developed the idea that everyone should get married in their twenties and be lovers for a half-century or more. The traditional *Leave it to Beaver* marriage of the 1950s, with defined gender roles, reflected this idealized vision of enduring love (Amato and others, 2007; Cherlin, 2004; Coontz, 1992).

In the last third of the twentieth century, ideas about marriage in the West took another dramatic turn. The women's movement told us that women should have careers and husbands and wives should equally share the child care. As a result of the 1960s lifestyle revolution, which stressed personal fulfillment, we rejected the idea that people should stay in an unhappy marriage for life (Cherlin, 2004). We could get divorced, decide to have babies without being married, and even choose not to get married at all.

From the 1950s stay-at-home mom to the two-career marriage with fully engaged dads—over the last third of the twentieth century, a revolution occurred in our ideas about married life. How do you feel about these lifestyle changes?

The outcome was a late-twentieth-century change that social scientists call the **deinstitutionalization of marriage**. This phrase means that today marriage has been transformed from the standard adult "institution" into a more optional choice (Thornton, Binstock, & Ghmire, 2008).

Table 11.2 shows statistics related to this transformation in the United States: a tremendous rise in divorce and more people living alone or cohabiting without a wedding ring. Perhaps the most telling shift relates to the standard idea that marriage must come before a baby carriage. During the 1950s, if a U.S. woman dared to reverse that order by getting pregnant without a spouse, her humiliated family typically shipped her off to a home for unwed mothers, or insisted that she marry the dad (the infamously named " shotgun marriage"). A mere half-century later, in a national 2005 poll, most U.S. adults reported they would "not be particularly embarrassed" if their family member had that baby on her own (Mollborn, 2009).

Still, it's important to understand that our attitudes today about every aspect of marriage—including thoughts about whether it's OK to have a baby "out of wedlock"—vary dramatically from person to person and, especially, from culture to culture. To get insights specifically into this incredible global diversity, let's travel to the Middle East and then visit Scandinavia again.

Traditional Middle Eastern Model: Male-Dominated Marriage

The 1960s lifestyle revolution has not penetrated Islamic nations, such as Egypt and Iran, where getting married is still the *only* acceptable life path. It's a mistake to think that Islam frowns on women who are highly educated. In Iran—as is true in the

---

TABLE 11.2: Some "Symptoms" of the Deinstitutionalization of Marriage in the United States

Sign	1960–1970 (percent)*	Early Twenty-First Century (percent)
Childbirths outside of marriage	5	30+
Probability of marriage ending in divorce	about 14	about 50
Percentage of married couples	71	53
Children living with one parent	9	40
People living alone	17	27

*Rough data from 1960 and 1970.
Sources: U.S. Department of Commerce, 2007; U.S Census Bureau, 2008; Fields & Casper, 2001; Furstenberg & Cherlin, 1991.

deinstitutionalization of marriage The decline in marriage and the emergence of alternate family forms that occurred during the last third of the twentieth century.

If you talked to this couple living in Cairo and then visited this Scandinavian family enjoying a picnic by a lake, the difference in scenery would be symbolic of a totally different approach to men's and women's roles and married life. In fact, there would be a fifty-fifty chance that the Swedish parents would not be married at all!

United States—more females enroll in universities than men (Abbas-Shavazi, Mohammad, & McDonald, 2008). However, according to Islamic law, when a woman gets married, she is expected to stay at home. In Iran and Egypt, as in many Middle Eastern countries, people do not subscribe to the Western view that each sex should have equal rights (Moghadam, 2004). Husbands can forbid their wives to work if they feel that the woman's job will interfere with family life. While getting a divorce is extremely difficult for females—involving lengthy court battles—until recently, if a man wanted to end his marriage, he could simply tell his partner, "I no longer want you around" (Abbas-Shavazi, Mohammad, & McDonald, 2008; Yount & Agree, 2004).

Given these conditions, it is no wonder that a young, unmarried Egyptian woman in an interview study gave this unromantic answer when a researcher asked what she hoped for from married life: "I don't believe in love. The only kind of love [I know] is for my mother and sister . . . I want to marry a man who is rich, successful and able to take responsibility" (Amin & Al-Bassusi, 2004, p. 1295).

Scandinavian Social Norm: Marriage Doesn't Matter

In comparison, Scandinavian ideas about marriage seem to be from a different planet. With more than one-half of all babies being born to single mothers in Norway, Sweden, and Denmark, in these Northern European nations, having children has become totally irrelevant to getting a wedding ring (Cherlin, 2004). With rates of cohabitation topping 50 percent in Sweden, in this country, the deinstitutionalization of marriage is virtually complete (see Figure 11.1). It's not that Scandinavian adults are anti-marriage. They simply see getting married as one among a number of *equally acceptable* alternatives for living a fulfilling life (Kiernan, 2002, 2004).

The United States: Dreaming of Marriage for Life

Where do we stand in the United States? Given the dismal divorce statistics, you might think our interest in getting married would have declined. You would be wrong. Polls regularly show roughly 8 out of 10 U.S. young people want to be married—the same fraction as in the past (Manning, Longmore, & Giordano, 2007; Martin and others, 2003). Although we understand that it's perfectly possible to live rich, fulfilling lives and stay single, in the United States, we still firmly believe

FIGURE 11.1: Married and cohabiting couples aged 30–39, selected E.U. countries: Rates of marriage versus cohabitation among people in their prime marriage years vary a good deal in different European nations. Notice that, in Sweden, among couples in their thirties, living together is just as common as being married.

Source: Adapted from Kiernan (2004), p. 982.

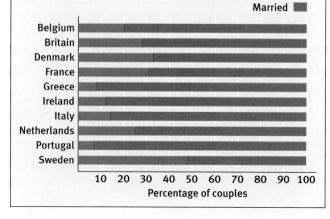

that being married is the ideal way to construct an adult life (Cherlin, 2004; Waite & Gallagher, 2000). However, Americans are realists. Before deciding on a wedding, we want to have certain foundations in place.

Take a minute to think about your requirements for getting married if you are single—or, if you are married, think of your personal goals before you were wed. In addition to finding the right person, if you are like most people, you probably believe that entering this kind of commitment demands reaching a certain place in your development. It's important to have a solid sense of identity (see Chapter 10). It's a good idea to be fairly financially secure (Edin, Kefalas, & Reed, 2004; Gibson-Davis, 2009). Therefore, as you saw in Chapter 10, because we select partners according to *homogamy*, the marriage market for low-income adults—both male and female—is poor (Gibson-Davis, 2009; Schoen & Cheng, 2006). Even when couples are committed to each other, they can find it difficult to move from living together to getting engaged.

Read what Candace, a 25-year-old, had to say about her marriage plans:

> Um, we have certain things that we want to do before we get married. We both want very good jobs. . . . He's been looking out for jobs everywhere and we— . . . we're trying. We just want to have—we gotta have everything before we say, "Let's get married."

(quoted in Smock, Manning, & Porter, 2005, p. 690)

And 30-year-old Donald put it more bluntly:

> [I would marry her] if I was to hit the lottery and could take her somewhere and we wouldn't have to worry about no problems for the rest of our life.

(quoted in Smock and others, 2005, p. 691)

As these comments imply, rather than pointing the blame at a general "culture of irresponsibility," the lack of decent jobs may be a major reason why many low-income fathers and mothers never wed (Gibson-Davis, 2009). Actually, today, for poverty-level women having children—and being the best possible mother—has become the main marker of adulthood. Getting married, although it is yearned for, can seem like a hazy, far in the future, unattainable goal (Edin & Kefalas, 2005).

Another goal that can seem hard to attain—for everyone, rich or poor—lies in managing to stay married for life. I got insights into the awe young people feel about this achievement when a college-student server came up to my husband and me at a local restaurant and shyly asked for our secret when we said we had been married for 30 years.

Is our dream of finding a soul mate for life too idealistic, given that we never expected people to stay madly in love for 50 or more years? How can we fulfill our dream of staying together for decades when there are so many alternatives to marriage and it is so easy to get divorced? In the next section, I'll focus on this crucial question as we look at the insights that social science research offers about how to have enduring, happy relationships. Let's begin, however, by examining what *typically* happens over time, as we trace how marital happiness normally changes through the years.

The Main Marital Pathway: Downhill and Then Up

Many of us enter marriage (or any love relationship) with blissful expectations. Then, disenchantment sets in. Hundreds of studies conducted over the past 40 years in Western countries show that marital satisfaction is at its peak during the honeymoon and then begins to decrease (Blood & Wolfe, 1960; Glenn, 1990). As the decline—statistically speaking—is steepest during the first few years, some researchers believe that, if people make it beyond four years of marriage, they have passed the main danger zone for getting divorced (Bradbury & Karney, 2004; Hetherington & Kelly, 2002).

Notice the interesting similarity to John Bowlby's ideas about the different attachment phases. In the first year or two of their relationship, people are in the phase of

Andrew Olney/Masterfile

The so-called "difficulties" of the empty nest are highly overrated. In fact, many couples find that, when the children leave, they can joyously rekindle marital love!

clear-cut attachment, when they are madly in love and see their significant other as the absolute center of their lives. As they move into the *working model* phase of their relationship—developing more separate lives, getting involved in the wider world—they face the risk of becoming more disconnected from their spouse.

Couples who pass the four-year mark are not out of the woods. During the next decade, as spouses cope with the pressures of work and the stresses of raising children, on average, there is a steady (but slower) decline in love. A first child's reaching puberty produces another dip in happiness, as parents wrestle with the emotional upheavals of the early teenage years (Whiteman, McHale, & Crouter, 2007; also see Chapters 8 and 9).

I must emphasize, however, that these are overall trends. Relationships, as you will see below, differ dramatically in the way they change. Moreover, for *most* married couples, there is a real positive change to look forward to later on. According to the **U-shaped curve of marital satisfaction,** after it dips to a low point, couples get happier at the empty nest, when the children leave the house and husbands and wives have the luxury of focusing on each other again (White & Edwards, 1990; Glenn, 1990). And, as people move up the age ranks into retirement, the curve can upswing even more. Compared to middle-aged couples, elderly spouses fight less. When discussing problem issues in their marriage, they relate in kinder, less combative ways (Carstensen and others, 1996; Carstensen, Levinson, & Gottman, 1995). As we reach the end of our lives, every moment gets more precious; we minimize our upsetting emotions and narrow our life focus to our mate (more about this fascinating change in emotional priorities in Chapter 13). Talk to elderly family members and you may hear comments like: "My main mission is making your grandma (or grandpa) happy" or "Nothing is more important than my husband or wife."

Understanding the general marital pathway is useful. But as we are all aware, marriages—at every life stage—are very different. Some of you may know elderly couples (perhaps in your own family!) who stay together miserably or even get divorced after 40 or 50 years of married life. For some inspiring couples, the U downswing never occurs. At least 1 in 3 husbands and wives rate their marriage as "very happy," even at the 16-year mark (Glenn, 1990). Every survey shows that, yes, it's possible to remain intensely, *romantically* involved for decades or more (Acevedo & Aron, 2009). Why do some relationships stay passionate for a lifetime while others fall apart? Why might marital happiness often (but not always!) tend to decline? To help us answer these questions, let's now turn to a contemporary psychologist's conceptualizations about love.

The Triangular Theory Perspective on Happiness

According to Robert Sternberg's (1986, 1988, 2004) **triangular theory of love,** we can break adult love relationships into three components: passion (sexual arousal), intimacy (feelings of closeness), and commitment (typically marriage, but also exclusive, lifelong cohabiting relationships). When we arrange them on a triangle, as you can see in Figure 11.2, we get a portrait of the different kinds of relationships in life.

With passion alone, we have a crush. This is the wonderful fantasy obsession for the girl down the street or a handsome professor we don't really know. With intimacy alone, we have the warm feelings of caring that we have for a best friend. *Romantic love* combines these two qualities. Walk around your campus and you can immediately see this type of relationship. Couples are passionate and clearly know each other well but have probably not made a final commitment to get married or to form a lifelong, exclusive bond.

On the marriage side of the triangle, commitment alone results in what some observers call "empty marriages." In these emotionally barren, loveless marriages (luckily, fairly infrequent today), people stay together physically but live totally separate lives. Intimacy plus commitment produces *companionate marriages*, the best-friend relationships that long-married couples may have after passion is gone. Finally, notice from the bottom of the diagram that a few married couples stay together because they share sexual passion and nothing else. The ideal in our culture is the relationship you can see at the center of the triangle —

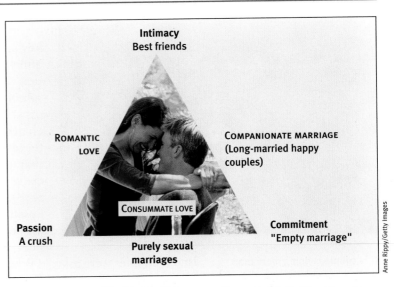

FIGURE 11.2: **Sternberg's triangle: The different types of love:** The three facets of love form the points of this triangle. The relationships along the triangle's sides reflect combinations of the facets. At the center is the ideal relationship: consummate love.

Source: Adapted from Sternberg (1988).

one that combines passion, intimacy, and commitment. Sternberg calls this ideal state **consummate love**.

Why is consummate love so fragile? One reason, according to Sternberg, is that as familiarity increases, passion naturally falls off. It's hard to keep lusting after your mate when you wake up together day after day for years (Klusmann, 2002). As couples enter into the working-model phase of their marriage, and genuinely move out into the world, intimacy can also decline. You and your partner don't talk the way you used to. Work or the children are more absorbing. There is a danger of becoming "ships passing in the night."

Sternberg's theory beautifully alerts us to why marriages naturally tend to get less happy over time. But it does not offer clues as to how we can beat the odds and stay romantically connected to our partner for life. As I mentioned earlier, a fraction of couples (roughly 1 in 10 people) do stay passionate for decades (Acevedo & Aron, 2009). What are these marital role models doing right? For answers, researchers decided to decode the inner experience of falling in love.

When we fall in love, they discovered, our self-concept expands enormously. Efficacy feelings are intense. We feel powerful, competent, special; capable of doing wonderful things (Aron and others, 2002). Given that romantic love causes a joyous feeling of self-expansion, couldn't we teach people to preserve passion and intimacy by encouraging couples to share exciting activities that expand the self?

To test this proposition, the psychologists asked married volunteers to list their most exciting activities—the passions that gave them a sense of flow (see Chapter 10). Then, they instructed one group of husbands and wives to engage in the stimulating activities *both* partners had picked out (for example, going to concerts or skiing) very frequently over 10 weeks. As they predicted, marital happiness rose dramatically among these couples compared to control groups who were told to engage in pleasant but not especially interesting activities (such as going out to dinner) or just to follow their normal routine (Reissman, Aron, & Bergen, 1993).

So, to stay passionate for decades, people may not need to take trips to Tahiti, or even have candlelit dinners with a mate. The secret is to simply *continue* to engage in the exciting, flow-inducing activities that brought couples together in the first place. For instance, since David and Doreen connected through their spirituality, they might do mission work together as the years pass. The problem, however, is that during the working-model phase of a relationship, the activities that give us a sense of flow tend to migrate outside of married life. When work does become more compelling (or flow-inducing), people may find their partner dull. Worse yet, they may fall in love with someone who is on the scene to witness their most efficacious self emerge: "My co-worker understands who I really am!" Keeping passions *within* a marriage may help keep marital passion alive.

U-shaped curve of marital satisfaction The most common pathway of marital happiness in the West, in which satisfaction is highest at the honeymoon, declines during the child-rearing years, then rises after the children grow up.

triangular theory of love Robert Sternberg's categorization of love relationships into three facets: passion, intimacy, and commitment. When arranged at the points of a triangle, their combinations describe all the different kinds of adult love relationships.

consummate love In Robert Sternberg's triangular theory of love, the ideal form of love, in which a couple's relationship involves all three of the major facets of love: passion, intimacy, and commitment.

This couple is doing more than sharing a wonderful experience—they are actually "working" on their relationship. Engaging in mutually exciting activities helps preserve marital passion.

But perhaps this advice is too idealistic. When, as you saw in the vignette, couples are working full time and juggling child care, how many hours are left to share activities that provide both partners a sense of flow? One solution might be to discuss your personal flow-inducing experiences with a mate. In an interesting diary study charting couples' daily moods, researchers found that, on the evenings when romantic partners came home and shared an exciting event from their day, they felt especially happy, close, and upbeat (Hicks & Diamond, 2008). (You might be interested to know that sharing an upsetting experience was a net "neutral"—neither making for more closeness nor driving people apart.) Consider this quotation from an interview study in which Israeli couples were asked, "What makes you feel especially close?"

Wife (who had just gotten a job as a yoga teacher): *There are nights when I come home after class fully energized and excited. . . . I don't know why, but on those nights I just want to be with him. . . . I want him to be around me so I can share . . . my excitement.*

Husband: *I love those Tuesday nights. I wait for them. I know she will come home so energetic. . . . It is contagious. It makes us like a couple on a honeymoon."*

(quoted in Ben-Ari & Lavee, 2007, p. 635)

Couple Communications and Happiness

Watch happy couples, like this husband and wife, and you will be struck with the way they relate. Like mothers and babies enjoying the dance of attachment, happy couples listen carefully. They openly share feelings. They are playful, affectionate. They

Their delighted facial expressions tip us off that this young married man and woman are blissfully in love. But, *specifically*, how do happy couples communicate when they talk? (The answers are listed to the right.)

use humor to signal, "I love you," even when they disagree (Driver & Gottman, 2004). But have you ever spent an evening with newlyweds and had the uneasy feeling, "I don't think this marriage will work out"? By simply listening to people talk about issues in their relationship, researchers can tell, with uncanny accuracy, whether a marriage will become unglued, even at the engagement stage. Here are three communication styles that distinguish relationships that are thriving from those that are fated for serious problems down the road (Driver and others, 2003; Gottman, 1994, 1999; Noller & Feeney, 2002):

- *Happy couples engage in a high ratio of positive to negative comments.* People can fight a good deal and still have a happy marriage. The key is to make sure that the number of caring, loving comments *strongly* outweighs the critical ones. In videotaping couples discussing problems in his "love lab," relationship researcher John Gottman (1994) has discovered that anytime the ratio of positive to negative interactions dips well below 5 to 1, the risk of getting divorced escalates.

- *Happy couples never get contemptuous and personally hurtful when they disagree.* When happily married couples fight, they confine themselves to the problem: "I don't like it when I come home and the house is messy. What can we do?" Unhappy couples personalize their conflicts: They use put-downs and sarcasm. They look disgusted. They roll their eyes. Expressions of contempt for the other person as a human being are poisonous to married life.

- *Happy couples don't get into a "demand-withdrawal pattern" of relating.* Another classic way of interacting that signals a marriage is in trouble occurs when one partner regularly pushes for more emotional involvement and the other tries to back off (Eldridge & Christensen, 2002; Noller and others, 2005). As this **demand–withdrawal interaction** escalates, it takes a bitter, personal turn:

WIFE (WORRIED VOICE): Is there something wrong, honey?

HUSBAND (DISTANT VOICE): Nope. Not a thing.

WIFE: I can tell that you are annoyed at me—I can see it in your face. What's wrong?

HUSBAND (SOUNDING ANNOYED): I already told you, there's nothing wrong. Will you lay off of me? I just need some time to myself.

WIFE (DISGUSTEDLY): Oh, you are impossible. You never talk to me.

HUSBAND (CONTEMPTUOUSLY): You are such a terrible nag!

(adapted from Gottman, 1994, p. 138)

You would not be surprised to learn that—as in the example above—women typically demand more involvement. Wives tend to want to talk about feelings; husbands withdraw and attempt to shut the discussion off (Eldridge & Christensen, 2002). But if we look more deeply, the real issue here is that the "demander"—whether male or female—is not responding sensitively by giving the other person space. This person is hypersensitive to being rejected. She has a *preoccupied/ambivalent attachment style*. Her partner has an *avoidant/dismissive approach*.

The bottom-line message is that when couples fall into these unproductive ways of communicating, their mate has been transformed from a loving ally into a potential enemy. People who adopt these poisonous ways of relating are insecurely attached (Feeney & Noller, 2002; Murray and others, 2003).

Commitment: A Core Quality in Relationship Success

Now that we know what concrete behaviors signal secure and insecure attachments, can we target an inner attitude that helps keep couples closely attached in the face of the natural pull toward less intimacy and passion that occur over time? One group of family researchers believes we can.

According to Frank Fincham and his colleagues, the internal glue that cements happy, enduring marriages is surprisingly similar to the one your beloved grandma might spell out: It's having a sense of commitment; that is, being dedicated to *the relationship*, above yourself (Fincham, Stanley, & Beach, 2007). For religious adults, like David and Doreen, this dedication may come from a sense of "sanctification," believing your marriage is blessed by God. For any couple—religious or not—commitment involves sacrifice, giving up what you want to further the other person's joy. Rather than seeing sacrifice as a negative thing, these psychologists argue, when people give up their needs for their partner, they see themselves as investing in the relationship. Sacrificing for the other person is *essential* in feeling closely attached.

A final requirement for commitment is the ability to forgive. People have to be willing to let go of their anger when their partner, as in any human relationship, may not be optimally sensitive or acts in a disappointing way.

Forgiveness—or teaching people to "let go" of their hurt feelings—is a new, popular approach to helping cure

demand–withdrawal communication A pathological type of interaction in which one partner, most often the woman, presses for more intimacy and the other person, most often the man, tends to back off.

Imagine how this father-to-be feels when he pampers his wife and you will understand why the thrill of "sacrificing" for a loved one helps relationships lovingly survive.

dysfunctional relationships (Bonach, 2007; Wade, Johnson, & Meyer, 2008). Moreover, being unable to reach out and forgive is another symptom signaling that "this person is insecurely attached" (Burnette and others, 2009). Can forgiveness really work? As one study showed, forgiveness has personal benefits. People who reported forgiving their significant other after an incident of being let down (provided they felt generally happy with their partner and the person apologized!) felt happier about their own lives (Bono, McCullough, & Root, 2008). Another study suggested that *not forgiving* may have long-term negative consequences for how couples act.

Researchers asked husbands and wives to write about how they reacted after an incident when their spouse disappointed them. Did they "do something to even the score" or "forgive"? Then, they looked at these couples' conflict-resolution skills a year later. When wives, in particular, reported holding on to their anger, partners were more prone to engage in the kinds of counterproductive arguments in the previous section—even when they had been relating well before (Fincham, Beach, & Davila, 2007). So, at the root of those poisonous interactions, which escalate into hurtful personal comments, may be "hurts" that are nursed and rehearsed and never forgiven—disappointments that lie simmering and waiting to re-erupt.

INTERVENTIONS: Staying Together Happily for Life

How can you draw on *all* of these research insights to have an enduring happy relationship? Understand the natural time course of love. Take steps to preserve intimacy and passion by sharing exciting activities you both enjoy. Make a special effort to share the uplifting, flow-inducing events in your life. Be very, very positive after you get negative. Avoid getting personal when you fight. Beware of falling into the demand–withdrawal pattern. Most important, be committed to your relationship. Act on that feeling of commitment by sacrificing for your loved one and being predisposed to forgive. Table 11.3 offers a checklist based on these points to evaluate your current relationship or to keep on hand for the love relationships you will have as you travel through life.

As a final caution, however, I must emphasize that sacrifice or forgiveness is sometimes seriously misplaced. One key to sacrificing is reciprocity. You need to know your partner will sacrifice for you, too. In fact, another family expert, Paul Amato (2007), believes a basic reason why Western marriages flounder is that one person (often the wife) feels she is doing all of the sacrificing: "My partner is not pulling his own weight" (more about this issue in the next section).

TABLE 11.3: Evaluating Your Close Relationship: A Checklist

Answer these questions as honestly as you can. The more "yes" boxes you check, the stronger your relationship is likely to be.

	Yes	No
1. Do you have realistic expectations about your relationship—realizing that passion and intimacy don't magically last forever?	☐	☐
2. Do you engage in activities that your partner feels as passionate about as you do and make time to share your exciting experiences at the end of the day?	☐	☐
3. Are you affectionate and positive with your mate?	☐	☐
4. Do you solve differences of opinion in a constructive way—not getting personal when you fight?	☐	☐
5. Do you and your partner try to sacrifice your own needs for the good of the relationship?	☐	☐
6. Are you both willing to let go and forgive, or do you hold onto hurts?	☐	☐
7. Are the two of you truly *committed* to your relationship, for better or for worse?	☐	☐

Forgiveness is clearly unwarranted if a person's violations are chronic and/or severe. Women who stay in abusive relationships, for instance, tend to be *too* forgiving. As one battered woman explained in an interview study: "Every single time I thought: Ok maybe . . . he's going through a bad patch . . . he will change" (quoted in Boonzaier, 2008, p. 93; see also Wade, Meyer, & Johnson, 2008). When couples regularly engage in the contempt-filled arguments I talked about in the previous section, forgiveness tends to backfire and excusing destructive comments leads to further verbal abuse (McNulty, 2008). If a person is being degraded, treated with contempt, or being taken advantage of, it's time to reconsider one's commitment and contemplate divorce.

Divorce

Researchers stress that, just as we saw in Chapter 7 when I described its impact on children, in looking at divorce, we need to think of this major life change as having specific phases.

When people consider divorce, they weigh the costs of leaving against the benefits (Hopper, 1993; Kelly, 2000). You and your spouse are not getting along, but perhaps you should just hang on. One deterrent is financial: "Can I afford the loss in income after a divorce?" But if the couple has children, money issues are trumped by a more critical concern: "How will divorce affect my parenting?" "Will this damage my daughter or son?" (Poortman & Seltzer, 2007.)

Couples typically cite communication problems such as those I've been discussing, lack of "attachment," and the weight of daily stresses as the main reasons for their divorce (Bodenmann and others, 2007). Often, what tips the balance in favor of leaving, however, is an extramarital affair. In a national study tracking the lives of thousands of U.S. couples, researchers found, among husbands and wives who eventually divorced, that 2 out of 3 people reported having had an affair around the time their relationship was breaking up (Amato and Hohmann-Marriott, 2007). But they also discovered that the stereotype that an affair breaks up an otherwise happy marriage is false. When people have an affair, it is a symptom that they are *already* unhappy in their married lives. However, there is a bidirectional process in operation here. Having an affair also works to widen the emotional chasm that already exists between a husband and wife (Previti & Amato, 2004).

Once a couple actually separates, they experience an overload of other changes. There is the need to move, perhaps find a different, better-paying job. There are the legal hassles, anxieties about the children, and telling other loved ones, "How will my friends and family feel?" As people adjust to their new lives, the stress does lessen (Barnet, 1990; Mitchell-Flynn & Hutchinson, 1993). Support from specific attachment figures and one's general "social network" eases the pain (Krumrei and others, 2007). But imagine regularly battling with your spouse over the children and you can see why psychologists have labeled divorce "a chronic stressor" in women's lives (Bursik, 1991).

Still, divorce can produce emotional growth and enhanced efficacy feelings as people learn they can they cope with making it on their own (Hetherington & Kelly, 2002; Young, Stewart, & Miner-Rubino, 2001). Dealing with this life change can energize women politically, making them more sensitive to social issues and women's concerns (Fahs, 2007). And, of course, for both men and women, ending a terrible marriage can come as a welcome relief.

Who feels relieved, or better emotionally, after a divorce? Fascinating insights come from looking at the reasons why people separate in the first place. In that huge national survey tracking U.S. married couples mentioned earlier in this section, researchers put the subset of couples who later divorced into two distinct categories: People who had reported being miserable in their marriage, and couples who divorced, even though they had previously judged their marital happiness as "fairly good" (Amato & Hohmann-Marriott, 2007).

The fact that their marriage is so full of conflict suggests that this couple may feel much better after they decide to divorce—but simply splitting up because you find your relationship "somewhat unfulfilling" predicts feeling more depressed after a marriage breaks up.

People in very unhappy marriages did feel much better after divorcing. But relatively satisfied couples who later divorced, perhaps thinking, "I just don't find our relationship extremely fulfilling, so maybe its time to split," reported subsequent declines in well-being! Given this finding, family expert Paul Amato (2007) suggests that perhaps our cultural fantasy of finding a life soul mate (or the sense that something is missing if we don't *automatically* have intimacy and passion for life) might be luring a whole group of people to leave a marriage when they would be better off remaining with their spouse. And what about the impact on children when couples make this choice? If your house is really a battleground, as I described in Chapter 7, it's probably better for the children's mental health for you to divorce. But imagine being shocked to learn that your beloved dad is suddenly moving out when you always believed your parents' marriage was perfectly fine.

This brings up the gender dimension of divorce. Because women still typically get primary custody of the children after a divorce, there is a tendency for many men to disengage from their families by not paying child support or perhaps not seeing the children at all (Furstenberg & Cherlin, 1991; Graham & Beller, 2002; Lamb, 2002). While the temptation is to blame men for "opting out," the Experiencing the Lifespan box on the facing page poignantly shows how difficult it can be to be a full-fledged father when you have the standard twice-a-week visitation schedule. Worse yet, for some dads, as my interview reveals, arriving to get the children can be fraught with anxieties: "Will my daughter or son be there this time?"

What often happens is that, after a divorce, as with David in the chapter-opening vignette, men remarry, have other children, and/or become stepfathers. They try to construct new relationships to make up for those they may have lost. However, as two experts beautifully put it: "Stepparent and child meet as strangers. They may or may not find common ground" (quoted in Wallerstein & Lewis, 2007, p. 457). Stepfathers also have to deal with the issue of whether they qualify as "real fathers," even when they want to take a fully involved parenting role. As one man complained in an interview study, "Sometimes I feel like I'm on the outside looking in because—sometimes I wish she was mine. . . . In my heart I feel like I'm her father" (quoted in Marsiglio, 2004, p. 31).

The same kinds of boundary issues face stepmothers. For instance, one woman in another interview study reported asking her husband for guidelines: "Was . . . I supposed to be a mom or not a mom?" (Quoted in Whiting and others, 2007, p. 103.) But despite this lack of clarity, parental emotions can kick in. Another stepmother commented to the researchers: "I don't look at her as a stepdaughter because that implies

Noncustodial fathers may have trouble staying involved because they have to struggle to be on the scene during important times during their children's lives. Imagine how hard it may have been for this divorced dad to get the chance to attend his daughter's Thanksgiving school play since that event took place on his "ex-wife's day."

EXPERIENCING THE LIFESPAN: VISITOR FATHER

Fatherhood is the critical experience of Henry's life. When Joanna was a preschooler, their destination was the zoo or the playground. As she grew older, Henry took Joanna for music lessons and taught her sports. His presence was hard won and, he feels, too rare. Henry had been demoted from father to person with visitation rights.

Henry and his wife separated when Joanna was almost 2. According to their divorce agreement, the child was supposed to be available every two weeks; but, often, Henry's ex-wife took off with the baby or gave him some excuse when he came to pick his daughter up. Henry never knew for sure if Joanna would be waiting there when he arrived.

Henry felt his only option was to sue for joint custody, the right to have Joanna on weekends and every other day. When they met in court, however, to Henry's astonishment, the judge ordered a psychiatric evaluation to determine if *he* was emotionally fit. One judge asked point blank: "Why would a man want to take care of a 2-year-old?" Eventually,

Henry won the right to have Joanna one afternoon per week, every other weekend, alternate holidays, and the month of July.

Over the next 10 years, Henry went to court periodically to try to force a greater role in his daughter's life. Once he sued for full custody. While no one denied that Henry was a good father, a psychologist testified that a child needed a mother during the early years.

For years, Henry felt terrible about not being able to see his daughter every day. His work suffered. He was often upset. Now that Joanna is 12, he has adjusted. His daughter has her own room in his apartment. He feels secure that she knows this is her second home. Henry feels he reached an emotional landmark when, during "his time" this past summer, he was able to let go and allow Joanna to attend sleep-away camp. Still, the heartache of not being on the scene to watch his child grow up never really goes away.

they are not . . . your child . . . she's my only child and I just accept the fact that she has another mother as well" (quoted in Whiting and others, 2007, p. 102). And a stepdad put it even more bluntly: "I don't introduce her as my stepdaughter because I didn't step on her. I introduce her, 'This is my daughter.' . . . I'd go crazy if something happened to her" (quoted in Marsiglio, 2004, p. 32).

Now, we explore the intense feelings these men and women were experiencing as we turn directly to parenthood, that second important adult role.

TYING IT ALL TOGETHER

1. Jared is making the case that, during the late twentieth century, there was an historic "deinstitutionalization of marriage." Which *two* of the following phenomena should Jared use to support this argument?

   a. Today, 1 of every 2 marriages ends in divorce.
   b. Today, most U.S. adults don't get very upset about "out-of-wedlock" motherhood.
   c. Today, marital satisfaction declines over the first few years of marriage.

2. Three couples are celebrating their silver anniversaries. Which relationship has followed the "classic" marital pathway?

   a. After being extremely happy with each other during the first three years, Ted and Elaine now find that their marriage has gone steadily downhill.
   b. Steve and Betty's marriage has had many unpredictable ups and downs over the years.
   c. Dave and Erika's marital satisfaction declined, especially during the first four years, but has dramatically improved now that their children have left home.

3. Describe the triangular theory to a friend and give an example of (a) romantic love, (b) consummate love, and (c) a companionate marriage. Can you think of couples who fit each category? At what stage of life are couples most likely to have companionate marriages?

4. Jennifer bitterly complains about Mark: "He clams up when he gets upset, which makes me paranoid; and then he gets furious and starts yelling at me when I try to get him to open up and discuss what's wrong." Jennifer is describing a _____ interaction, which suggests that this couple may have *secure/insecure* attachment styles.

5. You are a marriage counselor. Drawing on the research with regard to 1) keeping passion alive, 2) couple communications, and 3) commitment attitudes, formulate one suggestion for "homework" that you might give couples who come to your office for help.

6. Your best friend says, "I really like Kevin as a person, but I don't feel all that fulfilled in my marriage. Maybe I should get a divorce." Given the information in this section, what advice might you give?

Answers to the Tying It All Together questions can be found on the last page of this chapter.

Parenthood

I have never felt the joy that my daughter brings me when I wake up and see her . . . when you are laying there and . . . and feel this little hand tapping on your hand . . . that has been the most joyful thing I ever have experienced. . . . I've never been able to get that type of joy anywhere else.

(quoted in Palkovitz, 2002, p. 96)

Setting the Context: More Parenting Possibilities, Fewer Children

Take an informal poll of the parents you know and you will hear similar comments: "The love and joy you have with children is impossible to describe." The great benefit of the 1960s lifestyle revolution is that we have expanded the number of people who can fully participate in this life-changing experience, from stepparents, to gay couples, to never-married adults. Our twenty-first-century tapestry of nontraditional families, described in Chapter 7, offers many chances to fulfill this core identity of adult life.

At the same time, people have more freedom *not* to be parents—and increasing numbers of adults are making that choice. One sign of the times is the dramatic decline in **fertility rates**, or the average number of births per woman, in many developed countries. And whatever happened to those huge Spanish or Italian or Greek families? As you can see in Figure 11.3, adults in these southernmost European nations have some of the lowest fertility rates in the world.

Why has fertility dropped well below the level to keep the population constant (2.1 births) in every European nation, as well as in Russia, and countries such as Korea and Japan (Lestheghe & Surkyn, 2008)? A major cause, at least in Western Europe, may lie in the slower progress people are making toward adulthood. Remember from Chapter 10 that, in Italy and Spain, for instance, many people are well into their thir-

In the past, gay couples such as these women could never have hoped to be parents. In fact, they would have had to hide their relationship from the outside world. Today, they have the benefits of living in a society where this crucial life dream can be fulfilled.

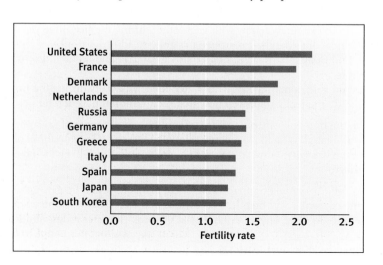

FIGURE 11.3: **Fertility rates in selected developed countries, 2008:** This chart reveals just why declining fertility is a crucial concern in Western Europe, where fertility rates are now below the replacement level (2.1 children) in every country. Notice, also, that childbearing rates are especially low in the southernmost European nations, Russia, and several Asian countries.

Source: Central Intelligence Agency, World Fact Book.

ties before they have the financial resources to leave home and marry. Moreover, when a comparatively poor, developed nation has extreme income inequalities (such as exist in Russia), or a government offers few social supports for new parents (such as in South Korea), young people are particularly unwilling to bring babies into the world.

Alarmed by their shrinking populations, a few elected officials in places like Italy have resorted to giving "baby bonuses" (that is, money) to couples who conceive. (But our discussion in Chapter 10 suggests that these nations might be better off if they promoted young people's transition to adulthood by providing them with decent jobs!) Newspapers in some European countries bombard twenty-something's with accusations of being self-indulgent, and offer dire warnings that choosing a childless life is destined to lead to an unhappy old age (Brown & Ferree, 2005). Not true! Studies suggest that people who decide not to have children are not more narcissistic (Gerson, Posner, & Morris, 1991). Provided they have freely made this choice, childless adults are just as happy later in life as people who do become parents (Connidis & McMullin, 1993). Moreover, the stereotype that having children makes a marriage stronger (or that having a child saves an unhappy marriage) is equally false. How does having a baby *really* change married life?

The Transition to Parenthood

To get a portrait of how becoming parents affects a marriage, researchers have conducted numerous longitudinal studies, selecting couples when the wife is pregnant and then tracking those families for a few years after the baby's birth. Understanding that parenthood arrives via many routes, social scientists have explored how having a child affects the bond between lesbian partners, too (Goldberg & Sayer, 2006). Here are the conclusions of these studies exploring *the transition to parenthood*:

- *Parenthood makes couples less intimate and happy.* Look back to the infancy chapters—especially the discussion of infant sleep in Chapter 3—and you will immediately see why a baby's birth is apt to change marital passion and intimacy for the worse. In fact, look at any couple struggling with an infant at your local restaurant and you will understand why researchers find that feelings about one's spouse shift from lover to "fellow worker" after the baby arrives (Belsky, Lang, & Rovine, 1985; Belsky & Rovine, 1990). One father aptly summarized what happens when he commented: "Instead of channeling our love towards just each other . . . we have channeled our love together towards them" (adapted from Palkovitz, 2002, p. 176).

- *Parenthood produces more traditional (and potentially conflict-ridden) marital roles.* If the couple is heterosexual, having children tends to make gender roles more distinct. Even when spouses have been sharing the household tasks equally, women often take over most of the housework and child care after the baby is born (Lawrence and others, 2008). Typically, this occurs because, after having children, the wife decides to leave her job or reduce her hours at work (Halrynjo, 2009; Singley & Hynes, 2005). However, even when both spouses work full time, mothers tend to do more of the diaper changing and household chores than fathers. This change can provoke conflicts centered on **marital equity**, or feelings of unfairness: Wives get angry at their husbands for not doing their share around the house (Feeney and others, 2001).

What compounds the sense of over-sacrificing are clashes centered on differing parenting styles (recall Chapter 7). One unhappy wife described this kind of disagreement when she informed her husband: "What's really getting to me . . . is that we hardly ever agree on how to handle [the baby]. I think you are too rough, and you think I'm spoiling her, and none of us wants to change" (quoted in Cowan & Cowan, 1992, p. 112).

These examples show how the stress of the baby's birth can work to poison the atmosphere between a husband and wife. However, most people adapt to this change in their relationship, although every study shows, *on average*, marital satisfaction does

fertility rate The average number of children a woman in a given country has during her lifetime.

marital equity Fairness in the "work" of a couple's life together. If a relationship lacks equity, with one partner doing significantly more than the other, the outcome is typically marital dissatisfaction.

Will this young couple's relationship seriously deteriorate after the baby? Will it improve? To answer these questions, we need to look at what their marriage was like *before* having a child.

tend to decline (Belsky & Rovine, 1990; Cowan & Cowan, 1992; Doss and others, 2009; Feeney and others, 2001; Houts and others, 2008; Keeton, Perry-Jenkins, & Sayer, 2008; Lawrence and others, 2008). Still, about one in three couples reports that having a child has *increased* their feelings of love for their spouse (Belsky & Rovine, 1990).

To predict which marriages completely deteriorate, decline slightly, or improve, we can look to specific demographic signs. For instance, it helps if the new parents are older, but *only* if they have been married a longer time before the birth (Bouchard, Lachance-Grzela, & Goguen, 2008). (That's why we may hear people advise newlyweds to "spend some time alone with your spouse before you conceive.") However, our best clues to how couples will cope come from looking *directly* at the pre-baby relationship. Are the parents-to-be securely attached? (See Feeney and others, 2003; Paley and others, 2005.) Did this husband and wife argue a good deal before the child arrived? (Kluwer & Johnson, 2007.) Have these people been slipping into the destructive communication styles I described in the previous section? (Houts and others, 2008.) In the words of one research team, "The transition to parenthood seems to act as an amplifier, tuning couples into their strengths and turning up the volume on existing difficulties in managing their . . . [love]" (Cowan & Cowan, 1992, p. 206).

Now that we've looked at its impact on a marriage, let's turn to the experience of parenthood from mothers' and fathers' points of view.

Exploring Motherhood

I've already talked about the incredible love that mothers feel for their children, especially in the infancy section of this book. But motherhood has its downside. National surveys show that mothers of young children report the *lowest* levels of day-to-day happiness, compared to women who are not parents or those who are in the empty-nest stage of life (McLanahan & Adams, 1989; Umberson & Gove, 1989). Moreover, unfortunately, it's a myth that simply becoming a parent makes us more mature. In fact, especially during the early childhood years—one longitudinal study showed—people typically become less calm and more emotionally stressed out than before they were moms (Jokela and others, 2009). Now, let's look at some reasons why.

The Motherhood Experience

Does becoming a mother really make people more tolerant, empathic, and mature? Just look at this photo and you will understand why—particularly when a woman has young children—that stereotype definitely doesn't fit the facts!

Motherhood, as one revealing poll showed, is tailor-made to destroy basic conceptions women have about themselves (Genevie & Margolies, 1987). In this U.S. study, 1 in 2 mothers admitted that they had trouble controlling their temper. Among the situations that made them most irate, challenges to their authority ranked first. Disobedience, disrespect, and even typical behaviors such as a child's whining might provoke reactions bordering on rage. When confronted with real-life children, these mothers found that their ideal of being calm, empathetic, and always in control came tumbling down (Genevie & Margolies, 1987).

Given the bidirectional quality of the parent–child bond, it should come as no surprise that a main force in this survey that affected how closely a woman fit her motherhood ideal lay in the quality of her attachment with a given child. Children who were temperamentally difficult provoked more irritation and lowered a mother's self-esteem. An easy child (recall Chapter 4) had the opposite effect, by evoking loving feelings and making that mother feel competent in her role. As one woman wrote:

> Lee Ann has been my godsend. My other two have given me so many problems and are rude and disrespectful. Not Lee Ann. . . . I disciplined her in the same way . . . except that she seemed to require less of it. Usually she just seemed to do the right thing. She is . . . my chance for supreme success after two devastating failures.

(quoted in Genevie & Margolies, 1987, pp. 220–221)

These emotions destroy another ideal that we have about motherhood: Mothers are supposed to love all their children equally. Although they said they tried not to let their preferences show, many women in this study did admit they had favorites. Typically, a favorite child was "easy" and successful in the wider world. However, what was most important, again, was the quality of the attachment relationship, the feeling of being totally loved by a particular child. As one woman reported:

> There will always be a special closeness with Darrell. He likes to test my word. . . . There are times he makes me feel like pulling my hair out. . . . But when he comes to "talk" to mom that's an important feeling to me.

(quoted in Genevie & Margolies, 1987, p. 248)

Not only does the experience of motherhood vary dramatically from child to child, it shifts from minute to minute and day to day:

> Good days are getting hugs and kisses and hearing "I love you." The bad days are hearing "you are not my friend." Good days are not knowing the color of the refrigerator because of the paintings and drawings all over it. Bad days are seeing a new drawing on a just painted wall.

(quoted in Genevie & Margolies, 1987, p. 412)

In sum, motherhood is incredibly wonderful and absolutely terrible. It evokes the most uplifting emotions *and* offers intensely painful insights into the self. Now, drawing on this study, let's explore how outside influences—the media, friends, family members, and some experts—can amplify mothers' distress.

Expectations and Motherhood Stress

The world provides women with an airbrushed view of motherhood—from the movie stars who wax enthusiastic about the joys of having babies ("much better than that terrible old career") to the family members who gush at bleary-eyed new mothers who haven't slept for weeks: "How wonderful you must feel!" By portraying motherhood as total bliss, are we doing women a disservice when they realize that their own experience does not live up to this glorified image? (See Douglas & Michaels, 2004.)

What compounds the problem are unrealistic performance pressures. Good children, as you saw in the above quotation, make a mother feel competent. "Difficult" children can make a woman feel like a failure. Despite all we know about the crucial role of genetics, peers, and the wider society in affecting development, mothers still bear the weight of responsibility for the way their children turn out (Coontz, 1992; Crittenden, 2001; Douglas & Michaels, 2004; Garey & Arendell, 2001).

Single mothers face the most intense pressures as they struggle to cope with poverty, working full time, plus trying to fulfill the "blissful" mom ideal. But *every* woman is subject to the heavy demands of contemporary motherhood: the need to be infinitely patient, to cram in the right amount of reading, to take children to lessons—to produce a perfect child. Critics talk in anguished terms about how today's working mothers are not giving children the attention they received in "the good old days." Stressed-out mothers berate themselves for not spending enough time with their daughters and sons (Bianchi, Robinson, & Milkie, 2006).

But these images about an epidemic of uninvolved mothers can be subjected to scientific scrutiny. And we have concrete data that *proves* that mother bashing is wrong. When developmentalists compared diary reports of mothers' involvement over the past 40 years, they discovered, to their astonishment, that mothers today spend *more* time with their children than their counterparts did a generation ago (Bianchi, Robinson, & Milkie, 2006; Sayer, Bianchi, & Robinson, 2004). In particular, notice from Figure 11.4 on page 344 the dramatic increase in the amount of time mothers spent teaching and playing. This cohort of young-adult mothers—including those

The blissful image of a mother and baby is nothing like contending with the reality of continual sleep deprivation and a screaming newborn—explaining why the idealized media images can make the first months of new motherhood come as a total shock.

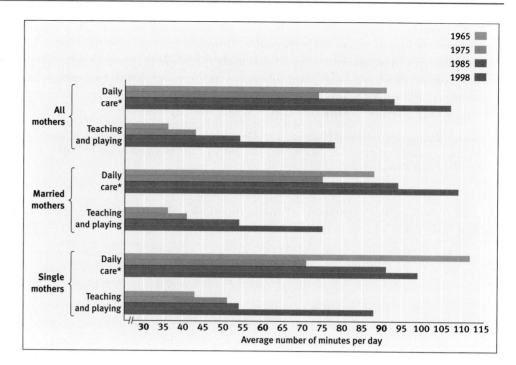

FIGURE 11.4: **Minutes per day devoted to hands-on child care by U.S. mothers:** Notice in particular that, in contrast to our myths, during the past 15 years, mothers are spending much more time teaching and playing with their children than in previous decades.

Source: Adapted from Sayer, Bianchi, & Robinson (2004).

*Refers to routine kinds of care, such as helping the child get dressed.

This photograph shows the reality of motherhood today. Young working mothers are spending much *more* time teaching their children than their own stay-at-home mothers did in the past!

new nurturer father Late-twentieth-century, middle-class idea in Western countries that fathers should do hands-on nurturing and share the child care equally with wives.

remarkable single moms—is spending almost *twice as much time* engaging in child cognition-stimulating activities as their own mothers spent with them!

Given that the average U.S. working mother clocks in about 39 hours a week at a job, what is giving way? The diary studies show major cutbacks in hours spent at housework (that's probably a good thing!) and less time devoted to community activities and with friends. A more ominous casualty for married women is a loss of time spent with their spouse (Amato and others, 2007; Bianchi, Robinson, & Milkie, 2006). One cost of the heroic dual focus on mothering and working, as you saw in the introductory vignette, is that marriages are at risk of suffering as people become "ships passing in the night."

Where are dads in his picture? Earlier, when I talked about equity issues during the transition to parenthood, I might have given you the impression that contemporary fathers are slacking off. Not so! The diary studies suggest that when we count hours at work plus what they do at home, fathers spend just as much total time "sacrificing" for the family as do mothers (Bianchi, Robinson, & Milkie, 2006). Actually, many of today's fathers are making valiant efforts to be involved parents, too (Halrynjo, 2009).

Exploring Fatherhood

When women first entered the workforce in large numbers in the 1970s, it became a badge of honor for fathers, in addition to fulfilling the traditional *breadwinner* role, to change the diapers and to be intensively involved in their children's lives. What social scientists called the **new nurturer father** became a masculine ideal. Furthermore, according to psychologists, we expect fathers to be good sex-role models, giving children a road map for how men should ideally behave. Sometimes, we even want them to be ultimate authority figures, the people responsible for laying down the family rules (as in the old saying: "Wait until your father gets home!").

The lack of clear guidelines leaves contemporary fathers with contradictory demands (Lamb, 1986, 1997). "Should I be strict or nurturing, sensitive or strong? Should I work full time to feed my family or stay home to feed my child?" As a perfect sign of the times, when college students in Finland were asked to list the characteristics of an ideal father, they seemed totally stumped (Perala-Littunen, 2007). Given that there may be no "right" way to be a father, how do contemporary men carry out their parental role?

How Fathers Act

As we would expect from the principle that they should be good sex-role models, fathers, on average, spend more time with their sons than their daughters (Bronstein, 1988). They play with their children in classically "male," rough-and-tumble ways (see Chapter 6). Fathers run, wrestle, and chase. They dangle infants upside down (Belsky & Volling, 1987). Although children adore this whirl-the-baby-around-by-the-feet kind of play (in our house we called it "going to Six Flags"), it can give mothers palpitations as they wonder: "Help! Is my baby going to be hurt?"

How much hands-on nurturing do today's fathers really perform? As you can see in Figure 11.5, the diary studies show that, in many Western countries, a genuine father-as-caregiver revolution occurred about 20 years ago (Bianchi, Robinson, & Milkie, 2006; Dribe & Stanfors, 2009). In the 1970s, men did not respond all that well to the call to be new nurturers. By the mid-1980s, they suddenly started to step in far more. At the turn of the century, many fathers *fully* embraced the nurturer role.

Statistically speaking, however, twenty-first-century child care remains a mainly female role. Though the percentages vary slightly from nation to nation, on average, in Canada, Western Europe, and the United States, women do roughly twice as much hands-on child care as do men (Bianchi, Robinson, & Milkie, 2006). Furthermore, the diary studies don't tell us which parent is taking bottom-line responsibility for managing the children—making that dentist appointment, arranging for a babysitter, planning the meals, and being on call when a child is sick. Having bottom-line responsibility may not translate into many hours spent physically with a daughter or son, but the weight and worry make this aspect of parenting a 24/7 job.

On the basis of our earlier discussion of society's expectations, it seems likely that mothers typically continue to take bottom-line responsibility. When we look at where the parenting buck stops, the gender dimension of being a parent is fully revealed (Lamb, 1997).

Variations in Fathers' Involvement

If you look at the fathers you know, however, you will be struck by their diversity (Halrynjo, 2009). There are divorced men who never see their children, as well as traditional "I never touch a diaper" dads. There also are fathers who take on *all* of the care (for instance, roughly 5 percent of American households are headed by single dads). What statistical forces predict how involved a given father is likely to be?

In two-parent families, one strong clue, researchers find, comes from looking at the man's gender-role conceptions. A father with a more traditional, authoritarian view of women's roles is far less likely to be willing to pitch in around the house (Bulanda, 2004; Gaertner and others, 2007). As one uninvolved father explained the situation, "Well, she's the housewife and she's the emotional one. I go to work . . . and I'm the disciplinarian guy" (quoted in Matta & Knudson-Martin, 2006, p. 27). Another influence lies in the other demands placed on the couple's lives. As women earn more (Gupta, 2007) or increase their time at work, men often respond by doing more child care and household chores (Amato and others, 2007).

And a third force depends on the attitudes of the partner in the parenthood duet: the woman. When a wife makes fun of her husband's diaper-changing abilities, or

Think back to the thrilled expressions on the faces of the boys engaged in rough-and-tumble play in Chapter 6 and you can understand why this male "hang 'em upside down" play style is a compelling bonding experience for *both* fathers and their sons. It's also clear why "daddy play" is apt to give moms fits.

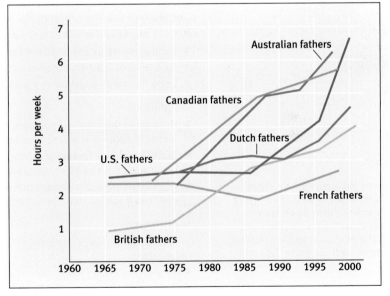

FIGURE 11.5: **Trends in father's primary activity time spent in child care in five countries:** Notice from this chart that, although the amount of time fathers spend in child care differs from nation to nation in interesting ways, in general, there has been a dramatic increase in "hands-on" fathering during the last 15 years of the twentieth century

Source: Adapted from Bianchi, Robinson, & Milkie (2006), p.160.

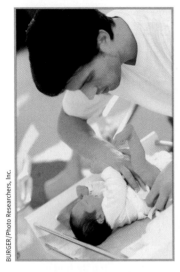

BURGER/Photo Researchers, Inc.

Contemporary fathers differ dramatically in how willing they are to change diapers. To explain this young man's behavior, we would predict that he has "father as nurturer" gender-role ideas and—very important—a wife who has been praising him, rather than making fun of his diaper-changing skills.

gets angry with him for being too rough, or shows signs of being jealous of her husband's relationship with the children, the message gets across. Women can be crucial gatekeepers. If wives are discouraging or set impossibly high standards, they put up serious barriers to their husbands' hands-on care (Cowan & Bronstein, 1988; Schoppe-Sullivan and others, 2008). This is a shame because fathers—even when they are not married to the mother of their child—feel much happier when they take a hands-on role in their child's life (Knoester, Petts, & Eggebeen, 2007).

In sum, to understand how men approach being fathers, once again, we need to adopt the *developmental systems theory perspective*. We should look at how a man views his role. We also need to understand how his wife *actually* acts when her husband does the child care. We may want to find out if the father has daughters or sons. We would definitely need to know about the demands of a couple's working lives.

This last consideration brings up the greatest barrier that traditionally has kept today's fathers from being completely involved: the need to fulfill the breadwinner role. As I will emphasize at the end of this chapter, for all our talk about "equal family roles," being able to support a family may remain at the core of many men's identities as adults. So having a demanding work schedule can force the most passionately interested man to be less involved with the children than he wants to be (Willott & Griffin, 2004; see Halrynjo, 2009). How much do career pressures *really* impinge on family life? First, let's sum up the messages in this parenthood section in Table 11.4. Then, I'll tackle this question and others as we turn to the third vital adult role: work.

TABLE 11.4: Advice for Parents: A Checklist

Coping with the Transition to Parenthood
- Don't expect your romantic feelings about each other to stay the same—they won't.
- Try to agree on your respective roles—who is going to do what around the house.
- Work on your communication skills before the baby arrives.
- Enjoy—and work together as a team!

For Mothers
- Understand that *you won't and can't be the perfect mother*—in fact, sometimes you will be utterly terrible—and accept yourself for being human!
- Don't buy into the fantasy of producing a perfect child. Children cannot be micromanaged into being perfect. Focus on enjoying and loving your child as he or she is (see also Chapter 7).
- Don't listen to people who say that working outside the home automatically means that you can't be an involved mother. Remember the findings discussed in this section.

For Fathers
- Understand that your role is full of contradictions—and that there is no "perfect" way to be a dad.
- Do what makes you feel comfortable, but also be flexible and responsive to the needs of your partner and the conditions of your life.
- Know your priorities. If fulfilling the breadwinner role is most important to you, don't beat yourself up for spending long hours at a job; but also take care to fully communicate and explain your feelings to your spouse and children.

❀ TYING IT ALL TOGETHER

1. Jenna and Charlie are expecting their first child, and Jenna plans to keep working full time. According to the research on the transition to parenthood, how is this couple prone to act after the baby is born?

2. Akisha, a new mother, is feeling unexpectedly stressed and unhappy. She and other mothers might cope better if they experienced which *two* of the following?

   a. got a less rosy, more accurate picture about motherhood from the media

   b. had more experts giving them parenting advice
   c. had less pressure placed on them from the outside world to "be perfect"

3. Your grandmother is lamenting that children today don't get the attention from their parents that they got in the "good old days." How should you respond, based on this chapter? Be specific with regard to both mothers and fathers.

4. Construct a questionnaire to predict how heavily involved in child care a particular man is likely to be, and give it to some fathers you know.

Answers to the Tying It All Together questions can be found on the last page of this chapter.

Work

How has the world of work been changing in the United States, and how do careers differ for men and women? Are there normal developmental changes in how people feel about their careers? Who tends to be successful at their jobs, and how can you construct a fulfilling work life?

Setting the Context: The Changing Landscape of Work

Let's begin our discussion by exploring the changing career landscape and examining women's versus men's careers.

General Trends: More Variability, Greater Work Fragility, and Longer Hours

You can see one major change in careers during the late twentieth century in the Experiencing the Lifespan box on page 348. Forty years ago, Mike would never have found his ideal job in middle age. Right after high school or college, men typically settled into their permanent life's work. Once in a job, they often stayed in the same organization until they retired (Super, 1957).

Today, this pattern, called the **traditional stable career**, is atypical. Like Mike, today, people move from job to job, or totally change direction, starting new careers as they travel through life. In fact, if you are like today's typical younger baby boomer, you can expect to have an astonishing 11 jobs, just from age 18 to 42 (U.S. Bureau of Labor Statistics, 2009)! In the twenty-first century, adults experience a shifting work pattern called **boundaryless careers** (DeFillippi & Arthur, 1994; Stahl, Miller, & Tung, 2002).

This more variable career path has many advantages. People are not locked into a single occupation. They have more freedom to flexibly tailor their careers to find a sense of flow in their work (Mirvis & Hall, 1994). But, as we all know, the boundaryless career has become common for a negative reason: greater job insecurity.

Job insecurity has been a concern for segments of the U.S. workforce since the late twentieth century, with outsourcing, globalization, and cutbacks in the mid-twentieth-century mega-corporations such as General Motors, which had previously hired many thousands of workers for life. But, as I am writing this chapter, the issue, "Will I keep my job?" is center stage for workers in every industry as the economy sputters and unemployment has rapidly taken off (see Figure 11.6 on page 348). How do anxious employees cope with the thought of getting laid off?

The answer, not unexpectedly, is that it depends on their options. Younger workers and people who feel more confident about their skills tend to disengage mentally from their "threatened position" and go back to school for further training or search out new work. However, if a person is late middle aged (like Mike in the Experiencing the Lifespan box), has been with a company for decades, or does not have sought-after skills, it is hard to mute the anxiety by sending out resumes or even vowing, "I'll

traditional stable career A career path in which people settle into their permanent life's work in their twenties and often stay with the same organization until they retire.

boundaryless career Today's most common career path for Western workers, in which people change jobs or professions periodically during their working lives.

EXPERIENCING THE LIFESPAN: FINDING AN IDEAL CAREER AT 50

To get insights into the "new boundaryless career"—to be described on the next page—read my interview with Mike:

I've put in a lot of mileage in my 25 years at work. In 1980, I dropped out of high school to work as a manager at Pizza Hut. Then, six years later, I was robbed and realized: "I've got to look for a calmer job!" I went into the steel pipe industry, loading trucks. I sold clothes for J.C. Penney. Then, I got my GED and finally got a job at Honeywell, selling heating and air-conditioning systems. It was like I was in heaven. I had a secretary, profit sharing, a great medical plan. The work was so easy. I could cold call and within a few months I was being invited for dinner. Then, management decided on cost-cutting measures. We'd just had a sales contest and, out of 169 reps, I'd come in second. That Tuesday, I went into the office expecting my boss to commend me. I was devastated when he said, "Mike, there's no easy way to tell you this. I have to lay you off."

My next job was selling medical equipment. Then, I worked for another heating and air-conditioning firm. Manufacturing went on strike and they laid off the sales force. I was desperate. A friend at the police department helped me get this job.

I've been a police officer for the past three years. I hope to make commander before I turn 55. Police officers are always on display. You're emotionally on the job 24 hours a day. I'm basically a trusting person. Training teaches you not to trust people. Being a deputy sheriff in a rural county, I go out on patrol without a partner. Last week, I pulled over a car that was driving all over the road. When I asked for the driver's license, the man gets out of the car and starts coming at me. I got lucky. When I pulled my gun, he backed down. I'm basically a nonviolent person. I hope until the day I die that I never have to take a life.

Much of what we do involves helping people. I've had several women call and say, "Thank you, officer, for saving my life." It's those times when I know the disappointments had a purpose. Finally, at age 50, I'm in the perfect career. Still, I am worried. Tennessee took in fewer taxes this quarter than ever, and government departments are facing cutbacks. It would be terrible to get laid off again—now that I'm toward the end of my working career—especially when I've just found my ideal job.

get trained in another field." The main strategy is to try, if possible, to work longer and harder than ever, in the hopes that your own position will be saved (Cheng & Chan, 2008; De Cuyper and others, 2008).

Actually, it is not even true that, in the days when men were the sole breadwinners, they worked longer and harder than they do today. Men (and, of course, women) are putting in more hours at their jobs than their parents or grandparents did.

Consider findings from the National Survey of the Changing Workforce (NSCW), a U.S. poll that has regularly monitored the hours that workers put in at their jobs (Families and Work Institute, 2009). This survey documents the fact that, as you saw with David in the introductory vignette, the 40-hour workweek is a relic of the past. In 2002, the typical male worker spent an average of 49 hours a week on his so-called 40-hour-a-week job (Galinsky and others, 2005).

Why has work expanded well beyond 9 to 5? One reason is that, in a more cut-throat economy, the competitive pressures and reinforcements favor working longer

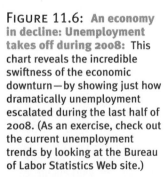

FIGURE 11.6: **An economy in decline: Unemployment takes off during 2008:** This chart reveals the incredible swiftness of the economic downturn—by showing just how dramatically unemployment escalated during the last half of 2008. (As an exercise, check out the current unemployment trends by looking at the Bureau of Labor Statistics Web site.)

Source: News: Adapted from U.S. Bureau of Labor Statistics, United States Department of Labor, *The Employment Situation*, February, 2009.

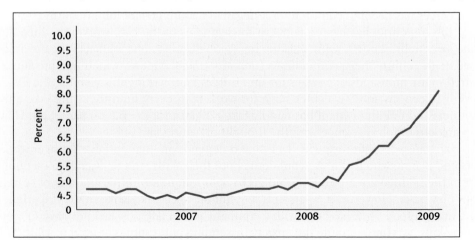

hours. Your co-worker starts regularly staying at the office until 7 P.M. In order to be promoted, you feel compelled to stay at your desk an extra hour or two. Soon, anyone who leaves the office at 5 is defined as slacking off (Schor, 1991). Furthermore, as companies continue to shed parts of their labor force, each individual worker has more to do. Since your company got rid of so many employees, everyone *must* work well into dinnertime to take up the slack.

The technology revolution has played its own part, with people able to stay in touch with their work 24/7 via handheld devices, cell phones, and pagers. In the 2002 NSCW survey, 1 in 3 U.S. workers reported being contacted after hours at least once a week via one of these "labor-saving devices" (Galinsky and others, 2005).

Having the flexibility to work at home is definitely a double-edged sword. Not only are you tempted to keep working on assignments when you should be putting your child to bed, but you are probably working far longer hours than if you had gone to the office.

In high-level, knowledge-based jobs, technology offers us more flexibility in setting our own schedule. As the managers in a software company exulted: "We are . . . very good at *letting* people work from home. As long as we hit certain targets, then people can do almost what they want. . . ." (MacEachen, Polzer, & Clarke, 2008, p. 1024). However, this blurring of work and home time has emotional costs. Yes, not having to go into the office allows you to take the kids to the dentist or pick them up from school, but you are potentially on the job 24 hours a day. In fact, in one national U.S. poll, workers who reported working 50-plus hours per week had the most flexible work schedules of all (Golden, 2008)!

Women's Work

Women face the same twenty-first-century work conditions and pressures as do men. However, their career paths differ from men's in the following ways:

- **Women have less continuous careers than men.** Because, as you saw earlier, they are often the primary nurturers, women are more likely to move in and out of the workforce or to work part time for significant periods during their lives (U.S. Bureau of Labor Statistics, 2009). So a woman decides to give up teaching for a few years, or to cut down her hours at the law firm, when she has her baby. Most often, it is after her second child that she simply feels that she *must* give up her job. These periodic "off ramps" with work potentially give women more flexibility to design genuinely creative boundaryless careers (Shapiro, Ingols, & Blake-Beard, 2008). However, taking time off can have enduring economic consequences, leading to lower lifetime earnings and a greater chance of sliding into poverty in old age (Belsky, 2001; O'Rand, 1988).

- **Women have different occupations and get lower wages.** Compounding their more erratic work lives are the facts that jobs are still segmented by gender and that stereotypically female jobs pay comparatively low wages. About 98 percent of secretaries, clerks, and childcare workers are female (Charles, 1992; Cohen, 2004; Reskin, 1993). Even in nations such as Sweden, where the government provides incentives for companies to hire women in traditionally male fields, there are very few female chemists or engineers (Anker, Malkas, & Korten, 2003).

To what degree is this **occupational segregation**—separation of men and women into different kinds of jobs—due to nature (biologically driven preferences) or nurture (socialization pressures in the wider world)? Whatever the answer, these

occupational segregation
The separation of men and women into different kinds of jobs and career paths.

Have you ever been astonished to see a woman climb into the cockpit of your plane? If so, you have had a vivid reminder that *occupational segregation* is still prevalent in many jobs today.

FIGURE 11.7: **Entry-level wages of male and female college graduates, 1973–2005:** Notice that, while the wage differential has waxed and waned, female college graduates still, on average, earn significantly less than men when they first enter the labor force.

Source: Mishel, Bernstein, & Allegretto (2007).

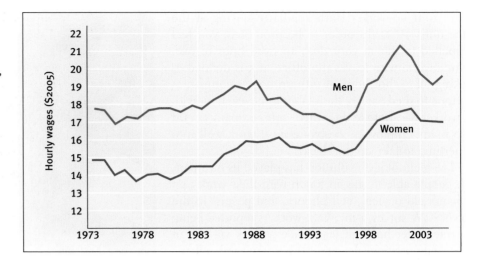

male/female differences take their toll in terms of pay. Statistically speaking, females have a real educational edge over men. In 2006, roughly 1 in 3 U.S. women in their late twenties had a B.A. compared to 1 in 4 males (U.S. Census Bureau News, 2008). In fact, currently about half of all female 21-year-olds are in college, compared to slightly more than 1 in 3 men (U.S. Bureau of Labor Statistics, 2009).

Still, the male/female wage gap remains. As of late 2008, the average weekly salary of a U.S. woman who worked full time was only roughly 80 percent that of man's (U.S. Bureau of Labor Statistics, CPS retrieved, March 22, 2009). You can see an even more stark comparison in Figure 11.7. Notice that the entry-level wage gap for male and female college graduates has remained substantial for over 40 years.

Now that we have a bird's-eye view of the overall trends, let's focus on people as they actually *travel* through their careers, by first spelling out a theory that charts predictable stages in our work lives, and then offering a crystal-ball look at the qualities that help predict career success.

Charting People's Careers Through Life

In his classic **lifespan theory of careers**, Donald Super (1957) spells out four general phases to our working lives. During adolescence and emerging adulthood, we are in a period of *moratorium*, actively searching for the right career. Once we have found our work identity, we enter the *establishment* phase. During this time, typically lasting from our twenties into our early forties, we are working hard to advance in our career. In our late forties and fifties, we reach the *maintenance* phase, as we enjoy being at our career peak, become more interested in nurturing the younger generation, and care more about ethical concerns at work (Pogson and others, 2003). Finally, we enter the *decline* phase, during which we retire and disengage from the world of work.

Although Super developed his ideas in the 1950s, they resonate today. U.S. workers in their twenties and thirties do report being more interested in working hard to get ahead in their careers than do middle-aged employees or workers about to retire (Galinsky and others, 2005).

Super's theory also fits our *social clock norms*—general ideas about what activities are appropriate at different adult stages (see Chapter 10). Even in our less age-stratified society, we expect people to be at specific places in their careers at certain times of life. Working as a salesperson at Target is "on target" for a 20-year-old. It is less appropriate if a worker is 45—especially if that person is male. My mid-life students who have returned to school to get training for a new career must cope with their anxiety about being seriously *off time* (see Chapter 10) in their career social clock: "Am I too old to get hired in my new field?" So despite the growth of boundaryless careers, there *are* predictable changes related to age in our attitudes about work.

lifespan theory of careers
Donald Super's identification of four career phases: *moratorium* in adolescence and emerging adulthood; *establishment* in young adulthood; *maintenance* in midlife; and *decline* in late life.

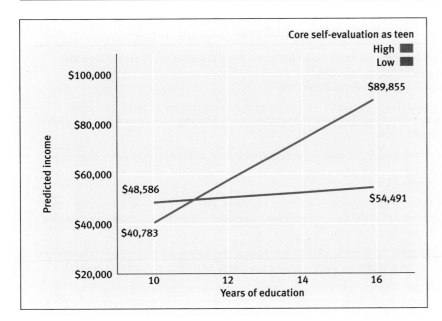

FIGURE 11.8: **How core self-evaluations measured in youth related to average income in early midlife for people with different amounts of education in the National Longitudinal Survey of Youth:** Notice that, as the number of years of schooling increases, feeling confident, efficacious, and happy as a teen translates into greater earning power. But, among people with low core self-evaluations, years of schooling make no difference. Bottom line: The best educational credentials only translate into economic success when people feel good about themselves and basically happy in life.

Source: Judge & Hurst (2007).

Super's ideas offer insights into the general shape of our working lives. But his theory doesn't address that important question: *Who* tends to do well in the work world? It's a no-brainer to say that socioeconomic status and education matters. Having the right educational credentials and coming from an affluent family gives people a platform on which to succeed. But some of you may know Harvard Ph.D.s or people with millionaire parents who are failing miserably to live up to their career potential. A huge U.S. study helps spell out what these adults may be missing in life.

For more than 30 years, the National Longitudinal Study of Youth has been tracking the lives of thousands of U.S. young people as they move from adolescence through adult life. At their first teenage evaluation in 1979, the researchers measured what they called "core self-evaluations": whether a person had high self-esteem; whether that individual was happy or depressed; and whether that teenager felt in control of his life. For adolescents with life advantages, this *single* evaluation, decades earlier, predicted economic success by early midlife!

Figure 11.8 shows the findings specifically for education. Notice that core self-evaluations did not translate into higher income in the face of poor educational credentials. But, as people got more well educated, having these inner attitudes had a powerful impact on later wages. In fact, if a young person had poor self-esteem, felt depressed, and had low self-efficacy, there were *no* income advantages of having an education at all.

So it's not true that Ph.D.s or people with wealthy parents have it made. In order to capitalize on these advantages, you need to feel generally happy and good about yourself.

Finding Career Happiness

This fascinating finding reminds us that who we are as people (our enduring personality) goes a long way to determining our career success. In fact, some psychologists persuasively argue that being a generally happy, self–confident person predicts satisfaction at a wide variety of jobs (Boehm & Lyubomirsky, 2008; Judge, Heller, & Klinger, 2008). But we also know from the last chapter that finding the right kind of work can also change people's personalities for the better during the emerging adult years. So let's look now at two specific strategies for finding the optimum person–environment fit at work.

Strategy 1: Find a Career That Fits Your Personality

According to John Holland's (1985) classic theory, the key to finding career fulfillment is to match our job to our personality. People who are sociable should not work in

> **TABLE 11.5: Holland's Six Personality Types**
>
> **Realistic type:** These people enjoy manipulating machinery or working with tools. They like physical activity and being outdoors. If you fit this profile, your ideal career might be in construction, appliance repair, or car repair.
>
> **Investigative type:** These people like to find things out through doing research, analyzing information, and collecting data. If you fit this pattern, you might get special satisfaction in some scientific career.
>
> **Artistic type:** These people are creative and nonconforming, and they love to freely express themselves in the arts. If this is your type, a career as a decorator, dancer, musician, or writer might be ideal.
>
> **Social type:** These people enjoy helping others and come alive when they are interacting with other human beings. If this description fits you, a career as a bartender, practicing physician, or social worker might be right.
>
> **Entrepreneurial type:** These people like to lead others, and they enjoy working on organizational goals. As this kind of person, you might find special joy as a company manager or in sales.
>
> **Conventional type:** These people have a passion for manipulating data and getting things organized. If you fit this type, you would probably be very happy as an accountant, administrative assistant, or clerk.
>
> Take a minute to think about your three-letter code. Can you use this framework to come up with your ideal career?

solitary cubicles. Someone strong in Howard Gardner's naturalistic intelligence (recall Chapter 7) should search for a profession that involves working with nature, perhaps choosing landscaping or working with animals, over slaving 50 stories up in a corporate tower. The closer we get to our ideal personality—career fit, Holland argues, the more satisfied and successful we will be at our jobs.

To promote this fit, Holland classifies six personality types, described in Table 11.5, and fits them to occupations. Based on their answers to items on a career inventory, people get a three–letter code, showing the three main categories into which they fit, in descending order of importance. If a person's ranking is SAE (social, artistic, and entrepreneurial), that individual might find fulfillment directing an art gallery or setting up and managing a beautiful restaurant. If your code is SIE (social, investigative, and entrepreneurial), you might be better off developing and marketing a medicine for heart disease, or spending your work life as a practicing veterinarian.

Still, even when people have found work that fits their personality, there is no guarantee that they will be happy at a job. What if your job as a gallery manager involves mountains of paperwork and very little time exercising your creative or social skills? In predicting career happiness, it is vital to consider the demands of the actual workplace, too.

Strategy 2: Find a Workplace That Fits Your Needs

What specific qualities constitute an ideal work environment? On this point, experts (Blustein, 2008) and U.S. workers are clear. People want jobs that expand their skills. They want autonomy to exercise their creativity. They want to have input into decision–making at work. They want caring colleagues and employers who are sensitive to their needs. Remember from Chapter 7 that these very qualities—autonomy, nurturing, and relatedness—define ideal school environments. Workers are looking for **intrinsic career rewards**—work that is fulfilling in and of itself.

Extrinsic career rewards, or external reinforcers, such as salary, can also be crucial, depending on a person's life situation. While, as you will see in the next chapter, money does not make for happiness, at the lower ends of the economic spectrum, family income has a dramatic impact on overall well–being (North and others, 2008).

intrinsic career rewards Work that provides inner fulfillment and allows people to satisfy their needs for creativity, autonomy, and relatedness.

extrinsic career rewards Work that is performed for external reinforcers, such as prestige or a high salary.

So for the 47–plus millions of near poor U.S. workers who are currently struggling to make it from paycheck to paycheck (see Newman & Chen, 2007), salary *is* a prime job concern. As I am writing this chapter, with so many 2009 developed–world layoffs, another extrinsic concern that should rank highly on any person's list of career priorities is job security (Gilboa and others, 2008). Unfortunately, having the luxury of viewing work as an intrinsically gratifying, flow–inducing experience depends on having our "security needs" satisfied or knowing we can economically survive (see Blustein, 2008).

Remember from Chapter 10 that flow states require that our skills match the demands of a given task. Therefore, it should come as no surprise that various surveys show that the most poisonous job–related stress is "role ambiguity," or a lack of clear work demands (Gilboa and others, 2008). If you are unsure of what is expected at your job, or have no guidelines as to how you can be effective, there is simply no chance of feeling competent and "in flow." Feeling a sense of unfairness—that other less–competent people are getting ahead at your job—is tailor–made to produce burnout and frustration, too (Maslach & Leiter, 2008). Another problem that impairs flow states is **role overload**—having way too much to do to do an effective job. A related issue is feeling a sense of **role conflict**—being torn between competing life demands (such as family and work).

How common is work–family conflict? Very, according to studies in the Western world (see Galinsky, 2002; Halryno, 2009). People are less likely to worry about their family interfering with their job responsibilities. They want their work to give them more time for their family lives (Galinsky, 2007). Interestingly, although balancing career and family is a concern for both genders, the most recent NSCW survey showed that men— because they work such long hours—are most upset about being deprived of family time (see Families and Work Institute, 2009, first report, retrieved, March 27, 2009).

If you are a male reader, how would you feel (or do you feel) about having a wife who is incredibly career-oriented and perhaps makes more money than you? If you said, "That's great" or "I'd love it," and you are in your twenties, you are far from alone. According to the most recent 2008 NSCW poll, today, for the first time, both men and women in their twenties are equally interested in advancing at a career. Today, for the first time, only a minority (41 percent) of adults agree that "it's better if the man earns the money and the woman stays at home." This sea change in gender attitudes is coming at just the right time. We may be experiencing a sea change in Western world career concerns and male/female roles.

Imagine what it's like to leave this screaming baby every morning and go to your job and you will understand why work-family conflict is a special torture for many women today. What's particularly interesting, though, is that contemporary dads may feel even guiltier than moms about not spending enough time with their kids.

Summing Things Up and a Few Future Family/Work Speculations

A basic message of this chapter has been that until now the main role problem for U.S. adults is "too much to do." Couples are working too hard to spend enough quality time with each other. Women and men are struggling heroically to be involved with the children while working more than full time. Now, I'd like to offer two speculations about how an ongoing economic downturn *might* change the landscape of work/family life.

- **A new family worry: concerns about keeping a job.** Should the developed world unemployment rate remain high or—heaven forbid—increase, the main, contemporary family concern is apt to shift from "I'm working too much" to "I'm working

role overload A job situation that places so many requirements or demands on workers that it becomes impossible to do a good job.

role conflict A situation in which a person is torn between two or more major sets of responsibilities—for instance, parent and worker—and cannot do either job adequately.

While his wife works, this twenty-something, temporarily jobless husband seems to be enjoying juggling the laundry and doing the child care. Do you think many more men will become househusbands in the future? How would the men you know adjust to being stay-at-home fathers, should they find themselves out of a job?

too little." Faced with job losses and/or declining income, will divorce rates escalate as couples get overwhelmed by financial stress? Or will husbands and wives become closer—given that they may have more time to spend together and with the children—if one or both partners gets laid off or needs to work part-time?

- **A new family alignment: more stay-at-home men.** Another underlying theme of this chapter is that, no matter how much gender roles have changed, until now, men have typically been the primary breadwinners. Males start out earning considerably more than females, right after graduation. The gender-wage gap remains throughout the working years. But, in our current economy, "male-type jobs" (factory, construction, financial services positions, for instance) are especially vulnerable to layoffs. Higher-paying, predominantly male managerial or corporate jobs are often the ones being cut. The two laid-off husbands—both in their forties, with employed wives—I wanted to talk to in preparing this chapter refused to be interviewed about their rapid shift from main breadwinner to househusband. (Were they too ashamed?) How will men and women generally cope with what may be dramatic shakeups in their standard family roles?

TYING IT ALL TOGETHER

1. Michael is unhappy about his job. His grandfather is trying to make him feel better by contrasting the career situation today with "the good old days." Which of the statements below can this grandfather legitimately say, based on what you read in this chapter?

   a. "Your problem isn't so bad! In my day people had to stick with their careers, even if they didn't really like them."
   b. "Your problem isn't so bad! In my day most people worked much longer hours than today."
   c. "Your problem isn't so bad! In my day we had much less job security."

2. Which of the men described below does *not* fit into any of Super's phases in his life-span theory of careers, but instead is following a work pattern common in today's world?

   a. Ethan, a 30-year-old, is working very hard to advance in his career.
   b. Brad, a 40-year-old, is looking for a whole new career.
   c. Tom, a 50-year-old, has risen through the ranks of the company and is now enjoying being at the peak of his career.
   d. John, a 60-year-old, is thinking about retirement.

3. In the previous question, which person clearly has a traditional, stable career, and which person has a boundaryless career?

4. Vanessa, a bubbly, outgoing 30-year-old, has what her friends see as a perfect job: She's a researcher in a one-person office, with flexible hours; she has a large, quiet workspace; a boss who is often away; job security; and great pay. Yet Vanessa is unhappy with the job. According to Holland's theory, what is the problem?

5. How have changes in the economy affected families today? Look up data relating to my two speculations above and then rewrite this last section of the chapter to reflect CURRENT family/work trends.

Answers to the Tying It All Together questions can be found on the last page of this chapter.

Final Thoughts

In this chapter, I put our adult roles center stage. In the next chapter, I'll return to exploring our inner self, from the emerging adult years through middle age. Can we target an attitude that explains why parenthood is incredibly joyful, one that naturally makes people more likely to forgive? How exactly do people change intellectually, and in terms of personality, as they move from the late twenties through the sixties? These are some of the compelling topics I'll tackle in the next chapter, as I continue to explore that important question "What are some keys to having a successful, fulfilling adult life?" and also tackle a few role changes specific to middle age.

SUMMARY

Marriage

Marriages used to be practical unions often arranged by families. In the early twentieth century, as life expectancy increased dramatically, we developed the modern idea that couples should be best friends and lovers for 50 years. During the late twentieth century, with the women's movement and the increasing acceptability of divorce and unwed motherhood, marriage became **deinstitutionalized**—less of a standard path in the Western world. In contrast to the Middle East, with its male-dominated marriages, and Scandinavia, where not getting married is perfectly fine, in the United States we still care deeply about getting married—but are reluctant to enter that state unless we feel fairly financially secure. Couples can expect a decline in marital happiness, especially during the first four years of married life; but, for those who stay together, there is often a **U-shaped curve of marital satisfaction**, with happiness rising at the empty-nest stage. It's important to understand, however, that variability characterizes marriages and that some couples stay blissfully happy throughout life.

According to Robert Sternberg's **triangular theory of love**, married couples start out with **consummate love**, but passion and intimacy can decline as partners construct separate lives. To preserve passion and intimacy, one strategy may be to share one's passions with one's mate. Happy couples make a high ratio of positive to negative comments and don't get personally hurtful or engage in **demand–withdrawal communications**. Having an inner sense of commitment, wanting to sacrifice for a marriage, and forgiving is important to having a happy, enduring relationship, too.

Divorce, that common adult event, has several phases. There is a pre-divorce phase of marital unhappiness—possibly accompanied by an affair—then the upheaval of the separation. Although divorce is very stressful, it can cause emotional growth, and lead to future happiness, but primarily if couples were very distressed earlier on (versus simply feeling "a bit" unfulfilled with their mates). Because mothers usually get custody of the children, divorced dads often face the problem of losing their children and go on to remarry and have new families. Both men and women struggle with the challenges and joys of step-parenthood.

Parenthood

Although many more people *can* become parents in our twenty-first-century society, more people are choosing not to have children. A major concern in Europe is declining **fertility rates**.

Despite our negative stereotypes, adults who choose not to have children are not more self-centered or unhappy in old age.

The transition to parenthood tends to lessen romance and intimacy. Gender roles become more traditional. Conflicts centered on **marital equity** can arise. Still, there is tremendous variability with some couples growing closer after the baby is born. The quality of a couple's relationship before becoming parents predicts how a marriage will fare after the baby arrives.

Motherhood has extreme lows as well as highs—and this experience is tailor-made to destroy women's idealized images of themselves. Society conveys a sanitized view of what motherhood is like. We tend to blame mothers for their children's "deficiencies," and we sometimes berate working women for not spending enough time with their children. In contrast to our images of an epidemic of uninvolved mothers, twenty-first-century women spend much more time (especially teaching time) with their children than in the past. Contemporary mothers (and fathers) are giving their children unparalleled attention and love—even while they hold down jobs.

Fathers are expected to be breadwinners and nurturers, as well as good sex-role models and, sometimes, the disciplinarians. During the past 20 years, men have stepped in as genuine caregiving partners, although women still typically do more and especially have bottom-line responsibility for directing children's lives. Fathers play with their children in traditionally male, active ways, and they vary in their involvement, depending on their sex-role attitudes, the attitudes of their spouse toward their getting involved, and the couple's work schedules. Feeling committed to the male role of breadwinner, and needing to work long hours, can interfere with men's (and women's) "child-care time."

Work

We used to have **traditional stable careers**. Today, partly due to job insecurity, we are likely to have **boundaryless careers**. How workers respond to the threat of being laid off depends on their possible new job-finding options. Today, however, the general pattern for full-time workers is to work much more than 40 hours. Technological advances, while they offer more flexibility with regard to needing to physically be on a job, contribute to this trend. Women have less continuous careers than men and **occupational segregation** and lower pay for women are still prevalent in the world of work.

Super's **lifespan theory of careers**, with *moratorium, establishment, maintenance,* and *decline* phases of work, explains our overall career path. For young people with advantages, happiness and self-confidence, even measured during adolescence, predicts economic success in midlife. Although being a happy, confident person sets people up to be happy at work, finding the right job matters, too.

One key to finding work happiness is to choose a career that fits our personality. Another is having a work environment that permits creativity and autonomy. U.S. workers are mainly looking for **intrinsic career rewards**, but **extrinsic career rewards**, such as pay, become paramount especially during economic downturns, when people need to work just to survive.

Forces that impair intrinsic career satisfaction include unclear job requirements, feeling a sense of unfairness, and **role overload**—having too much to do. **Role conflict**, being pulled between work and family, is also very common today—even more so for men as they still are most often the primary breadwinners. In recent years, the main family/work concern has been working too hard. Will worries about working too little and rapid shifts in traditional family roles—with more stay-at-home-husbands—become issues in a new era of economic decline?

KEY TERMS

deinstitutionalization of marriage, p. 329

U-shaped curve of marital satisfaction, p. 332

triangular theory of love, p. 332

consummate love, p. 333

demand–withdrawal communication, p. 335

fertility rate, p. 340

marital equity, p. 341

new nurturer father, p. 344

traditional stable career, p. 348

boundaryless career, p. 348

occupational segregation, p. 349

lifespan theory of careers, p. 350

intrinsic career rewards, p. 352

extrinsic career rewards, p. 352

role overload, p. 353

role conflict, p. 353

ANSWERS TO TYING IT ALL TOGETHER QUIZZES

Marriage

1. a and b.

2. c.

3. According to Sternberg, by looking at three dimensions—passion, intimacy, and commitment—and exploring their combinations we can get a portrait of all the partner love relationships that exist in life. By exploring how these facets change over time, we can also understand why marital happiness might naturally decline over the years. (a) This couple is extremely emotionally involved (has intimacy and passion) but has not decided to get married or enter a fully committed relationship. (b) This couple has it all: intimacy, passion, and commitment. Most likely, they are newlyweds. (c) This couple is best friends (intimate) and married (committed) but no longer passionate. Couples who have been married for decades are most likely to have companionate marriages.

4. demand/withdrawal interaction; *insecure* attachment styles.

5. (1) Spend time together doing exciting activities you both enjoy. (2) Keep disagreements to the topic. Never get personal when fighting. (3) Reach out and give to each other. If you are really committed, sacrificing for your partner should give you special joy.

6. You should advise *against* this!

Parenthood

1. Statistically speaking, Jenna will end up doing most of the childcare—which unfortunately may cause conflicts around marital equity.

2. a and c.

3. Tell grandma that's not true! Parents are spending more time with their children than in the past. Moms do far more hands-on teaching—even when they have full-time jobs. And

of course, fathers are also much more involved. Not only are dads spending more time teaching and playing with their daughters, and particularly sons, they are even doing more of the routine care.

4. My questions (but you can think of others!): 1) Do you think child care is basically a woman's job, or should couples equally share this responsibility? 2) Are females basically more superior at childrearing than men? 3) Does your wife make fun of your caregiving skills and/or seem jealous when you really step in to care for the kids? 4) How important is it to you to be the primary breadwinner, and how demanding is your job? 5) Does your wife work full time, and how much does she earn compared to you?

Work

1. a.
2. b.
3. Tom has a traditional stable career. Brad has a boundaryless career.
4. Vanessa's isolated work environment doesn't fit her sociable personality. She needs ample chances to interact with people during the day.
5. Here are some general sources for finding these data: 1) the U.S. Census Bureau (which offers regular updates on U.S. living arrangements, as well as unemployment and salaries); 2) the U.S. Bureau of Labor Statistics.

Chapter 12

Midlife

Today, at age 52, I am calm, in control, confident about my ideas. There is some regret about the wrinkles and the added pounds—but you might be surprised at how minor these concerns are. Getting through menopause was a problem, but now that it's over, I feel wonderful. Sex with David is better than before. My fear relates to my mind. After years spent crunching numbers as an accountant, I want to go back to school to get a social work degree. I've always volunteered on weekends at church. Now, it's time to devote myself full time during these next precious decades to helping "at risk" young people succeed. Having grown up during the Civil Rights movement here in Nashville, I learned social activism at a young age. But can I make it in the classroom at my age? Am I too old to get a job?

Then, there are the anxieties about time. Cotonia and Joshua recently moved in after the divorce. David wants to reduce his hours at O'Charley's to watch our precious grandbaby while my daughter is at work—but I can't put that responsibility totally on my husband. Child care is a grandma's job!

Still, my life experience will help me cope with these challenges, and I can rely on my life love, David, to cheer me on. In many ways, I'm basically the same person that I was at 20, just as caring, energetic, and outgoing—but much more responsible and better able to roll with the punches. And it's now or never. I feel the clock ticking when I look around. My good friend Susan just died of cancer. My baby brother Jay retired after having his stroke last year. I get my inspiration from Mom, at age 75 still running the beauty shop six days a week. Mom—well, she's supposed to be old, but she's really middle-aged.

When you think of middle age, what images come to your mind? As is true of Doreen, you might imagine people at the peak of their powers: wise, mature, competently mastering adult life. You might envision adults taking on new challenges, such as going back to school for a second career, but you also might think of menopause, sexual decline, and possible mental loss. You could imagine vigorous, happy grandparents, or people overburdened by caring for their parents in old age. In this chapter, devoted to the long life stage that psychologist Carl Jung (1933) poetically labeled "the afternoon of life," I'll explore these joys and heartaches, challenges, and changes.

Let's start by setting some boundaries. When exactly *are* people middle-aged?

Setting the Context

If you are like most people reading this chapter, you probably believe we enter middle age at about age 40 and exit this stage of life at age 60 or 65 (Etaugh & Bridges, 2006; Lachman, 2004). Your parents or grandparents might not agree. In U.S. surveys,

roughly *half* of all people in their late sixties and seventies call themselves middle-aged (Lachman, 2004). They may be right. When a woman, such as Doreen's mother, or the dance instructors in this photo, are healthy and working in their seventies, should we call them middle-aged or old? When someone is just starting a family at age 45 or 50, is that individual middle-aged or a young adult?

At the other extreme, you may know a middle-aged person who qualifies as "old": a relative in his fifties coping with serious heart disease; someone, like Doreen's brother, who was forced by poor health to retire at a too young, *off-time* age.

To complicate matters further, we might expect that people would have different perspectives about aging during early versus late middle age (the forties compared to the late fifties). We would be right—but in a somewhat surprising way. In one U.S. poll, people approaching 60 were just as likely to see the future as full of opportunities as adults in their early forties. But they also were more likely than the forty-somethings to agree with the statement "I have the sense that time is running out" (Cate & John, 2007).

So just as you saw with emerging adulthood, middle age is a hazy, ill-defined life stage, with different *social clock* feelings associated with its entry point and end. Moreover, people who fit into this chronological category are an incredibly diverse group—in their lifestyles, perceptions, and everything else. Diversity—of changes, and from person to person—*plus* consistency is the basic message of the chapter you are about to read.

Although the calendar would clearly categorize these seventy-something dance instructors as "senior citizens," they would almost certainly say, "No, we are middle-aged." When people are healthy and active, middle age can extend well into later life!

The Evolving Self

Do we get more mature as we age, or are we the same people at age 50 as at 25? Is Doreen right to be worried about going back to school in her fifties, and how do our intellectual abilities really change as we travel through adult life? These questions have been hotly debated for decades. The reasons for the controversies will become clear as we explore the following compelling questions: "How will I change as a person during adulthood?" "How can I have a happy, fulfilling adult life?"

Exploring Personality

We actually have *contradictory* views about how our personalities change over the years. One is that we basically don't change: "If Calista is bossy and self-centered in college, she will be bossy and self-centered in the nursing home." Another is that entering new stages of life, or having life-changing experiences, produces radical transformations in our basic self: "Since giving birth to my child, I'm a completely different person." "Coming close to death in my car accident last summer totally transformed how I think about the world." Then, there is the change that we all hope for, the one that Doreen describes and many middle-aged and older women also report (Zucker, Ostrove, & Stewart, 2002). As we get older, we grow more competent, confident, happier, and self-assured. Which point of view is true? The answer, as developmentalists have discovered, is *each* idea, depending on which aspect of personality we chart!

We Don't Change Much (on Average): Exploring the "Big Five"

Today, one popular way of measuring personality is by ranking people according to five core temperamental predispositions. As you read the following list, take a minute to think of where you stand on these dimensions, which psychologists label the **Big Five traits**:

- *Neuroticism* refers to our general tendency toward mental health versus psychological disturbance. Are you basically resilient, stable, and well-adjusted, someone who bounces back after setbacks and copes well with stress? Or are you hostile, high-strung, and hysterical, a person who others might label as psychologically disturbed? (Children with serious externalizing and internalizing tendencies, for instance, would rank high on neuroticism.)

- *Extraversion* describes outgoing attitudes, such as warmth, gregariousness, activity, and assertion. Are you sociable, friendly, a real "people person," someone who thrives on meeting new friends and going to parties? Or are you most comfortable curling up alone with a good book? Do you get antsy when you are by yourself, thinking "I've got to get out and be with people," or do you prefer living a reflective, solitary life?

- *Openness to experience* refers to our tendency to be risk-takers and seek out new experiences. Do you love traveling the world, sampling different cuisines, taking chances, having people shake up your preconceived ideas? Do you think life should be a continual adventure, and relish getting out of your comfort zone? Or are you basically cautious, risk averse, and comfortable mainly with what you already know?

- *Conscientiousness* describes having the kind of industrious worker personality described in Chapter 10. Are you hardworking, self-disciplined, and reliable, someone others count on to take on demanding jobs and get things done? Or are you erratic and irresponsible, prone to renege on obligations and forget appointments, a person your friends and co-workers really can't trust?

- *Agreeableness* has to do with kindness, empathy, and the ability to compromise. Are you pleasant, loving, and easy to get along with? Or are you stubborn, hot-tempered, someone who continually seems offended and gets into fights? (Agreeable people, for instance, have secure attachment styles.)

Where you rank these Big Five dimensions has consequences for your life. Extraverts tend to be upbeat and happy (Lucas, Le, & Dyrenforth, 2008). People high on neuroticism are stressed out, anxious, and sad. Conscientious adults tend to live longer (Martin, Friedman, & Schwartz, 2007). Because people with this trait are more responsible and health aware, conscientiousness even predicts the progression of diseases such as HIV (O'Cleirigh and others, 2007). Moreover, as you might expect, being conscientious, agreeable, and not neurotic makes for success in relationships. People who score high on these particular Big Five traits are more likely to be happily married, less prone to divorce. Plus, in one study, scores on extraversion, conscientiousness, agreeableness, and neuroticism, measured during very early adulthood, even predicted career achievement 46 years later (reported in Roberts and others, 2007).

This brings up a critical issue. How much do our Big Five rankings change during adult

Big Five traits Five core psychological predispositions—neuroticism, extraversion, openness to experience, conscientiousness, and agreeableness—that underlie personality.

Look at these exuberant women enjoying themselves at a party and you will understand why extraverts are *generally* happy (and also why simply being around a "people person" makes us generally feel more upbeat). How would you rank yourself on extraversion, and each of the other Big Five traits I just described?

Bob Daemmrich/Photo Edit

life? The good news is that positive traits, like agreeableness and, especially, conscientiousness, tend to strengthen with age. Think "unreliable teenager" versus "responsible grandma" and you can see why, in one mammoth, cross-sectional survey, the average difference in conscientiousness between 16-year-olds and 80-year-olds was huge (Allemand, Zimprich, & Hendriks, 2008). The bad news is that by the mid-twenties, on average, our relative rankings on all five dimensions tend to stabilize. So, if your 30-year-old friend is very unreliable, you can predict that this person will grow *somewhat* more responsible as the years pass, but still probably fall short compared to his peers. After emerging adulthood, the bottom-line prediction, based on the Big Five, to the question "How much will my personality change?" is "Not much" (Costa & McCrae, 2002; Schaie, Willis, & Caskie, 2004).

The idea that our basic personality doesn't change much may fit in with your personal experience. Contact a college acquaintance decades later, and you will probably be amazed at how much of the same person reemerges: "She's just as much a party animal at 60 as she was at 25!" "He's got the same problems with wife number three as he had with wife number one!"

Let's now follow the same approach I have been using throughout this book, exploring how "nature evokes nurture" forces might work to solidify our basic personality tendencies and make us *more* like ourselves as we age.

Take Sara, in her mid-twenties, who ranks high on conscientiousness. Her *worker* personality ensures that she does well in college and gets an excellent first job. As she travels through the work world, she is regularly praised for her industriousness, and eventually is promoted to an executive position at a firm. Sara is a committed, loyal friend who works hard on her marriage, and—because we match up by *homogamy*—has an equally conscientious mate. At age 55, Sara's life is a testament to the power of hard work in building a fulfilling life. She is the treasured rock on which her family and employees depend.

Now, imagine José, a friend of yours, who ranks low on agreeableness at age 30. Because José is so hostile, he continually loses jobs and has had several failed marriages. At age 60, when you bump into José after not seeing him for decades, he seems just as bitter, demoralized, and depressed.

But these are *average* tendencies. When developmentalists conduct longitudinal studies, they find some people change a good deal over the years (Roberts and others, 2007). What causes these core dimensions of personality to shift? In following men from late middle age into their sixties, researchers found that changes in basic temperamental traits most often occur in response to *other* major changes (Mroczek & Spiro, 2003). A lifelong extrovert might become much less outgoing after developing serious memory problems. A disagreeable 60-year-old could act mellower after finding a loving new mate (Small and others, 2003). So, yes, in general, you can predict that a 30-year-old extrovert will still love to socialize at 50 or 65. But you could be very wrong.

Robert Brenner/Photo Edit

This temperamentally disagreeable, middle-aged man has probably been inciting these kinds of angry encounters for decades, explaining why our Big Five personality rankings tend to remain stable, and—in this particular case—showing that disagreeable people may get even angrier as they travel through life.

Knowing that someone is extroverted, conscientious, or disagreeable gives us the basic outlines of personality. But it tells us little about the specifics of a given person's life. Think of several friends you would rank high on conscientiousness. One person might be a committed, full-time mother; another might be a company manager; yet another might have found the outlet for her conscientiousness through being a nurse. In order to really understand what makes human beings tick, we have to move in closer and interview people about their lives. This is the strategy that Dan McAdams has been using to explore personality during the adult years. Let's eavesdrop on one of McAdams's interviews:

I was living in a rural North Dakota town and was the mother of a 4-year-old son. One summer afternoon . . . Jeff left without me and was hit by a car. When I got there, he was lying in the street unconscious . . . . I felt sure he was dying, and I didn't know of anything I could do to preserve his life. My friend did, though, and today [Jeff] is 18 years old and very healthy. That feeling of being helpless and hopeless while I was sure I was watching my son die was a turning point. I decided I would never feel it again and I became an E.M.T.

(quoted in McAdams, de St. Aubin, & Logan, 1993, p. 228)

When he listened to these kinds of life stories, McAdams came to drastically different conclusions about how much our personality changes. Although this woman might have always ranked relatively high in conscientiousness, the *specific* path her life took was responsive to this life-changing event. In McAdams's opinion, once we fill in the rich details of human experience, we do see lives being transformed.

We Do Change: Examining Generativity

In addition to exploring the twists and turns of our human journey through asking people to reflect on their lives, McAdams has devoted his career to scientifically testing the ideas of the pioneering theorist who *does* believe that we change dramatically at different life stages: Erik Erikson. Does **generativity**, or nurturing the next generation, become our main priority during midlife? Is Erikson (1969) correct that fulfilling our generativity is the key to feeling happy during "the afternoon" of life? When people in their forties or fifties don't feel generative, are they stagnant, at loose ends, demoralized, and depressed? (See Table 12.1.)

To capture Erikson's complex concept, McAdams's research team devised three types of measures: They constructed a questionnaire designed to measure generative attitudes. (You can see the first ten items on this scale in Table 12.2 on page 364.) They explored people's generative goals or priorities (for example by telling them to "list the main agendas in your life now"). They questioned adults about specific generative activities, asking them, for instance, "Have you volunteered to help the homeless or taught someone else a skill within the past two months?" (See McAdams, 2001a.)

When these developmentalists gave their measures to young, middle-aged, and elderly people, they found few age differences in generative attitudes or activities. People were just as likely to care about making a difference in the world and doing good works at age 20 or 50 or 85. The researchers did discover striking age differences in generative *priorities*—with emerging adults ranking very low on this particular scale (McAdams, Hart, & Maruna, 1998). Young people's goals were centered on identity

TABLE 12.1: Erikson's Psychosocial Stages	
Life Stage	**Primary Task**
Infancy (birth to 1 year)	Basic trust versus mistrust
Toddlerhood (1 to 2 years)	Autonomy versus shame and doubt
Early childhood (3 to 6 years)	Initiative versus guilt
Late childhood (6 years to puberty)	Industry versus inferiority
Adolescence (teens into twenties)	Identity versus role confusion
Young adulthood (twenties to early forties)	Intimacy versus isolation
Middle adulthood (forties to sixties)	**Generativity versus stagnation**
Late adulthood (late sixties and beyond)	Integrity versus despair

generativity In Erikson's theory, the seventh psychosocial task, in which people in midlife find meaning from nurturing the next generation, caring for others, or enriching the life of others through their work. According to Erikson, when midlife adults have not achieved generativity, they feel stagnant, without a sense of purpose in life.

TABLE 12.2: McAdams's Generative Concern Scale

True	False	
☐	☐	1. I try to pass along the knowledge I have gained through my experiences.
☐	☐	2. I do not feel that other people need me.
☐	☐	3. I think I would like the work of a teacher.
☐	☐	4. I feel as though I have made a difference to many people.
☐	☐	5. I do not volunteer to work for a charity.
☐	☐	6. I have made and created things that have had an impact on other people.
☐	☐	7. I try to be creative in most things that I do.
☐	☐	8. I think that I will be remembered for a long time after I die.
☐	☐	9. I believe that society cannot be responsible for providing food and shelter to all homeless people.
☐	☐	10. Others would say that I have made unique contributions to society.

Answers: 1. T, 2. F, 3. T, 4. T, 5. F, 6. T, 7. T, 8. T, 9. F, 10. T

Source: McAdams & de St. Aubin (1992), pp. 1003–1015.

How do you score on this scale measuring overall generative motivations?

issues. A 20-year-old might say, "I want to make my job more interesting" or "My plan is to figure out what I want to do with my life." Midlife and older adults were more likely to report: "I want to be a positive role model," "My mission is to help my teenage son," or "My goal is to work for justice and peace in the world."

This makes sense. Remember from Chapter 6 that prosocial behaviors are in full swing by early childhood. There is no reason to think that our basic human drive to be nurturing changes at any particular life stage. But, just as Erikson would predict, we need to resolve issues related to our personal development before our primary concern shifts to giving to others in the wider world.

Is Erikson correct when he says that fulfilling our generativity is the key to happiness during adult life? As you will see later in this section, generative people do tend to be highly satisfied with many aspects of their lives. Still, when we think of outstandingly generative role models such as Martin Luther King, Jr. or Mother Theresa, words such as "happy" or "satisfied" do not come to mind. What comes to mind is having a deep sense of purpose and living a meaningful life. And yes, generative people do report having tremendously meaningful, fulfilling adult lives (Grossbaum & Bates, 2002; Zucker, Ostrove, & Stewart, 2002).

Moreover, when people are not fulfilling their generative impulses, their lives lack meaning. As Erikson described, they feel *stagnant*—purposeless and at loose ends. Read what one developmentalist had to say about a woman named Deborah, who scored very low on generativity in his longitudinal study of women's lives:

In response to a question about career wishes, Deborah, who at the time was in her late forties, wrote, "I have yet to think this one out fully. . . . Luck has always played a major role in my life." In reference to the birth of her first child, Deborah wrote, "All actions automatic. No emotional involvement . . . ; totally self-preserving but very unpleasant." After many years of marriage, Deborah underwent a difficult divorce. She began to work in a "blur of meaningless jobs."

(adapted from Peterson, 1998, p. 12)

Adults of every age get great pleasure from engaging in generative activities. But now that he has already made it professionally (or fulfilled himself in his work), this older Hispanic man is cultivating a community garden that will provide poor people with free vegetables—and being generative now ranks as his number one priority in life.

Michael Newman/Photo Edit, Inc.

As this case history suggests, having children does not automatically evoke generativity. You can give birth and be totally non-generative and uninvolved. But reaching Erikson's midlife milestone has long-term consequences for being a parent and, also, for the quality of other relationships in your life.

For instance, in the longitudinal study I mentioned above, if a woman in her early fifties ranked as highly generative (unlike Deborah in the previous quote), ten years later she was likely to say that being a grandparent was a peak life experience. As one woman commented, "Falling in love is putting it too mildly" (quoted in Peterson & Duncan, 2007, p. 415). In their early sixties, generative women reported feeling more nurtured and loved by their partners. In contrast to their less generative peers, they had no worries about growing old (Peterson & Duncan, 2007). Furthermore, being generative may make for effective parenting in one especially vital area of life—transmitting one's values.

Through sensitively consoling her disappointed teenager, this generative mom is doing more than simply making her daughter feel better. She is providing a compelling role model that can motivate her daughter to construct a generative, fulfilling life.

Researchers asked teenagers to tell a story about how their parents had taught them values (Pratt and others, 2008). Then, they related these midlife adults' generativity scores to the kinds of events their adolescent children described. Teens with highly generative parents gave examples that were more specific, interactive (dealing with an issue directly involving the teen), and had more caring themes. In addition, these teachable moments were more likely to have a profound emotional impact. As one 20-year-old recalled: "I got a 38 percent on (a test). I was devastated. . . . I showed it to her (my mom) and she said, 'Honey, don't cry about this. . . . I know you did your best. It just matters that you tried.' So that really influenced me. . . . She was completely accepting. . . . If I ever get the chance with my children, I would love to tell them that." (Quoted in Pratt and others, 2008, p. 187.)

What about the childhood experiences of highly generative people? Do their personal life histories differ from those of less generative adults? To answer this question, McAdams's research team selected community leaders who scored at the upper ends of their Generative Concern Scale (see page 364) and asked them to tell their life stories. Would these autobiographies differ from those of adults such as Deborah in my earlier example, who ranked low on fulfilling Erikson's midlife task?

The answer was yes. The life stories of unusually generative adults had a cluster of themes demonstrating what the researchers called a **commitment script**: They often described early memories of feeling especially fortunate, or "blessed": "I was my grandmother's favorite"; "I was a miracle child who should not have survived." They reported feeling sensitive to the suffering of others, from a young age. They also talked about having an identity revolving around generative values that never wavered from their teenage years. A 50-year-old minister in one of McAdams's studies was a teenage prostitute, then a con artist, who spent two years in a federal prison; but throughout her life, she reported, "I was always doing ministry."

The most striking characteristic of generative adults' life stories were **redemption sequences**—examples of devastating events that turned out in a positive way (McAdams, 2006; McAdams & Bowman, 2001). For instance, in the example I just mentioned, the woman minister might view the humiliation of being sent to prison as the best thing that ever happened, the experience that turned her life around. According to McAdams (2008), early memories of feeling personally blessed, an enduring sensitivity to others' misfortunes, basic caring values, and, especially, being able to turn one's tragedies into growth experiences are the core ingredients of the commitment script and the main correlates of constructing a generative adult life.

commitment script In Dan McAdams's research, a type of autobiography produced by highly generative adults that involves childhood memories of feeling special, being unusually sensitive to others' misfortunes, having a strong, enduring generative mission from adolescence, and redemption sequences.

redemption sequence In Dan McAdams's research, a characteristic theme of highly generative adults' autobiographies, in which they describe tragic events that turned out for the best.

Exceptionally generative people—especially prize-winning community activists cited for their good works—have other attributes. Because taking action to improve society involves being confident and assertive (recall that this quality is also involved in acting prosocially during childhood), generative role models have a strong sense of "agency," or personal power, as well as the motivation to do good (Walker & Frimer, 2007). In fact, as McAdams (2008) insightfully points out, taking action to improve, or "repair," the world is our ultimate vehicle for *extending* the self. While they may be greatly troubled by humanity's disrepair, generative people are, at heart, optimistic. They believe that change is possible and that human beings are basically good (McAdams, 2008; Walker & Frimer, 2007). One sign of this faith in people is that, in dealing with disappointments from their parents, generative adults are more forgiving (Pratt and others, 2008), highlighting, again, why researchers target "forgiveness" as crucial to having relationships that lovingly endure (recall Chapter 11).

While the motivation to be generative is probably universal in the human experience, McAdams (2006, 2008) makes the interesting point that the redemption sequence discussed earlier may be unique to our individualistic society. Our cultural

heroes are people who overcome personal adversity: the prostitutes who become ministers, the Lance Armstrongs who conquer cancer and win races, the battered women who set up shelters and/or manage million-dollar foundations and parade across *The Oprah Winfrey Show*. In collectivist societies (where people are discouraged from thinking about their personal achievements), this theme of individual suffering leading to triumph is probably not part of the cultural generativity script.

This brings up a tantalizing ethnic difference in generativity in our own society. When McAdams's research team searched out their generative role models, they found that African American men and women were overrepresented in the group of exceptionally generative adults (Hart and others, 2001; McAdams, 2006). Does their history of coping with discrimination—plus their strong grounding in the church—make African Americans unusually sensitive to suffering and more prone to devoting their lives to "repairing" the world? In support of this possibility, themes stressing steady progress toward overcoming adversity were central in highly generative African Americans' autobiographies (McAdams & Bowman, 2001).

Do you believe that dealing with adversity makes us more giving, generative people? Did some painful experience in your own life change your priorities, transforming you into a more loving human being? If so, you might agree with the adults in one study who highlighted a crucial *negative* experience as the defining event that caused them to become wise (Bluck & Glück, 2004).

The idea that coping with life's setbacks produces emotional growth may underlie our third idea about personality change described at the beginning of this section: Twenty-year-olds don't have enough real-world experience to handle life's disappointments in a calm, competent way. As we age, we expect to become more self-confident, emotionally secure, and better able to handle stress. Do people really become more confident as they move into midlife? Do we get happier as the years pass?

Do We Get More Mature (and Happier) with Age?

According to one classic longitudinal study, the answer to both questions is yes. In tracking the personalities of graduates from Mills College (a selective, private, all-girls college in California) from their senior year up to their sixties, researchers found that, as these women got older, they became more self-assured (Helson, Jones, & Kwan, 2002). Amazingly, by midlife, all of the people who had been rated as excessively clingy in their love relationships during their twenties were now ranked as securely attached! Moreover, in contrast to the old stereotype of menopausal women as

Karen Kasmauski/Corbis

This group project to restore the oldest black Baptist church in South Carolina is typical in the African American experience, where a mission to be of service—especially in a caring community that revolves around the church—is standard.

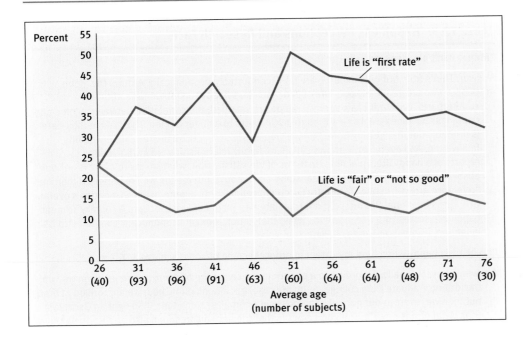

FIGURE 12.1: Satisfaction with life peaks among women in their fifties*: Notice from this chart that, in their fifties, women were most likely to describe life as "first rate."

Source: Mitchell & Helson (1990). Copyright 1990, reprinted with permission of Cambridge University Press.

*The graphs for each curve do not add up to 100 percent because they do not include responses that fell into an intermediate category.

depressed and demoralized, as you can see in Figure 12.1, the Mills women felt better about their lives in their fifties than at *any* other age (Mitchell & Helson, 1990). Yes, the Mills study did confirm that the awareness of being older sets in during late middle age. But, surprisingly, sensing one's limitations ("I know I don't have much time left") didn't signal feelings of sadness or any sense of loss. Life satisfaction among the Mills women was actually highest at age 61 (Helson & Soto, 2005).

Why might people feel happier when they are entering their last decades of life? Take a minute to list some possibilities. As I discuss this fascinating phenomenon in the next chapter, you'll see if your speculations agree with the ideas of a prominent contemporary gerontologist. For now, I want to assure you that this trend to get happier with age is not simply limited to "the elite," that is, privileged women, such as the Mills College graduates. It is backed up by cross-sectional studies exploring different dimensions of life.

For instance, consider the results of the poll sampling faith in humanity among adults of different ages described in Chapter 1. You may remember that, in this study, 20-year-olds felt most cynical about human nature. People in their sixties and early seventies had the most upbeat, benevolent worldview (Poulin & Silver, 2008). The same positive feelings about people extend into personal relationships. Recall from Chapter 11 that elderly couples tend to relate in more caring, loving ways than do middle-aged adults. In a study directly tracking age differences in emotional states, researchers discovered that the frequency of upsetting emotions lessened and the number of upbeat feelings rose from people's twenties to their early seventies (Mroczek, 2001). This is important because, as you can see in Table 12.3 on page 368, experts view the ratio of positive to negative emotions as a basic barometer of overall well-being. (Check out Table 12.3 for other fascinating research facts about happiness.)

Actually, one study even suggested that, among people with the most negative personality traits—those low in agreeableness and extraversion and high in neuroticism—the frequency of distressing emotions may decline most in later life (Ready & Robinson, 2008). True, temperamentally gloomy and disagreeable older adults may not qualify as happy, but at least in their older years, they seem able to mute their worst emotional states. Therefore, at least in our society, the twenties are highly overrated as life's happiest stage! On average, we can expect to get more self-confident, happier, plus develop greater emotional control as we age.

But averages don't apply to everyone. There are clearly many depressed, grumpy elderly people. When I gave talks on successful aging at local senior citizens centers

TABLE 12.3: Happiness Perceptions and Research Facts

"Money can't buy happiness."

Answer: That's true, but only once we are fairly comfortable economically. Around the globe, people who are genuinely poor *are* significantly less happy than their more affluent counterparts. Once our basic survival needs are satisfied, the correlation between income and happiness becomes weaker—although it still exists to a minor degree. The main reason here is probably not that getting more "things" matters, but that extra money can buy quality family time. And every study shows satisfying family relationships are *highly* related to reports of a happy life. Final note: In terms of life satisfaction, what seems relevant is not our absolute affluence (how many McMansions we can buy), but feeling we are better off than our "reference group." In one 15-country European comparison, a general rise in a nation's overall GNP (Gross National Product) did not translate into higher life satisfaction. A country's "mean happiness scores" did rise, however, when that nation took off economically compared to its neighbors (Bjornskov, Gupta, & Pedersen, 2008).

"I'll be truly happy when I get my career in order; become famous; achieve X, Y, Z goal."

Answer: Sorry, not really. According to a phenomenon called the *hedonic treadmill*, when we win the lottery, graduate from college, or (in my case) get a book published, we are thrilled at first; but then we revert to our normal happiness set point after some time ("So I got an Oscar last year. What else is new?"). The good news is that the hedonic treadmill also applies to negative events. We adjust, and then, eventually, our "natural" happiness returns. Unfortunately, however, with major traumas such as chronic unemployment or widowhood, we may never quite reach our prior happiness set point.

"You can't 1) measure happiness or 2) teach people to be happy."

Answer: Point 1 is totally false; point 2 is complicated—neither totally true nor false. Research shows that we *can* concretely quantify what it takes to be happy. Once people get above a ratio of 2.9 positive to negative emotions, they generally feel good about their lives. Therefore, some experts suggest we might increase this positive ratio by teaching people to savor the moment, count their blessings, or feel gratitude. Still, the best strategy for achieving happiness is probably *not* to spend time monitoring that internal state. When we are generative and live fully, a natural by-product is having a happy life.

Sources: Biswas-Diener, 2008; Diener, 2008; Drakopoulos, 2007; Emmons, 2008; Fredrikson, 2008; Fredrickson & Losada, 2005; Larsen & Prizmic, 2008; Lucas, 2008; North and others, 2008.

Rolf Bruderer/Masterfile

Like many people in their late fifties, this woman is at the peak of her powers. If you met her at age 25, could you see the seeds of the amazingly self-assured, competent older woman in this photograph? Given that young people who are already mature tend to grow the most with age, the answer is probably yes.

in my thirties (some gall!), I vividly recall one 89-year-old woman who put me in my place: "Wait till you are my age, young lady. Then, you'll *really* understand how terrible it is to be old!" Perhaps you have a middle-aged friend, like Deborah in my earlier example of low generativity, who remains mired in stagnation. The teenage football hero, or beauty queen, who descend into depression and drug abuse as they become older are classic life stories, too.

Can we predict who is likely to grow happier and more mature? When the Mills Study researchers gave the women a test that measured maturity, they found that the people who ranked high on that scale during their emerging-adult years were most likely to grow emotionally as they aged (Helson & Roberts, 1994).

The bottom-line message is that personality really matters in shaping the quality of our lives. Moreover, to a large degree, our basic personality endures. People who tend to grow most emotionally over the years are apt to think about life in a mature way in their twenties. Adults who are exceptionally generative report always having had generative identities. Where we stand on the Big Five as emerging adults predicts our chance of succeeding or having trouble with relationships and in a career. However, change is possible—and positive development really occurs. The basic thrust, as we age, is to get better in terms of personality well into later life!

Wrapping up Personality

Now, let's summarize *all* of these messages. Having read this chapter, here is what you might tell an emerging-adult friend who wants insights into the person she can expect to be at age 40 or 55:

- You are likely to become somewhat more reliable and agreeable; although, in general, your basic personality probably will not change much over the years.

- Your priorities will probably shift toward more generative concerns.

- You are likely to cope better with stress and to feel more self-confident and happier, especially if you are relatively mature right now.

- Still, take these predictions with a grain of salt. People vary in generativity and in the extent to which they change and grow. Life-changing experiences at every time of life can set you on a different life path.

Consistency from youth to later life, diversity from person to person, and different pathways of change, depending on the way we conceptualize personality—we can see these same themes when we explore how people develop intellectually during adult life.

Wechsler Adult Intelligence Scale (WAIS) The standard test to measure adult IQ, involving verbal and performance scales, each of which is made up of various subtests.

Exploring Intelligence

Remember from Chapter 7 that, when psychologists measure intelligence during childhood, they look mainly at how elementary schoolers perform on standard intelligence tests. Sometimes, they spell out different ideas about what it means to be smart, such as Gardner's multiple intelligences or Sternberg's successful intelligence. Developmentalists use standard IQ tests and nontraditional strategies to trace adult intelligence, too.

Taking the Traditional Approach: Looking at Standard IQ Tests

Think of your intellectual role model. Most likely, your mind will immediately gravitate to someone who is 50 or 80—not a person who is 20 or 25. In fact, if you are like most adults, you probably assume that, in general, people get more intelligent over the years (Sternberg & Berg, 1992).

Mid-twentieth-century psychologists had a different idea: They believed that people reach their intellectual peak in their twenties, and then intelligence steadily declines (Botwinick, 1967). They based these disturbing conclusions on studies using the (at the time) newly developed Wechsler Adult Intelligence Scale.

The **Wechsler Adult Intelligence Scale (WAIS)**, the standard test measuring adult IQ, has the same format as the WISC, the parallel scale for children, described in Chapter 7. It has verbal and performance scales. The verbal scale measures different types of knowledge, such as vocabulary and adults' ability to solve math problems. The performance scale asks test-takers to perform relatively unfamiliar activities, such as putting together puzzles or arranging blocks. On this part of the test, speed is essential. People must complete the performance scale items within a limited time.

When psychologists tested adults to derive their standards for how people should normally perform on the WAIS at different ages, they discovered that, starting in the twenties, in each older age group, average scores declined. They also found the interesting pattern that you can see in Figure 12.2. While verbal scores stayed stable or declined to a lesser degree, average scores on the performance scale steadily slid down, starting in people's twenties (Botwinick, 1967).

These findings would not give Doreen or any other midlife student confidence about venturing into a college classroom full of 20-year-olds. Luckily, however, the researchers were making a serious error. They were not taking into account the huge educational differences between different cohorts during that particular time in

FIGURE 12.2: Age-related changes in mean scores on the performance and verbal scales of the WAIS: This chart shows the pattern of decline from a study using the early form of the WAIS. Notice how average scores on the performance scale regularly slid down starting in the twenties, while scores on the verbal scale remained more stable with age.

Source: Botwinick (1967).

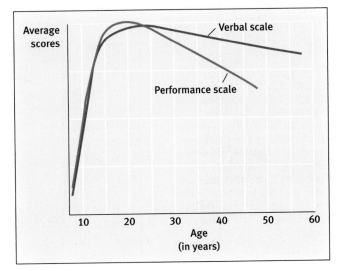

How will this young woman's cognitive abilities change as she ages? By comparing how adults of different ages performed on intelligence tests, early researchers came to the dismal conclusion that this twenty-something adult might be at her mental peak today.

Seattle Longitudinal Study The definitive study of the effect of aging on intelligence, carried out by K. Warner Schaie, involving simultaneously conducting and comparing the results of cross-sectional and longitudinal studies carried out with a group of Seattle volunteers.

U.S. history. While virtually all of the young people taking the test had gone to high school, many middle-aged or elderly people taking the original WAIS had probably left school in the seventh or eighth grade. So the psychologists were comparing apples to oranges—adults with far less education to those with much more.

How does our performance on standard intelligence tests *really* change as we travel through adult life? To answer this question, in the early 1960s, researchers began the **Seattle Longitudinal Study**—the definitive study of intelligence and age (Schaie, Willis, & Caskie, 2004; Schaie & Zanjani, 2006).

Imagine being a twentieth-century researcher interested in charting how people change intellectually during adulthood. If you were to carry out a cross-sectional study—comparing different age groups at the same time—your findings would be biased in a negative way. Older cohorts would be at a disadvantage, not having had as much experience taking tests, typically having gone to school for far fewer years. But if you carried out a longitudinal study, you would end up with a far-too-positive portrait of how the *average* person changes. The volunteers who enrolled in your study would probably be highly educated. Over the years, as people dropped out of your research, you would be left with an increasingly self-selected group, the tiny fraction of older people who were especially proud of proving their intellectual capacities and—as they reached their seventies—those healthy enough to take your tests (Baltes & Smith, 1997).

Faced with these contrasting biases (longitudinal research will be too positive; cross-sectional research will be biased in a negative way), the researchers devised a brilliant solution: They combined the two kinds of studies, then factored out the biases of each research method and isolated the "true" impact of age on IQ.

First, the research team selected people enrolled in a Seattle health organization who were 7 years apart in age, tested them, and compared their scores. Then, they followed each group longitudinally, testing them at 7-year intervals. At each evaluation, the psychologists selected another cross-sectional sample, some of whom they also followed over time.

Using an IQ test that, unlike the WAIS, measured five basic cognitive abilities, the researchers got a more encouraging portrait of how we change intellectually—one that fits our intuitive sense of how we should perform. Notice in looking at Figure 12.3 that, on this measure—involving tests such as vocabulary and our ability to mentally rotate designs in space—overall, we can expect to reach our intellectual peak during our forties and early fifties (Schaie, 1996; Schaie, Willis, & Caskie, 2004). Still, the Seattle study showed the same pattern researchers first found on the WAIS. On tests measuring people's store of knowledge, such as vocabulary, scores improve till at least age 60 (Larsen, Hartmann, & Nyborg, 2008).

FIGURE 12.3: **Changes in a few intellectual abilities over the decades in the Seattle Longitudinal Study:** Although various abilities show different age-related patterns, depending on the mix of fluid and crystallized skills (to be discussed on the next page), in general, notice that we reach our intellectual peak during the late forties and early fifties.

Source: Schaie (1996).

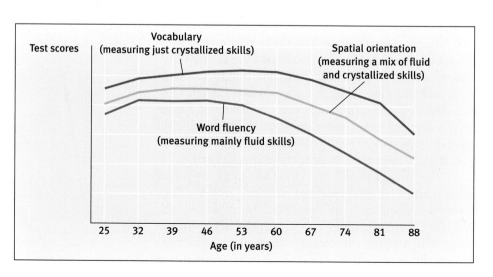

Test scores

Vocabulary (measuring just crystallized skills)

Spatial orientation (measuring a mix of fluid and crystallized skills)

Word fluency (measuring mainly fluid skills)

25   32   39   46   53   60   67   74   81   88

Age (in years)

Actually, even 90-year-olds, on average, perform better on some vocabulary tests than the typical young adult (Bowles & Salthouse, 2008)! But any time a test involves doing something new very fast (such as arranging puzzles or blocks within a time limit), losses start as early as the thirties (Ardila, 2007). Now, let's look at a theory that makes sense of these findings and tells us a good deal about our intellectual abilities in the real world.

Two Types of Intelligence: Crystallized and Fluid Skills

Psychologists today often divide intelligence into two basic categories. **Crystallized intelligence** refers to our knowledge base, the storehouse of information that we have accumulated over the years. The verbal scale of the WAIS, with its tests of vocabulary and math, mainly measures crystallized skills. **Fluid intelligence** involves our ability to reason quickly when facing totally new intellectual challenges. The WAIS performance scale, with its emphasis on putting together blocks or puzzles within a time limit, tends to measure fluid skills.

Fluid intelligence—because it depends on our nervous system being at its biological peak—is at its high point in our twenties and then declines. Because it measures the knowledge that we have amassed over years, crystallized intelligence follows a different path. This type of intelligence tends to increase as we age, until about the late fifties, when many crystallized skills begin to slowly fall off (Kaufman, 2001). The reason is that, at this time in life, our rate of forgetting outpaces the amount of new knowledge that we can absorb.

The great news for baby boomers like me is that, with regard to crucial crystallized skills, such as the ability to solve relationship-oriented problems, older adults do better than the young (Blanchard-Fields, Mienaltowski, & Seay, 2007). Moreover, the losses on fluid intelligence are not as great for my cohort as for my parent's generation (Zelinski & Kennison, 2007), showing that staying healthier or possibly being generally more well educated may even improve these biologically based skills. The bad news is that the fluid losses on IQ tests are a symptom of an overall slowing of information processing that extends to many areas of life.

So, in *any* situation requiring quick multitasking, people may notice their abilities declining at a relatively young age. For instance, in your late thirties it seems harder to dribble a basketball when you have to keep your attention on the opposing team. You realize that you are having more trouble juggling cooking and having conversations with guests at your dinner party than you did in your younger years. These fluid losses, as you will see in Chapter 14, gradually progress to the point where they interfere with many aspects of living when we reach old age.

The distinction between fluid and crystallized intelligence explains a good deal about the lifespan path of careers. It accounts for why people in fast-paced jobs, such as air-traffic controllers, worry about being over the hill in their forties. It makes sense of why airline CEOs can still be at their professional peak in their early sixties (although not much later!). Anytime an activity depends heavily on quickness and new learning, age presents problems. Whenever an intellectual challenge involves stored knowledge or experience, people can continue to improve well into their fifties and beyond.

Suppose you are an artist or a writer. When can you expect to do your finest work? Researchers find that the age for optimum creativity differs, depending on the specific art form. When a type of creative activity is heavily dependent on being totally original, such as dancing or writing poetry, people tend to

crystallized intelligence A basic facet of intelligence, consisting of a person's knowledge base, or storehouse of accumulated information.

fluid intelligence A basic facet of intelligence, consisting of the ability to quickly master new intellectual activities.

As their job demands speedy mental processing, thinking on their feet, and responding quickly, these professional hockey players may feel "aged" in their thirties. But this 60-year-old professor will probably feel his skills are better than ever today because teaching depends almost exclusively on crystallized skills.

Don Mason/Corbis

AP Images

FIGURE 12.4: Age-related changes in the career paths of geniuses and of less eminent creators: These charts show that people reach their peak period of creativity at different points in midlife, depending on when they start their creative careers. However, the most gifted geniuses stand head and shoulders above their contemporaries at every age.

Source: Simonton (1997).

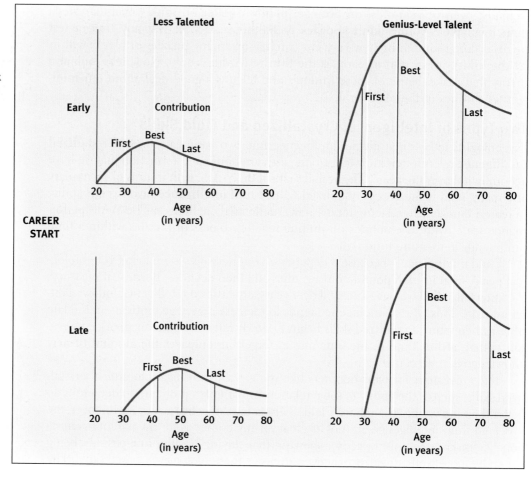

Is the middle-aged fashion designer on the left at his creative peak? According to the research, the answer is yes. How proficient will this young man watching ultimately be at designing suits? For answers, we would want to look at this person's creative talents right now.

perform best in their thirties (see Simonton, 2007). If the form of creativity depends just on crystallized experience, such as writing nonfiction or history or, in my case, producing college textbooks (yes!), people perform at their best in their early sixties (Simonton, 1997, 2002). But in tracing the lives of people famous for their creative work, one researcher discovered that who we are *as people,* or our enduring abilities, outweighs the changes that occur with age. As you can see in Figure 12.4, true geniuses outshine everyone else at *any* age (Simonton, 1997).

So, with regard to creativity or any type of intellectually challenging work, expect to reach your creative peak in middle age (in most fields). Still, as you saw earlier with personality, expect to be the same person—to a large degree—that you were when you were younger. If you are exceptionally competent and creative at 30, you can stay exceptionally competent and creative at 70, or even 95. To illustrate this point, here are quotations from an interview study of creative people over age 60 (Csikszentmihalyi, 1996).

Anthony Hecht, a 70-year-old poet, commented:

I'm not as rigid as I was. And I can feel this in the quality and texture of the poems themselves. They are freer metrically, they are freer in general design. The earliest poems that I wrote were almost rigid in their eagerness not to make any errors. I'm less worried than that now.

(p. 215)

And the historian C. Vann Woodward, in his mid-eighties, said:

Well, [today] I have . . . changed my mind and the reasons and conclusions about what I have written. For example, that book on Jim Crow. I have done four editions of it and I am thinking of doing a fifth, and each time it changes. And they come

Bettmann/Corbis

Fred Stein/Pix Inc./Time Life Pictures/Getty Images

Grandma Moses, who gained artistic fame in old age and died at age 101, and Frank Lloyd Wright, shown here lecturing at the young age of 91, are testaments to the fact that people can be exceptionally creative until the very limit of human life.

largely from criticisms that I have received. I think the worst mistake you could make as a historian is to be indifferent or contemptuous of what is new. You learn that there is nothing permanent in history. It's always changing.

(p. 216)

From Sigmund Freud, who kept putting forth masterpieces in psychology well into his eighties, to Frank Lloyd Wright, who was still actively designing world-class buildings into his ninth decade of life, history is full of examples showing that creativity can burn bright well into old age.

Staying IQ Smart

Returning to normally creative people, such as you and me, what qualities might help *any* person stay cognitively sharp well into later life? What forces might cause our IQ scores and our real-life intellectual capacities to decline at a younger-than-normal age?

Spending hours each day for your whole adult life fashioning a rock garden into waves seems incredibly boring. But his heart-healthy diet and the physical exercise this elderly Japanese monk is getting while he carries out this Zen-like task may be doing wonders at keeping him mentally sharp.

HEALTH MATTERS. The Seattle researchers discovered that one key to staying intelligent with age, as you might imagine, lies in keeping healthy. Specifically, men and women diagnosed with heart problems during their fifties lost points earlier on every one of the Seattle tests than did the other volunteers (Schaie, 1996). Even symptoms of impaired heart function, like high blood pressure, impair performance on fluid IQ tests (Raz and others, 2009). As you will see in Chapter 14, because these chronic diseases limit blood flow to the brain, cardiovascular problems actually cause frontal lobe atrophy and neural loss (see Raz and others, 2007).

Catherine Karnow/Corbis

The most interesting evidence that serious illness affects IQ relates to an eerie phenomenon called **terminal drop**. While conducting the earliest longitudinal studies of intelligence, developmentalists were astonished to discover that they could predict which older people were more likely to die or become seriously ill within the next few years by "larger than expected" losses in their verbal IQ (Cooney, Schaie, & Willis, 1988; Riegel & Riegel, 1972). If a person's scores on tests of vocabulary and other crystallized measures dramatically declined, these changes were an ominous early warning signal of a soon-to-be-diagnosed life-threatening disease. As you can see in the fascinating chart in Figure 12.5 on page 374, another, more recent, longitudinal study showed we can even use dramatic dips in life satisfaction among elderly people to predict impending death.

terminal drop A research phenomenon in which a dramatic decline in an older person's scores on vocabulary tests and other measures of crystallized intelligence predicts having a terminal disease.

FIGURE 12.5: Prior changes in life satisfaction among elderly German adults who later died, as a function of years from death: This 22-year-long study, tracking roughly 16,000 German older people, showed that the "terminal drop" phenomenon that applies to IQ has a counterpart in our emotional life. Notice that, starting at about 4 years prior to death, there is a steep decline in life satisfaction. Could we also look to the onset of depression to suggest that an elderly loved one might have an undiagnosed terminal disease?

Source: Gerstoff and others (2008).

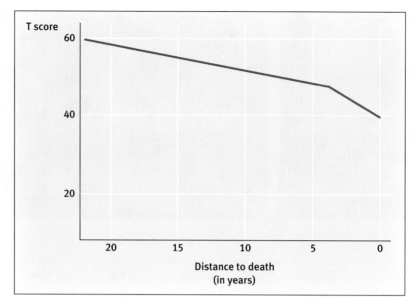

These studies haunted me the summer when I noticed that my father had suddenly aged mentally. My dad, who was always an intellectual whiz, had lost interest in the world. He was disoriented, depressed, and unable to remember basic facts, such as where I lived. A few months later, my worst fears were confirmed: My father was diagnosed with liver cancer, the illness that was to quickly end his life.

MENTAL EXERCISE MAY MATTER. Because, as you may recall from Chapter 3, environmental stimulation promotes synaptogenesis, the second key to keeping our IQ fine-tuned should be a no-brainer: Exercise your mind! The most interesting research supporting this idea relates to a topic in the previous chapter: work environments. Our impulse to search for intrinsically motivating jobs may have long-term cognitive benefits. People who work in complex jobs become more intellectually flexible as the years pass. Routine work, such as flipping hamburgers, is associated with earlier-than-normal cognitive decline (Schooler, 1999, 2001; Schooler, Mulatu, & Oates, 2004). Carmi Schooler (2007), the developmentalist who conducted these studies, has even extended his findings to performing complex household tasks. Engaging in mentally enriching activities—from reading, to attending lectures, to struggling to balance the challenges of parenting and work—helps *everyone* become more mentally flexible with age.

Having the fast-paced, difficult challenge of designing the Chinese edition of *Vogue* (like figuring out where to put these photos to highlight the main points in this chapter!) is the kind of intellectually complex work that is tailor-made to help these Shanghai women stay mentally flexible as they age.

Still, we need to be cautious. People who search out complex professions, or want to stretch their minds, are probably *already* intellectually motivated (and upper middle class) to begin with. Given that who we are as people endures—and, as we know, socioeconomic status matters a great deal—we would need to conduct an impossible experiment to *prove* that mental stimulation causes IQ to rise (or prevents decline): Randomly assign one group of young adults to "exercise their minds" for decades and compare their IQs to those of a control group in later middle age. Without this defining "clinical trial," one expert specializing in cognitive aging has pronounced the "use your brain or lose it" principle unproved (Salthouse, 2006, 2007).

But wait a second! We do have concrete evidence proving that providing enriched environments promotes synaptogenesis in laboratory rats (Dhanushkodi and others, 2007). When neuroscientists put rats in a large cage with a variety of wheels and swings and compared their cortexes with those of control groups, the animals exposed to this "treatment" had thicker, heavier brains! (Diamond, 1988, 1993.) Let's tentatively accept the idea, then, that, just as physical exercise strengthens our muscles, mental exercise *may* make for a more resilient brain.

In sum, people in their forties and fifties are at the peak of their mental powers. But they will have much more trouble mastering totally new cognitive challenges (those involving fluid skills) when they are under time pressure. To preserve their cognitive capacities as they age, people need to take care of their health and make sure to challenge their minds. And you can tell any worried older friend who—like Doreen in the chapter-opening vignette—is considering going back to school that she should definitely go for it!

INTERVENTIONS: **Keeping a Fine-Tuned Mind**

Now, let's look at the lessons the research offers for any person, whether middle-aged or young, who wants advice about how to stay mentally sharp as the years pass.

- Develop a hobby or passion that challenges your mind—preferably when you are young. Keep practicing your passion as you age.

- Throughout life, put yourself in intellectually challenging situations. If your job is not mentally stimulating, search out a more intrinsically rewarding career. If you are unable to find flow-inducing work, exercise your mental capacities outside your job, through volunteer work or hobbies that stretch your mind.

- As you age, watch your physical health. In particular, guard against developing cardiovascular disease.

- Understand that, as you get older, new activities involving complex information processing will be more difficult. To cope with the losses you experience, you might adopt the following three-part strategy advocated by Paul Baltes called **selective optimization with compensation**.

As we move into the older years and notice we cannot function as well as we used to, Baltes believes that we need to (1) *selectively* focus on our most important activities, shedding less important priorities; (2) *optimize*, or work harder, to perform at our best in these most important areas of life; and (3) *compensate*, or rely on external aids, when we cannot cope on our own (Baltes, 2003; Baltes & Carstensen, 2003; Krampe & Baltes, 2003).

Let's take the example of a woman whose passion is gourmet cooking. As she reaches her fifties, she might decide to give up some less important interest such as gardening, conserving her strength for the hours she spends at the stove (*selection*). She would need to work harder to prepare complex dishes demanding split-second timing, such as her prize-winning soufflés (*optimization*). She might put a chair in the kitchen rather than stand for hours while preparing meals, or give up preparing elaborate dinner party feasts all by herself and rely on her guests to bring an appetizer or dessert (*compensation*).

Although Baltes originally spelled out these guidelines to apply to successful aging, they are relevant to anyone coping with the hectic demands of daily life (Freund & Baltes, 2002; Wiese, Freund, & Baltes, 2002). For instance, when parents who are experiencing high levels of work-family conflict use selection, optimization, and compensation, they feel far less stressed out (Young, Baltes, & Pratt, 2007). Because this strategy helps us live effectively at *any* age, Table 12.4 on page 376 offers a selective-optimization-with-compensation checklist to complete, to help you enhance your life.

selective optimization with compensation Paul Baltes's three principles for successful aging (and living): (1) selectively focusing on what is most important, (2) working harder to perform well in those top-ranking areas, and (3) relying on external aids to cope effectively.

What can this white-haired female college student do to ensure that she can keep up with her twenty-something classmates in this computer course? She can try to take just this one class, rather than four or five, this term (selection); spend more time studying (optimization); and perhaps ask the instructor if she can tape the lectures, so she doesn't have to just rely on her notes (compensation).

Bill Aaron/Photo Edit, Inc.

TABLE 12.4: **Using Selective Optimization with Compensation to Construct a Fulfilling Life**

Selection: List your top-ranking priorities. Estimate how much time you spend on these agendas.

1. _____ hrs _____

2. _____ hrs _____

3. _____ hrs _____

Can you increase the time you spend on these most critical agendas and decrease the time you spend on less important concerns?

Optimization: List several strategies that you could use to perform better in your top-priority areas.

1. _____

2. _____

3. _____

Compensation: List some external aids that might help you be more successful in managing your time or succeeding.

1. _____

2. _____

3. _____

List the people to whom you can turn to help you when you feel overloaded. Think of friends and family who can take over some of your less important jobs.

1. _____

2. _____

3. _____

Taking a Nontraditional Approach: Examining Postformal Thought

So far, I have been talking about the insights related to intelligence that we've derived from exploring traditional IQ tests. But look back at the quotations from the older poet Anthony Hecht and the historian C. Vann Woodward, on pages 372–373. The qualities these creative people were describing have nothing to do with putting together puzzles or blocks. What stands out about these men is their passion for learning, their receptiveness to new ideas, and their sensitivity to their own inner lives. Given that standard IQ tests were devised to predict performance in school, perhaps it would make sense to come up with a test to capture the qualities that are central to being intelligent during adult life.

Jean Piaget, as we know, devoted his career to describing qualitative changes in cognition that occur in children as they age. So developmentalists decided to draw inspiration from this master theorist to construct an adult-relevant measure of IQ (Labouvie-Vief, 1992; Rybash, Hoyer, & Roodin, 1986; Sinnott, 2003).

Piaget, you may recall, believed that we develop cognitively through hands-on experience with the world. Although Piaget believed that the pinnacle of mental development occurs when we reach formal operations, and reason like "real scientists" during the teenage years, wouldn't adults' years of life experience produce a more advanced kind of reasoning called **postformal thought**? Let's look at the qualities that may differentiate this special adult intelligence from Piaget's final teenage stage.

postformal thought A uniquely adult form of intelligence that involves being sensitive to different perspectives, making decisions based on one's inner feelings, and being interested in exploring new questions.

POSTFORMAL THOUGHT IS RELATIVISTIC. As you saw in Chapter 9, adolescents in formal operations can argue rationally with their parents about absolute rights and wrongs. As we grow older and acquire more life experience, however, we realize that most real-world problems do not have clear-cut answers. Postformal thinkers accept the validity of different perspectives. They embrace the ambiguities of life.

This awareness that the truth is relative does not mean that postformal thinkers avoid making decisions or having strong beliefs. As you saw with C. Vann Woodward, people who reason postformally make better decisions precisely *because* they are open to changing their ideas when faced with the ambiguities of life.

POSTFORMAL THOUGHT IS FEELING-ORIENTED. Teenagers in formal operations feel that by using logic, they can make sense of the world. Postformal thinkers go beyond rationality to reason in a different way. Because there is often no objectively "right" answer to many of life's dilemmas, thinking postformally means relying more on one's gut feelings as the basis for making decisions. As with Anthony Hecht, people who reason postformally are less rigid, more open to new experiences, fully in touch with their inner lives.

POSTFORMAL THOUGHT IS QUESTION-DRIVEN. Adolescents want to get the correct answers and finish or solve tasks. Postformal thinkers are less focused on solutions. They thrive on developing new questions and reconsidering their opinions. As you saw with both Anthony Hecht and Dr. Woodward, people who think postformally enjoy coming up with new, interesting ways of looking at the world.

Clearly, we cannot measure this kind of intelligence by giving people tests in which each question has a single correct answer. We need to adopt the strategy that Lawrence Kohlberg used with his moral dilemmas: Present people with every-day situations and examine the *way* they reason about life. How would you respond to this sample situation the researchers devised?

John is known to be a heavy drinker, especially when he goes to parties. Mary, John's wife, warns him that if he gets drunk one more time, she will leave him and take the children. John goes to an office party and comes home drunk. Does Mary leave him? How sure are you of your answer?

The developmentalists originally predicted that, if you are in your twenties, you will answer this question in a rigid way: "Mary said she would leave, so of course she should. Yes, I am sure I am right." Middle-aged or elderly people, in contrast, would think through the consequences of leaving for Mary, for John, and for the children. They would realize that any answer they gave would be a judgment call.

Unfortunately, however, these psychologists' prediction that postformal thinking would increase in middle age and later life was wrong. This type of thinking is indeed lower during the teens. (Young adolescents, you may recall, have special trouble thinking through their actions when they are with their peers.) However, emerging adults are just as likely to reason postformally as people of any other age (Sinnott, 1989). Have you noticed yourself using this relativistic, person-centered kind of thinking when facing some complex real-world issue? Do you agree with the psychologists who believe that reasoning postformally is important to constructing a fulfilling adult life?

This brings us back to the compelling question I posed early in this chapter: How can you have a fulfilling adult life? Table 12.5 on page 378 summarizes *all* of this chapter's lessons in a chart that offers tips for flourishing during your own adult years.

Until this point, I have been discussing issues that are relevant to everyone—people in their twenties, their forties and fifties, and even adults aged 95. In this next section, I'll explore transitions that are unique to the middle years.

Setting up an innovative business demands postformal thinking—being able to look at issues from multiple perspectives, relying on your gut feelings about what may work, and coming up with creative new ways of looking at the world. But, according to the research, if he is lucky, this young entrepreneur does not need to wait until middle age to develop this mature adult thought.

> **TABLE 12.5:** How to Flourish During Adulthood: A Summary Table
>
> 1. Develop a generative mission. If you feel that you're at loose ends or that your life lacks purpose, try volunteering or helping others—it's addictive!
>
> 2. Try to view your failures and upsetting life experiences as learning lessons. Understand that life's tragedies and disappointments offer us our best opportunities to grow.
>
> 3. To keep your mind fine-tuned as you age, take care of your physical health. In particular, avoid heart disease.
>
> 4. In general, be interested in learning and developing as a person.
>
> 5. When you feel in role overload or role conflict, establish priorities, work hard in your most important areas, and rely on external aids to help you perform at your best.
>
> 6. Think postformally: Be open to different perspectives; question your established ideas and ways of thinking; be aware of your inner feelings and use them as a guide to make wise life choices.

TYING IT ALL TOGETHER

1. Tim is going to the thirtieth reunion of his college graduating class, and he can't wait to find out how his classmates have changed. Statistically speaking, which *two* changes is Tim likely to find in his undergraduate old friends?

   a. They will be less introverted and more outgoing.
   b. They will have different life priorities, caring more about nurturing the next generation.
   c. They will be more self-assured, confident, and happier.
   d. They will be more depressed and burned out.

2. You are interviewing your role model, your mother, about her life. She's your role model because she has always been the most caring, nurturing person you know. In describing her life, is your mom most likely to describe (a) negative life events that turned out for the best, (b) a life full of happy events, or (c) a life full of depressing events?

3. Andres is an air traffic controller and Mick is a historian. Pick out which man is likely to reach his career peak earlier, and explain the reasons why.

4. Your author is writing another textbook on lifespan development. She is also learning a new video game. Identify each type of intellectual skill involved and describe how my abilities in each of these areas are likely to change as I move into my sixties.

5. Rick says, "I've got way too much on my plate. I can't seem to do anything well." Sara says, "I don't feel my life has much meaning—I'm stagnating." Which theories of ideal development discussed in this chapter would be most helpful in addressing each of these problems, and what might each theory advise?

6. Kayla is considering whether to break up with her boyfriend, Mark, because, she says, "He doesn't give me the attention I need." Name the advice a postformal thinker would certainly *not* give to Kayla.

   a. "Leave the bum!"
   b. "Think of what is going on from Mark's perspective—for instance, is he overworked?"
   c. "Whatever choice you make, be sure to look at all the angles."
   d. "There may be no 'right decision.' Go with your gut."

Answers to the Tying It All Together questions can be found on the last page of this chapter.

Midlife Roles and Issues

As I mentioned at the beginning of this chapter, midlife transitions can be both sources of incredible joy and issues for concern. On the uplifting side, there is the chance to have that unparalleled life experience called grandparenthood. The

downside may be the need to care for disabled aged parents, and to face the reality of sexual decline. Let's now look at these "aging phase of life" joys and concerns one by one.

Grandparenthood

The grandparents always took . . . at least the first grandchild to raise because that's always the way the Lakota did it. They think that . . . they're more mature and have had more experience and they could teach the children a lot more than the young parents . . . . I'm still trying to carry on that tradition because my grandmother raised me most of the time up until I was nine years old. . . .

(quoted in Weibel-Orlando, 1999, p. 187)

This comment from Mrs. Big Buffalo, a Native American grandmother living in South Dakota, reminds us that every adult role, from spouse, to parent, to worker, to grandparent, is shaped by our culture. In our society, if we saw grandparents stepping in to raise a grandchild, we would probably assume that there was a serious problem with the parents' ability to provide care.

Still, even in the contemporary United States, our sense of the appropriate roles for grandparents differs by ethnic group. African American grandparents see their mission as providing considerable hands-on care—often at great personal cost (Winston, 2006). Middle-class European Americans have traditionally adopted a more removed stance. But with so many single parents and working mothers, these ethnic distinctions are breaking down. Today, grandparents *in general* tend to do more hands-on child care than they did even a few decades ago (Kulik, 2007). Actually, much more than simply being obligated to help out is involved. In European nations where the government offers free child care, grandparents are often heavily involved in taking care of the grandchildren, too (Hank & Buber, 2009).

Grandparenting Functions

What specifically are the functions of grandparents? In subsistence societies, grandparents literally help the youngest generation survive. Remember from my interview in the Experiencing the Lifespan box in Chapter 3 that, in Ghana, it's often the grandma who steps in to take care of the rest of the family, so her daughter can make the weekly trek to the clinic to stave off death in a young, malnourished child. Therefore, in Africa, simply the presence of a grandmother reduces the risk of mortality during the early years of life (Gibson & Mace, 2005).

In our culture, grandparents often serve as **family watchdogs** by stepping in during a crisis to stabilize the family. At these times, their true value shines through. Grandparents are the family's safety net (Troll, 1983).

Grandparents' mission to "be there" as family watchdogs is highlighted by tracing what happens during a divorce. After a divorce, grandparents often make an effort to see the grandchildren more frequently (Ehrenberg & Smith, 2003). As David and Doreen in the chapter-opening vignette did, they may have their newly single child and the grandchildren move in with them for a time.

As you might imagine, having a caring watchdog grandma or grandpa is especially important for children growing up in any "at-risk," that is, non-traditional family. In one survey of teens, having an involved grandparent didn't make a huge difference if a young person was living in a two-parent biological family; but it made for far fewer mental health problems if an adolescent was being raised by a stepparent or a single mom (Attar-Schwartz and others, 2009).

Actually, in *every family*, grandparents perform important watchdog roles. Grandparents often serve as mediators, helping the younger generations within the family resolve their differences (Kulik, 2007). Grandparents are the cement that keeps the extended family close. They are the command center for family news: "Hey, Mom. How are my little sister Amy and her children *really* doing since the divorce? Is there

family watchdogs A basic role of grandparents, which involves monitoring the younger family's well-being and intervening to provide help in a crisis.

anything I can do to help?" From Christmas holiday get-togethers to Thanksgiving dinners, "Grandma's house" is often the central meeting point—the place where brothers and sisters gather to regularly reconnect with one another during their adult years. As one developmentalist beautifully put it:

Grandparents serve as symbols of connectedness within and between lives; as people who can listen and have the time to do so; as reserves of time, help, and attention; as links to the unknown past; as people who are sufficiently varied, flexible, and complex to defy easy categories and clear-cut roles.

(Hagestad, 1985, p. 48)

You may notice this complexity and flexibility in action in your own family. One of your grandparents might be a shadowy figure, while another qualifies as a second mother or best friend. Some grandparents love to jump on trampolines with the grandchildren; others show their love in traditional, "baking cookies" ways. You may have an "intellectual grandma" who takes you to lectures and a "fishing grandpa" who takes you out on the lake.

From jumping on trampolines to taking the grandchildren to the local lake, grandparents fulfill this joyous life role in their own distinctive, personal ways.

Which Grandparents Are More or Less Involved?

In terms of being involved in their grandchildren's lives, what forces determine how active a particular grandparent is likely to be? Gender matters. Just as they do with their own children, women often tend to take a more hands-on approach with their grandchildren than do men (Reitzes & Mutran, 2004). Physical proximity makes a difference. If you live in rural Iowa, your grandparents are more likely to be a major presence in your life, because—living in a less mobile community—they are more likely to live nearby (King and others, 2003). Another predictor of involvement is age. Middle-aged grandparents are more likely to be "very active." Grandparents who are elderly tend to be more peripherally involved (Cherlin & Furstenberg, 1985).

Generative feelings are important. In fact, at *any* level of involvement, generative people thrive in the grandparent role (Thiele & Whelan, 2008). As one woman gushed, "I cannot tell you how wonderful it is to take care of the grandchildren every Friday afternoon. My whole world lights up when they walk in the room. And the fact that I don't have to be there every day to discipline Karen and Matt makes being a grandma pure joy."

Grandparent Problems

Grandparents love their freedom to "spoil" the grandchildren and send them back to Mom and Dad. As you saw earlier, they view their mission as "being there" for the younger generation (the family watchdog role). But they also believe they shouldn't interfere with how the grandchildren are being raised (Mason, May, & Clarke, 2007). This imperative to "never criticize," however, means that grandparents have to monitor their natural impulses to speak up or risk being cut off from visits. Moreover, always "being there" puts grandparents in a position of being either more or less involved than they want. Bottom line: Grandparents are really *not* free at all. Their relationship with the grandchildren depends on the generation in between.

Imagine the situation if you are a paternal grandmother, the mother of a son. Because women are naturally closer to their own mothers (versus their mothers-in-law) and tend to control the family's social relationships, around the world, maternal grandparents tend to be more heavily involved with the grandchildren (Hodgson,

1992; Monserud, 2008; Bernal & Anuncibay, 2008). Therefore, the problem for paternal grandparents is "not being there" as much as they would like.

Being the mother of a son produced heartache for a friend of mine. Her daughter-in-law decided to move across the country to be close to her own mother in Seattle, rather than stay in New York City—transforming my friend into the distant grandma she never wanted to be.

The allegiance to one's own family of origin can have devastating effects after a divorce. When the wife gets custody, she may prevent her ex-husband's parents from *ever* seeing the grandchildren again. In this case, paternal grandparents have to petition for visitation privileges, rights that are granted only when the court deems it in the best interest of the children (Henderson, 2005). So any paternal grandmother who wants to be closely involved must do what may not always come naturally: go out of her way to be a supportive, nurturing mother-in-law! (See Fingerman, 2004.)

Mothers of daughters may have the opposite problem. They may end up being there *too* much. Let's spell out a typical scenario: Your daughter wants you to watch the baby while she is at work. You don't want to disappoint your child, but you want to have your own life. The role conflict and feelings of ambivalence are especially intense when grandparents must assume an even more demanding job—needing to become full-time parents again.

Caregiving grandparents take full responsibility for raising their grandchildren. In recent decades, the ranks of these totally involved grandparents have swelled. Of the 6.1 million U.S. grandparents who lived with their grandchildren as of 2006, roughly 40 percent, or 2.5 million, were responsible for a child's basic care. Although they span the socioeconomic spectrum, caregiving grandparents tend to be relatively poor. Many are struggling to raise a grandchild plus work full-time (U.S. Department of Commerce, 2008). In the most extreme cases, these front-line caregivers must petition the court for custody or take steps to formally adopt a granddaughter or grandson.

How does it feel to take this difficult step? As you might expect, custodial grandparents are typically deeply distressed, mourning the fact that their own son or daughter—often because of drug or alcohol problems—is incapable of performing this job (Baird, 2003; Kelley & Whitley, 2003). They may feel angry at being forced into this "off-time" role. But they often feel a passionate, generative, "watchdog" mission to protect their flesh and blood (Hayslip & Patrick, 2003). Here is what one woman had to say to the police after her drug-abusing daughter took off with a grandchild and stole her car:

> [The police in a different state] said to me, "Ma'am, if you don't get here in 72 hours, then your grandson will be put in the [state protective services system] and you will have to fight to get him." I said, "I will fight from the moment I get there if my grandson is not there for me."

(quoted in Climo, Terry, & Lay, 2002, p. 25)

And another woman summed up the general feeling of the custodial grandmothers in this interview study when she blurted out: "Nobody is going to take [my grandson] away from me. I have done everything except give birth to him" (quoted in Climo, Terry, & Lay, 2002, p. 25).

These women, who were mainly in their late fifties, complained about feeling physically drained: "Some days I feel really old, like I just can't keep up with him" (quoted in Climo, Terry, & Lay, 2002, p. 23). They had mixed emotions about their situation: "Some days I feel real blessed by it, other days I want to sit and cry" (p. 25). They sometimes described redemption sequences, too: "God has given me this wonderful little boy to raise and I'm thinking, 'How many people get the opportunity to do it a second time?'" (p. 26).

caregiving grandparents Grandparents who have taken on full responsibility for raising their grandchildren.

parent care Adult children's care for their disabled elderly parents.

intergenerational solidarity Middle-aged adults' feeling of loving obligation to both the older and the younger generations.

Parent Care

Ask friends and family members and they will tell you that becoming a grandparent is one of the main joys of being middle-aged. Words such as *joy* and *fulfillment* do not come to mind with regard to the second classic midlife role: caring for elderly parents. Researchers who study **parent care** speak in terms of *burden, strain, hassles,* as well as impaired physical and mental health (Hunt, 2003; Son and others, 2007; Zarit, Reever, & Bach-Peterson, 1980).

Caring for parents violates the basic principle in Western cultures that parents give to their children, not the reverse (Belsky, 1999). It can heighten the feelings of role conflict when a woman is working and must reduce her hours at a job (Marks, 2008; Roberto & Jarrot, 2008). If, as is increasingly true, a caregiving daughter is in her sixties or seventies, parent care may interfere with a person's retirement plans or the need to care for her own frail, disabled spouse. More rarely, a woman is pulled between two intergenerational commitments, simultaneously caring for elderly parents and watching the grandchildren full time.

At this point, I need to set the record straight: The stereotype of a stressed-out "sandwich generation"—women pulled between caring for children and disabled parents—is *not* a common middle-aged role. (Same goes for the popular concept of a "midlife crisis." It simply doesn't exist for most adults.) However, when either the older or younger generation needs care, there is one generalization I can make: Men do take over more responsibility if there are no sisters and the father needs care (Daire, 2002; Kramer & Thompson, 2002). However, parent care is typically a daughter's or daughter-in-law's job (Kinsella & Velkoff, 2001; Spitzer and others, 2003).

What forces make this mainly female job easier? One factor, as you might imagine, is having an enduring, loving attachment to that parent (Marks and others, 2008; Silverstein and others, 2002). The intensity of the older person's needs also

matters. Caring for an aged parent is especially difficult when that person is highly irritable and/or has that difficult condition called Alzheimer's disease (Okamoto, Hasbe, & Harasawa, 2007; Tooth and others, 2008; see Chapter 14). We also need to look at how much help the caregiver gets from outside services (Iecovich, 2008), as well as whether she feels that the burden is unfair. Even when a specific child has willingly taken on the designated caregiver role, resentful feelings arise when that person feels her siblings are not doing their fair share: "Why don't they help at all?" (Merrill, 1996.)

Still, some children find that caring for a disabled parent offers its own redemption sequence. It is a chance to repay a beloved

Will this middle-aged child find parent care a labor of love or an impossible stress? Keys lie in whether this daughter and her mother have always had a close, loving attachment, how "difficult" her mom's symptoms are now, and—very important—whether this woman feels her siblings are doing their fair share.

mother or father for years of love (Kramer & Thompson, 2002). And just as with other difficult life challenges, confronting the trauma of caring for a parent—especially when that mom or dad has Alzheimer's disease—ultimately helps people grow emotionally as human beings (Leipold, Schacke, & Zank, 2008).

How can midlife adults balance their strong sense of **intergenerational solidarity**, or loving obligation, to their parents and children with the need to have their own lives? This is the question that women such as Doreen struggle with as they strive to be generative with both the grandchildren and their parents, and, at the same time, live autonomous lives.

Body Image, Sex, and Menopause

Physical disabilities lie far in the future for most midlife adults. Still, as you can see in the Experiencing the Lifespan box below, fifty-something adults take great pleasure in cataloguing each sign of bodily decay. Take it from me—these external signs of aging are unimportant. Remember from my discussion of teenage body image in Chapter 8 that *we* determine our own beauty. Furthermore, as women move into midlife and develop more generative priorities, they become less obsessed with looking physically perfect. Especially when they are happily married, older women report being less anxious about appearance issues related to aging than the young (Barrett & Robbins, 2008). You might be interested to know that several studies show that female college students tend to feel *worse* about their bodies than their middle-aged counterparts (see Greenleaf, 2005; McKinley, 2006). However, when we are 20 or 30, the thought of developing gray hair, wrinkles, or sagging skin can be alarming because these changes seem to signal the end of our sexual self. What *really* happens sexually to both men and women as they age?

The physiological findings for middle-aged men are actually somewhat depressing. According to classic studies, as they get older, males need more time to develop an erection. They are more likely to lose an erection before ejaculation occurs. Their ejaculations become less intense. By their fifties, most men are not able to have another erection for 12 to 24 hours after having had sex (Masters & Johnson, 1966).

I must emphasize that this slower arousal to ejaculation tempo has advantages. At a minimum, because it blocks those infamous one-minute lovemaking events of youth, it tends to make men superior sexual partners as they age. But it also explains the popularity of the billion-dollar market for erection-stimulating drugs such as Viagra. Desire remains, but by late middle age, many men feel they need some extra help to implement their plans.

EXPERIENCING THE LIFESPAN: CONFRONTING AN AGING FACE

Letty Pogrebin, a feminist and founding editor of *Ms.* magazine, has written a humorous book exposing the female body on "the far side of 50." Here is her frank account of her 55-year-old image as witnessed in the mirror—and some comments on what set her straight:

> Remember the opening scene from Mommie Dearest, when the aging Joan Crawford wakes up, takes off her lubricated sleep mask, . . . and plunges her face into a bowl of steaming hot water and then into a sink full of ice cubes? Well, I have what she was trying to prevent.

> Under my eyes are puffy fat pads surrounded by dark circles, each unfortunate feature trying its best to call attention to the other. My wrinkles materialized almost overnight when I was 49. Now the lines in my face remind me of my palms. When I raise my eyebrows, my forehead pleats, and when my eyebrows come down the pleats stay. . . . The cheerful parentheses at the corners of my smile have started looking downtrodden, and my top lip is beginning to produce those spidery . . . creases that soak up lipstick. . . .

> Just this year, my jaw, the Maginot Line of facial structure, surrendered to the force of gravity. On each side of my chin the muscles have pulled loose from the bone. Once I had a right-angle profile; now there's a hypotenuse between my chin and neck. . . . Which brings me, regrettably, to my neck, with its double choker of lines; and my chest, creased like crepe paper; and my shoulders and arms, which are holding their own for now except for the elbows, which are rough enough to shred a carrot. I don't yet have loose skin on the underside of my upper arm—you know, the part that keeps waving after you've stopped—but I can see it coming.

> These days I'm into the truth and the truth is I'm not crazy about my looks but I can live with them. . . . What jolted me out of my low-grade Body Image Blues was the death of friends felled by cancer in the prime of their lives. After the third funeral . . ., I saw my body, not as face, skin, hair, figure, but as the vehicle through which I could experience everything my friend would never know again. . . . Ordinary pleasures seemed so precious that I vowed to set my priorities straight before some fatal illness did it for me. Since then I have been trying to focus on the things that really matter. And I can assure you that being able to wear a bikini isn't one of them.

Source: Pogrebin (1996), pp. 128–129, 153.

menopause The age-related process, occurring at about age 50, in which ovulation and menstruation stop due to the loss of estrogen.

In contrast, females reach their desire peak in their early thirties (Schmitt and others, 2002). But by late middle age, most women do report having considerably less interest in sex than men (McHugh, 2007). One reason is not so hard to guess: fewer sexual signals coming in from the outside world.

As they move into their fifties, more women are likely to be without a partner (due to widowhood or divorce). Or they may be in a long-term *companionate* relationship with an older spouse. (Recall from the last chapter that, over time, sexual desire naturally tends to decline in any relationship.) Moreover, just as signals from the outside world accentuate our first feelings of sexual desire during puberty, when the outer world stops viewing older women as sexual human beings, desire tends to turn off (Kenrick and others, 1993). Menopause takes a toll on sexuality, too.

Menopause typically occurs at about age 50, when estrogen production falls off dramatically and women stop ovulating. Specifically, the defining marker of having reached menopause is not having menstruated for a year. As estrogen production declines and a woman approaches this milestone, the menstrual cycle becomes more irregular. During this sexual winding-down period, which is called *perimenopause,* some women experience minor mood changes and other physical symptoms, such as night sweats and hot flashes (sudden sensations of heat) (see Table 12.6).

Although some women sail through menopause without any symptoms, this estrogen loss produces changes in the reproductive tract. Normally, the walls of the vagina have thick folds that expand to admit a penis and to accommodate childbirth. After menopause, the vaginal walls thin out and become more fragile. The vagina shortens, and its opening narrows. The size of the clitoris and labia decreases. It takes longer after arousal for lubrication to begin (Masters & Johnson, 1966). Women don't produce as much fluid as before. These changes can make having intercourse so painful that some women stop having sex.

If women lose interest in sex after menopause, is this due to pain during intercourse, the fact that society doesn't react to older women as sexual human beings, or simply that, in long-term relationships, sexual desire declines (Birnbaum, Cohen, & Werthemer, 2007; Hillman, 2008)? Whatever the answer, once again, diversity is the main message with regard to sexuality (McHugh, 2007). As you saw in the chapter-opening vignette,

---

TABLE 12.6: Stereotypes and Facts About Menopause

1. **The stereotype:** Women have terrible physical symptoms while going through menopause.

   The facts: In longitudinal studies, researchers find that an upsurge of minor physical complaints does occur during the few years preceding menopause: lack of energy, backaches, and joint stiffness. Anywhere from 30 to 70 percent of U.S. women experience hot flashes and some sleeplessness. Still, there is tremendous variability. Women are most likely to report considerable physical and psychological distress during menopause, when they are undergoing other life stresses (Avis and others, 2003).

2. **The stereotype:** Women are very moody while going through menopause.

   The facts: Statistically speaking, women do show an increase in minor symptoms of anxiety and depression as they approach menopause, when estrogen levels are waning (Avis and others, 2004). However, these changes do not affect all people, and, after reaching menopause, many women report feeling better than they ever have. Remember that the Mills College study (described in the text) showed that most women see their lives as highly satisfying during their early fifties.

3. **The stereotype:** Women feel empty, "dried up," old, and asexual after menopause.

   The facts: Many women actually respond to menopause with a sense of relief. For instance, one-third of the women in Taiwan and almost half of all Australian women in a cross-cultural study said that they were happy not to have to deal with menstruation every month (Fu, Anderson, & Courtney, 2003). In another Danish study, at menopause most women felt that they were entering a new, freer stage of life. Some said that their sex life was much better now that they had no worries about getting pregnant (Hvas, 2001).

TABLE 12.7: Staying Passionate About Sex with Age

For Men

Problem	Solutions
Trouble maintaining or achieving an erection.	1. Understand that some physiological slowing down is normal, and do not be alarmed by occasional problems performing. Sexual relations need to occur more slowly; manual stimulation may be necessary to fully achieve erection and orgasm. 2. Stay healthy. Avoid sexually impairing conditions such as heart disease. If possible, avoid medications that have clear sexual side effects (such as antidepressants and blood pressure pills). 3. If troubled by chronic problems performing, explore the medicines that are now available for treating these problems (e.g., Viagra).

For Women

Problem	Solutions
No sexual signals coming from the outside world.	1. Stay sexy, be conscious of your physical appearance 2. Try to find a partner who really appreciates you as a sexual human being.
Decline in estrogen levels makes having sexual intercourse painful.	1. Consider using lubricants, such as K-Y Jelly, when having sex. 2. Consider hormone replacement therapy (but discuss this with your doctor).

some women find sex more exciting after menopause (Hillman, 2008). Some couples are very sexually active into their seventies and beyond (Brecher and *Consumer Reports* editors, 1984; Wiley & Bortz, 1996). Table 12.7 summarizes the male/female changes described in this section and offers some advice for staying passionate about sex.

TYING IT ALL TOGETHER

1. Juanita has two grandmothers, Karen and Louisa. Grandma Karen is much more involved with Juanita than is Grandma Louisa. List several characteristics that might explain why Karen is the more active, hands-on grandmother.

2. Poll your class. Do most people report being closest to their maternal grandmother (or grandfather)? For the students who were closer to a paternal grandparent, explore why that might be.

3. Kim is caring for her elderly mother, who just had a stroke. Each of the following factors should make Kim's job feel easier *except*:
   a. Kim and her mother were very close when Kim was growing up.
   b. Kim's mother has a mellow personality.
   c. Kim has several siblings.

4. For the following statements regarding age changes in sexuality, select the right gender: *Males/Females* decline the most physiologically at a younger age, but *male/female* age changes in sexuality are most affected by social issues (such as not having a partner). As they reach their fifties, *males/females* report having less interest in sex. *Males/Females* have the most untapped sexual potential in later life.

5. If Joselyn is going through menopause, she will *definitely*:
   a. experience mood swings.
   b. lose interest in sex.
   c. undergo reproductive tract changes, such as a thinning of her vaginal walls.

Answers to the Tying It All Together questions can be found on the last page of this chapter.

Yes, the secret is that many couples do stay passionate well into middle age and beyond—provided they make staying sexy and interested in sex a life priority!

Andy Ryan/Getty Images

Final Thoughts

The bottom-line message of this chapter is that from intelligence to developing new, generative roles, the middle years can be a high point of life. Readers in their twenties should look forward to their forties and fifties with joy! We also have interesting hints that old age may not be nearly as bad as the stereotypes suggest. How *do* we change physically, cognitively, and personality-wise during life's last stage? Stay tuned for answers as we move into the next section of the book.

SUMMARY

The Evolving Self

Although the boundaries of middle age span from about age 40 to the early sixties, many older adults describe themselves as middle aged. Diversity—among people and change processes—plus consistency are the defining characteristics of the middle years.

Research on the **Big Five traits** shows our scores on these core dimensions of personality predict a variety of life outcomes. Also, our relative rankings on these traits don't change much after age 30, unless we experience other major life changes. Interviews paint a different picture, suggesting that we change a good deal as we travel through life. Dan McAdams's research exploring Erikson's **generativity** shows that our priorities shift to "other-centered concerns" during midlife. Generativity predicts being a successful, fulfilled parent, and fulfilling Erikson's midlife task is intimately tied to having a meaningful adult life.

In their autobiographies, highly generative adults produce a **commitment script** and describe **redemption sequences**—negative events that turned out for the best. Although central to our individualistic culture's generativity script, the redemption sequence may not appear in more collectivist societies. Perhaps because they need to struggle with adversity, many African Americans are exceptionally generative.

A classic longitudinal study showed that women become more self-confident and happier as they move into midlife. Other cross-sectional studies show this trend to get happier (and control our emotions better) continues into old age. Yes, personality remains basically consistent in many ways. However, the overall message is "we get better" personality-wise as we travel through adult life.

Early studies using the **Wechsler Adult Intelligence Scale (WAIS)** found that people reach their intellectual peak in their twenties—although scores on the timed performance scale tests declined more rapidly than did scores on the verbal scale. The **Seattle Lon-**

gitudinal Study—which controlled for the biases of this research—showed the same change pattern, but it also indicated that we reach our intellectual peak in midlife.

Fluid intelligence, the capacity to master unfamiliar cognitive challenges quickly, is at its height early in adulthood, and then it declines. **Crystallized intelligence**, our knowledge base, rises or stays stable until well into middle age. In professions that heavily depend on crystallized knowledge—versus fast information processing—people do well into their sixties. Creativity reaches its peak in midlife, although our basic talents are the best predictors of our creative accomplishments at any age.

Staying healthy and stimulating our mind are two keys to preventing age-related cognitive decline. **Terminal drop**, a significant loss on verbal (crystallized) tests, can indicate that a person has a fatal disease. Using **selective optimization with compensation** helps people to successfully cope with age-related losses and to live more successfully at any life stage.

Postformal thinkers are sensitive to diverse perspectives, interested in exploring questions, and attuned to their inner feelings in making life decisions. While there are no systematic age differences in this type of thinking after emerging adulthood, the ability to think postformally may be very helpful in constructing a fulfilling adult life.

Midlife Roles and Issues

Grandparents often act as the **family watchdogs**, stepping in when their children and grandchildren need help. Gender, proximity to the grandchildren, and personality shape how people carry out this joyous but surprisingly constrained life role. Because women tend to be closer to their own mothers, paternal grandmothers are at risk of being less involved with the grandchildren than they want to be. The problem for maternal grandparents lies in being pressured to do too much. The extreme case

of taking "too much care" occurs when people become **caregiving grandparents** or must take full custody and raise the child.

Parent care is another family role that middle-aged daughters may have to assume. While often stressful, a variety of forces affect how people feel when caring for a disabled parent. Midlife adults feel a strong sense of **intergenerational solidarity** with their parents, their grandchildren, and their children.

Another midlife concern involves declining sexuality. For males, erectile capacity steadily declines. Although women tend to feel most passionate in their thirties, **menopause** has the side effect of making intercourse more painful. Because of this pain, as well as the fact that they may not have interested partners, many older women may lose interest in sex. Still, women (and men) can stay very sexually active well into later life.

ANSWERS TO TYING IT ALL TOGETHER QUIZZES

The Evolving Self

1. b and c.

2. a.

3. Andres will reach his career peak far earlier than Mick because his job is heavily dependent on fluid skills. A historian's job depends almost exclusively on crystallized skills.

4. Textbook writing is a crystallized skill, so I should be just as good at my life passion during my sixties—provided I don't get ill! Playing video games depends heavily on fluid skills, so I will be far worse now than at a younger age, and I would deteriorate further in my sixties.

5. The theory that applies to Rick's problem—"too much on his plate"— is Baltes's selective optimization with compensation: He needs to (1) prioritize and shed less important jobs, (2) work harder in his top-ranking areas, and (3) use external aids to help him cope whenever possible. Sara's difficulty seems to be a lack of generativity. She should get involved in activities that involve making a difference in the world—volunteering, helping family and friends, and so on.

6. a.

Midlife Roles and Issues

1. Karen may be younger, live closer to Emma, and be a more generative person. Most likely she is a maternal grandma.

2. Answers here will vary.

3. c.

4. *Males* decline most physiologically at a younger age; *female* sexuality is most affected by social issues (such as the lack of a partner). As they reach their fifties, *females* report having less interest than males in sex. *Females* have the most untapped sexual potential in later life.

5. c.

Later Life

This two-chapter section, devoted to life's last stage, highlights how we develop and change as we move through senior citizenhood (our sixties and beyond). Chapter 13 covers issues relevant to both the young-old and old-old years. Chapter 14 emphasizes concerns that become pressing priorities in advanced old age.

Chapter 13—**Later Life: Cognitive and Socioemotional Development** begins with an in-depth look at memory in later life. During this discussion, you will not only learn how memory changes with age, but also get insights into how to improve your memory at any age. Then, we look at personality. Here, I'll outline a provocative theory suggesting that our emotional priorities shift during later life, decode whether (or when) old age is the best or worst life stage, and offer tantalizing tips about living meaningfully during life's last stage. The second half of this chapter tackles those major later-life transitions: retirement and widowhood.

Chapter 14—**The Physical Challenges of Old Age** begins by describing the aging process and how it progresses into disease and disability. Then, I'll explore late-life sensory and motor changes and offer a detailed look at that most feared, old-age disease: dementia. At the end of this chapter, you will learn about the living arrangements and health-care options available to people when old-age frailties strike. This chapter will open your eyes to the challenges of age-related disabilities and, hopefully, sensitize you to the need to change the wider world to promote an ideal older adult-environment fit.

Chapter 15—In **Death and Dying**, my focus extends to *all* stages of life. Here, I'll explore how we have approached this ultimate milestone throughout history and in different cultures, look at death from the perspective of the person and the health-care system, and offer an in-depth analysis of issues related to that critical contemporary twenty-first century concern: taking control of how (and when) we die.

Chapter 13

Later Life: Cognitive and Socioemotional Development

When Theresa and Sal were 63, they both retired. They were healthy, active, and (at the time)—with Sal's investments and their pensions—remarkably well off. They were passionate to enjoy these final decades, to focus on the moment, to revel in their life. Sal loved being president of the bank, but he was getting burnt out. He wanted to retire to pursue his other love—traveling. Theresa and Sal never had children, but they had their nieces and nephews and many friends. In particular, they had their second family in Dr. Jane, her children, and her grand-kids. Theresa met Dr. Jane, the first female African American principal in their Pennsylvania town, during a 1960s Civil-Rights-era march. When Dr. Jane hired Theresa right out of college as the learning specialist at Pine Ridge Middle School, this cemented a relationship as best friends and older and younger "sisters in spirit" that lasted for almost 40 years.

For Theresa and Sal, retirement meant spending more time with their very closest friends, like Dr. Jane. It meant devoting weekdays to volunteering at church, and especially, taking those long awaited cruises to Mexico, the Mediterranean, and Marrakesh. Most of all, it meant having the joy of just being together as a couple, free from the demands of work. Sal's heart disease—first diagnosed in his mid sixties—lent a special poignancy to their shared life. As it turned out, their retirement years were priceless, but they were over too soon. At age 73, Sal died of a massive heart attack.

It has been hard for Theresa to function. How can you go on without your high school sweetheart, your best friend for over 50 years? Theresa takes comfort from her widowed friends, particularly Dr. Jane. Theresa and Sal were there for Jane when she lost her husband, Carl, to cancer at age 61. Now, it is Jane's turn—spry and vigorous at age 83—to envelop Theresa in her loving family and serve as a caring sounding board for Theresa to talk (or not talk) about Sal.

Theresa feels Sal's comforting presence in the house. She even finds herself mentally consulting her husband for advice. But for the most part (bless the Lord), she's been amazed at her inner strength. After being hit with Sal's medical bills, Theresa found that her income was alarmingly low. She scoured the county for jobs, thinking, "Who would want to hire an old lady of 75?" She was wrong and will start her job as a children's learning consultant at Barnes & Noble next week. Tonight, she plans to celebrate by opening a bottle of champagne with Sal!

Theresa's life changed dramatically from the time she entered retirement until after Sal became ill and died. These two chapters capture the developmental shifts people experience as they travel through the young-old (sixties and seventies) and old-old (over age 80) years. In the current chapter, I'll focus on cognition and the socioemotional side of later life. In Chapter 14, I'll be following Theresa as she moves into her eighties and confronts the physical frailties of advanced old age.

Theresa and Sal's lives differ dramatically from those of elderly people around the globe—in religion, in lifestyle, in having the freedom to travel the world. Still, in one way, they are the same as every person their age: Their cohort is the fastest-growing life stage.

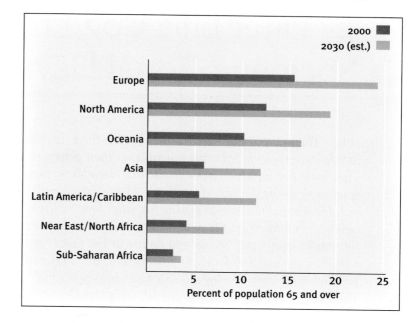

FIGURE 13.1: **Percent of elderly in selected regions, 2000 and 2030:** The elderly population is mushrooming in most areas of the world. In 20 years, an amazing one in four people in Europe will be over age 65.

Source: Adapted from Kinsella & Velkoff (2001), Table 2-1, p. 9.

median age The age at which 50 percent of a population is older and 50 percent is younger.

late-life life expectancy The number of additional years a person in a given country can expect to live once reaching age 65.

young-old People in their sixties and seventies.

old-old People age 80 and older.

Setting the Context

Theresa and Sal are members of an expanding army. By the turn of this century, in North America, about 1 of every 9 people was over age 65. In Europe, the percent was an astonishing 1 in 6. The developing world is beginning to catch up. Notice from Figure 13.1 that, during the first brief three decades of the twenty-first century, the percentage of older people in the population will more than double in Asia and Latin America (Kinsella & Velkoff, 2001).

What accounts for this amazing increase in older adults? One force, as you learned in Chapter 1, lies in our remarkable twentieth-century life expectancy advances. A second influence, particularly in North America and Europe, is the baby boom cohort now flooding into later life. Today, the leading edge of the baby boomers are in their sixties. By 2030, this mammoth cohort will all be well into their elderly years.

Finally, the decrease in fertility, discussed in Chapter 11, is also making for a new older world. When birth rates decline, the **median age** of a nation—meaning the cutoff age at which half of the population is older and half is younger—tends to rise. With childbearing rates decreasing so dramatically in Europe and Asia, as Figure 13.2

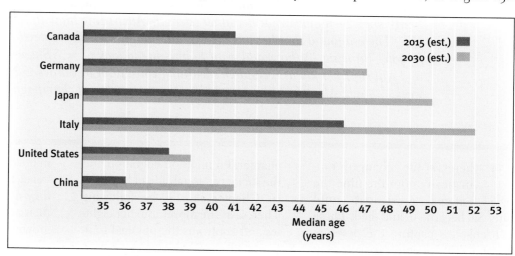

FIGURE 13.2: **Predicted median age of the population, selected countries, in 2015 and 2030:** A few years from now, the median age of the population—the point at which half the people are younger and half are older—will be 45-plus in Italy, Germany, and Japan. Also, notice how high the median ages in these nations will be in two decades. How do you think living in these "most-aged nations" will affect residents' daily lives?

Source: Kinsella & Velkoff (2001).

implies, the median age of the population in many developed countries is now well into middle age.

Life expectancy, the baby boomers, and low fertility set the stage for our new older world. Now, let's offer some predictions about what life will look like two decades from now. In 2030 in Japan, where average life expectancy now tops age 81 and fertility rates are among the lowest in the world, the median age of the population will be roughly age 50. In Italy, 1 out of *every* 2 people will be at least 52. And in that same year, roughly 1 in every 5 Americans and 1 in 4 Europeans will be over age 65 (Kinsella & Velkoff, 2001, National Center for Health Statistics, Health United States, 2007).

What will it be like to live in a nation where the people with walkers may outnumber the babies in strollers you see on your neighborhood streets? To answer this question, I need to re-emphasize the crucial fact about later life spelled out early in this book: Just as an emerging adult has little in common with an eighth grader, being age 90—statistically speaking—is very different from being age 60 or 65.

We celebrate our amazing twentieth-century progress in raising life expectancy at birth. A less well-known statistic concerns the increase in **late-life life expectancy**. This phrase refers to the number of years we can expect to live once we have turned 65. When they reached their sixty-fifth birthdays, contemporary U.S. adults, such as Theresa and Sal, had a fifty-fifty chance of surviving for almost 20 more years (National Center for Health Statistics, Health United States, 2007). Because these decades traveling through later life are very different, as you learned in Chapter 1, developmentalists divide the elderly into two groups: The **young-old**, people in their sixties and seventies, are typically healthy and relatively well off financially. The **old-old**, people over age 80, are far more likely to suffer from old-age disabilities (or use those walkers) and be poor.

The differences between being young-old and the old-old may explain our strange contradictory stereotypes about later life. There is the image of the wealthy senior citizen cruising the world and the portrait of the frail aged person in a nursing home; the vision of the upbeat, vigorous older adult going back to school, and the depressed, institutionalized elder who suffers from a dementing disease. At this point, you might take a minute to complete the "Is It True about the Elderly?" questionnaire in Table 13.1. Are you having trouble answering some of these questions simply because being age 60 is so different from being 95?

Rising life expectancy, declining fertility, the baby boomers reaching old age—all of these forces explain why the median age of the population is increasing and why, in the decades to come, more people will look closer in age to this elderly woman than her 22-year-old granddaughter.

The expressions on the faces of this joyous 65-year-old and dour 90-year-old say it all. In terms of lifestyle, personality, memory, health, and everything else, we cannot stereotype "the elderly," and there is a world of difference between being young-old and old-old.

TABLE 13.1: Is It True about the Elderly?

1. People treated the elderly better in "the good old days."

2. As people get older, memory dramatically declines.

3. There is little that can be done about memory problems in later life.

4. Older people are unhappy, demoralized, and depressed.

5. Older people are less stressed-out than younger adults.

6. It's impossible to live a fulfilling life if you live in a nursing home.

7. Older workers are more rigid and difficult to supervise.

8. People who have an extremely happy marriage, have the most trouble adjusting to widowhood.

9. Compared to late-life vision difficulties, hearing losses in old age are "a piece of cake."

10. No one who has Alzheimer's disease can live a meaningful life.

(Items 1–8 are discussed in this chapter; items 9 and 10 in Chapter 14.)

(Answers 1. F, 2. T and F, 3. F, 4. T and F, 5. T, 6. F, 7. F, 8. F, 9. F, 10. F)

The hair is gray. . . . The brows are gone, the eyes are blear . . . The nose is hooked and far from fair. . . . The ears are rough and pendulous. . . . The face is sallow, dead and drear. . . . The chin is purs'd . . . the lips hang loose. . . . Aye such is human beauty's lot! . . . Thus we mourn for the good old days . . . , wretched crones, huddled together by the blaze. . . . With many a man 'tis just the same.

(excerpted from an Old English poem called "Lament of the Fair Heaulmiere" [or Helmet-maker's girl], quoted in Minois, 1989, p. 230)

Many of us assume that people had better values and attitudes toward old age in "the good old days." Poems such as the one above show that we need to give that stereotype a much closer look.

In ancient times, old age was seen as a miracle of nature because it was so rare. Where there was no written language, older people were greatly valued for their knowledge. However, this elevated status applied only to a few people—typically men—who were upper class. For slaves, servants, and women, old age was often a cruel time. Moreover, just as we do today, many cultures made a clear distinction between active, healthy older people and those who were disabled and ill.

In many traditional cultures, for instance, the same person who had been revered several years earlier was subjected to barbaric treatment once he outlived his usefulness—that is, became decrepit or senile. Samoans killed their elderly in elaborate ceremonies in which the victim was required to participate. Other societies left their older people to die of neglect. Michelangelo and Sophocles, who were revered as old men, stand as symbols of the age-friendly attitudes of the cultures in which they lived. However, the images portrayed in their creative works celebrated youth and beauty. Even in Classical Greece and Renaissance Italy—societies known for being extremely enlightened—people believed old age was the worst time of life.

As historian Georges Minois (1989) concluded in a survey of how Western cultures treated their elders, "It is the tendency of every society to live and go on living: it extols the strength and fecundity that are so closely linked to youth and it dreads the . . . decrepitude of old age. Since the dawn of history . . . young people have regretted the onset of old age. The fountain of youth has always constituted Western man's most irrational hope" (p. 303).

(The information in this box is taken from Minois, 1989, and Fischer, 1977.)

In this section of the book, as we tour the triumphs and trials of life's last stage(s), you will realize why the answers to several items in Table 13.1 are both somewhat true and somewhat false. Let's begin by exploring stereotype number one: the widespread idea that—unlike in our contemporary, youth-obsessed age—there was a magic time in the past when the elderly were revered. As you can see in the Experiencing the Lifespan box above, that image is *totally* false. Ironically, because we are not killing off our frail elderly, our age may actually be the most age-friendly historical era of all!

Now, keeping in mind that age 60 is very different from 95, let's begin where we left off in the last chapter—exploring the developing self.

The Evolving Self

What happens to memory as we grow old? Are there changes in our emotional priorities that occur in later life? Are older people calm and together, or unhappy and depressed? Now, we look at these topics and many more.

Memory

When we think of our overall intellectual abilities as we get older, we can look forward to many positive changes: expanding our crystallized skills, becoming more competent and in control of life (recall Chapter 12). These upbeat feelings do not extend to memory. With memory, when everyone looks to old age, they see only decline (see, for instance, Lineweaver, Berger, & Hertzog, 2009). People worry about these losses well before they reach age 65. How often do you hear a 50-year-old say, "I'm having a senior moment," or, "Sorry, I forgot. . . . It's my Alzheimer's kicking in"?

For older adults, memory loss is a top-ranking fear (Dixon and others, 2007). The outside world can be on high alert for memory problems, too.

In a classic study, psychologists demonstrated this mindset by filming actors aged 20, 50, and 70 reading an identical speech. During the talk, each person made a few references to memory problems, such as "I forgot my keys." Volunteers then watched only the young, middle-aged, or older actor and wrote about what the person was like. Many of the people who saw the 70-year-old described him as forgetful. No one who heard the identical words read by the younger adults even mentioned memory (Rodin & Langer, 1980)!

So once someone is over age 65 or 75 or 80, we are especially attuned to memory lapses. We see memory failures in a more ominous light. When a young person forgets something, we pass off the problem as due to external forces: "He was distracted" or "She had too much else going on." When that person is old, we think: "Perhaps this is the beginning of Alzheimer's disease" (Erber & Prager, 1999). When you last were with an elderly family member and she forgot a name or appointment, did the idea that "grandma is declining mentally" cross your mind?

Scanning the Facts

Are older people's memory abilities *really* worse than those of younger adults? Unfortunately, according to hundreds of laboratory studies, the answer is yes. In testing everything from our ability to recall unfamiliar faces to the names of new places, from remembering the content of paragraphs to recalling where objects are located in space, the elderly perform more poorly than the young (see Dixon and others, 2007).

As a memory task gets more difficult, the performance gap between young and old people expands. When psychologists ask people to recognize a photograph they have previously seen, older people often do as well as the typical 20-year-old (Craik & McDowd, 1987). The elderly score comparatively worse when they need to come up with names of people pictured in those photos completely on their own. (The distinction here is analogous to taking a multiple-choice exam versus a short-answer test.) Older people perform even more dismally when they have to recall a face and connect it to a specific situation (Dennis and others, 2008; Old & Naveh-Benjamin, 2008): "Yes, I recognize that guy . . . but was he the cable repairman or a guest at Claire's commencement party last month?"

While connecting faces to places, or remembering exactly *where* you heard some bit of information, is especially difficult in old age, this task is not easy at any life stage. I'll never forget when a twenty-something student server blew me away with this comment: "I remember you very well, Dr. Belsky. I learned so much in your *English Literature class* three years ago."

The elderly also have unusual trouble with **divided-attention tasks**—situations in which they need to memorize material or perform an activity while simultaneously monitoring something else. Talking on your cell phone while writing a paper, remembering to check the clock while you are studying so that you don't miss your 3 P.M. class—these challenges also are difficult for people of any age. But while, after training, young people can learn to effortlessly master this kind of multitasking, the elderly have *permanent* problems focusing on more than one thing at a time (Gothe, Oberauer, & Kliegal, 2008).

More depressing, when researchers pile on the memory demands and add time pressures, deficits show up decades before later life. In fact, with the most difficult memory tasks, losses begin as early as the late twenties (Borella, Carretti, & De Beni, 2008; Salthouse, 2003). Returning to the previous chapter, it makes sense that when people are asked to remember completely new, random bits of information very fast, we should see age losses soon after youth. These requirements are prime examples of *fluid intelligence tasks.*

divided-attention task A difficult memory challenge involving memorizing material while simultaneously monitoring something else.

Rick Gomez/Masterfile

Shifting her attention from scanning a computer, remembering what is on the screen, and taking notes on what she just read is a piece of cake for this young woman. But this kind of *divided-attention* task, researchers find, can be difficult, or virtually impossible, when we reach later life.

What is going wrong with memory as we age? Let's get insights from examining two different ways of conceptualizing "a memory": the information-processing and memory-systems approaches.

An Information-Processing Perspective on Memory Change

Remember from Chapter 5 that developmentalists who adopt an *information-processing theory* perspective on cognition see memory as progressing through defined stages. The gateway system, in which we take action to transform information into more permanent storage, is called *working memory.*

Working memory, as I mentioned in Chapter 5, contains a limited memory-bin space—the amount of information we can keep in our awareness at a single time. It includes an executive processor that controls our attention and works to transform the contents of this temporary storage facility into material we can recall later on. You may recall that during childhood, as the frontal lobes mature, working memory dramatically improves. Unfortunately, as we travel through adulthood, working memory works worse and worse (Borella, Carretti, & De Beni, 2008; Salthouse, 2003).

What explains this decline? Today, many experts target deficits with the executive processor, that hypothetical structure responsible for focusing our attention and manipulating material into the permanent memory store. As we age, this master controller doesn't filter out irrelevant information as well, and we have more trouble selectively attending to what we need to learn (Hasher & Zacks, 1988; Rowe, Hasher, & Turcotte, 2008). One symptom of this selective attention deficit is that the elderly have unusual trouble memorizing information when there are distractions, such as irrelevant speech (Bell, Buchner, & Mund, 2008). Another is that, as I just described, older people have so much trouble mastering divided-attention tasks.

Remembering the speaker's messages at this senior citizen center lecture is going to be especially hard—because being surrounded by all these other women is destined to produce high levels of distracting noise.

When we think of *executive functions,* such as selective attention, a particular brain structure comes to mind. Later-life memory deficits, according to current thinking, mainly reflect age-related neural deterioration in our master planner, the frontal lobes (Park & Reuter-Lorenz, 2009). Neuroscientists can document this frontal lobe atrophy using brain-imaging techniques (Beason-Held, Kraut, & Resnick, 2008; Head and others, 2008). How does the older brain adapt? Brain imaging techniques give us information about this issue, too.

Brain scans offer insights into the intensity of neural activity when adults are given a variety of laboratory memory tasks. Even with easy memory challenges, like remembering a few items, as you can vividly see in Figure 13.3, older adults show a broader pattern of frontal-lobe activity compared to young adults. So to cope with frontal-lobe deterioration, older people must use more of their cortex to compensate (Park & Reuter-Lorenz, 2009; Reuter-Lorenz & Cappell, 2008).

This finding seems very depressing. Does our brain have to work on overdrive to remember *everything* in later life? Luckily, the answer is no. It is only in *specific* memory situations that older people need to engage in this intense mental work.

A Memory-Systems Perspective on Change

Think of the amazing resilience of some memories and the incredible vulnerability of others. Why do you automatically remember how to hold a tennis racquet even though you have not been on a court for years? Why is "George Washington," the name of our first president, locked in your mind while you are incapable of remembering what you had for dinner three days ago? These kinds of memories seem to differ in ways that go beyond how much effort went into embedding them into our minds. These types of memory seem qualitatively different in a fundamental way.

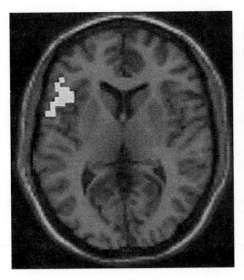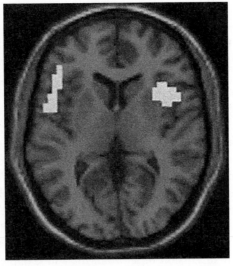

FIGURE 13.3: **Frontal lobe activation in young (left) and older adults (right) in a memory study:** In this fMRI study, researchers measured activation in the frontal lobes when older and younger adults were given a relatively easy laboratory memory task. Notice on the left photo that, while regions of the left hemisphere alone are activated in young adults, the older brains (right image) are working harder to master this task—as here activation occurs in both brain hemispheres.

Source: Reuter-Lorenz & Cappell (2008).

According to the **memory-systems perspective** (Craik, 2000; Tulving, 1985), there are three basic types of memory:

- **Procedural memory** refers to information that we automatically remember, without conscious reflection or thought. An important real-life example involves physical skills. Once we have learned a complex motor activity, such as how to hit a tennis ball, we automatically remember how to perform that skill once we are in that situation again.

- **Semantic memory** is our fund of basic factual knowledge. Remembering that George Washington was our first president and knowing what a tennis racquet is are examples of the kinds of information in this well-learned, crystallized database.

- **Episodic memory** refers to the ongoing events of daily life. When you remember getting on the tennis court last Thursday or what you had for dinner last night, or when a psychologist asks you to recall random names in a memory experiment, you are drawing on episodic memory.

As you can see in these examples and those described in Table 13.2, episodic memory is by far the most fragile system. A month or year from now you will still

memory-systems perspective A framework that divides memory into three types: procedural, semantic, and episodic memory.

procedural memory In the memory-systems perspective, the most resilient (longest-lasting) type of memory; refers to material, such as well-learned physical skills, that we automatically recall without conscious awareness.

semantic memory In the memory-systems perspective, a moderately resilient (long-lasting) type of memory; refers to our ability to recall basic facts.

episodic memory In the memory-systems perspective, the most fragile type of memory, involving the recall of the ongoing events of daily life.

TABLE 13.2: **Examples of the Differences Among Procedural, Semantic, and Episodic Memory**

Procedural Memory	Semantic Memory	Episodic Memory
You get into your blue Toyota and automatically know how to drive.	You know that you have a blue Toyota.	You memorize where you left your blue Toyota in the parking lot of the amusement park.
You automatically find yourself singing the words to "Jingle Bells" when the melody comes on the radio.	You remember that "Jingle Bells" is a song.	You remember the last time you heard "Jingle Bells."
You begin to get excited as you approach your college campus for the fall semester of your senior year.	You know that you are a student at *X* University and that you are a psychology major.	You memorize the locations of classrooms and your professors' names during the first week of the new semester.
I unconsciously find the letters I am typing now on my computer.	I know that I am writing a book called *Experiencing the Lifespan*.	I remember that today I must go to the library and photocopy an article on memory that I will need in preparing this chapter.

remember who George Washington was (semantic memory). You will recall how to hold the tennis racquet and hit the ball (procedural memory). However, even a week later you are likely to forget what you had for dinner on a particular night. Remembering any isolated event—from what day we last played tennis, to what we ate last Tuesday, to the paragraph you are reading right now—is especially vulnerable to the passage of time.

The good news is that on tests of semantic memory older people typically do as well as the young (Dixon and others, 2007). Procedural memory is amazingly long lasting, as we know when we get on the tennis court after not having played for years, and effortlessly hit the ball. The real age loss occurs in episodic memory—our ability to remember the ongoing details of daily life.

This decline in episodic memory is what people notice in their forties when they realize they are having more trouble remembering the name of a person at a party or where they parked the car. Our databank of semantic memories, or crystallized information, stays intact until well into later life, unless we have a fatal disease (recall my discussion of *terminal drop* in Chapter 12). People with Alzheimer's disease can retain procedural memories after the other memory systems are largely gone. They can walk, dress themselves, and even remember (to the horror of caregivers) how to turn on the ignition and drive a car after losing their ability to recall basic facts, such as where they live.

The incredible resilience of procedural memory explains why your 85-year-old aunt, who was an accomplished musician, can still beautifully play tunes on the

Why can this elegant 85-year-old pianist still beautifully entertain you, even though she is beginning to forget basic facts about her life? Because her talents have migrated into *procedural memory*—the final memory system to go.

piano, even though she is now totally incapable of remembering any family members' names. Why is this particular system the last to go? The reason, according to neuropsychologists, is that the information in procedural memory resides in a different region of the brain. When we first learn a complex motor skill, such as driving or playing an instrument, our frontal lobes are heavily involved. Then, after we have thoroughly learned that activity, this knowledge becomes automatic and migrates to a lower brain center, which frees up our frontal cortex for mastering other higher-level thinking tasks (Friedman, 2003). Actually, this is all to the good. If I had to focus on remembering how to type these words on my computer, would I ever be able to simultaneously do the enormously complicated mental work of figuring out how to clearly describe the concepts I am explaining right now?

In sum, the message with regard to age and memory is both worse and also far better than we might have thought: As you get older, you do not have to worry much about being able to remember basic facts. Your storehouse of crystallized knowledge is "really there." However, you will have more trouble memorizing bits of new information, and these losses in episodic memory will show up at a surprisingly early age.

INTERVENTIONS: Keeping Memory Fine-Tuned

What should people do when they notice that their ability to remember life's ongoing details is getting worse? Let's now look at three approaches:

USE SELECTIVE OPTIMIZATION WITH COMPENSATION The first strategy is to use Baltes's three-step process, spelled out in Chapter 12: (1) Selectively focus on what you want to remember—that is, don't let your working memory bins get clogged with irrelevant thoughts. (2) Optimize, or work hard to manipulate material in this system into permanent memory. (3) Use compensation, or external memory aids, when you do not feel confident about remembering information without help.

For example, to remember where you parked your car at the airport: (1) Actively focus on *where* you are parking when you slide your car into the spot. Don't daydream or get distracted by the need to catch the plane. (2) Work hard to encode that specific location in your brain. (3) Write yourself a note or send yourself a text message "G6, bus stop 4"so you won't have to remember that specific place all on your own.

As two memory heads are better than one, older adults can extend Baltes's compensation step to their social partners (Dixon and others, 2007): "I'm going to write this down; but just in case I forget, dear, could you remember where we parked?" Or, as my own social partner (my husband) recently pointed out: "It's 6 P.M., Janet. Don't you teach that Wednesday Aging class tonight?" (Whoops!) Now, let's look at what people can do on their own to slide information through their memory bins.

USE MNEMONIC TECHNIQUES Have you ever noticed that some episodic events are locked in memory (such as your wedding day or the time you and your significant other had that terrible fight), while others quickly fade? Emotional events embed themselves solidly into memory because they activate wider regions of the brain (Dolcos & Cabeza, 2002). Therefore, the key to memorizing any isolated bit of information is to make that material stand out emotionally.

Mnemonic techniques are strategies to make information emotionally vivid. When you use the jingle "Thirty days has September . . ." to remember the number of days in a particular month or, when introduced to a person, you realize, "I won't forget this person's name because my sister is also named Alice," you are enhancing the meaning of bits of random episodic data by using a mnemonic technique.

One way of making material stand out is to conjure up a striking visual image. To remember where you parked at the airport, take a visual snapshot of the location: "Here's the marker G6 right over my head." To remember G6, imagine your 6-year-old niece, Gina, driving your Toyota.

The fact that we learn emotionally vivid information without much effort may explain why our memories vary in such puzzling ways in real life. A history buff soaks up every detail about the Civil War but remains clueless about where he left his socks. Because your passion is developmental science, you do well with very little studying in this course, but it takes you hours to memorize a single page in your biology text. In fact, when they are asked to remember emotionally vivid material, older people actually tend to perform almost as well as the young! (See Kensinger, Krendl, & Corkin, 2006.)

ENHANCE MEMORY SELF-EFFICACY Because we learn emotionally relevant material best, this brings up the thought that standard laboratory memory tests may be unfair to older adults. These studies involve learning random bits of episodic information. So they highlight only the type of memory that dramatically declines with age. Furthermore, because older people have no hands-on experience memorizing meaningless items, they are less likely to spontaneously use mnemonic strategies than the expert-learner college students to whom they are often compared. I must emphasize that everyone—old and young—benefits from being taught mnemonic techniques. But when different age groups are given instructions such as "use imagery to remember that word," this training tends to boost older adults' performance most (Luo, Hendriks, & Craik, 2007; Naveh-Benjamin, Brav, & Levy, 2007).

Then, there is the poisonous, memory-impairing impact of self-doubt. If you were 70 or 80, imagine how you would feel if you entered a traditional-memory study. Wouldn't you be frightened, thinking, "Perhaps this test might show I have Alzheimer's disease"?

Therefore, a critical third strategy for improving memory in old age is to promote memory self-efficacy (Cavanaugh, 2000; West, Bagwell, & Dark-Freudeman, 2008). Older people should take the data referring to neural loss very lightly. Understand that with extra effort *anyone's* memory can be really good. Just as believing that

Ronnie Kaufman/Getty Images

Although his main goal is to greet this woman in a warm, personal way, in order to remember his new friend's name, this elderly man might want to step back and use the mnemonic strategy of forming a mental image, thinking, "I'll remember it's Mrs. Silver because of her hair."

mnemonic technique A strategy for aiding memory, often by using imagery or enhancing the emotional meaning of what needs to be learned.

socioemotional selectivity theory A theory of aging (and the lifespan) put forth by Laura Carstensen, describing how the time we have left to live affects our priorities and social relationships. Specifically, Carstensen believes that as people reach later life, they focus on enhancing the quality of the present and place priority on spending time with their closest attachment figures.

intelligence is a fixed genetic entity hurts children, when the elderly think they have a basic brain deficit—and so withdraw from challenging learning situations—they *ensure* that their memory will be poor!

Actually, in a rare, real-world memory study, older adults proved that motivation matters a great deal in daily life. Psychologists asked elderly and young adult groups to remember to perform an action in the future: "Call me on Sunday at three o'clock." Here, the more conscientious older people performed just as well as the young (Kvavilashvili & Fisher, 2007)! After all, despite firmly believing that memory is "deficient" in old age, who would you trust more to remember to feed your cat when you are on vacation—the teenager next door or your elderly neighbor down the street?

Personality

Everyone believes that memory declines with age. But think about our contradictory stereotypes about late life personality. Are elderly people demoralized and distressed or upbeat, together, and calm? Let's first look at an interesting theory that makes the case for late life as the happiest life stage, then explore under which conditions this upbeat perspective can be very right or very wrong, and finally target some keys to feeling fulfilled in old age.

Focusing on Time Left to Live: Socioemotional Selectivity Theory

Imagine that, like Theresa and Sal, you are elderly and well aware that you may have only a few years left to live. How might your priorities about what is important in life change? The idea that our place on the lifespan alters our agendas and goals is the basic premise of Laura Carstensen's **socioemotional selectivity theory.**

According to Carstensen (1995), during the first half of adult life, our basic push is to look to the future. We are eager to make it in the wider world. We want to reach a better place at some later date. As we grow older and realize that our future is limited, we refocus our priorities. We want to make the most of our present life.

Carstensen believes that this focus on making the most of every moment means that old age has the potential to be the *happiest* time of life. When our agenda lies in the future, we often forgo our immediate desires in the service of a later goal. Instead of telling off the professor or boss who insults us, we hold our tongue because this authority figure holds the key to getting ahead. We are nice to that nasty person, or go to that dinner party we would rather pass up in order to advance socially or in

Socioemotional selectivity theory, with its principle that older people focus only on the activities they really love, makes perfect sense of why we see young people looking bored because they feel they "must" go to a party (when they would rather stay home), while the elderly couple on the right are passionately getting into the swing of things.

Shannon Fagan/Getty Images

Martin Barraud/Getty Images

our career. We accept the anxiety-ridden months we face when we first move to an unfamiliar city or begin a new job because we expect to feel better than ever in a year or two.

In later life, we are less interested in where we *will* be going. So we refuse to let insulting remarks pass, waste time with unpleasant people, or enter anxiety-provoking situations because they may have a payoff at some later point. Almost unconsciously, we decide, "I don't have that long to live. I have to spend my time doing what makes me feel good emotionally *right now*."

Furthermore, when our passion lies in making the most of the present, Carstensen argues, our social priorities change. During childhood, adolescence, and emerging adulthood our basic thrust is to leave our attachment figures. We want to expand our social horizons, form new close relationships, and connect with exciting new people who can teach us new things. Once we have achieved our life goals, we are less interested in developing new close attachments. We already have our family and network of caring friends. So we center our lives on our spouse, our best friends, our children—the people we love the most.

To test whether this age-related shift really does occur, Carstensen's research team asked elderly and young people, "Who would you rather spend time with—a close family member, a recent acquaintance, or the author of a recent book?" Young people's choices were spread among the three possible partners. Older people chose overwhelmingly to be with the family member, their closest attachment figure in life (Fung, Lai, & Ng, 2001).

Socioemotional selectivity theory, with its principle that, in old age, we choose to spend as much time as possible with our closest attachment figures, explains why simply spending time with each other and their grandchild is this elderly Japanese couple's passion in life.

When Do We Prioritize the Present Regardless of Our Life Stage?

But is this shift in priorities *simply* a function of being old? The answer is no. People with AIDS also voted to spend an evening with a familiar close person. So did people who were asked to imagine that they were about to move across the country alone. According to Carstensen, whenever we see our future as limited, we selectively pare down our social contacts, spending as much time as possible with the people we care about the most.

Socioemotional selectivity theory explains why—although normally we are content to live a continent away—when we are in danger of losing a loved one, we want to be physically close. You fly in from California to spend time with your beloved grandma in New York when she is seriously ill. You insist on spending the weekend with your high school friend who is leaving for a tour of duty in the military in some dangerous part of the world.

The theory accounts for the choices my cousin Clinton made when he was diagnosed with lymphoma in his early twenties. An exceptionally gifted architect, Clinton gave up his promising career and retired to rural New Hampshire to build houses, hike, and ski for what turned out to be another quarter-century of life. Clinton's funeral, when he died at age 50, was an unforgettable celebration—a testament to a person who, although his life was shorter than most, was able to live fully for longer than many people who survive to twice this age. Have you ever seen the principles of socioemotional selectivity theory in operation in your own life?

Old Age: The Best and Worst of Life Stages

This passion to make the most of every moment and to spend time with loved ones when we see our future as limited makes good psychological sense. As you might predict, based on Baltes's principle of selection, studies around the world confirm that in old age people pare down their social contacts. They either focus just on their family (Shaw and others, 2007); or, in individualistic societies such as ours, where friendships are important, prioritize their family and closest friends (Yeung & Fung, 2007). But is Carstensen correct that people are *happiest* in later life?

As you saw in the last chapter, a surprising amount of research suggests yes. Contrary to our stereotypes, one huge U.S. epidemiological study showed that people over age 65 had *lower* rates of emotional problems than adults of any other age (Weissman and others, 1985). Remember that the elderly have a more upbeat view of human nature. During the sixties, the ratio of positive emotions to negative emotions reaches its life peak.

What is happening here? The answer, according to recent laboratory research, may be that older people are skilled at minimizing their negative emotional states (Scheibe & Blannchard-Fields, 2009). In one study involving risk-taking for monetary rewards, Carstensen and her colleagues found that an elderly group felt just as happy as young adults when they expected to win money. But in dramatic contrast to the young, the older people didn't get upset *at all* when they believed they would lose (Neilson, Knutson, & Carstensen, 2008). People of every age, as we know from the previous section, recall emotional information best. However, the elderly perform especially poorly (compared to younger people) when they need to remember upsetting images, words, or facts (Grühn, Scheibe, and Baltes, 2007; Lockenhoof & Carstensen, 2007; Murphy & Isaacowitz, 2008; Tomaszczyk, Fernandes, & MacLeod, 2008).

Conversely, when the challenge involves shutting out disturbing stimuli, older adults do exceptionally well. Psychologists told older and young volunteers to "think about something that makes you feel good." Then, the groups watched an upsetting video and were instructed to use this refocusing technique (think about pleasant images). In mastering this emotion management task, the elderly people were far superior to the young (Phillips and others, 2008).

It seems logical that, over years of living, the crucial internal skill of regulating our emotions would improve. But there also are concrete external reasons why old age should be a worry-free life stage. Imagine no longer having the hassles of raising children or being liberated from the gut-churning pressures to perform at work. Older people report fewer day-to-day stresses than the young (Charles & Almeida, 2007; von Hipple, Henry, & Matovic, 2008). An added bonus is that, in old age, the outside world may treat you with special care. In one study, when researchers asked adults how they would react in a difficult interpersonal situation, people said they would be prone to hold off confronting someone if that individual was old (Fingerman, Miller, & Charles, 2008). An elderly guest alerted my class to this interesting perk when he mentioned, "The best thing about being 88 is that everyone is incredibly nice!" If strangers took time to open doors for you, people forgave your foibles, and everyone made a special effort to be kind, wouldn't you feel better about the human race?

But at this point, you may be thinking, "Something is wrong with this picture." What about the millions of older people who the world *doesn't* treat so kindly—the aged who are socially isolated and left to languish in poverty during their so-called "golden years"? When societies marginalize their older citizens economically or when older people feel marginalized, isolated, and unloved, old age can be a terrible time (Krause, 2007; Rothermund & Brandstadter, 2003).

Most important, there is a difference between being young-old and old-old. Yes, depression rates are low among people in their sixties, but the prevalence of this problem climbs dramatically after age 75 (Rothermund & Brandstadter, 2003). In advanced old age, people *are* more vulnerable to being cut off socially (Li and Liang, 2007). As we know, of course, during the old-old years, people are far more likely to be in poor health.

So yes, late life is wonderful when people can fully *enjoy* their present lives. Happiness is common among healthy young-old people such as

Having help putting your jacket on is likely to be a new life experience for this man. How would you feel about "the goodness of humanity," if at 80 or 90, people started treating you in this kind of unusually caring way?

Theresa and Sal, who have the funds to travel the world. When the disabilities of advanced old age strike, or, as you saw in the last chapter, when death looms on the horizon, people can become seriously depressed. One 90-year-old nursing-home resident named Sophia described to a researcher just how meaningless life can be at the very end of the lifespan when she anguished: "I want my life to end now. No one talks to me except for you…. I just lie here sick, and all I do is think of old times" (Dwyer, Nordenfelt, & Ternestedt, 2008, p. 102). Soon after this interview, Sophia got her wish. She died in her sleep.

Still, let's not stereotype every 90- or 100-year-old person as in a dismal holding pattern, waiting for death. As you can see in my interview with Jules, in the Experiencing the Lifespan box, some people do live exceptionally gratifying lives well into advanced old age.

EXPERIENCING THE LIFESPAN: FULLY FUNCTIONING AT AGE 94

It was a hot August morning at Vanderbilt University as friends, colleagues, and students from their twenties to their seventies gathered to celebrate the publication of his book. Their voices often cracked with emotion as they rose to testify: "You changed my life. You are an inspiration—the best therapist and supervisor I've ever had." Frail, bent over, beginning to doze—suddenly, 94-year-old Jules came to life. "My book traces the development of my ideas about ideal mental health. It's been a 60-year journey to identify the 'fully-functioning person' that I'm still trying to get right today." Who is this revered role model (and my very own therapist)? What made Jules the person he is, and what is his philosophy about aging and life? Let's listen in to this interview.

My mother took the last boat to leave Europe before the First World War broke out, to join my father and brothers in the United States. So in 1915, I was lucky enough to actually arrive in this world (or be born). As the third of four boys growing up in Baltimore, we children were incredibly close because, as the only Jewish family in our neighborhood, we were living in an alien world, a noxious world. We were surrounded by other immigrants who believed that only Christians had the right ideas. I vividly remember the neighborhood kids regularly taunting us as Jesus killers as we walked to school. So we learned from an early age that the world can be a dangerous place. What this experience did was to take us all in the opposite direction . . . to see every person as precious, to develop attitudes that were really worldwide.

When I was a teenager, and asked myself, "What is important in life?" two things came to me. One was the simple word "relationships," . . . to have a fundamental faith in people. It was clear that human beings had a long way to go to reach maturity, because there was so much violence in the world. But you need to act ethically and lovingly and, above all, reach out. I also looked to the Bible for guidance, asking myself, "What do the ancient prophets tell us about living an ethical life?" During the Second World War my brothers and I took the stand that we would never participate in violence, and so all four of us were conscientious objectors. I knew I could never pick up a gun and kill another human being.

I started out my work life as a public school teacher in Baltimore, which was very fulfilling. I had no desire to get a Ph.D., but when I read a paper by Carl Rogers* in 1948, who was developing his client-centered therapy, I was electrified: Understand the person from his own framework; don't be judgmental; look beyond the diagnosis to the real human being. By listening empathically and relating unconditionally, you can guide a person toward health. Those years with Carl (with our group sharing my ideas about the fully-functioning person) were incredibly exciting—principles that defined my work and my relationships in life.

I'm still the same person I always was, the same adolescent now hiding in the body of a 94-year-old man—but with much more experience in living! The main difference is that, physically, I am handicapped [with congestive heart failure] and so I use a shorter horizon in my thinking. Instead of thinking about a year ahead, I might think about a week, because of the greater uncertainty. . . . I am well aware that I could die any time. But it's unthinkable to me not to continue to do therapy, because when I'm with a person, I'm in relationship with them. I'm incomplete if I am not expressing my passion in life.

It's important never to put life in the past tense. You don't wrap it up. There is no such thing as "aging" or "retirement." You are always learning and developing. When I was younger and looked to the prophets of the Bible for guidance, I gravitated to the book of Micah. Micah sums up my philosophy for living in this one sentence: "What doeth the lord require of me but to do justly, to love mercy, and to walk humbly with thy god."

*Rogers was one of the premier twentieth-century psychologists.

integrity Erik Erikson's eighth psychosocial stage in which elderly people decide that their life missions have been fulfilled and so accept impending death.

©Radius Images/Corbis

Notice this man's quiet sense of pleasure at realizing: "Yes, I still can get around!" If older people feel "efficacious" about important life activities, they can keep their *joie de vivre,* even when they need a walker and live in a nursing home.

Decoding Some Keys to Happiness in Old Age

Do you have an old-age role model such as Jules, someone who is living vigorously at age 90 or 94? What makes these special people stand out? For one thing, notice that Jules doesn't define himself as "old." He believes that we keep developing as people until the day we die. In fact, in one longitudinal study, older adults who felt that aging meant further development were more likely to live longer than those who believed that aging equaled decline (Wurm, Tesh-Romer, & Tomasik, 2007). Another striking quality about Jules is his incredible generativity and the fact that he has clearly reached Erikson's final milestone of **integrity** (see Table 13.3). Jules knows he has lived according to the prophetic guidelines that he views at the core of having a meaningful life.

Erikson believed that, to reach integrity, older people must review their lives and make peace with what they have previously done. But as you saw with Sophia, the demoralized nursing-home resident, happiness in old age involves more than simply focusing on one's past. As with Jules, it means feeling a sense of usefulness (generativity) and meaning in your *present* life. Longitudinal studies also suggest that older people who don't feel useful tend to become disabled and die at a younger age (Gruenewald and others, 2007, 2009). A related key to living fully during old age is having a sense of self-efficacy. If older people feel in control in a life domain they care deeply about, they feel a strong sense of personal meaning in life (Krause & Shaw, 2003).

Some amazing elderly people, such as Jules, derive their self-efficacy and sense of personal meaning from continuing to do therapy or publishing a book at age 94. Others find fulfillment in achieving simpler goals. Listen to Alice, another aged resident living at the same nursing home as Sophia, who—unlike this woman—derived considerable pleasure in her life: "Do you know what makes me happy? To be able to go the toilet on my own. . . . I'm so grateful that I can take care of myself as much as I can." (quoted in Dwyer, Nordenfelt, & Ternestedt, 2008, p. 101).

TABLE 13.3: **Erikson's Psychosocial Stages and Tasks**

Life Stage	Primary Task
Infancy (birth to 1 year)	Basic trust versus mistrust
Toddlerhood (1 to 2 years)	Autonomy versus shame and doubt
Early childhood (3 to 6 years)	Initiative versus guilt
Middle childhood (6 years to puberty)	Industry versus inferiority
Adolescence (teens into twenties)	Identity versus role confusion
Young adulthood (twenties to early forties)	Intimacy versus isolation
Middle adulthood (forties to sixties)	Generativity versus stagnation
Late adulthood (late sixties and beyond)	**Integrity versus despair**

According to Erikson, our task in later adulthood is to look back over our life to see if we accomplished what we set out to do. Older people who know they have lived fully are not afraid to die. When older adults have serious regrets about their lives, they may be terrified of death and feel a sense of despair.

The bottom-line message: Feel competent in a critical life domain, be generative, stay "in relationship," continue to see yourself as growing as a human being—these are some keys to successfully aging well into advanced old age. (They also are good tips for living successfully during any stage of adult life!)

INTERVENTIONS: Using the Memory and Personality Research at Home and Work

Now, let's summarize *all* of these research messages. How can we help older people improve their memory skills? How should you think about the relationship priorities of older loved ones, and when should you worry about their emotional states? Here are some suggestions:

- As late-life memory difficulties are most likely to show up in situations where there is "lots going on" and when it's difficult to focus, give older people ample time to learn material and provide them with a non-distracting environment (more about this environmental engineering in Chapter 14).

- Don't stereotype older adults as having a "bad" memory. Remember that semantic memory stays stable with age, and teaching mnemonic strategies works. Help older people develop a sense of self-efficacy by suggesting this chapter's memory tips. Also, however, be realistic. Tell the older person, "If you notice a decline in your ability to attend to life's details (episodic memory), that's normal. It does NOT mean you have Alzheimer's disease" (Dixon and others, 2007).

- Give older adults chances to exercise their personal passions. Remember that when we are emotionally engaged, information slides more effortlessly through our working memory bins.

- Using the insights that socioemotional selectivity theory offers, don't expect older people to automatically want to socialize or make new friends. When an elderly loved one says, "I don't want to go to the senior citizen center. All I care about is my family," she may be making an age-appropriate response.

- Don't imagine that older people are unhappy. Actually, assume the reverse is true, especially in the young-old years. However, be alert to depression in someone who is old-old, physically frail, and socially isolated. The key to preventing depression in old age is the same as at any age: being generative, feeling competent, and having a sense of meaning and purpose in life.

TYING IT ALL TOGETHER

1. Dwayne is planning on teaching lifespan development at the senior center. He's excited, but until now, he's taught only younger people. He is concerned about older people and memory and wonders what he might do differently. Based on your understanding of which memory situations give older people the most trouble, suggest some changes Dwayne might make in his teaching.

2. Classify each of the following memory challenges as involving episodic memory, semantic memory, or procedural memory:

    a. Someone asks you your street address.
    b. Someone asks you what you just read in this chapter.
    c. You go bike riding.

3. Which of the abilities in the previous question (a) will an older loved one retain the longest if she gets Alzheimer's disease, and (b) which memory ability may start to decline relatively early in life?

4. You are eavesdropping on three elderly friends at a local café as they discuss their feelings about life. According to socioemotional selectivity theory, which *two* of the following comments might you expect to hear?

   a. Frances says, "Now that I've gotten older, I want to start meeting as many new people as possible."
   b. Allen reports, "I've been enjoying life in the past few years more than ever. I'm taking time to savor every moment—and what a pleasure it is to do just what I want!"
   c. Milly mentions, "I've been trying to spend as much time as possible with my family. These are the people who matter to me the most."

5. A counselor friend tells you that, based on Erikson's theory, in treating older people, she focuses on getting older clients to review their lives. Based on this chapter, critique your friend's therapeutic approach and suggest some other strategies that might be more beneficial to help older adults at risk for depression.

Answers to the Tying It All Together questions can be found on the last page of this chapter.

Later-Life Transitions

Now, let's look at how people derive a sense of meaning as they confront the major life transitions of retirement and widowhood.

Retirement

When they retired in their early sixties, Theresa and Sal were right on target for the recently standard social clock norms. Over the last half of the twentieth century, at the same time that late-life life expectancy was floating upward, the average retirement age was sliding down. In 1950, 3 out of every 4 U.S. workers stayed at their jobs until at least age 65. By the beginning of the twenty-first century, the real U.S. average retirement age was close to 62, and only 1 in 4 U.S. adults was still in the labor force by the "traditional" retirement age (Kinsella & Velkoff, 2001). Moreover, in 1950, the typical American worker could expect to spend only six years in the retired state before he died. A half-century later, a new retiree could expect to live for almost two extra decades of life! (See Hardy, 2002.)

What caused retirement to expand to a full life stage, and what does this transition look like around the world? How is the landscape of U.S. retirement changing? Why do people retire, and what happens when they take that step? What are some core retirement issues that we currently face in our economy "in transition" as the baby boomers flood into their older years?

Setting the Context: Scanning the Global Economic Scene

Retirement is a socially constructed life stage. It became possible when governments began to provide a financial cushion for their older citizens to live without working. As government income-support programs proliferated during the last half of the twentieth century, retirement became a full stage of life in much of the developed world (see Figure 13.4).

This cushion, however, does not exist in some developing countries, where people must continue to work until they are disabled or die. In Bangladesh, Jamaica, and Mexico, more than half of all people over age 65 are in the labor force. Compare this to Italy, where life expectancy is far higher, but almost everyone retires by their early sixties or before (Zappala and others, 2008).

Actually, because of their lavish government income-support programs, Western Europeans exit the workforce at a surprisingly young age. By their late fifties and early sixties, 2 out of 3 E.U. workers has already retired (Taylor, 2007). However, among fairly affluent nations, government-funded retirement programs vary dramatically

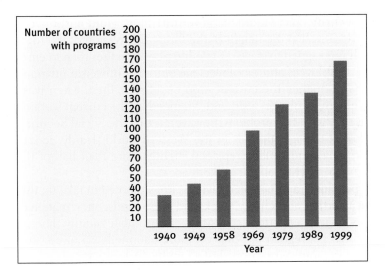

FIGURE 13.4: **Number of countries with government-funded old-age retirement programs, 1940–1999:** Notice that, by the end of the twentieth century, many countries provided their citizens with income-support programs for the elderly (and other needy groups). Notice also that the number of governments that established these programs began to rapidly take off in the 1960s.

Source: Kinsella & Velkoff (2001), Figure 11-2, p. 117.

from extensive to nil. For insights into these differences, let's first visit Germany, stop in the Far East, and then conclude by focusing on the United States.

GERMANY: MORE COMFORTABLE AFTER RETIREMENT THAN BEFORE. Germany stands out as a model of what the government can provide to retirees. In fact, in the late nineteenth century, Germany instituted the first public government-funded retirement program in the world. Retirement in Germany is mainly financed by employee and employer payroll taxes, in a system similar to the one we have in the United States. Unlike the United States, however, here the guiding philosophy has always been to keep people financially *comfortable* during their older years. When the typical German worker retires, the government replaces roughly three-fourths of that person's working income for life. In Germany, workers have no worries about falling into poverty in old age. Because the government stipend rises depending on increases in the cost of living, older people in this nation typically have had *more* spending power as they travel further into their retirement years (Hungerford, 2003).

CHINA: RELYING ON FAMILY AND FEELING INSECURE. At the opposite extreme is China, which encourages its citizens to save for retirement by setting up personal pensions but does not currently offer any structured, government-funded retirement plan (Calvo & Williamson, 2007). Aging adults in this traditionally collectivist country are in a difficult position. Historically, Chinese children were required to support their parents in old age. But today, this nation is making the transition to a more modern, Western point of view, in which the younger generation no longer feels compelled to "honor thy parents' financial needs."

Late-middle-aged people living in Hong Kong (that affluent, Westernized, largely autonomous Chinese city), caught in these cultural crosswinds, express special anxiety about their old-age fate. Many have not saved for retirement. They fear they can no longer rely on their children for help. They know the government will not step in. They are looking forward, with trepidation, to what will happen to them when they get old (Lee & Law, 2004).

THE UNITED STATES: DETERIORATING PENSIONS AND SAVINGS AND SOME GUARANTEED GOVERNMENT HELP. The United States lies midway between these extremes. Our nation does offer the famous guaranteed old-age insurance program called Social Security. But the income Social Security provides does not allow for a comfortable retirement. Our nation does strongly encourage workers to save for retirement through private pension plans, but this cushion is now far less generous. An increasing number of American adults enter retirement with no pensions at all.

Social Security The U.S. government's national retirement support program.

private pensions The major source of nongovernmental income support for retirees, in which the individual worker and the employer put a portion of each paycheck into an account to help finance retirement.

Social Security, the landmark government program instituted by President Franklin D. Roosevelt at the height of the Great Depression of the 1930s, operates as a safety net. It is designed to stave off late-life poverty rather than to ensure a comfortable old age. Employees and employers pay into this universal program during their working years to finance the current crop of retirees; then, when it is their turn to retire, these elderly adults get a stipend, financed by the current working population, for as long as they live. The problem, however, is that the Social Security system offers one of the lowest old-age stipends in the Western world (Hardy, 2002). On average, Social Security has traditionally replaced slightly more than half of the typical person's income at work (Kinsella & Velkoff, 2001).

Private pensions (and personal savings) are supposed to take up the slack. Workers put aside a portion of each paycheck, and these funds, often matched by employer contributions, go into a tax-free account that accumulates equity. Then, when people retire, they either get regular pay-outs or, more often today, a lump sum on which to live. Furthermore, some employers (but a rapidly declining number) offer health-care coverage to their retired employees (Johnson, 2009).

The central role of private pensions in financing retirement reflects the premium that the United States has historically placed on individual initiative. As with our reluctance to provide universal health care, traditionally, we have been leery about the expense and welfare-state implications of a federal government plan. We prefer to provide tax incentives that work to encourage workers to plan for retirement on their own.

The problem is that, in recent decades, U.S. pension plans have been restructured to shift the burden to save for retirement to individual workers. Moreover, during the 2008 economic crisis, baby boomers witnessed the value of their pensions and of their major asset—their homes—dramatically erode. Bankruptcies have been soaring among the age group in their fifties (Thorne, Warren, & Sullivan, 2008). The classic middle-class, privately financed retirement cushion has become patchy and frayed. People in low-wage jobs, such as servers or the cashiers at your local convenience store, are worse off. They enter retirement without any pensions or savings at all (Stanford & Usita, 2002).

This man would probably rather be sunning at a beach than sweating over these beef patties. But given Social Security's meager allotment, and having no retirement nest egg, this low-wage job may be his only option during his so-called "golden" retirement years.

Today, these considerations are changing the age at which people expect to retire. Even before the 2008 financial meltdown, many U.S. baby boomers said they would have to continue working past 65 because they could not afford to leave their jobs (Mermin, Johnson, & Murphy, 2007; see also Johnson, 2009). Actually, especially for low-income elderly—primarily women and rural residents—retirement at age 65 is *currently* a fantasy. Of the more than 1 in 4 U.S. workers who work into their late sixties (Johnson, 2009), one national poll showed a significant percentage were employed in minimum-wage jobs to make ends meet (Slack & Jensen, 2008). Affluent retirees, like Theresa and Sal, who left work well before the 2008 financial crisis hit, are not out of the economic woods. As people move further into retirement and their pension income and savings get depleted, they depend on Social Security for a larger chunk of their income. This spells financial trouble. The result: U.S. retirees typically experience declining living standards in their old-old years (Hungerford, 2003).

The bottom-line message is that, in the United States, retirement may be turning into a shorter, more fragile phase of life. Moreover, the U.S. income inequalities highlighted throughout this book persist into the older years. Economic hardship during middle age foreshadows economic difficulties during later life (Hungerford, 2007). Even people who have entered retirement as firmly middle class are vulnerable to sliding into poverty as they travel into their eighties and beyond.

Now that I have sketched out the often negative financial forces affecting retirement, it's time to explore some other influences that go into the mix.

Exploring the Complex Push/Pull Retirement Decision

Imagine that you are in your late fifties or early sixties and considering retiring. As I've suggested, your primary consideration is economic: "Do I have enough money to take this step?" (Mermin, Johnson, & Murphy, 2007). However, a second force that comes into play, particularly for low-income workers, is health: "Am I physically capable of continuing at my job?" (Szinovacz, 2003; Taylor & Doverspike, 2003). There may be another, insidious influence prompting your decision: age discrimination at work.

FOCUS ON A TOPIC: THE IMPACT OF AGE DISCRIMINATION

Age discrimination in the United States is illegal. People cannot be laid off because of their age (see Neumark, 2009). But despite the law, especially in large companies, there can be immense pressures to "get rid of" older employees.

Put yourself in the position of the CEO of a corporation. Your older, long-standing employees have higher salaries. They cost you more in benefits, such as health care. You cannot simply fire these people for being "old." What do you do?

One strategy is to offer these workers a special carrot, a one-shot pension incentive to retire. However, there can be an implicit threat: Retire now and get these benefits—or get laid off. As one early retiree who worked for Bethlehem Steel reported:

> *"They said if we didn't leave the company voluntarily (taking the early retirement incentive), they would have to reduce the work force at their discretion. Ordinarily we were a two-man office, but when my boss retired a year before, he was not replaced. . . . After vacation you would have twice as much work because it wasn't being done by anyone else.*

> (quoted in Williamson, Rinehart, & Blank, 1992, p. 43)

Encouraging early retirement via a special buyout and/or making the job so onerous that long-standing employees "want" to leave are well-established techniques for propelling people to "go gently" into their retirement years. But experts believe the most widespread, pernicious form of age discrimination may relate not to getting rid of existing employees, but to choosing *whom* to hire (Dennis & Thomas, 2007).

In many ways, older workers make superior employees. Studies show they are more ethical, more reliable, more safety conscious. Contrary to our stereotypes, they are even more compliant and less likely to take time off for being sick (Ng & Feldman, 2008; Streb, Voelpel, & Leibold, 2008). Still, these traits may not matter much when it comes down to deciding whom to employ (Dennis & Thomas, 2007). It's practically impossible to prove that "too old" was the reason for a given applicant being consigned to the "won't hire" pile (Newmark, 2009). However, laboratory studies suggest that, given hypothetical older and younger job seekers, employers routinely go for the younger adult (see Dennis & Thomas, 2007).

How does this bias affect real people in the real world? Consider the fate of my close friend Justine, fired from her sales manager job at age 50. Justine, a single mom with a teenager, has been unable to find work for months, even in a lower-status job, and recently was forced to apply for food stamps. Suppose you were a thirty-something employer who needed to hire a sales associate at your store. Look into your heart and be honest. Would you feel more comfortable hiring Justine or a job applicant your own age?

age discrimination Illegally laying off workers or failing to hire or promote them on the basis of age.

So far, I've been focusing on the dismal forces that affect retirement: Financial problems keep people in the workforce unwillingly. Age discrimination or health issues push older workers reluctantly to retire. I've been neglecting the fact that deciding to retire or not retire is often an active, efficacious, *positive* choice. Many baby boomers say they want to keep working after age 65 because they love their jobs (Galinsky, 2007). Many people, like Theresa and Sal, can't wait to retire in order to enter an exciting, new phase of life.

Who is passionate to stay in the labor force until their seventies or up to age 85? As you might imagine, these elderly workers often are healthy and highly educated (McNamara & Williamson, 2004; Rix, 2002). They are people, such as Jules in the Experiencing the Lifespan box on page 403, who find tremendous flow in their careers. One survey suggested that these older people are right. For white-collar workers, working full time after retirement tends to stave off depression in the older years (Christ and others, 2007). But what about people who do retire? Are they depressed or thrilled after taking this step?

Life as a Retiree

The answer is "it depends." People who have left their jobs unwillingly—those who would rather still be working—tend to feel unhappy after they retire (Calvo, Haverstick, & Sass, 2009; Solinge & Henkins, 2008). Having serious money worries or health concerns, as you might imagine, also works to poison the retirement years. Actually, the main qualities that make for happiness during retirement are identical to the attributes that make later life a *generally* happy life stage. Retirement smiles on people who are healthy, who are married, and who have the economic resources to really enjoy life (Pinquart & Schindler, 2007; van Solinge & Henkins, 2008). So you can predict whether a relative is going to be satisfied in retirement by knowing two facts: Did this person *want* to leave work? What are the overall conditions of this individual's life?

You also might want to look to personal qualities. Is your relative intrinsically motivated, interested in learning or developing as a person? If so, that person is likely to see retirement as a challenging new phase of life (Stephan, Fouquereau, & Fernandez, 2008). Does your family member have a compelling, serious leisure interest such as drama or dancing (Brown, McGuire, & Voelkl, 2008)? If your answer is yes, that individual has a built-in gift to enjoy the retirement years. Has this person been volunteering before she left work (Pinquart & Schindler, 2007)? Volunteering in midlife and during retirement—but not overdoing it—is associated with happiness, too (Nimrod, Janke, & Kleiber, 2009; Windsor, Anstey, & Rodgers, 2008). As you saw in Chapter 12, who we are as adults is relatively consistent. So it makes sense that how people act as retirees has much in common with who they were during their working lives (Atchley, 1989; Nimrod, Janke, & Kleiber, 2009; see Table 13.4 for a summary of these forces).

As you might imagine, one key to finding special joy in retirement is to follow Baltes's principle of "selective optimization": Focus on your top-ranking preferred activities; spend more time engaged in those labors of love (Nimrod, Janke, & Kleiber, 2009). It's a mistake, however, to imagine that, after retiring, those top-ranking labors of love must remain exactly the same. Retirement can also be all about new beginnings and life change. In fact, this life stage has many similarities to emerging

---

TABLE 13.4: Four Questions to Ask to Predict if a Person Will Be Happy as a Retiree: A Section Summary

1. Did this person *want to* retire, or was he forced out of the workforce?

2. Is this person married (happily!), in good health, and does she have sufficient income?

3. Is this individual intellectually interested, and/or does she have an absorbing hobby?

4. Does this person like to volunteer and/or want to use his time to get involved in a new activity or go back to school?

adulthood. It is a time to construct new identities, to test out other lifestyles, to discover different aspects of the self.

Some people, like Theresa and Sal, travel. Others take up new passions, like skydiving, or try to fulfill generative impulses that have been placed on hold during their working years (Savishinsky, 2004). A social activist joins the Peace Corps or works for Amnesty International. A business executive volunteers his services at SCORE (Senior Corps of Retired Executives), advising young people about setting up small businesses. A committed Catholic, such as Theresa, spends her days helping at church. Some people may choose to construct a new late-life identity as a student or scholar.

These older people are enrolled in an English class in a special senior citizens college in Japan. Because many people use their retirement years to devote themselves to the human passion for learning, special educational programs such as Elderhostel are flourishing in nations around the world.

A dazzling array of options are available to older adults who use retirement as a time for expanding their minds, from reduced-cost programs for returning students at universities to special older-adult institutes, such as **Elderhostel**. Here is what one joyous participant had to say about his experience at this international education-travel program, in which, for one exciting summer week, people age 55 and over can choose to enroll in courses taught by professors on campuses around the world.

After my program at the University of Notre Dame in Indiana I have an overwhelming memory. It was simply wonderful. . . . Dr. James Ellis . . . made mankind come alive, showed us how our species is swiftly and not wisely changing the world. His illustrations were stunning: "We Americans are using 75 percent of the world's calories." (And I didn't want to make him a liar as I passed through the cafeteria line.) . . . Next, Sandy Vanslinger put us through our paces in the aerobics class. . . . With my damaged ticker I was concerned, but . . . I felt great. . . . The quality of the program was so magnificent that I felt I was in heaven. . . . Notre Dame, I won't forget you!

(quoted in Mills, 1993, pp. 108–111)

As these examples show, in our society retiring from work can be the opposite of retiring from life. These years are for vigorously connecting to the world (Ekerdt, 1986). However, there is a different cultural model of retirement. In the Hindu perspective, later life is a time to disengage from worldly concerns. Ideally, people become wandering ascetics, renouncing their connections to loved ones and earthly pleasures in preparation for death (Savishinsky, 2004). Although this goal of disengagement is rarely followed in practice (after all, our need to be closely attached is a basic human drive!), let's not assume that our "do not go gently into the sunset," keep-active retirement ideal applies around the world.

Summing Things Up: Social Policy Retirement Issues

Now, let's summarize these section messages by focusing on some critical social issues with regard to the retirement years.

- *Retirement is an at-risk life stage.* In the United States, the decline in pension income and savings is the immediate force that threatens to make the once-standard practice of retiring for decades obsolete. Another troubling economic issue, however, relates to the solvency of Social Security, as the massive baby boom cohort fully marches into later life. In 1950, there were about 16 workers for every U.S. retiree. Over the next two decades, the **old-age dependency ratio,** or proportion of working adults to retirees, will decline to almost 2 to 1 (Johnson, 2009). Social Security was never intended to finance an entire stage of life. It was instituted when life expectancy was far shorter, as a cushion when physical problems made it impossible for people to work. The U.S. government has already increased the age of eligibility for full Social Security benefits to 67. Will retirement return to its original meaning as a support for old-age incapacity as the twenty-first century unfolds?

Elderhostel An education-travel program that offers people age 55 and older special learning experiences at universities and other locations across the United States and around the world.

old-age dependency ratio The fraction of people over age 60 to younger working-age adults (ages 15 to 59). This ratio is expected to rise dramatically as the baby boomers retire.

- *Older workers are an at-risk group of employees.* From people being offered pension incentives to retire early to not hiring older workers—as you vividly saw—implicit age discrimination at work is alive and well (Neumark, 2009; Palmore, 1990a; Rix, 2002; Rosen & Jerdee, 1995). But there is a silver lining. Until recently, employers have had their pick from a huge pool of workers. When the massive baby boom cohort retires, there will no longer be the same inexhaustible labor supply. Given that many baby boomers will need to work during retirement, will employers respond by changing their negative attitudes toward older employees?

- *Older people may be more at risk of being poor.* During the 1960s and 1970s, the United States took the landmark step of dramatically reducing poverty among older adults. Congress extended Social Security benefits. Our nation passed that crucial government-funded health-care program called Medicare. Old-age economic hardship is currently the fate for pockets of older adults (see Vartanian & McNamara, 2002)—low-wage workers who need to keep working during their "so-called" retirement years; middle-class retirees faced with sharply declining income as they travel into their eighties and beyond. Will poverty become a common life state among the over-65 population *in general* in future years?

Widowhood

Although we may worry about its future, many of us look forward to retirement with joy. That emotion does not apply to widowhood. In a classic study of life stress, researchers ranked the death of a spouse as life's most traumatic change (Holmes & Rahe, 1967). Today's baby boom adults will have some built-in lifestyle preparation for coping with this trauma because they may have lived alone for some time after being divorced. However, as with Theresa and Sal, people who are currently in their late seventies and eighties often got married in their early twenties and then stayed married for life.

Imagine losing your life partner after 50 or 60 years. You are unmoored and adrift, cut off from your main attachment figure. Tasks that may have been totally foreign, such as understanding the finances or fixing the faucet, fall on you alone. You must remake an identity whose central focus has been "married person" since your emerging-adult years. British psychiatrist Colin Parkes (1987) beautifully described how the world tilts: "Even when words remain the same, their meaning changes. The family is no longer the same as it was. Neither is home or a marriage" (p. 93).

How do people mourn this life loss and adapt over time to losing a partner? How do widows and widowers cope, and what specific strategies seem to help?

Exploring Mourning

During the early days and months after a loved one dies, people are often obsessed with the events surrounding the final event (Lindemann, 1944; Parkes, 1972). Especially if the death was relatively sudden, husbands and wives often report repeatedly going over a spouse's final days or hours. They may feel the impulse to search for their beloved, even though they know intellectually that they are being irrational. Notice that these responses have uncanny similarities to those of a toddler who frantically searches for a caregiver when she leaves the room. With widowhood—as some of the poignant comments of the women in the Experiencing the Lifespan box on the facing page show—John Bowlby's *clear-cut attachment response* reemerges at full force.

Many experts dislike using the word "recovery" to describe bereavement. They believe that adopting this term transforms mourning, a normal life process, into a pathological state (Sandler, Wolchik, & Ayers, 2008). They point out that when we lose a spouse we do not simply "get better" in the sense of returning to the person we were before. We emerge from this trauma as qualitatively different, hopefully more resilient human beings (Balk, 2008a, 2008b; Tedeschi & Calhoun, 2008). Still, at some point, let's say after a year or two, we do expect widowed people to "improve"

continuing bonds A widow's or widower's ongoing sense of the deceased spouse's presence "in spirit."

What is it like to lose your mate? What are some of the hardest things to endure in the first year after a spouse dies? Here are the responses I got when I visited a local support group for widowed people and asked the women in the room these kinds of questions:

"I've noticed that even when I'm in a crowd, I feel lonely."

"I find the weekends and evenings hard, especially now that it gets dark so early."

"Sundays are my worst. You sit in church by yourself. People avoid you when you are a widow."

"I think the hardest thing is when you had a handyman and then you lose your handyman. You would be amazed at how much fixing there is that you didn't know about. My hardest jobs were George's jobs. For instance, every time I have a car problem I break down and cry."

"I was married to a handyman and a cook. He spoiled me rotten. You don't realize it until they are gone."

"For me, it's the incessant doctors' bills. I got one yesterday. It's that continual painful reminder of the death."

"And you get all this stuff from Medicare, from Social Security. This year will be the last I file with him."

"You just don't know what to do. I didn't know anything, didn't know how much money we had . . . didn't know about the insurance. . . . My friends would help me out but, you know, it's funny—you don't ask."

"You have friends, but you can't really talk to them. You don't bring him up, and neither does anyone else."

"The thing that upsets me is that I'm scared that no one but me will remember that he was alive."

in the sense of being able to remake a satisfying new life (Rando, 1992–1993). People still care deeply about their spouses. Their emotional connection to a partner remains. However, this mental image is incorporated into the survivor's evolving identity as the widowed person continues to travel through life (Silverman & Klass, 1996).

What Helps Widowed People Cope?

As they struggle to come to terms with their loss, people often say that they have the sense their spouse is still "really" there (Field and others, 1999; Klass & Walter, 2001). Experts believe that this palpable sense of connection, which they refer to as **continuing bonds**, provides mourners with a sense of self-efficacy and mutes the feelings of grief (Dannenbaum & Kinner, 2009). One widowed friend described this sense of solace when she wrote: "I am never lonely. . . . I feel that my husband is now part of my heart and inner self."

Continuing bonds may allow widows and widowers to disconnect gradually from their spouse and give them the strength to grapple with the difficult task of reconstructing a new life: "My husband would want me to be happy"; "I need to reach out to others for his sake" (Dannenbaum & Kinnier, 2009). What else helps people adjust, and how do these influences change as men and women move from early bereavement into what attachment theorists might label the *working model*—or constructing an independent life—phase of widowhood? (Recall my discussion of Bowlby's stages of infant attachment in Chapter 4.)

To answer these questions, developmentalists conducted an ambitious longitudinal study. They evaluated the personalities of more than 1500 married couples and then followed the small subset of people who became widowed over the next four years (Brown & others, 2004; Ha, 2008).

THE IMPACT OF RELIGION. One force that the researchers felt might help people cope was faith in God. Do people become more religious after a spouse dies? Does religion help widows and widowers adjust?

Interestingly, during the first six months after the death, people did attend religious services more frequently and felt more spiritually connected to God. However, this rise in religiosity (or religious signs) was temporary. It declined to the pre-bereavement level at 24 months.

Chuck Savage/Corbis

Now that she is in the *working-model* phase of widowhood, this woman can take tremendous pleasure in this family party. But while enjoying a dance with her grandson, she might get sad as she thinks, "Wouldn't my husband be thrilled to be here?" Maybe she even believes that her husband is there "in spirit," looking down on everyone on this joyous day.

widowhood mortality effect
The slightly elevated risk of death that occurs among surviving spouses— particularly men—in the first months after being widowed.

Did turning to religion mute the pain? The answer here was also a qualified yes. Widowed people who felt more spiritually connected to God did grieve less intensely, although they were no less depressed than their counterparts who did not turn for comfort to their faith in a higher being.

THE IMPACT OF OTHER ATTACHMENTS. A second influence the research team examined was "significant others." What roles do friends and family play at different points in time in helping the bereaved (Ha, 2008)?

Here, too, there were tantalizing differences between early and later widowhood. At the six-month evaluation, people reported that they and their children had become especially close. Moreover, relationships with sons and daughters were less ambivalent and more harmonious than before (Ha & Ingersoll-Dayton, 2008). At the 18-month point, there was a return to pre-bereavement levels in terms of closeness and parent/child harmony; but widowed people reported leaning more on their friends.

This makes sense. During the early phase of intense mourning, children rally around; families grieve together; they share memories. Sons and daughters make a special effort to shower their bereaved parent with love. But after a while, it's normal to think, "Mom or Dad should be feeling better. . . . It's time for me to return to my normal life." Now, it's important for widows and widowers to reach out to friends— the companions they will be counting on day to day to construct a new, satisfying life. Who may have special trouble constructing this satisfying new life?

Having Trouble Moving On

> *It's been two years and I still can't get Joanne out of my mind. The children live miles away. I never see my old buddies from the plant . . . and after all, being men, we never were that close. How do you go on when everything you had is completely lost?*

As the quotation above suggests, intuitively we might think one group of at-risk adults might be men. Women are more emotionally embedded in relationships. They can use their loving attachments with their children and grandchildren and, more easily, draw comfort from their widowed friends. Just as having a friend at age 5 helps ease the trauma of the first day at school, especially for women, a nurturing network of friends can reach out at age 75 and smooth the person's passage into the widowed state.

This intuition seems accurate when we consider the **widowhood mortality effect.** Both men and women are at a slightly higher risk of dying, particularly during the first month or so of bereavement. But the odds of death—either through suicide or natural causes—are more than 10 times as great for males as for the other sex

Lost in loneliness, spending your days staring out at sea, this classic image of the elderly widower says it all. Men—especially when they are old-old—have special trouble after losing their life mate.

Chuck Franklin/Alamy

(Stroebe, Schut, & Stroebe, 2007). Because their remarriage options are limited and they are closer to dying, the most vulnerable group is old-old widowed men. Imagine losing your life mate at age 80 or 85 and you will understand why, for elderly men living alone, in particular, suicide is a major concern (Stroebe, Schut, & Stroebe, 2007).

However, rather than making generalizations based on gender and age in predicting who adjusts best, once again, we need to look at a complex set of personal forces. How emotionally resilient is the widowed person? Does that individual have other attachments or a life passion to cushion the blow? (See Carr, 2004.) We also need to look at the person's married attachment style. People who are securely attached to their partner tend to have other secure attachments in the wider world. Men and women who are insecurely attached, because they generally have more trouble relating, may have trouble forming new close relationships to make up for their loss (Bonanno and others, 2002; Field, Gal-Oz, & Bonanno, 2003).

Ironically, this suggests that having an extremely satisfying marriage might set people up to rebound from this trauma. And, in fact, in the longitudinal study following those couples I have been discussing, if a husband or wife reported that "my spouse is my closest confidant," that individual was more likely to develop another close one-to-one relationship after the partner died (Ha, 2008).

This is not to minimize the role of the wider environment in fostering adjustment. Widowhood is a more devastating economic blow for women, especially Hispanic and African American women, because they tend to be less well off prior to their husbands' death (Angel, Jimenez, & Angel, 2007). In one fascinating study, researchers found that, if older adults were living in an area with a relatively high concentration of widowed people, their odds of dying after being widowed were significantly reduced (Subramanian, Elwert, & Christakis, 2008). So moving as a couple to a senior-citizen community with all those widows and widowers may have an unexpected long-term survivor bonus in later life!

Finally, we also need to look to the way widowed people are treated by society as a whole. To take the most extreme case, let's travel to a place where being widowed (for women) can have nightmarish aspects that go well beyond losing a spouse.

Among the Igbo of West Africa, new widows must "prove" that they did not kill their spouse by sleeping with their husband's corpse. Because property rights revert to the paternal side of the family, after the man's death, his relatives feel perfectly free to take the newly bereaved woman's possessions and force her off her land (Cattell, 2003; Sossou, 2002). Given this totally male-dominated tilt to their society, it is no wonder that an African widow in her sixties made this comment: "I've had so much of this bossing by men. I have my house, my garden. Why should I have a man take my money and spend it on drink and other women? I am the boss now" (quoted in Cattell, 2003, p. 59)!

It's obvious from her determined expression that encouraging this woman to "emote about her grief" at a widowed persons' group would not be the best policy. Stay tuned for how to approach this new widow and any other recently bereaved person at the end of this section.

Widowed People Are Resilient

So far, I have highlighted the trauma of widowhood, except for this last ecstatic quote. However, we may be making a serious error in overemphasizing the pain (Bonanno, 2004). Most people—male or female—who lose a spouse cope very well (Bonanno and others, 2002). Support groups for widowed people, such as the one in the Experiencing the Lifespan box on page 413, are not useful unless a person is having considerable trouble adjusting to the person's death (Bonanno & Lilienfeld, 2008).

The most interesting evidence that widowhood has mixed effects comes once again from the longitudinal study that tracked older people from marriage

Darren Hauck/AP Images

through widowhood. In exploring personality, the researchers found, to their surprise, that wives with the lowest self-esteem during their marriage got *more* self-confident after their husbands died (Carr, 2004). Were these particular husbands infantilizing these wives or putting them down during their married lives? The answer is probably no. Women, such as Theresa, who have lived in a marriage for their whole adult life, may not realize how well they can cope on their own. When you discover that, yes, you *can* prepare the tax return or fix the faucet and you do not fall apart when finding yourself suddenly single after 50 or 60 years, you have learned an important lesson about who you are. As the Chinese proverb puts it: Within the worst crisis lies an opportunity (or, in Chapter 12's terminology, a potential redemption sequence). Life's traumas, handled successfully, can promote emotional growth.

Furthermore, this study had a lesson for all of us. Widows who reported having the most help from friends and family did not feel better. They actually had lower self-worth (Carr, 2004). So perhaps we need to apply Chapter 5's childhood principles of scaffolding to widowhood: Give people the support they need, but don't overprotect them. Don't rob widows or widowers of the chance to learn self-efficacy and connect with their confident, newly single selves. Table 13.5 summarizes these section messages by offering guidelines to surviving widowhood.

What can you say to a widowed loved one or any person who has been recently bereaved? Let's end this discussion with a study that offers answers to this delicate question, one that asked adults who had recently experienced a loved one's death, "What responses would help you most?" The answer: Listen openly; "be there"; express your care and concern; don't give advice (Rack & others, 2008). In other words, adopt Jules's strategy described in the Experiencing the Lifespan box on page 403 for living "in relationship" in a person-centered way.

> ***TABLE 13.5:*** **Advice for Surviving Widowhood: A Summary Table**
>
> 1. Develop a network of attachments and fulfilling identities outside of your marriage before being widowed, to cushion the loss of your life love.
>
> 2. You might want to draw on your faith in God, particularly in the first months, and use the feeling that your spouse is with you as you struggle to remake a competent new life.
>
> 3. Take comfort from your children, but understand that, after some time, they will need to go on with their own lives. Your challenge is to reach out to friends in order to help you construct meaning day by day.
>
> 4. Graciously accept emotional support—but don't let loved ones take over your life.
>
> 5. Try to see this tragedy as a challenge, an opportunity for understanding that you can function on your own. You may find that you are more resilient than you ever thought.

 TYING IT ALL TOGETHER

1. Joe, a fifty-something baby boomer, is looking forward to retiring from his job as a public school teacher. How might Joe's experience differ from that of a 70-year-old colleague who retired from the same school district a decade ago? (Here, pick out the *false* statement.)

   a. Joe may be entering retirement with a lower financial (that is, pension and savings) cushion.
   b. Joe may have to retire at an older age than his colleague.
   c. Joe's superintendent will probably be spending more time urging him not to retire.
   d. After retirement, Joe may have to go back to work in order to make ends meet.

2. Your dad plans to retire in the next few years. Based on this chapter, give him some advice for happily adjusting to this life transition.

3. Many social policy experts believe that we will soon need to increase the age of eligibility for getting full Social Security benefits to 70. Discuss the pros and cons of this idea.

4. Isabella's husband, Frank, just died, and her friends are especially worried because, during her 52-year marriage, Isabella was very dependent on Frank for practical things like handling the finances and doing home repairs. Should Isabella's friends (a) immediately step in to take over these jobs or (b) offer Isabella a good deal of emotional support but be careful to let her try to learn these tasks on her own?

5. An elderly relative of yours has just been widowed. List the signals mentioned in the chapter that might set off alarm bells that this person is at risk for having a rocky time. Then, in one sentence, describe how your relative might want you to best approach her when discussing the loss.

Answers to the Tying It All Together questions can be found on the last page of this chapter.

Final Thoughts

As we turn in this next chapter to explore physical aging, I'll be continuing to highlight similar themes: Look beyond the illness to the inner person; old-age impairments are not the tragedy they seem from an outsider's view; don't infantilize frail older people or minimize their ability to live fully; understand that older adults often confront the challenges of physical aging in a proactive, efficacious way. Most important, be aware that the wider world—from socioeconomic status, to culture, to the government support a society provides to its elderly citizens—is vital in determining how people function physically in their older years.

SUMMARY

Setting the Context: Scanning the New Older World

The **median age** of the population is rising, **late-life life expectancy** is expanding, and the baby boomers are moving into later life; all these forces are converging to make the twenty-first century the "age of the old." The most important fact to know about the elderly population is that there is a dramatic difference between being **young-old** and being **old-old**.

The Evolving Self

Everyone believes that as people get older, memory declines. Elderly people do perform less well than the young on most memory tasks. Memory challenges that are more difficult—such as linking faces to specific situations, remembering bits of information quickly, and **divided-attention tasks**—produce the most severe deficits, and losses in these situations begin at a surprisingly young age.

Using the information-processing perspective, researchers find that as people age, working memory-bin capacity declines because the executive processor is less able to screen out task-irrelevant thoughts. Using the **memory-systems perspective**, studies reveal few age-related losses in **semantic memory** or **procedural memory** but dramatic declines in **episodic memory**. To improve memory in old age (or at any age), use selective optimization with compensation, employ **mnemonic techniques**, and foster memory self-efficacy.

Socioemotional selectivity theory suggests that in old age (or at any age), when people see their future as limited, they focus on maximizing the quality of their current life, and prefer to be with their closest attachment figures. According to this interesting theory, we have the potential to be happier in later life than at any other age. Research confirms that the elderly are superior at minimizing negative emotions and experience less daily stress. Affluent young-old people are indeed likely to be happier than adults of other ages. But during advanced old age, when physical limitations (and life losses) make enjoying the present difficult, unhappiness can become a common life state. The keys to aging successfully, even in advanced old age, are feeling generative, seeing oneself as always developing as a person, and feeling a sense of meaning and control in one's current life.

Later-Life Transitions

Government programs offering older people financial support have made retirement a full stage of life in much of the developed world. Germany provides such generous old-age funding that the average retiree in that nation actually gets more financially comfortable over the years. In China and Hong Kong, where the government does not offer old-age assistance, people approach retirement full of anxiety.

In the United States, our main sources of retirement income are **Social Security** and **private pensions** and savings. Because Social Security only provides a meager income and the value of pensions have seriously eroded in our current economy, an increasing number of people may need to work after 65 to make ends meet. Even affluent older people, who enter retirement with ample pensions and savings, are vulnerable to falling into poverty as they travel into their old-old years and depend mainly on Social Security to live.

Most people base their retirement choice on financial considerations, but, especially at the lower ends of the economic spectrum, health concerns also come into play. **Age discrimination**, although illegal, can push people to leave work—and is a particular threat to middle-aged workers trying to find jobs. Despite these negatives, the decision to retire (or not to retire) is often a happy, positive choice. People who choose to work into their 70s tend to be healthy and well-educated, and hate the idea of leaving work.

People tend to be happy in retirement when they willingly made this decision, have few health and money worries, are intrinsically motivated, and have an enduring lifelong passion to pursue. People use this time to be generative, to further their education (through programs such as **Elderhostel**), and to develop new identities and interests, too. The current declining pension and savings retirement cushion, an increase in the **old-age dependency ratio**, workforce discrimination against older employees,

and especially looming old-age poverty are serious social policy retirement issues.

Widowhood qualifies as the number-one life stress, especially for this cohort of old-old people who have lived their whole adult lives in the married state. The early symptoms of bereavement have much in common with the separation response of an infant whose caregiver leaves the room. By about the second year after being widowed, people typically begin to recover, in the sense of beginning to construct a satisfying new life. **Continuing bonds**, or having a sense of the deceased partner's presence, can offer people comfort. Religion and the support of one's children seem particularly important in the early months; and friends help most during the later phases of widowhood.

Because they have a richer web of close attachments, women may cope better with the death of a spouse than men. The **widowhood mortality effect** hits males hardest, and the most at-risk group is old-old men. Having a close marriage predicts resilience, as does having other attachments to cushion the blow. Cultural forces shape the experience of widowhood, too. Finally, we need to beware of seeing widowhood as an *impossible* trauma. Don't overprotect widowed people. Listen to them sensitively. Let them connect with their "efficacious" self.

KEY TERMS

median age, p. 392
late-life life expectancy, p. 393
young-old, p. 393
old-old, p. 393
divided-attention task, p. 395

memory-systems perspective, p. 397
procedural memory, p. 397
semantic memory, p. 397
episodic memory, p. 397
mnemonic technique, p. 399

socioemotional selectivity theory, p. 400
Social Security, p. 408
private pensions, p. 408
age discrimination, p. 409
Elderhostel, p. 411

old-age dependency ratio, p. 411
continuing bonds, p. 413
widowhood mortality effect, p. 414

ANSWERS TO TYING IT ALL TOGETHER QUIZZES

The Evolving Self

1. Dwayne should present concepts more slowly (but not talk down to his audience) and refrain from presenting a good deal of information in a single session. He should explicitly tie the course content into older adults' knowledge base or crystallized skills and strive to make the material relevant personally. He must teach in a distraction-free environment. He might offer tips on using mnemonic techniques. He should continually stimulate self-efficacy: "With your incredible life experience, learning this stuff should be a piece of cake!"

2. a. semantic memory b. episodic memory c. procedural memory

3. c. Bike riding, that automatic skill, is "in" procedural memory. b. Remembering the material in this chapter since it is in the most fragile system, episodic memory.

4. b and c.

5. Rather than simply encouraging people to think about the past, tell your friend that her therapeutic goal should be the same as with depressed adults of any age—enabling people to find fulfillment in their *present* lives. Explore what might

give clients meaning. Foster self-efficacy and generative activities. Get people to develop close attachments or to reconnect with people they love. To counter ideas like "I'm too old to do X, Y, and Z, or change at my age," keep stressing the point that personal growth is possible at every age.

Later-Life Transitions

1. c.

2. First and foremost, tell your dad he must enter retirement with a decent nest egg and conserve some cash for his old-old years. Suggest allotting ample time to his top-ranking, enduring passions, but also using his time to explore new life dreams. Might your dad want to use his years of experience to "be of service"(generative)? Does he want to expand his mind by taking advantage of the many educational opportunities for older adults? Can he spend special time just being with his family during these precious years?

3. Pros: Raising the retirement age to 70 will help keep Social Security solvent, encourage older people to be productive for longer, and get society used to the fact that people can be highly productive well into later life. Cons: No longer will retirement remain a joyous, *extended* life stage. Having older adults stay in the labor force longer will make it more difficult for young people to get jobs or advance at work. For workers in their sixties who *must* retire for health reasons, cutting off this source of income may have devastating consequences.

4. b.

5. Risk factors for a rocky bereavement: Being male, especially an old-old man; being socially isolated; having few interests or attachments outside of the marriage; having an insecure married attachment style; in general, not having the internal or external resources to construct a satisfying new life. Best strategy for approaching your newly widowed relative: be there; show you care; listen; don't give advice.

Chapter 14

CHAPTER OUTLINE

The Physical Challenges of Old Age

At age 76, Theresa was vigorous and fit. She walked a mile each day and worked full time at the bookstore. She was the most beloved employee they had. However, because of her night vision problem, Theresa no longer drove after dusk. Unfortunately, her medical checkups showed ominous signs. Theresa's atherosclerosis was progressing. The bone loss that had first shown up on the scan in her fifties was getting much worse. By age 79, Theresa felt uncomfortable driving down Main Street during rush hour. When she realized it was impossible to see the titles of some paperback books, she knew it was time to quit her job.

Two years later, at age 81, Theresa was having trouble cooking and cleaning. She began to worry: "What will happen when I can't take care of myself?" Dr. Jane, now 90, still spry and caring for a sister with Alzheimer's, plus a 59-year-old son with heart disease, suggested that Theresa move in with her. Jane's children and grandchildren agreed: "It's our mission to 'honor thy father and mother.' As Theresa is our second mom, we'd consider it a privilege to help." Theresa politely said no. She was determined to actively plan for her future, and that future did not involve burdening loved ones with her care. It was time to check out the new advances in long-term care. But after going online to scan the assisted-living facilities in her area, Theresa almost had a heart attack. The average rates at some facilities ($4000 a month) were higher than at a four-star hotel! Eventually, she located a nursing home at the forefront of geriatric care. The St. Mary Center was only 50 miles away and, best of all, had a priest on staff. Theresa immediately put her name on the waiting list—and none too soon. Three years later, she fell, breaking her hip, and could no longer live at home.

Today Theresa uses a walker. She needs help getting dressed and using the toilet. However, when I visited her, she was surprisingly upbeat. True, Theresa admits that life at 87 can be difficult—not simply because of a person's physical state. The real problem is losing your life partner after 55 wonderful years. Still, the facility is wonderful. She loves the activities and many of her helpers. Ladies can hang on to their passions, too. The St. Mary's book club that Theresa formed—which uses books on tape—just won a national prize!

What enemy is Theresa battling? How does physical aging turn into disease, disability, and sometimes the need for a nursing home? This chapter offers answers to this compelling question and many more.

In the following pages, I'll be exploring the kinds of problems that some gerontologists (for example, Rowe & Kahn, 1998) label as "unsuccessful aging," describing what *can* go seriously physically wrong during the old-old years. I believe that equating "successful aging" with walking miles at age 90 is equally wrong. Successful aging means drawing on what gives your life meaning to live fully no matter how your body behaves. It is epitomized by 94-year-old Jules, described in the last chapter, who—although he can barely take a step without stumbling—is still sensitively doing therapy and writing books.

Aging successfully means having Jules's internal sense of self-efficacy and enduring generative mission. But successful aging also depends on whether the wider world offers older people the support they need to function at their best. The real issue in later life is not so much being ill, but living as fully as possible in the face of chronic disease. The way people function in later life depends on their personal capacities (or nature) combined with nurture—having the right person–environment fit.

How can we engineer the right person–environment fit for older loved ones? Let's begin our search for answers by charting the aging process itself.

This alert, vigorous 93-year-old, enjoying a swim, seems to have little in common with the same-aged, confused, and wheelchair-bound woman suffering from Alzheimer's disease. However, their aging process is identical. Although aging progresses at different rates, normal aging changes are predictable, biologically programmed into being human, and advance in tandem with the advancing years.

Tracing Physical Aging

Theresa has atherosclerosis, or fatty deposits on her artery walls. She has trouble seeing at night and has been losing density in her bones. These are just a few of the many body signs called **normal aging changes.**

Normal aging changes vary in their time of onset. Some, such as Theresa's bone density loss and night vision troubles, begin in midlife. Others, such as atherosclerosis and the losses in mental processing speed that I described in Chapters 12 and 13, become evident in our thirties or even before. But all normal aging changes have similar features: They are universal and genetically programmed into our DNA. They occur in every member of our species to some degree. They are progressive, growing more pronounced as the years pass.

Three Basic Principles of Age-Related Disease

Over time, as the following principles reveal, normal aging changes shade into disease, then disability, and finally—by a specific barrier age—universal death.

Chronic disease is often normal aging "at the extreme." Many physical losses, when they occur to a moderate degree, are called normal. When these changes become more extreme, they have a different label: **chronic disease.** Theresa's bone density loss and atherosclerosis are a perfect case in point. These changes, as they progress, produce those familiar old-age illnesses—osteoporosis and heart disease.

The National Health Interview Survey (NHIS), an annual government poll of health conditions among the U.S. population, tells us other interesting illness facts. Notice from scanning Figure 14.1 that arthritis is the top-ranking chronic illness in later life (CDC, 2009). As we travel up the age ladder, our chance of having a variety of illnesses increases. Like arthritis, many age-related diseases are not fatal. They interfere with the ability to function in the world. So the outcome of chronic illness is not just death, but what gerontologists call **ADL (activities of daily living) problems**—difficulties handling life.

ADL impairments are a serious risk during the old-old years. ADL limitations come in two categories. **Instrumental ADL problems** refer to difficulties in performing tasks required for living independently, such as the troubles with cooking and cleaning that Theresa had before her fall. **Basic ADL limitations** mean being inca-

normal aging changes The universal, often progressive signs of physical deterioration intrinsic to the aging process.

chronic disease Any long-term illness that requires ongoing management. Most chronic diseases are age-related and are the endpoint of normal aging changes.

ADL (activities of daily living) problems Difficulty in performing everyday tasks that are required for living independently. ADLs are classified as either basic or instrumental.

instrumental ADL problems Difficulties in performing everyday household tasks, such as cooking and cleaning.

basic ADL problems Difficulty in performing essential self-care activities, such as rising from a chair, eating, and getting to the toilet.

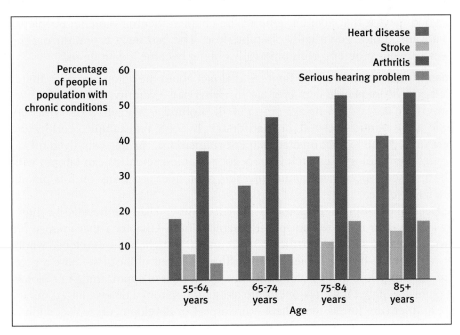

FIGURE 14.1: **Prevalence of selected chronic health conditions among U.S. adults in middle and later life (percentages):** As people travel into their 70s and 80s, the rates of common age-related chronic diseases rise, sometimes dramatically. Although every chronic illness can impair the ability to fully enjoy life, many common chronic diseases don't actually result in death.

Sources: CDC (2009); National Center for Health Statistics (2008).

pable of performing fundamental self-care activities such as standing or getting to the bathroom or feeding oneself. When people have these very severe disabilities, they need full-time caregiving help.

Notice from Figure 14.2 that the risk of developing instrumental ADL impairments rises dramatically by people's late seventies. It's fifty-fifty over age 85. Even more ominous, in the age group over 85, roughly 1 in 6 adults living in their own homes has a basic ADL problem or elemental life difficulty, such as walking to the toilet or dressing themselves (CDC, 2009). The fraction of very old people with these serious problems is actually higher because, as you saw with Theresa, these are the kinds of difficulties that cause people to enter a nursing home.

Here, you can see the real enemy in old age: It's ADL impairments, not specific illnesses. Moreover, if this 85-year-old man's difficulties walking independently to the toilet are permanent, he may be forced to enter a nursing home.

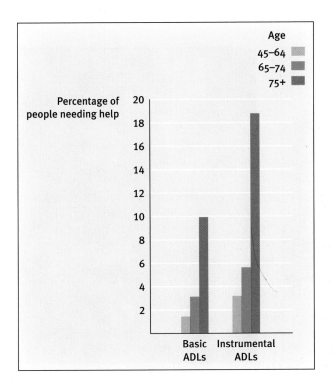

FIGURE 14.2: **Percentages of people needing assistance with instrumental ADLs and basic ADLs in middle and later life:** Although in middle age and even in the young-old years the fraction of people with ADLs is relatively small, the risk of having these kinds of problems increases dramatically over age 75. (Over age 85, roughly 1 in 6 people living in the community has a basic ADL problem.)

Source: National Center for Health Statistics (2005).

The good news is that, like Dr. Jane in the chapter-opening vignette, people *do* live into advanced old age virtually disability free. The bad news is that during the old-old years, major problems with physically coping become a definite risk.

The human lifespan has a defined limit. A final fact about the aging process is that it has a fixed end. More people than ever are surviving past a century. Actually, the 100-plus group is the fastest-growing age group of all (Robine & Michel, 2004). But very few people make it much beyond that barrier age. In 2008, for example, world wide, there were only about 70 documented "super-centenarians," people who lived till 110 (Los Angeles Gerontology Research Group, 2007). Unless scientists can tamper with our built-in, species-specific *maximum lifespan*, soon after a century on this planet, we all are fated to die.

The fact that our human lifespan lasts about a century makes our twentieth-century longevity strides even more remarkable. Remember from Chapter 1 that *average life expectancies* have now zoomed into the upper seventies throughout the developed world. So at this moment in history, babies born in affluent regions of the globe have a good chance of surviving close to the outer limit of life. Our odds of approaching this biological end point are higher if we *personally* are affluent, not from a disadvantaged minority group, and female. Just as they affect every aspect of development, socioeconomic status, along with ethnicity and gender, dramatically shape our physical aging path.

Socioeconomic Status, Aging, and Disease

Throughout this book, I have highlighted the impact that socioeconomic status has on many aspects of life. Now, it's time to explore the influence this basic marker has on the rate at which we age and die.

Specifically, within each nation, researchers have documented a **socioeconomic/health gap**. As people move up the social-status ladder, they tend to live healthier and to survive for a longer time.

The fact that *each* step up in social status translates into a longer lifespan was first discovered in Great Britain more than 30 years ago. Researchers were surprised to find that they could predict a male British government worker's risk of dying from heart disease by looking at his ranking on the civil service hierarchy (Batty and others, 2003; Reid and others, 1974). Since this classic study was published, social scientists have documented a similar socioeconomic/health gap in nations around the globe (Jen,

Although our species-specific human maximum lifespan is about 100 to 105 years, a minuscule number of people (one out of many millions!) make it to super-centenarian status, living to 110. Here is a photograph of a Lebanese woman who in 2004 was working and—at an amazing 126 years old—qualified as the oldest person on earth.

Jamal Saidi/Reuters/Corbis

Comparing this elegant, well-dressed, 100-year-old San Francisco man to this impoverished 60-something Polish woman, begging for change on the street, vividly brings home the basic message of this section: Statistically speaking, socioeconomic status is closely related to the rate at which we age and die.

Kevin Horan/Getty Images

© Peter Turnley/CORBIS

Jones, & Johnston, 2009; Smits & Monden, 2009). From Iceland (Olafsdotter, 2007) to Denmark (Osler and others, 2009) to Bangladesh (Kabir & others, 2003), people who are more affluent live longer and enjoy better health.

The relationship between income and illness becomes stronger during midlife, when normal aging changes are progressing to chronic diseases. You can get hints of what is happening by looking around. Notice how by their late thirties people start to show clear differences in their aging rates. Although there are many exceptions, notice also that people who appear to be poor often look physically older than their chronological age.

We can trace the origins of this accelerated aging process back to the beginning of life. Remember from Chapter 2 that low birth weight—which is linked to social class—sets babies up for obesity and generally poor health. Recall from Chapter 5 that childhood obesity and so elevated blood pressure (see Marin, Chen, & Miller, 2008) and early-onset diabetes (those major risk factors for heart disease and stroke) are far more common among boys and girls at the lower end of the socioeconomic scale. Even illnesses such as asthma—which disproportionately affect disadvantaged children—weaken the body and later make people more susceptible to age-related chronic disease (Dowd, Zajacova, & Aiello, 2009). What really seems to happen is that, over time, the *many* health-impairing forces linked to growing up poor—from diet, to illness, to life stress—accumulate to eventually produce dramatic differences in disability and death rates during adult life (Wilson, Shuey, & Elder, 2007).

Actually, for low-income U.S. adults, the statistical death and disability differences are stark. Expect an average life expectancy about five years shorter than your affluent counterparts (Manchester & Topoleski, 2008). Expect to develop ADL difficulties at a younger than normal age. In fact, among the most economically disadvantaged U.S. men and women, "old-age" illnesses, not infrequently, qualify as problems of midlife (CDC, 2009).

These alarming figures, however, are correlations. They don't tell us about causes. Suppose you were frequently ill during childhood. You would tend to miss school, be less likely to go to college, and so be set up to earn less during adult life (Haas, 2006). Or imagine developing heart disease in your forties. You could lose your job. You would have tremendous medical bills. You would probably find yourself sliding down the socioeconomic scale. In addition to poverty producing illness, wouldn't living with illness *cause* people to become poor? Keeping in mind that the poverty–illness relationship is bidirectional, let's now scan the forces linked to low socioeconomic status that accelerate physical aging and smooth the path to chronic disease.

Low-income adults are more likely to engage in high-risk behaviors such as smoking (CBO, 2008; Fagan and others, 2007). They are less likely to regularly exercise (Grzywacz & Marks, 2001). Who has time to go work out (or afford the gym!) if you are working two jobs to feed your family? They eat less nutritious foods than their upper-middle-class counterparts do. The next time you are at the supermarket, check out the prices of packaged foods such as chips or cookies, compared to fresh carrots, strawberries, or plums. What food choices would you make if you had to worry about saving every dime?

Then, there is the devastating impact of stress on the body itself—working at a dangerous job or being laid off from work (see Eliason & Storrie, 2009; Krieger and others, 2008), coping with the challenges of single parenthood, living in a crime-ridden, "toxic" neighborhood (Beard and others, 2009). In one interesting study, even reports of pain in old age were linked to the general socioeconomic status of the neighborhood in which a person lived (Fuentes, Hart-Johnson, & Green, 2007).

socioeconomic/health gap The disparity, found in nations around the world, between the health of the rich and poor. At every step up on the socioeconomic ladder, people survive longer and enjoy better health.

© Owen Franken/CORBIS

Just venturing out of his doorway is likely to be a stressful, demoralizing experience for this man. So it's no wonder that in addition to all of the other life-shortening forces linked to being poor, his neighborhood may also promote premature disability and death.

Now, imagine concerns surrounding being seen for medical care. Especially if you are an immigrant or an impoverished African American, you may not feel comfortable visiting a health-care provider: "How can I talk to that White, upper-middle-class, male doctor? The medical system is surely biased against people like me" (see Klonoff, 2009). You may not be fully aware that a symptom such as the pain in your chest or the lump in your breast needs to be looked at right away.

There can also be worries related to simply being diagnosed with a disease. Suppose you found out you were ill and had to take time off from work (medical leaves for low-wage hourly work are unpaid), or, worse yet, suppose your employer, after discovering your diagnosis, laid you off. Or imagine being among the 1 in 6 U.S. adults without health insurance as of 2008 (CDC, 2009). Would you make the effort to have a pain in your chest or lump in your breast checked out, especially if there was little you could do if you did learn the worst?

Ethnicity, Aging, and Disease

Hispanic Americans and African Americans face a double whammy. They are more likely to live in poverty, endure the stress-inducing impact of discrimination (see Mays, Cochran, & Barnes, 2007), as well as get less adequate medical care (Klonoff, 2009; Williams & Mohammed, 2009). But there is a fascinating health difference between these two major U.S. minority groups. Hispanic Americans seem relatively resistant to the disease-promoting effects of poverty. At the lower ends of the socioeconomic spectrum, they actually outlive Whites (Turra & Goldman, 2007). Are less acculturated Latino immigrants more insulated from the "toxic" effects of poverty because they are less prone to smoke or drink and more imbedded in two-parent families than other low-income groups (recall the immigrant statistics table in Chapter 7)?

This compelling photo offers one reason for what researchers call the "Hispanic paradox" (the fact that disadvantaged Latino heritage adults tend to live a surprisingly long time): a culture immersed in intergenerational adoration and respect. The lesson: As a caring, involved grandchild of *any* cultural background, you might be "working" to help extend a beloved elderly family member's life!

Whatever the answer, this resilience does not apply to African Americans. From heart disease, to diabetes, to cancer, Black Americans are more susceptible to illness and premature death than *any* other ethnic group (Chu, Miller, & Springfield, 2007; Yao & Robert, 2008). The racial health gap is especially alarming with regard to cardiovascular illnesses. African Americans, for instance, are roughly twice as likely to die of strokes than the U.S. population at large (Mays, Cochran, & Barnes, 2007).

When I worked in a nursing home, I vividly saw these statistics in operation in a 60-year-old African American patient, totally incapacitated by a stroke. The youngest person in our facility, this formerly vigorous, strapping railroad worker was incredibly angry and depressed. The staff was not sympathetic. Why didn't this man stop abusing alcohol? Why didn't he take the simple step of having his blood pressure checked? In truth, however, my patient was recently divorced and had just lost his job. From biological susceptibility to life stress, the deck was stacked against this man.

Our immediate impulse is to blame adults who develop so-called preventable conditions such as a stroke or heart disease at atypically early ages. "These people should have taken better care of their health." But our discussion reminds us that the issue with regard to poor health habits and illness is more complex. Suppose, like my patient, you were coping with a divorce and felt out of control of your life. How hard would it be for you to resist that classic stress reducer, alcohol, or visit the doctor? Yes, we need to empower people to follow good health habits. But the common practice of blaming the victim—for heart disease, for cancer, or for obesity (see Chapter 5)—when the reinforcers *all* converge to promote unhealthy living also seems shortsighted and unfair.

Who tends to be blamed for being ill? As with my patient, the answer, more often, is men. Males are more susceptible to so-called "preventable" age-related illnesses. Males, as you saw with my patient, are less likely to carefully watch their health.

Gender, Aging, and Disease

Women, as you learned in Chapter 2, are the more biologically resilient sex. Their second X chromosome gives them a survival advantage from the time they are in the womb. During adulthood, the main reason for this superior survival can be summed up in one phrase: fewer early heart attacks. Illnesses of the cardiovascular system (the arteries and their pump, the heart) are the top-ranking killers for both women and men. Heart disease alone accounts for more than one in four U.S. deaths (National Center for Health Statistics, 2009). However, because estrogen helps to slow the natural process by which fat deposits clog the arteries, men are roughly twice as likely as women to die of a heart attack in midlife (American Heart Association, 2001).

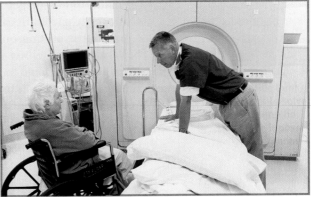

Their increased biological susceptibility to early heart attacks means men tend to "die quicker and sooner." For women, the aging pattern is "surviving longer but being more frail."

It makes sense that more disability is the price of traveling to the lifespan train's final stops. However, you might be interested to know that the phrase "living sicker" applies to women *throughout* adult life. At every stage of adulthood, in every nation, females report being in poorer health than males (Cummings & Jackson, 2008; Jen, Jones, & Johnston, 2009; Zunzunegui and others, 2009).

Years of experience with the medical system, being sensitive to her body's signals, understanding that "When I don't feel well, I need to go for tests such as this MRI"—all of these forces explain why this woman may be likely to have her cancer diagnosed at an early stage and so outlive the average man her age.

To explain this interesting paradox—higher life expectancy in the face of more sickness—we can look to nature forces. During the first half of adulthood, only women experience the physical ailments related to pregnancy and menstruation. In their older years, females are more susceptible to arthritis as well as the famous bone condition osteoporosis—illnesses that produce ADL problems but do not directly result in death.

We need to look to nurture forces, too. In their role as the family health protectors, as I suggested with Dr. Jane in the introductory vignette, women are generally more comfortable seeing doctors and sensitive to illness in their loved ones and themselves (von Bothmer & Fridlund, 2005). To explore this gender difference directly, you might want to take the poll in Table 14.1 and compare your ratings with

TABLE 14.1: Rate Your "Health Orientation"

	Never/ Unimportant		Always/ Very Important		
Health Practices					
1. Interest in exercising	1	2	3	4	5
2. Interest in healthful eating	1	2	3	4	5
Sensitivity Toward Illness					
3. Interest in seeing a doctor regularly	1	2	3	4	5
4. Tendency to stay in bed when sick	1	2	3	4	5
5. Use of over-the-counter medications	1	2	3	4	5
Overall Interest in Health Issues					
6. Read magazine articles related to health	1	2	3	4	5
7. Watch TV programs and visit Web sites related to health	1	2	3	4	5
8. Think about my health	1	2	3	4	5

What do your answers tell you about your overall interest in health?

those of class members of the opposite sex. Does the fact that men are more resistant to staying in bed or seeing a doctor (another symptom of the asking-for-directions issue) partly explain why women throughout the developed world outlive men by roughly five years?

INTERVENTIONS: Taking a Broader View of What Causes Disease

My discussion clearly implies that, to slow the progression from normal aging to illness to ADL problems, we should intervene at the first stage. Efforts to prevent premature births or get children to become more physically fit will have health and longevity payoffs decades down the road (see Kvaavik and others, 2009).

But is putting out the message to follow good health practices really enough? What good is telling someone to exercise when that person is working two jobs and cannot afford to go to the gym or buy healthful, high-cost foods? Why post public service advertisements on buses telling Black Americans to "Visit the doctor to have your blood pressure checked" if these very adults may have trouble getting adequate medical care? Now that I have documented the racial and socioeconomic/health gap, what can we do to reduce the *real* root cause of early chronic disease and premature death: the many toxic influences related to being minority and poor? (See Isaacs & Schroeder, 2004.)

Figure 14.3 provides a timeline illustrating a pathway from normal aging to disease to ADL problems to death and shows how that pattern can statistically vary by gender and social class. Now that we understand the overall process, let's spotlight two major causes of ADL impairments: sensory-motor declines and dementia.

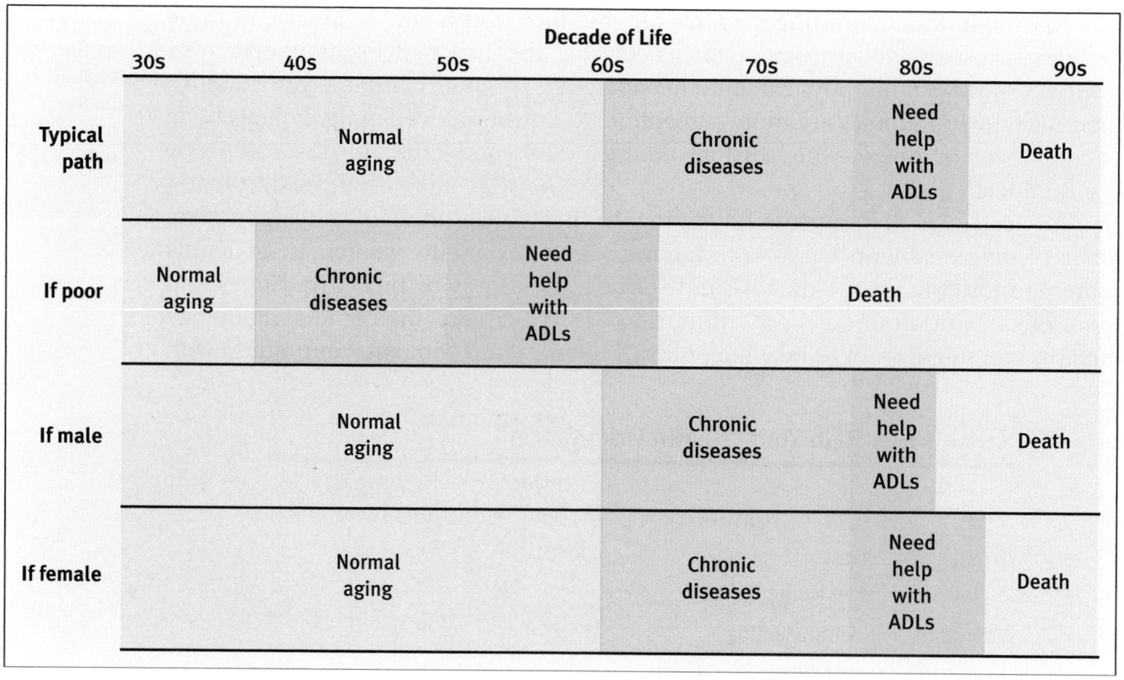

FIGURE 14.3: **The theoretical pathway from normal aging changes to death, and how that path can vary by socioeconomic status and gender**

TYING IT ALL TOGETHER

1. In her late fifties, Edna's doctor found considerable bone erosion and atherosclerosis during a checkup. At 70, Edna's been diagnosed with osteoporosis and heart disease. Did Edna a) suddenly develop these diseases, or b) have normal aging changes slowly progressed into these chronic diseases?

2. Marjorie has problems cooking and cleaning the house. Sara cannot dress herself or get out of bed without someone's help. Marjorie has _____ problems and Sara has _____ problems.

3. Statistically speaking, which man will be most likely to die of a heart attack at the youngest age?

    a. a hard-driving, upper-middle-class executive
    b. a first-generation immigrant from Mexico, living in poverty
    c. an African American man

4. Nico and Hiromi are arguing about men's versus women's health. Nico says that women are healthier during adult life; Hiromi thinks that it's men. Who is correct?

    a. Nico is right: Women live longer and are healthier during adult life.
    b. Hiromi is right: Men live longer and are healthier during adult life.
    c. Nico and Hiromi are each partly right: Women tend to live longer, but men tend to be healthier during adult life.

Answers to the Tying It All Together questions can be found on the last page of this chapter.

> **presbyopia** Age-related midlife difficulty with near vision, caused by the inability of the lens to bend.

Sensory-Motor Changes

What happens to vision, hearing, and motor abilities as we grow old, and how can people take action to minimize sensory-motor declines?

Our Windows on the World: Vision

One way aging affects our sight becomes evident during midlife. By their late forties and fifties, people have trouble seeing close objects. The year I turned 50, this change struck like clockwork and I had to buy glasses to read.

Presbyopia, the term for age-related difficulties with seeing close objects, is one of those classic signs, like gray hair, showing that people are no longer young. When I squint to make out sentences, the fact of my age crosses my consciousness. I imagine my students have this same thought ("Dr. Belsky is older") when they see me struggle with this challenge in class.

Other age-related changes in vision progress more gradually. Older people have special trouble seeing in dim light. They are more bothered by *glare*, a direct beam of light hitting the eye. They cannot distinguish certain colors as clearly or see visual stimuli as distinctly as before.

What is it like to be in the earlier stages of this progression? It can be annoying to ask the server what the impossibly faint restaurant bill comes to or to fumble your way into a neighbor's seat at a darkened movie theater. For me, the most hair-raising experiences relate to driving at night. Once, a curve of the highway exit ramp loomed out of the dark and I was inches from death. But apart from some hesitation about night driving, especially on unfamiliar roads, these problems have virtually no effect on my life or the lives of most middle-aged adults.

Unfortunately, this may not be true a few decades from now. As Figure 14.4 illustrates, seeing in glare-filled environments such as a lighted medicine cabinet, or even making out the print on a white page, can be a real challenge during the old-old years.

Nicole Villamora

FIGURE 14.4: How an 85-year-old might see the world: Age-related visual losses, such as sensitivity to glare, make the world look fuzzier at age 80 or 85. So, as these images show, everything from finding a bottle of pills in the medicine cabinet to reading the print in books such as this text can be a difficult task.

All of these signs of normal aging—presbyopia, problems seeing in the dark, and increased sensitivity to glare—are mainly caused by changes in a structure toward the front of the eye called the **lens** (see Figure 14.5). The disk-shaped lens allows us to see close objects by bending or curving outward. As people reach midlife, the transparent lens thickens and develops impurities, and so can no longer bend. This clouding and thickening not only produces presbyopia, but also limits vision in dimly lit places where people need as much light as possible to see.

These changes also make older adults far more sensitive to glare. Notice how, when sunlight hits a dirty window, the rays scatter and it becomes impossible for you to see out. Because they are looking at the world through a cloudier lens, older people see far less well when a beam of light shines in their eye. When this normal, age-related lens clouding becomes so pronounced that the person's vision is seriously impaired, the outcome is that familiar late-life chronic condition—a *cataract*.

The good news is that cataracts are curable. The physician simply removes the defective lens and inserts a contact lens. The bad news is that the other three top-ranking old-age vision conditions—*macular degeneration* (deterioration of the receptors promoting central vision), *glaucoma* (a buildup of pressure that can damage the visual receptors), and *diabetic retinopathy* (a leakage from the blood vessels of the retina into the body of the eye)—do tend to permanently impair sight.

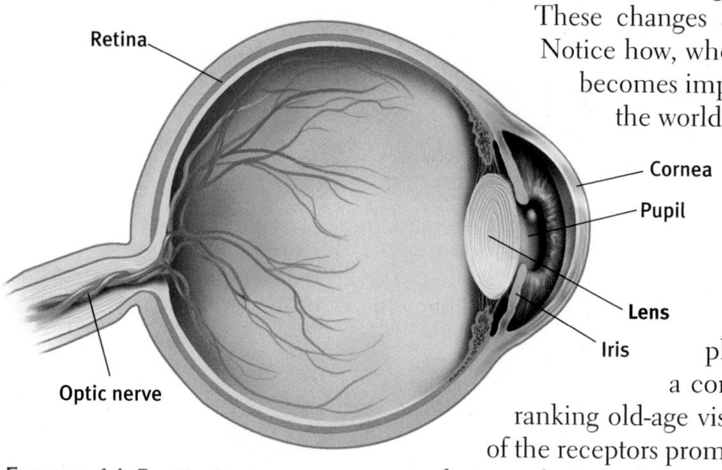

FIGURE 14.5: **The human eye:** Deterioration in many structures of the eye contributes to making older adults' vision poor. However, as discussed in the text, it is changes in the lens, shown here, that are responsible for presbyopia and also contribute greatly to impaired dark vision and sensitivity to glare—the classic signs of "aging vision."

lens A transparent, disk-shaped structure in the eye, which bends to allow us to see close objects.

presbycusis Age-related difficulty in hearing, particularly high-pitched tones, caused by the atrophy of the hearing receptors located in the inner ear.

INTERVENTIONS: Clarifying Sight

To lessen the impact of the normal vision losses basic to getting old, the key is to modify the wider world. People should make sure their homes are well lit but avoid overhead light fixtures, especially fluorescent bulbs shining down directly on a bare floor, as these produce glare. Appliances should be designed with non-reflective materials and adjustable lighting. Putting enlarged letters and numbers on appliances will make items such as the stove and computer keyboard easier to use.

If the person's problems have progressed to the chronic disease stage, it's important to explore the medical interventions that are continually being developed. Then, if impairments are genuinely permanent, the best policy is to adopt Paul Baltes's *compensation* mode. People need to rely on external aids to help them function to their best.

Vision impairments are a prime cause of ADL problems because they make everything from cooking, to walking, to working, a challenging task (Whitson and others, 2007). The loss of independence can hit people particularly hard. As one man in an interview study anguished: "I feel so embarrassed by letting the wife do things . . . I can't even change a fuse, and it's embarrassing, belittling" (quoted in Girdler, Packer, & Boldy, 2008, p. 113). So it's no wonder that researchers find impaired vision can seriously impair late-life satisfaction or make older people depressed (Chou, 2008; Good, 2008).

Therefore, to preserve their quality of life, avid readers, such as Theresa, might experiment with low-vision aids or books on tape or search out programs and services to help them function on their own. In confronting their situation, older adults can draw on their superior emotion regulation skills to cope. Ideally, people make lemonade when life hands them lemons, or, in developmental science terms, find *redemption sequences* in their losses (Girdler, Packer, & Boldy, 2008):

I bought large-print books, then used magnifiers. To me, trying books on tape meant giving up and admitting my vision was terribly poor; but since my local librarian convinced me to take home a tape, I've become addicted. It's like a gifted parent is reading to you . . . and now I can tune in to the world of literature, even while doing housework or relaxing in the tub.

Our Bridge to Others: Hearing

It's natural to worry most about losing our sight in old age. You might be surprised to know that hearing impairments can present just as many barriers to living fully in later life. The reason is that while poor vision limits our contact with the physical world, hearing losses prevent us from understanding language, our bridge to other minds. So when we lose the ability to hear, we are deprived of fully entering the human world.

Unfortunately, hearing problems are very common as we age. In one study among a random group of U.K. adults over age 50, about 2 out of 3 people tested showed mild evidence of hearing loss (St. Claire & He, 2009). The statistics are particularly alarming for men. Around the world, males are several times more likely than women to develop hearing losses in midlife (Belsky, 1999).

The main reason is that hearing impairments have a clear environmental cause: exposure to noise. Men are more likely to be construction workers; they operate heavy machinery, ride motorcycles, and go to NASCAR races. These high-noise environments set people up to develop hearing handicaps at an unusually young age. Government regulations mandate hearing protection devices for workers in noisy occupations—as you may have noticed when you last glanced at the ground crew before your plane took off. But people must take responsibility for protecting their hearing on their own. Ominously, rates of age-associated hearing problems have doubled since the 1970s (Strawbridge and others, 2000). From being surrounded by the jangle of horns when we are stalled in traffic, to the continual chatter of cell phones, the reason is that today we have noisier daily lives.

Presbycusis—the characteristic age-related hearing loss—is caused by the atrophy or loss of the hearing receptors, located in the inner ear (see Figure 14.6). So this condition is permanent. The receptors encoding our perception of high-pitched tones are most vulnerable. This means older people have special difficulties hearing tones that are of higher pitch. (For instance, if musicians are playing a guitar and a drum *equally* loudly, to an older person, the guitarist's melody will sound more faint.)

Put yourself in the place of someone with presbycusis. Because of your problem hearing higher-pitched sounds, listening to conversations feels a bit like hearing a radio that is filled with static. (That's why older people complain: "I can hear you, but I can't

Lon C. Diehl/Photo Edit, Inc.

Being in a wheelchair seriously compromises anyone's quality of life. But this woman's hearing impairment, which makes having a conversation with her husband practically impossible, may be even more important in cutting her off from the outside world.

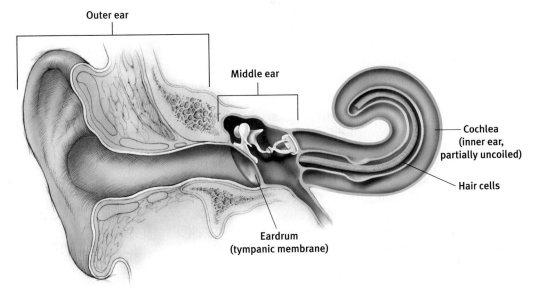

Outer ear

Middle ear

Cochlea (inner ear, partially uncoiled)

Hair cells

Eardrum (tympanic membrane)

FIGURE 14.6: **The human ear:** Presbycusis is caused by the selective loss of the hearing receptors in the inner ear—called hair cells—that allow us to hear high-pitched tones—so these changes are permanent.

Even though this aged woman may have spent her life as a Shakespeare scholar or a well-known scientist, her emerging-adult granddaughter will be tempted to talk to her frail, tiny grandma in *elderspeak*. How often have you used this patronizing type of speech with a cognitively sharp person in her eighties or nineties just because she looked as if she *might* be impaired?

elderspeak A style of communication used with an older person who seems to be physically impaired, involving speaking loudly and with slow, exaggerated pronunciation, as if talking to a baby.

reaction time The speed at which a person can respond to a stimulus. A progressive increase in reaction time is universal to aging.

osteoporosis An age-related chronic disease in which the bones become porous, fragile, and more likely to break. Osteoporosis is most common in thin women and so most common in females of European and Asian descent.

understand you," Tremblay and Ross, 2007). Because your impairment has been progressing gradually, you may not be sure you *have* a problem, thinking, "Other people are talking too softly." If you are like many older adults, unless family members pressure you, you probably don't want to buy a hearing aid (Duijvestijn and others, 2003; Hietanen and others, 2004). Hearing aids are hard to manage, and they do not work all that well—or so you have been told (Stephens, Vetter, & Lewis, 2003). Besides, these devices are for "old people." And after all, you can hear fairly well in quiet situations. It's only when it gets noisy that you can't hear at all.

Think of the pitch of the background noises surrounding you right now: the hum of a computer, the slamming of a door, the sound of a car motor starting up. These sounds are all lower in pitch than speech. This explains why hearing-impaired people are prone to complain about "all that noise." Background sounds overpower the higher-pitched conversations they are trying to understand. Moreover, because, as you learned in the previous chapter, in noisy environments the elderly *generally* have more problems mentally processing information, hearing-impaired older people are forced to rely on their "frontal cortex" to make simple judgments like "What did that person say?" (See Wong and others, 2009.)

Imagine having a conversation with a relative who cannot hear well—having to repeat your sentences, needing to shout to make yourself understood. Although you still may love your grandpa dearly, you now find yourself withdrawing when he enters the room. Now, imagine that you are a hearing-impaired person who must work hard to make sense of every statement or continually say "Please repeat that," and you will understand why this ailment can provoke feelings of isolation (Barlow and others, 2007). Hearing losses block our ability to participate fully in the human world.

INTERVENTIONS: Amplifying Hearing

Because the level of background noise is important in determining how well older people hear, the solution is to choose one's social settings with special care. Don't go to a noisy restaurant. Try to avoid places with low ceilings or bare floors, as they magnify sound. Install wall-to-wall carpeting in the house because it will help absorb background noise. Get rid of noisy appliances, such as a rattling air conditioner or fan.

When having a conversation with an older adult with a hearing problem, speak clearly. Enunciate words distinctly. Face the person. Perhaps use gestures so the person can take advantage of multiple sensory cues (Diederich, Colonius, & Schomburg, 2008). Your loved one will make better sense of your messages as she gets more experience reading your lips (Rosenblum, Miller, & Sanchez, 2007). But try to avoid *elderspeak*, the tendency to talk more slowly and in exaggerated tones ("HOW *ARE* YOU, *DARLING*? WHAT IS FOR *DINNER* TODAY?").

Elderspeak—a mode of communication we tend to naturally fall into when an older person looks physically (and so mentally) impaired—has unfortunate similarities to infant-directed speech. We use simpler phrases and grammar, and employ infantile "loving" words, such as *darling*, that we would never adopt when formally addressing a "real" adult (Kemper & Mitzner, 2001). I'll never forget going out to dinner with a friend in his late eighties who needed to use a walker, and cringing at how the 18-year-old server treated this intellectual man like a 2-year-old!

For your own future hearing, the message rings out loud and clear. *Avoid high-noise environments and cover your ears when you pass by noisy places.* Why do we hear so much about the need to exercise, and yet there is a deafening silence about the need to protect our hearing? How many of you religiously work out to prevent later life health problems like heart attacks but then attend rock concerts without a thought? Think of the noise level at your fitness center. Could the very place where you are going to improve your health be insidiously producing this very common age-related disease?

You are at the bank. You need to get to work, and at the head of this long line is a slow, elderly person. Experiences such as these are what cause us to dislike old people and automatically link "old age" with an image of being annoyingly slow.

Motor Performances

Late-life hearing loss tends to present problems when we talk to individual older adults. What everyone finds distressing when we think of the general category "old person" lies in the motor realm. The elderly are so slow!

Slowness puts older people out of sync with the physical world. It can make driving or getting across the street a challenging feat. It causes missteps in the world of relationships, too. If you find yourself behind an elderly person at the supermarket checkout counter or an older driver going 40 in a 65-mile-per-hour zone, notice that your immediate reaction is to get annoyed. Age-related slowing alone may help explain why our fast-paced, time-oriented society has such negative prejudices against the old.

The slowness that is so emblematic of old age is mainly caused by the loss in information-processing speed that starts decades earlier, in young adulthood, as described in Chapters 12 and 13. This slowed **reaction time**—or decline in the ability to respond quickly to sensory input—affects every action, from accelerating when the traffic light turns green, to counting change at the checkout counter, to performing well on a fluid IQ test.

Age changes in the skeletal structures propelling action compound the slowness: With *osteoarthritis*, the joint cartilage wears away, making everything from opening a jar to running for the bus an endurance test. With **osteoporosis**, the bones become porous, brittle, and fragile, and tend to break easily. Although men can also develop osteoporosis, women, as is well known, are more susceptible to this disease. The main reason is that females have frailer, smaller bones. Small-boned, slender women (therefore, most often females of Asian and European descent) are at highest risk of developing osteoporosis. With this illness, the fragile bones break at the slightest pressure and cannot knit themselves back together. Hip fractures are a special danger. As you saw with Theresa in the chapter-opening vignette, falling and breaking a hip is one of the primary reasons for needing to enter a nursing home (Jette and others, 1998).

The simple act of going down steps can be an ordeal when people have ADL impairments. Imagine being this woman and knowing that, because of your osteoporosis—graphically shown in the small image at the lower left—any misstep might land you in a nursing home.

INTERVENTIONS: Managing Motor Problems

Once again, when these difficulties strike, the solution is to achieve a delicate person–environment fit: Exercise moderately, as this strategy can help prevent falling (Lin and others, 2007; Stott, Langhorne, & Knight, 2008), and keep ADL problems from developing or getting worse (Mian and others, 2007). Encourage the older

person to go outside, as retreating to one's home ensures further physical decline (Kono and others, 2007). If an older adult is religious, push her to attend church regularly. This activity in itself may help protect against later ADL problems down the road (Park and others, 2008).

Another approach is to remodel one's house (Stott, Langhorne, & Knight, 2008): Provide the best possible indirect lighting and install low-pile, wall-to-wall carpeting to prevent tripping. Put grab bars in places such as the bathtub, where falls are likely to occur. To make activities such as cooking easier, install cabinet doors that open to the touch, and place shelves within easy reach.

Consider asking an older person's health-care provider to reduce the patient's medications because many drugs have a side effect of causing dizziness. Moreover, the elderly spend less time in the deepest stages of sleep, are prone to wake up often during the night, and so get drowsy during the day (see Vaz Fragoso and others, 2008)—which also suggests that the wider environment should be rearranged to minimize the impact of falls.

Table 14.2 summarizes the main points of this sensory-motor section, with special emphasis on highlighting what older adults and their loved ones can personally do to produce the right person–environment fit at home. I also must emphasize, however, that older people with ADL problems are highly creative at managing their environment in ways that go beyond just modifying their homes. As one study in Sweden showed, they have an innovative "can do" attitude that extends to staying independent in every life realm (Johannson, Josesphsson, & Lilja, 2009). How do the elderly handle that special environmental challenge so important to staying independent: Driving?

TABLE 14.2: Age-Related Sensory-Motor Changes and Interventions: A Summary

Changes	Interventions
Vision	
Problems with seeing in dimly lit places, sensitivity to glare	• Use strong, indirect light, and avoid using fluorescent bulbs.
	• Look for home appliances with large letters, nonreflective surfaces, and adjustable lighting.
	• Consider giving up driving at night or in the rain.
	• If your eyesight becomes severely impaired, use low-vision aids.
Hearing	
Loss of hearing for high-pitched tones	• Reduce background noise.
	• Speak distinctly, facing the person, but avoid elderspeak.
	• Install wall-to-wall carpeting and double-paned windows in a home.
Motor abilities	
Slower reaction time	• Be careful in speed-oriented situations.
Osteoporosis and osteoarthritis	• Exercise moderately, but don't overdo it.
	• Modify your home to prevent falls.
	• Install low-pile carpeting to prevent tripping.
	• Install grab bars and other assistive devices.
	(The lighting interventions suggested above will also help prevent falls.)

FOCUS ON A TOPIC: DRIVING IN OLD AGE

Imagine that you are an older adult, such as Theresa. You know your vision problems are making driving dangerous. So you stop driving during rush hour. For years you have been uncomfortable driving at night and in the rain. But even if you are well aware of having problems, if you are like many older people, you cannot imagine giving up your car (Lindstrom-Forneri, Tuokko, & Rhodes, 2007). Abandoning driving means confronting the crucial loss of independent selfhood that you first gained when you got your license as a teen. You would need to agonize over managing basic life activities, such as getting to the doctor or going to the store (Dupuis, Weiss, & Wolfson, 2007). You would be at risk of getting depressed (Satariano, 2007). Giving up driving might even lead to abandoning your home and entering a nursing home.

Actually, driving is a special concern for older adults because it involves many sensory and motor skills. In addition to demanding adequate vision, driving is affected by hearing losses because we become alert to the location of other cars partly by their sound. To drive well, people must have the muscle strength to push down the pedals and the joint flexibility to turn the wheel. And, as anyone behind an older driver when the light turns green immediately realizes, driving is especially sensitive to increases in reaction time.

The good news is that people, like Theresa, who are experiencing vision and motor problems naturally limit how much they drive (Ross and others, 2009). So when researchers look just at age-group differences in crashes, older adults have far lower accident rates than do drivers aged 18 to 25. The bad news is that, as you can see in Figure 14.7, when we consider the number of accidents per miles driven, driving—among people over 75—is a perilous practice indeed (Stamatiadis, 1996; see also Ross, 2009).

What steps should society take to reduce these hazards? Some experts advocate yearly license renewals accompanied by vision tests for people once they are over a certain age (Stamatiadis, Agent, & Ridgeway, 2003). Still, a simple eye screening might not pick up the deficits. Older people have trouble quickly processing the changing array of visual stimuli we encounter while on the road (Ball & Rebok, 1994; Roenker and others, 2003). As many wrecks are caused by cognitive impairments (Lafont and others, 2008), to really weed out dangerous drivers we might need to give older adults a battery of neuropsychological tests (Bieliauskas, 2005). Should we rely on family members or ask physicians to report impaired older drivers? Would you have the courage to rob an older loved one of his adult status by taking away his keys?

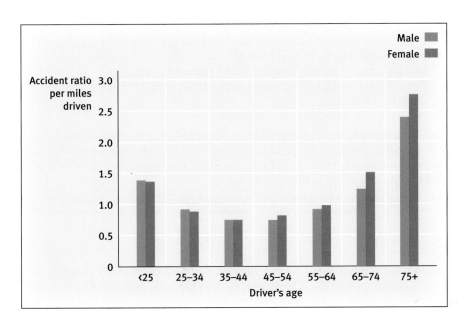

FIGURE 14.7: **Accident rates in U.S. urban areas, by age and gender:** Driving is especially dangerous for drivers age 75 and over. Notice from the chart that if we look at per-person miles driven, by this age accident rates are far higher than they are for even that other high-risk population—teenagers and emerging adults.

Source: Stamatiadis (1996).

Vision problems, hearing diffi-culties, slowed reaction time—and especially cognitive losses—combine to make this 80-year-old a more dangerous driver. Can you think of some ways to change the environment so that this man can either drive more safely or be able to stay independent without having to engage in this stressful activity?

None of these interventions speaks to the larger issue: "If I can't drive, I may have to leave my home." We need to redesign the driving environment by putting adequate light-ing on road signs, streets, highways, and, especially, exit ramps. We might extend the yellow light signal time and pro-vide more traffic lights, reducing the need for those left turns into traffic that are an accident waiting to happen for people of any age. As most crashes occur at intersections, we might build more roundabouts (circular structures, with traffic flowing in the same way) (Lord and others, 2006).

Most importantly, we need to construct less car-dependent communities: Have stores located within walking distance of homes; invest in cost-efficient mass transit—but make these systems easy for the frail elderly to use. This mandate is mandatory to tackle our energy crisis and the obesity epidemic, as well as make way for that huge cohort accelerating down the highway into later life—the baby boomers.

On your way home today, try to identify the most hazardous places for older drivers. Think of how you could redesign lights, signals, and intersections to make them more user-friendly for older adults—both pedestrians and drivers. This need to provide the right person–environment fit, as you will see in the next section, is also crucial when dealing with the most devastating problem of later life: dementing diseases.

 TYING IT ALL TOGETHER

1. Roy, who is 55, is having trouble seeing in the dark and in glare-filled environments. Roy's problem is caused by the clouding of his (cornea/iris/lens). At age 75, when Roy's condition has progressed to the point where he can't see much at all, he will have (a cataract/diabetic retinopathy/macular degeneration), a condition that (cannot/can) be cured by surgery.

2. Dr. Jones has just given a 45-year-old a diagnosis of presbycusis. All of the following predictions about this patient are accurate *except* (pick out the false statement):

   a. the patient is likely to be a male.
   b. the patient has probably been exposed to high levels of noise.
   c. the patient is at risk for becoming socially isolated.
   d. the patient will hear best in noisy environments.

3. Your 75-year-old grandma asks you for advice about how to remodel her home to make it safer. Which of the following modifications should you suggest?

   a. Install low-pile carpeting on your floors and put grab bars in your bathroom.
   b. Put fluorescent lights in your ceilings.
   c. Buy appliances with larger numerals and nonreflective surfaces.
   d. Put a skylight in the bathroom that allows direct sunlight to shine down on your medicine cabinet.
   e. Get rid of your noisy air conditioners and fans.

4. Your state legislature is considering a law to require annual eye exams for drivers over the age of 65. Using the points in this section, explain to the lawmakers why such a law may not be very effective and offer some alternate strategies that might minimize the dangers of needing to drive in old age.

Answers to the Tying It All Together questions can be found on the last page of this chapter.

Dementia

dementia The general term for any illness that produces serious, progressive, usually irreversible cognitive decline.

Dementia is the general label for any illness that produces serious, progressive, often irreversible cognitive decline. Dementia involves the total erosion of our personhood, the complete unraveling of the inner self. Younger people can also develop a dementing disease if they experience a brain injury or an illness such as AIDS. However, because—as you will see later in our discussion—dementias are typically produced by two illnesses basic to the aging process, these conditions almost always strike people in later life.

What are the general symptoms of *any* later-life dementia? As the first-person account in the Experiencing the Lifespan box below poignantly reveals, even in the earlier stages of these diseases, people forget basic *semantic information*. They cannot recall core facts about their lives, such as the name of their town or how to get home. Impairments in *executive functions*, such as the ability to inhibit one's actions, are prominent (Storandt, 2008). A conscientious person may start behaving erratically. A lifelong extrovert could turn sour and depressed (Duchek and others, 2007).

EXPERIENCING THE LIFESPAN: AN INSIDER'S PORTRAIT OF ALZHEIMER'S DISEASE

Hal is handsome, distinguished, a young-looking 69. He warmly welcomes me into his immaculate apartment at the assisted-living facility. Copies of National Geographic *and* Scientific American *are neatly laid out in stacks on the coffee table. Labeled photos of family members adorn the walls. Index cards organized in piles on the desk list his daughters' names and phone numbers, and provide reminders about the city and the state where he lives.*

Hal taught university chemistry for years. After his wife died, he kept active with volunteer work and church activities. About two years ago, his mind began to unravel. In addition to the forgetfulness, his children worried about the rambling conversations, the disorganized letters, and long-distance calls at all hours of the night. Concerned about Hal's ability to keep living on his own, his daughters planned to move him to Tennessee this coming fall. Their plans were cut short when Hal set out to drive across the country to Nashville but could not remember where he was going or who he was going to see. Luckily, Hal had the presence of mind to check himself into a local hospital, where he learned that he had the illness whose symptoms he graciously consents to describe:

I first noticed that I had a problem giving short speeches. All of a sudden you have a blank and like . . . what do I put in there . . . and I couldn't do it. I can speak. You are listening to me and you don't hear any pauses, but if you get me into something. . . . I just had one of these little pauses. I knew what I wanted to say and I couldn't get into it, so I think a little bit and wait and try to get around to it. It's there . . . I know it's there . . . but where do I use it? . . . Then, you have to sit down and think and sort. I went to the hospital because I knew there was something wrong. When I got there, they wanted to know about my life. I said: "If you provide me with some information about what you think will happen to me and if I find that it's a good argument, then I'll tell you about myself." When I was told I had Alzheimer's, I thought, "Oh, brother, this is a terrible place to be." The psychiatrist, Dr. West—

Oh, I got that right!—helped me a lot. Now, I tell everyone what I have. They are kind of shocked, but it doesn't bother me. I'm not ashamed of my Alzheimer's and I'm not ashamed of anyone else's Alzheimer's.

It's ups and downs; and then one day you are in a deep valley. You can't get tied up in the hills and valleys because they just lead you around and it makes you more frustrated than ever. . . . If I can't get things, I just give up and then try to calm down and come back to it. You have to work very hard to get back to where you were. Like, when I read, I get confused; but then I just stop and try again a month later. Or the people here: I know them by face, by sight, by what they wear, but I cannot get that focus down to memorize any names. I remember things from when I was five. It's what's happening now that doesn't make a lot of sense. Now, I think it's time for us to stop and let me show you the pictures on my wall and tell you who these people are. . . .

As we walk to my car after this interview, Hal's daughter fills me in:

My father seems a lot happier now that he is here. The big problem is the frustration, when he tries to explain things and I can't understand and neither of us connects. Then he gets angry, and I get angry. My father has always been a very organized, very intellectual person, so feeling dependent and out of control is overwhelming for him. We had to get a power of attorney [a legal order declaring guardianship]. I think he understood it conceptually, but he hasn't come to grips emotionally with it. The fact that he can't write checks is devastating. He has days where he gets paranoid, decides that there is a conspiracy out for him. It's tiny things. A letter came to the wrong place and he went down and exploded at the people at the desk.

The good news is that we put him on medication that seems to help. Also, they can handle this here. If we get home health services to come in, they will keep him until he gets very bad. For me the worst thing is remembering how my father was. You expect a certain response from him and you get this strange response. It's like there's a different person inside.

As the symptoms progress, every aspect of thinking is affected. Abstract reasoning becomes difficult. People can no longer think through options when making decisions. Their language abilities are compromised. People may be unable to name common objects, such as a shoe or a bed. Judgment is gone. Older adults often act inappropriately—undressing in public, running out in traffic, yelling in the street. They wander aimlessly and behave recklessly, unaware that they are endangering their lives.

As these diseases reach their later stages, there is the loss of all functions. People may be unable to speak or move. Ultimately, they are bedridden, unable to remember how to eat or even swallow. At this point, complications such as infections or pneumonia often occur and lead to death.

The Dimensions of Dementia

How long does this devastating decline process take? As you will see later, there is an in-between period between experiencing moderate memory problems and having full-blown symptoms. So it's hard to clearly define when dementia actually begins (Khachaturian, 2008). The deterioration progresses at different rates from person to person and also varies depending on the specific dementing disease. But in general, dementia amply deserves the label *chronic* disease. On average, the time from diagnosis until death is approximately four to eight years (Rivas-Vazquez and others, 2004).

The good news is that dementias are typically illnesses of *advanced* old age. Among the young-old, the prevalence of these diseases is in the low single digits; by age 85 people have a significant chance of developing memory problems this severe (Alzheimer's Association, 2009, see Figure 14.8). Is dementia the inevitable price of living a very long time? Luckily, the answer is no. When Danish researchers evaluated the cognitive capacities of every person in that nation who had their hundredth birthday during 1996, they discovered that one in three centenarians showed *no* signs of memory impairment (Andersen-Ranberg, Vasegaard, & Jeune, 2001). So yes, as you saw with Jules in the previous chapter, people do live sound in mind (as well as in body) until the limit of human life.

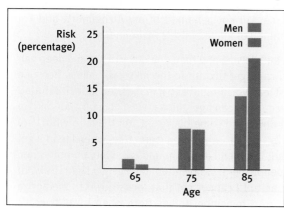

FIGURE 14.8: **Estimated risks for dementia in a major U.S. study, by age and sex:** The good news is that the chance of getting dementia by age 65 is minuscule. The bad news is that, by age 85—especially for females—there is a significant risk of developing these diseases.
Source: Alzheimer's Association (2009).

Dementia's Two Main Causes

What illnesses produce these terrible symptoms? Although there are a host of rarer dementing diseases, typically the older person will be diagnosed with *Alzheimer's disease* or *vascular dementia* or some combination of those two illnesses.

Vascular dementia refers to impairments in the vascular (blood) system, or network of arteries feeding the brain. Here, the person's cognitive problems are caused by multiple small strokes.

Alzheimer's disease directly attacks the core structure of human consciousness, our neurons. With this illness the neurons literally decay or wither away. They are replaced by strange wavy structures called **neurofibrillary tangles** and thick, bullet-shaped bodies of protein called **senile plaques**. These pathological signs of deterioration progress like a plague. They first show up in the hippocampus (an area of the brain solely responsible for memory), then move out to blanket the cortex as a whole (Bondi and others, 2008).

Vascular problems—because they limit the blood supply nourishing the brain—accelerate the neural loss. Particularly in advanced old age when a person develops the symptoms of dementia, stroke plus Alzheimer's changes are typically working together to produce the intense mental decline (Langa, Foster, & Larson, 2004).

vascular dementia A type of age-related dementia caused by multiple small strokes.

Alzheimer's disease A type of age-related dementia characterized by neural atrophy and abnormal by-products of that atrophy, such as senile plaques and neurofibrillary tangles.

neurofibrillary tangles Long, wavy filaments that replace normal neurons and are characteristic of Alzheimers' disease.

senile plaques Thick, bullet-like amyloid-laden structures that replace normal neurons and are characteristic of Alzheimer's disease.

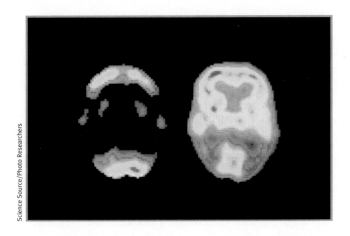

This photo shows PET-scan images of the metabolic activity of a normal brain (right) and one with advanced Alzheimer's (left). Notice how the neural devastation described in the text has literally shut down a person's brain.

Science Source/Photo Researchers

As you just saw, the number one risk factor for developing dementia is being old-old. But there is a genetic marker that significantly raises the risk for Alzheimer's disease. Roughly 15 percent of the U.S. population possesses the APOE-4 marker. Being in this unlucky group doubles a person's chance of getting Alzheimer's in the older years (Blacker & Lovestone, 2006; Blennow, de Leon, & Zetterberg, 2006; Cole & Vassar, 2008). Interestingly, during infancy and childhood, having this genetic marker seems to promote superior cognitive performance. But the same gene that helps boost IQ early in development can have devastating effects in later life (Han & Bondi, 2008).

This breakthrough in the genetics of Alzheimer's poses a dilemma. Children who have witnessed a parent develop this illness are (no surprise) terrified of getting the disease. Knowing they don't have the genetic marker would ease their minds. But having the APOE-4 allele does not mean that a given individual will definitely get Alzheimer's. It only shows that person is at higher risk. Would you decide to be tested? The answer, if you are like many people, might hinge on whether there are strategies to ward off the blow. Where *are* we today in terms of preventing and treating Alzheimer's disease?

Targeting the Beginnings: The Quest to Nip Alzheimer's in the Bud

The main front in the war to prevent Alzheimer's disease centers around a protein called amyloid, a fatty substance that is the basic constituent of the senile plaques. According to much current scientific thinking, as the amyloid-laden plaques accumulate in the brain, inflammation occurs, which promotes further plaque and tangle formation and accelerates the cortical decay (Vasto and others, 2008). So far, efforts to dissolve the plaques in the brains of people with existing Alzheimer's have been unsuccessful. The challenge is to ward off this amyloid cascade and halt the neural decay at the earliest possible stage (Khachaturian and others, 2008).

This means early diagnosis is crucial. We need to identify Alzheimer's before its full-blown symptoms arrive (Bain and others, 2008; Khachaturian and others, 2008). Unfortunately, scientists cannot look into the brain to actually see the individual neurons. So the current classic way of diagnosing Alzheimer's is to: (1) Look for a history of steady mental deterioration (rapid mental confusion signals a state called *delirium* which, in the elderly, may be due to anything from the side-effects of medications, to dietary imbalances, to a heart attack); (2) rule out other physical and psychological causes; and (3) explore performance on a battery of neuropsychological tests.

Still, a few cutting-edge biological techniques exist: Blood levels of amyloid may be an early marker for Alzheimer's (Luis and others, 2009). Brain imaging techniques can reveal cortical atrophy and plaque formation and so also possibly provide clues into beginning signs of the disease (Chetelat and others, 2008; Davatzikos and others, 2008; Eustache & Chetelat, 2008; Frisoni and others, 2008; Hall and others, 2008;

Villemange and others, 2008). Scientists are examining cerebrospinal fluid of at-risk older people for the by-products of amyloid, too (Ewers and others, 2008; Lewczuk and others, 2008; Kawarabayaski & Shoji, 2008).

Older adults diagnosed with *mild cognitive impairment* are center stage in this research effort. These people show serious learning impairments in the laboratory (Broder and others, 2008), but they have not crossed the line to Alzheimer's disease (Khachaturian, 2008; Villemagne and others, 2008). Not everyone labeled with mild cognitive impairment makes the transition to Alzheimer's. However, a good fraction (roughly 1 in 2 people) is destined to develop the illness within a few years (Alzheimer's Association, 2009; Guarch and others, 2008; Manly and others, 2008). How does the brain function and neuropsychological test performance of these people differ from that of normal older adults? (Bondi and others, 2008; Davatzikos, 2008.) And what about middle-aged adults with the APOE-4 marker? Do they manifest slowed EEGs or other atypical brain changes that may foreshadow the possible onset of the disease? (Ponomareva, Korovaitseva, & Rogaev, 2008; Trivedi and others, 2008.) Once we have developed these "biomarkers" of incipient Alzheimer's, we then can focus on the laborious process of testing out drugs that might stop the illness in its tracks (Alzheimer's Association, 2009; Khachaturian and others, 2008.)

Joel Rafkin/Photo Edit

These seventy-something dancers in the photo you saw at the beginning of Chapter 12, are not only likely to see themselves as young—but their favorite activity may actually help prevent Alzheimer's disease!

In the meantime, is there anything you and I can do? Unfortunately, there is no specific anti-Alzheimer's diet. Some scientists tout the potential of anti-inflammatory drugs, such as aspirin (Christen, 2008; Vasto and others, 2008). But so far, the value of these medicines is unproved. It's a good policy, as you saw in the last chapters, to generally keep mentally active. But despite a blossoming brain-stimulating-gadget industry aimed at anxious baby boomer consumers, there is *no evidence* that doing mental exercises will stave off any dementing disease. However, longitudinal studies suggest that people who dance or work out regularly have a lower risk of developing late-life dementia (Abbott and others, 2004). Even more tantalizing, exercise (via treadmills or running wheels) stimulates neurogenesis in the hippocampi of laboratory rats (Van der Borght and others, 2007; Lou and others, 2008; Pietropaolo and others, 2008). So if I had to vote, my number-one candidate for an anti-Alzheimer's strategy would be *physical exercise*. Even if it doesn't help construct new neurons in our species, at a minimum, regularly going to the gym or walking will help stave off the vascular component of a dementing illness (and many other diseases).

INTERVENTIONS: Dealing with Dementing Diseases

What about the efficacy of those anti-Alzheimer's drugs we hear about on TV? Yes, medications can slow the downward progression of symptoms; but they cannot halt the underlying disease process once it has begun (Alzheimer's Association, 2009). Therefore, as of this writing (mid-2009) with dementia, the main interventions still are environmental. They involve providing the best disease–environment fit for the person and helping dementia's second casualty—caregivers.

FOR THE PERSON WITH DEMENTIA: USING EXTERNAL AIDS AND MAKING LIFE PREDICTABLE AND SAFE. Creative external aids such as Hal's strategy of using note cards can be used to jog memory, particularly when people are in the beginning stages of the illness (Kasl-Godley & Gatz, 2000). To preserve performance in these vital ADL activities, it helps to carefully put shoes right next to socks or the coffee pot by the cup, and verbally remind the person what to do. A prime concern is safety. To prevent people from wandering off (or driving off!), caregivers need to double-lock or put buzzers on doors. They must deactivate dangerous appliances, such as the stove, and put toxic substances, such as household cleaners, out of reach. Some nursing facilities have innovative specialized Alzheimer's units, with living environments designed to promote cognitive capacities and staff skilled in dealing with dementing diseases. At every stage of the illness, the goals are to (1) protect people and keep them functioning as well as possible for as long as possible and (2) be caring and offer loving support.

So far, I have mainly discussed what others can do for dementia—as if the disease process had magically evaporated a human being. This assumption is wrong. The real profiles in courage are the people in the early stages of these illnesses, getting together to problem-solve and offer each other support. What does it feel like to be losing your basic anchor, your inner self? We already got insights from Hal in the Experiencing the Lifespan box. Now, let's read what other people with early Alzheimer's have to say:

> Well the first word that comes to my mouth is fear; becoming an infant, incontinence, not knowing who you are . . . I can go on and on, with those kinds of expressions.
>
> (quoted in MacRae, 2008, p. 400)

Outsiders can compound this terror when they develop their own kind of memory problem—centering only on the label and forgetting about the real human being inside. A woman named Bea vividly described this situation when she was first told her diagnosis:

> The last person who interviewed me was the neurologist. He was very indifferent and said it was just going to get worse. . . . He had no feelings for me. . . . Health-care professionals need to be compassionate. . . . There but for the grace of God go I.
>
> (quoted in Snyder, 1999, pp. 17–18)

Can people with Alzheimer's courageously face down their diagnosis and keep their sense of self-efficacy intact? Listen to a man named Ed:

> Life is a challenge . . . life is something you have to continually affirm, you know I am alive and I'm going to live life to the best I can. (If) people want to (say) oh what's the point in living? Well they've stopped living. And I think you only get one chance and this is it. Make the most of it.
>
> (quoted in McRae, 2008, p. 401)

Another man named Gorman went even further:

> This early diagnosis has given me time to enjoy the life I have now. . . .: A beautiful sunset, a tree in the spring, the rising sun over the city. Yes having Alzheimer's has changed my life; it has made me appreciate life more. I no longer take things for granted.
>
> (quoted in McRae, 2008, p. 401)

Can people with dementia give us other inspiring insights into what it means to be fully mature? Judge for yourself, as you read what a loving dad named Booker has to say about the cycle of life:

> I'm blessed to have a wonderful daughter. I sent her to . . . school and college and now she takes care of all of my business. . . . I'm in her hands. I'm in my baby phase now, so to speak. So sometimes I call her "my mumma." . . . Yes, she's my mumma now. [Booker smiled appreciatively.] . . . She's my backbone. She's such a blessing to me.
>
> (quoted in Snyder, 1999, p. 103)

FOR THE CAREGIVER: COPING WITH LIFE TURNED UPSIDE DOWN. Imagine suspecting that your beloved father or spouse has dementia. You know that the illness is permanent. You must helplessly witness your loved one deteriorate. It's no wonder that many family members report initially denying what is happening: "She never had much of a memory." "He's just getting old" (Carpentier and others, 2008). Then, after getting the diagnosis, the response is shock, grief, and uncertainty: "What can I expect?" (Laakkonen and others, 2008.) As the disease progresses to its middle stage, the challenge is to deal with a human being who has turned alien, where the tools used in normal encounters no longer apply. The person may be physically and verbally abusive. She may be agitated and wake and wander in the night. When the older adult becomes incontinent and needs total care, people typically suffer the guilt of putting their family member in a nursing home. Or they decide to put their life on hold for years as they care for the person every minute of the day.

What strategies do people use to cope? One study with African American caregivers revealed that many people rely on their faith for solace: "This is my mission from God" (Dilworth-Anderson, Boswell, & Cohen, 2007). Others turn to the vast array of Alzheimer's caregiver support groups and Internet chat rooms for advice: "She seems to get worse during the night." "What works for you?" "My husband hit me the other day, and I was devastated." "Keep telling yourself it's the illness. People with dementia can't help how they act."

Another key lies in changing your orientation to the wider world:

> *Accept the fact that the patient won't be able to live up to even minimum standards of behavior. . . . Let it go. . . . I realized I never knew what would happen but I . . . decided that wasn't a reason not to do things. He was happier and I was happier if the ordinary standards of life just didn't apply.*

(quoted in Aneshensel and others, 1995, p. 170)

And—most of all—you can simply relish the time together you have left:

> *(Tom and Jane, married for 63 years, who were being interviewed about the illness) sat close to one another on the couch . . . and shared a great deal of smiles and giggles... and at times it felt they were the only people in the room . . . Although the stories Jane told did not always make sense, her eyes lit up whenever a question was asked about her marriage to Tom . . . What cannot be easily captured on paper were the warm interactions . . . The investigators felt privileged to be part of such a rich process in which one couple had the opportunity to share the story of their relationship together.*

(quoted in Daniels, Lamson, & Hodgson, 2007, p. 167)

Yes, dealing with a loved one with dementia is often intensely embarrassing (Montoro-Rodriguez and others, 2009). It's terribly stressful and depressing, too. But this life experience offers its own *redemption sequence.* Dementia caregivers, as you can see above, tend to grow emotionally and think about life in more complex ways (Leipold, Schake, & Zank, 2009). Most important, coping with this illness teaches people what is really important in life. (Table 14.3 summarizes these messages in a list of caregiving tips.)

Until this point, I've been exploring how older people and their loved ones can personally take action to promote the best person–environment fit when old-age frailties strike. In the next section, I'll look at what society is doing to help.

TABLE 14.3: Tips for Helping People with Dementia

1. Provide clear cues to alert the person to the surroundings, such as using note cards with important names and addresses and labeling rooms and objects around the home (for example, use a picture of the toilet and tub at the door to the bathroom); use strong, contrasting colors to highlight the difference between different rooms in the house.

2. Protect the person from getting injured by double-locking the doors, turning off the stove, and taking away the keys to the car.

3. Offer a highly predictable, structured daily routine.

4. Don't take insulting comments personally. Try to understand that "it's the disease talking."

5. *Remember that there is a real person in there.* Respect the individual's personhood.

6. Try to see the silver lining; this is a time to understand what's really important in life, to grow as a person and show your love.

7. Definitely join a caregiver support group—and contact the Alzheimer's Association (www. Alzheimer's Association).

TYING IT ALL TOGETHER

1. Your grandmother has just been diagnosed with dementia. Describe the two disease processes that typically cause this condition.

2. Mary, age 50, is terrified of getting a dementing disease. Which statement can you make that is both accurate and comforting?

   a. Don't worry. Dementia is typically an illness of the "old-old" years.
   b. Don't worry. Very few people have dementia even in their nineties.
   c. Don't worry. Scientists can cure dementing illnesses when the illnesses are caught at their earliest stages.

3. You are giving a status report to a senate committee on biomedical efforts to prevent dementia. First, target the main research problem scientists face. Then, offer a tip to the worried elderly senators about a strategy that *might* help ward off the disease.

4. Mrs. Jones has just been diagnosed with early Alzheimer's disease. Her relatives might help by:

   a. taking steps to keep her safe in her home.
   b. encouraging her to attend an Alzheimer's patient support group.
   c. treating her like a human being.
   d. doing all of the above.

Answers to the Tying It All Together questions can be found on the last page of this chapter.

Options and Services for the Frail Elderly

Suppose that, like Theresa in the chapter-opening vignette, you are developing ADL problems. Cooking and cleaning are difficult. You start out by using selection and optimization. You focus on your most essential activities. You spend more time on each important life task. You are determined to live independently for as long as possible. But you know that the time is coming when you will enter Baltes's full-fledged compensation mode. You will need to depend on other people for your daily needs. Where can you turn?

Setting the Context: Scanning the Global Elder-Care Scene

For most of human history and in many regions of the developing world today, older people would never confront this challenge. Families lived in multigenerational households. When the oldest generation needed help, loving caregivers were right on the scene.

Today, however, with women in the labor force and the younger generations moving from the villages to cities to find work, this support network is fraying. So today, especially residents of newly affluent nations such as South Korea and China are turning to Western society-wide models of providing elder care (Chow and others, 2004).

The Scandinavian countries, in particular, offer excellent models for the kinds of comprehensive services an advanced society can provide. In Sweden, Norway, and Denmark, government-funded home health services swing into operation to help impaired older people "age in place"—meaning stay in their own homes. Residents can get cash grants to remodel their homes in the ways discussed earlier in this chapter (see Johansson, Josephsson, & Lilja, 2009). Innovative elderly housing alternatives dot the countryside—from multigenerational villages with a central community center providing health care to small nursing facilities with attractive private rooms (Johri, Beland, & Bergman, 2003).

In Scandinavia—as in every nation—families still take on the main responsibility of caring for the older generation. But because their governments fully fund services designed to help their disabled older citizens, elderly people living in these countries (and other Western E.U. nations) do not have to worry about what will happen to them should they get physically impaired.

Alternatives to Institutions in the United States

In the United States, we do have these worries. The reason is that **Medicare**, our health insurance system for the elderly, pays only for services defined as cure-oriented. It does not cover help with activities of daily living—the very ongoing services with cooking or cleaning or bathing that might keep people out of a nursing home when they are having some trouble functioning in life.

What choices do disabled older people in the United States (and people who love them) have *other* than going to a nursing home? Here are the main **alternatives to institutionalization** that exist today:

- A **continuing-care retirement community** is a residential complex that provides different levels of services from independent apartments to nursing home care. Continuing care is designed to provide people with the ultimate person—environment fit. Residents arrive in relatively good health and then get the appropriate type of care as their physical needs change. With this type of housing, older adults are purchasing peace of mind. They don't have to worry about burdening their children if they develop ADL problems. They know exactly where they will be going if and when they need nursing home care.

- An **assisted-living facility** is specifically for people who are currently experiencing ADL limitations but do not have the kinds of problems with dressing or feeding themselves that require full-time, 24-hour care. Assisted living—which has mushroomed in popularity in the United States over the past decade—offers care in a less medicalized, homey setting. Residents often have private rooms with their own furniture. The staff is attuned to older adults' need for independence. These settings do not have the overtones of an anonymous, institutional "old-age home" (Phillips & Hawes, 2005).

- **Day-care programs** are specifically for older people who live with their families. Much like its namesake for children, adult day care provides activities and a place for an impaired older person to go when family members are at work and feel uncomfortable about leaving that person alone. Because this service allows relatives—especially caregiving children—to care for a frail parent in their own home without having to give up their other responsibilities—day care puts off the need for a nursing home (Cho, Zarit, & Chirboga, 2009; Schacke & Zank, 2006).

- **Home health services** help people age "in place" (at home). Paid caregivers come to the house to cook, clean, and help the older adult with personal care activities such as bathing.

Assisted living has become an enticing option for upper-middle-class people with ADL impairments. The breathtaking atrium in this photo shows that top-of-the-line housing of this type often looks like a luxurious hotel.

Jim Wilson/The New York Times/Redux

With their homey atmosphere and services, assisted-living and continuing-care facilities can be marvelous places to spend your final years of life (I'm planning on going to one of these facilities myself!)—especially if you enjoy the food and connect with your fellow residents (Street and others, 2007). The problem is that—as you saw in the opening vignette—these housing alternatives are not covered by Medicare and so are mainly available to older adults with means (Ball and others, 2009). Can you devise some innovative, low-cost options for helping frail older people? We are in especially dire need of housing that bridges the gap from living independently to the need for a setting specially tailored for people who *are* severely physically impaired—the nursing home.

Nursing Home Care

Nursing homes, or **long-term-care facilities,** provide shelter and services to people with basic ADL problems—individuals who really do require 24-hour intensive caregiving help. Although adults of every age live in nursing homes, it should come as no surprise that the main risk factor for entering these institutions is being very old. The average nursing home resident is in his—or, I should say, her—late eighties and nineties. Because, as we know, females live sicker well into advanced old age, women make up the vast majority of residents in long-term-care (Belsky, 2001).

What causes people to enter nursing homes? Often, as you saw in the chapter-opening vignette, an older adult arrives after some physically incapacitating event, such as falling and breaking a hip. Given that dementia requires such daunting 24/7 care, roughly half of the nursing home population has been diagnosed with some dementing disease.

In predicting who ends up in a nursing home, both nature and nurture forces are involved. Yes, the person's biology (or physical state) does matter a good deal. But so does the environment, specifically whether family members are available to provide care. A spouse is the first line of defense against a nursing home. Children, particularly caregiving daughters, as you saw in Chapter 12, come second. People such as Theresa, who have no close living relatives, are at very high risk of ending their lives in long-term care (Belsky, 2001).

Just as the routes by which people arrive differ, residents take different paths once they enter nursing homes. Sometimes, a nursing home is a short stop before returning home. Or it may be a short interlude before death. Some residents live for years in long-term care.

You might be surprised to learn who is paying for these residents' care. Because people start out paying the huge costs out of their own pockets and "spend down" until they are impoverished, it is *Medicaid*, the U.S. health-care system specifically for the poor that finances our nation's nursing homes.

Evaluating Nursing Homes

Nursing homes are often viewed as dumping grounds where residents are abused or left to languish unattended until they die. How accurate are these stereotypes? Many times, the generalizations are unfair. Some nursing homes are rich in services, with state-of-the-art features, such as private rooms and a full complement of activities specifically tailored to residents' needs. There is a vigorous movement underway to change the nursing-home culture to make it more person-centered, or attentive to residents' individual needs (Rahman & Schnelle, 2008). But unfortunately, the disturbing images can also ring true. Surveys suggest 1 in 4 U.S. nursing homes provides seriously substandard care (Wiener, 2003). Even the best nursing home has psychological liabilities. Residents must suffer from the identity-eroding losses basic to living in any institution. Imagine having to share a small room with a stranger. You are required to eat the foods the facility serves at predetermined hours (Kane, 1995–1996). You can't just decide to lie in bed or refuse to take a medicine. Your every action—from sitting in a chair to being taken to the bathroom—is dependent on the health-care workers who are providing care (Solum, Slettebo, & Hauge, 2008).

Medicare The U.S. government's program of health insurance for elderly people.

alternatives to institutionalization Services and settings designed to keep older people who are experiencing age-related disabilities that don't merit intense 24-hour care from having to enter nursing homes.

continuing-care retirement community A housing option characterized by a series of levels of care for elderly residents, ranging from independent apartments to assisted living to nursing home care. People enter the community in relatively good health and move to sections where they can get more care when they become disabled.

assisted-living facility A housing option providing care for elderly people who have instrumental ADL impairments and can no longer live independently but may not need a nursing home.

day-care program A service for impaired older adults who live with relatives, in which the older person spends the day at a center offering various activities.

home health services Nursing–oriented and housekeeping help provided in the home of an impaired older adult (or any other impaired person).

nursing home/long-term-care facility A residential institution that provides shelter and intensive caregiving, primarily to older people who need help with basic ADLs.

certified nurse assistant or aide The main hands-on care provider in a nursing home, who helps elderly residents with basic ADL problems.

This brings up the health-care worker who is the main front-line care-provider in the nursing home—the **certified nurse assistant or aide**. Just as during life's early years, caregiving at the upper end of the lifespan is low-status work. Nursing home aides, like their counterparts in day-care centers, make poverty-level wages. Facilities are chronically understaffed (Quadagno & Stahl, 2003; Teeri and others, 2008). So even when an aide loves what she does, the conditions of the job can make it difficult to provide adequate care. Having worked in long-term care, I can testify that residents are sometimes left lying in urine for hours. They wait inordinately long for help getting fed. One reason is that it can take hours to feed the eight or so people in your care when dinner arrives!

Still, although they hate the pay and complain about the low status (Teeri and others, 2008), people get a real sense of satisfaction from this job. In one survey of U.S. aides, on the dimension of "work quality," the average ranking was close to 8 on a 10-point scale (Castle, 2007). Listen to what Jayson, a mellow, six-foot-tall, 200-pound giant says about his job as an activities director at a Philadelphia nursing home:

> At first I was put off by the smells. . . . Then I got moved to the Alzheimer's unit . . . and I found this to be like . . . the best task I ever had. . . . If you just come in here and say, "Okay, I got a job to do and I'm just doing my job," . . . then you're in the wrong field. . . . When somebody here dies, we all talk, we say how much we miss the person. . . . Some of them cry. . . . Some of them go to their funerals. . . . I actually spoke at some of the funerals. . . . I say how much this person meant to me.
>
> (quoted in Black & Rubinstein, 2005, pp. S-4–6)

For Jayson, who, after being shot and lingering near death, reported seeing an angel visit him in the form of a little old man, his career is a calling from God. At age 36, he is flourishing in this consummately generative job. What about nursing home residents? Can people get it together within this most unlikely setting of life? For uplifting answers, check out the Experiencing the Lifespan box.

EXPERIENCING THE LIFESPAN: GETTING IT TOGETHER IN THE NURSING HOME

A few years ago, I attended an unforgettable memorial service at a Florida nursing home. Person after person rose to eulogize this woman, a passionate advocate who had worked with immense self-efficacy to make a difference in her fellow residents' lives. Then Mrs. Alonzo's son told his story. He said that he had never really known his mother. When he was young, she became schizophrenic and was shunted from institution to institution. Then, at age 68, Mrs. Alonzo entered the nursing home to await death. It was only in this place, where life is supposed to end, that she blossomed as a human being.

If you think that this story is unique, that personal growth is virtually impossible in a nursing home, listen to this friend of mine, a psychologist who, like Jayson, finds her generativity in nursing home work:

My most amazing success entered treatment two years ago. This severely depressed resident had had an abusive childhood and marriage and suffered from enduring feelings of powerlessness and low self-esteem, and yet was very bright. I think that being sent to our institution allowed this woman to make the internal changes that she had been incapable of before. She began to look at her past and see how her experiences had shaped her poor sense of self and then to see her inner strengths. She and I formed a very close, very strong relationship.

So then she decided to work on becoming closer to her children. She had been aloof as a mother, and she told me that once her younger child had asked her to say that she loved her and she couldn't get the words out. Now, at age 89, she called this daughter, told her that she did love her and that she was sorry she couldn't say it before. Her daughters said that I had presented them with a miracle, the loving mother they always wanted. The nurses marveled at how my patient had been transformed. She made friends on the floor and became active in the residents' council. In the time we saw one another she used to tell me, "I never believed I could change at this age."

As she finished her story, my friend's eyes filled with tears: "My patient died a few months ago, and I still miss her so much."

 TYING IT ALL TOGETHER

1. You are a geriatric counselor, and an 85-year-old woman and her family come to your office for advice about the best arrangement for her care. Match the letter of each item below with the number of the suggestion that would be most appropriate if this elderly client:

    a. is affluent, worried about living alone, and has no ADL problems.
    b. has ADL impairments (but can still get around) and is living with the family—who want to continue to care for her at home.
    c. has instrumental ADL impairments (but can still perform basic self-care activities), can no longer live alone, and has a good amount of money.
    d. has basic ADL impairments.
    e. is beginning to have ADL impairments, lives alone, and has very little money (but does not qualify for Medicaid).

        (1) a continuing-care retirement facility
        (2) an assisted-living facility
        (3) a day-care program
        (4) a nursing home
        (5) There are no good alternatives you can suggest; people in this situation must struggle to cope at home.

2. Joey and Jane now realize that their mother needs to go a nursing home. Which of the following statements about this mother's situation—and nursing homes in general—is *not* true?

    a. Their mom is probably old-old and widowed.
    b. Medicare will completely cover their mom's expenses.
    c. The quality of the facilities their mom will possibly go to can vary greatly.
    d. The caregivers their mom will have probably hate their jobs.

3. Given the future explosion of the old-old, devise a few innovative solutions to the issue of caring for the frail elderly, other than the ones described in this chapter.

Answers to the Tying It All Together questions can be found on the last page of this chapter.

Final Thoughts

Dealing with the physical challenges of old age is a major social challenge we must confront in the developed world in roughly a decade as the baby boomers begin to move into their old-old years. Unfortunately, we cannot rely on medical miracles to magically erase the impairments that are the downside of our progress in getting so many people close to the biological maximum of life. We need to make preparations for the looming old-old army right now.

Our personal challenge, as you learned in these later life chapters, is to take steps to live fully as long as we are alive. The Experiencing the Lifespan box you just read highlights the fact—again—that yes, it is possible to flourish even in a nursing home. It underlines the importance of close attachments or relationships in promoting a meaningful life. Plus, the story of this woman who got it together in the nursing home enriches Erikson's masterful ideas that have guided our lifespan tour: It's never too late to accomplish developmental tasks that we may have missed. People can find their real identity (or authentic self), fulfill their generativity, and so reach integrity in their final months of life!

In the next chapter, I'll continue this theme of inner development and also stress the crucial importance of making connections with loved ones as I focus directly on life's endpoint—death.

SUMMARY

Tracing Physical Aging

Normal aging changes progress into **chronic disease** and finally, during the old-old years, may result in impairments in **activities of daily living (ADLs),** either less incapacitating **instrumental ADL problems** or **basic ADL problems**—troubles with basic self-care. Although living much beyond a century is impossible, the statistical odds of getting fairly close to our maximum lifespan are good when people live in an affluent country, rank high on that nation's socioeconomic status ladder, are not a member of a disadvantaged ethnic minority, and are female.

The **socioeconomic/health gap** refers to the fact that as social status rises—within each nation—people live healthier for a longer time. A variety of forces, from health-compromising lifestyles to stress, to inadequate medical care, make low income a major risk factor for early disability and death. African Americans are at a higher risk of dying (particularly from cardiovascular diseases) than any other ethnic group. Another risk factor for dying earlier is being male. Men tend to die quicker primarily because they have heart attacks at younger ages. Women live longer but report more health problems at every stage of adult life. The female "health orientation," or sensitivity to illness, may help promote longevity, too.

Sensory-Motor Changes

The classic age-related vision problems—**presbyopia** (impairments in near vision), difficulties seeing in dim light, and problems with glare—are caused by a rigid, cloudier **lens.** Modifying lighting can help compensate for these losses. Cataracts, the endpoint of a cloudy lens, can be easily treated, although the other major age-related vision impairments often result in a more permanent loss of sight. If vision losses are permanent people often rely on external aids and their own emotional resources to cope.

The old-age hearing impairment **presbycusis** presents special problems because it limits a person's contact with the human world. Because chronic exposure to noise causes this selective loss for high-pitched tones, men are at higher risk of having hearing handicaps, especially at younger ages. To help a hearing-impaired person, limit low-pitched background noise and speak distinctly—but avoid **elderspeak,** the impulse to talk to the older person like a baby. For your own future hearing, protect yourself against excessive noise.

"Slowness" in later life is due to age-related changes in **reaction time** and skeletal conditions such as osteoarthritis and **osteoporosis** (thin, fragile bones). Osteoporosis is a special concern because falling and breaking a hip is a major reason for entering a nursing home. With mobility problems, the key is to keep as active as possible and take care to modify one's home to reduce the risk of falls and injury.

Although older people drive less often, accident rates per miles driven rise sharply among drivers over age 75. Solutions to the problem, such as mandatory vision testing over a certain age, may not work so well, as driving involves many sensory, motor, and cognitive skills. Modifying the driving environment and especially developing a more car-free society is a critical challenge today.

Dementia

Dementia, the most feared old-age condition, is typically caused by **Alzheimer's disease** (neural atrophy accompanied by **senile plaques** and **neurofibrillary tangles**) and/or **vascular dementia** (small strokes). These diseases typically erupt during the old-old years and progress gradually, with the person losing all functions. Scientists are trying to prevent the accumulation of the plaques (the hallmark of Alzheimer's disease) by targeting this illness at its very earliest stage, and studying people with a genetic marker that makes them more prone to this disease. Today, Alzheimer's cannot be prevented or cured, although physical exercise *may* possibly help ward off its onset. The key is to make environmental modifications to keep the person safe—and understand that older adults with dementia are still people. Caregivers' accounts and the testaments of people with early stage dementia offer profiles in what human courage is all about.

Options and Services for the Frail Elderly

Elderly people in developed countries live apart from their families. In many developing nations, they traditionally lived in multigenerational households, with a built-in family support network when they became frail—but no more. We now need formal (non-family) structures to help seriously ADL impaired older people handle life. In the United States the major **alternatives to institutionalization**—**continuing-care retirement communities, assisted-living facilities, day-care programs,** and **home health services**—are typically fairly costly. These options are not covered by **Medicare.** We need creative services to keep frail older people from prematurely entering that setting designed for the most impaired older adults—the nursing home.

Being female and very old, and not having available family members, are the main risk factors for entering **nursing homes,** or **long-term-care facilities.** Nursing homes vary dramatically in quality, but in general there are tremendous "independence" losses intrinsic to living in long-term care. The **certified nursing assistant or aide,** the main caregiver, while very poorly paid, can find a generative mission in nursing home work. Society needs to prepare for the onslaught of baby boomers as they enter their old-old years. People can develop as human beings even in a nursing home, and reach every Eriksonian milestone during their final years—or months—of life.

KEY TERMS

normal aging changes, p. 422

chronic disease, p. 422

ADL (activities of daily living) problems, p. 422

instrumental ADL problems, p. 422

basic ADL limitations, p. 423

socioeconomic/health gap, p. 424

presbyopia, p. 429

lens, p. 430

presbycusis, p. 431

elderspeak, p. 432

reaction time, p. 433

osteoporosis, p. 433

dementia, p. 436

vascular dementia, p. 438

Alzheimer's disease, p. 438

neurofibrillary tangles, p. 438

senile plaques, p. 438

Medicare, p. 444

alternatives to institutionalization, p. 444

continuing-care retirement community, p. 444

assisted-living facility, p. 444

day-care program, p. 444

home health services, p. 444

nursing home/long-term-care facility, p. 445

certified nurse assistant or aide, p. 446

ANSWERS TO TYING IT ALL TOGETHER QUIZZES

Tracing Physical Aging

1. b.

2. Margery has *instrumental ADL problems*. Sara has *basic ADL problems*.

3. c.

4. c.

Sensory-Motor Changes

1. lens; a cataract; can be cured by surgery

2. d.

3. a, c, and e. (All of the other suggestions will make grandma's eyesight worse.)

4. Tell the lawmakers that relying just on an eye exam won't be effective because driving is dependent on many sensory and motor skills, and cognitive impairments are especially prone to cause wrecks. Suggest sponsoring bills to change roads and highways by putting adequate lighting on exit ramps, more traffic signals at intersections (especially left-turn signals), and exploring other ways to make the driving environment more age-friendly. Most important, foster initiatives that don't depend on driving: Invest in public transportation. Give tax incentives to developers to locate shopping embedded in residential neighborhoods, and to stimulate businesses that promote alternatives to cars.

Dementia

1. The illnesses are Alzheimer's disease, which involves deterioration of the neurons and their replacement with senile plaques and tangles, and vascular dementia, which involve small strokes. (If grandma is old-old, she's likely to have both illnesses.)

2. a.

3. The main problem scientists face is diagnosing incipient Alzheimer's before it progresses to the disease stage—so that we can develop treatments to ward off the illness. Tell the worried senators that they should start a fitness regimen now! While we don't have definitive evidence, there are strong hints that regular exercise may help stave off dementia.

4. d.

Options and Services for the Frail Elderly

1. *a*, 1; *b*, 3; *c*, 2; *d*, 4; *e*, 5.

2. b and d.

3. Here, you can use your own creativity. My suggestions: 1. Develop a government-funded program whereby people get cash incentives to care for frail elders in their homes. 2. Build small, intergenerational living communities, with a centrally located home option specifically for the frail elderly. Residents who buy houses here would commit to taking care of the older adults in their midst. 3. House frail elderly on college campuses; have students do hands-on service learning with this group. 4. Establish a nationwide scholarship program (perhaps called the "Belsky Grant"!) whereby your tuition and college expenses are paid if you commit to caring for frail elders in the community.

Chapter 15

Death and Dying

I was getting in the car to drive to work when Amy screamed, "Stewart! Come listen to the news!" We figured out pretty quickly that it came in right about the floor where she worked, the 96th. By the time the tower came down, we knew for sure that she died. With a normal death, you prepare for the grieving process. With a shocking death, it hits you by surprise. My wife was about to give birth to our first child, and my mother had plane tickets to come down on Friday. You get into the part of it where you mentally play back the events. Mom (typical, for her) had gone in to work early so she could leave for a dentist appointment. If she'd been a less responsible person, she would not have been there at 8:46. The other weird part of it is, like, the whole country feels they own pieces of this tragedy and need to constantly remind you about it. So it doesn't go away.

My mom didn't have young children, but she was looking forward to retirement, to being a grandmother, and so she was cheated of all those things. Not only did she die in this horrible way—she died at an unacceptably early age.

. . .

In his seventies my father seemed immortal. While he often joked about being an "old man," he had no major infirmities. At age 81, mortality hit. For a few months Dad had been listless—not his old self, suddenly looking old. Then came the unforgettable call: "The doctor says that it's cancer of the liver. Jan, I'm going to die."

Because medicine never admits defeat, the plan was three rounds of chemotherapy, punctuated by "recovery" at home. The doctor said, "Maybe we can lick this thing," but the treatments were agonizing. Worse yet, recovery never happened. My father got weaker. After a few months he could barely walk. Then, before going into the hospital for the third round, my mother called: "Last night we cried together and decided not to continue. We're calling in hospice. I think it's time for you to come down." My father had two more weeks to live.

A day or two before you die, you slip into a coma. It's the preceding week or two that lasts for years. Everyone has been summoned to bustle around a train that cannot be derailed. Yes, you can talk, but what do you say? My father was never a verbal man. Then, as if on cue, the disease picks up speed. From the wheelchair to becoming bedridden, the voice that mutates into a whisper, followed by waiting . . . for what? You force yourself to be at the bedside when the breathing gets slow and rattled, but you are terrified. You have never seen a dying person. You don't know how things will go. Above all, you hope that things go quickly. You can't stand to see your father suffer anymore.

My father died in the "normal" late-twentieth-century way. Although we knew nothing about the actual process by which people die, we had plenty of time to plan for the event. Dad's death came at the "right" time, at the end of a long life. The kind of death Stewart's mother faced on September 11 was horrifying, unexpected— totally outside the norm. How does death *really* happen today? How did people die in centuries past?

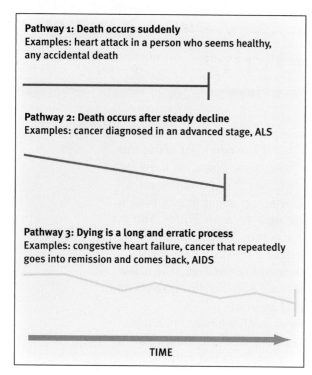

Pathway 1: Death occurs suddenly
Examples: heart attack in a person who seems healthy, any accidental death

Pathway 2: Death occurs after steady decline
Examples: cancer diagnosed in an advanced stage, ALS

Pathway 3: Dying is a long and erratic process
Examples: congestive heart failure, cancer that repeatedly goes into remission and comes back, AIDS

TIME

FIGURE 15.1: **Three pathways to death:** Although some people die suddenly, the pattern in blue and especially that in yellow are the most common pathways by which people die today.

For most of human history, death was ever present—"up close and personal"—and occurred in the midst of normal life. Here is an eighteenth-century painting entitled "The Dying Request," in which a dying young woman is offering her final words to her spouse.

THE DYING REQUEST.

Mary Evans Picture Library/The Image Works

Setting the Context

Today, as Figure 15.1 suggests, our pathways to death take distinctly different forms (Enck, 2003; Field, 2009). As happened most dramatically in the World Trade Center tragedy, roughly 1 out of every 6 or 7 people in developed nations dies without any warning—as a result either of an accident or, more often, of a sudden, fatal, age-related event, such as a heart attack or stroke (Enck, 2003; see the red line in Figure 15.1). My father's death fit the pattern when illnesses such as cancer are discovered at an advanced stage. Here, as you can see in the blue line, a person is diagnosed with a fatal disease and then steadily declines.

The prolonged, erratic pattern shown in yellow, however, is probably the most common dying pathway in our contemporary age of extended chronic disease. After developing cancer, kidney problems, or heart disease, people battle that condition for years, helped by medical technology until death eventually occurs.

So today, deaths in affluent countries typically occur slowly. They are dominated by medical procedures. They have a protracted, uncertain course (Field, 2009). For most of human history, people died in a very different way.

A Short History of Death

She contracted a summer cholera. After four days she asked to see the village priest, who came and waited to give her the last rites. "Not yet, M. le Curé, I'll let you know when the time comes." Two days later: "Go and tell M. le Curé to bring me Extreme Unction."

(reported in Walter, 2003, p. 213)

As you can see in this nineteenth-century description of the death of a French peasant woman, before modern medicine, death typically arrived quickly. People let nature take its course. There was nothing they could do. Dying was familiar, predictable, and normal. It was firmly embedded in daily life (Wood & Williamson, 2003).

According to the historian Philippe Ariès (1974, 1981), while life in the Middle Ages was unimaginably horrid and "wild," death was often "tame." Famine, childbirth, and infectious disease ensured that death was an expected presence throughout the lifespan. People died, as they lived, in full view of the community and then were buried in the churchyard in the center of town.

During the eighteenth and nineteenth centuries, death began to move off center stage when—because of fears about disease—villagers decided to relocate burial sites to cemeteries outside of town (Kastenbaum, 2004). Then, a more dramatic change took place about a century ago, when doctors began to vigorously wage war against disease. The early-twentieth-century conquest of many infectious illnesses moved dying toward the end of the lifespan, relocating it to old age (Field, 2009). Today, with 3 out of 4 deaths in the United States taking place among people over age 65 (and often happening in our eighties and nineties), the actors in the death drama are often a marginal, atypical group—nothing like you or me.

Moreover, as medicine took over, the scene of dying shifted to hospitals and nursing homes, so the actual physical process was removed from view. Now, when a person dies, often in the inner recesses of the intensive care unit, we immediately shroud the body and erase all signs of its presence as we ship it to the funeral home (Kastenbaum, 2004). According to one social critic, by the middle of the twentieth century, death had become the new "pornography"—disgusting, abnormal, never to be seen or talked about (Gorer, 1965).

The word pornographic still may fit our twenty-first-century feelings about confronting dying in the flesh. However, beginning with the 1960s lifestyle revolutions, Western ideas related to *talking* about death totally changed. Suddenly, university courses on **thanatology** (death and dying) became the rage (Doka, 2003; Wass, 2004). Doctors did a total turnaround from the earlier practice of concealing a devastating diagnosis (never mentioning, for instance, the "C word") in favor of honestly telling people, "Yes, you have cancer, and there is not much we can do" (see Bradley & Brasel, 2008). Today, we no longer see planning the way people die as ghoulish. We vigorously urge everyone to document in writing their personal preferences for "a good, dignified death."

thanatology The study of death and dying.

Cultural Variations on a Theme

But while the mainstream societal message stresses full disclosure and active planning for our "final act," death attitudes differ dramatically from person to person and culture to culture in the contemporary United States. To demonstrate this point, let's scan the practices of a group for whom dying remains *very* up close and personal, but for whom death is never openly discussed: the Hmong.

The Hmong, persecuted for centuries in China and Southeast Asia, migrated to North America after the Vietnam War and number close to a million U.S. residents today. According to Hmong tradition, discussing dying "will unlock the gate of evil spirits." So when a person enters the terminal phase of life, no one is permitted to discuss that fact. However, when death is imminent, the family becomes intimately involved. Relatives flock around and dress the ill person in the traditional burial garment—a black robe or suit. After death arrives, they lovingly wash and groom the corpse, preparing it to be viewed.

If, contrary to Hmong custom, the person dies in a hospital, it's crucial that the body *not* be immediately sent to the morgue. The reason is that the family is required to congregate at the bedside to wail and caress the corpse for hours. Then, after a lavish four-day funeral ceremony, during which the partly shrouded body remains in full view, the deceased is lovingly dressed in warm clothing to guard against the cold, and the feet are encased in special blue shoes for the journey to the next world. At the gravesite, the coffin is reopened for a final viewing before being permanently closed (Gerdner and others, 2007). Would you be able to participate in these activities? Could you give your relative the personal, hands-on care that the Hmong and other societies routinely provided throughout history to prepare loved ones for the grave?

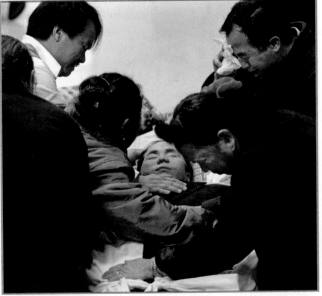

Even today, small pockets of the U.S. population adopt an intensely hands-on approach to death. Here, you can see phase one in the carefully orchestrated days-long Hmong funeral ceremony—the body, dressed in its traditional garments, being caressed by distraught family members.

This chapter explores what dying is like in the twenty-first-century West, an age of open communications, death-defying treatments, and extended chronic disease. First, I'll examine the feelings of the dying person; then, turn to the health-care system; and then, return to the person to tackle those challenging issues related to controlling the timing of when we die. As you just saw with the Hmong, however, it's crucial to remember that—just as dying pathways differ—with death and dying *in general*, diversity is the main theme. We all bring unique, *equally* valid perspectives to that ultimate universal event of human life.

TYING IT ALL TOGETHER

1. Imagine that you were born in the seventeenth or eighteenth century. Which of the following statements about your dying pathway would *not* be true?

   a. You would probably have died relatively quickly of an infectious disease.
   b. You would have died in a hospital.
   c. You would have seen death all around you from a young age.
   d. You would probably have died at a relatively young age.

2. If you follow the typical twenty-first-century pattern, as you approach death, you can expect to decline (quickly/slowly and erratically) due to (an accident/an age-related chronic disease).

3. Margaret says that, today, we live in a death-denying society. Ella says, "No, that's not true. Today, we are more accepting of death than ever." First, make Ella's case and then Margaret's, referring to the information in this section.

Answers to the Tying It All Together questions can be found on the last page of this chapter.

The Dying Person

How do people react when they are diagnosed with a fatal illness? What are their emotions as they struggle with this devastating news? The first person to scientifically study these topics was a young psychiatrist named Elisabeth Kübler-Ross.

Kübler-Ross's Stages of Dying: Description and Critique

While working as a consultant at a Chicago hospital during the 1960s, Kübler-Ross became convinced that the health-care system was neglecting the emotional needs of the terminally ill. As part of a seminar for medical students, she got permission to interview dying patients about their feelings. Many people, she found, were relieved to talk about their diagnosis. Many, she discovered, knew that their condition was terminal, even though the medical staff and family members had made valiant efforts to conceal that fact. Kübler-Ross published her discovery that open communication was important to dying people in *On Death and Dying*, a slim best-seller that ushered in a revolution in the way we treat the terminally ill.

Kübler-Ross (1969), in her **stage theory of dying**, originally proposed that we progress through five distinctive emotions in coming to terms with death: *denial, anger, bargaining, depression,* and *acceptance.* Let's now briefly look at each emotional state:

When a person first gets some terrible diagnosis, such as "You have advanced lung cancer," her immediate reaction is denial. She thinks, "There must be a mistake," and takes trips to doctor after doctor, searching for a new, more favorable set of tests. When these efforts fail, denial gives way to anger.

In the anger stage, the person lashes out, bemoaning her fate, railing at other people. One patient may get enraged at a physician: "He should have picked up my illness earlier on!" Others may direct their fury at a friend or family member: "Why did I get lung cancer at 55, while my brother, who has smoked a pack of cigarettes a day since he was 20, remains in perfect health?"

Eventually, this emotion yields to a more calculating one: bargaining. Now, the person pleads for more time, promising to be good if she can put off death a bit. Kübler-Ross (1969) gives this example of a woman who begged God to let her live long enough to attend the marriage of her oldest son:

> *The day preceding the wedding she left the hospital as an elegant lady. Nobody would have believed her real condition. She . . . looked radiant. I wondered what her reaction would be when the time was up for which she had bargained. . . . I will never forget the moment*

Kübler-Ross's stage theory of dying The landmark theory, developed by psychiatrist Elisabeth Kübler-Ross, that people who are terminally ill progress through five stages in confronting their death: denial, anger, bargaining, depression, and acceptance.

> *she returned to the hospital. She looked tired and somewhat exhausted and before I could say hello, said, "Now don't forget I have another son."*
>
> (1969, p. 83)

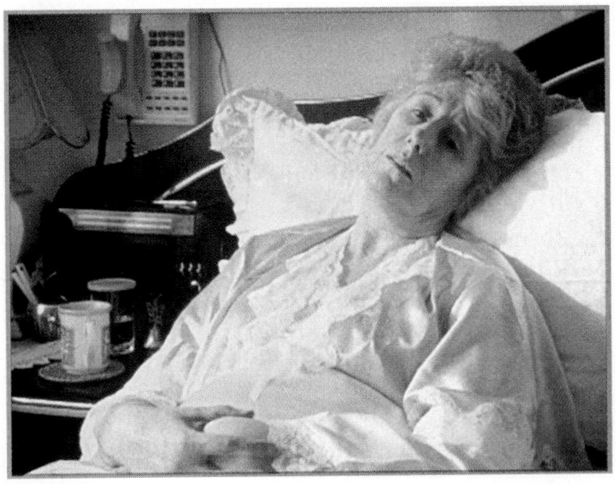

AFP/Getty Images

According to Kübler-Ross's famous *stage theory of dying,* we would label this terminally ill woman as being in the "depression phase" and then expect her to reach acceptance. But do people really die in this patterned way? As you can see here, the answer is no.

Then, once reality fully sinks in, the person gets depressed and, ultimately, reaches acceptance. By this time, the individual is quite weak and no longer feels upset, angry, or depressed. She may even look forward to the end.

Kübler-Ross deserves enormous credit for alerting us to the fact that there is a living, breathing person inside the diagnosis "terminal cancer" or "end-stage heart disease." The problem is that her original ideas were embraced in an overly rigid, simplistic way. Here are three reasons why we *cannot* take this famous theory as the final word about death:

TERMINALLY ILL PEOPLE DO *NOT* ALWAYS WANT TO DISCUSS THEIR SITUATION. Although she never intended this message, many people read into Kübler-Ross's theory the idea that all patients want to talk about impending death. This is emphatically not true (Baile, Aaron, & Parker, 2009; Shih and others, 2009; Wells-di Gregorio, 2008). When one researcher directly asked a group of terminally ill patients about their feelings about "death talk," she found that people broach this subject selectively—and often reluctantly. In the words of one respondent: "They're scary subjects and . . . we don't want to touch on it too much. . . . It's very personal" (quoted in McGrath, 2004, p. 836). Patients avoid these discussions to protect loved ones: "Because you don't want them to . . . get really upset so you . . . hold everything back. . . . My sister is good but I couldn't load off onto her, she would just break" (quoted in McGrath, 2004, p. 837). Sometimes, they shy away from this topic to emotionally protect themselves: "I think I've got as much as I can cope with. So I can't get her upset . . . and then have to try to calm her down" (quoted in McGrath, 2004, p. 839).

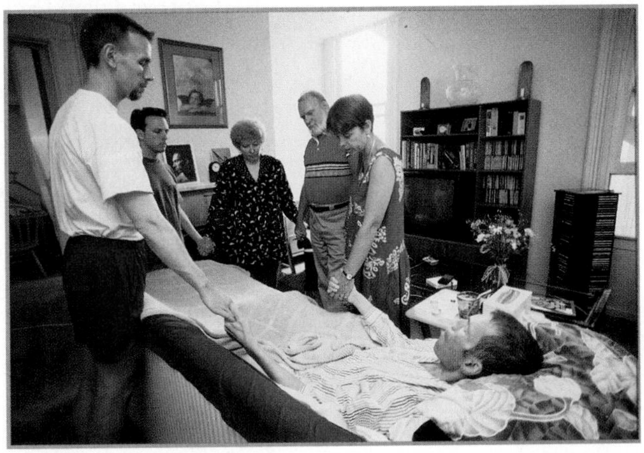

Karen Kasmauski/Corbis

Having members of a congregation praying by one's bedside can offer solace and a sense of connection during a person's final days. But to be really sensitive, this minister and church members would also need to respect this man's privacy, taking their cues from him as to whether he *really* wanted to discuss his impending death.

The bottom line is that people who are dying behave just as they do when they are fully living (which they are!). They are leery about bringing up painful subjects. People don't shed their sensitivity to others and feelings about what topics are appropriate to discuss when they have a terminal disease. Actually, as life is drawing to a close, preserving the quality of our attachment relationships is a *paramount* agenda—and this, as you will see, is a main message I will highlight later in our discussion.

NOT EVERY CULTURE OR PERSON OR FAMILY FEELS IT'S BEST TO SPELL OUT "THE FULL TRUTH." As you saw earlier with the Hmong, the idea that we must inform terminally ill patients about their prognosis is also far from universally accepted. In collectivist cultures that stress social harmony, such as China and Japan, for instance, doctors and families do not routinely follow the Western practice of telling patients when they have a fatal disease (Chan, 2004; Long, 2004). Surveys in the West suggest that, yes, most patients in our individualistic society do want to generally know about their illness. But people differ in how much *specific information* they desire (Baile, Aaron, & Parker, 2009; Innes & Payne, 2009). Families sometimes go further: "Don't tell my loved one anything at all!" Here is how one social worker described how she reacted when she received this plea from some loving sons:

> *"Hurting and sad, (after learning their mom's diagnosis of inoperable cancer). . . . The older sons rushed to the clinic to make me privy to the decision. . . . 'Our mother doesn't know anything and that's how we want to keep it.' I could see their behavior as denial and discuss the western ethic of patient responsibility. But I did not. I knew their children were protecting their mother from what they saw as worse than death: The expectation of nearing death.*
>
> (quoted in Kannai, 2008, pp. 146–147)

middle knowledge The idea that terminally ill people can know that they are dying yet at the same time not completely grasp or come to terms emotionally with that fact.

As this sensitive woman realized, the approach that Kübler-Ross and our contemporary culture spells out as caring can sometimes be unloving, insensitive, and rude.

PEOPLE DO *NOT* PASS THROUGH DISTINCTIVE STAGES IN ADJUSTING TO DEATH. Most important, Kübler-Ross's theory turns out to be wrong! People facing death do *not* progress emotionally in a stage-to-stage, cookie-cutter way. In fact, uncritically accepting Kübler-Ross's stages can be dangerous if it encourages us to distance ourselves from dying loved ones (Kastenbaum, 2004). Instead of understanding that becoming depressed is a reasonable reaction when facing a life-threatening illness, if friends and family see this feeling as "a phase," they might view this response as somehow not real. It's perfectly understandable for an ill person to get angry when others respond insensitively or don't call; but if we view this response through the lens of stage theory, we might dismiss these natural feelings of hurt as "predictable" signs of the anger stage.

Therefore, experts view Kübler-Ross's contributions with mixed emotions. Yes, she pioneered an important topic. But her theory inadvertently encouraged its own kind of insensitivity to the terminally ill (Kastenbaum, 2004).

The More Realistic View: Many Different Emotions

People who are dying *do* get angry, bargain, deny their illness, and become depressed. However, as one psychiatrist argues, it's more appropriate to view these feelings as "a complicated clustering of intellectual and affective states, some fleeting, lasting for a moment, or a day" (Schneidman, 1976, p. 6). Even when people "know" that their illness is terminal, the awareness that "I am dying" may not fully penetrate in a definitive way (Groopman, 2004). This emotional state, called **middle knowledge**, is beautifully highlighted in this description of Rachel, a 17-year-old who knew she had end-stage cystic fibrosis:

> *Rachel said very seriously that when she is to die, she wanted to be here in Canuck Place (the hospice), surrounded by friends and family . . . and the nurses and doctors that can help her feel not scared. And then she said "but I have another way that I'd like to die . . . sitting on my front porch wrapped in an afghan in a rocking chair and my husband holding my hand."*

(Liben, Papadatou, & Wolfe, 2008, p. 858)

Moreover, as Rachel's final heart-wrenching comment suggests, even when people realize that they are very close to death, an emotion that often burns strong is hope

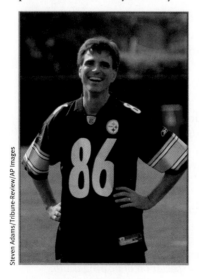

Diagnosed with fatal pancreatic cancer in the prime of life (his mid-forties), beloved Carnegie Mellon Computer Science Professor Randi Pausch captivated the world with his Last Lecture, entitled "Fulfilling Your Childhood Dreams," and viewed on YouTube by over six million people, and wrote a best-selling book in the months before he died. Pausch's final inspirational year of life is a testament that joy and future plans can remain very much alive when people know that they are dying. Here, you can see Pausch being granted a childhood dream he mentioned in the lecture—becoming a Pittsburgh Steeler for a day.

Steven Adams/Tribune-Review/AP Images

(Groopman, 2004; Little & Sayers, 2004; see also Innes & Payne, 2009). If people are religious, their hopes may hinge on divine intervention: "God will provide a miraculous cure." Others may pin their hopes on meditation, alternative therapies, or exercise. Another source of hope—as Kübler-Ross suggested—is the idea that the medical predictions can be wrong: "True, I have that diagnosis, but I know of cases where a doctor told a person with my illness she had six months left and she has been living for 10 years."

Hope is a complex emotion. It doesn't necessarily mean hoping for a long life. It may mean hoping to die surrounded by your loved ones or, as you saw in the earlier Kübler-Ross quotation, hoping to live "till I see my son married." It can mean hoping that your love lives on in your family or that your life work will make a difference in the world. (Remember, that's what being generative is all about.) Contrary to what Kübler-Ross implies, even reaching acceptance has nothing to do with abandoning hope. People can fully understand—"I'm dying"—and still have many goals and plans.

Moreover, in an era when our illness-to-death path can last for decades, being diagnosed with an ultimately fatal illness may even *provoke* new long-term life plans. It can energize people, foster further development, and stimulate the search for new, more satisfying identities and generative missions in life. Let's read what two young men with AIDS had to say (quoted in Sandstrom, 2003):

> I feel like AIDS has sort of been a blessing, because, well, it's helped me grow a lot as a person. I've come out of my shell emotionally. . . . I mean it's ironic . . . but because of AIDS I've learned how to enjoy life and enjoy people. . . . It's been a very positive experience.
>
> (p. 470)

> One of my concerns is that I haven't made a dent in the world. And so I've decided to do some advocacy things . . . and that's . . . helped take the focus off the fact that I might be dying. . . . It's made me feel like I'm finally making a contribution to the world.
>
> (p. 471)

The bottom line is that people react to the challenges of dying in the same ways as they react to the challenges of living. They get anxious and depressed, feel angry and "in denial." They may accept their fate and also feel hopeful and full of plans. Sometimes, they feel fully alive for the first time in life.

AIDS, being an extended chronic disease, is typical of the common twenty-first-century pathway to death I discussed at the beginning of this chapter. Patients are in limbo, unsure if they are really dying. They have good days and bad days. They can live for a long time in the shadow of death. But AIDS is unusual because it often strikes at an age that is clearly *off-time* in terms of our social clock—during the young adult years.

Drawing on Erik Erikson's theory, we might predict that facing death in our twenties or thirties is uniquely difficult and painful. How can you reach integrity, or the sense that you have accomplished your life goals, if you have not fully found your identity, mastered intimacy, or discovered your generative path? The elderly—although they may be just as afraid of the pain of dying as younger people are—almost always say that they are not afraid of death (Cicirelli, 2007).

Being robbed of the chance to be a loving husband and father at the threshold of adult life is impossibly unfair. Imagine being at this funeral of a private who, right after getting married to his 18-year-old sweetheart (shown here), left for Iraq and was killed by a roadside bomb at the terribly off-time age of 23.

Actually, we have concrete experimental evidence that making it to our older years really does mute the terror of death. In the psychology laboratory, researchers find that it's standard for younger people to react to reminders of their mortality by developing harsh moral judgments. However, the elderly show no signs of this classic unconscious "terror management" response (Maxfield and others, 2007). An 80-year-old colleague of mine with an inoperable brain tumor beautifully summed up this message when he explained why he rejected the chemotherapy that could buy him extra months of life: "At my age, you *really* understand: Life is a play with a beginning, middle, and end."

Still, while living a full lifespan may make our own death acceptable, it does not erase the fear of a loved one's dying. Because there is no event more distressing than the death of a child, let's now pause briefly to look at this horrendous off-time event.

FOCUS ON A TOPIC: THE DEATH OF A CHILD

My first son passed away at age 24 from bone cancer. It's been over 40 years since he died, but not a day goes by when I don't miss him. My younger boy just died from heart disease, last month, at age 62. I don't understand it. I'm 90. Why didn't the Lord take me instead?

When I worked in a nursing home, I realized that the death of a child outweighs any other loss. It doesn't matter whether their "baby" dies at age 6 or in his sixties; parents never fully come to terms with that unnatural event (Hayslip & Hansson, 2003). People do eventually go on to construct a fulfilling life. However, when a child dies, it's hard to move on to the *working-model,* "recovery" stage of mourning described in Chapter 13. Parents are typically immobilized by intense grieving for several years (Hayslip & Hansson, 2003; Singg, 2003). In one study, even 18 years later, parents who had experienced the death of a child had poorer health and higher rates of depression than a comparison group (Rogers and others, 2008).

As you just saw in the quotation above, a child's death may evoke powerful feelings of survivor guilt: "Why am I still alive?" If the death occurred suddenly due to an accident, there is disbelief and possibly guilt at having failed in one's fundamental mission as a parent: "I couldn't protect my baby!" (Cole & Singg, 1998). If the death was expected, for instance, a child died of an incurable genetic disorder such as cystic fibrosis, or after a long illness such as cancer, parents seem better able to cope. But even when they are confident that medically everything possible has been done, mothers and fathers may still have nagging concerns: "Maybe I *could* have done something else emotionally for my daughter or son."

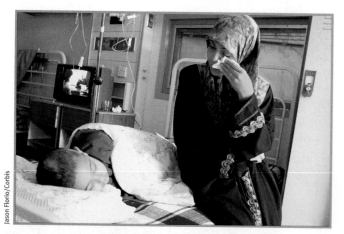

This photograph from Iraq of a terminally ill cancer patient and his grieving mother has its own universal theme. No event is harder to cope with than the death of a child.

When a child has inoperable cancer *and seems to understand that he is dying,* should parents explicitly talk about death? To thoroughly explore this question, Swedish researchers interviewed *every* family who had lost a child to cancer in that country over a period of several years (Kreicbergs and others, 2004). No parent who reported having a conversation about death with an ill daughter or son had any regrets. In contrast, more than half of the mothers and fathers who believed that their child understood what was happening but never discussed this topic felt guilty later on.

Other research has a similar message: If parents feel satisfied that they said goodbye to their child, this helps lessen the pain. Moreover, not discussing what is happening can produce enduring regrets:

I wish I had him back so that we could hug and kiss and say goodby" (said one anguished mother). "We never said goodby. We faked the whole thing. . . . I just feel there was no ending, no finish . . . Yet he never took the lead . . . he never said, 'Ma, I'm dying.'

(quoted in Wells-di Gregorio, 2008, p. 252)

Clearly, the events surrounding a child's death may have lifelong ramifications for a family's mental health (Liben, Papadatou, & Wolfe, 2008). What can health professionals do to help? Attend the funeral. Write condolence letters to honor the struggle of the parents and the courage of the child (Wolfe, 2004). Listen to people share their stories (Rallison & Moules, 2004). And prior to death, when the child's illness reaches its advanced stage, sensitively broach the possibility of dying, while not destroying feelings of hope (Liben, Papadatou, & Wolfe, 2008). Moreover, based on the research above, when death becomes imminent, invite the parents to *actively* participate in the hands-on care. After watching a man pace the room helplessly, his hands clenched together as his son was dying of AIDS, here is how one nurse gave a father one last chance to be a parent in the final moments of his son's life:

I adjusted the damp cloth on the young man's head and the father asked if he could do that. I handed him the cloth, and as he stroked his son's face with it, he told me about the times he had bathed his son when he was a little boy and prepared him for bed. I asked if he would like to do this now. . . . He then proceeded to bathe his son, who died later that evening. At the wake, the father came up to me, smiled and said proudly that his son had died in clean pajamas. . . . [Along with his pain] he will always have [that] memory.

(quoted in Brabant, 2003, pp. 480–481)

Because it is clearly off-time, most of us would never see the death of a child as appropriate or right. What qualities are involved in having what psychologists call "a good death"?

In Search of a Good Death

We can get interesting insights into the core dimensions of "a good death" by turning to religious sources, such as Old Testament writings (Spronk, 2004). According to the Bible, death is appropriate after a long life, making sense of why deaths that occur in childhood and early adult life cause special pain. The Bible specifies that death should be peaceful, explaining why surveys reveal that people—no matter what their religion—dislike the idea of dying after being "tortured" by machines and don't want to die after years of suffering from extended chronic illnesses, such as Alzheimer's disease (Long, 2004; Walter, 2003). Death is "best" when it occurs in the "homeland" (not far away), accounting for why—around the globe—people say they want to die at home surrounded by their loved ones and reject the sanitized, impersonal dying that takes place in the recesses of intensive care (Prevost & Wallace, 2009; Shih and others, 2009).

The principle that good deaths must occur "near the homeland" is embedded in many religious traditions—not just Judeo-Christian ones. This nineteenth-century depiction shows a Hindu funeral ceremony, with the deceased making his final passage surrounded by loving community members while being carried ceremoniously to the grave.

My personal example of a good death came to my grandmother, Lillian Sheerr, one beautiful summer day. Grandma, at age 98, was just beginning to get slightly frail. One afternoon, before preparing dinner for her visiting grandchildren and great-grandchildren (which she insisted on doing), she got in her car to drive to the hairdresser and—on leaving the driveway—was hit by an oncoming car. Of the eight people involved in the accident, no one was hurt but Grandma, who was killed instantly. They said she never felt any pain. My grandma got the death she deserved—because she was a saint in her life.

Given that our chances of being killed instantly in an accident at our doorstep, without any frailties at the limit of human life, are almost nil, how can we expand on the criteria mentioned above to spell out more specific dimensions of a good death? One psychologist offers the following guidelines (Corr, 1991–1992):

1. We want to minimize our physical distress, to be as free as possible from debilitating pain.

2. We want to maximize our psychological security, reduce fear and anxiety, and feel in control of how we die.

3. We want to enhance our relationships and be as close as possible emotionally to the people we care about most.

4. We want to foster our spirituality and have the sense that there was integrity and purpose to our lives.

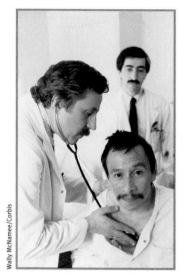

Did this relatively young cancer patient (who later died) have a "good death"? According to the research, much depended on whether he believed he had fulfilled his generative life-mission, and so reached Erikson's integrity, accepting the fact that his personal death was a natural part of the cycle of life.

Minimize pain and fear; be close to loved ones; enhance spirituality; feel that my life has meaning—these are messages of the few studies in which researchers actually explore the qualities that constitute "a good death" (Breitbart and others, 2004; Nakashima & Canda, 2005; Shih and others, 2009; Tang, Aaronson, & Forbes, 2004). Yes, many people classified as having optimum deaths do tend to have a strong religious faith (Kacela, 2004; Nakashima & Canda, 2005). But it's not necessary to believe in an afterlife or any specific religion. Actually, in one study conducted with terminally ill people, the main dimension that related to feeling comfortable about dying was having had a sense of purpose in life (Ardelt & Koenig, 2006).

So again, Erikson seems right in saying that the key to accepting death is fulfilling our life tasks and, especially, our generative missions. And in Erikson's (1963) poetic words, appreciating that one's "individual life is the accidental coincidence of . . . one lifecycle within . . . history" (p. 268) can be important in embracing death, too:

> Barbara turned on the lamp beside her bed. Her eyes were sunken and her skin was pale. It would not be long, I thought. . . . "Are you afraid?" I asked. "You know, not really, not as much as I thought. . . . I have strange comforting thoughts. . . . When fear starts to creep up on me, I conjure up the idea that millions and millions of people have passed away before me, and millions more will pass away after I do . . . I guess if they all did it, so can I."

(Groopman, 2004, pp. 137–138)

What are your priorities for a good death? Table 15.1 offers an expanded checklist based on the principles in this section, to help you evaluate your top-ranking death goals. In the next section, we turn to how well the health-care system is doing at helping people fulfill their plans for a dignified death.

TABLE 15.1: Evaluating Your Priorities for a Good Death: A Checklist

When you think about dying, rank how important each of these criteria might be to you as: (1) of utmost importance; (2) important, but not primary; or (3) relatively unimportant.

_____ 1. Not being a burden to my family.

_____ 2. Being at peace with death—that is, not being anxious about dying.

_____ 3. Not being in physical pain.

_____ 4. Having control over *where* I die—that is, being able to choose whether to die at home or in the hospital.

_____ 5. Having control over *how* I die—that is, being able to choose whether to be kept alive through medical interventions or to die naturally. Being able to end my life if I am terminally ill and in great pain.

_____ 6. Feeling close to my loved ones.

_____ 7. Feeling close to God.

_____ 8. Feeling that I have fulfilled my mission on earth or made a difference in the world.

Do your top-ranking priorities for dying tell you anything about your priorities for living?

TYING IT ALL TOGETHER

1. Sara is arguing that Kübler-Ross's conceptions about dying are "fatally flawed." Pick out the argument she should *not* use to make her case (that is, identify the false alternative):

   a. People who are dying do not necessarily want to talk about that fact.
   b. People don't necessarily feel it's best to be "up front" about a terminal diagnosis.
   c. People do not go through "stages" in adjusting to impending death.
   d. People who are dying simply accept that fact.

2. If your uncle has recently been diagnosed with advanced lung cancer, he should feel (*many different emotions/only depressed/only angry*), but in general, he should have (*hope/a lot of anger*).

3. You are a psychologist who works with the terminally ill and their families. All other things being equal, which client is likely to find it easiest to cope with impending death: a 16-year-old girl, a 30-year-old man, an 80-year-old woman, a parent of a dying 8-year-old child?

4. As a hospital administrator, outline some steps you might take to help patients have a good death by reducing their fear and increasing their feelings of having control over how they die.

Answers to the Tying It All Together questions can be found on the last page of this chapter.

The Health-Care System

How does the health-care system deal with dying patients? In this section, I'll first take a critical look at standard hospital terminal care and then explore some new health-care options designed to tame twenty-first-century death.

What's Wrong with Traditional Hospital Care for the Dying?

Most of us, as I mentioned earlier, will die in a hospital (Prevost & Wallace, 2009). But social scientists have known for a half century that the traditional hospital approach to dying has glaring flaws. Consider the findings of this pathbreaking 1960s study in which sociologists entered hospitals and observed how the medical staff organized "the work" of terminal care (Glaser & Straus, 1968).

The researchers found that, when a person was admitted to the hospital, nurses and doctors set up predictions about what pattern that individual's dying was likely to follow. This implicit **dying trajectory** then governed how the staff acted.

There actually were several dying trajectories. In "the expected swift death," for instance, a patient would arrive (usually in the emergency room) whose death was imminent, perhaps from an accident or heart attack, and who had no chance of surviving. "Expected lingering while dying" was another pathway. In this case, a man or woman would enter the hospital with advanced cancer or end-stage heart disease and slowly decline. Or the patient might follow the "entry–reentry" path that is typical of contemporary chronic diseases: admitted and stabilized medically, then discharged, to return periodically until the final crisis before death.

The problem, however, was that dying schedules could not always be predicted. When someone mistakenly categorized as "expected to linger" was moved to a unit in the hospital where she was not carefully monitored, this mislabeling tended, not infrequently, to hasten death. An interesting situation happened when "expected swift death" changed to "lingering." Doctors would call loved ones to the bedside to say goodbye, only to find that the person began to improve. This "final goodbye" scenario could play out time and time again. The paradox, as you can see in the following example, was that if it was "off schedule," *living* might be transformed into a negative event!

> One patient who was expected to die within four hours had no money, but needed a special machine in order to last longer. A private hospital at which he had been a frequent paying patient for 30 years agreed to receive him as a charity patient. He did not die immediately but started to linger indefinitely, even to the point where there was some hope he might live. The money problem, however, created much concern among both family members and the hospital administrators. . . . The doctor continually had to reassure both parties that the patient (who lived for six weeks) would soon die; that is, to try to change their expectations back to "certain to die on time."

(Glaser & Straus, 1968, pp. 11–12)

dying trajectory The fact that hospital personnel make projections about the particular pathway to death that a seriously ill patient will take and organize their care according to that assumption.

The bottom-line message is that deaths don't occur according to a pre-programmed timetable. Hospitals are structured according to the assumption that they do. This incompatibility makes for an inherently messy dance of terminal care.

palliative care Any intervention designed not to cure illness but to promote dignified dying.

end-of-life care instruction Courses in medical and nursing schools devoted to teaching health-care workers how to provide the best palliative care to the dying.

palliative-care service A service or unit in a hospital that is devoted to end-of-life care.

Unfortunately, since this study was conducted, conditions have not changed. Doctors and nurses still have a poor scorecard for accurately predicting the date of dying (Cicirelli, 2007; Twomey, O'Leary, & O'Brien, 2008). So families, not infrequently, suffer the trauma of being caught "off guard" when a loved one dies (Wells-di Gregario, 2008). When dying proceeds according to schedule (or as expected), health-care personnel classify the death as "good." As one resident in a study exploring physicians' perceptions reported: "I felt good that he died in a comfortable way. . . . I guess I just knew it would happen in 24 hours so it doesn't come as a shock" (quoted in Good and others, 2004, p. 944). When trajectories are mislabeled, the death is defined as "bad": "She came in for a bone marrow transplant to cure her [cancer] . . . and got pulmonary toxicity and died" (p. 945). Good deaths happen when there is smooth communication between the medical team and patients' families. Bad deaths are rife with disagreements, anger, and hurt (see Wells-di Gregario, 2008). In fact, because of the potential for miscommunication, traditional hospital dying may be more turbulent in the twenty-first century than ever before.

One reason is that, today, patients do not typically spend weeks or months in a hospital. They often enter this setting when they are within days of death. Therefore, the health-care professionals on the death scene may not be as emotionally involved with the person (Good and others, 2004). They may have little understanding of patients' and families' needs.

Disagreements between various members of the health-care team add to this problem. Physicians make the final decisions about treatments; but nurses, the front-line caregivers *on* the scene, really know the patient's and family's wishes best. Nurses—one survey showed—want to advocate for dying patients but are afraid of being disciplined if they do speak up (Thacker, 2008). Compounding these professional conflicts are issues related to living in our multicultural society (Wells-di Gregario, 2008). Suppose the attending doctor on the floor where your relative is dying is a recent immigrant from Beijing or Bangladesh, or your parents only speak Spanish or Swahili. How would it be possible for everyone to really communicate at this intensely emotional time?

What underlies many of these conflicts is the quantum leap in our death-defying technologies that extends life well beyond the time that nature would intend. Physicians can offer nutrition to people through a tube into the stomach, effectively bypassing the body's normal signal to stop eating in preparation for death. They can put critically ill patients on ventilators, machines that breathe for the person, after the lungs would have given out. Caring doctors may agonize about using these heroic measures. They worry about causing dying people unnecessary pain (Liben, Papadatou, & Wolfe, 2008). But as the following comment shows, their mission to cure makes it difficult to resist the lure of the machines:

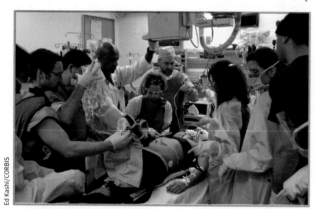

Is it right to vigorously intervene to artificially keep this patient alive? Some members of this health-care team may believe the answer is no. But unfortunately, the nurses and other health-care workers in this photo will be forced to squelch these moral concerns and obey what the attending physician dictates.

We were realizing that we were going to hurt him [a 40-year-old lung cancer patient who had had multiple surgeries and several strokes] if we, for example, . . . kept trying to keep a body alive that was not wanting to be alive. And everyone figured "what the heck, give it a shot."

(quoted in Good and others, 2004, p. 945)

Today, health-care workers are faced with agonizing ethical choices: How long do you vigorously wage war against death, and when should you say, "enough is enough"? Shifting from the cure-at-all-costs mode can be very difficult. To paraphrase one observer, it's like "deciding to play baseball while the football game is in full swing" (Chapple, 1999). With the understanding that we can never take the mess out of dying, just as we can never take the mess out of living, let's now explore how the traditional health-care system is taking action to tame death today.

INTERVENTIONS: Providing Superior Palliative Care

Palliative care refers to any strategy designed, not to cure people, but to promote dignified dying. Palliative care includes educating health-care personnel about how to deal with dying patients; modifying the hospital structure; or providing that well-known alternative to dying in a hospital, hospice care. Let's now scan and critique each of these interventions one by one.

Educating Health-Care Providers

In recent decades, **end-of-life care instruction** has become one component of medical and nursing training. Courses cover everything from the best drugs to control pain without "knocking the person out" to the ethics of withdrawing treatment, from tips on talking about death with patients, to ways of providing sensitive end-of-life care to people from different cultural groups.

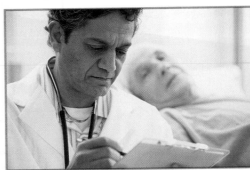

Unfortunately, however, this training is surprisingly spotty. In one hospital survey, although nurses reported dealing with death on a daily basis, less than half said they had any training in end-of-life care within the previous three years (Thacker, 2008). In another medical school poll, most deans described death education as valuable, but admitted that this topic was given insufficient emphasis at their school. They blamed this problem on "time constraints" and not having faculty members with that expertise (Sullivan and others, 2004).

Training in being sensitive to the needs of seriously ill patients and families is really vital. From the physicians who (perhaps out of their own fear) decide to take Kübler-Ross's concept of "honesty" literally, saying, "Your illness is terminal and there's nothing we can do," to the story of the woman in Chapter 14 whose neurologist coldly delivered the news, "You have Alzheimer's disease," many of us have horror stories about health-care providers who—when delivering a devastating diagnosis—totally left their humanity behind.

Imagine being this doctor and knowing the terminally ill patient whose chart you are reading is about to ask, "What is my prognosis?" Wouldn't it be helpful to have some *end-of-life care instruction* during your training to guide you about how best to respond?

Still, even the most humane physician will have trouble bucking an institutional structure where the push to provide a cure at all costs impedes good end-of-life care. Therefore, modern medical centers have developed a new in-hospital alternative designed to promote the best possible death.

Changing Hospitals: Palliative-Care Units

A **palliative-care service** is a special unit or service within a traditional hospital that is devoted to end-of-life care. Here, certain groups of inpatients—for instance, old-old people with multiple chronic illnesses and people with advanced cancer—have their care managed by a team of providers specifically trained in when to shift from "football to baseball mode" (recall the analogy mentioned earlier). Patients enrolled in the palliative-care service are not denied cure-oriented interventions. However, as their illness progresses and becomes terminal, the vigor of life-prolonging treatments shifts to providing the best possible "comfort care."

Palliative-care services, with their focus on pain control and letting patients spend their final days in a more natural setting, provide an alternative to dying in the medicalized recesses of intensive care. In this palliative-care unit, a nurse is taking the blood pressure of a patient who has had a stroke and is suffering from end-stage heart disease.

Families give palliative care high marks, compared to traditional end-of-life care (Garcia-Perez and others, 2009). Palliative-care services are "cost-effective," too (Meier & Beresford, 2009). So these services are thriving in Great Britain (Doyle, 2007; Morgan, 2008) and—as you can see in Figure 15.2 on page 464—becoming widespread in the United States (Dobbins, 2007). The global view, however, is bleak. Yes, some people in affluent nations are lucky to have access to exceptional end-of-life care. But of the roughly one million human beings who die each week worldwide, a large fraction spend their final days in agony, without access to even over-the-counter medicines to control their pain (Clark, 2007).

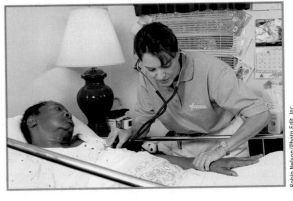

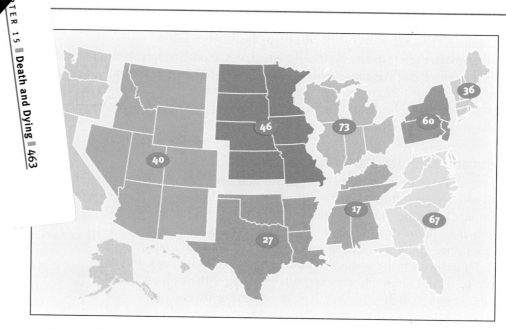

State-of-the art, hospital-based palliative-care services are a welcome trend. But it still seems unfair to ask health-care professionals to fully embrace the enemy. Physicians in particular may shy away from dying patients because it means they failed in their mission to cure—and they are human like the rest of us (Prevost & Wallace, 2009). As one resident admitted in a survey, because of his own feelings of failure and powerlessness, even "To go into the (dying) patient's room . . . becomes tough!" (quoted in Luthy and others, 2009, p. 62). Therefore, the best way to ensure dignified dying might be to remove that process completely from the doctors with their cure-oriented focus and death-defying machines.

Unhooking Death from Doctors and Hospitals: Hospice Care

This is the philosophy that underlies the **hospice movement**, which gained momentum in the 1970s, along with the natural childbirth movement. Like birth, hospice activists argued, death is a natural process. We need to let this natural process occur in the most personal, pain-free, natural way (Corr, 2007).

Hospice workers are skilled in techniques to minimize patients' physical discomfort. They are trained in providing a humanistic, supportive psychological environment, one that assures patients and family members that they will not be abandoned in the face of approaching death (Monroe and others, 2008).

Initially, hospice care was delivered only in an inpatient setting called a hospice, much like the palliative-care hospital services described above. Although there are exceptional inpatient hospice facilities (Addington-Hall & O'Callaghan, 2009), the current emphasis of the hospice movement—at least in the United States—is on providing backup care that allows people to die with dignity at home (Connor, 2007). As you can see in the Experiencing the Lifespan box on the facing page, multidisciplinary hospice teams go into the person's home, offering care on a part-time, scheduled, or daily basis. They provide 24-hour help in a crisis, giving family caregivers the support they need to allow their relative to spend his final days at home. Their commitment does not end after the person dies: An important component of hospice care is bereavement counseling.

Hospice has struck a tremendous chord (Corr, 2007). As I mentioned earlier in this chapter, surveys show most people want to spend their final days of life at home. Since the first American hospice was established in Connecticut in 1974, the hospice movement has also mushroomed (see Figure 15.3). As of 2006, more than 1 in 3 people who died in the United States spent their final days in hospice care (Corr, 2007; NHPCO facts and figures, 2007).

hospice movement A movement, which became widespread in recent decades, focused on providing palliative care to dying patients outside of hospitals and especially on giving families the support they need to care for the terminally ill at home.

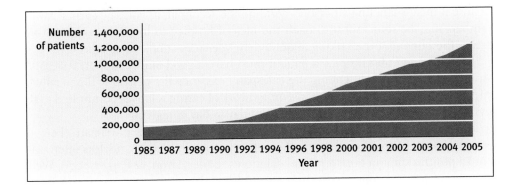

FIGURE 15.3: Increase in number of hospice patients in the United States (since 1985): The number of people enrolling in hospice has grown exponentially in recent years.

Source: Connor, 2007, p. 92.

Entering a hospice program is simple: It merely requires a physician to certify that the person is within six months of death. People even have the option of entering hospice without abandoning curative care. Moreover, as Medicare fully covers this service, hospice is available to people on every economic rung. Still, there are segments of the U.S. population who could theoretically benefit, but do not enroll. Ethnic and racial minorities, in particular, are less likely than European Americans to use this service (Connor, 2007; Grunier and others, 2007). Why might people avoid hospice even when they say they want to die in a natural way?

Barriers to Hospice Care

One reason is that, as we saw earlier, it's natural for human beings to hold on to hope. Making the decision to enter hospice means admitting, "I am going to die." People of color—those who have not always gotten the best curative care from the medical system (recall the previous chapter)—may have the perception that "I'll be abandoning my best shot at treatment if I enter hospice care" (Ardelt, 2003; Dresser, 2004).

EXPERIENCING THE LIFESPAN: HOSPICE TEAM

What is hospice care really like? How do people who work in hospice feel about what they do? For answers, here are some excerpts from an interview I conducted with the team (nurse, social worker, and volunteer coordinator) who manages our local hospice.

Usually, we get referrals from physicians. People may have a wide support system in the community or be new to the area. Even when there are many people involved, there is almost always one primary caregiver, typically a spouse or adult child.

We see our role as empowering families, giving them the support to care for their loved ones at home. We go into the home as a team to make our initial assessment: What services does the family need? We provide families training in pain control, in making beds, in bathing. A critical component of our program is respite services. Volunteers come in for part of each day. They may take the children out for pizza, or give the primary caregiver time off, or bathe the person, or just stay there to listen.

Families will say initially, "I don't think I can stand to do this." They are anxious because it's a new experience they have never been through. At the beginning, they call a lot. Then, you watch them really gain confidence in themselves. We see them at the funeral and they thank us for helping them give their loved one this experience. Sometimes, the primary caregiver can't bear to keep the person at home to the end. We respect that, too.

The whole thing about hospice is choice. Some people want to talk about dying. Others just want you to visit, ask about their garden, talk about current affairs. We take people to see the autumn leaves, to see Santa Claus. Our main focus is: What are your priorities? We try to pick up on that. We had a farmer whose goal was to go to his farm one last time and say goodbye to his tractor. We got together egg crates, a big tank of oxygen, and carried him down to his farm. We have one volunteer who takes a client to the mall.

We keep in close touch with the families for a year after, providing them counseling or referring them to bereavement groups in the community. Some families keep in contact with notes for years. We run a camp each summer for children who have lost a parent.

We have an unusually good support system among the staff. In addition to being with the families at 3 A.M., we call one another at all times of the night. Most of us have been working here for years. We feel we have the most meaningful job in the world.

Because it means labeling a person's condition as terminal, as you saw earlier, family members may be reluctant to broach the idea of hospice to loved ones. In cultures such as the Hmong, even talking about a dying person's condition is taboo.

Moreover, to enter hospice a patient must have a good family support system. As you just read in the Experiencing the Lifespan box, since the person will typically be dying at home, there must be a spouse or network of caring relatives committed to the physically and emotionally draining tasks of day-to-day caregiving.

Another barrier may lie in the hospice gatekeeper—the physician (Feeg & Elebiary, 2005). Even when they are theoretically open to hospice, doctors often want to put a positive spin on even terminal diagnoses (Baile, Aaron, & Parker, 2009; Wells-di Gregorio, 2008). As one physician put it, "A tumor has not always read the textbook, and a treatment can have an unexpectedly dramatic effect" (quoted in Groopman, 2004, p. 210). The good news is that—because dying trajectories *are* unpredictable—providing hope is perfectly compatible with telling the truth!

For these reasons, as was true of my father in the chapter-opening vignette, people typically enter hospice when their death is fairly imminent. In 2005, one in three hospice patients died within a week of enrollment. In that year, the median time spent in hospice before death occurred was 20 days (Connor, 2007).

As you saw in the Experiencing the Lifespan box, hospice care can offer tremendous solace to the dying person and loved ones, allowing families to offer one last demonstration of love as they care for the patient at home. Without minimizing these benefits, so beautifully described by the hospice team, let's point out some cautions about actually dying at home.

The Case Against Dying at Home

Deciding to care for a loved one at home demands a daunting commitment. True, hospice volunteers do come to relieve the family periodically, but if you are a spouse or caregiving child, you are basically on call 24/7. You may need to take time off from work, perhaps for months. Even with the backup provided by the hospice team, it may be too anxiety-provoking to manage the crises associated with impending death, so you may need to transfer your loved one to an inpatient setting in his final days.

There are problems from the patient's perspective, too. Imagine spending your final weeks of life being totally taken care of by your family. You don't have any privacy. Loved ones must bathe you and dress you; they must care for your every need. You may be embarrassed about being seen naked and incontinent; you may want time alone to cry out, to vent your anguish and pain. In a hospital, care is impersonal. At home, there is the humiliation of having to depend on the people you love most for each intimate bodily act.

Most importantly, care by strangers equals care that is free from guilt. As I described earlier in this chapter, when people are approaching death, they often want to emotionally protect their loved ones—to shield them from pain. Witnessing the toll that your disease is taking on your family may multiply the pain of dying itself.

For these reasons, when researchers actually *ask* seriously ill people about their preferences, they find less than overwhelming enthusiasm about dying at home (Thomas, Morris, & Clark, 2004). In one interview study, when women with advanced breast cancer were questioned, many people suggested they were ambivalent about taking that route (Hays and others, 2001). One patient said, "I guess it would depend on if you are not in great pain." Another was uncomfortable about the idea of blood—"Hemorrhaging concerns me. That would be so frightening [to my children]" (p. 9). A widow mentioned that she definitely wanted to die in the hospital because "I would not want my son to come into the bedroom one day and find me dead. That would be too traumatic for a 16-year-old" (p. 10).

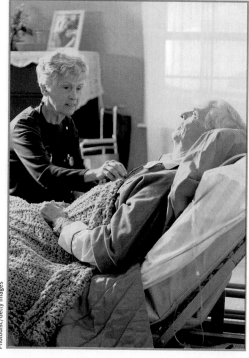

Although this wife probably would say she wouldn't have it any other way, caring for a beloved husband at home puts a tremendous burden on the caregiver and can be difficult from the perspective of the dying person as well.

Photodisc/Getty Images

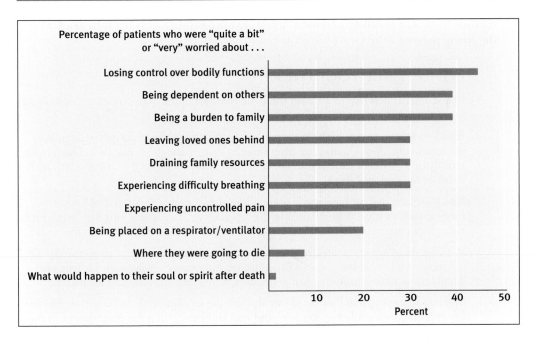

FIGURE 15.4: **Family reports of major worries of 63 dying patients:** As people are dying, worries about attachment-related issues outweigh everything else. (Losing control over bodily functions is in itself a "relationship issue," as patients want to spare their loved ones the need to care for them should they become incontinent.)

Source: Hickman, Tilden, & Tolle (2004).

Actually, when people are dying, concerns centering on one's physical state are paramount. It's "the pain," "my trouble breathing," and shame about "my inability to control my body" (Shah and others, 2008; Wijk & Grimby, 2008). Notice from the reports in Figure 15.4 that people also worry about the kinds of attachment-related issues described above—being a burden, draining family resources, feeling dependent. (Hawkins and others, 2005; Hickman, Tilden, & Tolle, 2004; Shih and others, 2009) (Now, you might want to see how this research compares with your responses to the death anxieties checklist you completed in Table 15.1 on page 460.) If preserving our connections to loved ones is crucially important at the end of life—and controlling physical discomfort looms large—the best choice may *not* necessarily be to die at home.

Table 15.2 summarizes these section points by comparing the pros and cons of home and hospital deaths. Now that we have surveyed the health-care possibilities,

TABLE 15.2: Hospital Death Versus Home Death: Pros and Cons

The case for dying in a hospital

1. Potential for better management of the physical aspects of dying.

2. No fear of burdening your family with your care.

3. Privacy to vent your feelings, without family members around.

4. Avoiding the embarrassment of depending on loved ones for help with your intimate body functions.

The case for dying at home

1. Avoiding having life-prolonging machines used on you.

2. Spending your final days surrounded by the people you care about most.

3. Spending your final days in the physical setting you love best.

4. Having full freedom to follow your own cultural and religious preferences relating to dying.

Given these considerations, where would you prefer to meet death—in a hospital or at home?

it's time to continue our search for a "good" twenty-first-century death by returning to the dying person.

TYING IT ALL TOGETHER

1. In a sentence, describe to a friend the basic message of the classic research describing the various dying trajectories discussed on page 461.

2. Based on this section, which statement most accurately reflects doctors' reactions to the terminally ill? a. Doctors are insensitive to dying patients' needs; or b. Doctors feel terribly upset when a patient is dying, and reluctantly feel forced to use modern technologies to "prolong" death.

3. Sara is arguing that we have made tremendous strides in improving end-of-life care in medical settings such as hospitals. Martha says no—we have a very long way to go. First, make Sara's case and, then, make Martha's, citing the evidence discussed in this section.

4. Which patient are you *most* likely to find enrolled in a U.S. hospice program: An old-old man who lives alone/a man with end-stage lung cancer living with his wife and daughters/an ethnic minority, first-generation immigrant who has had a stroke?

5. Melanie is arguing that there's no way she will die in a hospital. She wants to end her life at home, surrounded by her husband and children. Using the information in this section, try to convince Melanie that there might be a downside to spending her final days at home.

6. Your grandmother is dying. According to the text, her main priorities are likely to be (pick two alternatives):

   a. feeling close to her attachment figures—you and your parents.
   b. dying at home.
   c. having her pain controlled and worrying about body related issues.

Answers to the Tying It All Together questions can be found on the last page of this chapter.

The Dying Person: Taking Control of How We Die

In this section, I'll explore two strategies people can use to control their final passage and so promote a "good death." The first is an option that our society strongly encourages: People should make their wishes known in writing about their treatment preferences, in case they become permanently mentally incapacitated. The second approach is very controversial: People should be allowed to get help if they want to end their lives.

Giving Instructions: Advance Directives

An **advance directive** is the name for any written document spelling out instructions with regard to life-prolonging treatment when people are irretrievably ill and cannot communicate their wishes. There are four basic types of advance directives: two that the individual drafts and two that are filled out by other people, called *surrogates*, when the ill person is already seriously mentally impaired.

- In the **living will**, mentally competent individuals leave instructions about their treatment wishes for life-prolonging strategies should they become comatose or permanently incapacitated. Although people typically fill out living wills in order to refuse aggressive medical interventions, it is important to point out that this document can also specify that every possible heroic measure be carried out.

- In a **durable power of attorney for health care**, individuals designate a specific surrogate, such as a spouse or a child, to make end-of-life decisions "in their spirit" when they are incapable of making those choices known.

advance directive Any written document spelling out instructions with regard to life-prolonging treatment if individuals become irretrievably ill and cannot communicate their wishes.

living will A type of advance directive in which people spell out their wishes for life-sustaining treatment in case they become permanently incapacitated and unable to communicate.

durable power of attorney for health care A type of advance directive in which people designate a specific surrogate to make health-care decisions if they become incapacitated and are unable to make their wishes known.

- A **Do Not Resuscitate (DNR) order** is filled out when the sick person is already mentally impaired, usually by the doctor in consultation with family members. This document, most often placed in a nursing home or hospital chart, stipulates that, if a cardiac arrest takes place, health-care professionals should not try to revive the patient.

- A **Do Not Hospitalize (DNH) order** is specific to nursing homes. It specifies that, in case of a medical crisis, a mentally impaired resident should not be transferred to a hospital for emergency care.

Advance directives have an admirable goal. Ideally, they provide a road map so that family members and doctors are not forced to guess what care the permanently incapacitated person *might* want. However, there are serious issues, especially with regard to the most well-known advance directive—the living will (Cicirelli, 2007).

One difficulty is that people are reluctant to plan for their death in writing. Do you or your parents have a living will? Estimates suggest that only about 5 to 25 percent of the U.S. population does (Pevey, 2003). Doctors don't do much better. In one survey of thousands of Finnish physicians, only 13 percent had filled out a living will (Hildén, Louhiala, & Palo, 2004).

The concept of putting one's personal plans in writing flies in the face of the cultural norm to not talk about death. Therefore, urging advance directives on groups like the Hmong might be considered insulting, or worse. Other minorities may legitimately be leery of filling out these documents. Imagine, for instance, that you are an African American and well aware of the sordid history of health discrimination against your group. Would you want to write a living will telling medical personnel what *not* to do? The bottom line is that, in the United States, people who fill out living wills tend to be European American, well-educated, and affluent—those most at risk of getting "too much care" (Laakkonen and others, 2004; Pevey, 2003).

The main problem, however, is that these documents don't work all that well (Cicirelli, 2007; Dobbins, 2007)! Somehow, Grandma's living will gets lost in the transition to the hospital, or family members override the document and say, "Grandma really wanted (or didn't want) that particular intervention." The information in the typical living will is very vague (Cicirelli, 2007). Does "no aggressive treatments" mean not putting in the feeding tube that has allowed my aunt to survive for a year after brain surgery? What exactly does "no heroic measures" mean?

The solution has been to press for more specificity (" I don't want to be on a ventilator, but I do want a feeding tube"), but would that be feasible? Yes, before you get Alzheimer's disease, you might think, "Let me die if I become like that," but you've never been there. Perhaps if you were in this state, you would want modern medicine to pull out all the stops to keep you alive. A related issue is ignorance. How many of you *really* know what being on a ventilator or having a feeding tube entails? So it makes sense that, in surveys, older people—even those with a living will—say they prefer to leave the details of their care to experts (Hawkins and others, 2005; Reisfield & Wilson, 2004). They want physicians to make the final decision in consultation with family members on the scene.

This suggests that the most useful advance directive is the durable power of attorney (Hawkins and others, 2005). Granted, deciding on a single family member to carry out one's wishes can lead to jealousy ("Why did Mom give power of attorney to my brother and not me?"). Mistakes about what is really wanted do occur, even between spouses ("I didn't know my wife would want to be kept alive at all costs") (Zettel-Watson and others, 2008). So people need to sit down and *talk* to their designated family member about their

Do Not Resuscitate (DNR) order A type of advance directive filled out by surrogates (usually a doctor in consultation with family members) for impaired individuals, specifying that if they go into cardiac arrest, efforts should not be made to revive them.

Do Not Hospitalize (DNH) order A type of advance directive put into the charts of impaired nursing home residents, specifying that in a medical crisis they should not be transferred to a hospital for emergency care.

This elderly woman completing a *living will* is probably not aware that her preferences may not be fulfilled. She would be better off discussing her end-of-life wishes with family members, and designating a specific child as her *durable power of attorney*.

wishes, rather than have that person read their mind. Still, having a specific surrogate can reduce the potential for the kinds of conflicts that may crop up, especially when a parent is elderly and widowed and there are several siblings. Suppose you believe that Mom's suffering should not be prolonged, while your brother insists that treatment continue at all costs. Issues such as these can poison family relationships for years (or life).

By now, some readers may be getting uneasy, not so much about keeping people alive too long, but about the opposite problem—letting them die too soon. Let's ratchet up the anxiety a few notches as we move to the next step in the search for death with dignity: actively helping people take their own lives.

Deciding When to Die: Active Euthanasia and Physician-Assisted Suicide

Dr. Cox, a British rheumatologist, had a warm relationship with Mrs. Boyles, who had been his patient for 13 years. Mrs. Boyles was terminally ill, in excruciating pain and had repeatedly begged Dr. Cox to end her life: "Her pain was . . . grindingly severe. . . . [It] did not respond to increasingly large doses of opioids. Dr. Cox had reassured her that she would not be allowed to suffer terrible pain during her final days but was unable to honor that pledge. . . . As an act of compassion, he injected two ampoules of potassium chloride (a fatal drug). . . . The patient died a few minutes later peacefully in the presence of her (grateful) sons. . .". Then the ward sister, out of a sense of duty . . . reported the action to the police. Told to "disregard the doctor's motives" but only rule on his "intent to kill," a jury eventually convicted Dr. Cox "amid scenes of great emotional distress in the court."

(as reported in Begley, 2008, quotes are from pp. 436 and 438)

How do you feel about this doctor's decision, the reaction of his nurse, and the jury's judgment? If you were like many people in Great Britain, you would have been outraged, believing that Dr. Cox was a hero because he acted on his mission to relieve human suffering rather than follow an unjust law (recall Kohlberg's *post-conventional stage*, in Chapter 9).

Let's first make some distinctions. **Passive euthanasia**, withdrawing potentially life-saving interventions, such as a feeding tube, is perfectly legal. (That's what advance directives specify.) But the step Dr. Cox took qualified as **active euthanasia**—taking *action* to help a person die. Active euthanasia is illegal in every nation except Belgium, Luxembourg, and the Netherlands (see Table 15.3). However, a variation on active euthanasia called **physician-assisted suicide** is legal in Switzerland and the state of Oregon. Under very strict conditions, at a terminally ill patient's request, physicians can prescribe a medication the individual can personally take to bring on death.

As the judge in the above trial spelled out, the distinction between the two types of euthanasia lies in intentions (Dickens, Boyle, & Ganzini, 2008). When we with-

During the 1990s, Dr. Jack Kevorkian ignited a nationwide controversy when he reported having helped many terminally ill patients die and made numerous media appearances proudly showing off this "suicide machine." For the reasons to be discussed in the text, many people reacted with horror, and sentenced the man dubbed "Dr. Death" to serve time in prison for second-degree murder!

AP Photo/Richard Sheinwald

TABLE 15.3: Euthanasia and Physician-Assisted Suicide: A Fact Sheet on the Experience in the Netherlands and in Oregon

The Netherlands*

In 2001, both active euthanasia (physicians can administer a lethal injection) and physician-assisted suicide (a doctor can prescribe a lethal medication for the patient to take) were legalized in this country.

Requirements: People do not have to be terminally ill, but a physician must certify that the individual's suffering is "unbearable." The patient must persistently request that his life be terminated in repeated discussions with the primary physician, report that his suffering is unbearable, and state that he wants to die. An independent doctor must also confirm that the patient's suffering is permanent and incurable. Finally, after the death, the primary physician must submit a full report to the coroner, and a pathologist must perform an autopsy and report the findings to a review committee.

Additional facts:

- Slightly more than half of the doctors in the Netherlands have performed this procedure; 12 percent say that they would refuse to do so.
- In 2005, this nation reported 1933 cases of active euthanasia and physician-assisted suicide.

Oregon†

Oregon's Death with Dignity Act was approved by the state legislature in 1994, but due to legal proceedings, its implementation was put off until 1997. In Oregon, *only* physician-assisted suicide is legal, and doctors can prescribe a lethal medication only when the person is terminally ill.

Requirements: The person must make two requests to the prescribing doctor at least 15 days apart and make one written request witnessed by two people. Two doctors must confirm that the patient is within six months of death, mentally capable, and not depressed. The prescribing doctor must inform the patient of alternative choices and must have given the prescription to the Oregon Health Department.

Additional facts:

- In 2005, 38 people utilized this option.
- Compared to the overall population of deaths, people who used this approach were younger, more apt to be Asian American, divorced, and well educated. People with cancer or amyotrophic lateral sclerosis (ALS) were most likely to decide to end their lives in this way.
- Although a slim majority of Oregon doctors said that they approved of the legislation, only 1 in 3 said that they would be willing to prescribe a lethal medication themselves.

*Belgium is the only other country in which active euthanasia is fully legal.

†Physician-assisted suicide is also legal in Switzerland.

Sources: Ardelt (2003); Associated Press (2006); Pietsch (2004); and State of Oregon Department of Human Services (n.d.).

draw some heroic measure, we don't specifically wish for death. When doctors give a patient a lethal dose of a drug or, as in physician-assisted suicide, prescribe a lethal substance for a terminally ill person, they *want* that individual to die.

Although active euthanasia is almost universally against the law, studies suggest that these kinds of practices that hasten death do occur (Bilsen and others, 2004; Seale, 2009). Polls in the United States and other Western countries show that large majorities of the public do believe in "restricted," active euthanasia—if an individual is terminally ill and in great pain (Dickens, Boyle, & Ganzini, 2008). However, there is considerable resistance to actually making these practices legal. Why?

One reason is that killing violates the principle that only God can give or take a life. This is why highly religious people tend to passionately oppose both physician-assisted suicide and active euthanasia (Ardelt, 2003; Seale, 2009; Walker, 2003). Apart from religious considerations, there are other reasons many of us might be leery about taking this step.

passive euthanasia Withholding potentially life-saving interventions that might keep a terminally ill or permanently comatose patient alive.

active euthanasia A deliberate intervention that helps a terminally ill patient die.

physician-assisted suicide A type of active euthanasia in which a physician prescribes a lethal medication to a terminally ill person who wants to die.

By agreeing to legalize these practices, critics fear, we may be opening the gates to involuntary euthanasia, allowing doctors and families to "pull the plug" on people who are impaired but don't want to die (Ardelt, 2003; Walker, 2003). Even when someone requests help to end his life, we don't know whether the patient is being pressured into that decision by unscrupulous relatives who are anxious to get their inheritance or want to be spared the expense of waiting for the person to die.

Another issue relates to trusting the patient's *own* current feelings and thoughts. People who request physician-assisted suicide are almost always depressed (Wilson and others, 2007). If the depression were treated, they might feel differently about ending their lives. One psychiatrist cited the case of a young man in his thirties diagnosed with leukemia and given a 25 percent chance of survival. Fearing both the side effects of the treatment and being a burden to his family, he begged for assistance in killing himself:

> *Once the young man and I could talk about the possibility of his dying—what separation from his family and the destruction of his body meant to him—his desperation subsided. He accepted medical treatment and used the remaining months of his life to become closer to his wife and parents. Two days before he died, he talked about what he would have missed without the opportunity for a loving parting.*

(quoted in Hendin, 1994, Dec. 16, p. A19)

There are also excellent arguments on the other side. Should patients be forced to unwillingly endure the pain and humiliation of dying when physicians have the tools to mercifully end life? Knowing the agony that terminal disease can cause, is it really humane to stand by and let nature gradually take its course? Do you believe that legalizing active euthanasia or physician-assisted suicide is a true advance in caring for the dying or its opposite, the beginning of a "slippery slope" that might end in sanctioning the killing of anyone whose quality of life is impaired?

A Looming Social Issue: Age-Based Rationing of Care

There is an age component to the "slippery slope" of withholding care. As I suggested earlier, people with DNR or DNH orders in their charts are typically elderly, near the end of their natural lives. We already use passive euthanasia at the upper end of the lifespan on a case-by-case basis, holding off from giving aggressive treatments to people we deem "too frail." Should we formally adopt the principle "don't use death-defying strategies" for people after they reach a certain age?

Daniel Callahan (1988), a prominent biomedical ethicist, has taken the position that the answer must be yes. There is a time when "the never-to-be-finished fight against death" must stop. According to Callahan, waging total war for everyone might be acceptable if we all had equal access to health care. But in the United States, Medicare pays for expensive life-prolonging strategies, while, at the time of this writing, millions of younger Americans have no health insurance at all. Let's read Callahan's arguments in favor of **age-based rationing of care:**

1. *After a person has lived out a natural lifespan, medical care should no longer be oriented to resisting death.* While stressing that no precise cutoff age can be set, Callahan puts this marker at around the eighties. This does not mean that life at this age has no value, but rather that when people reach their old-old years, death in the near future is inevitable and this process cannot be vigorously defied.

2. *The existence of medical technologies capable of extending the lives of elderly persons who have lived out a natural lifespan creates no presumption that the technologies must be used for that purpose.* Callahan believes that the proper

age-based rationing of care The controversial idea that society should not use expensive life-sustaining technologies on people in their old-old years.

goal of medicine is to stave off premature death. We should not become slaves to our death-defying technology by blindly using each intervention on every person, no matter what that individual's age.

Is Callahan "telling it like it should be" from a logical, rational point of view, or do his proposals give you chills? As you consider this issue, you might be interested to know that we already practice age-based rationing of health care at the opposite end of the lifespan. At a major medical center in my city, babies born before the "cutoff" date of 25 weeks of pregnancy are given no heroic measures. If they survive in the uterus to 26 weeks, however, doctors pull out all the stops. Age-based rationing of care—and when to use aggressive medical measures—is an issue that applies to both the very beginning and the very end of life!

TYING IT ALL TOGETHER

1. Your mother asks you whether she should fill out an advance directive. Given what you now know from this chapter, what should your answer be?
   a. Go for it! The best thing to do is to fill out a living will so you can be sure your preferences will be fulfilled.
   b. Go for it! But the best alternative might be to carefully discuss your preferences with one of us and complete a durable power of attorney.
   c. Avoid advance directives like the plague, because your preferences will never be fulfilled.

2. Latoya and Jamal are arguing about legalizing physician-assisted suicide. Jamal is furious that this practice is not legal and feels that "people should have the right to die." Latoya is terribly worried about formally institutionalizing this practice. Using the points in this section, first make Jamal's case, and then support Latoya's argument.

3. Poll your class: How would your fellow students vote if they were on the jury deciding Dr. Cox's case? If you were the ward nurse, would you have reported this doctor's decision to the police?

Answers to the Tying It All Together questions can be found on the last page of this chapter.

Final Thoughts

Age-based rationing of health care is a major social challenge looming on the horizon. Expect these kinds of conversations to continue in the coming decades as the huge baby boom cohort enters its old-old years.

But the basic message of this chapter takes us back to the heart of our universal human concern. As we approach death, notice that our life comes full circle, and we care only about what mattered during our first year of life—being connected to the people we most love. Okay, during most of the lifespan, self-efficacy is important. But when we come right down to it, attachment trumps everything else!

SUMMARY

The Dying Person

Today, we have three major pathways to death: We may die suddenly, without warning; we may steadily decline; and, most often, we may battle an ultimately fatal, chronic condition for a prolonged time. Before modern medicine, people died quickly and everyone had a good deal of hands-on experience with death. Today, we have "moved" death to old age and keep the act of dying hidden from view. The physical process of dying is still "off the horizon"; but during the late twentieth century, **thanatology** became a major topic of study. Doctors now openly tell patients their illness may be terminal, and we urge people to discuss their

dying preferences, although talking about death is still forbidden in some cultural groups.

Elisabeth Kübler-Ross, in her **stage theory of dying**, proposed that people pass through *denial, anger, bargaining, depression,* and *acceptance* when they learn they have a fatal disease. However, we cannot take this landmark theory as the final truth. Not every person wants to talk about impending death. Many people disagree with Kübler-Ross that we should be totally honest with dying people. Furthermore, terminally ill people feel many different emotions—especially hope—rather than emotionally approaching death in "stages." They may experience a state called **middle knowledge**, both knowing and not fully comprehending their fate. It's possible to fully "accept death" and still have life goals. A fatal illness may also provoke people to get their lives together and approach living in a different way.

Parents have an enormously difficult time coping with that off-time event, the death of a child. When parents openly discuss death (if the child knows he or she is dying) and say goodbye to their child, they seem to adjust better to this trauma. Health-care workers can help families by attending the funeral, sensitively bringing up the possibility of death when the illness enters its terminal phase, and inviting parents to share in the hands-on care during a child's final hours.

The Old Testament injunction, that dying at peace after a long life and being surrounded by our loved ones is the best possible way for life to end, resonates today. Most people want to die at home and reject being kept artificially alive by medical interventions. Specifically, people want to end their lives relatively free of pain and anxiety, feel in control of how they die, and die feeling close to loved ones. Believing that we have fulfilled our purpose in living and appreciating that our death is part of the universal human cycle of life is also important in accepting death.

The Health-Care System

A classic study of **dying trajectories** showed that because dying doesn't proceed according to a predetermined plan but medical personnel assume it does, the way hospitals manage death leaves much to be desired. Communication problems among patients, families, and medical personnel, along with the fact that medical technologies can extend life well beyond the time the body "wants" to die, increase the potential for undignified hospital deaths. Interventions to provide better **palliative care** include: (1) offering **end-of-life care instruction** to health-care personnel; (2) establishing hospital-based **palliative-care services**; and (3) removing the scene of dying from hospitals to the hospice.

The **hospice movement** offers backup services that allow families to let their loved ones spend their final months dying naturally, typically at home. Although more people than ever use hospice care, this well-established program has not caught on with ethnic minorities. Enrolling in hospice means labeling the patient as definitely dying. It also demands that family members be committed to providing hands-on care. Home deaths may not always be the best choice when we understand that pain control and attachment-related issues such as not burdening one's family matter most to people who are dying.

The Dying Person: Taking Control of How We Die

Advance directives—the **living will** and **durable power of attorney for health care**, filled out by the individual in health, and the **Do Not Resuscitate (DNR)** and **Do Not Hospitalize (DNH)** orders, filled out by surrogates when the person is mentally impaired—provide information about whether to use heroic measures when individuals cannot make their treatment wishes known. As there are special problems with the living will, the best advance directive may be the durable power of attorney, which gives a specific surrogate decision-making power to direct one's care.

With **active euthanasia** and **physician-assisted suicide**, physicians move beyond **passive euthanasia** (withdrawing treatments) to actively take steps that promote the death of seriously ill people who want to end their lives. Paramount among the objections to legalizing active euthanasia is the idea that we may be opening the door to killing people who don't really want to die. A related issue is **age-based rationing of care**, whether to hold off on using expensive death-defying technologies with people who are in their old-old years. The bottom-line message of this chapter is that love (or, in developmental science terminology, our attachments) matters more than anything else.

ANSWERS TO TYING IT ALL TOGETHER QUIZZES

Setting the Context

1. b.

2. slowly and erratically; an age-related chronic disease

3. Ella's case: Today, we openly discuss dying with seriously ill patients and try to get everyone to document their wishes for a dignified death. We also routinely offer death education classes and make active efforts to think about how to take good care of the terminally ill. Margaret's case: We still are completely disconnected from—and frightened about—the physical reality of death. Our euphemisms for death, like "passing away," clearly show that we still live in an incredibly death-denying culture.

The Dying Person

1. d.

2. many different emotions; hope

3. an 80-year-old woman

4. Use your creativity here. My suggestions: provide counselors on call 24/7 so that terminally ill people on the units can express their fears and concerns. At entry to the hospital, ask seriously ill patients "what exactly do you want in terms of care?" and make sure that their preferences—with regard to family visits, pain control, and everything else—are fulfilled by the staff.

The Health-Care System

1. Although medical personnel set up predictions about how patients are likely to die, death doesn't always go according to schedule—so these prognostications are often very wrong!

2. b.

3. Sara's case: We now routinely provide death education courses to health professionals and, increasingly, have

established hospital-based palliative-care services. Martha's case: Death education is still not a priority, and palliative-care services are still not the norm. Moreover, health-care personnel still often feel compelled to use aggressive medical measures even when they are concerned about the ethics of doing so. The whole hospital system is cure-oriented, making it very difficult to shift to palliative care.

4. A man with end-stage lung cancer living with his wife and daughters

5. Here's what you might say to Melanie: Would you feel comfortable about burdening your family 24/7 with the job of nursing you for months or having them manage the terrifying health crises that would surely occur? How would you feel having loved ones see you naked and incontinent—would you want that to be their last memory of you? And, also, wouldn't it be better to be in a setting where trained professionals could manage your intense physical pain?

6. a and c.

The Dying Person: Taking Control of How We Die

1. b.

2. Jamal's case: We are free to make decisions about how to live our lives, so it doesn't make logical sense that we can't decide when our lives should end. Plus, it's cruel to torture fatally ill people, forcing them to suffer fruitless, unwanted pain when we can easily provide a merciful death. Latoya's argument: I'm worried that greedy relatives might pressure ill people into deciding to die "for the good of the family" (that is to save the family money). I believe that legalizing physician-assisted suicide leaves the door open to society deciding to kill people when *we think* the quality of their life is not good. Furthermore, only God can take a life!

3. Here your answers may vary in interesting ways. Enjoy the discussion!

Glossary

accommodation: In Piaget's theory, enlarging our mental capacities to fit input from the wider world.

acculturation: Among immigrants, the tendency to become more similar in terms of attitudes and practices to the mainstream culture after time spent living in a new society.

achievement tests: Measures that evaluate a child's knowledge in specific school-related areas.

active euthanasia: A deliberate intervention that helps a terminally ill patient die.

active forces: The nature-interacts-with-nurture principle that our genetic temperamental tendencies and predispositions cause us to actively choose to put ourselves into specific environments.

ADL (activities of daily living) problems: Difficulty in performing everyday tasks that are required for living independently. ADLs are classified as either basic or instrumental.

adolescence-limited turmoil: Antisocial behavior that, for most teens, is specific to adolescence and does not persist into adult life.

adolescent egocentrism: David Elkind's term for the tendency of young teenagers to feel that their actions are at the center of everyone else's consciousness.

adoption study: Behavioral genetic research strategy, designed to determine the genetic contribution to a given trait, that involves comparing adopted children with their biological and adoptive parents.

adrenal androgens: Hormones produced by the adrenal glands that program various aspects of puberty, such as growth of body hair, skin changes, and sexual desire.

adult attachment styles: The different ways in which adults relate to romantic partners, based on Mary Ainsworth's infant attachment styles. (Adult attachment styles are classi-fied as secure, or preoccupied/ambivalent insecure, or avoidant/dismissive insecure.)

adult development: The scientific study of the adult part of life.

advance directive: Any written document spelling out instructions with regard to life-prolonging treatment if individuals become irretrievably ill and cannot communicate their wishes.

age discrimination: Illegally laying off workers or failing to hire or promote them on the basis of age.

age norms: Cultural ideas about the appropriate ages for engaging in particular activities or life tasks.

age of viability: The earliest point at which a baby can survive outside the womb.

age-based rationing of care: The controversial idea that society should not use expensive life-sustaining technologies on people in their old-old years.

aggression: Any hostile or destructive act.

alternatives to institutionalization: Services and settings designed to keep older people who are experiencing age-related disabilities that don't merit intense 24-hour care from having to enter nursing homes.

altruism: Prosocial behaviors that we carry out for selfless, non-egocentric reasons.

Alzheimer's disease: A type of age-related dementia characterized by neural atrophy and abnormal by-products of that atrophy, such as senile plaques and neurofibrillary tangles.

amniocentesis: A second-trimester procedure that involves inserting a syringe into a woman's uterus to extract a sample of amniotic fluid, which is tested for a variety of genetic and chromosomal conditions.

amniotic sac: A bag-shaped, fluid-filled membrane that contains and insulates the fetus.

analytic intelligence: In Robert Sternberg's framework on successful intelligence, the facet of intelligence involving performing well on academic-type problems.

animism: In Piaget's theory, the preoperational child's belief that inanimate objects are alive.

anorexia nervosa: A potentially life-threatening eating disorder characterized by pathological dieting (resulting in severe weight loss and extreme thinness) and by a distorted body image.

A-not-B error: In Piaget's framework, a classic mistake made by infants in the sensorimotor stage, whereby babies approaching age 1 go back to the original hiding place to look for an object even though they have seen it get hidden in a second place.

anxious-ambivalent attachment: An insecure attachment style characterized by a child's intense distress at separation and by anger and great difficulty being soothed when reunited with the primary caregiver in the Strange Situation.

Apgar scale: A quick test used to assess a just-delivered baby's condition by measuring heart rate, muscle tone, respiration, reflex response, and color.

artificialism: In Piaget's theory, the preoperational child's belief that human beings make everything in nature.

assimilation: In Jean Piaget's theory, the first step promoting mental growth, involving fitting environmental input to our existing mental capacities.

assisted reproductive technology (ART): Any infertility treatment in which the egg is fertilized outside the womb.

assisted-living facility: A housing option providing care for elderly people who have instrumental ADL impairments and can no longer live independently but may not need a nursing home.

attachment in the making: The second phase of John Bowlby's developmental attachment sequence, lasting from about 4 to 7 months of age, when infants show a slight preference for their primary caregiver.

attachment theory: Theory formulated by John Bowlby centering on the crucial importance to our species' survival of being closely connected with a caregiver during early childhood and being attached to a significant other during all of life.

attachment: The powerful bond of love between a caregiver and child (or between any two individuals).

attention deficit/hyperactivity disorder (ADHD): The most common childhood learning disorder in the United States, disproportionately affecting boys, characterized by excessive restlessness and distractibility at home and at school.

authoritarian parents: In the parenting-styles framework, a type of childrearing in which parents provide plenty of rules but rank low on child-centeredness, stressing unquestioning obedience.

authoritative parents: In the parenting-styles framework, the best possible child-rearing style, in which parents rank high on both nurturance and discipline, providing both love and clear family rules.

autobiographical memories: Recollections of events and experiences that make up one's life history.

autonomy: Erikson's second psychosocial task, when toddlers confront the challenge of understanding that they are separate individuals.

average life expectancy: A person's fifty-fifty chance at birth of living to a given age.

avoidant attachment: An insecure attachment style characterized by a child's indifference to the primary caregiver when they are reunited in the Strange Situation.

avoidant/dismissive insecure attachment: A standoffish, excessively disengaged style of relating to loved ones.

axon: A long nerve fiber that usually conducts impulses away from the cell body of a neuron.

B

babbling: The alternating vowel and consonant sounds that babies repeat with variations of intonation and pitch and that precede the first words.

baby boom cohort: The huge age group born between 1946 and 1964.

baby-proofing: Making the home safe for a newly mobile infant.

basic ADL problems: Difficulty in performing essential self-care activities, such as rising from a chair, eating, and getting to the toilet.

behavioral genetics: Field devoted to scientifically determining the role that hereditary forces play in determining individual differences in behavior.

bidirectionality: The crucial principle that people affect one another, or that interpersonal influences flow in both directions.

Big Five traits: Five core psychological predispositions—neuroticism, extraversion, openness to experience, conscientiousness, and agreeableness—that underlie personality.

biracial or multiracial identity: How people of mixed racial backgrounds come to terms with who they are as people in relation to their heritage.

birth defect: A physical or neurological problem that occurs prenatally or at birth.

blastocyst: The hollow sphere of cells formed during the germinal stage in preparation for implantation.

body mass index (BMI): The ratio of weight to height; the main indicator of overweight or underweight.

boundaryless career: Today's most common career path for Western workers, in which people change jobs or professions periodically during their working lives.

bulimia nervosa: An eating disorder characterized by cycles of bingeing and purging (by inducing vomiting or taking laxatives) in an obsessive attempt to lose weight.

bullying: A situation in which one or more children (or adults) harass or target a specific child for systematic abuse.

C

caregiving grandparents: Grandparents who have taken on full responsibility for raising their grandchildren.

centering: In Piaget's conservation tasks, the preoperational child's tendency to fix on the most visually striking feature of a substance and not take other dimensions into account.

cephalocaudal sequence: The developmental principle that growth occurs in a sequence from head to toe.

cerebral cortex: The outer folded mantle of the brain, responsible for thinking, reasoning, perceiving, and all conscious responses.

certified nurse assistant or aide: The main hands-on care provider in a nursing home, who helps elderly residents with basic ADL problems.

cervix: The neck, or narrow lower portion, of the uterus.

cesarean section (c-section): A method of delivering a baby surgically by extracting the baby through incisions in the woman's abdominal wall and in the uterus.

child development: The scientific study of development from birth through adolescence.

child maltreatment: Any act that seriously endangers a child's physical or emotional well-being.

childhood obesity: A body mass index at or above the 95th percentile compared to the U.S. norms established for children in the 1970s.

chorionic villus sampling (CVS): A relatively risky first-trimester pregnancy test for fetal genetic disorders.

chromosome: A threadlike strand of DNA located in the nucleus of every cell that carries the genes, which transmit hereditary information.

chronic disease: Any long-term illness that requires ongoing management. Most chronic diseases are age-related and are the endpoint of normal aging changes.

circular reactions: In Piaget's framework, repetitive action-oriented schemas (or habits) characteristic of babies during the sensorimotor stage.

class inclusion: The understanding that a general category can encompass several subordinate elements.

clear-cut attachment: The critical period for human attachment, lasting from roughly 7 months of age through toddlerhood, characterized by separation anxiety, the need to have a caregiver physically close, and stranger anxiety.

clique: A small peer group composed of roughly six teenagers who have similar attitudes and who share activities.

cognitive behaviorism (social learning theory): A behavioral worldview that emphasizes that people learn by watching others and that our thoughts about the reinforcers determine our behavior. Cognitive behaviorists focus on charting and modifying people's thoughts.

cohabitation: Sharing a household in an unmarried romantic relationship.

cohort: The age group with whom we travel through life.

colic: A baby's frantic, continual crying during the first three months of life; caused by an immature nervous system.

collaborative pretend play: Fantasy play in which children work together to develop and act out the scenes.

collectivist cultures: Societies that prize social harmony, obedience, and close family connectedness over individual achievement.

commitment script: In Dan McAdams's research, a type of autobiography produced by highly generative adults that involves childhood memories of feeling special, being unusually sensitive to others' misfortunes, having a strong, enduring generative mission from adolescence, and redemption sequences.

concrete operational thinking: In Piaget's framework, the type of cognition characteristic of children aged 8 to 11, marked by the ability to reason about the world in a more logical, adult way.

conservation tasks: Piagetian tasks that involve changing the shape of a substance to see whether children can go beyond the way that substance visually appears to understand that the amount is still the same.

consummate love: In Robert Sternberg's triangular theory of love, the ideal form of love, in which a couple's relationship involves all three of the major facets of love: passion, intimacy, and commitment.

contexts of development: Fundamental markers, including cohort, socioeconomic status, culture, and gender, that shape how we develop throughout the lifespan.

continuing bonds: A widow's or widower's ongoing sense of the deceased spouse's presence "in spirit."

continuing-care retirement community: A housing option characterized by a series of levels of care for elderly residents, ranging from independent apartments to assisted living to nursing home care. People enter the community in relatively good health and move to sections where they can get more care when they become disabled.

conventional level of morality: In Lawrence Kohlberg's theory, the intermediate level of moral reasoning, in which people respond to ethical issues by considering the need to uphold social norms.

corporal punishment: The use of physical force to discipline a child.

correlational study: A research strategy that involves relating two or more variables.

co-sleeping: The standard custom, in collectivist cultures, of having a child and parent share a bed.

creative intelligence: In Robert Sternberg's framework on successful intelligence, the facet of intelligence involved in producing novel ideas or innovative work.

cross-sectional study: A developmental research strategy that involves testing different age groups at the same time.

crowd: A relatively large teenage peer group.

crystallized intelligence: A basic facet of intelligence, consisting of a person's knowledge base, or storehouse of accumulated information.

cyberbullying: Victimizing or targeting a specific child (or adult) for systematic abuse either on-line or via e-mail messages.

D

day-care center: A day-care arrangement in which a large number of children are cared for at a licensed facility by paid providers.

day-care program: A service for impaired older adults who live with relatives, in which the older person spends the day at a center offering various activities.

decentering: In Piaget's conservation tasks, the concrete operational child's ability to look at several dimensions of an object or substance.

deinstitutionalization of marriage: The decline in marriage and the emergence of alternate family forms that occurred during the last third of the twentieth century.

demand–withdrawal communication: A pathological type of interaction in which one partner, most often the woman, presses for more intimacy and the other person, most often the man, tends to back off.

dementia: The general term for any illness that produces serious, progressive, usually irreversible cognitive decline.

dendrite: A branching fiber that receives information and conducts impulses toward the cell body of a neuron.

depth perception: The ability to see (and fear) heights.

developed world: The most affluent countries in the world.

developing world: The more impoverished countries of the world.

developmental disorders: Learning impairments and behavioral problems during infancy and childhood.

developmental systems perspective: An all-encompassing outlook on development that stresses the need to embrace a variety of theories, and the idea that all systems and processes interrelate.

developmentalists (developmental scientists): Researchers and practitioners whose professional interest lies in the study of the human lifespan.

deviancy training: Socialization of a young teenager into delinquency through conversations centered on performing antisocial acts.

disorganized attachment: An insecure attachment style characterized by responses such as freezing or fear when a child is reunited with the primary caregiver in the Strange Situation.

divided-attention task: A difficult memory challenge involving memorizing material while simultaneously monitoring something else.

DNA (deoxyribonucleic acid): The material that makes up genes, which bear our hereditary characteristics.

Do Not Hospitalize (DNH) order: A type of advance directive put into the charts of impaired nursing home residents, specifying that in a medical crisis they should not be transferred to a hospital for emergency care.

Do Not Resuscitate (DNR) order: A type of advance directive filled out by surrogates (usually a doctor in consultation with family members) for impaired individuals, specifying that if they go into cardiac arrest, efforts should not be made to revive them.

dominant disorder: An illness that a child gets by inheriting one copy of the abnormal gene that causes the disorder.

Down syndrome: The most common chromosomal abnormality, causing mental retardation, susceptibility to heart disease, and other health problems; and distinctive physical characteristics, such as slanted eyes and stocky build.

durable power of attorney for health care: A type of advance directive in which people designate a specific surrogate to make health-care decisions if they become incapacitated and are unable to make their wishes known.

dying trajectory: The fact that hospital personnel make projections about the particular pathway to death that a seriously ill patient will take and organize their care according to that assumption.

dyslexia: A learning disability that is characterized by reading difficulties, lack of fluency, and poor word recognition that is often genetic in origin.

E

early childhood: The first phase of childhood, lasting from age 3 through kindergarten, or about age 5.

Early Head Start: A federal program that provides counseling and other services to low-income parents and children under age 3.

eating disorder: A pathological obsession with getting and staying thin. The two best-known eating disorders are *anorexia nervosa* and *bulimia nervosa*.

egocentrism: In Piaget's theory, the preoperational child's inability to understand that other people have different points of view from their own.

Elderhostel: An education-travel program that offers people age 55 and older special learning experiences at universities and other locations across the United States and around the world.

elderspeak: A style of communication used with an older person who seems to be physically impaired, involving speaking loudly and with slow, exaggerated pronunciation, as if talking to a baby.

embryonic stage: The second stage of prenatal development, lasting from week 3 through week 8.

emerging adulthood: The phase of life that begins after high school, tapers off toward the late twenties, and is devoted to constructing an adult life.

emerging adulthood: The phase of life that begins after high school, tapers off toward the late twenties, and is devoted to constructing an adult life.

emotion regulation: The capacity to manage one's emotional state.

empathy: Feeling the exact emotion that another person is experiencing.

end-of-life care instruction: Courses in medical and nursing schools devoted to teaching health-care workers how to provide the best palliative care to the dying.

episodic memory: In the memory-systems perspective, the most fragile type of memory, involving the recall of the ongoing events of daily life.

Erikson's psychosocial tasks: In Erik Erikson's theory, each challenge that we face as we travel through the eight stages of the lifespan.

ethnic identity: How people come to terms with who they are as people relating to their unique ethnic or racial heritage.

event-driven relationship: An erratic love relationship characterized by dramatic shifts in feelings and sense of commitment, with couples repeatedly breaking up, then getting back together again.

evocative forces: The nature-interacts-with-nurture principle that our genetic temperamental tendencies and predispositions evoke, or produce, certain responses from other people.

evolutionary psychology: Theory or worldview highlighting the role that inborn, species-specific behaviors play in human development and life.

executive functions: Any frontal-lobe ability that allows us to inhibit our responses and to plan and direct our thinking.

experience-sampling technique: A research procedure designed to capture moment-to-moment experiences by having people carry pagers and take notes describing their activities and emotions whenever the signal sounds.

externalizing tendencies: A personality style that involves acting on one's immediate impulses and behaving disruptively and aggressively.

extrinsic career rewards: Work that is performed for external reinforcers, such as prestige or a high salary.

extrinsic motivation: The drive to take an action because that activity offers external reinforcers such as praise, money, or a good grade.

F

face-perception studies: Research using preferential looking and habituation to explore what very young babies know about faces.

fallopian tube: One of a pair of slim, pipe-like structures that connect the ovaries with the uterus.

family day care: A day-care arrangement in which a neighbor or relative cares for a small number of children in her home for a fee.

family watchdogs: A basic role of grandparents, which involves monitoring the younger family's well-being and intervening to provide help in a crisis.

fantasy play: Play that involves making up and acting out a scenario; also called *pretend play*.

fertility rate: The average number of children a woman in a given country has during her lifetime.

fertilization: The union of sperm and egg.

fetal alcohol syndrome (FAS): A cluster of birth defects caused by the mother's alcohol consumption during pregnancy.

fetal stage: The final period of prenatal development, lasting seven months, characterized by physical refinements, massive growth, and the development of the brain.

fine motor skills: Physical abilities that involve small, coordinated movements, such as drawing and writing one's name.

flow: Csikszentmihalyi's term for feeling total absorption in a challenging, goal-oriented activity.

fluid intelligence: A basic facet of intelligence, consisting of the ability to quickly master new intellectual activities.

formal operational stage: Jean Piaget's fourth and final stage of cognitive development, reached at around age 12 and characterized by teenagers' ability to reason at an abstract, scientific level.

frontal lobes: The area at the uppermost front of the brain, responsible for reasoning and planning our actions.

G

gang: A close-knit, delinquent peer group. Gangs form mainly under conditions of economic deprivation; they offer their members protection from harm and engage in a variety of criminal activities.

gender schema theory: An explanation for gender-stereotyped behavior that emphasizes the role of cognitions; specifically, the idea that once children know their own gender label (girl or boy), they selectively watch and model their own sex.

gender-segregated play: Play in which boys and girls associate only with members of their own sex—typical of childhood.

gene: A segment of DNA that contains a chemical blueprint for manufacturing a particular protein.

generativity: In Erikson's theory, the seventh psycho-social task, in which people in midlife find meaning from nurturing the next generation, caring for others, or enriching the life of others through their work. According to Erikson, when midlife adults have not achieved generativity, they feel stagnant, without a sense of purpose in life.

genetic counselor: A professional who counsels parents-to-be about their own or their children's risk of developing genetic disorders, as well as about available treatments.

genetic testing: A blood test to determine whether a person carries the gene for a given genetic disorder.

germinal stage: The first 14 days of prenatal development, from fertilization to full implantation.

gerontology: The scientific study of the aging process and older adults.

gestation: The period of pregnancy.

gifted: The label for superior intellectual functioning characterized by an IQ score of 130 or above, showing that a child ranks in the top 2 percent of his age group.

gonads: The sex organs—the ovaries in girls and the testes in boys.

goodness of fit: An ideal parenting strategy that involves arranging children's environments to suit their temperaments, minimizing their vulnerabilities and accentuating their strengths.

grammar: The rules and word-arranging systems that every human language employs to communicate meaning.

gross motor skills: Physical abilities that involve large muscle movements, such as running and jumping.

growth spurt: A dramatic increase in height and weight that occurs during puberty.

guilt: Feeling upset about having caused harm to a person or about having violated one's internal standard of behavior.

H

habituation: The predictable loss of interest that develops once a stimulus becomes familiar; used to explore infant sensory capacities and thinking.

Head Start: A federal program offering high-quality day care at a center and other services to help preschoolers aged 3 to 5 from low-income families prepare for school.

holophrase: First clear evidence of language, when babies use a single word to communicate a sentence or complete thought.

home health services: Nursing-oriented and housekeeping help provided in the home of an impaired older adult (or any other impaired person).

homogamy: The principle that we select a mate who is similar to us.

homophobia: Intense fear and dislike of gays and lesbians.

hormones: Chemical substances released in the bloodstream that target and change organs and tissues.

hospice movement: A movement, which became widespread in recent decades, focused on providing palliative care to dying patients outside of hospitals and especially on giving families the support they need to care for the terminally ill at home.

hostile attributional bias: The tendency of highly aggressive children to see motives and actions as threatening when they are actually benign.

HPG axis: The main hormonal system programming puberty; it involves a triggering hypothalamic hormone that causes the pituitary to secrete its hormones, which in turn cause the ovaries and testes to develop and secrete the hormones that produce the major body changes.

I

identity achievement: An identity status in which the person decides on a definite adult life path after searching out various options.

identity confusion: Erikson's term for a failure in identity formation, marked by the lack of any sense of a future adult path.

identity constancy: In Piaget's theory, the preoperational child's inability to grasp that a person's core "self" stays the same despite changes in external appearance.

identity diffusion: An identity status in which the person is aimless or feels totally blocked, without any adult life path.

identity foreclosure: An identity status in which the person decides on an adult life path (often one spelled out by an authority figure) without any thought or active search.

identity statuses: Marcia's four categories of identity formation: identity diffusion, identity foreclosure, moratorium, and identity achievement.

identity: In Erikson's theory, the life task of deciding who to be as a person in making the transition to adulthood.

imaginary audience: David Elkind's term for the tendency of young teenagers to feel that everyone is watching their every action; a component of adolescent egocentrism.

implantation: The process in which a blastocyst becomes embedded in the uterine wall.

in vitro fertilization: An infertility treatment in which conception occurs outside the womb; the developing cell mass is then inserted into the woman's uterus so that pregnancy can occur.

individualistic cultures: Societies that prize independence, competition, and personal success.

induction: The ideal discipline style for socializing prosocial behavior, involving getting a child who has behaved hurtfully to empathize with the pain he has caused the other person.

industry versus inferiority: Erik Erikson's term for the psychosocial task of middle childhood, involving the capacity to work for one's goals.

infant mortality: Death during the first year of life.

infant-directed speech (IDS): The simplified, exaggerated, high-pitched tones that adults and children use to speak to infants that function to help teach language.

infertility: The inability to conceive after a year of unprotected sex. (Includes the inability to carry a child to term.)

information-processing theory: A perspective on cognition in which the process of thinking is divided into steps, components, or stages much like those a computer operates.

inner speech: In Vygotsky's theory, the way by which human beings learn to regulate their behavior and master cognitive challenges, through silently repeating information or talking to themselves.

insecure attachment: A deviation from the normally joyful response to being reunited with the primary caregiver in the Strange Situation, signaling a problem in the caregiver–child relationship.

instrumental ADL problems: Difficulties in performing everyday household tasks, such as cooking and cleaning.

instrumental aggression: A hostile or destructive act initiated to achieve a goal.

integrity: Erik Erikson's eighth psychosocial stage in which elderly people decide that their life missions have been fulfilled and so accept impending death.

intergenerational solidarity: Middle-aged adults' feeling of loving obligation to both the older and the younger generations.

internalizing tendencies: A personality style that involves intense fear, social inhibition, and often depression.

intimacy: Erikson's first adult task, involving connecting with a partner in a mutual loving relationship.

intrinsic career rewards: Work that provides inner fulfillment and allows people to satisfy their needs for creativity, autonomy, and relatedness.

intrinsic motivation: The drive to act based on the pleasure of taking that action in itself, not for an external reinforcer or reward.

joint attention: The first sign of "getting human intentions," when a baby looks at an object an adult is pointing to or follows a person's gaze.

K

kangaroo care: Carrying a young baby in a sling close to the caregiver's body. This technique is useful for soothing an infant.

Kübler-Ross's stage theory of dying: The landmark theory, developed by psychiatrist Elisabeth Kübler-Ross, that people who are terminally ill progress through five stages in confronting their death: denial, anger, bargaining, depression, and acceptance.

L

language acquisition device (LAD): Chomsky's term for a hypothetical brain structure that enables our species to learn and produce language.

late-life life expectancy: The number of additional years a person in a given country can expect to live once reaching age 65.

learned helplessness: A state that develops when a person feels incapable of affecting the outcome of events, and so gives up without trying.

lens: A transparent, disk-shaped structure in the eye, which bends to allow us to see close objects.

life-course difficulties: Antisocial behavior that, for a fraction of adolescents, persists into adult life.

lifespan development: The scientific field covering all of the human lifespan.

lifespan theory of careers: Donald Super's identification of four career phases: *moratorium* in adolescence and emerging adulthood; *establishment* in young adulthood; *maintenance* in midlife; and *decline* in late life.

little-scientist phase: The time around age 1 when babies use tertiary circular reactions to actively explore the properties of objects, experimenting with them like "scientists."

living will: A type of advance directive in which people spell out their wishes for life-sustaining treatment in case they become permanently incapacitated and unable to communicate.

longitudinal study: A developmental research strategy that involves testing an age group repeatedly over many years.

low birth weight (LBW): A body weight at birth of less than 5 1/2 pounds.

low income: According to child advocates, the real minimum income it takes for a family to decently make ends meet in the United States; defined as twice the poverty line.

M

marital equity: Fairness in the "work" of a couple's life together. If a relationship lacks equity, with one partner doing significantly more than the other, the outcome is typically marital dissatisfaction.

mass-to-specific sequence: The developmental principle that large structures (and movements) precede increasingly detailed refinements.

maximum lifespan: The biological limit of human life (about 105 years).

mean length of utterance (MLU): The average number of morphemes per sentence.

means–end behavior: In Piaget's framework, performing a different action to get to a goal—an ability that emerges in the sensorimotor stage as babies approach age 1.

median age: The age at which 50 percent of a population is older and 50 percent is younger.

Medicare: The U.S. government's program of health insurance for elderly people.

memory-systems perspective: A framework that divides memory into three types: procedural, semantic, and episodic memory.

menarche: A girl's first menstruation.

menopause: The age-related process, occurring at about age 50, in which ovulation and menstruation stop due to the loss of estrogen.

mentally retarded: The label for significantly impaired intellectual functioning, defined as when a child (or adult) has an IQ of 70 or below accompanied by evidence of deficits in learning abilities.

micronutrient deficiency: Chronically inadequate level of a specific nutrient important to development and disease prevention, such as Vitamin A, zinc, and/or iron.

middle childhood: The second phase of childhood, covering the elementary school years, from about age 6 to 11.

middle knowledge: The idea that terminally ill people can know that they are dying yet at the same time not completely grasp or come to terms emotionally with that fact.

miscarriage: The naturally occurring loss of a pregnancy and death of the fetus.

mnemonic technique: A strategy for aiding memory, often by using imagery or enhancing the emotional meaning of what needs to be learned.

modeling: Learning by watching and imitating others.

moratorium: An identity status in which the person actively searches out various possibilities to find a truly solid adult life path. A mature style of constructing an identity.

morpheme: The smallest unit of meaning in a particular language—for example, *boys* contains two morphemes: *boy* and the plural suffix *s*.

multiple intelligences theory: In Howard Gardner's perspective on intelligence, the principle that there are eight separate kinds of intelligence—verbal, mathematical, interpersonal, intrapersonal, spatial, musical, kinesthetic, naturalist—plus a possible ninth form, called spiritual intelligence.

myelination: Formation of a fatty layer encasing the axons of neurons. This process, which speeds the transmission of neural impulses, continues from birth to early adulthood.

N

natural childbirth: A general term for labor and birth without medical interventions.

naturalistic observation: A measurement strategy that involves directly watching and coding behaviors.

nature: Biological or genetic causes of development.

neonatal intensive care unit (NICU): A special hospital unit that treats at-risk newborns, such as low-birth-weight and very-low-birth-weight babies.

nest-leaving: Moving out of a childhood home and living independently.

neural tube: A cylindrical structure that forms along the back of the embryo and develops into the brain and spinal cord.

neurofibrillary tangles: Long, wavy filaments that replace normal neurons and are characteristic of Alzheimer's disease.

neuron: A nerve cell.

new nurturer father: Late-twentieth-century, middle-class idea in Western countries that fathers should do hands-on nurturing and share the child care equally with wives.

non-normative transitions: Unpredictable or atypical life changes that occur during development.

nonsuicidal self-injury: Cutting, burning, or purposely injuring one's body to cope with stress.

normal aging changes: The universal, often progressive signs of physical deterioration intrinsic to the aging process.

normative transitions: Predictable life changes that occur during development.

nursing home/long-term-care facility: A residential institution that provides shelter and intensive caregiving, primarily to older people who need help with basic ADLs.

nurture: Environmental causes of development.

O

object permanence: In Piaget's framework, the understanding that objects continue to exist even when we can no longer see them, which gradually emerges during the sensorimotor stage.

occupational segregation: The separation of men and women into different kinds of jobs and career paths.

off time: Being too late or too early in a culture's timetable for achieving adult life tasks.

old-age dependency ratio: The fraction of people over age 60 to younger working-age adults (ages 15 to 59). This ratio is expected to rise dramatically as the baby boomers retire.

old-old: People age 80 and older.

on time: Being on target in a culture's timetable for achieving adult life tasks.

operant conditioning: According to the traditional behavioral perspective, the law of learning that determines any voluntary response. Specifically, we act the way we do because we are reinforced for acting in that way.

osteoporosis: An age-related chronic disease in which the bones become porous, fragile, and more likely to break. Osteoporosis is most common in thin women and so most common in females of European and Asian descent.

ovary: One of a pair of almond-shaped organs that contain a woman's ova, or eggs.

overextension: An error in early language development in which young children apply verbal labels too broadly.

overregularization: An error in early language development, in which young children apply the rules for plurals and past tenses even to exceptions, so irregular forms sound like regular forms.

ovulation: The moment during a woman's monthly cycle when an ovum is expelled from the ovary.

ovum: An egg cell containing the genetic material contributed by the mother to the baby.

P

palliative care: Any intervention designed not to cure illness but to promote dignified dying.

palliative-care service: A service or unit in a hospital that is devoted to end-of-life care.

parent care: Adult children's care for their disabled elderly parents.

parenting style: In Diana Baumrind's framework, how parents align on two dimensions of childrearing: nurturance (or child-centeredness) and discipline (or structure and rules).

passive euthanasia: Withholding potentially life-saving interventions that might keep a terminally ill or permanently comatose patient alive.

permissive parents: In the parenting-styles framework, a type of childrearing in which parents provide few rules but rank high on child-centeredness, being extremely loving but providing little discipline.

personal fable: David Elkind's term for the tendency of young teenagers to believe that their lives are special and heroic; a component of adolescent egocentrism.

person–environment fit: The extent to which the environment is tailored to our biological tendencies and talents. In developmental science, fostering this fit between our talents and the wider world is an important goal.

phoneme: The sound units that convey meaning in a given language—for example, in English, the c sound of cat and the b sound of bat.

physician-assisted suicide: A type of active euthanasia in which a physician prescribes a lethal medication to a terminally ill person who wants to die.

Piaget's cognitive developmental theory: Jean Piaget's principle that from infancy to adolescence, children progress through four qualitatively different stages of intellectual growth.

placenta: The structure projecting from the wall of the uterus during pregnancy through which the developing baby absorbs nutrients.

plastic: Malleable, or capable of being changed (used to refer to neural or cognitive development).

postconventional level of morality: In Lawrence Kohlberg's theory, the highest level of moral reasoning, in which people respond to ethical issues by applying their own moral guidelines apart from society's rules.

postformal thought: A uniquely adult form of intelligence that involves being sensitive to different perspectives, making decisions based on one's inner feelings, and being interested in exploring new questions.

power assertion: An ineffective socialization strategy that involves yelling, screaming, or hitting out in frustration at a child.

practical intelligence: In Robert Sternberg's framework on successful intelligence, the facet of intelligence involved in knowing how to act competently in real-world situations.

preattachment phase: The first phase of John Bowlby's developmental attachment sequence, during the first three months of life, when infants show no visible signs of attachment.

preconventional level of morality: In Lawrence Kohlberg's theory, the lowest level of moral reasoning, in which people approach ethical issues by considering the personal punishments or rewards of taking a particular action.

preferential-looking paradigm: A research technique to explore early infant sensory capacities and cognition, drawing on the principle that we are attracted to novelty and prefer to look at new things.

preoccupied/ambivalent insecure attachment: An excessively clingy, needy style of relating to loved ones.

preoperational thinking: In Piaget's theory, the type of cognition characteristic of children aged 2 to 7, marked by an inability to step back from one's immediate perceptions and think conceptually.

presbycusis: Age-related difficulty in hearing, particularly high-pitched tones, caused by the atrophy of the hearing receptors located in the inner ear.

presbyopia: Age-related midlife difficulty with near vision, caused by the inability of the lens to bend.

preschool: Teaching-oriented child-care setting, serving children aged 3 to 5.

primary attachment figure: The closest person in a child's or adult's life.

primary circular reactions: In Piaget's framework, the first infant habits during the sensorimotor stage, centered on the body.

primary labor market: A category of jobs offering good salaries and benefits such as health care and retirement plans.

primary sexual characteristics: Physical changes of puberty that directly involve the organs of reproduction, such as the growth of the penis and the onset of menstruation.

private pensions: The major source of nongovernmental income support for retirees, in which the individual worker and the employer put a portion of each paycheck into an account to help finance retirement.

procedural memory: In the memory-systems perspective, the most resilient (longest-lasting) type of memory; refers to material, such as well-learned physical skills, that we automatically recall without conscious awareness.

prosocial behavior: Sharing, helping, and caring actions.

proximity-seeking behavior: Acting to maintain physical contact or to be close to an attachment figure.

proximodistal sequence: The developmental principle that growth occurs from the most interior parts of the body outward.

puberty rite: A "coming of age" ritual, usually beginning at some event such as first menstruation, held in traditional cultures to celebrate children's transition to adulthood.

puberty: The hormonal and physical changes by which children become sexually mature human beings.

Q

qualitative research: Occasional developmental science data-collection strategy that involves interviewing people to obtain information that cannot be quantified on a numerical scale.

quantitative research: Standard developmental science data-collection strategy that involves testing groups of people and using numerical scales and statistics.

quickening: A pregnant woman's first feeling of the fetus moving inside her body.

R

reaction time: The speed at which a person can respond to a stimulus. A progressive increase in reaction time is universal to aging.

reactive aggression: A hostile or destructive act carried out in response to being frustrated or hurt.

recessive disorder: An illness that a child gets by inheriting two copies of the abnormal gene that causes the disorder.

redemption sequence: In Dan McAdams's research, a characteristic theme of highly generative adults' autobiographies, in which they describe tragic events that turned out for the best.

reflex: A response or action that is automatic and programmed by non-cortical brain centers.

rehearsal: A learning strategy in which people repeat information to embed it in memory.

reinforcement: Behavioral term for reward.

rejecting-neglecting parents: In the parenting-styles framework, the worst child-rearing approach, in which parents provide little discipline and little nurturing or love.

relational aggression: A hostile or destructive act designed to cause harm to a person's relationships.

reliability: In measurement terminology, a basic criterion of a test's accuracy that scores must be fairly similar when a person takes the test more than once.

REM sleep: The phase of sleep involving rapid eye movements, when the EEG looks almost like it does during waking. REM sleep decreases as infants mature.

representative sample: A group that reflects the characteristics of the overall population.

resilient children: Children who rebound from serious early life traumas to construct successful adult lives.

reversibility: In Piaget's conservation tasks, the concrete operational child's knowledge that a specific change in the way a given substance looks can be reversed.

role conflict: A situation in which a person is torn between two or more major sets of responsibilities—for instance, parent and worker—and cannot do either job adequately.

role overload: A job situation that places so many requirements or demands on workers that it becomes impossible to do a good job.

role phase: In Murstein's theory, the final mate-selection stage, in which committed partners work out their future life together.

role: The characteristic behavior that is expected of a person in a particular social position, such as student, parent, married person, worker, or retiree.

rooting reflex: Newborns' automatic response to a touch on the cheek, involving turning toward that location and beginning to suck.

rough-and-tumble play: Play that involves shoving, wrestling, and hitting, but in which no actual harm is intended; especially characteristic of boys.

S

scaffolding: The process of teaching new skills by entering a child's zone of proximal development and tailoring one's efforts to that person's competence level.

school-to-work transition: The change from the schooling phase of life to the work world.

Seattle Longitudinal Study: The definitive study of the effect of aging on intelligence, carried out by K. Warner Schaie, involving simultaneously conducting and comparing the results of cross-sectional and longitudinal studies carried out with a group of Seattle volunteers.

secondary circular reactions: In Piaget's framework, habits of the sensorimotor stage lasting from about 4 months of age to the baby's first birthday, centered on exploring the external world.

secondary labor market: A category of low-wage jobs providing few benefits and little security.

secondary sexual characteristics: Physical changes of puberty that are not directly involved in reproduction.

secular trend in puberty: A century-long decline in the average age at which children reach puberty in the developed world.

secure attachment: The genuine intimacy that is ideal in love relationships.

secure attachment: The ideal attachment response, when a 1-year-old child responds with joy at being reunited with the primary caregiver in the Strange Situation.

selective attention: A learning strategy in which people manage their awareness so as to attend only to what is relevant and to filter out unneeded information.

selective optimization with compensation: Paul Baltes's three principles for successful aging (and living): (1) selectively focusing on what is most important, (2) working harder to perform well in those top-ranking areas, and (3) relying on external aids to cope effectively.

self-awareness: The ability to observe our abilities and actions from an outside frame of reference and to reflect on our inner state.

self-conscious emotions: Feelings of pride, shame, or guilt, which first emerge around age 2 and show the capacity to reflect on the self.

self-efficacy: According to cognitive behaviorism, an internal belief in our competence that predicts whether we initiate activities or persist in the face of failures, and predicts the goals we set.

self-esteem: Evaluating oneself as either "good" or "bad" as a result of comparing the self to other people.

self-report strategy: A measurement strategy that involves having people report on their feelings and activities through questionnaires.

self-soothing: Children's ability, usually beginning at about 6 months of age, to put themselves back to sleep when they wake up during the night.

semantic memory: In the memory-systems perspective, a moderately resilient (long-lasting) type of memory; refers to our ability to recall basic facts.

semantics: The meaning system of a language—that is, what the words stand for.

senile plaques: Thick, bullet-like amyloid-laden structures that replace normal neurons and are characteristic of Alzheimer's disease.

sensitive period: The time when a body structure is most vulnerable to damage by a teratogen, typically when that organ or process is rapidly developing or coming "on line."

sensorimotor stage: Piaget's first stage of cognitive development, lasting from birth to age 2, when babies' agenda is to pin down the basics of physical reality.

separation anxiety: The main signal of clear-cut attachment at about 7 months of age, when a baby gets visibly upset by a primary caregiver's departure.

seriation: The ability to put objects in order according to some principle, such as size.

sex-linked single-gene disorder: An illness, carried on the mother's X chromosome, that typically leaves the female offspring unaffected but has a fifty-fifty chance of striking each male child.

sexual double standard: A cultural code that gives men greater sexual freedom than women. Specifically, society expects males to want to have intercourse and expects females to remain virgins until they marry and to be more interested in relationships than in having sex.

shame: A feeling of being personally humiliated.

single-gene disorder: An illness caused by a single gene.

social clock: The concept that we regulate our passage through adulthood by an inner timetable that tells us which life activities are appropriate at certain ages.

social cognition: Any skill related to understanding feelings and negotiating interpersonal interactions.

social referencing: A baby's practice of checking back and monitoring a caregiver's expressions for cues as to how to behave in potentially dangerous exploration situations; linked to the onset of crawling and clear-cut attachment.

Social Security: The U.S. government's national retirement support program.

social smile: The first real smile, occurring at about 2 months of age.

social-interactionist view: An approach to language development that emphasizes its social function, specifically that babies and adults have a mutual passion to communicate.

socialization: The process by which children are taught to obey the norms of society and to behave in socially appropriate ways.

socioeconomic status (SES): A basic marker referring to status on the educational and—especially—income rungs.

socioeconomic/health gap: The disparity, found in nations around the world, between the health of the rich and poor. At every step up on the socioeconomic ladder, people survive longer and enjoy better health.

socioemotional selectivity theory: A theory of aging (and the lifespan) put forth by Laura Carstensen, describing how the time we have left to live affects our priorities and social relationships. Specifically, Carstensen believes that as people reach later life, they focus on enhancing the quality of the present and place priority on spending time with their closest attachment figures.

specific learning disability: The label for any impairment in language or any deficit related to listening, thinking, speaking, reading, writing, spelling, or understanding mathematics; diagnosed when a score on an intelligence test is much higher than a child's performance on achievement tests.

spermarche: A boy's first ejaculation of live sperm.

stimulus phase: In Murstein's theory, the initial mate-selection stage, in which we make judgments about a potential partner based on external characteristics such as appearance.

stimulus-value-role theory: Murstein's mate-selection theory that suggests similar people pair up and that our path to commitment progresses through three phases (called the stimulus, value-comparison, and role phases).

"storm and stress": G. Stanley Hall's phrase for the intense moodiness, emotional sensitivity, and risk-taking tendencies that characterize the life stage he labeled *adolescence*.

Strange Situation: A procedure developed by Mary Ainsworth to measure variations in attachment security at age 1, involving a series of planned separations and reunions with a primary caregiver.

stranger anxiety: A signal of the onset of clear-cut attachment at about 7 months of age, when a baby becomes wary of unfamiliar people and refuses to be held by anyone other than a primary caregiver.

stunting: Excessively short stature in a child, caused by chronic lack of adequate nutrition.

successful intelligence: In Robert Sternberg's framework, the optimal form of cognition, involving having a good balance of analytic, creative, and practical intelligence.

sucking reflex: The automatic, spontaneous sucking movements newborns produce, especially when anything touches their lips.

sudden infant death syndrome (SIDS): The unexplained death of an apparently healthy infant, often while sleeping, during the first year of life.

swaddling: Wrapping a baby tightly in a blanket or garment. This technique is calming during early infancy.

sympathy: A state necessary for acting prosocially, involving feeling upset *for* a person who needs help.

synapse: The gap between the dendrites of one neuron and the axon of another, over which impulses flow.

synaptogenesis: Forming of connections between neurons at the synapses. This process, responsible for all perceptions, actions, and thoughts, is most intense during infancy and childhood but continues throughout life.

synchrony: The reciprocal aspect of the attachment relationship, with a caregiver and infant responding emotionally to each other in a sensitive, exquisitely attuned way.

syntax: The system of grammatical rules in a particular language.

T

telegraphic speech: First stage of combining words in infancy, in which a baby pares down a sentence to its essential words.

temperament: A person's characteristic, inborn style of dealing with the world.

teratogen: A substance that crosses the placenta and harms the fetus.

terminal drop: A research phenomenon in which a dramatic decline in an older person's scores on vocabulary tests and other measures of crystallized intelligence predicts having a terminal disease.

tertiary circular reactions: In Piaget's framework, "little-scientist" activities of the sensorimotor stage, beginning around age 1, involving flexibly exploring the properties of objects.

testes: Male organs that manufacture sperm.

testosterone: The hormone responsible for the maturation of the organs of reproduction and other signs of puberty in men, and for hair and skin changes during puberty and for sexual desire in both sexes.

thanatology: The study of death and dying.

theory of mind: Children's first cognitive understanding, which appears at about age 4, that other people have different beliefs and perspectives from their own.

theory: Any perspective explaining why people act the way they do. Theories allow us to predict behavior and also suggest how to intervene to improve behavior.

toddlerhood: The important transitional stage after babyhood, from roughly 1 year to 2 1/2 years of age; defined by an intense attachment to caregivers and by an urgent need to become independent.

traditional behaviorism: The original behavioral worldview that focused on charting and modifying only "objective," visible behaviors.

traditional stable career: A career path in which people settle into their permanent life's work in their twenties and often stay with the same organization until they retire.

triangular theory of love: Robert Sternberg's categorization of love relationships into three facets: passion, intimacy, and commitment. When arranged at the points of a triangle, their combinations describe all the different kinds of adult love relationships.

trimester: One of the 3-month-long segments into which pregnancy is divided.

true experiments: The only research strategy that can determine that something causes something else; involves randomly assigning people to different treatments and then looking at the outcome.

twentieth-century life expectancy revolution: The dramatic increase in average life expectancy that occurred during the first half of the twentieth century in the developed world.

twin study: Behavioral genetic research strategy, designed to determine the genetic contribution of a given trait, that involves comparing identical twins with fraternal twins (or with other people).

twin/adoption studies: Behavioral genetic research strategy that involves comparing the similarities of identical twin pairs adopted into different families, to determine the genetic contribution to a given trait.

U

ultrasound: In pregnancy, an image of the fetus in the womb that helps to date the pregnancy, assess the fetus's growth, and identify abnormalities.

umbilical cord: The structure that attaches the placenta to the fetus, through which nutrients are passed and fetal wastes are removed.

underextension: An error in early language development in which young children apply verbal labels too narrowly.

undernutrition: A chronic lack of adequate food.

U-shaped curve of marital satisfaction: The most common pathway of marital happiness in the West, in which satisfaction is highest at the honeymoon, declines during the child-rearing years, then rises after the children grow up.

uterus: The pear-shaped muscular organ in a woman's abdomen that houses the developing baby.

V

validity: In measurement terminology, a basic criterion for a test's accuracy involving whether that measure reflects the real-world quality it is supposed to measure.

value-comparison phase: In Murstein's theory, the second mate-selection stage, in which we make judgments about a partner on the basis of similar values and interests.

vascular dementia: A type of age-related dementia caused by multiple small strokes.

very low birth weight (VLBW): A body weight at birth of less than 3 1/4 pounds.

visual cliff: A table that appears to "end" in a drop-off at its midpoint; used to test for infant depth perception.

W

Wechsler Adult Intelligence Scale (WAIS): The standard test to measure adult IQ, involving verbal and performance scales, each of which is made up of various subtests.

widowhood mortality effect: The slightly elevated risk of death that occurs among surviving spouses—particularly men—in the first months after being widowed.

WISC (Wechsler Intelligence Scale for Children): The standard intelligence test used in childhood, consisting of a Verbal Scale (questions for the child to answer), a Performance Scale (materials for the child to manipulate), and a variety of subtests.

working memory: In information-processing theory, the limited-capacity gateway system, containing all the material that we can keep in awareness at a single time. The material in this system is either processed for more permanent storage or lost.

working model: According to Bowlby's theory, the mental representation of a caregiver that allows children beyond age 3 to be physically apart from a primary caregiver and predicts their behavior in relationships.

Y

young-old: People in their sixties and seventies.

youth development program: Any after-school program, or structured activity outside of the school day, that is devoted to promoting flourishing in teenagers.

Z

zone of proximal development: In Vygotsky's theory, the gap between a child's ability to solve a problem totally on his own and his potential knowledge if taught by a more accomplished person.

zygote: A fertilized ovum.

References

Abbassi, V. (1998). Growth and normal puberty. *Pediatrics, 102,* 507–511.

Abbasi-Shavazi, J., Mohammad J., & McDonald, P. (2008). Family change in Iran: Religion, revolution, and the state. In R. Jayakody, A. Thornton, & W. Axinn (Eds.), *International family change: Ideational perspectives* (pp. 177–198). New York, NY: Taylor & Francis Group/Lawrence Erlbaum Associates.

Abbott, R. D., White, L. R., Ross, G. W., Masaki, K. H., Curb, J. D., & Petrovitch, H. (2004). Walking and dementia in physically capable elderly men. *Journal of the American Medical Association, 292,* 1447–1453.

Abelev, M. S. (2009). Advancing out of poverty: Social class worldview and its relation to resilience. *Journal of Adolescent Research, 24,* 114–141.

Abramson, L. Y., Seligman, M. E., & Teasdale, J. D. (1978). Learned helplessness in humans: Critique and reformulation. *Journal of Abnormal Psychology, 87,* 49–74.

Acevedo, B. P., & Aron, A. (2009). Does a long-term relationship kill romantic love? *Review of General Psychology, 13,* 59–65.

Adair, L. S. (2008). Child and adolescent obesity: Epidemiology and developmental perspectives. *Physiology & Behavior, 94,* 8–16.

Addington-Hall, J. M., & O'Callaghan, A. C. (2009). A comparison of the quality of care provided to cancer patients in the UK in the last three months of life in inpatient hospices compared with hospitals, from the perspective of bereaved relatives: Results from a survey sing the VOICES questionnaire. *Palliative Medicine, 23,* 190–197.

Adolph, K. E. (2008). Learning to move. *Current Directions in Psychological Science 17*(3), 213–218.

Adolph, K., & Berger, S. E. (2006). Motor development. In D. Kuhn, R. S. Siegler, W. Damon, & R. M. Lerner (Eds.), *Handbook of child psychology: Vol. 2, cognition, perception, and language* (6th ed.), pp. 161–213. Hoboken, NJ: John Wiley & Sons Inc.

Agrawal, A., & Lynskey, M. T. (2008). Are there genetic influences on addiction: Evidence from family, adoption, and twin studies. *Addiction, 103,* 1069–1081.

Ahnert, L., Pinquart, M., & Lamb, M. (2006). Security of children's relationships with nonparental care providers: A meta-analysis. *Child Development, 74*(3), 664–679.

Ainsworth, M. D. S. (1967). *Infancy in Uganda: Infant care and the growth of love.* Baltimore: Johns Hopkins Press.

Ainsworth, M. D. S. (1973). The development of infant-mother attachment. In B. M. Caldwell & H. N. Ricciuti (Eds.), *Review of child development research* (Vol. 3, pp. 1–94). Chicago: University of Chicago Press.

Ainsworth, M. D. S., Blehar, M. C., Waters, E., & Wall, S. (1978). *Patterns of attachment: A psychological study of the strange situation.* Hillsdale, NJ: Erlbaum.

Akerman, A., Williams, M. E., & Meuniser, J. (2007). Perception versus reality: An exploration of children's measured body mass in relation to caregivers' estimates. *Journal of Health Psychology, 12*(6), 871–882.

Aksan, N., & Kochanska, G. (2004). Links between systems of inhibition from infancy to preschool years. *Child Development, 75,* 1477–1490.

Aldred, H. E. (1997). *Pregnancy and birth sourcebook: Basic information about planning for pregnancy, maternal health, fetal growth and development.* Detroit, MI: Omnigraphics.

Aliyu, M. H., Wilson, R. E., Zoorob, R., Chakrabarty, S., Alio, A. P., Kirby, R. S., & Salihu, H. M. (2008). Alcohol consumption during pregnancy and the risk of early stillbirth among singletons. *Alcohol, 42,* 369–374.

Allemand, M., Zimprich, D., & Hendricks, A. A. J. (2008). Age differences in five personality domains across the life span. *Developmental Psychology, 44*(3), 758–770.

Allen, J. P., McElhaney, K. B., Land, D. J., Kuperminc, G. P., Moore, C. W., O'Beirne-Kelly, H., & Kilmer, S. L. (2003). A secure base in adolescence: Markers of attachment security in the mother-adolescent relationship. *Child Development, 74,* 292–307.

Allen, J. P., Porter, M., McFarland, C., McElhaney, K. B., & Marsh, P. (2007). The relation of attachment security to adolescents' paternal and peer relationships, depression, and externalizing behavior. *Child Development, 78*(4), 1222–1239.

Alzheimer's Association. (2009). *2009 Alzheimer's Disease, Facts and Figures,* p. 14.

Alzheimer's Disease Education & Referral Center [ADEAR]. (2004). Estrogen-alone hormone therapy could increase risk of dementia in older women. Retrieved January 13, 2006, from http://www.alzheimers.org/nianews/nianews66.html

Amato, P. R. (2000). The consequences of divorce for adults and children. *Journal of Marriage & the Family, 62,* 1269–1287.

Amato, P. R. (2001). Children of divorce in the 1990s: An update of the Amato and Keith (1991) meta-analysis. *Journal of Family Psychology, 15,* 355–370.

Amato, P. R. (2007). Transformative processes in marriage: Some thoughts from a sociologist. *Journal of Marriage and Family, 69*(2), 305–309.

Amato, P. R., & Hohmann-Marriott, B. (2007). A comparison of high- and low-distress marriages that end in divorce. *Journal of Marriage and Family, 69*(3), 621–638.

Amedi, A., Raz, N., Pianka, P., Malach, R., & Zohary, E. (2003). Early 'visual' cortex activation correlates with superior verbal memory performance in the blind. *Nature Neuroscience, 6,* 758–766.

American Academy of Pediatrics [AAP], Committee on Adolescence. (2003). Identifying and treating eating disorders. *Pediatrics, 111,* 204–211.

American Academy of Pediatrics [AAP], Committee on Drugs. (2000). Use of psychoactive medication during pregnancy and possible effects on the fetus and newborn. *Pediatrics, 105,* 880–887.

American Academy of Pediatrics [AAP], Section on Breastfeeding. (2005). Breastfeeding and the use of human milk. *Pediatrics, 115,* 496–506.

American Heart Association. (2001). *2002 heart and stroke statistical update.* Dallas, TX: American Heart Association.

Amin, S., & Al-Bassusi, N. H. (2004). Education, wage work, and marriage: Perspectives of Egyptian working women. *Journal of Marriage and Family, 66,* 1287–1299.

Andero, A. A., & Stewart, A. (2002). Issue of corporal punishment: Re-examined. *Journal of Instructional Psychology, 29,* 90–96.

Anders, T., Goodlin-Jones, B., & Zelenko, M. (1998). Infant regulation and sleep-wake state development. *Zero to Three, 19*(2), 9–14.

Andersen-Ranberg, K., Vasegaard, L., & Jeune, B. (2001). Dementia is not inevitable: A population-based study of Danish centenarians. *Journals of Gerontology: Series B: Psychological Sciences and Social Sciences, 56B*, P152–P159.

Anderson, D. I., Campos, J. J., & Barbu-Roth, M. A. (2004). A developmental perspective on visual proprioception. In G. Bremner & A. Slater (Eds.), *Theories of infant development* (pp. 30–69). Malden, MA: Blackwell.

Anderson, J. W. (1972). Attachment behaviour out of doors. In N. Blurton Jones (Ed.), *Ethological studies of child behaviour* (pp. 199–215). Oxford, England: Cambridge University Press.

Anderson, R., & Mitchell, E. M. (1984). Children's health and play in rural Nepal. *Social Science & Medicine, 19*, 735–740.

Andrade, B. F., Brodeur, D. A., Waschbusch, D. A., Stewart, S. H., & Mcgee, R. (2009). Selective and sustained attention as predictors of social problems in chiildren with typical and disordered attention abilities. *Journal of Attention Disorders, 12*(4), 341–352.

Aneshensel, C. S., Pearlin, L. I., Mullan, J. T., Zarit, S. H., & Whitlatch, C. J. (1995). *Profiles in caregiving: The unexpected career.* San Diego, CA: Academic Press.

Angel, J. L., Jimenez, M. A., & Angel, R. J. (2007). The economic consequences of widowhood for older minority women. *The Gerontologist, 47*(2), 224–234.

Anglin, D. M., & Wade, J. C. (2007). Racial socialization, racial identity, and black student's adjustment to college. *Cultural Diversity and Ethnic Minority Psychology, 13*(3), 207–215.

Anker, R., Malkas, H., & Korten, A. (2003). *Gender-based occupational segregation in the 1990's* (Declaration/WP/16/2003). Geneva, Switzerland: International Labour Office.

Apfelbacher, C. J., Cairns, J., Bruckner, T., Mohrenschlager, M., Behrendt, H., Ring, J., & Kramer, U. (2008). Prevalence of overweight and obesity in East and West German children in the decade after reunification: Population-based series of cross-sectional studies. *Journal of Epidemiology and Community Health, 62*(2), 125–130.

Aquilino, W. S. (2006). Family relationships and support systems in emerging adulthood. In J. J. Arnett, & J. L. Tanner (Eds.), *Emerging adults in America: Coming of age in the 21st century* (pp. 193–217). Washington, DC, US: American Psychological Association.

Archibald, A. B., Graber, J. A., & Brooks-Gunn, J. (2003). Pubertal processes and physiological growth in adolescence. In G. R. Adams & M. D. Berzonsky (Eds.), *Blackwell handbook of adolescence* (pp. 24–47). Malden, MA: Blackwell.

Arcus, D. (2001). Inhibited and uninhibited children: Biology in the social context. In T. D. Wachs & G. A. Kohnstamm (Eds.), *Temperament in context* (pp. 43–60). Mahwah, NJ: Erlbaum.

Ardelt, M. (2003). Physician-assisted death. In C. D. Bryant (Ed.), *Handbook of death & dying* (pp. 424–434). Thousand Oaks, CA: Sage.

Ardelt, M., & Koenig, C. S. (2006). The role of religion for hospice patients and relatively healthy older adults. *Research on Aging, 28*, 184–215.

Ardila, A. (2007). Normal aging increases cognitive heterogeneity: Analysis of dispersion in WAIS-III scores across age. *Archives of Clinical Neuropsychology, 22*, 1003–1011.

Ardley, J., & Ericson, L. (2002). "We don't play like that here!": Understanding aggressive expressions of play. In C. R. Brown & K. C. Marchant (Eds.), *Play in practice: Case studies in young children's play* (pp. 35–48). St. Paul, MN: Redleaf.

Arias, D. F., & Hernandez, A. M. (2007). Emerging adulthood in Mexican and Spanish youth. *Journal of Adolescent Research, 22*(5).

Ariès, P. (1962). *Centuries of childhood: A social history of family life.* New York: Knopf.

Ariès, P. (1974). *Western attitudes toward death: From the Middle Ages to the present* (P. M. Ranum, Trans.). Baltimore: Johns Hopkins University Press.

Ariès, P. (1981). *The hour of our death* (H. Weaver, Trans.). New York: Knopf.

Arnett, J. J. (1999). Adolescent storm and stress, reconsidered. *American Psychologist, 54*, 317–326.

Arnett, J. J. (2000). Emerging adulthood: A theory of development from the late teens through the twenties. *American Psychologist, 55*, 469–480.

Arnett, J. J. (2004). *Emerging adulthood: The winding road from the late teens through the twenties.* New York: Oxford University Press.

Arnett, J. J. (2007a). The long and leisurely route: Coming of age in Europe today. *Current History: A Journal of Contemporary Affairs, 106*, 130–136.

Arnett, J. J. (2007b). Socialization in emerging adulthood: From the family to the wider world, from socialization to self-socialization. In J. E. Grusec & P. D. Hastings (Eds.), *Handbook of socialization: Theory and research* (208–230). New York, NY: Guilford Press.

Arnett, J. J. (2007c). Suffering, selfish, slackers? Myths and reality about emerging adults. *Journal of Youth Adolescence, 36*, 23–29.

Aron, A., Norman, C. C., Aron, E. N., & Lewandowski, G. (2002). Shared participation in self-expanding activities: Positive effects on experienced marital quality. In P. Noller & J. A. Feeney (Eds.), *Understanding marriage: Developments in the study of couple interaction* (pp. 177–194). New York: Cambridge University Press.

Arriaga, X. B. (2001). The ups and downs of dating: Fluctuations in satisfaction in newly formed romantic relationships. *Journal of Personality and Social Psychology, 80*, 754–765.

Ashford, J., Smit, F., van Lier, P. A. C., Cuijpers, P., & Koot, H. M. (2008). Early risk indicators of internalizing problems in late childhood: A 9-year longitudinal study. *Journal of Child Psychology and Psychiatry, 49*, 774–780.

Associated Press. (2006). Euthanasia on the rise in Netherlands. Retrieved October 18, 2006, from The Christian Post Web site: http://world.christianpost.com/-article.htm?aid=8565&dat=20060502

Astin, A. W. (1993). *What matters in college? Four critical years revisited.* San Francisco: Jossey-Bass.

Astin, A. W. (1999). How the liberal arts college affects students. *Daedalus, 128*(1), 77–100.

Attar-Schwartz, S., Buchnan, A., Tan, J., Flouri, E., & Griggs, J. (2009). Grandparenting and adolescent adjustment in two-parent biological, lone parent, and step-families. *Journal of Family Psychology, 23*, 67–75.

Austin, W. G. (2008). Relocation, research, and forensic evaluation, part I: Effects of residential mobility on children on divorce. *Family Court Review, 46*(1), 137–150.

AVERT. (2005, November 22, 2005). AIDS and HIV statistics for Sub-Saharan Africa. Retrieved January 24, 2006, from http://www.avert.org/subaadults.htm

Avis, N. E., Assmann, S. F., Kravitz, H. M., Ganz, P. A., & Ory, M. (2004). Quality of life in diverse groups of midlife women: Assessing the influence of menopause, health status and psychosocial and demographic factors. *Quality of Life Research, 13*, 933–946.

Avis, N. E., Ory, M., Matthews, K. A., Schocken, M., Bromberger, J., & Colvin, A. (2003). Health-related quality of life in a multiethnic sample of middle-aged women: Study of Women's Health Across the Nation (SWAN). *Medical Care, 41*, 1262–1276.

Baddeley, A. D. (1992). Working memory: The interface between memory and cognition. *Journal of Cognitive Neuroscience, 4*, 281–288.

Baile, W. F., Aaron, J., & Parker, P. A. (2009). Practitioner-patient communication in cancer diagnosis and treatment. In S. M. Miller, D. J. Bowen, R. T. Croyle, & J. H. Rowland (Eds.), *Handbook of cancer control and behavioral science: A resource for researchers, practitioners, and policymakers* (pp. 327–346). Washington, DC, US: American Psychological Association.

Baillargeon, R. (1987). Young infants' reasoning about the physical and spatial properties of a hidden object. *Cognitive Development, 2*, 179–200.

Baillargeon, R. (1993). The object concept revisited: New direction in the investigation of infants' physical knowledge. In C. Granrud (Ed.), *Visual perception and cognition in infancy* (pp. 265–315). Hillsdale, NJ: Erlbaum.

Baillargeon, R., & DeVos, J. (1991). Object permanence in young infants: Further evidence. *Child Development, 62*, 1227–1246.

Baillargeon, R., & Graber, M. (1987). Where's the rabbit? 5.5-month-old infants' representation of the height of a hidden object. *Cognitive Development, 2*, 375–392.

Bain, L. J., Barker, W., Loewenstein, D. A., & Duara, R. (2008). Towards an earlier diagnosis of Alzheimer's disease. *Alzheimer's Disease and Associated Disorders, 22*(2), 99–110.

Baird, A. H. (2003). Through my eyes: Service needs of grandparents who raise their grandchildren, from the perspective of a custodial grandmother. In B. Hayslip, Jr. & J. H. Patrick (Eds.), *Working with custodial grandparents* (pp. 59–65). New York: Springer.

Baird, A. L., & Grieve, F. G. (2006). Exposure to male models in advertisements leads to a decrease in men's body satisfaction. *North American Journal of Psychology, 8*, 115–121.

Baker, A. J. L. (2005). The long-term effects of parental alienation on adult children: A qualitative research study. *American Journal of Family Therapy, 33*, 289–302.

Bakermans-Kranenburg, M. J., van IJzendoorn, M. H., Pijlman, F. T. A., Mesman, J., & Juffer, F. (2008). Experimental evidence for differential susceptibility: Dopamine D4 Receptor Polymorphism (DRD4) moderates intervention effects on toddlers' externalizing behavior in a randomized controlled trial. *Developmental Psychology, 44*(1), 293–300.

Balk, D. E. (2008a). A modest proposal about bereavement and recovery. *Death Studies, 32*, 84–93.

Balk, D. E. (2008b). Special issue on bereavement, outcomes, and recovery: Guest editor's opening remarks. *Death Studies, 32*, 1–5.

Ball, H. (2007). Bed-sharing practices of initially breastfed infants in the first 6 months of life. *Infant and Child Development, 16*, 387–401.

Ball, K., & Rebok, G. W. (1994). Evaluating the driving ability of older adults. *Journal of Applied Gerontology, 13*, 20–38.

Ball, M. M., Perkins, M. M., Hollingsworth, C., Whittington, F. J., & King, S. V. (2009). Pathways to assisted living: The influence of race and class. *Journal of Applied Gerontology, 28*, 81–108.

Baltes, M. M., & Carstensen, L. L. (2003). The process of successful aging: Selection, optimization and compensation. In U. M. Staudinger & U. Lindenberger (Eds.), *Understanding human development: Dialogues with lifespan psychology* (pp. 81–104). Dordrecht, Netherlands: Kluwer Academic.

Baltes, P. B. (2003). On the incomplete architecture of human ontogeny: Selection, optimization, and compensation as foundation of developmental theory. In U. M. Staudinger & U. Lindenberger (Eds.), *Understanding human development: Dialogues with lifespan psychology* (pp. 17–43). Boston: Kluwer Academic Publishers.

Baltes, P. B., & Smith, J. (1997). A systemic-wholistic view of psychological functioning in very old age: Introduction to a collection of articles from the Berlin Aging Study. *Psychology and Aging, 12*, 395–409.

Bandura, A. (1977). *Social learning theory.* Englewood Cliffs, NJ: Prentice Hall.

Bandura, A. (1986). *Social foundations of thought and action: A social cognitive theory.* Englewood Cliffs, NJ: Prentice-Hall.

Bandura, A. (1989). Human agency in social cognitive theory. *American Psychologist, 44*, 1175–1184.

Bandura, A. (1992). Exercise of personal agency through the self-efficacy mechanism. In R. Schwarzer (Ed.), *Self-efficacy: Thought control of action* (pp. 3–38). Washington, DC: Hemisphere.

Bandura, A. (1997). *Self-efficacy: The exercise of control.* New York: Freeman.

Bandy, T., & Moore. K. A. (2008). *The parent-child relationship: A family strength.* (Child Trends publication #2008-27). Washington DC: Child Trends.

Barboza, G. E., Schiamberg, L. B., Oehmke, J., Korzeniewski, S. J., Post, L. A., & Heraux, C. G. (2009). Individual characteristics and the multiple contexts of adolescent bullying: An ecological perspective. *Journal of Youth and Adolescence, 38*, 101–121.

Barkin, S., Scheindlin, B., Ip, E. H., Richardson, I., & Finch, S. (2007). Determinants of parental discipline practices: A national sample from primary care practices. *Clinical Pediatrics, 46*(1), 64–69.

Barkley, R. A. (1998). *Attention-deficit hyperactivity disorder: A handbook for diagnosis and treatment* (2nd ed.). New York: Guilford Press.

Barkley, R. A. (2003). Attention-deficit/hyperactivity disorder. In E. J. Mash & R. A. Barkley (Eds.), *Child psycho-pathology* (2nd ed., pp. 75–143). New York: Guilford Press.

Barkley, R. A., & Murphy, K. R. (2006). *Attention-deficit hyperactivity disorder: A clinical workbook* (3rd ed.). New York: Guilford Press.

Barlow, J. H., Turner, A. P., Hammond, C. L., & Gailey, L. (2007). Living with late deafness: Insight from between worlds. *International Journal of Audiology, 46*, 442–448.

Barnes, G. M., Hoffman, J. H., Welte, J. W., Farrell, M. P., & Dintcheff, B. A. (2007). Adolescents' time use: Effects on substance use, delinquency and sexual activity. *Journal of Youth and Adolescence, 36*, 697–710.

Barnet, H. S. (1990). Divorce stress and adjustment model: Locus of control and demographic predictors. *Journal of Divorce, 13*, 93–109.

Barnett, S. M., Ceci, S. J., & Williams, W. M. (2006). Is the ability to make a bacon sandwich a mark of intelligence?, and other issues: Some reflections on Gardner's theory of multiple intelligences. In J. A. Schaler (Ed.) *Howard Gardner under fire: The rebel psychologist faces his critics* (pp. 95–114). Chicago, IL: Open Court Publishing Co.

Baron-Cohen, S. (1999). The evolution of a theory of mind. In M. C. Corballis & S. E. G. Lea (Eds.), *The descent of mind: Psychological perspectives on hominid evolution* (pp. 261–277). New York: Oxford University Press.

Barr, R. G. (2000). Excessive crying. In A. J. Sameroff, M. Lewis, & S. M. Miller (Eds.), *Handbook of developmental psychopathology* (2nd ed., pp. 327–350). Dordrecht, Netherlands: Kluwer.

Barrett, A.E., & Robbins, C. (2008). The multiple sources of women's aging anxiety and their relationship with psychological distress. *Journal of Aging and Health, 20*(1), 32–65.

Barry, R. A., Kochanska, G., & Philibert, R. A. (2008). G × E interaction in the organization of attachment: Mother's responsiveness as a moderator of children's genotypes. *Journal of Child Psychology and Psychiatry, 49*, 1313–1320.

Bartolini, V., & Lunn, K. (2002). "Teacher, they won't let me play!": Strategies for improving inappropriate play behavior. In C. R. Brown & K. C. Marchant (Eds.), *Play in practice: Case studies in young children's play* (pp. 13–20). St. Paul, MN: Redleaf.

Batty, G. D., Shipley, M. J., Marmot, M. G., & Smith, G. D. (2003). Leisure time physical activity and disease-specific mortality among men with chronic bronchitis: Evidence from the Whitehall Study. *American Journal of Public Health, 93*, 817–821.

Bauermeister, J. J., Shrout, P. E., Chavez, L., Rubio-Stipec, M., Ramirez, R., Padilla, L., Anderson, A., Garcia, P., & Canino, G. (2007). ADHD and gender: Are risks and sequel of ADHD the same for boys and girls? *Journal of Child Psychology and Psychiatry, 48*(8), 831–839.

Baumrind, D. (1971). Current patterns of parental authority. *Developmental Psychology, 4*(1, Pt. 2), 1–103.

Baumrind, D., Larzelere, R. E., & Cowan, P. A. (2002). Ordinary physical punishment: Is it harmful? Comment on Gershoff (2002). *Psychological Bulletin, 128*, 580–589.

Bayless, S., & Stevenson, J. (2007). Executive functions in school-age children born very prematurely. *Early Human Development, 83*(4), 247–254.

Bayless, S., Cate, I. M. P., & Stevenson, J. (2008). Behaviour difficulties and cognitive function in children born very prematurely. *International Journal of Behavioral Development, 32*(3), 199–206.

Beard, J. R., Blaney, S., Cerda, M., Frye, V., Lovasi, G. S., Ompad, D., Rundle, A., Vlahov, D. (2009). Neighborhood characteristics and disability in older adults. *Journal of Gerontology: Social Sciences, 64B*, 252–257.

Beason-Held, L. L., Kraut, M. A., & Resnick, S. M. (2008). Temporal patterns of longitudinal change in aging brain function. *Neurobiology of Aging, 29*(4), 497–513.

Beaver, K. M., Wright, J. P., & Delisi, M. (2007). Self-control as an executive function: Reformulating Gottfreson and Hirschi's parental socialization thesis. *Criminal Justice and Behavior, 34*(10), 1345–1361.

Beckmann, C. R. B., Ling, F. W., Laube, D. W., Smith, R. P., Barzansky, B. M., & Herbert, W. N. P. (2002). *Obstetrics and gynecology* (4th ed.). Baltimore: Lippincott Williams & Wilkins.

Beebe, B., Badalamenti, A., Jaffe, J., Feldstein, S., Marquette, L., Helbraun, E., Demetri-Friedman, D., Flaster, C., Goodman, P., Kaminer, T., Kaufman-Balamuth, L., Putterman, J., Stepakoff, S., & Ellman, L. (2008). Distressed mothers and their infants use a less efficient timing mechanism in creating expectancies of each other's looking patterns. *Journal of Psycholinguistic Research, 37*(5), 293–307.

Beernick, A. C. E., Swinkels, S. H. N., & Buitelaar, J. K. (2007). Problem behavior in a community sample of 14- and 19-month-old children. *European Child Adolescent Psychiatry, 16*, 271–280.

Begley, A. M. (2008). Guilty but good: Defending voluntary active euthanasia from a virtue perspective. *Nursing Ethics, 15* (4), 434–445.

Bell, J. H., & Bromnick, R. D. (2003). The social reality of the imaginary audience: A ground theory approach. *Adolescence, 38*, 205–219.

Bell, R., Buchner, A., & Mund, I. (2008). Age-related differences in irrelevant-speech effects. *Psychology and Aging, 23*(2), 377–391.

Bellenir, K. (ed.). (2004). *Genetic disorders sourcebook* (3rd ed.). Detroit, MI: Omnigraphics.

Bellinger, D., Leviton, A., Waternaux, C., Needleman, H., & Rabinowitz, M. (1987). Longitudinal analyses of prenatal and postnatal lead exposure and early cognitive development. *New England Journal of Medicine, 316*, 1037–1043.

Belsky, J. K. (1999). *The psychology of aging: Theory, research, and interventions* (3rd ed.). Pacific Grove, CA: Brooks/Cole.

Belsky, J. K. (2001). Aging. In J. Worell (ed.), *Encyclopedia of women and gender: Sex similarities and differences and the impact of society on gender* (Vol. 1, pp. 95–108). San Diego, CA: Academic Press.

Belsky, J., & Rovine, M. (1990). Patterns of marital change across the transition to parenthood: Pregnancy to three years postpartum. *Journal of Marriage & the Family, 52*, 5–19.

Belsky, J., & Volling, B. L. (1987). Mothering, fathering, and marital interaction in the family triad during infancy: Exploring family system's processes. In P. W. Berman & F. A. Pedersen (Eds.), *Men's transitions to parenthood: Longitudinal studies of early family experience* (pp. 37–63). Hillsdale, NJ: Erlbaum.

Belsky, J., Lang, M. E., & Rovine, M. (1985). Stability and change in marriage across the transition to parenthood: A second study. *Journal of Marriage and the Family, 47*, 855–865.

Belsky, J., Steinberg, L., & Draper, P. (1991). Childhood experience, interpersonal development, and reproductive strategy: An evolutionary theory of socialization. *Child Development, 62*, 647–670.

Belsky, J., Steinberg, L. D., Houts, R. M., Friedman, S. L., DeHart, G., Cauffman, E., Roisman, G. I., Halpern-Felsher, B. L., & Susman, E. (2007). Family rearing antecedents of pubertal timing. *Child Development, 78*(4), 1302–1321.

Belsky, J., Vandell, D. L., Burchinal, M., Clarke-Stewart, K. A., McCartney, K., Owen, M. T., & The NICHD Early Child Care Research Network. (2007). Are there long-term effects of early child care? *Child Development, 78*(2), 681–701.

Bem, S. L. (1981). Gender schema theory: A cognitive account of sex typing. *Psychological Review, 88*, 354–364.

Ben-Ari, A., & Lavee, Y. (2007). Dyadic closeness in marriage: From the inside story to a conceptual model. *Journal of Social and Personal Relationships, 24*(5), 627–644.

Bengtson, V. L. (1989). The problem of generations: Age group contrasts, continuities and social change. In V. L. Bengtson & K. W. Schaie (Eds.), *The course of later life: Research and reflections* (pp. 25–54). New York: Springer.

Benjet, C., & Kazdin, A. E. (2003). Spanking children: The controversies, findings and new directions. *Clinical Psychology Review, 23,* 197–224.

Benson, L., Baer, H. J., & Kaelber, D. C. (2009). Trends in the diagnosis of overweight and obesity in children and adolescents: 1999–2007. *Pediatrics, 123,* 153–158.

Beran, T. N., & Lupart, J. (2009). The relationship between school achievement and peer harassment in canadian adolescents: The importance of mediating factors. *School Psychology International, 30,* 75–91.

Berg, E. Z. (2004). Gender and its effects on psychopathology. *American Journal of Psychiatry, 161,* 179.

Berger, S. E., Theuring, C., & Adolph, K. E. (2007). How and when infants learn to climb stairs. *Infant Behavior & Development 30*(1), 36–49.

Berk, L. E., & Winsler, A. (1999). *NAEYC research into practice series: Vol. 7. Scaffolding children's learning: Vygotsky and early childhood education.* Washington, DC: National Association for the Education of Young Children.

Berko, J. (1958). The child's learning of English morphology. *Word, 14,* 150–177.

Berkowitz, R. I., & Stunkard, A. J. (2002). Development of childhood obesity. In T. A. Wadden & A. J. Stunkard (Eds.), *Handbook of obesity treatment* (pp. 515–531). New York: Guilford Press.

Bernal, J. G., & Anuncibay, R. D. (2008). Intergenerational grandparent/grandchild relations: The socioeducational role of grandparents. *Educational Gerontology, 34,* 67–88.

Bersamin, M., Bourdeau, B., Fisher, D. A., Hill, D. L., Walker, S., Grube, J. W., & Grube, E. L. (2008). *Casual partnerships: Media exposure and relationship status at last oral sex and vaginal intercourse.* Paper presented at the Biennial Meeting, Society for Research in Adolescence, Chicago, 2008.

Bertenthal, B. I., Campos, J. J., & Kermoian, R. (1994). An epigenetic perspective on the development of self-produced locomotion and its consequences. *Current Directions in Psychological Science, 3,* 140–145.

Berthelsen, D., & Brownlee, J. (2007). Working with toddlers in child care: Practitioners' beliefs about their role. *Early Childhood Research Quarterly, 22,* 347–362.

Bhandari, N., Bahl, R., Mazumdar, S., Martines, J., Black, R. E., & Bhan, M. K. (2003). Effect of community-based promotion of exclusive breastfeeding on diarrhoeal illness and growth: A cluster randomised controlled trial. *Lancet, 361,* 1418–1423.

Bianchi, S., Robinson, J. R., & Milkie, M. A. (2006). *Changing rhythms of American family life.* New York: Russell Sage Foundation.

Bieliauskas, L. A. (2005). Neuropsychological assessment of geriatric driving competence. *Brain Injury, 19,* 221–226.

Billy, J. O., & Udry, J. R. (1985). The influence of male and female best friends on adolescent sexual behavior. *Adolescence, 20,* 21–32.

Bilsen, J. J. R., Vander Stichele, R. H., Mortier, F., & Deliens, L. (2004). Involvement of nurses in physician-assisted dying. *Journal of Advanced Nursing, 47,* 583–591.

Birnbaum, G. E., Cohen, O., & Wertheimer, V. (2007). Is it all about intimacy? Age, menopausal status, and women's sexuality. *Personal Relationships, 14,* 167–185.

Birren, J. E., & Birren, B. A. (1990). The concepts, models, and history of the psychology of aging. In J. E. Birren & K. W. Schaie (Eds.), *Handbook of the psychology of aging* (3rd ed., pp. 3–20). San Diego, CA: Academic Press.

Bissada, A., & Briere, J. (2001). Child abuse: Physical and sexual. In J. Worell (Ed.), *Encyclopedia of women and gender: Sex similarities and differences and the impact of society on gender* (pp. 219–232). San Diego, CA: Academic Press.

Biswas-Diener, R. M. (2008). Material wealth and subjective well-being. In M. Eid & R. J. Larsen (eds.), *The Science of Subjective Well-Being* (307–322). New York: The Guilford Press.

Bizumic, B., Reynols, K. J., Turner, J. C., Bromhead, D., & Subasic, E. (2009). The role of the group in individual functioning: School identification and the psychological well-being of staff and students. *Applied Psychology: An International Review, 58,* 171–192.

Bjorklund, D. F. (2005). *Children's thinking: Cognitive development and individual differences* (4th ed.). Belmont, CA: Wadsworth.

Bjorklund, D. F., & Harnishfeger, K. K. (1995). The evolution of inhibition mechanisms and their role in human cognition and behavior. In F. N. Dempster & C. J. Brainerd (Eds.), *Interference and inhibition in cognition*

(pp. 141–173). San Diego, CA: Academic Press.

Bjorklund, D. F., & Pellegrini, A. D. (2002). *The origins of human nature: Evolutionary developmental psychology.* Washington, DC: American Psychological Association.

Bjorklund, D. F., & Rosenblum, K. E. (2001). Children's use of multiple and variable addition strategies in a game context. *Developmental Science, 4,* 184–194.

Black, H. K., & Rubinstein, R. L. (2005). Direct care workers' response to dying and death in the nursing home: A case study. *Journals of Gerontology: Series B: Psychological Sciences and Social Sciences, 60B,* S3-S10.

Blacker, D., & Lovestone, S. (2006). Genetics and dementia nosology. *Journal of Geriatric Psychiatry and Neurology, 19,* 186–191.

Blackwell, C. C., Moscovis, S. M., Gordon, A. E., Al Madani, O. M., Hall, S. T., Gleeson, M., Scott, R. J., Roberts-Thomson, J., Weir, D. M., & Busuttil, A. (2004). Ethnicity, infection and sudden infant death syndrome. *FEMS Immunology and Medical Microbiology, 42,* 53–65.

Blake, W. (1794). The schoolboy. Retrieved October 21, 2006, from University of Dundee Web site: http://www.dundee.ac.uk/english/wics/blake/blake2.htm#e25

Blakemore, S. (2008). Development of the social brain during adolescence. *The Quarterly Journal of Experimental Psychology, 61*(1), 40–49.

Blanchard-Fields, F., Mienaltowski, A., & Seay, R. B. (2007). Age differences in everyday problem-solving effectiveness: Older adults select more effective strategies for interpersonal problems. *Journal of Gerontology: Psychological Sciences, 62B*(1), 61–64.

Blatney, M., Jelinek, M., & Osecka, T. (2007). Assertive toddler, self-efficacious adult: Child temperament predicts personality over forty years. *Personality and Individual Differences, 43,* 2127–2136.

Blennow, K., de Leon, M. J., & Zetterberg, H. (2006). Alzheimer's disease. *Lancet, 368,* 387–403.

Blodgett Salafia, E. H., Gondoli, D. M., Corning, A. F., McEnery, A. M., & Grundy, A. M. (2007). Psychological distress as a mediator of the relation between perceived maternal parenting and normative maladaptive eating among adolescent girls. *Journal of Counseling Psychology, 54*(4), 434–446.

Blood, R. O., & Wolfe, D. M. (1960). *Husbands and wives: The dynamics of family living.* Oxford, England: Free Press Glencoe.

Bluck, S., & Glück, J. (2004). Making things better and learning a lesson: Experiencing wisdom across the lifespan. *Journal of Personality, 72,* 543–572.

Blum, D. (2002). *Love at Goon Park: Harry Harlow and the science of affection.* Cambridge, MA: Perseus.

Blustein, D. L. (2008). The role of work in psychological health and well-being: A conceptual, historical, and public policy perspective. *American Psychologist, 63*(4), 228–240.

Bodenhorn, N., & Lawson, G. (2003). Genetic counseling: Implications for community counselors. *Journal of Counseling & Development, 81,* 497–501.

Bodenmann, G., Charvos, L., Bradbury, T. N., Bertoni, A., Iafrate, R., Giuliani, C., Banse, R., & Behling, J. (2007). The role of stress in divorce: A three-national retrospective study. *Journal of Social and Personal Relationships, 24*(5), 707–728.

Boehm, J. K., & Lyubomirsky, S. (2008). Does happiness promote career success? *Journal of Career Assessment, 16*(1), 101–116.

Bogaert, A. F. (2005). Age at puberty and father absence in a national probability sample. *Journal of Adolescence, 28,* 541–546.

Bohnert, A. M., Aikins, J. W., & Edidin, J. (2007). The role of organized activities in facilitating social adaptations across transition to college. *Journal of Adolescent Research, 22*(2), 189–208.

Boland, A. M., Haden, C. A., & Ornstein, P. A. (2003). Boosting children's memory by training mothers in the use of an elaborative conversational style as an event unfolds. *Journal of Cognition and Development, 4,* 39–65.

Bonach, K. (2007). Forgiveness intervention model: Application to coparenting post-divorce. *Journal of Divorce & Remarriage, 48*(1/2), 105–123.

Bonanno, G. A. (2004). Loss, trauma, and human resilience: Have we underestimated the human capacity to thrive after extremely aversive events? *American Psychologist, 59,* 20–28.

Bonanno, G. A., & Lilienfeld, S. O. (2008). Let's be realistic: When grief counseling is effective and when it's not. *Professional Psychology: Research and Practice, 39*(3), 377–380.

Bonanno, G. A., Wortman, C. B., Lehman, D. R., Tweed, R. G., Haring, M., Sonnega, J., Carr, D., & Nesse, R. M. (2002). Resilience to loss and chronic grief: A prospective study from preloss to 18-months postloss. *Journal of Personality and Social Psychology, 83,* 1150–1164.

Bondi, M. W., Jak, A. J. Delano-Wood, L., Jacobson, M. W., Delis, D. C., & Salmon, D. P. (2008). Neuropsychological contributions to the early identification of Alzheimer's disease. *Neuropsychology Review, 18,* 73–90.

Bono, G., McCullough, M. E., & Root, L. M. (2008). Forgiveness, feeling connected to others, and well-being: Two longitudinal studies. *Personality and Social Psychology Bulletin, 34*(2), 182–195.

Bookwala, J. (2003). Being "single and unattached": The role of adult attachment styles. *Journal of Applied Social Psychology, 33,* 1564–1570.

Boonzaier, F. (2008). 'If the man says you must sit, then you must sit': The relationship construction of woman abuse: Gender, subjectivity and violence. *Feminism & Psychology, 18*(2), 183–206.

Booth-LaForce, C., & Oxford, M. L. (2008). Trajectories of social withdrawal from grades 1 to 6: Prediction from early parenting, attachment, and temperament. *Developmental Psychology, 44,* 1298–1313.

Borella, E., Carretti, B., & De Beni, R. (2008, May). Working memory and inhibition across the adult life-span. *Acta Psychologica, 128,* 33–44.

Borko, H., Wolf, S. A., Simone, G., & Uchiyama, K. P. (2003). Schools in transition: Reform efforts and school capacity in Washington state. *Educational Evaluation and Policy Analysis, 25,* 171–201.

Bornstein, M. H., & Tamis-LeMonda, C. S. (2001). Mother-infant interaction. In G. Bremner & A. Fogel (Eds.), *Blackwell handbook of infant development* (pp. 269–295). Malden, MA: Blackwell.

Bos, H. M. W., Sandfort, T. G. M., de Bruyn, E. H., & Hakvoort, E. M. (2008). Same-sex attraction, social relationships, psychosocial functioning, and school performance in early adolescence. *Developmental Psychology, 44*(1), 59–68.

Botwinick, J. (1967). *Cognitive processes in maturity and old age.* New York: Springer.

Bouchard, G., Lachance-Grzela, M., & Goguen, A. (2008). Timing of the transition to motherhood and union quality: The moderator role of union length. *Personal Relationships, 15,* 71-80.

Boucher, N., Bairam, A., & Beaulac-Baillargeon, L. (2008). A new look at the neonate's clinical presentation after in utero exposure to antidepressants in late pregnancy. *Journal of Clinical Psychopharmacology, 28*(3), 334–339.

Boute, V. M., Pancer, S. M., Pratt, M. W., Adams, G., Birnie-Lefcovitch, S., Polivy, J., & Wintre, M. G. (2007). The importance of friends: Friendship and adjustment among 1st-Year university students. *Journal of Adolescent Research, 22*(6), 665–689.

Bowlby, J. (1969). *Attachment and loss: Vol. 1. Attachment.* New York: Basic Books.

Bowlby, J. (1973). *Attachment and loss: Vol. 2. Separation: Anxiety and anger.* New York: Basic Books.

Bowlby, J. (1980). *Attachment and loss: Vol. 3. Loss: Sadness and depression.* New York: Basic Books.

Bowles, R. P., & Salthouse, T. A. (2008). Vocabulary test format and differential relations to age. *Psychology and Aging, 23,* 366–376.

Boyle, D. E., Marshall, N. L., & Robeson, W. W. (2003). Gender at play: Fourth-grade girls and boys on the playground. *American Behavioral Scientist, 46,* 1326–1345.

Bozick, R. (2007). Making it through the first year of college: The role of students' economic resources, employment, and living arrangements. *Sociology of Education, 80,* 261–285.

Brabant, S. (2003). Death in two settings: The acute care facility and hospice. In C. D. Bryant (Ed.), *Handbook of death & dying* (pp. 475–484). Thousand Oaks, CA: Sage.

Bradbury, T. N., & Karney, B. R. (2004). Understanding and altering the longitudinal course of marriage. *Journal of Marriage and Family, 66,* 862–879.

Bradley, C. T., & Brasel, K. J. (2008). Core competencies in palliative care for surgeons: Interpersonal and communication skills. *American Journal of Hospice & Palliative Medicine, 24* (6), 499–507.

Bradley, R. H., Corwyn, R. F., Burchinal, M., McAdoo, H. P., & Garcia Coll, C. (2001a). The home environments of children in the United States Part II: Relations with behavioral development through age thirteen. *Child Development, 72,* 1868–1886.

Breakstone, S., Dreiblatt, M., & Dreiblatt, K. (2009). *How to Stop Bullying and Social Aggression: Elementary Grade Lessons and Activities That Teach*

Empathy, Friendship, and Respect. Thousand Oaks: Corwin Press.

Brecher, E. M., & the editors of Consumer Reports books. (1984). *Love, sex, and aging: A Consumers Union report.* Boston: Little, Brown.

Breitbart, W., Gibson, C., Poppito, S. R., & Berg, A. (2004). Psychotherapeutic interventions at the end of life: A focus on meaning and spirituality. *Canadian Journal of Psychiatry, 49,* 366–372.

Brennan, A., Ayers, S., Ahmed, H., & Marshall-Lucette, S. (2007). A critical review of the Couvade syndrome: The pregnant male. *Journal of Reproductive and Infant Psychology, 25*(3), 173–189.

Bretherton, I. (2005). In pursuit of the internal working model construct and its relevance to attachment relationships. In K. E. Grossmann, K. Grossmann, & E. Waters (Eds.), *Attachment from infancy to adulthood: The major longitudinal studies* (pp. 13–47). New York: Guilford Press.

Bridges, L. J., Denham, S. A., & Ganiban, J. M. (2004). Definitional issues in emotion regulation research. *Child Development, 75,* 340–345.

Britt, D. W., & Evans, M. I. (2007). Sometimes doing the right task sucks: Frame combinations and multi-fetal pregnancy reduction decision difficulty. *Social Science & Medicine, 65,* 2342–2356.

Broder, A., Herwig, A., Teipel, S., & Fast, K. (2008). Different storage and retrieval deficits in normal aging and mild cognitive impairment: A multinomial modeling analysis. *Psychology and Aging, 23*(2), 353–365.

Brodhagen, A., & Wise, D. (2008). Optimism as a mediator between the experience of child abuse, other traumatic events, and distress. *Journal of Family Violence, 36,* 403–411.

Brody, G. H., Beach, S. R. H., Philibert, R. A., Chen, Y., & Murry, V. M. (2009). Prevention effects moderate the association of 5-HTTLPR and youth risk behavior initiation: Gene X environment hypotheses tested via a randomized prevention design. *Child Development, 80,* 645–661.

Brody, N. (2006). Geocentric theory: A valid alternative to Gardner's theory of intelligence. In J. A. Schaler (Ed.), *Howard Gardner under fire: The rebel psychologist faces his critics* (pp. 73–94). Chicago, IL: Open Court Publishing Co.

Bronfenbrenner, U. (1977). Toward an experimental ecology of human development. *American Psychologist, 32,* 513–531.

Bronstein, P. (1988). Father-child interaction: Implications for gender-role socialization. In P. Bronstein & C. P. Cowan (Eds.), *Fatherhood today: Men's changing role in the family* (pp. 107–124). Oxford, England: Wiley.

Brooks-Gunn, J., Newman, D. L., Holderness, C. C., & Warren, M. P. (1994). The experience of breast development and girls' stories about the purchase of a bra. *Journal of Youth and Adolescence, 23,* 539–565.

Brooks-Gunn, J., & Ruble, D. N. (1982). The development of menstrual-related beliefs and behaviors during early adolescence. *Child Development, 53,* 1567–1577.

Brooks-Gunn, J., & Warren, M. P. (1985). The effects of delayed menarche in different contexts: Dance and nondance students. *Journal of Youth and Adolescence, 14,* 285–300.

Brooks-Gunn, J., & Warren, M. P. (1988). The psychological significance of secondary sexual characteristics in nine- to eleven-year-old girls. *Child Development, 59,* 1061–1069.

Brotman, L. M., O'Neal, C. R., Huang, K., Gouley, K. K., Rosenfelt, A., & Shrout, P. E. (2009). An experimental test of parenting practices as a mediator of early childhood physical aggression. *Journal of Child Psychology and Psychiatry, 50*(3), 235–245.

Brown, C. A., McGuire, F. A., & Voelkl, J. (2008). The link between successful aging and serious leisure. *International Journal of Aging and Human Development, 66*(1), 73–95.

Brown, J. A., & Ferree, M. M. (2005). Close your eyes and think of England: Pronatalism in the British print media. *Gender & Society, 19,* 5–24.

Brown, J. D., Cai, H., Oakes, M. A., & Deng, C. (2009). Cultural similarities in self-esteem functioning: East is east and west is west, but sometimes the twain do meet. *Journal of Cross-Cultural Psychology, 40,* 140–157.

Brown, S. L., Nesse, R. M., House, J. S., & Utz, R. L. (2004). Religion and emotional compensation: Results from a prospective study of widowhood. *Personality and Social Psychology Bulletin, 30,* 1165–1174.

Brownell, K. D. (1991). Dieting and the search for the perfect body: Where physiology and culture collide. *Behavior Therapy, 22,* 1–12.

Buck Louis, G. M., Gray, L. E., Marcus, M., Ojeda, S. R., Pescovitz, O. H., Witchel, S. F., Sippell, W., Abbott, D. H., Soto, A., Tyl, R. W., Bourguignon, J. P., Skakkebaek, N. E., Swan, S. H.,

Golub, M. S., Wabitsch, M., Toppari, J., & Euling, S. Y. (2008). Environmental factors and puberty timing: Expert panel research needs. *Pediatrics, 121*(3), S192–207.

Bugental, D. B., Martorell, G. A., & Barraza, V. (2003). The hormonal costs of subtle forms of infant maltreatment. *Hormones and Behavior, 43,* 237–244.

Buhl, H. M., & Lanz, M. (2007). Emerging adulthood in Europe: Common traits and variability across five European countries. *Journal of Adolescent Research, 22*(5), 439–443.

Bukowski, W. M. (2001). Friendship and the worlds of childhood. In D. W. Nangle & C. A. Erdley (Eds.), *New directions for child and adolescent development: No. 91. The role of friendship in psychological adjustment* (pp. 93–105). San Francisco: Jossey-Bass.

Bulanda, R. E. (2004). Paternal involvement with children: The influence of gender ideologies. *Journal of Marriage and Family, 66,* 40–45.

Bureau of the Census. (2008). Current Population Survey, Annual Social and Economic Supplement. Retrieved November 22, 2008, from http://pubdb3.census.gov.

Burnette, J. L., Davis, D. E., Green, J. D., Worthington Jr., E. L., & Bradfield, E. (2009). Insecure attachment and depressive symptoms: The mediating role of rumination, empathy, and forgiveness. *Personality and Individual Differences, 49,* 276–280.

Burton, L. M. (2001). One step forward and two steps back: Neighborhoods, adolescent development, and unmeasured variables. In A. Booth & A. C. Crouter (Eds.), *Does it take a village? Community effects on children, adolescents, and families* (pp. 149–159). Mahwah, NJ: Erlbaum.

Bushnell, I. W. R. (1998). The origins of face perception. In F. Simion & G. Butterworth (Eds.), *The development of sensory, motor and cognitive capacities in early infancy: From perception to cognition* (pp. 69–86). Hove, England: Psychology Press.

Buttelmann, D., Call, J., & Tomasello, M. (in press). Do great apes use emotional expressions to infer desires? *Developmental Science.*

Calkins, S. D. (2004). Early attachment processes and the development of emotional self-regulation. In R. F. Baumeister & K. D. Vohs (Eds.), *Handbook of self-regulation: Research, theory, and applications* (pp. 324–339). New York: Guilford Press.

Calkins, S. D., Dedmon, S. E., Gill, K. L., Lomax, L. E., & Johnson, L. M. (2002). Frustration in infancy: Implications for emotion regulation, physiological processes, and temperament. *Infancy, 3,* 175–197.

Callahan, D. (1988). *Setting limits: Medical goals in an aging society.* New York: Simon and Schuster.

Calvo, E., & Williamson, J. B. (2007). Old-age pension reform and modernization pathways: Lessons for China from Latin America. *Journal of Aging Studies, 22,* 74–87.

Calvo, E., Haverstick, K., & Sass, S. A. (2009) Gradual retirement, sense of control, and retirees' happiness. *Research on Aging, 31,* 112–135.

Camaioni, L. (2001). Early language. In G. Bremner & A. Fogel (Eds.), *Blackwell handbook of infant development* (pp. 404–426). Malden, MA: Blackwell.

Campa, M. I., Bradshaw, C. P., Eckenrode, J., & Zielinski, D. S. (2008). Patterns of problem behavior in relation to thriving and precocious behavior in late adolescence. *J Youth Adolescence, 37,* 627–640.

Campos, J. J., Anderson, D. I., Barbu-Roth, M. A., Hubbard, E. M., Hertenstein, M. J., & Witherington, D. (2000). Travel broadens the mind. *Infancy, 1,* 149–219.

Campos, J. J., Langer, A., & Krowitz, A. (1970, October 9). Cardiac responses on the visual cliff in prelocomotor human infants. *Science, 170,* 196–197.

Canter, A. S. (1997). The future of intelligence testing in the schools. *School Psychology Review, 26,* 255–261.

Caplan, A. L., Blank, R. H., & Merrick, J. C. (Eds.). (1992). *Compelled compassion: Government intervention in the treatment of critically ill newborns.* Totowa, NJ: Humana Press.

Card, N. A., Stucky, B. D., Sawalani, G. M., & Little, T. D. (2008). Direct and indirect aggression during childhood and adolescence: A meta-analytic review of gender differences, intercorrelations, and relations to maladjustment. *Child Development, 79,* 1185–1229.

Caron, S. L., & Moskey, E. G. (2002). Changes over time in teenage sexual relationships: Comparing the high school class of 1950, 1975, and 2000. *Adolescence, 37,* 515–526.

Carpenter, R. G., Irgens, L. M., Blair, P. S., England, P. D., Fleming, P., Huber, J., Jorch, G., & Schreuder, P. (2004). Sudden unexplained infant death in 20 regions in Europe: Case control study. *Lancet, 363,* 185–191.

Carpentier, N., Ducharme, F., Kergoat, M., & Bergman, H. (2008). Social representations of barriers to care early in the care of caregivers of persons with Alzheimer's disease. *Research on Aging, 30*(3), 334–357.

Carr, D. (2004). Gender, preloss marital dependence, and older adults' adjustment to widowhood. *Journal of Marriage and Family, 66,* 220–235.

Carroll, J. S., Willoughby, B., Badger, S., Nelson, L. J., Barry, C. M., & Madsen, S. D. (2007). So close, yet so far away: The impact of varying marital horizons on emerging adulthood. *Journal of Adolescent Research, 22*(3), 219–247.

Carskadon, M. A., Acebo, C., & Jenni, O. G. (2004). Regulation of adolescent sleep: Implications for behavior. In R. E. Dahl & L. P. Spear (Eds.), *Adolescent brain development: Vulnerabilities and opportunities* (Vol. 1021, pp. 276–291). New York: New York Academy of Sciences.

Carstensen, L. L. (1995). Evidence for a life-span theory of socioemotional selectivity. *Current Directions in Psychological Science, 4,* 151–156.

Carstensen, L. L., Gottman, J. M., & Levenson, R. W. (l995). Emotional behavior in long-term marriage. *Psychology and Aging, 10,* 140–149.

Carstensen, L. L., Graff, J., Levenson, R. W., & Gottman, J. M. (1996). Affect in intimate relationships: The developmental course of marriage. In C. Magai, & S. H. McFadden (Eds.), *Handbook of emotion, adult development, and aging* (pp. 227–247). San Diego, CA: Academic Press.

Carver, L. J. & Vaccaro, B. G. (2007). 12-month-old infants allocate increased neural resources to stimuli associated with negative adult emotion. *Developmental Psychology, 43*(1), 54–69.

Casanueva, C. E., & Martin, S. L. (2007). Intimate partner violence during pregnancy and mothers' child abuse potential. *Journal of Interpersonal Violence, 22,* 603–622.

Case, R. (1999). Conceptual development. In M. Bennett (ed.), *Developmental psychology: Achievements and prospects* (pp. 36–54). New York: Psychology Press.

Cashmore, J., & Parkinson, P. (2008). Children's and parents' perceptions on children's participation in decision making after parental separation and divorce. *Family Court Review, 46*(1), 91–104.

Caspi, A., Begg, D., Dickson, N., Harrington, H., Langley, J., Moffitt, T. E., & Silva, P. A. (1997). Personality differences predict health-risk behaviors in young adulthood: Evidence from a longitudinal study. *Journal of Personality and Social Psychology, 73,* 1052–1063.

Caspi, A., Henry, B., McGee, R. O., Moffitt, T. E., & Silva, P. A. (1995). Temperamental origins of child and adolescent behavior problems: From age three to age fifteen. *Child Development, 66,* 55–68.

Caspi, A., Moffitt, T. E., Cannon, M., McClay, J., Murray, R., Harrington, H., Taylor, A., Arseneault, L., Williams, B., Braithwaite, A., Poulton, R., & Craig, I. W. (2005). Moderation of the effect of adolescent-onset cannabis use on adult psychosis by a functional polymorphism in the catechol-O-methyltransferase gene: Longitudinal evidence of a gene X environment interaction. *Biological Psychiatry, 57,* 1117–1127.

Caspi, A., Sugden, K., Moffitt, T. E., Taylor, A., Craig, I. W., Harrington, H., McClay, J., Mill, J., Martin, J., Braithwaite, A., & Poulton, R. (2003, July 18). Influence of life stress on depression: Moderation by a polymorphism in the 5-HTT gene. *Science, 301,* 386–389.

Castle, L., Aubert, R. E., Verbugge, R. R., Khalid, M., & Epstein, R. S. (2007). Trends in medication treatment for ADHD. *Journal of Attention Disorders, 10*(4), 335–342.

Castle, N. C. (2007). Assessing job satisfaction of nurse aids in nursing homes: The Nursing Home Nurse Aide Job Satisfaction Questionnaire. *Journal of Gerontological Nursing, 33*(5), 41–47.

Cate, R. A., & John, O. P. (2007). Testing models of the structure and development of future time perspective: Maintaining a focus on opportunities in middle age. *Psychology and Aging, 22*(1), 186–201.

Cattell, M. G. (2003). African widows: Anthropological and historical perspectives. *Journal of Women & Aging, 15,* 49–66.

Caulfield, L., Richard, S. A., Rivera, J. A., Musgrove, P., & Black, R. E. (2006). *Disease Control Priorities in Developing Countries* (2nd ed.). New York: Oxford University Press.

Cavanaugh, J. C. (2000). Metamemory from a social-cognitive perspective. In D. C. Park & N. Schwarz (Eds.), *Cognitive aging: A primer* (pp. 115–130). New York: Psychology Press.

Ceci, S. J., Rosenblum, T., de Bruyn, E., & Lee, D. Y. (1997). A bio-ecological model of intellectual development: Moving beyond h-sup-2. In R. J. Sternberg & E. L. Grigorenko (Eds.),

Intelligence, heredity, and environment (pp. 303–322). New York: Cambridge University Press.

Centers for Disease Control and Prevention. (2005). *Assisted Reproductive Technology (ART) report, National Summary*, retrieved, October 10, 2008.

Centers for Disease Control and Prevention. (2008). National Center for Health Statistics, *Fastats*, retrieved Oct. 14, 2008.

Centers for Disease Control and Prevention. (2009). Health Data Interactive, retrieved April 7, 2009.

Central Intelligence Agency. (2007). *The world factbook 2007*. Washington, DC: U.S. Government Printing Office.

Central Intelligence Agency. (2008). *The world factbook 2008*. Washington, DC: U.S. Government Printing Office.

Cesaroni, G., Forastieri, F., & Perucci, C. A. (2008). Are cesarean deliveries more likely for poorly educated parents? A brief report from Italy. *Birth, 35*(3), 241–244.

Chambers, W. C. (2007). Oral sex: Varied behaviors and perceptions in a college population. *Journal of Sex Research, 44*(1), 28–42.

Chan, H. M. (2004). Sharing death and dying: Advance directives, autonomy and the family. *Bioethics, 18*, 87–103.

Chapple, H. S. (1999). Changing the game in the intensive care unit: Letting nature take its course. *Critical Care Nurse, 19*, 25–34.

Charles, M. (1992). Cross-national variation in occupational sex segregation. *American Sociological Review, 57*, 483–502.

Charles, S. T., & Almeida, D. M. (2007). Genetic and environmental effects on daily life stressors: More evidence for greater variation in later life. *Psychology and Aging, 22*(2), 331–340.

Chavez, M., & Insel, T. R. (2007). Eating disorders: National institute of mental health's perspective. *American Psychologist, 62*(3), 159–166.

Chen, S. X., Benet-Martinez, V., & Bond, M. H. (2008). Bicultural identity, bilingualism, and psychological adjustment in multicultural societies: Immigration-based and globalization-based acculturation. *Journal of Personality, 76*(4), 803–838.

Chen, X., & French, D. C. (2008). Children's social competence in cultural context. *Annual Review of Psychology, 59*, 591–616.

Cheng, G. H-L., & Chan, D. K-S. (2008). Who suffers more from job insecurity? A

meta-analytic review. *Applied Psychology: An International Review, 57*, 272–303.

Cherlin, A., & Furstenberg, F. F. (1985). Styles and strategies of grandparenting. In V. L. Bengtson & J. F. Robertson (Eds.), *Grandparenthood* (pp. 97–116). Thousand Oaks, CA: Sage.

Cherlin, A. J. (2004). The deinstitutionalization of American marriage. *Journal of Marriage and Family, 66*, 848–861.

Chételat, G., Fouquet, M., Kalpouzos, G., Denghien, I., De la Sayette, V., Viader, F., Mezenge, F., Landeau, B., Baron, J. C., Eustache, F., & Desgranges, B. (2008). Three-dimensional surface mapping of hippocampal atrophy progression from MCI to AD and over normal aging assessed using voxel-based morphometry. *Neuropsychologia, 46*(6), 1721–1731.

Child Soldiers Global Report. (2008). Coalition to stop the use of child soldiers. http://www.Childsoldiersglobalreport.org.

Child Trends. (2008, August). Retrieved on August 20, 2009 from www.childtrends.org.

Child Trends Fact Sheet. (2008, August). *How much do you know about teen sexual behavior: A true-false quiz* (Publication No. 2008-31). Washington, DC: Holcombe, E., Peterson, K., & Manlove, J.

Child Welfare Information Gateway. (2008). Child abuse and neglect fatalities: Statistics and interventions. *Numbers and Trends*.

Chirkov, V. I., & Ryan, R. M. (2001). Parent and teacher autonomy-support in Russian and U. S. adolescents: Common effects on well-being and academic motivation. *Journal of Cross-Cultural Psychology, 32*, 618–635.

Choi, Y., He, M., & Harachi, T. W. (2008). Intergenerational cultural dissonance, parent-child conflict and bonding, and youth problem behaviors among Vietnamese and Cambodian immigrant families. *Journal of Youth Adolescence, 37*, 85–96.

Chou, K. (2008). Combined effect of vision and hearing impairment on depression in older adults: Evidence from the English Longitudinal Study of Ageing. *Journal of Affective Disorders, 106*, 191–196.

Chow, E. S. L., Kong, B. M. H., Wong, M. T. P., Draper, B., Lin, K. L., Ho, S. K. S., & Wong, C. P. (2004). The prevalence of depressive symptoms among elderly Chinese private nursing home residents in Hong Kong.

International Journal of Geriatric Psychiatry, 19, 734–740.

Christ, S. L., Lee, D. J., Fleming, L. E., LeBlanc, W. G., Arheart, K. L., Chung-Bridges, K., Caban, A. J., McCollister, K. E. (2007). Employment and occupation effects on depressive symptoms in older Americans: Does working past age 65 protect against depression? *Journal of Gerontology: SOCIAL SCIENCES, 62B*(6), S399–S403.

Christen, Y. (2008). Commentary on "A roadmap for the prevention of dementia: The inaugural Leon Thal Symposium." Prevention of dementia: A few heretical proposals. *Alzheimer's & Dementia, 4*, 167–168.

Christopher, J. C., & Bickhard, M. H. (2007). Culture, self and identity: Interactivist contributions to a metatheory for cultural psychology. *Culture and Psychology, 13*, 259–295.

Chu, K. C., Miller, B. A., & Springfield, S. A. (2007). Measures of racial/ethnic health disparities in cancer mortality rates and the influence of socioeconomic status. *Journal of the National Medical Association, 99*(10), 1092–1104.

Cicirelli, V. G. (2007). End of life decisions: Research findings and implications. In A. Tomer, P. T. Wong, & G. Eliason (Eds.), *Existential and spiritual issues in death attitudes* (pp. 115–138). Hillsdale, NJ: Lawrence Erlbaum.

Cillessen, A. H. N., & Mayeux, L. (2004). From censure to reinforcement: Developmental changes in the association between aggression and social status. *Child Development, 75*, 147–163.

Clark, D. (2007). End-of-life care around the world: Achievements to date and challenges remaining. *Omega, 56*(1), 101–110.

Clark, R. L., & Quinn, J. F. (2002). Patterns of work and retirement for a new century: Emerging trends and policy implications. *Generations, 26*(2), 17–24.

Clausen, J. S. (1991). Adolescent competence and the shaping of the life course. *American Journal of Sociology, 96*, 805–842.

Clay, M. M., & Cazden, C. B. (1992). A Vygotskian interpretation of Reading Recovery. In L. C. Moll (Ed.), *Vygotsky and education: Instructional implications and applications of sociohistorical psychology* (pp. 206–222). New York: Cambridge University Press.

Climo, J. J., Terry, P., & Lay, K. (2002). Using the double bind to interpret the experience of custodial grandparents. *Journal of Aging Studies, 16*, 19–35.

Cohen, P. N. (2004). The gender division of labor: "Keeping house" and occupational segregation in the United States. *Gender & Society, 18*, 239–252.

Cohen, P., Kasen, S., Chen, H., Hartmark, C., & Gordon, K. (2003). Variations in patterns of developmental transmissions in the emerging adulthood period. *Developmental Psychology, 39*, 657–669.

Coie, J. D., & Dodge, K. A. (1998). Aggression and antisocial behavior. In W. Damon (Series d.) & N. Eisenberg (Vol. ed.), *Handbook of child psychology: Vol 3. Social, emotional, and personality development* (5th ed., pp. 779–862). Hoboken, NJ: John Wiley & Sons Inc.

Cole, B., & Singg, S. (1998). *Relationship between parental bereavement reaction factors and selected psychosocial variables.* Paper presented at the Annual Meeting of the American Psychological Society, Washington, DC.

Cole, D. A., Ciesla, J. A., Dallaire, D. H., Jacquez, F. M., Pineda, A. Q., LaGrange, B., Truss, A. E., Folmer, A. S., Tilghman-Osborne, C., & Felton, J. W. (2008). Emergence of attributional style and its relation to depressive symptoms. *Journal of Abnormal Psychology, 117*(1), 16–31.

Cole, S. L., & Vassar, R. (2008). BACE1 structure and function in health and Alzheimer's disease. *Current Alzheimer Research, 5*, 100–120.

Coles, R. (1970). *Erik H. Erikson: The growth of his work.* Boston: Little, Brown.

Collins, R. L., Elliott, M. N., Berry, S. H., Kanouse, D. E., Kunkel, D., Hunter, S. B., & Miu, A. (2004). Watching sex on television predicts adolescent initiation of sexual behavior. *Pediatrics, 114*, e280–289.

Compian, L., Gowen, L. K., & Hayward, C. (2004). Peripubertal girls' romantic and platonic involvement with boys: Associations with body image and depression symptoms. *Journal of Research on Adolescence, 14*, 23–47.

Condon, J. T., Boyce, P., & Corkindale, C. J. (2004). The First-Time Fathers Study: A prospective study of the mental health and wellbeing of men during the transition to parenthood. *Australian and New Zealand Journal of Psychiatry, 38*, 56–64.

Connell-Carrick, K. (2006). Trends in popular parenting books and the need for parental critical thinking. *Child Welfare, 85*(5), 819–836.

Connidis, I. A., & McMullin, J. A. (1993). To have or have not: Parent status and the subjective well-being of older men and women. *Gerontologist, 33*, 630–636.

Connor, S. R. (2007). Development of hospice and palliative care in the United States. *Omega, 56*(1), 89–99.

Cook, T. D., & Furstenberg, F. F. (2002). Explaining aspects of the transition to adulthood in Italy, Sweden, Germany, and the United States: A cross-disciplinary, case synthesis approach. *Annals of the American Academy of Political & Social Science, 580*, 257–287.

Cook, T. D., Deng, Y., & Morgano, E. (2007). Friendship influences during early adolescence: The special role of friends' grade point average. *Journal of Research on Adolescence, 17*(2), 325–356.

Cooley, E., Toray, T., Wang, M. C., & Valdez, N. N. (2008). Maternal effects on daughters' eating pathology and body image. *Eating Behaviors, 9*, 52–61.

Cooney, T. M., Schaie, K. W., & Willis, S. L. (1988). The relationship between prior functioning on cognitive and personality dimensions and subject attrition in longitudinal research. *Journals of Gerontology, 43*, P12-P17.

Coontz, S. (1992). *The way we never were: American families and the nostalgia trap.* New York: Basic Books.

Coplan, R. J., Closson, L. M., & Arbeau, K. A. (2007). Gender differences in the behavioral associates of loneliness and social dissatisfaction in kindergarten. *Journal of Child Psychology and Psychiatry, 48*(10), 988–995.

Corr, C. A. (1991–1992). A task-based approach to coping with dying. *Omega: Journal of Death and Dying, 24*, 81–94.

Corr, C. A. (2007). Hospice: Achievements, legacies, and challenges. *Omega, 56*(1), 111–120.

Corsaro, W. A. (1985). *Friendship and peer culture in the early years.* Norwood, NJ: Ablex.

Corsaro, W. A. (1997). *The sociology of childhood.* Thousand Oaks, CA: Pine Forge Press/Sage.

Costa, P. T., & McCrae, R. R. (2002). Looking backward: Changes in the mean levels of personality traits from 80 to 12. In D. Cervone & W. Mischel (Eds.), *Advances in personality science* (pp. 219–237). New York: Guilford Press.

Costos, D., Ackerman, R., & Paradis, L. (2002). Recollections of menarche: Communication between mothers and daughters regarding menstruation. *Sex Roles, 46*, 49–59.

Côté, J., & Bynner, J. M. (2008). Changes in the transition to adulthood in the UK and Canada: The role of structure and agency in emerging adulthood. *Journal of Youth Studies, 11*, 251–268.

Cotterell, J. (1996). *Social networks and social influences in adolescence.* New York: Routledge.

Cowan, C. P., & Bronstein, P. (1988). Fathers' roles in the family: Implications for research, intervention, and change. In P. Bronstein & C. P. Cowan (Eds.), *Fatherhood today: Men's changing role in the family* (pp. 341–347). Oxford, England: Wiley.

Cowan, C. P., & Cowan, P. A. (1992). *When partners become parents: The big life change for couples.* New York: Basic Books.

Cozzarelli, C., Karafa, J. A., Collins, N. L., & Tagler, M. J. (2003). Stability and change in adult attachment styles: Associations with personal vulnerabilities, life events, and global construals of self and others. *Journal of Social & Clinical Psychology, 22*, 315–346.

Crade, M., & Lovett, S. (1988). Fetal response to sound stimulation: Preliminary report exploring use of sound stimulation in routine obstetrical ultrasound examinations. *Journal of Ultrasound in Medicine, 7*, 499–503.

Craik, F. I. M. (2000). Age-related changes in human memory. In D. C. Park & N. Schwarz (Eds.), *Cognitive aging: A primer* (pp. 75–92). New York: Psychology Press.

Craik, F. I. M., & McDowd, J. M. (1987). Age differences in recall and recognition. *Journal of Experimental Psychology: Learning, Memory, and Cognition, 13*, 474–479.

Cramer, P. (2008). Identification and the development of competence: A 44-year longitudinal study from late adolescence to late middle age. *Psychology and Aging, 23*, 410–421.

Crick, N. R., & Dodge, K. A. (1996). Social information-processing mechanisms on reactive and proactive aggression. *Child Development, 67*, 993–1002.

Crick, N. R., & Rose, A. J. (2000). Toward a gender-balanced approach to the study of social-emotional development: A look at relational aggression. In P. H. Miller & E. Kofsky Scholnick (Eds.), *Toward a feminist developmental psychology* (pp. 153–168). Florence, KY: Taylor & Frances/Routledge.

Crittenden, A. (2001). *The price of motherhood: Why the most important job in the world is still the least valued.* New York: Metropolitan Books.

Crockenberg, S. C. (2003). Rescuing the baby from the bathwater: How gender and temperament (may) influence how child care affects child development. *Child Development, 74,* 1034–1038.

Crockenberg, S. C., & Leerkes, E. M. (2005). Infant temperament moderates associations between childcare type and quantity and externalizing and internalizing behaviors at 2 1/2 years. *Infant Behavior & Development, 28,* 20–35.

Crowell, J. A., Fraley, R. C., & Shaver, P. R. (1999). Measurement of individual differences in adolescent and adult attachment. In J. Cassidy & P. R. Shaver (Eds.), *Handbook of attachment: Theory, research, and clinical applications* (pp. 434–465). New York: Guilford Press.

Csikszentmihalyi, M. (1990). *Flow: The psychology of optimal experience.* New York: Harper & Row.

Csikszentmihalyi, M. (1996). *Creativity: Flow and the psychology of discovery and invention.* New York: HarperCollins.

Csikszentmihalyi, M., & Larson, R. (1984). *Being adolescent: Conflict and growth in the teenage years.* New York: Basic Books.

Csikszentmihalyi, M., & Schneider, B. L. (2000). *Becoming adult: How teenagers prepare for the world of work.* New York: Basic Books.

Cummings, J. L., & Jackson, P. B. (2008). Race, gender, and SES disparities in self-assessed health, 1974–2004. *Research on Aging, 30,* 137–168.

Cummins, D. D., & Allen, C. (Eds.). (1998). *The evolution of mind.* New York: Oxford University Press.

CysticFibrosis.com. (n.d.). CysticFibrosis.com. Retrieved January 20, 2006, from http://www.cysticfibrosis.com/info/index.html

Dahl, R. E. (2004). Adolescent brain development: A period of vulnerabilities and opportunities. In R. E. Dahl & L. P. Spear (Eds.), *Adolescent brain development: Vulnerabilities and opportunities* (Vol. 1021, pp. 1–22). New York: New York Academy of Sciences.

Daire, A. P. (2002). The influence of parental bonding on emotional distress in caregiving sons for a parent with dementia. *Gerontologist, 42,* 766–771.

Daniels, K. J., Lamson, A. L., & Hodgson, J. (2007). An exploration of the marital relationship and Alzheimer's disease:

One couple's story. *Families, Systems, & Health, 25*(2), 162–177.

Dannenbaum, S. M., & Kinnier, R. T. (2009). Imaginal relationships with the dead: Applications for psychotherapy. *Journal of Humanistic Psychology, 49,* 100–113.

Darwich, L., Hymel, S., Pedrini, L., Sippel, J., & Waterhouse, T. (2008, March). *Lesbian, gay, bisexual, and questioning adolescents: Their social experiences and the role of supportive adults in high school.* Prepared for the Biennial Meeting for the Society of Research on Adolescence, Chicago, IL.

Dasen, P. R. (1977). *Piagetian psychology: Cross-cultural contributions.* New York: Gardner Press.

Dasen, P. R. (1984). The cross-cultural study of intelligence: Piaget and the Baoule. *International Journal of Psychology, 19,* 407–434.

Davatzikos, C., Fan, Y., Wu, X., Shen, D., & Resnick, S. M. (2008). Detection of prodromal Alzheimer's disease via pattern classification of magnetic resonance imaging. *Neurobiology of Aging, 29*(4), 514–523.

David, S., & Knight, B. G. (2008). Stress and coping among gay men: Age and ethnic differences. *Psychology and Aging, 23*(1), 62–69.

Davila, J., & Kashy, D. A. (2009). Secure Base Processes in couples: Daily associations between support experiences and attachment security. *Journal of Family Psychology, 23,* 76–88.

DeAngelis, T. (2008). Priming for a new role. *Monitor on Psychology, 39*(8), 29–31.

de Boysson-Bardies, B., Sagart, L., & Durand, C. (1984). Discernible differences in the babbling of infants according to target language. *Journal of Child Language, 11,* 1–15.

DeCasper, A. J., & Fifer, W. P. (1980, June 6). Of human bonding: Newborns prefer their mothers' voices. *Science, 208,* 1174–1176.

De Cuyper, N., Bernhard-Oettel, C., Berntson, E., De Wiite, H., & Alarco, B. (2008). Employability and employees' well-being: Mediation by job insecurity. *Applied Psychology: An International Review, 57*(3), 488–509.

DeFillippi, R. J., & Arthur, M. B. (1994). The boundaryless career: A competency-based perspective. *Journal of Organizational Behavior, 15,* 307–324.

de Moor, J., Didden, R., & Korzilius, H. (2007). Parent-reported feeding and feeding problems in a sample of Dutch

toddlers. *Early Child Development and Care, 177*(3), 219–234.

DeNavas-Walt, C., Proctor, B. D., & Smith, J. C. (2008). U.S. Census Bureau, Current Population Reports, P60-235, *Income, Poverty, and Health Insurance Coverage in the Unites States: 2007.* Washington, DC: U.S. Government Printing Office.

de Schipper, E. J., Riksen-Walraven, J. M., & Geurts, S. A. E. (2006). Effects of child-caregiver ratio on the interactions between caregivers and children in child-care centers: An experimental study. *Child Development, 77*(4), 861–874.

De Schipper, J. C., Tavecchio, L. W. C., & van IJzendoorn, M. H. (2008). Children's attachment relationships with day care caregivers: Associations with positive caregiving and the child's temperament. *Social Development, 17*(3), 454–470.

DeWall, C. N., Twenge, J. M., Gitter, S. A., & Baumeister R. F. (2009). It's the thought that counts: The role of hostile cognition in shaping aggressive responses to social exclusion. *Journal of Personality and Social Psychology, 96,* 45–59.

Dean, R. S., & Davis, A. S. (2007). Relative risk of perinatal complications in common childhood disorders. *School Psychology Quarterly, 22*(1), 13–23.

Dearing, E. (2004). The developmental implications of restrictive and supportive parenting across neighborhoods and ethnicities: Exceptions are the rule. *Journal of Applied Developmental Psychology, 25,* 555–575.

Deary, I. J., Whalley, L. J., Lemmon, H., Crawford, J. R., & Starr, J. M. (2000). The stability of individual differences in mental ability from childhood to old age: Follow-up of the 1932 Scottish Mental Survey. *Intelligence, 28,* 49–55.

Deater-Deckard, K. (1996). Within family variability in parental negativity and control. *Journal of Applied Developmental Psychology, 17,* 407–422.

Deater-Deckard, K., Ivy, L., & Smith, J. (2005). Resilience in gene-environment transactions. In S. Goldstein, & R. B. Brooks (Eds.), *Handbook of resilience in children* (pp. 49–63). New York: Kluwer Academic/Plenum Publishers.

Deater-Deckard, K., Ivy, L., & Smith, J. (2005). Resilience processes in development: Fostering positive adaptation in the context of adversity. In S. Goldstein & R. B. Brooks (Eds.), *Handbook of Resilience in Children.* (pp. 49–63). New York: Kluwer Academic/Plenum Publishers.

Deci, E. L., & Ryan, R. M. (1985). The general causality orientations scale: Self-determination in personality. *Journal of Research in Personality, 19,* 109–134.

Deci, E. L., & Ryan, R. M. (2000). The "what" and "why" of goal pursuits: Human needs and the self-determination of behavior. *Psychological Inquiry, 11,* 227–268.

Declercq, E., Cunningham, D., Johnson, C., & Sakala, C. (2008). Mothers' reports of postpartum pain associated with vaginal and cesarean deliveries: Results of a national survey. *Birth, 35*(1), 16–24.

Degnan, K. A., & Fox, N. A. (2007). Behavioral inhibition and anxiety disorders: Multiple levels of resilience process. *Development and Psychopathology, 19,* 729–746.

Dempster, F. N. (1981). Memory span: Sources of individual and developmental differences. *Psychological Bulletin, 89,* 63–100.

Denham, S. A. (1998). *Emotional development in young children.* New York: Guilford Press.

Denham, S. A., Blair, K. A., DeMulder, E., Levitas, J., Sawyer, K., Auerbach-Major, S., & Queenan, P. (2003). Preschool emotional competence: Pathway to social competence. *Child Development, 74,* 238–256.

Dennis, H., & Thomas, K. (2007). Ageism in the workplace. *Generations, 31*(1), 84–89.

Dennis, N. A., Hayes, S. M., Prince, S. E., Madden, D. J., Huettel, S. A., & Cabeza, R. (2008). Effects of aging on the neural correlates of successful item and source memory encoding. *Journal of Experimental Psychology: Learning, Memory, and Cognition, 34*(4), 791–808.

Dennissen, J. J. A., Asendorpf, J. B., & van Aken, M. A. G. (2008). Childhood personality predicts long-term trajectories of shyness and aggressiveness in the context of demographic transitions in emerging adulthood. *Journal of Personality, 76*(1), 67–99.

Der, G., Batty, G. D., & Deary, I. J. (2006). Effect of breast feeding on intelligence in children: Prospective study, sibling pairs analysis, and meta-analysis. *British Medical Journal,* 1–6.

Deveci, S. E., Acik, Y., & Ayar, A. (2008). A survey of rate victimization and attitudes towards physical violence among school-aged children in Turkey. *Child: Care, Health and Development, 43*(1), 25–31.

Dezoete, J., MacArthur, B., & Tuck, B. (2003). Prediction of Bayley and Stanford-Binet scores with a group of very low birthweight children. *Child: Care, Health and Development, 29,* 367–372.

Dhanushkodi, A., Bindu, B., Raju, T. R., & Kutty, B. M. (2007). Exposure to enriched environment improves spatial learning performances and enhances cell density but not choline acetyltranserase activity in the hippocampus of ventral subicular-lesioned rats. *Behavioral Neuroscience, 121*(3), 491–500.

Diamanti, A., Basso, M. S., Castro, M., Bianco, G., Ciacco, E., Calce, A., Caramadre, A. M., Noto, C., & Gambarara, M. (2008). Clinical efficacy and safety of parental nutrition in adolescent girls with anorexia nervosa. *Journal of Adolescent Health, 42,* 111–118.

Diamantopoulou, S., Rydell, A., & Henricsson, L. (2008). Can both low and high self-esteem be related to aggression in children? *Social Development, 17,* 682–698.

Diamond, A. (2009). The interplay of biology and the environment broadly defined. *Developmental Psychology, 45,* 1–8.

Diamond, A., Kirkham, N., & Amso, D. (2002). Conditions under which young children can hold two rules in mind and inhibit a prepotent response. *Developmental Psychology, 38,* 352–362.

Diamond, L. M., & Savin-Williams, R. C. (2003). Explaining diversity in the development of same-sex sexuality among young women. In L. D. Garnets & D. C. Kimmel (Eds.), *Psychological perspectives on lesbian, gay, and bisexual experiences* (2nd ed., pp. 130–148). New York: Columbia University Press.

Diamond, M. C. (1988). *Enriching heredity: The impact of the environment on the anatomy of the brain.* New York: Free Press.

Diamond, M. C. (1993). An optimistic view of the aging brain. *Generations, 17*(1), 31–33.

Diaz, M. A., Le, H-N., Cooper, B. A., & Muñoz, R. F. (2007). Interpersonal factors and perinatal depressive symptomatology in a low-income Latina sample. *Cultural Diversity and Ethnic Minority Psychology, 13*(4), 328–333.

Dickens, B. M., Boyle, J. M., & Ganzini, L. (2008). Euthanasia and assisted suicide. In P. A. Singer, & A. M. Viens (Eds.), *The Cambridge textbook of bioethics* (pp. 72–77). New York, NY, US: Cambridge University Press.

Diederich, A., Colonius, H., & Schomburg, A. (2008). Assessing age-related multisensory enhancement with the time-window-of-integration model. *Neuropsychologia, 46,* 2556–2562.

Diener, E. (2008). Myths in the science of happiness, and directions for future research. In M. Eid, & R. L. Larsen (Eds.) *The science of subjective well-being* (pp. 493–514). New York, NY, US: Guilford Press.

Dilworth-Anderson, P., Boswell, G., & Cohen, M. D. (2007). Spiritual and religious coping values and beliefs among African American caregivers: A qualitative study. *Journal of Applied Gerontology, 26*(4), 355–369.

Dishion, T. J., McCord, J., & Poulin, F. (1999). When interventions harm: Peer groups and problem behavior. *American Psychologist, 54,* 755–764.

Dixon, R. A., Rust, T. B., Feltmate, S. E., & See, S. K. (2007). Memory and aging: Selected research directions and application issues. *Canadian Psychology, 48*(2), 67–76.

Dixon, S. V., Graber, J. A., & Brooks-Gunn, J. (2008). The roles of respect for parental authority and parenting practices in parent-child conflict among African American, Latino, and European American families. *Journal of Family Psychology, 22*(1), 1–10.

Dobbins, E. H. (2007). End-of-life decisions: Influence of advance directives on patient care. *Journal of Gerontological Nursing, 33,* 50–56.

Dodge, K. A., Coie, J. D., & Lynam, D. (2006). Aggression and antisocial behavior in youth. In N. Eisenberg, W. Damon, & R. M. Lerner (Eds.), *Handbook of child psychology: Vol. 3, Social, emotional, and personality development* (6th ed.) (pp. 719–788). Hoboken, NJ: John Wiley & Sons Inc.

Doka, K. J. (2003). The death awareness movement: Description, history, and analysis. In C. D. Bryant (Ed.), *Handbook of death & dying* (pp. 50–55). Thousand Oaks, CA: Sage.

Dolcos, F., & Cabeza, R. (2002). Event-related potentials of emotional memory: Encoding pleasant, unpleasant, and neutral pictures. *Cognitive, Affective & Behavioral Neuroscience, 2,* 252–263.

Dombrowski, S. C., & Martin, R. P. (2007). Perinatal exposure in later psychological and behavioral disabilities. *School Psychology Quarterly, 22*(1), 1–7.

Dominguez, T. P., Dunkel-Schetter, C., Glynn, L. M., Hobel, C., & Sandman, C. A. (2008). Racial differences in birth outcomes: The role of general, pregnancy, and racism stress. *Health Psychology, 27*(2), 194–203.

Donnellan, M. B., Conger, R. D., & Burzette, R. G. (2007). Personality development from late adolescence to young adulthood: Differential stability, normative maturity, and evidence for the maturity-stability hypothesis. *Journal of Personality, 75*(2), 237–263.

Donohue, P. K., Maurin, E., Kimzey, L., Allen, M. C., & Strobino, D. (2008). Quality of life of caregivers of very-low-birthweight infants. *Birth: Issues in Perinatal Care, 35*(3), 212–219.

Donovan, W., Leavitt, L., Taylor, N., & Broder, J. (2007). Maternal sensory sensitivity, mother-infant 9-month interaction, infant attachment status: Predictors of mother-toddler interaction at 24 months. *Infant Behavior & Development, 30,* 336–352.

Doss, B. D., Rhoades, G. K., Stanley, S. M., & Markman H. J. (2009). The effect of the transition to parenthood on relationship quality: An 8-year prospective study. *Journal of Personality and Social Psychology, 96,* 601–619.

Doucet, S., Soussignan, R., Sagot, P., & Schaal, B. (2007). The "smallscape" of mother's breast: Effects of odor masking and selective unmasking on neonatal arousal, oral and visual responses. *Developmental Psychobiology, 49,* 129–138.

Douglas, S. J., & Michaels, M. W. (2004). *The mommy myth: The idealization of motherhood and how it has undermined women.* New York: Free Press.

Douglas-Hall, A., & Chau, M. (2008). *Basic facts about low-income children: Birth to age 6.* National Center for Children in Poverty, Columbia University Mailman School of Public Health.

Dowd, J. B., Zajacova, A., & Aiello, A. (2009). Early origins of health disparities: Burden of infection, health, and socioeconomic status in U.S. children. *Social Science and Medicine, 68,* 699–707.

Doyle, D. (2007). Palliative medicine in Britain. *Omega, 56*(1), 77–88.

Drakopoulos, S. A. (2007). The paradox of happiness: Towards an alternative explanation. *Journal of Happiness Studies, 9,* 303–315.

Dresser, R. (2004). Death with dignity: Contested boundaries. *Journal of Palliative Care, 20,* 201–206.

Dribe, M., & Stanfors, M. (2009). Does parenthood strengthen a traditional household division of labor? Evidence from Sweden. *Journal of Marriage and Family, 71,* 33–45.

Driver, J., & Gottman, J. M. (2004). Daily marital interactions and positive affect during marital conflict among newlywed couples. *Family Process, 43*(3), 301–314.

Driver, J., Tabares, A., Shapiro, A., Nahm, E. Y., & Gottman, J. M. (2003). Interactional patterns in marital success and failure: Gottman laboratory studies. In F. Walsh (Ed.), *Normal family processes: Growing diversity and complexity* (3rd ed., pp. 493–513). New York: Guilford Press.

DuBois, D. L., Felner, R. D., Brand, S., & George, G. R. (1999). Profiles of self-esteem in early adolescence: Identification and investigation of adaptive correlates. *American Journal of Community Psychology, 27,* 899–932.

Dubois, L., & Girard, M. (2005). Breast-feeding, day-care attendance and the frequency of antibiotic treatments from 1.5 to 5 years: A population-based longitudinal study in Canada. *Social Science & Medicine, 60,* 2035–2044.

DuBose, K. D., Mayo, M. S., Gibson, C. A., Green, J. L., Hill, J. O., Jacobsen, D. J., Smith, B. K., Sullivan, D. K., Washburn, R. A., & Donnelly, J. E. (2008). Physical activity across the curriculum (PAAC): Rationale and design. *Contemporary Clinical Trials, 29*(1), 83–93.

Dubowitz, H., & Bennett, S. (2007). Physical abuse and neglect of children. *Lancet, 369*(9576), 1891–1899.

Duchek, J. M., Balota, D. A., Storandt, M., & Larsen, R. (2007). The power of personality in discriminating between healthy aging and early-stage Alzheimer's disease. *Journal of Gerontology, 62B*(6), P353–P361.

Duijvestijn, J. A., Anteunis, L. J. C., Hoek, C. J., van den Brink, R. H. S., Chenault, M. N., & Manni, J. J. (2003). Help-seeking behaviour of hearing-impaired persons aged 55 years; effect of complaints, significant others and hearing aid image. *Acta Oto-Laryngologica, 123,* 846–850.

Duncan, G. J., & Brooks-Gunn, J. (2000). Family poverty, welfare reform, and child development. *Child Development, 71,* 188–196.

Dungy, C. I., McInnes, R. J., Tappin, D. M., Wallis, A. B., & Oprescu, F. (2008). Infant feeding attitudes and knowledge among socioeconomically disadvantaged women in Glasgow. *Maternal and Child Health Journal 12*(3), 313–322.

Dunn, J., & Hughes, C. (2001). "I got some swords and you're dead!": Violent fantasy, antisocial behavior, friendship, and moral sensibility in young children. *Child Development, 72,* 491–505.

Dunn, J., Wooding, C., & Hermann, J. (1977). Mothers' speech to young children: Variation in context. *Developmental Medicine & Child Neurology, 19,* 629–638.

Dunphy, D. C. (1963). The social structure of urban adolescent peer groups. *Sociometry, 26,* 230–246.

Dupuis, J., Weiss, D. R., & Wolfson, C. (2007). Gender and transportation access among community-dwelling seniors. *Canadian Journal on Aging, 26*(2), 149–158.

Durston, S., & Konrad, K. (2007). Integrating genetic, psychopharmacological and neuroimaging studies: A converging methods approach to understanding the neurobiology of ADHD. *Developmental Review, 27*(3), 374–395.

Dweck, C. S. (1986). Motivational processes affecting learning. *American Psychologist, 41,* 1040–1048.

Dworkin, J. B., Larson, R., & Hansen, D. (2003). Adolescents' accounts of growth experiences in youth activities. *Journal of Youth and Adolescence, 32,* 17–26.

Dwyer, L-L., Nordenfelt, L., & Ternestedt, B-M. (2008). Three nursing home residents speak about meaning at the end of life. *Nursing Ethics, 15*(1), 97–109.

Earle, S. (2002). Factors affecting the initiation of breastfeeding: Implications for breastfeeding promotion. *Health Promotion International, 17,* 205–214.

Ebbeling, C. B., Pawlak, D. B., & Ludwig, D. S. (2002). Childhood obesity: Public-health crisis, common sense cure. *Lancet, 360,* 473–482.

Ebling, F. J. P. (2005). The neuroendocrine timing of puberty. *Reproduction, 129,* 675–683.

Eccles, J. S., & Midgley, C. (1989). Stage-environment fit: Developmentally appropriate classrooms for young adolescents. In C. Ames & R. Ames (Eds.), *Research on motivation in education: Vol. 3. Goals and cognitions* (pp. 13–44). New York: Academic Press.

Eccles, J. S., & Roeser, R. W. (2003). Schools as developmental contexts. In G. R. Adams & M. D. Berzonsky (Eds.), *Blackwell handbook of adolescence* (pp. 129–148). Malden, MA: Blackwell.

Edin, K., & Kefalas, M. (2005). *Promises I can keep: Why poor women put motherhood before marriage.* Berkeley: University of California Press.

Edin, K., Kefalas, M. J., & Reed, J. M. (2004). A peek inside the black box: What marriage means for poor unmarried parents. *Journal of Marriage and Family, 66,* 1007–1014.

Egeland, B. (2009). Taking stock: Childhood emotional maltreatment and developmental psychopathology. *Child Abuse & Neglect, 33,* 22–26.

Ehrenberg, M. F., & Smith, S. T. L. (2003). Grandmother-grandchild contacts before and after an adult daughter's divorce. *Journal of Divorce & Remarriage, 39,* 27–43.

Eichorn, D. H., Clausen, J. A., Haan, J., Honzik, M. P., & Mussen, P. H. (eds.). (1981). *Present and past in middle life.* New York: Academic Press.

Eisenberg, N. (1992). *The caring child.* Cambridge, MA: Harvard University Press.

Eisenberg, N. (2003). Prosocial behavior, empathy, and sympathy. In M. H. Bornstein, L. Davidson, C. L. M. Keyes, & K. A. Moore (Eds.), *Well-being: Positive development across the life course* (pp. 253–265). Mahwah, NJ: Erlbaum.

Eisenberg, N., & Fabes, R. A. (1998). Prosocial development. In W. Damon (Series ed.) & N. Eisenberg (Vol. ed.), *Handbook of child psychology: Vol 3. Social, emotional, and personality development* (5th ed., pp. 701–778). Hoboken, NJ: John Wiley & Sons Inc.

Eisenberg, N., Guthrie, I. K., Murphy, B. C., Shepard, S. A., Cumberland, A., & Carlo, G. (1999). Consistency and development of prosocial dispositions: A longitudinal study. *Child Development, 70,* 1360–1372.

Eisner, E. W. (2004). Multiple intelligences: Its tensions and possibilities. *Teachers College Record, 106,* 31–39.

Ekerdt, D. J. (1986). The busy ethic: Moral continuity between work and retirement. *Gerontologist, 26,* 239–244.

Elder, G. H., & Caspi, A. (1988). Economic stress in lives: Developmental perspectives. *Journal of Social Issues, 44,* 25–45.

Eldridge, K. A., & Christensen, A. (2002). Demand-withdraw communication during couple conflict: A review and analysis. In P. Noller & J. A. Feeney (Eds.), *Understanding marriage: Developments in the study of couple interaction* (pp. 289–322). New York: Cambridge University Press.

Eliason, M., & Storrie, D. (2009). Job loss is bad for your health: Swedish evidence on cause-specific hospitalization following involuntary job loss. *Social Science and Medicine, 68,* 1396–1406.

Elkind, D. (1968). Cognitive development in adolescence. In J. F. Adams (Ed.), *Understanding adolescence* (pp. 128–158). Boston: Allyn and Bacon.

Elkind, D. (1978). Understanding the young adolescent. *Adolescence, 13,* 127–134.

Ellis, B. J. (2004). Timing of pubertal maturation in girls: An integrated life history approach. *Psychological Bulletin, 130,* 920–958.

Elshafie, M., Fouad, G., Shaaban, M., Helmi, A., & Ewies, A. (2008). The effect of leptin on maturation of the ovarian compartments of albino rats: An ultrastructural and histological study. *Gynecological Endocrinology, 24,* 67–78.

El-Sheikh, M., Cummings, E. M., Kouros, C. D., Elmore-Staton, L., & Buckhalt, J. (2008). Marital psychological and physical aggression and children's mental and physical health: Direct, mediated, and moderated effects. *Journal of Consulting and Clinical Psychological, 76*(1), 138–148.

Emmons, R. A. (2008). Gratitude, subjective well-being, and the brain. In M. Eid & R. J. Larsen (Eds.), *The Science of Subjective Well-Being* (469–492). New York: The Guilford Press.

Enck, G. E. (2003). The dying process. In C. D. Bryant (Ed.), *Handbook of death & dying* (pp. 457–467). Thousand Oaks, CA: Sage.

Engle, S. (n.d.). Degree attainment rates at colleges and universities: College completion declining, taking longer, UCLA study shows. Retrieved September 6, 2006, from Higher Education Research Institute Web site: http://www.gseis.ucla.edu/heri/darcu_pr.html

Englund, K. T., & Behne, D. M. (2005). Infant directed speech in natural interaction—Norwegian vowel quantity and quality. *Journal of Psycholinguistic Research, 34,* 259–280.

Englund, M. M., Egeland, B., Olivia, E. M., & Collins, W. A. (2008). Childhood and adolescent predictors of heavy drinking and alcohol use disorders in early adulthood: A longitudinal development analysis. *Addiction, 103* (Suppl. 1), 23–35.

Erber, J. T., & Prager, I. G. (1999). Age and memory: Perceptions of forgetful young and older adults. In T. M. Hess & F. Blanchard-Fields (Eds.), *Social cognition and aging* (pp. 197–217). San Diego, CA: Academic Press.

Erikson, E. H. (1950). *Childhood and society.* Oxford, England: Norton.

Erikson, E. H. (1963). *Childhood and society* (2nd ed.). New York: Norton.

Erikson, E. H. (1968). *Identity: Youth and crisis.* New York: Norton.

Erikson, E. H. (1969). *Gandhi's truth: On the origins of militant nonviolence.* New York: Norton.

Erikson, E. H. (1980). *Identity and the life cycle.* New York: Norton.

Etaugh, C. A., & Bridges, J. S. (2006). Midlife transitions. In J. Worell & C. D. Goodheart (Eds.), *Handbook of girls' and women's psychological health: Gender and well-being across the lifespan* (pp. 359–367). New York: Oxford University Press.

Euling, S. Y., Selevan, S. G., Pescovitz, O. H., & Skakkebaek, N. E. (2008). Role of environmental factors in the timing of puberty. *Pediatrics, 121*(3), S167–171.

EUROCAT. (2004). *EUROCAT special report: A review of environmental risk factors for congenital anomalies.* Newtownabbey, Northern Ireland: Author.

Eustache, F., & Chételat, G. (2008). Picturing the brain from different perspectives: The neuroimaging of early AD. *Neuropsychologia, 46,* 1595–1596.

Evans, G. W. (2006). Child development and the physical environment. *Annual Review of Psychology, 57,* 423–451.

Ewers, M., Zhong, Z., Bürger, K., Wallin, A., Blennow, K., Teipel, S. J., Shen, Y., & Hampel, H. (2008). Increased CSF-BACE 1 activity is associated with ApoE-4 genotype in subjects with mild cognitive impairment and Alzheimer's disease. *Brain: A Journal of Neurology, 131,* 1252–1258.

Fabes, R. A., Eisenberg, N., Smith, M. C., & Murphy, B. C. (1996). Getting angry at peers: Associations with liking of the provocateur. *Child Development, 67,* 942–956.

Fabes, R. A., Martin, C. L., & Hanish, L. D. (2003). Young children's play qualities in same-, other-, and mixed-sex peer groups. *Child Development, 74,* 921–932.

Fadjukoff, P., Kokko, K., & Pulkkinen, L. (2007). Implications of timing of entering adulthood for identity achievement. *Journal of Adolescent Research, 22*(5).

Fagan, J. F. (1988). Evidence for the relationship between responsiveness to visual novelty during infancy and later intelligence: A summary. *Cahiers de*

Psychologie Cognitive/Current Psychology of Cognition, 8, 469–475.

Fagan, J. F. (2000). A theory of intelligence as processing: Implications for society. *Psychology, Public Policy, and Law, 6,* 168–179.

Fagan, P., Moolchan, E. T., Lawrence, D., Fernander, A., & Ponder, P. K. (2007). Identifying health disparities across the tobacco continuum. *Addiction, 102*(Suppl. 2), 5–29.

Fahs, B. (2007). Second shifts and political awakenings: Divorce and the political socialization of middle-aged women. *Journal of Divorce & Remarriage, 47*(3/4), 43-64.

Families and Work Institute. (2009). Times are changing: Gender and generation at work and at home. www.familiesandwork.org.

Farquhar, J. C., & Wasylkiw, L. (2007). Media images of men: Trends and consequences of body conceptualization. *Psychology of Men & Masculinity, 8*(3), 145–160.

Farroni, T., Massaccesi, S., & Simion, F. (2002). La direzione dello sguardo di un'altra persona puo dirigere l'attenzione del neonato? [Can the direction of the gaze of another person shift the attention of a neonate?]. *Giornale Italiano di Psicologia, 29,* 857–864.

Farroni, T., Menon, E., & Johnson, M. H. (2006). Factors influencing newborns' preference for faces with eye contact. *Journal of Experimental Child Psychology 95*(4), 298–308.

Fass, S., & Cauthen, N. K. (2007). *Who are America's Poor Children? The Official Story.* New York, NY: Columbia University. National Center for Children in Poverty.

Fauth, R. C., Leventhal, T., & Brooks-Gunn, J. (2007). Welcome to the neighborhood? Long term impacts of moving to low-poverty neighborhoods on poor children's and adolescents' outcomes. *Journal of Research on Adolescence, 17*(2), 249–284.

Feeg, V. D., & Elebiary, H. (2005). Exploratory study on end-of-life issues: Barriers to palliative care and advance directives. *American Journal of Hospice and Palliative Medicine, 22,* 119–124.

Feeney, J. A. (1999). Adult romantic attachment and couple relationships. In J. Cassidy & P. R. Shaver (Eds.), *Handbook of attachment: Theory, research, and clinical applications* (pp. 355–377). New York: Guilford Press.

Feeney, J. A., Hohaus, L., Noller, P., & Alexander, R. P. (2001). *Becoming parents: Exploring the bonds between mothers, fathers, and their infants.* New York: Cambridge University Press.

Feeney, J. A., & Noller, P. (2002). Allocation and performance of household tasks: A comparison of new parents and childless couples. In P. Noller & J. A. Feeney (Eds.), *Understanding marriage: Developments in the study of couple interaction* (pp. 411–436). New York: Cambridge University Press.

Feldman, R., & Eidelman, A. I. (2003b). Skin-to-skin contact (kangaroo care) accelerates autonomic and neurobehavioural maturation in preterm infants. *Developmental Medicine & Child Neurology, 45,* 274–281.

Feng, X., Shaw, D. S., & Silk, J. S. (2008). Developmental trajectories of anxiety symptoms among boys across early and middle childhood. *Journal of Abnormal Psychology, 117*(1), 32–47.

Fernald, A., Pinto, J. P., Swingley, D., Weinberg, A., & McRoberts, G. W. (1998). Rapid gains in speed of verbal processing by infants in the 2nd year. *Psychological Science, 9,* 228–231.

Fernandez, M., Blass, E. M., Hernandez-Reif, M., Field, T., Diego, M., & Sanders, C. (2003). Sucrose attenuates a negative electroencephalographic response to an aversive stimulus for newborns. *Journal of Developmental & Behavioral Pediatrics, 24,* 261–266.

Field, A. E., Austin, S. B., Camargo, C. A., Jr., Taylor, C. B., Striegel-Moore, R. H., Loud, K. J., & Colditz, G. A. (2005). Exposure to the mass media, body shape concerns, and use of supplements to improve weight and shape among male and female adolescents. *Pediatrics, 116,* e214–220.

Field, M. J. (2009). How people die in the United States. *Decision Making Near the End of Life: Issues, Developments, and Future Directions,* 63–75.

Field, N. P., Gal-Oz, E., & Bonanno, G. A. (2003). Continuing bonds and adjustment at 5 years after the death of a spouse. *Journal of Consulting and Clinical Psychology, 71,* 110–117.

Field, N. P., Nichols, C., Holen, A., & Horowitz, M. J. (1999). The relation of continuing attachment to adjustment in conjugal bereavement. *Journal of Consulting and Clinical Psychology, 67,* 212–218.

Field, T., Diego, M., & Hernandez-Reif, M. (2007). Massage therapy research. *Developmental Review, 27,* 75–89.

Fields, J. (2003). *Children's living arrangements and characteristics: March 2002* (Current Population Reports P20-547). Washington, DC: U.S. Census Bureau.

Fields, J., & Casper, L. M. (2001). *America's families and living arrangements: March 2000* (Current Population Reports P20-537). Washington, DC: U.S. Census Bureau.

Fincham, F. D., Beach, S. R. H., & Davila, J. (2007). Longitudinal relations between forgiveness and conflict resolution in marriage. *Journal of Family Psychology, 21*(3), 542–545.

Finchman, F. D., Stanley, S. M., & Beach, S. R. (2007). Transformative processes in marriage: An analysis of emerging trends. *Journal of Marriage and Family, 69*(2), 275–292.

Fingerman, K. L. (2004). The role of offspring and in-laws in grandparents' ties to their grandchildren. *Journal of Family Issues, 25,* 1026–1049.

Fingerman, K. L., Miller, L., & Charles, S. (2008). Saving the best for last: How adults treat social partners of different ages. *Psychology and Aging, 23*(2), 399–409.

Finkel, D., & Pedersen, N. L. (2004). Processing speed and longitudinal trajectories of change for cognitive abilities: The Swedish Adoption/Twin Study of Aging. *Aging, Neuropsychology, and Cognition, 11,* 325–345.

Fischer, D. H. (1977). *Growing old in America.* New York: Oxford University Press.

Flavell, J. H. (1963). *The developmental psychology of Jean Piaget.* New York: Van Nostrand.

Flavell, J. H., Beach, D. R., & Chinsky, J. M. (1966). Spontaneous verbal rehearsal in a memory task as a function of age. *Child Development, 37,* 283–299.

Flower, K. B., Willoughby, M., Cadigan, R. J., Perrin, E. M., & Randolph, G. (2008). Understanding breastfeeding initiation and continuation in rural communities: A combined qualitative/quantitative approach. *Maternal and Child Health Journal 12*(3), 402–414.

Fluke, J. D., Shusterman, G. R., Hollinshead, D. M., & Yuan, Y. T. (2008). Longitudinal analysis of repeated child abuse reporting and victimization: Multistate analysis of associated factors. *Child Maltreatment, 13*(1), 76–88.

Ford, D. H., & Lerner, R. M. (1992). *Developmental systems theory: An integrative approach.* Newbury Park, CA: Sage.

Ford, J. D. (2005). Treatment implications of altered affect regulation and information processing following child maltreatment. *Psychiatric Annals, 35,* 410–419.

Fouad, N. A., & Bynner, J. (2008). Work transitions. *American Psychologist, 63*(4), 241–251.

Frazier, T. W., Youngstrom, E. A., & Naugle, R. I. (2007). The latent structure of attention-deficit/hyperactivity disorder in a clinic-referred sample. *Neuropsychology, 21*(1), 45–64.

Fredrickson, B. L. (2008). Promoting positive affect. In M. Eid & R. J. Larsen (Eds.), *The science of subjective well-being* (449–468). New York: The Guilford Press.

Fredrickson, B. L., & Losada, M. F. (2005). Positive affect and the complex dynamics of human flourishing. *American Psychologist, 60*(7), 678–686.

Freedman, D. S., Khan, L. K., Serdula, M. K., Dietz, W. H., Srinivasan, S. R., & Berenson, G. S. (2002). Relation of age at menarche to race, time period, and anthropometric dimensions: The Bogalusa Heart Study. *Pediatrics, 110,* e43.

Freund, A. M., & Baltes, P. B. (2002). Life-management strategies of selection, optimization and compensation: Measurement by self-report and construct validity. *Journal of Personality and Social Psychology, 82,* 642–662.

Frey, K. S., & Ruble, D. N. (1985). What children say when the teacher is not around: Conflicting goals in social comparison and performance assessment in the classroom. *Journal of Personality and Social Psychology, 48,* 550–562.

Frey, K. S., & Ruble, D. N. (1990). Strategies for comparative evaluation: Maintaining a sense of competence across the life span. In R. J. Sternberg & J. Kolligian, Jr. (Eds.), *Competence considered* (pp. 167–189). New Haven, CT: Yale University Press.

Friedman, D. (2003). Cognition and aging: A highly selective overview of event-related potential (ERP) data. *Journal of Clinical and Experimental Neuropsychology, 25,* 702–720.

Frischen, A., Bayliss, A. P., & Tipper, S. P. (2007) Gaze cueing of attention: Visual attention, social cognition, and individual differences. *Psychological Bulletin, 133*(4), 694–724.

Frisoni, G. B., Henneman, W. J., Weiner, M. W., Scheltens, P., Vellas, B., Reynish, E., Hudecova, J., Hampel, H., Burger, K., Blennow, K., Waldermar, G., Johannsen, P., Wahlund, L., Zito, G., Rossini, P. M., Winblad, B., & Barkhof, F. (2008). The pilot European

Alzheimer's Disease Neuroimaging Initiative of the European Alzheimer's Disease Consortium. *Alzheimer's and Dementia, 4*(4), 255–264.

Fu, G., Xu, F., Cameron, C. A., Heyman, G., & Lee, K. (2007). Cross-cultural differences in children's choices, categorizations, and evaluations of truth and lies. *Developmental Psychology, 43*(2), 278–293.

Fu, S.-Y., Anderson, D., & Courtney, M. (2003). Cross-cultural menopausal experience: Comparison of Australian and Taiwanese women. *Nursing & Health Sciences, 5,* 77–84.

Fuentes, M., Hart-Johnson, T., & Green, C. R. (2007). The association among neighborhood socioeconomic status, race and chronic pain in back and white older adults. *Journal of the National Medical Association, 99*(10), 1160–1169.

Fung, H. H., Lai, P., & Ng, R. (2001). Age differences in social preferences among Taiwanese and mainland Chinese: The role of perceived time. *Psychology and Aging, 16,* 351–356.

Furstenberg, F. F., & Cherlin, A. J. (1991). *Divided families: What happens to children when parents part.* Cambridge, MA: Harvard University Press.

Fussenegger, D., Pietrobelli, A., & Widhalm, K. (2007). Childhood obesity: Political developments in Europe and related perspectives for future action on prevention. *Obesity Reviews, 9,* 76–82.

Gaertner, B. M., Spinard, T. L., Eisenberg, N., & Greving, K. A. (2007). Parental childrearing attitudes as correlates of father involvement during infancy. *Journal of Marriage and Family, 69*(4), 962–976.

Gagne, M. H., Tourigny, M., Joly, J., & Pouliot-Lapointe, J. (2007). Predictors of adult attitudes toward corporal punishment of children. *Journal of Interpersonal Violence, 22*(10), 1285–1304.

Gajic-Veljanosky, O., & Stewart, D. E. (2007). Women trafficked into prostitution: Determinants, human rights, and health needs. *Transcultural Psychiatry, 44*(3), 338–358.

Galinsky, E. (2007). The changing landscape of work. *Generations, 31*(1), 16–22.

Galinsky, E., Bond, J. T., Kim, S., Backon, L., Brownfield, E., & Sakai, K. (2005). *Overwork in America: When the way we work becomes too much.* New York: Families and Work Institute.

Gallimore, R., & Tharp, R. (1992). Teaching mind in society: Teaching,

schooling, and literate discourse. In L. C. Moll (ed.), *Vygotsky and education: Instructional implications and applications of sociohistorical psychology* (pp. 175–205). New York: Cambridge University Press.

García-Pérez, L., Linertová, R., Martín-Olivera, P., Serrano-Aguilar, P., & Benítez-Rosario, M. P. (2009). A systematic review of specialised palliative care for terminal patients: Which model is better? *Palliative Medicine, 23,* 17–22.

Gardner, F., Shaw, D. S., Dishion, T. J., Burton, J., & Supplee, L. (2007). Randomized prevention trail for early conduct problems: Effects on proactive parenting and links to toddler disruptive behavior. *Journal of Family Psychology, 21*(3), 398–406.

Gardner, H. (1998). A multiplicity of intelligences. *Scientific American Presents, 9*(4), 18–23.

Gardner, H. (2004). *Frames of mind: The theory of multiple intelligences.* New York: Basic Books.

Gardner, H., & Moran, S. (2006). The science of multiple intelligences theory: A response to Lynn Waterhouse. *Educational Psychologist, 41*(4), 227–232.

Gardner, M., & Steinberg, L. (2005). Peer influence on risk taking, risk preference, and risky decision making in adolescence and adulthood: An experimental study. *Developmental Psychology, 41,* 625–635.

Gardner, M., Roth, J., & Brooks-Gunn, J. (2008). Adolescents' participation in organized activities and developmental success 2 and 8 years after high school: Do sponsorship, duration, and intensity matter? *Developmental Psychology, 44,* 814–830.

Garey, A. I., & Arendell, T. (2001). Children, work, and family: Some thoughts on "mother blame". In R. Hertz & N. L. Marshall (Eds.), *Working families: The transformation of the American home* (pp. 293–303). Berkeley, CA: University of California Press.

Garner, P. W., Dunsmore, J. C., & Southam-Gerrow, M. (2008). Mother-child conversations about emotions: Linkages to child aggression and prosocial behavior. *Social Development, 17,* 259–277.

Garon, N., Bryson, S. E., & Smith, I. M. (2008). Executive function in preschoolers: A review using an integrative framework. *Psychology Bulletin, 134*(1), 31–60.

Gath, A. (1993). Changes that occur in families as children with intellectual disability grow up. *International Journal* of *Disability, Development and Education, 40,* 167–174.

Gavin, J., Rodham, K., & Poyer, H. (2008). The presentation of "pro-anorexia" in online group interactions. *Qualitative Health Research, 18*(3), 325–33.

Gazelle, H. (2008). Behavioral profiles of anxious solitary children and heterogeneity in peer relations. *Developmental Psychology, 44,* 1604–1624.

Gazelle, H., & Ladd, G. W. (2003). Anxious solitude and peer exclusion: A diathesis-stress model of internalizing trajectories in childhood. *Child Development, 74,* 257–278.

Gazelle, H., & Spangler, T. (2007). Early childhood anxious solitude and subsequent peer relationships: Maternal and cognitive moderators. *Journal of Applied Developmental Psychology, 28*(5-6), 515–535.

Ge, X., Elder, G. H., Regnerus, M., & Cox, C. (2001). Pubertal transitions, perceptions of being overweight, and adolescents' psychological maladjustment: Gender and ethnic differences. *Social Psychology Quarterly, 64,* 363–375.

Geary, D. C. (1998). *Male, female: The evolution of human sex differences.* Washington, DC: American Psychological Association.

Geary, D. C., & Flinn, M. V. (2001). Evolution of human parental behavior and the human family. *Parenting: Science and Practice, 1,* 5–61.

Genevie, L. E., & Margolies, E. (1987). *The motherhood report: How women feel about being mothers.* New York: Macmillan.

Gerber, E. B., Whitebook, M., & Weinstein, R. S. (2007). At the heart of child care: Predictors of teacher sensitivity in center-based child care. *Early Childhood Research Quarterly, 22,* 327–346.

Gerdner, L. A., Cha, D., Yang, D., & Tripp-Reimer, T. (2007). The circle of life: End-of-life care and death rituals for Hmong-American elders. *Journal of Gerontological Nursing, 33*(5), 20–29.

Germo, G. R., Chang, E. S., Keller, M. A., & Goldberg, W. A. (2007). Child sleep arrangements and family life: Perspectives from mothers and fathers. *Infant and Child Development, 16,* 433–456.

Gershoff, E. T. (2002). Corporal punishment by parents and associated child behaviors and experiences: A meta-analytic and theoretical review. *Psychological Bulletin, 128,* 539–579.

Gerson, M.-J., Posner, J.-A., & Morris, A. M. (1991). The wish for a child in couples eager, disinterested, and conflicted about having children. *American Journal of Family Therapy, 19,* 334–343.

Gerstoff, D., Ram, N., Estabrook, R., Schupp, J., Wagner, G., & Lindenberger, U. (2008). Life Satisfaction shows terminal decline in old age: Longitudinal evidence from the German Socio-Economic Panel Study (SOEP). *Developmental Psychology, 44,* 1148–1159.

Gibbins, S., & Stevens, B. (2001). Mechanisms of sucrose and non-nutritive sucking in procedural pain management in infants. *Pain Research & Management, 6,* 21–28.

Gibson, E. J., & Walk, R. D. (1960). The "visual cliff." *Scientific American, 202*(4), 64–71.

Gibson, M. A., & Mace, R. (2005). Helpful grandmothers in rural Ethio-pia: A study of the effect of kin on child survival and growth. *Evolution and Human Behavior, 26,* 469–482.

Gibson-Davis, C., & Brooks-Gunn, J. (2007). Breastfeeding and verbal ability of 3 year olds in a multicity sample. *Journal of Developmental & Behavioral Pediatrics, 28*(1), 72.

Gibson-Davis, C. M. (2009). Money, marriage, and children: Testing the financial expectations and family formation theory. *Journal of Marriage and Family, 71,* 146–160.

Giedd, J. N. (2008, March). *The teen brain: Insights from neuroimaging.* Presented at 12th Biennial Meeting of Society for Research on Adolescence, Chicago, IL.

Gilbert-Barness, E. (2000). Maternal caffeine and its effect on the fetus. *American Journal of Medical Genetics, 93,* 253.

Gilboa, S., Shirom, A., Fried, Y., & Cooper, C. (2008). A meta-analysis of work demand stressors and job performance: Examining main and moderating effects. *Personnel Psychology, 61*(2), 227–272.

Gilissen, R., Bakermans-Kranenburg, M. J., van IJzendoorn, M. H., & van der Veer, R. (2008). Parent-child relationship, temperament, and physiological reactions to fear-inducing film clips: Further evidence for differential susceptibility. *Journal of Experimental Child Psychology, 99*(3), 182–195.

Gill, S. L., Reifsnider, E., & Lucke, J. F. (2007). Effects of support on the initiation and duration of breastfeeding.

Western Journal of Nursing Research, 29(6), 708–723.

Gilman, R., Huebner, E. S., Tian, L., Park, N., O'Byrne, J., Schiff, M., Sverko, D., & Langknecht, H. (2008). Cross-national adolescent multidimensional life satisfaction reports: Analysis of mean scores and response style differences. *Journal of Youth Adolescence, 37,* 142–154.

Ginsburg, H., & Opper, S. (1969). *Piaget's theory of intellectual development: An introduction.* Englewood Cliffs, NJ: Prentice-Hall.

Girdler, S., Packer, T. L., & Boldy, D. (2008). The impact of age-related vision loss. *OTJR: Occupation, Participation, and Health, 28,* 110–120.

Glaser, B. G., & Strauss, A. L. (1968). *Time for dying.* Chicago: Aldine.

Glazier, R., Elgar, F., Goel, V., & Holzapfel, S. (2004). Stress, social support and emotional distress in a community sample of pregnant women. *Journal of Psychosomatic Obstetrics & Gynecology, 25,* 247–255.

Glenn, N. (1990). Quantitative research on marital quality in the 1980s: A critical review. *Journal of Marriage and the Family, 52,* 818–831.

Glynn, L. M., Schetter, C. D., Hobel, C. J., & Sandman, C. A. (2008). Pattern of perceived stress and anxiety in pregnancy predicts preterm birth. *Health Psychology, 27*(1), 43–51.

Goede, I. H. D., Branje, S. J. T., & Meeus, W. H. J. (2009). Developmental changes in adolescents' perceptions of relationships with their parents. *Journal of Youth and Adolescence, 38,* 75–88.

Goldberg, A. E., & Sayer, A. (2006). Lesbian couples' relationship quality across the transition to parenthood. *Journal of Marriage and Family, 68,* 87–100.

Goldberg, W. A., & Keller, M. A. (2007). Parent-infant co-sleeping: Why the interest and concern? *Infant and Child Development, 16,* 331–339.

Golden, L. (2008). Limited access: Disparities in flexible work schedules and work-at-home. *Journal of Family Economic Issues, 29,* 86–109.

Goldscheider, F. K., & Goldscheider, C. (1999). *The changing transition to adulthood: Leaving and returning home.* Thousand Oaks, CA: Sage.

Goldstein, S. E., Davis-Kean, P. E., & Eccles, J. S. (2005). Parents, peers, and problem behavior: A longitudinal investigation of the impact of relationship perceptions and characteristics on the development of adolescent problem behavior. *Developmental Psychology, 41*, 401–413.

Golombok, S., Perry, B., Burston, A., Murray, C., Mooney-Somers, J., Stevens, M., & Golding, J. (2003). Children with lesbian parents: A community study. *Developmental Psychology, 39*, 20–33.

Golub, M. S., Collman, G. W., Foster, P. M., Kimmel, C. A., Rajpert-De Meyts, E., Reiter, E. O., Sharpe, R. M., Skakkebaek, N. E., & Toppari, J. (2008). Public health implications of altered puberty timing. *Pediatrics, 121*(3), S218–230.

Good, G. A. (2008). Life satisfaction and quality of life of older New Zealanders with and without impaired vision: A descriptive, comparative study. *European Journal of Ageing, 5*, 223–231.

Good, M.-J. D., Gadmer, N. M., Ruopp, P., Lakoma, M., Sullivan, A. M., Redinbaugh, E., Arnold, R. M., & Block, S. D. (2004). Narrative nuances on good and bad deaths: Internists' tales from high-technology work places. *Social Science & Medicine, 58*, 939–953.

Goodlin-Jones, B. L., Burnham, M. M., & Anders, T. F. (2000). Sleep and sleep disturbances: Regulatory processes in infancy. In A. J. Sameroff, M. Lewis, & S. M. Miller (Eds.), *Handbook of developmental psychopathology* (2nd ed., pp. 309–325). Dordrecht, Netherlands: Kluwer.

Goodlin-Jones, B. L., Burnham, M. M., Gaylor, E. E., & Anders, T. F. (2001). Night waking, sleep-wake organization, and self-soothing in the first year of life. *Journal of Developmental & Behavioral Pediatrics, 22*, 226–233.

Goodman, G. S., Emery, R. E., & Haugaard, J. J. (1998). Developmental psychology and law: Divorce, child maltreatment, foster care and adoption. In W. Damon (Series ed.) & I. E. Sigel & K. A. Renninger (Vol. eds.), *Handbook of child psychology: Vol. 4. Child psychology in practice* (5th ed., pp. 775–874). Hoboken, NJ: John Wiley & Sons Inc.

Gore, T., & Dubois, R. (1998). The "Back to Sleep" campaign. *Zero To Three, 19*(2), 22–23.

Gorer, G. (1965). *Death, grief, and mourning in contemporary Britain.* London: Cresset Press.

Gothe, K., Oberauer, K., & Kliegl, R. (2008). Age differences in dual-task performance after practice. *Psychology and Aging, 22*(3), 596–606.

Gottlieb, B. H., Still, E., & Newby-Clark, I. R. (2007). Types and precipitants of growth and decline in emerging

adulthood. *Journal of Adolescent Research, 22*(2), 132–155.

Gottman, J. (1994). *Why marriages succeed or fail: And how you can make yours last.* New York: Simon & Schuster.

Gottman, J. M. (1999). *The marriage clinic: A scientifically based marital therapy.* New York: Norton.

Gould, S. J. (1981). *The mismeasure of man.* New York: Norton.

Graber, J. A., Petersen, A. C., & Brooks-Gunn, J. (1996). Pubertal processes: Methods, measures, and models. In J. A. Graber, J. Brooks-Gunn, & A. C. Petersen (Eds.), *Transitions through adolescence: Interpersonal domains and context* (pp. 23–53). Hillsdale, NJ: Erlbaum.

Graham, J. W., & Beller, A. H. (2002). Nonresident fathers and their children: Child support and visitation from an economic perspective. In C. S. Tamis-LeMonda & N. Cabrera (Eds.), *Handbook of father involvement: Multidisciplinary perspectives* (pp. 431–453). Mahwah, NJ: Erlbaum.

Grandmaison, E., & Simard, M. (2003). A critical review of memory stimulation programs in Alzheimer's disease.

Greenfield, G. K., & Kerr, W. C. (2008). Alcohol measurement methodology in epidemiology: Recent advances and opportunities. *Addiction, 103*, 1082–1099.

Greenleaf, C. (2005). Self-objectification among physically active women. *Sex Roles, 52*, 51–62.

Gregory, A. M., Caspi, A., Eley, T. C., Moffitt, T. E., O'Connor, T. G., & Poulton, R. (2005). Prospective longitudinal associations between persistent sleep problems in childhood and anxiety and depression disorders in adulthood. *Journal of Abnormal Child Psychology, 33*, 157–163.

Gregory, A. M., Light-Häusermann, J. H., Rijsdijk, F., & Eley, T. C. (2009). Behavioral genetic analyses of prosocial behavior in adolescents. *Developmental Science, 12*, 165–174.

Grello, C. M., Welsh, D. P., & Harper, M. S. (2006). No strings attached: The nature of casual sex in college students. *The Journal of Sex Research, 43*(3), 255–267.

Grogan-Kaylor, A., & Otis, M. D. (2007). The predictors of parental use of corporal punishment. *Family Relations, 56*, 80–91.

Groopman, J. E. (2004). *The anatomy of hope: How patients prevail in the face of illness.* New York: Random House.

Grossbaum, M. F., & Bates, G. W. (2002). Correlates of psychological well-being at midlife: The role of generativity, agency and communion, and narrative themes. *International Journal of Behavioral Development, 26*, 120–127.

Grossmann, K., Grossmann, K. E., & Kindler, H. (2005). Early care and the roots of attachment and partnership representations: the Bielefeld and Regensburg longitudinal studies. In K. E. Grossmann, K. Grossmann, & E. Waters (Eds.), *Attachment from infancy to adulthood: The major longitudinal studies* (pp. 98–136). New York: Guilford Press.

Grossmann, K. E., Grossmann, K., & Zimmermann, P. (1999). A wider view of attachment and exploration: Stability and change during the years of immaturity. In J. Cassidy & P. R. Shaver (Eds.), *Handbook of attachment: Theory, research, and clinical applications* (pp. 760–786). New York: Guilford Press.

Grotevant, H. D., & Cooper, C. R. (1998). Individuality and connected-ness in adolescent development: Review and prospects for research on identity, relationships, and context. In E. E. A. Skoe & A. L. von der Lippe (Eds.), *Personality development in adolescence: A cross national and life span perspective* (pp. 3–37). New York: Routledge.

Grube, J. W., Bourdeau, B., Fisher, D. A., & Bersamin, M. (2008). *Television exposure and sexuality among adolescents: A longitudinal survey study.* Paper presented at the Biennial Meeting, Society for Research in Adolescence, Chicago, 2008.

Gruenewald, T. L., Karlamangla, A. S., Greendale, G. A., Singer, B. H., & Seeman, T. E. (2007). Feelings of usefulness to others, disability, and mortality in older adults: The MacArthur study of successful aging. *The Journals of Gerontology: Series B: Psychological Sciences and Social Sciences, 62B*(1), 28–37.

Gruenewald, T. L., Karlamangla, A. S., Greendale, G. A., Singer, B. H., & Seeman, T. E. (2009). Increased mortality risk in older adults with persistently low or declining feelings of usefulness to others. *Journal of Aging and Health, 21*, 398–425.

Grühn, D., Scheibe, S., & Baltes, P. B. (2007). Reduced negativity effect in older adults' memory for emotional pictures: The heterogeneity-homogeneity list paradigm. *Psychology and Aging, 22*, 644–649.

Grunier, A., Mor, V., Weitzen, S., Truchil, R., Teno, J., & Roy, J. (2007). Where people die: A multilevel approach to understanding influences on site of death in America. *Medical Care Research and Review, 64* (4), 351–378.

Grzywacz, J. G., & Marks, N. F. (2001). Social inequalities and exercise during adulthood: Toward an ecological perspective. *Journal of Health and Social Behavior, 42,* 202–220.

Guarch, J., Marcos, T., Salamero, M., Gastó, C., & Blesa, R. (2008). Mild cognitive impairment: A risk indicator of later dementia, or a preclinical phase of the disease? *International Journal of Geriatric Psychiatry, 23,* 257–265.

Guendelman, S., Kosa, J. L., Pearl, M., Graham, S., Goodman, J., & Kharrazi, M. (2009). Juggling work and breastfeeding: Effects of maternity leave and occupational characteristics. *Pediatrics, 123,* e38–e46.

Guerrini, I., Thomson, A. D., & Gurling, H. D. (2007). The importance of alcohol misuse, malnutrition and genetic susceptibility on brain growth and plasticity. *Neuroscience and Biobehavioral Reviews, 31,* 212–220.

Gupta, S. (2007). Autonomy, dependence, or display? The relationship between married women's earnings and housework. *Journal of Marriage and Family, 69*(2), 399–417.

Gutman, L. M., & Eccles, J. S. (2007). Stage-environment fit during adolescence: Trajectories of family relations and adolescent outcomes. *Developmental Psychology, 43*(2), 522–537.

Guttmacher Institute. (2006). *State policies in brief: Sex and STD/HIV education.* New York: Author.

Guttmacher Institute. (2007). *Facts on American teens' sexual and reproductive health.* www.guttmacher.org/sections/adolescents.

Ha, J-H. (2008). Changes in support from confidants, children, and friends following widowhood. *Journal of Marriage and Family, 70,* 306–318.

Ha, J-H, & Ingersoll-Dayton, B. (2008). The effect of widowhood on international ambivalence. *Journal of Gerontology: SOCIAL SCIENCES, 63B*(1), S49–S58.

Haan, N., Millsap, R., & Hartka, E. (1986). As time goes by: Change and stability in personality over fifty years. *Psychology and Aging, 1,* 220–232.

Haas, S. A. (2006). Health selection and the process of social stratification: The effect of childhood health on socioeconomic attainment. *Journal of Health and Social Behavior, 47*(4), 339–354.

Hagestad, G. O. (1985). Continuity and connectedness. In V. L. Bengtson & J. F. Robertson (Eds.), *Grandparenthood* (pp. 31–48). Thousand Oaks, CA: Sage.

Hale, T. S., Bookheimer, S., McGough, J., Phillips, J. M., & McCracken. J. Y. (2007). Atypical brain activation during simple and complex levels of processing in adult ADHD. *Journal of Attention Disorders, 11*(2), 125–140.

Hall, A. M., Moore, R. Y., Lopez, O. L., Kuller, L., & Becker, J. T. (2008). Basal forebrain atrophy is a presymptomatic marker for Alzheimer's disease. *Alzheimer's and Dementia, 4*(4), 271–279.

Hall, G. S. (1969). *Adolescence.* New York: Arno Press. (Original work published 1904.)

Halpern-Felsher, B. L., Cornell, J. L., Kropp, R. Y., & Tschann, J. M. (2005). Oral versus vaginal sex among adolescents: Perceptions, attitudes, and behavior. *Pediatrics, 115,* 845–851.

Halrynjo, S. (2009). Men's work-life conflict: Career, care, and self-realization: Patterns of privileges and dilemmas. *Gender, Work, and Organization, 16.*

Hamlin, J. K., Wynn, K., & Bloom, P. (2007). Social evaluation by preverbal infants. *Nature, 450,* 557–559.

Han, S. D., & Bondi, M. W. (2008). Revision of the apolipoprotein E compensatory mechanism recruitment hypothesis. *Alzheimer's and Dementia, 4*(4), 251–254.

Hank, K., & Buber, I. (2009). Grandparents caring for their grandchildren: Findings from the 2004 Survey of Health, Ageing, and Retirement in Europe. *Journal of Family Issues, 30,* 53–73.

Hansen, M., Janssen, I., Schiff, A., Zee, P. C., & Dubocovich, M. L. (2005). The impact of school daily schedule on adolescent sleep. *Pediatrics, 115,* 1555–1561.

Hansen, M., Kurinczuk, J. J., Bower, C., & Webb, S. (2002). The risk of major birth defects after intracytoplasmic sperm injection and in vitro fertilization. *New England Journal of Medicine, 346,* 725–730.

Hardy, M. A. (2002). The transformation of retirement in twentieth-century America: From discontent to satisfaction. *Generations, 26*(2), 9–16.

Hargreaves, D., & Tiggemann, M. (2003). The effect of "thin ideal" television commercials on body dissatisfaction and schema activation during early adolescence. *Journal of Youth and Adolescence, 32,* 367–373.

Harley, K., & Reese, E. (1999). Origins of autobiographical memory. *Developmental Psychology, 35,* 1338–1348.

Harlow, C. M. (Ed.). (1986). *From learning to love: The selected papers of H. F. Harlow.* New York: Praeger.

Harlow, H. F. (1958). The nature of love. *American Psychologist, 13,* 673–685.

Harlow, H. F., Harlow, M. K., Dodsworth, R. O., & Arling, G. L. (1966). Maternal behavior of rhesus monkeys deprived of mothering and peer associations in infancy. *Proceedings of the American Philosophical Society, 110,* 58–66.

Harris, J. R. (1995). Where is the child's environment? A group socialization theory of development. *Psychological Review, 102,* 458–489.

Harris, J. R. (1998). *The nurture assumption: Why children turn out the way they do.* New York: Free Press.

Harris, J. R. (2002). Beyond the nurture assumption: Testing hypotheses about the child's environment. In J. G. Borkowski, S. L. Ramey, & M. Bristol-Power (Eds.), *Parenting and the child's world: Influences on academic, intellectual, and social-emotional development* (pp. 3–20). Mahwah, NJ: Erlbaum.

Harris, J. R. (2006). *No two alike: Human nature and human individuality.* New York, NY: W. W. Norton & Co.

Harrist, A. W., Thompson, S. D., & Norris, D. J. (2007). Defining quality child care: Multiple stakeholder perspectives. *Early Education and Development, 18*(2), 305–336.

Hart, H. M., McAdams, D. P., Hirsch, B. J., & Bauer, J. J. (2001). Generativity and social involvement among African Americans and White adults. *Journal of Research in Personality, 35,* 208–230.

Harter, S. (1981). A new self-report scale of intrinsic versus extrinsic orientation in the classroom: Motivational and informational components. *Developmental Psychology, 17,* 300–312.

Harter, S. (1999). *The construction of the self: A developmental perspective.* New York: Guilford Press.

Harter, S. (2006). Developmental and individual difference perspectives on self-esteem. In D. K. Mroczek, & T. D. Little (Eds.), *Handbook of personality development* (pp. 311–334). Mahwah, NJ: Lawrence Erlbaum Associates Publishers.

Harter, S., & Pike, R. (1984). The Pictorial Scale of Perceived Competence and Social Acceptance for Young Children. *Child Development, 55,* 1969–1982.

Hartup, W. W., & Stevens, N. (1997). Friendships and adaptation in the life course. *Psychological Bulletin, 121,* 355–370.

Hasher, L., & Zacks, R. T. (1988). Working memory, comprehension, and aging: A review and a new view. In G. H. Bower (Ed.), *Advances in research and theory: Vol. 22. The psychology of learning and motivation* (pp. 193–225). San Diego, CA: Academic Press.

Hauck, Y., Hall, W. A., & Jones, C. (2007). Prevalence, self-efficacy and perceptions of conflicting advice and self-management: Effects of a breastfeeding journal. *Journal of Advanced Nursing, 57*(3), 306–317.

Hawkins, N. A., Ditto, P. H., Danks, J. H., & Smucker, W. D. (2005). Micromanaging death: Process preferences, values, and goals in end-of-life medical decision making. *Gerontologist, 45,* 107–117.

Hawley, P. H., Johnson, S. E., Mize, J. A., & McNamara, K. A. (2007). Physical attractiveness in preschoolers: Relationships with power, status, aggression, and social skills. *Journal of School Psychology, 45,* 499–521.

Hawley, P. H., Little, T. D., & Card, N. A. (2008). The myth of the alpha male: A new look at dominance-related beliefs and behaviors among adolescent males and females. *International Journal of Behavioral Development, 32*(1), 76–88.

Hay, D. F. (2007). The gradual emergence of sex differences in aggression: alternative hypotheses. *Psychological Medicine, 37,* 1527–1537.

Hayslip, B., Jr., & Hansson, R. O. (2003). Death awareness and adjustment across the life span. In C. D. Bryant (Ed.), *Handbook of death & dying* (pp. 437–447). Thousand Oaks, CA: Sage.

Hayslip, B., Jr., & Patrick, J. H. (Eds.). (2003). *Working with custodial grandparents.* New York: Springer.

Hazan, C., & Shaver, P. (1987). Romantic love conceptualized as an attachment process. *Journal of Personality and Social Psychology, 52,* 511–524.

Head, D., Rodrigue, K. M., Kennedy, K. M., & Raz, N. (2008). Neuroanatomical and cognitive mediators of age-related differences in episodic memory. *Neuropsychology, 22*(4), 491–507.

HealthLink. (2002). Bad news about hormone replacement therapy. Retrieved September 24, 2006, from

Medical College of Wisconsin Web site: http://healthlink.mcw.edu/article/1025191125.html

Heatherington, L., & Lavner, J. A. (2008). Coming to terms with coming out: Review and recommendations for family systems-focused research. *Journal of Family Psychology, 22*(3), 329–343.

Heaven, P. C. L., Ciarrochi, J., & Vialle, W. (2008). Self-nominated peer crowds, school achievement, and psychological adjustment in adolescents: Longitudinal analysis. *Personality and Individual Differences, 44,* 977–988.

Heckhausen, J., Chang, E. S., & Chen, E. (2007). *Optimistic goal selection and control striving during the transition after high school.* Unpublished manuscript, University of California, Irvine.

Heimann, M., Strid, K., Smith, L., Tjus, T., Ulvund, S. E., & Meltzoff, A. N. (2006). Exploring the relation between memory, gestural communication, and the emergence of language in infancy: A longitudinal study. *Infant and Child Development, 15,* 233–49.

Heine, S. J., & Hamamura, T. (2007). In search of East Asian self-enhancement. *Personality and Social Psychology Review, 11,* 1–24.

Helson, R., Jones, C., & Kwan, V. S. Y. (2002). Personality change over 40 years of adulthood: Hierarchical linear modeling analyses of two longitudinal samples. *Journal of Personality and Social Psychology, 83,* 752–766.

Helson, R., & Roberts, B. W. (1994). Ego development and personality change in adulthood. *Journal of Personality and Social Psychology, 66,* 911–920.

Helson, R., & Soto, C. J. (2005). Up and down in middle age: Monotonic and nonmonotonic changes in roles, status, and personality. *Journal of Personality and Social Psychology, 89*(2), 194–204.

Henderson, T. L. (2005). Grandparent visitation rights: Successful acquisition of court-ordered visitation. *Journal of Family Issues, 26,* 107–137.

Hendin, H. (1994, December 16). Scared to death of dying [Op-Ed]. *New York Times,* p. A19.

Heron, M. P., Hoyert, D. L., Murphy, S. L., Xu, J. Q., Kochanek, K. D., & Tejuda-Vera, B. (2009). *Deaths: Final Data for 2006.* National vital statistics reports, vol.57, no. 14. Hyattsville, MD: National Center for Health Statistics, retrieved. August 14, 2009.

Herrnstein, R. J., & Murray, C. A. (1994). *The bell curve: Intelligence and class structure in American life.* New York: Free Press.

Hertzog, C. (1996). Research design in studies of aging and cognition. In J. E. Birren, K. W. Schaie, R. P. Abeles, M. Gatz, & T. A. Salthouse (Eds.), *Handbook of the psychology of aging* (4th ed., pp. 24–37). San Diego, CA: Academic Press.

Hetherington, E. M. (1999). *Coping with divorce, single parenting, and remarriage: A risk and resiliency perspective.* Mahwah, NJ: Erlbaum.

Hetherington, E. M., & Kelly, J. (2002). *For better or for worse: Divorce reconsidered.* New York: Norton.

Hickman, S. E., Tilden, V. P., & Tolle, S. W. (2004). Family perceptions of worry, symptoms, and suffering in the dying. *Journal of Palliative Care, 20,* 20–27.

Hicks, A. M., & Diamond, L. M. (2008). How was your day? Couples' affect when telling and hearing daily events. *Personal Relationships, 15,* 205–228.

Hietanen, A., Era, P., Sorri, M., & Heikkinen, E. (2004). Changes in hearing in 80-year-old people: A 10-year follow-up study. *International Journal of Audiology, 43,* 126–135.

Hildén, H. M., Louhiala, P., & Palo, J. (2004). End of life decisions: Attitudes of Finnish physicians. *Journal of Medical Ethics, 30,* 362–365.

Hillman, J. (2008). Sexual issues and aging within the context of work with older adult patients. *Professional Psychology: Research and Practice, 39*(3), 290–297.

Hinde, R. A. (2005). Ethology and attachment theory. In K. E. Grossmann, K. Grossmann, & E. Waters (Eds.), *Attachment from infancy to adulthood: The major longitudinal studies* (pp. 1–12). New York: Guilford Press.

Hinduja, S., & Patchin, J. W. (2008). Cyberbullying: An exploratory analysis of factors related to offending and victimization. *Deviant Behavior, 29,* 129–156.

Hirsh-Pasek, K., & Golinkoff, R. M. (1991). Language comprehension: A new look at some old themes. In N. A. Krasnegor, D. M. Rumbaugh, R. L. Schiefelbusch, & M. Studdert-Kennedy (Eds.), *Biological and behavioral determinants of language development* (pp. 301–320). Hillsdale, NJ: Erlbaum.

Hla, M. M., Novotny, R., Kieffer, E. C., Mor, J., & Thiele, M. (2003). Early weaning among Japanese women in Hawaii. *Journal of Biosocial Science, 35,* 227–241.

Hodgson, L. G. (1992). Adult grandchildren and their grandparents: Their enduring bond. *International*

Journal of Aging & Human Development, 34, 209–225.

Hoff-Ginsberg, E. (1997). *Language development.* Belmont, CA: Brooks/Cole.

Hoffman, M. L. (1994). Discipline and internalization. *Developmental Psychology, 30,* 26–28.

Hoffman, M. L. (2001). Toward a comprehensive empathy-based theory of pro-social moral development. In A. C. Bohart & D. J. Stipek (Eds.), *Constructive & destructive behavior: Implications for family, school, & society* (pp. 61–86). Washington, DC: American Psychological Association.

Hofstede, G. (1981). Cultures and organizations. *International Studies of Management and Organization, 10(4),* 15–41.

Hofstede, G. (2001). *Culture's consequences: Comparing values, behaviors, institutions, and organizations across nations* (2nd ed.). Thousand Oaks, CA: Sage.

Holmes, T. H., & Rahe, R. H. (1967). The social readjustment rating scale. *Journal of Psychosomatic Research, 11,* 213–218.

Hopper, J. (1993). The rhetoric of motives in divorce. *Journal of Marriage & the Family, 55,* 801–813.

Houts, R. M., Barnett-Walker, K. C., Paley, B., & Cox, M. J. (2008). Patterns of couple interaction during the transition to parenthood. *Personal Relationships, 15,* 103–122.

Hrdy, S. B. (1999). *Mother nature: A history of mothers, infants, and natural selection.* New York: Pantheon Books.

Hu, S., & Kuh, G. D. (2003). Diversity experiences and college student learning and personal development. *Journal of College Student Development, 44,* 320–334.

Huddleston, J., & Ge, X. (2003). Boys at puberty: Psychosocial implications. In C. Hayward (Ed.), *Gender differences at puberty* (pp. 113–134). New York: Cambridge University Press.

Hughes, C., & Ensor, R. (2007). Executive function and theory of mind: Predictive relations from ages 2 to 4. *Developmental Psychology, 43(6),* 1447–1459.

Hungerford, T. L. (2003). Is there an American way of aging? Income dynamics of the elderly in the United States and Germany. *Research on Aging, 25,* 435–455.

Hungerford, T. L. (2007). The persistence of hardship over the life course. *Research on Aging, 29,* 491–511.

Hunt, C. E. (2005). Gene-environment interactions: Implications for sudden unexpected deaths in infancy. *Archives of Disease in Childhood, 90,* 48–53.

Hunt, C. K. (2003). Concepts in caregiver research. *Journal of Nursing Scholarship, 35,* 27–32.

Hunter, J. P., & Csikszentmihalyi, M. (2003). The positive psychology of interested adolescents. *Journal of Youth and Adolescence, 32,* 27–35.

Huttenlocher, J., Vasilyeva, M., Waterfall, H. R., Vevea, J. L., & Hedges, L. V. (2007). The varieties of speech to young children. *Developmental Psychology, 43(5),* 1062–1083.

Huttenlocher, P. R. (2002). *Neural plasticity: The effects of environment on the development of the cerebral cortex.* Cambridge, MA: Harvard University Press.

Hvas, L. (2001). Positive aspects of menopause: A qualitative study. *Maturitas, 39,* 11–17.

Iecovich, E. (2008). Caregiver burden, community services, and quality of life of primary caregivers of frail elderly persons. *Journal of Applied Gerontology, 27(3),* 309–330.

Innes, S., & Payne, S. (2009). Advanced cancer patients' prognostic information preferences: A review. *Palliative Medicine, 23,* 29–39.

Ireland, T. O., & Smith, C. A. (2009). Living in partner-violent families: Developmental links to antisocial behavior and relationship violence. *Journal of Youth and Adolescence, 38,* 323–339.

Isaacs, S. L., & Schroeder, S. A. (2004). Class—The ignored determinant of the nation's health. *New England Journal of Medicine, 351,* 1137–1142.

Islam, M. K., & Gerdtham, U.-G. (2006). *The costs of maternal-newborn illness and mortality.* Geneva, Switzerland: World Health Organization.

Ito, M., & Sharts-Hopko, N. C. (2002). Japanese women's experience of childbirth in the United States. *Health Care for Women International, 23,* 666–677.

Jackson, T., & Chen, H. (2008). Predicting changes in eating disorder symptoms among Chinese adolescents: A 9-month prospective study. *Journal of Psychosomatic Research, 64,* 87–95.

Jacobson, J. L., & Jacobson, S. W. (1994). Prenatal alcohol exposure and neurobehavioral development: Where is the threshold? *Alcohol Health & Research World, 18,* 30–36.

Jaffee, S. A., Caspi, A., Moffitt, T. E., Polo-Tomas, M., & Taylor, A. (2007). Individual, family, and neighborhood factors distinguish resilient from non-resilient maltreated children: A cumulative stressors model. *Child Abuse & Neglect, 31,* 231–253.

Jen, M. H., Jones, K., & Johnston R. (2009). Global variations in health: Evaluating Wilkinson's income inequality hypothesis using the World Values Survey. *Social Science & Medicine. 68,* 643–653.

Jenkins, J. M., & Astington, J. W. (2000). Theory of mind and social behavior: Causal models tested in a longitudinal study. *Merrill-Palmer Quarterly, 46,* 203–220.

Jenkins, J. M., Turrell, S. L., Kogushi, Y., Lollis, S., & Ross, H. S. (2003). A longitudinal investigation of the dynamics of mental state talk in families. *Child Development, 74,* 905–920.

Jenson, W. R., Olympia, D., Farley, M., & Clark, E. (2004). Positive psychology and externalizing students in a sea of negativity. *Psychology in the Schools, 41,* 67–79.

Jesse, D. E., Schoneboom, C., & Blanchard, A. (2007). The effect of faith or spirituality in pregnancy: a content analysis. *Journal of Holistic Nursing, 25(3),* 159.

Jette, A. M., Assmann, S. F., Rooks, D., Harris, B. A., & Crawford, S. (1998). Interrelationships among disablement concepts. *Journals of Gerontology: Series A: Biological Sciences and Medical Sciences, 53A,* M395–M404.

Joesch, J. M., Gossman, G. L., & Tanfer, K. (2008). Primary cesarean deliveries prior to labor in the United States, 1979–2004. *Maternal Child Health Journal, 12,* 323–331.

Johansson, K., Josephsson, S., & Lilja, M. (2009). Creating possibilities for action in the presence of environmental barriers in the process of 'ageing in place.' *Ageing & Society, 29,* 49–70.

Johnson, B., & Chavkin, W. (2007). Policy efforts to prevent ART-related preterm birth. *Maternal Child Health Journal, 11,* 219–225.

Johnson, F., & Wardle, J. (2005). Dietary restraint, body dissatisfaction, and psychological distress: A prospective analysis. *Journal of Abnormal Psychology, 114,* 119–125.

Johnson, K. A., & Tyler, K. A. (2007). Adolescent sexual onset: An intergenerational analysis. *Journal of Youth Adolescence, 36,* 939–949.

Johnson, M. H. (2001). Functional brain development during infancy. In G. Bremner & A. Fogel (eds.), *Blackwell handbook of infant development* (pp. 169–190). Malden, MA: Blackwell.

Johnson, R. W. (2009), Employment opportunities at older ages: Introduction to the special issue. *Research on Aging, 31,* 3–16.

Johnson, W., Hicks, B. M., McGue, M., & Iacono, W. G. (2007). Most of the girls are alright, but some aren't: Personality trajectory groups from ages 14 to 24 and some associations with outcomes. *Journal of Personality and Social Psychology, 93*(2), 266–284.

Johnston, C., Hommerson, P., & Seipp, C. M. (2009). Maternal attributions and child oppositional behavior: A longitudinal study of boys with and without attention-deficit/hyperactivity disorder. *Journal of Consulting and Clinical Psychology, 77,* 189–195.

Johnston, L. D., O'Malley, P. M., Bachman, J. G., & Schulenberg, J. E. (2009). *Monitoring the future national results on adolescent drug use: Overview of key findings, 2008* (NIH Publication No. 09-7401). Bethesda, MD: National Institute on Drug Abuse, 73 pp.

Johri, M., Beland, F., & Bergman, H. (2003). International experiments in integrated care for the elderly: A synthesis of the evidence. *International Journal of Geriatric Psychiatry, 18,* 222–235.

Jokela, M., Kivimaki, M., Elovainio, M., & Keltikangas-Jarvinen, L. (2009). Personality and having children: A two-way relationship. *Journal of Personality and Social Psychology, 96,* 218–230.

Joussemet, M., Vitaro, F., Barker, E. D., Côté, S., Nagin, D. S., Zoccolillo, M., Tremblay, R. E. (2008). Controlling parenting and physical aggression during elementary school. *Child Development, 79,* 411–425.

Judge, T. A., Heller, D., & Klinger, R. (2008). The dispositional sources of job satisfaction: A comparative test. *Applied Psychology: An International Review, 57*(3), 361–372.

Judge, T. A., & Hurst, C. (2007). Capitalizing on one's advantages: Role of core self-evaluations. *Journal of Applied Psychology, 92*(5), 1212–1227.

Jung, C. G. (1933). *Modern man in search of a soul.* Oxford, England: Harcourt.

Kabir, Z. N., Tishelman, C., Agüero-Torres, H., Chowdhury, A. M. R.,

Winblad, B., & Höjer, B. (2003). Gender and rural-urban differences in reported health status by older people in Bangladesh. *Archives of Gerontology and Geriatrics, 37,* 77–91.

Kacela, X. (2004). Religious maturity in the midst of death and dying. *American Journal of Hospice & Palliative Care, 21,* 203–208.

Kagan, J. (1984). *The nature of the child.* New York: Basic Books.

Kagan, J. (1994). *Galen's prophecy: Temperament in human nature.* New York: Basic Books.

Kagan, J. (1998). *Galen's prophecy: Temperament in human nature.* Boulder, CO: Westview Press.

Kaitz, M. (2007). Maternal concerns during early parenthood. *Child: Care, Health and Development, 33*(6), 720–727.

Kaltiala-Heino, R., Kosunen, E., & Rimpela, M. (2003). Pubertal timing, sexual behaviour and self-reported depression in middle adolescence. *Journal of Adolescence, 26,* 531–545.

Kane, R. A. (1995–1996). Transforming care institutions for the frail elderly: Out of one shall be many. *Generations, 14*(4), 62–68.

Kannai, R. (2008). Zohara. *Patient Education and Counseling, 71,* 145–147.

Kaplowitz, P. B. (2008). Link between body fat and the timing of puberty. *Pediatrics, 121*(3), S208–217.

Karen, R. (1998). *Becoming attached: First relationships and how they shape our capacity to love.* London: Oxford University Press.

Karns, J. T. (2001). Health, nutrition, and safety. In G. Bremner & A. Fogel (Eds.), *Blackwell handbook of infant development* (pp. 693–725). Malden, MA: Blackwell.

Karraker, K. H., & Young, M. (2007). Night waking in 6-month-old infants and maternal depressive symptoms. *Journal of Applied Developmental Psychology, 28*(5–6), 493–498.

Kasl-Godley, J., & Gatz, M. (2000). Psychosocial intervention for individuals with dementia: An intergration of theory, therapy, and a clinical understanding of dementia. *Clinical Psychology Review, 20,* 755–782.

Kastenbaum, R. (2004). *On our way: The final passage through life and death.* Berkeley, CA: University of California Press.

Kato, K., & Pedersen, N. L. (2005). Personality and coping: A study of twins

reared apart and twins reared together. *Behavior Genetics, 35,* 147–158.

Kaufman, A. S. (2001). WAIS-III IQs, Horn's theory, and generational changes from young adulthood to old age. *Intelligence, 29,* 131–167.

Kawarabayashi, T., & Shoji, M. (2008). Plasma biomarkers of Alzheimer's disease. *Current Opinion in Psychiatry, 21,* 260–267.

Keefe, M. R., Karlsen, K. A., Lobo, M. L., Kotzer, A. M., & Dudley, W. N. (2006). Reducing parenting stress in families with irritable infants. *Nursing Research, 55*(3), 198–205.

Keel, P. K., Baxter, M. G., Heatherton, T. F., & Joiner, T. E. (2007). A 20-year longitudinal study of body weight, dieting, and eating disorder symptoms. *Journal of Abnormal Psychology, 116*(2), 422–432.

Keeton, C. P., Perry-Jenkins, M., & Sayer, A. G. (2008). Sense of control predicts depressive and anxious symptoms across the transition to parenthood. *Journal of Family Psychology, 22,* 212–221.

Keller, H., Abels, M., Borke, J., Lamm, B., Lo, W., Su, Y., Wang, Y., & Lo, W. (2007). Socialization environments of Chinese and Euro-American middle-class babies: Parenting behaviors, verbal discourses, and ethnotheories. *International Journal of Behavioral Development, 31,* 210–217.

Keller, M. A., & Goldberg, W. A. (2004). Co-sleeping: Help or hindrance for young children's independence? *Infant and Child Development, 13,* 369–388.

Kelley, S. J., & Whitley, D. M. (2003). Psychological distress and physical health problems in grandparents raising grandchildren: Development of an empirically-based intervention model. In B. Hayslip, Jr. & J. H. Patrick (Eds.), *Working with custodial grandparents* (pp. 127–144). New York: Springer.

Kellman, P. J., & Banks, M. S. (1998). Infant visual perception. In W. Damon (Series ed.) & D. Kuhn & R. S. Siegler (Vol. eds.), *Handbook of child psychology: Volume 2: Cognition, perception, and language* (pp. 103–146). Hoboken, NJ: John Wiley & Sons Inc.

Kelly, D. J., Quinn, P. C., Slater, A. M., Lee, K., Ge, L., & Pascalis, O. (2007). The other-race effect develops during infancy: Evidence of perceptual narrowing. *Psychological Science, 18*(12), 1084–1089.

Kelly, J. B. (2000). Children's adjustment in conflicted marriage and divorce: A decade review of research. *Journal of the American Academy of Child & Adolescent Psychiatry, 39,* 963–973.

Kelly, J. B. (2003). Changing perspectives on children's adjustment following divorce: A view from the United States. *Childhood: A Global Journal of Child Research, 10,* 237–254.

Kemper, S., & Mitzner, T. L. (2001). Language production and comprehension. In J. E. Birren & K. W. Schaie (Eds.), *Handbook of the psychology of aging* (5th ed., pp. 378–398). San Diego, CA: Academic Press.

Kenrick, D. T., Groth, G. E., Trost, M. R., & Sadalla, E. K. (1993). Integrating evolutionary and social exchange perspectives on relationships: Effects of gender, self-appraisal, and involvement level on mate selection criteria. *Journal of Personality and Social Psychology, 64,* 951–969.

Kensinger, E. A., Krendl, A. C., & Corkin, S. (2006). Memories of an emotional and a nonemotional event: Effects of aging and delay interval. *Experimental Aging Research, 32,* 23–45.

Kerckhoff, A. C. (2002). The transition from school to work. In J. T. Mortimer & R. W. Larson (Eds.), *The changing adolescent experience: Societal trends and the transition to adulthood* (pp. 52–87). New York: Cambridge University Press.

Keys, C. L. (2007). Promoting and protecting mental health as flourishing: A complementary strategy for improving national mental health. *American Psychologist, 61,* 95–108.

Khachaturian, Z. S., Petersen, R. C., Gauthier, S., Buckholtz, N., Corey-Bloom, J. P., Evans, B., Fillit, H., Foster, N., Greenberg, B., Grundman, M., Sano, M., Simpkins, J., Schneider, L. S., Weiner, M. W., Galasko, D., Hyman, B., Kuller, L., Schenk, D., Snyder, S., Thomas, R. G., Tuszynski, M. H., Vellas, B., Wurtman, R. J., Snyder, P. J., Frank, R. A., Albert, M., Doody, R., Ferris, S., Kaye, J., Koo, E., Morrison-Bogorad, M., Reisberg, B., Salmon, D. P., Gilman, S., Mohs, R., Aisen, P. S., Breitner, J. C. S., Cummings, J. L., Kawas, C., Phelps, C., Poirier, J., Sabbagh, M., Touchon, J., Khachaturian, A. S., & Bain, L. J. (2008). A roadmap for the prevention of dementia: The inaugural Leon Thal Symposium. *Alzheimer's & Dementia, 4,* 156–163.

Kiang, L., & Fuligni, A. J. (2009). Ethnic identity and family processes among adolescents from Latin American, Asian, and European backgrounds. *Journal of Youth and Adolescence, 38,* 228–241.

Kiernan, K. (2002). Cohabitation in Western Europe: Trends, issues, and implications. In A. Booth & A. C. Crouter (Eds.), *Just living together: Implications of cohabitation on families, children, and social policy* (pp. 3–31). Mahwah, NJ: Erlbaum.

Kiernan, K. (2004). Redrawing the boundaries of marriage. *Journal of Marriage and Family, 66,* 980–987.

King, V., Silverstein, M., Elder, G. H., Bengtson, V. L., & Conger, R. D. (2003). Relations with grandparents: Rural midwest versus urban Southern California. *Journal of Family Issues, 24,* 1044–1069.

Kinsella, K., & Velkoff, V. A. (2001). *An aging world: 2001* (Series P95/01-1). Washington, DC: U.S. Census Bureau.

Kinsley, C. H., & Lambert, K. G. (2008). Reproduction-induced neuroplasticity: Natural behavioural and neuronal alterations associated with the production and care of offspring. *Journal of Neuroendocrinology. 20*(4), 515–525.

Kisilevsky, B. S., Muir, D. W., & Low, J. A. (1992). Maturation of human fetal responses to vibroacoustic stimulation. *Child Development, 63,* 1497–1508.

Kitahara, M. (1989). Childhood in Japanese culture. *Journal of Psychohistory, 17,* 43–72.

Kitzinger, S. (2000). *Rediscovering birth.* New York: Pocket Books.

Klass, D., & Walter, T. (2001). Processes of grieving: How bonds are continued. In M. S. Stroebe, R. O. Hansson, W. Stroebe, & H. Schut (Eds.), *Handbook of bereavement research: Consequences, coping, and care* (1st ed., pp. 431–448). Washington, DC: American Psychological Association.

Klein, J. D., & Committee on Adolescence. (2005). Adolescent pregnancy: Current trends and issues. *Pediatrics, 116,* 281–286.

Klonoff, E. A. (2009). Disparities in the provision of medical care: An outcome in search of an explanation. *Journal of Behavioral Medicine, 32,* 48–63.

Klusmann, D. (2002). Sexual motivation and the duration of partnership. *Archives of Sexual Behavior, 31,* 275–287.

Kluwer, E. S., & Johnson, M. D. (2007). Conflict frequency and relationship quality across the transition to parenthood. *Journal of Marriage and Family, 69*(5), 1089–1106.

Knafo, A., & Plomin, R. (2006). Prosocial behavior from early to middle childhood: Genetic and environmental influences on stability and change. *Developmental Psychology, 42*(5), 771–786.

Knoester, C., Petts, R. J., & Eggebeen, D. J. (2007). Commitments to fathering and the well-being and social participation of new, disadvantaged fathers. *Journal of Marriage and Family, 69*(4), 991–1004.

Kochanska, G., Barry, R. A., Aksan, N., & Boldt, L. J. (2008). A developmental model of maternal and child contributions to disruptive conducts: The first six years. *The Journal of Child Psychology and Psychiatry, 49,* 1220–1227.

Kochanska, G., & Coy, K. C. (2002). Child emotionality and maternal responsiveness as predictors of reunion behaviors in the Strange Situation: Links mediated and unmediated by separation distress. *Child Development, 73,* 228–240.

Kochanska, G., Coy, K. C., & Murray, K. T. (2001). The development of self-regulation in the first four years of life. *Child Development, 72,* 1091–1111.

Kochanska, G., & Knaack, A. (2003). Effortful control as a personality characteristic of young children: Antecedents, correlates, and consequences. *Journal of Personality, 71,* 1087–1112.

Kohlberg, L. (1966). Moral education in the schools: A developmental view. *School Review, 74,* 1–30.

Kohlberg, L. (1981). *The meaning and measurement of moral development.* Worcester, MA: Clark University Press.

Kohlberg, L. (1984). *The psychology of moral development: The nature and validity of moral stages.* San Francisco: Harper & Row.

Kono, A., Kai, I., Sakato, C., & Rubenstien, L. Z. (2007). Frequency of going outdoors predicts long-range functional change among ambulatory frail elders living at home. *Archives of Gerontology and Geriatrics, 45,* 233–242.

Kosir, K., & Pecjak, S. (2005). Sociometry as a method for investigating peer relationships: What does it actually measure? *Educational Research, 47,* 127–144.

Kovács, Á. M. (2009). Early bilingualism enhances mechanisms of false-belief reasoning. *Developmental Science, 12*(1), 45–54.

Kozol, J. (1988). *Rachel and her children: Homeless families in America.* New York: Crown.

Kozol, J. (2005). *The shame of the nation: The restoration of apartheid schooling in America.* New York: Crown.

Kramer, B. J., & Thompson, E. H. (2002). *Men as caregivers: Theory, research, and service implications.* New York: Springer.

Krampe, R. T., & Baltes, P. B. (2003). Intelligence as adaptive resource development and resource allocation: A new look through the lenses of SOC and expertise. In R. J. Sternberg & E. L. Grigorenko (Eds.), *The psychology of abilities, competencies, and expertise* (pp. 31–68). New York: Cambridge University Press.

Krause, N. (2007). Longitudinal study of social support and meaning in life. *Psychology and Aging, 22*(3), 456–469.

Krause, N., & Shaw, B. A. (2003). Role-specific control, personal meaning, and health in late life. *Research on Aging, 25*(6), 559–586.

Kreader, J. L., Ferguson, D., & Lawrence, S. (2005). *Infant and Toddler Child Care Arrangements.* National Center for Children in Poverty, Columbia University Mailman School of Public Health.

Kreicbergs, U., Valdimarsdóttir, U., Onelöv, E., Henter, J.-I., & Steineck, G. (2004). Talking about death with children who have severe malignant disease. *New England Journal of Medicine, 351,* 1175–1186.

Krieger, N., Chen, J. T., Waterman, P. D., Hartman, C., Stoddard, A. M., Quinn, M. M., Sorensen, G., Barbeau, E. M. (2008). The inverse hazard law: Blood pressure, sexual harassment, racial discrimination, workplace abuse and occupational exposures in US low-income black, white, and Latino workers. *Social Science & Medicine, 67,* 1970–1981.

Kroger, J. (2000). *Identity development: Adolescence through adulthood.* Thousand Oaks, CA: Sage.

Krumm, J. (2002). Genetic discrimination: Why Congress must ban genetic testing in the workplace. *Journal of Legal Medicine, 23,* 491–521.

Krumrei, E., Coit, C., Martin, S., Fogo, W., & Mahoney, A. (2007). Post-divorce adjustment and social relationships: A meta-analytic review. *Journal of Divorce & Remarriage, 46*(3/4), 145–166.

Kübler-Ross, E. (1969). *On death and dying.* New York: Macmillan.

Kuhn, D. (1989). Children and adults as intuitive scientists. *Psychological Review, 96,* 674–689.

Kulik, L. (2007). Contemporary midlife grandparenthood. In V. Muhlbauer, & J. C. Chrisler (Eds.), *Women over 50: Psychological perspectives* (pp. 131–146).

New York, NY: Springer Science + Business Media.

Kunkel, C. D. (2009). Schooling built on the multiple intelligences. *School Administrator, 66,* 24–25.

Kurtines, W. M., Montgomery, M. J., Ferrer-Wreder, L., Berman, S. L., Lorente, C. C., & Silverman, W. K. (2008). Promoting positive youth development: Implications for future directions in developmental theory methods, and research. *Journal of Adolescent Research, 23,* 359–378.

Kvaavik, E., Klepp, K., Tell, G. S., Meyer, H. E., & Batty, G. D. (2009). Physical fitness and physical activity at age 13 years as predictors of cardiovascular disease risk factors at ages 15, 25, 33, and 40 years: Extended follow-up of the Oslo youth study. *Pediatrics, 123,* e80–e86.

Kvavilashvili, L., & Fisher, L. (2007). Is time-based prospective remembering mediated by self-initiated rehearsals? Role of incidental cues, ongoing activity, age, and motivation. *Journal of Experimental Psychology: General, 136*(1), 112–132.

Laakkonen, M.-L., Pitkälä, K. H., Strandberg, T. E., Berglind, S., & Tilvis, R. S. (2004). Living will, resuscitation preferences, and attitudes towards life in an aged population. *Gerontology, 50,* 247–254.

Laakkonen, M.-L., Raivio, M. M., Eloniemi-Sulkava, U., Saarenheimo, M., Pietilä, M., Tilvis, R. S., & Pitkälä, K. H. (2008). How do elderly spouse care givers of people with Alzheimer's disease experience the disclosure of dementia diagnosis and subsequent care? *Journal of Medical Ethics, 34,* 427–430.

Labouvie-Vief, G. (1992). A neo-Piagetian perspective on adult cognitive development. In R. J. Sternberg & C. A. Berg (Eds.), *Intellectual development* (pp. 197–228). New York: Cambridge University Press.

Labouvie-Vief, G. (2006). Emerging structures of adult thought. In J. J. Arnett & J. L. Tanner (Eds.), *Emerging adults in America: Coming of age in the 21st century* (pp. 59–84). Washington, DC: American Psychological Association. xxii, 340 pp.

Lachman, M. E. (2004). Development in midlife. *Annual Review of Psychology, 55,* 305–331.

Ladd, G. W., Herald-Brown, S. L., & Reiser, M. (2008). Does chronic classroom peer rejection predict the development of children's classroom participation during the grade school

years? *Child Development, 79,* 1001–1015.

Lafont, S., Laumon, B., Helmer, C., Dartigues, J., & Fabrigoule, C. (2008). Driving cessation and self-reported car crashes in older drivers: The impact of cognitive impairment and dementia in population-based study. *Journal of Geriatric Psychiatry and Neurology, 21,* 171–182.

Laible, D. J. (2004). Mother-child discourse surrounding a child's past behavior at 30 months: Links to emotional understanding and early conscience development at 36 months. *Merrill-Palmer Quarterly, 50,* 159–180.

Lamb, M. E. (1986). The changing role of fathers. In M. E. Lamb (Ed.), *The father's role: Applied perspectives* (pp. 3–27). New York: John Wiley & Sons Inc.

Lamb, M. E. (1997). *The role of the father in child development* (3rd ed.). Hoboken, NJ: John Wiley & Sons Inc.

Lamb, M. E. (2002). Infant-father attachments and their impact on child development. In C. S. Tamis-LeMonda & N. Cabrera (Eds.), *Handbook of father involvement: Multidisciplinary perspectives* (pp. 93–117). Mahwah, NJ: Erlbaum.

Lambert, S., Sampaio, E., Mauss, Y., & Scheiber, C. (2004). Blindness and brain plasticity: Contribution of mental imagery? An fMRI study. *Cognitive Brain Research, 20,* 1–11.

Lamerz, A., Kuepper-Nybelen, J., Wehle, C., Bruning, N., Trost-Brinkhues, G., Brenner, H., Hebebrand, J., & Herpertz-Dahlmann, B. (2005). Social class, parental education, and obesity prevalence in a study of six-year-old children in Germany. *International Journal of Obesity, 29,* 373–380.

Langa, K. M., Foster, N. L., & Larson, E. B. (2004). Mixed dementia: Emerging concepts and therapeutic implications. *Journal of the American Medical Association, 292,* 2901–2908.

Lanz, M., & Tagliabue, S. (2007). Do I really need someone in order to become an adult? Romantic relationships during emerging adulthood in Italy. *Journal of Adolescent Research, 22*(5), 531–549.

Larsen, L., Hartmann, P., & Nyborg, H. (2007). The stability of general intelligence from early adulthood to middle age. *Intelligence, 36*(1), 29–34.

Larsen, R. E., & Prizmic, Z. (2008). Regulation of emotional well-being: Overcoming the hedonic treadmill. In M. Eid, & R. J. Larsen (Eds.), *The Science of subjective well-being*

(258–289). New York: The Guilford Press.

LaRusso, M. D., Romer, D., & Selman, R. L. (2008). Teachers as builders of respectful school climates: Implications for adolescent drug use norms and depressive symptoms in high school. *Journal of Youth Adolescence, 37,* 386–398.

Larzelere, R. E., & Kuhn, B. R. (2005). Comparing child outcomes of physical punishment and alternative disciplinary tactics: A meta-analysis. *Clinical Child and Family Psychology Review, 8,* 1–37.

Latz, S., Wolf, A. W., & Lozoff, B. (1999). Cosleeping in context: Sleep practices and problems in young children in Japan and the United States. *Archives of Pediatrics & Adolescent Medicine, 153,* 339–346.

Laursen, B., & Collins, W. A. (1994). Interpersonal conflict during adolescence. *Psychological Bulletin, 115,* 197–209.

Lawrence, E., Rothman, A. D., Cobb, R. J., Rothman, M. T., & Bradbury, T. N. (2008). Marital satisfaction across the transition to parenthood. *Journal of Family Psychology, 22*(1), 41–50.

Lawson, M. A. (2003). School-family relations in context: Parent and teacher perceptions of parent involvement. *Urban Education, 38,* 77–133.

Leavitt, J. W. (1986). *Brought to bed: Childbearing in America, 1750 to 1950.* New York: Oxford University Press.

Lecanuet, J. P., Graniere-Deferre, C., Jacquet, A. Y., & DeCasper, A. J. (2000). Fetal discrimination of low-pitched musical notes. *Developmental Psychobiology, 36,* 29–39.

LeClere, F. B., & Wilson, J. B. (1997). *Advance data from vital and health statistics: No. 288. Smoking behavior of recent mothers, 18–44 years of age, before and after pregnancy: United States, 1990* (PHS 97-1250). Hyattsville, MD: National Center for Health Statistics.

Lee, B. J., & Mackey-Bilaver, L. (2007). Effects of WIC and food stamp program participation on child outcomes. *Children and Youth Services Review, 29*(4), 501–517.

Lee, C., & Gramotnev, H. (2007). Life transitions and mental health in a national cohort of young Australian women. *Developmental Psychology, 43*(4), 877–888.

Lee, J. (2008). "A kotex and a smile": Mothers and daughters at menarche. *Journal of Family Issues, 29,* 1325–1347.

Lee, J., Super, C. M., & Harkness, S. (2003). Self-perception of competence in Korean children: Age, sex and home influences. *Asian Journal of Social Psychology, 6,* 133–147.

Lee, V. E., & Burkam, D. T. (2002). *Inequality at the starting gate: Social background differences in achievement as children begin school.* Washington, DC: Economic Policy Institute.

Lee, W. K. M., & Law, K. W. K. (2004). Retirement planning and retirement satisfaction: The need for a national retirement program and policy in Hong Kong. *Journal of Applied Gerontology, 23,* 212–233.

Leipold, B., Schacke, C., & Zank, S. (2008). Personal growth and cognitive complexity in caregivers of patients with dementia. *European Journal of Ageing, 5,* 203–214.

Lepper, M. R., Corpus, J. H., & Iyengar, S. S. (2005). Intrinsic and extrinsic motivational orientations in the classroom: Age differences and academic correlates. *Journal of Educational Psychology, 97,* 184–196.

Lepper, M. R., Greene, D., & Nisbett, R. E. (1973). Undermining children's intrinsic interest with extrinsic reward: A test of the "overjustification" hypothesis. *Journal of Personality and Social Psychology, 28,* 129–137.

Lerner, R. M. (1998). Theories of human development: Contemporary perspectives. In W. Damon (Series ed.) & R. M. Lerner (Vol. ed.), *Handbook of child psychology: Vol. 1: Theoretical models of human development* (5th ed., pp. 1–24). Hoboken, NJ: John Wiley & Sons Inc.

Lerner, R. M., Dowling, E. M., & Anderson, P. M. (2003). Positive youth development: Thriving as the basis of personhood and civil society. *Applied Developmental Science, 7,* 172–180.

Lerner, R. M., Dowling, E., & Roth, S. L. (2003). Contributions of lifespan psychology to the future elaboration of developmental systems theory. In U. M. Staudinger & U. Lindenberger (Eds.), *Understanding human development: Dialogues with lifespan psychology* (pp. 413–422). Dordrecht, Netherlands: Kluwer Academic.

Lerner, R. M., Lerner, J. V., Almerigi, J. B., Theokas, C., Phelps, E., Gestsdottir, S., Naudeau, S., Jelicic, H., Alberts, A., Ma, L., Smith, L. M., Bobek, D. L., Richman-Raphael, D., Simpson, I., Christiansen, E. D., & von Eye, A. (2005). Positive youth development, participation in community youth development programs, and community contributions of fifth-grade adolescents: Findings from the first wave of the 4-H Study of Positive Youth Development. *Journal of Early Adolescence, 25,* 17–71.

Lesthaeghe, R., & Surkyn, J. (2008). When history moves on: The foundations and diffusion of a second demographic transition. In R. Jayakody, A. Thornton, & W. Axinn (Eds.) *International family change: Ideational perspectives* (pp. 81–117). New York: Taylor & Francis Group/Lawrence Erlbaum Associates.

Levin, S., Taylor, P. L., & Caudle, E. (2007). Interethnic and interracial dating in college: A longitudinal study. *Journal of Social and Personal Relationships, 24*(3), 323–341.

Levitt, H. M. (2006). How I ended up in a happy relationship: Women's process of successful partnering. *Journal of Humanistic Psychology, 46*(4), 449–473.

Li, L. W., & Liang, J. (2007). Social exchanges and subjective well-being among older Chinese: Does age make a difference? *Psychology and Aging, 22*(2), 386–391.

Liben, S., Papadatou, D., & Wolfe, J. (2008). Paediatric palliative care: Challenges and emerging ideas. *Lancet, 371,* 852–864.

Lieberman, A. F. (1993). *The emotional life of the toddler.* New York: Free Press.

Light, R. J. (2001). *Making the most of college: Students speak their minds.* Cambridge, MA: Harvard University Press.

Lightfoot, C. (1997). *The culture of adolescent risk-taking.* New York: Guilford Press.

Li-Grining, C. P. (2007). Effortful control among low-income preschoolers in three cities: Stability, change, and individual differences. *Developmental Psychology, 43*(1), 208–221.

Lillard, A. S. (1998). Playing with a theory of mind. In O. N. Saracho & B. Spodek (Eds.), *Multiple perspectives on play in early childhood education* (pp. 11–33). Albany, NY: State University of New York Press.

Lim, S. L., Yeh, M., Liang, J., Lau, A. S., & McCabe, K. (2009) Acculturation gap, intergenerational conflict, parenting style, and youth distress in immigrant Chinese American families. *Marriage & Family Review, 45,* 84–106.

Lin, M., Wolf, S. L., Hwang, H., Gong, S., & Chen, C. (2007). A randomized, controlled trial of fall prevention programs and quality of life in older fallers. *Journal of the American Geriatrics Society, 55,* 499–506.

Lindemann, E. (1944). Symptomatology and management of acute grief.

American Journal of Psychiatry, 101, 141–148.

Lindstrom-Forneri, W., Tuokko, H., & Rhodes, R. E. (2007). "Getting around town": A preliminary investigation of the theory of planned behavior and intent to change driving behaviors among older adults. *Journal of Applied Gerontology,* 26(4), 385–398.

Lineweaver, T. T., Berger, A. K., & Hertzog, C. (2009). Expectations about memory change across the life span are impacted by aging stereotypes. *Psychology and Aging, 24,* 169–176.

Linver, M. R., Roth, J. L., & Brooks-Gunn, J. (2009). Patterns of Adolescents' Participation in Organized Activities: Are sports best when combined with other activities? *Developmental Psychology, 45,* 354–367.

Lipsitt, L. P. (2003). Crib death: A bio-behavioral phenomenon? *Current Directions in Psychological Science, 12,* 164–170.

Little, M., & Sayers, E.-J. (2004). While there's life . . . hope and the experience of cancer. *Social Science & Medicine, 59,* 1329–1337.

Lobel, M., & DeLuca, R. S. (2007). Psychosocial sequelae of cesarean delivery: Review and analysis of their causes and implications. *Social Science & Medicine, 64,* 2272–2284.

LoBue, V. (2009). More than just another face in the crowd: Superior detection of threatening facial expressions in children and adults. *Developmental Science, 12,* 305–313.

Löckenhoff, C. E., & Carstensen, L. L. (2007). Aging, emotion, and health-related decision strategies: Motivational manipulations can reduce age differences. *Psychology and Aging, 22,* 134–146.

Loessi, B., Valerius, G., Kopasz, M., Hornyak, M., Riemann, D., & Voderholzer, U. (2008). Are adolescents chronically sleep-deprived? An investigation of sleep habits of adolescents in the southwest of Germany. *Child: Care, Health, and Development, 34,* 549–556.

Lonardo, R. A., Giordano, P. C., Longmore, M. A., & Manning, W. D. (2009). Parents, friends, and romantic partners: Enmeshment in deviant networks and adolescent delinquency involvement. *Journal of Youth and Adolescence, 38,* 367–383.

Long, S. O. (2004). Cultural scripts for a good death in Japan and the United States: Similarities and differences. *Social Science & Medicine, 58,* 913–928.

Lord, D., Schalkwyk, I., Chrysler, S., & Staplin, L. (2006). A strategy to reduce older driver injuries at intersections using more accommodating roundabout design practices. *Accident Analysis & Prevention,* 39(3), 427–432.

Lorenz, K. (1935). Der Kumpan in der Umwelt des Vogels. Der Artgenosse als auslosendes Moment sozialer Verhaltungsweisen. [The companion in the bird's world. The fellow-member of the species as releasing factor of social behavior.]. *Journal fur Ornithologie. Beiblatt. (Leipzig), 83,* 137–213.

Los Angeles Gerontology Research Group (LA-GRG). (2007). Validated worldwide supercentenarians, living and recently deceased. *Rejuvenation Research, 10,* 113–116.

Lou, S., Liu, J., Chang, H., & Chen, P. (2008). Hippocampal neurogenesis and gene expression depend on exercise intensity in juvenile rats. *Brain Research, 1210,* 48–55.

Lowenstein, L. F. (2005). Causes and associated features of divorce as seen by recent research. *Journal of Divorce & Remarriage, 42,* 153–171.

Lucas, R. E. (2008). Personality and subjective well-being. In M. Eid & R. J. Larsen (Eds.), *The science of subjective well-being* (171–194). New York: The Guilford Press.

Lucas, R. E., Le, K., & Dyrenforth, P. S. (2008). Explaining the extraversion/positive affect relation: Sociability cannot account for extraverts' greater happiness. *Journal of Personality,* 76(3), 386–414.

Lugo-Gil, J., & Tamis-LeMonda, C. S. (2008). Family resources and parenting quality: Links to children's cognitive development across the first 3 years. *Child Development,* 79(4), 1065–1085.

Luis, C. A., Abdullah, L., Paris, D., Quadros, A., Mullan, M., Mouzon, B., & Ait-Ghezala, G. (2009). Serum I2-amyloid correlates with neuropsychological impairment. *Aging, Neuropsychology, and Cognition, 16,* 203–218.

Luo, L., Hendriks, T., & Craik, F. I. M. (2007). Age differences in recollection: Three patterns of enhanced encoding. *Psychology and Aging,* 22(2), 269–280.

Luo, Z., Jose, P. E., Huntsinger, C. S., & Pigott, T. D. (2007). Fine motor skills and mathematics achievement in East Asian American and European American kindergartners and first graders. *British Journal of Developmental Psychology, 25,* 595–614.

Luthy, C., Cedraschi, C., Pautex, S., Rentsch, D., Piguet, V., & Allaz, A. F. (2009). Difficulties of residents in training in end-of-life care: A qualitative study. *Palliative Medicine, 23,* 59–65.

Maccoby, E. E. (1990). Gender and relationships: A developmental account. *American Psychologist, 45,* 513–520.

Maccoby, E. E. (1998). *The two sexes: Growing up apart, coming together.* Cambridge, MA: Belknap Press of Harvard University Press.

Maccoby, E. E. (2002). Gender and group process: A developmental perspective. *Current Directions in Psychological Science, 11,* 54–58.

Maccoby, E. E., & Martin, J. A. (1983). Socialization in the context of the family: Parent-child interaction. In P. H. Mussen (Series ed.) & E. M. Hethenington (Vol. ed.), *Handbook of child psychology: Vol. 4. Socialization, personality, and social development* (4th ed., pp. 1–101). New York: John Wiley & Sons Inc.

MacEachen, E., Polzer, J., & Clarke, J. (2008). "You are free to set your own hours": Governing worker productivity and health through flexibility and resilience. *Social Science & Medicine, 66,* 1019–1033.

Macek, P., Bejcek, J., & Vanickova, J. (2007). Contemporary Czech emerging adults: Generation growing up in the period of social changes. *Journal of Adolescent Research,* 22(5), 444–474.

MacFarlane, A. (1975). Olfaction in the development of social preferences in the human neonate, *Ciba Foundation Symposium: Vol. 33. Parent-infant interactions* (pp. 103–117). New York: Elsevier.

MacRae, H. (2008). Making the best you can of it: Living with early-state Alzheimer's disease. *Sociology of Health & Wellness,* 30(3), 396–412.

Maggs, J. L., Patrick, M. E., & Feinstein, L. (2008). Childhood and adolescent predictors of alcohol use and problems in adolescence and adulthood in the National Child Development Study. *Addiction, 103* (Suppl. 1), 7–22.

Males, M. (2009). Does the adolescent brain make risk taking inevitable? *Journal of Adolescent Research 24,* 3–20.

Manchester, J., & Topoleski, J. (2008). *Growing disparities in life expectancy. Economic and Budget Issue Brief.* Washington, DC: Congressional Budget Office.

Mandler, J. M. (2007). On the origins of the conceptual system. *American Psychologist,* 62(8), 741–751.

Maner, J. K., Rouby, D. A., & Gonzaga, G. C. (2008). Automatic inattention to attractive alternatives: The evolved psychology of relationship maintenance. *Evolution and Human Behavior, 29,* 343–349.

Manfra, L., & Winsler, A. (2006). Preschool children's awareness of private speech. *International Journal of Behavioral Development, 30*(6), 537–549.

Manly, J. J., Tang, M., Schupf, N., Stern, Y., Vonsattel, J. G., & Mayeux, R. (2008). Frequency and course of mild cognitive impairment in a multiethnic community. *Annals of Neurology, 63*(4), 494–506.

Manning, W. D., Giordano, P. C., & Longmore, M. A. (2006). Hooking up: The relationship contexts of "nonrelationship" sex. *Journal of Adolescent Research, 21*(5), 459–483.

Manning, W. D., Longmore, M. A., & Giordano, P. C. (2007). The changing institution of marriage: Adolescents' expectation to cohabit and to marry. *Journal of Marriage and Family, 69*(3), 559–575.

Mao, A., Burnham, M. M., Goodlin-Jones, B. L., Gaylor, E. E., & Anders, T. F. (2004). A comparison of the sleep-wake patterns of cosleeping and solitary-sleeping infants. *Child Psychiatry & Human Development, 35,* 95–105.

Marcia, J. E. (1966). Development and validation of ego-identity status. *Journal of Personality & Social Psychology, 3,* 551–558.

Marcia, J. E. (1987). The identity status approach to the study of ego identity development. In T. Honess & K. Yardley (Eds.), *Self and identity: Perspectives across the lifespan* (pp. 161–171). New York: Routledge.

Marieb, E. N. (2004). *Human anatomy & physiology* (6th ed.). New York: Pearson Education.

Marin, B. V., Kirby, D. B., Hudes, E. S., Coyle, K. K., & Gomez, C. A. (2006). Boyfriends', girlfriends' and teenagers' risk of sexual involvement. *Perspectives on Sexual and Reproductive Health, 38,* 76–83.

Marin, T. J., Chen, E., & Miller, G. E. (2008). What do trajectories of childhood socioeconomic status tell us about markers of cardiovascular health in adolescence? *Psychosomatic Medicine, 70,* 152–159.

Markey, P. M., & Markey, C. N. (2007). Romantic ideals, romantic obtainment, and relationship experiences: The complementarity of interpersonal traits among romantic partners. *Journal of Social and Personal Relationships, 24*(4), 517–533.

Marks, N. F., Lambert, J. D., Jun, H., & Song, J. (2008). Psychosocial moderators of the effects of transitioning into filial caregiving on mental and physical health. *Research on Aging, 30*(3), 358–389.

Markstrom, C. A., & Iborra, A. (2003). Adolescent identity formation and rites of passage: The Navajo Kinaaldá ceremony for girls. *Journal of Research on Adolescence, 13,* 399–425.

Marlier, L., Schaal, B., & Soussignan, R. (1998). Neonatal responsiveness to the odor of amniotic and lacteal fluids: A test of perinatal chemosensory continuity. *Child Development, 69,* 611–623.

Marsh, H. W., Hau, K. T., Sung, R. Y. T., & Yu, C. W. (2007). Childhood obesity, gender, actual-ideal body image discrepancies, and physical self-concept in Hong Kong children: Cultural differences in the value moderation. *Developmental Psychology, 43*(3), 647–662.

Marsiglio, W. (2004). When stepfathers claim stepchildren: A conceptual analysis. *Journal of Marriage and Family, 66,* 22–39.

Martin, C. L., & Dinella, L. M. (2002). Children's gender cognitions, the social environment, and sex differences in cognitive domains. In A. McGillicuddy-De Lisi & R. De Lisi (Eds.), *Biology, society, and behavior: The development of sex differences in cognition* (pp. 207–239). Westport, CT: Ablex.

Martin, C. L., & Fabes, R. A. (2001). The stability and consequences of young children's same-sex peer interactions. *Developmental Psychology, 37,* 431–446.

Martin, J. A., Hamilton, B. E., Menacker, F., Sutton, P. D., & Mathews, T. J. (2005, November 15). *Preliminary births for 2004: Infant and maternal health.* Hyattsville, MD: National Center for Health Statistics.

Martin, J. A., Hamilton, B. E., Sutton, P. D., Ventura, S. J., Menacker, F., & Munson, M. L. (2003, December 17). Births: Final data for 2002. *National Vital Statistics Reports, 52*(10).

Martin, K. A. (1996). *Puberty, sexuality, and the self: Boys and girls at adolescence.* New York: Routledge.

Martin, L. R., Friedman, H. S., & Schwartz, J. E. (2007). Personality and mortality risk across the life span: The importance of conscientiousness as a biopsychosocial attribute. *Health Psychology, 26*(4), 428–436.

Martin, P. D., Specter, G., Martin, D., & Martin, M. (2003). Expressed attitudes of adolescents toward marriage and family life. *Adolescence, 38,* 359–367.

Maslach, C., & Leiter, M. P. (2008). Early predictors of job burnout and engagement. *Journal of Applied Psychology, 93*(3), 498–512.

Mason, J., May, V., & Clarke, L. (2007). Ambivalence and the paradoxes of grandparenting. *Sociological Review, 55*(4), 687–706.

Masten, A. S. (2004). Regulatory processes, risk, and resilience in adolescent development. In R. E. Dahl & L. P. Spear (eds.), *Adolescent brain development: Vulnerabilities and opportunities* (Vol. 1021, pp. 310–319). New York: New York Academy of Sciences.

Masten, M. L., Guyer, A. E., Hogdon, H. B., McClure, E. B., Charney, D. S., Ernst, M., Kaufman, J., Pine, D. S., & Monk, C. S. (2008). Recognition of facial emotions among maltreated children with high rates of post-traumatic stress disorder. *Child Abuse & Neglect, 32,* 139–153.

Masters, W. H., & Johnson, V. E. (1966). *Human sexual response.* Boston: Little, Brown.

Mathews, B., & Kenny, M. C. (2008). Mandatory reporting legislation in the United States, Canada, and Australia: A cross-jurisdictional review of key features, differences, and issues. *Child Maltreatment, 13*(1), 50–63.

Matsumoto, D., Yoo, S. H., Fontaine, J., Anguas-Wong, A., Arriola, M., Ataca, B., et al. (2008). Mapping expressive differences around the world: The relationship between emotional display rules and individualism versus collectivism. *Journal of Cross-Cultural Psychology, 39,* 55–74.

Matta, D. S., & Knudson-Martin, C. (2006). Father responsivity: Couple processes and the coconstruction of fatherhood. *Family Process, 45,* 19–37.

Matychuk, P. (2004). A case study on the role of child-directed speech (CDS) in child language acquisition. *Dissertation Abstracts International, 64*(8), 2864A. (UMI No. AAI3100465)

Maxfield, M., Pyszczynski, T., Kluck, B., Cox, C. R., Greenberg, J., Solomon, S., & Weise, D. (2007). Age-related differences in responses to thoughts of one's own death: Mortality salience and judgments of moral transgressions. *Psychology and Aging, 22,* 341–353.

Maxwell, L. E. (2007). Competency in child care settings. *Environment and Behavior, 39*(2), 229–245.

Mayberry, M. L., & Espelage, D. L. (2007). Associations among empathy, social competence, & reactive/proactive aggression subtypes. *Journal of Youth and Adolescence, 36,* 787–798,

Mayeux, L., & Cillessen, A. H. N. (2008). It's not just being popular, it's knowing it, too: The role of self-perceptions of status in the associations between peer status and aggression. *Social Development, 17,* 871–888.

Maynard, A. E., & Greenfield, P. M. (2003). Implicit cognitive development in cultural tools and children: Lessons from Maya Mexico. *Cognitive Development, 18,* 489–510.

Mays, V. M., Cochran, S. D., & Barnes, N. W. (2007). Race, race-based discrimination, and health outcomes among African Americans. *Annual Review of Psychology, 58,* 201–225.

Maziak, W., Ward, K. D., & Stockton, M. B. (2008). Childhood obesity: Are we missing the big picture? *Obesity Reviews, 9,* 35–42.

McAdams, D. (2008). Generativity, the redemptive self, and the problem of a noisy ego in American life. In H. A. Wayment & J. J. Bauer (Eds.), *Transcending Self-Interest: Psychological Explorations of the Quiet Ego* (235–242). American Psychological Association.

McAdams, D. P. (2001a). Generativity in midlife. In M. E. Lachman (Ed.), *Handbook of midlife development* (pp. 395–443). Hoboken, NJ: John Wiley & Sons Inc.

McAdams, D. P. (2001b). The psychology of life stories. *Review of General Psychology, 5,* 100–122.

McAdams, D. P. (2006). *The redemptive self: Stories Americans live by.* New York: Oxford University Press.

McAdams, D. P., & Bowman, P. J. (2001). Narrating life's turning points: Redemption and contamination. In D. P. McAdams, R. Josselson, & A. Lieblich (Eds.), *Turns in the road: Narrative studies of lives in transition* (pp. 3–34). Washington, DC: American Psychological Association.

McAdams, D. P., & de St. Aubin, E. (1992). A theory of generativity and its assessment through self-report, behavioral acts, and narrative themes in autobiography. *Journal of Personality and Social Psychology, 62,* 1003–1015.

McAdams, D. P., de St. Aubin, E., & Logan, R. L. (1993). Generativity among young, midlife, and older adults. *Psychology and Aging, 8,* 221–230.

McAdams, D. P., Hart, H. M., & Maruna, S. (1998). The anatomy of generativity.

In D. P. McAdams & E. de St. Aubin (Eds.), *Generativity and adult development: How and why we care for the next generation* (pp. 7–43). Washington, DC: American Psychological Association.

McCabe, M. P., & Ricciardelli, L. A. (2005). A longitudinal study of body image and strategies to lose weight and increase muscles among children. *Journal of Applied Developmental Psychology, 26,* 559–577.

McCartney, K. (2004). Current research on child care effects. In *Encyclopedia on Early Childhood Development.* USA: Center of Excellence for Early Childhood Development.

McCartney, K., Dearing, E., Beck, A. T., & Bub, K. L. (2007). Quality child care supports the achievement of low-income children: Direct and indirect pathways through caregiving and the home environment. *Journal of Applied Developmental Psychology, 28(5–6),* 411–426.

McClintock, M. K., & Herdt, G. (1996). Rethinking puberty: The development of sexual attraction. *Current Directions in Psychological Science, 5,* 178–183.

McCreight, B. S. (2004). A grief ignored: Narratives of pregnancy loss from a male perspective. *Sociology of Health and Illness, 26,* 326–350.

McDowell, D. J., & Parke, R. D. (2009). Parental correlates of children's peer relations: An empirical test of a tripartite model. *Developmental Psychology, 45,* 224–235.

McElwain, N. L., Halberstadt, A. G., & Volling, B. L. (2007). Mother- and father-reported reactions to children's negative emotions: Relations to young children's emotional understanding and friendship quality. *Child Development, 78(5),* 1407–1425.

McElwain, N. L., & Volling, B. L. (2004). Attachment security and parental sensitivity during infancy: Associations with friendship quality and false-belief understanding at age 4. *Journal of Social and Personal Relationships, 21,* 639–667.

McGrath, P. (2004). Affirming the connection: Comparative findings on communication issues from hospice patients and hematology survivors. *Death Studies, 28,* 829–848.

McIntosh, H., Metz, E., & Youniss, J. (2005). Community service and identity formation in adolescents. In J. L. Mahoney, R. W. Larson, & J. S. Eccles (Eds.), *Organized activities as contexts of development: Extracurricular activities, after-school and community programs* (pp. 331–351). Mahwah, NJ: Erlbaum.

McKenna, J. J., & Volpe, L. E. (2007). Sleeping with baby: An internet-based sampling of parental experiences, choices, perceptions, and interpretations in a western industrialized context. *Infant and Developmental Psychology, 16,* 359–385.

McKinley, N. M. (2006). The developmental and cultural contexts of objectified body consciousness: A longitudinal analysis of two cohorts of women. *Developmental Psychology, 42,* 679–687.

McLanahan, S., & Adams, J. (1989). The effects of children on adults' psychological well-being: 1957–1976. *Social Forces, 68,* 124–146.

McLeod, B. R., Wood, J. J., & Weisz, J. R. (2007). Examining the association between parenting and childhood anxiety: A meta-analysis. *Child Psychology Review, 27(2),* 155–172.

McLoyd, V. C., Kaplan, R., Hardaway, C. R., & Wood, D. (2007). Does endorsement of physical discipline matter? Assessing moderating influences on the maternal and child psychological correlates of physical discipline in African American families. *Journal of Family Psychology, 21,* 165–175.

McNamara, T. K., & Williamson, J. B. (2004). Race, gender, and the retirement decisions of people ages 60 to 80: Prospects for age integration in employment. *International Journal of Aging & Human Development, 59,* 255–286.

McNulty, J. K. (2008). Forgiveness in marriage: Putting the benefits into context. *Journal of Family Psychology, 22,* 171–175.

Meier, D. E., & Beresford, L. (2009). Palliative care cost research can help other palliative care programs make their case. *Journal of Palliative Medicine, 23,* 15–20.

Meltzer, L. J., & Mindell, J. A. (2007). Relationship between child sleep disturbances and maternal sleep, mood and parenting stress: A pilot study. *Journal of Family Psychology, 21(1),* 67–73.

Meltzoff, A. N., & Moore, M. K. (1977, October 7). Imitation of facial and manual gestures by human neonates. *Science, 198,* 75–78.

Menard, J. L., & Hakvoort, R. M. (2007). Variations of maternal care alter offspring levels of behavioral defensiveness in adulthood: Evidence for a threshold model. *Behavioral Brain Research, 176,* 302–313.

Meno, C. A., Hannum, J. W., Espelage, D. E., & Low, K. S. D. (2008). Familial and individual variables as predictors of dieting concerns and binge eating in college females. *Eating Behaviors, 9,* 91–101.

Mermin, G. B. T., Johnson, R. W., & Murphy, D. P. (2007). Why do boomers plan to work longer? *Journal of Gerontology: SOCIAL SCIENCES, 62B*(5), S286–S294.

Merrell, K. W., Buchanan, R., & Tran, O. K. (2006). Relational aggression in children and adolescents: A review with implications for school settings. *Psychology in the Schools, 43,* 345–360.

Merrill, D. M. (1996). Conflict and cooperation among adult siblings during the transition to the role of filial caregiver. *Journal of Social and Personal Relationships, 13*(3), 399–413.

Meyer, T. A., & Gast, J. (2008). The effects of peer influence on disordered eating behavior. *The Journal of School Nursing, 24*(1), 36–42.

Mian, O. S., Baltzopoulos, V., Minetti, A. E., & Narici, M. V. (2007). The impact of physical training on locomotor function in older people. *Sports Med, 37*(8), 683–701.

Michael, A., & Eccles, J. S. (2003). When coming of age means coming undone: Links between puberty and psychosocial adjustment among European American and African American girls. In C. Hayward (Ed.), *Gender differences at puberty* (pp. 277–303). New York: Cambridge University Press.

Mikulincer, M., Florian, V., Cowan, P. A., & Cowan, C. P. (2002). Attachment security in couple relationships: A systemic model and its implications for family dynamics. *Family Process, 41,* 405–434.

Milkie, M. A. (1999). Social comparisons, reflected appraisals, and mass media: The impact of pervasive beauty images on black and white girls' self concepts. *Social Psychology Quarterly, 62,* 190–210.

Miller, D., & Daniel, B. (2007). Competent to cope, worthy of happiness? How the duality of self-esteem can inform a resilience-based classroom environment. *School Psychology International, 28*(5), 605–622.

Miller, K. E., Merrill, J. M., Barnes, G. M., Sabo, D., & Farrell, M. P. (2007). Athletic involvement and adolescent delinquency. *Journal of Youth Adolescence, 36,* 711–723.

Miller, L. (2008). Spirituality and resilience in adolescent girls. In K. K. Kline (Ed.), *Authoritative communities: The scientific cases for nurturing the whole child* (pp. 295–302). New York: Springer-Verlag.

Miller, S. D. (2003). How high and low challenge tasks affect motivation and learning: Implications for struggling learners. *Reading & Writing Quarterly: Overcoming Learning Difficulties, 19,* 39–57.

Miller-Loncar, C., Bigsby, R., High, P., Wallach, M., & Lester, B. (2004). Infant colic and feeding difficulties. *Archives of Disease in Childhood, 89,* 908–912.

Mills, E. S. (1993). *The story of Elderhostel.* Hanover, NH: University Press of New England.

Miniño, A. M., Arias, E., Kochanek, K. D., Murphy, S. L., & Smith, B. L. (2002, September 16). Deaths: Final data for 2000. *National Vital Statistics Reports, 50*(16).

Minois, G. (1989). *History of old age: From antiquity to the Renaissance* (S. H. Tenison, Trans.). Chicago: University of Chicago Press.

Mintz, S. (2004). *Huck's raft: A history of American childhood.* Cambridge, MA: Belknap Press of Harvard University Press.

Mirvis, P. H., & Hall, D. T. (1994). Psychological success and the boundaryless career. *Journal of Organizational Behavior, 15,* 365–380.

Mishel, L., Bernstein, J., & Allegretto, S. (2007). *The State of Working America 2006/2007.* An Economic Policy Institute Book, Ithaca, NY: ILR Press, and imprint of Cornell University Press.

Mistry, J., Chaudhuri, J., & Diez, V. (2003). Ethnotheories of parenting: Integrating culture and child development. In R. M. Lerner, F. H. Jacobs, & D. Wertlieb (Eds.), *Handbook of applied developmental science: Promoting positive child, adolescent, and family development through research, policies, and programs* (pp. 233–256). Thousand Oaks, CA: Sage.

Mistry, R. S., Biesanz, J. C., Taylor, L. C., Burchinal, M., & Cox, M. J. (2004). Family income and its relation to preschool children's adjustment for families in the NICHD Study of Early Child Care. *Developmental Psychology, 40,* 727–745.

Mitchell, V., & Helson, R. (1990). Women's prime of life: Is it the 50s? *Psychology of Women Quarterly, 14,* 451–470.

Mitchell-Flynn, C., & Hutchinson, R. L. (1993). A longitudinal study of the problems and concerns of urban divorced men. *Journal of Divorce & Remarriage, 19,* 161–182.

Modell, J. (1989). *Into one's own: From youth to adulthood in the United States, 1920–1975.* Berkeley, CA: University of California Press.

Moehler, E., Kagan, J., Oelkers-Ax, R., Brunner, R., Poustka, L., Haffner, J., & Resch, F. (2008). Infant predictors of behavioural inhibition. *British Journal of Developmental Psychology, 26*(1), 145–150.

Moffitt, T. E. (1993). Adolescence-limited and life-course-persistent antisocial behavior: A developmental taxonomy. *Psychological Review, 100,* 674–701.

Moffitt, T. E., Caspi, A., Belsky, J., & Silva, P. A. (1992). Childhood experience and the onset of menarche: A test of a sociobiological model. *Child Development, 63,* 47–58.

Moghadam, V. M. (2004). Patriarchy in transition: Women and the changing family in the Middle East. *Journal of Comparative Family Studies, 35,* 137–162.

Molden, D. C., & Dweck, C. S. (2006). Finding "meaning" in psychology: A lay theories approach to self-regulation, social perception, and social development. *American Psychologist, 61,* 192–203.

Moll, H., & Tomasello, M. (2007). How 14- and 18-month-olds know what others have experienced. *Developmental Psychology, 43*(2), 309–317.

Mollborn, S. (2009). Norms about nonmarital pregnancy and willingness to provide resources to unwed parents. *Journal of Marriage and Family, 71,* 122–134.

Monastra, V. J. (2008). *Unlocking the potential of patients with ADHD: A model for clinical practice.* Washington, DC: American Psychological Association.

Monroe, B., Hansford, P., Payne, M., & Sykes, N. (2008). St. Christopher's and the future. *Omega: Journal of Death and Dying. Special Issue: "Hospice heritage" In memory of Dame Cicely Saunders, 56,* 63–75.

Monserud, M. A. (2008). Intergenerational relationships and affectual solidarity between grandparents and young adults. *Journal of Marriage and Family, 70*(1), 182–195.

Montemayor, R. (1983). Parents and adolescents in conflict: All families some of the time and some families most of the time. *Journal of Early Adolescence, 3,* 83–103.

Montoro-Rodriguez, J., Kosloski, K., Kercher, K., & Montgomery, R. J. V. (2009). The impact of social embarrassment on caregiving distress in a multicultural sample of caregivers. *Journal of Applied Geontology, 28,* 195–217.

Moore, K. A. (2008). Teen births: Examining the recent increase. *The National Campaign to Prevent Teen and Unplanned Pregnancy.*

Moore, L. L., Gao, D., Bradlee, M. L., Cupples, L. A., Sundarajan-Ramamurti, A., Proctor, M. H., Hood, M. Y., Singer, M. R., & Ellison, R. C. (2003). Does early physical activity predict body fat change throughout childhood? *Preventive Medicine: An International Journal Devoted to Practice and Theory, 37,* 10–17.

Moorman, E. A., & Pomerantz, E. M. (2008). The role of mothers' control in children's mastery orientation: A time frame analysis. *Journal of Family Psychology, 22,* 734–741.

Morawska, A., & Sanders, M. R. (2007). Concurrent predictors of dysfunctional parenting and maternal confidence: Implications for parenting interventions. *Child: Care, Health and Development, 33*(6), 757–767.

Morgan, H. J., & Shaver, P. R. (1999). Attachment processes and commitment to romantic relationships. In J. M. Adams & W. H. Jones (Eds.), *Handbook of interpersonal commitment and relationship stability* (pp. 109–124). Dordrecht, Netherlands: Kluwer Academic.

Morgan, J. (2008). End-of-life care in UK critical care units—a literature review. *Nursing in Critical Care, 13*(3), 152–161.

Mortensen, E. L., Michaelsen, K. F., Sanders, S. A., & Reinisch, J. M. (2002). The association between duration of breastfeeding and adult intelligence. *Journal of the American Medical Association, 287,* 2365–2371.

Mosko, S., Richard, C., & McKenna, J. (1997). Maternal sleep and arousals during bedsharing with infants. *Sleep: Journal of Sleep Research & Sleep Medicine, 20,* 142–150.

Moss, E., Cyr, C., Bureau, J.-F., Tarabulsy, G. M., & Dubois-Comtois, K. (2005). Stability of attachment during the preschool period. *Developmental Psychology, 41,* 773–783.

Mouihate, A., Harre, E. M., Martin, S., & Pittman, Q. J. (2008). Suppression of the febrile response in late gestation: Evidence, mechanisms and outcomes. *Journal of Neuroendocrinology, 20,* 508–514.

Mroczek, D. K. (2001). Age and emotion in adulthood. *Current Directions in Psychological Science, 10,* 87–90.

Mroczek, D. K., & Spiro, A. (2003). Modeling intraindividual change in personality traits: Findings from the Normative Aging Study. *Journals of Gerontology: Series B: Psychological Sciences and Social Sciences, 58B,* P153–P165.

Mrug, S., Hoza, B., Gerdes, A. C., Hinshaw, S., Arnold, E. L., Hechtman, L., & Pelham, W. E. (2009). Discriminating between children with ADHD and classmates using peer variables. *Journal of Attention Disorders, 12,* 372–380.

Mueller, C. M., & Dweck, C. S. (1998). Praise for intelligence can undermine children's motivation and performance. *Journal of Personality and Social Psychology, 75*(1), 33–52.

Mulvaney, M. K., & Mebert, C. J. (2007). Parental corporal punishment predicts behavior problems in early childhood. *Journal of Family Psychology, 21*(3), 389–397.

Mundy, P., Block, J., Delgado, C., Pomares, Y., Van Hecke, A. V., & Parlade, M. V. (2007). Individual differences and the development of joint attention in infancy. *Child Development, 78*(3), 938–954.

Murphy, K. (2005). Psychosocial treatments for ADHD in teens and adults: A practice-friendly review. *Journal of Clinical Psychology, 61,* 607–619.

Murphy, N. A., & Isaacowitz, D. M. (2008). Preferences for emotional information in older and younger adults: A meta-analysis of memory and attention tasks. *Psychology and Aging, 23*(2), 263–286.

Murray, S. L., & Holmes, J. G. (1997). A leap of faith? Positive illusions in romantic relationships. *Personality and Social Psychology Bulletin, 23,* 586–604.

Murray, S. L., Bellavia, G. M., Rose, P., & Griffin, D. W. (2003). Once hurt, twice hurtful: How perceived regard regulates daily marital interactions. *Journal of Personality and Social Psychology, 84,* 126–147.

Murray, S. L., Holmes, J. G., Bellavia, G., Griffin, D. W., & Dolderman, D. (2002). Kindred spirits? The benefits of egocentrism in close relationships. *Journal of Personality and Social Psychology, 82,* 563–581.

Murray, S. L., Holmes, J. G., Dolderman, D., & Griffin, D. W. (2000). What the motivated mind sees: Comparing friends' perspectives to married partners' views of each other. *Journal of Experimental Social Psychology, 36,* 600–620.

Murstein, B. I. (1970). Stimulus-value-role: A theory of marital choice. *Journal of Marriage & the Family, 32,* 465–481.

Murstein, B. I. (1999). The relationship of exchange and commitment. In J. M. Adams & W. H. Jones (Eds.), *Handbook of interpersonal commitment and relationship stability* (pp. 205–219). Dordrecht, Netherlands: Kluwer Academic.

Murstein, B. I., Reif, J. A., & Syracuse-Siewert, G. (2002). Comparison of the function of exchange in couples of similar and differing physical attractiveness. *Psychological Reports, 91,* 299–314.

Must, A., Naumova, E. N., Phillips, S. M., Blum, M., Dawson-Hughes, B., & Rand, W. M. (2005). Childhood overweight and maturational timing in the development of adult overweight and fatness: The Newton Girls Study and its follow-up. *Pediatrics, 116,* 620–627.

Muuss, R. E. (1986). Adolescent eating disorder: Bulimia. *Adolescence, 21,* 257–267.

Nakashima, M., & Canda, E. R. (2005). Positive dying and resiliency in later life: A qualitative study. *Journal of Aging Studies, 19,* 109–125.

National Center for Health Statistics. (2005). *Health, United States, 2005: With chartbook on trends in the health of Americans.* Hyattsville, MD: National Center for Health Statistics.

National Center for Health Statistics. (2007). *Health, United States, 2007 with chartbook on trends in the health of Americans,* Hyattsville, MD: National Center for Health Statistics.

National Center for Health Statistics. (2007). *Health, United States, 2007 with chartbook on trends in the health of Americans* (PHS Publication No. 2007–1232). Hyattsville, MD: U.S. Government Printing Office.

National Center for Health Statistics. (2008). *Health, United States, 2007, with chartbook on trends in the health of Americans.* Hyattsville, MD: National Center for Health Statistics.

National Center for Health Statistics. (CDC Faststats). Hyattsville, MD. Retrieved online on April 2, 2009, at cdcinfo[a]cdc.gov.

National Clearinghouse on Child Abuse and Neglect Information. (2005). Child maltreatment 2003: Summary. Retrieved October 20, 2005, from National Clearinghouse on Child Abuse and Neglect Information Web site:

http://www.acf.hhs.gov/programs/cb/pubs/cm03/index.htm

National Health and Nutrition Examination Survey. (2004). Clinical growth charts. Retrieved October 4, 2006, from National Center for Health Statistics (U.S. Department of Health & Human Services [USDHHS]) Web site: http://www.cdc.gov/nchs/about/major/nhanes/growthcharts/clinical_charts.htm

Natsuaki, M., Ge, X., & Wenk, E. (2008). Continuity and changes in the developmental trajectories of criminal career: Examining the roles of timing of first arrest and high school graduation. *Journal of Youth and Adolescence, 37,* 431–444.

Naveh-Benjamin, M., Brav, K. T., & Levy, O. (2007). The associative memory deficit of older adults: The role of strategy utilization. *Psychology and Aging, 22*(1), 202–208.

Nayak, A., & Kehily, M. J. (2008). *Gender, Youth and Culture: Young Masculinities and Femininities.* Basingstoke (England): Palgrave MacMillan.

Negriff, S., Fung, M. T., & Trickett, P. K. (2008). Self-rated pubertal development, depressive symptoms and delinquency: Measurement issues and moderation by gender and maltreatment. *Journal of Youth and Adolescence, 37,* 736–746.

Nelson, C. A., & Thomas, K. M. (2008). New advances in understanding sensitive periods in brain development. *Current Directions in Psychological Science, 17*(1), 1–5.

Nelson, C. A., Thomas, K. M., & de Haan, M. (2006). Neural bases of cognitive development. In D. Kuh, R. S. Siegler, W. Damon, & R. M. Lerner (Eds.), *Handbook of child psychology, Vol. 2: Cognition, perception, and language* (6th ed.), pp. 3–57. Hoboken, NJ: John Wiley & Sons Inc.

Nelson, K. (1974). Concept, word, and sentence: Interrelations in acquisition and development. *Psychological Review, 81,* 267–285.

Nelson, K. (1999). The developmental psychology of language and thought. In M. Bennett (Ed.), *Developmental psychology: Achievements and prospects* (pp. 185–204). New York: Psychology Press.

Nelson, K. (2000). Narrative, time and the emergence of the encultured self. *Culture & Psychology, 6,* 183–196.

Nelson, K., & Fivush, R. (2004). The emergence of autobiographical memory: A social cultural developmental theory. *Psychological Review, 111,* 486–511.

Nelson, L. J., Padilla-Walker, L. M., Carroll, J. S., Madsen, S. D., Barry, C. M., & Badger, S. (2007). "If you want me to treat you like an adult, start acting like one!" Comparing the criteria that emerging adults and their parents have for adulthood. *Journal of Family Psychology, 21*(4), 665–674.

Neugarten, B. (1972). Personality and the aging process. *Gerontologist, 12*(1, Pt. 1), 9–15.

Neugarten, B. L. (1979). Time, age, and the life cycle. *American Journal of Psychiatry, 136,* 887–894.

Neumark, D. (2009). The age discrimination in employment act and the challenge of population aging. *Research on Aging, 31,* 41–68.

Newcomb, A. F., & Bagwell, C. L. (1995). Children's friendship relations: A meta-analytic review. *Psychological Bulletin, 117,* 306–347.

Newman, K. S., & Chen, V. T. (2007). *The missing class: Portraits of the near poor in America.* Boston: Beacon Press.

Ng, F. F., Pomerantz, E. M., & Lam, S. (2007). European American and Chinese parents' responses to children's success and failure: Implications for children's responses. *Development Psychology, 43*(5), 1239–1255.

Ng, T. W. H., & Feldman, D. C. (2008). The relationship of age to ten dimensions of job performance. *Journal of Applied Psychology, 93*(2), 392–423.

NHPCO Facts and Figures. *Hospice care in America.* (2007, Nov.) Retrieved on August 20, 2009 from www.nhpco.org/research.

NICHD Early Child Care Research Network. (2003). Does amount of time spent in child care predict socioemotional adjustment during the transition to kindergarten? *Child Development, 74,* 976–1005.

NICHD Early Child Care Research Network. (2004). Type of child care and children's development at 54 months. *Early Childhood Research Quarterly, 19,* 203–230.

NICHD Early Child Care Research Network. (2006). Child-care effect sizes for the NICHD Study of Early Child Care and Youth Development. *American Psychologist, 61,* 99–116.

NICHD Early Child Care Research Network. (2009). Study of Early Child Care and Youth Development. Retrieved August 15, 2009, from http://secc.rti.org/summary.

NICHD. (2009, Aug.). Study of early child care and youth development. Retrieved on August 15, 2009 from https://secc.rti.org/summary.

Nielsen, L., Knutson, B., & Carstensen, L. L. (2008). Affect dynamics, affective forecasting, and aging. *Emotion, 8*(3), 318–330.

Nierop, A., Wirtz, P. H., Bratsikas, A., Zimmermann, R., & Elhert, U. (2008). Stress-buffering effects of psychosocial resources on physiological and psychological stress response in pregnant women. *Biological Psychology, 78*(3), 261–268.

Nimrod, G., Janke, M. C., & Kleiber, D. A. (2009). Expanding, reducing, concentrating, and diffusing: Activity patterns of recent retirees in the United States. *Leisure Sciences, 31,* 37–52.

Noller, P., & Feeney, J. A. (2002). Communication, relationship concerns, and satisfaction in early marriage. In A. L. Vangelisti, H. T. Reis, & M. A. Fitzpatrick (Eds.), *Stability and change in relationships* (pp. 129–155). New York: Cambridge University Press.

Noller, P., Feeney, J. A., Roberts, N., & Christensen, A. (2005). Withdrawal in couple interactions: Exploring the causes and consequences. In R. E. Riggio & R. S. Feldman (Eds.), *Applications of nonverbal communication* (pp. 195–213). Mahwah, NJ: Erlbaum.

North, R. J., Holahan, C. J., Moos, R. H., & Cronkite, R. C. (2008). Family support, family income, and happiness: A 10-year perspective. *Journal of Family Psychology, 22*(3), 475–483.

Nunner-Winkler, G. (2007). Development of moral motivation from childhood to early adulthood. *Journal of Moral Education, 36*(4), 399–414.

O'Cleirigh, C., Ironson, G., Weiss, A., & Costa, P. T., Jr. (2007). Conscientiousness predicts disease progression (CD4 number and viral load) in people living with HIV. *Health Psychology, 26*(4), 473–480.

O'Connor, E., & McCartney, K. (2007). Attachment and cognitive skills: An investigation of mediating mechanisms. *Journal of Applied Developmental Psychology, 28*(5–6), 458–476.

O'Rand, A. M. (1988). Convergence, institutionalization, and bifurcation: Gender and the pension acquisition process. In G. L. Maddox & M. P. Lawton (Eds.), *Annual review of gerontology and geriatrics, Vol. 8: Varieties of aging* (pp. 132–155). New York: Springer.

Offer, D., Ostrov, E., Howard, K. I., & Atkinson, R. (1988). *The teenage world: Adolescents' self-image in ten countries.* New York: Plenum.

Ogden, C. L., Carroll, M. D., & Flegal, K. M. (2008). High body mass index for age among U.S. children and adolescents, 2003–2006. *Journal of the American Medical Association, 299,* 2401–2405.

Okamoto, K., Hasebe, Y., & Harasawa, Y. (2007). Caregiver psychological characteristics predict discontinuation of care for disabled elderly at home. *International Journal of Geriatric Psychiatry, 22,* 1110–1114.

Old, S. R., & Naveh-Benjamin, M. (2008). Memory for people and their actions: Further evidence for an age-related associative deficit. *Psychology and Aging, 23*(2), 467–472.

Olfson, M., Gameroff, M. J., Marcus, S. C., & Jensen, P. S. (2003). National trends in the treatment of attention deficit hyperactivity disorder. *American Journal of Psychiatry, 160,* 1071–1077.

Olthof, T., & Goossens, F. A. (2008). Bullying and the need to belong: Early adolescents' bullying-related behavior and the acceptance they desire and receive from particular classmates. *Social Development, 17*(1), 24–46.

Olweus, D., Limber, S., & Mihalic, S. F. (1999). *Blueprints for violence prevention, Book 9: Bullying prevention program.* Boulder, CO: Center for the Study and Prevention of Violence, Institute of Behavioral Science, University of Colorado at Boulder.

Omar, H., McElderry, D., & Zakharia, R. (2003). Educating adolescents about puberty: What are we missing? *International Journal of Adolescent Medicine and Health, 15,* 79–83.

Onishi, K. H., & Baillargeon, R. (2005, April 8). Do 15-month-old infants understand false beliefs? *Science, 308,* 255–258.

Ornstein, P. A., Naus, M. J., & Liberty, C. (1975). Rehearsal and organizational processes in children's memory. *Child Development, 46,* 818–830.

Osler, M., Madsen, M., Andersen A. N., Avlund, K., Mcgue, M., Jeune, B., & Christensen, K. (2009). Do childhood and adult socioeconomic circumstances influence health and physical function in middle-age? *Social Science and Medicine, 68,* 1425–1431.

Ott, M. A., Millstein, S. G., Ofner, S., & Halpern-Felsher, B. L. (2006). Greater expectations: Adolescents' positive motivations for sex. *Perspectives on Sexual and Reproductive Health, 38,* 84–89.

Paikoff, R. L., & Brooks-Gunn, J. (1991). Do parent-child relationships change during puberty? *Psychological Bulletin, 110,* 47–66.

Pajer, K. (2008). Externalizing disorders: Beyond psychosocial and biological correlates. *Journal of the American Academy of Child and Adolescent Psychiatry, 47*(7), 734–762.

Palkovitz, R. J. (2002). *Involved Fathering and Men's Adult Development: Provisional Balances.* Mahwah, NJ: Erlbaum.

Palladino, G. (1996). *Teenagers: An American history.* New York: Basic Books.

Palmore, E. B. (1990a). *Ageism: Negative and positive.* New York: Springer.

Panksepp, J. (1998). Attention deficit hyperactivity disorders, psychostimulants and intolerance of childhood playfulness: A tragedy in the making? *Current Directions in Psychological Science, 7,* 91–98.

Pantsiotou, S., Papadimitriou, A., Douros, K., Priftis, K., Nicolaidou, P., & Fretzayas, A. (2008). Maturational tempo differences in relation to the timing of the onset of puberty in girls. *Acta Paediatrica, 97*(2), 217–220.

Parault, S. J., Davis, H. A., & Pellegrini, A. D. (2007). The social context of bullying and victimization. *Journal of Early Adolescence, 27*(2), 145–174.

Parent, A.-S., Teilmann, G., Juul, A., Skakkebaek, N. E., Toppari, J., & Bourguignon, J.-P. (2003). The timing of normal puberty and the age limits of sexual precocity: Variations around the world, secular trends, and changes after migration. *Endocrine Reviews, 24,* 668–693.

Park, D. C., & Reuter-Lorenz, P. (2009). The adaptive brain: Aging and neurocognitive scaffolding. *The Annual Review of Psychology, 60,* 173–196.

Park, N. S., Klemmack, D. L., Roff, L. L., Parker, M. W., Koenig, H. G., Sawyer, P., & Allman, R. M. (2008). Religiousness and longitudinal trajectories in elders' functional status. *Research on Aging, 30*(3), 279–298.

Parkes, C. M. (1972). *Bereavement: Studies of grief in adult life.* New York: International Universities Press.

Parkes, C. M. (1987). *Bereavement: Studies of grief in adult life* (2nd ed.). Madison, CT: International Universities Press.

Pascalis, O., de Schonen, S., Morton, J., Deruelle, C., & Fabre-Grenet, M. (1995). Mother's face recognition by neonates: A replication and an extension. *Infant Behavior & Development, 18,* 79–85.

Pascual-Leone, J. (1970). A mathematical model for the transition rule in Piaget's developmental stages. *Acta Psychologica, Amsterdam, 32,* 301–345.

Patall, E. A., Cooper, H., & Robinson, J. C. (2008). The effects of choice on intrinsic motivation and related outcomes: A meta-analysis of research findings. *Psychological Bulletin, 134*(2), 270–300.

Paulussen-Hoogeboom, M. C., Stams, G. J. J. M., Hermanns, J. M. A., & Peetsma, T. T. D. (2007). Child negative emotionality and parenting from infancy to preschool: A meta-analytic review. *Developmental Psychology, 43*(2), 438–453.

Peck, S. C., Roeser, R. W., Zarrett, N., & Eccles, J. S. Exploring the roles of extracurricular activity quantity and quality in the educational resilience of vulnerable adolescents: Variable- and pattern-centered approaches. *Journal of Social Issues, 64,* 135–155.

Peck, S. C., Vida, M., & Eccles, J. S. (2008). Adolescent pathways to adulthood drinking: Sport activity involvement is not necessarily risky or protective. *Addiction, 103* (Suppl. 1), 69–83.

Pedersen, N. L. (1996). Gerontological behavior genetics. In J. E. Birren, K. W. Schaie, R. P. Abeles, M. Gatz, & T. A. Salthouse (Eds.), *Handbook of the psychology of aging* (4th ed., pp. 59–77). San Diego, CA: Academic Press.

Pedro-Carroll, J. L. (2005). Fostering resilience in the aftermath of divorce: The role of evidence-based programs for children. *Family Court Review, 43,* 52–64.

Pellegrini, A. D. (2006). The development and function of rough-and-tumble play in childhood and adolescence: A sexual selection theory perspective. In A. Göncü, & S. Gaskins (Eds.), *Play and development: Evolutionary, sociocultural, and functional perspectives. The Jean Piaget Symposium Series* (pp. 77–98). Mahwah, NJ: Lawrence Erlbaum Associates Publishers.

Pellegrini, A. D. (2008). The roles of aggressive and affiliative behaviors in resource control: A behavioral ecological perspective. *Developmental Review, 28,* 461–487.

Pellegrini, A. D., Dupuis, D., & Smith, P. K. (2007). Play in evolution and development. *Developmental Review*, 27, 261–276.

Pellegrini, A. D., Long, J. D., Roseth, C. J., Bohn, C. M., & Van Ryzin, M. (2007a). A short-term longitudinal study of preschoolers' (homo sapiens) sex segregation: The role of physical activity, sex, and time. *Journal of Comparative Psychology, 121*(3), 282–289.

Pellegrini, A. D., Roseth, C. J., Miller, S., Bohn, C. M., Van Ryzin, M., Vance, N., Cheatham, C. L., & Tarullo, A. (2007b). Social dominance in preschool classrooms. *Journal of Comparative Psychology, 121*(1), 54–64.

Perala-Littunen, S. (2007). Gender equality or primacy of the mother? Ambivalent descriptions of good parents. *Journal of Marriage and Family, 69*(2), 341–351.

Perner, J., Rendl, B., & Garnham, A. (2007). Objects of desire, thought and reality: Problems of anchoring discourse referents in development. *Mind & Language, 22*(5), 475–513.

Perry, J. A., Silvera, D. H., Neilands, T. B., Rosenvinge, J. H., & Hanssen, T. (2008). A study of the relationship between parental bonding, self-concept and eating disturbances in Norwegian and American college populations. *Eating Behaviors, 9*, 13–24.

Peskin, J. (1992). Ruse and representations: On children's ability to conceal information. *Developmental Psychology, 28*, 84–89.

Peterson, B. D., Gold, L., & Feingold, T. (2007). The experience and influence of infertility; Considerations for couple counselors. *The Family Journal: Counseling and Therapy for Couples and Families, 15*(3), 251–257.

Peterson, B. E. (1998). Case studies of midlife generativity: Analyzing motivation and realization. In D. P. McAdams & E. de St. Aubin (Eds.), *Generativity and adult development: how and why we care for the next generation* (pp. 101–131). Washington, DC: American Psychological Association.

Peterson, B. E., & Duncan, L. E. (2007). Midlife women's generativity and authoritarianism: Marriage, motherhood, and 10 years of aging. *Psychology and Aging, 22*(3), 411–419.

Pevey, C. (2003). Living wills and durable power of attorney for health care. In C. D. Bryant (Ed.), *Handbook of death & dying* (pp. 891–898). Thousand Oaks, CA: Sage.

Phelan, P., Davidson, A. L., & Yu, H. C. (1998). *Adolescents' worlds: Negotiating family, peers, and school.* New York: Teachers College Press.

Phillips, C. D., & Hawes, C. (2005). Care provision in housing with supportive services: The importance of care type, individual characteristics, and care site. *Journal of Applied Gerontology, 24*, 55–67.

Phillips, L. H., Henry, J. D., Hosie, J. A., & Milne, A. B. (2008). Effective regulation of the experience and expression of negative affect in old age. *Journal of Gerontology: PSYCHOLOGICAL SCIENCES, 63B*(3), P138–P145.

Phinney, J. S. (2006). Acculturation is not an independent variable: Approaches to studying acculturation as a complex process. In M. H. Bornstein, & L. R. Cote (Eds.), *Acculturation and parent-child relationships: measurement and development* (pp. 79–95). Mahwah, NJ: Lawrence Erlbaum Associates Publishers.

Phinney, J. S., Kim-Jo, T., Osorio, S., & Vilhjalmsdottir, P. (2005). Autonomy and relatedness in adolescent-parent disagreements: Ethnic and developmental factors. *Journal of Adolescent Research, 20*, 8–39.

Piaget, J. (1950). *The psychology of intelligence.* Oxford, England: Harcourt.

Piaget, J. (1962). *Play, dreams and imitation in childhood.* New York: Norton. (Original work published 1951)

Piaget, J. (1965). *The moral judgment of the child* (Paperback ed.). New York: Free Press.

Piaget, J. (1971). *The psychology of intelligence.* London: Routledge & Kegan Paul. (Original work published 1950)

Pietropaolo, S., Sun, Y., Li, R., Brana, C., Feldon, J., & Yee, B. K. (2008). The impact of voluntary exercise on mental health in rodents: A neuroplasticity perspective. *Behavioural Brain Research, 192*, 42–60.

Pietsch, J. H. (2004). Health care decision making and physician-aid-in-dying in Hawaii. *Journal of Legal Medicine, 25*, 303–332.

Pinquart, M., & Schindler, I. (2007). Changes of life satisfaction in the transition to retirement: A latent-class approach. *Psychology and Aging, 22*(3), 442–455.

Pitkanen, T., Kokko, K., Lyyra, A., & Pulkkinen, L. (2008). A developmental approach to alcohol drinking behaviour in adulthood: A follow-up study from age 8 to 42. *Addiction, 103* (Suppl. 1), 48–68.

Pitkanen, T., Lyyra, A. L., & Pulkkinen, L. (2005). Age of onset of drinking and the use of alcohol in adulthood: A follow-up study from age 8–42 for females and males. *Addiction, 100*, 652–661.

Pizzolato, J. E. (2007). Impossible selves: Investigating students' persistence decisions when their career-possible selves border on impossible. *Journal of Career Development, 33*(3), 201–223.

Plomin, R., & Bergeman, C. S. (1991). The nature of nurture: Genetic influence on "environmental" measures. *Behavioral and Brain Sciences, 14*, 373–427.

Plomin, R., & Spinath, F. M. (2004). Intelligence: Genetics, genes, and genomics. *Journal of Personality and Social Psychology, 86*, 112–129.

Plomin, R., DeFries, J. C., Craig, I. W., & McGuffin, P. (2003). Behavioral genomics. In R. Plomin, J. C. DeFries, I. W. Craig, & P. McGuffin (Eds.), *Behavioral genetics in the postgenomic era* (pp. 531–540). Washington, DC: American Psychological Association.

Pogrebin, L. C. (1996). *Getting over getting older: An intimate journey.* Boston: Little, Brown.

Pogson, C. E., Cober, A. B., Doverspike, D., & Rogers, J. R. (2003). Differences in self-reported work ethic across three career stages. *Journal of Vocational Behavior, 62*, 189–201.

Poirier, F. E., & Smith, E. O. (1974). Socializing functions of primate play. *American Zoologist, 14*, 275–287.

Ponomareva, N. V., Korovaitseva, G. I., & Rogaev, E. I. (2008). EEG alterations in non-demented individuals related to apolipoprotein E genotype and to risk of Alzheimer disease. *Neurobiology of Aging, 29*(6), 819–827.

Poortman, A. R., & Seltzer, J. A. (2007). Parents' expectations about childrearing after divorce: Does anticipating difficulty deter divorce? *Journal of Marriage and Family, 69*(1), 254–269.

Potter, J. E., Hopkins, K., Faundes, A., & Perpetuo, I. (2008). Women's autonomy and scheduled cesarean sections in Brazil: A cautionary tale. *Birth, 35*(1), 33–39.

Poulin, M., & Silver, R. (2008). World benevolence beliefs and well being across the lifespan. *Psychology and Aging, 23*, 19.

Prakash, K., & Coplan, R. J. (2007). Socioemotional characteristics and school adjustment of socially withdrawn children in India. *International Journal of Behavioral Development, 31*(2), 123–132.

Pratt, M. W., Norris, J. E., Hebblethwaite, S., & Arnold, M. L. (2008). Intergenerational transmission of values:

Family generativity and adolescents' narratives of parent and grandparent value teaching. *Journal of Personality, 76*(2), 171–198.

Pressley, M., Mohan, L., Raphael, L. M., & Fingeret, L. (2007). How does Bennett Woods Elementary School produce such high reading and writing achievement? *Journal of Educational Psychology, 99*(2), 221–240.

Preston, S. H. (1991). *Fatal years: Child mortality in late nineteenth-century America.* Princeton, NJ: Princeton University Press.

Previti, D., & Amato, P. R. (2004). Is infidelity a cause or a consequence of poor marital quality? *Journal of Social and Personal Relationships, 21,* 217–230.

Prevost, S. S., & Wallace, J. B. (2009). Dying in institutions. In J. L. Werth, & D. Blevins (Eds.), *Decision making near the end-of-life: Issues, developments, and future directions. Series in death, dying and bereavement* (pp. 189–208). New York: Routledge/Taylor & Francis Group.

Prinstein, M. J., & Cillessen, A. H. N. (2003). Forms and functions of adolescent peer aggression associated with high levels of peer status. *Merrill-Palmer Quarterly, 49,* 310–342.

Prinstein, M. J., & La Greca, A. M. (2002). Peer crowd affiliation and internalizing distress in childhood and adolescence: A longitudinal follow-back study. *Journal of Research on Adolescence, 12,* 325–351.

Proctor, M. H., Moore, L. L., Gao, D., Cupples, L. A., Bradlee, M. L., Hood, M. Y., & Ellison, R. C. (2003). Television viewing and change in body fat from preschool to early adolescence: The Framingham Children's Study. *International Journal of Obesity, 27,* 827–833.

Pruett, M. K., Insabella, G. M., & Gustafson, K. (2005). The collaborative divorce project: A court-based intervention for separating parents with young children. *Family Court Review, 43,* 38–51.

Pugzles Lorch, E., Eastham, D., Milich, R., Lemberger, C. C., Polley Sanchez, R., Welsh, R., & van den Broek, P. (2004). Difficulties in comprehending causal relations among children with ADHD: The role of cognitive engagement. *Journal of Abnormal Psychology, 113,* 56–63.

Puhl, R. M., & Latner, J. D. (2007). Stigman, obesity, and the health of the nation's children. *Psychological Bulletin, 133*(4), 557–580.

Putallaz, M., Grimes, C. L., Foster, K. J., Kupersmidt, J. B., Coie, J. D., &

Dearing, K. (2007). Overt and relational aggression and victimization: Multiple perspectives within the school setting. *Journal of School Psychology, 45,* 523–547.

Quadagno, J., & Stahl, S. M. (2003). Challenges in nursing home care: A research agenda. *Gerontologist, 43,* 4–6.

Quinlan, R. J. (2003). Father absence, parental care, and female reproductive development. *Evolution and Human Behavior, 24,* 376–390.

Rack, J. J., Burleson, B. R., Bodie, G. D., Holstrom, A. J., & Servaty-Seib, H. (2008). Bereaved adults' evaluations of grief management messages: Effects of message person centeredness, recipient individual differences, and contextual factors. *Death Studies, 32,* 399–427.

Rahman, A. N., & Schnelle, J. F. (2008). The nursing home culture-change movement: Recent past, present, and future directions for research. *The Gerontologist, 48*(2), 142–148.

Rahman, A., Iqbal, Z., & Harrington, R. (2003). Life events, social support and depression in childbirth: Perspectives from a rural community in the developing world. *Psychological Medicine, 33,* 1161–1167.

Raikes, H. A., & Thompson, R. A. (2006). Family emotional climate, attachment security and young children's emotion knowledge in a high risk sample. *British Journal of Developmental Psychology, 24,* 89–104.

Rallison, L., & Moules, N. J. (2004). The unspeakable nature of pediatric palliative care: Unveiling many cloaks. *Journal of Family Nursing, 10,* 287–301.

Rando, T. A. (1992–1993). The increasing prevalence of complicated mourning: The onslaught is just beginning. *Omega: Journal of Death and Dying, 26,* 43–59.

Raz, N., Rodrigue, K. M., Kennedy, K. M., & Acker, J. D. (2007). Vascular health and longitudinal changes in brain and cognition in middle-aged and older adults. *Neuropsychology, 21*(2), 149–157.

Raz, N., Rodrigue, K. M., Kennedy, K. M., & Land, S. (2009). Genetic and vascular modifiers of age-sensitive cognitive skills: Effects of COMT, DNF, APOE, and hypertension. *Neuropsychology, 23,* 105–116.

Reading, R. (2008). Comment on the impact of exposure to domestic violence on children and young people: A review of the literature. *Child Care, Health and Development, 34,* 840–841.

Ready, R. E., & Robinson, M. D. (2008). Do older individuals adapt to their traits?: Personality-emotion relations among younger and older adults. *Journal of Research in Personality, 42*(4), 1020–1030.

Reese, E., & Newcombe, R. (2007). Training mothers in elaborative reminiscing enhances children's autobiographical memory and narrative. *Child Development, 78*(4), 1153–1170.

Reese, E., Haden, C. A., & Fivush, R. (1993). Mother-child conversations about the past: Relationships of style and memory over time. *Cognitive Development, 8,* 403–430.

Reid, D. D., Brett, G. Z., Hamilton, P. J., Jarrett, R. J., Keen, H., & Rose, G. (1974). Cardiorespiratory disease and diabetes among middle-aged male civil servants. A study of screening and intervention. *Lancet, 1,* 469–473.

Reijneveld, S. A., van der Wal, M. F., Brugman, E., Sing, R. A. H., & Verloove-Vanhorick, S. P. (2004). Infant crying and abuse. *Lancet, 364,* 1340–1342.

Reimer, J., Paolitto, D. P., & Hersh, R. H. (1983). *Promoting moral growth: From Piaget to Kohlberg* (2nd ed.). New York: Longman.

Reimer, K. (2003). Committed to caring: Transformation in adolescent moral identity. *Applied Developmental Science, 7,* 129–137.

Reinders, H., & Youniss, J. (2006). School-based required community service and civic development in adolescents. *Applied Developmental Science, 10,* 2–12.

Reis, M., & Kallen, B. (2008). Maternal use of antipsychotics in early pregnancy and deliver outcome. *Journal of Clinical Psychopharmacology, 28*(3), 279–288.

Reisfield, G. M., & Wilson, G. R. (2004). Advance care planning redux: It's time to talk. *American Journal of Hospice & Palliative Care, 21,* 7–9.

Reissman, C., Aron, A., & Bergen, M. R. (1993). Shared activities and marital satisfaction: Causal direction and self-expansion versus boredom. *Journal of Social and Personal Relationships, 10,* 243–254.

Reitzes, D. C., & Mutran, E. J. (2004). Grandparenthood: Factors influencing frequency of grandparent-grandchildren contact and grandparent role satisfaction. *Journals of Gerontology: Series B: Psychological Sciences and Social Sciences, 59B,* S9-S16.

Reskin, B. (1993). Sex segregation in the workplace. *Annual Review of Sociology, 19,* 241–270.

Reuter-Lorenz, P. A., & Cappell, K. A. (2008). Neurocognitive aging and the compensation hypothesis. *Current Directions in Psychological Science, 17*(3), 177–182.

Rhoades, K. A. (2008). Children's responses to interparental conflict: A meta-analysis of their associations with child adjustment. *Child Development, 79,* 1942–1956.

Ricciardelli, L. A., & McCabe, M. P. (2004). A biopsychosocial model of disordered eating and the pursuit of muscularity in adolescent boys. *Psychological Bulletin, 130,* 179–205.

Ridgway, A., Northup, J., Pellegrin, A., LaRue, R., & Hightsoe, A. (2003). Effects of recess on the classroom behavior of children with and without Attention-Deficit Hyperactivity Disorder. *School Psychology Quarterly, 18,* 253–268.

Riegel, K. F., & Riegel, R. M. (1972). Development, drop, and death. *Developmental Psychology, 6,* 306–319.

Righetti, P., Dell'Avanzo, M., Grigio, M., & Nicolini, U. (2005). Maternal/paternal antenatal attachment and fourth-dimensional ultrasound technique: A preliminary report. *British Journal of Psychology, 96,* 129–137.

Rivas-Vazquez, R. A., Mendez, C., Rey, G. J., & Carrazana, E. J. (2004). Mild cognitive impairment: New neuropsychological and pharmacological target. *Archives of Clinical Neuropsychology, 19,* 11–27.

Rix, S. E. (2002). The labor market for older workers. *Generations, 26*(2), 25–30.

Roberto, K. A., & Jarrot, S. E. (2008). Family caregivers of older adults: A life span perspective. *Family Relations, 57*(1), 100–111.

Roberts, B. W., Kuncel, N. R., Shiner, R., Caspi, A., & Goldberg, L. R. (2007). The power of personality: The comparative validity of personality traits, socioeconomic status, and cognitive ability for predicting important life outcomes. *Perspectives on Psychological Science, 2,* 313–335.

Robine, J.-M., & Michel, J.-P. (2004). Looking forward to a general theory on population aging. *Journals of Gerontology: Series A: Biological Sciences and Medical Sciences, 59A,* 590–597.

Rodin, J., & Langer, E. J. (1980). Aging labels: The decline of control and the fall of self-esteem. *Journal of Social Issues, 36,* 12–29.

Roenker, D. L., Cissell, G. M., Ball, K. K., Wadley, V. G., & Edwards, J. D. (2003). Speed-of-processing and driving simulator training result in improved driving performance. *Human Factors, 45,* 218–233.

Roffwarg, H. P., Muzio, J. N., & Dement, W. C. (1966, April 29). Ontogenetic development of the human sleep-dream cycle. *Science, 152,* 604–619.

Rogers, C. H., Floyd, F. J., Seltzer, M. M., Greenberg, J., & Hong, J. (2008). Long-term effects of the death of a child on parents' adjustment in midlife. *Journal of Family Psychology, 22* (2), 203–211.

Rogoff, B. (1990). *Apprenticeship in thinking: Cognitive development in social context.* New York: Oxford University Press.

Rogoff, B., Paradise, R., Arauz, R. M., Correa-Chavez, M., & Angelillo, C. (2003). Firsthand learning through intent participation. *Annual Review of Psychology, 54,* 175–203.

Roisman, G. I. (2007). The psychophysiology of adult attachment relationships: Autonomic reactivity in marital and premarital interactions. *Developmental Psychology, 43*(1), 39–53.

Roisman, G. I., Clausell, E., Holland, A., Fortuna, K., & Elieff, C. (2008). Adult romantic relationships as contexts of human development: A multimethod comparison of same-sex couples with opposite-sex dating, engaged and married dyads. *Developmental Psychology, 44*(1), 91–101.

Rose, A. J., & Asher, S. R. (2000). Children's friendships. In C. Hendrick & S. S. Hendrick (Eds.), *Close relationships: A sourcebook* (pp. 47–57). Thousand Oaks, CA: Sage.

Rosen, B., & Jerdee, T. H. (1995). *The persistence of age and sex stereotypes in the 1990s.* Washington, DC: American Association of Retired Persons.

Rosenbaum, J. E. (2001). *Beyond college for all: Career paths for the forgotten half.* New York: Russell Sage Foundation.

Rosenbaum, J. E. (2009). Patient teenagers? A comparison of the sexual behavior of virginity pledgers and matched nonpledgers. *Pediatrics, 123,* 110–120.

Rosenblum, L. D., Miller, R. M., & Sanchez, K. (2007). Lip-read me now, hear me better later: Cross-modal transfer of talker-familiarity effects. *Psychological Science, 18*(5), 392–396.

Rosenfield, R. L., Lipton, R. B., & Drum, M. L. (2009). Thelarche, pubarche, and menarche attainment in children with normal and elevated body mass index. *Pediatrics, 123,* 84–88.

Roseth, C. J., Pellegrini, A. D., Bohn, C. M., Van Ryzin, M., & Vance, N. (2007). Preschoolers' aggression, affiliation, and social dominance relationships: An observational, longitudinal study. *Journal of School Psychology, 45,* 479–497.

Ross, L. A., Clay, O. J., Edwards, J. D., Ball, K. K., Wadley, V. G., Vance, D. E., Cissell, G. M., Roenker, D. L., & Joyce, J. J. (2009). Do older drivers at-risk for crashes modify their driving over time? *Journal of Gerontology: Psychological Sciences, 64B,* 163–170.

Rothermund, K., & Brandtstädter, J. (2003). Depression in later life: Cross-sequential patterns and possible determinants. *Psychology and Aging, 18,* 80–90.

Rowe, D. C. (1981). Environmental and genetic influences on dimensions of perceived parenting: A twin study. *Developmental Psychology, 17,* 203–208.

Rowe, D. C. (1983). A biometrical analysis of perceptions of family environment: A study of twin and singleton sibling kinships. *Child Development, 54,* 416–423.

Rowe, D. C. (2003). Assessing genotype-environment interactions and correlations in the postgenomic era. In R. Plomin, J. C. DeFries, I. W. Craig, & P. McGuffin (Eds.), *Behavioral genetics in the postgenomic era* (pp. 71–86). Washington, DC: American Psychological Association.

Rowe, G., Hasher, L., & Turcotte, J. (2008). Age differences in visuospatial working memory. *Psychology and Aging, 23*(1), 79–84.

Rowe, J. W., & Kahn, R. L. (1998). *Successful aging.* New York: Pantheon Books.

Rowe, M. L., Levine, S. C., Fisher, J. A., & Goldin-Meadow, S. (2009). Does linguistic input play the same role in language learning for children with and without early brain injury? *Developmental Psychology, 45,* 90–102.

Royal College of Obstetricians and Gynaecologists [RCOG]. (1999). Alcohol consumption in pregnancy. Retrieved January 25, 2006, from http://www.rcog.org.uk/index.asp?PageID=509

Rubertsson, C., Waldenström, U., & Wickberg, B. (2003). Depressive mood in early pregnancy: Prevalence and women at risk in a national Swedish sample. *Journal of Reproductive and Infant Psychology, 21,* 113–123.

Rubin, K. H., Bukowski, W. M., & Parker, J. G. (2006). Peer interactions, relationships, and groups. In N. Eisenberg, W. Damon, & R. M. Lerner (Eds.), *Handbook of child psychology, Vol. 3: Social, emotional, and personality development* (6th ed.) (pp. 571–645). Hoboken, NJ: John Wiley & Sons Inc.

Rubin, K., Fredstrom, B., & Bowker, J. (2008). Future directions in . . . friendship in childhood and early adolescence. *Social Development, 17,* 1085–1096.

Ruble, D. N., Martin, C., & Berenbaum, S. A. (2006). Gender development. In N. Eisenberg, W. Damon, & R. M. Lerner (Eds.), *Handbook of child psychology, Vol. 3: Social, emotional, and personality development* (6th ed.) (pp. 858–932). Hoboken, NJ: John Wiley & Sons Inc.

Ruffman, T., Perner, J., Naito, M., Parkin, L., & Clements, W. A. (1998). Older (but not younger) siblings facilitate false belief understanding. *Developmental Psychology, 34,* 161–174.

Rumbaut, R., (2008, Mar.). *Divergent destinies: Acculturation, social mobility, and adult transitions among children of Latin American and Asian immigrants.* Paper presented at the Annual Meeting of the Society for Research in Adolescence, Chicago, IL.

Rumbaut, R. G. (2008, March). *Divergent destinies: Acculturation, social mobility, and adult transitions among children of Latin American and Asian immigrants.* Presented at 12th Biennial Meeting of Society for Research on Adolescence, Chicago, IL.

Rusbult, C. E., Kumashiro, M., Kubacka, K. E., & Finkel, E. J. (2009). "The part of me that you bring out": Ideal similarity and the Michelangelo phenomenon. *Journal of Personality and Social Psychology, 96,* 61–82.

Rushton, J. P., & Jensen, A. R. (2005). Thirty years of research on race differences in cognitive ability. *Psychology, Public Policy, and Law, 11,* 235–294.

Rutters, F., Nieuwenhuizen, A. G., Vogels, N., Bouwman, F., Mariman, E., & Westerterp-Plantenga, M. S. (2008). Leptin-adiposity relationship changes, plus behavioral and parental factors, are involved in the development of body weight in a Dutch children cohort. *Physiology & Behavior, 93*(4–5), 967–974.

Ryan, R. M., Deci, E. L., Grolnick, W. S., & La Guardia, J. G. (2006). The significance of autonomy and autonomy support in psychological development and psychopathology. In D. Cicchetti &

D. J. Cohen (eds.), *Developmental psychopathology, Vol. 1: Theory and method* (2nd ed., pp. 795–849). Hoboken, NJ: John Wiley & Sons Inc.

Rybash, J. M., Hoyer, W. J., & Roodin, P. (1986). *Adult cognition and aging: Developmental changes in processing, knowing, and thinking.* New York: Pergamon Press.

Saarni, C. (1999). *The development of emotional competence.* New York: Guilford Press.

Sagi, A., Koren-Karie, N., Gini, M., Ziv, Y., & Joels, T. (2002). Shedding further light on the effects of various types and quality of early child care on infant-mother attachment relationship: The Haifa Study of Early Child Care. *Child Development, 73,* 1166–1186.

Sagi-Schwartz, A., & Aviezer, O. (2005). Correlates of attachment to multiple caregivers in kibbutz children from birth to emerging adulthood: The Haifa Longitudinal Study. In K. E. Grossmann, K. Grossmann, & E. Waters (Eds.), *Attachment from infancy to adulthood: The major longitudinal studies* (pp. 165–197). New York: Guilford Press.

Salisbury, A., Law, K., LaGasse, L., & Lester, B. (2003). Maternal-fetal attachment. *Journal of the American Medical Association, 289,* 1701.

Salmela-Aro, K., & Suikkari, A. M. (2008). Letting go of your dreams—Adjustment of child-related goal appraisals and depressive symptoms during infertility treatment. *Journal of Research in Personality, 42,* 988–1003.

Salmela-Aro, K., Aunola, K., & Nurmi, J. E. (2007). Personal goals during emerging adulthood: A 10-year follow up. *Journal of Adolescent Research, 22*(6), 690–715.

Salthouse, T. A. (2003). Memory aging from 18 to 80. *Alzheimer's Disease and Associated Disorders, 17,* 162–167.

Salthouse, T. A. (2006). Mental exercise and mental aging. *Perspectives on Psychological Science, 1,* 68–87.

Sandler, I. N., Wolchik, S. A., & Ayers, T. S. (2008). Resilience rather than recovery: A contextual framework on adaptation following bereavement. *Death Studies, 32,* 59–73.

Sandstrom, K. L. (2003). On coming to terms with death and dying: Neglected dimensions of identity work. In C. D. Bryant (Ed.), *Handbook of death & dying* (pp. 468–474). Thousand Oaks, CA: Sage.

Santesso, D. L., Schmidt, L. A., Trainor, L. J. (2007). Frontal brain electrical activity (EEG) and heart rate in response to affective infant-directed (ID) speech in 9-month-old infants. *Brain and Cognition, 65,* 14–21.

Satariano, W. A. (2007). Driving and the promotion of safe mobility in order populations. *Journal of Gerontology, 62A*(10), 1111–1112.

Sattler, J. M. (2001). *Assessment of children: Cognitive applications* (4th ed.). La Mesa, CA: Jerome M. Sattler.

Savage, C. L., Anthony, J., Lee, R., Kappesser, M. L., & Rose, B. (2007). The culture of pregnancy and infant care in African American women: An ethnographic study. *Journal of Transcultural Nursing, 18*(3), 215–223.

Savin-Williams, R. C. (2001). *Mom, dad, I'm gay. How families negotiate coming out.* Washington, DC: American Psychological Association.

Savin-Williams, R. C. (2008). Then and now: Recruitment, definition, diversity, and positive attributes of same-sex populations. *Developmental Psychology, 44*(1), 135–138.

Savin-Williams, R. C., & Ream, G. L. (2003). Sex variations in the disclosure to parents of same-sex attractions. *Journal of Family Psychology, 17,* 429–438.

Savishinsky, J. (2004). The volunteer and the Sannyasin: Archetypes of retirement in America and India. *International Journal of Aging & Human Development, 59,* 25–41.

Sayer, L. C., Bianchi, S. M., & Robinson, J. P. (2004). Are parents investing less in children? Trends in mothers' and fathers' time with children. *American Journal of Sociology, 110,* 1–43.

Scarr, S. (1997). Behavior-genetic and socialization theories of intelligence: Truce and reconciliation. In R. J. Sternberg & E. L. Grigorenko (eds.), *Intelligence, heredity, and environment* (pp. 3–41). New York: Cambridge University Press.

Schacke, C., & Zank, S. R. (2006). Measuring the effectiveness of adult day care as a facility to support family caregivers of dementia patients. *Journal of Applied Gerontology, 25,* 65–81.

Schaie, K. W. (1996). Intellectual development in adulthood. In J. E. Birren, K. W. Schaie, R. P. Abeles, M. Gatz, & T. A. Salthouse (Eds.), *Handbook of the psychology of aging* (4th ed., pp. 266–286). San Diego, CA: Academic Press.

Schaie, K. W., & Zanjani, F. A. K. (2006). Intellectual development across adulthood. In C. Hoare (ed.), *Handbook of adult development and learning* (pp. 99–122). New York: Oxford University Press.

Schaie, K. W., Willis, S. L., & Caskie, G. I. L. (2004). The Seattle longitudinal study: Relationship between personality and cognition. *Aging, Neuro-psychology, and Cognition, 11*, 304–324.

Scheibe, S., & Blanchard-Fields, F. (2009). Effects of regulating emotions on cognitive performance: What is costly for young adults is not so costly for older adults. *Psychology and Aging, 24*, 217–223.

Schirduan, V., & Case, K. (2004). Mindful curriculum leadership for students with attention deficit hyperactivity disorder: Leading in elementary schools by using multiple intelligences theory (SUMIT). *Teachers College Record, 106*, 87–95.

Schlegel, A. (1995). The cultural management of adolescent sexuality. In P. R. Abramson & S. D. Pinkerton (eds.), *Sexual nature, sexual culture* (pp. 177–194). Chicago: University of Chicago Press.

Schlegel, A., & Barry, H., III. (1991). *Adolescence: An anthropological inquiry.* New York: Free Press.

Schlinger, H. D. (2003). The myth of intelligence. *Psychological Record, 53*, 15–32.

Schmitt, D. P., Shackelford, T. K., Duntley, J., Tooke, W., Buss, D. M., Fisher, M. L., Lavellée, M., & Vasey, P. (2002). Is there an early-30s peak in female sexual desire? Cross-sectional evidence from the United States and Canada. *Canadian Journal of Human Sexuality, 11*, 1–18.

Schneidman, E. (Ed.). (1976). *Death: Current perspectives.* Palo Alto, CA: Mayfield.

Schoen, R., & Cheng, Y.-H. A. (2006). Partner choice and the differential retreat from marriage. *Journal of Marriage and Family, 68*, 1–10.

Scholte, R. H. J., Overbeek, G., Brink, G. B., Rommes, E., de Kemp, R. A. T., Goossens, L., & Engels, R. C. M. E. (2009). The significance of reciprocal and unilateral friendships for peer victimization in adolescence. *Journal of Youth and Adolescence, 38*, 89–100.

Schooler, C. (1999). The workplace environment: Measurement, psychological effects, and basic issues. In S. L. Friedman & T. D. Wachs (Eds.), *Measuring environment across the life span: Emerging methods and concepts* (pp. 229–246). Washington, DC: American Psychological Association.

Schooler, C. (2001). The intellectual effects of the demands of the work environment. In R. J. Sternberg & E. L. Grigorenko (Eds.), *Environmental effects on cognitive abilities* (pp. 363–380). Mahwah, NJ: Erlbaum.

Schooler, C. (2007). Use it and keep it, longer, probably: A reply to Salthouse (2006). *Perspectives on Psychological Science, 2*(1), 24–29.

Schooler, C., Mulatu, M. S., & Oates, G. (2004). Occupational self-direction, intellectual functioning, and self-directed orientation in older workers: Findings and implications for individuals and societies. *American Journal of Sociology, 110*, 161–197.

Schooler, D. (2008). Real women have curves: A longitudinal investigation of TV and body image development of Latina adolescents. *Journal of Adolescent Research, 23*(2), 132–153.

Schoppe-Sullivan, S. J., Brown, G. L., Cannon, E. A., Mangelsdorf, S. C., & Sokolowski, M. S. (2008). Maternal gatekeeping, coparenting quality, and fathering behavior in families with infants. *Journal of Family Psychology, 22*(3), 389–398.

Schor, J. (1991). *The overworked American: The unexpected decline of leisure.* New York: Basic Books.

Schulenberg, J. E., & Zarrett, N. R. (2006). Mental health during emerging adulthood: Continuity and discontinuity in courses, causes, and functions. In J. J. Arnett, & J. L. Tanner (Eds.), *Emerging adults in America: Coming of age in the 21st century* (pp. 135–172). Washington, DC: American Psychological Association.

Schupf, N., Pang, D., Patel, B. N., Silverman, W., Schubert, R., Lai, F., Kline, J. K., Stern, Y., Ferin, M., Tycko, B., & Mayeux, R. (2003). Onset of dementia is associated with age at menopause in women with Down's syndrome. *Annals of Neurology, 54*, 433–438.

Schwartz, A. N., Campos, J. J., & Baisel, E. J. (1973). The visual cliff: Cardiac and behavioral responses on the deep and shallow sides at five and nine months of age. *Journal of Experimental Child Psychology, 15*, 86–99.

Schwartz, C. E., Wright, C. I., Shin, L. M., Kagan, J., & Rauch, S. L. (2003, June 20). Inhibited and uninhibited infants "grown up": Adult amygdalar response to novelty. *Science, 300*, 1952–1953.

Scrimsher, S., & Tudge, J. (2003). The teaching/learning relationship in the first years of school: Some revolutionary implications of Vygotsky's theory. *Early Education and Development, 14*, 293–312.

Seale, C. (2009). Legalisation of euthanasia or physician-assisted suicide: survey of doctors' attitudes. *Palliative Medicine, 23*, 205–212.

Seifer, R., Sameroff, A. J., Dickstein, S., Hayden, L. C., & Schiller, M. (1996). Parental psychopathology and sleep variation in children. *Child and Adolescent Psychiatric Clinics of North America, 5*, 715–727.

Self-Brown, S. R., & Mathews, S. (2003). Effects of classroom structure on student achievement goal orientation. *Journal of Educational Research, 97*, 106–111.

Shah, M., Quill, T., Norton, S., Sada, Y., Buckley, M., & Fridd, C. (2008). "What bothers you most?" Initial responses from patients receiving palliative care consultation. *American Journal of Hospice & Palliative Medicine, 25* (2), 88–92.

Shapiro, M., Ingols, C., & Blake-Beard, S. (2008). Confronting career double blinds: Implications for women, organizations, and career practitioners. *Journal of Career Development, 34*(3), 309–333.

Shaw, B. A., Krause, N., Liang, J., & Bennett, J. (2007). Tracking changes in social relations throughout late life. *Journal of Gerontology: SOCIAL SCIENCES, 62B*(2), S90–S99.

Shay, N. L., & Knutson, J. F. (2008). Maternal depression and trait anger as risk factors for escalated physical discipline. *Child Maltreatment, 13*(1), 39–49.

Shaywitz, S. E., Morris, R., & Shaywitz, B. A. (2008). The education of dyslexic children from childhood to young adulthood. *Annual Review of Psychology, 59*, 451–475.

Shearer, C. L., Crouter, A. C., & McHale, S. M. (2005). Parents' perceptions of changes in mother-child and father-child relationships during adolescence. *Journal of Adolescent Research, 20*, 662–684.

Shelden, R. G., Tracy, S. K., & Brown, W. B. (1997). *Youth gangs in American society.* Belmont, CA: Wadsworth.

Shernoff, D. J., Csikszentmihalyi, M., Shneider, B., & Shernoff, E. S. (2003). Student engagement in high school classrooms from the perspective of flow theory. *School Psychology Quarterly, 18*, 158–176.

Shih, F., Lin, H., Gau, M., Chen, C., Hsiao, S., Shih, S., Sheu, S. J. (2009). Spiritual needs of Taiwan's older patients with terminal cancer. *Oncology Nursing Forum, 36,* e31–e38.

Shonkoff, J. P., & Phillips, D. A. (2000b). Growing up in child care. In J. P. Shonkoff & D. A. Phillips (Eds.), *From neurons to neighborhoods: The science of early childhood development* (pp. 297–327). Washington, DC: National Academy Press.

Shulruf, B., Morton, S., Goodyear-Smith, F., O'Loughlin, L., & Dixon, R. (2007). Designing multidisciplinary longitudinal studies of human development: Analyzing past research to inform methodology. *Evaluation & the Health Professions, 30,* 207–228.

Siegler, A. L. (2005). Home is where the hurt is: Developmental consequences of domestic conflict and violence on children and adolescents. In L. Gunsberg & P. Hymowitz (Eds.), *A handbook of divorce and custody: Forensic, developmental, and clinical perspectives* (pp. 61–80). Hillsdale, NJ: Analytic Press.

Siklos, S., & Kerns, K. A. (2004). Assessing multitasking in children with ADHD using a modified Six Elements Test. *Archives of Clinical Neuropsychology, 19,* 347–361.

Silventoinen, K., Haukka, J., Dunkel, L., Tynelius, P., & Rasmussen, F. (2008). Genetics of pubertal timing and its associations with relative weight in childhood and adult height: The Swedish young male twins study. *Pediatrics, 121*(4), 885–891.

Silverman, P. R., & Klass, D. (1996). Introduction: What's the problem? In D. Klass, P. R. Silverman, & S. L. Nickman (Eds.), *Continuing bonds: New understandings of grief* (pp. 3–27). Washington, DC: Taylor & Francis.

Silverstein, M., Conroy, S. J., Wang, H., Giarrusso, R., & Bengtson, V. L. (2002). Reciprocity in parent-child relations over the adult life course. *Journals of Gerontology: Series B: Psychological Sciences and Social Sciences, 57B,* S3–S13.

Simmons, R. G., & Blyth, D. A. (1987). *Moving into adolescence: The impact of pubertal change and school context.* Hawthorne, NY: Aldine.

Simonton, D. K. (1997). Creative productivity: A predictive and explanatory model of career trajectories and landmarks. *Psychological Review, 104,* 66–89.

Simonton, D. K. (2002). Longitudinal changes in creativity. In D. K. Simonton (ed.), *Great psychologists and their times: Scientific insights into psychology's history* (pp. 67–101). Washington, DC: American Psychological Association.

Simonton, D. K. (2007). Creative life cycles in literature: Poets versus novelists or conceptualists versus experimentalists? *Psychology of Aesthetics, Creativity, and the Arts, 1*(3), 133–139.

Simpson, J. A., Collins, W. A., Tran, S., & Hayden, K. C. (2007). Attachment and the experience and expression of emotions in romantic relationships: A developmental perspective. *Journal of Personality and Social Psychology, 92*(2), 355–367.

Singg, S. (2003). Parents and the death of a child. In C. D. Bryant (Ed.), *Handbook of death & dying* (pp. 880–884). Thousand Oaks, CA: Sage.

Singley, S., & Hynes, K. (2005). Transitions to parenthood: Work-family policies, gender, and the couple context. *Gender & Society, 19,* 376–397.

Sinnott, J. D. (1989). General systems theory: A rationale for the study of everyday memory. In L. W. Poon, D. C. Rubin, & B. A. Wilson (Eds.), *Everyday cognition in adulthood and late life* (pp. 59–70). New York: Cambridge University Press.

Sinnott, J. D. (2003). Postformal thought and adult development: Living in balance. In J. Demick & C. Andreoletti (Eds.), *Handbook of adult development* (pp. 221–238). New York: Kluwer/Plenum.

Sirois, S., & Jackson, I. (2007). Social cognition in infancy: A critical review of research on higher order abilities. *European Journal of Developmental Psychology. Special Issue: Social Cognition During Infancy, 4,* 46–64.

Sisk, C. L., & Foster, D. L. (2004). The neural basis of puberty and adolescence. *Nature Neuroscience, 7,* 1040–1042.

Skinner, B. F. (1960). *The behavior of organisms: An experimental analysis.* New York: Appleton-Century-Crofts.

Skinner, B. F. (1974). *About behaviorism.* New York: Knopf.

Slack, T., & Jensen, L. (2008). Employment hardship among older workers: Does residential and gender inequality extend into older age? *Journal of Gerontology: SOCIAL SCIENCES, 63B*(1), S15–S24.

Slater, A. (2001). Visual perception. In G. Bremner & A. Fogel (Eds.), *Blackwell handbook of infant development* (pp. 5–34). Malden, MA: Blackwell.

Slater, A., Von der Schulenburg, C., Brown, E., Badenoch, M., Butterworth, G., Parsons, S., & Samuels, C. (1998). Newborn infants prefer attractive faces. *Infant Behavior & Development, 21,* 345–354.

Slobin, D. I. (1972). Children and language: They learn the same way all around the world. *Psychology Today, 6*(2), 71–74, 82.

Small, B. J., Hertzog, C., Hultsch, D. F., & Dixon, R. A. (2003). Stability and change in adult personality over 6 years: Findings from the Victoria Longitudinal Study. *Journals of Gerontology: Series B: Psychological Sciences and Social Sciences, 58B,* P166-P176.

Smart, J., & Hiscock, H. (2007). Early infant crying and sleeping problems: A pilot study of impact on parental well-being and parent-endorsed strategies for management. *Journal of Paediatrics and Child Health, 43,* 284–290.

Smeets, E., Roefs, A., van Furth, E., & Jansen, A. (2008). Attentional bias for body and food in eating disorders: Increased distraction, speeded detection, or both? *Behavior Research and Therapy, 46,* 229–238.

Smetana, J. G., Campione-Barr, N., & Metzger, A. (2006). Adolescent development in interpersonal and societal contexts. *Annual Review of Psychology, 57,* 255–284.

Smetana, J. G., Daddis, C., & Chuang, S. S. (2003). "Clean your room!" A longitudinal investigation of adolescent-parent conflict and conflict resolution in middle-class African American families. *Journal of Adolescent Research, 18,* 631–650.

Smetana, J. G., Kochanska, G., & Chuang, S. (2000). Mothers' conceptions of everyday rules for young toddlers: A longitudinal investigation. *Merrill-Palmer Quarterly, 46,* 391–416.

Smith, A. B., Taylor, E., Brammer, M., Halari, R., & Rubia, K. (2008). Reduced activation in right lateral prefrontal cortex and anterior cingulated gyrus in medication-naïve adolescents with attention deficit hyperactivity disorder during time discrimination. *The Journal of Child Psychology and Psychiatry, 49,* 977–985.

Smith, M. C. (1998). Sibling placement in foster care: An exploration of associated concurrent preschool-aged child functioning. *Children and Youth Services Review, 20,* 389–412.

Smith, M. E. (1926). An investigation of the development of the sentence and the extent of vocabulary in young children. *University of Iowa Studies: Child Welfare, 3,* 92.

Smith, P. K., Cowie, H., Olafsson, R. F., Liefooghe, A. P. D., Almeida, A., Araki, H., del Barrio, C., Costabile, A., Dekleva, B., Houndoumadi, A., Kim, K., Olaffson, R. P., Ortega, R., Pain, J., Pateraki, L., Schafer, M., Singer, M., Smorti, A., Toda, Y., Tomasson, H., & Wenxin, Z. (2002a). Definitions of bullying: A comparison of terms used, and age and gender differences, in a fourteen-country international comparison. *Child Development, 73,* 1119–1133.

Smith, P. K., Smees, R., Pellegrini, A. D., & Menesini, E. (2002b). Comparing pupil and teacher perceptions for playful fighting, serious fighting, and positive peer interaction. In J. L. Roopnarine (Ed.), *Conceptual, social-cognitive, and contextual issues in the fields of play* (pp. 235–245). Westport, CT: Ablex.

Smits, J., & Monden, C. (2009). Length of life inequality around the globe. *Social Science and Medicine, 68,* 1114–1123.

Smock, P. J., & Gupta, S. (2002). Cohabitation in contemporary North America. In A. Booth & A. C. Crouter (Eds.), *Just living together: Implications of cohabitation on families, children, and social policy* (pp. 53–84). Mahwah, NJ: Erlbaum.

Smock, P. J., Manning, W. D., & Porter, M. (2005). "Everything's there except money": How money shapes decisions to marry among cohabitors. *Journal of Marriage and Family, 67,* 680–696.

Smolucha, L., & Smolucha, F. (1998). The social origins of mind: Post-Piagetian perspectives on pretend play. In O. N. Saracho & B. Spodek (Eds.), *Multiple perspectives on play in early childhood education* (pp. 34–58). Albany, NY: State University of New York Press.

Snarey, J. R. (1985). Cross-cultural universality of social-moral development: A critical review of Kohlbergian research. *Psychological Bulletin, 97,* 202–232.

Snyder, L. (1999). *Speaking our minds: Personal reflections from individuals with Alzheimer's.* New York: Freeman.

Soderlund, G., Sikstrom, S., & Smart, A. (2007). Listen to the noise: Noise is beneficial for cognitive performance in ADHD. *Journal of Child Psychology and Psychiatry, 48*(8), 840–847.

Sodian, B., & Thoermer, C. (2008). Precursors to a theory of mind in infancy: Perspectives for research on autism. *The Quarterly Journal of Experimental Psychology, 61*(1), 27–39.

Solum, E. M., Slettebo, A., & Hauge, S. (2008). Prevention of unethical actions in nursing homes. *Nursing Ethics, 15*(4), 536–548.

Son, J., Erno, A., Shea, G., Femia, E. E., Zarit, S. H., & Stephens, M. P. (2007). The caregiver stress process and health outcomes. *Journal of Aging and Health, 19,* 871–887.

Sossou, M.-A. (2002). Widowhood practices in West Africa: The silent victims. *International Journal of Social Welfare, 11,* 201–209.

Spear, L. P. (2008). The psychology of adolescence. In K. K. Kline (Ed.), *Authoritative Communities: The Scientific Cases for Nurturing the Whole Child* (pp. 263–280). New York: Springer-Verlag.

Spinath, B., & Steinmayr, R. (2008). Longitudinal analysis of intrinsic motivation and competence beliefs: Is there a relation over time? *Child Development, 49,* 1555–1569.

Spitzer, D., Neufeld, A., Harrison, M., Hughes, K., & Stewart, M. (2003). Caregiving in transnational context: "My wings have been cut; where can I fly?" *Gender & Society, 17,* 267–286.

Spitzer, R. L. (2003). Can some gay men and lesbians change their sexual orientation? 200 participants reporting a change from homosexual to heterosexual orientation. *Archives of Sexual Behavior, 32,* 403–417.

Spronk, K. (2004). Good death and bad death in ancient Israel according to biblical lore. *Social Science & Medicine, 58,* 985–995.

Sroufe, L. A. (2000). Early relationships and the development of children. *Infant Mental Health Journal, 21,* 67–74.

Sroufe, L. A., Egeland, B., Carlson, E., & Collins, W. A. (2005). Placing early attachment experiences in developmental context: The Minnesota Longitudinal Study. In K. E. Grossmann, K. Grossmann, & E. Waters (Eds.), *Attachment from infancy to adulthood: The major longitudinal studies* (pp. 48–70). New York: Guilford Press.

St. Claire, L., & He, Y. (2009). How do I know if I need a hearing aid? Further support for the self-categorisation approach to symptom perception. *Applied Psychology: An international review, 58,* 24–41.

St. James-Roberts, I. (2007). Helping parents to manage infant crying and sleeping: A review of the evidence and its implications for services. *Child Abuse Review, 16,* 47–69.

Stacks, A. M. (2007). Defensive dysregulation in preschool children's attachment story narratives and its relation to attachment classification and externalizing behaviour. *School Psychology International, 28*(3), 294–312.

Stahl, G. K., Miller, E. L., & Tung, R. L. (2002). Toward the boundaryless career: A closer look at the expatriate career concept and the perceived implications of an international assignment. *Journal of World Business, 37,* 216–227.

Stamatiadis, N. (1996). Gender effect on the accident patterns of elderly drivers. *Journal of Applied Gerontology, 15,* 8–22.

Stamatiadis, N., Agent, K. R., & Ridgeway, M. (2003). Driver license renewal for the elderly: A case study. *Journal of Applied Gerontology, 22,* 42–56.

Stanford, E. P., & Usita, P. M. (2002). Retirement: Who is at risk? *Generations, 26*(2), 45–48.

Stanton, C., Ronsman, C., & Baltimore Group on Cesarean. (2008). Recommendations for routine reporting on indications for cesarean delivery in developing countries. *Birth, 35*(3), 204–211.

State of Oregon Department of Human Services. (n.d.). Death with dignity act. Retrieved October 17, 2006, from http://oregon.gov/DHS/ph/pas/

Stattin, H., & Magnusson, D. (1990). *Pubertal maturation in female development.* Hillsdale, NJ: Erlbaum.

Stebbins, H., & Knitzer, J. (2007). *State early childhood policies.* New York, NY: Columbia University. National Center for Children in Poverty.

Steele, S., Joseph, R. M., & Tager-Flusberg, H. (2003). Brief report: Developmental change in theory of mind abilities in children with autism. *Journal of Autism and Developmental Disorders, 33,* 461–467.

Stein, J. H., & Reiser, L. W. (1994). A study of White middle-class adolescent boys' responses to "semenarche" (the first ejaculation). *Journal of Youth and Adolescence, 23,* 373–384.

Steinberg, L. (2001). We know some things: Parent-adolescent relationships in retrospect and prospect. *Journal of Research on Adolescence, 11,* 1–19.

Steinberg, L. (2005). Cognitive and affective development in adolescence. *Trends in Cognitive Sciences, 9,* 69–74.

Steinberg, L. (2008). A social neuroscience perspective on adolescent risk-taking. *Developmental Review, 28,* 78–106.

Steinberg, L. D., & Hill, J. P. (1978). Patterns of family interaction as a function of age, the onset of puberty, and formal thinking. *Developmental Psychology, 14,* 683–684.

Steinberg, L., Albert, D., Cauffman, E., Banich, M., Graham, S., & Woolard, J. (2008). Age differences in sensation seeking and impulsivity as indexed by behavior and self-report: Evidence for a dual systems model. *Developmental Psychology, 44,* 1764–1778.

Steinberg, L., Graham, S., O'Brien, L., Woolard, J., Cauffman, E., & Banich, M. (2009). Age differences in future orientation and delay discounting. *Child Development, 80,* 28–44.

Steinberg, L., & Monahan, K. C. (2007). Age differences in resistance to peer influence. *Developmental Psychology, 43*(6), 1531–1543.

Stephan, Y., Fouquereau, E., & Fernandez, A. (2008). The relation between self-determination and retirement satisfaction among active retired individuals. *International Journal of Aging and Human Development, 66*(4), 329–345.

Stephens, D., Vetter, N., & Lewis, P. (2003). Investigating lifestyle factors affecting hearing aid candidature in the elderly. *International Journal of Audiology, 42*(Suppl. 2), 2S33–32S38.

Sternberg, R. J. (1984). Toward a triarchic theory of human intelligence. *Behavioral and Brain Sciences, 7,* 269–315.

Sternberg, R. J. (1986). A triangular theory of love. *Psychological Review, 93,* 119–135.

Sternberg, R. J. (1988). Triangulating love. In R. J. Sternberg & M. L. Barnes (Eds.), *The psychology of love* (pp. 119–138). New Haven, CT: Yale University Press.

Sternberg, R. J. (1996). *Successful intelligence: How practical and creative intelligence determine success in life.* New York: Simon & Schuster.

Sternberg, R. J. (1997). The triarchic theory of intelligence. In D. P. Flanagan, J. L. Genshaft, & P. L. Harrison (Eds.), *Contemporary intellectual assessment: Theories, tests, and issues* (pp. 92–104). New York: Guilford Press.

Sternberg, R. J. (2004). A triangular theory of love. In H. T. Reis & C. E. Rusbult (Eds.), *Close relationships: Key readings* (pp. 213–227). Philadelphia: Taylor & Francis.

Sternberg, R. J. (2007). Who are the bright children? The cultural context of being and acting intelligent. *Educational Researcher, 36*(3), 148–155.

Sternberg, R. J., & Berg, C. A. (1992). *Intellectual development.* New York: Cambridge University Press.

Sternberg, R. J., & Grigorenko, E. L. (2007). *Teaching for successful intelligence: To increase student learning and achievement* (2nd ed.). Thousand Oaks, CA: Corwin Press.

Sternberg, R. J., Grigorenko, E. L., & Bundy, D. A. (2001). The predictive value of IQ. *Merrill-Palmer Quarterly, 47,* 1–41.

Sternberg, R. J., Grigorenko, E. L., & Kidd, K. K. (2005). Intelligence, race, and genetics. *American Psychologist, 60,* 46–59.

Sternberg, R. J., Torff, B., & Grigorenko, E. L. (1998). Teaching for successful intelligence raises school achievement. *Phi Delta Kappan, 79,* 667–669.

Stewart, A. L., Dean, M. L., & Gregorich, S. E. (2007). Race/ethnicity, socioeconomic status and the health of pregnant women. *Journal of Health Psychology, 12*(2), 285–300.

Stewart-Knox, B., Gardiner, K., & Wright, M. (2003). What is the problem with breast-feeding? A qualitative analysis of infant feeding perceptions. *Journal of Human Nutrition and Dietetics, 16,* 265–273.

Stice, E., & Whitenton, K. (2002). Risk factors for body dissatisfaction in adolescent girls: A longitudinal investigation. *Developmental Psychology, 38,* 669–678.

Stice, E., Marti, C. N., Spoor, S., Presnell, K., & Shaw, H. (2008). Dissonance and healthy weight eating disorder prevention programs: Long-term effects from a randomized efficacy trial. *Journal of Consulting and Clinical Psychology, 76*(2), 329–340.

Stipek, D. J. (1996). Motivation and instruction. In D. C. Berliner & R. C. Calfee (Eds.), *Handbook of educational psychology* (pp. 85–113). New York: Macmillan Library Reference.

Stipek, D. J. (1997). Success in school— For a head start in life. In S. S. Luthar, J. A. Burack, D. Cicchetti, & J. R. Weisz (Eds.), *Developmental psychopathology: Perspectives on adjustment, risk, and disorder* (pp. 75–92). New York: Cambridge University Press.

Stone, M. R., & Brown, B. B. (1998). In the eye of the beholder: Adolescents' perceptions of peer crowd stereotypes. In R. E. Muuss & H. D. Porton (Eds.), *Adolescent behavior and society: A book of readings* (5th ed., pp. 158–169). New York: McGraw-Hill.

Storandt, M. (2008). Cognitive deficits in the early stages of Alzheimer's disease [Abstract]. *Current Directions in Psychological Science, 17*(3), 198–202.

Stott, D. J., Langhorne, P., & Knight, P. V. (2008). Multidisciplinary care for elderly people in the community. *Lancet, 371,* 699–700.

Straus, M. A., & Donnelly, D. A. (1994). *Beating the devil out of them: Corporal punishment in American families.* New York: Lexington Books.

Straus, M. A., & Stewart, J. H. (1999). Corporal punishment by American parents: National data on prevalence, chronicity, severity, and duration, in relation to child and family characteristics. *Clinical Child and Family Psychology Review, 2,* 55–70.

Strauss, B. (2002). *Involuntary childlessness: Psychological assessment, counseling, and psychotherapy.* Seattle, WA: Hogrefe & Huber.

Strawbridge, W. J., Wallhagen, M. I., Shema, S. J., & Kaplan, G. A. (2000). Negative consequences of hearing impairment in old age: A longitudinal analysis. *Gerontologist, 40,* 320–326.

Streb, C. K., Voelpel, S. C., & Leibold, M. (2008). Managing the aging workforce: Status quo and implications for the advancement of theory and practice. *European Management Journal, 26,* 1–10.

Street, D., Burge, S., Quadagno, J., & Barrett, A. (2007). The salience of social relationships for resident well-being in assisted living. *Journal of Gerontology, 62B*(2), S129–S134.

Striegel-Moore, R. H., & Bulik, C. M. (2007). Risk factors for eating disorders. *American Psychologist, 62*(3), 181–198.

Stroebe, M., Schut, H., & Stroebe, W. (2007). Health outcomes of bereavement. *Lancet, 370,* 1960–1973.

Sturm, R. (2004). The economics of physical activity: Societal trends and rationales for interventions. *American Journal of Preventive Medicine, 27*(Suppl. 3), 126–135.

Subrahmanyam, K., Greenfield, P. M., & Tynes, B. (2004). Constructing sexuality and identity in an online teen chat room. *Journal of Applied Developmental Psychology, 25,* 651–666.

Subrahmanyam, K., Greenfield, P. M., & Tynes, B. (2004). Constructing sexuality and identity in an online teen chat room. *Journal of Applied Developmental Psychology. Special Issue: Developing Children, Developing Media: Research from Television to the Internet from the Children's Digital Media Center, 25,* 651–666.

Subramanian, S. V., Elwert, G., & Christakis, N. (2008). Widowhood and mortality among the elderly: The modifying role of neighborhood concentration of widowed individuals. *Social Science & Medicine, 66*(4), 873–884.

Sullivan, A. M., Warren, A. G., Lakoma, M. D., Liaw, K. R., Hwang, D., & Block, S. D. (2004). End-of-life care in the curriculum: A national study of medical education deans. *Academic Medicine, 79,* 760–768.

Sullivan, H. S. (1953). *The interpersonal theory of psychiatry.* New York: Norton.

Sun, S. S., Schubert, C. M., Chumlea, W. C., Roche, A. F., Kulin, H. E., Lee, P. A., Himes, J. H., & Ryan, A. S. (2002). National estimates of the timing of sexual maturation and racial differences among U.S. children. *Pediatrics, 110,* 911–919.

Suomi, S. J. (2004). How gene-environment interactions shape biobehavioral development: Lessons from studies with rhesus monkeys. *Research in Human Development, 1,* 205–222.

Super, C. M., & Harkness, S. (2003). The metaphors of development. *Human Development, 46,* 3–23.

Super, D. E. (1957). *The psychology of careers: An introduction to vocational development.* New York: Harper.

Surra, C. A., & Hughes, D. K. (1997). Commitment processes in accounts of the development of premarital relationships. *Journal of Marriage & the Family, 59,* 5–21.

Surra, C. A., Hughes, D. K., & Jacquet, S. E. (1999). The development of commitment to marriage: A phenomenological approach. In J. M. Adams & W. H. Jones (Eds.), *Handbook of interpersonal commitment and relationship stability* (pp. 125–148). Dordrecht, Netherlands: Kluwer Academic.

Sussman, S., Pokhrel, P., Ashmore, R. D., & Brown, B. B. (2007). Adolescent peer group identification and characteristics: A review of the literature. *Addictive Behaviors, 32,* 1602–1627.

Sutcliffe, P. A., Bishop, D. V. M., & Houghton, S. (2006). Sensitivity of four subtests of the Test of Everyday Attention for Children (TEA-Ch) to stimulant medication in children with ADHD. *Educational Psychology, 26,* 325–337.

Swann, W. B., Chang-Schneider, C., & McClarty, K. L. (2007). Do people's self-views matter? *American Psychologist, 62*(2), 84–94.

Szinovacz, M. E. (2003). Caring for a demented relative at home: Effects on parent-adolescent relationships and family dynamics. *Journal of Aging Studies, 17,* 445–472.

Tadmor, C. T., Tetlock, P. E., & Peng, K. (2009). Acculturation strategies and integrative complexity: The cognitive implications of biculturalism. *Journal of Cross-Cultural Psychology, 40,* 105–139.

Tamis-LeMonda, C. S., Way, N., Hughes, D., Yoshikawa, H., Kalman, R. K., & Niwa, E. Y. (2008). Parents' goals for children: The dynamic coexistence of individualism and collectivism in cultures and individuals. *Social Development, 17*(1), 183–209.

Tang, W.-R., Aaronson, L. S., & Forbes, S. A. (2004). Quality of life in hospice patients with terminal illness. *Western Journal of Nursing Research, 26,* 113–128.

Tangney, J. P. (2003). Self-relevant emotions. In M. R. Leary & J. P. Tangney (Eds.), *Handbook of self and identity* (pp. 384–400). New York: Guilford Press.

Tanner, J. L. (2006). Recentering during emerging adulthood: A critical turning point in life span human development. In J. J. Arnett, & J. L. Tanner (Eds.), *Emerging adults in America: Coming of age in the 21st century* (pp. 21–55). Washington, DC: American Psychological Association.

Tanner, J. M. (1955). *Growth at adolescence.* Oxford, UK: Blackwell.

Tanner, J. M. (1978). *Foetus into man: Physical growth from conception to maturity.* Cambridge, MA: Harvard University Press.

Taylor, M. A., & Doverspike, D. (2003). Retirement planning. In G. A. Adams & T. A. Beehr (Eds.), *Retirement: Reasons, processes, and results* (pp. 53–82). New York: Springer.

Taylor, P. (2007). Older workers and the labor market: Lessons from abroad. *Generations, 31(1),* 96–101.

Teachman, J. D. (2008). The living arrangements of children and their educational well-being. *Journal of Family Issues, 29,* 734–761.

Tedeschi, R. G., & Calhoun, L. G. (2008). Beyond the concept of recovery: Growth and the experience of loss. *Death Studies, 32,* 27–39.

Teeri, S., Valimaki, M., Katajisto, J., & Leino-Kilpi, H. (2008). Maintenance of parents' integrity in long-term institutional care. *Nursing Ethics, 15*(4), 523–535.

Teisl, M., & Cicchetti, D. (2007). Physical abuse, cognitive and emotional processes, and aggressive/disruptive behavior problems. *Social Development, 17*(1), 1–23.

Thacker, K. S. (2008). Nurses' advocacy behaviors in end-of-life nursing care. *Nursing Ethics, 15*(2), 174–185.

Thiele, D. M., & Whelan, T. A. (2008). The relationship between grandparent satisfaction, meaning, and generativity. *International Journal of Aging & Human Development, 66,* 21–48.

Thiessen, E. D., Hill, E. A., & Saffran, J. R. (2005). Infant-directed speech facilitates word segmentation. *Infancy, 7,* 53–71.

Thomaes, S., Stegge, H., & Olthof, T. (2007). Externalizing shame responses in children: The role of fragile-positive self-esteem. *British Journal of Developmental Psychology, 25*(4), 559–577.

Thoman, E. B., & Whitney, M. P. (1990). Behavioral states in infants: Individual differences and individual analyses. In J. Colombo & J. W. Fagen (Eds.), *Individual differences in infancy: Reliability, stability, prediction* (pp. 113–135). Hillsdale, NJ: Erlbaum.

Thomas, A., & Chess, S. (1977). *Temperament and development.* Oxford, England: Brunner/Mazel.

Thomas, A., Chess, S., & Birch, H. G. (1968). *Temperament and behavior disorders in children.* Oxford, England: New York University Press.

Thomas, C., Morris, S. M., & Clark, D. (2004). Place of death: Preferences among cancer patients and their carers. *Social Science & Medicine, 58,* 2431–2444.

Thomas, J. R., & French, K. E. (1985). Gender differences across age in motor performance: A meta-analysis. *Psychological Bulletin, 98,* 260–282.

Thomas, S. V., Ajaykumar, B., Sindhu, K., Nair, M. K. C., George, B., & Sarma, P. S. (2008). Motor and mental development of infants exposed to antiepileptic drugs in utero. *Epilepsy & Behavior, 13,* 229–236.

Thompson, E. M., & Morgan, E. M. (2008). "Mostly straight" young women: Variations in sexual behavior and identity development. *Developmental Psychology, 44*(1), 15–21.

Thorell, L. B., & Rydell, A-M. (2008) Behaviour problems and social competence deficits associated with symptoms of attention-deficit/hyperacivity disorder: Effects of age and gender. *Child Care, Health & Development, 34*, 584–595.

Thorne, B. (1993). *Gender play: Girls and boys in school.* New Brunswick, NJ: Rutgers University Press.

Thorne, D., Warren, E., & Sullivan, T. (2008). *Generations of struggle.* (AARP Research Report #2008-11). Washington, DC: AARP.

Thornton, A., Binstock, G., & Ghimire, D. (2008). International dissemination of ideas about development and family change. In R. Jayakody, A. Thornton, & W. Axinn (Eds.), *International family change: Ideational perspectives* (pp. 19–44). New York, NY: Taylor & Francis Group/Lawrence Erlbaum Associates.

Timimi, S. (2004). A critique of the International Consensus Statement on ADHD. *Clinical Child and Family Psychology Review, 7*, 59–63.

Tinto, V. (1987). *Leaving college: Rethinking the causes and cures of student attrition.* Chicago: University of Chicago Press.

Tither, J. M., & Ellis, B. J. (2008). Impact of fathers on daughters' age at menarche: A genetically and environmentally controlled sibling study. *Developmental Psychology, 44*, 1409–1420.

Tolman, D. L., Spencer, R., Harmon, T., Rosen-Reynoso, M., & Striepe, M. (2004). Getting close, staying cool: Early adolescent boys' experiences with romantic relationships. In N. Way & J. Y. Chu (Eds.), *Adolescent boys: Exploring diverse cultures of boyhood* (pp. 235–255). New York: New York University Press.

Tomaszczyk, J. C., Fernandes, M. A., & Macleod, C. M. (2008). Personal relevance modulates the positivity bias in recall of emotional pictures in older adults. *Psychonomic Bulletin & Review, 15*(1), 191–196.

Tomlinson, M., Cooper, P., & Murray, L. (2005). The mother-infant relationship and infant attachment in a South African peri-urban settlement. *Child Development, 76*, 1044–1054.

Tooth, L., Russell, A., Lucke, J., Byrne, G., Lee, C., Wilson, A., & Dobson, A. (2008). Impact of cognitive and physical impairment on career burden and quality of life. *Quality of Life Research, 17*, 267–273.

Torquati, J. C., Raikes, H., & Huddleston-Casas, C. A. (2007). Teacher education, motivation, compensation, workplace support, and links to quality of center-based child care and teachers' intention to stay in the early childhood profession.

Early Childhood Research Quarterly, 22, 261–275.

Tremblay, K., & Ross, B. (2007). Effects of age and age-related hearing loss on the brain. *Journal of Communication Disorders, 40*, 305–312.

Triandis, H. C. (1995). *Individualism & collectivism.* Boulder, CO: Westview Press.

Trickett, P. K., Kurtz, D. A., & Pizzigati, K. (2004). Resilient outcomes in abused and neglected children: Bases for strengths-based intervention and prevention policies. In K. I. Maton, C. J. Schellenbach, B. J. Leadbeater, & A. L. Solarz (Eds.), *Investing in children, youth, families, and communities: Strengths-based research and policy* (pp. 73–95). Washington, DC: American Psychological Association.

Trivedi, M. A., Schmitz, T. W., Ries, M. L., Hess, T. M., Fitzgerald, M. E., Atwood, C. S., Rowley, H. A., Asthana, S., Sager, M. A., & Johnson, S. C. (2008). fMRI activation during episodic encoding and metacognitive appraisal across the lifespan: Risk factors for Alzheimer's disease. *Neuropsychologia, 46*, 1667–1678.

Troll, L. E. (1983). Grandparents: The family watchdog. In T. H. Brubaker (Ed.), *Family relationships in later life* (pp. 63–74). Beverly Hills, CA: Sage.

Trommsdorff, G., Friedlmeier, W., & Mayer, B. (2007). Sympathy, distress, and prosocial behavior of preschool children in four cultures. *International Journal of Behavioral Development, 31*(3), 284–293.

Tulving, E. (1985). How many memory systems are there? *American Psychologist, 40*, 385–398.

Turkheimer, E., Haley, A., Waldron, M., D'Onofrio, B., & Gottesman, I. I. (2003). Socioeconomic status modifies heritability of IQ in young children. *Psychological Science, 14*, 623–628.

Turkington, C., & Alper, M. M. (2001). *The encyclopedia of fertility and infertility.* New York: Facts On File.

Turner, S., & Alborz, A. (2003). Academic attainments of children with Down's syndrome: A longitudinal study. *British Journal of Educational Psychology, 73*, 563–583.

Turra, C. M., & Goldman, N. (2007). Socioeconomic differences in mortality among U.S. adults: Insights into the Hispanic paradox. *Journal of Gerontology, 62B*(3), S184–S192.

Twomey, F., O'Leary, N., & O'Brien, T. (2008). Prediction of patient survival by healthcare professionals in a specialist

palliative care inpatient unit: A prospective study. *American Journal of Hospice & Palliative Medicine, 25*(2), 139–145.

Tyler, C., Johnston, C. A., Dalton III, W. T., & Foreyt, J. P. (2009). Relationship between weight and body dissatisfaction, body esteem, and teasing in African American girls. *Journal of Black Psychology, 35*, 125–132.

U. S. Department of Health and Human Services, Administration for Children and Families (2005, May). *Head Start impact study: First year findings.* Washington, DC.

U.S. Bureau of Labor Statistics (2009, February). *The Employment Situation.* United States Department of Labor.

U.S. Census Bureau. (2008). *Unmarried and single Americans week.* Washington, D.C.: U.S. Census Bureau News.

U.S. Department of Agriculture Economic Research Service. (2009). Food Security in the United States, 2007. Retrieved August 14, 2009.

U.S. Department of Commerce. (2007). *Single-parent households showed little variation since 1994, Census Bureau reports.* Washington, D.C.: U.S. Census Bureau News.

U.S. Department of Commerce. (2008). *Grandparents Day 2008: Sept. 7.* Washington, D.C.: U.S. Census Bureau News.

U.S. Department of Education. (2008). *Enrollment in postsecondary institutions, fall 2006; graduation rates, 2000 & 2003 cohorts; and financial statistics, fiscal year 2006.* (NCES 2008-173). Washington DC: IPEDS.

U.S. Department of Health and Human Services (n.d.). *Child Maltreatment 2006: Summary.* Retrieved February 15, 2009, from http://www.acf.hhs.gov/programs/cb/pubs/cm06/summary.htm.

U.S. Department of Health and Human Services Administration for Children and Families. (2005). *Head Start impact study: First year findings.* Retrieved March 28, 2006, from http://www.acf.hhs.gov/programs/opre/hs/-impact_study/reports/first_yr_finds/-first_yr_finds.pdf

U.S. Department of Health and Human Services Administration for Children and Families. (May 2005). *Head Start Impact Study: First Year Findings.* Washington, D.C.

U.S. Department of Health and Human Services Administration for Children and Families. (2006). *Summary: Child maltreatment, 2006.* Washington, D.C.: United States Children's Bureau.

Udry, J. R. (1990). Biosocial models of adolescent problem behaviors. *Social Biology, 37,* 1–10.

Udry, J. R. (2000). Biological limits of gender construction. *American Sociological Review, 65,* 443–457.

Udry, J. R., & Campbell, B. C. (1994). Getting started on sexual behavior. In A. S. Rossi (Ed.), *Sexuality across the life course* (pp. 187–207). Chicago: University of Chicago Press.

Umberson, D., & Gove, W. R. (1989). Parenthood and psychological well-being: Theory, measurement, and stage in the family life course. *Journal of Family Issues, 10,* 440–462.

UNICEF (United Nations Children's Fund). (2002a). *The state of the world's children 2003.* New York: Author.

UNICEF (United Nations Children's Fund.) (2002b). *Profiting from abuse* (No. E.01.XX.14). New York: Author.

USDA, Economic Research Service. (2007, Aug.) *Food security in the United States.* Retrieved August 14, 2009.

Vaillancourt, T., Miller, J. L., Fagbemi, J., Côté, S., & Tremblay, R. E. (2007). Trajectories and predictors of indirect aggression: Results from a nationally representative longitudinal study of Canadian children aged 2–10. *Aggressive Behavior, 33,* 314–326.

van Aken, C., Junger, M., Verhoeven, M., van Aken, M. A. G., & Deković, M. (2008). The longitudinal relations between parenting and toddlers' attention problems and aggressive behaviors. *Infant Behavior and Development, 31,* 432–446.

van den Berg, M., Timmermans, D. R. M., Knol, D. L., van Eijk, J. T. M., de Smit, D. J., van Vugt, J. M. G., & van der Wal, G. (2008). Understanding pregnant women's decision making concerning prenatal screening. *Health Psychology, 27*(4), 430–437.

Van der Borght, K., Havekes, R., Bos, T., Eggen, B. J., & Van der Zee, E. A. (2007). Exercise improves memory acquisition and retrieval in the Y-maze task: Relationship with hippocampal neurogenesis. *Behavioral Neuroscience, 121*(2), 324–334.

van IJzendoorn, M. H., & Sagi, A. (1999). Cross-cultural patterns of attachment: Universal and contextual dimensions. In J. Cassidy & P. R. Shaver (Eds.), *Handbook of attachment: Theory, research, and clinical applications* (pp. 713–734). New York: Guilford Press.

van Solinge, H., & Henkens, K. (2008). Adjustment to and satisfaction with retirement: Two of a kind? *Psychology and Aging, 23*(2), 422–434.

Vando, J., Rhule-Louie, D. M., McMahon, R. J., & Spieker, S. J. (2008). Examining the link between infant attachment and child conduct problems in grade 1. *Journal of Child and Family Studies, 17,* 615–628.

Vando, J., Rhule-Louie, D. M., McMahon, r. J., & Spieker, S. J. (2008). Examining the link between infant attachment and child conduct problems in grade 1. *Journal of Child and Family Studies, 17*(5), 615–628.

Vartanian, T. P., & McNamara, J. M. (2002). Older women in poverty: The impact of midlife factors. *Journal of Marriage and Family, 64,* 532–547.

Vasto, S., Candore, G., Listi, F., Balistreri, C. R., Colonna-Romano, G., Malavolta, M., Lio, D., Nuzzo, D., Mocchegiani, E., Bona, D. D., & Caruso, C. (2008). Inflammation, genes and zinc in Alzheimer's disease. *Brain Research Reviews, 58*(1), 96–105.

Vaz Fragoso, C. A., Araujo, K. L., Van Ness, P. H., & Marottoli, R. A. (2008). Prevalence of sleep disturbances in a cohort of older drivers. *Journal of Gerontology, 63A*(7), 715–723.

Vianna, E., & Stetsenko, A. (2006). Embracing history through transforming it: Contrasting Piagetian versus Vygotskian (activity) theories of learning and development to expand constructivism within a dialectical view of history. *Theory & Psychology, 16*(1), 81–108.

Vielwerth, S. E., Jensen, R. B., Larsen, T., & Greisen, G. (2007). The impact of maternal smoking on fetal and infant growth. *Early Human Development, 83,* 491–495.

Villemagne, V. L., Pike, K. E., Darby, D., Maruff, P., Savage, G., Ng, S., Ackermann, U., Cowie, T. F., Currie, J., Chan, S. G., Jones, G., Tochon-Danguy, H., O'Keefe, G., Masters, C. L., & Rowe, C. C. (2008). Aβ deposits in older non-demented individuals with cognitive decline are indicative of preclinical Alzheimer's disease. *Neuropsychologia, 46*(6), 1688–1697.

von Bothmer, M. I. K., & Fridlund, B. (2005). Gender differences in health habits and in motivation for a healthy lifestyle among Swedish university students. *Nursing & Health Sciences, 7,* 107–118.

von Hippel, W., Henry, J. D., & Matovic, D. (2008). Aging and social satisfaction:

Offsetting positive and negative effects. *Psychology and Aging, 23,* 435–439.

Von Raffler-Engel, W. (1994). *The perception of the unborn across the cultures of the world.* Seattle, WA: Hogrefe & Huber.

Votruba-Drzal, E. (2006). Economic disparities in middle childhood development: Does income matter? *Developmental Psychology, 42*(6), 1154–1167.

Vygotsky, L. S. (1962). *Thought and language* (E. Hanfmann & G. Vakar, Eds. & Trans.). New York: MIT Press and Wiley. (Original work published 1934)

Vygotsky, L. S. (1978). *Mind in society: The development of higher psychological processes.* Cambridge, MA: Harvard University Press. (Original work published 1935)

Vygotsky, L. S. (1978). *Mind in society: The development of higher psychological processes* (M. Cole, V. John-Steiner, S. Scribner, & E. Souberman, Eds.). Cambridge, MA: Harvard University Press. (Original work published 1935)

Vygotsky, L. S. (1986). *Thought and language* (A. Kozulin, Ed., E. Hanfmann & G. Vakar, Trans., Revised ed.). Cambridge, MA: MIT Press. (Original work published 1934)

Wade, N. G., Johnson, C. V., & Meyer, J. E. (2008). Understanding concerns about interventions to promote forgiveness: A review of the literature. *Psychology Theory, Research, Practice, Training, 45*(1), 88–102.

Wadsworth, B. J. (1996). *Piaget's theory of cognitive and affective development: Foundations of constructivism* (5th ed.). White Plains, NY: Longman.

Wadsworth, M. E., & Santiago, C. D. (2008). Risk and resiliency processes in ethnically diverse families in poverty. *Journal of Family Psychology, 22,* 399–410.

Wadsworth, M. E., & Santiago, C. D. (2008). Risk and resiliency processes in ethnically diverse families in poverty. *Journal of Family Psychology, 22*(3), 399–410.

Wagner, T. (2000). *How schools change: Lessons from three communities revisited* (2nd ed.). New York: RoutledgeFalmer.

Waite, L. J., & Gallagher, M. (2000). *The case for marriage: Why married people are happier, healthier, and better off financially.* New York: Doubleday.

Waldman, I. D. (2007). Gene-environment interactions reexamined: Does mother's marital stability interact with the dopamine receptor D2 gene in the etiology of childhood attention deficit/hyperactivity disorder? *Development and Psychopathology, 19*(4), 1117-1128.

Walker, G. C. (2003). Medical euthanasia. In C. D. Bryant (Ed.), *Handbook of death & dying* (pp. 405–423). Thousand Oaks, CA: Sage.

Walker, L. J., & Frimer, J. A. (2007). Moral personality of brave and caring exemplars. *Journal of Personality and Social Psychology, 93*(5), 845–860.

Wallerstein, J., & Lewis, J. M. (2007). Sibling outcomes and disparate parenting and stepparenting after divorce: Report from a 10-year longitudinal study. *Psychoanalytic Psychology, 24,* 445–458.

Walsh, J. L. (2008, March). *Magazine reading as a longitudinal predictor of your women's sexual norms and behaviors.* Paper presented at 12th Biennial Meeting of Society for Research on Adolescence, Chicago, IL.

Walter, T. (2003, July 24). Historical and cultural variants on the good death. [INII]BMJ, 327,[FFO] 218–220.

Wang, S., & Kohne, L. (2007). Visual experience enhances infants' use of task-relevant information in an action task. *Developmental Psychology, 43,*1513–1522.

Wang, S., & Kohne, L. (2007). Visual experience enhances infants' use of task-relevant information in an action task. *Developmental Psychology 43*(6), 1513–1522.

Wapner, R., Thom, E., Simpson, J. L., Pergament, E., Silver, R., Filkins, K., Platt, L., Mahoney, M., Johnson, A., Hogge, W., Wilson, R., Mohide, P., Hershey, D., Krantz, D., Zachary, J., Snijders, R., Greene, N., Sabbagha, R., MacGregor, S., Hill, L., Gagnon, A., Hallahan, T., & Jackson, L. (2003). First-trimester screening for trisomies 21 and 18. *New England Journal of Medicine, 349,* 1405–1413.

Ward, R. A., & Spitze, G. D. (2007). Nestleaving and coresidence by young adult children: The role of family relations. *Research on Aging, 29*(3), 257-277.

Warr, M. (2007). The tangled web: Delinquency, deception, and parental attachment. *Journal of Youth Adolescence, 36,* 607–622.

Wass, H. (2004). A perspective on the current state of death education. *Death Studies, 28,* 289–308.

Waterman, A. S. (1999). Identity, the identity statuses, and identity status development: A contemporary statement. *Developmental Review, 19,* 591–621.

Watson, J. B. (1930). *Behaviorism* (Revised ed.). New York: W. W. Norton.

Watson, J. B. (1998). *Behaviorism.* New Brunswick, NJ: Transaction. (Original work published 1924)

Watson, J. B. (with the assistance of Watson, R. R.). (1972). *Psychological care of infant and child.* New York: Arno Press. (Original work published 1928)

Wechsler, D. (1991). *Wechsler intelligence scale for children (WISC-III).* San Antonio, TX: The Psychological Corporation.

Wedding, D., Kohout, J., Mengel, M. B., Ohlemiller, M., Ulione, M., Cook, K., Rudeen, K., & Braddock, S. (2007). Psychologists' knowledge and attitudes about fetal alcohol syndrome, fetal alcohol spectrum disorders, and alcohol use during pregnancy. *Professional Psychology: Research and Practice, 38*(2), 208–213.

Weese-Mayer, D. E., Berry-Kravis, E. M., Zhou, L., Maher, B. S., Curran, M. E., Silvestri, J. M., & Marazita, M. L. (2004). Sudden infant death syndrome: Case-control frequency differences at genes pertinent to early autonomic nervous system embryologic development. *Pediatric Research, 56,* 391–395.

Weibel-Orlando, J. (1999). Powwow princess and gospelettes: Growing up in grandmother's world. In M. Schweitzer (Ed.), *Indian grandparenthood* (pp. 181–202). Albuquerque, NM: University of New Mexico Press.

Weigel, D. J., Lowman, J. L., & Martin, S. S. (2007). Language development in the years before school: A comparison of developmental assets in home and child care settings. *Early Child Development and Care, 177*(6–7), 719–734.

Weinberg, J., Sliwowska, J. H., Lan, N., & Hellemans, K. G. C. (2008). Prenatal alcohol exposure: Foetal programming, the hypothalamic-pituitary-adrenal axis and sex differences in outcome. *Journal of Neuroendocrinology, 20,* 470–488.

Weinfield, N. S., Sroufe, L. A., Egeland, B., & Carlson, E. A. (1999). The nature of individual differences in infant-caregiver attachment. In J. Cassidy & P. R. Shaver (Eds.), *Handbook of attachment: Theory, research, and clinical applications* (pp. 68–88). New York: Guilford Press.

Weisfeld, G. (1997). Puberty rites as clues to the nature of human adolescence. *Cross-Cultural Research: The Journal of Comparative Social Science, 31,* 27–54.

Weissman, M. M., Myers, J. K., Tischler, G. L., Holzer, C. E., 3rd, Leaf, P. J., Orvaschel, H., & Brody, J. A. (1985). Psychiatric disorders (DSM-III) and cognitive impairment among the elderly in a U.S. urban community. *Acta Psychiatrica Scandinavica, 71,* 366–379.

Wellman, B. (1990). The place of kinfolk in personal community networks. *Marriage & Family Review, 15,* 195–228.

Wells-di Gregorio, S. W. (2009). Family end-of-life decision making. In J. Werth & D. Blevins (eds.), *Decision Making Near the End of Life: Recent Developments and Future Directions.* Routledge Publishing, 2008.

Werth, B., & Tsiaras, A. (2002). *From conception to birth: A life unfolds.* New York: Doubleday.

Wertz, R. W., & Wertz, D. C. (1989). *Lying-in: A history of childbirth in America* (expanded ed.). New Haven: Yale University Press.

West, R. L., Bagwell, D. K., & Dark-Freudeman, A. (2008). Self-efficacy and memory aging: The impact of a memory intervention based on self-efficacy. *Aging, Neuropsychology, and Cognition, 15,* 302–329.

Westermann, G., Mareschal, D., Johnson, M. H., Sirois, S., Spratling, M. W., & Thomas, M. S. C. (2007). Neuroconstructivism. *Developmental Science, 10*(1), 75–83.

Whitaker, D. J., Lutzker, J. R., & Shelley, G. A. (2005). Child maltreatment prevention priorities at the Centers for Disease Control and Prevention. *Child Maltreatment: Journal of the American Professional Society on the Abuse of Children, 10,* 245–259.

White, J. (2006). Multiple invalidities. In J. A. Schaler (Ed.), *Howard Gardner under fire: The rebel psychologist faces his critics* (pp. 45–71). Chicago, IL, US: Open Court Publishing Co.

White, L., & Edwards, J. N. (1990). Emptying the nest and parental well-being: An analysis of national panel data. *American Sociological Review, 55,* 235–242.

White, N. R. (2002). "Not under my roof!" Young people's experience of home. *Youth & Society, 34,* 214–231.

Whiteman, S. D., McHale, S. M., & Crouter, A. C. (2007). Longitudinal changes in marital relationships: The role of offspring's pubertal development. *Journal of Marriage and Family, 69*(4), 1005–1020.

Whiting, J. B., Smith, D. R., Barnett, T., & Grafsky, E. L. (2007). Overcoming the Cinderella myth: A mixed methods study of successful stepmothers. *Journal of Divorce & Remarriage*, 47(1/2), 95–109.

Whitson, H. E., Cousins, S. W., Burchett, B. M., Hybels, C. F., Pieper, C. F., & Cohen, H. J. (2007). The combined effect of visual impairment and cognitive impairment on disability in older people. *Journal of the American Geriatrics Society*, 55, 885–891.

Wiener, J. M. (2003). An assessment of strategies for improving quality of care in nursing homes. *Gerontologist*, 43, 19–27.

Wiese, B. S., Freund, A. M., & Baltes, P. B. (2002). Subjective career success and emotional well-being: Longitudinal predictive power of selection, optimization and compensation. *Journal of Vocational Behavior*, 60, 321–335.

Wijk, H. & Grimby, A. (2008). Needs of elderly patients in palliative care. *American Journal of Hospice & Palliative Medicine*, 25 (2), 106–111.

Wiley, D., & Bortz, W. M., II. (1996). Sexuality and aging—Usual and successful. *Journals of Gerontology: Series A: Biological Sciences and Medical Sciences*, 51A, M142-M146.

Williams, A. L., & Merten, M. J. (2008). A review of online social networking profiles by adolescents: implications for future research and intervention. *Adolescence*, 43, 253–274.

Williams, D. R., & Mohammed, S. A. (2009) Discrimination and racial disparities in health: Evidence and needed research. *Journal of Behavioral Medicine*, 32, 20–47.

Williams, J. (2008). Working toward a neurobiological account of ADHD: Commentary on Gail Tripp and Jeff Wickens, dopamine transfer deficit. *The Journal of Child Psychology and Psychiatry*, 49, 705–711.

Williamson, R. C., Rinehart, A. D., & Blank, T. O. (1992). *Early retirement: Promises and pitfalls*. New York: Insight Books/Plenum Press.

Willott, S., & Griffin, C. (2004). Redundant men: Constraints on identity change. *Journal of Community & Applied Social Psychology*, 14, 53–69.

Wilson, A. E., Shuey, K. M., & Elder, G. H. (2007). Cumulative advantage: processes as mechanisms of inequity in life course health. *American Journal of Sociology*, 112(6), 1886–1924.

Wilson, K. G., Chochinov, H. M., McPherson, C. J., Skirko, M. G., Allard, P., Chary, S., Gagnon, P. R., Macmillan, K., De Luca, M., O'Shea, F., Kuhl, D., Fainsinger, R. L., Karam,

A. M., & Clinch, J. J. (2007). Desire for euthanasia or physician-assisted suicide in palliative cancer care. *Health Psychology*, 26, 314–323.

Wilson, P. A., & Yoshikawa, H. (2004). Experiences of and responses to social discrimination among Asian and Pacific Islander gay men: Their relationship to HIV risk. *AIDS Education and Prevention*, 16, 68–83.

Wilson, S. M., Ngige, L. W., & Trollinger, L. J. (2003). Connecting generations: Paths to Maasai and Kamba marriage in Kenya. In R. R. Hamon & B. B. Ingoldsby (Eds.), *Mate selection across cultures* (pp. 95–118). Thousand Oaks, CA: Sage.

Wimmer, H., & Perner, J. (1983). Beliefs about beliefs: Representation and constraining function of wrong beliefs in young children's understanding of deception. *Cognition*, 13, 103–128.

Windsor, T. D., Anstey, K. J., & Rodgers, B. (2008). Volunteering and psychological well-being among young-old adults: How much is too much? *The Gerontologist*, 48(1), 59–70.

Winston, C. A. (2006). African American grandmothers parenting AIDS orphans: Grieving and coping. *Qualitative Social Work: Research and Practice*, 5, 33–43.

Wolchik, S. A., Sandler, I. N., Winslow, E., & Smith-Daniels, V. (2005). Programs for promoting parenting of residential parents: Moving from efficacy to effectiveness. *Family Court Review*, 43, 65–80.

Wolfe, L. (2004). Should parents speak with a dying child about impending death? *New England Journal of Medicine*, 351, 1251–1253.

Wong, P. C. M., Jin, J. X., Gunasekera, G. M., Abel, R., Lee, E. R., & Dhar, S. (2009). Aging and cortical mechanisms of speech perception in noise. *Neuropsychologia*, 47, 693–703.

Wood, D., Bruner, J. S., & Ross, G. (1976). The role of tutoring in problem solving. *Journal of Child Psychology and Psychiatry*, 17, 89–100.

Wood, D., Larson, R. W., & Brown, J. R. (2009). How adolescents come to see themselves as more responsible through participation in youth programs. *Child Development*, 80, 295–309.

Wood, W. R., & Williamson, J. B. (2003). Historical changes in the meaning of death in the western tradition. In C. D. Bryant (ed.), *Handbook of death & dying* (pp. 14–23). Thousand Oaks, CA: Sage.

Woodland, M. H. (2008). Watcha doin' after school? A review of the literature

on the influence of after-school programs on young black males. *Urban Education*, 43, 537–560.

World Health Organization [WHO]. (2003a). *Global strategy for infant and young child feeding*. Geneva, Switzerland: World Health Organization.

World Health Organization [WHO]. (2003b). *Kangaroo mother care: A practical guide*. Geneva, Switzerland: Dept. of Reproductive Health and Research, World Health Organization.

Wright, M. O., & Masten, A. S. (2005). Resilience processes in development: Fostering positive adaptation in the context of adversity. In S. Goldstein, & R. B. Brooks (eds.), *Handbook of resilience in children* (pp. 17–37). New York, NY, US: Kluwer Academic/Plenum Publishers.

Wright, M. O., & Masten, A. S. (2005). Resilience processes in development: Fostering positive adaptation in the context of adversity. In S. Goldstein & R. B. Brooks (Eds.), *Handbook of Resilience in Children*. (pp. 17–37). New York: Kluwer Academic/Plenum Publishers.

Wu, T., Mendola, P., & Buck, G. M. (2002). Ethnic differences in the presence of secondary sex characteristics and menarche among U.S. girls: The Third National Health and Nutrition Examination Survey, 1988–1994. *Pediatrics*, 110, 752–757.

Wurm, S., Tesch-Romer, C., & Tomasik, M. J. (2007). Longitudinal findings on aging-related cognitions, control beliefs, and health in later life. *Journal of Gerontology: PSYCHOLOGICAL SCIENCES*, 62B(3), P156–P164.

Xia, Y. R., & Zhou, Z. G. (2003). The transition of courtship, mate selection, and marriage in China. In R. R. Hamon & B. B. Ingoldsby (Eds.), *Mate selection across cultures* (pp. 231–246). Thousand Oaks: Sage.

Yancey, G. (2007). Homogamy over the net: Using internet advertisements to discover who interracially dates. *Journal of Social and Personal Relationships*, 24(6), 913–930.

Yancey, G. A., & Yancey, S. W. (2002). *Just don't marry one: Interracial dating, marriage, and parenting*. Valley Forge, PA: Judson Press.

Yang, C. K., & Hahn, H. M. (2002). Cosleeping in young Korean children. *Journal of Developmental & Behavioral Pediatrics*, 23, 151–157.

Yao, L., & Robert, S. A. (2008). The contributions of race, individual socioeconomic status, and neighborhood socioeconomic context on the self-rated health trajectories and morality of older adults. *Research on Aging, 30*(2), 251–273.

Yates, M., & Youniss, J. (1998). Community service and political identity development in adolescence. *Journal of Social Issues, 54*, 495–512.

Yates, T. M., Allison, J. T., & Luthar, S. S. (2008). Nonsuicidal self-injury among "privileged" youths: Longitudinal and cross-sectional approaches to developmental process. *Journal of Counseling and Clinical Psychology, 76*(1), 52–62.

Yeoh, B. H., Eastwood, J., Phung, H., & Woolfenden, S. (2007). Factors influencing breastfeeding rates in south-western Sydney. *Journal of Paediatrics and Child Health, 43*, 249-255.

Yeung, G. T. Y., & Fung, H. H. (2007). Social support and life satisfaction among Hong Kong Chinese older adults: Family first? *European Journal of Ageing, 4*, 219–227.

Young, L. M., Baltes, B. B., & Pratt, A. K. (2007). Using selection, optimization, and compensation to reduce job/family stressors: Effective when it matters. *Journal of Business and Psychology, 21*(4), 511–539.

Yount, K. M., & Agree, E. M. (2004). The power of older women and men in Egyptian and Tunisian families. *Journal of Marriage and Family, 66*, 126–146.

Zaichkowsky, L. D., & Larson, G. A. (1995). Physical, motor, and fitness development in children and adolescents. *Journal of Education, 177*, 55–79.

Zappalà, S., Depolo, M., Fraccaroli, F., Guglielmi, D., & Sarchielli, G. (2008). Postponing job retirement? Psychosocial influences on the preference for early or late retirement. *Career Development International, 13*, 150–167.

Zarit, S. H., Reever, K. E., & Bach-Peterson, J. (1980). Relatives of the impaired elderly: Correlates of feelings of burden. *Gerontologist, 20*, 649–655.

Zelinski, E. M., & Kennison, R. F. (2007). Not your parents' test scores: Cohort reduces psychometric aging effects. *Psychology and Aging, 22*(3), 546–557.

Zeskind, P. S., & Lester, B. M. (2001). Analysis of infant crying. In L. T. Singer & P. S. Zeskind (eds.), *Biobehavioral assessment of the infant* (pp. 149–166). New York: Guilford Press.

Zettel-Watson, L., Ditto, P. H., Danks, J. H., & Smucker, W. D. (2008). Actual and perceived gender differences in the accuracy of surrogate decisions about life-sustaining medical treatment among older spouses. *Death Studies, 32*, 273–290.

Zettergren, P. (2007). Cluster analysis in sociometric research: A pattern-oriented approach to identifying temporally stable peer status groups of girls. *The Journal of Early Adolescence, 27*, 90–114.

Zigler, E., & Finn-Stevenson, M. (2007). From research to policy and practice: The school of the 21st century. *American Journal of Orthopsychiatry, 77*(2), 175–181.

Zimmer-Gembeck, M. J., & Helfand, M. (2008). Ten years of longitudinal research on U.S. adolescent sexual behavior: Developmental correlates of sexual intercourse, and the importance of age, gender and ethnic background. *Developmental Review, 28*, 153–224.

Zucker, A. N., Ostrove, J. M., & Stewart, A. J. (2002). College-educated women's personality development in adulthood: Perceptions and age differences. *Psychology and Aging, 17*, 236–244.

Zunzunegui, M., Alvarado, B., Beland, F., & Vissandjee, B. (2009). Explaining health differences between men and women in later life: A cross-city comparison in Latin America and the Caribbean. *Social Science & Medicine, 68*, 235–242.

Name Index

Jensen, L., 408
Jenson, W. R., 184
Jerdee, T. H., 412
Jesse, D. E., 35
Jette, A. M., 433
Jeune, B., 438
Jimenez, M. A., 415
Joesch, J. M., 63
Johansson, K., 434, 443
John, O. P., 360
Johnson, B., 59
Johnson, C. V., 336, 337
Johnson, F., 251
Johnson, K. A., 255
Johnson, M. D., 342
Johnson, M. H., 76, 91
Johnson, R. W., 408, 409, 411
Johnson, V. E., 383, 384
Johnson, W., 307
Johnston, C., 307
Johnston, L. D., 272
Johnston, R., 424–425, 427
Johri, M., 443
Jokela, M., 342
Jones, C., 80, 366
Jones, K., 424–425, 427
Joseph, R. M., 166
Josephsson, S., 434, 443
Joussemet, M., 184
Judge, T. A., 351
Jung, C. G., 359

K

Kabir, Z. N., 425
Kacela, X., 460
Kaelber, D. C., 144
Kagan, J., 116, 127, 129, 208
Kaitz, M., 123
Kallen, B., 50
Kaltiala-Heino, R., 246
Kane, R. A., 445
Kannai, R., 455
Kaplowitz, P. B., 238, 243
Karen, R., 16
Karney, B. R., 331
Karns, J. T., 80, 88
Karraker, K. H., 86
Kashy, D. A., 320, 321
Kasl-Godley, J., 440
Kastenbaum, R., 452, 453, 456
Kato, K., 18
Kaufman, A. S., 371
Kawarabayashi, T., 440
Keefe, M. R., 83
Keel, P. K., 251
Keeton, C. P., 342
Kefalas, M. J., 331
Kehily, M. J., 258
Keller, H., 10
Keller, M. A., 87
Kelley, S. J., 381
Kellman, P. J., 91
Kelly, D. J., 191

Kelly, J., 331, 337
Kelly, J. B., 213, 337
Keltikangas-Jarvinen, L., 342
Kemper, S., 432
Kennison, R. F., 371
Kenny, M. C., 212
Kenrick, D. T., 384
Kensinger, E. A., 399
Kerckhoff, A. C., 310
Kermoian, R., 92
Kerr, W. C., 52
Kevorkian, J., 470
Keys, C. L., 276
Khachaturian, Z. S., 438, 439, 440
Kiang, L., 300
Kidd, K. K., 216
Kiernan, K., 8, 330
King, V., 380
Kinnier, R. T., 413
Kinsella, K., 7, 382, 392, 393, 406, 408
Kinsley, C. H., 45
Kirkham, N., 157
Kisilevsky, B. S., 42
Kitahara, M., 87
Kitzinger, S., 36, 58, 61
Kivimaki, M., 342
Klass, D., 413
Kleiber, D. A., 410
Klein, J. D., 258
Kliegl, R., 395
Klinger, R., 351
Klonoff, E. A., 426
Klusmann, D., 333
Kluwer, E. S., 342
Knaack, A., 128, 130
Knafo, A., 180
Knight, B. G., 315
Knight, P. V., 433, 434
Knitzer, J., 122, 125
Knoester, C., 346
Knutson, B., 402
Knutson, J. F., 211
Kochanska, G., 20, 116, 122, 127, 128, 130
Koenig, C. S., 460
Kohlberg, L., 190, 267–269, 377
Kohne, L., 100
Kono, A., 434
Konrad, K., 158
Korovaitseva, G. I., 440
Korten, A., 349
Korzilius, H., 79
Kosir, K., 193
Kosunen, E., 246
Kovács, Á. M., 166
Kozol, J., 121, 122
Kramer, B. J., 382
Krampe, R. T., 375
Krause, N., 402, 403
Kraut, M. A., 396
Kreader, J. L., 123

Kreicbergs, U., 458
Krendl, A. C., 399
Krieger, N., 425
Kroger, J., 266
Krowitz, A., 92
Krumm, J., 55
Krumrei, E., 337
Kübler-Ross, E., 454
Kuh, G. D., 312
Kuhn, B. R., 210
Kuhn, D., 267
Kulik, L., 379
Kunkel, C. D., 222
Kurtines, W. M., 280
Kurtz, D. A., 212
Kvaavik, E., 428
Kvavilashvili, L., 400
Kwan, V. S. Y., 366

L

Laakkonen, M.-L., 441, 469
Labouvie-Vief, G., 307, 376
Lachance-Grzela, M., 342
Lachman, M. E., 7
Ladd, G. W., 193, 194, 196
Lafont, S., 435
LaGasse, L., 45
La Greca, A. M., 286, 287
Lai, P., 401
Laible, D. J., 153
Lam, S., 177
Lamb, M, 124, 125
Lamb, M. E., 338, 344, 345
Lambert, K. G., 45
Lambert, S., 77
Lamerz, A., 142
Lamson, A. L., 442
Lang, M. E., 341
Langa, K. M., 438
Langer, A., 92
Langer, E. J., 395
Langhorne, P., 433, 434
Lanz, M., 297, 298, 323
Larsen, L., 370
Larsen, R. E., 368
Larson, E. B., 438
Larson, G. A., 141
Larson, R., 274, 275, 280, 282, 283, 284
Larson, R. W., 280
LaRusso, M. D., 280
Larzelere, R. E., 210
Latner, J. D., 143, 144
Latz, S., 87
Laursen, B., 283
Lavee, Y., 334
Lavner, J. A., 317
Law, K., 45
Law, K. W.-K., 407
Lawrence, E., 341, 342
Lawson, M. A., 215
Lay, K., 381
Le, K., 361

Leavitt, J. W., 61
Lecanuet, J. P., 90
LeClere, F. B., 51
Lee, C., 298, 299
Lee, J., 173, 245
Lee, V. E., 215, 216
Lee, W. K. M., 407
Leerkes, E. M., 125
Leibold, M., 409
Leipold, B., 382
Leitner, M. P., 353
Lepper, M. R., 225
Lerner, R. M., 4, 24, 280
Lester, B., 45
Lester, B. M., 83
Lesthaeghe, R., 340
Levenson, R. W., 332
Leventhal, T., 288, 289
Levin, S., 315
Levitt, H. M., 320
Levy, O., 399
Lewis, J. M., 338
Lewis, P., 432
Li, L. W., 402
Liang, J., 402
Liben, S., 456, 458, 462
Liberty, C., 156
Light, R. J., 312
Lightfoot, C., 271, 272, 274
Li-Grining, C. P., 121
Lilja, M., 434, 443
Lillard, A. S., 164
Lim, S. L., 285
Limber, S., 195
Lin, M., 433
Lincoln, A., 207
Lindemann, E., 412
Lindstrom-Forneri, W., 435
Lineweaver, T. T., 435
Linver, M. R., 280
Lipsitt, L. P., 88
Lipton, R. B., 242, 243
Little, M., 456
Little, T. D., 182, 193
Lobel, M., 63
Lobue, V., 113
Locke, J., 5
Löckenhoff, C. E., 402
Loessi, B., 281
Logan, R. L., 363, 364
Lonardo, R. A., 286
Long, S. O., 455, 459
Longmore, M. A., 256, 330
Lord, D., 436
Lorenz, K., 110
Losada, M. F., 368
Louhiala, P., 469
Lovestone, S., 439
Lovett, S., 42
Low, J. A., 42
Lowenstein, L. F., 213
Lowman, J. L., 122
Lozoff, B., 87